To THE MILLIONS of people now using the carefully edited POCKET BOOKS, INC., we prepared by The University of Chicago. The accuracy and authenticity of this Spanish-English, English-Spanish Dictionary will, we sincerely hope, demonstrate again our aim to present "the finest books at the lowest possible price."

UNIVERSIDAD DE CHICAGO

DICCIONARIO

ESPAÑOL-INGLÉS e INGLÉS-ESPAÑOL

*Un Nuevo y Conciso Diccionario Que Contiene las Voces
y Locuciones Básicas de Ambos Idiomas*

RECOPILACIÓN
DE
CARLOS CASTILLO y OTTO F. BOND
Universidad de Chicago

CON LA AYUDA DE
BARBARA M. GARCÍA
Mills College

POCKET BOOKS, INC.
NEW YORK

THE UNIVERSITY OF CHICAGO

SPANISH-ENGLISH, ENGLISH-SPANISH

DICTIONARY

*A New Concise Dictionary of Words and Phrases Basic
to the Written and Spoken Languages of Today*

COMPILED BY

CARLOS CASTILLO & OTTO F. BOND

The University of Chicago

WITH THE ASSISTANCE OF

BARBARA M. GARCIA

Mills College

POCKET BOOKS, INC.

NEW YORK

The University of Chicago Spanish-English, English-Spanish Dictionary

University of Chicago edition published 1948

POCKET BOOK edition published October, 1950

CARDINAL edition published August, 1953
30th printing.........................May, 1960

L

CARDINAL editions are distributed in the U.S. by Affiliated Publishers, Inc., 630 Fifth Avenue, New York 20, N.Y.

FOREWORD

THE *University of Chicago Spanish-English, English-Spanish Dictionary* has been compiled for the general use of the American learner of Spanish and the Spanish learner of English, with special reference in either case to New World usages as found in the United States and in Latin America.

With this particular purpose in mind, the editors have selected the words to be defined according to the relative frequency of their occurrence. The Spanish-English section, therefore, contains all the items listed in Buchanan's *Graded Spanish Word Book* (Toronto: University of Toronto Press, 1929); all the idioms found in Keniston's *Standard List of Spanish Words and Idioms* (Boston: D. C. Heath & Co., 1941); and the words and idioms used in the Heath-Chicago series of *Graded Spanish Readers* (Boston: D. C. Heath & Co., 1936——), supplemented by many words occurring in a number of textbooks used in the United States at the elementary and intermediate levels of Spanish instruction, in Spanish-American newspapers and commercial correspondence, and in technical use by the average layman.

Similarly, in the English-Spanish section the words selected for definition have been taken from the first nine thousand entries in Thorndike and Lorge's *Teacher's Word Book of 30,000 Words* (New York: Bureau of Publications, Teachers College, Columbia University, 1944), supplemented by residual words in the combined word lists of Eaton, Buckingham-Dolch, and the *Interim Report on Vocabulary Selection* (London: P. S. King & Co., 1936).

In order to equalize the two parts and not leave undefined words used in a definition, it has been necessary to introduce into each section a number of secondary entries which are a by-product of the primary definitions, bringing the total number of entries for the *Dictionary* to approximately 30,000 words.

The New World application of the *Dictionary* is further emphasized by its acceptance of American standards of speech in indicating the pronunciation of the English entries and by the inclusion of American and Latin-American equivalents and usages throughout. The latter values have been identified by the use of the abbreviation "*Am.*"

It should be noted, however, that the abbreviation "*Am.*" may mean that the word is exclusively Spanish American or that a certain meaning is exclusively Spanish American or that the word is relatively common in Spanish America but is obsolete or obsolescent in Spain or that the word or meaning may be known locally or regionally in Spain, as well as in Spanish America, although the *Dictionary* of the Spanish Academy fails to recognize it.

Certain auxiliary data have been provided at the beginning of each section, such as a list of abbreviations; an explanation of speech sounds; a summary of the use and value of suffixes; a list of numerals; a brief treatment of nouns, adjectives, and adverbs; and a table of irregular verb forms. In the Spanish-English section a superior number following a verb entry refers to a similarly numbered verb listed in the table preceding the section.

A dictionary should be an instrument for the better understanding between peoples. It is the earnest wish of the editors of this one that it may serve to that end.

THE EDITORS

PART ONE
SPANISH-ENGLISH

PART ONE

SPANISH-ENGLISH

LIST OF ABBREVIATIONS ix
SPANISH PRONUNCIATION ix
THE NOUN xv
THE ADJECTIVE AND ADVERB xvii
COMMON SPANISH SUFFIXES xix
SPANISH IRREGULAR AND ORTHOGRAPHIC CHANGING VERBS xxiii
NUMERALS xxxviii

LIST OF ABBREVIATIONS

adj.	adjective	*m.*	masculine noun
adv.	adverb	*math.*	mathematics
Am.[1]	Americanism	*neut.*	neuter
arith.	arithmetic	*num.*	numeral
conj.	conjunction	*p.p.*	past participle
contr.	contraction	*pers.*	personal
def.	definite	*pers. pron.*	personal pronoun
def. art.	definite article	*pl.*	plural
dem.	demonstrative	*poss.*	possessive
dem. adj.	demonstrative adjective	*prep.*	preposition
dem. pron.	demonstrative pronoun	*pron.*	pronoun
etc.	et cetera	*refl.*	reflexive
f.	feminine noun	*refl. pron.*	reflexive pronoun
fam.	familiar	*rel.*	relative
indef.	indefinite	*rel. adv.*	relative adverb
indef. art.	indefinite article	*rel. pron.*	relative pronoun
inf.	infinitive	*sing.*	singular
interj.	interjection	*subj.*	subjunctive
interr.	interrogative	*v.*	verb
irr.	irregular	*v. irr.*	irregular verb

SPANISH PRONUNCIATION

The Spanish alphabet consists of twenty-eight letters: *a, b, c, ch, d, e, f, g, h, i, j, l, ll, m, n, ñ, o, p, q, r, rr, s, t, u, v, x, y, z* (*k* and *w* are found only in words of foreign origin).

I. THE VOWELS AND DIPHTHONGS

Each Spanish vowel has one *fundamental* sound.

1. **i**, like *i* in police. Examples: **hilo, camino, piso.**

   a) When **i** is the first member of a diphthong, it is a semicon-

---

[1] This abbreviation placed before a word or phrase *does not apply* to definitions beyond the semicolon.

sonant and is pronounced like the English *y* in *year, yes:* ie, ia, io, iu. Examples: bien, diablo, sabio, ciudad.

b) When i is the second member of a diphthong, it is a semivowel: ei, ai, oi, ui. (At the end of a word the first three diphthongs are written: ey, ay, oy.) They have the following approximate English equivalents: ei, like the *ey* in *they;* ai, like the *i* in *wife;* oi, like the *oy* in *toy;* ui, like *we.* Note that the i in these diphthongs is closer and more tense than in English. Examples: aceite, ley; baile, hay; heroico, hoy; cuida.

2. e, like *e* in *they,* but without diphthongal glide. Examples: tela, mesa, este. However, it is more open before rr and before r plus consonant: perro, terco, cerdo.

3. a, like the first *a* in *mama* (if accented on first syllable). Examples: caso, cano; ¡ah!

4. o, like the *o* in *low,* but without diphthongal glide. Examples: boda, hablo, modo. However, it is more open before rr and before r plus consonant: corro, porte, torpe.

5. u, like the *u* in *rude,* or *oo* in *fool.* Examples: cura, agudo, uno.

a) Note that the u is silent in the following combinations: qui, que, gui, gue.

b) When u is the first member of a diphthong, it is a semiconsonant and is pronounced like the English *w* in *wet:* ui, ue, ua, uo. Examples: cuida, cuento, cuadro, cuota.

c) When u is the second member of a diphthong, it is a semivowel and has the following approximate English equivalents: iu, like the *ew* in *few;* au, like the *ou* in *foul;* eu has no equivalent. Note that the u in these diphthongs is closer and more tense than in English. Examples: ciudad, deuda, causa.

II. THE CONSONANTS

1. p

Spanish p has *approximately* the same sound as in English, but it is weaker and less explosive. It is similar to the English *p* in *open, April.* Examples: padre, capa, apuro, punto.

NOTE—
a) In ordinary speech p is generally omitted in septiembre, séptimo, suscriptor.
b) It is not pronounced, except in affected speech, in the initial group ps: psicología.

2. b and v

These two letters have identically the same sound in Spanish.

a) When initial in a breath group,[1] or when preceded by **m** or **n**, Spanish **b** or **v** is pronounced by bringing the lips lightly together. In English the lips are tightly pressed in pronouncing the *b*, but in Spanish there is only a slight pressure, except in emphatic utterance. It is similar to the English *b* in an unstressed syllable, as in *abolition*. Examples: **bomba, en vez de, vine, invierno.**

b) When not initial in a breath group, and when within a word (except after **m** or **n**), Spanish **b** or **v** is like neither English *b* nor English *v*. It is pronounced by bringing the lips as near together as possible without completely closing them. Examples: **hablar, haba, la vaca, la bella, hervir.**

3. m

Spanish **m** has approximately the same sound as the English *m* in *much*. Examples: **madre, mano, cama.** Final **m** is generally pronounced as an **n** in such foreign or learned words as: **álbum, memorándum.**

4. f

Spanish **f** is similar to the English *f* in *few, floor*. Examples: **fuente, afán, flor.**

5. t

In the articulation of Spanish **t** the tongue touches the inner surface of the upper front teeth, while in English the tongue touches slightly above the gums. The *t*-sound in Spanish is more vigorous, tense, and precise and is not pronounced with audible breath as in English. It is similar to the English *t* in *stun, astonish, stupid*. Examples: **tela, tino, tinta.**

6. d

Spanish **d** has three sounds:

a) When initial in a breath group, or when preceded by **l** or **n**, Spanish **d** is somewhat like English *d*, but it is less explosive. It is similar to the *d* in *colder, elude, idle, yesterday*. Examples: **donde, falda, conde.**

b) When not initial in a breath group, and when within a word (except after **l** or **n**), **d** is like the English *th* in *then*, but it is pronounced by projecting the tongue out between the teeth, leaving a small opening for the air to escape so that the ar-

[1] A "breath group" is a word or group of words pronounced between pauses or breaths.

ticulation is very feeble. Examples: **hado, cuerda, hablado.** Note that **d** has this sound also in intervocalic **dr: padre, cuadro.**

c) When at the end of a word, it has the same sound as inter-vocalic **d**, but it is pronounced weakly and half-whispered. Examples: **abad, Madrid.**

7. z

In Castilian Spanish **z** is similar to the *th* in *thin*; but in Spanish America it is commonly pronounced as the *s* in *sane*. This sound is represented in Spanish by **z** before **a, o, u,** and **c** before **e** and **i: ci, ce, za, zo, zu.** The letter **z** is very seldom used before **e** or **i.** Examples: **ciento, cerro, zagal, zorro, azul.**

8. s

Spanish **s** has two sounds:

a) When initial or intervocalic, **s** is approximately the same as the English *s* in *son* or the *ss* in *essence*, but the articulation is more feeble. When final in a syllable or word, **s** is weak and brief; in certain regions it is hardly pronounced. Examples: **sonido, sano, cosa, casas, hasta.**

b) When **s** is followed by a voiced consonant (**b, v, d, m, n, l, g, r**), it is similar to the English *s* in *rose*, but it is only half-voiced and brief and is never prolonged as in English. In certain regions this Spanish voiced **s** is reduced to a breath sound or *h*. Examples: **mismo, desde, es verde, los labios.**

9. l

Spanish **l** has practically one sound, whether it is initial, inter-vocalic, or final. It is similar to the English *l* when initial, as in *late, light*, but it is pronounced more precisely and forcefully. Examples: **lado, ala, farol.**

10. n

Spanish **n** has four sounds:

a) Spanish **n**, except in the cases listed below, has approximately the same sound as the English *n* in *no* or *enter*; however, the intervocalic **n** is more tense and precise in Spanish than in English. Examples: **no, nada, mano.**

b) Before **b, v,** or **p** it is pronounced like an **m: envidia, en vez de, en Barcelona, en paz.**

c) Before **f** it is similar to the English *m* in *comfort*. Examples: **enfermo, confiado.**

d) Before **ca, co, cu, que, qui, g** and **j** it is similar to the English *n* in *ankle, angle.* Examples: **anca, banco, aunque, tengo, mango, conjugar.**

11. **ll**

This symbol represents one sound. The nearest English equivalent is a blending of *l* and *y* as in *will you*, pronounced rapidly. This sound is often reduced to a *y* as in *York*. Examples: **calle, pillo.** In certain regions **ll** is pronounced like the *y* in paragraph 14,*b*.

12. **ñ**

Spanish **ñ** is formed by the blending of *n* and *y* as in *can you.* The tongue must be placed in the *y* position and the *n* and *y* sounded at the same time. Examples: **cañón, año.**

13. **ch**

Spanish **ch** has approximately the same sound as the English *ch* in *choose, choice, cheek.* Examples: **chato, chaleco, mucho.**

14. **y**

a) Spanish **y** is similar to the English *y* in *yawn*, but it is pronounced with a stronger palatal friction. Examples: **ayer, leyes.** The combination **hie** is equal to **ye: hierba (yerba).**

b) In some regions the **y** is similar to a sound midway between the *j* in *joy* and the *z* in *azure.* This tendency is especially noticeable in Argentina and Uruguay.

c) For the pronunciation of final **y** see paragraph 1,*b*.

15. **x**

a) Spanish **x** between vowels in emphatic pronunciation is similar to the English *x* in *axle.* Note that the **x** in **México** is pronounced like a **j**. See paragraph 20.

b) Before a consonant **x** is given the sound of *gss* by careful speakers. In ordinary speech it is pronounced like the *s* in *sane.* Examples: **explicar, exterminar.**

16. **c**

Spanish **c** has two sounds:

a) Spanish **c** before **a, o, u** (or before **l** or **r**) is similar to the English *k* sound, but it is less explosive. Examples: **casa, cosa, cuna, aclamar, crudo.** This *k* sound before **e** and **i** is represented by **qu: quinto, queso.** Before **t** or **c** in ordinary speech, **c** is pronounced like a soft *k*, so that **acto** sounds like *agto*, **recto** like *regto*.

b) For the pronunciation of the **c** before **e** and **i** see paragraph 7.

17. k

There is no letter **k** in Spanish except in words of foreign deriva-
tion: **kilo, kilómetro.** This sound is represented in Spanish by
c before **a, o, u,** and by **qu** before **e** and **i: ca, co, cu, qui,
que.** See paragraph 16,*a.*

18. q

This letter is used only in the combinations **qui, que.** See paragraph 16,*a.*

19. g

Spanish **g** has three sounds:

a) g before **a, o, u,** when initial in a breath group, or after **n,** has
approximately the sound of the English *g* in *agony:* **gato,
goma, guarda, mango, tengo.** The **u** is not sounded in
gue or **gui** unless these syllables are written **güe, güi: guerra,
guitarra; agüero, argüir.**

b) When not initial of a breath group and when within a word
(except after **n**), the Spanish **g** has no equivalent in English.
The articulation of this sound is similar to the initial **g,** but
the contact of the tongue with the palate is loose, and the breath
passing through the narrow passage produces a slight friction.
Examples: **la guerra, agua, lago, averigüe, fragua.**

c) For the pronunciation of **g** before **e** or **i** see paragraph 20.

20. j

Spanish **j** has no exact equivalent in English. It is a strongly
aspirated *h* or a guttural sound, produced by forcing voiceless
breath through a loose contact of the back of the tongue with
the soft palate. The sound is represented by **j** before **a, o, u,** (and
occasionally before **e** or **i**) and by **g** before **e** and **i: gi, ge, ja, jo,
ju.** Examples: **giro, gema, jalar, jovial, jugo.**

21. h

This letter is not pronounced in Spanish.

22. r and rr

Spanish **r** has little in common with English *r.* It has two sounds:

a) Within a word (when not preceded by **l, n,** or **s**), **r** is similar
in articulation to English **tt** as in **kitty** pronounced rapidly. The
articulation requires one single flip of the tongue tip against
the ridge of the gums. Examples: **caro, farol, mero.**

b) Single **r** at the beginning of a word, **rr** within a word, and **r** preceded by **l**, **n**, or **s** have the same position of formation as the **r** described above, but they are strongly trilled. Examples: **rico, ronda, alrededor, honra, Enrique, correr.**

III. ACCENT OR STRESS

1. *Syllabic stress*

   a) Words ending in a vowel, or in **n** or **s**, are accented on the next to the last syllable: **madre, hablan, campos.**

   b) Words ending in a consonant other than **n** or **s** are accented on the last syllable: **farol, calidad, hablar.**

   c) Words that do not conform to the above rules must have the written accent over the vowel to be stressed: **café, cortés, acción, alemán, teléfono, último, cónsul.**

   d) The written accent is also used to distinguish words that are written alike but have different meanings: **de** (the preposition "of"), **dé** (subjunctive of **dar**); **este** (the demonstrative adjective "this"), **éste** (the demonstrative pronoun "this one", "the latter"); **el** (the definite article "the"), **él** (the pronoun "he").

2. *Syllable division*

   a) When consonant and vowel alternate, the division is always after the vowel: **ma-má, ca-lle, ni-ño, ca-mi-no, mu-cho.**

   b) Generally, two consonants within a word are divided as follows: **cal-ma, cos-ta, pal-co, ac-ción.** (Note that **s** plus a consonant cannot begin a syllable in Spanish). These groups, however, are pronounced with the following vowel: **pl, pr, bl, br, fl, fr, tl, tr, dr, cl, cr, gl, gr.** Examples: **a-fli-gir, co-fre, a-pla-nar, pa-dre, a-bra-zo.**[1]

   c) Three adjacent consonants are always divided, the last two going with the following vowel whenever possible: **hom-bre, com-pren-der, cons-tan-te.** (Note that **s** plus a consonant cannot begin a syllable in Spanish.)

THE NOUN

I. GENDER[3]

A. *Masculine Gender*

1. Names of male beings are naturally masculine: **el hombre** the

---

[1] In printing it is customary to avoid leaving a lone vowel at the end of a line Divide thus: **afli-gir, apla-nar, abra-zo.**

[3] There is no general rule for the gender of nouns that are not treated in this section.

man; **el muchacho** the boy; **el tío** the uncle; **el rey** the king;
el buey the ox.

2. Nouns ending in **-o** are masculine: **el libro** the book; **el banco**
the bank. *Exception*: **la mano** the hand.

3. Days of the week, months, rivers, oceans, and mountains are
masculine: **el martes** Tuesday; **enero** January; **el Pacífico** the
Pacific; **el Rin** the Rhine; **los Andes** the Andes.

4. Many nouns ending in **-l** or **-r**, and nouns of Greek origin ending
in **-ma** are masculine: **el papel** the paper; **el azúcar** the sugar;
el favor the favor; **el drama** the drama. *Common exceptions*: **la
miel** the honey; **la sal** the salt; **la catedral** the cathedral; **la
flor** the flower. Note that **mar** is both masculine and feminine.

B. *Feminine Gender*

1. Names of female persons or animals are naturally feminine: **la
mujer** the woman; **la muchacha** the girl; **la tía** the aunt; **la
vaca** the cow.

2. Nouns ending in **-a** are feminine: **la pluma** the pen; **la carta**
the letter; **la casa** the house. *Common exceptions*: **el día** the day;
el mapa the map; nouns of Greek origin ending in **-ma**:
el dogma the dogma; **el programa** the program.

3. Letters of the alphabet are feminine: **la e**, **la s**, **la t**.

4. Nouns ending in **-ión**, **-tad**, **-dad**, **-tud**, **-umbre** are feminine:
la canción the song; **la facultad** the faculty; **la ciudad** the city;
la virtud the virtue; **la muchedumbre** the crowd. *Exceptions*:
el gorrión the sparrow; **el sarampión** the measles.

C. *Formation of the Feminine*

1. Nouns ending in **-o** change **o** to **a**: **tío** uncle, **tía** aunt; **niño**
boy, **niña** girl.

2. Nouns ending in **-ón**, **-or**, and **-án** add **a**: **patrón** patron, **patrona** patroness; **pastor** shepherd, **pastora** shepherdess; **holgazán** lazy man, **holgazana** lazy woman.

3. Certain nouns have a special form for the feminine: **el poeta, la
poetisa; el cantante, la cantatriz; el sacerdote, la sacer-
dotisa; el emperador, la emperatriz; el abad, la abadesa;
el conde, la condesa; el duque, la duquesa.**

Note that (*a*) some nouns have different genders according to their meanings: **el corte** the cut or the cutting edge; **la corte** the court; **el guía** the
guide; **la guía** the guidebook; **el capital** the capital (money); **la capital**
the capital (city); (*b*) some nouns have invariable endings which are used
for both the masculine and the feminine: **artista** (and all nouns ending in

-ista), amante, mártir, testigo, reo, demócrata, aristócrata, intérprete, consorte, comensal, homicida, suicida, indígena, cómplice,
cliente.

II. PLURAL OF NOUNS[1]

1. Nouns ending in an unaccented vowel add -s to form the plural:
   el libro, los libros; la casa, las casas.

2. Nouns ending in a consonant, in -y, or in an accented vowel
   add -es: el papel, los papeles; la canción, las canciones: la
   ley, las leyes; el rubí, los rubíes. The accepted plural, however, of papá is papás, and of mamá is mamás.

3. Nouns ending in unaccented -es and -is do not change in the
   plural: el lunes Monday, los lunes Mondays; la tesis the
   thesis, las tesis the theses.

   Note that (a) nouns ending in -z change z to c before -es: lápiz, lápices;
   (b) nouns ending in -ión lose the written accent in the plural: canción,
   canciones.

THE ADJECTIVE AND ADVERB

I. THE ADJECTIVE

A. *Agreement.* The adjective in Spanish agrees in gender and number
with the noun it modifies: el lápiz rojo the red pencil; la casa blanca
the white house; los libros interesantes the interesting books; las
muchachas hermosas the beautiful girls.

B. *Formation of the plural.* Adjectives follow the same rules as nouns
for the formation of the plural: pálido, pálidos pale; fácil, fáciles
easy; cortés, corteses courteous; capaz, capaces capable.

C. *Formation of the feminine.*

1. Adjectives ending in -o change o to a: blanco, blanca.

2. Adjectives ending in other vowels are invariable: verde green;
   fuerte strong; indígena indigenous, native; pesimista pessimistic;
   baladí trivial.

3. Adjectives ending in a consonant are invariable: fácil easy; cortés
   courteous. *Exceptions:* (a) adjectives ending in -ón, -án, -or (except comparatives) add a to form the feminine: holgazán, holgazana lazy; preguntón, preguntona inquisitive; hablador, habladora talkative (Note that mayor, mejor, menor, peor, superior, inferior, exterior, interior, anterior, and posterior are
   invariable. Superior adds an a when it is used as a noun meaning

[1] The plurals of certain masculine nouns may include the masculine and
feminine genders: los padres the father(s) and mother(s), the parents; los tíos
the uncle(s) and aunt(s); los reyes the king(s) and queen(s).

"mother superior.") (b) adjectives of nationality ending in a consonant add a to form the feminine: **francés, francesa** French; **español, española** Spanish; **alemán, alemana** German; **inglés, inglesa** English.

II. THE ADVERB

Many adverbs are formed by adding **-mente** to the feminine form of the adjective: **claro, claramente; lento, lentamente; fácil, fácilmente.**

III. COMPARISON OF ADJECTIVES AND ADVERBS

A. *Comparative of inequality.* The comparative of inequality is formed by placing **más** or **menos** before the positive form of the adjective or adverb: **más rico que** richer than; **menos rico que** less rich than; **más tarde** later; **menos tarde** less late. The superlative is formed by placing the definite article **el** before the comparative: **el más rico** the richest; **el menos rico** the least rich. Note the position of the article in the following examples: **la niña más linda** or **la más linda niña** the prettiest girl.

The following adjectives and adverbs have in addition irregular forms of comparison:

Positive	Comparative	Superlative
bueno	mejor	el (la) mejor
malo	peor	el (la) peor
grande	mayor	el (la) mayor
pequeño	menor	el (la) menor
alto	superior	supremo
bajo	inferior	ínfimo
mucho	más	
poco	menos	

B. *Comparative of equality.* With adjectives and adverbs the comparative of equality is formed with **tan ... como: tan fácil como** as easy as; **tan bien como** as well as; with nouns the comparative of equality is formed with **tanto (tanta, tantos, tantas) ... como: tanto dinero como** as much money as; **tantas personas como** as many people as.

C. *Absolute superlative of adjectives.* The absolute superlative of adjectives is formed by placing **muy** (very) before the adjective or by adding the suffix **-ísimo:**

Positive	Absolute Superlative
feliz	muy feliz, felicísimo
fácil	muy fácil, facilísimo
importante	muy importante, importantísimo

Positive	*Absolute Superlative*
limpio	muy limpio, limpísimo
feo	muy feo, feísimo
rico	muy rico, riquísimo
largo	muy largo, larguísimo
notable	muy notable, notabilísimo

A few adjectives have, in addition, other forms derived from the Latin superlatives:

bueno	muy bueno, bonísimo[1], óptimo
malo	muy malo, malísimo, pésimo
grande	muy grande, grandísimo, máximo
pequeño	muy pequeño, pequeñísimo, mínimo

Some adjectives ending in **-ro** or **-re** revert to the corresponding Latin superlative:

acre	muy acre, acérrimo
célebre	muy célebre, celebérrimo
mísero	muy mísero, misérrimo
salubre	muy salubre, salubérrimo

D. *Absolute superlative of adverbs.* The absolute superlative of adverbs not ending in **-mente** is formed in the same manner as that of adjectives:

tarde	muy tarde, tardísimo
pronto	muy pronto, prontísimo
mucho	muchísimo
poco	poquísimo
cerca	muy cerca, cerquísima
lejos	muy lejos, lejísimos

Superlative adverbs ending in -mente are formed by adding the suffix -ísima to the corresponding feminine adjective:

claramente	muy claramente, clarísimamente
noblemente	muy noblemente, nobilísimamente

COMMON SPANISH SUFFIXES

I. DIMINUTIVES

The most common diminutive endings in Spanish are:

-ito, -ita	(-cito, -cita, -ecito, -ecita). Examples: **librito** (from **libro**), **casita** (from **casa**), **corazoncito** (from **corazón**), **mujercita** (from **mujer**), **cochecito** (from **coche**), **florecita** (from **flor**).
-illo, -illa	(-cillo, -cilla, -ecillo, -ecilla). Examples: **corderillo** (from **cordero**), **dolorcillo** (from **dolor**), **viejecillo** (from **viejo**), **piedrecilla** (from **piedra**).

[1] Also buenísimo.

-ico, -ica	(**-cico, -cica, -ecico, -ecica**). Examples: **niñico** (from **niño**), **hermanica** (from **hermana**), **corazoncico** (from **corazón**), **mujercica** (from **mujer**), **pobrecico** (from **pobre**).
-uelo, -uela	(**-zuelo, -zuela, -ezuelo, -ezuela**). Examples: **arroyuelo** (from **arroyo**), **mozuela** (from **moza**), **mujerzuela** (from **mujer**), **reyezuelo** (from **rey**), **piedrezuela** (from **piedra**).
-ete, -eta.	Examples: **vejete** (from **viejo**), **vejeta** (from **vieja**).
-uco, -uca.	Example: **casuca** (from **casa**).
-ucho, -ucha.	Examples: **serrucho** (from **sierra**), **casucha** (from **casa**).

II. Augmentatives

The most common augmentative endings in Spanish are:

-acho, -acha.	Example: **ricacho** (from **rico**).
-azo, -aza.	Examples: **gigantazo** (from **gigante**), **bribonazo** (from **bribón**), **manaza** (from **mano**), **bocaza** (from **boca**).
-ón, -ona.	Examples: **hombrón** (from **hombre**), **mujerona** (from **mujer**), **almohadón** (from **almohada**), **borrachón** (from **borracho**).
-ote, -ota.	Examples: **grandote** (from **grande**), **muchachote** (from **muchacho**), **muchachota** (from **muchacha**).

III. Depreciatives

The most common depreciative endings in Spanish are:

-aco, -aca.	Example: **pajarraco** ugly bird.
-ejo, -eja.	Example: **librejo** old, worthless book.

Note that a depreciative or ironic connotation is often conveyed by many of the augmentatives and by the diminutive endings **-uelo, -ete, -uco, -ucho, -illo.**

IV. Other Suffixes

-ada	*a*) is sometimes equal to the English suffix *-ful:* **cucharada** spoonful; **palada** shovelful;
	b) often indicates a blow: **puñada** blow with the fist; **puñalada** stab or blow with a dagger; **topetada** butt, blow with the head;

	c) indicates a group or a crowd of: **peonada** a group or crowd of peons; **indiada** a group or crowd of Indians.
-al, -ar	denote a grove, field, plantation or orchard: **naranjal** orange grove; **cauchal** rubber plantation; **pinar** pine grove.
	indicates a blow or explosion: **puñetazo** blow with the fist; **topetazo** butt, blow with the head; **escobazo** blow with a broom; **cañonazo** cannon shot.
-dad, -tad	are suffixes forming many abstract nouns and are usually equivalent to the English suffix -*ty*: **fraternidad** fraternity; **facultad** faculty; **cantidad** quantity; **calidad** quality.
-dizo	is an adjective-forming suffix which means sometimes *tending to*, or *in the habit of*: **resbaladizo** slippery; **olvidadizo** forgetful; **enojadizo** irritable, easily angered; **asustadizo** easily frightened, scary, timid; **movedizo** movable.
-ería	*a*) denotes a place where something is made or sold: **panadería** bakery; **librería** bookstore; **zapatería** shoestore; **pastelería** pastry shop; *b*) indicates a profession, business or occupation: **carpintería** carpentry; **ingeniería** engineering; *c*) means sometimes a collection: **pastelería** pastry, pastries; *d*) is sometimes equivalent to English suffix -*ness*; it also suggests a single act or action: **tontería** foolishness; foolish act; **niñería** childishness; childish act.
-ero	*a*) indicates a person who makes, sells, or is in charge of: **panadero** baker; **librero** bookseller; **zapatero** shoemaker; **carcelero** jailer; **cajero** cashier; *b*) is an adjective-forming suffix: **parlero** talkative; **guerrero** warlike.
-ez, -eza	are used to make abstract nouns: **vejez** old age; **niñez** childhood; **viudez** widowhood; **grandeza** greatness.
-ía	*a*) is the ending of the names of many arts and

sciences: **geología** geology; **geometría** geometry; **biología** biology;

b) see **-ería.**

-iento indicates a *resemblance*, or a *tendency to*: **ceniciento** ashlike; **soñoliento** sleepy, drowsy.

-ísimo is the ending of the absolute superlative: **hermosísimo** very beautiful.

-izo is a suffix meaning *tending to* or *somewhat*: **rojizo** reddish. See **-dizo.**

-mente is the adverbial ending attached to the feminine form of the adjective: **generosamente** generously; **claramente** clearly.

-ón *a)* is an augmentative suffix;

b) is also a suffix without an augmentative force, meaning *in the habit of*, or *full of*: **juguetón** playful; **preguntón** full of questions, inquisitive; **llorón** tearful; crybaby;

c) indicates suddenness or violence of an action: **estirón** pull, tug, jerk; **apretón** squeeze.

-or, -dor *a)* are equivalent to the English suffixes *-or, -er,* and indicate the agent or doer: **hablador** talker; **regulador** regulator;

b) may also be used as adjectives: **hablador** talkative; **regulador** regulating.

-oso is an adjective-forming suffix which usually means *having, full of,* or *characterized by*: **rocoso** rocky; **tormentoso** stormy; **fangoso** muddy; **herboso** grassy; **lluvioso** rainy; **maravilloso** marvelous; **famoso** famous.

-udo is an adjective-forming suffix meaning *having* or *characterized by*: **zancudo** long-legged; **peludo** hairy; **panzudo** big-bellied; **caprichudo** stubborn.

-ura is a suffix forming many abstract nouns: **negrura** blackness; **blancura** whiteness; **altura** height; **lisura** smoothness.

-uzco indicates *resemblance* or *a tendency to*; it is akin to the English suffix *-ish*: **blancuzco** whitish; **negruzco** blackish.

SPANISH IRREGULAR AND ORTHOGRAPHIC CHANGING VERBS

The superior number, or numbers, after a verb entry indicate that it is conjugated like the model verb in this section which has the corresponding number. Only the tenses which have irregular forms or spelling changes are given. The irregular forms and spelling changes are shown in bold-face type.

1. pensar (if stressed, the stem vowel e becomes ie)

    Pres. Indic. **pienso, piensas, piensa,** pensamos, pensáis, **piensan.**

    Pres. Subj. **piense, pienses, piense,** pensemos, penséis, **piensen.**

    Imper. **piensa** tú, **piense** Vd., pensemos nosotros, pensad vosotros, **piensen** Vds.

2. contar (if stressed, the stem vowel o becomes ue)

    Pres. Indic. **cuento, cuentas, cuenta,** contamos, contáis, **cuentan.**

    Pres. Subj. **cuente, cuentes, cuente,** contemos, contéis, **cuenten.**

    Imper. **cuenta** tú, **cuente** Vd. contemos nosotros, contad vosotros, **cuenten** Vds.

3. *a)* sentir (if stressed, the stem vowel e becomes ie; if unstressed, the stem vowel e becomes i when the following syllable contains stressed a, ie, or ió)

    Pres. Indic. **siento, sientes, siente,** sentimos, sentís, **sienten.**

    Pres. Subj. **sienta, sientas, sienta, sintamos, sintáis, sientan.**

    Pret. Indic. sentí, **sentiste,** sintió, sentimos, sentisteis, **sintieron.**

    Imp. Subj. **sintiera** or **sintiese, sintieras** or **sintieses, sintiera** or **sintiese, sintiéramos** or **sintiésemos, sintierais** or **sintieseis, sintieran** or **sintiesen.**

    Imper. **siente** tú, **sienta** Vd., **sintamos** nosotros, sentid vosotros, **sientan** Vds.

    Pres. Part. **sintiendo.**

    b) erguir (this verb has same vowel changes as *sentir*, but the initial i of the diphthong ie is changed to y. For regular spelling changes see No. 12,*a*)

    Pres. Indic. **yergo, yergues, yergue,** erguimos, erguís, **yerguen.**

    Pres. Subj. **yerga, yergas, yerga, irgamos, irgáis, yergan.**

    Pret. Indic. erguí, erguiste, **irguió,** erguimos, erguisteis, **irguieron.**

    Imp. Subj. **irguiera** or **irguiese, irguieras** or **irguieses, irguiera** or **irguiese, irguiéramos** or **irguiésemos, irguierais** or **irguieseis, irguieran** or **irguiesen.**

Imper. **yergue** tú, **yerga** Vd., **irgamos** nosotros, erguid vosotros, **yergan** Vds.
Pres. Part. **irguiendo.**

4. dormir (if stressed, the stem vowel **o** becomes **ue**; if unstressed,
   the stem vowel **o** becomes **u** when the following syllable contains
   stressed **a, ie,** or **ió**)
   Pres. Indic. **duermo, duermes, duerme,** dormimos, dormís,
      duermen.
   Pres. Subj. **duerma, duermas, duerma, durmamos, durmáis,**
      duerman.
   Pret. Indic. dormí, dormiste, **durmió,** dormimos, dormisteis,
      durmieron.
   Imp. Subj. **durmiera** or **durmiese, durmieras** or **durmieses,**
      durmiera or **durmiese, durmiéramos** or **durmié-**
      semos, durmierais or **durmieseis, durmieran** or
      durmiesen.
   Imper. **duerme** tú, **duerma** Vd., **durmamos** nosotros, dormid
      vosotros, **duerman** Vds.
   Pres. Part. **durmiendo.**

5. pedir (if stressed, the stem vowel **e** becomes **i**; if unstressed, the
   stem vowel **e** becomes **i** when the following syllable contains
   stressed **a, ie,** or **ió**)
   Pres. Indic. **pido, pides, pide,** pedimos, pedís, **piden.**
   Pres. Subj. **pida, pidas, pida, pidamos, pidáis, pidan.**
   Pret. Indic. pedí, pediste, **pidió,** pedimos, pedisteis, **pidieron.**
   Imp. Subj. **pidiera** or **pidiese, pidieras** or **pidieses, pidiera** or
      pidiese, pidiéramos or **pidiésemos, pidierais** or
      pidieseis, pidieran or **pidiesen.**
   Imper. **pide** tú, **pida** Vd., **pidamos** nosotros, pedid vosotros,
      pidan Vds.
   Pres. Part. **pidiendo.**

6. buscar (verbs ending in **car** change **c** to **qu** before **e**)
   Pres. Subj. **busque, busques, busque, busquemos, bus-**
      quéis, busquen.
   Pret. Indic. **busqué,** buscaste, buscó, buscamos, buscasteis,
      buscaron.
   Imper. busca tú, **busque** Vd., **busquemos** nosotros, buscad
      vosotros, **busquen** Vds.

7. llegar (verbs ending in **gar** change the g to gu before **e**)
   Pres. Subj. **llegue, llegues, llegue, lleguemos, lleguéis, lleguen.**
   Pres. Indic. **llegué,** llegaste, llegó, llegamos, llegasteis, llegaron.
   Imper. llega tú, **llegue** Vd., lleguemos nosotros, llegad vosotros, **lleguen** Vds.

8. averiguar (verbs ending in **guar** change the gu to gü before **e**)
   Pres. Subj. **averigüe, averigües, averigüe, averigüemos, averigüéis, averigüen.**
   Pret. Indic. **averigüé,** averiguaste, averiguó, averiguamos, averiguasteis, averiguaron.
   Imper. averigua tú, **averigüe** Vd., **averigüemos** nosotros, averiguad vosotros, **averigüen** Vds.

9. abrazar (verbs ending in **zar** change z to c before **e**)
   Pres. Subj. **abrace, abraces, abrace, abracemos, abracéis, abracen.**
   Pret. Indic. **abracé,** abrazaste, abrazó, abrazamos, abrazasteis, abrazaron.
   Imper. abraza tú, **abrace** Vd., **abracemos** nosotros, abrazad vosotros, **abracen** Vds.

10. *a)* convencer (verbs ending in **cer** preceded by a consonant change **c** to **z** before a and o)
    Pres. Indic. **convenzo,** convences, convence, convencemos, convencéis, convencen.
    Pres. Subj. **convenza, convenzas, convenza, convenzamos, convenzáis, convenzan.**
    Imper. convence tú, **convenza** Vd., **convenzamos** nosotros, convenced vosotros, **convenzan** Vds.

    b) esparcir (verbs ending in **cir** preceded by a consonant change **c** to **z** before a and o)
    Pres. Indic. **esparzo,** esparces, esparce, esparcimos, esparcís, esparcen.
    Pres. Subj. **esparza, esparzas, esparza, esparzamos, esparzáis, esparzan.**
    Imper. esparce tú, **esparza** Vd., **esparzamos** nosotros, esparcid vosotros, **esparzan** Vds.

    c) mecer (some verbs ending in **cer** preceded by a vowel change **c** to **z** before a and o; see No. 13)
    Pres. Indic. **mezo,** meces, mece, mecemos, mecéis, mecen.

Pres. Subj. **meza, mezas, meza, mezamos, mezáis, mezan.**
Imper. mece tú, **meza** Vd., **mezamos** nosotros, meced vosotros, **mezan** Vds.

11. *a*) dirigir (verbs ending in **gir** change **g** to **j** before **a** and **o**)
   Pres. Indic. **dirijo,** diriges, dirige, dirigimos, dirigís, dirigen.
   Pres. Subj. **dirija, dirijas, dirija, dirijamos, dirijáis, dirijan.**
   Imper. dirige tú, **dirija** Vd., **dirijamos** nosotros, dirigid vosotros, **dirijan** Vds.

   b) coger (verbs ending in **ger** change **g** to **j** before **o** and **a**)
   Pres. Indic. **cojo,** coges, coge, cogemos, cogéis, cogen.
   Pres. Subj. **coja, cojas, coja, cojamos, cojáis, cojan.**
   Imper. coge tú, **coja** Vd., **cojamos** nosotros, coged vosotros, **cojan** Vds.

12. *a*) distinguir (verbs ending in **guir** drop the **u** before **o** and **a**)
   Pres. Indic. **distingo,** distingues, distingue, distinguimos, distinguís, distinguen.
   Pres. Subj. **distinga, distingas, distinga, distingamos, distingáis, distingan.**
   Imper. distingue tú, **distinga** Vd., **distingamos** nosotros, distinguid vosotros, **distingan** Vds.

   b) delinquir (verbs ending in **quir** change **qu** to **c** before **o** and **a**)
   Pres. Indic. **delinco,** delinques, delinque, delinquimos, delinquís, delinquen.
   Pres. Subj. **delinca, delincas, delinca, delincamos, delincáis, delincan.**

13. *a*) conocer (verbs ending in **cer** when preceded by a vowel insert **z** before **c** when **c** is followed by **o** or **a**; see No. 10,*c*)
   Pres. Indic. **conozco,** conoces, conoce, conocemos, conocéis, conocen.
   Pres. Subj. **conozca, conozcas, conozca, conozcamos, conozcáis, conozcan.**
   Imper. conoce tú, **conozca** Vd., **conozcamos** nosotros, conoced vosotros, **conozcan** Vds.

   b) lucir (verbs ending in **cir** when preceded by a vowel insert **z** before **c** when **c** is followed by **o** or **a**; see No. 25)
   Pres. Indic. **luzco,** luces, luce, lucimos, lucís, lucen.
   Pres. Subj. **luzca, luzcas, luzca, luzcamos, luzcáis, luzcan.**
   Imper. luce tú, **luzca** Vd., **luzcamos** nosotros, lucid vosotros, **luzcan** Vds.

14. creer (unstressed i between vowels is regularly changed to y)
    Pret. Indic. creí, creíste, creyó, creímos, creísteis, creyeron.
    Imp. Subj. creyera or creyese, creyeras or creyeses, creyera
          or creyese, creyéramos or creyésemos, creyerais
          or creyeseis, creyeran or creyesen.
    Pres. Part. creyendo.

15. reír (like No. 5, except that when the i of the stem would be
    followed by ie or ió the two i's are reduced to one)
    Pres. Indic. río, ríes, ríe, reímos, reís, ríen.
    Pres. Subj. ría, rías, ría, riamos, riáis, rían.
    Pret. Indic. reí, reíste, rió, reímos, reísteis, rieron.
    Imp. Subj. riera, or riese, rieras or rieses, riera, or riese, riéra-
          mos or riésemos, rierais or rieseis, rieran or riesen.
    Imper. ríe tú, ría Vd., ríamos nosotros, reíd vosotros, rían Vds.
    Pres. Part. riendo.

16. podrir or pudrir
    Pres. Indic. pudro, pudres, pudre, podrimos or pudrimos, po-
          drís or pudrís, pudren.
    Pres. Subj. pudra, pudras, pudra, pudramos, pudráis,
          pudran.
    Imp. Indic. pudría or podría, etc. (Seldom *podría* because of con-
          fusion with *poder*)
    Pret. Indic. podrí or pudrí, podriste or pudriste, pudrió, podri-
          mos or pudrimos, podristeis or pudristeis, pudrieron.
    Imp. Subj. pudriera or pudriese, pudrieras or pudrieses,
          pudriera or pudriese, pudriéramos or pudriése-
          mos, pudrierais or pudrieseis, pudrieran or
          pudriesen.
    Fut. Indic. pudriré or podriré, etc.
    Cond. pudriría or podriría, etc.
    Pres. Part. pudriendo.
    Past. Part. podrido or pudrido.

17. enviar
    Pres. Indic. envío, envías, envía, enviamos, enviáis, envían.
    Pres. Subj. envíe, envíes, enviemos, enviéis, envíen.
    Imper. envía tú, envíe Vd., enviemos nosotros, enviad vosotros,
          envíen Vds.

18. continuar

    Pres. Indic. continúo, continúas, continúa, continuamos, conti-
nuáis, continúan.

    Pres. Subj. continúe, continúes, continúe, continuemos, conti-
nuéis, continúen.

    Imper. continúa tú, continúe Vd., continuemos nosotros, conti-
nuad vosotros, continúen Vds.

19. gruñir (i of the diphthong ie or ió is lost after ñ)

    Pret. Indic. gruñí, gruñiste, **gruñó**, gruñimos, gruñisteis, gru-
ñeron.

    Imp. Subj. gruñera or gruñese, gruñeras or gruñeses, gru-
ñera or gruñese, gruñéramos or gruñésemos, gru-
ñerais or gruñeseis, gruñeran or gruñesen.

    Pres. Part. gruñendo.

20. bullir (i of the diphthong ie or ió is lost after ll)

    Pret. Indic. bullí, bulliste, **bulló**, bullimos, bullisteis, **bulleron**.

    Imp. Subj. bullera or bullese, bulleras or bulleses, bullera or
bullese, bulléramos or bullésemos, bullerais or
bulleseis, bulleran or bullesen.

    Pres. Part. bullendo.

21. andar

    Pret. Indic. anduve, anduviste, anduvo, anduvimos, andu-
visteis, anduvieron.

    Imp. Subj. anduviera or anduviese, anduvieras or andu-
vieses, anduviera or anduviese, anduviéramos
anduviésemos, anduvierais or anduvieseis, andu-
vieran or anduviesen.

22. asir

    Pres. Indic. asgo, ases, ase, asimos, asís, asen.

    Pres. Subj. asga, asgas, asga, asgamos, asgáis, asgan.

    Imper. ase tú, asga Vd., asgamos nosotros, asid vosotros, as-
gan Vds.

23. caber

    Pres. Indic. quepo, cabes, cabe, cabemos, cabéis, caben.

    Pres. Subj. quepa, quepas, quepa, quepamos, quepáis,
quepan.

    Pret. Indic. cupe, cupiste, cupo, cupimos, cupisteis, cu-
pieron.

Imp. Subj. · cupiera or cupiese, cupieras or cupieses, cupiera
          or cupiese, cupiéramos or cupiésemos, cupierais
          or cupieseis, cupieran or cupiesen.
Fut. Indic. cabré, cabrás, cabrá, cabremos, cabréis, cabrán.
Cond. cabría, cabrías, cabría, cabríamos, cabríais, cabrían.
Imper. cabe tú, quepa Vd., quepamos nosotros, cabed vo-
          sotros, quepan Vds.

24. caer
Pres. Indic. caigo, caes, cae, caemos, caéis, caen.
Pres. Subj. caiga, caigas, caiga, caigamos, caigáis, caigan.
Pret. Indic. caí, caiste, cayó, caímos, caísteis, cayeron.
Imp. Subj. · cayera or cayese, cayeras or cayeses, cayera or
          cayese, cayéramos or cayésemos, cayerais or
          cayeseis, cayeran or cayesen.
Imper. cae tú, caiga Vd., caigamos nosotros, caed vosotros,
          caigan Vds.
Pres. Part. cayendo.

25. conducir (all verbs ending in **ducir** have the irregularities of
          conducir)
Pres. Indic. conduzco, conduces, conduce, conducimos, con-
          ducís, conducen.
Pres. Subj. conduzca, conduzcas, conduzca, conduzcamos,
          conduzcáis, conduzcan.
Pret. Indic. conduje, condujiste, condujo, condujimos, con-
          dujisteis, condujeron.
Imp. Subj. condujera or condujese, condujeras or condu-
          jeses, condujera or condujese, condujéramos or
          condujésemos, condujerais or condujeseis, con-
          dujeran or condujesen.
Imp. conduce tú, conduzca Vd., conduzcamos nosotros, con-
          ducid vosotros, conduzcan Vds.

26. dar
Pres. Indic. doy, das, da, damos, dais, dan.
Pres. Subj. dé, des, dé, demos, deis, den.
Pret. Indic. dí, diste, dió, dimos, disteis, dieron.
Imp. Subj. diera or diese, dieras or dieses, diera or diese, dié-
          ramos or diésemos, dierais or dieseis, dieran or
          diesen.

27. decir

Pres. Indic. digo, dices, dice, decimos, decís, dicen.
Pres. Subj. diga, digas, diga, digamos, digáis, digan.
Pret. Indic. dije, dijiste, dijo, dijimos, dijisteis, dijeron.
Imp. Subj. dijera or dijese, dijeras or dijeses, dijera or dijese, dijéramos or dijésemos, dijerais or dijeseis, dijeran or dijesen.
Fut. Indic. diré, dirás, dirá, diremos, diréis, dirán.
Cond. diría, dirías, diría, diríamos, diríais, dirían.
Imper. di tú, diga Vd., digamos nosotros, decid vosotros, digan Vds.
Pres. Part. diciendo.
Past. Part. dicho.

NOTE. The compound verbs of *decir* have the same irregularities with the exception of the following:

a) The future and conditional of the compound verbs *bendecir* and *maldecir* are regular: *bendeciré, maldeciré*, etc.; *bendeciría, maldeciría*, etc.
b) The familiar imperative is regular: *bendice tu, maldice tu, contradice tu*, etc.
c) The past participles of *bendecir* and *maldecir* are regular when used with *haber*: *bendecido, maldecido*; when used as an adjective with *estar*, the forms are: *bendito, maldito*.

28. errar (like No. 1, except that the initial *ie* is spelled *ye*)

Pres. Indic. yerro, yerras, yerra, erramos, erráis, yerran.
Pres. Subj. yerre, yerres, yerre, erremos, erréis, yerren.
Imper. yerra tu, yerre Vd., erremos nosotros, errad vosotros, yerren Vds.

29. estar

Pres. Indic. estoy, estás, está, estamos, estáis, están.
Pres. Subj. esté, estés, esté, estemos, estéis, estén.
Pret. Indic. estuve, estuviste, estuvo, estuvimos, estuvisteis, estuvieron.
Imp. Subj. estuviera or estuviese, estuvieras or estuvieses, estuviera or estuviese, estuviéramos or estuviésemos, estuvierais or estuvieseis, estuvieran or estuviesen.
Imper. está tú, esté Vd., estemos nosotros, estad vosotros, estén Vds.

30. haber

Pres. Indic. he, has, ha, hemos, habéis, han.
Pres. Subj. haya, hayas, haya, hayamos, hayáis, hayan.

Pret. Indic. hube, hubiste, hubo, hubimos, hubisteis, hu-
bieron.

Imp. Subj. hubiera or hubiese, hubieras or hubieses, hubiera
or hubiese, hubiéramos or hubiésemos, hubierais
or hubieseis, hubieran or hubiesen.

Fut. Indic. habré, habrás, habrá, habremos, habréis, habrán.

Cond. habría, habrías, habría, habríamos, habríais, habrían.

31. hacer

Pres. Indic. hago, haces, hace, hacemos, hacéis, hacen.

Pres. Subj. haga, hagas, haga, hagamos, hagáis, hagan.

Pret. Indic. hice, hiciste, hizo, hicimos, hicisteis, hicieron.

Imp. Subj. hiciera or hiciese, hicieras or hicieses, hiciera or
hiciese, hiciéramos or hiciésemos, hicierais or
hicieseis, hicieran or hiciesem.

Fut. Indic. haré, harás, hará, haremos, haréis, harán.

Cond. haría, harías, haría, haríamos, haríais, harían.

Imper. haz tú, haga Vd., hagamos nosotrós, haced vosotros,
hagan Vds.

Past. Part. hecho.

32. a) huir

Pres. Indic. huyo, huyes, huye, huimos, huís, huyen.

Pres. Subj. huya, huyas, huya, huyamos, huyáis, huyan.

Pret. Indic. huí, huiste, huyó, huimos, huisteis, huyeron.

Imp. Subj. huyera or huyese, huyeras or huyeses, huyera
or huyese, huyéramos or huyésemos, huyerais
or huyeseis, huyeran or huyesen.

Imper. huye tú, huya Vd., huyamos nosotros, huid vosotros,
huyan Vds.

Pres. Part. huyendo.

b) argüir

Pres. Indic. arguyo, arguyes, arguye, argüimos, argüís, ar-
guyen.

Pres. Subj. arguya, arguyas, arguya, arguyamos, arguyáis,
arguyan.

Pret. Indic. argüí, argüiste, arguyó, argüimos, argüisteis, ar-
guyeron.

Imp. Subj. arguyera or arguyese, arguyeras or arguyeses,
arguyera or arguyese, arguyéramos or arguyé-

semos, **arguyerais** or **arguyeseis, arguyeran** or
arguyesen.

Imper. **arguye** tú, **arguya** Vd., **arguyamos** nosotros, argüid
vosotros, **arguyan** Vds.

Pres. Part. **arguyendo.**

33. ir

Pres. Indic. **voy, vas, va, vamos, vais, van.**

Pres. Subj. **vaya, vayas, vaya, vayamos, vayáis, vayan.**

Imp. Indic. **iba, ibas, iba, íbamos, ibais, iban.**

Pret. Indic. **fuí, fuiste, fué, fuimos, fuisteis, fueron.**

Imp. Subj. **fuera** or **fuese, fueras** or **fueses, fuera** or **fuese,
fuéramos** or **fuésemos, fuerais** or **fueseis, fueran**
or **fuesen.**

Imper. **ve** tú, **vaya** Vd., **vayamos** (**vamos**) nosotros, id vosotros,
vayan Vds.

Pres. Part. **yendo.**

34. jugar (cf. Nos. 2 and 7)

Pres. Indic. **juego, juegas, juega,** jugamos, jugáis, **juegan.**

Pres. Subj. **juegue, juegues, juegue,** juguemos, juguéis,
jueguen.

Pret. Indic. **jugué,** jugaste, jugó, jugamos, jugasteis, jugaron.

Imper. **juega** tú, **juegue** Vd., juguemos nosotros, jugad vosotros, **jueguen** Vds.

35. adquirir

Pres. Indic. **adquiero, adquieres, adquiere,** adquirimos, ad-
quirís, **adquieren.**

Pres. Subj. **adquiera, adquieras, adquiera,** adquiramos, ad-
quiráis, **adquieran.**

Imper. **adquiere** tú, **adquiera** Vd., adquiramos nosotros, ad-
quirid vosotros, **adquieran** Vds.

36. oír

Pres. Indic. **oigo, oyes, oye,** oímos, oís, **oyen.**

Pres. Subj. **oiga, oigas, oiga, oigamos, oigáis, oigan.**

Pret. Indic. oí, oíste, **oyó,** oímos, oísteis, **oyeron.**

Imp. Subj. **oyera** or **oyese, oyeras** or **oyeses, oyera** or oyese,
oyéramos or **oyésemos, oyerais** or **oyeseis, oyeran**
or **oyesen.**

Imper. **oye** tú, **oiga** Vd., **oigamos** nosotros, oíd vosotros, **oigan**
Vds.

Pres. Part. **oyendo.**

37. oler (like No. 2, except that initial **ue** is spelled **hue**)
   Pres. Indic. **huelo, hueles, huele,** olemos, oléis, **huelen.**
   Pres. Subj. **huela, huelas, huela,** olamos, oláis, **huelan.**
   Imper. **huele tú, huela Vd.,** olamos nosotros, oled vosotros, **huelan Vds.**

38. placer
   Pres. Indic.: **plazco,** places, place, placemos, placéis, placen.
   Pres. Subj.: **plazca, plazcas, plazca, plazcamos, plazcáis, plazcan.** (There are also the antiquated forms, **plegue** and **plega,** used now only in the third person in poetic language.)
   Pret. Indic. In addition to the regular forms, there is the antiquated form **plugo,** used now only in poetic language.
   Imp. Subj. In addition to the regular forms, there are the antiquated forms, **pluguiera** and **pluguiese,** used now only in poetic language.

39. poder
   Pres. Indic. **puedo, puedes, puede,** podemos, podéis, **pueden.**
   Pres. Subj. **pueda, puedas, pueda,** podamos, podáis, **puedan.**
   Pret. Indic. **pude, pudiste, pudo, pudimos, pudisteis, pudieron.**
   Imp. Subj. **pudiera** or **pudiese, pudieras** or **pudieses, pudiera** or **pudiese, pudiéramos** or **pudiésemos, pudierais** or **pudieseis, pudieran** or **pudiesen.**
   Fut. Indic. **podré, podrás, podrá, podremos, podréis, podrán.**
   Cond. **podría, podrías, podría, podríamos, podríais, podrían.**
   Pres. Part. **pudiendo.**

40. poner
   Pres. Indic. **pongo,** pones, pone, ponemos, ponéis, ponen.
   Pres. Subj. **ponga, pongas, ponga, pongamos, pongáis, pongan.**
   Pret. Indic. **puse, pusiste, puso, pusimos, pusisteis, pusieron.**
   Imp. Subj. **pusiera** or **pusiese, pusieras** or **pusieses, pusiera** or **pusiese, pusiéramos** or **pusiésemos, pusierais** or **pusieseis, pusieran** or **pusiesen.**
   Fut. Indic. **pondré, pondrás, pondrá, pondremos, pondréis, pondrán.**
   Cond. **pondría, pondrías, pondría, pondríamos, pondríais, pondrían.**

Imper. **pon** tú, **ponga** Vd., **pongamos** nosotros, poned vosotros, pongan Vds.

Past Part. **puesto.**

41. querer

Pres. Indic. **quiero, quieres, quiere,** queremos, queréis, quieren.

Pres. Subj. **quiera, quieras, quiera,** queramos, queráis, **quieren.**

Pret. Indic. **quise, quisiste, quiso, quisimos, quisisteis, quisieron.**

Imp. Subj. **quisiera** or **quisiese, quisieras** or **quisieses, quisiera** or **quisiese, quisiéramos** or **quisiémos, quisierais** or **quisieseis, quisieran** or **quisiesen.**

Fut. Indic. **querré, querrás, querrá, querremos, querréis, querrán.**

Cond. **querría, querrías, querría, querríamos, querríais, querrían.**

Imper. **quiere** tú, **quiera** Vd., queramos nosotros, quered vosotros, quieran Vds.

42. saber

Pres. Indic. **sé,** sabes, sabe, sabemos, sabéis, saben.

Pres. Subj. **sepa, sepas, sepa, sepamos, sepáis, sepan.**

Pret. Indic. **supe, supiste, supo, supimos, supisteis, supieron.**

Imp. Subj. **supiera** or **supiese, supieras** or **supieses, supiera** or **supiese, supiéramos** or **supiésemos, supierais** or **supieseis, supieran** or **supiesen.**

Fut. Indic. **sabré, sabrás, sabrá, sabremos, sabréis, sabrán.**

Cond. **sabría, sabrías, sabría, sabríamos, sabríais, sabrían.**

Imper. sabe tú, sepa Vd., **sepamos** ñosotros, sabed vosotros, sepan Vds.

43. salir

Pres. Indic. **salgo,** sales, sale, salimos, salís, salen.

Pres. Subj. **salga, salgas, salga, salgamos, salgáis, salgan.**

Fut. Indic. **saldré, saldrás, saldrá, saldremos, saldréis, saldrán.**

Cond. **saldría, saldrías, saldría, saldríamos, saldríais, saldrían.**

Imper. **sal** tú, **salga** Vd., **salgamos** nosotros, salid vosotros, salgan Vds.

NOTE. The compound *sobresalir* is regular in the familiar imperative: sobresale tú.

44. ser

> *Pres. Indic.* soy, eres, es, somos, sois, son.
> *Pres. Subj.* sea, seas, sea, seamos, seáis, sean.
> *Imp. Indic.* era, eras, era, éramos, erais, eran.
> *Pret. Indic.* fuí, fuiste, fué, fuimos, fuisteis, fueron.
> *Imp. Subj.* fuera or fuese, fueras or fueses, fuera or fuese,
> fuéramos or fuésemos, fuerais or fueseis, fueran
> or fuesen.
> *Imper.* sé tú, sea Vd., seamos nosotros, sed vosotros, sean Vds.

45. tener

> *Pres. Indic.* tengo, tienes, tiene, tenemos, tenéis, tienen.
> *Pres. Subj.* tenga, tengas, tenga, tengamos, tengáis, tengan.
> *Pret. Indic.* tuve, tuviste, tuvo, tuvimos, tuvisteis, tuvieron.
> *Imp. Subj* tuviera or tuviese, tuvieras or tuvieses, tuviera or
> tuviese, tuviéramos or tuviésemos, tuvierais or
> or tuvieseis, tuvieran or tuviesen.
> *Fut. Indic.* tendré, tendrás, tendrá, tendremos, tendréis,
> tendrán.
> *Cond.* tendría, tendrías, tendría, tendríamos, tendríais, ten-
> drían.
> *Imper.* ten tú, tenga Vd., tengamos nosotros, tened vosotros,
> tengan Vds.

46. traer

> *Pres. Indic.* traigo, traes, trae, traemos, traéis, traen.
> *Pres. Subj.* traiga, traigas, traiga, traigamos, traigáis, trai-
> gan.
> *Pret. Indic.* traje, trajiste, trajo, trajimos, trajisteis, tra-
> jeron.
> *Imp. Subj.* trajera or trajese, trajeras or trajeses, trajera or
> trajese, trajéramos or trajésemos, trajerais or
> trajeseis, trajeran or trajesen.
> *Imper.* trae tú, traiga Vd., traigamos nosotros, traed vosotros,
> traigan Vds.
> *Prés. Part.* trayendo.

47. valer

> *Pres. Indic.* valgo, vales, vale, valemos, valéis, valen.
> *Pres. Subj.* valga, valgas, valga, valgamos, valgáis, valgan.
> *Fut. Indic.* valdré, valdrás, valdrá, valdremos, valdréis,
> valdrán.

Cond. **valdría, valdrías, valdría, valdríamos, valdríais, val-
    drían.**
Imper. **val** or **vale tú, valga Vd., valgamos** nosotros, valed voso-
    tros, **valgan** Vds.

48. venir
  Pres. Indic. **vengo, vienes, viene,** venimos, venís, **vienen.**
  Pres. Subj. **venga, vengas, venga, vengamos, vengáis; vengan.**
  Pret. Indic. **vine, viniste, vino, vinimos, vinisteis, vinieron.**
  Imp. Subj. **viniera** or **viniese, vinieras** or **vinieses, viniera** or
      viniese, viniéramos or **viniésemos, vinierais** or
      vinieseis, vinieran or **viniesen.**
  Fut. Indic. **vendré, vendrás, vendrá, vendremos, vendréis,
      vendrán.**
  Cond. **vendría, vendrías, vendría, vendríamos, vendríais,
      vendrían.**
  Imper. **ven tú, venga Vd., vengamos** nosotros, venid vosotros,
      vengan Vds.
  Pres. Part. **viniendo.**

49. ver
  Pres. Indic. **veo, ves, ve,** vemos, veis, **ven.**
  Pres. Subj. **vea, veas, vea, veamos, veáis, vean.**
  Imp. Indic. **veía, veías, veía, veíamos, veíais, veían.**
  Imper. **ve tú, vea Vd., veamos** nosotros, ved vosotros, **vean** Vds.
  Past Part. **visto.**

50. yacer
  Pres. Indic. **yazco** or **yazgo,** yaces, yace, yacemos, yacéis, yacen.
  Pres. Subj. **yazca** or **yazga, yazcas** or **yazgas, yazca** or **yazga,
      yazcamos** or **yazgamos, yazcáis** or **yazgáis, yaz-
      can** or **yazgan.**
  Imper. **yace tú, yazca** or **yazga Vd., yazcamos** or **yazgamos**
      nosotros, yaced vosotros, **yazcan** or **yazgan** Vds.

51. DEFECTIVE VERBS
  a) The following verbs are used only in the forms that have an **i**
      in the ending: abolir, agredir, aterirse, empedernir, transgredir.
  b) atañer
      This verb is used only in the third person. It is most frequently
      used in the present indicative: atañe, atañen.
  c) concernir

This verb is used only in the third person of the following tenses:

Pres. Indic. **concierne, conciernen.**

Pres. Subj. **concierna, conciernan.**

Imp. Indic. concernía, concernían.

Imp. Subj. concerniera or concerniese, concernieran or concerniesen.

Pres. Part. concerniendo.

d) soler

This verb is used most frequently in the present and imperfect indicative. It is less frequently used in the present subjunctive.

Pres. Indic. **suelo, sueles, suele,** solemos, soléis, **suelen.**

Pres. Subj. **suela, suelas, suela,** solamos, soláis, **suelan.**

Imp. Indic. solía, solías, solía, solíamos, solíais, solían.

The preterit is seldom used. Of the compound tenses, only the present perfect is commonly used: he solido, etc. The other tenses are very rare.

e) roer

This verb has three forms in the first person of the present indicative: **roo, royo, roigo,** all of which are infrequently used. In the present subjunctive the preferable form is **roa, roas, roa,** etc., although the forms **roya** and **roiga** are found.

52. Irregular Past Participles

abrir—**abierto**

absorber—absorbido, **absorto**

bendecir—bendecido, **bendito**

componer—**compuesto**

cubrir—**cubierto**

decir—**dicho**

deponer—**depuesto**

descomponer—**descompuesto**

describir—**descrito**

descubrir—**descubierto**

desenvolver—**desenvuelto**

deshacer—**deshecho**

devolver—**devuelto**

disolver—**disuelto**

encubrir—**encubierto**

entreabrir—**entreabierto**

entrever—**entrevisto**

envolver—**envuelto**

escribir—**escrito**

freir—**frito,** freído

hacer—**hecho**

imprimir—**impreso**

inscribir—**inscrito, inscripto**

maldecir—maldecido, **maldito**

morir—**muerto**

poner—**puesto**

prescribir—**prescrito, prescripto**

proscribir—**proscrito, proscripto**

proveer—proveído, **provisto**

resolver—**resuelto**

revolver—**revuelto**

romper—rompido, **roto**

satisfacer—**satisfecho**

subscribir—**subscrito**

ver—**visto**

volver—**vuelto**

NUMERALS—NUMEROS

Cardinal Numbers		Números Cardinales	Ordinal Numbers	Números Ordinales[1]
1	one	uno, una	first	primero
2	two	dos	second	segundo
3	three	tres	third	tercero
4	four	cuatro	fourth	cuarto
5	five	cinco	fifth	quinto
6	six	seis	sixth	sexto
7	seven	siete	seventh	séptimo
8	eight	ocho	eighth	octavo
9	nine	nueve	ninth	noveno, nono
10	ten	diez	tenth	décimo
11	eleven	once	eleventh	undécimo
12	twelve	doce	twelfth	duodécimo
13	thirteen	trece	thirteenth	décimotercio
14	fourteen	catorce	fourteenth	décimocuarto
15	fifteen	quince	fifteenth	décimoquinto
16	sixteen	dieciseis, diez y seis	sixteenth	décimosexto
17	seventeen	diecisiete, diez y siete	seventeenth	décimoséptimo
18	eighteen	dieciocho, diez y ocho	eighteenth	décimoctavo
19	nineteen	diecinueve, diez y nueve	nineteenth	décimonono
20	twenty	veinte	twentieth	vigésimo
21	twenty-one	veintiuno, veinte y uno	twenty-first	vigésimo primero
30	thirty	treinta	thirtieth	trigésimo
40	forty	cuarenta	fortieth	cuadragésimo
50	fifty	cincuenta	fiftieth	quincuagésimo
60	sixty	sesenta	sixtieth	sexagésimo
70	seventy	setenta	seventieth	septuagésimo
80	eighty	ochenta	eightieth	octogésimo
90	ninety	noventa	ninetieth	nonagésimo
100	one hundred	ciento	(one) hundredth	centésimo
101	one hundred and one	ciento (y) uno	(one) hundred and first	centésimo primo
200	two hundred	doscientos	two-hundredth	ducentésimo
300	three hundred	trescientos	three-hundredth	tricentésimo
400	four hundred	cuatrocientos	four-hundredth	cuadringentésimo
500	five hundred	quinientos	five-hundredth	quingentésimo
600	six hundred	seiscientos	six-hundredth	sexagésimo
700	seven hundred	setecientos	seven-hundredth	septingentésimo
800	eight hundred	ochocientos	eight-hundredth	octingentésimo
900	nine hundred	novecientos	nine-hundredth	noningentésimo
1000	one thousand	mil	(one) thousandth	milésimo
100,000	one hundred thousand	cien mil	(one) hundred thousandth	cienmilésimo
1,000,000	one million	un millón	(one) millionth	millonésimo

1. The ordinals beyond the "tenth" are less used in Spanish than in English. They are often replaced by the cardinals: *Alfonso the Thirteenth* **Alfonso trece.**

A

a *prep.* to; in, into; on; by.

abacería *f.* grocery; grocery store; **abacero** *m.* grocer.

abad *m.* abbot; **abadía** *f.* abbey.

abajarse *v.* to lower oneself, humiliate oneself.

abajo *adv.* down, below; downstairs.

abalanzar⁶ *v.* to balance; to hurl, impel; **-se** to hurl oneself; to rush (upon), swoop down (upon); *Am.* to rear, balk.

abandonamiento = abandono.

abandonar *v.* to abandon, desert; to give up.

abandono *m.* abandon; desertion; neglect.

abanicar⁶ *v.* to fan.

abanico *m.* fan.

abaratar *v.* to cheapen, lower the price of.

abarcar⁶ *v.* to embrace, contain, include; *Am.* to buy up, monopolize.

abarrotería *f. Am.* grocery, grocery store; **abarrotero** *m. Am.* grocer.

abarrotes *m. pl.* small packages (*in hold of a ship*); *Am.* groceries; **tienda de — *Am.* grocery store.**

abastecer¹³ *v. irr.* to supply.

abastecimiento *m.* supply; provisions.

abasto *m.* supply; **no dar — a** to be unable to cope with.

abatido *adj.* dejected, depressed, crestfallen, humbled; fallen; lowered.

abatimiento *m.* discouragement, dejection, depression; descent, swoop, drop.

abatir *v.* to lower; to knock down; to depress; to humble; **-se** to become discouraged; to swoop down.

abdicar⁶ *v.* to abdicate.

abdomen *m.* abdomen.

abecedario *m.* alphabet; primer.

abedul *m.* birch.

abeja *f.* bee; **abejera** *f.* beehive; **abejón** *m.* drone; bumblebee; **abejorro** *m.* bumblebee.

aberración *f.* aberration, mental or moral deviation.

abertura *f.* aperture, opening, hole, slit.

abeto *m.* fir (*tree and wood*).

abierto *p.p. of* **abrir** opened; *adj.* open; frank; *Am.* proud, self-satisfied; *Am.* generous.

abigarrado *adj.* motley; multicolored; variegated.

abismado *p.p.* absorbed, buried in thought; overwhelmed.

abismar *v.* to overwhelm; to depress; **-se** to be plunged (into); to bury oneself (*in thought, grief, etc.*).

abismo *m.* abyss, precipice, chasm.

ablandar *v.* to soften.

abnegación *f.* abnegation, self-denial, self-sacrifice.

abnegado *adj.* self-sacrificing.

abnegarse⁷ *v.* to deny oneself, sacrifice oneself.

abobado *adj.* stupid, silly.

abochornar *v.* to overheat; to embarrass; **-se** to get overheated; to blush; to be embarrassed.

abofetear *v.* to slap.

abogado *m.* lawyer.

abogar⁷ *v.* to advocate, plead in favor of; to intercede.

abolengo *m.* lineage, ancestry; inheritance, patrimony.

abolición *f.* abolition.

abolir⁵¹, *v.* to abolish; to repeal.

abolsarse *v.* to bag (*said of trousers, skirts, etc.*).

abollado *p.p. & adj.* dented; bumped; bruised.

abolladura *f.* dent, bump.

abollar *v.* to dent; to bump; to crush, crumple; to bruise.

abominable *adj.* abominable, detestable.

abominar *v.* to abominate, abhor, detest.

abonado *m.* subscriber; *p.p. of* **abonar.**

abonar *v.* to credit with; to make a payment; to indorse, back (*a person*); to fertilize (*soil*); **-se** to subscribe.

abonaré *m.* promissory note; I.O.U.

abono *m.* payment; installment; indorsement, guarantee; fertilizer; subscription.

abordar *v.* to board (*a ship*); to dock, put into port; to approach; to undertake, take up (*a matter, problem, etc.*).

aborigen *adj.* aboriginal, indigenous, native; **aborígenes** *m. pl.* aborigines, primitive inhabitants.

aborrascarse⁶ *v.* to become stormy.

aborrecer¹³ *v. irr.* to abhor, hate, detest.

aborrecible *adj.* abominable, hateful.

aborrecimiento *m.* abhorrence; hatred.

abortar *v.* to miscarry, have a miscarriage; to give birth prematurely; to fail.

aborto *m.* abortion, miscarriage; monster.

abotagarse⁷ *v.* to bloat; to swell.

abotonador *m.* buttonhook.

abotonar *v.* to button, button up; to bud; **-se** to button up.

abovedar *v.* to vault, cover with a vault; to arch.

abozalar *v.* to muzzle.

abra *f.* cove; mountain gap or pass; dale; *Am.* breach (*in the jungle*); *Am.* leaf (*of a door*).

abrasador *adj.* burning, very hot.

abrasar *v.* to burn; to parch; **-se** to

burn up, be consumed.

abrazar[9] v. to hug, embrace; to include.

abrazo m. hug, embrace.

abrelatas m. can opener.

abrevadero m. drinking trough; watering place for cattle.

abrevar v. to water (*livestock*).

abreviación f. abbreviation.

abreviar v. to abbreviate, shorten, condense.

abreviatura f. abbreviation.

abrigar[7] v. to shelter, cover, protect; to wrap up; to harbor (*fear*), cherish (*hope*); -se to find shelter; to wrap oneself up.

abrigo m. shelter, cover, protection; wrap; overcoat.

abril m. April.

abrillantar v. to polish, shine; to glaze.

abrir[52] v. to open; to unlock.

abrochar v. to button; to clasp; to fasten.

abrogación f. repeal.

abrogar[7] v. to abrogate, repeal, annul.

abrojo m. thistle, thorn; -s reef.

abrumador adj. crushing, overwhelming; oppressive; fatiguing.

abrumar v. to crush, overwhelm; to trouble, annoy; -se to become foggy.

abrupto adj. abrupt, steep.

absceso m. abscess.

absolución f. absolution; acquittal.

absoluto adj. absolute; unconditional.

absolver[2,52] v. irr. to absolve, free from guilt; to pardon, acquit.

absorbente adj. & m. absorbent.

absorber[52] v. to absorb.

absorción f. absorption.

absorto p.p. irr. of **absorber** & adj. absorbed, engrossed; amazed.

abstenerse[45] v. irr. to abstain, refrain.

abstinencia f. abstinence; fasting.

abstracción f. abstraction; reverie.

abstracto adj. abstract.

abstraer[46] v. irr. to abstract; to withdraw, remove; -se to be lost in thought.

abstraído adj. lost in thought, absentminded; aloof.

absuelto p.p. of **absolver** absolved, acquitted.

absurdo adj. absurd, ridiculous, senseless; m. absurdity.

abuela f. grandmother.

abuelo m. grandfather; -s grandparents; ancestors.

abulia f. abulia, loss of will power.

abultado adj. bulky, bulgy.

abultar v. to bulge; to be bulky; to enlarge.

abundancia f. abundance, plenty.

abundante adj. abundant, plentiful.

abundar v. to abound, be plentiful.

aburrido p.p. & adj. bored; boring, tiresome; weary.

aburrimiento m. weariness, dullness, boredom.

aburrir v. to bore, vex; -se to become bored or vexed.

abusar v. to abuse, mistreat; to misuse; — de to take unfair advantage of; to impose upon.

abuso m. abuse; misuse.

acá adv. here, over here; this way, hither.

acabamiento m. finish, completion, end; death; Am. exhaustion, physical decline.

acabar v. to end, finish, complete; — de (+ inf.) to have just; — por (+ inf.) to end by; — con to put an end to, make short work of; to destroy; -se to be over, finished; to be consumed; Am. to wear oneself out; Am. to age or decline in health.

academia f. academy; a special school; a scientific, literary, or artistic society.

académico adj. academic; m. academician, member of an academy.

acaecer[13] v. irr. to happen, occur.

acaecimiento m. event, happening.

acalorado adj. heated, excited, angry.

acaloramiento m. heat, ardor, excitement.

acalorar v. to heat, warm; to excite; -se to get overheated, get excited.

acallar v. to silence; to calm, quiet.

acampar v. to encamp; to camp.

acanalar v. to groove; to flute (*as a column*); to form a channel in.

acantilado adj. sheer, steep (*cliff*); m. bluff, cliff.

acantonar v. to quarter (*troops*).

acaparar v. to corner (*the market*); to monopolize; to gather in (*for one's gain or profit*).

acariciar v. to caress, pet; to cherish (*a hope or illusion*).

acarreador m. carter; carrier.

acarrear v. to cart, transport; to bring about (*harm, disaster*).

acarreo m. cartage, carriage, transport, haul.

acaso adv. perhaps; by chance; por si — just in case; m. chance, accident.

acatamiento m. homage, reverence, respect.

acatar v. to revere, respect; to pay homage to; Am. to realize; Am. to notice, pay attention.

acatarrar v. to chill; Am. to bother, annoy; -se to get chilled, catch cold; Am. to get tipsy.

acaudillar v. to lead, command.

acceso m. access; entrance, admittance; attack; fit (of madness, anger, etc.).

accesorio adj. & m. accessory.

accidentado adj. seized with a fit; in a swoon; rough, uneven (ground).

accidental adj. accidental, casual.

accidentarse v. to have a seizure or fit; to swoon, faint.

accidente m. accident, mishap; chance; sudden fit, swoon.

acción f. action; act; gesture; battle; stock, share; — de gracias thanksgiving.

accionar v. to gesticulate, make gestures; Am. to act, be active.

accionista m. & f. shareholder, stockholder.

acechanza f. snare; ambush.

acechar v. to lurk; to spy.

acecho m. ambush; spying; al (or en) — waiting in ambush, lying in wait.

acedo adj. rancid; acid; sour; harsh, disagreeable.

aceitar v. to oil, grease.

aceite m. oil; — alcanforado camphorated oil; — de hígado de bacalao codliver oil; — de oliva olive oil; — de ricino castor oil.

aceitera f. oil can; oil cruet (bottle for the table).

aceitoso adj. oily.

aceituna f. olive; aceitunado adj. olive green.

aceleración f. acceleration.

acelerador m. accelerator.

acelerar v. to accelerate, speed up; to quicken; to hurry, hasten.

acémila f. pack mule.

acendrado adj. pure, without blemish; purified.

acendrar v. to refine (metals); to purify, cleanse.

acento m. accent; emphasis.

acentuar[18] v. to accentuate, emphasize; to accent; -se to become worse (as an illness).

acepción f. acceptation, usual meaning.

acepillar v. to brush; to plane.

aceptación f. acceptance; approval.

aceptar v. to accept; to approve; to admit.

acequia f. irrigation canal or ditch; Am. small stream; Am. sewer.

acera f. sidewalk.

acerado adj. steely, made of steel; steel-like; sharp.

acerar v. to steel.

acerbo adj. bitter; harsh, cruel.

acerca de prep. about, concerning.

acercamiento m. approach; approaching; rapprochement (coming together).

acercar[6] v. to bring near, draw up; -se to get near, approach.

acero m. steel.

acérrimo adj. very sour, very tart; very harsh; very strong, stanch, stalwart, steadfast.

acertar[1] v. irr. to hit, (the mark); to hit upon, find by chance; to guess right; — a (+ inf.) to happen to.

acertijo m. riddle.

aciago adj. ill-fated, unlucky.

acicalado p.p. & adj. polished; dressed up; adorned; trim, neat.

acicalar v. to polish; to adorn; -se to dress up, doll up.

acicate m. spur; incentive.

acidez f. acidity, sourness.

ácido m. acid; adj. acid, sour.

acierto m. right guess; lucky hit; good aim; good judgment; con — effectively, successfully.

aclamación f. acclamation, applause.

aclamar v. to acclaim, cheer, hail, applaud.

aclaración f. explanation.

aclarar v. to clarify, explain; to clear up; to rinse; to dawn.

aclimatar v. to acclimatize, accustom to a climate or new environment.

acobardar v. to frighten, intimidate.

acoger[11] v. to receive; to give shelter; -se to take refuge.

acogida f. reception, welcome; refuge.

acogimiento m. reception, welcome.

acojinar v. to cushion; to quilt.

acolchar v. to quilt.

acólito m. acolyte, altar boy.

acometer v. to attack; to undertake.

acometida f., acometimiento m. attack, assault.

acomodado adj. well-off, wealthy; suitable, convenient; p.p. of acomodar.

acomodador m. usher (in a theater).

acomodar v. to arrange, adjust; to place; to accommodate, lodge; to place; to give employment to; -se to make oneself comfortable; to adapt oneself.

acomodo m. occupation, employment; arrangement.

acompañador m. companion; accompanist.

acompañamiento m. accompaniment; retinue, company.

acompañante m. companion; escort; attendant; accompanist.

acompañar v. to accompany; to escort; to enclose (in a letter).

acompasado adj. rhythmical; measured;

slow, deliberate.

acondicionado *adj.* conditioned; comfortable; air-conditioned; *Am.* adequate, suitable.

acondicionar *v.* to condition; to prepare; to arrange; -se to become conditioned or prepared.

acongojar *v.* to grieve; -se to grieve; to be distressed.

aconsejar *v.* to advise, counsel.

acontecer[13] *v. irr.* to happen, occur.

acontecimiento *m.* event, happening.

acopiar *v.* to gather, accumulate, store up.

acopio *m.* storing; accumulation; stock, store, supply.

acoplamiento *m.* coupling; joint, connection.

acoplar *v.* to couple, connect; to fit or join together; to yoke; to pair, mate.

acorazado *m.* armored ship, battleship.

acorazar[9] *v.* to armor.

acordar[3] *v. irr.* to agree; to decide; to tune, put in harmony (*stringed instruments*); *Am.* to grant; -se to remember.

acorde *adj.* in harmony; in tune; *m.* chord.

acordelar *v.* to measure with a cord; to rope off, put a cord around.

acordonar *v.* to tie with a cord, string or rope; to rope off, tie a rope around (*a place*); to mill (*a coin*).

acornear *v.* to gore, wound with a horn; to butt.

acorralar *v.* to corral; to surround.

acortamiento *m.* shortening.

acortar *v.* to shorten, diminish; -se to shrink; to be shy, bashful.

acosar *v.* to pursue, harass.

acostado *adj.* reclining, lying down, in bed; tilted.

acostar[3] *v. irr.* to put to bed; to lay down; -se to lie down, go to bed; to tilt.

acostumbrado *adj.* accustomed, used; usual, habitual.

acostumbrar *v.* to accustom, train; to be used to, be accustomed to; -se to get accustomed.

acotación *f.* marginal note; stage directions (*for a play*); boundary mark; mark on a map showing altitude.

acotar *v.* to mark off (*with boundary marks*); to make marginal notes or citations; to put the elevation marks on (*maps*).

acre *adj.* sour, tart, sharp; rude, harsh; *m.* acre.

acrecentamiento *m.* growth, increase.

acrecentar[1] *v. irr.* to increase; to advance, promote.

acreditar *v.* to credit; to bring fame or credit to; to accredit, authorize; -se to win credit or fame.

acreedor *adj.* worthy, deserving; *m.* creditor.

acribillar *v.* to riddle; to perforate; to pierce.

acróbata *m. & f.* acrobat.

acta *f.* minutes (*of a meeting*); document; **levantar** — to write the minutes.

actitud *f.* attitude; posture, pose.

activar *v.* to activate, make active; to speed up, hasten.

actividad *f.* activity; energy.

activo *adj.* active, lively; *m.* assets.

acto *m.* act; action, deed; ceremony; — **continuo** (*or* **seguido**) immediately after; **en el** — immediately.

actor *m.* actor; **actriz** *f.* actress.

actuación *f.* action; intervention, participation, performance; -es legal proceedings.

actual *adj.* present (*time*); of the present month; -**mente** *adv.* at present, nowadays.

actualidad *f.* present time; -es latest news, fashions, or events; **de** — current, up-to-date.

actuar[18] *v.* to act, perform a function or act; to set in motion, cause to act.

acuarela *f.* water color.

acuario *m.* aquarium.

acuartelar *v.* to quarter (*troops*).

acuático *adj.* aquatic; **deportes** -**s** water sports.

acuchillar *v.* to knife; to stab; to slash.

acudir *v.* to go or come (*to aid, or in response to a call*); to attend, be present; to resort or turn to for help.

acueducto *m.* aqueduct, water channel or pipe.

acuerdo *m.* agreement; decision, resolution; opinion; remembrance; **estar de** — to be in agreement; **ponerse de** — to come to an agreement; **tomar un** — to take a decision.

acullá *adv.* yonder, over there.

acumulación *f.* accumulation.

acumulador *m.* storage battery.

acumular *v.* to accumulate, gather, pile up.

acuñación *f.* coinage, minting; wedging.

acuñar *v.* to mint, coin; to wedge.

acuoso *adj.* watery.

acurrucarse[6] *v.* to cuddle, nestle; to huddle.

acusación *f.* accusation, charge.

acusado *p.p. & adj.* accused; *m.* defendant.

acusar v. to accuse, denounce; to acknowledge (receipt).

acuse m. acknowledgment (of receipt).

acústica f. acoustics (science of sound).

achacar⁶ v. to impute, attribute.

achacosó adj. sickly.

achaparrado adj. scrub, of shrub size; squat, squatty.

achaque m. slight chronic illness; excuse; pretext; infirmity.

achicar⁶ v. to shorten; to make small; to bail (water); to humiliate; Am. to kill; Am. to tie, fasten; -se to get smaller; to shrink.

adagio m. adage, proverb, wise saying; adagio (musical Spanish America).

adaptar v. to adapt, fit, adjust.

adecuado adj. adequate, fit, suitable.

adecuar v. to fit, adapt.

adefesio m. absurdity, nonsense; ridiculous sight, dress, or person.

adelantado p.p. & adj. anticipated; advanced; ahead; forward, bold; por — in advance; m. governor of a province (in colonial Spanish America).

adelantamiento m. advancement, progress, betterment.

adelantar v. to advance; to move forward; to progress; to better; -se to get ahead.

adelante adv. forward, ahead; en — from now on.

adelanto m. advance; advancement; progress; betterment.

adelgazar⁹ v. to thin out, taper; -se to get thin, slender.

ademán m. gesture, gesticulation; attitude.

además adv. moreover, besides; — de prep. in addition to, besides.

adentro adv. within, inside; tierra — inland; mar — out to sea; hablar para sus -s to talk to oneself.

aderezamiento m. dressing; adornment, decoration.

aderezar⁹ v. to fix up, adorn, beautify, to garnish (food); to season; to prepare; to starch, stiffen.

aderezo m. adornment; garnish; trappings; finery; set of jewels; dressing; seasoning; starch, stiffener, filler (used in cloth).

adestrado adj. trained, skilled.

adestrar¹ v. irr. to train; to guide.

adeudado adj. indebted; in debt; p.p. of adeudar.

adeudar v. to owe; to debit, charge; -se to run into debt.

adeudo m. debt, indebtedness; duty (on imports); debit, charge.

adherencia f. adherence; attachment.

adherir³ v. irr. to adhere, stick.

adhesión f. adhesion; attachment.

adicto adj. addicted; devoted; m. addict; follower.

adiestrado = adestrado.

adiestramiento m. training; drill.

adiestrar = adestrar.

adinerado adj. wealthy.

¡adiós! interj. good-bye!; farewell! Am. you don't say!

aditamento m. addition; annex.

adivinación f. divination, prediction; guess.

adivinanza f. conundrum, riddle.

adivinar v. to guess.

adivino m. fortuneteller; soothsayer.

adjetivo m. & adj. adjective.

adjudicar⁶ v. to adjudge, award, assign; -se to appropriate.

adjunto adj. adjoining; attached, enclosed.

adminículo m. accessory; gadget.

administración f. administration, management; headquarters; Am. extreme unction, last sacrament.

administrador m. administrator, manager.

administrar v. to administer; to manage; -se Am. to receive the extreme unction or last sacrament.

administrativo adj. administrative.

admirable adj. admirable, wonderful.

admiración f. admiration, wonder; punto de — exclamation point.

admirador m. admirer.

admirar v. to admire; -se to be astonished or amazed; to wonder.

admisión f. admission; acceptance; acknowledgment.

admitir v. to admit; to let in; to accept; to allow, permit.

adobar v. to fix, cook, prepare (food); to tan (hides); to pickle (meats, fish).

adobe m. adobe, sun-dried mud brick.

adobo m. mending; sauce for seasoning or pickling; mixture for dressing skins or cloth; rouge.

adoctrinamiento m. indoctrination, teaching, instruction.

adoctrinar v. to indoctrinate, teach, instruct.

adolecer¹³ v. irr. to suffer (from an illness, defect, etc.).

adolescencia f. adolescence.

adolescente adj. adolescent.

adonde rel. adv. where; ¿adónde? interr. adv. where to?; where?

adoptar v. to adopt; to accept (an opinion).

adoptivo *adj.* adoptive, related by adoption; adopted.

adoración *f.* adoration, worship.

adorar *v.* to adore, worship.

adormecer[18] *v. irr.* to make sleepy or drowsy; to lull; -se to get sleepy; to get numb; to fall asleep.

adormilado *adj.* drowsy.

adornar *v.* to adorn, decorate, ornament.

adorno *m.* adornment, ornament, decoration.

adquirir[35] *v. irr.* to acquire, gain, win, obtain.

adquisición *f.* acquisition; attainment.

adrede *adv.* on purpose, intentionally.

aduana *f.* customhouse.

aduanero *m.* customhouse officer; *adj.* customhouse.

aduar *m.* gypsy camp; *Am.* Indian camp or ranch.

aducir[35] *v. irr.* to cite, allege, offer as proof.

adueñarse *v.* to take possession.

adulación *f.* flattery.

adulador *m.* flatterer.

adular *v.* to flatter.

adulterar *v.* to adulterate, corrupt, make impure.

adulterio *m.* adultery.

adúltero *m.* adulterer.

adulto *m. & adj.* adult.

adusto *adj.* stern, severe, austere.

advenedizo *m.* newcomer, stranger; upstart; *Am.* novice, beginner; *adj.* newly arrived; upstart; *Am.* inexperienced.

advenimiento *m.* advent, arrival, coming.

adverbio *m.* adverb.

adversario *m.* adversary, opponent; foe.

adversidad *f.* adversity; calamity.

adverso *adj.* adverse; contrary; unfavorable.

advertencia *f.* notice; warning; advice.

advertir[3] *v. irr.* to notice; to warn; to advise.

adyacente *adj.* adjacent.

aéreo *adj.* aerial; airy; **correo —** air mail.

aeródromo *m.* airport.

aeronave *f.* airship.

aeroplano *m.* airplane.

aeropuerto *m.* airport.

afabilidad *f.* friendliness, pleasantness, courtesy; affable *adj.* affable, pleasant, courteous.

afamado *adj.* famous.

afán *m.* eagerness, anxiety, ardor.

afanar *v.* to urge, press; -se to hurry; to worry; to work eagerly; to toil.

afear *v.* to make ugly; to disfigure; to blame, censure, condemn.

afección *f.* affection, fondness; disease.

afectado *p.p. & adj.* affected; *Am.* hurt, harmed; *Am.* **estar — del corazón** to have heart trouble.

afectar *v.* to affect, move; to pretend to have or feel; *Am.* to injure, hurt, harm.

afecto *m.* affection; *adj.* fond; **— a** fond of; given to, prone to.

afectuoso *adj.* affectionate, tender.

afeitada *f.* *Am.* shave, shaving.

afeitar *v.* to shave; -se to shave oneself; to put on make-up.

afeite *m.* make-up, cosmetics.

afeminado *adj.* effeminate.

aferrado *adj.* stubborn, obstinate; *p.p.* of aferrar.

aferramiento *m.* grasping, seizing; attachment; stubbornness; tenacity.

aferrar *v.* to seize, grasp, grapple; -se to take or seize hold of; to cling; -se a una opinión to cling to an opinion.

afianzar[9] *v.* to fasten, secure; to steady; to give bail or bond.

afición *f.* taste, inclination; fondness, affection.

aficionado *adj.* fond; *m.* amateur, fan.

aficionar *v.* to inspire a liking or fondness; -se a to become fond of.

afilador *m.* grinder, sharpener.

afilar *v.* to sharpen; to grind; *Am.* to make love to, woo; *Am.* to flatter; *Am.* **— con** to flirt with.

afín *adj.* kindred, related; **ideas afines** related ideas.

afinador *m.* piano tuner.

afinar *v.* to refine, polish; to tune.

afinidad *f.* affinity; similarity; relationship.

afirmación *f.* affirmation, assertion.

afirmar *v.* to affirm, assert; to make firm; *Am.* **— un golpe** to deal a blow.

afirmativa *f.* affirmative.

afirmativo *adj.* affirmative.

aflicción *f.* affliction, trouble, pain, grief.

afligir[11] *v.* to afflict, trouble, grieve; *Am.* to mistreat, harm, beat, strike; -se to worry, grieve.

aflojar *v.* to slacken; to loosen, unfasten; to let go; *Am.* to let go of money, spend easily; *Am.* **— un golpe** to give a blow.

afluente *m.* tributary; *adj.* abundant.

afluir[32] *v. irr.* to flow (into).

afortunado *adj.* fortunate; lucky.

afrenta *f.* affront, offense, insult.

afrentar *v.* to insult, offend, dishonor.

afrentoso *adj.* outrageous, shameful, disgraceful.

africano *adj. & m.* African.

afrontar v. to face; to confront.

afuera adv. out, outside; -s f. pl. out-skirts.

agachar v. to lower; to bend down; -se to stoop, bend down, duck; to crouch; Am. to give in, yield; Am. -se con algo to make away with or steal something.

agalla f. gill; tonsil; Am. greed; tener -s to have guts, have courage; Am. to be unscrupulous and bold in business deals; Am. to be greedy or stingy; Am. to be smart, astute, cunning.

agarrar v. to seize, grasp, grab; -se to cling, hold on.

agarro m. clench, clutch, grasp, grip, grab; agarrón m. tight clench, sudden grasp, grab; Am. pull, tug.

agasajar v. to entertain; to flatter.

agasajo m. entertainment; kind reception; friendliness; flattery.

agazapar v. to nab, seize (a person); -se to crouch; to squat.

agencia f. agency; Am. pawnshop.

agenciar v. to negotiate; to procure by negotiation; to promote.

agente m. agent; Am. officer, official.

ágil adj. agile, nimble, limber.

agilidad f. agility, nimbleness.

agitación f. agitation; excitement.

agitador m. agitator; adj. agitating; stirring.

agitar v. to agitate, excite; to stir; to wave; to shake.

aglomeración f. conglomeration, heap, pile, mass.

aglomerar v. to mass together; to cluster; -se to crowd together, pile up.

agobiar v. to oppress, weigh down; to overwhelm.

agolparse v. to crowd together, jam.

agonía f. agony.

agonizante adj. dying; m. dying person.

agonizar[9] v. to be dying.

agorero adj. ominous, of bad omen; prophetic; m. augur, prophet, fortune-teller.

agostar v. to parch, dry up; to pasture; to plow (in August).

agosto m. August; harvest; hacer su — to make hay while the sun shines.

agotado adj. & p.p. exhausted; out-of-print.

agotamiento m. exhaustion; draining.

agotar v. to exhaust, use up; to drain off; -se to be exhausted, used up.

agraciado adj. graceful; m. winner (of a favor, prize, etc.).

agraciar v. to grace; to adorn.

agradable adj. agreeable, pleasant.

agradar v. to please, be agreeable (to).

agradecer[13] v. irr. to thank for; to be grateful for.

agradecido adj. thankful, grateful.

agradecimiento m. gratitude, thankfulness.

agrado m. agreeableness; liking, pleasure; de su — to his liking.

agrandar v. to enlarge, to aggrandize, make greater.

agravar v. to aggravate, make worse; to make heavier; to oppress; -se to get worse.

agraviar v. to offend, insult, affront.

agravio m. offense, insult, affront.

agredir[51] v. to assail, assault, attack.

agregado m. attaché, person attached to a staff; aggregate, collection.

agregar[7] v. to add; to join; to attach.

agresivo adj. aggressive, offensive.

agresor m. aggressor; assailant.

agreste adj. rustic; wild (fruit, flower, etc.).

agriar[17] v. to sour, make sour; -se to sour, turn sour, become sour.

agrícola adj. agricultural.

agricultor m. agriculturist, farmer.

agricultura f. agriculture.

agridulce adj. bittersweet, tart.

agrietarse v. to crack; to chap (said of the skin).

agrimensura f. survey, surveying (of land).

agrio adj. sour; disagreeable.

agrupación f. group; bunch; grouping; gathering.

agrupar v. to group, bunch up.

agrura f. sourness.

agua f. water; rain; — abajo downstream; — arriba upstream.

aguacate m. Am. avocado, alligator pear, Am. avocado tree; Am. phlegmatic person.

aguacero m. shower.

aguada f. watering place; supply of drinking water; flood in a mine; wall wash; water color.

aguadero m. watering place.

aguado adj. watery; watered; Am. soft, unstarched; Am. weak, limp; Am. insipid, uninteresting, dull; sopa aguada thin soup; p.p. of aguar.

aguantar v. to endure, bear; to resist; -se to be silent, restrain oneself.

aguante m. endurance, fortitude, resistance.

aguar[9] v. to water, dilute with water; to spoil (pleasure); Am. to water (livestock); -se to become diluted; to get watery; to fill up with water; se aguó

7

la fiesta the party was spoiled.

aguardar v. to wait; to wait for.

aguardentoso adj. alcoholic; hoarse, raucous.

aguardiente m. brandy, hard liquor; — de caña rum.

aguarrás m. turpentine, oil of turpentine.

aguazal m. marsh, swamp.

agudeza f. sharpness; keenness; wit; witty remark or saying.

agudo adj. sharp; sharp-pointed; keen, witty; acute; shrill.

agüero m. augury, prediction; sign, omen; Am. fortuneteller.

aguijar v. to prick, spur, goad; to encourage, incite.

aguijón m. prick; sting; spur, goad.

aguijonear v. to goad; to prick.

águila f. eagle; es un — he is a shark.

aguileño adj. aquiline; eaglelike.

aguinaldo m. Christmas or New Year's gift.

aguja f. needle; crochet hook; watch hand; church spire; railroad switch.

agujerear v. to pierce, perforate; to riddle.

agujero m. hole; needle peddler; needle box; pincushion.

aguzar v. to sharpen; to goad, stimulate; — las orejas to prick up one's ears.

ahí adv. there; por — over there.

ahijado m. godchild.

ahinco m. effort, eagerness, zeal.

ahogar v. to drown; to choke, strangle; to smother; to quench, extinguish.

ahogo m. suffocation; breathlessness; anguish, grief.

ahondar v. to deepen; to dig; to penetrate, go deep into.

ahora adv. now; — mismo right now; por — for the present; — que Am. as soon as; ahorita instantly, this very minute; ahoritica, ahoritita Am. this very second, in a jiffy.

ahorcar v. to hang, kill by hanging.

ahorrar v. to save; to spare; to avoid.

ahorro m. saving, economy; caja de -s savings bank.

ahuecar v. to make hollow; to hollow out; — la voz to speak in a hollow voice; Am. ¡ahueca! get out of here!; -se to become puffed up, get conceited.

ahuehuete m. Am. a Mexican cypress.

ahumado adj. smoked; smoky.

ahumar v. to smoke; to fume.

ahuyentar v. to drive away; to scare away; -se to go away, flee; Am. to stop frequenting a place.

aindiado adj. Indian-like.

airar v. to annoy, irritate; -se to get

angry.

aire m. air; wind; tune; appearance; conceit; -cito m. breeze; a little tune; a certain air or appearance.

airear v. to air, ventilate.

airoso adj. windy; airy; graceful, elegant; lively, spirited.

aislador m. insulator; isolator; adj. insulating; isolating.

aislamiento m. isolation; insulation.

aislar v. to isolate, place apart; to insulate.

ajar v. to crumple, wither.

ajedrez m. chess

ajeno adj. another's; unaware; oblivious; alien; — a mi voluntad beyond my control;—de cuidados free from cares.

ajetrearse v. to hustle and bustle; to get tired out.

ajetreo m. bustle, hustle; hubbub; fuss; fatigue.

ají m. Am. chili pepper, chili sauce.

ajo m. garlic; garlic clove; garlic sauce swear word.

ajuar m. furniture set; trousseau, bride's oufit; bride's portion or dowry.

ajustado adj. tight, fitting tight; agreed upon (as a price); — a la ley in accordance with the law; p.p. of ajustar.

ajustamiento m. adjustment.

ajustar v. to adjust; to fit tight; to regulate; to tighten; to settle (accounts); to hire (a person); to stint, scrimp, save; Am. — una bofetada to give a good slap; Am. hoy ajusta quince años he is just fifteen years old today; -se to come to an agreement.

ajuste m. adjustment, fit; agreement; settlement (of accounts).

ajusticiar v. to execute, put to death.

al = a + el to the.

ala f. wing; hat brim.

alabanza f. praise.

alabar v. to praise.

alacena f. cupboard; closet; Am. booth, stall, market stand.

alacrán m. scorpion.

alado adj. winged.

alambicado p.p. & adj. distilled; over-refined, over-subtle (applied to style).

alambique m. still.

alambrada f. wire entanglement.

alambrado m. wire fence; wire screening; wiring.

alambre m. wire.

alameda f. poplar grove; park.

álamo m. poplar.

alancear v. to lance, spear.

alano m. mastiff.

alarde m. boast, bluff, brag.

alardear v. to boast, brag.

alargar[7] v. to lengthen; to prolong; to stretch out, extend.

alarido m. shout, scream, howl.

alarma f. alarm.

alarmar v. to alarm.

alazán adj. chestnut-colored; sorrel.

alba f. dawn; alb (white robe worn by priest).

albacea m. executor.

albañal m. sewer.

albañil m. mason, brickmason; albañilería f. masonry.

albaricoque m. apricot; albaricoquero m. apricot tree.

albayalde m. white lead.

albazo m. Am. early morning serenade; Am. bad surprise, surprise attack at dawn.

albear v. to show white (in the distance); Am. to rise at dawn.

albedrío m. free will.

albéitar m. veterinary.

alberca f. water reservoir, tank; pool.

albergar[7] v. to house, shelter, lodge; -se to take shelter; to lodge.

albo adj. white; Am. white-footed (horse).

albóndiga f. meat ball; fish ball.

albor f. dawn; whiteness.

alborada f. dawn; reveille (morning bugle call).

alborear v. to dawn.

alborotador m. agitator, troublemaker.

alborotar v. to disturb, upset; Am. to excite, arouse enthusiasm; -se to get upset; to mutiny; to riot; Am. to get excited; Am. to rear, balk (said of a horse).

alboroto m. uproar, disturbance; riot; Am. excitement, enthusiasm; Am. popcorn, candied popcorn ball.

alborozado adj. elated, excited.

alborozar[9] v. to gladden; -se to rejoice.

alborozo m. joy, delight.

albricias f. pl. good news; reward (for good news).

alcachofa f. artichoke; Am. sock, blow.

alcahuete m. procurer, pander; go-between; alcahueta f. bawd, procuress, go-between.

alcaide m. warden (of a fortress, prison, etc.).

alcalde m. mayor; justice of the peace; — mayor mayor.

alcance m. reach; scope; talent, capacity; last minute news, newspaper extra; cortos -s meagre intellect; dar — a to catch up with.

alcancía f. money box (with slit for coin); savings bank.

alcanfor m. camphor.

alcanzado adj. needy; broke, short of funds.

alcanzar[9] v. to reach; to overtake; to obtain; to befall; to be enough; Am. to hand, pass, put within reach.

alcayata f. wall hook; meat hook.

alcázar m. castle, fortress.

alcoba f. alcove, bedroom.

alcohol m. alcohol; alcohólico adj. alcoholic.

alcor m. hill.

alcornoque m. cork tree; cork wood; blockhead, dunce.

alcuza f. oil can; cruet, oil bottle.

aldaba f. knocker (of a door); crossbar, bolt, latch; handle (of a door, chest, etc.); tener buenas -s to have "pull"; influential connections.

aldabón m. large iron knocker; large handle; aldabonazo m. knock, knocking.

aldea f. village; aldehuela f. little village, hamlet.

aldeano adj. rustic, countrified; m. villager; peasant.

aleación f. alloy; alloying.

alear v. to alloy, mix (metals); to flutter; to flap (wings, arms, etc.).

aleccionar v. to coach; to teach, instruct; to train; to drill.

aledaños m. pl. borders, frontiers.

alegar[7] v. to allege, assert; Am. to argue, dispute.

alegato m. allegation; assertion.

alegrar v. to cheer up, gladden; to brighten; -se to be glad, rejoice; to get tipsy.

alegre adj. merry, gay, joyful, cheerful, bright; tipsy.

alegría f. joy, mirth, gaiety, merriment.

alejamiento m. withdrawal; retirement; aloofness.

alejar v. to remove, move away from; -se to move away; to withdraw, be aloof.

aleiado adj. stupefied, open-mouthed; silly.

alemán adj. & m. German.

alentar[1] v. irr. to breathe; to encourage, cheer, cheer up; -se to take heart; Am. to recover (from illness).

alergia f. allergy.

alero m. eaves; projecting edge.

alerto adj. alert, watchful; ¡alerta! attention! look out!; estar alerta to be on the alert.

aleta f. small wing; flap; fin (of a fish).

aletargado adj. drowsy, sluggish.

aletargarse[7] v. to fall into a state of

lethargy; to become drowsy.

aletazo *m.* flap, blow with a wing.

aletear *v.* to flap, flutter.

aleteo *m.* flapping, flutter (*of wings*).

aleve *adj.* treacherous.

alevosía *f.* treachery.

alevoso *adj.* treacherous.

alfabeto *m.* alphabet.

alfalfa *f.* alfalfa; **alfalfar** *m.* alfalfa field.

alfarería *f.* pottery; **alfarero** *m.* potter.

alfeñicar *v.* to frost with sugar (*a cake, cookie, etc.*); -se to get frail, delicate; to act affectedly.

alfeñique *m.* sugar paste; delicate person.

alférez *m.* ensign; second lieutenant.

alfil *m.* bishop (*in chess*).

alfiler *m.* pin; brooch; -es pin money; **ponerse de veinticinco** -es to dress up, dress up.

alfombra *f.* carpet; **alfombrilla** *f.* small carpet, rug; measles; *Am.* plant of the vervain family; *Am.* black smallpox; *Am.* skin eruption.

alforja *f.* saddlebag; knapsack; food provisions for a trip; *Am.* **pasarse a la otra —** to take undue liberties.

alforza *f.* tuck, fold, pleat; scar.

algarabía *f.* jargon; chatter; uproar.

algarrobo *m.* locust tree; carob tree.

algazara *f.* clamor; shouting; uproar.

álgebra *f.* algebra.

algo *pron.* something; *adv.* somewhat.

algodón *m.* cotton; **algodonal** *m.* cotton plantation.

alguacil *m.* policeman, constable.

alguien *pron.* somebody, someone.

algún(o) *adj.* some; any; *pron.* someone.

alhaja *f.* jewel.

alharaca *f.* rumpus, clamor, racket.

aliado *adj.* allied; *m.* ally.

alianza *f.* alliance, union; *Am.* wedding ring; *Am.* mixture of liquors.

aliar *v.* to ally; to unite; -se to form an alliance; to unite.

alicaído *adj.* crestfallen, downcast, discouraged; drooping.

alicates *m. pl.* pliers, small pincers.

aliciente *m.* inducement, incentive, attraction.

alienista *m.* alienist (*doctor who treats mental diseases*).

aliento *m.* breath; encouragement.

aligerar *v.* to lighten; to hasten.

alimentación *f.* nourishment, food, nutrition; feeding.

alimentar *v.* to feed, nourish.

alimenticio *adj.* nutritious, nourishing.

alimento *m.* food.

alinear *v.* to line up, put into line; to range; -se to fall in line, form into a line.

aliño *m.* ornament, decoration; neatness; condiment, dressing, seasoning.

alisar *v.* to smooth; to polish; to plane.

alistamiento *m.* enlistment; enrollment.

alistar *v.* to enlist; to enroll; to make ready; -se to enlist; to get ready; *Am.* to dress up.

aliviar *v.* to lighten; to alleviate, relieve, remedy, soothe; -se to get better, recover.

alivio *m.* relief, remedy; aid, help; improvement.

aljibe *m.* cistern, reservoir, tank; water tanker; *Am.* well, artesian well, spring.

alma *f.* soul, spirit; inhabitant.

almacén *m.* warehouse; department store; store.

almacenaje *m.* storage.

almacenar *v.* to store, store up; to put in storage.

almacenista *m. & f.* department store owner; warehouse owner or manager; wholesale merchant.

almanaque *m.* almanac, calendar.

almeja *f.* clam.

almendra *f.* almond; **almendrado** *m.* almond paste; **almendro** *m.* almond tree.

almíbar *m.* syrup.

almidón *m.* starch; *Am.* paste (*for gluing*).

almidonar *v.* to starch.

alminar *m.* turret.

almirante *m.* admiral.

almirez *m.* metal mortar.

almohada *f.* pillow; **almohadón** *m.* large cushion or pillow.

almohaza *f.* currycomb (*for grooming horses*).

almoneda *f.* auction.

almorzar [2, 9] *v. irr.* to lunch, eat lunch.

almuerzo *m.* lunch.

alojamiento *m.* lodging.

alojar *v.* to lodge; to house; to quarter (*troops*); -se to lodge, room.

alondra *f.* lark.

alpaca *f.* alpaca (*sheeplike animal of South America*); alpaca wool; alpaca cloth.

alpargata *f.* sandal (*usually of canvas and with hemp sole*).

alquería *f.* farmhouse.

alquilar *v.* to rent; to hire; -se to hire out.

alquiler *m.* rent, rental; **de —** for rent, for hire.

alquitrán *m.* tar.

alrededor *adv.* about, around; **— de**

prep. around; **-es** *m. pl.* environs, outskirts.

altanería *f.* haughtiness.

altanero *adj.* haughty, proud.

altar *m.* altar; **— mayor** high altar.

altavoz *m.* loud-speaker.

alteración *f.* alteration, change; disturbance.

alterar *v.* to alter, change; to disturb.

altercar *v.* to argue, dispute; to quarrel.

alternar *v.* to alternate; to take turns; **— con** to rub elbows with, be friendly with.

alternativa *f.* alternative, choice, option.

alternativo *adj.* alternating, alternative.

alterno *adj.* alternate.

alteza *f.* highness (*title*); lofty height.

altibajo *m.* downward thrust (*in fencing*); **-s** ups and downs; uneven ground.

altiplanicie *f.* upland; high plateau.

altiplano *m. Am.* high plateau.

altisonante *adj.* high-sounding.

altitud *f.* altitude.

altivez *f.* haughtiness, arrogance.

altivo *adj.* haughty, proud, arrogant.

alto *adj.* high; tall; loud; *adv.* loud; *m.* height; story (*of a building*); halt; *Am.* heap, pile; **-s** *Am.* upper floors; **hacer —** to halt, stop; **pasar por —** to omit, overlook; **¡ —!** halt!

altoparlante *m.* loud-speaker.

altura *f.* height, altitude.

alud *m.* avalanche.

aludir *v.* to allude, refer indirectly.

alumbrado *m.* lighting; *adj.* lit, lighted; tipsy.

alumbramiento *m.* childbirth; lighting.

alumbrar *v.* to light, give light; to enlighten; to give birth; **-se** to get tipsy.

aluminio *m.* aluminum.

alumno *m.* student.

alusión *f.* allusion.

alza *f.* rise; lift (*for shoes*).

alzada *f.* height (*of a horse*).

alzamiento *m.* raising, lifting; uprising, insurrection.

alzar *v.* to lift, raise; to cut (*cards*); **-se** to rebel, rise up in arms; *Am.* to puff up with pride; **-se con algo** to run off with something, steal something.

allá *adv.* there, over there; **más —** farther.

allanar *v.* to level, even off; to invade, break into (*a house*); to raid; **— una dificultad** to smooth out a difficulty.

allegado *adj.* near; related; allied; *m.* relative; partisan, follower.

allegar *v.* to accumulate, heap up, gather.

allende *adv.* on the other side; beyond; **— el mar** across the sea, overseas.

allí *adv.* there; **por —** through that place, around there.

ama *f.* mistress, owner; **— de leche** wet nurse; **— de llaves** housekeeper.

amabilidad *f.* kindness, courtesy.

amable *adj.* kind, amiable.

amador *m.* lover.

amaestrar *v.* to teach, coach, train.

amagar *v.* to threaten; to feint, make a threatening motion; to strike at.

amago *m.* threat; indication.

amalgamar *v.* to amalgamate, combine, mix, blend.

amamantar *v.* to nurse, suckle.

amanecer *v. irr.* to dawn; **— malo** to wake up ill; *m.* dawn, sunrise.

amanecida *f.* dawn, sunrise.

amansar *v.* to tame; to subdue; to pacify.

amante *m.* lover; **— de** fond of.

amapola *f.* poppy.

amar *v.* to love.

amargar *v.* to embitter, make bitter.

amargo *adj.* bitter; *m.* bitters; *Am.* mate (*Paraguayan tea*) without sugar.

amargor *m.* bitterness.

amargura *f.* bitterness; grief.

amarillear *v.* to show or have a yellowish tinge; to turn yellow.

amarillento *adj.* yellowish.

amarillo *adj.* yellow.

amarra *f.* cable; rope; strap.

amarrar *v.* to tie, fasten, rope; to moor (*a ship*); *Am.* **amarrárselas** to get "tight," drunk.

amasar *v.* to knead, mix; to mash; *Am.* to amass, accumulate (*a fortune*).

amatista *f.* amethyst.

ambages *m. pl.* circumlocutions; **hablar sin —** to go straight to the point, speak plainly, not to beat about the bush.

ámbar *m.* amber; **ambarino** *adj.* amber; like amber.

ambición *f.* ambition; aspiration.

ambicionar *v.* to seek, aspire after; to covet.

ambicioso *adj.* ambitious, eager; greedy, grasping.

ambiente *m.* atmosphere, environment.

ambigüedad *f.* ambiguity.

ambiguo *adj.* ambiguous; uncertain, doubtful.

ámbito *m.* precinct, enclosure.

ambos *adj. & pron.* both.

ambulancia *f.* ambulance; field hospital.

ambulante *adj.* walking; itinerant; moving; wandering.

amedrentar *v.* to scare, frighten.

amenaza *f.* menace, threat.

amenazador, amenazante *adj.* threatening.

amenazar⁹ *v.* to menace, threaten.

amenguar⁹ *v.* to lessen, diminish; to defame, dishonor.

amenidad *f.* pleasantness.

amenizar⁹ *v.* to make pleasant, cheer, brighten.

ameno *adj.* pleasant, agreeable.

americana *f.* suit coat.

americano *adj. & m.* American.

ametrallador *m.* gunner; ametralladora *f.* machine gun.

amigable *adj.* friendly; affable, pleasant.

amígdala *f.* tonsil; amigdalitis *f.* tonsilitis.

amigo *m.* friend; — de fond of.

aminorar *v.* to lessen.

amistad *f.* friendship; friendliness.

amistoso *adj.* friendly.

amo *m.* master, owner, boss.

amodorrado *adj.* drowsy.

amodorrar *v.* to make drowsy; -se to become drowsy.

amolador *m.* grinder, sharpener; *adj.* grinding; sharpening.

amolar² *v. irr.* to hone, sharpen, grind; to annoy; *Am.* to ruin, harm; -se *Am.* to go to rack and ruin.

amoldar *v.* to mold; to shape; to adjust; to adapt.

amonestación *f.* admonition, advice, warning; -es marriage bans (*or* banns).

amonestar *v.* to admonish, advise, warn.

amoníaco *m.* ammonia.

amontonamiento *m.* accumulation, pile, heap.

amontonar *v.* to heap up, pile up, crowd up.

amor *m.* love; — propio self-esteem.

amoratado *adj.* livid, bluish, purplish.

amordazar⁹ *v.* to gag; to muzzle.

amorío *m.* love affair; love-making.

amoroso *adj.* loving, tender, affectionate.

amortajar *v.* to shroud.

amortiguador *m.* shock absorber; silencer, muffler.

amortiguar⁸ *v.* to muffle; to deafen (*a sound*); to deaden (*a blow or sound*); to soften, tone down (*a color or sound*).

amortizar⁹ *v.* to pay on account; to liquidate, pay (*a debt*); to provide a sinking fund.

amoscarse⁶ *v.* to get peeved, annoyed; *Am.* to blush, be inhibited or em-

barrassed.

amostazar⁹ *v.* to anger, irritate; -se to get angry or irritated.

amotinar *v.* to incite to rebellion; -se to mutiny; to riot.

amparar *v.* to protect; to defend; *Am.* to grant mining rights; -se to seek protection or refuge; to protect oneself.

amparo *m.* protection; habeas corpus (*protection against imprisonment*); *Am.* mining rights.

ampliación *f.* enlargement, widening.

ampliar¹⁷ *v.* to enlarge, widen.

amplificar⁶ *v.* to amplify, expand, extend, enlarge; to magnify.

amplio *adj.* ample, wide, large, roomy.

amplitud *f.* breadth, extent, width.

ampolla *f.* blister; water bubble; narrow-necked bottle or vase; cruet; electric-light bulb; ampolleta *f.* small vial; small cruet.

ampollar *v.* to blister; -se to blister.

ampuloso *adj.* inflated, wordy, bombastic, pompous.

amputar *v.* to amputate, cut off.

amueblar *v.* to furnish (*with furniture*).

ánade *m. & f.* duck; anadeja *f.* duckling.

anadear *v.* to waddle.

anales *m. pl.* annals, historical records.

analfabeto *adj. & m.* illiterate; analfabetismo *m.* illiteracy.

análisis *m.* analysis.

analizar⁹ *v.* to analyze, examine.

analogía *f.* analogy, similarity.

análogo *adj.* analogous, similar, comparable.

ananá, ananás *f.* pineapple. *See* piña.

anaquel *m.* shelf; bookshelf; anaquelería *f.* shelves, bookshelves, library stacks.

anaranjado *adj.* orange-colored; *m.* orange color.

anarquía *f.* anarchy.

anatomía *f.* anatomy.

anca *f.* haunch, hind quarter, rump; *Am.* popcorn.

ancianidad *f.* old age.

anciano *adj.* old, aged; *m.* old man.

ancla *f.* anchor.

anclar *v.* to anchor.

ancho *adj.* wide; broad; loose; roomy; *Am.* self-satisfied, conceited; a sus anchas at one's ease; comfortable; leisurely; *m.* width.

anchoa, anchova *f.* anchovy.

anchura *f.* width, breadth; comfort, ease.

anchuroso *adj.* vast, extensive; spacious.

andada *f. Am.* walk, stroll; -s track,

footprints; **volver a las -s** to fall back into one's old ways or habits.
andadura *f.* gait, pace.
andaluz *adj.* Andalusian, of or pertaining to Andalusia, Spain; *m.* Andalusian, native of Andalusia.
andamiada *f.*, **andamiaje** *m.* scaffolding; framework.
andamio *m.* scaffold, scaffolding.
andanada *f.* grandstand; broadside *(discharge of the guns on one side of a ship)*; **soltar una —** to discharge a broadside; to reprimand.
andante *adj.* walking; errant, wandering; moderately slow *(music)*; **caballero —** knight-errant.
andanzas *f. pl.* rambles, wanderings.
andar[11] *v. irr.* to walk; to go, go about; to run *(as a watch or machinery)*; **— con cuidado** to be careful; **anda en quince años** he is about fifteen; **a todo —** at full (walking) speed; **a más —** walking briskly; **¡anda!** move on!; **¿qué andas haciendo?** what are you doing?; *Am.* **— andando** to be walking around; *Am.* **¡ándale!** hurry!
andariego *adj.* fond of walking; roving; *m.* walker.
andas *f. pl.* portable platform; litter.
andén *m.* railway station platform.
andino *adj.* Andean, of or from the Andes.
andrajo *m.* rag.
andrajoso *adj.* ragged, in rags.
anécdota *f.* anecdote, story.
anegar[7] *v.* to drown; to flood.
anejo *m.* annexed, attached.
anestésico *m. & adj.* anesthetic.
anexar *v.* to annex.
anexo *m.* annex; *adj.* annexed, joined.
anfiteatro *m.* amphitheater.
anfitrión *m.* generous host.
ángel *m.* angel.
angélico *adj.* angelic.
angina *f.* angina, inflammation of the throat; *Am.* tonsil; **— del pecho** angina pectoris.
anglosajón *adj. & m.* Anglo-Saxon.
angostar *v.* to narrow; **-se** to narrow, become narrow; to contract.
angosto *adj.* narrow.
angostura *f.* narrowness; narrows *(narrow part of a river, valley, strait, etc.)*.
anguila *f.* eel.
angular *adj.* angular; **piedra —** cornerstone.
ángulo *m.* angle, corner.
anguloso *adj.* angular, sharp-cornered.
angustia *f.* anguish, sorrow, grief, worry.
angustiar *v.* to distress, grieve, worry.

angustioso *adj.* anguished, worried, grievous; distressing.
anhelante *adj.* anxious, desirous, longing; panting.
anhelar *v.* to long for; to breathe hard; to pant.
anhelo *m.* longing.
anheloso *adj.* anxious; eager.
anidar *v.* to nest; to nestle; to dwell, to shelter.
anillo *m.* ring.
ánima *f.* soul, spirit.
animación *f.* animation, liveliness, life.
animal *m.* animal; *adj.* animal; stupid; beastly; **animalejo** *m.* little animal; **animalucho** *m.* insignificant animal; hideous little beast.
animar *v.* to animate, give life to; to inspire, encourage.
ánimo *f.* spirit, mind; courage, valor; intention.
animosidad *f.* animosity, ill will; courage, energy.
animoso *adj.* spirited; courageous.
aniñado *adj.* boyish; childish; **aniñada** girlish.
aniquilar *v.* to annihilate, wipe out, destroy completely.
aniversario *m.* anniversary.
anoche *adv.* last night.
anochecer[13] *v. irr.* to grow dark; to be or arrive at nightfall; *m.* nightfall.
anochecida *f.* nightfall.
anonadar *v.* to annihilate; to humiliate.
anónimo *adj.* anonymous; nameless; *m.* anonymous letter or note.
anormal *adj.* abnormal.
anotación *f.* annotation; note.
anotar *v.* to annotate, provide with notes; to write down.
anquilosado *adj.* stiff-jointed; gnarled.
anquilosarse *v.* to become stiff in the joints; to become mentally stagnant.
ansia *f.* anxiety, anguish; longing, eagerness; **-s** anguish; *Am.* nausea.
ansiar[17] *v.* to long for, desire eagerly.
ansiedad *f.* anxiety; worry.
ansioso *adj.* anxious, troubled; eager.
antagonismo *m.* antagonism.
antagonista *m. & f.* antagonist, adversary, opponent.
antaño *adv.* yesteryear, formerly; **días de —** days of old.
ante *prep.* before, in the presence of; **— todo** above all; *m.* elk; buckskin.
anteanoche *adv.* night before last.
anteayer *adv.* day before yesterday.
antebrazo *m.* forearm.
antecámara *f.* antechamber, waiting room.

13

antecedente *m.* antecedent; *adj.* antecedent, preceding.

antecesor *m.* ancestor; predecessor.

antedicho *adj.* aforesaid.

antelación *f.* precedence, priority (*in time*).

antemano: de — beforehand.

antena *f.* antenna (*of a radio or wireless*); lateen yard (*of a ship*); **-s** antennae, feelers.

antenoche = anteanoche.

anteojera *f.* blinder.

anteojo *m.* spyglass; small telescope; cyeglass; **-s** spectacles; **-s de larga vista** field glasses.

antepasado *adj.* passed; **año —** year before last; *m.* ancestor.

antepecho *m.* sill, railing.

anteponer[10] *v. irr.* to place before; to prefer.

antepuesto *p.p. of* anteponer.

anterior *adj.* front, toward the front; earlier, previous; **el día —** the day before.

antes *adv.* before, formerly; **— de** *prep.* before; **— (de) que** *conj.* before.

antesala *f.* anteroom, waiting room.

antiaéreo *adj.* antiaircraft.

anticipación *f.* anticipation, expectation; **con —** in advance.

anticipado *adj.* early, ahead of time; advanced (*payment*); **por —** in advance; *p.p. of* anticipar anticipated.

anticipar *v.* to anticipate; to advance, pay in advance; **-se** to get ahead (of).

anticipo *m.* advance, advance payment.

anticlericalismo *m.* anticlericalism (*opposition or antagonism to the clergy*).

anticuado *adj.* antiquated, out-of-date.

antídoto *m.* antidote.

antigualla *f.* antique; anything old.

antigüedad *f.* antiquity, ancient times; **-es** antique objects, antiques.

antiguo *adj.* ancient, old; antique.

antílope *m.* antelope.

antiparras *f. pl.* goggles; spectacles.

antipatía *f.* antipathy, dislike; mutual antagonism.

antipático *adj.* disagreeable; unlikeable, unpleasant.

antiséptico *adj. & m.* antiseptic.

antojadizo *adj.* fanciful, whimsical.

antojarse *v. :* **antojársele a uno** to take a notion or fancy to; to strike one's fancy; to want, desire.

antojo *m.* whim, notion, fancy.

antorcha *f.* torch.

antracita *f.* anthracite, hard coal.

anual *adj.* annual, yearly.

anuario *m.* annual, yearbook.

anublar *v.* to cloud; to dim, obscure; **-se** to become cloudy.

anudar *v.* to knot; **anudársele a uno la garganta** to choke up with emotion.

anulación *f.* voiding, cancellation.

anular *v.* to annul, void, cancel, abolish.

anunciador *m.* announcer; advertiser; *adj.* announcing; advertising.

anunciante *m. & f.* announcer, advertiser.

anunciar *v.* to announce; to advertise.

anuncio *m.* announcement; advertisement.

anzuelo *m.* fishhook; lure, attraction.

añadidura *f.* addition.

añadir *v.* to add.

añejado *adj.* aged (*wine, cheese, etc.*).

añejo *adj.* old; of old vintage; stale.

añicos *m. pl.* bits, shatters, fragments; **hacer(se) —** to shatter, break into a thousand pieces.

añil *m.* indigo (*plant*); indigo blue.

año *m.* year; **— bisiesto** leap year; **¿cuántos -s tiene Vd.?** how old are you?

añoranza *f.* nostalgia, longing.

añorar *v.* to long for, yearn for, be homesick for; to make reminiscences.

añoso *adj.* old, aged.

aojar *v.* to bewitch; to cast the evil eye.

apabullar *v.* to crush, crumple.

apacentar[1] *v. irr.* to graze, pasture; to feed (*the spirit, desires, passions, etc.*); **-se** to graze, pasture.

apacibilidad *f.* gentleness, mildness, pleasantness; **apacible** *adj.* pleasant, quiet, gentle.

apaciguamiento *m.* appeasement.

apaciguar[8] *v.* to pacify, calm, appease; **-se** to calm down.

apachurrar *v. Am.* to crush. *See* despachurrar.

apadrinar *v.* to sponsor; to act as a godfather; to act as a second in a duel.

apagar[7] *v.* to put out, extinguish; to deafen (*a sound*).

apalabrar *v.* to speak for, engage, reserve; **-se con** to make a verbal agreement with.

apalear *v.* to beat up, thrash; to thresh.

aparador *m.* sideboard; cupboard; showcase; show window; workshop.

aparato *m.* apparatus; pomp.

aparatoso *adj.* pompous, ostentatious.

aparcero *m.* co-owner of land; *Am.* pal, comrade.

aparear *v.* to mate; to match; to pair; **-se** to mate; to match; to pair.

aparecer[13] *v. irr.* to appear, show up.

aparecido *m.* ghost, specter, phantom

aparejar *v.* to prepare; to harness; to rig; to equip.

aparejo *m.* harness; packsaddle; rigging (*of a boat*); preparation; fishing tackle; **-s** equipment, tools.

aparentar *v.* to appear, seem; to pretend, feign, affect.

aparente *adj.* apparent.

aparición *f.* apparition, ghost; appearance.

apariencia *f.* appearance.

apartado *m.* compartment; — **postal** post office letter box; *p.p. of* **apartar.**

apartamento *m.* apartment.

apartamiento *m.* separation; retirement; aloofness; retreat, refuge; *Am.* apartment, flat.

apartar *v.* to set apart, separate; to remove; *Am.* — **las reses** to sort out cattle; **-se** to withdraw; to step aside; to go away.

aparte *adv.* apart; aside; *m.* aside (*in a play*); new paragraph; *Am.* sorting out of cattle.

apasionado *adj.* passionate; very fond (of); impassioned, emotional.

apasionar *v.* to arouse passion; to fill with passion; **-se** to become impassioned; to fall ardently in love.

apatía *f.* apathy, indolence, indifference.

apático *adj.* apathetic, indifferent, indolent.

apear *v.* to dismount, to lower, take down; to shackle (*a horse*); to fell (*a tree*); *Am.* to fire, dismiss from a position; — **el tratamiento** to omit the title (*in addressing a person*); **-se** to get off, alight; *Am.* **-se por la cola** (*or* **por las orejas**) to go off at a tangent, make an irrelevant remark.

apechugar[7] *v.* to push with the chest; to push ahead; — **con** to accept reluctantly; to go through with (*something*) courageously; *Am.* to snatch, take possession of.

apedrear *v.* to stone, hit with stones.

apegado *adj.* devoted, attached; *p.p. of* **apegarse.**

apegarse[7] *v.* to become attached (to); to become fond (of).

apego *m.* attachment, fondness.

apelación *f.* appeal.

apelar *v.* to appeal.

apelotonar *v.* to form or roll into a ball; to pile up, bunch together.

apellidar *v.* to call, name; **-se** to be named; to have the surname of.

apellido *m.* surname.

apenar *v.* to grieve, afflict; **-se** to be grieved, *Am.* to feel embarrassed,

feel ashamed,

apenas *adv.* hardly, scarcely; *conj.* as soon as.

apéndice *m.* appendix.

apercibir *v.* to prepare beforehand; to supply; to warn, advise; to perceive; **-se a la pelea** to get ready to fight; *Am.* **-se de** to notice.

apergaminado *adj.* parchment-like, dried up.

aperitivo *m.* aperitif, appetizer; cocktail.

aperlado *adj.* pearly, pearl-colored.

apero *m.* farm equipment; **-s** tools, implements; *Am.* saddle and trappings.

apertura *f.* opening (*act of opening or beginning*).

apestar *v.* to infect; to corrupt; to sicken; to stink; **-se** to turn putrid, become corrupted; *Am.* to catch cold.

apestoso *adj.* putrid, foul-smelling.

apetecer[13] *v. irr.* to desire, crave.

apetecible *adj.* desirable; appetizing.

apetencia *f.* hunger, appetite; desire.

apetito *m.* appetite; hunger.

apetitoso *adj.* appetizing; gluttonous.

apiadarse *v.* to pity; — **de** to pity, take pity on.

ápice *m.* apex, top, summit.

apilar *v.* to pile up, stack, heap.

apiñado *p.p. of* **apiñar** & *adj.* crowded, jammed; cone-shaped, shaped like a pine cone.

apiñamiento *m.* crowd, jam (*of people or animals*); crowding together.

apiñar *v.* to cram together; to crowd; **-se** to pile up, crowd together

apio *m.* celery.

apisonar *v.* to pack down, flatten by pounding.

aplacar[6] *v.* to appease, pacify, soothe.

aplanamiento *m.* flattening, leveling; dejection, depression.

aplanar *v.* to level; to flatten; to astonish, *Am.* — **las calles** to tramp the streets; **-se** to be flattened out; to be leveled to the ground; to lose one's strength; *Am.* to give in, yield.

aplastar *v.* to squash, crush, flatten; *Am.* to tire out, break (*a horse*); **-se** *Am.* to plump oneself down; *Am.* to overstay a call (*remaining seated*).

aplaudir *v.* to applaud, clap; to approve, praise.

aplauso *m.* applause; praise, approval.

aplazamiento *m.* postponement; adjournment.

aplazar[9] *v.* to postpone; to adjourn.

aplicable *adj.* applicable, suitable, fitting.

aplicación *f.* application; effort, diligence; -es appliqué (*trimming laid on a dress*).

aplicado *adj.* industrious, diligent.

aplicar[6] *v.* to apply; to put on, lay on; -se to apply oneself, work hard.

aplomado *adj.* gray, lead-colored; *p.p. of* **aplomar.**

aplomar *v.* to plumb (*a wall*); to make vertical; to make heavier; -se *Am.* to become ashamed or embarrassed; *Am.* to be slow

aplomo *m.* assurance, confidence, self-possession, serenity; **estar —** to be plumb, vertical.

apocado *adj.* cowardly; timid; *p.p. of* **apocar.**

apocamiento *m.* timidity; bashfulness; belittling.

apocar[6] *v.* to lessen, to belittle, give little importance to; -se to humble oneself.

apodar *v.* to nickname.

apoderado *m.* attorney; proxy, substitute.

apoderar *v.* to empower, give power of attorney; -se de to take possession of, seize.

apodo *m.* nickname.

apogeo *m.* apogee (*point at which a planet is at the greatest distance from the earth*); highest point, height (*of glory, fame, etc.*).

apolillado *adj.* moth-eaten; worm-eaten.

apología *f.* apology

apoplejía *f.* apoplexy, stroke.

aporrear *v.* to beat; to maul; *Am.* to beat (*in a game*), defeat.

aportación *f.* contribution.

aportar *v.* to bring; to contribute; to arrive in port; to reach an unexpected place (*after having gone astray*); -se *Am.* to appear, approach.

aporte *m.* contribution

aposento *m.* room; lodging.

apostar[2] *v irr.* to bet; to post, station.

apóstol *m.* apostle; religious leader.

apostólico *adj.* apostolic (*pertaining to the apostles, or to the Pope and his authority*).

apostura *f.* elegant bearing, graceful carriage.

apoyar *v.* to lean, rest; to back, support; to aid, favor; to confirm; -se to lean (on)

apoyo *m.* support; favor, protection.

apreciable *adj.* appreciable, noticeable; estimable, esteemed; valuable; appraisable.

apreciación *f.* appreciation, valuation; estimation.

apreciar *v.* to appreciate, value, esteem; to price, fix the price of; to appraise.

aprecio *m.* esteem, high regard; appraisal, valuation, estimate; *Am.* **hacer —** to notice, pay attention.

aprehender *v.* to apprehend, seize, arrest.

aprehensión, aprensión *f.* apprehension; fear, dread; seizure, arrest; *Am.* prejudice.

aprehensor, aprensor *m.* captor.

apremiante *adj.* pressing, urgent.

apremiar *v.* to press, urge onward, hurry.

apremio *m.* pressure; urgency

aprender *v.* to learn.

aprendiz *m.* apprentice.

aprendizaje *m.* apprenticeship; learning (*act of learning*).

apresar *v.* to seize, grab; to capture; to imprison.

aprestar *v.* to prepare, make ready; -se to get ready.

apresto *m.* preparation; readiness.

apresurado *adj.* hasty.

apresurar *v.* to hurry, hasten; -se to hurry, hasten.

apretado *adj.* tight; compact; stingy, miserly; difficult, dangerous; *p.p. of* **apretar.**

apretar[1] *v. irr.* to press, squeeze, tighten; to urge on; *Am.* to increase in strength or intensity (*as rain, wind, etc.*); *Am.* to redouble one's effort; **— a correr** to start to run; -se *Am.* to gorge, overeat.

apretón *m.* sudden pressure; squeeze; dash, short run; **— de manos** handshake.

apretura *f.* jam, crush; tight squeeze, narrow place; difficulty, predicament; dire poverty.

aprieto *m.* tight spot, difficulty.

aprisa *adv.* quickly, fast, speedily

aprisco *m.* sheepfold.

aprisionar *v.* to imprison; to tie, fasten.

aprobación *f.* approbation, approval; consent; pass, passing grade.

aprobar[2] *v. irr.* to approve; to pass (*in an examination*).

aprontar *v.* to make ready; to expedite; to hand over without delay; *Am.* to pay in advance.

apropiación *f.* appropriation; confiscation.

apropiado *adj.* appropriate, proper, fitting, suitable; *p.p. of* **apropiar.**

apropiar *v.* to fit; to adapt; -se to take possession (of); to confiscate.

aprovechable *adj.* available; usable, fit

to use.

aprovechado *adj.* diligent, industrious; *p.p.* of **aprovechar**.

aprovechamiento *m.* use, utilization; exploitation; profit, benefit; progress.

aprovechar *v.* to profit, be profitable; to progress, get ahead; to utilize; **-se de** to take advantage of; **¡que aproveche!** may you enjoy it!

aproximado *adj.* approximate; near; nearly correct.

aproximar *v.* to place or bring near; to approximate; **-se** to get near, approach.

aproximativo *adj.* approximate.

aptitud *f.* aptitude, capacity, ability.

apto *adj.* apt; competent.

apuesta *f.* bet, wager.

apuesto *adj.* smart, stylish; good-looking.

apuntación *f.* note; memorandum; musical notation, set of musical symbols or signs.

apuntalar *v.* to prop; to shore up.

apuntar *v.* to point; to aim; to write down; to prompt (*an actor*); to sharpen; to stitch, mend; to begin to show (*as a mustache or beard on a young face*); — **el día** to begin to dawn; **-se** *Am.* to sprout (*said of wheat, corn, etc.*)

apunte *m.* note, memorandum.

apuñalar *v.* to stab.

apuración *f.* worry; trouble.

apurado *adj.* worried; needy, difficult; dangerous; in a hurry.

apurar *v.* to drain to the last drop; to exhaust (*a subject*); to press, hurry; to worry, annoy; **-se** to be or get worried; to hurry up.

apuro *m.* need; worry; predicament; *Am.* rush, hurry.

aquejar *v.* to grieve, afflict.

aquel, aquella *dem. adj.* that (*at a distance*); **aquellos, aquellas** those; **aquél, aquélla** *m.*, *f. dem. pron.* that one; the former; **aquello** that, that thing; **aquéllos, aquéllas** *m.*, *f. pl.* those; the former.

aquí *adv.* here; **por —** this way; through here; around here.

aquietar *v.* to quiet, calm, to hush; **-se** to calm down, become calm.

aquilón *m.* north wind.

ara *f.* altar.

árabe *adj.* & *m.* Arab; Arabic.

arado *m.* plow; *Am.* plowed land, piece of cultivated land.

aragonés *adj.* Aragonese, of or from Aragón, Spain; *m.* Aragonese.

arancel *m.* tariff; **— de aduanas** customs, duties; **arancelario** *adj.* pertaining to tariff.

araña *f.* spider; chandelier.

arañar *v.* to scratch; to claw.

araño *m.* scratch; **arañazo** *m.* big scratch.

arar *v.* to plow.

arbitración *f.* arbitration.

arbitrador *m.* arbitrator, referee, umpire.

arbitraje *m.* arbitration.

arbitrar *v.* to arbitrate, to umpire.

arbitrario *adj.* arbitrary.

arbitrio *m.* free will; scheme, means, compromise, arbitration; sentence (*of a judge*); judgment.

árbitro *m.* arbitrator, sole judge, umpire.

árbol *m.* tree; mast; **arbolado** *adj* wooded; *m.* grove of trees.

arboleda *f.* grove.

arbusto *m.* shrub.

arca *f.* ark; chest, coffer, **arcón** *m* large coffer or chest, bin.

arcada *f.* arcade; archway.

arcaico *adj.* archaic.

arcano *adj.* hidden, secret; *m.* secret, mystery.

arce *m.* maple, maple tree.

arcilla *f.* clay.

arco *m.* arc; arch; bow; violin bow; — **iris** rainbow.

archipiélago *m.* archipelago (*group of many islands*).

archisabido *adj.* very well-known.

archivo *m.* archives; file; public records; *Am.* office, business office; **archivero** *m.* keeper of archives; city clerk.

arder *v.* to burn; to be consumed (*with fever or passion*); *Am.* to smart, sting.

ardid *m.* trick, scheme.

ardiente *adj.* ardent, burning, fervent; passionate; fiery.

ardilla *f.* squirrel.

ardite *m.* ancient coin of small value; bit, trifle; **no valer un —** not to be worth a penny.

ardor *m.* ardor; heat; fervor, eagerness.

ardoroso *adj.* ardent, fiery.

arduo *adj.* arduous, hard, difficult.

área *f.* area.

arena *f.* sand; arena; **-s** kidney stones, **arenal** *m.* sand pit.

arenga *f.* address, speech.

arenisco *adj.* sandy; gritty; **piedra arenisca** sandstone.

arenoso *adj.* sandy; gritty.

arenque *m.* herring.

arete *m.* earring.

argamasa *f.* mortar.

argentar *v.* to plate (*with silver*); to polish.

argentino *adj.* silvery; Argentine; *m.* Argentine; Argentine gold coin worth 5 pesos.

argolla *f.* large iron ring, *Am.* plain finger ring, engagement ring; *Am.* **tener — to be lucky.**

argucia *f.* cunning, astuteness; scheme; subtlety.

argüir[52] *v. irr.* to argue; to deduce, infer.

argumentación *f.* argumentation, argument, reasoning.

argumento *m.* argument, reasoning; subject matter, resumé (*of a play or story*).

aridez *f.* barrenness; dryness; drought.

árido *adj.* arid, dry, barren; **-s** *m. pl.* grains and dry vegetables; **medida para -s** dry measure.

ariete *m.* ram, battering ram; — **hidráulico** hydraulic ram.

arisco *adj.* gruff, harsh, unsociable; *Am.* shy, distrustful.

arista *f.* sharp edge; ridge; beard (*of wheat or corn*).

aristocracia *f.* aristocracy.

aristócrata *m. & f.* aristocrat.

aristocrático *adj.* aristocratic.

aritmética *f.* arithmetic.

arma *f.* arm, weapon; branch (*of the army*); **-s** armed forces; — **arrojadiza** missile weapon; — **blanca** sword; **de -s tomar** ready for any emergency; ready to fight.

armada *f.* armada, fleet.

armador *m.* shipbuilder; assembler.

armadura *f.* armor; armature (*of a generator or dynamo*); framework; mounting.

armamento *m.* armament; equipment.

armar *v.* to arm; to set up, assemble, rig up; — **una pendencia** to start a quarrel; *Am.* — **un trique** to lay a snare, set a trap; *Am.* **-se** to balk; to be stubborn; *Am.* **-se con alguna cosa** to refuse to return something.

armario *m.* wardrobe, clothes closet; cabinet.

armatoste *m.* unwieldy object or machine; clumsy thing; heavy, clumsy fellow.

armazón *f.* framework, skeleton; *m.* skeleton (*of an animal*); *Am.* shelf, set of shelves.

armella *f.* staple; screw eye.

armiño *m.* ermine.

armisticio *m.* armistice.

armonía *f.* harmony.

armónico *adj.* harmonic; harmonious.

armonioso *adj.* harmonious, musical.

armonizar[9] *v.* to harmonize.

arnés *m.* harness; coat of mail; **-es** harness and trappings; equipment, outfit.

aro *m.* hoop; rim (*of a wheel*); *Am.* finger ring; *Am.* earring.

aroma *f.* aroma, scent, perfume.

aromático *adj.* aromatic, fragrant, spicy; **sales aromáticas** smelling salts.

arpa *f.* harp.

arpía *f.* shrew.

arpón *m.* harpoon, spear.

arqueado *adj.* arched.

arquear *v.* to arch.

arquitecto *m.* architect.

arquitectónico *adj.* architectural.

arquitectura *f.* architecture.

arrabal *m.* outlying district; **-es** outskirts, suburbs.

arracada *f.* earring.

arraigar[7] *v.* to root, take root; **-se** to become rooted, attached.

arrancar[6] *v.* to uproot; to pull out; to start, start out; *Am.* to flee, run away.

arranque *m.* start, pull; uprooting; automobile starter; — **de ira** fit or outburst of anger; **punto de** — starting point.

arrasar *v.* to level; to tear down, raze; to fill to the brim; **-se** to clear up (*said of the sky*); **-se de lágrimas** to fill up with tears.

arrastrado *adj.* poor, destitute; mean, vile; wretched; rascally; **llevar una vida arrastrada** to lead a dog's life.

arrastrar *v.* to drag, haul; *Am.* to harrow (*land*); **-se** to drag along, crawl.

arrayán *m.* myrtle.

¡arre! *interj.* gee! get up there!

arrear *v.* to drive (*mules, cattle*); *Am.* to rustle, steal cattle; *Am.* **-le a uno una bofetada** to give a person a slap.

arrebatamiento *m.* snatch; ecstasy; rage.

arrebatar *v.* to snatch away; **-se de cólera** to have a fit of anger.

arrebatiña *f.* grab, snatch; scramble; **arrebatón** *m.* quick or violent grab.

arrebato *m.* rage; rapture, ecstacy; fit.

arrebol *m.* red color of the sky; rouge; **-es** red clouds.

arreciar *v.* to increase in intensity, get stronger.

arrecife *m.* reef.

arredrar *v.* to frighten, intimidate; **-se** to be or get scared.

arreglar *v.* to arrange, put in order; to regulate; to fix; to adjust, settle; *Am.* to pay (*a debt*); *Am.* to correct, punish; **-se** to doll up, fix oneself up; to settle differences, come to an agreement.

arreglo *m.* arrangement; adjustment;

18

settlement; conformity, agreement; con — a according to.

arrellanarse v. to sprawl, lounge; to be self-satisfied.

arremangado adj. & p.p. turned up; **nariz arremangada** turned up nose.

arremangar[7] v. to tuck up, turn up, roll up (the sleeves, trousers, etc.); -se to roll up one's sleeves; -se los pantalones to roll up one's trousers.

arremeter v. to attack, assail, assault.

arremetida f. thrust, push, attack.

arremolinarse v. to whirl, swirl; to eddy; to mill around.

arrendamiento m. renting; lease; rental, rent.

arrendar[1] v. irr. to rent, lease, let; to hire; to tie (a horse); to bridle; Am. to head for.

arrendatario m. renter, tenant.

arreo m. raiment; ornament; Am. driving of horses or mules; Am. drove of horses or mules; -s trappings; equipment; finery; adv. uninterruptedly, without interruption.

arrepentido adj repentant; p.p. of arrepentirse.

arrepentimiento m. repentance, regret.

arrepentirse[3] v. irr. to repent, regret.

arrestado adj. daring, rash; p.p. of arrestar.

arrestar v. to arrest; Am. to return, strike back (a ball); Am. to reprimand; -se to dare, venture.

arresto m. arrest, imprisonment; detention; daring, rashness; rash act.

arriar[17] v. to haul down, lower (the flag); to lower (the sails); to slacken (a rope).

arriba adv. above; upstairs; de — abajo from top to bottom; up and down; río — upstream; ¡ — ! hurrah!

arribada f. arrival; Am. back talk, impudent answer.

arribar v. to arrive; to put into port; Am. to prosper, better one's lot.

arribo m. arrival.

arriendo = arrendamiento.

arriero m. muleteer.

arriesgado adj. risky, daring.

arriesgar[7] v. to risk; -se to dare, run a risk.

arrimar v. to bring or place near; to lay aside; to strike (a blow); -se to lean (on); to get near; to seek shelter.

arrinconar v. to corner; to put in a corner; to lay aside; to slight, neglect; -se to retire; to live a secluded life.

arriscado adj. bold; daring; brisk; spirited (horse); craggy, rugged.

arriscar[6] v. to risk, venture; Am. to roll up, curl up, tuck up, fold back; Am. to have vim and vigor; Am. — a to reach, amount to; -se to get angry; Am. to dress up, doll up.

arroba f. weight of 25 pounds.

arrobamiento m. trance, rapture.

arrobarse v. to be entranced; to be in a trance; to be enraptured.

arrodillarse v. to kneel.

arrogancia f. arrogance, pride.

arrogante adj. arrogant, haughty, proud.

arrogarse[7] v. to appropriate, usurp, assume (power or rights).

arrojadizo adj. missile; **arma arrojadiza** missile weapon.

arrojado adj. daring, rash, fearless; p.p. of arrojar.

arrojar v. to throw, hurl, cast; to expel; Am. to throw up, vomit; — un saldo de to show a balance of; -se a to hurl oneself upon or at; to dare to.

arrojo m. boldness, daring.

arrollador adj. sweeping, overwhelming, violent; winding (that serves to wind or roll up).

arrollar v. to roll up; to sweep away; to trample upon; to destroy.

arropar v. to wrap, cover; Am. to snap up, accept on the spot (a deal); -se to wrap up, cover up.

arrostrar v. to face, defy; -se to dare, dare to fight face to face.

arroyada f. gully, valley of a stream; bed (formed by a stream); river flood.

arroyo m. brook, small stream, rivulet; gutter; **arroyuelo** m. rivulet.

arroz m. rice; **arrozal** m. rice field.

arruga f. wrinkle.

arrugar[7] v. to wrinkle; Am. to bother, annoy; -se to get wrinkled; Am. to crouch with fear, be afraid.

arruinar v. to ruin, destroy; -se to become ruined; Am. to go "broke", lose all one's fortune.

arrullar v. to lull, to coo.

arrullo m. lullaby; cooing.

arrumbar v. to lay aside (as useless), put away in a corner, discard; to dismiss, remove (from office or a position of trust); to take bearings; — a su adversario to corner one's opponent, overpower him.

arsenal m. arsenal; navy yard.

arsénico m. arsenic.

arte m. & f. art; skill, ability; cunning; craft; por — de by way or means of; **bellas** -s fine arts.

artefacto m. piece of workmanship; manufactured object; handiwork; contrivance.

arteria f. artery.

artero adj. crafty, astute.

artesa f. trough.

artesano m. artisan, craftsman; artesanía f. arts and crafts; workmanship, craftsmanship.

artesonado m. ceiling decorated with carved panels.

ártico adj. arctic.

articulación f. articulation; pronunciation; joint.

articular v. to articulate; to join, unite.

artículo m. article; — de fondo editorial.

artífice m. artisan, craftsman.

artificial adj. artificial.

artificio m. artifice, clever device; craft, skill; cunning, deceit.

artificioso adj. cunning, astute, deceitful; skilful.

artillería f. artillery, gunnery; — de plaza (or de sitio) heavy artillery; — de montaña light mountain artillery.

artillero m. artilleryman, gunner.

artimaña f. trick.

artista m. & f. artist.

artístico adj. artistic.

arzobispo m. archbishop.

arzón m. saddletree.

as m. ace.

asa f. handle.

asado m. roast; p.p. & adj. roasted.

asador m. spit (for roasting).

asaltador m. assailant; highway robber.

asaltar v to assault, attack; -le a uno una idea to be struck by an idea; Am — la casa de un amigo to give a surprise party.

asalto m. assault, attack; Am. surprise party.

asamblea f assembly, legislature; meeting.

asar v. to roast; -se to roast; to feel hot.

asaz adv. enough, very.

ascendencia f. ancestry, origin.

ascendente adj. ascendent, ascending, upward, rising.

ascender[1] v. irr. to ascend, climb; to promote; to amount (to).

ascendiente m. ancestor; influence.

ascensión f. ascension; ascent.

ascenso m. ascent, rise; promotion.

ascensor m. elevator.

asco m. disgust, loathing; nausea, me da — it makes me sick; it disgusts me; Am. poner a uno del — to call a person all kinds of bad names; to soil.

ascua f. ember.

aseado adj. clean, neat; p.p. of asear.

asear v. to adorn; to make neat and clean; -se to clean oneself up.

asechanza = acechanza.

asediar v. to besiege, attack.

asedio m. siege.

asegurar v. to assure; to secure; to affirm; to insure; -se to make sure; to hold on; to get insured.

asemejar v. to liken, compare; -se a to resemble.

asentaderas f. pl. buttocks.

asentador m. razor strop.

asentar[1] v. irr. to set; to put down in writing; to assert; to iron out; to hone, strop; to establish, -se to settle.

asentimiento m. assent, acquiescence, agreement.

asentir[3] v. irr. to assent, agree.

aseo m. neatness, cleanliness.

asequible adj. obtainable, available.

aserción f. assertion, affirmation.

aserradero m. sawmill.

aserrar[1] v. irr. to saw.

aserrín m. sawdust.

aserto m. assertion.

asesinar v. to assassinate, murder.

asesinato m. assassination, murder.

asesino m. assassin, murderer; adj. murderous.

asestar v. to point, aim, direct; — un golpe to deal a blow; — un tiro to fire a shot.

aseveración f. assertion, affirmation, contention.

aseverar v. to assert, affirm.

asfalto m. asphalt.

asfixia f. suffocation.

asfixiar v. to suffocate, smother.

así adv. so, thus, like this; therefore; — so-so; — que so that; — que (or como) conj. as soon as; Am. — no más so-so; just so

asiático adj. & m. Asiatic

asidero m. handle; hold

asiduo adj assiduous, diligent, persevering.

asiento m. seat; site, location; bottom; entry (in bookkeeping), -s dregs, sediment.

asignación f assignment, allowance

asignar v. to assign; to allot, to attribute; to appoint.

asilado m. inmate (of an asylum).

asilar v. to house, shelter; to put in an asylum.

asilo m. asylum, refuge, shelter

asimilar v to assimilate, digest, absorb; to liken, compare.

asimismo adv. likewise, also

asir[22] v. irr to seize, take hold of.

asistencia f. presence; attendance; assistance, help; *Am.* sitting room; **-s** allowance; *Am.* **casa de —** boarding house.

asistente m. assistant; helper; military orderly; *Am.* servant; **los -s** those present.

asistir v. to attend, be present; to help; *Am.* to board, serve meals.

asno m. ass, donkey.

asociación f. association.

asociado m. associate.

asociar v. to associate; **-se** to join; to associate.

asolamiento m. devastation, ravage, havoc, destruction.

asolar[2] v. irr. to raze; to lay waste; to parch; to dry up, become parched; to settle (*as liquids*).

asoleado adj. sunny; p.p. of **asolear**.

asolear v. to sun; **-se** to bask in the sun; to get sunburnt.

asomar v. to show, appear; **— la cabeza** to stick one's head out; **-se** to look out (*of a window*); to peep out (*or into*); *Am.* to draw near, approach.

asombrar v. to astonish, amaze; to frighten; to cast a shadow; to darken; **-se** to be astonished, be amazed.

asombro m. astonishment, amazement; fright.

asombroso adj. astonishing, amazing.

asomo m. sign, indication; conjecture, suspicion; **ni por —** by no means.

aspa f. wing of a windmill; blade (*of a propeller*); reel (*for winding yarn*).

aspecto m. aspect, look, appearance.

aspereza f. roughness, ruggedness; harshness; severity.

áspero adj. rough, uneven, harsh; gruff.

aspiración f. aspiration, ambition, longing; inhalation, breathing in.

aspirante m. & f. applicant; candidate.

aspirar v. to aspire, long for, seek, to inhale, breathe in; to aspirate (*pronounce an* h *sound*).

asquear v. to disgust, nauseate, sicken.

asqueroso adj. loathsome, disgusting, sickening; filthy.

asta f. horn; antler; mast, pole, staff, flagstaff; lance; **a media —** at half mast.

asterisco m. asterisk, star (*used in printing*).

astilla f. chip; splinter; splint.

astillar v. to chip; to splinter; **-se** to splinter, break into splinters.

astillero m. dry dock; shipyard; lumber yard; rack (*for lances or spears*)

astro m. star; planet.

astronomía f. astronomy; **astrónomo** m. astronomer.

astucia f. shrewdness, cunning; trick.

asturiano adj. Asturian, of or from Asturias, Spain; m. Asturian.

astuto adj. astute, shrewd, wily, crafty.

asueto m. recess, vacation; **día de —** holiday.

asumir v. to assume.

asunto m. topic, subject matter; business; affair.

asustadizo adj. shy, scary, easily frightened, jumpy.

asustar v. to frighten, scare.

atacante m. attacker; adj. attacking.

atacar[6] v. to attack; to tighten, fasten; to ram; to plug, wad (*a gun*).

atadura f. tie, knot; fastening.

atajar v. to intercept; to interrupt, cut off; to take a short cut; to cross out.

atajo m. short cut; interception; *Am.* drove. See **hatajo**.

atalaya f. lookout, watchtower; m. lookout, watchman, guard.

atañer[19, 51] v. to concern.

ataque m. attack; fit.

atar v. to tie, fasten; **-se** to get tied up, to be puzzled or perplexed.

atareado adj. busy, over-worked.

atarear v. to overwork, load with work; **-se** to toil, work hard; to be very busy.

atascadero m. muddy place; obstruction.

atascar[6] v. to stop up; to jam, obstruct; **-se** to get stuck; to stick; to jam, get obstructed; to stall.

ataúd m. coffin.

ataviar[17] v. to attire, deck, adorn; **-se** to dress up, doll up.

atavío m. attire, costume; ornaments, finery.

atemorizar[9] v. to frighten, scare.

atención f. attention, care, thought; courtesy; **-es** business, affairs; **en —** a having in mind, considering.

atender[1] v. irr. to heed, pay attention, to attend to, take care of; to take into account or consideration.

atendido adj. *Am.* attentive, courteous.

atenerse[45] v. irr. to rely (on); to accept, abide (by).

atenido adj. *Am.* habitually dependent on another; p.p. of **atenerse**.

atentado m. offense, violation, crime, violence.

atentar[1] v. irr. to attempt, try; **— contra la vida de alguien** to attempt the life of someone.

atento adj. attentive, courteous, polite.

atenuar[18] v. to attenuate, lessen; to tone down, to dim; to make thin or

21

slender.

ateo m. atheist; adj. atheistic.

aterciopelado adj. velvety.

aterido adj. stiff, numb from cold.

aterirse[3,61] v. irr. to become numb with cold.

aterrador adj. terrifying, appalling.

aterrar v. to terrify, frighten.

aterrizaje m. landing (of a plane); **pista de —** landing strip.

aterrizar[9] v. to land (said of a plane).

aterronar v. to make lumpy, form into lumps; **-se** to lump, form into lumps, become lumpy.

aterrorizar[9] v. to terrify, frighten, appall.

atesorar v. to treasure; to hoard, lay up, accumulate.

atestado adj. crowded, jammed, stuffed; witnessed; p.p. of atestar.

atestar v. to attest, testify, witness; to fill up, cram, stuff, crowd; **-se de** to stuff oneself with; to get stuffed with.

atestiguar[8] v. to testify, witness; to attest.

atiborrar v. to stuff; **-se** to stuff oneself.

atiesar v. to stiffen.

atildado adj. spruce, trim; painstaking in dress or style.

atinar v. to hit the mark; to guess right.

atisbar v. to spy, look cautiously; to watch, pry; to catch a glimpse of; to peek.

atisbo m. glimpse; insight; peek; spying.

atizar[9] v. to poke, stir (the fire); to kindle, rouse; to trim (a wick); **— un bofetón** to give a wallop.

atlántico adj. Atlantic; **el Atlántico** the Atlantic.

atlas m. atlas.

atleta m. & f. athlete.

atlético adj. athletic.

atletismo m. athletics.

atmósfera f. atmosphere, air.

atmosférico adj. atmospheric.

atole m. Am. Mexican drink made of corn meal.

atolondrado p.p. & adj. confused, muddled; stunned; heedless, harebrained, thoughtless.

atolondramiento m. thoughtlessness, recklessness; confusion, perplexity.

atolondrar v. to confuse, muddle, perplex; to stun; **-se** to get muddled, confused; to get stunned.

átomo m. atom; small particle, tiny bit.

atónito adj. astonished, amazed.

atontado adj. stupefied, stupid, stunned.

atontar v. to stupefy, stun, to confuse.

atorar v. to jam; to stop up, clog; Am. to hold up, stop; **-se** to get stuck (in

the mud); to get clogged; to get jammed; to choke (with food).

atormentar v. to torment; to worry, afflict; to tease, bother, vex.

atornasolado = tornasolado.

atornillar v. to screw, Am. to bother, torment.

atorrante m. & f. Am. vagabond, tramp.

atrabancar[6] v. to rush awkwardly; to run over; **-se** Am. to get involved in difficulties; Am. to rush into things.

atrabiliario adj. melancholy; bad-tempered.

atracar[6] v. to cram, stuff; to moor; to approach land; to hold up, assault; Am. to seize; Am. to pursue, harass; Am. to treat severely; Am. to thrash, beat; **— al muelle** to dock, moor to the wharf; **-se** to stuff oneself, overeat; Am. to have a fist fight; Am. to falter, stutter; **-se a** to come alongside of (a ship).

atracción f. attraction.

atraco m. holdup, assault; Am. **darse un — de comida** to stuff oneself, gorge.

atracón m. stuffing, gorging; Am. violent quarrel; **darse un — de comida** to stuff oneself, gorge.

atractivo adj. attractive; m. attractiveness, charm.

atraer[46] v. irr. to attract.

atragantarse v. to gobble up; to choke (with food).

atrancar[6] v. to bolt, fasten with a bolt; Am. **-le una cosa** to face something, stand up against something; **-se** to get crammed, obstructed; Am. to be stubborn, stick to one's opinion; Am. to stuff oneself, choke (with food).

atrapar v. to trap, ensnare; to seize, grab; to overtake.

atrás adv. back; behind; backward; Am. **echarse — (or para —)** to back out, go back on one's word.

atrasado adj. late; behind time; backward; behind (in one's work, payments, etc.); slow (said of a clock); p.p. of atrasar.

atrasar v. to delay; to be slow or behind time; **-se** to get behind, lose time; Am. to suffer a setback (in one's health or fortune).

atraso m. backwardness; delay; setback; **-s** arrears.

atravesar[1] v. irr. to cross; to walk across; to go through; to pierce; Am. to buy wholesale.

atreverse v. to dare, risk; to be insolent, saucy.

atrevido *adj.* bold, daring; insolent.

atrevimiento *m.* boldness, daring; insolence.

atribuir [32] *v. irr.* to attribute, ascribe, impute.

atribular *v.* to grieve, distress; -se to grieve; to be distressed.

atributo *m.* attribute, quality.

atril *m.* lectern, reading desk, book stand, music stand.

atrincherar *v.* to intrench, fortify with trenches; -se to intrench oneself.

atrio *m.* court, patio in front of a church; entrance hall.

atrocidad *f.* atrocity.

atronador *adj.* thunderous, deafening.

atronar [2] *v. irr.* to deafen; to stun.

atropellar *v.* to run over, run down, knock down; to trample upon; to insult; — **por** to knock down, overcome with violence; -se to rush.

atropello *m.* violent act; insult; outrage; trampling.

atroz *adj.* atrocious, awful; inhuman.

atún *m.* tunny fish, tuna fish.

aturdido *adj. & p.p.* stupid, awkward; stunned, bewildered.

aturdimiento *m.* daze, bewilderment, confusion.

aturdir *v.* to stun; to deafen; to bewilder.

audacia *f.* daring, boldness.

audaz *adj.* daring, bold.

audiencia *f.* audience, hearing; court of justice.

auditor *m.* judge advocate.

auditorio *m.* audience.

auge *f.* boom (*in the market*); boost (*in prices*); topmost height (*of fortune, fame, dignity, etc.*); **estar** (*or* **ir**) **en** — to be on the increase.

augurar *v.* to foretell, predict.

augusto *adj.* venerable; majestic.

aula *f.* schoolroom, classroom; lecture hall.

aullar *v.* to howl; to shriek; to bawl.

aullido *m.* howl.

aumentar *v.* to augment, increase.

aumento *m.* increase, advance, rise

aun (aún) *adv.* even, still, yet.

aunque *conj.* though, although.

aura *f.* breeze; favor, applause; *Am.* bird of prey, buzzard, vulture.

áureo *adj.* golden.

aureola *f.* aureole, halo.

aurora *f.* dawn; beginning; — **boreal** aurora borealis, northern lights.

auscultar *v.* to sound, examine by listening to (*the chest, lungs, heart, etc.*).

ausencia *f.* absence.

ausentarse *v.* to absent oneself; to be absent; to leave

ausente *adj.* absent.

auspicios *m. pl.* auspices, patronage; omens.

austeridad *f.* austerity, severity, sternness, harshness.

austero *adj.* austere, stern, strict, harsh.

austral *adj.* southern

austríaco *adj. & m.* Austrian

austro *m.* south wind.

auténtico *adj.* authentic, true, genuine

auto *m.* auto, automobile; one-act play, writ, order; — **sacramental** one-act religious play; —**s** proceedings.

autobús *m.* bus, autobus.

autóctono *adj.* indigenous, native.

automático *adj.* automatic.

automotriz *adj.* automotive, self-moving.

automóvil *m.* automobile, auto

automovilista *m. & f.* motorist.

autonomía *f.* autonomy.

autor *m.* author.

autoridad *f.* authority.

autoritario *adj.* authoritative; authoritarian, domineering; bossy.

autorización *f.* authorization, sanction

autorizar [9] *v.* to authorize, give power (to).

auxiliar *v.* to aid, help; *adj.* auxiliary, helping, assisting; *m.* assistant.

auxilio *m.* aid, help.

avaluación *f.* valuation, appraisal, assessment.

avaluar [18] *v.* to value, appraise

avalúo *m.* valuation, appraisal.

avance *m.* advance, progress, headway; advanced payment; attack.

avanzada *f.* advance guard; outpost; advanced unit, spearhead.

avanzar [9] *v.* to advance.

avaricia *f.* avarice, greed.

avariento *adj.* avaricious, miserly; *m* miser.

avaro *adj.* miserly, greedy; *m.* miser.

avasallar *v.* to subject, dominate, subdue.

ave *f.* bird; fowl; — **de corral** domestic fowl; — **de rapiña** bird of prey.

avecindarse *v.* to settle, locate, establish oneself, take up residence (*in a community*)

avellana *f.* hazelnut; **avellano** *m.* hazel; hazelnut tree; **avellanado** *adj.* hazel, light brown.

avena *f.* oats.

avenencia *f.* harmony, agreement; conformity

avenida *f.* avenue; flood.

avenir [48] *v. irr.* to adjust; to reconcile;

-se a to adapt oneself to; -se con alguien to get along with someone.

aventador m. fan (for fanning a fire); ventilator; winnower (machine for separating wheat from chaff).

aventajar v. to excel; to be ahead (of), -se a to get ahead of.

aventar¹ v. irr. to fan, to winnow, blow chaff from grain; to throw out, expel; Am. to pitch, throw; Am. to dry sugar (in the open); Am. to rouse (game); -se to be full of wind; to flee, run away; Am. to attack, hurl oneself (on someone)

aventura f. adventure; risk, danger; chance.

aventurado adj. adventurous, risky; bold, daring.

aventurar v. to venture, risk, -se a to risk, run the risk of; to dare

aventurero adj. adventurous, m adventurer.

avergonzar².⁹ v. irr to shame, -se to feel ashamed.

avería f. damage; aviary, birdhouse; Am. misfortune; Am. mischief.

averiar¹⁷ v. to damage, spoil, hurt; -se to become damaged; to spoil.

averiguar⁹ v. to find out; to investigate.

aversión f. aversion, dislike, reluctance.

avestruz m. ostrich.

avezado p.p. & adj accustomed; trained, practiced

aviación f. aviation

aviador m. aviator, flyer, purveyor, provider, Am moneylender (to miners or laborers), promoter

aviar¹⁷ v. to equip, to supply, to prepare, make ready, Am to lend money or equipment, estar aviado to be surrounded by difficulties; to be in a fix

ávido adj. eager, greedy

avinagrado adj. sour, acid, cross.

avinagrar v. to sour, make sour or acid; -se to sour, become sour.

avío m. provision, supply; preparation; Am. loan of money or equipment; -s equipment; -s de pescar fishing tackle.

avión m. airplane; martin (a bird similar to a swallow).

avisar v. to inform, give notice, advise; to announce, to warn.

aviso m. notice, advice, announcement; warning.

avispa f. wasp; avispero m. wasp's nest; avispón m. hornet.

avispado adj lively, keen, clever, wideawake; Am. frightened, scared

avispar v. to spur, incite; -se to be on the alert; to be uneasy; Am. to become

frightened, scared

avistar v. to glimpse, catch sight of, -se to see each other, meet.

avivar v. to enliven, give life to, to revive; to brighten; to quicken.

avizor adj. alert, watchful.

avizorar v. to spy, watch closely.

aya f. child's nurse, governess, ayo m. tutor, guardian.

ayer adv. yesterday.

ayuda f. aid, help.

ayudante m. assistant.

ayudar v. to aid, help.

ayunar v. to fast.

ayunas, en — fasting, en — de totally ignorant of

ayuno m fast, — de wholly ignorant of

ayuntamiento m municipal government; town hall.

azabache m. jet; -s jet ornaments.

azada f. spade; hoe, azadón m. hoe.

azafrán m. saffron.

azahar m. orange or lemon blossom.

azar m. hazard; chance; accident; disaster

azogue m. quicksilver.

azolvar v. to clog, obstruct, -se to clog, get clogged

azorar v. to disturb, startle, to bewilder; -se to be startled, astonished, to be bewildered, perplexed; to be uneasy

azotaina f flogging, lashing, beating

azotar v. to whip, lash, beat, Am to thresh (rice); — las calles to "beat the pavement," walk the streets

azote m. whip; lash with a whip; scourge; affliction, calamity

azotea f. flat roof.

azteca adj., m. & f Aztec

azúcar m. sugar

azucarar v. to sugar, to sweeten, -se to become sweet, Am. to crystallize, turn to sugar.

azucarera f. sugar bowl; sugar mill.

azucarero adj. sugar (used as adj.), m. sugar manufacturer, producer or dealer; sugar bowl.

azucena f. white lily.

azufre m. sulphur.

azul adj. blue; — celeste sky-blue; — marino navy blue; — turquí indigo; Am. tiempos -es hard times.

azulado adj. bluish.

azular v. to dye or color blue.

azulejo m. glazed tile, Am. bluebird; adj. bluish.

azuzar⁹ v. to urge, egg on, to incite.

B

baba f drivel, slaver, saliva; slime, slimy secretion, Am. small alligator.

babear v. to drivel; to slobber
babero m. baby's bib.
babor m. port, port side (of a ship)
babosear v. to slaver, drivel; to keep one's mouth open; to act like a fool.
baboso adj. driveling, slobbering; slimy; foolishly sentimental; Am. silly, idiotic, foolish; **babosa** f. slug (creature like a snail, but without a shell).
babucha f. slipper, Am. a — pickaback, on the back or shoulders.
bacalao, bacallao m. codfish
bacilo m. bacillus.
bacín m. pot, chamber pot; **bacinica** f. chamber pot.
bacteria f. bacterium; -s bacteria.
bacteriología f. bacteriology.
bacteriológico adj. bacteriological, pertaining to bacteriology.
báculo m. staff, cane; aid, support.
bache m. rut, hole in the road.
bachiller m. bachelor (one who holds degree); talkative person; **bachillerato** m. bachelor's degree; studies for the bachelor's degree.
badajo m. clapper of a bell, foolish talker.
badana f. sheepskin.
bagaje m. baggage, army pack mule.
bagatela f. trifle.
bagazo m. waste pulp (of sugarcane, olives, grapes, etc.)
bagual adj. Am. wild, untamed, unruly; Am. rude, discourteous; Am. lanky, awkward; m. Am. wild horse.
bahía f. bay, harbor.
bailador m. dancer; adj. dancing.
bailar v. to dance, to spin around
bailarín m. dancer, **bailarina** f. dancer.
baile m. dance, ball; ballet.
bailotear v. to jig, jiggle; to dance poorly; to dance around.
baja f. fall (of prices), war casualty, **dar de —** to discharge, muster out.
bajada f. descent; slope, dip (on a road), **de —** on the way down; **subidas y -s** ups and downs.
bajar v. to go down, to drop (as price or value); to lower; to take or carry down; to humble; **-se** to get down or off; to alight; Am. to stop at a hotel.
bajel m. boat, ship.
bajeza f. vile act or remark, meanness; baseness; degradation.
bajío m. shoal, sand bank; Am. lowland.
bajo adj. low; short; soft, bass (tone or voice); shallow (water); subdued (color); humble; base; **piso — first floor**, ground floor; prep. under, underneath;

m. bass.
bala f. bullet, shot, ball; bale (of cotton).
balada f. ballad.
baladí adj. trivial; flimsy
balance m. balance; equilibrium; balance sheet; rocking, rolling.
balancear v. to balance; to rock, roll, to swing, sway; to waver.
balanceo m. rocking, rolling, swinging; balancing; wavering; wabbling.
balanza f. balance, scale.
balar v. to bleat.
balaustrada f. balustrade, banisters, railing.
balaustre m. banister
balazo m. shot; bullet wound; adj. Am. clever, cunning.
balbucear v. to stammer, stutter, to babble.
balbuceo m. babble.
balcón m. balcony.
baldado m. cripple; adj. & p.p. crippled.
baldar v. to cripple; to trump (a card).
balde m. pail; bucket; **de —** free of charge; **en —** in vain.
baldío adj. barren; fallow, uncultivated; m. fallow land; wasteland
baldón m. infamy, insult.
baldosa f. floor tile; paving stone
balido m. bleat, bleating.
balneario m. bathing resort, adj. pertaining to bathing resorts or medicinal springs.
balompié m. football
balota f. ballot.
balotar v. to ballot, vote.
balsa f. pond, pool, raft, Am. marsh, Am. a species of ceiba (a tropical tree).
bálsamo m. balsam, balm.
baluarte m. bulwark.
ballena f. whale, whalebone.
bambolear v. to sway, swing, rock, -se to stagger; to sway
bambú m. bamboo.
banana f. banana, **banano** m. banana tree.
banasta f. large basket.
banca f. bench; card game, banking, banking house.
bancario adj. bank, pertaining to a bank.
bancarrota f. bankruptcy, failure, collapse.
banco m. bank; bench; stool; school (of fish); Am. pile of grain; Am. small hill on a plain.
banda f. band; ribbon, sash, gang; group, party; flock; side, edge, border.
bandada f. flock of birds; Am. gang.
bandeja f. tray; Am. bowl.

bandera f. banner, flag; Am. parar uno — to take the lead, be a gangleader.

banderilla f. dart with a small flag or streamers (used in bullfights); clavar a uno una — to goad or taunt someone; Am. pegar una— to touch for a loan.

banderillero m. bullfighter who sticks the banderillas into the bull.

banderín m. small flag; signal flag; recruiting office.

banderola f. streamer, small banner or flag; pennant.

bandidaje m. banditry, highway robbery; bandits.

bandido m. bandit, gangster.

bando m. decree, proclamation; party, faction.

bandolero m. bandit.

bandurria f. bandore (stringed instrument); Am. a species of wading bird.

banquero m. banker.

banqueta f. bench (without a back), stool, footstool; Am sidewalk.

banquete m. banquet.

banquetear v. to banquet, feast.

banquillo m. bench, stool.

bañada f. shower, spray; dip, bath.

bañar v. to bathe, wash, to dip; -se to take a bath.

bañera f. bathtub.

bañista m & f. bather.

baño m. bath, bathtub, cover, coating; — de María double boiler, Am. — ruso steam bath.

baqueta f. rod; whip, -s drumsticks; tratar a la — to treat scornfully, despotically

baquiano, baqueano m. Am. native guide (through the wilderness, Pampas, etc.); adj. Am. having an instinctive sense of direction

bar m bar, taproom, tavern.

baraja f. pack of cards.

barajar v. to shuffle, to mix, jumble together; to scuffle, wrangle; Am. to hinder, obstruct.

baranda f. railing; **barandal** m. banister, railing.

barandilla f balustrade, rail, railing.

barata f. barter, exchange, Am. bargain sale; Am. cockroach.

baratear v. to sell cheap; to cheapen; to cut the price of.

baratija f. trinket, trifle.

barato adj. cheap; m. bargain sale; money given by the winning gambler.

baratura f. cheapness.

baraúnda f. clamor, uproar, clatter.

barba f. chin; beard; -s whiskers.

barbacoa f. Am. barbecue; barbecued meat.

barbado adj. bearded.

barbaridad f. cruelty, brutality, rudeness; una — de a lot of; ¡que — ! what nonsense!; what an atrocity!

barbarie f. barbarousness; savagery; lack of culture, ignorance; cruelty, brutality.

bárbaro adj. barbarous, cruel, savage; crude, coarse; m. barbarian.

barbechar v. to plow; to fallow.

barbecho m. first plowing; plowed land; fallow, fallow land.

barbería f. barbershop.

barbero m. barber; Am. flatterer.

barbilla f. point of the chin.

barbón, barbudo adj. bearded.

barca f. boat, launch, barge.

barco m. boat, ship.

bardo m. bard, minstrel, poet.

barniz m. varnish; glaze; printer's ink.

barnizar v. to varnish; to glaze.

barómetro m. barometer.

barquero m. boatman; bargeman.

barquillo m. rolled wafer.

barquinazo m. tumble, bad fall, hard bump, somersault; Am. lurch (of a vehicle or boat).

barra f. bar; rod; railing; sand bar; — de jabón bar of soap.

barrabasada f. mischief, mean prank; rash, hasty act.

barraca f. hut, cabin, Am. large shed, warehouse.

barranca f., **barranco** m. ravine, gorge, Am. cliff.

barreminas m. mine-sweeper.

barrena f. auger, drill; gimlet (small tool for boring holes); spinning dive (of a plane)

barrenar v. to drill, bore; to scuttle (a ship), to blast (a rock).

barrendero m. sweeper.

barrer v. to sweep, to sweep away; Am. to defeat, Am. al — altogether, as a whole.

barrera f. barrier, obstacle

barreta f. small iron bar; Am. pick, pickaxe.

barrica f cask, keg.

barrida f. Am. sweep, sweeping.

barrido m. sweep, sweeping; sweepings, p.p. of **barrer**.

barriga f. belly; bulge.

barrigón, barrigudo adj. big-bellied.

barril m. barrel, keg.

barrio m. district, neighborhood, quarter; -s bajos slums.

barro m. mud, clay; pimple; Am. hacer (or cometer) un — to commit a blunder.

barroso *adj.* muddy; pimply; reddish.

barrote *m.* short, thick bar; brace; rung (*of a ladder or chair*).

barruntar *v.* to foresee; to have a presentiment; to conjecture.

barrunto *m.* foreboding, presentiment; guess; hint, indication, sign.

hártulos *m. pl.* household goods; implements, tools.

barullo *m.* hubbub, racket, disorder.

basa *f.* base, pedestal; basis, foundation.

basar *v.* to base; to put on a base.

basca *f.* nausea, sickness to one's stomach; **tener -s** to be nauseated, sick to one's stomach.

báscula *f.* scale (*for weighing*), platform scale.

base *f.* base, basis, foundation.

básico *adj.* basic.

basquear *v.* to heave, try to vomit; to be nauseated, sick to one's stomach.

basquetbol *m.* basketball.

bastante *adj.* enough, sufficient; *adv.* enough.

bastar *v.* to be enough; to suffice.

bastardilla *f.* italic type, italics.

bastardo *adj.* bastard.

bastidor *m.* wing (*of a stage*); frame; embroidery frame; window sash; easel (*support for a picture, blackboard, etc.*); **entre -es** behind the scenes, off stage.

bastilla *f.* hem.

bastimento *m.* supply, provisions; vessel, ship.

basto *adj.* coarse; *m.* club (*in cards*); *Am.* saddle pad.

bastón *m.* cane, walking stick.

basura *f.* rubbish, scraps; garbage; refuse.

basurero *m.* garbage or rubbish dump; manure pile; garbage man, rubbish man; street cleaner.

bata *f.* lounging robe; housecoat, wrapper, dressing gown; smock; **batín** *m.* smock.

batahola *f.* hubbub, racket, uproar.

batalla *f.* battle; struggle.

batallar *v.* to battle, fight, struggle.

batallón *m.* battalion.

batata *f.* sweet potato.

bate *m.* *Am.* baseball bat.

batea *f.* tray; trough; bowl; barge; *Am.* washtub.

bateador *m.* *Am.* batter (*in baseball*).

batear *v.* *Am.* to bat.

batería *f.* battery (*military, naval, or electric*); **— de cocina** set of kitchen utensils; *Am.* **dar —** to raise a rumpus; to plod, work hard.

batidor *m.* beater; scout.

batintín *m.* gong.

batir *v.* to beat, whip; to defeat; to reconnoiter, explore; to flap; *Am.* to rinse (*clothes*); *Am.* to denounce; **-se** to fight; **— palmas** to clap, applaud.

baturrillo *m.* medley, mixture; hodgepodge.

batuta *f.* orchestra conductor's baton or wand; **llevar la —** to lead; to be the leader.

baúl *m.* trunk, chest; **— mundo** large trunk.

bautismo *m.* baptism, christening; **nombre de —** Christian name.

bautista *m. & f.* Baptist; baptizer.

bautizar *v.* to baptize, christen.

bautizo *m.* christening, baptism.

baya *f.* berry.

bayeta *f.* flannel, flannelette; **bayetón** *m.* thick wool cloth; *Am.* long poncho lined with flannel.

bayo *adj.* bay, reddish-brown.

baza *f.* trick (*cards played in one round*); **meter —** to meddle; to butt into a conversation; **no dejar meter —** not to let a person put a word in edgewise.

bazar *m.* bazaar; department store.

bazo *m.* spleen.

bazofia *f.* scraps, refuse, garbage; dregs.

beatitud *f.* bliss, blessedness.

beato *adj.* blessed; beatified; devout; overpious; hypocritical.

bebé *m.* baby.

bebedero *m.* drinking trough; watering place; spout.

bebedor *m.* drinker; drunkard.

beber *v.* to drink; to drink in, absorb.

bebida *f.* drink, beverage; **dado a la —** given to drink.

beca *f.* scholarship, fellowship; sash worn over the academic gown.

becario *m.* scholar, fellow, holder of a scholarship.

becerro *m.* young bull; calf; calfskin.

becuadro *m.* natural sign (*in music*).

befa *f.* scoff, jeer.

befar *v.* to scoff, jeer at, mock.

bejuco *m.* cane; **silla de —** cane chair.

beldad *f.* beauty.

belga *adj.*, *m. & f.* Belgian.

bélico *adj.* warlike.

beligerante *adj.*, *m. & f.* belligerent.

bellaco *adj.* sly, deceitful; *m.* villain; rascal.

bellaquear *v.* to cheat; to play tricks; *Am.* to rear, stand up on the hind legs; *Am.* to balk; *Am.* to be touchy, over-sensitive.

bellaquería *f.* cunning, trickery; sly

act or remark.

belleza f. beauty.

bello adj. beautiful.

bellota f. acorn.

bendecir[27,52] v. irr. to bless.

bendición f. benediction, blessing; Am. echarle la — a una cosa to give something up for lost.

bendito adj. blessed; saintly; es un — he is a saint, he is a simple soul; p.p. of bendecir.

benefactor m. benefactor; patron.

beneficencia f. beneficence, kindness, charity.

beneficiar v. to benefit, do good; to cultivate (land); to exploit (a mine); to treat (metals); Am. to slaughter (cattle) for marketing.

beneficio m. benefit; profit; exploitation of a mine; land cultivation; Am. fertilizer; Am. slaughtering (of cattle).

benéfico adj. beneficent, good, kind.

benemérito m. worthy, notable; adj. worthy.

benevolencia f. benevolence, kindness.

benévolo adj. benevolent, good, kindly.

benigno adj. benign, gentle, mild, kind.

beodo adj. drunk; m. drunkard.

berenjena f. eggplant; Am. kind of squash; berenjenal m. eggplant patch; meterse uno en un — to get into a mess.

bergantín m. brigantine, brig (square-rigged ship with two masts).

bermejo adj. crimson, bright red.

bermellón adj. vermilion (bright red).

berrear v. to bellow; to scream; to sing off key.

berrido m. bellow, bellowing; scream.

berrinche m. fit of anger; tantrum.

berza f. cabbage.

besar v. to kiss.

beso m. kiss.

bestia f. beast.

bestialidad f. bestiality, brutality.

besugo m. sea bream (a fish).

besuquear v. to kiss repeatedly.

betabel f. Am. beet.

betún m. bitumen (combustible mineral); black pitch; shoeblacking.

Biblia f. Bible.

bíblico adj. Biblical.

biblioteca f. library; set of volumes; bookcase.

bibliotecario m. librarian.

bicicleta f. bicycle; **biciclista, bicicletista** m. & f. bicyclist, bicycle rider.

bicho m. insect, bug; any small animal; an insignificant person.

bien adv. well; — que although; **ahora**

— now then; **más** — rather; **si** — although; m. good, benefit; -es property; -es inmuebles real estate; -es raíces real estate.

bienaventurado adj. blessed, happy.

bienaventuranza f. blessedness; beatitude; bliss.

bienestar m. well-being, comfort, welfare.

bienhechor m. benefactor.

bienvenida f. welcome.

bienvenido adj. welcome.

biftec, bistec, bisté m. beefsteak.

bifurcación f. fork, forking, branching out; railway junction; branch railroad.

bifurcarse[2] v. to fork, branch off, divide into two branches.

bigamía f. bigamy.

bigote m. mustache.

bilis f. bile.

billar m. billiards; billiard room.

billete m. ticket; note; bill, banknote.

billón m. billion.

bimestre m. two-month period; bimonthly salary, rent, etc; adj. bimonthly; **bimestral** adj. bimonthly.

biografía f. biography.

biología f. biology.

biombo m. folding screen.

birlar v. to snatch away; to steal; to kill or knock down with one blow.

bisabuelo m. great-grandfather; **bisabuela** f. great-grandmother.

bisagra f. hinge.

bisiesto adj. leap (year).

bisojo adj. squint-eyed.

bisturí m. bistoury, surgical knife.

bitoque m. barrel plug, stopper; Am. faucet; Am. injection point (of a syringe).

bizarría f. gallantry, bravery; generosity.

bizarro adj. gallant, brave; generous.

bizco adj. cross-eyed.

bizcocho m. hardtack, hard biscuit; cooky; — borracho cake dipped in wine.

biznieto m. great-grandson; **biznieta** f. great-granddaughter.

blanco adj. white; m. white man; blank; blank sheet; target, aim, goal; — del ojo white of the eye.

blancura f. whiteness.

blancuzco, blanquecino, blanquizco adj. whitish.

blandir v. to brandish, flourish, swing.

blando adj. bland, smooth; soft; **blanducho** adj. flabby; soft.

blandura f. softness; mildness, gentleness.

blanquear v. to whiten, bleach; to whitewash; to show white; to begin to turn white.

blanqueo m. whitening, bleach, bleaching.

blanquillo adj. whitish; white (flour); m. Am. egg; Am. white peach.

blasfemar v. to blaspheme, curse, swear.

blasfemia f. blasphemy

blasón m. coat of arms; honor, glory.

blasonar v. to boast.

blindaje m. armor, armor plating.

blindar v. to armor.

bloc m. Am. tablet, pad of paper.

blondo adj. blond.

bloque m. block (of stone, wood, etc.); Am. tablet, pad of paper; Am. political block.

bloquear v. to blockade.

bloqueo m. blockade.

blusa f. blouse.

boato m. pomp, ostentation.

bobada f. foolishness, folly.

bobalicón adj. foolish, silly; m. simpleton, blockhead, dunce.

bobear v. to act like a fool; to fool around; to gawk, stare foolishly.

bobería f. foolishness, folly; nonsense; foolish remark.

bobina f. bobbin (spool or reel for holding thread); electric coil.

bobo adj. simple, foolish, stupid; m. booby, fool, dunce.

boca f. mouth; opening; — **abajo** face downward; — **arriba** face upward; a — **de jarro** at close range; **bocaza** f. large mouth.

bocacalle f. street intersection.

bocado m. mouthful, morsel, bite; bit (of a bridle); **bocadillo, bocadito** m. snack; sandwich; tidbit; Am. piece of candy.

bocanada f. mouthful; puff (of smoke).

boceto m. sketch; outline; skit.

bocina f. horn; trumpet; automobile horn; speaking tube; megaphone.

bochorno m. sultry weather; suffocating heat; blush, flush; embarrassment.

bochornoso adj. sultry; embarrassing.

boda f. marriage, wedding; — **de negros** a noisy party; —**s de Camacho** lavish feast, banquet.

bodega f. cellar; wine cellar; storeroom; warehouse; Am. grocery store; **bodeguero** m. keeper of a wine cellar; liquor dealer; Am. grocer.

bodoque m. wad; lump; dunce; Am. bump, swelling.

bofe m. lung; Am. snap, easy job; **echar uno los —s** to throw oneself into a job;

to work hard; Am. **ser un —** to be a bore; to be repulsive

bofetada f. slap; **bofetón** m. big slap, blow, hard sock, wallop.

boga f. vogue, fashion; rowing; m. rower.

bogar v. to row.

bohemio adj. & m. Bohemian.

bohío m. Am. cabin, shack, hut.

boina f. cap.

bola f. ball; game of bowling; fib, lie; shoe polish; Am. brawl, disturbance, riot, revolution; **no dar pie con —** not to do things right; not to hit the mark; to make mistakes; Am. **darle a la —** to hit the mark.

boleada f. Am. lassoing with **boleadoras**; Am. hunting expedition (with **boleadoras**); Am. shoeshine; Am. affront, insult.

boleadoras f. pl. Am. lasso with balls at the ends.

bolear v. to play billiards; to bowl; to lie, fib; Am. to lasso with **boleadoras**; Am. to entangle; Am. to polish (shoes); Am. to dismiss; Am. to blackball, vote against; Am. to flunk; **-se** Am. to rear, balk (said of a horse); Am. to blush, be ashamed.

boleta f. certificate; pass; pay order; Am. ballot; Am. first draft of a deed.

boletín m. bulletin.

boleto m. Am. ticket; **boletería** f. Am. ticket office.

boliche m. bowl (wooden ball for bowling); bowling alley; Am. cheap tavern; Am. gambling joint; Am. cheap store or shop, notions' store, variety store.

bolita f. small ball; Am. ballot (small ball used in voting); Am. marble; Am. armadillo.

bolo m. one of the ninepins (used in bowling); dunce, stupid fellow; **-s** bowls, bowling; **jugar a los -s** to bowl.

bolsa f. bag, purse; stock exchange; Am. pocket.

bolsillo m. pocket; pocketbook.

bolsista m. stockbroker, market operator.

bollo m. bun, muffin; bump, lump; puff (in a dress); tuft (on upholstery); Am. loaf of bread; Am. a kind of tamale; **-s** Am. difficulties, troubles.

bomba f. bomb; pump; lamp globe; Am. false news; Am. stanza improvised by a dancer; Am. firecracker, skyrocket; Am. satirical remark; Am. large drum; — **para incendios** fire engine; Am. **estar con una —** to be drunk; **bombita** f. soap bubble; Am. shame, embarrassment.

29

bombachas *f. pl. Am.* loose-fitting breeches.

bombacho *adj.* loose-fitting (*trousers or breeches*).

bombardear *v.* to bomb.

bombardeo *m.* bombardment, bombing; **avión de —** bomber, bombing plane.

bombardero *m.* bombardier; bomber.

bombear *v.* to bomb; to praise, extol; *Am.* to pump; *Am.* to fire, dismiss; *Am.* to puff hard on a cigar or cigarette.

bombero *m.* fireman; pumper.

bombilla *f.* electric-light bulb; *Am.* kerosene lamp tube; *Am.* small tube for drinking mate.

bombo *m.* large drum; base drum; player on a bass drum; *Am.* pomp, ostentation; *Am.* buttocks, rump; **dar —** to praise, extol (*in the press or newspapers*); *Am.* **darse —** to put on airs; *Am.* **irse uno al —** to fail; *adj.* stunned; *Am.* lukewarm; *Am.* slightly rotten; *Am.* stupid, silly, simple; *Am.* **fruta bomba** papaya (*tropical fruit*).

bombón *m.* bonbon, candy; **— de altea** marshmallow.

bonachón *adj.* good-natured; naive, simple.

bonanza *f.* fair weather; prosperity; rich vein of ore.

bondad *f.* goodness.

bondadoso *adj.* good, kind.

boniato *m. Am.* sweet potato.

bonito *adj.* pretty; *m.* striped tunny (*a fish*).

bono *m.* certificate; bond.

boñiga *f.* dung, manure.

boqueada *f.* gape, gasp.

boquear *v.* to open one's mouth; to gape, gasp; to be dying.

boquete *m.* breach, gap, hole, opening.

boquiabierto *adj.* openmouthed.

boquilla *f.* little mouth; small opening; cigarette or cigar holder; mouthpiece (*of a wind instrument*).

borbollón, borbotón *m.* spurt; spurting; big bubble; bubbling up; **a -es** in spurts.

borbotar *v.* to bubble up; to spurt, gush forth; to boil over.

bordado *m.* embroidery.

bordadura *f.* embroidery.

bordar *v.* to embroider.

borde *m.* border, edge.

bordear *v.* to skirt, go along the edge of; *Am.* to trim with a border; *Am.* to make a **bordo** (*small, temporary dam*); **-se** *Am.* to approach, get near.

bordo *m.* board, side of a ship; tack (*of a ship*); *Am.* ridge (*of a furrow*); *Am.*

small dam; **a —** on board.

borla *f.* tassel; doctor's cap; doctor's degree; tuft; powder puff; **tomar uno la —** to get a doctor's degree.

borlarse *v. Am.* to get a doctor's degree.

borrachera *f.* drunkenness; drunken spree.

borrachín *m.* toper.

borracho *adj.* drunk; *m.* drunkard; **borrachón** *m.* drunkard, heavy drinker.

borrador *m.* rough draft; *Am.* rubber eraser.

borrar *v.* to blot out; to erase.

borrasca *f.* storm, tempest.

borrascoso *adj.* stormy.

borrego *m.* lamb; fool, simpleton; *Am.* false news.

borrico *m.* donkey, ass; fool; sawhorse.

borrón *m.* blotch (*of ink*), blot.

borronear *v.* to blot, blotch; to scribble; to blur; to make a rough sketch.

boruca *f.* racket, noise.

boscaje *m.* grove, thicket, woods; landscape (*picture of natural scenery*).

bosque *m.* forest, woods; **bosquecillo** *m.* small forest, grove.

bosquejar *v.* to sketch; to outline.

bosquejo *m.* sketch, plan, outline, rough draft.

bostezar *v.* to yawn.

bostezo *m.* yawn.

bota *f.* leather wine bag; boot; *adj. Am.* stupid, clumsy; *Am.* drunk.

botar *v.* to launch; to fling; to throw away; to bounce; *Am.* to waste, squander; *Am.* to fire, dismiss; **-se** *Am.* to lie down.

botarate *m.* fool; braggart; *Am.* spendthrift.

bote *m.* small jar; boat; bounce; blow; jump; *Am.* liquor bottle; *Am.* jail; **estar de — en —** to be crowded, completely filled up.

botella *f.* bottle.

botica *f.* drugstore.

boticario *m.* druggist.

botija *f.* earthern jug; fat person; *Am.* buried treasure; *Am.* belly; *Am.* **poner a uno como — verde** to dress down, scold, insult a person.

botín *m.* booty, plunder; high shoe; *Am.* sock.

botiquín *m.* medicine cabinet; medicine kit; *Am.* liquor store, wine shop.

botón *m.* bud; button; knob; handle; **-es** bellboy.

bóveda *f.* arched roof; vault, underground cellar; burial place.

boxeador *m.* boxer.

boxear v. to box, fight with the fists.
boxeo m. boxing.
boya f. buoy; float net; Am. crease, dent; Am. rich mineral vein; Am. **estar en la buena —** to be in good humor.
bozal m. muzzle; bells on a harness; novice, beginner; **negro** native of Africa; Am. headstall (of a halter); Am. person (especially a negro) who speaks broken Spanish; Am. coarse, crude individual, adj. green, inexperienced; wild, untamed; stupid.
bozo m. down (on the upper lip); mustache; outside part of the mouth; headstall (of a halter).
bracear v. to swing one's arms; to struggle; to crawl, swim with a crawl.
bracero m. laborer; **de —** arm in arm; **servir de — a una señora** to serve as an escort, give a lady one's arm.
bracete: de — arm in arm.
bramante m. hemp cord, hemp string; Brabant linen; adj. roaring, bellowing.
bramar v. to bellow, roar, howl; to rage.
bramido m. roar; howl; bellow.
brasa f. red-hot coal.
brasero m. brazier (pan for burning coal), grate; hearth; Am. brick cooking stove.
bravata f. bravado, boastfulness, defiance.
bravear v. to bluster; to bully.
bravío adj. savage, wild; rustic.
bravo adj. brave; wild, ferocious; harsh; ill-tempered; Am. angry; Am. hot, highly seasoned.
bravura f. fierceness; courage; bravado; show of boldness.
braza f. fathom.
brazada f. armful; movement of the arms; **a una —** at arm's length.
brazalete m. bracelet.
brazo m. arm; branch; **-s** day laborers; Am. **de —** arm in arm; **luchar a — partido** to wrestle; to fight hand to hand.
brea f. pitch; tar; canvas.
brecha f. breach, gap.
bregar v. to struggle; to fight.
breña f. rough, craggy ground covered with brambles; bramble; **breñal** m. brambles; bush country.
breve adj. brief, short; **en —** shortly.
brevedad f. brevity; shortness.
bribón adj. idle, indolent; m. rascal, rogue; **bribonazo** m. scoundrel, cheat.
brida f. bridle; rein.
brigada f. brigade.
brillante adj. brilliant, bright; m. diamond.

brillantez f. brilliance, dazzle.
brillar v. to shine.
brillo m. luster, sparkle, shine.
brincar v. to hop, skip, jump, bounce.
brinco m. hop, skip, bounce, leap.
brindar v. to toast, drink to the health of; to offer.
brindis m. toast (to a person's health).
brío m. vigor, liveliness; valor, courage.
brioso adj. lively; brave.
brisa f. breeze.
británico adj. British.
brizna f. particle, chip, fragment; blade of grass.
brocal m. curb, curbstone (of a well).
brocha f. painter's brush; loaded dice; **cuadro de — gorda** badly done painting; **pintor de — gorda** house painter; **brochada** f. stroke of the brush, brush stroke; **brochazo** m. blow with a brush; brush stroke.
broche m. brooch; clasp, clip, fastener; hook and eye.
broma f. jest, joke; fun, merriment; Am. disappointment, irritation; **de —** in jest; **fuera de —** all joking aside.
bromear v. to joke, jest.
bronca f. quarrel, dispute, wrangle; **armar una —** to cause a disturbance, raise a rumpus.
bronce m. bronze.
bronceado adj. bronzed; bronze-colored; m. bronze finish.
bronco adj. hoarse; raspy, harsh; coarse, rough; uncouth; wild, untamed (horse).
broquel m. buckler, shield (worn on the arm).
brotar v. to shoot forth; to bud; to break out (on the skin); to gush, flow; to spring forth.
broza f. brushwood, underbrush; rubbish, refuse, trash; coarse, hard brush.
bruces: de — face downward.
bruja f. witch; hag; owl; adj. Am. broke, poor; **brujo** m. sorcerer, magician, wizard.
brújula f. compass; magnetic needle; peephole; gun sight.
bruma f. mist, fog; **brumoso** adj. foggy, misty, hazy.
bruñir v. irr. to burnish, polish; to put on make-up.
brusco adj. blunt, rude, abrupt.
brutal adj. brutal, beastly, savage.
brutalidad f. brutality.
bruto adj. brutal; stupid; coarse, rough; **peso —** gross weight; **diamante en —** diamond in the rough, unpolished diamond; m. brute, beast.

bucal *adj.* oral, pertaining to the mouth.

bucear *v.* to dive; to dive into, plunge into; to explore thoroughly a subject.

bucle *m.* curl, ringlet.

buche *m.* crop (*of a bird*); mouthful (*of water*); wrinkle, bag (*in clothes*); *Am.* goiter.

budín *m.* pudding.

buen(o) *adj.* good; kind; useful; well, in good health; **de buenas a primeras** all of a sudden, unexpectedly, on the spur of the moment; **por la(s) buena(s) o por la(s) mala(s)** willingly or unwillingly, by hook or crook.

buey *m.* ox.

búfalo *m.* buffalo.

bufanda *f.* muffler, scarf.

bufar *v.* to snort; to puff with anger; **-se** *Am.* to swell, bulge (*as a wall*).

bufete *m.* desk, writing table; lawyer's office.

bufido *m.* snort.

bufón *m.* buffoon, jester, clown; *adj.* comical, funny; **bufonada** *f.* wisecrack; jest.

bufonear *v.* to clown; to jest.

buhardilla *f.* garret, attic; skylight.

buho *m.* owl.

buhonero *m.* peddler.

buitre *m.* vulture.

bujía *f.* candle; candle power; candlestick; spark plug.

bula *f.* bull (*papal document*); papal seal.

bulevar *m.* boulevard.

bulto *m.* bulk, volume; lump, swelling; shadow, body; bundle; *Am.* briefcase; **a — haphazardly, by guess; escurrir el — to dodge; imagen de —** statue, sculpture; **una verdad de —** an evident truth.

bulla *f.* shouting, uproar; noisy crowd.

bullicio *m.* noise, uproar.

bullicioso *adj.* boisterous, noisy; gay, lively; turbulent, stormy.

bullir[26] *v. irr.* to boil; to buzz about; to bustle; to stir, move; *Am.* to deride.

buñuelo *m.* fritter; botch, poor piece of work.

buque *m.* ship, boat.

burbuja *f.* bubble.

burdo *adj.* coarse.

burgués *adj.* bourgeois, middle-class.

burla *f.* jest, mockery; **de — in jest.**

burlador *m.* practical joker; jester; scoffer; seducer.

burlar *v.* to mock, ridicule, deceive; **-se de** to scoff at; to make fun of.

burlón *m.* jester, teaser.

burro *m.* ass, donkey; *Am.* stepladder; *adj.* stupid; **burrito** *m.* small donkey;

Am. saddle rack.

busca *f.* search; hunting party; *Am.* **-s** profit on the side; graft.

buscar[6] *v.* to seek, search, look for; *Am.* to provoke.

búsqueda *f.* search.

busto *m.* bust (*upper part of body*).

butaca *f.* armchair; orchestra seat; **butacón** *m.* large armchair.

buzo *m.* diver.

buzón *m.* mailbox; letter drop.

C

cabal *adj.* complete, entire; exact; **estar uno en sus -es** to be in one's right mind.

cabalgar[7] *v.* to ride, mount (*a horse*); to ride horseback.

caballa *f.* horse mackerel.

caballada *f.* herd of horses; *Am.* nonsense, stupidity, blunder.

caballejo *m.* nag; poor horse.

caballeresco *adj.* gentlemanly; knightly; chivalrous, gallant.

caballería *f.* cavalry; horsemanship; mount, horse; knighthood; chivalry.

caballeriza *f.* stable; horses of a stable.

caballerizo *m.* groom, stableman.

caballero *m.* gentleman; knight, horseman; *adj.* gentlemanly.

caballerosidad *f.* chivalry, gentlemanly conduct.

caballeroso *adj.* chivalrous, gentlemanly.

caballete *m.* small horse; sawhorse; easel; ridge of a roof; bridge of the nose; *Am.* knife and fork rest.

caballo *m.* horse; knight (*in chess*); *Am.* stupid or brutal person; **a — on horseback; caballuco** *m.* nag.

cabaña *f.* hut, cabin; *Am.* cattle ranch.

cabecear *v.* to nod; to shake the head; to pitch (*as a boat*); *Am.* to begin to rise or fall (*said of a river*).

cabeceo *m.* nodding; pitching (*of a boat*).

cabecera *f.* head (*of bed or table*); seat, chief city (*of a district*).

cabecilla *f.* small head; *m.* ringleader.

cabellera *f.* head of hair, long hair; wig; tail of a comet.

cabello *m.* hair; **traer algo por los -s** to bring in a far-fetched fact or quotation; **-s de angel** cotton candy.

cabelludo *adj.* hairy; **cuero — scalp.**

caber[23] *v. irr.* to fit into, go into; to have enough room for; to befall; **no cabe duda** there is no doubt; **no cabe más** there is no room for more; **no — uno en sí** to be puffed up with pride; **no cabe en lo posible** it is absolutely impossible.

cabestro *m.* halter; leading ox; *Am.* rope, cord; *Am.* advance payment; **cabestrillo** *m.* sling (*for an arm*).

cabeza *f.* head; chief, leader; upper part; capital (*of a district*); *Am.* source (*of a river*); — **de playa** beachhead; — **de puente** bridgehead.

cabezada *f.* butt (*with the head*); bump on the head; nod, shake of the head; pitching (*of a ship*); headgear (*of a harness*).

cabezazo *m.* butt (*with the head*); bump on the head.

cabezudo *adj.* big-headed; hard-headed, pig-headed, stubborn, headstrong.

cabezón *adj.* big-headed; pig-headed, stubborn; *Am.* strong (*liquor*); *m.* large head; cavesson (*iron noseband used in breaking a horse*); *Am.* rapids or whirlpool in a river.

cabida *f.* space, room, capacity; **tener — con alguien** to have influence with someone.

cabildo *m.* cathedral chapter; municipal council; council room; town hall.

cabina *f.* cabin (*of an airplane*).

cabizbajo *adj.* crestfallen, downcast; pensive.

cable *m.* cable.

cablegrafiar[17] *v.* to cable.

cablegrama *m.* cablegram.

cabo *m.* end, tip, handle; piece of rope; cape, headland; corporal; **al — finally**; **al fin y al — anyway**, in the long run; **de — a rabo** from beginning to end; **estar al — de** to be well informed about; **llevar a — to** carry out, finish.

cabra *f.* goat; *Am.* fraud, trick; *Am.* loaded dice; *Am.* light two-wheeled carriage; **cabrillas** *f. pl.* whitecaps (*small waves with white crests*); Pleiades (*constellation*); game of skipping stones on the water.

cabrío *adj.* goatish; **macho — he-goat**; *m.* herd of goats.

cabriola *f.* caper, leap, hop, skip; somersault; **hacer -s** to cut capers; to prance.

cabriolar *v.* to prance; to caper; to romp, frolic, frisk.

cabrito *m.* kid; **cabritilla** *f.* kid, kidskin.

cabrón *m.* he-goat; cuckold (*man whose wife is unfaithful*).

cacahuate *m.* peanut.

cacao *m.* cocoa.

cacarear *v.* to cackle; to boast; *Am.* to run away from a fight.

cacareo *m.* cackle.

cacería *f.* hunt, hunting.

cacerola *f.* saucepan.

cacique *m.* chief; political boss; *Am.* tyrant; *Am.* one who leads an easy life.

caciquismo *m.* political bossism (*rule by political bosses*).

cacto *m.* cactus.

cacumen *m.* acumen, keen insight.

cacharro *m.* earthen pot or vase; broken piece of a pot; crude utensil; *Am.* cheap trinket.

cachaza *f.* slowness; calm; rum.

cachazudo *adj.* slow, easy going.

cachetada *f. Am.* slap on the face.

cachete *m.* cheek; slap on the cheek.

cachivache *m.* piece of junk; worthless fellow; *Am.* trinket.

cachorro *m.* cub; small pistol; *Am.* rude, ill-bred person.

cachucha *f.* cap; rowboat; popular Andalusian dance, song and music; *Am.* slap.

cada *adj.* each, every; — **uno** each one; — **y cuando que** whenever; *Am.* **a — nada** every second.

cadalso *m.* gallows; scaffold, platform.

cadáver *m.* corpse; **cadavérico** *adj.* deadly, ghastly, pale, like a corpse.

cadena *f.* chain.

cadencia *f.* cadence.

cadencioso *adj.* rhythmical.

cadera *f.* hip.

cadete *m.* cadet.

caducar[6] *v.* to dote, be in one's dotage; to lapse, expire; to become extinct, fall into disuse.

caduco *adj.* decrepit, very old, feeble; perishable.

caer[24] *v. irr.* to fall; to fall down; to fall off; **-se** to fall down, tumble; — **a to** face, overlook; — **bien** to fit, be becoming; — **en cama** to fall ill; — **en la cuenta** to catch on, get the point; — **en gracia** to please; **al — de la noche** at nightfall; **dejar — to** drop.

café *m.* coffee; café; *Am.* annoyance, bad time.

cafeína *f.* caffein.

cafetal *m.* coffee plantation.

cafetera *f.* coffeepot; woman café owner, coffee vendor or merchant; coffee-bean picker.

cafetero *adj.* pertaining to coffee; *m.* coffee grower; coffee merchant; owner of a café or coffee-house; *Am.* coffee drinker.

cafeto *m.* coffee tree.

caída *f.* fall, drop; descent; **a la — del sol** (*or* **de la tarde**) at sunset.

caimán *m.* cayman, alligator.

caja *f.* case, box; — de ahorros savings bank; — de píldora pillbox; — fuerte safe; echar a uno con -s destempladas to give someone the gate.

cajero *m.* cashier; box maker.

cajetilla *f.* small box; package of cigarettes.

cajón *m.* large box, chest; drawer; vendor's booth or stand; *Am.* narrow canyon; — de muerto coffin; *Am.* — de ropa dry-goods and clothing store.

cal *f.* lime (*mineral*).

calabaza *f.* pumpkin, squash; gourd; an ignorant person; dar -s to jilt, turn down (*a suitor*); to flunk, fail.

calabozo *m.* dungeon; prison cell.

calado *m.* drawn work; openwork (*in wood, metal, linen, etc.*), fretwork; draft (*of a ship*).

calamar *m.* squid, cuttlefish.

calambre *m.* cramp.

calamidad *f.* calamity, misfortune.

calandria *f.* lark, skylark.

calar *v.* to pierce, penetrate; to soak through; to make openwork (*in cloth, metal*); to cut out a sample of; to probe, search into; -se el sombrero to put on one's hat; to pull down one's hat.

calavera *f.* skull; *Am.* tail light; *m.* madcap, reckless fellow.

calcar[6] *v.* to trace; to copy, imitate.

calceta *f.* hose, stocking; hacer — to knit; calcetería *f.* hosiery shop; hosiery (*business of making hose*).

calcetín *m.* sock.

calcinar *v.* to burn, char, heat.

calcio *m.* calcium.

calco *m.* tracing, traced copy; exact copy; imitation.

calcular *v.* to calculate, figure, estimate.

cálculo *m.* calculation, estimate; calculus; gravel (*in the gall bladder, kidney, etc.*).

caldear *v.* to heat; to weld; -se *Am.* to become overheated, excited; *Am.* to get "lit up", get drunk.

caldera *f.* boiler; caldron, kettle; calderilla *f.* copper coin.

caldo *m.* broth; gravy.

calefacción *f.* heat, heating.

calendario *m.* calendar; almanac.

caléndula *f.* marigold.

calentador *m.* heater.

calentar[1] *v. irr.* to warm, heat; to spank; *Am.* to annoy, bother; -se to warm oneself; to become heated, excited; to be in heat; *Am.* to become angry.

calentura *f.* fever; *Am.* fit of temper; — de pollo feigned illness; calenturón *m.* high fever.

calenturiento *adj.* feverish; *Am.* tubercular.

caletre *m.* judgment, acumen, keen insight.

calibrar *v.* to gauge, measure; to measure the caliber of.

calibre *m.* caliber; bore, gauge (*of a gun*); diameter (*of a pipe, tube, wire*).

calicanto *m.* stone masonry.

calicó *m.* calico, cotton cloth.

calidad *f.* quality.

cálido *adj.* warm, hot.

caliente *adj.* warm, hot; heated; fiery; *Am.* angry; *Am.* bold, brave; *m. Am.* brandy in hot water; calientito *adj.* nice and warm.

calificación *f.* qualification; grade, mark (*in a course or examination*); judgment.

calificar[6] *v.* to qualify; to rate, consider, judge; to grade; *Am.* to compute (*election returns*); -se *Am.* to qualify or register (*as a voter*).

caligrafía *f.* penmanship.

calina *f.* haze, mist.

cáliz *m.* chalice, communion cup; cup, goblet; calyx (*of a flower*).

calma *f.* calm, quiet.

calmante *adj.* soothing; *m.* sedative.

calmar *v.* to calm, quiet, soothe.

calmo *adj.* calm, quiet.

calmoso *adj.* calm; soothing; phlegmatic, slow.

calor *m.* heat, warmth; ardor.

calorífero *m.* heater, radiator.

calofrío, calofrío *m.* chill.

calumnia *f.* slander.

calumniar *v.* to slander.

caluroso *adj.* hot, warm; heated, excited; cordial, enthusiastic.

calva *f.* bald head; bald spot; barren spot.

calvario *m.* Cavalry, place of the Cross; suffering, tribulation.

calvo *adj.* bald; barren.

calza *f.* wedge; shoehorn; *Am.* gold inlay, tooth filling; -s breeches.

calzada *f.* paved road; highway; *Am.* wide avenue.

calzado *m.* footwear.

calzador *m.* shoehorn.

calzar[9] *v.* to put on (*shoes, gloves, spurs*); to put a wedge under a wheel; *Am.* to fill (*a tooth*).

calzón *m.* (*or* calzones) breeches, short trousers; *Am.* drawers; *Am.* white cotton trousers; calzoncillos *m. pl.* drawers, men's shorts.

callado *adj.* silent, quiet.

callar v. to be silent; to hush; **-se** to be or keep silent.

caile f. street.

calleja f. small street, alley, lane; **callejuela** f. small, narrow street; lane.

callejear v. to walk the streets, ramble.

callejero m. street-rambler, street-stroller; street-loiterer; adj. fond of walking the streets; rambling.

callejón m. alley; lane; narrow pass; **— sin salida** blind alley.

callo m. callus, corn; **-s** tripe (food).

calloso adj. callous, hard.

cama f. bed, couch, cot; litter; **caer en —** to fall ill; **guardar —** to be confined to bed; **Am. tenderle uno la — a otro** to help one in his love affairs; to set a trap for someone; **camastro** m. poor, uncomfortable bed.

camada f. litter; brood.

cámara f. chamber, hall, parlor; house (of a legislative body); cabin, stateroom; chamber (of a gun); **— de aire** inner tube; **— fotográfica** camera.

camarada m. comrade; **camaradería** f. comradeship, companionship.

camarera f. waitress; chambermaid; stewardess.

camarero m. waiter; chamberlain; steward; valet.

camarilla f. political lobby; small group of politicians; "kitchen cabinet," group of unofficial advisers; small room.

camarón m. shrimp.

camarote m. cabin, stateroom.

cambalache m. swap, barter, exchange.

cambalachear v. to swap, barter, exchange.

cambiador m. barterer; money changer; Am. switchman.

cambiante adj. changing; exchanging; **-s** m. pl. iridescent colors.

cambiar v. to change; to exchange; to shift; **— de marcha** to shift gears.

cambiavía m. Am. railway switchman. See **guardagujas** and **cambiador**.

cambio m. change; exchange; railway switch; **libre —** free trade; **en —** on the other hand; in exchange.

cambista m. exchange broker, banker; Am. railway switchman.

camello m. camel.

camilla f. stretcher; cot; **camillero** m. stretcher bearer.

caminante m. & f. walker, traveler.

caminar v. to travel; to walk; Am. to progress, prosper.

caminata f. long walk; hike; jaunt.

camino m. road; course; Am. table runner; Am. hall·runner; **— de hierro**

railroad; **— real** highway; **de — on** the way.

camión m. truck; wagon; Am. bus; **camionero** m. truck driver; **camioneta** f. small truck; Am. bus.

camisa f. shirt; **— de fuerza** strait jacket; **meterse en — de once varas** to attempt more than one can manage, bite off more than one can chew; **camiseta** f. undershirt.

camisón m. long shirt; Am. nightgown; Am. gown, dress.

camote m. Am. a kind of sweet potato.

campamento m. encampment; camp.

campana f. bell; Am. spy, lookout (for thieves); **campanada** f. stroke of a bell; Am. **por — de vacante** once in a blue moon, very seldom.

campanario m. bell tower.

campanilla f. small bell; bubble; uvula; tassel; bell-flower.

campanillazo m. loud ring of a bell.

campanilleo m. ringing; tinkling.

campaña f. level, open country; campaign; period of active service.

campear v. to pasture; to grow green (said of the fields); to excel; to be prominent, stand out; to be in the field; Am. to search the plains for lost cattle; Am. to act the bully.

campechano adj. frank, open.

campeón m. champion; defender.

campeonato m. championship.

campesino adj. rural, rustic; m. peasant, countryman; farmer.

campestre adj. rural, rustic.

campiña f. large field; open country.

campo m. country; field; camp; **a — raso** in the open; **a — traviesa** (or **travieso**) cross-country.

camposanto m. churchyard, cemetery.

camuesa f. pippin (a variety of apple).

camuflaje m. camouflage.

can m. dog; trigger (of a gun).

cana f. white hair, grey hair; Am. a kind of palm; **echar una — al aire** to go out for a good time; to go out on a fling.

canadiense adj., m. & f. Canadian.

canal m. canal, channel; f. eaves trough.

canalla f. rabble, mob; m. mean fellow.

canana f. cartridge belt; **-s** Am. handcuffs.

canapé m. couch, lounge, sofa; settee.

canario m. canary; native of the Canary Islands; interj. great Scott!

canasta f. basket; crate.

cancelación f. cancellation.

cancelar v. to cancel.

canciller m. chancellor.

canción f. song; a kind of lyric poem; **volver a la misma —** to repeat, harp on the same thing.

cancha f. court (*for tennis, etc.*); sports ground or field; cockpit, enclosure for cockfights; *Am.* roasted corn or beans; *Am.* ¡**abran —** ! gangway!; make room!

candado m. padlock; *Am.* goatee.

candela f. candle; fire, forest fire; light.

candelero m. candlestick.

candente adj. incandescent, white-hot, red-hot.

candidato m. candidate.

candidatura f. candidacy.

candidez f. candor, simplicity.

cándido adj. candid, simple, innocent; white.

candil m. lamp; *Am.* chandelier; **candileja** f. small oil lamp; oil receptacle (*of a lamp*); **-s** footlights (*of a stage*).

candor m. candor, simplicity, innocence; frankness, sincerity.

canela f. cinnamon; an exquisite thing.

cangrejo m. crab.

canguro m. kangaroo.

caníbal m. cannibal.

canica f. marble (*small glass or marble ball*).

canilla f. long bone (*of the arm or leg*); cock (*of a barrel*), faucet; spool (*for a sewing maching*); *Am.* slender leg; *Am.* calf (*of the leg*); *Am.* **tener —** to have physical strength; **canillita** m. *Am.* newspaper boy.

canino adj. canine; **tener un hambre canina** to be ravenous; to be hungry as a dog.

canje m. interchange, exchange.

canjear v. to exchange, interchange.

cano adj. grey-headed, grey-haired.

canoa f. canoe.

canon m. canon; precept, rule, principle.

canónigo m. canon (*churchman*).

canonizar[9] v. to canonize, saint.

canoso adj. grey, grey-haired.

cansado adj. tired; tiresome, boring.

cansancio m. fatigue, weariness.

cansar v. to tire, fatigue; **-se** to get tired.

cantar v. to sing; to squeal, confess; *Am.* **— alto** to ask a high price; **— claro** (or **-las claras**) to speak with brutal frankness; m. song, epic poem.

cántaro m. pitcher, jug.

cantatriz f. singer.

cantera f. quarry; *Am.* stone block.

cántico m. canticle, religious song.

cantidad f. quantity.

cantilena f. song, ballad; monotonous repetition.

cantimplora f. canteen; metal vessel for cooling water; *Am.* flask for carrying gunpowder.

cantina f. mess hall; wine cellar; wine shop; canteen; *Am.* barroom, tavern; *Am.* saddlebag.

cantinela = **cantilena**.

cantinero m. bartender; tavern keeper.

canto m. song; singing; canto (*division of a long poem*); stone; edge; *Am.* lap; *Am.* piece.

cantón m. canton, region; corner; *Am.* cotton cloth.

cantor m. singer; song bird.

canturrear, canturriar v. to hum, sing softly.

canturreo m. hum, humming.

caña f. cane, reed; tall, thin glass; stem; *Am.* sugar-cane brandy; *Am.* a kind of dance; *Am.* bluff, boast.

cañada f. narrow canyon, dale, dell, gully, ravine; *Am.* brook.

cáñamo m. hemp; hemp cloth; *Am.* hemp cord, rope; **cañamazo** m. canvas.

cañaveral m. cane field; reed patch; sugar-cane plantation.

cañería f. conduit, pipe line; tubing, piping; gas or water main.

caño m. pipe, tube; spout; sewer; narrow channel; *Am.* branch of a river, stream.

cañón m. cannon, gun; barrel (*of a gun*); ravine, gorge, canyon; tube, pipe; beard stubble; pinfeather; quill (*of a feather*); chimney shaft; **cañonazo** m. cannon shot.

cañonear v. to cannonade, bombard.

cañoneo m. cannonade; bombardment.

cañonero m. gunboat; gunner; **lancha cañonera** gunboat.

caoba f. mahogany.

caos m. chaos, confusion.

capa f. cape, cloak; covering, coating; layer; scum; **so — de** under the guise of, under pretense of.

capacidad f. capacity; ability

capacitar v. to enable, prepare, fit, qualify; *Am.* to empower, authorize.

capataz m. boss, foreman, overseer.

capaz adj. capable, able, competent; spacious, roomy.

capellán m. chaplain, priest, clergyman.

caperuza f. pointed hood.

capilla f. chapel; hood.

capirote m. hood; **tonto de —** dunce, plain fool.

capital m. capital, funds; f. capital, capital city; adj. capital; **capitalismo** m. capitalism; **capitalista** m. & f.

36

capitalist; *adj.* capitalistic.
capitalizar[9] *v.* to capitalize.
capitán *m.* captain.
capitanear *v.* to command, lead.
capitolio *m.* capitol.
capitular *v.* to surrender; to come to an agreement.
capítulo *m.* chapter.
caporal *m.* boss, leader; *Am.* foreman in a cattle ranch.
capote *m.* cloak (*with sleeves*); bullfighter's cloak; *Am.* thrashing, beating; **decir para su —** to say to oneself; *Am.* de — in an underhanded way; *Am.* dar — to get ahead; to deceive.
capricho *m.* caprice, whim, notion.
caprichoso *adj.* capricious, whimsical; changeable, fickle.
caprichudo *adj.* whimsical; stubborn, willful.
cápsula *f.* capsule; percussion cap, cartridge shell; metal cap (*on bottles*).
captar *v.* to win, attract; to captivate; *Am.* to get, tune in on (*a radio station*).
captura *f.* capture.
capturar *v.* to capture, arrest.
capucha *f.* hood.
capullo *m.* cocoon, bud; acorn cup.
cara *f.* face; expression, countenance; front; de — opposite; echar (*or* dar) en — to reproach, blame; sacar la — por alguien to take someone's part, defend him.
carabina *f.* carbine, rifle.
caracol *m.* snail; winding stairs, *Am.* embroidered blouse; *Am.* curl.
caracolear *v.* to caper, prance around (*said of horses*); *Am.* to muddle, entangle; *Am.* to sidestep an obligation.
caracoleo *m.* prancing around; winding, turn.
carácter *m.* character; temper.
característico *adj.* characteristic, característica *f.* characteristic, trait.
caracterizar[9] *v.* to characterize.
¡caramba! *interj.* great guns! great Scott!
carámbano *m.* icicle.
caramelo *m.* caramel
caramillo *m.* reed pipe, small flute; armar un — to raise a rumpus, create a disturbance.
carancho *m. Am.* hawk, buzzard.
carátula *f.* mask; *Am.* title page of a book; *Am.* dial, face of a watch.
caravana *f.* caravan.
carbólico *adj.* carbolic.
carbón *m.* carbon; coal; — de leña charcoal; carbono *m.* carbon.
carbonera *f.* coal bin; coal cellar; woman coal or charcoal vendor; *Am.* coal

mine; **carbonero** *m.* coal dealer; charcoal vendor; *adj.* coal, relating to coal or charcoal.
carburador *m.* carburetor.
carcajada *f.* loud laughter, peal of laughter.
cárcel *f.* jail, prison.
carcelero *m.* jailer; *adj.* relating to a jail.
carcomido *adj.* worm-eaten; decayed.
cardar *v.* to card (*wool*).
cardenal *m.* cardinal; cardinal bird; bruise.
cárdeno *adj.* dark-purple.
cardo *m.* thistle; a kind of cactus.
carear *v.* to confront, bring face to face, to compare; -se to meet face to face.
carecer[13] *v.* to lack, be in need of.
carencia *f.* lack, want.
carente *adj.* lacking.
carero *adj.* overcharging; profiteering; *m.* profiteer.
carestía *f.* dearth, scarcity; high price.
careta *f.* mask.
carga *f.* load, burden; freight; cargo, charge of gunpowder; **volver a la —** to insist again and again.
cargado *p.p. & adj.* loaded; strong (*as tea or coffee*); cloudy, sultry; — de espaldas round-shouldered, stoop-shouldered.
cargador *m.* loader; stevedore; *Am.* carrier, errand boy, mover.
cargamento *m.* cargo.
cargar[7] *v.* to load; to charge; to bother, annoy; *Am.* to carry, lug; *Am.* to punish; — con to carry away; to assume (*responsibility*); — con el muerto to get the blame (*unjustly*).
cargo *m.* charge, position, duty, burden; loading; accusation; hacerse — de to take charge of; to realize.
carguero *adj.* load-carrying; freight-carrying; *m. Am.* beast of burden; *Am.* skilled loader of pack animals; *Am.* patient, long-suffering person.
caribe *adj.* Caribbean; *m.* Carib, Caribbean Indian; cannibal; savage.
caricatura *f.* caricature; cartoon.
caricia *f.* caress.
caridad *f.* charity; alms.
caries *f.* decay (*of a bone*), tooth decay.
cariño *m.* affection, love; *Am.* gift.
cariñoso *adj.* affectionate, loving.
caritativo *adj.* charitable.
carmesí *adj. & m.* crimson.
carmín *m.* crimson.
carnal *adj.* carnal, sensual.
carnaval *m.* carnival.

carne *f.* meat; flesh; — **de gallina** "goose flesh", "goose pimples"; **echar -s** to put on weight, get fat; *Am.* — **de res** beef.

carneada *f. Am.* butchering, slaughtering.

carnear *v. Am.* to butcher; *Am.* to kill.

carnero *m.* ram, male sheep; mutton; *Am.* a weak-willed person; *Am.* waste basket; *Am.* — **de la tierra llama** (*or any fleece-bearing animal*); *Am.* **cantar uno el** — to die.

carnicería *f.* meat market; butchery, slaughter; *Am.* slaughterhouse.

carnicero *m.* butcher; *adj.* carnivorous, flesh-eating; cruel.

carnívoro *adj.* carnivorous.

carnosidad *f.* fleshiness, fatness; abnormal growth (*on animal or plant tissues*).

carnoso *adj.* fleshy, meaty; pulpy.

caro *adj.* expensive; dear; *adv.* at a high price.

carona *f.* saddle pad.

carozo *m.* cob, corncob.

carpa *f.* carp (*fresh-water fish*), *Am.* canvas tent, circus tent; — **dorada** goldfish.

carpeta *f.* table cover; desk pad, portfolio, letter case or file; *Am.* office desk; *Am.* bookkeeping department; **carpetazo: dar** — **to table** (*a motion*); to set aside, pigeonhole or dismiss.

carpintería *f.* carpentry; carpenter's workshop.

carpintero *m.* carpenter; **pájaro** — woodpecker.

carraspear *v.* to cough up, to clear one's throat; to be hoarse.

carraspera *f.* hoarseness.

carrera *f.* career; race, run, course; stocking run.

carreta *f.* long, narrow wagon; cart; *Am.* wheelbarrow.

carretaje *m.* cartage (*transporting by cart, truck, etc.*); price paid for cartage.

carrete *m.* spool; reel.

carretel *m.* reel, spool, bobbin, fishing reel; log reel (*of a boat*).

carretera *f.* highway.

carretero *m.* carter, teamster; cart maker; **camino** — highway.

carretilla *f.* wheelbarrow; small cart; baggage truck; *Am.* wagon; *Am.* jaw; *Am.* string, series (*of lies, blunders, etc.*); *Am.* firecracker; **repetir de** — to rattle off, repeat mechanically.

carretón *m.* truck; wagon, cart.

carril *m.* rail; rut; furrow.

carrillo *m.* cheek; pulley; small cart.

carro *m.* cart; cartload *Am.* car, auto, streetcar, coach; *Am.* **pararle a uno el** — to restrain someone; *Am.* **pasarle a uno el** — to suffer an injury or misfortune; **carroza** *f.* large and luxurious carriage; chariot.

carroña *f.* dead and decaying flesh, putrid, decaying carcass.

carruaje *m.* carriage, vehicle.

carta *f.* letter; playing card; charter; map; — **blanca** full authority, freedom to act; — **de naturaleza** naturalization papers; — **de venta** bill of sale; *Am.* **retirar** — to repent, back down; *Am.* **ser la última** — **de la baraja** to be the worst or most insignificant person or thing.

cartearse *v.* to correspond, write to each other.

cartel *m.* poster, handbill; cartel, written agreement; **cartela** *f.* tag, slip of paper, small card, piece of cardboard; **cartelera** *f.* billboard; **cartelón** *m.* large poster.

cartera *f.* wallet; briefcase, desk pad, portfolio, position of a minister or cabinet member.

cartero *m.* mailman, letter carrier, postman.

cartilla *f.* primer; note, short letter; **leerle a uno la** — to scold, lecture someone concerning his duties.

cartografiar[17] *v.* to chart; to make charts.

cartón *m.* cardboard, pasteboard; **cartulina** *f.* fine cardboard.

cartuchera *f.* cartridge belt.

cartucho *m.* cartridge; roll of coins; paper cone or bag.

casa *f.* house, home; household; business firm; square (*of a chessboard*); *Am.* bet, wager; — **de empeños** pawnshop; — **de huéspedes** boardinghouse; **echar la** — **por la ventana** to spend recklessly, squander everything; **poner** — to set up housekeeping.

casabe, cazabe *m. Am.* cassava; *Am.* cassava bread.

casaca *f.* long military coat; **volver** — to be a turncoat, change sides or parties.

casamiento *m.* wedding; marriage.

casar *v.* to marry; to match; *Am.* to graft (*trees*); **-se** to get married.

cascabel *m.* jingle bell, tinkle bell; snake's rattle; *Am.* rattlesnake; **cascabela** *f. Am.* rattlesnake.

cascada *f.* cascade, waterfall.

cascajo *m.* coarse gravel; crushed stone;

pebble; fragment; rubbish.

cascanueces m. nutcracker.

cascar[6] v. to crack, break; **-se** to crack or break open.

cáscara f. shell, husk, hull, rind; bark of a tree; Am. **dar a uno — de novillo** to give someone a whipping; **cascarudo** adj. having a thick husk; having a thick rind.

cascarrabias m. & f. crab, grouch, ill-tempered person; adj. grouchy, cranky, irritable.

casco m. helmet, hoof; skull; broken piece of earthenware; cask; empty bottle; hull of a ship; Am. compound, main buildings of a farm; **caliente de -s** hot-headed; **ligero de -s** light-headed, frivolous; **romperse los -s** to rack one's brain.

caserío m. hamlet, small settlement.

casero adj. domestic; homemade; m. landlord; janitor, caretaker; Am. customer; Am. delivery boy; **casera** f. landlady; housekeeper.

caseta f. small house, cottage; booth, stall

casi adv. almost.

casilla f. stall, booth; square (of a checkerboard); pigeonhole; post-office box; **sacarle a uno de sus -s** to change someone's way of life or habits; to irritate, annoy, try someone's patience; **salirse de sus -s** to lose one's temper; to do something out of the way.

casino m. club, society, clubhouse; recreation hall.

caso m. case; point; matter; event; — **que** (or **en — de que**) in case that; **dado —** supposing; **hacer — de** to pay attention to; **hacer — omiso de** to omit; **no viene al —** that is not to the point.

casorio m. wedding, marriage.

caspa f. dandruff.

casta f. race, breed; caste, distinct class; quality, kind.

castaña f. chestnut; jug; knot or roll of hair; Am. small barrel; Am. trunk, large suitcase.

castañetear v. to rattle the castanets; to chatter (said of the teeth); to crackle (said of the knees or joints); — **con los dedos** to snap one's fingers.

castañeteo m. rattle or sound of castanets; chatter, chattering (of the teeth).

castaño m. chestnut (tree and wood); adj. chestnut-colored.

castañuela f. castanet.

castellano adj. & m. Castilian.

castidad f. chastity.

castigar[7] v. to chastise, punish.

castigo m. punishment; correction.

castillo m. castle.

castizo adj. pure, correct (language); pure-blooded.

casto adj. chaste, pure.

castor m. beaver; beaver cloth.

casual adj. casual, accidental.

casualidad f. chance, accident.

casuca f. little house; hut, shanty.

casucha f. hut, hovel, shack.

catadura f. aspect, appearance.

catalán adj. Catalan, Catalonian, of or from Catalonia, Spain; m. Catalan.

catalogar[7] v. to catalogue.

catálogo m. catalogue.

catar v. to look at, examine; to taste, sample.

catarata f. cataract; waterfall.

catarro m. catarrh, cold.

catástrofe f. catastrophe, mishap.

catear v. to explore, look around; Am. to search or raid (a home); Am. to explore for ore; Am. to test, try.

catecismo m. catechism.

cátedra f. class; subject; chair, professorship.

catedral f. cathedral.

catedrático m. professor.

categoría f. category, rank; kind, class.

categórico adj. categorical, positive.

catequizar[9] v. to catechize, give religious instruction (to); to induce, persuade.

católico adj. Catholic; universal; m. Catholic; **catolicismo** m. Catholicism.

catre m. cot, small bed; Am. raft, float; Am. camp stool, folding stool; — **de tijera** folding cot.

catrín m. Am. dandy; adj. Am. over-elegant, dressy.

cauce m. river bed.

caución f. precaution; security, guarantee; bail.

cauchero m. Am. rubber gatherer; Am. rubber producer; adj. Am. rubber, pertaining to rubber.

caucho m. rubber; Am. rubber tree; Am. rubber raincoat or cloak; **cauchal** m. rubber grove or plantation.

caudal m. wealth; river current; volume of water.

caudaloso adj. wealthy; abundant.

caudillaje m. military leadership; Am. political bossism; Am. tyranny.

caudillo m. leader, chief; Am. political boss.

causa f. cause; case, lawsuit; Am. light lunch, snack.

causar v. to cause.

cautela f. caution; cunning, craftiness; trick, deception.

cauteloso adj. cautious; crafty.

cautivar v. to capture; to charm, fascinate.

cautiverio m. captivity.

cautivo m. captive, war prisoner.

cauto adj. cautious.

cavar v. to dig, spade; to excavate.

caverna f. cavern, cave.

cavernoso adj. cavernous, like a cavern; hollow; **voz cavernosa** deep, hollow voice.

cavidad f. cavity.

cayado m. shepherd's crook, staff

cayo m. key, island reef.

caza f. hunt, hunting; wild game; **dar — to** pursue, track down.

cazador adj. hunting; m. hunter.

cazar v. to chase, hunt; to track down.

cazatorpedero m. destroyer, torpedo-boat.

cazo m. dipper; pot, pan.

cazuela f. stewing pan; earthenware cooking pan; topmost theatre gallery; Am. stewed hen; Am. candied sweet potatoes with spices.

cebada f. barley; Am. brewing of mate; **cebadal** m. barley field.

cebar v. to feed, fatten (animals); to encourage, nourish (a passion); to prime (a gun, pump, etc.); to bait (a fishhook); Am. to brew and serve mate or tea; **-se** to vent one's fury.

cebo m. feed (for animals); bait; incentive.

cebolla f. onion.

cecear v. to lisp.

ceceo m. lisp, lisping.

cecina f. dried beef, jerked beef.

cedazo m. sieve.

ceder v. to cede, transfer; to yield, surrender, submit; to diminish, abate.

cedro m. cedar.

cédula f. slip of paper; certificate; **— de vecindad** (or **— personal**) official identification card.

céfiro m. zephyr, soft breeze; Am. fine muslin.

cegar [1,7] v. irr. to blind; to become blind; to confuse; to fill up, stop up (a hole).

ceguedad, ceguera f. blindness.

ceiba f. Am. ceiba, silk-cotton tree.

ceja f. eyebrow; brow of a hill.

cejar v. to go backward; to back; to back down, give in, yield; to slacken.

cejijunto adj. frowning; with knitted eyebrows.

celada f. ambush, snare, trap.

celaje m. colored clouds; skylight; presage, portent; Am. shadow, ghost; Am. **como un — like** lightning.

celar v. to guard, watch; to watch over jealously; to conceal.

celda f. cell.

celebración f. celebration.

celebrar v. to celebrate; to praise, honor; to be glad.

célebre adj. famous; funny, witty; Am. graceful, pretty (woman).

celebridad f. fame, renown; celebrity, famous person; celebration.

celeridad f. swiftness, speed.

celeste adj. celestial, heavenly.

celestial adj. celestial, heavenly, divine.

célibe adj. unmarried; m. & f. unmarried person.

celo m. zeal, ardor; envy; heat (sexual excitement in animals); **-s** jealousy, suspicion, **tener -s** to be jealous.

celosía f. window lattice; Venetian blind.

celoso adj. jealous; zealous, eager; suspicious.

célula f. cell.

celuloide m. celluloid.

cellisca f. sleet; rain and snow.

cementar v. to cement.

cementerio m. cemetery.

cemento m. cement; **— armado** reinforced concrete.

cena f. supper.

cenagal m. quagmire, muddy ground, swamp.

cenagoso adj. muddy, miry.

cenar v. to eat supper.

cencerrada f. racket, noise (with cowbells, tin cans, etc.); tin pan serenade.

cencerrear v. to make a racket (with cowbells, tin cans, etc.).

cencerro m. cowbell.

cendal m. gauze; thin veil.

cenicero m. ash tray; ash pit; ash pan

ceniciento adj. ashen, ash-colored.

cenit m. zenith.

ceniza f. ashes, cinders.

cenizo adj. ash-colored.

censo m. census.

censor m. censor.

censura f. censure, criticism, disapproval; censorship.

censurador m. censor, critic; critical person; adj. critical.

censurar v. to censure, criticize, reprove; to censor.

centavo m. cent.

centella f. lightning, flash; spark.

centelleante adj. sparkling; flashing.

centellear v. to twinkle; to sparkle,

glitter; to flash.

centelleo *m.* glitter, sparkle.

centenar *m.* one hundred; field of rye.

centenario *m.* centennial, one hundredth anniversary; *adj.* centennial; old ancient.

centeno *m.* rye.

centésimo *adj. & m.* hundredth.

centímetro *m.* centimeter (*one hundredth part of a meter*).

céntimo *m.* one hundredth part of a peseta.

centinela *m.* sentry, sentinel.

central *adj.* central; *f.* main office; headquarters; *Am.* main sugar mill or refinery.

centrar *v.* to center.

céntrico *adj.* central.

centro *m.* center, middle.

ceñidor *m.* girdle, belt, sash.

ceñir⁵, ¹⁹ *v. irr.* to gird, girdle; to tighten; to encircle; to diminish; to limit; -**se** a to limit oneself to.

ceño *m.* frown; scowl; **fruncir el** — to frown; to scowl.

cepa *f.* stump, stub (*of a tree or plant*); vinestock; origin, stock (*of a family*); *Am.* mass of plants growing from a common root; *Am.* excavation (*for a building*), hole, pit (*for planting trees*); **de buena** — of good stock.

cepillo *m.* brush; alms box; carpenter's plane; *Am.* flatterer; — **de dientes** toothbrush.

cera *f.* wax.

cerámica *f.* ceramics, pottery.

cerca *adv.* near, near by; — **de** *prep.* near, nearly; *f.* fence, low wall.

cercado *m.* enclosure; fenced-in garden; fence; *Am.* Peruvian political division; *p.p. of* **cercar**.

cercanía *f.* proximity; -**s** surroundings, vicinity.

cercano *adj.* near; neighboring.

cercar⁶ *v.* to fence, enclose; to surround; to besiege.

cercenar *v.* to clip off; to curtail, diminish, reduce.

cerciorar *v.* to assure, affirm; -**se** to ascertain, find out.

cerco *m.* fence, enclosure; siege; circle; *Am.* small farm or orchard.

cerda *f.* bristle; *Am.* **ir en** -**s** to go halves or share in a deal.

cerdo *m.* hog, pig; pork.

cerdoso *adj.* bristly.

cereal *m.* cereal, grain.

cerebro *m.* brain.

ceremonia *f.* ceremony.

ceremonial *adj. & m.* ceremonial.

ceremonioso *adj.* ceremonious.

cereza *f.* cherry; **cerezo** *m.* cherry tree; cherry wood.

cerilla *f.* wax taper; wax match; earwax.

cerillo *m. Am.* match.

cerner¹ *v. irr.* to sift; to drizzle; *Am.* to strain through a sieve; -**se** to hover (*as a bird or plane*).

cero *m.* zero; nothing.

cerquita *adv.* quite near, nice and near.

cerrado *adj.* closed; cloudy; thick (*beard*); reserved (*person*); dull; *Am.* stubborn.

cerradura *f.* locking, closing; lock; — **de golpe** spring lock.

cerrajería *f.* locksmith's shop; locksmith's trade.

cerrajero *m.* locksmith.

cerrar¹ *v. irr.* to close, shut, lock; -**se** to close; -**se el cielo** to become overcast or cloudy.

cerrazón *f.* cloudiness, darkness.

cerro *m.* hill.

cerrojo *m.* latch, bolt.

certamen *m.* contest, literary contest; debate; competition.

certero *adj.* accurate, exact; well-aimed; **tirador** — good shot.

certeza *f.* certainty.

certidumbre *f.* certainty.

certificado *adj.* certified, registered; *m.* certificate.

certificar⁶ *v.* to certify; to register (*a letter*).

cervato *m.* fawn, young deer.

cerveza *f.* beer; **cervecería** *f.* beer tavern; brewery.

cesante *adj.* unemployed.

cesar *v.* to cease, stop; to quit.

cesta *f.* basket; a kind of racket for playing jai alai (*Basque ball game*).

cesto *m.* large basket, hamper.

cetrino *adj.* greenish-yellow, lemon-colored; citronlike; melancholy, gloomy.

cetro *m.* scepter, staff.

cicatero *adj.* miserly, stingy.

cicatriz *f.* scar.

cicatrizar⁹ *v.* to heal, close (*a wound*).

ciclo *m.* cycle; period of time; school term.

ciclón *m.* cyclone.

ciego *adj.* blind; **a ciegas** blindly; *m.* blindman.

cielo *m.* sky; heaven; — **de la boca** palate; **poner en el** — to praise, extol; **poner el grito en el** — to "hit the ceiling"; **cielito** *m. Am.* gaucho group dance and tune.

ciempiés, cientopiés *m.* centipede.

ciénaga f. swamp, bog, quagmire, marsh.

ciencia f. science; learning; skill; a (or de) — cierta with certainty.

cieno m. mud, mire.

científico adj. scientific; m. scientist.

cierre m. clasp, fastener; closing, fastening, locking; method of closing.

cierto adj. certain, true, sure; por — certainly; Am. ciertas hierbas so-and-so (person not named).

ciervo m. deer; cierva f. doe, hind, female deer.

cierzo m. north wind.

cifra f. cipher, number; abridgment, summary; code; monogram; emblem.

cifrar v. to write in code; to summarize; — la esperanza en to place one's hope in.

cigarra f. cicada, locust.

cigarrera f. cigar or cigarette case; woman cigar maker or vendor.

cigarrillo m. cigarette.

cigarro m. cigar; cigarette.

cigüeña f. stork; crank, handle (for turning).

cilíndrico adj. cylindrical.

cilindro m. cylinder; Am. hand organ.

cima f. peak, summit, top; dar — to complete, carry out.

cimarrón adj. Am. wild, untamed; Am. mate — black, bitter mate.

cimarronear v. Am. to drink mate without sugar.

cimbrar, cimbrear v. to 'brandish, flourish, swing; to shake; to bend; Am. to swing around, change suddenly one's direction; — a uno de un golpe to knock a person down with a blow; -se to swing, sway; to vibrate, shake.

cimiento m. foundation, base; source, root; abrir los -s to break ground for a building.

cinc m. zinc.

cincel m. chisel.

cincelar v. to chisel; to engrave.

cincha f. cinch, girth; Am. blows with the flat of a sword; Am. a revienta -s unwillingly; hurriedly; at breakneck speed.

cinchar v. to cinch, tighten the saddle girth; Am. to hit with the flat of a sword.

cine, cinema m. cinema, motion picture, movie; cinematógrafo m. motion picture.

cíngulo m. girdle, cord, belt.

cínico adj. cynical, sarcastic, sneering; m. cynic.

cinta f. ribbon, band; tape; strip; movie film; coarse fishing net; Am. tin can.

cintarada f. beating, flogging; cintarazo m. blow with the flat of a sword.

cintilar v. to sparkle, twinkle; to glimmer.

cinto m. belt; girdle.

cintura f. waist; meter en — to subdue, subject.

cinturón m. belt, — de seguridad safety belt.

ciprés m. cypress.

circo m. circus.

circuito m. circuit.

circulación f. circulation; traffic.

circular v. to circulate; to circle; adj. circular; f. circular letter, notice.

círculo m. circle; group; club; clubhouse.

circundante adj. surrounding.

circundar v. to surround.

circunferencia f. circumference.

circunlocución f. circumlocution, roundabout expression.

circunspección f. circumspection, decorum, prudence, restraint.

circunspecto adj. circumspect, prudent.

circunstancia f. circumstance.

circunstante adj. surrounding; present; -s m. pl. bystanders, onlookers, audience.

circunvecino adj. neighboring, surrounding.

cirio m. wax candle.

ciruela f. plum; prune; — pasa prune, dried prune; ciruelo m. plum tree.

cirugía f. surgery.

cirujano m. surgeon.

cisne m. swan; Am. powder puff.

cisterna f. cistern.

cita f. date, appointment; citation, summons; quotation.

citación f. citation, quotation; summons.

citar v. to make a date or appointment with; to cite, quote; to summon; to incite, provoke (a bull).

ciudad f. city.

ciudadano m. citizen; resident of a city; adj. of or pertaining to a city; ciudadanía f. citizenship.

ciudadela f. citadel.

cívico adj. civic.

civil adj. civil; polite, courteous.

civilidad f. civility, courtesy.

civilización f. civilization.

civilizador adj. civilizing; m. civilizer.

civilizar⁹ v. to civilize.

cizaña f. weed; vice; discord; sembrar — to sow discord.

clamar v. to clamor, shout; to whine.

clamor m. clamor, shout; whine; knell.

clamoreo m. clamoring; shouting.

42

clamorear v. to clamor, shout; to toll, knell.

clandestino adj. clandestine, underhanded, secret.

clara f. white of egg; bald spot; thin spot (in a fabric); **a las -s** clearly, openly, frankly.

claraboya f. skylight.

clarear v. to clarify, make clear; to grow light, begin to dawn; to clear up; Am. to pierce through and through; **-se** to become transparent; to reveal oneself.

claridad f. clarity, clearness; blunt remark, slam; fame.

claridoso adj. Am. blunt, outspoken, plainspoken.

clarificar[6] v. to clarify, make clear.

clarín m. bugle; bugler; organ stop; Am. song bird.

clarinete m. clarinet; clarinet player.

clarito adj. & adv. quite clear, nice and clear.

clarividencia f. clairvoyance; keen insight.

claro adj. clear; light (color); illustrious; adv. clearly; m. skylight; space, gap; clearing (in a forest); **pasar la noche de — en —** not to sleep a wink; Am. **en —** without eating or sleeping; Am. **poner en —** to copy (a rough draft).

clase f. class; classroom; kind, sort.

clásico adj. classic, classical.

clasificación f. classification.

clasificar[6] v. to classify.

claustro m. cloister; meeting of a university faculty; **— de profesores** university faculty.

cláusula f. clause.

clausura f. closing; seclusion, monastic life.

clavar v. to nail; to fix; to deceive, cheat; **-se to** be deceived; Am. to fall into a trap.

clave f. key, code; keystone; clef.

clavel m. carnation, pink.

clavetear v. to nail; to stud with nails.

clavija f. peg; electric plug; peg (of a stringed instrument).

clavijero m. hat or clothes rack.

clavo m. nail; clove (spice); sharp pain or grief; sick headache; Am. rich mineral vein; Am. bother, worry; Am. surprise, disappointment; Am. drug on the market (unsaleable article); **dar en el —** to hit the nail on the head; Am. **meter a uno en un —** to put a person in a predicament; Am. **ser un —** to be punctual, exact.

clemencia f. mercy; **clemente** adj. merciful.

clerical adj. clerical, of a clergyman or the clergy.

clérigo m. clergyman.

clero m. clergy.

cliente m. & f. client; customer; **clientela** f. clientele, clients; customers.

clima m. climate.

clímax m. climax.

clínica f. clinic.

clíper m. clipper.

cloaca f. sewer.

cloquear v. to cluck.

cloqueo m. cluck, clucking.

cloro m. chlorine.

club m. club, society.

clueca f. brooding hen.

coacción f. compulsion, force; enforcement.

coagular v. to coagulate, thicken, clot; to curd, curdle; **-se** to coagulate, clot; to curd, curdle.

coágulo m. coagulation, clot.

coartar v. to restrain, limit.

coba f. flattery; fib; **dar —** to flatter; to tease.

cobarde adj. cowardly; timid; weak; m. coward.

cobardía f. cowardice.

cobertizo m. shed; shanty.

cobertor m. bedcover, quilt.

cobertura f. cover, covering.

cobija f. cover; shelter; roof; Am. blanket; Am. shawl, serape, poncho; **-s** Am. bedclothes.

cobijar v. to cover; to shelter.

cobrador m. collector; ticket collector.

cobranza f. collection (of a sum of money); cashing.

cobrar v. to collect (bills, debts); to charge; to cash (a draft, check, etc.); to recover, regain; to gain, acquire; Am. to demand payment; **— cariño a** to take a liking to.

cobre m. copper; copper kitchen utensils; Am. copper coin; **-s** brass musical instruments; **batir el —** to hustle, work with energy; Am. **mostrar el —** to show one's worse side.

cobrizo adj. coppery, copper-colored.

cobro m. collection (of bills); **poner en —** to put in a safe place; **ponerse en —** to take refuge, get to a safe place.

coca f. Am. coca (South American shrub and its leaves); Am. cocaine; Am. coca tea; Am. eggshell; Am. fruit skin or rind; Am. **de —** free of charge; in vain.

cocaína f. cocaine.

cocear v. to kick.

cocer[2,10] v. irr. to cook; to boil; to bake.

cocido m. Spanish stew; p.p. of cocer.

cociente m. quotient.

cocimiento m. cooking; baking; liquid concoction (generally made of medicinal herbs).

cocina f. kitchen; cuisine, cooking; — económica stove, range.

cocinar v. to cook.

cocinero m. cook.

coco m. coconut; coconut palm; bogyman, goblin; Am. derby hat; Am. head; Am. blow on the head; hacer -s a to make eyes at, flirt with; Am. pelar a — to crop the hair; cocotal m. grove of coconut palms; coconut plantation; cocotero m. coconut palm.

cocodrilo m. crocodile.

coche m. coach; car; taxi.

cochero m. coachman; cabman; taxi driver.

cochinada f. filth, filthiness; filthy act or remark; dirty trick; herd of swine.

cochino m. hog, pig; dirty person; Am. stingy person; Am. — de monte wild boar; adj. filthy, dirty; Am. miserly, stingy.

codazo m. nudge; poke (with the elbow).

codear v. to elbow; to nudge; -se con alguien to rub elbows with someone.

codicia f. greed; greediness.

codiciar v. to covet.

codicioso adj. covetous, greedy.

código m. code of laws.

codo m. elbow; bend; alzar (or empinar) el — to drink too much; hablar por los -s to talk too much; meterse (or estar metido) hasta los -s to be up to the elbows, be very busy.

codorniz f. partridge.

coetáneo adj. contemporary.

cofrade m. & f. fellow member (of a brotherhood, club, society, etc.).

cofradía f. brotherhood; sisterhood; guild; trade union.

cofre m. coffer, jewel box; chest, trunk.

coger[11] v. to seize; to catch; to grasp; to gather; Am. -se una cosa to steal something.

cogote m. nape, back of the neck.

cohechar v. to bribe.

coheredero m. joint heir.

coherente adj. coherent; connected.

cohete m. skyrocket; rocket; Am. al — in vain, uselessly.

cohibición f. repression, inhibition, restraint.

cohibido p.p. & adj. inhibited; embarrassed, uneasy.

cohibir v. to restrain, repress; to inhibit.

coincidencia f. coincidence.

coincidir v. to coincide.

cojear v. to limp; cojeamos del mismo pie we both have the same weakness.

cojera f. limp, lameness.

cojín m. cushion; pad; cojincillo m. pad.

cojinete m. small pillow or cushion, pad; bearing, ball bearing.

cojo adj. lame, crippled; one-legged.

col f. cabbage; — de Bruselas Brussels sprouts.

cola f. tail; line of people; train of a dress; glue; hacer — to stand in line; Am. comer — to be the last one in a contest.

colaboración f. collaboration, mutual help.

colaborar v. to collaborate, work together.

coladera f. colander, strainer, sieve; Am. drain.

colar[2] v. irr. to strain, filter; to bleach with lye; -se to slip in or out, sneak in.

colcha f. quilt; bedspread; -s Am. saddle and trappings; Am. gaucho clothing.

colchón m. mattress.

colear v. to wag the tail; to grab a bull by the tail and throw him over; Am. to flunk (a student); Am. to trail, tag behind (a person); Am. to bother, nag, harass; Am. to smoke one cigarette after another.

colección f. collection; set; gathering.

coleccionista m. & f. collector (of stamps, curios, etc.).

coleccionar v. to collect, make a collection.

colecta f. collection of voluntary gifts; assessment; collect (a short prayer of the mass).

colectivo adj. collective; m. Am. small bus.

colector m. collector; water pipe, drain.

colega m. & f. colleague, fellow worker.

colegiatura f. college fellowship or scholarship; Am. tuition in a college.

colegio m. boarding school; school, academy; college, body of professional men.

colegir[6, 11] v. to gather; to conclude, infer.

cólera f. anger, rage; m. cholera (disease).

colérico adj. irritable; angry.

coleto m. leather jacket; one's inner self; Am. impudence, shamelessness; decir

para su — to say to oneself; **echarse al —** to drink down; to devour.

colgadero m. hanger; hook, peg; hat or clothes rack.

colgadura f. drape, hanging; drapery; tapestry.

colgante adj. hanging; dangling; **puente —** suspension bridge.

colgar², ⁷ v. irr. to hang, suspend; to dangle; to drape (walls); to impute, attribute; Am. to flunk, fail (a student); Am. -se to fall behind.

colibrí m. hummingbird.

coliflor f. cauliflower.

coligarse⁷ v. to league together, band together.

colilla f. small tail; butt (of a cigarette), stub (of a cigar).

colina f. hill.

colindante adj. contiguous, neighboring, adjacent.

colindar v. to border (on); to be adjoining.

colisión f. collision, clash.

colmar v. to fill to the brim; **— de** to fill with; to shower with (gifts, favors, etc.); **-le a uno el plato** to exhaust one's patience.

colmena f. beehive; Am. bee.

colmillo m. eyetooth, canine tooth; tusk; fang.

colmo m. overfullness; limit; **— de la locura** height of folly; **¡ eso es el —!** that's the limit! adj. overfull, filled to the brim.

colocación f. placing, arrangement; position, job.

colocar⁶ v. to place; to put in place, arrange; to give employment to.

colombiano adj. Colombian, of or pertaining to Colombia, South America.

colon m. colon (of the large intestine).

colonia f. colony; silk ribbon; Am. city district; Am. sugar plantation.

coloniaje m. Am. colonial period.

colonial adj. colonial.

colonización f. colonization.

colonizador m. colonizer, colonist; adj. colonizing.

colonizar⁹ v. to colonize.

colono m. colonist, settler; tenant farmer; Am. owner of a sugar plantation; Am. bootlicker, flatterer.

coloquio m. conversation, talk; literary dialogue; Am. street comedy, farce.

color m. color; coloring; paint; rouge; **so — de** under the pretext of.

coloración f. coloring.

colorado adj. red, reddish; colored; **ponerse —** to blush.

colorante adj. & m. coloring.

colorar v. to color; to stain; to dye.

colorear v. to color; to redden; to give color to.

colorete m. rouge.

colorido m. coloring; color; adj. colored; colorful.

colosal adj. colossal, huge.

columbrar v. to see faintly; to glimpse.

columna f. column.

columpiar v. to swing; **-se** to swing; to sway.

columpio m. swing.

collado m. hillock, knoll.

collar m. necklace; dog collar; Am. collar (of a draft horse); **collera** f. collar (for draft animals).

coma f. comma; m. coma, stupor, prolonged unconsciousness.

comadre f. gossip; woman friend; midwife; name used to express kinship between mother and godmother; **comadrona** f. midwife.

comadreja f. weasel.

comandancia f. command; position and headquarters of a commander.

comandante m. major; commander.

comandar v. to command (troops).

comandita f. silent partnership; **sociedad en —** limited company.

comando m. military command.

comarca f. district, region.

comba f. bulge, warp.

combar v. to warp, bend, twist; **-se** to warp; to sag; to bulge.

combate m. combat, battle, fight.

combatiente m. combatant, fighter.

combatir v. to combat; to fight.

combinación f. combination.

combinar v. to combine, unite.

combustible adj. combustible; m. fuel.

combustión f. combustion.

comedero m. trough (for feeding animals); adj. edible, eatable.

comedia f. comedy; farce.

comediante m. actor, comedian.

comedido adj. courteous, polite; obliging; p.p. of **comedirse**.

comedirse⁵ v. irr. to be civil, polite, obliging; Am. to meddle; Am. **— a hacer algo** to volunteer to do something.

comedor m. dining room; great eater.

comelón m. Am. big eater. See **comilón**.

comendador m. commander (of certain military orders).

comensal m. & f. table companion; dinner guest.

comentador m. commentator.

comentar v. to comment.

comentario *m.* commentary, explanation.

comentarista *m. & f.* commentator.

comenzar[1, 9] *v. irr.* to begin.

comer *v.* to eat; to dine; to take (*in chess or checkers*); **dar de** — to feed; **ganar de** — to earn a living; **-se** to eat; to eat up; to skip (*a letter, syllable, word, etc.*); *Am.* **-se uno a otro** to deceive each other.

comercial *adj.* commercial.

comerciante *m.* merchant; storekeeper.

comerciar *v.* to trade; to have dealings (with).

comercio *m.* commerce, trade.

comestible *adj.* edible, eatable; **-s** *m. pl.* food, groceries.

cometa *m.* comet; *Am.* person seldom seen; *f.* kite.

cometer *v.* to commit; to entrust; to use (*a figure of speech*).

cometido *m.* commission, assignment, charge; task, duty.

comezón *f.* itch.

comicios *m. pl.* primaries, elections.

cómico *adj.* comic, of comedy; comical, funny, amusing; *m.* comedian, actor.

comida *f.* meal; dinner; food; gossip; **la comidilla** *f.* small meal; gossip; **la comidilla de la vecindad** the talk of the town.

comienzo *m.* beginning; origin.

comilitona *f.* spread, big feast.

comilón *m.* big eater.

comillas *f. pl.* quotation marks.

comisario *m.* commissary, deputy, delegate; manager; *Am.* police inspector.

comisión *f.* commission; committee.

comisionado *adj.* commissioned, charged, delegated; *m.* commissioner; *Am.* constable.

comisionar *v.* to commission.

comistrajo *m.* mess, strange food concoction, mixture.

comité *m.* committee, commission.

comitiva *f.* retinue, group of attendants or followers.

como *adv. & conj.* as, like, such as; if, provided that, since, when; *Am.* about, approximately; **¿cómo?** *interr. adv.* how?; what (did you say)?; *Am.* **¡cómo no!** yes, of course!

cómoda *f.* bureau, chest of drawers.

comodidad *f.* comfort; convenience.

cómodo *adj.* comfortable; convenient; *m. Am.* bedpan.

compacto *adj.* compact

compadecer[13] *v. irr.* to pity, sympathize with; **-se con** to be in harmony with; **-se de** to take pity on.

compadrazgo *m.* compaternity (*spirit-*

ual affinity between the godfather and the parents of a child); friendship; relationship; clique, group of friends.

compadre *m.* co-sponsor; crony, pal, comrade; *name used to express kinship between father and godfather.*

compañero *m.* companion; partner; mate; **compañerismo** *m.* companionship.

compañía *f.* company; *Am.* — **del ahorcado** silent companion, poor company.

comparación *f.* comparison.

comparar *v.* to compare.

comparativo *adj.* comparative.

comparecer[13] *v. irr.* to appear (*before a judge or tribunal*).

compartimiento *m.* compartment.

compartir *v.* to share; to divide into shares.

compás *m.* compass; measure; beat; **llevar el** — to beat time.

compasión *f.* compassion, pity.

compasivo *adj.* compassionate, sympathetic.

compatible *adj.* compatible, in harmony

compatriota *m. & f.* compatriot, fellow countryman.

compeler *v.* to compel, force.

compendiar *v.* to abstract, summarize, condense.

compendio *m.* summary, condensation.

compensación *f.* compensation; recompense.

compensar *v.* to balance; to make equal; to compensate, recompense.

competencia *f.* competition, rivalry; competence, ability.

competente *adj.* competent; capable; adequate.

competidor *m.* competitor; rival; *adj.* competing.

competir[5] *v. irr.* to compete, vie.

compilar *v.* to compile.

compinche *m.* chum, pal, comrade.

complacencia *f.* complacency, satisfaction, contentment.

complacer[38] *v. irr.* to please, humor; to comply; **-se** to take pleasure or satisfaction (in).

complaciente *adj.* obliging, agreeable, willing to please.

complejidad *f.* complexity.

complejo *adj. & m.* complex.

complemento *m.* complement; object (*of a verb*).

completamiento *m.* completion.

completar *v.* to complete; to finish.

completo *adj.* complete, full, perfect.

complicar[6] v. to complicate.

cómplice m. & f. accomplice, companion in crime.

complot m. plot, conspiracy; intrigue.

componenda f. adjustment; compromise.

componente adj. component, constituent; m. component, essential part.

componer[40] v. irr. to fix, repair; to fix up; to adorn, trim; to compose, to set up (type); to settle (a dispute); Am. to set (bones).

comportamiento m. conduct, behavior.

composición f. composition; settlement.

compositor m. composer.

compostura f. repair; composure, dignity; neatness; composition; settlement, adjustment.

compota f. fruit preserves; — de manzana applesauce.

compra f. purchase; buying; ir de -s to go shopping.

comprador m. buyer, purchaser.

comprar v. to buy, purchase.

comprender v. to understand, grasp, comprehend; to comprise, embrace.

comprensible adj. comprehensible, understandable.

comprensión f. understanding; comprehension); keenness.

comprensivo adj. comprehensive; understanding.

compresión f. compression.

comprimir v. to compress; to repress.

comprobación f. confirmation, check, proof, test.

comprobante adj. proving, verifying; m. proof; evidence; certificate; voucher; warrant.

comprobar[2] v. irr. to verify; to check; to prove.

comprometer v. to compromise; to endanger; to bind; -se to promise, bind oneself; to become engaged; to compromise oneself.

compromiso f. compromise; engagement; appointment; predicament, trouble.

compuerta f. sluice (gate to control the flow of water), floodgate.

compuesto p.p. of **componer** & adj. repaired; fixed, adorned; composed; composite; compound; m. composite, compound.

compungirse[11] v. to feel regret or remorse.

computar v. to compute, calculate.

cómputo m. computation, calculation.

comulgar[7] v. to commune, take communion.

común adj. common; por lo — generally; m. toilet; el — de las gentes the majority of the people; the average person.

comunero adj. common, popular; Am. pertaining to a community; m. commoner (one of the common people); Am. member of an Indian community.

comunicación f. communication.

comunicar[6] v. to communicate, to notify; -se to communicate; to correspond; to be in touch (with); to connect.

comunicativo adj. communicative, talkative.

comunidad f. community; commonwealth; the common people; commonness; guild.

comunión f. communion; political party.

comunismo m. communism; **comunista** m. & f. communist; adj. communistic, communist.

con prep. with; — ser in spite of being; — tal que provided that; — todo however.

concavidad f. hollow, cavity; hollowness.

cóncavo adj. concave, hollow.

concebible adj. conceivable.

concebir[5] v. irr. to conceive; to imagine; to understand, grasp.

conceder v. to concede, grant; to admit.

concejal m. councilman, alderman.

concentración f. concentration.

concentrar v. to concentrate.

concepción f. conception.

concepto m. concept, idea, thought.

concernir[51] v. irr. to concern.

concertar[1] v. irr. to arrange, plan, settle; to conclude (a treaty or business deal); to harmonize; to agree.

concesión f. concession, grant; granting; acknowledgment.

conciencia f. conscience.

concienzudo adj. conscientious.

concierto m. concert; harmony; agreement; de — by common agreement.

conciliar v. to conciliate, win over; to reconcile, bring into harmony; — el sueño to get to sleep.

concilio m. council.

concisión f. coneiseness, brevity.

conciso adj. concise, brief.

conciudadano m. fellow citizen, fellow countryman.

concluir[32] v. irr. to conclude, finish; to infer.

conclusión f. conclusion.

concordancia f concord, agreement, harmony.

concordar³ *v. irr.* to agree; to be in harmony; to put in harmony.

concordia *f.* concord, harmony, agreement.

concretar *v.* to summarize, condense; to limit; **-se a** to limit oneself to.

concreto *adj.* concrete, real, specific; **en —** concretely; to sum up; *m. Am.* concrete.

concupiscente *adj.* sensual.

concurrencia *f.* gathering, audience; concurrence, simultaneous meeting or happening; competition.

concurrido *adj.* well-patronized, well-attended, much frequented.

concurrir *v.* to concur, meet together; to happen at the same time or place; to attend; to agree.

concurso *m.* gathering; contest; competitive examination; assistance.

concha *f.* shell; shellfish; prompter's box; *Am.* **tener —** to be indifferent, unruffled, tough.

conchabar *v.* to unite, join; *Am.* to hire (*labor*); **-se** to join, gang together; to conspire; *Am.* to hire oneself out, get a job.

conchabo *m. Am.* hiring of a laborer or servant; *Am.* job, menial job.

conde *m.* count; **condesa** *f.* countess.

condecoración *f.* decoration; badge, medal.

condecorar *v.* to decorate (*with a badge or medal*).

condena *f.* term in prison, sentence, penalty.

condenación *f.* condemnation; conviction (*of a prisoner or criminal*); damnation.

condenar *v.* to condemn; to sentence; *Am.* to annoy, irritate; **-se** to be damned, go to hell.

condensar *v.* to condense.

condescendencia *f.* condescension, patronizing attitude.

condescender¹ *v. irr.* to condescend; to comply, yield.

condición *f.* condition.

condimentar *v.* to season.

condimento *m.* condiment, seasoning.

condolerse² *v. irr.* to condole (with), sympathize (with), be sorry (for).

cóndor *m. Am.* condor, vulture; *Am.* gold coin of Ecuador, Chile and Colombia.

conducir²⁵ *v. irr.* to conduct, lead; to drive (*an auto*); **-se** to behave, act.

conducta *f.* conduct; behavior; convoy, escort; management.

conducto *m.* conduit, pipe, channel;

por — de through.

conductor *adj.* conducting; *m.* leader, guide; conductor (*electrical*); *Am.* conductor, ticket collector (*on trains, buses, streetcars*); *Am.* teamster, driver.

conectar *v.* to connect.

condiscípulo *m.* schoolmate, classmate.

conejera *f.* burrow; rabbit warren (*piece of land for breeding rabbits*); den, joint, dive (*of ill repute*).

conejo *m.* rabbit; *Am.* guinea pig; **conejillo de Indias** guinea pig.

conexión *f.* connection.

conexo *adj.* connected; coherent.

confección *f.* making; confection; manufactured article; workmanship; concoction, compound.

confeccionar *v.* to make; to manufacture; to mix, put up (*a prescription*).

confederación *f.* confederation, alliance, league.

confederar *v.* to confederate; **-se** to confederate, form into a confederacy.

conferencia *f.* lecture; conference, meeting.

conferenciante *m. & f.* lecturer.

conferencista *m. & f.* lecturer.

conferir² *v. irr.* to confer; to give, bestow.

confesar¹ *v. irr.* to confess.

confesión *f.* confession.

confesionario *m.* confessional, confessional box.

confesor *m.* confessor.

confiado *adj.* confident, trusting, credulous; presumptuous, self-confident.

confianza *f.* confidence, trust; familiarity; informality; **reunión de —** informal gathering or party.

confianzudo *adj.* over-friendly, over-familiar; *Am.* meddlesome.

confiar¹⁷ *v.* to confide, entrust; to trust, hope firmly.

confidencia *f.* confidence, trust; secret, confidential remark; **confidencial** *adj.* confidential.

confidente *m.* confidant; spy, secret agent; settee or sofa for two people, love seat; *adj.* faithful, trustworthy.

confín *m.* limit, border, boundary; *adj.* bordering, limiting.

confinar *v.* to border (upon); to confine, exile to a specific place.

confirmación *f.* confirmation.

confirmar *v.* to confirm.

confiscar⁶ *v.* to confiscate.

confitar *v.* to candy (*with sugar syrup*); to make into candy or preserves; to sweeten.

confite *m.* candy, bonbon; **confitería** *f.* confectionery; candy shop; **confitura**

f. confection.

conflicto *m.* conflict.

confluencia *f.* junction (*of two rivers*).

conformar *v.* to adapt, adjust; -se to conform, comply; to agree; to be resigned (to); to be satisfied.

conforme *adj.* in agreement; resigned, satisfied; alike, similar; — a in accordance with.

conformidad *f.* conformity; agreement, harmony; compliance; — con la voluntad de Dios resignation to the will of God; en — con in compliance with; estar de — con to be in accordance or agreement with.

confortar *v.* to comfort, console.

confraternidad *f.* brotherhood.

confrontar *v.* to confront; to face; to compare, check.

confundir *v.* to confound, confuse, mix up; to bewilder; to shame.

confusión *f.* confusion.

confuso *adj.* confused, bewildered; blurred; vague.

congelado *p.p.* & *adj.* frozen; icy.

congelar *v.* to congeal, freeze.

congenial *adj.* congenial.

congeniar *v.* to be congenial (with); to harmonize, be in harmony (with).

congoja *f.* anguish, grief, anxiety.

congratular *v.* to congratulate.

congregación *f.* congregation, assembly; religious fraternity.

congregar[7] *v.* to congregate, call together; to assemble; -se to congregate, assemble.

congresista *m.* congressman; *f.* congresswoman.

congreso *m.* congress, assembly; — de los Diputados House of Representatives.

conjetura *f.* conjecture, guess, surmise.

conjeturar *v.* to conjecture, guess, surmise.

conjugación *f.* conjugation; coupling, joining together.

conjugar[7] *v.* to conjugate.

conjunción *f.* conjunction; union, combination.

conjunto *m.* total, whole, entirety; en — as a whole; *adj.* joined; related, allied.

conjuración *f.* conspiracy, plot.

conjurado *m.* conspirator.

conjurar *v.* to conspire, plot; to join a conspiracy; to entreat; to conjure; to ward off.

conmemorar *v.* to commemorate.

conmemorativo *adj.* memorial, serving to commemorate.

conmigo with me.

conminación *f.* threat.

conminatorio *adj.* threatening.

conmoción *f.* commotion.

conmovedor *adj.* moving, touching; stirring.

conmover[2] *v. irr.* to move, touch, affect (*with emotion*); to stir (*emotions*).

conmutador *m.* electric switch; cuadro — switchboard.

connatural *adj.* inborn.

cono *m.* cone; pine cone.

conocedor *adj.* knowing, aware, expert; *m.* connoisseur, judge, expert; ser — de to be judge of.

conocer[13] *v. irr.* to know, be acquainted with; to recognize; to meet; se conoce que it is clear or evident that.

conocido *p.p.* & *adj.* known; well-known; *m.* acquaintance.

conocimiento *m.* knowledge, understanding; acquaintance; bill of lading; -s knowledge, learning; poner en — to inform.

conque *conj.* so then, well then, and so.

conquista *f.* conquest.

conquistador *m.* conqueror; *adj.* conquering, victorious.

conquistar *v.* to conquer, defeat; to win.

consabido *adj.* aforementioned, aforesaid.

consagración *f.* consecration.

consagrar *v.* to consecrate.

consciencia *f.* consciousness.

consciente *adj.* conscious.

consecución *f.* attainment.

consecuencia *f.* consequence; result; a — de as a result of; por (*or* en) — therefore; consequently.

consecuente *adj.* consequent, logical; consistent; *m.* consequence, result.

consecutivo *adj.* consecutive, successive.

conseguir[5, 12] *v. irr.* to get, obtain; to reach, attain

conseja *f.* old wives' tale, fable.

consejero *m.* adviser, counselor.

consejo *m.* counsel, advice; council; council hall.

consentimiento *m.* consent.

consentir[3] *v. irr.* to consent, permit; to pamper, spoil.

conserje *m.* janitor, caretaker.

conserva *f.* preserve; pickled fruit or vegetables; *Am.* filling (*for tarts or candy*).

conservación *f.* conservation.

conservador *m.* conservative; preserver; guardian; *adj.* conservative.

conservar *v.* to conserve, keep; to preserve.

considerable *adj.* considerable.

consideración *f.* consideration.

considerado *adj.* considerate, thoughtful; respected; prudent.

considerar *v.* to consider; to treat with consideration.

consigna *f.* watchword, password; *Am.* checkroom.

consignar *v.* to consign; to deliver; to deposit; to assign; to check (*baggage*).

consigo with oneself; with himself (herself, themselves).

consiguiente *adj.* consequent; *m.* consequence; **por** — consequently.

consistente *adj.* firm, substantial.

consistir *v.* to consist; to be based on; **¿en qué consiste?** why?; what is the explanation for it?

consocio *m.* associate, partner.

consolación *f.* consolation.

consolar[2] *v. irr.* to console, cheer.

consolidar *v.* to consolidate, make solid; to unite, combine.

consonante *adj.* perfect rhyme; *f.* consonant; *adj.* in harmony.

consorte *m. & f.* consort; mate; companion.

conspicuo *adj.* conspicuous.

conspiración *f.* conspiracy, plot.

conspirador *m.* conspirator, plotter.

conspirar *v.* to conspire, plot.

constancia *f.* constancy; perseverance; evidence, certainty; *Am.* documentary proof, record.

constante *adj.* constant; continual; firm, faithful.

constar *v.* to be evident, clear; to consist (of), be composed (of); to be on record.

constatación *f. Am.* proof, check, evidence.

constelación *f.* constellation.

constipado *adj.* suffering from a cold; *m.* cold in the head.

constipar *v.* to stop up (*the nasal passages*); to cause a cold; **-se** to catch cold.

constitución *f.* constitution.

constitucional *adj.* constitutional.

constituir[32] *v. irr.* to constitute, form; to set up, establish; **-se en** to set oneself up as.

constitutivo = constituyente.

constituyente *adj.* constituent.

constreñir[5, 19] *v. irr.* to constrain; to compel, oblige.

construcción *f.* construction; structure; building.

construir[32] *v. irr.* to construct, build

consuelo *m.* consolation, comfort; relief; cheer.

consuetudinario *adj.* habitual, customary; **derecho** — common law.

cónsul *m.* consul.

consulado *m.* consulate.

consulta *f.* consultation; opinion.

consultar *v.* to consult.

consultorio *m.* office for consultation; doctor's office or clinic.

consumado *p.p. of* **consumar;** *adj.* consummate, perfect, complete; accomplished.

consumar *v.* to consummate, complete.

consumidor *m.* consumer; *adj.* consuming.

consumir *v.* to consume; to waste; **-se** to be consumed; to burn out; to be exhausted; to waste away.

consumo *m.* consumption (*of food, provisions, etc*).

consunción *f.* consumption (*illness*).

contabilidad *f.* accounting; bookkeeping.

contacto *m.* contact.

contado : **al** — in cash; **de** — immediately; **por de** — of course; **contados** *adj.* few, scarce, rare.

contador *m.* accountant; purser, cashier; counter; meter (*for water, gas, or electricity*).

contaduría *f.* accountant's or auditor's office; box office; cashier's office; accounting.

contagiar *v.* to infect; to corrupt; to contaminate.

contagio *m.* contagion; infection.

contagioso *adj.* contagious; infectious.

contaminar *v.* to contaminate, defile; to corrupt.

contar[2] *v. irr.* to count; to tell, relate; **— con** to count on, rely on; **a —** **desde** starting from, beginning with.

contemplación *f.* contemplation; gazing; meditation.

contemplar *v.* to contemplate, gaze at; to examine; to meditate.

contemporáneo *adj.* contemporary.

contender[1] *v. irr.* to contend, fight; to compete.

contener[45] *v. irr.* to contain; to restrain, check; **-se** to refrain; to restrain oneself.

contenido *m.* contents; *adj.* restrained, moderate.

contentamiento *m.* contentment, joy.

contentar *v.* to give pleasure, make happy; **-se** to be satisfied, pleased; *Am.* to make up, renew friendship.

contento adj. content, contented, satisfied, glad; m. gladness, contentment.

contera f. metal tip (of a cane, umbrella, etc.); tip, end; refrain of a song; por — as a finishing touch.

contertulio m. fellow-member.

contestación f. answer, reply; argument.

contestar v. to answer, reply.

contextura f. texture, composition; structure (of animal or vegetable tissues).

contienda f. fight; dispute; contest.

contigo with you (with thee).

contiguo adj. contiguous, next, neighboring.

continental adj. continental.

continente m. continent; countenance; adj. continent, moderate, sober.

contingencia f. contingency, possibility; risk.

contingente adj. contingent, accidental; m. quota; military contingent.

continuación f. continuation; continuance; a — below, as follows.

continuar[18] v. to continue; to last.

continuidad f. continuity.

continuo adj. continuous, connected; continual; steady, constant.

contonearse v. to strut, swagger; to waddle.

contoneo m. strut; waddle.

contorno m. environs, surrounding country; contour, outline.

contra prep. against; **el pro y el** — the pro and con; f. opposition; Am. antidote, remedy; -s Am. play-off, final game (to determine the winner); **llevar a uno la** — to contradict a person, take the opposite view.

contraalmirante m. rear admiral.

contrabandear v. to smuggle.

contrabandista m. smuggler.

contrabando m. contraband; smuggled goods; smuggling.

contracción f. contraction; Am. diligence, application, devotion.

contradecir[27] v. irr. to contradict.

contradicción f. contradiction.

contradictorio adj. contradictory, contrary, opposing.

contradicho p.p. of **contradecir**.

contraer[46] v. irr. to contract; — **matrimonio** to get married; -se to shrink; to contract.

contrafuerte m. buttress; spur (of a mountain); -s secondary chain of mountains.

contrahacer[31] v. irr. to counterfeit; to forge; to copy, imitate; to mimic.

contrahecho p.p. of **contrahacer** & adj. counterfeit; forged; deformed.

contralor m. Am. controller or comptroller (of accounts or expenditures). See **controlador**.

contraorden f. countermand; cancellation of an order.

contrapelo : a — against the grain.

contrapesar v. to counterbalance, balance; to offset.

contrapeso m. counterpoise, counterweight, counterbalance; Am. fear, uneasiness.

contrariar[17] v. to oppose; to contradict; to irritate, vex.

contrariedad f. opposition; contradiction; bother, irritation; disappointment.

contrario adj. contrary; opposite; m. opponent.

contrarrestar v. to counteract; to resist, oppose; to strike back (a ball).

contraseña f. password, watchword; mark; check (for baggage); — **de salida** theatre check (to re-enter during the performance).

contrastar v. to contrast; to resist, oppose; to test (scales, weights, measures, etc.); to assay (metals).

contraste m. contrast; assay, test; assayer, tester; assayer's office.

contrata f. contract, bargain, agreement.

contratar v. to contract for; to trade; to engage, hire (men); -se to come to, or make, an agreement.

contratiempo m. accident, mishap.

contratista m. & f. contractor.

contrato m. contract.

contraventana f. shutter.

contribución f. contribution; tax.

contribuir[32] v. irr. to contribute.

contribuyente m. contributor; taxpayer; adj. contributing.

control m. Am. control.

controlador m. Am. controller.

controlar v. Am. to control.

controversia f. controversy.

contumacia f. stubbornness, obstinacy; contempt of court, failure to appear in court; rebelliousness.

contumaz adj. stubborn; rebellious.

contusión f. bruise.

convalecer[13] v. irr. to convalesce, recover from an illness.

convecino adj. near, neighboring; m. neighbor.

convencedor adj. convincing.

convencer[10] v. to convince.

convencimiento m. conviction, belief; convincing.

convención *f.* convention, assembly; pact, agreement; *Am.* political convention; **convencional** *adj.* conventional.

convenido *adj.* agreed; O.K., all right; *p.p.* of **convenir**.

conveniencia *f.* convenience; comfort; utility, profit.

conveniente *adj.* convenient, useful, profitable; fit, proper, suitable; opportune.

convenio *m.* pact, agreement.

convenir[48] *v. irr.* to agree; to convene, assemble; to be suitable, proper, advisable; to suit, fit; -se to agree.

conventillo *m. Am.* tenement house.

convento *m.* convent.

convergente *adj.* convergent, coming together.

converger,[11] **convergir**[11] *v.* to converge.

conversación *f.* conversation.

conversar *v.* to converse.

conversión *f.* conversion.

convertir[3] *v. irr.* to convert.

convicción *f.* conviction.

convicto *p.p. irr.* of **convencer**; convicted, guilty.

convidado *m.* guest; *Am.* — y con ollita guest who abuses hospitality.

convidar *v.* to invite; -se to volunteer one's services; to invite oneself.

convincente *adj.* convincing.

convite *m.* invitation; banquet.

convocación *f.* convocation.

convocar[6] *v.* to convoke, call together.

convoyar *v.* to convoy, escort.

convulsión *f.* convulsion.

convulsivo *adj.* convulsive; **tos convulsiva** whooping cough.

conyugal *adj.* conjugal, pertaining to marriage or a married couple; **vida** — married life.

cónyuge *m.* husband; *f.* wife.

cooperación *f.* cooperation.

cooperador *adj.* cooperating, cooperative; *m.* cooperator, co-worker.

cooperar *v.* to cooperate.

cooperativo *adj.* cooperative; **cooperativa** *f.* cooperative, cooperative society.

coordinación *f.* coordination.

coordinar *v.* to coordinate.

copa *f.* goblet; treetop; crown of a hat; card in the suit of **copas** (*in Spanish cards*); *Am.* **empinar la** — to drink, get drunk.

copartícipe *adj.* participant; *m. & f.* joint partner.

copete *m.* tuft; crest; top, summit; ornamental top on furniture; **de** — of

high rank, important; proud; **estar uno hasta el** — to be stuffed; to be fed up; **tener mucho** — to be arrogant, haughty.

copia *f.* copy; imitation; abundance.

copiar *v.* to copy.

copioso *adj.* copious, abundant.

copita *f.* little glass; little drink.

copla *f.* couplet; stanza (*of variable length and meter*); popular song.

copo *m.* snowflake; wad, tuft (*of wool or cotton*).

coqueta *f.* coquette, flirt.

coquetear *v.* to flirt.

coquetería *f.* coquetry, flirting.

coraje *m.* courage, valor; anger.

coral *m.* coral; *Am.* red poisonous snake; -es coral beads; *adj.* choral, pertaining to a choir; **coralino** *adj.* coral, like coral.

coraza *f.* cuirass, armor; armor plate or plating; shell (*of a turtle*).

corazón *m.* heart; core, center.

corazonada *f.* presentiment, foreboding; hunch.

corbata *f.* necktie; cravat; *Am.* colorful kerchief, scarf.

corcel *m.* charger, steed.

corcova *f.* hump, hunch; **corcovado** *adj.* hunchbacked; *m.* hunchback.

corcovear *v.* to prance about, leap; *Am.* to kick, protest against.

corcho *m.* cork; beehive; *adj. Am.* corklike, spongy.

cordel *m.* cord, rope.

cordero *m.* lamb; lambskin.

cordial *adj.* cordial, friendly; **dedo** — middle finger.

cordialidad *f.* cordiality, friendliness, warmth.

cordillera *f.* mountain range.

cordobés *adj.* Cordovan, of or pertaining to Cordova; *m.* native of Cordova.

cordón *m.* cord; braid; cordon, line of soldiers; *Am.* — **de la acera** curb, curbstone of the sidewalk; **cordonería** *f.* lace or cord maker's shop; collection of cords and laces; cord maker's work; braiding.

cordoncillo *m.* small cord, drawstring, lace, lacing; braid; mill (*ridged edge of a coin*); ridge, rib (*of certain fabrics*).

cordura *f.* good judgment, wisdom; sanity.

cornada *f.* goring; butt with the horns; **dar -s** to gore, horn, butt with the horns.

corneta *f.* cornet; bugle; horn; *m.* bugler.

cornisa *f.* cornice.

coro *m.* choir; chorus.

corona *f.* crown; wreath.

coronar *v.* to crown; to top.

coronel *m.* colonel.

coronilla *f.* small crown; crown of the head; **estar uno hasta la —** to be fed up, be satiated.

corpanchón *m.* large body; carcass.

corpiño *m.* bodice.

corporación *f.* corporation.

corporal *adj.* corporal, of the body; *m.* corporal (*small piece of linen used at Mass*).

corpóreo *adj.* corporeal, bodily; tangible, material.

corpulento *adj.* corpulent, fat, stout.

corral *m.* yard; corral, cattle yard; **corralón** *m.* large corral; *Am.* lumber warehouse.

correa *f.* leather strap; resistance; *Am.* -**s** leather blanket carrier; *Am.* **tener muchas -s** to be phlegmatic, calm.

corrección *f.* correction; correctness.

correcto *adj.* correct, proper.

corredizo *adj.* sliding, slipping; **nudo —** slip knot.

corredor *m.* runner; racer; corridor; gallery around a patio; broker; *Am.* covered porch; *Am.* beater of wild game; *adj.* running; speedy.

corregidor *m.* corrector; Spanish magistrate.

corregir[5, 11] *v. irr.* to correct; to reprove; to punish; -**se** to mend one's ways.

correligionario *adj.* of the same religion; of the same political party or sympathies; *m.* coreligionist.

correntada *f. Am.* strong river current.

correo *m.* mail; mail service; postman; post office; **— aéreo** air mail.

correón *m.* large strap.

correoso *adj.* flexible; leathery; tough; **correosidad** *f.* toughness; flexibility.

correr *v.* to run; to blow (*said of the wind*); to pass, elapse; to draw (*a curtain*); to race; to chase; *Am.* to dismiss, throw out; -**se** to slip through; to slide; to be embarrassed.

correría *f.* foray, raid for plunder; excursion, short trip; -**s** wanderings, travels; raids.

correspondencia *f.* correspondence; letters, mail; agreement; interchange.

corresponder *v.* to reciprocate, return (*love, favors*); to belong; to concern; to correspond (*one thing with another*).

correspondiente *adj.* corresponding, agreeing; respective; *m.* correspondent.

corresponsal *m.* correspondent; agent; newspaper reporter.

corretear *v.* to run around; to roam, rove; *Am.* to pursue, chase.

corrida *f.* race; *Am.* row, file; *Am.* night spree; *Am.* beating up of game; **— del tiempo** swiftness of time; **— de toros** bullfight; **de —** without stopping.

corrido *adj.* embarrassed, ashamed; worldly-wise; flowing, fluent; **de —** without stopping; *m. Am.* popular ballad.

corriente *adj.* running, flowing, fluent; usual, common, ordinary; *Am.* frank, open; **¡—!** all right! O.K.!; **el ocho del —** the eighth of the current month; **estar al —** to be up-to-date; to be well-informed (*about current news*); **poner a uno al —** to keep someone posted or well informed; *f.* current; flow; course; *Am.* **hay que llevarle la —** one must humor him.

corrillo *m.* circle or group of gossipers.

corro *m.* group of talkers or spectators.

corroer[51] *v. irr.* to corrode.

corromper *v.* to corrupt; to seduce; to bribe; -**se** to rot; to become corrupted.

corrompido *adj.* corrupt; rotten, spoiled; degenerate; *p.p.* of **corromper.**

corrupción *f.* corruption.

corrupto *adj.* corrupt, rotten.

cortada *f. Am.* cut, slash.

cortador *m.* cutter.

cortadura *m.* cut; gash; slash.

cortante *adj.* cutting; sharp.

cortaplumas *m.* penknife.

cortar *v.* to cut; to cut off; to cut out; to cut down; to interrupt; *Am.* to harvest, pick (*fruit*); to gossip, speak ill of someone; -**se** to be embarrassed, ashamed; to sour, curdle (*said of milk*); *Am.* to become separated, cut off; *Am.* to leave in a hurry; *Am.* to die.

corte *m.* cut; cutting; cutting edge; fit, style; *Am.* cut (*in cards*); *Am.* harvest; *Am.* weeding; *Am.* gracefulness in dancing *f.* royal court; retinue; *Am.* court of justice; -**s** Spanish parliament; **hacer la —** to court, woo; *Am.* **darse uno —** to put on airs.

cortedad *f.* smallness; timidity; bashfulness, shyness.

cortejar *v.* to court, woo.

cortejo *m.* cortege, procession; retinue; courtship; suitor.

cortés *adj.* courteous, polite.

cortesana *f.* courtesan, prostitute.

cortesano *m.* courtier; *adj.* courtlike; courteous.

cortesía f. courtesy, politeness.

corteza f. bark; crust; peel.

cortijo m. farmhouse.

cortina m. curtain.

corto adj. short; scanty; bashful.

corveta f. buck, leap, bound (of a horse); **hacer -s** to prance.

corvo adj. see **curvo.**

cosa f. thing; **— de** approximately, about; **no es —** it is not worth anything; **otra —** something else; **como si tal —** serene, as if nothing had happened; **Am. ni por una de estas nueve -s** absolutely not, not for anything in the world.

cosecha f. crop; harvest.

cosechar v. to reap; to harvest.

coser v. to sew; to stitch.

cosmético m. & adj. cosmetic.

cosquillas f. pl. ticklishness; tickling; **hacer —** to tickle; to excite (one's desire or curiosity); **tener —** to be ticklish.

cosquillear v. to tickle; to excite (one's curiosity or desire).

cosquilleo m. tickle, tickling sensation.

cosquilloso adj. ticklish; touchy.

costa f. coast; cost, expense, price; **a toda —** at all costs, by all means.

costado m. side; flank.

costal m. sack; **estar hecho un — de huesos** to be nothing but skin and bones; to be very thin.

costanero adj. coastal, relating to a coast; sloping.

costar[2] v. irr. to cost; **— trabajo** to be difficult.

costarricense adj., m. & f. Costa Rican.

coste, costo m. cost; expense.

costear v. to defray or pay costs; to pay, be profitable; to navigate along the coast; to go along the edge of; **no costea** it does not pay.

costero adj. coastal; **navegación costera** coastal navigation.

costilla f. rib; chop, cutlet.

costoso adj. costly, expensive.

costra f. crust; scab.

costroso adj. crusty, scabby.

costumbre f. custom, habit.

costura f. sewing; stitching; seam.

costurera f. seamstress.

costurero m. sewing table or cabinet; sewing box; sewing room.

costurón m. coarse stitching; large seam; patch, mend; big scar.

cotejar v. to confront, compare.

cotejo m. comparison.

cotense m. Am. burlap.

cotidiano adj. daily.

cotizable adj. quotable (price).

cotización f. quotation of prices; current price.

cotizar[9] v. to quote (prices); Am. to contribute one's share or quota; Am. to prorate, distribute proportionally.

coto m. enclosure; landmark; limitation; limit, boundary; **poner —** a to set a limit to; to put an end to.

cotorra f. small parrot; magpie; talkative person, chatterbox.

cotorrear v. to chatter; to gossip.

covacha f. small cave; grotto; Am. hut, shanty; Am. cubbyhole, small dark room.

coyote m. Am. coyote, prairie wolf; Am. shyster, tricky lawyer; Am. agent, broker (often illegal).

coyuntura f. joint; articulation; occasion; precise moment.

coz f. kick; recoil of a gun; butt of a firearm; **dar** (or **tirar**) **coces** to kick.

cráneo m. cranium, skull.

craso adj. fat; thick, coarse, gross; **ignorancia crasa** gross ignorance.

cráter m. crater of a volcano.

creación f. creation.

creador m. creator; adj. creating, creative.

crear v. to create.

crecer[13] v. irr. to grow; to increase; **-se** to swell (as a river); to become or feel important.

crecida f. river flood.

crecido adj. grown, increased; large; swollen.

creciente adj. growing, increasing; crescent (moon); f. river flood; m. crescent.

crecimiento m. growth, increase.

credenciales f. pl. credentials.

crédito m. credit; credence, belief; fame, reputation; letter of credit; **dar a —** to loan on credit.

credo m. creed; **en un —** in a jiffy, in a minute.

crédulo adj. credulous, too ready to believe.

creencia f. belief, faith.

creer[14] v. to believe; to think, suppose; **¡ya lo creo!** I should say so!; yes, of course!

creíble adj. credible, believable.

crema f. cream; custard; cold cream.

crepitar v. to crackle, snap; to creak; to rattle.

crepuscular adj. twilight.

crepúsculo m. twilight.

crespo adj. curly; artificial (style); angry; crisp.

crespón m. crepe.

cresta f. crest; top, summit; tuft, comb (of a bird).

cretona f. cretonne.

creyente m. & f. believer; adj. believing.

creyón m. Am. crayon.

cría f. brood; suckling; breeding.

criadero m. tree nursery; breeding place; hotbed; rich mine.

criado m. servant; adj. bred; **mal —** ill-bred; **criada** f. maid, servant.

criador m. breeder, raiser, rearer; creator; adj. creating, creative; breeding; nourishing.

crianza f. breeding; nursing; manners.

criar[17] v. to breed; to bring up, rear, educate; to nurse.

criatura f. creature; baby, child.

criba f. sieve.

cribar v. to sift.

crimen m. crime.

criminal adj., m. & f. criminal.

crin f. mane.

crinudo adj. Am. with a long or thick mane.

criollo m. Am. Creole; native of America (especially Spanish America); adj. Am. national, domestic (not foreign to Spanish America).

crisantema f., **crisantemo** m. chrysanthemum.

crisis f. crisis.

crisol m. crucible, melting pot; hearth of a blast furnace.

crispar v. to contract (muscles); to clench (fists); to put (nerves) on edge.

cristal m. crystal; glass; mirror; lens.

cristalería f. glassware shop or factory; glassware.

cristalino adj. crystalline, transparent, clear; m. lens of the eye.

cristalizar[9] v. to crystallize.

cristiandad f. Christianity; Christendom.

cristianismo m. Christianity.

cristiano m. Christian; person; **hablar en —** to speak clearly; adj. Christian

criterio m. criterion, rule, standard; judgment.

crítica f. criticism; censure; gossip.

criticador adj. critical; m. critic, faultfinder.

criticar[6] v. to criticize; to censure; to find fault with.

crítico adj. critical; m. critic, judge; Am. faultfinder, slanderer; **criticón** m. critic, knocker, faultfinder; adj. critical, over-critical, faultfinding.

croar v. to croak.

crónica f. chronicle, history; **cronista** m. & f. chronicler.

crónico adj. chronic.

cronómetro m. chronometer, timepiece.

croquis m. rough sketch.

cruce m. crossing; crossroads; crossbreeding.

crucero m. cross-bearer; crossing, crossroads; cruiser; transept (of a church); crossbeam; Cross (a constellation).

crucificar[6] v. to crucify.

crucifijo m. crucifix.

crucigrama m. crossword puzzle.

crudo adj. raw; uncooked; unripe; harsh; **agua cruda** hard water; **petróleo — crude** oil; Am. **estar —** to have a hang-over; **cruda** f. Am. hang-over.

cruel adj. cruel.

crueldad f. cruelty.

crujido m. creak, crack, creaking; rustle.

crujir v. to creak, crackle; to grate (one's teeth); to rustle; to crunch.

cruz f. cross.

cruzada f. crusade; holy war; campaign.

cruzado m. crusader; adj. crossed; cross, crosswise, transverse.

cruzamiento m. crossing; crossroads.

cruzar[9] v. to cross; Am. to fight, dispute; **-se con** to meet.

cuaco m. Am. horse; Am. cassava flour.

cuaderno m. notebook; memorandum book; booklet; Am. pamphlet.

cuadra f. hall, large room; stable; hospital or prison ward; Am. city block; Am. reception room.

cuadrado adj. square; m. square; square ruler; die, metal block or plate.

cuadrante m. dial, face of a clock or watch; sundial; quadrant (fourth part of circle; instrument used in astronomy).

cuadrar v. to square; to form into a square; to please; to conform, harmonize; Am. to be becoming (said of clothes); Am. to be ready; Am. to contribute a large sum; Am. to come out well, succeed; **-se** to stand at attention.

cuadricular v. to square off, divide into squares.

cuadrilla f. group, troupe, gang; armed band; quadrille, square dance.

cuadro m. square; picture; scene; frame; flower bed; Am. blackboard; Am. slaughterhouse.

cuajada f. curd.

cuajado p.p. & adj. coagulated, curdled; filled, covered; **— de** full or covered with (flowers, dew, etc.).

cuajar v. to coagulate, thicken, curd, curdle; to turn out well; to jell; to please; Am. to chatter, prattle; **-se** to coagulate, curd; to become crowded, be filled; **la cosa no cuajó** the thing did not work, did not jell.

cuajarón *m.* clot.

cual *rel. pron.* which; **cada —** each one; **— más, — menos** some people more, others less; **el —, la —, los -es, las -es** which; who; **lo —** which; *adv.* as, like; **¿cuál?** *interr. pron.* which one? what?

cualidad *f.* quality; trait.

cualquier(a) *indef. adj. & pron.* any, anyone; whichever; **un hombre cualquiera** any man whatever.

cuando *rel. adv. & conj.* when; **aun —** even though; **¿cuándo?** *interr. adv.* when?

cuantía *f.* quantity; rank, importance.

cuantioso *adj.* plentiful, abundant; numerous.

cuanto *rel. adj. & pron.* as much as, as many as; all that; **— antes** as soon as possible, immediately; **en —** *conj.* as soon as; **en — a** as for, with regard to; **unos -s** a few; **¿cuánto?** *interr. adj. & pron.* how much?; **¿cuántos?** how many?

cuarentena *f.* quarantine; forty units of anything; period of forty days, months, or years.

cuarentón *m.* man in his forties; **cuarentona** *f.* woman in her forties.

cuaresma *f.* Lent.

cuarta *f.* fourth, fourth part; span of a hand; *Am.* horse whip; *Am.* **echar —** to beat, flog.

cuartear *v.* to quarter, divide into quarters; *Am.* to whip; **-se** to crack, split (*said of walls or ceilings*); *Am.* to back down, go back on one's word.

cuartel *m.* quarter, one fourth; quarters, barracks; district; quarter, mercy; **no dar —** to give no quarter.

cuartelada *f.* military coup d'état, uprising, insurrection.

cuartelazo *m. Am.* military coup d'état, insurrection.

cuarterón *m.* quarter, fourth part; fourth of a pound; panel (*of a door or window*); *adj. & m.* quarter-breed (*one fourth Indian and three fourths Spanish*); quadroon (*person of quarter negro blood*).

cuarteto *m.* quartet; quatrain (*stanza of four lines*).

cuartilla *f.* sheet of paper; about 4 quarts; about 1½ pecks; fourth of an **arroba** (*about 6 pounds*); *Am.* three cents' worth; *Am.* **no valer uno —** not to be worth a penny.

cuartillo *m.* fourth of a peck; about a pint; fourth of a **real.**

cuarto *m.* room; quarter, one fourth; **tener -s** to have money; *adj.* fourth.

cuarzo *m.* quartz.

cuate *adj., m. & f. Am.* twin.

cuatrero *m.* horse thief, cattle thief; *Am.* Indian who speaks "broken" Spanish.

cuba *f.* cask, barrel; tub, vat; big-bellied person; drunkard.

cubano *adj. & m.* Cuban.

cubeta *f.* small barrel or keg; bucket, pail.

cúbico *adj.* cubic.

cubierta *f.* cover; covering; envelope; deck (*of a ship*); *Am.* sheath.

cubierto *p.p. of* **cubrir;** *m.* cover; place setting for one person at a table.

cubo *m.* cube; bucket, pail; hub of a wheel; mill pond; *Am.* finger bowl.

cubremesa *f.* table cover.

cubrir[52] *v.* to cover; to hide; to coat; to settle, pay (*a bill*); **-se** to cover oneself; to put on one's hat.

cucaracha *f.* cockroach.

cuclillas : **en —** in a squatting position; **sentarse en —** to squat.

cuclillo *m.* cuckoo.

cuco *adj.* dainty, cute; sly, shrewd; *m.* cuckoo; a kind of caterpillar; card game; *Am.* peach, peach tree; *Am.* **hacer — a** to make fun of; to fool.

cucurucho *m.* paper cone; *Am.* peak, summit; *Am.* cowl, cloak with a hood (*worn by penitents in Holy Week processions*).

cuchara *f.* spoon; scoop; *Am.* mason's trowel; **media —** mediocre person; *Am.* mason's helper; *Am.* **hacer —** to pout; *Am.* **meter uno su —** to butt into a conversation; to meddle; **cucharada** *f.* spoonful; scoop; **cucharón** *m.* large spoon; ladle; dipper; scoop.

cuchichear *v.* to whisper.

cuchicheo *m.* whispering, whisper.

cuchilla *f.* large knife, cleaver; blade (*of any cutting instrument*); *Am.* penknife; *Am.* mountain ridge; *Am.* gore (*in a garment*); *Am.* narrow tract of land.

cuchillada *f.* thrust with a knife, stab, slash; cut, gash.

cuchillo *m.* knife; gore (*in a garment*); **— de monte** hunting knife; **cuchillería** *f.* cutlery; cutlery shop.

cueca *f. Am.* a Chilean dance.

cuello *m.* neck; collar.

cuenca *f.* river basin; narrow valley; wooden bowl; socket of the eye.

cuenco *m.* earthen bowl.

cuenta *f.* count, calculation; bill; account; bead (*of a rosary or necklace*); **a fin de -s** in the final analysis; **caer en la —** to see, get the point; **darse — to realize**; *Am.* **de toda —** anyway; **eso corre de mi —** that is my responsibility; I'll take charge of that; **eso no me tiene —** that does not pay me; it is of no profit to me; **en resumidas -s** in short; *Am.* **hacerle — una cosa a uno** to be useful or profitable for one; **tomar en —** to take into account; **tomar una cosa por su —** to take charge of something, take the responsibility for it; **vamos a -s** let's understand or settle this.

cuentagotas *m.* dropper (*for counting drops*).

cuento *m.* story, tale; **— de nunca acabar** never-ending tale; **déjese de -s** come to the point; **no viene a —** it is not opportune or to the point.

cuerda *f.* cord, string, rope; chord; watch spring; **dar — a** to wind (*a watch*).

cuerdo *adj.* sane; wise.

cuereada *f. Am.* flogging, whipping; *Am.* skinning of an animal.

cuerear *v. Am.* to flog, whip; *Am.* to harm, dishonor; *Am.* to beat (*in a game*); *Am.* to skin (*an animal*).

cuerno *m.* horn; antenna, feeler; **poner -s a** to be unfaithful to, deceive (*a husband*); *Am.* **mandar al —** to send to the devil.

cuero *m.* hide, skin; leather; wineskin; *Am.* whip; **en -s** naked.

cuerpeada *f. Am.* dodge; evasion.

cuerpo *m.* body; bulk; corps; **en — ** without hat or coat; **luchar — a —** to fight in single combat; *Am.* **sacar el —** to dodge; to escape, avoid doing something.

cuervo *m.* crow; raven; *Am.* buzzard; *Am.* dishonest priest; *Am.* **hacer uno la del —** to leave abruptly and not return.

cuesta *f.* hill, slope; **a -s** on one's shoulders or back; in one's care; **— abajo** downhill; **— arriba** uphill.

cuestión *f.* question; controversy, dispute; problem, matter.

cuestionario *m.* questionnaire, list of questions.

cueva *f.* cave, cavern; cellar.

cuico *m. Am.* cop, policeman; *Am.* gossiper, tattletale, "squealer"; *Am.* half-breed; *Am.* short, chubby person.

cuidado *m.* care, attention; worry, misgiving; **al — de** in care of; **tener —** to be careful; **¡ — !** look out!; **be careful! ¡cuidadito!** be very careful!

cuidadoso *adj.* careful; attentive; anxious.

cuidar *v.* to take care of, look after, keep; to make or do carefully.

cuita *f.* grief, care, anxiety; misfortune; *Am.* bird dung.

cuitado *adj.* unfortunate; timid, shy.

culata *f.* haunch, buttock, rear, butt (*of a firearm*).

culatazo *f.* blow with the butt of a rifle; recoil, kick of a firearm.

culebra *f.* snake; coil; *Am.* money belt.

culebrear *v.* to zigzag; to twist, wriggle.

culminación *f.* culmination, climax.

culminar *v.* to culminate; to come to a climax.

culpa *f.* fault; guilt; blame; **echar la — a** to blame; **tener la —** to be to blame.

culpabilidad *f.* guilt; **culpable** *adj.* guilty.

culpar *v.* to blame; to declare guilty.

cultivación *f.* cultivation.

cultivador *m.* cultivator; **máquina cultivadora** cultivator.

cultivar *v.* to cultivate.

cultivo *m.* cultivation, culture.

culto *adj.* cultured; *m.* cult, worship; religious sect; **rendir — a** to pay homage to; to worship.

cultura *f.* culture; cultivation.

cumbre *f.* summit; top.

cumpleaños *m.* birthday.

cumplido *adj.* complete, full; perfect; courteous; *p.p.* fulfilled; due, fallen due; **tiene tres años -s** he is just over three years old; *m.* courtesy, attention; compliment.

cumplimentar *v.* to compliment; to congratulate; to pay a courtesy visit.

cumplimiento *m.* fulfilment; courtesy; completion; compliment; **de —** formal, ceremonious.

cumplir *v.* to fulfill; to comply; to carry out; to fall due; **— años** to have a birthday; to be (*so many*) years old.

cúmulo *m.* pile, heap; accumulation; cumulus (*mass of clouds*).

cuna *f.* cradle; origin; *Am.* dive, den (*for gambling and dancing*).

cundir *v.* to spread (*as news, disease, liquids*); to propagate, extend, multiply.

cuña *f.* wedge; splinter; *Am.* influential person.

cuñado *m.* brother-in-law; **cuñada** *f.* sister-in-law.

cuota f. quota; dues, fee; **— de entrada** admission fee.

cuotidiano adj. everyday, daily.

cupé m. coupé.

cupón m. coupon.

cúpula f. dome.

cura f. cure; m. curate, priest.

curación f. cure.

curandero m. healer (not a doctor); quack; medicine man (among Indians).

curar v. to cure, heal; to treat; to cure (meats, tobacco); to tan (skins); Am. to load (dice), fix (cards); **— de** to take care of; **-se** to cure oneself; to get well; Am. to get drunk.

curiosear v. to snoop, peek, peer, pry; to observe with curiosity.

curiosidad f. curiosity; neatness, daintiness.

curioso adj. curious; neat, dainty; **libros raros y -s** rare books.

curro adj. showy, gaudy, flashy; m. dandy.

currutaco m. fop, dandy; adj. affected (in one's dress).

cursi adj. common, in bad taste; cheap, ridiculous; **cursilería** f. bad taste, cheapness, false elegance; group of cheap, ridiculous people.

curso m. course, direction; scholastic year; course of study.

curtidor m. tanner.

curtiduría f. tannery.

curtir v. to tan; to harden, accustom to hardships; Am. to dirty, soil; **-se** to get tanned or sunburned; to become accustomed to hardships.

curva f. curve.

curvo adj. curved; bent, crooked; arched.

cúspide f. summit, peak, top; spire, steeple.

custodia f. custody; guard, guardian; monstrance (vessel in which the consecrated Host is exposed).

custodiar v. to guard, watch; to keep in custody.

custodio m. guardian, keeper.

cutícula f. cuticle.

cutis m. skin; complexion.

cuyo rel. poss. adj. whose, of whom, of which.

CH

chabacano adj. crude, unpolished; inartistic; cheap, in bad taste; m. Am. a variety of apricot.

chacota f. fun; jest; **echar a — to** take as a joke; **hacer — de** to make fun of.

chacotear v. to frolic, joke, make merry;

to be boisterous; to show off.

chacra f. Am. small farm; Am. cultivated field.

chagra f. Am. farm, piece of farm land; m. & f. Am. peasant; adj. uncivilized, unrefined.

chal m. shawl.

chalán m. horse trader; Am. broncobuster, horse breaker.

chaleco m. waistcoat, vest.

chalupa f. sloop, sailboat; launch; Am. canoe; Am. raft; Am. Mexican tortilla with sauce.

chamaco m. Am. boy; **chamaquito** m. Am. little boy.

chamarra f. coarse wool jacket or sweater; Am. sheepskin jacket, leather jacket; Am. heavy wool blanket.

chamarreta f. short loose jacket; Am. square poncho.

chambón adj. clumsy, awkward, unskillful; m. bungler, clumsy performer, awkward workman; clumsy player.

champaña f. champagne.

champú m. shampoo.

champurrado m. Am. a mixed drink of chocolate and atole; Am. a mixed alcoholic beverage.

champurrar, Am. champurrear v. to mix (drinks).

chamuscada, chamuscadura f. Am. singe, scorch.

chamuscar v. to scorch; to singe; to sear; Am. to sell at a low cost; **-se** to get scorched, singed, or seared; Am. to get peeved, offended.

chamusquina f. singe, scorch.

chancear v. to fool, joke, jest.

chancero m. jester, joker; adj. jolly.

chancla f. slipper; old shoe; **chancleta** f. slipper; m. Am. good-for-nothing.

chanclo m. galosh, overshoe; clog; rubber overshoe; **-s** rubbers.

changador m. Am. carrier, porter; Am. handy man, person who does odd jobs.

chantaje m. blackmail, blackmailing.

chanza f. joke, jest.

chapa f. metal plate; veneer (thin leaf of wood); rosy spot on the cheeks; Am. lock; Am. Indian spy; **-s** game of tossing coins; **hombre de —** serious, reliable man.

chapado adj. veneered (covered with a thin layer of wood or other material); **— a la antigua** old-fashioned.

chapalear = **chapotear.**

chaparro m. scrub oak; short, chubby person; Am. a kind of tropical shrub with rough leaves; Am. short whip; adj. Am. short, squatty.

chaparrón m. downpour, heavy shower.

chapitel m. spire, steeple; capital (of a column).

chapotear v. to splash, paddle in the water.

chapoteo m. splash.

chapucear v. to fumble; to botch, bungle, do or make clumsily; Am. to deceive, trick.

chapulín m. Am. grasshopper.

chapurrar v. to speak (a language) brokenly; to mix (drinks).

chapuz m. dive, duck, ducking.

chapuza f. botch, clumsy piece of work; Am. foul trick, fraud.

chapuzar² v. to duck; to dive.

chaqueta f. jacket; chaquetón m. long jacket, coat.

charamusca f. Am. twisted candy stick or cane; Am. brushwood, firewood; Am. hubbub, uproar.

charamusquero m. Am. candystick maker or vendor.

charca f. pond.

charco m. puddle, pool; pasar el — to cross the pond, cross the ocean.

charla f. chat, chatter, prattle.

charladuría f. chatter, gossip.

charlar v. to chat, chatter, prate.

charlatán m. chatterer, prater; gossiper; charlatan, quack.

charol m. varnish; patent leather; charola f. Am. tray.

charolar v. to varnish, polish.

charqui m. jerky, jerked beef.

charrúa m. & f. Am. Charruan Indian (Indian of Uruguay).

chascarrillo m. joke, funny story.

chasco m. joke, prank; surprise; disillusionment, disappointment; llevarse — to be disappointed, surprised or fooled; adj. Am. thick, curly (hair); Am. ruffled (plumage).

chasquear v. to play a trick on; to disappoint; to crack (a whip); to smack (the lips); to click (the tongue) to crack, snap; Am. to chatter (said of the teeth); Am. to munch (food); -se to be disappointed or disillusioned; to be tricked or fooled.

chasqui m. Am. courier, messenger.

chasquido m. crack of a whip; crackle; smack (of the lips); click (of the tongue).

chata f. bedpan; scow, barge, flat-bottomed boat; Am. platform wagon, platform car, flatcar; chatita f. Am. "honey," "cutie," "funny face."

chato adj. snub-nosed, flat-nosed; flat; flattened, squatty; Am. quedarse uno — to be left flat or in the lurch; to be disappointed.

chayote m. Am. vegetable pear (a tropical fruit growing on a vine); Am. dunce, silly fool.

che Am. word used in Argentina as a familiar form of address; ¡ — ! interj. Am. say! listen!

cheque m. check, bank check.

chica f. little girl; girl; maid, servant.

chicle m. Am. chicle; Am. chewing gum.

chico adj. small, little; m. child, boy; Am. each game of billiards; Am. = chicozapote (tropical fruit and tree from which chicle is extracted).

chicote m. cigar; piece of rope; Am. whip; Am. cigar butt.

chicotear v. Am. to lash, whip, flog; Am. to fight, quarrel; Am. to kill.

chicoteo m. Am. whipping; Am. shooting, killing; Am. crackling, rattling (as of machine guns); Am. quarreling.

chicha f. Am. chicha (a popular alcoholic beverage); Am. thick-soled shoe; no ser ni — ni limonada to be worth nothing, be neither fish nor fowl.

chícharo m. pea; Am. bad cigar; Am. apprentice.

chicharra f. cicada, locust; talkative person; Am. person with a shrill voice; Am. rickety, squeaky car; Am. harsh-sounding musical instrument or bell; Am. piece of fried pork skin.

chicharrón m. crackling, crisp piece of fried pork skin; burned piece of meat; sunburnt person; Am. dried-up, wrinkled person; Am. bootlicker, flatterer.

chichón m. bump, lump; Am. joker, jester; chichona adj. Am. large-breasted.

chiflado adj. "cracked", "touched", crazy; p.p. of chiflar.

chifladura f. craziness, mania; mockery, jest.

chiflar v. to whistle; to hiss; Am. to sing (said of birds); -se to lose one's head; to become unbalanced, crazy.

chiflido m. whistle; hiss; Am. en un — in a jiffy, in a second.

chile m. chili, red pepper.

chileno adj. & m. Chilean.

chillante adj. flashy, bright, showy, loud; shrieking.

chillar v. to shriek, scream; to hiss; Am. to shout, protest, moan; Am. to "squeal," turn informer; Am. no — not to say a word; Am -se to be piqued, offended. .

chillido m. shriek, scream.

chillón adj. shrieking, screaming; shrill;

loud, gaudy; *Am.* whining, discontented; *Am.* touchy.

chimenea *f.* chimney; fireplace, hearth.

china *f.* Chinese woman; pebble; porcelain; China silk or cotton; *Am.* girl, young woman (*usually half-breed or Indian*); *Am.* servant girl; *Am.* sweet orange; *Am.* spinning top; **chinita** *f. Am.* little Indian girl; darling.

chinche *f.* bedbug; thumbtack; tiresome person, bore; *Am.* touchy or irritable person; *Am.* plump, squatty person.

chino *adj.* Chinese; *Am.* curly; *m.* Chinese; Chinaman; *Am.* pig; *Am.* half-breed (*Negro and Indian, white and Indian*); *Am.* Indian; *Am.* house servant; *Am.* coarse, rough, ugly person; *Am.* curl.

chiquero *m.* pigsty, pigpen; pen for bulls; goat shelter.

chiquilín *m. Am.* tot, little boy; **chiquilina** *f. Am.* little girl.

chiquito *adj.* tiny, very small; *m.* tiny tot, tiny child; **chiquitico** *adj.* tiny.

chiripa *f.* stroke of good luck.

chiripá *m. Am.* loose riding trousers (*square of cloth draped from the waist and between the legs*).

chirola *f. Am.* "jug," jail; *Am.* coin of low value.

chirona *f.* "jug," jail.

chirriar[17] *v.* to squeak, creak; to sizzle; to chirp; to sing out of tune; *Am.* to go on a spree.

chirrido *m.* creak, squeak; chirp; squeaking, creaking; chirping.

chisguete *m.* squirt.

chisme *m.* gossip, piece of gossip; trifle, trinket, knickknack, gadget.

chismear *v.* to gossip; to tattle.

chismería *f.* gossiping, talebearing.

chismero *adj.* gossiping; *m.* gossip.

chismoso *adj.* gossiping; *m.* gossip, talebearer, tattletale.

chispa *f.* spark; small diamond; wit; *Am.* false rumor, lie; *Am.* two-wheeled cart; *Am.* brazen, shameless woman; *Am.* **da** — it clicks, works, functions; *Am.* **ponerse** — to get drunk.

chispeante *adj.* sparkling.

chispear *v.* to spark; to sparkle; to twinkle; to drizzle.

chisporrotear *v.* to sputter, throw off sparks.

chiste *m.* joke, jest; **dar en el** — to guess right, hit the nail on the head.

chistera *f.* top hat; fish basket.

chistoso *adj.* funny, amusing, humorous.

¡chito! ¡chitón! *interj.* hush!

chiva *f.* female goat; *Am.* goatee; **chi-**

vo *m.* he-goat; *Am.* fit of anger; *Am.* insulting remark; *Am.* **estar hecho un** — to be very angry; *adj. Am.* angry.

chocante *adj.* striking, surprising; shocking; disgusting; *Am.* tiresome, annoying, impertinent.

chocar[6] *v.* to bump, collide, clash; to fight; to shock, surprise, disgust; **me choca ese hombre** I loathe that man.

chocarrear *v.* to tell coarse jokes; to clown.

chocarrería *f.* coarse joke; **chocarrero** *adj.* coarse, vulgar; clownish.

choclo *m.* overshoe; clog; *Am.* low shoe or slipper; *Am.* ear of corn; *Am.* corn stew; *Am.* spike, ear of wheat.

chocolate *m.* chocolate.

chochear *v.* to be in one's dotage, act senile.

chochera, chochez *f.* senility, dotage; **chocheras, chocheces** senile actions or habits.

chocho *adj.* doting; *m.* childish old man.

chófer *m.* chauffeur.

cholo *m. Am.* half-breed; *Am.* half-civilized Indian; *adj. Am.* coarse, rude; *Am.* dark-skinned; *Am.* black (*dog*).

chopo *m.* black poplar; *adj. Am.* stupid.

choque *m.* collision, bump; shock; clash, conflict; dispute.

chorizo *m.* sausage; *Am.* string of things; *Am.* fool.

chorrazo *m.* spurt, large stream or jet.

chorrear *v.* to drip; to spout.

chorro *m.* spurt, jet; stream, flow; *Am.* strand of a whip; *Am.* river rapids.

choteador *m. Am.* joker, jester.

chotear *v. Am.* to make fun of, jeer, jest, mock, kid; *Am.* to idle, fool around; *Am.* to pamper.

choteo *m. Am.* joking, jeering, kidding.

choza *f.* hut, cabin.

chubasco *m.* squall, sudden shower; **aguantar el** — to weather the storm.

chuchería *f.* trifle, trinket; knickknack; tidbit.

chueco *adj. Am.* crooked, bent; *Am.* crook-legged, bow-legged, knock-kneed; *Am.* worn-out, dejected; *Am.* disgusted, annoyed; *Am.* **comerciar en** — to trade in stolen goods.

chuleta *f.* cutlet, chop; blow, slap.

chulo *m.* dandy; effeminate man; clownish fellow; bullfighter's assistant; *Am.* buzzard; *Am.* coarse, thick brush; *adj. Am.* good-looking, pretty.

chupada *f.* sucking; suction; suck, sip; *Am.* puff from a cigarette; *Am.*

big swallow of liquor.

chupador *m.* sucker; teething ring; *Am.* toper, heavy drinker; *Am.* smoker.

chupaflor, chuparrosa *m. Am.* hummingbird.

chupar *v.* to suck; to sip; to absorb, take in; *Am.* to smoke; *Am.* to drink, get drunk; -se to shrivel up.

churrasco *m. Am.* roasted meat; *Am.* barbecued meat; *Am.* large piece of meat for barbecuing.

churrasquear *v. Am.* to barbecue, roast over coals; *Am.* to prepare (*meat*) for barbecuing; *Am.* to eat barbecued meat.

churrasquito *m.* small piece of roast.

churrigueresco *adj.* baroque, ornate (*architecture*).

chuscada *f.* jest, joke.

chusco *adj.* funny, witty; ridiculous; *Am.* perro — mongrel dog.

chusma *f.* rabble, mob.

D

dable *adj.* feasible, possible.

daca = da acá.

dádiva *f.* gift.

dadivoso *adj.* liberal, generous.

dado *m.* die; -s dice.

dador *m.* giver.

daga *f.* dagger.

dama *f.* lady; jugar a las -s to play checkers.

damisela *f.* damsel, girl.

danza *f.* dance.

danzante *m. & f.* dancer.

danzar[9] *v.* to dance.

danzarina *f.* dancer.

dañar *v.* to harm, hurt, damage; -se to spoil, rot; to get hurt; to get damaged.

dañino *adj.* harmful; destructive.

daño *m.* damage, harm, loss.

dañoso *adj.* harmful.

dar[26] *v. irr.* to give; to strike, hit; to emit, give off; — a luz to give birth to; to publish; — con to encounter, find; — de comer to feed; — de sí to give, stretch; — en to hit upon; to persist in; — largas a un asunto to prolong or postpone a matter; *Am.* — cuero (guasca, puños) to beat, thrash, lash; lo mismo da it makes no difference; -se to give up; dárselas de to boast of.

dardo *m.* dart, arrow.

dares y tomares *m. pl.* give-and-take, dispute; dealings.

dársena *f.* dock, wharf.

datar *v.* to date; — de to date from.

dátil *m.* date (*fruit of the date palm*).

dato *m.* datum, fact; -s data.

de *prep.* of, from; about, concerning; in (*after a superlative*); if (*before inf.*); — no llegar if he does not arrive; el — la gorra azul the one with the blue cap; el mejor — América the best in America; más — lo que dice more than he says.

debajo *adv.* under, underneath; — de *prep.* under.

debate *m.* debate; dispute, quarrel.

debatir *v.* to debate, argue, discuss; to fight; -se to struggle.

debe *m.* debit.

debelar *v.* to subdue, defeat.

deber *v.* to owe; to have to (must, should, ought); debe de ser it must be, probably is; ¡me la debes! I have an account to settle with you!

deber *m.* duty, obligation; debt, debit, debit side (*in bookkeeping*).

debido *adj.* due, owing; just, appropriate.

débil *adj.* weak, feeble.

debilidad *f.* debility, weakness.

debilitación *f.*, **debilitamiento** *m.* weakening; weakness.

debilitar *v.* to weaken.

débito *m.* debt; debit.

debutar *v.* to make a debut, make a first public appearance.

década *f.* decade, ten years; series of ten.

decadencia *f.* decadence, decline, falling off.

decaer[24] *v. irr.* to decay, decline, wither, fade; to fall to leeward.

decaimiento *m.* decline, decay; dejection; weakness.

decano *m.* dean; senior member of a group.

decantado *p.p. & adj.* much talked about; overrated.

decapitar *v.* to behead.

decencia *f.* decency; decente *adj.* decent; respectable; fair

decenio *m.* decade.

decepción *f.* disillusion, disappointment.

decepcionante *adj.* disappointing.

decepcionar *v.* to disillusion, disappoint.

decidir *v.* to decide, resolve; -se a to make up one's mind to; to decide to.

décima *f.* tenth; tithe; stanza of ten octosyllabic lines.

décimo *adj.* tenth.

decir[27] *v. irr.* to say; to tell; to speak; es — that is; querer — to mean, signify.

decisión *f.* decision.

decisivo *adj.* decisive, final.

declamar *v.* to declaim, recite.

declaración *f.* declaration; statement; deposition, testimony.

declarar *v.* to declare, state, affirm; to testify; **-se** to propose, declare one's love; to give one's views or opinion.

declinar *v.* to decline; to go down; to lose vigor, decay; to bend down.

declive *m.* declivity, slope.

decoración *f.* decoration, ornament; stage setting.

decorar *v.* to decorate, adorn.

decorativo *adj.* decorative, ornamental.

decoro *m.* decorum, propriety, dignity; honor.

decoroso *adj.* decorous, becoming, proper, decent.

decrépito *adj.* decrepit, old, feeble.

decretar *v.* to decree.

decreto *m.* decree; decision, order.

dechado *m.* model, pattern, example.

dedal *m.* thimble.

dedicar[6] *v.* to dedicate; to devote; **-se** to apply oneself.

dedicatoria *f.* dedication, inscription.

dedo *m.* finger; toe; — **del corazón** middle finger; — **meñique** little finger; — **pulgar** thumb; **no mamarse el** — not to be easily fooled; **dedillo** *m.* small finger; **saber al dedillo** to know perfectly, know by heart.

deducción *f.* deduction; inference.

deducir[25] *v. irr.* to deduce, conclude; to deduct.

defecto *m.* defect, fault.

defectuoso *adj.* defective, faulty.

defender[1] *v. irr.* to defend.

defensa *f.* defense; *Am.* automobile bumper.

defensivo *adj.* defensive; *m.* defense, safeguard; **defensiva** *f.* defensive.

defensor *m.* defender.

deficiencia *f.* deficiency; **deficiente** *adj.* deficient.

déficit *m.* deficit, shortage.

definición *f.* definition.

definido *adj.* definite; *p.p. of* **definir.**

definir *v.* to define, explain; to determine.

definitivo *adj.* definitive, conclusive, final; **en definitiva** in short, in conclusion; definitely.

deformación *f.* deformation, deformity.

deformar *v.* to deform; **-se** to become deformed; to lose its shape or form.

deforme *adj.* deformed; ugly.

deformidad *f.* deformity.

defraudar *v.* to defraud, cheat, rob of.

defunción *f.* death, decease.

degenerado *adj.* & *m.* degenerate.

degenerar *v.* to degenerate.

deglución *f.* swallowing.

deglutir *v.* to swallow.

degollar[2] *v. irr.* to behead; to slash the throat; to cut (*a dress*) low in the neck.

degradar *v.* to degrade; to debase.

degüello *m.* beheading; throat-slashing.

dehesa *f.* pasture, grazing ground.

deidad *f.* deity.

dejadez *f.* lassitude, languor, listlessness; self-neglect, slovenliness.

dejado *adj.* indolent, listless; slovenly.

dejar *v.* to leave; to quit; to let go; to omit; to let, permit; to abandon; — **de** to stop, cease; — **caer** to drop; *Am.* **no -se** not to be an easy mark, not to let others pick on one.

dejo *m.* aftertaste; slight accent, peculiar inflection; slight taste.

del = **de** + **el** of the.

delantal *m.* apron.

delante *adv.* before, in front; — **de** *prep.* in front of.

delantera *f.* lead, forepart, front.

delantero *adj.* front, foremost, first.

delatar *v.* to denounce, accuse, inform against.

delator *m.* accuser, informer.

delegación *f.* delegation.

delegado *m.* delegate.

delegar[7] *v.* to delegate.

deleitable *adj.* delightful, enjoyable.

deleitar *v.* to delight, please.

deleite *m.* delight, joy, pleasure.

deleitoso *adj.* delightful.

deletrear *v.* to spell.

deleznable *adj.* perishable; brittle.

delgadez *f.* thinness; slimness; fineness.

delgado *adj.* thin, slender, slim.

deliberado *adj.* deliberate; *p.p. of* **deliberar.**

deliberar *v.* to deliberate, consider, ponder.

delicadeza *f.* fineness; delicacy; softness, exquisiteness.

delicado *adj.* delicate; weak, frail; exquisite, dainty; tender.

delicia *f.* delight.

delicioso *adj.* delicious, delightful.

delincuente *adj.*, *m.* & *f.* delinquent.

delineación *f.*, **delineamiento** *m.* delineation, design, outline, drawing; portrayal.

delinear *v.* to delineate, sketch, outline.

delirante *adj.* delirious, raving.

delirar *v.* to be delirious; to rave, talk wildly or foolishly.

delirio *m.* delirium, temporary madness; wild excitement; foolishness.

delito *m.* crime; misdemeanor.

demacrado *adj.* scrawny, emaciated, thin.

demanda *f.* demand; petition; question; claim; complaint; lawsuit.

demandado *m.* defendant; *p.p. of* **demandar.**

demandante *m. & f.* plaintiff.

demandar *v.* to demand; to petition; to sue, file a suit; to indict.

demás *indef. adj. & pron.* los — the rest; the others; las — **personas** the other people; lo — the rest; por — useless; uselessly; por lo — as to the rest; moreover.

demasía *f.* excess; boldness, insolence; offense, outrage; en — excessively.

demasiado *adv.* too much, excessively; too; *adj.* too much, excessive.

demente *adj.* demented, insane, crazy.

democracia *f.* democracy; **demócrata** *m. & f.* democrat; **democrático** *adj.* democratic.

demoler² *v.irr.* to demolish, tear down.

demonio *m.* demon, devil; evil spirit.

demontre *m.* devil; ¡ — ! the deuce!

demora *f.* delay.

demorar *v.* to delay; to retard; -se to linger; to be delayed.

demostración *f.* demonstration; proof, explanation.

demostrar² *v. irr.* to demonstrate, show, prove, explain.

demostrativo *adj.* demonstrative.

demovilizar⁹ *v.irr.* to demobilize.

demudar *v.* to change, alter; to disguise; -se to change color or one's facial expression; to turn pale.

dengoso, denguero *adj.* affected; finicky.

dengue *m.* primness; coyness, affectation; dengue, breakbone fever; *Am.* marigold; *Am.* zigzag; *Am.* swagger; hacer -s to act coy, make grimaces.

denigrar *v.* to blacken, defame, revile, insult.

denodado *adj.* dauntless, daring.

denominación *f.* denomination; name, title, designation.

denominar *v.* to name, call, entitle.

denostar² *v.irr.* to insult, outrage, revile.

denotar *v.* to denote, indicate, mean.

densidad *f.* density.

denso *adj.* dense, compact; thick.

dentado *adj.* toothed, notched.

dentadura *f.* set of teeth.

dentar¹ *v. irr.* to tooth, furnish (*a saw*) with teeth; to indent; to cut teeth, grow teeth (*referring to a child*).

dentellada *f.* bite; tooth mark; a -s with big bites.

dentición *f.* teething.

dentífrico *m.* dentifrice, tooth cleanser; **pasta dentífrica** toothpaste; **polvos dentífricos** toothpowder.

dentista *m.* dentist.

dentro *adv.* inside, within; — de *prep.* inside of; por — on the inside.

denuedo *m.* spirit, courage, daring.

denuesto *m.* affront, insult.

denuncia *f.* denunciation, condemnation, accusation; miner's claim.

denunciar *v.* to denounce, accuse; to proclaim, advise, give notice; to claim (*a mine*).

deparar *v.* to furnish, offer, supply.

departamento *m.* department; compartment; apartment.

departir *v.* to talk, converse.

dependencia *f.* dependence; dependency; branch office.

depender *v.* to depend, rely (on).

dependiente *m.* clerk; dependent, subordinate; *adj.* dependent.

deplorar *v.* to deplore, lament, regret.

deponer⁴⁰ *v. irr.* to set aside; to depose, remove (*an official*); to testify, declare; to have a bowel movement; *Am.* to vomit.

deportar *v.* to deport, banish.

deporte *m.* sport; pastime, recreation.

deportista *m.* sportsman; *f.* sportswoman.

deportivo *adj.* sport, sports (*used as an adj.*); copa **deportiva** loving cup.

deposición *f.* declaration, assertion; testimony; dismissal, removal (*from office or power*); bowel movement.

depositar *v.* to deposit; to deliver, intrust.

depositario *m.* receiver, trustee.

depósito *m.* deposit; storage; warehouse; — de agua reservoir.

depravado *adj.* depraved, corrupt, degenerate.

depravar *v.* to corrupt, pervert, contaminate.

depreciar *v.* to depreciate, lessen the value of.

depresión *f.* depression; dip, sag.

deprimente *adj.* depressing.

deprimir *v.* to depress; to press down; to humiliate, belittle.

depuesto *p.p. of* **deponer.**

depurar *v.* to purify.

derecha *f.* right hand; right side; right wing (*in politics*); a la — to the right.

derecho *adj.* right; straight; *m.* law; duty, tax; fee.

derechura *f.* straightness.

deriva *f.* drift (*of a boat or plane*); irse (*or andar*) a la — to drift, be drifting.

derivar v. to derive; to come (from).

derogar[7] v. to revoke, repeal, abolish.

derramamiento m. spill, spilling, shedding; overflow; scattering; — **de sangre** bloodshed.

derramar v. to spill; to spread, scatter; to shed.

derrame m. spill, spilling, shedding; overflow; discharge (of secretion, blood, etc.); slope.

derredor m. circuit; contour; **al —** around; **en —** around.

derrengado p.p. & adj. lame, crippled; dislocated (said of hip or spine).

derrengar[1, 7] v. irr. to dislocate or sprain (hip or spine); to cripple; to bend.

derretimiento m. thaw, thawing, melting.

derretir[5] v. irr. to melt, dissolve; -se to be consumed; to melt.

derribar v. to demolish, knock down, fell; to overthrow; -se to lie down, throw oneself down.

derrocamiento m. overthrow.

derrocar[6] v. to fling down; to fell; to overthrow.

derrochador m. squanderer, spendthrift; adj. wasteful, extravagant.

derrochar v. to waste; to squander.

derroche m. waste; dissipation, lavish spending.

derrota f. rout, defeat; ship's route or course.

derrotar v. to defeat; to squander; to destroy, ruin; to lose or shift its course (said of a ship).

derrotero m. course, direction; ship's course; book of marine charts.

derrumbadero m. precipice.

derrumbamiento m. landslide; collapse.

derrumbar v. to fling down; Am. to knock down; Am. to go down in a hurry; -se to crumble away; to topple over; Am. to dwindle (as a business).

derrumbe m. landslide; collapse.

desabotonar v. to unbutton.

desabrido adj. tasteless, insipid; harsh; sour.

desabrigar[7] v. to uncover; -se to uncover oneself.

desabrimiento m. tastelessness; harshness; sourness.

desabrochar v. to unfasten, unbutton, unclasp; -se to unbutton oneself, unfasten one's clothes.

desacato m. irreverence, disrespect; profanation.

desacierto m. mistake, error.

desacostumbrado adj. unaccustomed;

unusual; p.p. of desacostumbrar.

desacostumbrar v. to disaccustom, rid of a habit; -se to become unaccustomed; to lose a custom.

desacreditar v. to discredit; to disgrace.

desacuerdo m. disagreement; discord; blunder; forgetfulness.

desafiar[17] v. to challenge; to compete; to defy.

desafinado adj. out of tune.

desafinar v. to be discordant; to be out of tune; -se to get out of tune.

desafío m. challenge, defiance; duel; contest.

desafortunado adj. unfortunate, unlucky.

desafuero m. violation; outrage, abuse.

desagradable adj. disagreeable, unpleasant.

desagradar v. to displease.

desagradecido adj. ungrateful

desagrado m. displeasure; discontent.

desagraviar v. to make amends; to compensate for a damage or injury; to right a wrong; to apologize; to vindicate.

desagravio m. reparation; compensation for a wrong or injury; vindication; apology.

desaguadero m. drain, drain pipe, water outlet.

desaguar[8] v. to drain, draw off; to flow (into); Am. to wash (something) two or more times; Am. to extract the juice from; Am. to urinate; -se to drain.

desagüe m. drainage; drain.

desaguisado m. outrage, violence, wrong.

desahogado p.p. & adj. relieved; roomy, spacious; **estar —** to be in easy or comfortable circumstances; to be well-off.

desahogar[7] v. to relieve from pain or trouble; -se to find relief or release; to unbosom oneself, disclose one's feelings.

desahogo m. relief from pain or trouble; release; ease, comfort, relaxation; freedom, unrestraint.

desairar v. to slight, snub, disdain; to rebuff; to disappoint; to neglect.

desaire m. rebuff, snub, slight, disdain.

desalentar[1] v. irr. to put out of breath; to discourage; -se to get discouraged.

desaliento m. discouragement, dejection.

desaliñado adj. disheveled, slovenly, unkempt, untidy; disorderly.

desaliño m. sloven'iness, untidiness; neglect, carelessness; disorder.

desalmado *adj.* soulless, cruel, inhuman.

desalojar *v.* to dislodge; to evict, expel from a lodging; to vacate.

desamarrar *v.* to untie, unfasten; to unmoor (*a ship*).

desamparar *v.* to abandon, forsake.

desamparo *m.* desertion, abandonment.

desamueblado *adj.* unfurnished.

desangrar *v.* to bleed, draw blood from; to drain; **-se** to bleed, lose blood.

desanimado *adj.* discouraged; lifeless; dull (*said of a party, meeting, etc.*).

desanimar *v.* to dishearten, discourage.

desaparecer[13] *v. irr.* to disappear; to hide; **-se** to disappear, vanish.

desaparición *f.* disappearance.

desapasionado *adj.* dispassionate; free from passion; calm; impartial.

desapego *m.* aloofness, indifference, detachment.

desapercibido *adj.* unprepared; unprovided; unnoticed.

desaprobación *f.* disapproval.

desaprobar[2] *v. irr.* to disapprove.

desarmar *v.* to disarm; to dismount, take apart.

desarme *m.* disarmament.

desarraigar[7] *v.* to root out, uproot.

desarreglado *p.p.* & *adj.* disordered; disorderly; slovenly.

desarreglar *v.* to disarrange, disorder, disturb, upset.

desarreglo *m.* disorder, confusion.

desarrollar *v.* to unroll, unfold; to develop, explain; **-se** to develop; to unfold.

desarrollo *m.* development.

desaseado *adj.* unkempt, untidy.

desaseo *m.* sloverliness, untidiness.

desasir[22] *v. irr.* to loosen, unfasten; **-se** to get loose (from); to let go (of).

desasosiego *m.* unrest, uneasiness, restlessness.

desastrado *adj.* unfortunate, unhappy; ragged, dirty, untidy.

desastre *m.* disaster.

desastroso *adj.* disastrous, unfortunate.

desatar *v.* to untie, loosen; to dissolve; to unravel, clear up; **-se** to let loose, let go; to break loose; **-se en improperios** to let out a string of insults.

desatención *f.* inattention, lack of attention; discourtesy.

desatender[1] *v. irr.* to disregard, pay no attention (to); to slight, neglect.

desatento *adj.* inattentive; discourteous.

desatinado *adj.* senseless; reckless.

desatinar *v.* to act foolishly; to talk nonsense; to blunder; to rave; to lose one's bearings.

desatino *m.* blunder, error; folly, nonsense.

desatracar[6] *v.* to push off (*from shore or from another ship*); to cast off, unmoor.

desavenencia *f.* disagreement, discord; dispute, misunderstanding.

desayunarse *v.* to eat breakfast; **— con la noticia** to hear a piece of news for the first time.

desayuno *m.* breakfast.

desazón *f.* uneasiness, anxiety; insipidity, flatness, tastelessness; displeasure.

desbandarse *v.* to disband, scatter, disperse; to desert the army or a party.

desbaratar *v.* to destroy, ruin; to upset, disturb; to disperse, put to flight; to talk nonsense; **-se** to be upset, be in disorder; to fall to pieces.

desbocado *adj.* runaway (*horse*), dashing headlong; foul-mouthed, abusive; broken-mouthed (*jar, pitcher, etc.*).

desbordamiento *m.* overflow, flood.

desbordante *adj.* overflowing; *Am.* frantic.

desbordar *v.* to overflow, flood; **-se** to spill over; to get overexcited.

descabalar *v.* to break (*a given amount, making it thereby incomplete*).

descabezado *p.p.* beheaded; *adj.* headless; harebrained, thoughtless.

descabezar[9] *v.* to behead; to chop off the head or tip of; **— el sueño** to take a nap; **-se** to break one's head; to rack one's brain.

descaecido *adj.* feeble, weak; **— de ánimo** depressed, dejected, despondent.

descaecimiento *m.* languor, weakness; depression, dejection.

descalabradura *f.* blow or wound on the head; scar on the head.

descalabrar *v.* to wound on the head; to hurt, injure; to damage; **-se** to suffer a head wound or skull fracture.

descalabro *m.* loss, misfortune.

descalzar[9] *v.* to take off (*someone's*) shoes or (and) stockings; **-se** to take off one's shoes or (and) stockings; to lose a shoe (*said of horses*).

descalzo *adj.* barefoot; shoeless.

descaminar *v.* to mislead, lead astray; **-se** to go astray.

descamisado *adj.* shirtless; in rags; *m.* ragamuffin, ragged fellow.

descansar *v.* to rest.

descanso *m.* rest; staircase landing.

descarado *adj.* shameless, impudent, brazen.

descarga *f.* discharge; unloading.

descargar[7] *v.* to discharge; to unload.

descargo *m.* discharge (*of a duty or obligation*); unloading; relief.

descargue *m.* unloading; discharge.

descarnado *adj.* fleshless, scrawny.

descarnar *v.* to pull the flesh from the bone; to corrode, eat away; **-se** to become thin, emaciated.

descaro *m.* effrontery, shamelessness, impudence, audacity.

descarriar[17] *v.* to mislead, lead astray; to separate (*cattle*) from the herd; **-se** to stray; to go astray.

descarrilar *v.* to derail (*cause a train to run off the track*); to wreck (*a train*); **-se** to get or run off the track; to go astray.

descartar *v.* to discard; to put aside.

descascarado *p.p.* & *adj.* peeled off; chipped off.

descascarar *v.* to shell, hull, husk; to peel; to chip off (*plaster*); *Am.* to defame, discredit; *Am.* to flay; **-se** to chip off, peel off.

descendencia *f.* descent, lineage; descendants, offspring.

descendente *adj.* descending, downward.

descender[1] *v. irr.* to descend, go down; to get down; to come (from), originate.

descendiente *m.* & *f.* descendant; *adj.* descending.

descendimiento *m.* descent.

descenso *m.* descent; fall.

descifrar *v.* to decipher, puzzle out, figure out.

descolgar[2,7] *v. irr.* to unhang, take down; to let down; **-se** to climb down (*a rope, tree, etc.*); to drop in, appear unexpectedly.

descolorar *v.* to discolor; to fade; **-se** to fade, lose its color; to discolor.

descolorido *adj.* pale.

descollar[2] *v. irr.* to excel; to stand out, tower (above).

descomedido *adj.* rude, discourteous, impolite; unobliging.

descompletar *v.* to make incomplete, break (*a unit, sum, set, etc.*).

descomponer[40] *v. irr.* to upset, disturb; to put out of order; to decompose; **-se** to decompose, rot; to become upset, ill; to get out of order; *Am.* **se me descompuso el brazo** I dislocated my arm, my arm got out of joint.

descomposición *f.* decomposition; decay, corruption; disorder, confusion.

descompuesto *p.p. of* **descomponer**; *adj.* out of order; insolent; brazen; immodest.

descomunal *adj.* colossal, enormous, monstrous.

desconcertante *adj.* disconcerting, disturbing, confusing, baffling, embarrassing.

desconcertar[1] *v. irr.* to disconcert, bewilder, confuse; to disturb; **-se** to be confused, perplexed.

desconcierto *m.* disorder; confusion; disagreement; feeling of discomfort.

desconchadura *f.* chip (*chipped off place*); chipping off, peeling off (*of plaster, varnish, etc.*).

desconchar *v.* to scrape off (*plaster or stucco*); **-se** to peel off, chip off (*as plaster*).

desconectar *v.* to disconnect.

desconfiado *adj.* distrustful, suspicious.

desconfianza *f.* mistrust, distrust.

desconfiar[17] *v.* to distrust; to lose confidence.

desconocer[13] *v. irr.* to fail to recognize or remember; to disown; to disregard, slight; not to know.

desconocido *adj.* unknown; unrecognizable; *m.* stranger.

desconocimiento *m.* disregard; ignorance.

desconsolado *p.p.* & *adj.* disconsolate, forlorn; disheartened, grieved.

desconsolador *adj.* disheartening, saddening.

desconsolar[2] *v. irr.* to sadden, grieve; to discourage; **-se** to become disheartened, grieved.

desconsuelo *m.* dejection, sadness, distress.

descontar[2] *v. irr.* to discount, deduct; to allow for.

descontentadizo *adj.* discontented, fretful, hard to please.

descontentar *v.* to displease.

descontento *adj.* discontent, displeased; *m.* discontent, displeasure.

descorazonado *adj.* disheartened, discouraged, depressed.

descorchar *v.* to uncork; to remove the bark from (*a cork tree*); to force or break open.

descortés *adj.* discourteous, rude, impolite.

descortesía *f.* discourtesy, rudeness, impoliteness.

descortezar[9] *v.* to bark, strip the bark from (*trees*); to remove the crust or shell from; to peel; to civilize, remove the rough manners from.

descoser *v.* to rip, unsew, unstitch; **-se** to rip, come unstitched; to talk too much or indiscreetly.

descosido *m.* rip; *adj.* too talkative, indiscreet; disorderly, *p.p. of* **descoser.**

descostrar *v.* to flake; to scale off; to remove the crust from; **-se** to flake, scale off.

descoyuntado *p.p. & adj.* dislocated, out of joint.

descoyuntar *v.* to dislocate, put out of joint; **-se** to get out of joint.

descrédito *m.* discredit.

descreído *adj.* incredulous, unbelieving; *m.* unbeliever.

descreimiento *m.* unbelief, lack of faith.

describir[52] *v.* to describe.

descripción *f.* description.

descriptivo *adj.* descriptive.

descrito *p.p. irr. of* **describir.**

descuartizar[9] *v.* to quarter (*an animal*); to tear or cut into parts.

descubierto *p.p. of* **descubrir** *& adj.* discovered; uncovered; hatless; bareheaded; *m.* deficit, shortage; **al —** openly, in the open; **en —** uncovered, unpaid.

descubridor *m.* discoverer.

descubrimiento *m.* discovery; find; invention.

descubrir[52] *v.* to discover; to uncover; **-se** to uncover; to take off one's hat.

descuento *m.* discount; deduction.

descuidado *adj.* careless, negligent; untidy, slovenly; unaware; thoughtless.

descuidar *v.* to neglect; to overlook; to be careless or negligent; **-se** to be careless or negligent.

descuido *m.* carelessness; neglect; oversight; disregard; inattention; slip, error.

desde *prep.* from; since; **— luego** immediately; of course; **— que** *conj.* since, ever since.

desdecir[27] *v. irr.* to be out of harmony (with); to detract (from); **-se** to retract; to contradict oneself.

desdén *m.* disdain, scorn.

desdentado *adj.* toothless.

desdeñar *v.* to disdain, scorn.

desdeñoso *adj.* disdainful, scornful.

desdicha *f.* misfortune; misery, poverty.

desdichado *adj.* unfortunate; unhappy, wretched; miserable; *m.* wretch.

desdoblamiento *m.* unfolding.

desdoblar *v.* to unfold; to spread out.

desdorar *v.* to remove the gilt from; to tarnish; to dishonor.

desdoro *m.* tarnish, blemish; dishonor.

deseable *adj.* desirable.

desear *v.* to desire, want.

desecación *f.*, **desecamiento** *m.* drying; drainage.

desecar[6] *v.* to dry; to dry up; to drain (*land*).

desechar *v.* to discard; to reject; to refuse, decline; *Am.* to cut across, take a short cut.

desecho *m.* remainder, residue; waste material; piece of junk; discard; **-s** refuse, scraps, junk; **hierro —** scrap iron; **papel de —** wastepaper, scraps of paper.

desembalar *v.* to unpack.

desembarazar[9] *v.* to rid, free, clear; *Am.* to give birth; **-se** to get rid of.

desembarazo *m.* freedom, ease, naturalness; *Am.* childbirth.

desembarcadero *m.* dock, wharf, pier.

desembarcar[6] *v.* to disembark, land; to unload; to go ashore.

desembarco, desembarque *m.* landing; unloading.

desembocadura *f.* mouth (*of a river, canal, etc.*); outlet.

desembocar[6] *v.* to flow (into); to lead (to).

desembolsar *v.* to disburse, pay out.

desembolso *m.* disbursement, outlay, expenditure.

desembragar[7] *v.* to throw out the clutch; to disconnect.

desemejante *adj.* unlike.

desempacar[6] *v.* to unpack.

desempeñar *v.* to recover, redeem, take out of pawn; **— un cargo** to perform the duties of a position; **— un papel** to play a part; **-se** to get out of debt.

desempeño *m.* fulfilment, carrying out, discharge; performance (*of a duty*); acting (*of a role*); redeeming (*of a thing pawned*).

desempleado *adj.* unemployed.

desempleo *m.* unemployment.

desempolvar *v.* to dust, remove the dust from.

desencadenar *v.* to unchain, free from chains; to loosen, set free; **-se** to free oneself; to break loose.

desencajado *p.p. & adj.* disjointed; disfigured; sunken (*eyes*); emaciated.

desencantar *v.* to disillusion, disappoint.

desencanto *m.* disillusion, disappointment.

desenfado *m.* ease, freedom; calmness.

desenfrenado *p.p. & adj.* unbridled; wanton, reckless; loose, immoral.

desenganchar *v.* to unhitch; to unhook; to unfasten.

desengañador *adj.* disappointing, disillusioning.

desengañar *v.* to undeceive, disillusion, disappoint.

desengaño m. disillusion, disappointment, blighted hope.

desengranar v. to throw out of gear.

desenmarañar v. to untangle; to unravel.

desenmascarar v. to unmask.

desenredar v. to disentangle, unravel.

desenrollar v. to unroll.

desensartar v. to unstring; to unthread; to unfasten from a ring.

desensillar v. to unsaddle.

desentenderse[1] v. irr. to neglect, ignore, pay no attention to; to pretend not to see, hear or understand.

desentendido adj. unmindful, heedless; p.p. of **desentenderse; hacerse el —** to pretend not to notice.

desenterrar[1] v. irr. to unearth, dig up.

desentonado adj. inharmonious, out of tune.

desentonar v. to be out of tune; to be out of harmony; to sing off key, play out of tune.

desenvoltura f. freedom, ease, abandon; boldness, impudence.

desenvolver[2, 52] v. irr. to unroll, unfold: to unwrap; to develop.

desenvolvimiento m. development, unfolding.

desenvuelto adj. free, easy; forward, bold; shameless, brazen; p.p. of **desenvolver.**

deseo m. desire, wish.

deseoso adj. desirous, eager.

desequilibrado adj. unbalanced; p.p. of **desequilibrar.**

desequilibrar v. to unbalance; to derange.

desequilibrio m. lack of balance; derangement, mental disorder.

deserción f. desertion.

desertar v. to desert; to abandon; **-se de** to desert.

desertor m. deserter; quitter.

desesperación f. despair; desperation; fury.

desesperado adj. desperate; despairing; hopeless, p.p. of **desesperar.**

desesperanzado p.p. & adj. discouraged; hopeless; desperate, in despair.

desesperanzar[9] v. to discourage, deprive of hope; **-se** to be discouraged; to despair, lose one's hope.

desesperar v. to despair, lose hope; to make (someone) despair; **-se** to despair, be desperate; to be furious.

desfachatez f. shamelessness, effrontery, impudence.

desfalcar[6] v. to embezzle; to remove a part of.

desfalco m. embezzlement; diminution, decrease.

desfallecer[13] v. irr. to grow weak; to faint.

desfallecimiento m. faintness; weakness; languor; swoon, faint.

desfavorable adj. unfavorable.

desfigurar v. to disfigure; to deface; to distort.

desfiladero m. narrow passage, narrow gorge; road on the edge of a precipice.

desfilar v. to march, parade, pass by.

desfile m. parade.

desgana f. lack of appetite; reluctance.

desgarrado p.p. torn; adj. shameless; impudent.

desgarradura f. tear.

desgarrar v. to tear, rend; to expectorate, cough up; **-se** to tear; to separate oneself (from).

desgastar v. to waste, consume, wear away; **-se** to waste away, lose one's strength or vigor; to wear off.

desgaste m. waste; wear and tear.

desgracia f. misfortune, mishap; disgrace.

desgraciado adj. unfortunate, wretched.

desgranar v. to thrash, thresh (grain); to remove the grain from; to shell (peas, beans, etc.).

desgreñado adj. disheveled.

deshabitado adj. uninhabited, deserted; empty, vacant.

deshacer[31] v. irr. to undo; to dissolve; to destroy; to untie; **-se** to dissolve; to melt; to waste away; **-se de** to get rid of.

desharrapado, desarrapado adj. ragged, shabby, tattered.

deshecha f. simulation, pretense; **hacer la —** to feign, pretend.

deshecho p.p. of **deshacer** & adj. undone; ruined, destroyed, in pieces; violent (said of rainstorms); worn-out, fatigued; Am. disorderly, untidy.

deshelar[1] v. irr. to melt; to thaw; **-se** to melt; to thaw.

desherbar[1] v. irr. to weed.

deshielo m. thaw.

deshierbe m. weeding.

deshilachar v. to ravel, fray.

deshilar v. to unravel; **-se** to unravel; to fray.

deshojar v. to strip off the leaves, petals, or pages; **-se** to lose its leaves (said of a plant or book); to lose petals.

deshollejar v. to husk, hull; to peel, pare, skin; to shell (beans).

deshonesto adj. immodest; unchaste, lewd.

deshonra f. dishonor; disgrace.
deshonrar v. to dishonor, disgrace; to insult, offend; to seduce.
deshonroso adj. dishonorable; shameful.
deshora f. inopportune time; **a —** (or **a -s**) unexpectedly; **comer a —** to piece, eat between meals.
deshuesar v. to stone, remove the pits or stones from (fruits); to bone, remove the bones from (an animal).
desidia f. indolence, laziness.
desidioso adj. indolent, negligent, lazy; listless.
desierto adj. deserted, uninhabited; alone, lonely; m. desert, wilderness.
designación f. designation; appointment.
designar v. to designate, appoint, select; to design, plan, intend.
designio m. design, plan, purpose.
desigual adj. unequal; uneven; variable, changeable.
desigualdad f. inequality; unevenness; roughness (of the ground).
desilusión f. disillusion, disappointment.
desilusionar v. to disillusion, disappoint; -se to become disillusioned; to lose one's illusions.
desinencia f. termination, ending (of a word).
desinfectante adj. disinfecting; m. disinfectant.
desinfectar v. to disinfect.
desinflado adj. deflated, not inflated, flat.
desinterés m. disinterestedness, unselfishness, impartiality.
desinteresado adj. disinterested, unselfish, fair, impartial.
desistir v. to desist, stop, cease.
deslavado p.p. & adj. half-washed; weakened; faded; pale; saucy.
deslavar v. to wash away; to fade; to wash superficially.
desleal adj. disloyal, faithless.
desleír [15] v. irr. to dissolve; to dilute, make thin or weak; -se to become diluted.
deslindar v. to mark off, mark the boundaries of.
desliz m. slip, slide; error.
deslizador m. glider.
deslizamiento m. slip, slipping; glide; sliding, skidding.
deslizar [9] v. to slip, slide; -se to slip; to skid; to glide; to slip out.
deslucido p.p. & adj. tarnished; dull; discredited; dingy, shabby; awkward,

ungraceful; inelegant.
deslucir [13] v. irr. to tarnish, dull the lustre of; to discredit.
deslumbrador adj. dazzling, glaring.
deslumbramiento m. dazzle, glare; daze, confusion.
deslumbrar v. to dazzle.
deslustrado adj. & p.p. tarnished; dim, dull; opaque.
deslustrar v. to tarnish; to soil, stain (one's honor or reputation).
deslustre m. tarnish; disgrace.
desmadejado p.p. & adj. enervated, exhausted; depressed.
desmadejar v. to enervate, weaken.
desmán m. misconduct, abuse, insult; calamity, disaster.
desmantelar v. to dismantle, strip of furniture, equipment, etc.
desmañado adj. unskilful, awkward, clumsy.
desmayar v. to dismay; to lose strength, courage; -se to faint.
desmayo m. faint, swoon; dismay, discouragement.
desmazalado adj. dejected, depressed.
desmejorar v. to impair; to make worse; -se to grow worse; to waste away, lose one's health.
desmentir [3] v. irr. to contradict; to give the lie; -se to contradict oneself; to retract, take back one's word.
desmenuzar [9] v. to crumble, break into bits; to mince; to shred; -se to crumble, fall to pieces.
desmerecer [13] v. irr. to become unworthy of; to deteriorate, lose merit or value; to be inferior to.
desmigajar v. to crumb (bread); to crumble; -se to crumble.
desmochar v. to cut off, chop off (the top or tip).
desmolado adj. toothless, without molars.
desmontar v. to dismount; to cut down (a forest); to clear or level off (ground); to dismantle, take apart; to tear down -se to dismount, alight, get off.
desmoronar v. to crumble; -se to crumble down, fall gradually to pieces.
desnatar v. to skim, take the cream from (milk).
desnaturalizado adj. unnatural, cruel; **alcohol —** denatured alcohol (made unfit for drinking); **madre desnaturalizada** unnatural mother (one without motherly instincts).
desnudar v. to undress, uncover; -se to undress.
desnudez f. nudity, nakedness.

desnudo *adj.* nude, naked, bare.

desobedecer[15] *v. irr.* to disobey.

desobediencia *f.* disobedience; desobediente *adj.* disobedient.

desocupación *f.* unemployment; idleness; vacationing.

desocupado *adj.* unoccupied; unemployed, idle; empty, vacant.

desocupar *v.* to empty, vacate; -se de un negocio to get rid of, or not pay attention to, a business.

desoír[36] *v. irr.* to turn a deaf ear to, not to heed; to refuse (*a petition*).

desolación *f.* desolation; ruin; loneliness; anguish, affliction, grief.

desolado *adj.* desolate; *p.p. of* desolar.

desolar[2] *v. irr.* to lay waste, ruin; -se to be in anguish; to grieve.

desollar[2] *v. irr.* to skin, flay; to fleece, extort money from.

desorbitado *adj.* out of its orbit; out of place or proportion; decentered; *Am.* popeyed, with bulging eyes; *Am.* crazy, eccentric.

desorden *m.* disorder, confusion.

desordenado *adj.* disorderly; lawless; unsettled; *p.p. of* desordenar.

desordenar *v.* to disturb, confuse, upset.

desorientar *v.* to throw off one's bearings; to lead astray; to misdirect, mislead; to confuse; -se to lose one's bearings; to go astray, get lost.

despabilado *adj.* wakeful; wide-awake, bright, lively.

despabilar *v.* to snuff, trim the wick of (*a candle*); to enliven, awaken (*the mind*), sharpen (*the wits*); -se to wake up, rouse oneself, shake off drowsiness.

despacio *adv.* slowly.

despacioso *adj.* slow.

despachar *v.* to despatch; to send; to facilitate; to ship.

despacho *m.* dispatch; office, bureau; salesroom; message; official communication; sending, shipment; promptness; *Am.* country store, farm store.

despachurrar *v.* to crush, squash.

desparejo *adj.* unequal, uneven.

desparpajar *v.* to upset, disarrange; to rant, talk too much; *Am.* to disperse, scatter.

desparpajo *m.* ease, freedom of manner; freshness, pertness; *Am.* dispersion, scattering; *Am.* disorder, jumble.

desparramar *v.* to scatter, spread; to spill; to squander; -se to "spread" oneself, spend lavishly; to scatter; to spill.

desparramo *m. Am.* scattering, spreading, spilling; *Am.* disorder, commotion.

despatarrarse *v.* to sprawl; to fall sprawling to the ground.

despecho *m.* spite; grudge; despair; weaning; a — de in spite of.

despedazar[9] *v.* to break, cut, tear into pieces.

despedida *f.* farewell; departure; dismissal.

despedir[5] *v. irr.* to discharge, dismiss; to emit, throw off, give off; to see (*a person*) off (*at a station, airport, etc.*); -se to take leave, say good-bye.

despegar[7] *v.* to detach; to unfasten; to take off (*said of a plane*); *Am.* to unhitch; no — los labios not to say a word, not to open one's mouth; -se to grow apart; to come loose or detached.

despego = desapego.

despegue *m.* take-off (*of an airplane*).

despejado *adj.* clear, cloudless; smart, bright; *p.p. of* despejar.

despejar *v.* to clear; to remove obstacles from; -se to clear up (*as the sky*); to clear one's mind.

despellejar *v.* to skin, flay.

despensa *f.* pantry; storeroom (*for food*); food provisions.

despensero *m.* butler; steward.

despeñadero *m.* steep cliff, precipice.

despeñar *v.* to fling down a precipice; -se to fall down a precipice; to throw oneself down a cliff.

despepitar *v.* to seed, remove the seeds from; -se to talk or shout vehemently; to rave, talk wildly; -se por una cosa to long for something; to be crazy about something.

desperdiciado *adj.* wasteful; *p.p. of* desperdiciar.

desperdiciar *v.* to squander; to waste.

desperdicio *m.* waste; extravagance; -s leftovers, garbage; residue.

desperdigar[7] *v.* to disperse; to scatter; to strew.

desperezarse[9] *v.* to stretch oneself.

desperfecto *m.* damage; flaw, defect.

despertador *m.* alarm clock.

despertar[1] *v. irr.* to awaken; to wake up; -se to wake up.

despiadado *adj.* pitiless, heartless, cruel.

despierto *adj.* awake; wide-awake.

despilfarrado *adj.* wasteful, extravagant; ragged; *p.p. of* despilfarrar.

despilfarrar *v.* to squander; to waste.

despilfarro *m.* extravagance, squandering; waste.

despistar *v.* to throw off the track.

desplante *m.* arrogance; impudent remark or act.

desplazar[9] *v.* to displace.

desplegar[1,7] *v. irr.* to unfold; to unfurl; to show, manifest.

desplomar *v.* to cause (*a wall*) to lean; -se to slump; to topple over, tumble down, collapse.

desplome *m.* collapse; toppling over; landslide.

desplumar *v.* to pick, pluck (*a fowl*); to fleece, skin, rob, strip; -se to molt, shed the feathers.

despoblado *adj.* uninhabited, desolate; — de árboles treeless; *m.* open country; uninhabited place; wilderness.

despojar *v.* to despoil, rob; to strip (of), deprive (of); -se to undress; to deprive oneself.

despojo *m.* plundering, robbery; spoil, booty; leftover, scrap; -s remains.

desportilladura *f.* chip; nick.

desportillar *v.* to chip; to nick.

desposar *v.* to marry; -se to become formally engaged; to get married.

déspota *m. & f.* despot, tyrant.

despótico *adj.* despotic, tyrannical.

despotismo *m.* despotism, tyranny.

despreciable *adj.* contemptible; worthless; insignificant, negligible.

despreciar *v.* to despise, scorn.

desprecio *m.* scorn, contempt.

desprender *v.* to unfasten, loosen; to detach; -se to get loose, come unfastened; to climb down; to get rid (of); to be inferred, be deduced.

desprendimiento *m.* detachment; generosity; unfastening; landslide.

despreocupado *p.p. & adj.* unbiased; liberal, broadminded; unconventional, carefree; *Am.* careless, slovenly; *Am.* indifferent to criticism.

desprestigiar *v.* to discredit, harm the reputation of; -se to lose one's prestige.

desprestigio *m.* discredit, loss of prestige.

desprevenido *adj.* unprepared; unaware.

despropósito *m.* absurdity, nonsense.

después *adv.* after, afterward; then, later; — de *prep.* after; — (de) que *conj.* after.

despuntado *adj.* blunt, dull; *p.p.* of despuntar.

despuntar *v.* to blunt; to cut off (*a point*), nip; to bud or sprout; to be clever, witty; to excel; — el alba to begin to dawn.

desprovisto *adj.* destitute; lacking; devoid.

desquitar *v.* to retrieve, restore (*a loss*); -se to get even, take revenge; to win back one's money; to make up (for).

desquite *m.* retaliation, revenge; getting even; recovery of a loss; return game or match.

desrazonable *adj.* unreasonable.

destacado *adj.* outstanding; *p.p.* of destacar.

destacamento *m.* military detachment.

destacar[6] *v.* to detach (*troops*); to make stand out; to stand out; **hacer —** to emphasize; to make stand out; -se to stand out.

destapar *v.* to uncover; to uncork; *Am.* to start running; -se to uncover, get uncovered; to get uncorked; *Am.* to burst out talking.

destartalado *adj.* in disorder; in rack and ruin; dismantled, stripped of furniture.

destechado *adj.* roofless.

destellar *v.* to flash; to sparkle, twinkle; to gleam.

destello *m.* flash, sparkle, gleam.

destemplado *adj.* out of tune, out of harmony; immoderate; **sentirse —** not to feel well; to feel feverish.

desteñir[5,19] *v. irr.* to discolor; to fade; to bleach; -se to become discolored; to fade.

desternillarse *v.* — de risa to split one's sides with laughter.

desterrado *m.* exile; outcast; *p.p. & adj.* exiled, banished.

desterrar[1] *v.* to exile, banish; to remove earth (from).

destetar *v.* to wean.

destierro *m.* exile.

destilación *f.* distillation.

destiladera *f.* still; *Am.* filter.

destilar *v.* to distill; to drip, trickle; to filter.

destilería *f.* distillery.

destinación *f.* destination.

destinar *v.* to destine; to employ.

destinatario *m.* addressee.

destino *m.* destiny, fate; destination; employment, job.

destituido *adj.* destitute; *p.p.* of destituir.

destituir[32] *v. irr.* to deprive.

destornillador *m.* screwdriver.

destornillar *v.* to unscrew.

destrabar *v.* to unlock, unfasten; to untie; to separate; to unfetter.

destreza *f.* dexterity, skill, ability.

destronar *v.* to dethrone, depose, overthrow.

destrozar[9] *v.* to shatter, cut to pieces; to destroy; to squander.

destrozo *m.* destruction; ruin.

destrucción f. destruction.

destructivo adj. destructive.

destructor adj. destructive; m. destroyer.

destruir[33] v. irr. to destroy; to ruin.

desunir v. to divide, separate.

desusado adj. unusual, unaccustomed; obsolete, out of use.

desuso m. disuse; obsoleteness.

desvaído adj. lanky, tall and awkward; gaunt; dull, faded.

desvainar v. to shell (peas, beans, etc.).

desvalido adj. abandoned; destitute; helpless.

desvalijar v. to ransack the contents of a valise; to rob.

desván m. garret, attic.

desvanecer[18] v. irr. to fade, dissolve; to make vain; to make dizzy; -se to evaporate; to vanish; to fade out, disappear; to get dizzy.

desvanecido adj. dizzy, faint; proud, haughty; p.p. of desvanecer.

desvanecimiento m. dizziness, faintness; vanity.

desvariar[17] v. to rave, be delirious; to rant, talk excitedly; to talk nonsense.

desvarío m. raving; delirium; madness; inconstancy.

desvelado adj. sleepless, awake; watchful; p.p. of desvelar.

desvelar v. to keep (another) awake; -se to keep awake; to have insomnia, lose sleep; to be worried, anxious.

desvelo m. lack of sleep; restlessness; vigilance, watchfulness; worry, anxiety.

desvencijado adj. tottering, rickety, shaky, falling apart.

desventaja f. disadvantage.

desventura f. misfortune, unhappiness.

desventurado adj. unfortunate, unhappy, miserable, wretched.

desvergonzado adj. shameless, brazen.

desvergüenza f. shamelessness; disgrace; shame; insolence; impudent word.

desvestir[5] v. irr. to undress; -se to undress.

desviación f. deviation, turning aside, shift; detour.

desviar[17] v. to deviate, turn aside; to swerve; -se to shift direction; to branch off, turn off the main road; to swerve.

desvío m. deviation, turning aside; indifference, coldness; side track, railroad siding; detour.

desvirtuar[18] v. to impair, diminish the value or quality of.

desvivirse v. — por to long for; to be excessively fond of, be crazy about, to

make a fuss over; to do one's best for; **ella se desvive por complacerme** she does her utmost to please me.

desyerbar = desherbar.

detallar v. to detail, report in detail; to retail.

detalle m. detail; retail; ¡ahí está el — ! that's the point.

detallista m. & f. retailer; detailer, person fond of detail.

detective, detectivo m. detective.

detención f. detention, arrest; stop, halt; delay.

detener[45] v. irr. to detain, stop; to arrest; -se to halt; to delay oneself, stay.

detenimiento m. detention; delay; care, deliberation.

deteriorar v. to deteriorate, damage; -se to deteriorate, become impaired or damaged; to wear out.

deterioro m. deterioration, impairment.

determinación f. determination; firmness.

determinar v. to determine; to decide; -se to resolve, decide.

detestable adj. detestable; hateful.

detestar v. to detest.

detonación f. detonation, report (of a gun), loud explosion; pop.

detonar v. to detonate, explode with a loud noise; to pop.

detrás adv. behind; — de prep. behind; por — from the rear, by the rear, from behind.

deuda f. debt; indebtedness.

deudo m. relative, kinsman.

deudor m. debtor; adj. indebted, obligated.

devanar v. to spool, wind on a spool; -se los sesos to rack one's brain.

devaneo m. frenzy; dissipation; wandering; idle pursuit; giddiness.

devastar v. to devastate, lay waste, destroy.

devenir[48] v. irr. to befall; to become, be transformed into.

devoción f. devotion; piety; attachment.

devocionario m. prayer book.

devolución f. return, giving back; replacement.

devolver[2, 52] v. irr. to return, give back, pay back.

devorador adj. devouring; absorbing; ravenous; m. devourer.

devorar v. to devour, gobble up.

devoto adj. devout, religious, pious; very fond (of).

devuelto p.p. of devolver.

día *m.* day; **al otro —** on the next day; **hoy —** nowadays; **un — sí y otro no** every other day.

diablo *m.* devil, demon.

diablura *f.* deviltry, mischief, devilish prank.

diabólico *adj.* diabolic, devilish, fiendish.

diácono *m.* deacon.

diadema *f.* diadem, crown.

diáfano *adj.* transparent, clear; sheer.

diagnosticar[6] *v.* to diagnose.

diagrama *m.* diagram; graph.

dialecto *m.* dialect.

dialogar[7] *v.* to dialogue.

diálogo *m.* dialogue.

diamante *m.* diamond.

diámetro *m.* diameter.

diantre *m.* devil.

diapasón *m.* pitch (*of a sound*); tuning fork.

diario *adj.* daily; *m.* newspaper; daily expense; journal, diary.

diarrea *f.* diarrhea.

dibujante *m. & f.* draftsman; designer.

dibujar *v.* to draw, make a drawing; to delineate, depict, portray; to describe; **-se** to appear, show.

dibujo *m.* drawing; delineation, portrayal, picture; **— natural** drawing of the human figure, drawing from life.

dicción *f.* diction; word; choice of words, style.

diciembre *m.* December.

dictado *m.* dictation; title; dictate; **escribir al —** to take dictation.

dictador *m.* dictator.

dictadura *f.* dictatorship.

dictamen *m.* opinion, judgment.

dictaminar *v.* to give an opinion or judgment.

dictar *v.* to dictate.

dicha *f.* happiness; good luck.

dicharachero *adj.* fond of making wisecracks; witty.

dicharacho *m.* wisecrack, smart remark; malicious remark.

dicho *p.p.* of **decir** said; **— y hecho** no sooner said than done; *m.* saying, popular proverb.

dichoso *adj.* happy, lucky.

diente *m.* tooth; tusk; **— de león** dandelion; **de -s afuera** insincerely; *Am.* **pelar el —** to smile affectedly.

diestra *f.* right hand.

diestro *adj.* skilful; right; *m.* matador; skilful swordsman; halter.

dieta *f.* diet; assembly; salary, fee.

diezmo *m.* tithe.

difamación *f.* libel, slander.

difamador *m.* slanderer.

difamar *v.* to defame, libel, malign, slander.

difamatorio *adj.* scandalous, slandering.

diferencia *f.* difference.

diferenciar *v.* to differentiate, distinguish; to differ, disagree; **-se** to distinguish oneself; to become different.

diferente *adj.* different.

diferir[3] *v. irr.* to defer, put off, delay, to differ, disagree; to be different.

difícil *adj.* difficult.

dificultad *f.* difficulty.

dificultar *v.* to make difficult; **— el paso** to impede or obstruct the passage; **-se** to become difficult.

dificultoso *adj.* difficult, hard.

difteria *f.* diphtheria.

difundir *v.* to diffuse, spread out, scatter; to broadcast by radio.

difunto *adj.* deceased, dead; *m.* corpse.

difusión *f.* diffusion, spreading, scattering; wordiness; broadcasting.

difuso *adj.* diffuse; diffused, widespread.

digerible *adj.* digestible.

digerir[3] *v. irr.* to digest.

dignarse *v.* to deign, condescend.

dignatario *m.* dignitary (*person in a high office*).

dignidad *f.* dignity.

digno *adj.* worthy; dignified.

digresión *f.* digression.

dije *m.* trinket, small piece of jewelry; locket; woman of fine qualities, a "jewel"; *Am.* locket or charm of a watch chain.

dilación *f.* delay.

dilatado *adj.* vast, spacious; extensive; *p.p.* of **dilatar**.

dilatar *v.* to dilate, widen, enlarge; to expand; to lengthen, extend; to spread out; to defer, put off, retard; **-se** to expand; to be diffuse, wordy; *Am.* to delay oneself, take long.

diligencia *f.* diligence, care, industry; speed; stagecoach; business, errand.

diligente *adj.* diligent; quick, speedy.

diluir[32] *v. irr.* to dilute.

diluvio *m.* flood.

dimensión *f.* dimension.

dimes: — y diretes quibbling, arguing; **andar en — y diretes** to quibble, argue.

diminución *f.* diminution, decrease.

diminutivo *adj.* diminutive, tiny; diminishing; *m.* diminutive.

diminuto *adj.* tiny, little.

dimisión *f.* resignation (*from an office*).

dimitir *v.* to resign, give up (*a position, office, etc.*).

73

dinámica *f.* dynamics; **dinámico** *adj.* dynamic.

dinamismo *m.* vigor, forcefulness; dynamic force or energy.

dinamita *f.* dynamite.

dínamo *m.* dynamo.

dinastía *f.* dynasty.

dineral *m.* a lot of money.

dinero *m.* money; currency; *Am.* Peruvian silver coin equivalent to about ten cents; — **contante y sonante** ready cash, hard cash.

dios *m.* god; **Dios** God; **a la buena de** — without malice; without plan, haphazard, at random.

diosa *f.* goddess.

diplomacia *f.* diplomacy; tact.

diplomático *adj.* diplomatic; tactful; *m.* diplomat.

diputación *f.* deputation; committee.

diputado *m.* deputy; representative.

diputar *v.* to depute, delegate, commission.

dique *m.* dike; barrier; — **de carena** dry dock.

dirección *f.* direction, course; advice, guidance; management; board of directors; office of the board of directors; address.

directivo *adj.* directive, directing, guiding; **mesa directiva** board of directors.

directo *adj.* direct, straight.

director *m.* director, manager; *adj.* directing.

directorio *adj.* directory, directive, directing; *m.* directory, book of instructions; directorate, board of directors.

dirigente *adj.* directing, leading; *m.* leader, director.

dirigir[11] *v.* to direct, manage, govern; to guide; to address (*letters, packages*); to dedicate; **-se a** to address (*a person*); to go to or toward.

discernimiento *m.* discernment, keen judgment, insight, discrimination.

discernir[3] *v. irr.* to discern; to distinguish; to discriminate.

disciplina *f.* discipline, training; rule of conduct; order; any art or science; scourge, whip.

disciplinar *v.* to discipline, train; to drill; **-se** to discipline oneself; to scourge oneself.

discípulo *m.* pupil; disciple.

disco *m.* disk; discus; phonograph record.

díscolo *adj.* unruly, disobedient; unfriendly.

discordancia *f.* discord, disagreement.

discordia *f.* discord.

discreción *f.* discretion; keenness; wit; **darse** (*or* **rendirse**) **a** — to surrender unconditionally; **discrecional** *adj.* optional.

discrepancia *f.* discrepancy.

discreto *adj.* discreet, prudent; clever.

disculpa *f.* excuse; apology.

disculpable *adj.* excusable.

disculpar *v.* to excuse, free from blame; **-se** to excuse oneself, apologize.

discurrir *v.* to ramble about; to reason, think over; to invent, think out; to discuss.

discursear *v.* to make speeches.

discurso *m.* discourse; speech; reasoning; lapse of time.

discusión *f.* discussion.

discutible *adj.* debatable, questionable.

discutir *v.* to discuss.

disecar[6] *v.* to dissect; to stuff and mount (*the skins of animals*).

diseminación *f.* dissemination, spread, scattering.

diseminar *v.* to disseminate, scatter, spread.

disensión *f.* dissension, dissent, disagreement.

disentería *f.* dysentery.

disentir[3] *v. irr.* to dissent, differ, disagree.

diseñador *m.* designer.

diseñar *v.* to design; to sketch, outline.

diseño *m.* design; sketch, outline.

disertar *v.* to discourse, discuss.

disforme *adj.* deformed, ugly, hideous; out of proportion.

disfraz *m.* disguise, mask; masquerade costume.

disfrazar[9] *v.* to disguise, conceal; **-se** to disguise oneself; to masquerade.

disfrutar *v.* to enjoy; to reap benefit or advantage; to make use of.

disfrute *m.* enjoyment, benefit, use.

disgustar *v.* to disgust, displease; **-se** to get angry; to get bored.

disgusto *m.* displeasure; unpleasantness; annoyance; quarrel; grief; disgust.

disimulado *adj.* underhanded, sly, cunning; *p.p. of* **disimular.**

disimular *v.* to feign, hide, mask; to overlook, excuse.

disimulo *m.* dissimulation, feigning, pretense; slyness; reserve.

disipación *f.* dissipation; waste, extravagance.

disipar *v.* to dissipate, scatter; to squander; **-se** to vanish.

dislocar[6] *v.* to dislocate, put out of joint; **-se** to become dislocated, get out of joint.

disminución = diminución.

disminuir[32] v. irr. to diminish, decrease, lessen.

disociación f. dissociation, separation.

disociar v. to dissociate, separate.

disolución f. dissolution, breaking up; dissoluteness, lewdness.

disoluto adj. dissolute, loose, immoral, dissipated.

disolver[2, 52] v. irr. to dissolve; to melt.

disonancia f. discord.

disparada f. Am. rush, run.

disparar v. to shoot, fire, discharge; to throw; -se to run away, dart out.

disparatado adj. absurd, foolish, senseless.

disparatar v. to talk nonsense; to blunder; to act foolishly.

disparate m. nonsense, blunder.

disparidad f. inequality.

disparo m. shooting, discharge, explosion; shot; sudden dash, run.

dispensa f. dispensation; exemption.

dispensar v. to excuse, absolve, pardon; to grant, give.

dispensario m. dispensary; pharmaceutical laboratory; pharmacopoeia (book containing list and description of drugs).

dispersar v. to disperse, scatter.

dispersión f. dispersion, dispersal.

displicencia f. displeasure, discontent, dislike.

displicente adj. unpleasant, disagreeable, cross.

disponer[40] v. irr. to dispose; to arrange, put in order; to prepare; to order, command; -se to get ready; to make one's will and testament.

disponible adj. spare, available; on hand.

disposición f. disposition; arrangement; order, command; aptitude; disposal.

dispuesto p.p. of disponer & adj. disposed; ready; fit; smart, clever.

disputa f. dispute.

disputar v. to dispute.

distancia f. distance.

distante adj. distant.

distar v. to be distant, far (from).

distender[1] v. irr. to distend, stretch; to inflate; -se to distend, expand.

distinción f. distinction.

distinguido adj. & p.p. distinguished.

distinguir[12] v. to distinguish; -se to distinguish oneself, excel; to differ, be different.

distintivo adj. distinctive, distinguishing; m. distinguishing characteristic;

mark, sign; badge.

distinto adj. distinct, plain, clear; different.

distracción f. distraction; diversion; amusement; lack of attention.

distraer[46] v. irr. to distract; to divert, amuse; to lead astray; to divert (funds); -se to have a good time; to be absentminded; to be inattentive.

distraído adj. distracted; inattentive; absent-minded; Am. slovenly, untidy.

distribución f. distribution, apportionment.

distribuidor m. distributor; adj. distributing.

distribuir[32] v. irr. to distribute; to sort, classify.

distrito m. district; region.

disturbio m. disturbance.

disuelto p.p. of disolver.

divagación f. rambling, digression.

divagar[7] v. to ramble; to digress.

diván m. divan, sofa.

divergencia f. divergence; difference (of opinion).

divergir[11] v. to diverge; to differ.

diversidad f. diversity; variety.

diversión f. amusement.

diverso adj. diverse; different; -s several, various.

divertido adj. amusing, funny.

divertir[3] v. irr. to amuse, entertain; to divert, turn aside; -se to have a good time, amuse oneself.

dividendo m. dividend.

dividir v. to divide, split.

divinidad f. divinity, deity; ¡qué — ! what a beauty!

divino adj. divine.

divisa f. device, emblem.

divisar v. to sight; to make out, distinguish.

división f. division.

divorciar v. to divorce; to separate.

divorcio m. divorce.

divulgar[7] v. to divulge, spread, make public, give out.

diz = dice; dizque they say that . . .

dobladillar v. to hem.

dobladillo m. hem; — de ojo hemstitch.

doblar v. to bend, fold; to double; to toll, knell; Am. to knock down; — la esquina to turn the corner; -se to stoop; to bend down; to give in.

doble adj. double, twofold; double-faced, hypocritical; Am. broke, poor; m. fold; toll, tolling of bells, knell.

doblegar[7] v. to bend; to fold; -se to bend over; to stoop; to submit, yield.

doblez m. fold, crease; duplicity, hypocrisy.

docena *f.* dozen.

docente *adj.* teaching; educational.

dócil *adj.* docile, obedient, manageable, meek; flexible; **docilidad** *f.* obedience, meekness, gentleness; flexibility.

docto *adj.* learned; expert.

doctor *m.* doctor.

doctorar *v.* to grant a doctor's degree to; -se to get a doctor's degree.

doctrina *f.* doctrine.

documentar *v.* to document.

documento *m.* document.

dogal *m.* halter; noose.

dogma *m.* dogma; **dogmático** *adj.* dogmatic, pertaining to dogma; positive.

dolencia *f.* ailment; ache, aching.

doler[2] *v. irr.* to ache, hurt, cause pain; to cause grief; -se de to feel pity for, feel sorry for; to repent from.

doliente *adj.* sorrowful; suffering; aching; *m.* sick person, patient; mourner.

dolor *m.* pain, ache; sorrow, grief.

dolorido *adj.* aching, sore; afflicted; repentant; doleful.

doloroso *adj.* painful; sorrowful.

doma *f.* breaking of horses.

domador *m.* horsebreaker, broncobuster.

domar *v.* to tame, subdue.

domeñar *v.* to tame; to subdue; to dominate.

domesticar[6] *v.* to domesticate, tame.

doméstico *adj.* domestic; *m.* house servant.

domiciliar *v.* to house, lodge; *Am.* to address (a letter); -se to take up residence; to settle down; to dwell, reside.

domicilio *m.* home, dwelling.

dominación *f.* domination, rule, authority.

dominador *adj.* dominant, dominating; domineering, bossy; *m.* ruler, boss.

dominante *adj.* dominant; domineering; tyrannical; prevailing, predominant.

dominar *v.* to dominate, rule, lead; to stand out, tower above; to master.

dómine *m.* teacher; pedagogue; pedant.

domingo *m.* Sunday; — de ramos Palm Sunday.

dominio *m.* domain; dominion; authority; mastery (of a science, art, language, etc.).

dominó *m.* domino.

don *m.* gift; ability, knack; Don (title used only before Christian names of men).

donación *f.* donation; grant.

donador *m.* donor, giver.

donaire *m.* grace, elegance; wit; humor witty remark.

donairoso *adj.* elegant, graceful; witty.

donar *v.* to donate.

doncella *f.* virgin, maiden; maid servant; *Am.* felon (sore or inflammation near a finger or toe nail).

donde *rel. adv.* where, in which; a — (adonde) where, to which; *Am.* to the house of; de — from where, from which; en — where, in which; por — where, through which; wherefore; no otherwise; if not; ¿dónde? *interr. adv.* where?; ¿por — ? which way?

dondequiera *adv.* wherever; anywhere.

donoso *adj.* witty, gay; graceful.

doña *f.* Doña (title used only before Christian names of women).

dorado *p.p. & adj.* gilded, gilt; golden; *m.* gilding; *Am.* a kind of hummingbird; **doradillo** *adj. Am.* honeycolored, golden (applied to horses).

dorar *v.* to gild.

dormir[4] *v. irr.* to sleep; -se to go to sleep, fall asleep; to become numb.

dormitar *v.* to doze.

dormitorio *m.* dormitory; bedroom.

dorso *m.* back, reverse.

dosel *m.* canopy.

dosis *f.* dose.

dotación *f.* endowment, endowing; donation, foundation; dowry; complement (personnel of a warship); office force.

dotar *v.* to endow; to provide with a dowry.

dote *m. & f.* dowry; *f.* natural gift, talent, or quality.

draga *f.* dredge, dredging machine.

dragado *m.* dredging.

dragaminas *m.* mine sweeper.

dragar[7] *v.* to dredge.

dragón *m.* dragon.

drama *m.* drama.

dramático *adj.* dramatic; *m.* dramatic actor; playwright, dramatist.

dramatizar[9] *v.* to dramatize.

dramaturgo *m.* playwright, dramatist.

drenaje *m. Am.* drainage.

drenar *v. Am.* to drain.

dril *m.* drill (strong cotton or linen cloth).

droga *f.* drug, medicine; lie, fib; trick; bother, nuisance; *Am.* bad debt; *Am.* drug on the market, unsaleable article.

droguería *f.* drugstore; drug business.

droguero *m.* druggist; *Am.* cheat, debt evader.

droguista *m. & f.* druggist; cheat, crook.

ducha *f.* shower bath: douche.

ducho *adj.* expert, skilful.

duda f. doubt.
dadable adj. doubtful.
dadar v. to doubt; to hesitate.
dudoso adj. doubtful; uncertain.
duela f. stave (of a barrel); Am. long, narrow floor board.
duelo m. grief, sorrow; mourning; mourners; duel; **estar de —** to be in mourning; to mourn.
duende m. goblin.
dueña f. owner, landlady; duenna, chaperon or governess.
dueño m. owner; master.
dueto, duo m. duet.
dulce adj. sweet; pleasant, agreeable; fresh (water); soft (metal); m. sweet-meat; candy; preserves; Am. sugar, honey; **dulcería** f. candy shop.
dulcificar[6] v. to sweeten; to soften.
dulzón adj. over-sweet, sickeningly sweet.
dulzura f. sweetness; meekness.
duplicado adj. & m. duplicate; **por —** in duplicate; p.p. of **duplicar**.
duplicar[6] v. to duplicate, double; to repeat.
duplicidad f. duplicity, deceit, deceitfulness, treachery.
duque m. duke.
duquesa f. duchess.
durabilidad f. durability, durable quality, wear.
durable adj. durable.
duración f. duration.
duradero adj. durable, lasting.
durante prep. during, for.
durar v. to last, endure; to wear well.
durazno m. peach; peach tree; **duraznero** m. peach tree.
dureza f. hardness; harshness.
durmiente adj. sleeping; m. sleeper; crossbeam; Am. railroad tie.
duro adj. hard; firm, solid; strong, untiring; harsh; rigid; cruel; stubborn; stingy; **a duras penas** with difficulty; Am. **— y parejo** eagerly, tenaciously; Am. **hacer —** to resist stubbornly; m. **duro** (Spanish dollar).

E

e conj. and (before words beginning with i or hi).
ébano m. ebony.
ebrio adj. drunk.
ebullición f. boiling, bubbling up.
eclesiástico adj. ecclesiastic, belonging to the church; m. clergyman.
eclipsar v. to eclipse; to outshine, surpass.
écloga f. eclogue, pastoral poem, idyll.

eco m. echo.
economía f. economy; **— política** economics, political economy.
económico adj. economic; economical, saving; **economista** m. economist.
economizar[9] v. to economize, save.
ecuación f. equation.
ecuador m. equator.
echar v. to throw, cast; to expel, throw out, to give off; to sprout; **— a correr** to run away; **-(se) a perder** to spoil; **— a pique** to sink; **-(se) a reír** to burst out laughing; **— carnes** to get fat; **— de menos** to miss; **— de ver** to notice; to make out; **— mano** to seize; **— papas** to fib; **— raíces** to take root; **— suertes** to draw lots; **-se** to lie down; Am. **echársela** to boast.
edad f. age.
edén m. Eden, paradise.
edición f. edition; publication.
edificación f. edification (moral or spiritual uplift); construction.
edificar[6] v. to construct, build; to edify, uplift.
edificio m. edifice, building.
editar v. to publish.
editor m. publisher; adj. publishing.
editorial adj. publishing, editorial; m. editorial; f. publishing house.
edredón m. down quilt, comforter, quilted blanket.
educación f. education, training; breeding, manners.
educador m. educator; adj. educating.
educando m. pupil; inmate (of an orphanage, boarding school, etc.).
educar[6] v. to educate, teach, train, raise, bring up.
educativo adj. educational.
efectivo adj. effective; real; in operation, active; m. cash.
efecto m. effect, result; end, purpose; **-s** goods, personal property; **en —** in fact, actually; **llevar a —** to carry out; **surtir —** to come out as expected; to give good results.
efectuar[18] v. to effect, bring about.
eficacia f. efficacy; efficiency; effectiveness.
eficaz adj. effective; active; efficient.
eficiencia f. efficiency; **eficiente** adj. efficient.
efímero adj. ephemeral, short-lived, brief.
efluvio m. emanation, exhalation, vapors.
efusión f. effusion, unrestrained expression of feeling, gushy manner; **—**

de sangre bloodshed.

efusivo *adj.* effusive, too demonstrative, over-emotional.

egipcio *adj. & m.* Egyptian.

egocéntrico *adj.* egocentric, self-centered.

egoísmo *m.* selfishness.

egoísta *adj.* selfish; *m. & f.* selfish person.

egolatría *f.* self-worship.

eje *m.* axis; axle.

ejecución *f.* execution; carrying out.

ejecutar *v.* to execute; to carry out; to perform, do.

ejecutivo *adj.* executive; active; *m.* executive.

ejecutor *m.* executor; **— de la justicia** executioner.

ejemplar *adj.* exemplary, model; *m.* copy; specimen.

ejemplo *m.* example; model, pattern.

ejercer[10] *v.* to practice (*a profession*); to exert.

ejercicio *m.* exercise; practice; military drill; exercise (*of authority*); **hacer —** to take exercise.

ejercitar *v.* to practice, exercise; to drill, train; **-se** to train oneself; to practice.

ejército *m.* army.

ejido *m.* public land, common.

ejote *m. Am.* string bean.

el *def. art. m.* the; **— de** the one with, that one with; **— que** *rel. pron.* he who, the one that; **él** *pers. pron.* he; him, it (*after a prep.*).

elaborar *v.* to elaborate.

elasticidad *f.* elasticity.

elástico *adj.* elastic; flexible; *m.* elastic; elastic tape; wire spring; **-s** *Am.* suspenders.

elección *f.* election; choice.

electo *adj.* elect, chosen; *m.* elect, person chosen.

elector *m.* elector, voter; *adj.* electoral, electing.

electoral *adj.* electoral.

electricidad *f.* electricity.

electricista *m.* electrician; electrical engineer.

eléctrico *adj.* electric, electrical.

electrizar[9] *v.* to electrify; to thrill, excite; *Am.* to anger, irritate.

elefante *m.* elephant.

elegancia *f.* elegance, grace, distinguished manner.

elegante *adj.* elegant, graceful, polished; stylish.

elegir[5, 11] *v. irr.* to elect, choose.

elemental *adj.* elementary; elemental, fundamental.

elemento *m.* element; **-s** elements, fun-

damentals; *Am.* **ser** (*or* **estar**) **hecho un —** to be an idiot, a fool.

elevación *f.* elevation; height; rise; rapture.

elevador *m. Am.* elevator, hoist.

elevar *v.* to elevate, raise, lift; **-se** to go up; to soar.

eliminación *f.* elimination, removal

eliminar *v.* to eliminate.

elocuencia *f.* eloquence.

elocuente *adj.* eloquent.

elogiar *v.* to praise.

elogio *m.* praise.

elote *m. Am.* ear of corn, corn on the cob.

elucidación *f.* elucidation, explanation.

elucidar *v.* to elucidate, illustrate, explain.

eludir *v.* to elude, avoid, dodge.

ella *pers. pron.* she; her, it (*after a prep.*).

ello *pron.* it; **— es que** the fact is that.

emanación *f.* emanation, flow; fumes, vapor, odor; manifestation.

emanar *v.* to emanate, spring, issue.

emancipación *f.* emancipation.

emancipar *v.* to emancipate, set free; **-se** to become free.

embajada *f.* embassy; errand, mission.

embajador *m.* ambassador.

embalador *m.* packer.

embalaje *m.* packing.

embalar *v.* to pack; to bale, crate.

embaldosar *v.* to pave with flagstones or tiles.

embalsamar *v.* to embalm; to scent, perfume.

embarazar[9] *v.* to embarrass, hinder; to obstruct; to make pregnant; **-se** to become pregnant; to become embarrassed.

embarazo *m.* impediment, obstacle; pregnancy; embarrassment; bashfulness, awkwardness.

embarazoso *adj.* embarrassing; cumbersome, unwieldly.

embarcación *f.* ship, boat; embarkation.

embarcadero *m.* wharf, pier.

embarcador *m.* shipper.

embarcar[6] *v.* to embark; to ship; *Am.* to ship by train or any vehicle; **-se** to embark, sail; to engage (in); *Am.* to board, get on a train.

embarco *m.* embarkation.

embargar[7] *v.* to impede; to restrain; to attach, confiscate; to lay an embargo on; **estar embargado de emoción** to be overcome with emotion.

embargo *m.* embargo, restriction on commerce; attachment, confiscation;

sin — nevertheless.

embarque *m.* shipment.

embarrado *p.p. & adj.* smeared; plastered; muddy.

embarrar *v.* to smear, daub.

embaucador *m.* cheat, impostor.

embaucar⁶ *v.* to fool, trick, swindle, deceive.

embebecido *p.p. & adj.* absorbed; amused.

embebecimiento *m.* absorption; rapture.

embeber *v.* to imbibe, absorb; to soak; to shrink; -se to be fascinated; to be absorbed.

embelesar *v.* to enrapture, delight, charm.

embeleso *m.* delight, ecstasy.

embellecer¹³ *v. irr.* to embellish, beautify, adorn.

embestida *f.* sudden attack, onset, assault.

embestir⁵ *v. irr.* to attack, assail.

embetunar *v.* to cover with pitch; to black.

emblanquecer¹³ *v. irr.* to whiten; to bleach; to become white; -se to whiten, become white.

emblema *m.* emblem.

embobar *v.* to fool; to amuse; to fascinate; to amaze; -se to be amazed; to be fascinated.

embocadura *f.* mouth (*of a river*); entrance (*through a narrow passage*); mouthpiece (*of a wind instrument*); bit (*of a bridle*); taste, flavor (*said of wines*).

embolado *m.* bull whose horns have been tipped with balls; impotent, ineffectual person; *p.p. of embolar.*

embolar *v.* to tip a bull's horns with balls; to black, polish; -se *Am.* to get drunk.

émbolo *m.* piston; plunger (*of a pump*); embolus (*clot in a blood vessel*).

embolsar *v.* to put into a pocket or purse; -se to pocket, put into one's pocket.

emborrachar *v.* to intoxicate; -se to get drunk.

emborronar *v.* to blot; to scribble.

emboscada *f.* ambush.

emboscar⁶ *v.* to ambush; -se to lie in ambush; to go into a forest.

embotado *adj.* dull, blunt; *p.p. of embotar.*

embotamiento *m.* dullness, bluntness; dulling, blunting.

embotar *v.* to dull, blunt; to enervate, weaken.

embotellar *v.* to bottle; to bottle up; *Am.* to jail.

embozado *adj.* cloaked; muffled, covered up to the face.

embozar⁷ *v.* to muffle; to cloak, conceal, disguise; to muzzle; -se to muffle oneself, wrap oneself.

embragar⁷ *v.* to engage or throw in the clutch.

embrague *m.* clutch (*of a machine*); coupling.

embriagar⁷ *v.* to intoxicate; -se to get drunk, intoxicated.

embriaguez *f.* intoxication; drunkenness.

embrollar *v.* to involve, ensnare, entangle; to confuse.

embrollo *m.* confusion, tangle; trickery, lie, deception.

embromar *v.* to chaff, make fun of, "kid"; *Am.* to bother, molest; *Am.* to delay unnecessarily; *Am.* to ruin, harm; -se *Am.* to be bothered, disgusted; *Am.* to get delayed.

embrujar *v.* to bewitch, enchant.

embrujo *m.* charm, enchantment; glamour.

embrutecer¹³ *v. irr.* to stupefy, render brutish; to dull the mind, make insensible.

embudo *m.* funnel; trick.

embuste *m.* lie, fraud; trinket.

embustero *m.* liar; *adj.* deceitful, tricky.

embutido *m.* sausage; inlaid work; *Am.* insertion of embroidery or lace; *p.p. of embutir.*

embutir *v.* to insert, inlay; to stuff.

emerger¹¹ *v.* to emerge, come out.

emigración *f.* emigration.

emigrante *m. & f.* emigrant.

emigrar *v.* to emigrate; to migrate.

eminencia *f.* eminence; height.

eminente *adj.* eminent, high, lofty.

emisión *f.* issue (*of bonds, money, etc.*); radio broadcast.

emisor *adj.* emitting; broadcasting; *m.* radio transmitter; **emisora** *f.* broadcasting station.

emitir *v.* to emit, give off; to utter; to send forth; to issue; to broadcast.

emoción *f.* emotion.

emocional *adj.* emotional.

emocionante *adj.* moving, touching, thrilling.

emocionar *v.* to cause emotion, touch, move; -se to be touched, moved, stirred.

emotivo *adj.* emotional.

empacador *m.* packer.

empacar⁶ *v.* to pack up, wrap up, bale,

crate; *Am.* to goad, irritate (*an animal*); -se to be stubborn; to get angry; *Am.* to balk; *Am.* to put on airs.

empachado *p.p. & adj.* clogged; stuffed; upset from indigestion; embarrassed; bashful.

empachar *v.* to stuff, cram; to cause indigestion; -se to get upset; to get clogged; to be stuffed; to suffer indigestion; to get embarrassed.

empacho *m.* indigestion; bashfulness; **no tener — en** to have no objection to; to feel free to.

empalagar[7] *v.* to cloy; to pall on, become distasteful; to disgust.

empalagoso *adj.* cloying; sickeningly sweet; boring, wearisome.

empalizada *f.* stockade, palisade.

empalmar *v.* to splice; to join; **— con** to join (*as railroads or highways*).

empalme *m.* junction; joint, connection; splice.

empanada *f.* pie, meat pie; swindle, fraud.

empanizar[9] *v. Am.* to bread.

empañado *adj. & p.p.* tarnished; dim, blurred.

empañar *v.* to blur, dim, tarnish.

empapada *f. Am.* drench, soaking.

empapar *v.* to soak, drench, saturate.

empapelador *m.* paper hanger.

empapelar *v.* to paper; to wrap in paper.

empaque *m.* packing; looks, appearance, air; airs, importance; *Am.* impudence.

empaquetar *v.* to pack; to pack in; to make a package; -se to dress up, doll up.

emparedado *adj.* shut up, confined between walls; *m.* sandwich; prisoner confined in a narrow cell.

emparejar *v.* to even up, level off; to match; to pair off; to overtake, catch up with.

emparentado *adj. & p.p.* related by marriage.

emparentar *v.* to become related by marriage.

emparrado *m.* vine arbor.

empastar *v.* to paste; to fill (*a tooth*); to bind (*books*); -se *Am.* to get lost in the pasture; *Am.* to become overgrown with grass.

empaste *m.* tooth filling; binding (*of a book*).

empatar *v.* to tie (*in a game*), have an equal score; to have an equal number of votes; to hinder, obstruct; *Am.* to tie, join.

empate *m.* tie, draw, equal score, equal number of votes; hindrance, obstruction; *Am.* joint, junction.

empecinado *adj. Am.* stubborn.

empedernido *adj.* hardened, hardhearted.

empedernir[51] *v.* to harden, toughen; -se to become hardened.

empedrado *m.* cobblestone pavement; *p.p. & adj.* paved with stones.

empedrar[1] *v. irr.* to pave with stones.

empeine *m.* instep; groin (*hollow between lower part of abdomen and thigh*).

empellón *m.* push, shove; a -es by pushing.

empeñar *v.* to pawn; to oblige, compel; -se to persist, insist; to oblige oneself; to go into debt; -se por to plead for, intercede for; -se empeñaron en una lucha they engaged in a fight.

empeño *m.* pledge, pawn; persistence, insistence; perseverance; eagerness; *Am.* pawnshop; **tener — en** to be eager to.

empeorar *v.* to impair; to make worse; to grow worse; -se to grow worse.

empequeñecer[13] *v. irr.* to diminish, make smaller; to belittle.

emperador *m.* emperor; **emperatriz** *f.* empress.

emperifollar *v.* to decorate, adorn; -se to dress up, deck out, doll up.

empero *conj.* however, nevertheless.

empezar[1, 9] *v. irr.* to begin.

empiezo *m. Am.* beginning.

empinado *adj.* steep; lofty.

empinar *v.* to raise, lift; to incline, bend; **— el codo** to drink; -se to stand on tiptoes; to rear (*said of horses*); to rise high; *Am.* to overeat.

empiojado *adj.* lousy, full of lice.

emplasto *m.* plaster, poultice.

empleado *m.* employee; *p.p. of* **emplear.**

emplear *v.* to employ; to invest, spend; -se en to be employed in.

empleo *m.* employment, position, job; employ; occupation; aim; investment.

emplumar *v.* to feather; to adorn with feathers; to tar and feather; *Am.* to deceive; *Am.* to send away to a house of correction or prison; *Am.* **— con algo** to run away with something, steal it; *Am.* -las (*or* emplumárselas) to take to one's heels, flee, escape.

empobrecer[13] *v. irr.* to impoverish; -se to become poor.

empobrecimiento *m.* impoverishment.

empolvado *adj.* dusty, covered with dust or powder.

empolvar v. to sprinkle powder; to cover with dust; -se to get dusty; to powder one's face.

empollar v. to hatch, brood.

emponzoñar v. to poison.

emprendedor adj. enterprising.

emprender v. to undertake.

empreñar v. to impregnate, make pregnant.

empresa f. enterprise, undertaking; symbol; company, management.

empresario m. manager; impresario, promoter.

empréstito m. loan.

empujar v. to push, shove.

empuje m. push; shove; impulse; energy.

empujón m. shove, push.

empuñar v. to grasp, grab, clutch, seize.

émulo m. rival, competitor.

en prep. in, on, upon.

enaguas f. pl. underskirt, petticoat; short skirt.

enajenamiento m. trance; abstraction, absence of mind; transfer (of property); — mental mental disorder; — de los sentidos loss of consciousness.

enajenar v. to dispossess, transfer property; to enrapture, charm; to deprive (of one's senses); — el afecto de to alienate the affection of; -se to be enraptured, be in a trance.

enaltecer v. to extol, exalt.

enamorado adj. in love; m. lover.

enamorar v. to make love, woo, court; to enamor; -se to fall in love.

enano m. dwarf; adj. dwarfish, tiny, little.

enarbolar v. to hoist, lift, raise on high; to brandish (a sword, cane, etc.); -se to rear, balk.

enarcado p.p. arched.

enarcar v. to arch; to hoop (barrels, kegs, etc.); — las cejas to arch one's eyebrows.

enardecer v. irr. to excite, kindle, fire with passion; -se to become excited; to become passionate; to get angry.

enardecimiento m. ardor, passion, unbridled enthusiasm; inflaming.

encabezado m. headline; heading.

encabezamiento m. heading; headline; list or roll of taxpayers; registration of taxpayers.

encabezar v. to give a heading or title to; to head; to lead; to make up (a list or tax roll); to strengthen (wine).

encabritarse v. to rear, rise up on the hind legs.

encadenar v. to chain; to link together.

encajar v. to thrust in, fit into, insert; -se to squeeze into; to intrude, meddle.

encaje m. lace; adjustment; fitting together; socket, groove, hole; inlaid work.

encajonar v. to box (put or pack in a box).

encallar v. to strand, run aground; to get stuck.

encamado p.p. confined in bed.

encaminar v. to direct, guide; -se to betake oneself, go (toward); to start out on a road.

encanecer v. irr. to get grey, get grey-haired.

encanijado adj. emaciated, thin, sickly.

encanijarse v. to get thin, emaciated.

encantado p.p. & adj. delighted, charmed; enchanted.

encantador adj. charming; m. charmer, enchanter.

encantamiento m. enchantment.

encantar v. to charm, enchant.

encanto m. charm, enchantment, delight.

encapillar v. Am. to confine in the death cell.

encapotado p.p. & adj. cloaked; overcast, cloudy; in a bad humor.

encapotarse v. to become overcast, cloudy; to cover up, put on a cloak or raincoat; to frown.

encapricharse v. to persist in one's whims; to get stubborn.

encaramar v. to raise; to elevate; to extol; -se to climb; to climb upon, get upon, perch upon; Am. to be ashamed; Am. to go to one's head (said of liquor).

encarar v. to face; to aim; -se con to face; to confront.

encarcelación f. imprisonment.

encarcelamiento = encarcelación.

encarcelar v. to imprison, jail.

encarecer v. irr. to go up in value; to make dear, raise the price of; to exaggerate; to extol; to recommend highly; to enhance.

encarecidamente adv. earnestly.

encargar v. to put in charge; to entrust; to recommend, advise; to order; to commission; to beg; -se de to take charge of.

encargo m. recommendation, advice; charge; order; commission; errand.

encariñado adj. & p.p. attached, fond, enamored.

encariñamiento m. affection, fondness, attachment.

encariñar v. to awaken love or affection; -se to become fond (of), attached (to).

encarnado adj. flesh-colored; red; p.p. of **encarnar**.

encarnar v. to incarnate, embody; to bait (a fishhook).

encarnizado adj. bloody; hard-fought, fierce.

encarnizar[9] v. to infuriate, enrage; -se to get furious, enraged; to fight with fury.

encasillar v. to pigeonhole, put in a pigeonhole or compartment; to put in a stall; to classify, sort out.

encender[1] v. irr. to light, kindle; to set on fire; -se to take fire, be on fire; to get red.

encendido adj. red; p.p. of **encender**; m. ignition (of a motor).

encerado m. blackboard; oilcloth; wax coating; p.p. & adj. waxed; wax-colored; **papel** — wax paper.

encerar v. to wax; to thicken (lime).

encerramiento m. enclosure, confinement; locking up; retreat; prison.

encerrar[1] v. irr. to enclose; to lock up; to contain; -se to lock oneself up, go into seclusion.

encía f. gum (of the teeth).

enciclopedia f. encyclopedia.

encierro m. confinement; retreat; prison.

encima adv. above, overhead, over, on top; besides, in addition; — de on top of; **por** — **de** over; Am. **de** — besides, in addition; Am. **echárselo todo** — to spend everything on clothes.

encina f. live oak.

encinta adj. pregnant.

encintado m. curb (of a sidewalk).

enclaustrar v. to cloister.

enclavar v. to nail, fix, fasten.

enclenque adj. sickly, wan; weak, feeble.

encoger[11] v. to shrink, shrivel, shorten, contract; -se to shrink; to shrivel; -se de hombros to shrug one's shoulders.

encogido p.p. & adj. shrunk, shrivelled, timid, shy.

encogimiento m. shrinking; timidity; — de hombros shrug.

encolerizar[9] v. to anger; -se to get angry.

encomendar[1] v. irr. to charge, advise; to entrust; to recommend, commend; -se to put oneself in the hands (of); to send regards; to pray (to).

encomiar v. to extol, praise.

encomienda f. charge, commission; recommendation; royal land grant (including Indian inhabitants); Am. warehouse (for agricultural products); Am. parcel-post package.

encomio m. encomium, high praise.

enconado p.p. & adj. inflamed; infected; sore; angry.

enconar v. to inflame; to infect; to irritate; -se to become inflamed, infected; to get irritated.

encono m. rancor, animosity, ill will; Am. inflammation, swelling.

encontrado adj. opposite; opposing; contrary; p.p. of **encontrar**.

encontrar[2] v. irr. to encounter, meet; to find; -se to meet; to coincide; to be; to be found, be situated; to collide; to conflict; -se **con** to come across, meet up with.

encontrón, encontronazo m. bump, collision; **darse un** — to collide (with), bump (into); to bump into each other.

encordelar v. to string; to tie with strings.

encorvar v. to curve, bend; -se to bend down; to stoop.

encrespar v. to curl; to ruffle; to irritate; -se to curl; to get ruffled; to become involved or entangled (a matter or affair); to become rough (said of the sea).

encrucijada f. crossroads, street intersection; ambush.

encuadernación f. binding (of books).

encuadernar v. to bind (books).

encuadrar v. to enclose in a frame; to encompass; to fit (into); Am. to suit; Am. to summarize briefly, give a synthesis of.

encubierto p.p. of **encubrir**.

encubrir[52] v. to cover, hide.

encuentro m. encounter, meeting; find, finding; conflict, clash; collision; **salir al** — **de** to go out to meet; to make a stand against, oppose; Am. **llevarse de** — to run over, knock down; to drag along.

encuerado adj. Am. naked; Am. ragged.

encuerar v. Am. to strip of clothes; Am. to skin, fleece, strip of money; -se Am. to strip, get undressed.

encuesta f. search, inquiry, investigation.

encumbrado p.p. & adj. elevated; exalted; high, lofty.

encumbramiento m. elevation; exaltation; height; eminence.

encumbrar v. to elevate; to exalt, extol; -se to climb to the top; to rise up; to hold oneself high; to soar.

encurtido *m.* pickle; *p.p. of* **encurtir.**

encurtir *v.* to pickle.

enchilada *f. Am.* rolled **tortilla** served with chili.

enchuecar⁶ *v.* to bend, twist; **-se** *Am.* to get bent or twisted.

enchufar *v.* to plug in; to telescope; to fit. (*a tube or pipe*) into another.

enchufe *m.* socket, plug, electric outlet.

ende : por — hence, therefore.

endeble *adj.* weak, feeble; flimsy.

endemoniado *adj.* possessed by the devil; devilish, fiendish; mischievous.

endentar¹ *v. irr.* to indent, form notches in; to furnish (*a saw, wheel, etc.*) with teeth; to mesh.

enderezar⁹ *v.* to straighten; to set upright; to right, correct; to direct; to address; **-se** to go straight (to); to straighten up.

endeudado *p.p. & adj.* indebted; in debt.

endeudarse *v.* to get into debt, become indebted.

endiablado *adj.* devilish; possessed by the devil; ugly; mean; wicked; *Am.* dangerous, risky.

endomingado *p.p. & adj.* dressed up in one's Sunday, or best, clothes.

endosante *m.* indorser.

endosar *v.* to indorse (*a check, draft, etc.*).

endose, endoso *m.* indorsement.

endulzar⁹ *v.* to sweeten; to soften.

endurecer¹³ *v. irr.* to harden; **-se** to get hardened; to get cruel.

enemigo *m.* enemy; devil; *adj.* hostile; unfriendly; **ser — de una cosa** to dislike a thing.

enemistad *f.* enmity, hatred.

enemistar *v.* to cause enmity between; **-se con** to become an enemy of.

energía *f.* energy.

enérgico *adj.* energetic.

enero *m.* January.

enervar *v.* to enervate, weaken.

enfadar *v.* to anger; **-se** to get angry.

enfado *m.* anger, disgust.

enfadoso *adj.* annoying.

enfardar *v.* to bale, pack.

énfasis *m.* emphasis; **enfático** *adj.* emphatic.

enfermar *v.* to become ill; to make ill; to weaken; **-se** to become ill.

enfermedad *f.* sickness, illness.

enfermería *f.* infirmary.

enfermero *m.* male nurse; **enfermera** *f.* nurse (*for the sick*).

enfermizo *adj.* sickly; unhealthy.

enfermo *adj.* sick, ill; feeble; *m.* patient.

enflaquecer¹³ *v. irr.* to become thin; to make thin; to weaken.

enfocar⁶ *v.* to focus.

enfrenar *v.* to bridle; to brake, put the brake on; to check, curb.

enfrentar *v.* to put face to face; **-se con** to confront, face, meet face to face.

enfrente *adv.* in front, opposite; **— de** in front of, opposite.

enfriamiento *m.* cooling; chill; refrigeration.

enfriar¹⁷ *v.* to cool, chill; *Am.* to kill; **-se** to cool, cool off; to get chilled.

enfurecer¹³ *v. irr.* to infuriate, enrage; **-se** to rage; to get furious; to get rough, stormy (*said of the sea*).

enfurruñarse *v.* to get angry; to grumble.

engalanar *v.* to adorn, decorate; **-se** to dress up, primp.

enganchamiento = enganche.

enganchar *v.* to hitch; to hook; to ensnare; to draft; to attract into the army; *Am.* to hire (*labor with false promises*); **-se** to engage, interlock; to get hooked; to enlist in the army.

enganche *m.* hooking; coupling; draft (*into the army*); *Am.* enrolling of laborers (*for a rubber plantation or other risky business under false promises.*).

engañador *adj.* deceitful, deceiving; *m.* deceiver.

engañar *v.* to deceive; to while away (*time*); to ward off (*hunger or sleep*); **-se** to deceive oneself; to be mistaken.

engaño *m.* deceit, trick, fraud; mistake, misunderstanding; *Am.* bribe.

engañoso *adj.* deceitful; tricky; misleading.

engastar *v.* to mount, set (*jewels*).

engaste *m.* setting (*for a gem or stone*).

engatusar *v.* to coax, entice; to fool.

engendrar *v.* to engender, beget, produce; to cause.

engolfarse *v.* to get deep (into); to go deeply (into); to become absorbed, lost in thought.

engomar *v.* to gum; to glue.

engordar *v.* to fatten; to get fat; to get rich.

engorroso *adj.* cumbersome; bothersome.

engranaje *m.* gear, gears, gearing.

engranar *v.* to gear, throw in gear; to mesh gears.

engrandecer¹³ *v. irr.* to aggrandize, make greater; to magnify; to exalt.

engrane *m.* engagement (*of gears*).

engrasar *v.* to lubricate, grease; to stain with grease; to fertilize, manure; to dress (*cloth*).

engreído *adj.* & *p.p.* conceited, vain; *Am.* attached, fond.

engreír[15] *v. irr.* to make vain, conceited; -se to puff up, get conceited; *Am.* to become fond (of), become attached (to).

engrosar[2] *v. irr.* to enlarge; to thicken; to fatten; to get fat.

engrudo *m.* paste (*for gluing*).

engullir[20] *v.* to gobble, devour; to gorge.

enhebrar[7] *v.* to thread (*a needle*); to string (*beads*).

enhiesto *adj.* straight, upright, erect.

enhorabuena *f.* congratulation; *adv.* safely; well and good; all right; with much pleasure.

enigma *m.* enigma, riddle, puzzle.

enjabonar *v.* to soap; to soft-soap, flatter.

enjaezar[9] *v.* to harness.

enjalbegar[7] *v.* to whitewash; -se to paint (*one's face*).

enjambre *m.* swarm of bees; crowd.

enjaular *v.* to cage; to confine; to jail.

enjuagar[7] *v.* to rinse, rinse out.

enjuague *m.* mouth wash; rinse; rinsing; scheme, plot.

enjugar[7] *v.* to dry; to wipe; -se to dry oneself.

enjuiciar *v.* to indict; to prosecute, bring suit against; to try (*a case*); to judge.

enjundia *f.* substance, essence; fat; force, strength.

enjuto *adj.* dried; thin, skinny; -s *m. pl.* dry kindling.

enlace *m.* link; tie, bond; marriage.

enladrillado *m.* brick pavement or floor.

enladrillar *v.* to pave with bricks.

enlatar *v.* to can; *Am.* to roof with tin.

enlazar[9] *v.* to join, bind, tie; to rope; *Am.* to lasso; -se to join; to marry; to become related through marriage.

enlodar *v.* to cover with mud; to smear, sully, soil, dirty; -se to get in the mud; to get muddy.

enloquecer[13] *v. irr.* to make crazy; to drive mad; to lose one's mind; -se to go crazy.

enlosado *m.* flagstone pavement; *p.p.* of **enlosar**.

enlosar *v.* to pave with flagstones.

enmantecado *m. Am.* ice cream. *See* mantecado.

enmantecar[6] *v.* to butter; to grease (*with lard or butter*).

enmarañar *v.* to entangle; to snarl; to confuse, mix up.

enmascarar *v.* to mask; -se to put on a mask; to masquerade.

enmendar[1] *v. irr.* to amend, correct; to indemnify, compensate; -se to reform, mend one's ways.

enmienda *f.* correction; amendment; reform; indemnity, compensation.

enmohecer[13] *v.* to rust; to mold; -se to rust, become rusty; to mold.

enmudecer[13] *v. irr.* to silence; to remain silent; to lose one's voice; to become dumb.

ennegrecer[13] *v. irr.* to blacken; to darken; -se to become dark; to get cloudy.

ennoblecer[13] *v. irr.* to ennoble, dignify.

enojadizo *adj.* irritable, ill-tempered.

enojado *adj.* angry.

enojar *v.* to make angry, vex, annoy; -se to get angry.

enojo *m.* anger; annoyance.

enojoso *adj.* annoying, bothersome.

enorgullecer[13] *v. irr.* to fill with pride; -se to swell up with pride; to be proud.

enorme *adj.* enormous.

enramada *f.* arbor, bower; shady grove.

enrarecer[13] *v. irr.* to rarefy, thin, make less dense (*as air*); -se to become rarefied; to become scarce.

enrarecimiento *m.* rarity, thinness (*of the air*); rarefaction (*act of making thin, rare or less dense*).

enredadera *f.* climbing vine.

enredar *v.* to entangle, snare; to snarl; to mix up; to raise a rumpus; to wind (*on a spool*); -se to get tangled up, mixed up; to get trapped; -se con to have an affair with.

enredista *m. Am.* liar; *Am.* talebearer.

enredo *m.* tangle; confusion; lie; plot.

enredoso *adj.* tangled up; *Am.* tattler.

enrejado *m.* trellis; grating.

enrevesado *adj.* turned around; intricate, complicated; unruly.

enriquecer[13] *v. irr.* to enrich; to become rich; -se to become rich.

enrojecer[13] *v. irr.* to redden; -se to get red, blush.

enrollar *v.* to roll, roll up; to coil.

enronquecer[13] *v irr.* to make hoarse; to become hoarse; -se to become hoarse.

enroscar[6] *v.* to coil; to twist, twine; -se to coil; to curl up.

ensacar[6] *v.* to sack, bag, put in a bag or sack.

ensalada *f.* salad; hodgepodge, mixture.

ensalzar[9] *v.* to exalt, praise.

ensanchar *v.* to widen, enlarge; -se to expand; to puff up.

ensanche *m.* widening, expansion, extension.

ensangrentado *adj.* gory, bloody; *p.p.* of **ensangrentar.**

ensangrentar *v.* to stain with blood; **-se** to be covered with blood; to get red with anger.

ensartar *v.* to string; to thread; to link; to rattle off (*tales, stories, etc.*); *Am.* to tie to a ring; *Am.* to swindle, trick; **-se** *Am.* to fall into a trap.

ensayar *v.* to try; to attempt; to test; to rehearse; **-se** to practice, train oneself.

ensayo *m.* trial, attempt; rehearsal; test; experiment; essay.

ensenada *f.* small bay, cove.

enseñanza *f.* teaching; education, training.

enseñar *v.* to show; to teach; to train; to point out.

enseres *m. pl.* household goods; utensils; implements; equipment.

ensillar *v.* to saddle; *Am.* to abuse, mistreat, domineer; *Am.* **— el picazo** to get angry.

ensimismarse *v.* to become absorbed in thought; *Am.* to become conceited or vain.

ensoberbecer[13] *v. irr.* to make proud or haughty; **-se** to puff up with pride; to become haughty; to get rough, choppy (*said of the sea*).

ensordecer[13] *v. irr.* to deafen; to become deaf.

ensortijar *v.* to curl; to ring the nose of (*an animal*); **-se** to curl.

ensuciar *v.* to dirty, soil; to stain; **-se** to get dirty; to soil oneself.

ensueño *m.* illusion, dream.

entablar *v.* to board up; to plank; to splint; **— una conversación** to start a conversation; **— un pleito** to bring a lawsuit.

entablillar *v.* to splint; *Am.* to cut (*chocolate*) into tablets or squares.

entallar *v.* to fit closely (*a dress*); to carve.

entapizar[9] *v.* to cover with tapestry; to drape with tapestries; to upholster.

entarimar *v.* to floor (*with boards*).

ente *m.* entity, being; queer fellow.

enteco *adj.* sickly, skinny.

entender[1] *v. irr.* to understand; **— de** to know, be an expert in; **— en** to take care of; to deal with; **-se con** to have dealings or relations with; to have an understanding with.

entendido *p.p.* understood; *adj.* wise, prudent; well-informed; able, skilful; **no darse por —** to pretend not to

hear or understand; not to take the hint.

entendimiento *m.* understanding; intellect; mind.

enterado *p.p.* & *adj.* informed; aware.

enterar *v.* to inform, acquaint; to know, learn, find out; to understand, get the idea.

entereza *f.* entirety, integrity; fortitude; serenity; firmness; perfection.

enternecedor *adj.* touching, moving, pitiful.

enternecer[13] *v. irr.* to soften, touch, stir, move; **-se** to become tender; to be touched, stirred.

entero *adj.* entire, whole; just, right; firm; *m.* integer, whole number; *Am.* payment, reimbursement; *Am.* balance of an account; **caballo —** stallion.

enterramiento *m.* burial.

enterrar[1] *v. irr.* to bury; *Am.* to sink, stick into.

entibiar *v.* to make lukewarm; **-se** to become lukewarm.

entidad *f.* entity; unit, group, organization; **de —** of value or importance.

entierro *m.* burial; funeral; grave; *Am.* hidden treasure.

entintar *v.* to ink; to stain with ink; to dye.

entoldar *v.* to cover with an awning; **-se** to puff up with pride; to become overcast, cloudy.

entonación *f.* intonation.

entonar *v.* to sing in tune; to start a song (*for others to follow*); to be in tune; to harmonize; **-se** to put on airs.

entonces *adv.* then, at that time; **pues — ** well then.

entornado *adj.* half-open; half-closed, ajar.

entornar *v.* to half-open.

entorpecer[13] *v. irr.* to stupefy; to benumb, make numb; to delay, obstruct; to thwart, frustrate.

entorpecimiento *m.* numbness; dullness; delay, obstruction.

entrada *f.* entrance; entry; gate; opening; entering; admission; entrée (*dish or dinner course*); *Am.* attack, assault, goring; *Am.* beating; **-s** cash receipts.

entrambos *adj.* & *pron.* both.

entrampar *v.* to trap, ensnare; to trick; to burden with debts; **-se** to get trapped or entangled; to run into debt.

entrante *adj.* entering; incoming; **el año —** next year.

entraña *f.* entrail; innermost recess; heart; disposition, temper; **-s** entrails, "innards", insides; **hijo de mis -s** child of my heart; **no tener -s** to be cruel.

entrar v. to enter, go in, come in; to attack; **me entró miedo** I became afraid; **-se** to slip in, get in, sneak in; to enter.

entre prep. between; among: **dijo — sí** he said to himself; **— tanto** meanwhile; Am. **— más habla menos dice** the more he talks the less he says.

entreabierto p.p. of **entreabrir**; adj. ajar, half-open, partly open.

entreabrir[52] v. to half-open.

entreacto m. intermission; intermezzo (*entertainment between the acts*); small cigar.

entrecano adj. greyish.

entrecejo m. space between the eyebrows; **fruncir el —** to wrinkle one's brow.

entrecortado adj. hesitating, faltering (*speech*); breathless, choking; p.p. interrupted.

entrecortar v. to cut halfway through or in between; to interrupt at intervals.

entrecruzar[9] v. to intercross, cross; to interlace; **-se** to cross.

entredicho m. prohibition, injunction.

entrega f. delivery; surrender; instalment (*of a book*); **novela por -s** serial novel.

entregar[7] to deliver, hand over; **-se** to surrender, submit, give up; to devote oneself (to); to abandon oneself (to).

entrelazar[9] v. to interlace; to weave together.

entremés m. relish, side dish (*of olives, pickles, etc.*); one-act farce (*formerly presented between the acts of a play.*)

entremeter v. to insert; to place between; **-se** to meddle; to intrude.

entremetido adj. meddlesome; m. meddler; intruder.

entremetimiento m. intrusion, meddling.

entremezclar v. to intermix, intermingle.

entrenador m. Am. trainer.

entrenamiento m. Am. training, drill.

entrenar v. Am. to train, drill; **-se** Am. to train.

entresacar[6] v. to pick out, select.

entresuelo m. mezzanine; second floor.

entretanto adv. meanwhile.

entretejer v. to weave together; to intertwine.

entretener[45] v. irr. to delay, detain; to amuse, entertain; **-se** to amuse one-

self; to delay oneself; **— el tiempo** to while away the time.

entretenido adj. entertaining, amusing; p.p. of **entretener**.

entretenimiento m. entertainment; pastime; delay.

entrever[49] v. to glimpse, catch a glimpse of; to half-see, see vaguely.

entreverar v. to intermingle, intermix.

entrevista f. interview; date, appointment.

entrevistar v. to interview; **-se con** to have an interview with.

entrevisto p.p. of **entrever**.

entristecer[13] v. irr. to sadden, make sad; **-se** to become sad.

entrometer = **entremeter**.

entrometido = **entremetido**.

entumecer[13] v. irr. to make numb; **-se** to get numb; to surge; to swell.

entumido adj. numb, stiff; Am. timid, shy, awkward.

entumirse v. to get numb.

enturbiar v. to make muddy; to muddle; to disturb; to obscure; **-se** to get muddy; to get muddled.

entusiasmar v. to excite, fill with enthusiasm; **-se** to get enthusiastic, excited.

entusiasmo m. enthusiasm.

entusiasta m. & f. enthusiast; **entusiástico** adj. enthusiastic.

enumeración f. enumeration, counting.

enumerar v. to enumerate.

enunciar v. to express, state, declare.

envainar v. to sheathe.

envalentonar v. to make bold or haughty; **-se** to get bold; to brag, swagger.

envanecer[13] v. irr. to make vain; **-se** to become vain.

envasar v. to pack, put up in any container; to bottle; to can.

envase m. packing; container, jar, bottle, can (*for packing*).

envejecer[13] v. irr. to make old; to grow old, get old; **-se** to grow old, get old.

envenenamiento m. poisoning.

envenenar v. to poison; to infect.

envergadura f. span (*of an airplane*); spread (*of a bird's wings*); breadth (*of sails*).

envés m. back or wrong side.

enviado m. envoy.

enviar[17] v. to send; **— a uno a paseo** to give someone his walking papers.

enviciar v. to vitiate, corrupt; **-se** to become addicted (to), overly fond (of).

envidar v. to bid (*in cards*); to bet.

envidia f. envy.

envidiable adj. enviable, desirable.

envidiar v. to envy.

envidioso adj. envious.

envilecer[13] v. irr. to revile, malign, degrade; -se to degrade or lower oneself.

envilecimiento m. degradation, humiliation, shame.

envío m. remittance, sending; shipment.

envite m. bid; stake (in cards); offer; push.

envoltorio m. bundle, package.

envoltura f. wrapping, cover; wrapper.

envolver[2,52] v. irr. to involve, entangle; to wrap; to wind (a thread, rope, etc.); to surround; -se to become involved, entangled; to cover up, wrap up.

envuelto p.p. of envolver.

enyesar v. to plaster; to chalk.

enzolvar v. Am. to clog, obstruct; Am. -se to clog, get clogged. See azolvar.

¡epa! interj. Am. hey! listen! stop! look out!

épico adj. epic.

epidemia f. epidemic.

epidémico adj. epidemic.

episodio m. episode.

epístola f. epistle; letter.

epitafio m. epitaph.

época f. epoch.

epopeya f. epic poem.

equidad f. equity, justice, fairness.

equidistante adj. equidistant, equally distant, halfway, midway.

equilibrar v. to balance, poise.

equilibrio m. equilibrium, balance; poise.

equipaje m. baggage, luggage; equipment, outfit; crew.

equipar v. to equip, fit out; to man, equip and provision (a ship).

equipo m. equipment, equipping; outfit; work crew; sport team; — de novia trousseau.

equitación f. horsemanship; horseback riding.

equitativo adj. fair, just.

equivalente adj. equivalent.

equivaler[47] v. irr. to be equivalent.

equivocación f. error, mistake.

equivocado p.p. & adj. mistaken.

equivocar[6] v. to mistake; -se to be mistaken; to make a mistake.

equívoco adj. equivocal, ambiguous, vague; Am. mistaken; m. pun, play on words; Am. mistake, error.

era f. era, age; threshing floor.

erario m. public treasury.

erguido adj. erect; p.p. of erguir.

erguir[3] v. irr. to erect, set upright; to lift (the head); -se to sit up or stand erect; to become proud and haughty.

erial m. uncultivated land; adj. un-

plowed, untilled.

erigir[11] v. to erect, build; to found.

erizado adj. bristly, prickly; — de bristling with.

erizar[9] v. to set on end, make bristle; -se to bristle; to stand on end (hair).

erizo m. hedgehog, porcupine; thistle; — de mar sea urchin; ser un — to be irritable, harsh.

ermitaño m. hermit.

erosión f. erosion.

errabundo adj. wandering.

errado adj. mistaken, wrong, in error; p.p. of errar.

errante adj. errant, roving, wandering.

errar[28] v. irr. to err, make mistakes; to miss (target, road); to rove, wander.

errata f. misprint, printer's error.

erróneo adj. erroneous, mistaken, wrong, incorrect.

error m. error, fault, mistake.

eructar v. to belch.

eructo m. belch.

erudición f. erudition, learning.

erudito adj. erudite, scholarly, learned; m. scholar.

erupción f. eruption; outburst; rash.

esbelto adj. slender.

esbozar[9] v. to sketch, outline.

esbozo m. sketch, outline.

escabechar v. to pickle.

escabeche m. pickled fish; pickle (solution for pickling).

escabel m. stool; footstool.

escabrosidad f. roughness, unevenness; harshness; improper word or phrase.

escabroso adj. rough; rugged; scabrous, rather indecent.

escabullirse[20] v. irr. to slip away; to slip through; to scoot, scamper, scurry.

escala f. ladder; scale; port of call; stopover; hacer — en to stop over at; escalafón m. army register.

escalar v. to scale; to climb.

escaldar v. to scald; to make red-hot; -se to get scalded.

escalera f. stairs, staircase; ladder.

escalfar v. to poach (eggs).

escalinata f. flight of stairs (usually on the outside).

escalofriarse[17] v. to become chilled.

escalofrío m. chill; -s chills and fever.

escalón m. step (of a ladder or staircase); stepping stone; Am. -es tribe of quichua Indians.

escalonar v. to echelon (arrange in step-like formation); to terrace; -se to rise in terraces.

escama f. scale, fish scale; flake.

escamoso adj. scaly.

escamotear v. to whisk out of sight; to steal or snatch away with cunning; to conceal by a trick or sleight of hand.

escandalizar[9] v. to scandalize, shock; -se to be shocked.

escándalo m. scandal; bad example.

escandaloso adj. scandalous, shocking; *Am.* showy, loud (*color*).

escapada f. escape, flight.

escapar v. to escape, flee, avoid; -se to run away, escape.

escaparate m. show window; glass case, glass cabinet or cupboard.

escapatoria f. escape, loophole, excuse.

escape m. escape; vent, outlet; exhaust; a — rapidly, at full speed.

escarabajo m. black beetle.

escaramuza f. skirmish; quarrel.

escarbar v. to scrape, scratch; to dig out; to pry into, investigate.

escarcear v. *Am.* to prance.

escarcha f. frost; frosting.

escarchar v. to frost; to freeze.

escardar v. to weed; to weed out.

escarlata f. scarlet; scarlet fever; scarlet cloth; **escarlatina** f. scarlet fever

escarmentar[1] v. irr. to punish (*as an example or warning*); to profit by one's misfortunes, punishment, etc.; — en cabeza ajena to profit by another's mistake or misfortune.

escarmiento m. lesson, example, warning; punishment.

escarnecer[13] v. irr. to jeer, insult, mock.

escarnio m. scoff, jeer.

escarpa f. steep slope, bluff, cliff; scarp (*of a fortification*).

escarpado adj. steep; rugged.

escarpia f. hook (*for hanging something*).

escasear v. to be scarce; to grow less, become scarce; to stint.

escasez f. scarcity, lack, scantiness.

escaso adj. scarce, limited; scant; scanty; stingy.

escatimar v. to stint, skimp; to curtail.

escena f. scene; scenery; theatre, stage.

escenario m. stage.

escenificación f. dramatization, stage adaptation.

escepticismo m. scepticism; doubt, unbelief.

escéptico m. & adj. sceptic.

esclarecer[13] v. irr. to lighten, illuminate; to elucidate, make clear, explain.

esclarecimiento m. clarification, illumination, illustration; worth, nobility.

esclavitud f. slavery.

esclavizar[9] v. to enslave.

esclavo m. slave.

esclusa f. lock (*of a canal*); sluice, flood-

gate.

escoba f. broom.

escobazo m. blow with a broom.

escobilla f. whisk broom; small broom.

escocer[2, 10] v. irr. to sting, smart.

escocés adj. Scotch; m. Scotch; Scotchman.

escoger[11] v. to choose, select, pick out.

escolar adj. scholastic, academic; m. scholar, student.

escolástico adj. & m. scholastic.

escolta f. escort; convoy.

escoltar v. to escort; to convoy.

escollo m. reef; danger; obstacle.

escombro m. debris, rubbish; mackerel.

esconder v. to hide, conceal; -se to hide, go into hiding.

escondidas : a — on the sly, under cover; *Am.* jugar a las — to play hide-and-seek.

escondite m. hiding place; **jugar al —** to play hide-and-seek.

escondrijo m. hiding place.

escopeta f. shotgun.

escopetazo m. gunshot; gunshot wound; sudden bad news; *Am.* offensive or ironic remark.

escoplo m. chisel.

escoria f. slag; scum; **escorial** m. dump, dumping place; pile of slag.

escorpión m. scorpion.

escote m. low neck; **convite a —** Dutch treat (*where everyone pays his share*).

escotilla f. hatchway; **escotillón** m. hatch, hatchway; trap door.

escozor m. smarting sensation, sting.

escribano m. court clerk; lawyer's clerk; notary.

escribiente m. clerk, office clerk.

escribir[52] v. to write.

escrito p.p. of **escribir** written; m. writing, manuscript.

escritor m. writer.

escritorio m. desk; office.

escritura f. writing, handwriting; deed, document; **Sagrada Escritura** Holy Scripture.

escrúpulo m. scruple, doubt.

escrupuloso adj. scrupulous; particular, exact.

escrutador adj. scrutinizing, examining; peering; penetrating; m. scrutinizer, examiner; inspector of election returns.

escrutar v. to scrutinize.

escrutinio m. scrutiny, careful inspection.

escuadra f. squadron; fleet; square (*instrument for drawing or testing right angles*).

88

escuadrón *m.* squadron.

escualidez *f.* squalor.

escuálido *adj.* squalid, filthy; thin, emaciated.

escuchar *v.* to listen; to heed.

escudar *v.* to shield.

escudero *m.* squire.

escudo *m.* shield; escutcheon, coat of arms; gold crown (*ancient coin*); *Am.* Chilean gold coin.

escudriñar *v.* to scrutinize, search, pry into.

escuela *f.* school.

escuelante *m. & f. Am.* schoolboy; schoolgirl.

escueto *adj.* plain, unadorned, bare.

esculcar[6] *v. Am.* to search; *Am.* to frisk (*a person's pockets*).

esculpir *v.* to sculpture; to engrave.

escultor *m.* sculptor.

escultura *f.* sculpture.

escupir *v.* to spit.

escurrir *v.* to drip; to drain; to trickle; -se to ooze out, trickle; to slip out, sneak out.

ese, esa *dem. adj.* that; **esos, esas** those; **ése, ésa** *m., f. dem. pron.* that one; **ésos, ésas** *m., f. pl.* those.

esencia *f.* essence.

esencial *adj.* essential.

esfera *f.* sphere; clock dial.

esférico *adj.* spherical.

esforzado *adj.* strong; valiant; courageous.

esforzar[2,9] *v. irr.* to give or inspire strength; to encourage; -se to make an effort; to strive, try hard.

esfuerzo *m.* effort; spirit, courage, vigor; stress.

esfumar *v.* to shade, tone down; -se to vanish, disappear.

esgrima *f.* fencing.

esgrimir *v.* to fence; to brandish; to wield (*the sword or pen*).

eslabón *m.* link of a chain; steel knife sharpener; black scorpion; *Am.* a kind of lizard.

eslabonar *v.* to link; to join; to connect.

esmaltar *v.* to enamel; to beautify, adorn.

esmalte *m.* enamel; enamel work; smalt (*a blue pigment*).

esmerado *adj.* painstaking, careful, conscientious; *p.p. of* **esmerar.**

esmeralda *f.* emerald; *Am.* an eel-like fish; *Am.* hummingbird; *Am.* variety of pineapple.

esmerar *v.* to polish, clean; -se to strive, take special pains, use great care.

esmero *m.* care, precision.

esmoquin *m.* tuxedo, dinner coat.

eso *dem. pron.* that, that thing, that fact; **— es** that is it; **a — de** at about (*referring to time*); *Am.* ¡eso! that's right!

espaciar[17] *v.* to space; to spread; to expand; -se to enlarge (*upon a subject*); to relax, amuse oneself.

espacio *m.* space; interval; slowness, delay; *adv. Am.* slowly.

espacioso *adj.* spacious; slow.

espada *f.* sword; skilled swordsman; matador (*bull-fighter who kills the bull*); **-s** swords (*Spanish card suit*).

espalda *f.* back, shoulders; **-s** back, back part; **a -s** behind one's back; **de -s** on one's back; **dar la — a** to turn one's back on; **espaldilla** *f.* shoulder blade.

espaldar *m.* back (*of a chair*); trellis (*for plants*); backplate of a cuirass (*armor*).

espantadizo *adj.* scary, shy, timid.

espantajo *m.* scarecrow.

espantapájaros *m.* scarecrow.

espantar *v.* to frighten, scare; to scare away; *Am.* to haunt; -se to be scared; to be astonished; *Am.* **espantárselas** to be wide-awake, catch on quickly.

espanto *m.* fright, terror; astonishment; *Am.* ghost.

espantoso *adj.* frightful, terrifying; wonderful.

español *adj.* Spanish; *m.* Spaniard; Spanish language.

esparadrapo *m.* court plaster, adhesive tape. *See* **tela adhesiva.**

esparcir[10] *v.* to scatter, spread; -se to relax, amuse oneself.

espárrago *m.* asparagus.

esparto *m.* esparto grass (*used for making ropes, mats, etc.*).

espasmo *m.* spasm; horror.

especia *f.* spice.

especial *adj.* special; **en —** in particular, specially.

especialidad *f.* specialty.

especialista *m. & f.* specialist.

especializar[9] *v.* to specialize; -se en to specialize in.

especie *f.* species; kind, sort; pretext; idea.

especificar[6] *v.* to specify; to name.

específico *adj.* specific; *m.* specific (*medicine*).

espécimen *m.* specimen, sample.

espectacular *adj.* spectacular.

espectáculo *m.* spectacle.

espectador *m.* spectator.

espectro *m.* spectre, ghost; spectrum.
especulación *f.* speculation.
especulador *m.* speculator.
especular *v.* to speculate.
especulativo *adj.* speculative.
espejismo *m.* mirage; illusion.
espejo *m.* mirror; model; — de cuerpo entero full-length mirror.
espeluznante *adj.* hair-raising, terrifying.
espeluznarse *v.* to be terrified; to bristle with fear.
espera *f.* wait; stay (*granted by judge*), delay; extension of time (*for payment*); sala de — waiting room; estar en — de to be waiting for; to be expecting.
esperanza *f.* hope; expectation.
esperanzado *adj.* hopeful.
esperanzar⁹ to give hope to.
esperar *v.* to hope; to expect; to trust; to wait; to await, wait for; — en alguien to place hope or confidence in someone.
esperezarse = desperezarse.
esperpento *m.* ugly thing; nonsense.
espesar *v.* to thicken; to make dense; -se to thicken; to become thick or dense.
espeso *adj.* thick, dense; compact; slovenly; *Am.* bothersome, boring.
espesor *m.* thickness.
espesura *f.* density, thickness; thicket; thickest part (*of a forest*).
espetar *v.* to spring (*a joke, story, etc.*) on (*a person*), surprise with (*a joke, speech, story, etc.*); to pop (*a question*); to run a spit through (*meat, fish, etc. for roasting*); to pierce; -se to be stiff, pompous.
espía *m. & f.* spy.
espiar¹⁷ *v.* to spy; *Am.* -se to bruise the hoofs, get lame (*said of horses*).
espiga *f.* ear of wheat; peg; spike.
espigar⁷ *v.* to glean; to grow spikes (*said of corn or grain*); -se to grow tall and slender.
espina *f.* thorn; sharp splinter; fish bone; spine; fear, suspicion; darle a uno mala — to arouse one's suspicion.
espinaca *f.* spinach.
espinazo *m.* spine, backbone.
espinilla *f.* shin (*front part of leg*); blackhead (*on the skin*).
espino *m.* hawthorn; thorny shrub; thorny branch.
espinoso *adj.* thorny; difficult, dangerous.
espionaje *m.* espionage, spying.
espiral *adj. & f.* spiral.

espirar *v.* to exhale; to emit, give off; to die. See expirar.
espíritu *m.* spirit; soul; courage; vigor; essence; ghost.
espiritual *adj.* spiritual.
espita *f.* spigot, faucet, tap; toper, drunkard.
esplendidez *f.* splendor.
espléndido *adj.* splendid.
esplendor *m.* splendor.
esp.endoroso *adj.* resplendent, shining.
espliego *m.* lavender (*plant*).
espolear *v.* to spur; to incite.
espolón *m.* spur (*on a cock's leg*); ram (*of a boat*); spur, buttress.
espolvorear *v.* to powder, sprinkle with powder.
esponja *f.* sponge; sponger, parasite; *Am.* souse, habitual drunkard.
esponjado *adj.* fluffy; spongy; puffed up; *p.p. of* esponjar.
esponjar *v.* to fluff; to make spongy or porous; -se to fluff up; to become spongy or porous; to swell, puff up; to puff up with pride.
esponjoso *adj.* spongy.
esponsales *m. pl.* betrothal.
espontaneidad *f.* spontaneity, ease, naturalness.
espontáneo *adj.* spontaneous.
esposa *f.* wife; -s handcuffs.
esposo *m.* husband.
espuela *f.* spur.
espulgar⁷ *v.* to delouse, remove lice or fleas from; to scrutinize.
espuma *f.* foam, froth; scum; — de jabón suds.
espumar *v.* to skim; to froth, foam.
espumarajo *m.* froth, foam (*from the mouth*); echar -s to froth at the mouth; to be very angry.
espumoso *adj.* foamy.
esputo *m.* sputum, spit, saliva.
esquela *f.* note, letter; announcement
esqueleto *m.* skeleton; carcass; framework; *Am.* blank (*to fill out*); *Am.* outline.
esquema *f.* scheme, outline.
esquí *m.* ski.
esquiar¹⁷ *v.* to ski.
esquila *f.* small bell; cow bell; sheepshearing.
esquilar *v.* to shear; to clip; to crop.
esquina *f.* corner, angle; esquinazo *m.* corner; *Am.* serenade; dar esquinazo to avoid meeting someone; to "ditch" someone.
esquivar *v.* to avoid, dodge; to shun; -se to withdraw, shy away.
esquivez *f.* shyness; aloofness; disdain.

esquivo *adv.* reserved, unsociable; shy; disdainful, aloof.

estabilidad *f.* stability.

estable *adj.* stable, firm, steady.

establecer[13] *v. irr.* to establish; to found; to decree, ordain.

establecimiento *m.* establishment; foundation; statute, law.

establo *m.* stable; **establero** *m.* groom.

estaca *f.* stake, club; stick; picket.

estacada *f.* stockade; picket fence; *Am.* predicament.

estacar[6] *v.* to stake; to tie to a stake; to stake off, mark off with stakes; *Am.* to fasten down with stakes; -se to remain stiff or rigid.

estación *f.* station; season; railway station.

estacionar *v.* to station; to place; to park (*a car*); -se to remain stationary; to park.

estacionario *adj.* stationary; motionless.

estada *f.* sojourn, stay.

estadía *f.* detention, stay; stay in port (*beyond time allowed for loading and unloading*); *Am.* sojourn, stay (*in any sense*).

estadio *m.* stadium.

estadista *m.* statesman.

estadística *f.* statistics.

estado *m.* state, condition; station, rank; estate; — **mayor** army staff; **hombre de** — statesman; *Am.* **en** — **interesante** pregnant.

estadounidense *adj.* from the United States, American.

estafa *f.* swindle, fraud, trick.

estafador *m.* swindler, crook.

estafar *v.* to swindle, defraud, cheat.

estallar *v.* to explode, burst; to creak, crackle.

estallido *m.* explosion, outburst; crash; creaking; crack (*of a gun*), report (*of a gun or cannon*).

estambre *m.* woolen yarn; stamen (*of a flower*).

estampa *f.* image; print; stamp; cut, picture; footprint; figure, appearance.

estampado *m.* print, printed fabric; printing.

estampar *v.* to stamp, print.

estampida *f.* crack, sharp sound; *Am.* stampede (*sudden scattering of a herd of cattle or horses*).

estampido *m.* crack, sharp sound; report of a gun.

estampilla *f.* stamp, seal; *Am.* postage stamp.

estancar[6] *v.* to stem; to stanch; to stop the flow of; to corner (*a market*); -se to stagnate, become stagnant.

estancia *f.* stay; hall, room; mansion; *Am.* farm, cattle ranch; *Am.* main building of a farm or ranch.

estanciero *m.* *Am.* rancher, ranchowner, cattle raiser; *adj.* pertaining to an estancia.

estanco *m.* monopoly, government store (*for sale of monopolized goods such as tobacco, stamps and matches*); tank, reservoir; *Am.* liquor store.

estándar *m.* *Am.* standard, norm.

estandardizar, estandarizar[9] *v.* *Am.* to standardize.

estandarte *m.* standard, flag, banner.

estanque *m.* pond, pool, reservoir.

estanquillo *m.* tobacco store; *Am.* small store; *Am.* small liquor store, tavern.

estante *m.* shelf; bookshelf; *Am.* prop, support; **estantería** *f.* shelves; bookcases.

estaño *m.* tin.

estaquilla *f.* peg; spike.

estar[29] *v. irr.* to be; **-le bien a uno** to be becoming to one; — **de prisa** to be in a hurry; **¿a cuántos estamos?** what day of the month is it today?; -se to keep, remain.

estático *adj.* static; **estática** *f.* statics; radio static.

estatua *f.* statue.

estatura *f.* stature, height.

estatuto *m.* statute.

este, esta *dem. adj.* this; **estos, estas** these; **éste, ésta** *m., f. dem. pron.* this one, this thing; the latter; **esto** this, this thing; **éstos, éstas** *m., f. pl.* these; the latter.

este *m.* east; east wind.

estela *f.* wake of a ship.

estenógrafo *m.* stenographer.

estentóreo *adj.* loud, thundering (*voice*).

estepa *f.* steppe, treeless plain.

estera *f.* matting; mat.

estercolar *v.* to manure, fertilize with manure.

estercolero *m.* manure pile, manure dump; manure collector.

estéril *adj.* sterile, barren.

esterilidad *f.* sterility, barrenness.

esterilizar[9] *v.* to sterilize.

esterlina *adj.* sterling; **libra** — pound sterling.

estero *m.* estuary.

estertor *m.* death-rattle; snort.

estético *adj.* aesthetic; **estética** *f.* aesthetics.

estetoscopio m. stethoscope.

estibador m. stevedore, longshoreman.

estibar v. to stow (in a boat); to pack down, compress.

estiércol m. manure; fertilizer.

estigma m. stigma; brand, mark of disgrace; birthmark.

estilar v. to use, be accustomed to using;-se to be in style (said of clothes).

estilete m. stiletto, narrow-bladed dagger; stylet (instrument for probing wounds); long, narrow sword.

estilo m. style; fashion.

estima f. esteem.

estimación f. esteem, regard; valuation.

estimar v. to esteem, regard highly; to estimate, appraise; to judge, think.

estimulante adj. stimulant, stimulating; m. stimulant.

estimular v. to stimulate, excite, goad.

estímulo m. stimulation, incitement; stimulus.

estío m. summer.

estipulación f. stipulation, specification, provision, proviso.

estipular v. to stipulate, specify.

estirado p.p. & adj. stretched; extended, drawn out; stuck-up, conceited.

estirar v. to stretch, extend; — la pata to die; -se to stretch out; Am. to die.

estirón m. hard pull, tug; stretch; dar un — to grow suddenly (said of a child).

estirpe f. lineage, family, race.

estival adj. summer, relating to the summer.

estocada f. thrust, stab; stab wound.

estofa f. stuff, cloth; class, quality; gente de baja — low class people, rabble.

estofado m. stew, stewed meat; p.p. of estofar.

estofar v. to quilt; to stew.

estoico adj. & m. stoic.

estómago m. stomach.

estopa f. burlap; oakum (loose fiber of old ropes).

estoque m. long, narrow sword.

estorbar v. to hinder; to obstruct.

estorbo m. hindrance; nuisance, bother.

estornudar v. to sneeze.

estornudo m. sneeze.

estrado m. dais (platform for a throne, seats of honor, etc.); main part of a parlor or drawing room.

estragado p.p. & adj. corrupted; spoiled; ruined; tired, worn out.

estragar[7] v. to corrupt, contaminate; to spoil; to ruin.

estrago m. havoc, ruin; massacre.

estrangulador m. strangler, choke (of an automobile); adj. strangling.

estrangular v. to strangle; to choke, throttle.

estratagema f. stratagem, scheme.

estrategia f. strategy.

estratégico adj. strategic; m. strategist, person trained or skilled in strategy.

estrato m. stratum, layer (of mineral).

estratosfera f. stratosphere.

estrechar v. to tighten; to narrow down; to embrace, hug; — la mano to squeeze, grasp another's hand; to shake hands.

estrechez, estrechura f. narrowness; tightness; austerity; dire straits; poverty; closeness.

estrecho adj. narrow; tight; m. strait, narrow passage.

estrella f. star; — de mar starfish.

estrellado adj. starry; spangled with stars; huevos -s fried eggs.

estrellar v. to shatter; to dash to pieces; to star, spangle with stars; -se to shatter, break into pieces; to fail.

estremecer[13] v. irr. to shake; -se to shiver, shudder; to vibrate.

estremecimiento m. shiver, shudder; vibration; shaking.

estrenar v. to wear for the first time; to perform (a play) for the first time; to inaugurate; to begin.

estreno m. début, first appearance or performance.

estreñimiento m. constipation.

estreñir[5, 19] v. irr. to constipate; -se to become constipated.

estrépito m. racket, noise, crash.

estrepitoso adj. noisy; boisterous.

estriado p.p. & adj. fluted, grooved; streaked.

estriar[17] v. to groove; to flute (as a column).

estribación f. spur (of a mountain or mountain range).

estribar v. to rest (upon); eso estriba en que . . . the basis or reason for it is that . . .

estribillo m. refrain.

estribo m. stirrup; footboard, running board; support; brace; spur (of a mountain); perder los -s to lose one's balance; to lose control of oneself.

estribor m. starboard.

estricto adj. strict.

estrofa f. strophe, stanza.

estropajo *m.* fibrous mass (*for scrubbing*); **tratar a uno como un —** to treat someone scornfully.

estropear *v.* to spoil, ruin, damage; to cripple.

estructura *f.* structure.

estructural *adj.* structural.

estruendo *m.* clatter; clamor, din, racket.

estruendoso *adj.* thunderous, uproarious, deafening.

estrujamiento *m.* crushing, squeezing.

estrujar *v.* to squeeze, press, crush.

estrujón *m.* squeeze, crush; smashing.

estuario *m.* estuary.

estuco *m.* stucco.

estuche *m.* jewel box; instrument case, kit; small casket; sheath.

estudiante *m.* & *f.* student.

estudiar *v.* to study.

estudio *m.* study; studio.

estudioso *adj.* studious; *m.* learner.

estufa *f.* heater; stove; hothouse; steam room; steam cabinet.

estupefacto *adj.* stunned; speechless.

estupendo *adj.* stupendous, marvelous.

estupidez *f.* stupidity.

estúpido *adj.* stupid.

etapa *f.* stage, lap (*of a journey or race*); army food rations; epoch, period.

éter *m.* ether.

etéreo *adj.* ethereal; heavenly.

eternidad *f.* eternity.

eternizar[9] *v.* to prolong excessively; to perpetuate, make eternal.

eterno *adj.* eternal, everlasting.

ética *f.* ethics; **ético** *adj.* ethical, moral.

etiqueta *f.* etiquette; formality; tag; **de —** formal (*dress, function, etc.*).

eucalipto *m.* eucalyptus.

europeo *adj.* & *m.* European.

evacuación *f.* evacuation; bowel movement.

evacuar[18] *v.* to evacuate, empty; to vacate.

evadir *v.* to evade, elude; **-se** to slip away, escape.

evaluar[18] *v.* to evaluate, appraise.

evangelio *m.* gospel.

evaporar *v.* to evaporate; **-se** to evaporate; to vanish, disappear.

evasión *f.* evasion, dodge, escape.

evasiva *f.* evasion, dodge, escape.

evasivo *adj.* evasive.

evasor *m.* evader, dodger.

evento *m.* event.

evidencia *f.* evidence.

evidenciar *v.* to prove, show, make evident.

evidente *adj.* evident.

evitable *adj.* avoidable.

evitar *v.* to avoid, shun.

evocar[6] *v.* to evoke, call forth.

evolución *f.* evolution.

evolucionar *v.* to evolve; to perform maneuvers; to go through changes.

exacerbar *v.* to exasperate, irritate; to aggravate, make worse.

exactitud *f.* exactness, precision; punctuality.

exacto *adj.* exact, precise; punctual.

exagerar *v.* to exaggerate.

exaltación *f.* exaltation; excitement.

exaltado *adj.* elated; excited; hotheaded.

exaltar *v.* to exalt, elevate, glorify; to praise; **-se** to get excited; to become upset emotionally.

examen *m.* examination; inspection.

examinar *v.* to examine; to inspect.

exánime *adj.* lifeless, motionless; weak, faint.

exasperar *v.* to exasperate, irritate, annoy.

excavar *v.* to excavate, dig, dig out.

excedente *m.* surplus; *adj.* exceeding, extra.

exceder *v.* to exceed, surpass; to overdo; **-se** to go beyond the proper limit; to misbehave.

excelencia *f.* excellence, superiority; excellency (*title*).

excelente *adj.* excellent.

excelso *adj.* lofty, elevated; sublime; **El Excelso** the Most High.

excéntrico *adj.* eccentric; queer, odd.

excepción *f.* exception.

excepcional *adj.* exceptional, unusual.

excepto *adv.* except, with the exception of.

exceptuar[18] *v.* to except.

excesivo *adj.* excessive.

exceso *m.* excess; crime; **— de equipaje** excess baggage; **en —** in excess, excessively.

excitación *f.* excitement.

excitante *adj.* exciting; stimulating.

excitar *v.* to excite, stir; **-se** to get excited.

exclamación *f.* exclamation.

exclamar *v.* to exclaim.

excluir[32] *v.* *irr.* to exclude.

exclusivo *adj.* exclusive.

excomulgar[6] *v.* to excommunicate.

excomunión *f.* excommunication.

excrecencia, excrescencia *f.* excrescence (*abnormal growth or tumor*).

excremento *m.* excrement.

excursión *f.* excursion, tour, outing.

excusa *f.* excuse.

excusado p.p. & adj. excused; exempt; superfluous; unnecessary; reserved, private; m. toilet.

excusar v. to excuse; to avoid, shun; to exempt; -se to excuse oneself, apologize; to decline.

exención f. exemption.

exentar v. to exempt. See **eximir**.

exento adj. exempt, freed; free, unobstructed.

exequias f. pl. obsequies, funeral rites.

exhalar v. to exhale; to emit, give off; to breathe forth; -se to evaporate; to run away.

exhibición f. exhibition; exposition; Am. payment of an installment.

exhibir v. to exhibit; Am. to pay for in installments (stocks, policies, etc.); -se to exhibit oneself, show off.

exhortar v. to exhort, admonish.

exigencia f. demand; urgent want; emergency.

exigente adj. demanding, exacting; urgent.

exigir[11] v. to require; to demand; to exact.

exiguo adj. scanty, meager.

eximio adj. very distinguished.

eximir v. to exempt, except, excuse; -se de to avoid, shun.

existencia f. existence; -s stock on hand, goods; en — in stock, on hand.

existente adj. existent, existing; in stock.

existir v. to exist.

éxito m. outcome, result; success; tener buen (mal) — to be successful (unsuccessful).

éxodo m. exodus, emigration.

exonerar v. to exonerate, free from blame; to relieve of a burden or position; to dismiss.

exorbitante adj. exorbitant, excessive, extravagant.

exótico adj. exotic, foreign, strange; quaint.

expansión f. expansion; relaxation; recreation.

expansivo adj. expansive; demonstrative, effusive.

expatriar v. to expatriate, exile; -se to expatriate oneself, renounce one's citizenship; to emigrate.

expectación f. expectation.

expectativa f. expectation; hope, prospect; estar en — de algo to be expecting, or on the lookout for, something.

expectorar v. to expectorate, cough up.

expedición f. expedition; dispatch;

promptness; papal dispatch or bull.

expedicionario adj. expeditionary; m. member of an expedition; explorer.

expediente m. certificate; papers pertaining to a business matter; expedient, means; dispatch, promptness.

expedir[5] v. irr. to dispatch; to issue officially; to remit, send.

expeler v. to expel, eject.

experiencia f. experience; experiment.

experimentado adj. & p.p. experienced.

experimental adj. experimental.

experimentar v. to experiment, try, test; to experience, feel.

experimento m. experiment, trial.

experto adj. expert, skilful; m. expert.

expiación f. expiation, atonement.

expiar[17] v. to atone for; to make amends for; to purify.

expirar v. to die; to expire, come to an end.

explayar v. to extend; -se to become extended; to relax in the open air; to enlarge upon a subject; -se con un amigo to unbosom oneself, speak with utmost frankness with a friend.

explicable adj. explainable.

explicación f. explanation.

explicar[6] v. to explain; — una cátedra to teach a course; -se to explain oneself; to account for one's conduct.

explicativo adj. explanatory, explaining.

explícito adj. explicit, express, clear, definite.

exploración f. exploration.

explorador m. explorer, scout; adj. exploring.

explorar v. to explore.

explosión f. explosion.

explosivo adj. & m. explosive.

explotación f. exploitation; operation of a mine; development of a business; plant.

explotar v. to exploit, operate, develop; to utilize, profit by; to make unfair use of; Am. to explode.

exponer[40] v. irr. to expose, reveal; to show, exhibit; to display; to expose, leave unprotected; to explain, expound; -se a exponer oneself to; to run the risk of.

exportación f. exportation; export.

exportar v. to export.

exposición f. exposition; exhibition; explanation; exposure.

exprés m. Am. express; Am. express company.

expresar v. to express; -se to express oneself, speak.

expresión f. expression; utterance; -es

regards.

expresivo *adj.* expressive; affectionate.

expreso *adj.* expressed; express, clear, exact; fast; *m.* express train.

exprimir *v.* to squeeze, extract (*juice*); to wring out; to express, utter.

expuesto *p.p. of* **exponer** & *adj.* exposed; expressed; displayed; risky, dangerous; **lo** — what has been said.

expulsar *v.* to expel, eject.

expulsión *f.* expulsion, expelling.

exquisitez *f.* exquisiteness.

exquisito *adj.* exquisite.

extasiado *adj.* rapt, in ecstasy; *p.p. of* **extasiar.**

extasiar[17] *v.* to delight; **-se** to be in ecstasy; to be entranced.

éxtasis *m.* ecstasy.

extender[1] *v. irr.* to extend; to spread; to unfold; to draw up (*a document*); **-se** to extend, spread; to expatiate, be too wordy.

extensión *f.* extension; extent; expanse; expansion.

extensivo *adj.* extensive.

extenso *p.p. irr. of* **extender** extended; *adj.* extensive, vast, spacious; **por** — extensively, in detail.

extenuado *adj.* wasted, weak, emaciated.

exterior *adj.* exterior, outer; *m.* exterior; outside; outward appearance.

exterminar *v.* to exterminate.

exterminio *m.* extermination, destruction.

externo *adj.* external, outward.

extinguir[12] *v.* to extinguish, put out; to destroy.

extinto *adj.* extinct.

extirpar *v.* to eradicate, pull out by the roots, root out, remove completely; to destroy completely.

extorsión *f.* extortion.

extorsionar *v. Am.* to extort, extract money, blackmail.

extorsionista *m. Am.* extortioner, profiteer, racketeer.

extracto *m.* extract; abstract, summary.

extraer[46] *v. irr.* to extract.

extranjero *adj.* foreign; *m.* foreigner.

extrañamiento *m.* wonder, surprise, amazement.

extrañar *v.* to wonder at; to banish; *Am.* to miss (*a person or thing*); **-se** to marvel, be astonished.

extrañeza *f.* strangeness; surprise, astonishment; oddity, odd thing.

extraño *adj.* strange; rare; odd; *m.* stranger.

extraordinario *adj.* extraordinary.

extravagancia *f.* extravagance; folly.

extravagante *adj.* extravagant, fantastic; queer, odd.

extraviar[17] *v.* to lead astray; to strand; to misplace; **-se** to lose one's way; to get stranded; to get lost; to miss the road.

extravío *m.* deviation, straying; error; misconduct; damage.

extremado *adj.* extreme; extremely good or extremely bad; *p.p. of* **extremar.**

extremar *v.* to carry to an extreme; **-se** to take great pains, exert great effort.

extremidad *f.* extremity; extreme degree; remotest part; **-es** extremities, hands and feet.

extremo *adj.* extreme, last; farthest; excessive; utmost; *m.* extreme, highest degree or point; end, extremity; extreme care; **con** (**en o por**) — very much, extremely.

exuberante *adj.* exuberant; luxuriant.

F

fábrica *f.* manufacture; factory, mill; structure.

fabricación *f.* manufacture.

fabricante *m.* manufacturer, maker.

fabricar[6] *v.* to manufacture, make; to construct, build; to fabricate, make up, invent.

fabril *adj.* manufacturing.

fábula *f.* fable, tale; falsehood.

fabuloso *adj.* fabulous; false, imaginary.

facción *f.* faction, band, party; battle; **-es** features; **estar de** — to be on duty.

faceto *adj. Am.* cute, funny; *Am.* affected.

fácil *adj.* easy; docile, yielding, manageable; likely; probable.

facilidad *f.* facility, ease; opportunity.

facilitar *v.* to facilitate, make easy; to furnish, give; — **todos los datos** to furnish all the data.

facón *m. Am.* dagger, large knife; **faconazo** *m. Am.* stab.

factible *adj.* feasible.

factor *m.* factor; element; joint cause; commercial agent; baggage man.

factura *f.* invoice, itemized bill; make; workmanship, form; *Am.* roll, biscuit, muffin; — **simulada** temporary invoice, memorandum.

facturar *v.* to invoice, bill; to check (*baggage*).

facultad *f.* faculty; ability, aptitude; power, right; permission; branch of learning.

facultativo *m.* doctor, physician.

facundia *f.* eloquence, fluency, facility in speaking, gift of expression.

facha f. appearance, figure, aspect, looks.

fachada f. façade, front (of a building); title page.

fachenda f. ostentation, vanity.

fachendoso adj. vain, boastful, ostentatious.

faena f. task, job, duty; Am. extra job; Am. work crew, labor gang.

faja f. sash; girdle; band; Am. belt, waist band.

fajar v. to girdle; to bind, wrap, or bandage with a strip of cloth; Am. to beat, strike, thrash; Am. — un latigazo a uno to whip, thrash someone; -se to put on a sash or belt; to tighten one's sash or belt; Am. -se con to have a fight with, come to blows with.

fajo m. bundle; sheaf.

falaz adj. illusive, illusory; deceitful, deceiving.

falda f. skirt; lap; hat brim; foothill, slope; **faldón** m. coattail; shirttail.

faldear v. to skirt (a hill).

falsario m. crook, forger; liar.

falsear v. to falsify, misrepresent; to counterfeit; to forge; to pick (a lock); to flag, grow weak; to hit a wrong note.

falsedad f. falsehood, lie; deceit.

falsificación f. falsification, forgery; counterfeit.

falsificar[6] v. to falsify, make false; to counterfeit; to forge.

falso adj. false; untrue, unreal; deceitful; counterfeit; sham; Am. cowardly; m. inside facing of a dress; lining; Am. false testimony, slander; en — upon a false foundation; without proper security; Am. coger a uno en — to catch one lying.

falta f. lack, want; fault, mistake; defect; absence; misdemeanor, offense; a — de for want of; hacer — to be necessary; to be missing; me hace — I need it; sin — without fail.

faltar v. to be lacking, wanting; to be absent or missing; to fail, be of no use or help; to fail to fulfill (a promise or duty); to die; Am. to insult; — poco para las cinco to be almost five o'clock; ¡no faltaba más! that's the last straw!; why, the very idea!

falto adj. lacking; deficient; short; Am. foolish, stupid.

faltriquera f. pocket.

falla f. fault, defect; failure; fault (fracture in the earth's crust); Am. baby's bonnet.

fallar v. to render a verdict; to fail, be deficient; to default; to miss, fail to hit; to give way, break; to trump.

fallecer[13] v. irr. to die.

fallecimiento m. decease, death.

fallido adj. frustrated; bankrupt.

fallo m. verdict, judgment; decision; adj. lacking (a card, or suit, in card games); Am. silly, foolish.

fama f. fame, reputation; rumor, report; Am. bull's-eye, center of a target.

famélico adj. ravenous, hungry, starved.

familia f. family.

familiar adj. domestic, homelike; familiar, well-known; friendly, informal; colloquial (phrase or expression); m. intimate friend; member of a household; domestic servant; familiar spirit, demon; Am. relative.

familiaridad f. familiarity, informality.

familiarizar[9] v. to familiarize, acquaint; -se to acquaint oneself, become familiar (with).

famoso adj. famous; excellent.

fanal m. beacon, lighthouse; lantern; headlight; bell jar, glass cover.

fanático adj. & m. fanatic.

fanatismo m. fanaticism.

fanega f. Spanish bushel; — de tierra land measure (variable according to region).

fanfarrón m. braggart, boaster; bluffer.

fanfarronada f. boast, brag, swagger, bluff.

fanfarronear v. to bluff, brag; to swagger.

fango m. mud, mire.

fangoso adj. muddy, miry.

fantasear v. to fancy; to imagine.

fantasía f. fantasy, imagination, fancy, whim; -s string of pearls; Am. tocar por — to play by ear.

fantasma m. phantom, image; vision, ghost; f. scarecrow.

fantasmagórico adj. fantastic, unreal, illusory.

fantástico adj. fantastic.

fardel m. knapsack, bag; bundle.

fardo m. bundle; bale; Am. pasar el — to "pass the buck", shift the responsibility to someone else.

farmacéutico m. pharmacist, druggist; adj. pharmaceutical (pertaining to a pharmacy or pharmacists).

farmacia f. pharmacy; drugstore.

faro m. lighthouse; beacon; Am. headlight.

farol m. lantern; street lamp; conceit, self-importance; Am. balcony; Am. presumptuous man; Am. bluff; darse — to show off; to put on airs.

farolero *adj.* vain, ostentatious; *m.* lamp maker or vendor; lamplighter (*person*).

farra *f. Am.* spree, revelry, wild party, noisy merrymaking; *Am.* **ir de —** to go on a spree.

farsa *f.* farce; company of actors; sham, fraud.

farsante *m.* charlatan, bluffer; quack; comedian; wag.

fascinación *f.* fascination; glamour.

fascinador *adj.* fascinating, glamorous, charming,

fascinar *v.* to fascinate, bewitch, charm; to allure.

fase *f.* phase, aspect.

fastidiar *v.* to annoy, bother; to bore; *Am.* to hurt, harm, ruin.

fastidio *m.* boredom; disgust; nuisance, annoyance.

fastidioso *adj.* annoying, bothersome; boring, tiresome.

fatal *adj.* fatal; mortal, deadly; unfortunate.

fatalidad *f.* fatality, destiny; calamity, misfortune.

fatiga *f.* fatigue, weariness; toil; **-s** hardships.

fatigar[7] *v.* to fatigue, weary; to bother.

fatigoso *adj.* fatiguing, tiring.

fatuo *adj.* foolish, stupid; vain; **fuego —** will-o'-the-wisp.

favor *m.* favor; kindness; help, aid; protection; *Am.* ribbon bow; **a — de** in favor of; **hágame el —** please.

favorable *adj.* favorable.

favorecer[13] *v. irr.* to favor, help, protect.

favoritismo *m.* favoritism.

favorito *adj.* & *m.* favorite.

faz *f.* face.

fe *f.* faith; **— de bautismo** baptismal certificate.

fealdad *f.* ugliness, homeliness; foulness, foul or immoral action.

febrero *m.* February.

febril *adj.* feverish.

fécula *f.* starch.

fecundar *v.* to fertilize.

fecundo *adj.* fruitful, fertile, productive.

fecha *f.* date.

fechar *v.* to date.

fechoría *f.* misdeed, misdemeanor.

federación *f.* federation, union.

federal *adj.* federal.

felicidad *f.* happiness; **¡-es!** congratulations!

felicitación *f.* congratulation.

felicitar *v.* to congratulate.

feligrés *m.* parishioner.

feliz *adj.* happy; lucky.

felpudo *adj.* plushy, like plush; *m.* small plushlike mat; door mat.

femenil *adj.* womanly, feminine.

femenino *adj.* feminine.

fementido *adj.* false; treacherous.

fenecer[13] *v. irr.* to die; to finish, end.

fénix *m.* phoenix (*mythical bird*).

fenómeno *m.* phenomenon.

feo *adj.* ugly, homely; *Am.* bad (*referring to taste or odor*); **feote** *adj.* hideous, very ugly.

féretro *m.* bier; coffin.

feria *f.* fair; market; *Am.* change (*money*); *Am.* tip; **-s** *Am.* present given to servants or the poor during holidays.

feriante *m.* & *f.* trader at fairs; trader; peddler.

fermentar *v.* to ferment.

fermento *m.* ferment; yeast, leaven.

ferocidad *f.* ferocity, fierceness.

feroz *adj.* ferocious, wild, fierce.

férreo *adj.* ferrous (*pertaining to or derived from iron*); ironlike; harsh; **vía férrea** railroad.

ferretería *f.* hardware shop; hardware.

ferrocarril *m.* railroad.

ferroviario *adj.* railway, railroad (*used as adj.*); *m.* railroad man; railroad employee.

fértil *adj.* fertile, productive; **fertilidad** *f.* fertility.

fertilizar[9] *v.* to fertilize.

ferviente *adj.* fervent, ardent.

fervor *m.* fervor, zeal, devotion.

fervoroso *adj.* fervent, ardent; pious, devout; zealous.

festejar *v.* to feast, entertain; to celebrate; to woo; *Am.* to thrash, beat.

festejo *m.* entertainment, festival, celebration; courtship; *Am.* revelry.

festín *m.* feast; banquet.

festividad *f.* festival; holiday; holy day; festivity, gaiety, rejoicing.

festivo *adj.* festive, gay; **día —** holiday.

fétido *adj.* foul, foul-smelling.

fiado *p.p. of* **fiar; al —** on credit.

fiador *m.* guarantor, backer, bondsman; *Am.* chin strap, hat guard.

fiambre *m.* cold meat; cold or late news; *Am.* cold meat salad; *Am.* flop, failure (*referring to a party*).

fianza *f.* bond, security, surety, guarantee; bail.

fiar[17] to trust; to guarantee, back; *Am.* to borrow on credit; **-se de** to place confidence in.

fibra *f.* fiber; **fibroso** *adj.* fibrous.

ficción *f.* fiction.

ficticio *adj.* fictitious.

ficha f. chip; token; domino; file card; Am. check (used in barbershops and stores); Am. rascal, scamp; **fichero** m. file, card index, filing cabinet.

fidedigno adj. trustworthy, reliable.

fidelidad f. fidelity, faithfulness.

fideo m. vermicelli, thin noodle; thin person.

fiebre f. fever; excitement, agitation; Am. astute person.

fiel adj. faithful; true, accurate; m. public inspector; pointer of a balance or scale; pin of the scissors; **los -es** the worshipers, the congregation.

fieltro m. felt; felt hat; felt rug.

fiera f. wild beast; Am. go-getter, hustler; **ser una — para el trabajo** to be a demon for work.

fiereza f. ferocity, fierceness; cruelty; ugliness.

fiero adj. fierce, ferocious, wild; cruel; ugly, horrible; huge; m. threat; **echar** (or **hacer**) **-s** to threaten; to boast.

fierro m. Am. iron; Am. iron bar; Am. cattle brand; **-s** Am. tools, implements. See **hierro**.

fiesta f. festivity, celebration, entertainment; holiday; **estar de —** to be in a holiday mood; **hacer -s a uno** to fawn on a person.

fiestero adj. fond of parties, fond of entertaining; gay, festive; playful; m. merrymaker.

figón m. cheap eating house, "joint."

figura f. figure; shape, form; countenance; face card.

figurado adj. figurative.

figurar v. to figure; to form; to represent, symbolize; **-se** to imagine; **se me figura** I think, guess, or imagine.

figurín m. fashion plate; dandy.

fijar v. to fix, fasten; to establish; **-se** to settle; **-se en** to notice, pay attention to.

fijeza f. firmness, solidity, steadiness.

fijo adj. fixed; firm; secure.

fila f. row, tier; rank.

filamento m. filament.

filete m. edge, rim; fillet, tenderloin; snaffle bit (for horses); hem; screw thread.

filial adj. filial.

filmar v. to film, screen (a play or novel).

filo m. cutting edge; Am. hunger; **por —** exactly; Am. **de —** resolutely.

filón m. seam, layer (of metallic ore).

filoso adj. Am. sharp, sharp-edged.

filosofía f. philosophy.

filosófico adj. philosophic, philosoph-

ical.

filósofo m. philosopher.

filtrar v. to filter; **-se** to leak through, leak out; to filter.

filtro m. filter.

filudo adj. Am. sharp, sharp-edged.

fin m. end, ending; purpose; **al —** at last; **al — y al cabo** at last; anyway; in the end; **a — de que** so that; a **-es del mes** toward the end of the month; **en —** in conclusion; well; in short.

final adj. final; m. end.

finalizar[9] v. to finish; to end.

financiamiento m. Am. financing.

financiar v. Am. to finance.

financiero adj. financial; m. financier.

financista m. Am. financier.

finanza f. Am. finance; **-s** Am. public treasury, government funds.

finca f. real estate; property; country house; Am. ranch, farm.

fincar v. to buy real estate; Am. to rest (on), be based (on); Am. to build a farmhouse or country house.

fineza f. fineness; nicety; courtesy; favor, kindness; present.

fingimiento m. pretense, sham.

fingir[11] v. to feign, pretend, fake; to imagine.

finiquito m. settlement (of an account); quittance, final receipt; **dar —** to finish up.

fino adj. fine; nice; delicate; sharp; subtle; refined.

finura f. fineness; nicety; subtlety; courtesy, good manners.

firma f. signature; firm, firm name.

firmamento m. firmament, sky.

firmante m. & f. signer.

firmar v. to sign.

firme adj. firm; solid, hard; **de —** without stopping, hard, steadily.

firmeza f. firmness.

fiscal m. public prosecutor, district attorney; adj. fiscal.

fisgar[7] v. to pry; to snoop; to spy on.

fisgón m. snoop, snooper; adj. snooping; curious.

fisgonear v. to pry about; to snoop.

física f. physics.

físico adj. physical; Am. vain, prudish, affected; Am. real; m. physicist.

fisiología f. physiology.

fisiológico adj. physiological.

fisonomía f. face, features.

flaco adj. lean, skinny; frail, weak; **su lado —** his weak side, his weakness.

flacura f. thinness.

flama f. flame.

flamante *adj.* bright, shiny; brand-new.

flameante *adj.* flaming, flashing.

flamear *v.* to flame; to flap, flutter (*in the wind*).

flamenco *adj.* Flemish; *Am.* skinny; *m.* Flemish, Flemish language; flamingo.

flan *m.* custard.

flanco *m.* flank, side.

flanquear *v.* to flank.

flaquear *v.* to weaken, flag.

flaqueza *f.* thinness, leanness; weakness, frailty.

flauta *f.* flute; **flautista** *m.* & *f.* flute player.

fleco *m.* fringe; bangs, fringe of hair.

flecha *f.* arrow, dart.

flechar *v.* to dart, shoot (*an arrow*); to strike, wound or kill with an arrow; to cast an amorous or ardent glance; *Am.* to prick, sting; *Am.* to burn (said of the sun).

fletamento *m.* charter, charter party (of a ship).

fletar *v.* to charter (a ship); to freight; *Am.* to hire (pack animals); *Am.* to let loose (strong words); *Am.* to scatter (false rumors); **-se** *Am.* to run away, slip away; *Am.* to slip in uninvited; *Am.* **salir fletado** to leave on the run.

flete *m.* freight, freightage; cargo; load; *Am.* fine horse, race horse; *Am.* bother, nuisance; *Am.* **salir sin -s** to leave in a hurry.

flexibilidad *f.* flexibility; **flexible** *adj.* flexible.

flexión *f.* bending, bend; sag.

flojear *v.* to slacken; to weaken; to idle, be lazy.

flojedad *f.* laxity, looseness; slackness; laziness; slack.

flojera = flojedad.

flojo *adj.* lax; loose, slack; lazy; weak; *Am.* timid.

flor *f.* flower, blossom; compliment; — **de la edad** prime; — **de lis** iris (flower); — **y nata** the best, the cream, the chosen few; **a — de flush** with; **echar -es** to throw a bouquet; to compliment, flatter.

floreado *p.p.* & *adj.* flowered; made of the finest wheat.

florear *v.* to decorate with flowers; to brandish, flourish; to make a flourish on the guitar; to flatter, compliment; to bolt, sift out (the finest flour); *Am.* to flower, bloom; *Am.* to choose the best; **-se** *Am.* to shine, excel; *Am.* to burst open like a flower.

florecer[13] *v. irr.* to flower, bloom; to flourish, thrive.

floreciente *adj.* flourishing, thriving; prosperous.

florecimiento *m.* flourishing, flowering, bloom.

floreo *m.* flourish; idle talk; flattery, compliment.

florería *f.* florist's shop.

florero *m.* florist; flower vase; flatterer; *adj.* flattering.

floresta *f.* wooded place, grove; arbor.

florete *m.* fencing foil.

florido *adj.* flowery.

flota *f.* fleet; *Am.* **echar -s** to brag, boast.

flotador *m.* floater; float; pontoon (of a hydroplane); *adj.* floating.

flotante *adj.* floating; *m.* *Am.* bluffer, braggart.

flotar *v.* to float.

flote : **a** — afloat.

fluctuación *f.* fluctuation; wavering, hesitation.

fluctuar[18] *v.* to fluctuate; to waver; to hesitate.

fluente *adj.* fluent, flowing.

fluidez *f.* fluidity, easy flow, fluency.

flúido *adj.* fluid, flowing, fluent; *m.* fluid.

fluir[32] *v. irr.* to flow.

flujo *m.* flux; flow; flood tide.

flux *f.* flush (in cards); *Am.* suit of clothes; **hacer** — to use up one's funds, lose everything; *Am.* **tener uno** — to be lucky.

foca *f.* seal, sea lion.

foco *m.* focus, center; *Am.* electric-light bulb.

fofo *adj.* spongy, porous; light (in weight); soft.

fogata *f.* fire, blaze, bonfire.

fogón *m.* hearth, fireplace; grill (for cooking); vent of a gun; *Am.* fire, bonfire; **fogonazo** *m.* flash (of gunpowder).

fogoso *adj.* fiery, ardent; lively, spirited.

follaje *m.* foliage.

folletín *m.* small pamphlet; serial story.

folleto *m.* pamphlet.

fomentar *v.* to foment, encourage, promote, foster.

fomento *m.* promotion, encouragement; development; aid.

fonda *f.* inn; restaurant.

fondear *v.* to cast anchor; to sound, make soundings; to search (a ship); to sound out; **-se** *Am.* to save up for the future.

fondero *m.* *Am.* innkeeper.

fondillos *m. pl.* seat of trousers.

fondista *m.* & *f.* innkeeper.

fondo m. bottom; depth; background; back, rear end; nature, heart, inner self; fund; Am. underskirt; -s funds; **a** — thoroughly; **echar a** — to sink.

fonducho m. cheap eating place.

fonética f. phonetics, study of pronunciation.

fonógrafo m.. phonograph.

forajido m. outlaw, fugitive; highwayman, bandit.

foráneo adj. foreign; m. outsider, stranger.

forastero m. stranger; foreigner; outsider; adj. foreign.

forcejear, forcejar v. to struggle; to strive; to oppose, resist.

forja f. forge; forging; blacksmith's shop.

forjador m. forger (of metals); smith, blacksmith; inventor (of lies, stories, tricks, etc.).

forjar v. to forge; to form, shape; to invent, feign, fake.

forma f. form, shape, figure; manner; format (size and shape of a book); host (unleavened bread for communion).

formación f. formation.

formal adj. formal; serious, trustworthy, punctual; reliable.

formalidad f. formality; seriousness, reliability; gravity, dignity; punctuality; red tape.

formalismo m. formality, red tape (excess of formalities); **formalista** adj. fond of excessive formalities, fond of red tape.

formalizar v. to give proper form to; to legalize; to make official; -se to settle down, become serious.

formar v. to form; to shape, mold; -se to get into line; to be molded, educated; to take form.

formidable adj. formidable; fearful.

formón m. wide chisel.

fórmula f. formula.

formular v. to formulate, word.

fornido adj. stout, strong, sturdy.

foro m. stage; back, rear (of a stage); forum, court; bar (profession of law).

forraje m. forage, green grass, fodder, feed.

forrajear v. to forage, gather forage.

forrar v. to line; to cover, put a sheath, case, or covering on; -se Am. to eat well; Am. to supply oneself with provisions; Am. to save money.

forro m. lining; sheathing, casing; covering; book cover.

fortalecer v. irr. to fortify; to strengthen.

fortaleza f. fortress; fortitude; strength, vigor; Am. stench, stink.

fortificación f. fortification; fort.

fortificar v. to fortify.

fortuito adj. fortuitous, accidental, unexpected.

fortuna f. fortune; fate, chance; wealth; **por** — fortunately.

forzar v. irr. to force; to compel; to take (a fort); to rape; — **la entrada en** to break into.

forzozo adj. compulsory; necessary.

fosa f. grave; cavity.

fosco adj. dark; cross, irritable, frowning.

fosfato m. phosphate.

fosforecer, fosforescer v. to glow.

fósforo m. phosphorus; match.

fósil adj. & m. fossil.

foso m. hole, pit; stage pit; ditch.

fotografía f. photograph; photography.

fotografiar v. to photograph.

fotógrafo m. photographer.

fracasado adj. failed; m. failure.

fracasar v. to fail; to come to ruin; to crumble to pieces.

fracaso m. failure, ruin; calamity; crash.

fracción f. fraction.

fractura f. fracture; break, crack.

fracturar v. to fracture, break.

fragancia f. fragrance, scent, perfume.

fragante adj. fragrant; en — in the act.

fragata f. frigate.

frágil adj. fragile, breakable; frail, weak.

fragmento m. fragment.

fragor m. clang, din; crash.

fragoroso adj. deafening, thunderous.

fragoso adj. rugged, craggy, rough, uneven; noisy.

fragua f. forge; blacksmith's shop.

fraguar v. to forge; to scheme, hatch (a plot).

fraile m. friar; priest; **frailuco** m. little old friar.

frambuesa f. raspberry; **frambueso** m. raspberry bush.

francés adj. French; m. Frenchman; French language.

franco adj. frank, open, candid, sincere; free; exempt; m. franc; **francote** adj. very frank, blunt, outspoken.

franela f. flannel.

franja f. fringe, border; stripe; braid.

franquear v. to exempt; to free; to frank (a letter); to dispatch, send; to make grants; — **el paso** to permit the passage (of); -se to unbosom oneself, disclose one's innermost thoughts and feelings.

franqueo m. postage; franking (of a

letter); freeing (*of slaves or prisoners*).

franqueza *f.* frankness; freedom.

franquicia *f.* franchise, grant, privilege; freedom or exemption (*from fees*).

frasco *m.* flask, vial, small bottle.

frase *f.* phrase; sentence.

fraternal *adj.* fraternal, brotherly.

fraternidad *f.* fraternity; brotherhood.

fraude *m.* fraud.

fraudulento *adj.* fraudulent, tricky, deceitful, dishonest.

fray *m.* (*contr. of* fraile, *used before Christian name*) friar.

frazada *f.* blanket.

frecuencia *f.* frequency; **con — frequently.**

frecuentar *v.* to frequent.

frecuente *adj.* frequent.

fregadero *m.* sink.

fregado *m.* scrub, scrubbing; *p.p. of* fregar; *adj. Am.* bothersome, annoying; *Am.* stubborn; *Am.* brazen.

fregar[7] *v. irr.* to scour; to scrub; to rub; to wash (*dishes*); *Am.* to molest, annoy.

fregona *f.* scrub woman; dishwasher, kitchen maid.

freír[15] *v. irr.* to fry; to tease, bother.

frenesí *m.* frenzy, madness.

frenético *adj.* frantic; furious; **in a frenzy.**

freno *m.* bridle; brake; control; bit (*for horses*).

frente *f.* forehead; countenance; *m.* front; **en — de** in front of; **— a** in front of, facing; **hacer —** to face.

fresa *f.* strawberry.

fresca *f.* fresh air; fresh remark.

fresco *adj.* fresh; cool; calm, serene; forward, bold; *m.* coolness; cool air; fresco (*painting*); *Am.* refreshment; **al — in the open air; pintura al — painting in fresco.**

frescor *m.* freshness, coolness.

frescura *f.* freshness; coolness; calm; freedom, ease; boldness, impudence; impudent remark.

fresno *m.* ash, ash tree.

fresquecillo *adj.* nice and cool; *m.* cool air, fresh breeze; **fresquecito, fresquito** *adj.* nice and cool.

frialdad *f.* coldness; coolness, indifference.

fricción *f.* friction, rub, rubbing.

friccionar *v.* to rub; to massage.

friega *f.* rub, rubbing; *Am.* bother, nuisance, irritation; *Am.* flogging, beating.

frigorífico *adj.* freezing; *m.* refrigerator, icebox; *Am.* meat-packing house.

frijol *m.* bean; kidney bean, navy bean.

frío *adj.* cold; frigid; cool, indifferent; *m.* cold; **-s** *Am.* chills and fever; *Am.* malaria.

friolento *adj.* cold-blooded, sensitive to cold; chilly.

friolera *f.* trifle.

fritada *f.* dish of fried food.

frito *p.p. irr. of* freír fried; *m.* fry, dish of fried food.

tritura *f.* fry, dish of fried food; fritter.

frivolidad *f.* frivolity; **frívolo** *adj.* frivolous.

fronda *f.* leaf; fern leaf; foliage.

frondoso *adj.* leafy.

frontera *f.* frontier, border; **fronterizo** *adj.* frontier (*used as an adj.*); opposite, facing.

frontero *adj.* facing, opposite.

frontis *m.* façade, front (*of a building*).

frontispicio *m.* front, façade (*front of a building*); title page.

frontón *m.* main wall of a handball court; handball court.

frotación *f.* friction, rubbing.

frotar *v.* to rub; to scour.

frote *m.* rubbing; friction.

fructificar[6] *v.* to fruit, bear or produce fruit; to yield profit.

fructuoso *adj.* fruitful.

frugal *adj.* frugal, economical, saving, thrifty; **frugalidad** *f.* frugality, thrift.

fruncir[10] *v.* to wrinkle; to gather in pleats; to contract, shrivel; **— las cejas** to frown; to knit the eyebrows; **— los labios** to purse or curl the lips.

fruslería *f.* trifle, trinket.

frustración *f.* frustration; failure.

frustrar *v.* to frustrate, thwart, foil; **-se** to fail, be thwarted.

fruta *f.* fruit (*not a vegetable*); **frutería** *f.* fruit store.

frutero *m.* fruit vendor; fruit dish; *adj.* fruit (*used as adj.*); **buque —** fruit boat; **plato —** fruit dish.

fruto *m.* fruit (*any organic product of the earth*); result; benefit, profit.

¡fuche! *interj. Am.* phew! ugh! pew! phooey!

fuego *m.* fire; passion; skin eruption; *Am.* cold sore; **-s artificiales** fireworks; **hacer —** to fire, shoot; **estar hecho un —** to be very angry; **romper —** to begin to fire, start shooting.

fuelle *m.* bellows; pucker, wrinkle, fold; tattletale, windbag, gossiper.

fuente *f.* fountain; source, origin; spring; platter, serving dish.

fuera *adv.* outside, out; **— de** *prep* outside of; in addition to.

fuereño *m. Am.* outsider, stranger.

fuero *m.* law, statute; power, jurisdiction; code of laws; exemption, privilege.

fuerte *adj.* strong; loud; secure, fortified; grave, serious; excessive; *Am.* stinking; *m.* fort; forte, strong point; forte (*music*); *Am.* alcohol, liquor; *adv.* strongly; excessively; loud; hard.

fuerza *f.* force; power, strength; violence, compulsion; a — de by dint of; a la — (por —, por lá —, de por —, *Am.* de —) by force, forcibly; necessarily; ser — to be necessary.

fuete *m. Am.* whip; **fuetazo** *m. Am.* lash.

fuga *f.* flight, escape; leak, leakage; fugue (*musical composition*).

fugarse[7] *v.* to flee, escape.

fugaz *adj.* fleeing; fleeting, brief, passing.

fugitivo *adj.* fugitive; fleeting, passing; perishable; *m.* fugitive.

fulano *m.* so-and-so (*referring to person*).

fulgor *m.* radiance, brilliance.

fulgurar *v.* to gleam, flash, shine.

fulminar *v.* to thunder, thunder forth; to utter (*threats*).

fullero *m.* cardsharp; crooked gambler; cheat.

fumada *f.* puff, whiff (*of smoke*).

fumadero *m.* smoking room.

fumador *m.* smoker, habitual smoker.

fumar *v.* to smoke (*tobacco*); *Am.* -se a uno to swindle or cheat someone.

fumigar[7] *v.* to fumigate.

función *f.* function; functioning; office, occupation; show, performance; religious festival.

funcionamiento *m.* functioning, action, working, operation.

funcionar *v.* to function; to work, run (*said of machines*).

funcionario *m.* public employee, officer or official.

funda *f.* cover, case; *Am.* skirt; — de almohada pillowcase.

fundación *f.* foundation.

fundador *m.* founder.

fundamental *adj.* fundamental.

fundamento *m.* foundation, groundwork; basis; *Am.* skirt.

fundar *v.* to found, establish; to erect; to base, ground.

fundir *v.* to smelt, fuse, melt; to cast, mold; *Am.* to ruin; -se to fuse, melt together; to unite; *Am.* to be ruined.

fundo *m.* farm, country estate; property, land.

fúnebre *adj.* funeral; funereal, gloomy, dismal.

funeral *adj. & m.* funeral.

funeraria *f.* undertaking establishment, funeral parlor.

funesto *adj.* ill-fated, unlucky; sad, unfortunate.

fungosidad *f.* fungus, fungous growth.

furgón *m.* freight car, boxcar; **furgonada** *f.* carload.

furia *f.* fury, rage; speed.

furibundo *adj.* furious.

furioso *adj.* furious.

furor *m.* fury, rage, anger; frenzy.

furtivo *adj.* furtive, sly, secret.

fuselaje *m.* fuselage (*of an airplane*).

fusible *adj.* fusible; *m.* electric fuse.

fusil *m.* gun, rifle.

fusilar *v.* to shoot, execute.

fustigar[7] *v.* to lash, whip; to censure severely, scold sharply.

fútil *adj.* futile, useless; trivial; **futilidad** *f.* futility, uselessness.

futuro *adj.* future; *m.* fiancé, future husband; future.

G

gabacho *adj.* from or of the Pyrenees; Frenchlike; *Am.* me salió — it turned out wrong; *m.* Frenchman (*used depreciatively*).

gabán *m.* overcoat.

gabeta = **gaveta**.

gabinete *m.* cabinet (*of a government*); studio; study, library room; dressing room; sitting room; private room; dentist's office; laboratory; *Am.* glassed-in **mirador**.

gaceta *f.* gazette, official newspaper; professional periodical; *Am.* any newspaper.

gacetilla *f.* short newspaper article; column of short news items; gossip column; *m. & f.* newsmonger, tattletale; **gacetillero** *m.* newspaper reporter; newsmonger.

gacha *f.* watery mass or mush; *Am.* china or earthenware bowl; -s porridge, mush; caresses; -s de avena oatmeal.

gacho *adj.* drooping; bent downward; turned down; stooping; slouching; with horns curved downward; **sombrero** — slouch hat; **a gachas** on all fours; **con las orejas gachas** with drooping ears; crestfallen, discouraged.

gafas *f. pl.* spectacles; grappling hooks.

gaita *f.* flageolet, a kind of flute; -s good-for-nothing, lazy bum; — **gallega** bagpipe; **sacar la** — to stick out one's neck; **gaitero** *m.* piper, bagpipe player.

gaje m. fee; -s wages, salary; fees.

gala f. elegance; full dress or uniform; ostentation; *Am.* award, prize, tip; -s finery, regalia, best clothes; -s de novia trousseau; **hacer — de** to boast of.

galán m. gallant, lover; leading man (in a play).

galante adj gallant, attentive to ladies; polite.

galanteador m. gallant, lady's man; flatterer.

galantear v. to court, woo; to make love.

galanteo m. wooing, courtship.

galantería f. gallantry, compliment, attention to ladies; courtesy; gracefulness; generosity.

galardón m. recompense, reward.

galeote m. galley slave.

galera f. galley; large wagon; women's jail; printer's galley; *Am.* jail; *Am.* tall hat.

galerada f. galley, galley proof; wagon load, van load.

galería f. gallery; corridor.

galgo m. greyhound; adj. *Am.* gluttonous, always hungry.

galillo m. uvula.

galón m. galloon, braid, trimming; gallon.

galoneado adj. gallooned, trimmed with braid.

galopada f. gallop; **pegar una — to** break into a gallop.

galopar v. to gallop.

galope m. gallop; a (al or de) — at a gallop; speedily.

galopear = **galopar**.

galpón m. *Am.* large open shed.

gallardete m. streamer.

gallardía f. elegance; gracefulness; bravery.

gallardo adj. elegant, graceful; brave.

gallego adj. Galician, from or of Galicia, Spain; m. Galician; *Am* Spaniard (used as a nickname).

galleta f. cracker; hardtack, hard biscuit; hard cookie; blow, slap; small pot; *Am.* bread of coarse meal or bran; *Am.* reproof; *Am.* **colgarle la — a uno** to fire, dismiss someone; *Am.* **tener — to** have strength, muscle.

gallina f. hen; m. & f. chickenhearted person.

gallinero m. chicken coop, house, or yard; flock of chickens; basket for carrying chickens; poultryman; noisy gathering; top gallery of a theatre.

gallo m. cock, rooster; aggressive, bossy

person; cork float; false note (in singing); frog (in one's throat); *Am.* secondhand clothing; *Am.* fire wagon; *Am.* serenade.

gamo m. buck, male deer.

gamuza f. chamois, chamois skin (soft leather made from the skin of sheep, goats, deer, etc.).

gana f. desire, appetite; de buena (mala) — willingly (unwillingly); tener — (or -s) to feel like, want to; no me da la — I don't want to.

ganadero m. cattleman; cattle dealer; adj. cattle, pertaining to cattle.

ganado m. cattle; herd; livestock; — mayor cattle; horses; mules; — menor sheep; — de cerda swine.

ganador m. winner; adj. winning.

ganancia f. profit, gain; *Am.* something to boot, something extra.

ganancioso adj. winning; profitable; m. winner.

ganar v. to win; to profit, gain; to earn; to get ahead of.

gancho m. hook; hooked staff; *Am.* hairpin; *Am.* bait, lure, trick; aguja de — crochet hook; echar a uno el — to hook someone; tener — to be attractive, alluring.

gandul m. bum, loafer.

ganga f. bargain; snap, easy job; kind of prairie hen.

gangoso adj. twangy, nasal (voice).

gangrena f. gangrene.

gangrenar v. to gangrene, cause gangrene; -se to gangrene.

ganoso adj. desirous; *Am.* lively, spirited (horse).

ganso m. goose, gander; lazy, slovenly person; dunce.

ganzúa f. hook; picklock (tool for picking locks); m. & f. burglar.

garabato m. hook; scrawl, scribble; hacer -s to scribble, write poorly.

garaje m. garage.

garantía f. guaranty; security; bail, bond.

garantizar v. to guarantee, vouch for.

garañón m. jackass, male ass; male camel (for breeding); *Am.* stallion.

garapiñar v. to candy (almonds, fruits, etc.).

garbanzo m. chickpea.

garbo m. elegance, graceful air, good carriage.

garboso adj. graceful; elegant; sprightly.

garfio m. hook.

garganta f. throat, neck; gorge, ravine; **gargantilla** f. necklace.

gárgara f. gargling; -s *Am.* gargle, gargling solution; **hacer** -s to gargle.

gargarear v. *Am.* to gargle.

gargarismo m. gargling; gargle, gargling solution.

gargarizar[9] v. to gargle.

garita f. sentry box; watchman's booth; *Am.* vendor's booth.

garito m. gambling house, gambling joint; gambler's winnings.

garra f. claw, paw; hook; *Am.* strength; *Am.* leather or cloth remnant; *Am.* skinny person or animal; *Am.* margin of profit in a business deal; **echar la** — to arrest; to grab; *Am.* **hacer** -s to tear to pieces.

garrafa f. decanter; **garrafón** m. large decanter.

garrapata f. tick (*an insect*).

garrapatear v. to scribble, scrawl, write poorly.

garrocha f. pole; iron-pointed staff; *Am.* goad (*for goading oxen*).

garrote m. club, cudgel, heavy stick; *Am.* brake; **dar** — to strangle; *Am.* to brake, set the brakes; **garrotazo** m. blow with a club; huge stick.

garrotero m. *Am.* brakeman; *Am.* beater (*one who beats with a club*); adj. *Am.* stingy.

garrucha f. pulley.

garúa f. *Am.* drizzle.

garza f. heron.

garzo adj. blue, bluish; blue-eyed.

gas m. gas, vapor; *Am.* gasoline.

gasa f. gauze.

gaseosa f. soda water; soda pop.

gaseoso adj. gaseous.

gasolina f. gasoline.

gastador adj. lavish, extravagant, wasteful; m. spendthrift, lavish spender.

gastar v. to spend; to wear; to use; to waste; -se to wear out; to get old.

gasto m. expense, expenditure; wear.

gatas : a — on all fours; **andar a** — to creep, crawl; **salir a** — to crawl out of a difficulty.

gateado adj. catlike; veined, streaked; m. *Am.* light-colored horse with black streaks.

gatear v. to creep, crawl; to walk on all fours; to claw, scratch; to steal.

gatillo m. kitten; trigger; forceps (*for extracting teeth*); petty thief.

gato m. cat; moneybag; jack (*for lifting weights*); sneak thief; sly fellow; *Am.* trigger; *Am.* outdoor market; *Am.* hot-water bottle; *Am.* a gaucho song and tap dance (*by extension*, the dancer); *Am.* blunder.

gatuperio m. fraud, intrigue.

gauchada f. *Am.* gaucho deed or exploit.

gauchaje m. *Am.* band of Gauchos, Gaucho folk.

gauchesco adj. *Am.* relating to Gauchos.

gaucho m. *Am.* Gaucho, Argentine and Uruguayan cowboy; *Am.* good horseman; adj. *Am.* relating to Gauchos, Gaucho-like; *Am.* sly, crafty

gaveta f. drawer.

gavilla f. sheaf; gang, band (*of rogues, thieves, etc.*).

gaviota f. sea gull.

gaza f. loop; *Am.* noose of a lasso.

gazmoñería f. prudery, affected modesty; **gazmoño** adj. prudish, affected, coy.

gaznate m. windpipe; a kind of fritter; *Am.* a sweetmeat made of pineapple or coconut.

gelatina f. gelatin; jelly.

gema f. gem, jewel; bud.

gemelo m. twin; -s twins; binoculars, opera glasses, field glasses; cuff links.

gemido m. moan; wail, cry.

gemir[5] v. irr. to moan; to wail, cry.

gendarme m. *Am.* policeman.

generación f. generation.

general adj. & m. general; **por lo** — generally.

generalidad f. generality; majority.

generalizar[9] v. to generalize; -se to spread, become general.

género m. kind, sort, class, gender; goods, material, cloth; — **humano** human race.

generosidad f. generosity.

generoso adj. generous; best (*wine*).

genial adj. genial, jovial, pleasant.

genio m. genius; temperament, disposition; spirit.

gente f. people; crowd; race, nation; clan; *Am.* — **bien** upper-class or important person; *Am.* **ser** — to be a somebody; to be cultured; to be socially important.

gentil adj. graceful; genteel; courteous; gentile; m. pagan; gentile.

gentileza f. grace, courtesy; nobility; favor.

gentío m. crowd, throng.

gentuza f. rabble.

genuino adj. genuine.

geografía f. geography; **geográfico** adj. geographical.

geología f. geology; **geológico** adj. geological.

geometría f. geometry; **geométrico** adj. geometric.

geranio m. geranium.

gerencia f. management, administration.

gerente *m.* manager.

germen *m.* germ; origin, source.

germinar *v.* to germinate.

gerundio *m.* gerund; present participle.

gesticular *v.* to gesticulate.

gestión *f.* action, step, maneuver; intervention; -es negotiations.

gestionar *v.* to manage; to take steps; to negotiate or carry out (*a deal, transaction, etc.*).

gesto *m.* face, expression; grimace; gesture; estar de buen (*or* mal) — to be in a good (*or* bad) humor; hacer -s a to make faces at.

giba *f.* hump, hunch.

gigante *adj.* gigantic; *m.* giant.

gigantesco *adj.* gigantic.

gimnasia *f.* gymnastics; gimnasio *m.* gymnasium; German institute (*for secondary instruction*).

gimotear *v.* to whimper, whine.

gimoteo *m.* whimper, whining.

ginebra *f.* gin (*liquor*).

gira *f.* excursion, tour; outing, picnic.

girador *m.* drawer (*of a check or draft*).

girar *v.* to revolve, rotate, whirl; to send, issue, or draw (*checks, drafts, etc.*); to manage (*a business*).

girasol *m.* sunflower.

giratorio *adj.* rotary, revolving.

giro *m.* rotation; trend, bend, direction, turn; turn of phrase; line of business; draft; — postal money order; *adj.* yellowish (*rooster*); *Am.* black and white (*rooster*); *Am.* cocky.

gitano *adj.* gypsy; gypsylike; sly, clever, *m.* gypsy.

gitomate *Am.* = jitomate.

glacial *adj.* glacial, icy, very cold.

glaciar *m.* glacier.

glándula *f.* gland.

glasear *v.* to glaze (*paper, fruits, etc.*), make glossy.

globo *m.* globe, sphere; world; balloon.

gloria *f.* glory; gloria (*song of praise to God*).

gloriarse[17] *v.* to glory (in), delight (in), be proud (of); to boast (of).

glorieta *f.* arbor, bower; secluded nook in a park (*with benches*).

glorificar[6] *v.* to glorify; -se to glory (in), take great pride (in).

glorioso *adj.* glorious.

glosar *v.* to gloss, comment upon, explain (*a text*).

glosario *m.* glossary.

glotón *adj.* gluttonous; *m.* glutton.

glotonería *f.* gluttony.

gobernador *adj.* governing; *m.* governor, ruler.

gobernante *adj.* governing, ruling; *m.* governor, ruler.

gobernar[1] *v. irr.* to govern, rule; to lead, direct; to steer (*a boat*).

gobierno *m.* government; management; control; helm, rudder.

goce *m.* enjoyment; joy.

goleta *f.* schooner, sailing vessel.

golfo *m.* gulf; open sea; faro (*gambling game*); vagabond, bum, ragamuffin.

golondrina *f.* swallow; swallow fish.

golosina *f.* sweet, dainty, tidbit; trifle; appetite, desire.

goloso *adj.* sweet-toothed, fond of sweets; gluttonous.

golpazo *m.* bang, whack, heavy blow, hard knock.

golpe *m.* blow, hit, stroke; knock; beat; *Am.* facing (*of a garment*); *Am.* sledge hammer; — de fortuna stroke of good luck; — de gente crowd, throng; — de gracia death blow; finishing stroke; de — suddenly; de un — all at once; pestillo de — spring latch; *Am.* al — instantly, at once; *Am.* al — de vista at one glance.

golpear *v.* to strike, hit; to knock; to beat; *Am.* to knock at a door.

golpetear *v.* to tap, knock or pound continuously; to flap; to rattle.

golpeteo *m.* tapping, pounding, knocking; flapping; rattling.

gollería *f.* dainty, delicacy; superfluous thing.

goma *f.* gum; rubber; elastic; eraser; tire; — de repuesto spare tire; *Am.* estar de — to have a hang-over (*after excessive drinking*).

gomero *adj.* rubber, pertaining to rubber; *m. Am.* gum or rubber tree; *Am.* rubber producer; *Am.* rubber-plantation worker; *Am.* glue container or bottle.

gomífero *adj.* rubber-bearing, rubber-producing.

gomoso *adj.* gummy, sticky; *m.* dandy.

gordiflón *adj.* fat; chubby.

gordo *adj.* fat; plump; *m.* suet, fat; gorda *f. Am.* thick tortilla or cornmeal cake; se armó la gorda all hell broke loose; there was a big rumpus.

gordura *f.* fatness; stoutness; fat.

gorgojo *m.* weevil; puny person; *Am.* wood borer, wood louse; gorgojoso *adj.* infested with weevils.

gorila *m.* gorilla.

gorjeador *m.* warbler; *adj.* warbling; pájaro — warbler.

gorjear *v.* to warble; to chirp.

gorjeo *m.* warble; warbling.

gorra *f.* cap; bonnet; **de** — at another's expense; **vivir de** — to sponge, live at another's expense.

gorrión *m.* sparrow.

gorro *m.* cap; bonnet.

gorrón *m.* sponge, parasite; bum; rake (*dissolute fellow*).

gota *f.* drop; gout; **sudar la** — **gorda** to sweat profusely, toil, work hard.

gotear *v.* to drip; to leak; to dribble, trickle; to sprinkle, begin to rain; **-se** to leak.

goteo *m.* trickle, drip.

gotera *f.* leak, hole (*in the roof*); eaves trough; **-s** *Am.* surroundings, outskirts.

gotero *m.* *Am.* dropper (*for counting drops*).

gótico *adj.* Gothic; *m.* Goth; Gothic language.

gozar[9] *v.* to enjoy; to possess, have; **-se** to rejoice.

gozne *m.* hinge.

gozo *m.* pleasure, joy.

gozoso *adj.* joyful, glad, merry.

gozque, gozquejo, gozquecillo *m.* a small dog.

grabado *adj.* engraved; *m.* engraving; woodcut, print; — **al agua fuerte** etching.

grabar *v.* to engrave; to carve; to fix, impress; — **al agua fuerte** to etch.

gracejada *f.* *Am.* clownish act or expression.

gracejo *m.* grace; cuteness; humor, wit.

gracia *f.* grace; gracious act; favor; pardon; joke, witty remark; **caer en** — to please; **hacer** — to amuse, make (*someone*) laugh; **¡-s!** thanks!; **dar -s** to thank.

gracioso *adj.* graceful, attractive; witty, amusing; gracious; *m.* comedian, clown.

grada *f.* step of a staircase; harrow; **-s** steps; seats of an amphitheatre; bleachers.

gradación *f.* gradation.

gradería *f.* series of steps; rows of seats (*in an amphitheater or stadium*); — **cubierta** grandstand; **-s** bleachers.

grado *m.* degree; step; **de (buen)** — willingly, with pleasure; **de mal** — unwillingly; **de** — **en** — by degrees, gradually.

graduación *f.* graduation; military rank.

gradual *adj.* gradual; *m.* response sung at mass.

graduar[18] *v.* to graduate, give a diploma, rank or degree to; to gauge; to classify;

grade; **-se** to graduate, take a degree.

gráfico *adj.* graphic; vivid, lifelike; **gráfica** *f.* graph, diagram, chart.

grafito *m.* graphite.

grajo *m.* jay.

grama *f.* grama grass.

gramática *f.* grammar; **gramatical** *adj.* grammatical; **gramático** *adj.* grammatical; *m.* grammarian.

gramo *m.* gram.

gran *contr.* *of* **grande.**

grana *f.* cochineal, kermes (*insects used for producing a red dye*); scarlet color; scarlet cloth; any small seed.

granada *f.* pomegranate; grenade, shell, small bomb; — **de mano** hand grenade.

granado *m.* pomegranate tree; *adj.* notable; illustrious; select.

grande *adj.* large, big; great; grand; *Am.* **mamá (papá)** — grandmother (grandfather); *m.* grandee (*Spanish or Portuguese nobleman*); **en** — on a large scale.

grandeza *f.* greatness; grandeur, splendor; bigness; size; grandeeship; body of grandees.

grandiosidad *f.* grandeur, grandness; greatness; **grandioso** *adj.* grandiose, great, grand, magnificent.

granero *m.* granary; grain bin; country or region rich in grain.

granito *m.* granite; small grain; small pimple.

granizada *f.* hailstorm; shower, volley.

granizar[9] *v.* to hail.

granizo *m.* hail; hailstorm; web or film in the eye; *adj.* *Am.* spotted (*horse*).

granja *f.* grange, farm; country house.

granjear *v.* to earn, gain; to acquire, obtain; *Am.* to steal; **-se** to win for oneself (*favor, goodwill, esteem, etc.*).

granjería *f.* farming; business profit.

granjero *m.* farmer.

grano *m.* grain; seed; pimple; grain (*unit of measure*); **ir al** — to come to the point.

granuja *m.* ragamuffin, urchin; scamp.

granular *v.* to granulate; **-se** to become granulated; to break out with pimples.

grapa *f.* clamp.

grasa *f.* grease; fat; tallow; *Am.* shoe polish; *Am.* **dar** — to polish (*shoes*).

grasiento *adj.* greasy, oily.

grasoso *adj.* greasy, oily.

gratificación *f.* gratuity, bonus, tip; recompense, reward.

gratis *adv.* gratis, for nothing, free of charge.

gratitud *f.* gratitude.

grato adj. pleasing, pleasant; gratuitous; su grata your favor, your letter.

gratuito adj. gratuitous, free, free of charge.

grava f. gravel.

gravamen m. burden; mortgage.

grave adj. grave; serious; weighty, heavy; grievous; deep, low (in pitch).

gravedad f. gravity; seriousness; depth (of a sound).

gravoso adj. burdensome; serle a uno — to be burdensome; to weigh on one's conscience.

graznar v. to caw, croak, squawk, cackle, quack.

graznido m. caw, croak, squawk, cackle, quack.

greda f. clay, chalk; chalk cleaner.

gremio m. guild, society, brotherhood; trade union; fold (referring to the Church).

greña f. shock of hair, tangled mop of hair (usually greñas); greñudo adj. shaggy, with long, unkempt hair.

grey f. flock; congregation (of a church).

griego adj. Greek, Grecian; m. Greek.

grieta f. crevice; crack; fissure.

grifo m. faucet; Am. cheap tavern (where chicha is sold); Am. gas station; Am. colored person; Am. drug addict; Am. drunkard; adj. curly, kinky, woolly (hair); Am. vain, conceited; letra grifa script; ponerse — to bristle, stand on end (said of hair).

grillo m. cricket; sprout, shoot; -s fetters; obstacle, hindrance.

grima f. uneasiness; displeasure, disgust; Am. sadness, compassion, pity; Am. bit, small particle; dar — to disgust; to make uneasy; Am. to make sad, inspire pity.

gringo adj. Am. foreign (not Spanish); m. Am. foreigner (not Spanish); Am. Yankee or English-speaking person.

gripe f. grippe, flu, influenza.

gris adj. grey; grisáceo adj. greyish.

grita f. shouting, hooting; clamor, uproar.

gritar v. to shout, cry.

gritería f. shouting, clamor, uproar.

grito m. shout, cry; poner el — en el cielo to complain loudly, "hit the ceiling".

grosella f. currant; — blanca gooseberry; grosellero m. currant bush.

grosería f. rudeness; coarseness; crudeness; insult.

grosero adj. rough, coarse; rude, impolite.

grosor m. thickness.

grotesco adj. grotesque, fantastic; ab-

surd.

grúa f. crane, derrick.

gruesa f. gross, twelve dozen.

grueso adj. fat, stout; thick; coarse; bulky, big, heavy; gross, dense; m. thickness; bulk; density; main part; en — in gross, in bulk, by wholesale.

grulla f. crane (bird).

gruñido m. growl, grumble; grunt.

gruñir v. ir. to grunt; to growl; to snarl; to grumble.

gruñón adj. growling; grunting; grumbly; m. growler; grumbler.

grupa f. rump; volver -s to turn around (usually on horseback).

grupo m. group; set.

gruta f. grotto, cavern.

guacal m. Am. crate (for transporting fruit, vegetables, etc.). Also huacal.

guacamayo m. Am. macaw (large parrot); Am. flashily dressed person.

guacho m. birdling, chick; young animal; Am. orphan; Am. foundling, abandoned child; adj. Am. odd, not paired; Am. forlorn, alone, abandoned.

guadal m. Am. small dune, sand hill; Am. quagmire, bog, swamp; Am. growth of bamboo grass.

guadaña f. scythe.

guagua f. Am. bus; trifle, insignificant thing; m. & f. Am. baby; de — for nothing, gratis, free.

guaje m. Am. a species of gourd; Am. vessel or bowl made of a gourd; Am. simpleton, fool; Am. trifle, trinket, piece of junk; adj. Am. foolish; Am. hacerse uno — to play the fool; Am. hacer a uno — to fool, deceive someone.

guajiro m. Indian of the Guajira peninsula (in Venezuela and Colombia); Am. rustic, peasant.

guajolote m. Am. turkey; Am. fool.

guanaco m. Am. guanaco (a kind of llama); Am. tall, lanky, gawky person; Am. fool, simpleton.

guanajo m. Am. turkey; Am. fool, dunce.

guano m. Am. palm tree; Am. palm leaves (used for thatching); Am. guano, bird dung, fertilizer.

guantada f. wallop, blow, slap.

guante m. glove; Am. whip, scourge; echar el — a uno to seize or grab a person; guantelete m. gauntlet.

guapo adj. handsome, good-looking; ostentatious, showy; daring, brave; Am. harsh, severe; Am. angry; m. brawler, quarreler, bully.

guarache m. Am. Mexican leather sandal; Am. tire patch. Also huarache.

guaraní adj. pertaining to the Guarani Indians of Paraguay; m. & f. Guarani Indian.

guarapo m. Am. juice of the sugar cane; Am. sugar-cane liquor; Am. low grade brandy.

guarda m. & f. guard; keeper; Am. ticket collector on a streetcar; f. custody, care, keeping; observance of a law; -s outside ribs of a fan; flyleaves.

guardabarros, guardafango m. fender.

guardabosques m. forest ranger, forester, forest keeper.

guardabrisa f. windshield.

guardafrenos m. brakeman.

guardagujas m. switchman.

guardapapeles m. file, filing cabinet or box.

guardapelo m. locket.

guardar v. to guard, watch over; to keep; to store; to observe (laws, customs); -se de to guard against, keep from, avoid.

guardarropa m. wardrobe; cloakroom; keeper of a cloakroom.

guardia f. guard, body of guards; defense, protection; m. guard, guardsman.

guardiamarina f. midshipman.

guardián m. guardian, keeper; guardian, superior of a Franciscan monastery.

guarecer[13] v. irr. to protect, shelter; -se to take shelter.

guarida f. den, cave, lair.

guarismo m. number.

guarnecer[13] v. irr. to garnish, decorate; to adorn; to trim; to harness; to garrison; to set (jewels).

guarnición f. adornment; trimming; setting of a jewel; guard of a sword; garrison; -es trappings, harness.

guasca f. Am. leather thong; Am. rope, cord; Am. whip; Am. dar — to whip, beat, thrash.

guaso m. Am. stag, male deer; Am. peasant; Am. half-breed; Am. lasso; adj. rustic, peasantlike.

guasón adj. funny, comical; m. joker, jester.

guata f. Am. padding; Am. fib; Am. a species of potato; Am. paunch, belly; Am. echar — to get fat.

guatemalteco m. & adj. Guatemalan.

guayaba f. guava (pear-shaped tropical fruit); **guayabo** m. guava tree; Am. lie, fraud, trick.

gubernativo adj. governmental, administrative.

guedeja f. forelock; lock of hair; lion's mane.

güero adj. Am. blond; m. Am. cassava liquor. See huero.

guerra f. war; — a muerte war to the finish; dar — to bother, trouble.

guerrear v. to war; Am. to do mischief or to bother (said of children).

guerrero adj. warlike, martial; m. warrior, soldier.

guerrilla f. small war; skirmish; body of soldiers; band of fighters.

guerrillero m. guerrilla fighter.

guía m. & f. guide, leader; f. guidebook, directory; signpost; shoot, sprout; Am. garland of flowers.

guiar[17] v. to guide; to drive (a car).

guija f. pebble; **guijarro** m. pebble.

guijo m. gravel.

guinda f. a kind of cherry.

guiñada f. wink.

guiñapo m. tag, tatter, rag; ragamuffin, ragged person.

guiñar v. to wink.

guiño m. wink.

guión m. hyphen; repeat sign (in music); cross (carried before a prelate in a procession); guide, leader (among birds and animals); leader in a dance.

guirnalda f. garland, wreath.

guisa f. way, manner; a — de like, in the manner of.

guisado m. stew.

guisante m. pea; — de olor sweet pea.

guisar v. to cook; to prepare, arrange.

guiso m. dish, dish of food.

guitarra f. guitar.

gula f. gluttony.

gusano m. worm; caterpillar; — de la conciencia remorse; — de luz glowworm; Am. matar el — to satisfy a need or desire (particularly hunger or thirst).

gustar v. to taste; to experience; to please, be pleasing; -le a uno una cosa to like something — de to have a liking for, be fond of.

gusto m. taste; flavor; pleasure; whim, fancy; dar — to please; estar a — to be comfortable, contented; tener — en to be glad to; tomar el — a una cosa to become fond of something.

gustoso adj. tasty; pleasant; glad, merry; willing; adv. willingly.

H

haba f. large bean; Lima bean.

haber[30] v. irr. to have (auxiliary verb); habérselas con to have it out with; ha de llegar mañana he is to arrive tomorrow; ha de ser verdad it must

108

be true; **hay** (**había**, **hubo**, *etc.*) there is, there are (there was, there were, *etc.*); **hay que** (+ *inf.*) it is necessary; **no hay de qué** you are welcome; **¿qué hay?** what's the matter?

haber *m.* credit, credit side (*in book-keeping*); **―es** property, goods, cash, assets.

habichuela *f.* bean; ― **verde** string bean.

hábil *adj.* skilful, capable, able.

habilidad *f.* ability, skill.

habilitar *v.* to enable; to equip; to qualify.

habitación *f.* apartment; room; lodging.

habitante *m.* inhabitant; resident.

habitar *v.* to inhabit; to live, reside.

hábito *m.* habit; custom.

habitual *adj.* habitual, customary.

habituar[18] *v.* to accustom; **-se** to get used, accustomed.

habla *f.* speech; language, dialect; **al ―** within speaking distance; in communication (with).

hablador *m.* talker; gossip; *adj.* talkative.

habladuría *f.* gossip, rumor; empty talk; impertinent remark.

hablar *v.* to speak; to talk; ― **alto** (*or* **en voz alta**) to speak loud; ― **bajo** (**quedo** *or* **en voz baja**) to speak softly; ― **por los codos** to chatter constantly.

hablilla *f.* gossip, rumor, malicious tale.

hacedero *adj.* feasible.

hacedor *m.* maker; **el Supremo Hacedor** the Maker.

hacendado *m.* landholder; *Am.* owner of a farm, plantation, or ranch.

hacendoso *adj.* industrious, diligent.

hacer[31] *v. irr.* to do; to make; to form; to accustom; to cause, order (*followed by inf.*); ― **caso** to mind, pay attention; ― **frío** (**calor**) to be cold (warm); ― **la maleta** to pack one's suitcase; ― **un papel** to play a part; *Am.* ― **aprecio** to pay attention; *Am.* ― **caras** (*or* **caritas**) to flirt; **no le hace** it makes no difference; **-se** to become, grow, get to be; **-se a** to get used to; **-se de rogar** to want to be coaxed.

hacia *prep.* toward; about; ― **adelante** forward; ― **atrás** backward.

hacienda *f.* estate; property; finance; large farm; *Am.* cattle, livestock.

hacina *f.* shock (*of grain*), stack, pile.

hacinar *v.* to shock (*grain*); to stack, pile up; to accumulate.

hacha *f.* ax; hatchet; torch.

hachero *m.* axman, woodcutter.

hada *f.* fairy.

hado *m.* fate, fortune, destiny.

halagar[7] *v.* to coax; to flatter; to allure, attract.

halago *m.* flattery; caress; allurement.

halagüeño *adj.* alluring, attractive; flattering; promising.

halar = **jalar**.

halcón *m.* falcon.

hálito *m.* breath; vapor.

hallar *v.* to find; to discover, find out; **-se** to be; to fare, get along.

hallazgo *m.* find; discovery; reward (*for finding something*).

hamaca *f.* hammock.

hambre *f.* hunger; famine; appetite; **tener ―** to be hungry; **hambruna** *f. Am.* great hunger, starvation.

hambrear *v.* to starve; to be hungry.

hambriento *adj.* hungry; greedy; *Am.* stingy.

hampa *f.* underworld.

hangar *m.* hangar.

haragán *adj.* lazy, indolent; *m.* loafer, idler.

haraganear *v.* to lounge, loaf, be lazy.

haraganería *f.* laziness.

harapiento *adj.* tattered, ragged.

harapo *m.* rag, tatter; **andar hecho un ―** to be in tatters.

haraposo *adj.* tattered, ragged.

harina *f.* flour; **eso es ― de otro costal** that is something entirely different; **harinoso** *adj.* floury; flour-like.

harmonía *f.* harmony.

hartar *v.* to fill up, gorge; to sate, satiate; **-se** to have one's fill; to over-eat, eat too much.

harto *adj.* full; sated, satiated; fed up; too much; *adv.* too much; *Am.* much, very much.

hasta *prep.* till, until; up to; ― **luego** good-bye, see you later; *conj.* even; ― **que** until.

hastiar[17] *v.* to surfeit; to cloy, to disgust.

hastío *m.* surfeit, excess; boredom; loathing, disgust.

hato *m.* herd; flock; sheepfold; shepherd's hut; gang, crowd; pile; *Am.* cattle ranch.

haya *f.* beech; **hayuco** *m.* beechnut.

haz *f.* face; surface; *m.* fagot, bundle, bunch.

hazaña *f.* deed, exploit, feat.

he (*used with* **aquí** *or* **allí**) behold, here is, here you have; **heme aquí** here I am; **helo aquí** here it is.

hebilla *f.* buckle.

hebra *f.* thread; fiber; fine string; *Am.* de una — all at once, at one stroke, *Am.* ni — absolutely nothing; **hebroso** *adj.* fibrous, stringy.

hecatombe *m.* massacre, great slaughter; **hecatomb** (*sacrifice of 100 oxen*).

hechicera *f.* witch, enchantress; hag.

hechicería *f.* witchcraft; magic; charm; enchantment.

hechicero *adj.* bewitching, charming; *m.* magician; charmer; sorcerer.

hechizar[9] *v.* to bewitch; to charm.

hechizo *m.* charm; enchantment.

hecho *m.* fact; act, deed; de — in fact; *p.p. of* **hacer** done, made.

hechura *f.* make; shape, cut; workmanship.

heder[1] *v. irr.* to stink; to reek.

hediondez *f.* stink, stench.

hediondo *adj.* foul-smelling, stinking; filthy; *m. Am.* skunk.

hedor *m.* stink, stench.

helada *f.* frost.

helado *adj.* frozen; freezing; frosty; icy; *m.* ice cream; ice, sherbet; **heladería** *f. Am.* ice-cream parlor.

heladora *f.* freezer.

helar[1] *v. irr.* to freeze.

helecho *m.* fern.

hélice *f.* screw propeller; helix, spiral.

hembra *f.* female; staple; nut (*of a screw*); **macho y** — hook and eye.

hemisferio *m.* hemisphere.

henchir[5] *v. irr.* to swell, stuff, fill.

hendedura, hendidura *f.* crack, crevice, fissure.

hender[1] *v. irr.* to split, crack, cleave.

henequén *m. Am.* sisal, sisal hemp.

heno *m.* hay; **henil** *m.* hayloft.

heraldo *m.* herald.

herbazal *m.* field of grass.

herboso *adj.* grassy; weedy.

heredad *f.* parcel of land; rural property; estate.

heredar *v.* to inherit; to bequeath, leave in a will.

heredero *m.* heir; successor; **heredera** *f.* heiress.

hereditario *adj.* hereditary.

hereje *m.* heretic; **cara de** — hideous face.

herejía *f.* heresy; offensive remark.

herencia *f.* inheritance; heritage; heredity.

herida *f.* wound; injury.

herido *adj.* wounded; *m.* wounded man; *Am.* small drainage channel.

herir[3] *v. irr.* to wound; to hurt; to strike; to offend.

hermana *f.* sister.

hermanastro *m.* stepbrother, half brother; **hermanastra** *f.* stepsister, half sister.

hermandad *f.* brotherhood, fraternity.

hermano *m.* brother.

hermético *adj.* hermetic; airtight; tight-lipped; close-mouthed; **hermetismo** *m.* complete silence.

hermosear *v.* to beautify, adorn.

hermoso *adj.* beautiful, handsome.

hermosura *f.* beauty.

héroe *m.* hero; **heroína** *f.* heroine.

heroico *adj.* heroic.

heroísmo *m.* heroism.

herradura *f.* horseshoe.

herraje *m.* ironwork; iron trimmings; horseshoes and nails; *Am.* silver saddle trimmings; *Am.* horseshoe.

herramienta *f.* set of tools; iron tool.

herrar[1] *v. irr.* to shoe (*a horse*); to brand; to trim with iron.

herrería *f.* blacksmith's shop or trade; forge; ironworks.

herrero *m.* blacksmith.

hervidero *m.* bubbling sound (*of boiling water*); bubbling spring; swarm, crowd; **un** — **de gente** a swarm of people.

hervir[3] *v. irr.* to boil; — **de gente** to swarm with people.

hervor *m.* boiling; boiling point; **soltar el** — to come to a boil.

hez *f.* scum; **la** — **del pueblo** the scum of society; **heces** dregs, sediment.

hidalgo *m.* hidalgo (*Spanish nobleman*); *adj.* noble, courteous.

hidalguía *f.* nobility; generosity; courtesy.

hidráulico *adj.* hydraulic; **fuerza hidráulica** water power; **ingeniero** — hydraulic engineer.

hidroavión *m.* hydroplane, seaplane.

hidrógeno *m.* hydrogen.

hidroplano *m.* hydroplane.

hiedra *f.* ivy.

hiel *f.* gall, bile; bitterness.

hielo *m.* ice; frost.

hierba *f.* grass; herb; weed; *Am.* mate (*Paraguayan tea*); *Am.* marihuana (*a narcotic*); *Am.* **ciertas** -**s** so-and-so (*person not named*).

hierbabuena *f.* mint. *Also* **yerbabuena**.

hierro *m.* iron; brand; iron tool, instrument, or weapon; -**s** irons, chains, handcuffs.

hígado *m.* liver; courage, valor; **malos** -**s** ill will.

higiene *f.* hygiene; **higiénico** *adj.* hygienic, sanitary.

higo *m.* fig; **higuera** *f.* fig tree; hi-

guerilla f. Am. castor-oil plant.

hija f. daughter; native daughter.

hijo m. son; native son; offspring; fruit, result.

hilachas f. pl. lint; **mostrar uno la hilacha** to show one's worst side or nature; **hilachos** m. pl. Am. rags, tatters.

hilado m. yarn; p.p. of **hilar.**

hilandera f. spinner.

hilandería f. spinning mill; art of spinning; spinning.

hilandero m. spinner; spinning room.

hilar v. to spin, make into thread; — **muy delgado** to be very subtle.

hilas f. pl. lint, fine ravelings (for dressing wounds).

hilaza f. coarse thread; yarn.

hilera f. file, row, line; — **de perlas** strand or string of pearls.

hilo m. thread; fine yarn; string; filament; thin wire; linen; **a — without** interruption; **al — along the thread;** Am. very well, all right; **de — straight,** without stopping; Am. **de un — constantly,** without stopping; **tener el alma en un — to be frightened to** death; to be in great anxiety or suspense.

hilván m. basting stitch; basting; Am. hem.

hilvanar v. to baste; to put together, connect; to do hastily; Am. to hem.

himno m. hymn.

hincapié : hacer — ` to emphasize, stress; to insist (upon).

hincar⁴ v. to drive, thrust (into); **-se** (or **-se de rodillas**) to kneel down.

hinchado adj. & p.p. swollen; inflated; presumptuous.

hinchar v. to swell; **-se** to swell; to swell up, puff up.

hinchazón f. swelling; inflation; conceit; bombast, inflated style.

hinojos : de — on one's knees.

hipo m. hiccough; sob; longing; grudge, ill will.

hipocresía f. hypocrisy.

hipócrita adj. hypocritical, insincere; m. & f. hypocrite.

hipódromo m. race track.

hipoteca f. mortgage.

hipotecar⁶ v. to mortgage.

hipótesis f. hypothesis, theory.

hirviente adj. boiling.

hispano adj. Hispanic, Spanish; m. Spaniard.

hispanoamericano adj. Spanish-American.

histérico adj. hysterical.

historia f. history; story; tale, fable; **dejarse de -s** to stop fooling and come to the point; **historieta** f. story, anecdote.

historiador m. historian.

historial m. record, data (concerning a person or firm); adj. historic.

histórico adj. historic, historical.

hocico m. snout; **caer de -s** to fall on one's face; **meter el — en todo** to meddle, stick one's nose in everything.

hogaño adv. nowadays.

hogar m. hearth, fireplace; home.

hogareño adj. home-loving, domestic; homelike.

hoguera f. bonfire.

hoja f. leaf; petal; sheet of paper or metal; blade; — **de lata** tin plate.

hojalata f. tin plate.

hojaldre m. & f. puff pastry.

hojarasca f. fallen leaves; dry foliage; superfluous ornament; trash; useless words.

hojear v. to leaf, turn the pages of; to browse.

hojuela f. leaflet, small leaf; thin leaf (of metal); flake; thin pancake; — **de estaño** tin foil.

¡hola! interj. hello!; ho!; ah!

holandés adj. Dutch; m. Dutchman; Dutch language.

holgado adj. loose, wide; roomy, spacious; comfortable; free, at leisure; p.p. of **holgar.**

holgar²ᐟ¹ v. irr. to rest; to loaf; **-se** to be glad; to relax, have a good time; **huelga decir** needless to say.

holgazán m. idler, loafer; adj. lazy, idle.

holgazanear v. to loiter, lounge, idle, bum around.

holgazanería f. idleness, laziness.

holgorio m. spree.

holgura f. ease; rest, comfort; roominess, plenty of room.

holocausto m. holocaust, burnt offering, sacrifice.

hollar v. to tread, trample upon.

hollejo m. skin, peel; husk.

hollín m. soot.

hombrada f. manly act; show of bravery.

hombre m. man; **hombría** f. manliness, manly strength; — **de bien** honesty.

hombro m. shoulder; **arrimar** (or **meter**) **el — to help.**

hombruno adj. mannish, masculine.

homenaje m. homage, honor.

homicida m. murderer; f. murderess; adj. homicidal, murderous.

homicidio m. homicide, murder.

homogéneo adj. homogeneous, of the

same kind or nature.

honda *f.* sling, slingshot.

hondo *adj.* deep; low; *m.* bottom, depth.

hondonada *f.* hollow, dip, gully, ravine.

hondura *f.* depth; **meterse en —s** to go beyond one's depth; to get into trouble.

honestidad *f.* chastity, modesty, decency; decorum, propriety.

honesto *adj.* chaste, modest, decent; just; honest.

hongo *m.* mushroom; fungus; derby hat.

honor *m.* honor; glory; dignity.

honorario *m.* fee (*for professional services*); *adj.* honorary.

honorífico *adj.* honorary; **mención honorífica** honorable mention.

honra *f.* honor; reputation; **—s** obsequies, funeral rites.

honradez *f.* honesty, honor, integrity.

honrado *adj.* honest, honorable; honored.

honrar *v.* to honor; **—se** to be honored; to consider it an honor.

honroso *adj.* honorable; honoring.

hora *f.* hour; time; **—s** canonical hours, office (*required daily prayers for priests and nuns*); **es — de** it is time to; **no ver la — de** (+ *inf.*) to be anxious to; **¿qué — es?** what time is it?

horadar *v.* to pierce, bore, perforate.

horario *m.* schedule, timetable; hour hand.

horca *f.* gallows; pitchfork; forked prop; *Am.* birthday present; **— de ajos** string of garlic.

horcajadas: a — astride (*with one leg on each side*); **ponerse a —** to straddle.

horcón *m.* forked pole, forked prop; *Am.* post, roof support; *Am.* roof.

horda *f.* horde.

horizontal *adj.* horizontal.

horizonte *m.* horizon.

horma *f.* form, mold; block (*for shaping a hat*); shoe last; shoe tree.

hormiga *f.* ant.

hormigón *m.* concrete.

hormiguear *v.* to swarm; to be crawling with ants; **me hormiguea el cuerpo** I itch all over.

hormigueo *m.* itching, creeping sensation; tingle, tingling sensation.

hormiguero *m.* ant hill; ant nest; swarm; **oso —** anteater.

hornada *f.* batch of bread, baking.

hornear *v.* to bake (*in an oven*).

hornilla *f.* burner; grate (*of a stove*).

horno *m.* furnace; oven; kiln (*for baking bricks*).

horquilla *f.* hairpin; forked pole;

small pitchfork.

horrendo *adj.* horrible, hideous.

horrible *adj.* horrible.

horripilante *adj.* horrifying.

horror *m.* horror; atrocity; **dar — to** cause fright; to horrify; **tenerle —** a uno to feel a strong dislike for one.

horrorizar *v.* to horrify, shock, terrify.

horroroso *adj.* horrid; frightful, hideous.

hortaliza *f.* vegetables; vegetable garden.

hortelano *m.* gardener.

hosco = **fosco**.

hospedaje *m.* board and lodging; lodging.

hospedar *v.* to lodge, give lodging; **—se** to take lodging; to room; to stop (*at a hotel*).

hospedero *m.* innkeeper.

hospicio *m.* asylum; orphanage, orphan asylum; poorhouse; **hospiciano** *m.* inmate of a poorhouse or asylum.

hospital *m.* hospital; **— de primera sangre** first-aid station.

hospitalidad *f.* hospitality.

hostia *f.* host (*consecrated wafer*).

hostigar *v.* to harass, vex; to beat, lash; *Am.* to cloy.

hostil *adj.* hostile; **hostilidad** *f.* hostility.

hotel *m.* hotel; villa; **hotelero** *m.* hotel-keeper.

hoy *adv.* today; **— día** nowadays; **de — en adelante** from now on; **— por —** at present; **de — más** henceforth.

hoya *f.* pit, hole; grave; valley; *Am.* river basin.

hoyo *m.* hole; pit; grave; *Am.* dimple.

hoyuelo *m.* dimple; tiny hole.

hoz *f.* sickle; narrow ravine.

hozar *v.* to root, turn up the earth with the snout (*as hogs*).

huacal = **guacal**.

huarache = **guarache**.

huaso = **guaso**.

hueco *adj.* hollow; empty; vain, affected; puffed up; high-sounding; *m.* gap, space, hole.

huelga *f.* labor strike; rest; leisure; **declararse en —** to strike.

huelguista *m.* striker.

huella *f.* trace; footprint.

huérfano *adj. & m.* orphan.

huero *adj.* empty; rotten, spoiled (*egg*). See **güero**.

huerta *f.* orchard and vegetable garden; irrigated land.

huerto *m.* small orchard and vegetable garden; garden patch.

hueso *m.* bone; stone, pit; **la sin —** the tongue; **soltar la sin —** to talk too much; **no dejarle un — sano** to pick him to pieces.

huésped m. guest; host; **ser — en su casa** to be seldom at home.

hueste f. host, army, multitude.

huesudo adj. bony.

huevo m. egg; **— duro** hard-boiled egg; **— estrellado** fried egg; **— pasado por agua** soft-boiled egg; **-s revueltos** scrambled eggs; Am. **-s tibios** soft-boiled eggs; Am. **-s pericos** scrambled eggs; Am. **costar un —** to be very expensive.

huída f. flight; escape.

huír[53] v. irr. to flee, escape; to avoid, shun.

huizache m. Am. huisache (a species of acacia).

hule m. rubber; oilcloth; Am. rubber tree.

hulla f. soft coal.

humanidad f. humanity, mankind; humaneness; **-es** humanities, letters.

humanitario adj. humanitarian, humane, kind, charitable.

humano adj. human; humane; m. man, human being.

humareda f. cloud of smoke.

humeante adj. smoking, smoky; steaming.

humear v. to smoke, give off smoke; to steam; Am. to fumigate.

humedad f. humidity, moisture, dampness.

humedecer[13] v. irr. to moisten, wet, dampen.

húmedo adj. humid, moist, wet, damp.

humildad f. humility; humbleness; meekness.

humilde adj. humble, lowly, meek.

humillación f. humiliation; submission.

humillar v. to humiliate, humble, lower, crush; **-se** to humiliate oneself; to bow humbly.

humillos m. pl. airs, conceit, vanity.

humo m. smoke, fume, vapor; **-s** conceit, vanity.

humor m. humor; mood, disposition.

humorada f. pleasantry, witty remark; caprice, notion.

humorismo m. humor, humorous style.

humorístico adj. humorous.

humoso adj. smoky.

hundimiento m. sinking, collapse, cave-in.

hundir v. to sink, submerge; to crush, oppress; to destroy; **-se** to sink; to collapse, cave in.

huracán m. hurricane.

huraño adj. diffident, shy, bashful; unsociable.

¡hurra! interj. hurrah!

hurtadillas : a — on the sly, secretly, stealthily.

hurtar v. to steal, rob; **-se** to withdraw, slip away; to hide; **— el cuerpo** to dodge; to flee.

hurto m. robbery, theft; stolen article; **a —** stealthily, on the sly.

husmear v. to scent, smell, follow the track of; to nose, pry (into).

husmeo m. sniff, sniffing, smelling; prying.

huso m. spindle.

I

ibérico, ibero adj. Iberian; **iberoamericano** adj. Ibero-American (Spanish or Portuguese American).

ida f. departure; sally; **billete de — y vuelta** round-trip ticket; **-s y venidas** goings and comings.

idea f. idea; notion.

ideal m. & adj. ideal.

idealismo m. idealism.

idealista adj. idealistic; m. & f. idealist; dreamer.

idear v. to form an idea of; to devise, think out, plan.

ídem idem (abbreviation: id.), ditto, the same.

idéntico adj. identical.

identidad f. identity.

identificar[6] v. to identify.

idilio m. idyl.

idioma m. language, tongue.

idiota m. & f. idiot; adj. idiotic, foolish.

idiotismo m. idiom; idiocy.

idolatrar v. to idolize, worship.

ídolo m. idol.

idóneo adj. fit, suitable; qualified.

iglesia f. church.

ignición f. ignition.

ignominia f. infamy, shame, disgrace.

ignominioso adj. ignominious; infamous, shameful, disgraceful.

ignorancia f. ignorance.

ignorante adj. ignorant.

ignorar v. to be ignorant of, not to know.

ignoto adj. unknown, undiscovered.

igual adj. equal; even, smooth; uniform; constant; **serle — a uno** to be all the same to one, make no difference to one; m. equal; **al —** equally.

igualar v. to equal; to equalize; to match; to level, smooth; to adjust; to be equal.

igualdad f. equality.

igualitario adj. equalitarian (promoting the doctrine of equality).

ijada f. loin; flank (of an animal); pain

in the side; **ijar** *m.* flank (*of an animal*).
ilegal *adj.* illegal, unlawful.
ilegítimo *adj.* illegitimate; illegal.
ileso *adj.* unharmed, uninjured, unhurt, safe and sound.
ilícito *adj.* illicit, unlawful.
ilimitado *adj.* unlimited.
iluminación *f.* illumination.
iluminar *v.* to illuminate; to light; to enlighten.
ilusión *f.* illusion.
ilusivo *adj.* illusive.
iluso *adj.* deluded; *m.* visionary, dreamer.
ilusorio *adj.* illusive; deceptive; worthless.
ilustración *f.* illustration; elucidation, explanation.
ilustrador *m.* illustrator.
ilustrar *v.* to illustrate.
ilustre *adj.* illustrious, distinguished.
imagen *f.* image.
imaginable *adj.* imaginable, conceivable.
imaginación *f.* imagination.
imaginar *v.* to imagine.
imaginario *adj.* imaginary.
imaginativo *adj.* imaginative; **imaginativa** *f.* imagination.
imán *m.* magnet; attraction.
imbécil *adj.* imbecile, stupid.
imborrable *adj.* indelible, not erasable; unforgettable.
imbuir[23] *v. irr.* to imbue; to instill, infuse, inspire (with).
imitación *f.* imitation.
imitador *m.* imitator; follower; *adj.* imitative, imitating.
imitar *v.* to imitate.
impaciencia *f.* impatience.
impaciente *adj.* impatient.
impar *adj.* odd; **número —** odd number.
imparcial *adj.* impartial; **imparcialidad** *f.* impartiality, fairness, justice.
impasible *adj.* impassive, insensitive, insensible, unfeeling, unmoved.
impávido *adj.* fearless; calm; *Am.* impudent, brazen.
impedimento *m.* impediment, hindrance, obstacle.
impedir[5] *v. irr.* to impede, prevent, hinder.
impeler *v.* to impel, push; to incite, spur.
impenetrable *adj.* impenetrable; impervious; incomprehensible.
impensado *adj.* unforeseen, unexpected; offhand, done without thinking; **impensadamente** *adv.* offhand, without thinking; unexpectedly.
imperar *v.* to rule, command, dominate.

imperativo *adj.* imperative; urgent, compelling; *m.* imperative mood.
imperceptible *adj.* imperceptible.
imperdible *m.* safety pin; *adj.* safe, that cannot be lost.
imperecedero *adj.* imperishable, enduring, everlasting.
imperfecto *adj.* imperfect; *m.* imperfect tense.
imperial *adj.* imperial; *f.* coach top; top seats on a coach or bus.
impericia *f.* inexperience.
imperio *m.* empire; command, rule; sway, influence.
imperioso *adj.* imperious, arrogant, domineering; urgent.
impermeable *adj.* waterproof, impervious, rainproof; *m.* raincoat.
impersonal *adj.* impersonal.
impertinencia *f.* impertinence; impudence; insolent remark or act; **decir —s** to talk nonsense; to make insolent remarks.
impertinente *adj.* impertinent, impudent; meddlesome; irrelevant, not to the point; **-s** *m. pl.* lorgnette (*eyeglasses mounted on a handle*).
ímpetu *m.* impetus; violent force; impulse; *Am.* vehement desire; **— de ira** fit of anger.
impetuoso *adj.* impetuous, violent.
impío *adj.* impious, irreligious; profane.
implacable *adj.* implacable, relentless.
implantación *f.* implantation, establishment, introduction (*of a system*).
implantar *v.* to implant, establish, introduce.
implicar[4] *v.* to imply; to implicate, involve.
implorar *v.* to implore, entreat, beg.
imponente *adj.* imposing.
imponer[40] *v. irr.* to impose; to invest (*money*); **— miedo** to inspire fear; **— respeto** to inspire or command respect; **-se** to inspire fear or respect; to dominate; *Am.* **-se a** to get accustomed or used to.
importancia *f.* importance.
importante *adj.* important.
importar *v.* to be important; to matter; to amount to; to be necessary; to concern; to import.
importe *m.* amount, price, value.
importunar *v.* to importune, nag, tease, pester.
importuno *adj.* annoying, persistent.
imposibilidad *f.* impossibility.
imposibilitado *p.p. & adj.* disabled, unfit; helpless.
imposibilitar *v.* to make impossible; to

disable.

imposible adj. impossible; intolerable, unbearable; Am. disabled (because of illness); Am. slovenly, untidy.

imposición f. imposition; burden; tax.

impostor m. impostor, cheat; **impostura** f. imposture, fraud, deceit.

impotencia f. impotence.

impotente adj. impotent, powerless.

impreciso adj. vague, indefinite; inaccurate.

impregnar v. to impregnate, saturate.

imprenta f. press; printing shop; printing.

imprescindible adj. essential, indispensable.

impresión f. impression; printing; mark; footprint.

impresionante adj. impressive.

impresionar v. to impress; to move, affect, stir; -se to be stirred, moved.

impreso p.p. irr. of **imprimir** printed; impressed, imprinted; m. printed matter.

impresor m. printer.

imprevisión f. carelessness, lack of foresight.

imprevisto adj. unforeseen, unexpected.

imprimir v. to print; to imprint, impress.

improbable adj. improbable, unlikely.

improperio m. affront, insult.

impropio adj. improper; unsuitable.

improvisar v. to improvise.

improviso adj. unforeseen; de — suddenly; Am. en un — in a moment, in the twinkling of an eye.

imprudencia f. imprudence, indiscretion, rash act.

imprudente adj. imprudent; unwise; indiscreet.

impuesto p.p. of **imponer** imposed; informed; Am. estar — a to be used or accustomed to; m. tax, duty.

impulsar v. to impel, push, move; to force.

impulso m. impulse; push.

impureza f. impurity.

impuro adj. impure.

imputar v. to impute, attribute.

inacabable adj. unending, endless.

inacabado adj. unfinished.

inaccesible adj. inaccessible, unobtainable.

inacción f. inaction, inactivity, idleness.

inaceptable adj. unacceptable, unsatisfactory.

inactividad f. inactivity.

inactivo adj. inactive.

inadecuado adj. inadequate.

inadvertencia f. oversight; inattention, heedlessness.

inadvertido adj. careless, heedless; unnoticed.

inafectado adj. unaffected.

inagotable adj. inexhaustible.

inaguantable adj. insufferable, unbearable.

inalámbrico adj. wireless.

inalterable adj. unalterable, unchangeable.

inalterado adj. unchanged.

inamovible = **inmovible**.

inanición f. starvation.

inanimado adj. inanimate, lifeless.

inapetencia f. lack of appetite.

inaplicable adj. inapplicable, unsuitable; — al caso irrelevant.

inapreciable adj. invaluable; inappreciable, too small to be perceived, very slight.

inasequible adj. inaccessible, not obtainable; hard to attain or obtain.

inaudito adj. unheard-of; unprecedented.

inauguración f. inauguration.

inaugurar v. to inaugurate, begin, open.

incaico, incásico adj. Incan (of or pertaining to the Incas).

incalculable adj. incalculable; innumerable, untold.

incandescente adj. incandescent.

incansable adj. untiring, tireless.

incapacidad f. incompetence, inability, unfitness.

incapacitar v. to cripple, disable, handicap, unfit, make unfit.

incapaz adj. incapable, unable.

incauto adj. unwary, heedless, reckless.

incendiar v. to set fire to; -se to catch fire.

incendio m. conflagration, fire.

incentivo m. incentive, inducement.

incertidumbre f. uncertainty, doubt.

incesante adj. incessant.

incidental adj. incidental.

incidente adj. incidental; m. incident.

incienso m. incense.

incierto adj. uncertain, doubtful; unstable; unknown; untrue.

incisión f. incision, cut, slit, gash.

incitamiento m. incitement, inducement, incentive.

incitar v. to incite, rouse, stir up.

incivil adj. uncivil, rude, impolite.

inclemencia f. inclemency, severity, harshness; **inclemente** adj. unmerciful, merciless.

inclinación f. inclination, affection; tendency, bent; bow; incline, slope.

inclinar v. to incline; to persuade; **-se** to bow; to stoop; to incline, slope, slant; to lean, bend.

incluir[32] v. irr. to include; to inclose.

inclusive adv. inclusive, including; **inclusivo** adj. inclusive; comprehensive.

incluso adj. inclosed; included; including; even.

incógnito adj. unknown; **de —** incognito (with one's name or rank unknown); **incógnita** f. unknown quantity (in mathematics).

incoherente adj. incoherent, disconnected, rambling.

incoloro adj. colorless.

incombustible adj. incombustible; fireproof.

incomodar v. to inconvenience, disturb, trouble, annoy.

incomodidad f. inconvenience, discomfort; bother, annoyance.

incómodo adj. inconvenient, bothersome; uncomfortable.

incomparable adj. incomparable.

incompasivo adj. merciless, pitiless.

incompatible adj. incompatible; unsuitable, uncongenial.

incompetencia f. incompetence, inability, unfitness; **incompetente** adj. incompetent, unfit.

incompleto adj. incomplete.

incomprensible adj. incomprehensible.

incondicional adj. unconditional.

inconexo adj. unconnected; incoherent, disconnected.

inconfundible adj. unmistakable.

incongruente adj. unsuitable, not appropriate; not harmonious.

inconquistable adj. unconquerable.

inconsciencia f. unconsciousness; unawareness.

inconsciente adj. unconscious; unaware.

inconsecuente adj. inconsistent; illogical.

inconsiderado adj. inconsiderate, thoughtless.

inconstancia f. inconstancy, changeableness, fickleness.

inconstante adj. inconstant, fickle, changeable, variable.

incontable adj. countless, innumerable.

inconveniencia f. inconvenience; trouble.

inconveniente adj. inconvenient; improper; m. obstacle; objection.

incorporar v. to incorporate, unite; to embody; to include; **-se** to sit up; **-se a** to join.

incorrecto adj. incorrect.

incredulidad f. incredulity, unbelief.

incrédulo adj. incredulous, unbelieving; m. unbeliever.

increíble adj. incredible, unbelievable.

incremento m. increment, increase.

incrustar v. to inlay; to encrust (cover with a crust or hard coating); **-se en** to penetrate, impress itself deeply into.

inculcar[6] v. to inculcate, instill, impress.

inculto adj. uncultured; uncultivated; unrefined.

incumbencia f. concern, duty, obligation; **no es de mi —** it does not concern me, it is not within my province.

incurable adj. incurable.

incurrir v. to incur, fall (into); **— en un error** to fall into or commit an error; **— en el odio de** to incur the hatred of.

incursión f. raid, invasion.

indagación f. investigation, inquiry.

indagador m. investigator; inquirer; adj. investigating; inquiring.

indagar[7] v. to find out, investigate; to inquire.

indebido adj. undue, improper; illegal; **indebidamente** adv. unduly; illegally.

indecencia f. indecency, obscenity, indecent act or remark.

indecente adj. indecent, improper.

indecible adj. inexpressible, untold.

indeciso adj. undecided; doubtful, uncertain.

indefectible adj. unfailing; **-mente** unfailingly.

indefenso adj. defenseless, unprotected.

indefinible adj. indefinable.

indefinido adj. indefinite.

indeleble adj. indelible.

indemnización f. indemnity, compensation.

indemnizar[9] v. to indemnify, compensate.

independencia f. independence.

independiente adj. independent.

indescriptible adj. indescribable.

indeseable adj. undesirable, unwelcome.

indiada f. Am. community, group, or crowd of Indians; Am. an Indian-like remark or act; Am. an uncontrollable fit of anger.

indianista m. & f. student of Indian culture; adj. pertaining to Indian culture.

indiano adj. of or pertaining to the West or East Indies; m. Spaniard who goes back to settle in his country after having lived for some time in Spanish America.

indicación f. indication.

indicar[6] v. to indicate, show, point out.

116

indicativo *adj.* indicative; *m.* indicative, indicative mood.

índice *m.* index; catalogue; sign; pointer; forefinger.

indicio *m.* indication, sign.

indiferencia *f.* indifference.

indiferente *adj.* indifferent.

indígena *adj.* indigenous, native; *m. & f.* native inhabitant; *Am.* Indian.

indignación *f.* indignation.

indignado *p.p. & adj.* indignant, irritated, angry.

indignar *v.* to irritate, anger; **-se** to become indignant, angry.

indignidad *f.* indignity, affront, insult; unworthy or disgraceful act.

indigno *adj.* unworthy; low, contemptible.

indio *adj. & m.* Indian; Hindu.

indirecta *f.* hint, indirect remark, innuendo, insinuation.

indirecto *adj.* indirect.

indisciplinado *adj.* undisciplined, untrained.

indiscreto *adj.* indiscreet, imprudent, unwise, rash.

indiscutible *adj.* indisputable, unquestionable.

indispensable *adj.* indispensable.

indisponer[40] *v. irr.* to indispose; to make ill; — **a uno con otro** to prejudice someone against another; **-se** to become ill; **-se con** to fall out with, quarrel with.

indisposición *f.* indisposition, upset, slight illness; reluctance, unwillingness.

indispuesto *p.p. of* **indisponer** *& adj.* indisposed, unwilling; ill.

indisputable *adj.* unquestionable.

indistinto *adj.* indistinct, dim, vague, not clear.

individual *adj.* individual.

individualidad *f.* individuality.

individuo *adj.* individual; indivisible; *m.* individual; person; member.

indócil *adj.* unruly, disobedient, headstrong.

indocto *adj.* uneducated, ignorant.

índole *f.* disposition, temper; kind, class.

indolencia *f.* indolence, laziness; insensitiveness, indifference.

indolente *adj.* indolent, lazy; insensitive, indifferent.

indomable *adj.* indomitable, unconquerable; unmanageable; untamable.

indómito *adj.* untamed; uncontrollable, unruly.

inducir[25] *v. irr.* to induce; to persuade.

indudable *adj.* unquestionable, certain.

indulgencia *f.* indulgence, tolerance, forgiveness; remission of sins.

indulgente *adj.* indulgent, lenient.

indultar *v.* to pardon, set free; to exempt.

indulto *m.* pardon, forgiveness; exemption; privilege.

indumentaria *f.* costume, dress; manner of dressing.

industria *f.* industry; cleverness, skill; **de —** intentionally, on purpose.

industrial *adj.* industrial; *m.* industrialist; manufacturer.

industrioso *adj.* industrious.

inédito *adj.* unpublished.

inefable *adj.* ineffable, inexpressible.

ineficaz *adj.* ineffective; inefficient.

inepto *adj.* incompetent; unsuitable.

inequívoco *adj.* unmistakable.

inercia *f.* inertia, lifelessness; inactivity.

inerme *adj.* unarmed, defenseless.

inerte *adj.* inert; inactive, sluggish, slow.

inesperado *adj.* unexpected.

inestable *adj.* unstable; unsettled; unsteady.

inestimable *adj.* inestimable, invaluable.

inevitable *adj.* inevitable, unavoidable.

inexacto *adj.* inexact, inaccurate.

inexperiencia *f.* inexperience.

inexperto *adj.* unskilful, unskilled, inexperienced.

inexplicable *adj.* inexplicable.

inextinguible *adj.* inextinguishable, unquenchable.

infalible *adj.* infallible.

infame *adj.* infamous; *m.* scoundrel.

infamia *f.* infamy, dishonor; wickedness.

infancia *f.* infancy.

infante *m.* infant; infante (*royal prince of Spain, except the heir to the throne*); infantryman.

infantería *f.* infantry.

infantil *adj.* infantile, childlike, childish.

infatigable *adj.* tireless, untiring.

infausto *adj.* unfortunate; unhappy.

infección *f.* infection; **infeccioso** *adj.* infectious.

infectar *v.* to infect; to corrupt; **-se** to become infected.

infeliz *adj.* unhappy, unfortunate; *m.* poor wretch.

inferior *adj.* inferior; lower; *m.* inferior.

inferioridad *f.* inferiority.

inferir[3] *v. irr.* to infer; to imply; to inflict.

infernal *adj.* infernal.

infestar *v.* to infest, invade, overrun, plague; to corrupt, infect.

inficionar v. to infect; to contaminate.

infiel adj. unfaithful, faithless; infidel; inaccurate.

infierno m. hell; **en el quinto —** very far away.

infiltrar v. to filter through; -se to leak (into), filter (through), infiltrate.

infinidad f. infinity; **una — de** a large number of.

infinito adj. infinite; adv. infinitely; m. infinity.

inflamación f. inflammation.

inflamado p.p. & adj. inflamed; sore.

inflamar v. to inflame, excite; to kindle, set on fire; -se to become inflamed.

inflar v. to inflate; to exaggerate; -se to become inflated; to swell up with pride.

inflexible adj. inflexible, stiff, rigid; unbending.

inflexión f. inflection.

infligir[11] v. to inflict.

influencia f. influence.

influenza f. influenza, grippe, flu.

influir[32] v. irr. to influence.

influjo m. influence; influx, inward flow.

influyente adj. influential.

información f. information.

informal adj. informal; unconventional; unreliable, not dependable, not punctual.

informar v. to inform; to give form to; to give a report; to present a case; -se to find out.

informe m. report, account; information; brief; adj. formless, shapeless.

infortunio m. misfortune, mishap; misery.

infracción f. infraction, breach, violation (of a law, treaty, etc.).

infractor m. transgressor, lawbreaker, violator (of a law).

infrascrito m. undersigned, subscriber, signer (of a letter, document, etc.); **el — secretario** the secretary whose signature appears below.

infringir[11] v. to infringe, break, violate.

infructuoso adj. fruitless.

ínfulas f. pl. airs, false importance; **darse —** to put on airs.

infundado adj. groundless, without foundation.

infundir v. to infuse, inspire; to instill.

infusión f. infusion (liquid extract obtained by steeping); infusion, inspiration; **poner en —** to steep (as tea leaves).

ingeniería f. engineering.

ingeniero m. engineer.

ingenio m. genius; talent; ingenuity;

mentality, mental power, mind; wit; **— de azúcar** sugar refinery; sugar plantation.

ingeniosidad f. ingenuity, cleverness.

ingenioso adj. ingenious, clever.

ingenuidad f. candor, frankness; unaffected simplicity.

ingenuo adj. frank, sincere; simple, unaffected.

ingerir = **injerir**.

inglés adj. English; **a la inglesa** in the English fashion; Am. **ir a la inglesa** to go Dutch treat; m. Englishman; the English language.

ingobernable adj. ungovernable, unruly, uncontrollable.

ingratitud f. ingratitude.

ingrato adj. ungrateful, thankless; harsh; cruel; disdainful.

ingrediente m. ingredient.

ingresar v. to enter; **— en** to join (a society, club, etc.).

ingreso m. entrance; entry; -s receipts, profits; revenue.

inhábil adj. unskilled; unskilful; unfit.

inhabilidad f. inability; unfitness.

inhabilitar v. to disqualify; to unfit, disable.

inherente adj. inherent.

inhospitalario adj. inhospitable.

inhumano adj. inhuman, cruel.

iniciador m. initiator; pioneer; adj. initiating.

inicial adj. & f. initial.

iniciar v. to initiate; to begin.

iniciativa f. initiative.

inicuo adj. wicked.

iniquidad f. iniquity, wickedness; sin.

injerir[3] v. irr. to inject, insert; -se to interfere, meddle.

injertar v. to graft.

injuria f. affront, insult; harm, damage.

injuriar v. to insult, offend; to harm, damage.

injurioso adj. insulting, offensive; harmful.

injusticia f. injustice.

injustificado adj. unjustified; unjustifiable.

injusto adj. unjust, unfair.

inmaculado adj. immaculate, clean; pure.

inmediación f. vicinity; nearness; -es environs, outskirts.

inmediato adj. near, close; Am. **de —** immediately; suddenly; **inmediatamente** adv. immediately, at once.

inmensidad f. immensity, vastness; vast number.

inmenso adj. immense, vast, huge;

boundless.

inmersión f. immersion, dip.

inmigración f. immigration.

inmigrante adj., m. & f. immigrant.

inmigrar v. to immigrate.

inminente adj. imminent.

inmiscuir[32] v. irr. to mix; **-se** to meddle, interfere.

inmoble adj. motionless; unshaken.

inmoral adj. immoral; **inmoralidad** f. immorality.

inmortal adj. immortal; **inmortalidad** f. immortality.

inmovible adj. immovable, fixed; steadfast.

inmóvil adj. motionless, still; immovable.

inmundicia f. filth, dirt; nastiness.

inmundo adj. filthy, dirty; impure; nasty.

inmune adj. immune; exempt.

inmunidad f. immunity.

inmutable adj. unchangeable, invariable.

inmutar v. to alter, change; **-se** to show emotion (either by turning pale or blushing).

innato adj. innate, natural, inborn.

innecesario adj. unnecessary.

innegable adj. undeniable, not to be denied.

innocuo adj. innocuous, harmless; **innocuidad** f. harmlessness.

innovación f. innovation; novelty.

innumerable adj. innumerable.

inobservancia f. nonobservance, violation (of a law), lack of observance (of a law, rule, or custom).

inocencia f. innocence.

inocente adj. innocent; m. innocent person; **inocentón** adj. quite foolish or simple; easily fooled; m. dupe, unsuspecting victim.

inocular v. to inoculate.

inodoro adj. odorless; m. Am. toilet, water closet.

inofensivo adj. inoffensive; harmless.

inolvidable adj. unforgettable.

inopinado adj. unexpected.

inoportuno adj. inopportune, untimely, unsuitable.

inquietar v. to worry, disturb, make uneasy; **-se** to become disturbed, uneasy.

inquieto adj. restless; uneasy, anxious.

inquietud f. restlessness; anxiety, uneasiness; fear.

inquilino m. tenant, renter; lodger.

inquina f. aversion, grudge, dislike.

inquirir[35] v. irr. to inquire, investigate;

to find out.

inquisición f. inquisition; inquiry, investigation.

insaciable adj. insatiable, never satisfied, greedy.

insalubre adj. unhealthy, unhealthful, unwholesome.

insano adj. insane, crazy; unhealthy.

inscribir[52] v. to inscribe; to register, enroll; to record; **-se** to register.

inscripción f. inscription; registration.

inscripto, inscrito p.p. of **inscribir**.

insecto m. insect.

inseguro adj. insecure; unsafe; doubtful, uncertain.

insensato adj. senseless; foolish.

insensibilidad f. insensibility, unconsciousness; lack of feeling.

insensible adj. insensible; unfeeling; imperceptible.

inseparable adj. inseparable.

inserción f. insertion; insert.

insertar v. to insert.

inserto adj. inserted.

inservible adj. useless.

insidioso adj. insidious; sly, crafty.

insigne adj. famous.

insignia f. badge, medal, decoration; flag, pennant; **-s** insignia.

insignificante adj. insignificant.

insinuación f. insinuation; intimation, hint.

insinuar[18] v. to insinuate, hint; **-se** to insinuate oneself (into another's friendship); to creep (into) gradually.

insipidez f. flatness, tastelessness, dullness; **insípido** adj. insipid; tasteless.

insistencia f. insistence, persistence, obstinacy; **insistente** adj. insistent, persistent.

insistir v. to insist; to persist.

insociable adj. unsociable.

insolación f. sunstroke.

insolencia f. insolence.

insolentarse v. to sauce, become insolent, act with insolence.

insolente adj. insolent.

insólito adj. unusual; uncommon.

insolvente adj. insolvent, bankrupt.

insomne adj. sleepless.

insondable adj. fathomless, deep; impenetrable.

insoportable adj. unbearable.

insospechado adj. unsuspected.

inspección f. inspection.

inspeccionar v. to inspect.

inspector m. inspector; overseer.

inspiración f. inspiration; inhalation, breathing in.

inspirar v. to inspire; to inhale.

instalación f. installation.

instalar v. to install.

instancia f. instance, urgent request; petition; **a -s de** at the request of.

instantánea f. snapshot.

instantáneo adj. instantaneous; sudden.

instante m. instant, moment; **al —** at once, immediately; **por -s** continually; from one moment to another; adj. instant, urgent.

instar v. to urge, press; to be urgent.

instigar[1] v. to instigate, urge on, incite.

instintivo adj. instinctive.

instinto m. instinct.

institución f. institution; establishment, foundation; **-es** institutes, collection of precepts and principles.

instituir[32] v. irr. to institute; **— por heredero** to appoint as heir.

instituto m. institute; established principle, law, or custom; **— de segunda enseñanza** high school.

institutriz f. governess.

instrucción f. instruction; education.

instructivo adj. instructive.

instruir[32] v. irr. to instruct, teach; to inform.

instrumento m. instrument.

insuficiencia f. insufficiency, deficiency; incompetence; dearth, scarcity, lack.

insuficiente adj. insufficient.

insufrible adj. insufferable, unbearable.

ínsula f. island.

insultante adj. insulting, abusive.

insultar v. to insult; **-se** to be seized with a fit.

insulto m. insult; sudden fit or attack.

insuperable adj. insuperable; insurmountable.

insurgente adj., m. & f. insurgent.

insurrección f. insurrection, uprising, revolt.

insurrecto m. insurgent, rebel; adj. rebellious.

intacto adj. intact.

intachable adj. faultless, irreproachable.

integral adj. integral; f. integral (math).

integrante adj. integral; integrating.

integridad f. integrity; wholeness; honesty; purity.

íntegro adj. whole, complete; honest, upright.

intelecto m. intellect.

intelectual adj. intellectual.

inteligencia f. intelligence.

inteligente adj. intelligent.

intemperancia f. intemperance, excess.

intemperie f. open air; bad weather; **a la —** unsheltered, outdoors, in the open air; exposed to the weather.

intención f. intention; **intencional** adj. intentional.

intendente m. manager, superintendent, supervisor; *Am.* governor of a province; *Am.* police commissioner.

intensidad f. intensity.

intenso adj. intense; intensive; ardent, vehement.

intentar v. to attempt, try; to intend.

intento m. intent, purpose, intention; **de —** on purpose.

intercalar v. to insert, place between.

intercambio m. interchange; exchange.

interceder v. to intercede.

interceptar v. to intercept.

intercesión f. intercession, mediation.

interés m. interest.

interesante adj. interesting.

interesar v. to interest; to give an interest or share; **-se** to be or become interested.

interferencia f. interference.

ínterin m. interim, meantime; **en el —** in the meantime.

interino adj. acting, temporary.

interior adj. interior; inner; internal; m. interior, inside.

interjección f. interjection, exclamation.

interlocutor m. participant in a dialogue.

intermedio adj. intermediate; intervening; m. intermission; interval; **por — de** by means of, through the intervention of.

interminable adj. interminable, unending, endless.

intermisión f. intermission, interruption, pause, interval.

intermitente adj. intermittent, occurring at intervals; **calentura** (*or* **fiebre**) **—** intermittent fever.

internacional adj. international.

internar v. to intern, confine; **-se** to penetrate, go into the interior.

interno adj. internal; interior; m. boarding-school student.

interoceánico adj. interoceanic; transcontinental.

interpelar v. to interrogate, question, demand explanations; to ask the aid of.

interponer[40] v. irr. to interpose, put between, insert; to place as a mediator; **-se** to intervene, mediate.

interpretación f. interpretation.

interpretar v. to interpret.

intérprete m. & f. interpreter.

interpuesto p.p. of **interponer.**

interrogación f. interrogation, question; **signo de —** question mark.

interrogador *m.* questioner; *adj.* questioning.

interrogar[7] *v.* to interrogate, question.

interrogativo *adj.* interrogative.

interrogatorio *m.* interrogation, questioning.

interrumpir *v.* to interrupt.

interrupción *f.* interruption.

interruptor *m.* interrupter; electric switch.

intersección *f.* intersection.

intervalo *m.* interval.

intervención *f.* intervention; mediation; participation; auditing of accounts.

intervenir[48] *v. irr.* to intervene; to mediate; to audit (*accounts*).

interventor *m.* inspector; controller; comptroller; auditor.

intestino *m.* intestine; *adj.* intestine, internal.

intimación *f.* intimation; hint, insinuation, suggestion.

intimar *v.* to announce, notify; to intimate, hint; to become intimate, become friendly.

intimidad *f.* intimacy.

intimidar *v.* to intimidate.

íntimo *adj.* intimate.

intitular *v.* to entitle; to give a title to (*a person or a thing*); -se to be entitled, be called; to call oneself (*by a certain name*).

intolerable *adj.* intolerable.

intolerancia *f.* intolerance; **intolerante** *adj.* intolerant, narrow-minded.

intranquilo *adj.* disturbed, uneasy.

intranquilidad *f.* uneasiness, restlessness.

intransigencia *f.* uncompromising act or attitude; intolerance.

intransigente *adj.* uncompromising, unwilling to compromise or yield; intolerant.

intratable *adj.* unsociable; rude; unruly.

intravenoso *adj.* intravenous (*within a vein or the veins; into a vein*).

intrepidez *f.* fearlessness, courage.

intrépido *adj.* intrepid, fearless.

intriga *f.* intrigue; scheme; plot.

intrigante *m. & f.* intriguer, plotter; *adj.* intriguing.

intrigar[7] *v.* to intrigue.

intrincado *adj.* intricate, complicated, entangled.

introducción *f.* introduction.

introducir[25] *v. irr.* to introduce; -se to introduce oneself; to get in; to penetrate.

intromisión *f.* meddling; insertion.

intruso *adj.* intrusive, intruding; *m.* intruder.

intuición *f.* intuition.

intuir[32] *v. irr.* to sense, feel by intuition.

inundación *f.* inundation, flood.

inundar *v.* to inundate, flood.

inusitado *adj.* unusual, rare.

inútil *adj.* useless.

inutilidad *f.* uselessness.

inutilizar[9] *v.* to make useless, put out of commission, to disable; to ruin, spoil.

invadir *v.* to invade.

invalidar *v.* to render invalid; to void, annul.

inválido *adj.* invalid; void, null; sickly, weak; *m.* invalid.

invariable *adj.* invariable.

invasión *f.* invasion.

invasor *m.* invader; *adj.* invading; ejército — invading army.

invencible *adj.* invincible, unconquerable.

invención *f.* invention.

invendible *adj.* unsaleable.

inventar *v.* to invent.

inventariar[17] *v.* to inventory, take an inventory of.

inventario *m.* inventory.

inventiva *f.* inventiveness, power of inventing, ingenuity.

inventivo *adj.* inventive.

invento *m.* invention.

inventor *m.* inventor; storyteller, fibber.

invernáculo *m.* greenhouse, hothouse.

invernadero *m.* winter quarters; winter resort; winter pasture; greenhouse, hothouse.

invernal *adj.* wintry, winter.

invernar[1] *v. irr.* to winter, spend the winter.

inverosímil, inverisímil *adj.* unlikely, improbable.

inversión *f.* inversion; investment.

inverso *adj.* inverse, inverted; reverse; a (*or por*) la inversa on the contrary.

invertir[3] *v.* to invert; to reverse; to invest; to employ, spend (*time*).

investigación *f.* investigation.

investigador *m.* investigator; *adj.* investigating.

investigar[7] *v.* to investigate.

invicto *adj.* unconquered; always victorious.

invierno *m.* winter.

invisible *adj.* invisible.

invitación *f.* invitation.

invitar *v.* to invite.

invocar[6] *v.* to invoke.

involuntario *adj.* involuntary.

inyección *f.* injection.

inyectado p.p. injected; adj. bloodshot, inflamed.

inyectar v. to inject.

ir³³ v. irr. to go; to walk; — **corriendo** to be running; — **entendiendo** to understand gradually; to begin to understand; — **a caballo** to ride horseback; — **a pie** to walk; — **en automóvil** to drive, ride in an automobile; **no irle ni venirle a uno** to make no difference to one; **¿cómo le va?** how are you?; **no me va nada en eso** that doesn't concern me; **¡vamos! let's go!** come on!; **¡vaya!** well now!; **¡vaya un hombre!** what a man!; **-se** to go, go away; to escape; — **abajo** to fall down, topple over; to collapse; **-se a pique** to founder, sink.

ira f. ire, anger.

iracundo adj. irritable; angry.

iris m. iris (of the eye); **arco —** rainbow.

irisado adj. iridescent, rainbow-hued.

ironía f. irony.

irónico adj. ironic, ironical.

irracional adj. irrational, unreasonable.

irradiar v. to radiate.

irreal adj. unreal.

irreflexión f. thoughtlessness.

irreflexivo adj. thoughtless.

irrefrenable adj. uncontrollable.

irregular adj. irregular.

irreligioso adj. irreligious.

irremediable adj. irremediable; hopeless, incurable.

irreprochable adj. irreproachable, flawless.

irresistible adj. irresistible.

irresoluto adj. irresolute, undecided, hesitating.

irrespetuoso adj. disrespectful.

irreverencia f. irreverence.

irreverente adj. irreverent.

irrigación f. irrigation.

irrigar⁷ v. to irrigate.

irrisión f. mockery, ridicule, derision.

irritación f. irritation.

irritante adj. irritating.

irritar v. to irritate.

irrupción f. sudden attack, raid, invasion.

isla f. island.

isleño m. islander.

islote m. islet, small rocky island.

istmo m. isthmus.

italiano adj. & m. Italian.

itinerario m. itinerary; timetable, schedule; railroad guide.

izar⁹ v. to hoist; to heave.

izquierda f. left hand; left side; left wing (in politics); **a la —** to the left;

izquierdista m. & f. leftist, radical.

izquierdo adj. left; left-handed.

J

jabalí m. wild boar.

jabón m. soap; Am. fright, fear; **dar —** to soft-soap, flatter; **dar un —** to give a good scolding; to beat, thrash.

jabonadura f. washing, soaping; **-s** suds, lather; **dar a uno una —** to reprimand or scold someone.

jabonar v. to lather, soap; to scold, reprimand.

jabonera f. soap dish; woman soap vendor or maker.

jaca f. pony; small horse; **jaco** m. small nag; poor horse.

jacal m. Am. shack, adobe hut; **jacalucho** m. Am. poor, ugly shack.

jacinto m. hyacinth.

jactancia f. boast, brag; boasting.

jactancioso adj. braggart, boastful.

jactarse v. to brag, boast.

jaculatoria f. short, fervent prayer.

jadeante adj. breathless, panting, out of breath.

jadear v. to pant.

jadeo m. pant, panting.

jaez m. harness; kind, sort; **jaeces** trappings.

jalar v. to pull; to haul; to jerk; Am. to court, make love; Am. to flunk (a student); Am. **¡jala** (or **jálale**)! get going! get a move on there!; **-se** Am. to get drunk; Am. to go away, move away.

jalea f. jelly.

jalear v. to shout (to hunting dogs); to rouse, beat up (game); to shout and clap (to encourage dancers).

jaleo m. shouting and clapping (to encourage dancers); an Andalusian dance; revelry, merrymaking; jesting; gracefulness.

jaletina f. gelatin.

jalón m. marker (for boundaries); Am. pull, jerk, tug; Am. swallow of liquor; Am. stretch, distance.

jalonear v. Am. to pull, jerk.

jamás adv. never.

jamón m. ham; Am. fix, difficulty.

japonés adj. & m. Japanese.

jaque m. check (in chess); braggart, bully; — **mate** checkmate (in chess); **tener a uno en —** to hold someone under a threat.

jaqueca f. headache; sick headache.

jara f. rockrose (shrub); Am. reed; **jaral** m. bramble of rockroses; Am. reeds, clump of reeds.

jarabe m. syrup; sweet beverage; Am. a kind of tap dance; Am. song and musical accompaniment of the jarabe.

jarana f. merrymaking, revelry; trick; fib; jest; Am. small guitar; **ir de —** to go on a spree.

jarcia f. rigging (ropes, chains, etc. for the masts, yards and sails of a ship); fishing tackle; pile, heap; jumble of things.

jardín m. flower garden.

jardinero m. gardener.

jarra f. jar, vase, pitcher; **de** (or **en**) **-s** akimbo (with hands on the hips).

jarro m. jar, jug, pitcher.

jarrón m. large vase or jar.

jaspe m. jasper; veined marble; **jaspeado** adj. veined, streaked, mottled.

jaula f. cage; cagelike cell or prison; Am. roofless cattle car or freight car.

jauría f. pack of hounds.

jazmín m. jasmine.

jefatura f. position of chief; headquarters of a chief.

jefe m. chief, leader, head.

jengibre m. ginger.

jerez m. sherry wine.

jerga f. thick coarse cloth; straw mattress; jargon; slang; Am. saddle pad; Am. poncho made of coarse cloth.

jergón m. straw mattress; ill-fitting suit or dress; big clumsy fellow; Am. cheap coarse rug.

jerigonza f. jargon; slang.

jeringa f. syringe; **jeringazo** m. injection; squirt.

jeringar v. to inject; to squirt; to bother, molest, vex, annoy.

jesuita m. Jesuit.

jeta f. snout; thick lips.

jiba = giba.

jíbaro adj. Am. rustic, rural, rude, uncultured; m. Am. bumpkin, peasant.

jícara f. chocolate cup; Am. small bowl made out of a gourd; Am. any small bowl; Am. bald head.

jilguero m. linnet.

jinete m. horseman, rider.

jineteada f. Am. roughriding, horsebreaking.

jinetear v. to ride horseback; to perform on horseback; Am. to break in (a horse); Am. to ride a bronco or bull.

jira f. excursion, tour; outing, picnic; strip of cloth.

jirafa f. giraffe.

jitomate m. Am. tomato. Also gitomate.

jofaina f. basin, washbowl.

jolgorio = holgorio.

jornada f. day's journey; military expedition; working day; act (of a Spanish play).

jornal m. day's wages; bookkeeping journal; **a —** by the day.

jornalero m. day laborer.

joroba f. hump; nuisance, annoyance.

jorobado adj. hunchbacked; annoyed, bothered, in a bad fix; m. hunchback.

jorobar v. to bother, pester, annoy.

jorongo m. Am. Mexican poncho.

jota f. name of the letter j; iota (anything insignificant); Aragonese and Valencian dance and music; Am. (= **ojota**) leather sandal; **no saber una —** not to know anything.

joven adj. young; m. & f. youth; young man; young woman.

jovial adj. jovial, jolly, merry; **jovialidad** f. gaiety, merriment, fun.

joya f. jewel; piece of jewelry; **-s** jewels; trousseau.

joyería f. jeweler's shop.

joyero m. jeweler; jewel box.

juanete m. bunion.

jubilación f. retirement (from a position or office); pension.

jubilar v. to pension; to retire; **-se** to be pensioned or retired; to rejoice; Am. to decline, fall into decline; Am. to play hooky or truant.

jubileo m. jubilee; time of rejoicing; concession by the Pope of plenary (complete) indulgence.

júbilo m. joy, glee.

jubiloso adj. jubilant, joyful.

jubón m. jacket; bodice.

judía f. bean; string bean; Jewess; **-s tiernas** (or **verdes**) string beans.

judicial adj. judicial; **-mente** adv. judicially.

judío adj. Jewish; m. Jew.

juego m. game; play; sport; gambling; pack of cards; set; **— de palabras** pun, play on words; **— de te** tea set; **hacer —** to match; **poner en —** to coordinate; to set in motion.

juerga f. spree, revelry, wild festivity; **irse de —** to go out on a spree; **juerguista** m. & f. merrymaker.

jueves m. Thursday.

juez m. judge; juror, member of a jury; **— arbitrador** (or **árbitro**) arbitrator, umpire.

jugada f. play, move; stroke; trick.

jugador m. player; gambler; **— de manos** juggler.

jugar[34] v. irr. to play; to gamble; to toy; **— a la pelota** to play ball; Am. **— a dos cartas** to be double-faced.

jugarreta f. bad play, wrong play; mean trick; tricky deal; Am. noisy game.

ugo m. juice; sap.

ugosidad f. juiciness; **jugoso** adj. juicy.

juguete m. plaything, toy; jest, joke; cómico skit; **por** (or **de**) — jokingly.

juguetear v. to play around, romp, frolic; to toy; to tamper (with), fool (with).

juguetón adj. playful.

juicio m. judgment; sense, wisdom; opinion; trial; **perder el** — to lose one's mind, go crazy.

juicioso adj. judicious, wise; sensible.

julio m. July.

jumento m. ass, donkey.

junco m. rush, reed; junk (Chinese sailboat).

jungla f. Am. jungle.

junio m. June.

junquillo m. reed; jonquil (yellow flower similar to the daffodil), species of narcissus.

junta f. meeting, conference; board, council.

juntar v. to join, unite; to connect; to assemble; to collect; **-se** to assemble, gather; to be closely united; to associate (with).

junto adj. joined, united; **-s** together; adv. near; — **a** near to, close to; **en** — all together, in all; **por** — all together, in a lump; wholesale.

juntura f. juncture; junction; joint, seam.

jurado m. jury; juror, juryman; adj. & p.p. sworn.

juramentar v. to swear in; **-se** to take an oath, be sworn in.

juramento m. oath; vow; curse.

jurar v. to swear, vow; to take oath; to curse.

jurisconsulto m. jurist, expert in law; lawyer.

jurisdicción f. jurisdiction.

jurisprudencia f. jurisprudence, law.

juro: de — adv. certainly, of course.

justa f. joust, tournament, combat (between horsemen with lances); contest.

justicia f. justice; court of justice; judge; police.

justiciero adj. strictly just, austere (in matters of justice).

justificación f. justification.

justificante adj. justifying; m. voucher; written excuse; proof.

justificar[6] v. to justify; to vindicate, clear of blame.

justo adj. just; pious; exact, correct;

tight; adv. duly; exactly; tightly; m. just man; **los -s** the just.

juvenil adj. juvenile, young, youthful.

juventud f. youth; young people.

juzgado m. court, tribunal.

juzgar[7] v. to judge.

K

kerosena f. kerosene, coal oil.

kilo m. kilo, kilogram.

kilogramo m. kilogram.

kilometraje m. number of kilometers.

kilómetro m. kilometer.

L

la def. art. f. the; — **de** the one with, that one with; obj. pron. her; it; — **que** rel. pron. she who, the one that; which.

laberinto m. labyrinth, maze; labyrinth, internal ear.

labia f. fluency, talkativeness, gift of gab; **tener mucha** — to be a good talker.

labio m. lip.

labor f. labor, work; embroidery; needlework; tillage; — **de punto** knitting; **laborable** adj. workable; tillable; **día laborable** work day; **laboral** adj. pertaining to labor.

laboratorio m. laboratory.

laboriosidad f. laboriousness, industry.

laborioso adj. laborious; industrious.

labrado p.p. & adj. tilled, cultivated; wrought; carved; manufactured; m. carving; — **en madera** woodwork, carving; **-s** cultivated lands.

labrador m. farmer; peasant.

labranza f. farming, tillage, plowing; cultivated land, farm.

labrar v. to till, cultivate, farm; to plow; to carve; to embroider; to work (metals); to build (a monument).

labriego m. peasant.

laca f. lacquer; shellac.

lacayo m. lackey, footman, flunky.

lacio adj. withered; languid; limp; straight (hair).

lacra f. trace of an illness; blemish, defect; Am. sore, ulcer, scab, scar.

lacre m. red sealing wax; adj. Am. red.

lactar v. to nurse, suckle; to feed with milk.

lácteo adj. milky; **fiebre láctea** milk fever; **régimen** — milk diet; **Vía Láctea** Milky Way.

ladear v. to tilt, tip; to go along the slope or side of; to turn aside (from a way or course); **-se** to tilt; to sway; to incline or lean (towards); to move

to one side; *Am.* to fall in love.
ladeo *m.* inclination, tilt.
ladera *f.* slope.
ladino *adj.* crafty, sly, shrewd; conversant with two or three languages; *m. Am.* Spanish-speaking person (*as opposed to one who speaks an Indian language*); *Am.* mestizo, half-breed; *Am.* talker, talkative person.
lado *m.* side; al — near, at hand, at one's side; de — tilted, obliquely; sideways; — a side by side; ¡a un —! gangway! hacerse a un — to move over, step aside, move to one side; *Am.* echársela de — to boast.
ladrar *v.* to bark.
ladrido *m.* bark, barking.
ladrillo *m.* brick.
ladrón *m.* thief, robber; **ladronzuelo** *m.* petty thief.
lagartija *f.* small lizard.
lagarto *m.* lizard; rascal, sly fellow.
lago *m.* lake.
lágrima *f.* tear; **llorar a — viva** to weep abundantly.
lagrimear *v.* to weep, shed tears.
laguna *f.* lagoon; gap, blank space.
laico *adj.* lay; *m.* layman.
laja *f.* slab; flat stone.
lamedero *m.* salt lick (*for cattle*).
lamentable *adj.* lamentable, pitiful.
lamentación *f.* lamentation.
lamentar *v.* to lament, deplore; -se to moan, complain, wail.
lamento *m.* lament, moan, cry.
lamer *v.* to lick; to lap.
lamida *f. Am.* lick.
lámina *f.* metal plate; sheet of metal; engraving; book illustration.
lámpara *f.* lamp.
lampiño *adj.* hairless; beardless.
lana *f.* wool; *Am.* tramp, vagabond.
lanar *adj.* wool-bearing; of wool.
lance *m.* occurrence, event; cast, throw, move, turn; accident; quarrel; predicament.
lancear *v.* to lance, spear.
lancha *f.* launch; boat; slab; **lanchón** *m.* barge.
langosta *f.* lobster; locust.
languidecer[13] *v. irr.* to languish.
languidez *f.* languor, faintness, weakness.
lánguido *adj.* languid.
lanudo *adj.* wooly; *Am.* coarse, crude, ill-bred; *Am.* dull, slow, weak-willed.
lanza *f.* lance, spear; *Am.* swindler, cheat.
lanzada *f.* thrust (*with a spear*).
lanzadera *f.* shuttle.

lanzar[9] *v.* to fling, throw; to eject; to launch; -se to rush, fling oneself; to dart out.
lanzazo *m.* thrust with a lance.
lapicero *m.* pencil (*a mechanical pencil, one with an adjustable lead*).
lápida *f.* slab, tombstone; stone tablet.
lapidar *v.* to stone; *Am.* to cut precious stones.
lápiz *m.* pencil, crayon; — para los labios lipstick.
lapso *m.* lapse.
lardo *m.* lard.
largar[7] *v.* to loosen; to let go; to set free; to unfold (*a flag or sails*); *Am.* to hurl, throw; *Am.* to strike (*a blow*); *Am.* to give, hand over; -se to go away, slip away; to leave.
largo *adj.* long; generous; *m.* length; largo (*music*); a la larga in the long run; slowly; a lo — along; lengthwise; ¡ — de aquí! get out of here!
largor *m.* length.
largucho *adj.* lanky.
largueza *f.* generosity, liberality; length.
larguísimo *adj.* very long.
largura *f.* length.
laringe *f.* larynx.
larva *f.* larva.
las *def. art. f. pl.* the; *obj. pron.* them; — que *rel. pron.* those which; which.
lascivia *f.* lewdness.
lascivo *adj.* lascivious, lewd.
lástima *f.* pity; compassion, grief.
lastimadura *f.* sore, hurt.
lastimar *v.* to hurt; to offend; -se to get hurt; -se to feel pity for.
lastimero *adj.* pitiful; mournful.
lastimoso *adj.* pitiful.
lastre *m.* ballast, weight.
lata *f.* tin plate; tin can, can; thin board; small log; boring speech; annoyance; embarrassment; *Am.* gaucho saber; *Am.* prop.
latente *adj.* latent.
lateral *adj.* lateral, side.
latido *m.* palpitation, throb, beat; bark, howl.
latifundio *m.* large landed estate.
latigazo *m.* lash, stroke with a whip; crack of a whip; harsh reprimand; unexpected blow or offense.
látigo *m.* whip; *Am.* whipping, beating; *Am.* end or goal of a horse race.
latín *m.* Latin language.
latino *adj.* Latin; *m.* Latinist, Latin scholar; Latin.
latir *v.* to throb, beat, palpitate; to bark.
latitud *f.* latitude; extent, breadth.
latón *m.* brass.

latrocinio *m.* larceny, theft, robbery.
laúd *m.* lute; catboat (*long, narrow boat with a lateen sail*).
laudable *adj.* laudable, praiseworthy.
laurel *m.* laurel; laurel wreath.
lauro *m.* laurel; glory, fame.
lava *f.* lava; washing of minerals.
lavable *adj.* washable.
lavabo *m.* lavatory, washroom; washstand; washbowl.
lavadero *m.* washing place.
lavado *m.* wash, washing; laundry, laundry work.
lavador *m.* washer; cleaner; *adj.* washing; cleaning; lavadora *f.* washer, washing machine.
lavadura *f.* washing; slops, dirty water.
lavamanos *m.* lavatory, washbowl, washstand.
lavandera *f.* laundress, washerwoman.
lavandería *f.* laundry.
lavar *v.* to wash; to launder; to whitewash.
lavativa *f.* enema; syringe; bother, nuisance.
lavatorio *m.* washing (*act of washing*); wash (*liquid or solution for washing*); lavatory (*ceremonial act of washing*); washbowl, washstand; *Am.* washroom.
lavazas *f. pl.* slops, dirty water.
lazada *f.* bow, bowknot; *Am.* throwing of the lasso, lassoing.
lazar⁹ *v.* to rope, lasso; to noose.
lazarillo *m.* blindman's guide.
lazo *m.* bow, knot; slipknot; lasso, lariat; tie, bond; snare, trap; trick.
le *obj. pron.* him; you (*formal*); to him; to her; to you (*formal*).
leal *adj.* loyal.
lealtad *f.* loyalty.
lebrel *m.* greyhound.
lebrillo *m.* earthenware basin or tub.
lección *f.* lesson; reading; dar la — to recite the lesson; dar — to teach; tomarle a uno la — to have someone recite his lesson.
lector *m.* reader; lecturer.
lectura *f.* reading; libro de — reader.
lechada *f.* whitewash; *Am.* milking.
leche *f.* milk; *Am.* luck (*in games*).
lechería *f.* dairy, creamery; lechero *adj.* milk; milch, giving milk (*applied to animals*); *Am.* lucky (*in games of chance*); *m.* milkman; lechera *f.* milkmaid; milk can; milk pitcher.
lecho *m.* bed; river bed.
lechón *m.* suckling pig; pig.
lechoso *adj.* milky; *m.* papaya tree; lechosa *f.* papaya (*tropical fruit*).
lechuga *f.* lettuce.

lechuza *f.* screech owl, barn owl.
leer¹⁴ *v.* to read.
legación *f.* legation.
legado *m.* legacy; legate, representative, ambassador.
legal *adj.* legal, lawful; truthful; reliable; *Am.* excellent, best; *Am.* just, honest.
legalizar⁹ *v.* to legalize.
legar⁷ *v.* to will, bequeath; to send as a delegate.
legendario *adj.* legendary.
legión *f.* legion.
legislación *f.* legislation.
legislador *m.* legislator; *adj.* legislating, legislative.
legislar *v.* to legislate.
legislativo *adj.* legislative.
legislatura *f.* legislature, legislative assembly.
legítimo *adj.* legitimate; real, genuine.
lego *adj.* lay; ignorant; *m.* layman.
legua *f.* league (*about 3 miles*).
leguleyo *m.* shyster.
legumbre *f.* vegetable.
leída *f. Am.* reading. See lectura.
lejanía *f.* distance; distant place.
lejano *adj.* distant; remote.
lejía *f.* lye; harsh reprimand.
lejos *adv.* far, far away; a lo — in the distance; *Am.* a un — in the distance; de (or desde) — from afar; *m.* view, perspective; background.
lelo *adj.* silly, stupid, foolish.
lema *m.* motto; theme; slogan.
lencería *f.* dry goods; dry-goods store; linen room or closet.
lengua *f.* tongue; language; interpreter; — de tierra point, neck of land.
lenguado *m.* flounder, sole (*a fish*).
lenguaje *m.* language (*manner of expression*).
lenguaraz *adj.* talkative, loose-tongued.
lengüeta *f.* small tongue; lengüetada *f.* lick.
lente *m. & f.* lens; -s *m. pl.* eyeglasses.
lenteja *f.* lentil; lentil seed; lentejuela *f.* spangle.
lentitud *f.* slowness.
lento *adj.* slow; dull.
leña *f.* firewood; kindling; beating; leñera *f.* woodshed; woodbox.
leñador *m.* woodcutter, woodman.
leño *m.* log; timber; piece of firewood.
león *m.* lion; leona *f.* lioness; leonera *f.* lion's den or cage; dive, gambling joint; disorderly room.
leontina *f. Am.* watch chain.
leopardo *m.* leopard.
leopoldina *f. Am.* watch chain.
lerdo *adj.* dull, heavy, stupid, slow.

126

les *obj. pron.* to them; to you (*formal*).

lesión *f.* wound, injury.

lesionar *v.* to injure; to wound; to hurt; to damage.

lesna = **lezna**.

letargo *m.* lethargy, stupor, drowsiness.

letra *f.* letter (*of the alphabet*); printing type; hand, handwriting; letter (*exact wording or meaning*); words of a song; **— abierta** letter of credit; **— de cambio** draft, bill of exchange; **— mayúscula** capital letter; **— minúscula** small letter; **al pie de la —** literally; **-s** letters, learning.

letrado *adj.* learned; *m.* lawyer.

letrero *m.* notice, poster, sign; legend (*under an illustration*).

leva *f.* levy, draft; weighing anchor, setting sail; **echar —** to draft, conscript; *Am.* **echar -s** to boast.

levadura *f.* leaven, yeast.

levantamiento *m.* uprising, revolt, insurrection; elevation; lifting, raising; adjournment (*of a meeting*); **— de un plano** surveying.

levantar *v.* to raise, lift; to set up; to erect; to rouse, stir up; to recruit; *Am.* to break land, plow; **— el campo** to break camp; **— la mesa** to clear the table; **— la sesión** to adjourn the meeting; **— un plano** to survey, map out; **— falso testimonio** to bear false witness; **-se** to stand up, get up, rise; to rebel.

levante *m.* east; east wind.

levantisco *adj.* turbulent; rebellious.

levar *v.* to weigh (*anchor*); **— el ancla** to weigh anchor; **-se** to weigh anchor, set sail.

leve *adj.* light; slight, unimportant.

levita *f.* frock coat; *m.* Levite, member of the tribe of Levi.

léxico *m.* lexicon, dictionary; vocabulary; glossary.

ley *f.* law; rule; loyalty; standard quality; **de buena —** of good quality; **plata de —** sterling silver; **-es** jurisprudence, law; system of laws.

leyenda *f.* legend; reading; inscription.

lezna *f.* awl.

liar *v.* to tie, bind; to roll up; to deceive; **-se** to bind oneself; to get tangled up.

libelo *m.* libel.

libélula *f.* dragon fly.

liberación *f.* liberation; deliverance.

liberal *adj.* liberal; generous; **liberalidad** *f.* liberality; generosity.

libertad *f.* liberty.

libertador *m.* liberator, deliverer.

libertar *v.* to liberate, free, set free; **-se** to get free; to escape.

libertinaje *m.* license, licentiousness, lack of moral restraint.

libertino *m.* libertine (*person without moral restraint*).

libra *f.* pound; Libra (*sign of the Zodiac*).

librador *m.* drawer (*of a bill, draft, etc.*); deliverer, liberator; measuring scoop.

libranza *f.* bill of exchange, draft.

librar *v.* to free, set free; to issue; to draw (*a draft*); **— guerra** to wage war; **-se** to save oneself; to escape; **-se de** to get rid of, escape from.

libre *adj.* free; unmarried; loose; vacant.

librea *f.* livery (*uniform*).

librería *f.* bookstore.

librero *m.* bookseller; *Am.* bookcase, bookshelves.

libreta *f.* notebook, memorandum book.

libro *m.* book; **— de caja** cashbook; **— mayor** ledger.

licencia *f.* license; permission; furlough, leave; looseness; license to practice.

licenciado *m.* licenciate (*person having a degree approximately equivalent to a master's degree*); *Am.* lawyer.

licenciar *v.* to license; to give a license or permit; to dismiss, discharge (*from the army*); to confer the degree of **licenciado**; **-se** to get the degree of **licenciado**.

licenciatura *f.* degree of **licenciado**.

licencioso *adj.* licentious, lewd.

lícito *adj.* lawful; permissible; allowable.

licor *m.* liquid; liquor.

lid *f.* fight; contest.

líder *m. Am.* leader.

lidiar *v.* to fight; to combat; to contend.

liebre *f.* hare; coward.

lienzo *m.* cotton or linen cloth; canvas; painting.

liga *f.* league; alliance; garter; alloy (*mixture of metals*); birdlime.

ligadura *f.* binding; tie, bond.

ligar *v.* to bind, tie, unite; to alloy (*combine metals*); **-se** to unite, combine, form an alliance.

ligereza *f.* lightness; swiftness; flippancy; frivolity.

ligero *adj.* light; swift; nimble; flippant; *adv. Am.* quickly; **a la ligera** quickly, superficially.

lija *f.* sandpaper.

lijar *v.* to sandpaper.

lila *f.* lilac; pinkish-purple.

lima *f.* file; lime (*fruit*); finishing, polishing.

limar *v.* to file; to file down; to smooth, polish.

limeño *adj.* of or from Lima, Peru.
limitación *f.* limitation; district.
limitar *v.* to limit; to restrict; to bound.
límite *m.* limit; boundary.
limo *m.* slime.
limón *m.* lemon; lemon tree; **limonada** *f.* lemonade; **limonero** *m.* lemon tree; lemon dealer or vendor.
limosna *f.* alms, charity.
limpiabotas *m.* bootblack; *Am.* bootlicker, flatterer.
limpiadientes *m.* toothpick.
limpiar *v.* to clean; to wipe; to cleanse, purify; *Am.* to beat up, whip, lash.
límpido *adj.* limpid, clear.
limpieza *f.* cleanliness, neatness; purity; honesty.
limpio *adj.* clean; neat; pure; **poner en —** to make a clean copy; *Am.* **— y soplado** absolutely broke, wiped out.
linaje *m.* lineage, family, race.
linaza *f.* linseed.
lince *m.* lynx; sharp-sighted person.
linchar *v.* to lynch.
lindar *v.* to border, adjoin.
linde *m. & f.* limit, border, boundary; landmark.
lindero *adj.* bordering upon; *m. Am.* landmark; boundary.
lindeza *f.* prettiness; exquisiteness; neatness; witty act or remark.
lindo *adj.* pretty; **de lo —** wonderfully; very much; to the utmost.
línea *f.* line; limit.
lineal *adj.* lineal, linear.
lino *m.* linen; flax; **linón** *m.* lawn, thin linen or cotton.
linterna *f.* lantern.
lío *m.* bundle; fib; mess, confusion; **armar un —** to raise a rumpus; to cause confusion; **hacerse un —** to be confused, get tangled up; **meterse en un —** to get oneself into a mess.
liquidación *f.* liquidation; settlement (*of an account*).
liquidar *v.* to liquidate; to settle (*an account*).
líquido *m.* liquid.
lira *f.* lyre, small harp; a type of metrical composition; lira (*Italian coin*).
lírico *adj.* lyric, lyrical; *Am.* fantastic; *m. Am.* visionary, dreamer.
lirio *m.* lily.
lirismo *m.* lyricism (*lyric quality*); *Am.* idle dream, fantasy.
lisiado *adj.* lame, hurt, injured
liso *adj.* smooth, even; flat; evident, clear; *Am.* crafty, sly; *Am.* fresh, impudent.
lisonja *f.* flattery.

lisonjear *v.* to flatter; to fawn on; to please.
lisonjero *adj.* flattering, pleasing; *m.* flatterer.
lista *f.* list; strip; stripe; **pasar —** to call the roll.
listado *adj.* striped.
listar *v.* to register, enter in a list; *Am.* to stripe, streak.
listo *adj.* ready, prompt; clever; *Am.* mischievous.
listón *m.* ribbon, tape; strip.
lisura *f.* smoothness; sincerity, frankness; *Am.* freshness, impudence; *Am.* insulting or filthy remark.
litera *f.* berth (*on a boat or train*); litter (*for carrying a person*).
literario *adj.* literary.
literato *adj.* literary, learned; *m.* literary man, writer.
literatura *f.* literature.
litigio *m.* litigation, lawsuit.
litoral *adj.* seaboard, coastal; *m.* coast, shore.
litro *m.* liter (*about 1.05 quarts*).
liviandad *f.* lightness; frivolity; lewdness.
liviano *adj.* light; slight, unimportant; frivolous, fickle; lewd; unchaste.
lívido *adj.* livid, having a dull-bluish color; pale.
lo *obj. pron.* him; you (*formal*); it; so; *dem. pron.* **— de** that of, that affair of, that matter of; **— bueno** the good, what is good; **sé — bueno que Vd. es** I know how good you are; **— que** that which, what.
loable *adj.* laudable, worthy of praise.
loar *v.* to praise.
lobanillo *m.* growth, tumor.
lobo *m.* wolf.
lóbrego *adj.* dark, gloomy.
lobreguez *f.* darkness, gloominess.
local *adj.* local; *m.* place, quarters; site; premises.
localidad *f.* location; locality; town; place; seat (*in a theatre*).
localización *f.* localization, localizing.
localizar *v.* to localize.
loco *adj.* insane, mad, crazy; **— de remate** stark mad; *m.* lunatic, insane person.
locomotor *adj.* locomotive.
locomotora *f.* locomotive.
locuaz *adj.* loquacious, talkative.
locución *f.* phrase; diction.
locura *f.* madness, insanity.
locutor *m.* radio announcer.
lodazal *m.* muddy place; mire.
lodo *m.* mud; **lodoso** *adj.* muddy, miry.

logia *f.* lodge (*secret society*).

lógica *f.* logic; reasoning.

lógico *adj.* logical.

lograr *v.* to gain, obtain, accomplish; — (+ *inf.*) to succeed in; -se to succeed; to turn out well.

logrero *m.* usurer; profiteer.

logro *m.* profit, gain; usury; attainment; realization.

loma *f.* small hill; lomerío *m. Am.* group of hills.

lombriz *f.* earthworm.

lomo *m.* back (*of an animal, book, knife, etc.*); loin; ridge between two furrows; *Am.* hacer — to bear with patience, resign oneself.

lona *f.* canvas.

lonche *m. Am.* lunch; lonchería *f. Am.* lunchroom.

longaniza *f.* pork sausage.

longevidad *f.* longevity, long life; span of life, length of life.

longitud *f.* longitude; length.

longitudinal *adj.* longitudinal, lengthwise; -mente *adv.* longitudinally, lengthwise.

lonja *f.* exchange; market; slice of meat; leather strap; *Am.* raw hide.

lontananza *f.* background; en — in the distance, in the background.

loro *m.* parrot.

los *def. art. m. pl.* the; *obj. pron.* them; — que *rel. pron.* those which; which.

losa *f.* flagstone; slab; gravestone.

lote *m.* lot, share, part; *Am.* remnant lot; *Am.* swallow of liquor; *Am.* blockhead, dunce.

lotear *v. Am.* to subdivide into lots; *Am.* to divide into portions.

lotería *f.* lottery; raffle.

loza *f.* fine earthenware; crockery; — fina chinaware.

lozanía *f.* luxuriance (*rich foliage or growth*); vigor.

lozano *adj.* luxuriant; exuberant, vigorous, lusty.

lubricar[6] *v.* to lubricate, oil, grease.

lucero *m.* morning star; any bright star; star on the forehead of certain animals; splendor, brightness.

lúcido *adj.* lucid, clear; shining, bright.

luciente *adj.* shining, bright.

luciérnaga *f.* firefly; glowworm.

lucimiento *m.* splendor; brilliance; success.

lucir[13] *v. irr.* to shine; to excel; to illuminate; to brighten; to show off; -se to shine, be brilliant; to show off; to be successful.

lucrativo *adj.* lucrative, profitable.

lucro *m.* profit, gain.

luctuoso *adj.* sad, mournful, dismal.

lucha *f.* fight, struggle; dispute; wrestling match.

luchador *m.* fighter; wrestler.

luchar *v.* to fight; to wrestle; to struggle; to dispute.

luego *adv.* soon, presently; afterwards, then, next; desde — immediately, at once; naturally, — de afuera — que as soon as; hasta — good-bye, so long; — — right away.

luengo *adj.* long; -s años many years.

lugar *m.* place; site; town; space; position, employment; time, occasion, opportunity; dar — a to give cause or occasion for; hacer (*or* dar) — to make room; en — de instead of.

lúgubre *adj.* mournful, gloomy.

lujo *m.* luxury, extravagance.

lujoso *adj.* luxurious; elegant; showy.

lujuria *f.* lust, lewdness, sensuality.

lujurioso *adj.* lustful, lewd, sensual.

lumbre *f.* fire; brightness.

luminoso *adj.* luminous, bright, shining.

luna *f.* moon; mirror, glass for mirrors.

lunar *adj.* lunar; *m.* mole; blemish, spot.

lunático *adj. & m.* lunatic.

lunes *m.* Monday; *Am.* hacer San Lunes to lay off on Monday.

lustre *m.* luster, shine; glory.

lustroso *adj.* lustrous, glossy, shining.

luto *m.* mourning; sorrow, grief.

luz *f.* light; clarity; hint, guidance; dar a — to give birth; to publish; entre dos luces at twilight.

LL

llaga *f.* wound; ulcer, sore.

llama *f.* flame; llama (*a South American beast of burden*).

llamada *f.* call; beckon, sign; knock; reference mark (*as an asterisk*).

llamador *m.* knocker (*of a door*); caller.

llamamiento *m.* call, calling; calling together, appeal.

llamar *v.* to call; to summon; to name; to invoke; — a la puerta to knock at the door; -se to be called, named; *Am.* to break one's word or promise.

llamarada *f.* flash; sudden flame or blaze; sudden flush, blush.

llamativo *adj.* showy, loud, gaudy, flashy; thirst-exciting.

llameante *adj.* flaming.

llana *f.* mason's trowel.

llanero *m. Am.* plainsman.

llaneza *f.* simplicity; frankness; sincerity; plainness.

llano *adj.* plain, simple; even, smooth,

level; frank; *m.* plain, flat ground.

llanta *f.* tire; tire casing; rim of a wheel; *Am.* large sunshade (*used in Peruvian markets*).

llanto *m.* crying, weeping; tears.

llanura *f.* extensive plain; prairie; evenness, flatness.

llave *f.* key; faucet; clef; **— de tuercas** wrench; **— inglesa** monkey wrench; **— maestra** master key.

llavera *f. Am.* housekeeper.

llavero *m.* key ring; key maker; keeper of the keys.

llavín *m.* small key.

llegada *f.* arrival.

llegar[1] *v.* to arrive; to reach; to amount; **— a ser** to get or come to be; **— a las manos** to come to blows; **-se** to approach, get near.

llenar *v.* to fill; to stuff; **-se** to fill up; to overeat; **-se de** to get filled with; to get covered with, spattered with.

lleno *adj.* full; *m.* fullness, completeness; **de —** totally, completely; **un — completo** a full house (*said of a theater*).

llenura *f.* fullness; abundance.

llevadero *adj.* bearable, tolerable.

llevar *v.* to carry; to bear; to transport; to wear; to keep (*accounts*); to charge, ask a certain price; to take, lead; **— ventaja** to be ahead, have the advantage; **— un año** to be one year older than; **— un mes aquí** to have been here one month; **— un castigo** to suffer punishment; **-se** to carry away; **-se bien con** to get along with.

llorar *v.* to cry, weep.

lloriquear *v.* to whimper, whine, weep.

lloriqueo *m.* whimper, whining.

lloro *m.* weeping.

llorón *adj.* weeping; **sauce —** weeping willow; *m.* weeper, crybaby, whiner.

llorona *f.* weeping woman; **-s** *Am.* large spurs.

lloroso *adj.* tearful; weeping.

llovedizo *adj.* rain (*used as adj.*); **agua llovediza** rain water.

llover[2] *v. irr.* to rain, shower.

llovizna *f.* drizzle.

lloviznar *v.* to drizzle, sprinkle.

lluvia *f.* rain; shower.

lluvioso *adj.* rainy.

M

macana *f. Am.* club, cudgel, stick; *Am.* lie, absurdity, nonsense.

macarrón *m.* macaroon; **-es** macaroni.

maceta *f.* flowerpot; small mallet; stonecutter's hammer; handle of tools; *Am.* head; *adj.* slow.

macilento *adj.* thin, emaciated; pale.

macizo *adj.* solid, firm; massive; *m.* massiveness; firmness; thicket; clump.

machacar[6] *v.* to pound, crush; to insist, harp on.

machacón *adj.* persistent; tenacious.

machete *m.* machete, large heavy knife; **machetazo** *m.* large machete; blow with a machete.

macho *m.* male; he-mule; hook (*of a hook and eye*); abutment; pillar; stupid fellow; sledge hammer; *Am.* **pararle a uno el —** to halt or repress a person; *adj.* masculine, male; strong.

machucar[6] *v.* to pound, beat, bruise; *Am.* to crush; *Am.* to break (*a horse*).

machucón *m.* smash; bruise.

madeja *f.* skein; mass of hair; limp, listless person.

madera *f.* wood; timber; lumber; **maderero** *m.* lumberman, lumber dealer.

maderaje *m.* timber, lumber; timber work; woodwork.

maderamen *m.* timber; timber work; woodwork.

madero *m.* beam; plank; timber, piece of lumber; blockhead, dunce.

madrastra *f.* stepmother.

madre *f.* mother; womb; root, origin; river bed; **salirse de —** to overflow (*said of rivers*).

madrepeña *f. Am.* moss.

madreperla *f.* mother-of-pearl.

madreselva *f.* honeysuckle.

madriguera *f.* burrow; den, lair.

madrileño *adj.* Madrilenian, from or pertaining to Madrid; *m.* Madrilenian.

madrina *f.* godmother; bridesmaid; sponsor; prop; strap for yoking two horses; leading mare; *Am.* small herd of tame cattle (*used for leading wild cattle*).

madrugada *f.* dawn; early morning; **de —** at daybreak.

madrugador *m.* early riser.

madrugar[1] *v.* to rise early; to be ahead of others.

madurar *v.* to mature; to ripen.

madurez *f.* maturity; ripeness.

maduro *adj.* ripe; mature; prudent, wise; *Am.* bruised, sore.

maestría *f.* mastery; great skill.

maestro *m.* master, teacher; chief craftsman; *adj.* master; masterly, skilful; **llave maestra** master key; **obra maestra** masterpiece.

magia *f.* magic; charm.

mágico *adj.* magic; *m.* magician.

magín *m.* imagination, fancy.

magisterio *m.* teaching profession.

magistrado *m.* magistrate, judge.
magistral *adj.* masterly; masterful; authoritative.
magnánimo *adj.* magnanimous, noble, generous.
magnético *adj.* magnetic; attractive.
magnificencia *f.* magnificence, splendor.
magnífico *adj.* magnificent, splendid.
magnitud *f.* magnitude, greatness.
mago *m.* magician, wizard; **los tres Reyes Magos** the Three Wise Men.
magra *f.* slice of ham.
magro *adj.* lean.
maguey *m.* maguey, century plant.
magullar *v.* to bruise; to maul; to mangle; *Am.* to crumple.
mahometano *adj. & m.* Mohammedan.
maíz *m.* corn; **maizal** *m.* cornfield.
majada *f.* sheepfold; dung, manure; *Am.* flock of sheep or goats.
majadería *f.* foolishness, nonsense.
majadero *adj.* foolish; bothersome.
majar *v.* to pound; to crush; to bruise; to crumple; to mash; to annoy, bother.
majestad *f.* majesty; dignity.
majestuoso *adj.* majestic, stately.
majo *adj.* gaudy, showy; gaily attired; pretty; *m.* dandy; **maja** *f.* belle.
mal *m.* evil; illness; harm; wrong. *See* **malo.**
malabarista *m. & f.* juggler; *Am.* sly thief.
malacate *m.* hoist, hoisting machine; winch; *Am.* spindle (*for cotton*); *Am.* **parecer uno un —** to be constantly on the go, be in constant motion.
malandanza *f.* misfortune.
malaventura *f.* misfortune, disaster.
malazo *adj.* perverse, evil, wicked; vicious.
malbaratar *v.* to undersell, sell at a loss; to squander.
malcontento *adj.* discontented; *m.* malcontent, troublemaker.
malcriado *adj.* ill-bred, rude.
maldad *f.* badness, evil, wickedness.
maldecir[27, 52] *v. irr.* to curse; to damn.
maldición *f.* curse.
maldispuesto *adj.* unwilling, not inclined.
maldito *p.p. of* **maldecir** *& adj.* cursed; wicked; damned; *Am.* tricky; *Am.* bold, boastful.
maleante *m.* crook, rogue, rascal, villain.
malecón *m.* mole, dike.
maledicencia *f.* slander.
maleficio *m.* spell, charm, witchery.
maléfico *adj.* evil, harmful.
malestar *m.* indisposition; slight illness; discomfort.

maleta *f.* travelling bag; suitcase; *Am.* bundle of clothes; *Am.* hump (*on the back*); *Am.* saddlebag; *Am.* **rogue**, rascal; *Am.* lazy fellow.
maletín *m.* small valise, satchel.
malevo *adj. Am.* bad, wicked.
malévolo *adj.* bad, evil, wicked.
maleza *f.* underbrush; thicket; weeds.
malgastar *v.* to squander, waste.
malhechor *m.* malefactor, evildoer, criminal.
malhora *f. Am.* trouble, misfortune.
malhumorado *adj.* ill-humored.
malicia *f.* malice; wickedness; shrewdness; suspicion; *Am.* bit of brandy or cognac added to another drink.
maliciar *v.* to suspect.
malicioso *adj.* malicious; wicked; shrewd; suspicious.
maligno *adj.* malign, malignant; pernicious, harmful.
malmandado *adj.* disobedient; stubborn.
mal(o) *adj.* bad, evil; wicked; ill; difficult; *Am.* **a la mala** treacherously; *Am.* **de malas** by force; **estar de malas** to be out of luck; **por la mala** unwillingly, by force; **venir de malas** to come with evil intentions; **mal** *adv.* badly; poorly; wrongly.
malograr *v.* to waste, lose; **-se** to turn out badly; to fail.
malón *m.* mean trick; *Am.* surprise Indian raid; *Am.* tin-pan serenade, boisterous surprise party.
malpagar[7] *v.* to underpay, pay poorly.
malparto *m.* miscarriage, abortion.
malquerencia *f.* aversion, dislike, ill will.
malsano *adj.* unhealthy; sickly.
malta *f.* malt.
maltratar *v.* to treat badly; to misuse, abuse.
maltrato *m.* mistreatment, abuse.
maltrecho *adj.* battered, bruised, injured.
malvado *adj.* wicked; malicious.
malversación *f.* graft, corruption, misuse of public funds.
malversar *v.* to misuse (*funds in one's trust*); to embezzle.
malla *f.* mesh; coat of mail; *Am.* species of potato; **hacer —** to knit.
mamá *f.* mamma.
mamada *f.* suck, sucking.
mamar *v.* to suckle; to suck; to gorge; **-se** *Am.* to get drunk; *Am.* to go back on one's promise; *Am.* to fold up, crack up; **-se a uno** to get the best of someone, deceive someone;

Am. to kill someone.

mamífero *m.* mammal; *adj.* mammalian, of mammals.

mamón *adj.* suckling; *m.* suckling (*very young animal or child*); shoot, sucker (*of a tree*); *Am.* cherimoya (*tree and fruit*); *Am.* papaya (*tree and fruit*); *Am.* a kind of cake.

mampara *f.* screen.

mampostería *f.* masonry, stone masonry.

manada *f.* herd; drove; pack; flock.

manantial *m.* spring; source, origin.

manar *v.* to spring, flow (from); to abound.

manaza *f.* large hand.

manazo *m. Am.* slap. *See* **manotazo.**

mancarrón *m.* one-armed or one-handed man; cripple; old nag; *Am.* crude, clumsy fellow; *Am.* disabled workman; *Am.* dike, small dam.

mancebo *m.* youth, young man; bachelor.

mancera *f.* handle of a plough.

mancilla *f.* stain, spot; dishonor.

manco *adj.* one-armed; one-handed; maimed; lame (*referring to an arm or the front leg of an animal*); faulty, defective; *m. Am.* nag.

mancha *f.* spot, stain, blemish; *Am.* cloud, swarm; *Am.* roving herd of cattle.

manchar *v.* to stain, soil, spot; to tarnish.

manchego *adj.* of or belonging to La Mancha (*region of Spain*); *m.* inhabitant of la Mancha.

manchón *m.* large stain; large patch.

mandadero *m.* messenger, errand boy.

mandado *m.* command, order; errand; *p.p. of* **mandar; bien —** well-behaved; **mal —** ill-behaved.

mandamiento *m.* command, order; writ; commandment.

mandar *v.* to command, order; to send; to bequeath, will; to rule; *Am.* to throw, hurl; **— hacer** to have made, order; *Am.* **— una bofetada** to give a slap; *Am.* **— una pedrada** to throw a stone; **-se** *Am.* to be impudent; **-se mudar** *Am.* to go away.

mandatario *m.* attorney, representative; *Am.* magistrate, chief.

mandato *m.* mandate; order, command.

mandíbula *f.* jaw, jawbone.

mando *m.* command, authority, power.

mandón *adj.* bossy, domineering; *m.* bossy person; *Am.* boss or foreman of a mine; *Am.* race starter.

maneador *m. Am.* hobble, leather lasso

(*for the legs of an animal*); *Am.* whip; *Am.* halter.

manear *v.* to hobble, lasso, tie the legs of (*an animal*); **-se** *Am.* to get tangled up.

manecilla *f.* small hand; hand of a watch or clock.

manejable *adj.* manageable.

manejar *v.* to manage, handle; to drive (*a car*); **-se** to move about, get around (*after an illness or accident*); *Am.* to behave oneself.

manejo *m.* handling; management; trick, intrigue.

manera *f.* manner, way, mode; side opening in a skirt; front opening in breeches; **-s** customs; manners, behavior; **a — de** (*or* **a la — de**) like, in the style of; **de — que** so that; **sobre —** exceedingly; extremely.

manga *f.* sleeve; bag; hose (*for watering*); body of troops; *Am.* multitude, herd, swarm; *Am.* cattle chute (*narrow passageway*); *Am.* corral; **— de agua** waterspout, whirlwind over the ocean; *Am.* **— de hule** raincape; **por angas o por -s** by hook or crook, in one way or another.

mangana *f.* lariat, lasso.

manganeso *m.* manganese.

mango *m.* handle; *Am.* mango (*tropical tree and its fruit*).

manguera *f.* hose (*for water*); waterspout; *Am.* large corral (*for livestock*).

manguito *m.* muff; knitted half-sleeve (*worn on the forearm*); oversleeve.

maní *m. Am.* peanut; **manicero** *m. Am.* peanut vendor.

manía *f.* mania, frenzy; craze, whim.

maniatar *v.* to tie the hands; to handcuff; to hobble (*an animal*).

maniático *m.* crank, queer fellow; *adj.* cranky, queer, odd.

manicomio *m.* insane asylum.

manicura *f.* manicure; manicurist.

manicurar *v.* to manicure.

manido *adj.* rotting; *Am.* trite, commonplace.

manifestación *f.* manifestation; demonstration.

manifestar[1] *v. irr.* to manifest; to show.

manifiesto *adj.* manifest, clear, plain; *m.* manifesto, public declaration; customhouse manifest.

manigua *f. Am.* Cuban jungle or thicket; *Am.* **coger —** to get feverish; *Am.* **irse a la —** to rise up in rebellion.

manija *f.* handle; crank; fetter.

manilla *f.* small hand; bracelet; **-s de hierro** handcuffs.

maniobra f. maneuver; operation.

maniobrar v. to maneuver.

manipulación f. manipulation.

manipular v. to manipulate, handle.

maniquí m. manikin, model, dummy, figure of a person; puppet.

manivela f. crank.

manjar m. dish, food; choice bit of food.

mano f. hand; forefoot; clock hand; coat of paint or varnish; quire (25 *sheets*) of paper; *Am.* adventure, mishap; *Am.* handful; **— de obra** workmanship; labor; *Am.* to fondle; at hand; by hand; *Am.* **estamos a —** we are even, we are quits; *Am.* **doblar las -s** to give up; **ser —** to be first (*in a game*); to lead (*in a game*); **venir a las -s** to come to blows.

manojo m. handful; bunch.

manopla f. gauntlet; heavy glove; huge hand.

manosear v. to handle, touch, feel with the hand; *Am.* to fondle, pet, caress.

manotada f. slap, blow; sweep of the hand; *Am.* handful, fistful; **manotazo** m. slap.

manotear v. to gesticulate; to strike with the hands; *Am.* to embezzle, steal; *Am.* to snatch away (*what is given*).

mansalva: a — without danger or risk; treacherously; **matar a —** to kill without warning or without giving a person a chance to defend himself.

mansedumbre f. meekness; gentleness.

mansión f. sojourn, stay; abode, dwelling.

manso adj. meek; mild, gentle; tame; *Am.* cultivated (*plant*), civilized (*Indian*); m. leading sheep, goat, or ox.

manta f. blanket; large shawl; tossing in a blanket; *Am.* coarse cotton cloth; *Am.* poncho; *Am.* **— mojada** dull person, dunce; **darle a uno una —** to toss someone in a blanket.

mantear v. to toss (*someone*) in a blanket.

manteca f. fat; lard; butter; *Am.* **— de cacao** cocoa butter; *Am.* **— de coco** coconut oil; **mantequera** f. churn; butter dish; woman who makes or sells butter.

mantecado m. ice cream.

mantel m. tablecloth; altar cloth; *Am.* **estar de -es largos** to dine in style.

mantener[45] v. ir. to maintain; to support; to sustain; to defend; **-se** to continue, remain; to support oneself; **-se firme** to remain firm; stand firm; **-se quieto** to stay or keep quiet.

mantenimiento m. maintenance, support; sustenance; livelihood.

mantequilla f. butter; **mantequillería** f. *Am.* creamery, dairy (*for making butter*).

mantilla f. mantilla (*Spanish veil or scarf for the head*); saddlecloth.

manto m. mantle, cloak; cape; large mantilla; mantel, mantelpiece.

mantón m. large shawl; **— de Manila** embroidered silk shawl.

manuable adj. handy, easy to handle.

manual adj. manual; handy; m. manual, handbook.

manubrio m. crank; handle.

manufacturar v. to manufacture.

manufacturero adj. manufacturing; m. manufacturer.

manuscrito adj. written by hand; m. manuscript.

manutención f. maintenance; support; conservation.

manzana f. apple; block of houses; *Am.* Adam's apple; **manzano** m. apple tree.

maña f. skill, knack; cunning; **malas -s** bad tricks or habits.

mañana f. morning; *Am.* **media —** mid-morning snack; adv. tomorrow, in the near future; **pasado —** day after tomorrow; **muy de —** very early in the morning; m. morrow; **mañanitas** f. pl. *Am.* popular song sung early in the morning to celebrate a birthday, saint's day, etc.

mañanero m. early riser; adj. early rising; **mañanista** m. & f. *Am.* procrastinator, one who puts things off until tomorrow.

mañero adj. astute, artful, clever; *Am.* tricky; *Am.* shy (*animal*); *Am.* indolent, lazy (*child*).

mañoso adj. skilful; clever; sly; tricky; *Am.* slow, lazy; *Am.* greedy, gluttonous (*child*).

mapa m. map, chart.

mapache m. *Am.* raccoon.

mapurite, mapurito m. *Am.* skunk. See **zorrino, zorrillo**.

máquina f. machine; engine; **— de coser** sewing machine; **— de escribir** typewriter.

maquinación f. machination, scheming, plotting; plot, scheme.

maquinador m. schemer, plotter.

maquinal adj. mechanical, automatic; **-mente** adv. mechanically, automatically, in a mechanical manner.

maquinar v. to plot, scheme.

maquinaria f. machinery; mechanism; mechanics.

maquinista m. engineer, locomotive

engineer; machinist; mechanic.

mar *m. & f.* sea; — **alta** rough sea; — **llena** high tide (*see* **pleamar**); — **de fondo** swell; **a** -**es** abundantly; **baja** — low tide; **en alta** — on the high seas; **la** — **de cosas** a lot of things.

maraña *f.* tangle; snarl; thicket; maze; plot, intrigue.

maravedí *m.* maravedi (*an old Spanish coin*).

maravilla *f.* wonder, marvel; marigold; **a las mil** -**s** wonderfully, perfectly.

maravillar *v.* to astonish, dazzle; -**se** to wonder, marvel.

maravilloso *adj.* marvellous, wonderful.

marbete *m.* label, stamp; baggage tag or check.

marca *f.* mark, stamp; sign; brand, make; gauge, rule; march, frontier province; — **de fábrica** trademark; **de** — of excellent quality.

marcar[6] *v.* to mark, stamp, brand; to note, observe.

marcial *adj.* martial, warlike; frank, abrupt.

marco *m.* frame; mark (*German coin*); mark (*unit of weight, equal to 8 ounces*).

marcha *f.* march; course, progress; speed; gait; running, functioning; movement of a watch.

marchamo *m.* customhouse mark; *Am.* tax on each slaughtered animal.

marchante *m.* merchant, dealer; customer, regular client.

marchar *v.* to march, mark step; to walk; to parade; to run (*said of machinery*); -**se** to go away.

marchitar *v.* to wither; -**se** to wither; to fade; to shrivel up.

marchito *adj.* withered; faded; shrivelled up.

marea *f.* tide; *Am.* sea fog.

mareado *adj.* seasick; dizzy.

marear *v.* to navigate, sail; to annoy, upset (*a person*); -**se** to get sea-sick, nauseated.

mareo *m.* seasickness; nausea; vexation, annoyance.

marfil *m.* ivory; *Am.* fine-toothed comb.

margarita *f.* marguerite, daisy; pearl.

margen *m. & f.* margin, border; river bank; **dar** — **a** to give an occasion to.

maricón *adj.* sissy, effeminate; *m.* sissy.

marido *m.* husband.

marina *f.* sea coast, shore; marine, fleet; navy; seamanship; seascape; — **de guerra** navy; — **mercante** merchant marine.

marinero *m.* mariner, seaman, sailor.

marino *adj.* marine; *m.* mariner, seaman, sailor.

mariposa *f.* butterfly; moth; *Am.* blindman's buff (*a game*).

mariscal *m.* marshal; blacksmith; — **de campo** field marshal.

marisco *m.* shellfish.

marítimo *adj.* maritime, marine.

marmita *f.* kettle, boiler, teakettle.

mármol *m.* marble.

marmóreo *adj.* marble, of marble, like marble.

maroma *f.* rope; *Am.* somersault; *Am.* acrobatic performance; *Am.* sudden change of political views; **andar en la** — to walk the tightrope; **maromero** *m. Am.* acrobat.

marqués *m.* marquis.

marquesa *f.* marquise; *Am.* couch.

marrano *m.* pig, hog; filthy person.

marrazo *m. Am.* bayonet, dagger.

marrullero *adj.* sly, wily.

martes *m.* Tuesday; — **de carnestolendas** Shrove Tuesday (*Tuesday before Lent*).

martillar *v.* to hammer, pound.

martillo *m.* hammer.

martinete *m.* pile driver; drop hammer; hammer of a piano.

mártir *m. & f.* martyr.

martirio *m.* martyrdom; torture, torment.

martirizar[9] *v.* to martyr; to torture, torment.

marzo *m.* March.

mas *conj.* but.

más *adj.* more; most; *adv.* more; most; plus; — **bien** rather; — **de** more than, over; — **que** more than; **no . . .** — **que** only; **a** — **de** in addition to; **a lo** — at the most; **está de** — it is superfluous, unnecessary; *Am.* **no** — only; *Am.* **no quiero** — **nada** (*instead of* **no quiero nada** —) I don't want anything more.

masa *f.* mass; volume; crowd; dough, paste; mortar; — **coral** glee club, choral society; **agarrarle a uno con las manos en la** — to catch someone in the act; **masilla** *f.* putty.

masaje *m.* massage.

mascada *f.* chewing; *Am.* mouthful; *Am.* chew or quid of tobacco; *Am.* reprimand, scolding; *Am.* silk handkerchief, scarf.

mascar[6] *v.* to chew.

máscara *f.* mask; -**s** masquerade; *m. & f.* masquerader; **mascarada** *f.* masquerade.

masculino *adj.* masculine.

mascullar *v.* to mumble; to munch.

mason *m.* mason, freemason; **maso-neria** *f.* masonry, freemasonry.
masticar[6] *v.* to chew.
mástil *m.* mast; post.
mastín *m.* mastiff.
mastuerzo *m.* nasturtium; simpleton, fool.
mata *f.* shrub, plant, bush; grove; clump of trees; *Am.* thicket, jungle; — **de pelo** head of hair.
matadero *m.* slaughterhouse; hard work.
matador *m.* killer, murderer; bull-fighter who kills the bull.
matanza *f.* massacre, butchery; slaughter of livestock; *Am.* slaughterhouse.
matar *v.* to kill; to murder; **-se** to commit suicide; to overwork; **-se con alguien** to fight with somebody.
matasanos *m.* quack, quack doctor.
mate *m.* checkmate (*winning move in chess*); *Am.* Paraguayan tea (*used also in Argentina and Uruguay*); *Am.* teapot (*for mate*), any small pot; *Am.* bald head; *adj.* unpolished, dull (*surface*).
matear *v.* to plant seeds or shoots; to hunt among the bushes; *Am.* to drink mate; *Am.* to checkmate (*make the winning move in chess*).
matemáticas *f. pl.* mathematics.
matemático *adj.* mathematical; *m.* mathematician.
materia *f.* matter; material; subject; pus; — **prima** (*or* **primera** —) raw material.
material *adj.* material; rude, coarse; *m.* ingredient; material; equipment; *Am.* **de** — made of adobe.
maternal *adj.* maternal.
maternidad *f.* maternity, motherhood.
materno *adj.* maternal.
matinal *adj.* morning, of the morning.
matiné *m. Am.* matinée.
matiz *m.* tint, shade, color, hue; shading.
matizar[9] *v.* to blend (*colors*); to tint; to shade, tone down.
matón *m.* bully.
matorral *m.* thicket.
matoso *adj.* bushy; weedy, full of weeds.
matrero *adj.* astute, shrewd; cunning, sly; *m. Am.* trickster, swindler; *Am.* bandit, outlaw, cattle thief.
matrícula *f.* register, list; matriculation, registration; certificate of registration.
matricular *v.* to matriculate, enroll, register.
matrimonio *m.* matrimony, marriage; married couple.
matriz *f.* matrix, mold, form; womb;

screw nut; *adj.* main, principal, first.
matungo *m. Am.* nag, old worn-out horse.
matutino *adj.* morning, of the morning.
maullar *v.* to mew.
maullido, maúllo *m.* mew.
máxima *f.* maxim, rule; proverb.
máxime *adj.* principally, especially.
máximo *adj. & m.* maximum.
maya *f.* daisy; May queen; *m. & f.* Maya, Mayan Indian; *m.* Mayan language.
mayo *m.* May; Maypole; *Am.* Mayo Indian (*from Sonora, Mexico*); *Am.* language of the Mayo Indian.
mayonesa *f.* mayonnaise; dish served with mayonnaise.
mayor *adj.* greater; larger; older; greatest; largest; oldest; main; major; high (*altar, mass*); *m.* major; chief; **-es** elders; ancestors; — **de edad** of age; **por** — (*or* **al por** —) wholesale; *f.* major premise (*of a syllogism*).
mayoral *m.* head shepherd; stagecoach driver; foreman; overseer, boss.
mayorazgo *m.* primogeniture (*right of inheritance by the first-born*); first-born son and heir; family estate left to the eldest son.
mayordomo *m.* majordomo, steward, butler; manager of an estate.
mayorear *v. Am.* to wholesale, sell at wholesale.
mayoreo *m. Am.* wholesale.
mayoría *f.* majority.
mayorista *m. Am.* wholesale dealer.
mazmorra *f.* dungeon.
mazo *m.* mallet; sledge hammer; bunch, handful.
mazorca *f.* ear of corn; *Am.* tyrannical government; *Am.* cruel torture (*imposed by tyrants*).
me *obj. pron.* me; to me; for me; myself.
mecánico *adj.* mechanical; *m.* mechanic, machinist, repairman; driver, chauffeur.
mecanismo *m.* mechanism.
mecanografía *f.* stenography, typewriting.
mecanógrafo *m.* stenographer, typist.
mecate *m. Am.* rope, cord.
mecedor *m.* swing; *adj.* swinging, rocking.
mecedora *f.* rocking chair.
mecer[10] *v.* to swing, rock, sway; to shake.
mecha *f.* wick; lock of hair; fuse; strip of salt pork or bacon (*for larding meat*); *Am.* tip of a whip; *Am.* scare, fright; *Am.* fib; *Am.* jest, joke; *Am.* trifle,

worthless thing.

mechar v. to lard (*meat or fowl*).

mechero m. lamp burner; gas jet; candlestick socket; pocket lighter; large wick; *Am.* disheveled hair; *Am.* joker, jester.

mechón m. large wick; large lock of hair.

medalla f. medal.

médano m. dune, sand hill, sand bank; *Am.* sandy marshland.

media f. stocking; *Am.* — **corta** (or — —) sock.

mediación f. mediation.

mediador m. mediator.

mediados : a — de about the middle of.

medianero m. mediator; go-between; adj. mediating; intermediate; **pared medianera** partition wall.

medianía f. mediocrity; average; middle ground; moderate circumstances; moderation; *Am.* partition wall.

mediano adj. medium; moderate; middle-sized; average; mediocre.

medianoche f. midnight.

mediante adj. intervening; **Dios** — God willing; prep. by means of, through, with the help of.

mediar v. to mediate, intervene; to intercede; to arrive at, or be in, the middle.

medible adj. measurable.

medicamento m. medicament, medicine.

medicastro m. quack, quack doctor.

medicina f. medicine.

medicinar v. to doctor, treat, prescribe medicine for; **-se** to take medicine.

medición f. measurement; measuring.

médico m. doctor, physician; adj. medical.

medida f. measure; measurement; gauge, rule; — **para áridos** dry measure; a — **del deseo** according to one's desire; a — **que** as, in proportion as; at the same time as.

medio adj. half; middle; intermediate; medium, average; **media noche** midnight; **hacer una cosa a medias** to do something halfway; **ir a medias** to go halves; adv. half, not completely; m. middle; means, way; medium; environment; **-s** means, resources; **meterse de por** — to intervene, meddle in a dispute.

mediocre adj. mediocre; **mediocridad** f. mediocrity.

mediodía m. midday, noon; south.

medioeval, medieval adj. medieval.

medir[5] v. irr. to measure; to scan (*ver-*

ses); *Am.* — **las calles** to walk the streets, be out of a job; **-se** to measure one's words or actions; *Am.* **-se con otro** to try one's strength or ability against another; to fight with another.

meditación f. meditation.

meditar v. to meditate; to muse.

medrar v. to flourish, thrive; to prosper.

medroso adj. timid, faint-hearted; fearful, dreadful.

médula f. marrow; pith; — **oblongada** medulla oblongata (*the posterior part of the brain tapering off into the spinal cord*).

megáfono m. megaphone.

mejicano adj. Mexican; m. Mexican; the Aztec language; inhabitant of Mexico City. Also **mexicano**.

mejilla f. cheek.

mejor adj. better; **el** — the best; adv. better; a lo — suddenly, unexpectedly; **tanto** — so much the better.

mejora f. betterment; improvement.

mejoramiento m. improvement.

mejorar v. to better, improve; to get better, recover; **-se** to get better, recover.

mejoría f. betterment, improvement; superiority.

melado adj. honey-colored; m. sugarcane syrup; honey cake.

melancolía f. melancholy, gloom.

melancólico adj. melancholy, gloomy.

melaza f. molasses.

melena f. mane.

melindre m. affectation; affected act or gesture; whim; fritter; marzipan (*sweetmeat made of almond paste*).

melindroso adj. affected; too particular, finicky, fussy.

melocotón m. peach; **melocotonero** m. peach tree.

melodía f. melody; **melodioso** adj. melodious.

melón m. melon; cantaloupe; muskmelon; melon vine.

melosidad f. sweetness; softness, gentleness.

meloso adj. honeyed; soft, sweet; m. *Am.* honey-voiced person; *Am.* over-affectionate person.

mella f. nick; dent; **hacer** — to make a dent or impression; to cause pain, worry, or suffering.

mellar v. to notch; to nick; to dent; to impair, damage.

mellizo adj. & m. twin.

membrete m. heading; letterhead; memorandum.

membrillo m. quince (*tree and its fruit*).

membrudo *adj.* sinewy, robust, strong, muscular.

memorable *adj.* memorable, notable.

memorándum *m.* memorandum, note; memorandum book, notebook.

memoria *f.* memory; remembrance; reminiscence; memoir, note, account; memorándum; **de** — by heart; **hacer** — to remember, recollect, **de golio** poor memory; **-s** regards; memoirs.

memorial *m.* memorandum book; memorial, brief, petition.

mención *f.* mention.

mencionar *v.* to mention.

mendigar[7] *v.* to beg; to ask alms.

mendigo *m.* beggar.

mendrugo *m.* crumb of bread.

menear *v.* to move, shake, stir; to wiggle; to wag; **-se** to hustle about; to wag; to wiggle.

meneo *m.* shaking; swaying; wagging; wiggle; wiggling.

menester *m.* need; job, occupation; **-es** bodily needs; implements, tools; tasks, chores; **ser** — to be necessary.

menesteroso *adj.* needy, in want.

mengua *f.* diminution, decrease; waning; poverty, want; discredit.

menguar[8] *v.* to diminish, decrease; to wane.

menjurje *m.* stuff, mixture.

menor *adj.* smaller, lesser, younger; smallest, least, youngest; minor; *m. & f.* — **de edad** minor; *m.* minor (*music*); Minorite, Franciscan; *f.* minor premise (*of a syllogism*); **por** — (**al por** —) at retail; in small quantities.

menoría = **minoría**

menos *adv.* less; least; except; *adj. & pron.* less; least; *m.* minus; — **de** (or — **que**) less than; **a lo** — (**al** —, or **por lo** —) at least; **a** — **que** unless; **echar de** — to miss, feel or notice the absence of; **no puede** — **de hacerlo** he cannot help doing it; **venir a** — to decline; to become weak or poor.

menoscabar *v.* to diminish, lessen; to impair, damage; — **la honra de** to undermine the reputation of.

menoscabo *m.* impairment; damage; diminution, lessening.

menospreciar *v.* to despise, scorn; to underestimate.

menosprecio *m.* scorn, contempt; underestimation.

mensaje *m.* message.

mensajero *m.* messenger.

menstruo *m.* menstruation.

mensual *adj.* monthly.

mensualidad *f.* monthly allowance; monthly payment.

mensurable *adj.* measurable.

menta *f.* mint; peppermint; *Am.* rumor, hearsay; *Am.* **por -s** by hearsay; *Am.* **persona de** — famous person.

mentado *adj.* famous; *p.p.* mentioned.

mental *adj.* mental.

mentalidad *f.* mentality.

mentar[1] *v. irr.* to mention; to call, name.

mente *f.* mind; intellect.

mentecato *adj.* foolish, simple; *m.* fool.

mentir[3] *v. irr.* to lie, tell lies.

mentira *f.* lie, falsehood, fib; white spot on the fingernails.

mentiroso *adj.* lying; deceptive, false; *m.* liar, fibber; **mentirosillo** *m.* little fibber.

mentís: dar un — to give the lie (to).

mentón *m.* chin.

menú *m.* menu.

menudear *v.* to occur frequently; to repeat over and over; to fall incessantly (*as rain, stones, projectiles, etc.*); to tell in detail; *Am.* to retail, sell at retail; *Am.* to meet together often.

menudeo *m.* retail; **vender al** — to retail, sell at retail.

menudo *adj.* minute, small; insignificant; exact, detailed; **dinero** — change; **a** — often; **por** — in detail; retail; *m.* entrails, "innards"; change, small coins.

meñique *adj.* tiny, wee; **dedo** — little finger.

meollo *m.* marrow; pith; kernel; substance; brain; brains.

meple *m. Am.* maple.

merca *f.* purchase.

mercachifle *m.* peddler, vendor; cheap merchant; cheap fellow.

mercader *m.* trader, merchant.

mercadería *f.* merchandise; trade.

mercado *m.* market; mart.

mercancía *f.* merchandise; goods

mercantil *adj.* mercantile, commercial.

mercar[6] *v.* to purchase, buy.

merced *f.* **favor**; present, gift; mercy; **Vuestra Merced** Your Honor; **a** — **de** at the mercy of; at the expense of.

mercería *f.* notions (*pins, buttons, etc.*); notions store; *Am.* drygoods store.

mercurio *m.* mercury; quicksilver.

merecedor *adj.* worthy, deserving.

merecer[13] *v. irr.* to deserve.

merecido *adj. & p.p.* deserved; *m.* deserved punishment.

merecimiento *m.* merit.

merendar[1] *v. irr.* to have an afternoon

snack or refreshment; *Am.* **-se uno a alguien** to fleece or skin someone (*in a game or business deal*); to kill someone.

merendero *m.* lunchroom.

meridional *adj.* southern; *m.* southerner.

meridiano *adj.* & *m.* meridian.

merienda *f.* light afternoon meal; afternoon refreshments.

mérito *m.* merit; **de —** notable.

merito *dim. of* **mero.**

meritorio *adj.* meritorious, worthy, deserving; *m.* employee without salary (*learning trade or profession*).

merluza *f.* hake (*species of codfish*); drunken state.

merma *f.* reduction, decrease.

mermar *v.* to dwindle; to decrease, reduce.

mermelada *f.* marmalade.

mero *adj.* mere, pure; *Am.* exact, real; **la mera verdad** the real truth; *adv. Am.* very, very same, exactly; *Am.* soon; *Am.* only; *Am.* **una mera de las tres** only one of the three; *Am.* **ya —** (*or* **merito**) very soon; *Am.* **allí —** (*or* **merito**) right there; *m.* species of perch; *Am.* species of thrush.

merodear *v.* to rove in search of plunder.

mes *m.* month.

mesa *f.* table; executive board; staircase landing; mesa, plateau; **levantar la —** to clear the table; **poner la —** to set the table; *Am.* **quitar la —** to clear the table.

mesada *f.* monthly salary or allowance.

mesarse *v.* to tear (*one's hair or beard*).

mesero *m. Am.* waiter.

meseta *f.* plateau; staircase landing.

mesón *m.* inn (*usually a large one-story shelter for men and pack animals*).

mesonero *m.* innkeeper.

mestizo *adj.* half-breed; hybrid; **perro —** mongrel dog; *m.* mestizo, half-breed.

mesura *f.* moderation; composure; dignity; politeness.

mesurado *adj.* moderate, temperate; dignified.

meta *f.* goal; objective.

metáfora *f.* metaphor.

metal *m.* metal.

metálico *adj.* metallic, metal; *m.* specie, coined money; cash in coin.

metalurgia *f.* metallurgy.

metate *m. Am.* flat stone (*used for grinding corn, etc.*).

meteoro *m.* meteor.

meteorología *f.* meteorology; **meteoro-**

lógico *adj.* meteorological; **oficina meteorológica** weather bureau.

meter *v.* to put (in); to get (in); to insert; to smuggle; to make (*noise, trouble, etc.*); to cause (*fear*); *Am.* to strike (*a blow*); *Am.* **-le** to hurry up; **-se** to meddle, interfere; to plunge (into); **-se monja** (*Am.* **-se de monja**) to become a nun; **-se con** to pick a quarrel with.

metódico *adj.* methodical.

método *m.* method.

métrico *adj.* metric.

metro *m.* meter; subway.

metrópoli *f.* metropolis.

metropolitano *adj.* metropolitan; *m.* archbishop.

mexicano = mejicano. (*Pronounced identically*).

mezcal *m. Am.* mescal (*a species of maguey and an alcoholic beverage made from it*).

mezcla *f.* mixture; mortar; mixed cloth; **mezclilla** *f.* mixed cloth (*generally black and white*); tweed.

mezclar *v.* to mix, blend; **-se** to mix, mingle; to meddle.

mezcolanza *f.* jumble, mess, mixture.

mezquindad *f.* meanness; stinginess; dire poverty.

mezquino *adj.* poor, needy; mean, stingy; meager; small, tiny; *m. Am.* wart (*usually on a finger*).

mi *adj.* my.

mí *pers. pron.* (*used after prep.*) me, myself.

miaja = migaja.

miau *m.* mew.

microbio *m.* microbe.

micrófono *m.* microphone.

microscopio *m.* microscope; **microscópico** *adj.* microscopic.

miedo *m.* fear; dread; **tener —** to be afraid.

miedoso *adj.* afraid, fearful, timid.

miel *m.* honey; molasses.

miembro *m.* member; limb.

mientes *f. pl.* thought, mind; **parar en** to consider, reflect on; **traer a las —** to recall; **venírsele a uno a las —** to occur to one, come to one's mind.

mientras *conj.* while; **— que** while; **— tanto** in the meantime, meanwhile; **— más . . . — menos . . .** the more . . . the less . . . .

miércoles *m.* Wednesday.

mies *f.* ripe grain; harvest; **-es** fields of grain.

miga *f.* crumb; soft part of bread; substance; **-s** crumbs; fried crumbs of

138

bread; **hacer buenas -s** (*or* **malas -s**) **con** to get along well (*or* badly) with.

migaja *f.* crumb; bit, fragment, small particle.

migración *f.* migration.

milagro *m.* miracle; wonder.

milagroso *adj.* miraculous.

milicia *f.* militia; military science; military profession.

militar *adj.* military; *m.* soldier, military man; *v.* to serve in the army; to militate, fight (against).

milpa *f. Am.* cornfield.

milla *f.* mile.

millar *m.* thousand; **-es** thousands, a great number.

millón *m.* million; **millonario** *adj. & m.* millionaire; **millonésimo** *adj. & m.* millionth.

mimar *v.* to pamper, spoil, humor; to pet.

mimbre *m.* wicker; **mimbrera** *f.* willow.

mímico *adj.* mimic.

mimo *m.* pampering; caress; coaxing.

mimoso *adj.* tender, sensitive; delicate; finicky, fussy.

mina *f.* mine; source; fortune.

minar *v.* to mine; to undermine; to sow with explosive mines.

mineral *m.* mineral; mine; wealth, fortune; *adj.* mineral.

minería *f.* mining; miners.

minero *m.* miner; wealth, fortune; source; *adj.* mining; **compañía minera** mining company.

miniatura *f.* miniature.

mínimo *adj.* least, smallest; *m.* minimum.

minino *m.* kitten, kitty, pussy.

ministerio *m.* ministry; administration, ministering; portfolio (*office of a cabinet member*); minister's office.

ministrar *v.* to minister; to give (*money, aid, etc.*).

ministro *m.* minister; cabinet member; officer of justice.

minoría *f.* minority.

minoridad *f.* minority (*in age*).

minucioso *adj.* minute, detailed; scrupulous.

minúsculo *adj.* small; **letra minúscula** small letter.

minuta *f.* minutes; memorandum; first draft (*of a contract, deed, etc.*); memorandum list; lawyer's bill; *Am.* **a la —** breaded and fried (*said of meat or fish*).

minuto *m.* minute; **minutero** *m.* minute hand.

mío *poss. adj.* my, of mine; *poss. pron.*

mine; *Am.* **detrás —** behind me.

miope *adj.* shortsighted, nearsighted; *m. & f.* nearsighted person.

mira *f.* gun sight; guiding point; intention, design; lookout; **estar a la —** **de** to be on the lookout for; to be on the alert for; **poner la — en** to fix one's eyes on; to aim at.

mirada *f.* glance, gaze, look.

mirador *m.* mirador, enclosed balcony (*commanding an extensive view*); watchtower; onlooker, spectator; *Am.* penthouse (*small house built on a roof for recreation*).

miramiento *m.* consideration, respect, regard; reverence; circumspection, prudence.

mirar *v.* to look; to glance; to behold; to see; **— por alguien** to take care of someone; **¡mira (tú)!** look!

miríada *f.* myriad, multitude, great number.

mirlo *m.* blackbird.

mirón *m.* bystander, onlooker, spectator; *adj.* curious.

mirto *m.* myrtle.

misa *f.* mass; **— del gallo** midnight mass.

misceláneo *adj.* miscellaneous.

miserable *adj.* miserable, unhappy; forlorn; miserly, stingy; mean.

miseria *f.* misery; poverty; stinginess; bit, trifle.

misericordia *f.* mercy, compassion, pity.

misericordioso *adj.* merciful, compassionate.

mísero *adj.* miserable, unhappy; forlorn; stingy.

misión *f.* mission.

misionero *m.* missionary.

mismo *adj.* same; self, very; **ahora —** right away.

misterio *m.* mystery; secret.

misterioso *adj.* mysterious.

místico *adj.* mystical, mystic; *m.* mystic.

mitad *f.* half; middle.

mitigar[7] *v.* to mitigate, soften, soothe.

mitin *m.* meeting.

mito *m.* myth; **mitología** *f.* mythology.

mitra *f.* bishop's miter.

mixto *adj.* mixed; half-breed; *m.* composite; match; explosive compound.

mobiliario *m.* furniture.

moblaje = mueblaje

mocedad *f.* youth; youthfulness; youthful prank.

mocetón *m.* tall, robust lad.

moción *f.* motion.

mocoso *adj.* sniffling; *m.* brat, scamp;

sniffling boy.

mochar *v. Am.* to cut off, chop off, cut, trim (see **desmochar**); *Am.* to snitch, pilfer; *Am.* to depose, dismiss, put out of a job.

mochila *f.* knapsack; soldier's kit.

mocho *adj.* cut off; cropped, shorn; *Am.* maimed, mutilated; *Am.* reactionary, conservative; *m.* butt of a firearm; *Am.* nag; *Am.* cigar butt.

moda *f.* mode, custom, style, fashion; **de —** fashionable.

modelar *v.* to model.

modelo *m.* model, copy, pattern; *m.* & *f.* life model.

moderación *f.* moderation.

moderado *adj.* moderate; conservative.

moderar *v.* to moderate, temper; to regulate; to restrain.

moderno *adj.* modern.

modestia *f.* modesty.

modesto *adj.* modest.

módico *adj.* moderate, reasonable (price).

modificación *f.* modification.

modificar⁶ *v.* to modify.

modismo *m.* idiom.

modista *f.* dressmaker; milliner.

modo *m.* mode, manner, way; mood (grammar); **a** (or **al**) **— de** like, in the manner of; **de — que** so that; **and so; de todos -s** at any rate, anyway.

modorra *f.* drowsiness; gid (a disease of sheep).

modular *v.* to modulate, tone down.

mofa *f.* scoff, jeer, taunt; mockery.

mofar *v.* to mock, scoff, jeer; **-se de** to make fun of, scoff at.

moflete *m.* fat cheek; **mofletudo** *adj.* fat-cheeked.

mohín *m.* grimace; wry face.

mohino *adj.* moody, discontented, sad, melancholy; black (referring to a horse, cow, or bull).

moho *m.* rust; mold.

mohoso *adj.* musty, moldy; rusty.

mojada *f.* drench, drenching, wetting.

mojado *adj.* wet, damp, moist; *p.p.* of **mojar.**

mojadura *f.* wetting, dampening, drenching.

mojar *v.* to dampen, wet, moisten; *Am.* to accompany (a song); *Am.* to bribe; *Am.* to celebrate by drinking; *Am.* **mojársele a uno los papeles** to get things mixed up.

mojicón *m.* punch, blow; muffin, bun.

mojigatería *f.* prudery; false humility; affected piety.

mojigato *adj.* prudish; affectedly pious, overzealous (in matters of religion); hypocritical; *m.* prude; hypocrite.

mojón *m.* landmark; milestone; heap, pile.

molde *m.* mold, cast; form; pattern, model; **venir de —** to come pat, be to the point; **letras de —** printed letters; print.

moldear *v.* to mold; to cast; to decorate with moldings.

moldura *f.* molding.

mole *f.* mass, bulk; *adj.* soft, mild; *m. Am.* **— de guajolote** a Mexican dish of turkey served with a chili gravy.

molécula *f.* molecule.

moler² *v. irr.* to mill; to grind; to tire, fatigue; to wear out, destroy; to bother; **— a palos** to give a thorough beating.

molestar *v.* to molest, disturb; to bother, annoy.

molestia *f.* bother, annoyance; discomfort.

molesto *adj.* bothersome, annoying; uncomfortable.

molicie *f.* softness; fondness for luxury.

molienda *f.* grind, grinding, milling; portion to be, or that has been, ground; grinding season (for sugar cane or olives); fatigue, weariness; bother.

molinero *m.* miller.

molinete *m.* small mill; ventilating fan; pin wheel; twirl, whirl, flourish.

molinillo *m.* small mill or grinder; chocolate beater; restless person.

molino *m.* mill; restless person; **— de viento** windmill.

mollera *f.* crown of the head; judgment, good sense; **ser duro de —** to be stubborn; **no tener sal en la —** to be dull, stupid.

momentáneo *adj.* momentary; sudden, quick.

momento *m.* moment; importance; momentum; **al —** immediately, without delay; **a cada —** continually, frequently.

mona *f.* female monkey; mimic; drunkenness; **dormir la —** to sleep it off; **pillar una —** to get drunk.

monada *f.* monkeyshine; monkey face; cute little thing; cute gesture; nonsense; flattery.

monarca *m.* monarch.

monarquía *f.* monarchy.

monasterio *m.* monastery.

mondadientes *m.* toothpick.

mondar *v.* to pare; to peel; to prune;

to clean out; *Am.* to beat, thrash; *Am.* to beat, defeat; **-se los dientes** to pick one's teeth.

moneda *f.* coin; money; **— corriente** currency; **— menuda** (*or* **suelta**) change, small coins; **casa de —** mint.

monería *f.* monkeyshine, antic; trifle, trinket; cute little thing.

monetario *adj.* monetary, pertaining to money; financial.

monigote *m.* puppet, ridiculous figure; dunce.

monje *m.* monk.

monja *f.* nun.

mono *m.* monkey; silly fool; mimic; *Am.* pile of fruit or vegetables (*in a market*); **-s** *Am.* worthless household utensils and furniture; *Am.* **meterle a uno los -s en el cuerpo** to frighten, terrify someone; *adj.* pretty, neat, cute; *Am.* sorrel, reddish-brown; *Am.* blond.

monologar[7] *v.* to soliloquize, talk to oneself; to recite monologues; to monopolize the conversation.

monólogo *m.* monologue.

monopolio *m.* monopoly.

monopolizar[9] *v.* to monopolize; to corner (*a market*).

monosílabo *adj.* monosyllabic, of one syllable; *m.* monosyllable.

monotonía *f.* monotony; **monótono** *adj.* monotonous.

monserga *f.* gabble.

monstruo *m.* monster.

monstruosidad *f.* monstrosity; monster, freak.

monstruoso *adj.* monstrous.

monta *f.* amount, sum; value, importance; **de poca — of** little value or importance.

montaje *m.* assembly, assembling (*of machinery*); mount, support for a cannon.

montante *m.* broadsword; transom; upright; post; *Am.* sum, amount, cost; *f.* high tide.

montaña *f.* mountain; **— rusa** roller coaster.

montañés *adj.* mountain (*used as adj.*), of, from or pertaining to the mountains; *m.* mountaineer; native of the province of Santander, Spain.

montañoso *adj.* mountainous.

montar *v.* to mount; to ride horseback; to amount (to); to set (*jewels*); to cock (*a gun*); to assemble, set up (*machinery*); *Am.* to organize, establish.

montaraz *adj.* wild, primitive, uncivi-

lized; *m.* forester.

monte *m.* mount, mountain; forest; thicket; monte (*a card game*); *Am.* grass, pasture; *Am.* country, outskirts; **montecillo** *m.* mound, small hill; **montepío** *m.* pawnshop.

montera *f.* cap; *Am.* Bolivian coneshaped hat (*worn by Indians*).

montés *adj.* wild, mountain (*used as as adj.*); **cabra — mountain goat, gato —** wildcat.

montículo *m.* mound.

montón *m.* pile, heap; mass, great number; **a -es** in abundance, in heaps, by heaps.

montonera *f. Am.* band of mounted rebels or guerrilla fighters; *Am.* pile of wheat, hay, straw, etc.; *Am.* pile, heap (*of anything*).

montuoso *adj.* hilly; mountainous.

montura *f.* mount, horse; saddle and trappings.

monumento *m.* monument; **monumental** *adj.* monumental.

moño *m.* knot or roll of hair; bow of ribbon; crest, tuft of feathers; *Am.* forelock (*lock of hair on the fore part of the head*); *Am.* crest, peak (*of anything*); *Am.* whim; *Am.* **-s** a Colombian popular dance; **-s** frippery, gaudy ornaments; *Am.* **estar con el — torcido** to be in an ugly humor.

mora *f.* blackberry; mulberry; brambleberry; *Am.* blood pudding, sausage.

morada *f.* dwelling, residence; stay.

morado *adj.* purple.

morador *m.* dweller, resident.

moral *adj.* moral; *f.* ethics, moral philosophy; morale; *m.* mulberry tree; blackberry bush.

moraleja *f.* moral, lesson, maxim.

moralidad *f.* morality.

moralista *m. & f.* moralist.

morar *v.* to live, dwell, reside.

morbidez *f.* softness; mellowness.

mórbido *adj.* morbid, soft.

morboso *adj.* morbid, unhealthy, diseased.

morcilla *f.* blood pudding, blood sausage; gag (*an amusing remark by a comedian*).

mordacidad *f.* sharpness (*of tongue*).

mordaz *adj.* biting, cutting, sarcastic.

mordaza *f.* gag (*for the mouth*).

mordedor *adj.* biting; snappy *m.* biter; slanderer.

mordedura *f.* bite; sting.

mordelón *adj. Am.* biting, snappy; *m. Am.* biter; *Am.* public official who accepts a bribe.

morder³ *v. irr.* to bite; to nip; to gnaw; to corrode; to backbite, slander; *Am.* to swindle; *Am.* to "shake down", exact a bribe.

mordida *f. Am.* bite; *Am.* graft, money obtained by graft.

mordiscar⁶, **mordisquear** *v.* to nibble; to gnaw.

mordisco *m.* bite; nibble.

moreno *adj.* brown; dark, brunette; *m. Am.* colored person.

moretón *m.* bruise, black-and-blue mark.

morfina *f.* morphine; **morfinómano** *m.* morphine addict, drug fiend.

moribundo *adj.* dying.

morir⁴, ⁵² *v. irr.* to die; -se to die; to die out, be extinguished.

morisco *adj.* Moorish; Moresque, in the Moorish style; *m.* Morisco (*Christianized Moor*); language of the Moriscos.

moro *adj.* Moorish; *Am.* dappled, spotted (*horse*); *Am.* unbaptized; *m.* Moor; *Am.* frosted cookie. .

morral *m.* nose bag; knapsack; hunter's bag.

morriña *f.* melancholy, blues, sadness.

mortaja *f.* shroud; *Am.* cigarette paper.

mortal *adj.* mortal; fatal; deadly; *m.* mortal; **mortalidad** *f.* mortality; death rate.

mortandad *f.* mortality, death rate; massacre, slaughter.

mortecino *adj.* deathly pale; dying; **hacer la mortecina** to pretend to be dead.

morterete *m.* small mortar, small cannon.

mortero *m.* mortar (*for grinding*).

mortífero *adj.* deadly, fatal.

mortificar⁶ *v.* to mortify; to torment; to vex, annoy; -se to do penance; to be grieved; *Am.* to be embarrassed.

mortuorio *adj.* funeral; funereal, mournful; *m.* funeral, burial.

mosaico *adj.* & *m.* mosaic.

mosca *f.* fly; bore; bother; *Am.* sponger, parasite; *Am.* bull's-eye, center of a target; **moscón** *m.* large fly; *Am.* **ir de moscón** to go along as a chaperone.

mosquear *v.* to brush off or drive away flies; to whip, beat; *Am.* to rage, be furious; -se to show pique or resentment; *Am.* to go away.

mosquito *m.* mosquito; gnat; *Am.* Mosquito Indian of Nicaragua; **mosquitero** *m.* mosquito net.

mostacho *m.* mustache.

mostaza *f.* mustard; mustard seed;

bird shot.

mostrador *m.* demonstrator; store counter; clock dial.

mostrar² *v. irr.* to show; to demonstrate; to exhibit.

mostrenco *adj.* ownerless; homeless; stray (*animal*); slow, dull; fat, heavy; *m.* dunce; *Am.* worthless animal.

mota *f.* mote, speck; knot in cloth; slight defect; mound, knoll; *Am.* powder puff; *Am.* tuft.

mote *m.* motto; slogan; nickname; *Am.* stewed corn; *Am.* grammatical error (*made by illiterate people and children*); *Am.* — **pelado** hominy.

motear *v.* to speck, speckle; to spot; *Am.* to mispronounce, enunciate badly.

motejar *v.* to jeer at; to call bad names; to insult; to censure; — **de** to brand as.

motín *m.* mutiny; riot.

motivar *v.* to cause; to give a cause for.

motivo *m.* motive, reason; motif, theme; *m.* **con** — **de** because of; on the occasion of; *adj.* motive.

motocicleta *f.* motorcycle; **motociclista** *m.* & *f.* motorcyclist, motorcycle rider.

motor *m.* motor; *adj.* motor, causing motion.

motorista *m.* & *f.* motorist; motorman, motorwoman.

motriz *adj.* motive, impelling, driving; **fuerza** — power, driving force.

movedizo *adj.* movable; shaky; shifting; **arena movediza** quicksand.

mover² *v. irr.* to move; to persuade; to stir, excite; to touch, affect; -se to move.

movible *adj.* movable; mobile; fickle.

móvil *m.* motive, inducement, incentive; *adj.* mobile, movable; unstable.

movilización *f.* mobilization.

movilizar⁹ *v.* to mobilize.

movimiento *m.* movement; motion; commotion, disturbance.

moza *f.* maid; girl; last hand of a game; *Am.* last song or dance of a fiesta.

mozalbete *m.* youth, lad.

mozo *adj.* young; unmarried; *m.* youth; manservant; waiter; porter; errand boy; **buen** — handsome man.

mozuela *f.* lass, young girl.

mozuelo *m.* lad, young boy.

mucama *f. Am.* servant girl; **mucamo** *m. Am.* servant.

mucoso *adj.* mucous; slimy; **membrana mucosa** mucous membrane.

muchacha *f.* child; girl; servant, maid.

muchacho *m.* child; boy, lad.

muchedumbre *f.* multitude; crowd.

mucho *adj.* much, a lot of; long (*referring to time*); -s many; *adv.* much; a great deal; **ni con —** not by far, not by a long shot; **ni — menos** not by any means, nor anything like it; **por — que** no matter how much; **no es que it is no wonder that.**

muda *f.* change; change of clothes; molt (*act or time of shedding feathers*); *Am.* relay of draft animals.

mudable *adj.* changeable; fickle.

mudanza *f.* change; removal; inconstancy.

mudar *v.* to change; to remove; to molt; **— de casa** to move; **— de traje** to change one's suit or costume; **-se** to change one's clothes; to change one's habits; to move, change one's abode.

mudez *f.* muteness, dumbness.

mudo *adj.* mute, dumb; silent; *m.* dumb person.

mueblaje *m.* furniture.

mueble *m.* piece of furniture; **-s** furniture, household goods; *adj.* movable; **bienes -s** chattels, movable possessions.

mueca *f.* grimace; wry face.

muela *f.* molar tooth; millstone; grindstone; **— cordal** (*or* **— del juicio**) wisdom tooth.

muelle *adj.* soft; voluptuous; *m.* spring; wharf; loading platform; **— real** main spring of a watch.

muerte *f.* death.

muerto *p.p. of* **morir** & *adj.* dead; withered; faded; **naturaleza muerta** still life; *m.* corpse.

muesca *f.* notch; groove.

muestra *f.* sample; pattern, model; shop sign; sign, indication; presence, bearing; face, dial (*of a clock or watch*); **muestrario** *m.* book or collection of samples.

mugido *m.* moo; mooing, lowing of cattle.

mugir[11] *v.* to moo, low.

mugre *f.* dirt, grime.

mugriento *adj.* grimy, dirty.

mujer *f.* woman; wife.

mujeril *adj.* womanly, feminine; womanish, like a woman.

mula *f.* mule; *Am.* cushion for carrying loads; *Am.* worthless merchandise; *Am.* cruel, treacherous person; *Am.* **echar a uno la —** to give someone the dickens, scold someone.

muladar *m.* rubbish pile or dump; dunghill, pile of manure.

mulato *adj.* & *m.* mulatto.

muleta *f.* crutch; red cloth draped over a rod (*used by bullfighters*).

muletilla *f.* cane with a crutchlike handle; red cloth draped over a rod (*used by bullfighters*); cliché (*hackneyed or trite phrase*); refrain; repetitious word or phrase; braid frog (*fastener for a coat*).

mulo *m.* mule.

multa *f.* fine.

multicolor *adj.* many-colored, motley.

múltiple *adj.* multiple.

multiplicación *f.* multiplication.

multiplicar[6] *v.* to multiply.

multiplicidad *f.* multiplicity, manifold variety.

múltiplo *m.* multiple number.

multitud *f.* multitude; crowd.

mullido *adj.* soft; fluffy; *m.* stuffing for mattresses or pillows; soft cushion or mattress.

mullir[20] *v.* to fluff; to soften.

mundanal *adj.* worldly.

mundano *adj.* mundane, worldly.

mundial *adj.* universal; **la guerra —** the World War.

mundo *m.* world; trunk; **todo el —** everybody.

munición *f.* ammunition; buckshot; **-es de guerra** war supplies.

municipal *adj.* municipal; **municipalidad** *f.* municipality; town hall; city government.

municipio *m.* municipality.

muñeca *f.* doll; wrist; manikin (*figure for displaying clothes*); **muñeco** *m.* boy doll; dummy, puppet.

muñón *m.* stump (*of an arm or leg*).

muralla *f.* surrounding wall; rampart.

murciano *adj.* of or from Murcia, Spain; *m.* native of Murcia.

murciélago *m.* bat.

murga *f.* brass band.

murmullo *m.* murmur, rumor; whisper; muttering.

murmuración *f.* slander, gossip; grumbling.

murmurar *v.* to murmur; to slander, gossip; to whisper; to grumble.

muro *m.* wall.

murria *f.* sulkiness, sullenness, melancholy, blues; **tener —** to be sulky; to have the blues.

musa *f.* Muse; muse, poetic inspiration; poetry; **-s** fine arts.

muscular *adj.* muscular.

musculatura *f.* muscles; muscular system.

músculo m. muscle.

musculoso adj. muscular; sinewy.

muselina f. muslin.

museo m. museum.

musgo m. moss.

musgoso adj. mossy.

música f. music.

musical adj musical.

músico adj. musical; m. musician.

musitar v. to mutter, mumble; to whisper.

muslo m. thigh.

mustio adj. sad; withered; humble.

mutilar v. to mutilate; to butcher; to mar.

mutismo m. muteness, silence.

mutuo adj. mutual; reciprocal.

muy adv. very; greatly; most.

N

nabo m. turnip.

nácar m. mother-of-pearl; pearl color.

nacarado adj. pearly.

nacer[13] v. irr. to be born; to spring, originate; to bud; to sprout, grow (said of plants); **— de pie** (or **— de pies**) to be born lucky.

naciente adj. rising (sun); m. orient, east.

nacimiento m. birth; origin; beginning; descent; source; crèche (representation of the Nativity).

nación f. nation.

nacional adj. national; m. national, citizen.

nacionalidad f. nationality.

nada f. nothingness; indef. pron. nothing, not . . . anything; adv. not at all; **de —** you are welcome, don't mention it (as a reply to «gracias»); Am. a **cada —** constantly; **una nadita** a trifle, just a little.

nadada f. swim.

nadador m. swimmer; Am. fish-net float.

nadar v. to swim; to float.

nadería f. a mere nothing, trifle, worthless thing.

nadie indef. pron. nobody, no one, not . . . anyone.

nafta f. naphtha.

naguas = enaguas.

naipe m. playing card.

nalgas f. pl. buttocks; rump; **nalgada** f. spank; **-s** spanking.

nana f. grandma; lullaby; Am. child's nurse; Am. nice old lady.

naranja f. orange; **— tangerina** tangerine; **naranjada** f. orangeade; orange juice; orange marmalade;

naranjal m. orange grove; **naranjo** m. orange tree.

narciso m. narcissus; daffodil; fop, dandy.

narcótico adj. & m. narcotic.

narcotizar[9] v. to dope, drug with narcotics.

nariz f. nose; nostril; **narices** nostrils.

narración f. narration, account, story.

narrar v. to narrate, tell, relate.

narrativo adj. narrative; **narrativa** f. narrative.

nata f. cream; best part; scum; **-s** whipped cream with sugar; custard; **natoso** adj. creamy.

natal adj. natal; native; **natalicio** m. birthday; **natalidad** f. birth rate.

natillas f. pl. custard.

nativo adj. native.

natural adj. natural; native; simple, unaffected; m. & f. native; m. nature, disposition; **al —** without affectation; **del —** from nature, from life.

naturaleza f. nature; disposition; nationality; naturalization; **— muerta** still life.

naturalidad f. naturalness; simplicity; birthright.

naturalista adj. naturalistic; m. & f. naturalist.

naturalización f. naturalization.

naturalizar[9] v. to naturalize; to acclimatize, accustom to a new climate; **-se** to become naturalized.

naufragar[7] v. to be shipwrecked; to fail.

naufragio m. shipwreck; failure, ruin.

náufrago m. shipwrecked person.

náusea f. nausea; **dar -s** to nauseate, sicken; to disgust; **tener -s** to be nauseated, be sick to one's stomach.

nauseabundo adj. nauseating, sickening.

nauseado adj. nauseated, sick to one's stomach.

náutica f. navigation (science of navigation).

navaja f. jackknife, pocketknife; penknife; razor.

navajazo m. stab with a jackknife or razor; stab wound.

naval adj. naval.

navarro adj. Navarrese, of or pertaining to Navarre, Spain; m. Navarrese.

nave f. ship, boat; nave.

navegable adj. navigable.

navegación f. navigation; sea voyage; **— aérea** aviation.

navegador, navegante m. navigator; adj. navigating.

navegar[7] v. to navigate; to sail.

navidad f. Nativity; Christmas; -es Christmas season.

navío m. vessel, ship; — **de guerra** warship.

neblina f. fog, mist.

necedad f. foolishness, nonsense.

necesario adj. necessary.

neceser m. toilet case; sewing kit.

necesidad f. necessity, need, want.

necesitado adj. needy; in need, destitute, poor; p.p. of **necesitar**; m. needy person.

necesitar v. to need; to necessitate.

necio adj. stupid, ignorant; foolish; stubborn; Am. touchy.

nefando adj. abominable; wicked.

negación f. negation, denial; negative (*negative particle*).

negar[1],[7] v. irr. to deny; to refuse; to prohibit; to disown; -se to refuse, decline.

negativa f. negative; denial, refusal.

negativo v. negative.

negligencia f. negligence, neglect, carelessness.

negligente adj. negligent, neglectful, careless.

negociación f. negotiation; business; business house; management; transaction, deal.

negociante m. merchant, trader, dealer; businessman; adj. negotiating.

negociar v. to negotiate; to trade; to transact.

negocio m. business; business deal; negotiation, transaction; Am. store; **hombre de -s** businessman.

negrear v. to become black; to appear black, look black (*in the distance*).

negro adj. black; dark; sad, gloomy; unfortunate; m. black color; negro; Am. dear, darling; **negra** f. negress; Am. dear, darling.

negrura f. blackness.

negruzco adj. blackish.

nena f. baby girl; **nene** m. baby boy.

nervio m. nerve.

nervioso, nervoso adj. nervous; sinewy, strong.

nerviosidad, nervosidad f. nervousness; flexibility; vigor.

nervudo adj. sinewy, tough, powerful.

neto adj. clear, pure; net (*profit, price, etc*); **netamente** adv. clearly, distinctly.

neumático m. tire; adj. pneumatic.

neutralidad f. neutrality.

neutralizar[9] v. to neutralize, counteract.

neutro adj. neutral; neuter; sexless.

nevada f. snowfall.

nevado adj. snowy, white as snow; covered with snow.

nevar[1] v. irr. to snow.

nevasca f. snowstorm.

nevera f. icebox; refrigerator; ice storehouse; ice or ice-cream vendor (*woman*).

ni conj. & adv. nor; not even; neither; — **siquiera** not even.

nicho m. niche; recess, hollow in a wall.

nidada f. nestful of eggs; brood of chicks; hatch, brood.

nido m. nest; abode; Am. **patearle el** — **a alguien** to "upset the applecart", upset someone's plans.

niebla f. fog, mist; confusion.

nieto m. grandson, grandchild; **nieta** f. granddaughter.

nieve f. snow; Am. sherbet, ice cream; **tiempo de -s** snowy season.

nimio adj. miserly, stingy; Am. very small, insignificant.

ninfa f. nymph.

ningun(o) indef. adj. & pron. no one, none, not . . . any; nobody.

niña f. girl; Am. lady, mistress (*title of respect and endearment given to adults*); — **del ojo** pupil of the eye.

niñada f. childishness, childish act or remark.

niñera f. child's nurse.

niñería f. childish act; child's play; trifle; foolishness.

niñez f. infancy; childhood.

niño m. child, boy; infant; Am. master (*title of respect given to a young man by his servants*); adj. childlike, childish; very young, immature.

níquel m. nickel.

niquelado adj. nickel-plated; m. nickel plating; nickel plate.

nitidez f. clarity, clearness.

nítido adj. clear.

nitrato m. nitrate; saltpeter.

nitro m. niter, saltpeter.

nitrógeno m. nitrogen.

nivel m. level.

nivelar v. to level; to grade; to equalize.

no adv. no; not; nay; — **bien** as soon as; **un** — **sé qué** something indefinable; **por sí o por** — just in case, anyway.

noble adj. noble; m. nobleman.

nobleza f. nobility; nobleness.

noción f. notion, idea.

nocivo adj. noxious, harmful, injurious.

nocturno adj. nocturnal, nightly, nightly; m. nocturne (*musical or lyrical composition*).

noche f. night; darkness; **a la** — tonight; **de** — by (at) night; **por (en)**

la — at night, in the evening; **dejar a uno a buenas -s** to leave a person in the lurch.

Nochebuena f. Christmas Eve.

nocherniego m. night owl (person).

nodriza f. child's nurse; wet nurse.

nogal m. walnut (tree and wood).

nomás Am. = **no más** just; only.

nombradía f. renown, fame.

nombramiento m. nomination; appointment; naming.

nombrar v. to nominate; to name; to appoint.

nombre m. name; fame; noun; watchword; — **de pila** (or — **de bautismo**) Christian name.

nomeolvides f. forget-me-not.

nómina f. list (of names); pay roll.

nominación f. nomination; appointment.

nominal adj. nominal; **valor** — small, insignificant value.

nominar v. to nominate.

non adj. odd, uneven; m. odd number, uneven number; **estar** (or **quedar**) **de** — to be left alone, be left without a partner or companion.

nonada f. trifle, mere nothing.

nopal m. nopal, prickly pear tree (species of cactus).

nordeste adj. & m. northeast.

noria f. draw well; chain pump.

norma f. norm, standard, model.

normal adj. normal; standard; f. perpendicular line.

normalizar v. to normalize, make normal; to standardize.

noroeste adj. & m. northwest.

nortada f. strong north wind.

nortazo m. Am. sudden gust of wind, strong north wind.

norte m. north; north wind; guide; North Star; direction.

norteamericano adj. North American; American (from or of the United States).

norteño adj. northern; m. northerner.

noruego adj. & m. Norwegian.

nostalgia f. nostalgia, longing, homesickness.

nostálgico adj. homesick; lonesome; longing.

nota f. note; mark; fame.

notable adj. notable; noticeable.

notar v. to note, observe; to mark; to write down.

notario m. notary.

noticia f. notice, information; news; **recibir -s** to receive word, hear (from).

noticiario m. news sheet, news column,

news bulletin; **noticiero** m. = **noticiario**; adj. news (used as adj.); newsy, full of news.

noticioso adj. newsy, full of news; well-informed.

notificación f. notification, notifying; notice; summons.

notificar v. to notify.

notorio adj. well-known; obvious, evident.

novato m. novice, beginner.

novedad f. novelty; latest news, event, or fashion; change; newness; **hacerle a uno** — to seem strange or new to one; to excite one's curiosity or interest; **sin** — as usual; well.

novel adj. new, inexperienced.

novela f. novel; fiction.

novelesco adj. novelistic, fictional; fantastic.

novelista m. & f. novelist.

novia f. fiancée; sweetheart; bride.

noviazgo m. betrothal, engagement; courtship.

novicio m. novice; beginner; apprentice; adj. inexperienced.

noviembre m. November.

novilla f. heifer, young cow.

novillada f. herd of young bulls; bullfight (using young bulls).

novillo m. young bull; steer; **-s** bullfight (using young bulls); **hacer -s** to play hooky, cut classes; to play truant.

novio m. fiancé; sweetheart; bridegroom.

nubarrón m. large storm cloud.

nube f. cloud; film on the eyeball; **poner por las -s** to praise to the skies.

nublado m. storm cloud; imminent danger; adj. cloudy.

nublar v. to cloud; to darken, obscure; **-se** to grow cloudy.

nubloso adj. cloudy; gloomy.

nuca f. nape.

núcleo m. nucleus; kernel.

nudillo m. small knot; knuckle; loop, knitted stitch.

nudo m. knot; joint; union, bond, tie; crisis, turning point (of a play); knot, nautical mile; — **ciego** hard knot.

nudoso adj. knotty, gnarled, knotted.

nuera f. daughter-in-law.

nueva f. news.

nuevecito adj. nice and new, brand-new.

nuevo adj. new; newly arrived; **de** — again; ¿ **qué hay de** —? what's new? what's the news?

nuez f. walnut; nut; — (or — **de Adán**) Adam's apple; — **moscada** (or — **de especia**) nutmeg.

nulidad f. nullity (state or quality of

being null); incompetence; nonentity, a nobody.

nulo *adj.* null, void; useless.

numeral *adj. & m.* numeral.

numerar *v.* to number; to calculate; to enumerate.

numérico *adj.* numerical.

número *m.* number; numeral.

numeroso *adj.* numerous.

nunca *adv.* never; **no** . . . **—** not . . . ever; **más que** — more than ever.

nuncio *m.* herald, messenger; nuncio, Papal envoy.

nupcial *adj.* nuptial, relating to marriage or weddings.

nupcias *f. pl.* nuptials, wedding.

nutria *f.* otter.

nutrición *f.* nutrition; nourishment.

nutrido *adj.* full, abundant; substantial; *p.p.* of **nutrir.**

nutrimento, nutrimiento *m.* nutrition; nourishment, food.

nutrir *v.* to nourish, feed.

nutritivo *adj.* nutritious, nourishing.

Ñ

ñapa *f. Am.* additional amount, something extra; *Am.* **de** — to boot, in addition, besides.

ñato *adj. Am.* flat-nosed, pug-nosed, snub-nosed; *Am.* ugly, deformed; *Am.* insignificant.

ñoñería *f.* silly remark or action; *Am.* dotage.

ñoño *adj.* feeble-minded; silly; *Am.* old, decrepit, feeble; *Am.* old-fashioned, out of style.

O

o *conj.* or, either.

oasis *m.* oasis.

obedecer[13] *v. irr.* to obey; **— a cierta causa** to arise from, be due to, a certain cause; **esto obedece a que** . . . this is due to the fact that . . .

obediencia *f.* obedience.

obediente *adj.* obedient.

obertura *f.* musical overture.

obispo *m.* bishop; *Am.* **a cada muerte de (or por la muerte de un) —** once in a blue moon.

objeción *f.* objection.

objetar *v.* to object.

objetivo *adj.* objective; *m.* objective (*lens of a microscope*); objective.

objeto *m.* object, purpose, aim; thing.

oblea *f.* wafer.

oblicuo *adj.* oblique, slanting, bias.

obligación *f.* obligation; duty; bond, security; engagement.

obligar[7] *v.* to oblige; to obligate, bind, compel, put under obligation; **-se to** bind oneself, obligate oneself.

obligatorio *adj.* obligatory, compulsory; binding.

óbolo *m.* mite, small contribution.

obra *f.* work; act; labor, toil; book; building (*under construction*); repair; **— de** approximately; **por — de** through, by virtue or power of; **hacer mala —** to interfere, hinder; **poner por —** to undertake, begin; to put into practice.

obrar *v.* to work; to act; to operate; to function; to perform; to make; to do; **obra en nuestro poder** we are in receipt of; **la carta que obra en su poder** the letter that is in his possession.

obrero *m.* workman, laborer.

obscenidad *f.* obscenity.

obsceno *adj.* obscene.

obscurecer[13] *v. irr.* to obscure, darken; to tarnish; to grow dark; **-se** to get dark or cloudy.

obscuridad *f.* obscurity; darkness; dimness.

obscuro *adj.* obscure; dark; dim; **a obscuras (= a oscuras)** in the dark; *m.* shade (*in painting*).

obsequiar *v.* to regale, entertain; to court; *Am.* to give, make a present of.

obsequio *m.* attention, courtesy; gift; **en — de** for the sake of, in honor of.

obsequioso *adj.* attentive, courteous, obliging; obsequious, servile.

observación *f.* observation; remark.

observador *m.* observer; *adj.* observing.

observancia *f.* observance (*of a law, rule, custom, etc.*).

observante *adj.* observant (*of a law, custom, or rule*).

observar *v.* to observe; to watch; to remark.

observatorio *m.* observatory.

obsesión *f.* obsession.

obsesionar *v.* to obsess.

obstáculo *m.* obstacle.

obstante: no — notwithstanding; nevertheless.

obstar *v.* to hinder, impede, obstruct.

obstinación *f.* obstinacy, stubbornness.

obstinado *adj.* obstinate, stubborn.

obstinarse *v.* to persist (in); to be obstinate, stubborn (about).

obstrucción *f.* obstruction.

obstruir[32] *v. irr.* to obstruct, block.

obtener[45] *v. irr.* to obtain, get; to attain.

obtenible *adj.* obtainable, available.

obturador *m.* choke (*of an automobile*);

throttle; plug, stopper; **shutter** (*of a camera*).

obviar *v.* to obviate, clear away, remove.

obvio *adj.* obvious.

ocasión *f.* occasion, opportunity; cause; danger, risk; **de —** reduced, bargain; **avisos de —** want "ads" (*advertisements*); *Am.* **esta —** this time.

ocasional *adj.* occasional.

ocasionar *v.* to occasion, cause.

ocaso *m.* sunset; setting (*of any star or planet*); west; decadence, decline, end.

occidental *adj.* occidental, western.

occidente *m.* occident, west.

océano *m.* ocean.

ocio *m.* leisure, idleness; recreation, pastime.

ociosidad *f.* idleness, leisure.

ocioso *adj.* idle; useless.

octubre *m.* October.

ocular *adj.* ocular; **testigo —** eye witness; *m.* eyepiece, lens (*for the eye in a microscope or telescope*).

oculista *m. & f.* oculist; *Am.* flatterer.

ocultar *v.* to hide, conceal.

oculto *adj.* hidden, concealed; *m. Am.* species of mole (*small animal*).

ocupación *f.* occupation; employment.

ocupante *m. & f.* occupant.

ocupar *v.* to occupy; to employ; **-se en** (*Am.* **-se de**) to be engaged in; to pay attention to, be interested in.

ocurrencia *f.* occurrence, event; witticism, joke; bright or funny idea.

ocurrente *adj.* witty, funny, humorous; occurring.

ocurrir *v.* to occur.

ocurso *m. Am.* petition, application.

oda *f.* ode.

odiar *v.* to hate.

odio *m.* hatred.

odioso *adj.* odious, hateful.

oeste *m.* west; west wind.

ofender *v.* to offend; to displease; **-se** to get offended; to become angry, take offense.

ofensa *f.* offense.

ofensivo *adj.* offensive; obnoxious; attacking; **ofensiva** *f.* offensive.

ofensor *m.* offender; *adj.* offending.

oferta *f.* offer; promise.

oficial *m.* official, officer; skilled workman; *adj.* official.

oficiar *v.* to officiate, serve, minister, perform the duties of a priest or minister; to communicate officially; **— de** to serve as, act as.

oficina *f.* office; shop; **oficinesco** *adj.* clerical, pertaining to an office.

oficio *m.* office, position; trade; function; official communication; religious office (*prayers*).

oficioso *adj.* officious, meddlesome.

ofrecer[13] *v. irr.* to offer; to promise; **-se** to offer, occur, present itself; to offer oneself, volunteer; **¿qué se le ofrece a Vd?** what do you wish?

ofrecimiento *m.* offer; offering.

ofrenda *f.* offering, gift.

ofuscamiento *m.* clouded vision, blindness; cloudiness of the mind, bewilderment, mental confusion.

ofuscar[6] *v.* to darken, cast a shadow on; to blind; to cloud; to bewilder, confuse.

ogro *m.* ogre.

oído *m.* hearing; ear; **al —** confidentially; **de** (*or* **al**) **—** by ear; **de -s** (*or* **de oídas**) by hearsay or rumor.

oidor *m.* hearer, listener; judge.

oír[36] *v. irr.* to hear; to listen; to understand; **— misa** to attend mass; **— decir que** to hear that; **— hablar de** to hear about.

ojal *m.* buttonhole; hole.

¡ojalá! *interj.* God grant!; I hope so; **— que** would that, I hope that.

ojazo *m.* large eye.

ojeada *f.* glimpse, quick glance.

ojear *v.* to eye, stare; to bewitch; to beat up, rouse (*wild game*).

ojera *f.* dark circle under the eye; eyecup.

ojeriza *f.* grudge, spite.

ojeroso *adj.* with dark circles under the eyes.

ojiva *f.* pointed arch; **ojival** *adj.* pointed (*arch*); **ventana ojival** window with a pointed arch.

ojo *m.* eye; keyhole; hole; **¡ — !** careful! look out!; **a —** by sight, by guess; **a -s vistas** visibly, clearly; **mal (** *or* **mal de) —** evil eye; *Am.* **hacer —** to cast the evil eye; *Am.* **pelar el —** to be alert, keep one's eye peeled; *Am.* **poner a uno los -s verdes** to deceive someone; **tener entre -s** to have ill will toward, have a grudge against.

ojota *f. Am.* leather sandal.

ola *f.* wave.

oleada *f.* big wave; swell; surge; abundant yield of oil.

oleaje, olaje *m.* swell, surge, succession of waves.

oleo *m.* oil; holy oil; **pintura al —** oil painting.

oleoso *adj.* oily.

oler[37] *v. irr.* to smell; to scent; **— a** to smack of; to smell like; *Am.* **olérselas** to suspect it, "smell a rat".

olfatear v. to scent, sniff, smell.

olfateo m. sniff, sniffing.

olfato m. sense of smell.

oliva f. olive; olive tree; owl; olivar m. olive grove; olivo m. olive tree.

olmo m. elm.

olor m. smell, odor, fragrance; smack, trace, suspicion; Am. spice; olorcillo m. faint odor.

oloroso adj. fragrant.

olote m. Am. cob, corncob.

olvidadizo adj. forgetful.

olvidar v. to forget; to neglect; -se de to forget; olvidársele a uno algo to forget something.

olvido m. forgetfulness; oblivion; neglect; echar al — to cast into oblivion; to forget on purpose.

olla f. pot, kettle; olla (vegetable and meat stew); — podrida Spanish stew of mixed vegetables and meat.

ombligo m. navel; middle, center.

omisión f. omission; oversight; neglect.

omiso adj. careless, neglectful; Am. guilty; hacer caso — to omit.

omitir v. to omit; to overlook.

ómnibus m. omnibus, bus.

omnipotente adj. omnipotent, almighty.

onda f. wave; ripple; sound wave; scallop.

ondear v. to wave; to waver; to ripple; to sway, swing.

ondulación f. undulation, waving motion; wave; — permanente permanent wave.

ondulado p.p. & adj. wavy; scalloped (edge).

ondulante adj. wavy, waving.

ondular v. to undulate, wave.

onza f. ounce; ounce, wildcat; Am. small tiger.

opaco adj. opaque, dim, dull.

ópalo m. opal.

ópera f. opera.

operación f. operation; business transaction.

operador m. operator, surgeon.

operar v. to operate; to take effect, work; to speculate (in business); to manipulate, handle.

operario m. operator, workman, worker.

opereta f. operetta.

opinar v. to express an opinion; to think; to judge; to argue.

opinión f. opinion; reputation.

opio m. opium.

oponer[40] v. irr. to oppose; -se to disapprove; -se a to. oppose, be against.

oporto m. port wine.

oportunidad f. opportunity.

oportuno adj. opportune; convenient, timely.

oposición f. opposition; competition; -es competitive examinations.

opositor m. opponent; competitor.

opresión f. oppression.

opresivo adj. oppressive.

opresor m. oppressor.

oprimir v. to oppress; to crush; to press down.

oprobio m. infamy; insult; shame; dishonor.

optar v. to choose, select; — por to decide upon; to choose.

óptica f. optics.

óptico adj. optical, optic; m. optician.

optimismo m. optimism; optimista m. & f. optimist; adj. optimistic.

óptimo adj. very good, very best.

opuesto p.p. of oponer opposed; adj. opposite; contrary.

opulencia f. opulence, abundance, wealth.

opulento adj. opulent, wealthy.

oquedad f. cavity, hollow; chasm.

ora conj. now, then; whether; either.

oración f. oration; prayer; sentence.

oráculo m. oracle.

orador m. orator, speaker.

oral adj. oral.

orar v. to pray.

oratoria f. oratory, eloquence.

oratorio m. oratory, private chapel; oratorio (a religious musical composition); adj. oratorical, pertaining to oratory.

orbe m. orb, sphere, globe; the earth; world, universe.

órbita f. orbit; eye socket.

orden m. order; succession, series; class, group; relation; proportion; f. order, command; honorary or religious order; m. & f. sacrament of ordination; a sus órdenes at your service.

ordenado p.p. & adj. ordered; ordained; orderly; neat.

ordenanza f. ordinance, decree, law; command, order; m. orderly (military).

ordenar v. to arrange, put in order; to order, command; to ordain; -se to become ordained.

ordeña f. milking.

ordeñar v. to milk.

ordinariez f. commonness, lack of manners.

ordinario adj. ordinary; usual; common, coarse; m. ordinary (a bishop or judge); ordinary mail; daily household expense; de — usually, ordinarily.

orear *v.* to air; **-se** to be exposed to the air; to dry in the air.

oreja *f.* ear; hearing; loop; small flap; *Am.* handle (*shaped like an ear*); **orejano** *adj.* unbranded (*cattle*); *Am.* cautious; *m. Am.* aloof, unsociable person; **orejera** *f.* ear muff, ear flap; **orejón** *m.* pull by the ear; *Am.* rancher or inhabitant of the sabana; *adj. Am.* long-eared, long-horned; *Am.* unbranded (*cattle*); *Am.* coarse, crude, -uncouth.

orfandad *f.* orphanage (*state of being an orphan*).

orfanato *m.* orphanage, orphan asylum.

orfanatorio *Am.* = **orfanato**.

orfebre *m.* goldsmith; silversmith.

orfeón *m.* glee club, choir.

orgánico *adj.* organic.

organismo *m.* organism.

organización *f.* organization.

organizador *m.* organizer.

organizar[9] *v.* to organize; to arrange.

órgano *m.* organ; **organillo** *m.* hand organ.

orgía *f.* orgy, wild revel.

orgullo *m.* pride; haughtiness, arrogance.

orgulloso *adj.* proud; haughty, arrogant.

oriental *adj.* oriental, eastern.

orientar *v.* to orientate, orient; **-se** to orient oneself, find one's bearings.

oriente *m.* orient, east; east wind; source, origin.

orificación *f.* gold filling.

orificio *m.* orifice, small hole, aperture, outlet.

origen *m.* origin; source.

original *adj.* original; strange, quaint; *m.* original; manuscript, copy; queer person; **originalidad** *f.* originality.

originar *v.* to originate, cause to be; **-se** originate, arise.

orilla *f.* shore, bank; beach; edge, border; **-s** *Am.* outskirts, environs.

orillar *v.* to border, trim the edge of; to skirt, go along the edge of; to reach the edge or shore.

orín *m.* rust; **orines** *m. pl.* urine.

orina *f.* urine.

orinar *v.* to urinate.

oriol *m.* oriole.

oriundo *adj.* native; **ser — de** to hail from, come from.

orla *f.* border; trimming, fringe.

orlar *v.* to border, edge, trim with a border or fringe.

ornado *adj.* ornate; *p.p.* adorned, orna-

---

mented.

ornamentar *v.* to ornament, adorn.

ornamento *m.* ornament; decoration; **-s** sacred vestments.

ornar *v.* to adorn.

oro *m.* gold; gold ornament; **-s** "gold coins" (*Spanish card suit*).

orondo *adj.* self-satisfied, puffed up, vain; *Am.* serene, calm.

oropel *m.* tinsel.

orquesta *f.* orchestra.

orquídea *f.* orchid.

ortiga *f.* nettle.

ortografía *f.* orthography, spelling.

ortográfico *adj.* orthographic (*pertaining to orthography or spelling*).

oruga *f.* caterpillar.

orzuelo *m.* sty (*on the eyelid*).

osadía *f.* boldness, daring.

osado *adj.* bold, daring.

osar *v.* to dare, venture.

oscilación *f.* oscillation, sway; fluctuation, wavering.

oscilar *v.* to oscillate, swing, sway; to waver.

oscurecer = **obsurecer**.

oscuridad = **obsuridad**.

oscuro = **obscuro**.

oso *m.* bear; **— blanco** polar bear; **— hormiguero** anteater; **— marino** seal.

ostentación *f.* ostentation, show, display.

ostentar *v.* to display, show; to show off; to boast.

ostentoso *adj.* ostentatious, showy.

ostión *m.* large oyster.

ostra *f.* oyster.

otate *m. Am.* species of bamboo; *Am.* bamboo stick or cane.

otero *m.* hillock, small hill, knoll.

otoñal *adj.* autumnal, of autumn.

otoño *m.* autumn, fall.

otorgar[7] *v.* to grant; to promise; to consent to.

otro *adj.* another; **otra vez** again; *Am.* **como dijo el —** as someone said.

otrora *adv.* formerly, in other times.

ovación *f.* ovation, enthusiastic applause.

oval, ovalado *adj.* oval; **óvalo** *m.* oval.

oveja *f.* sheep.

ovejero *m.* shepherd; sheep dog.

ovejuno *adj.* sheep, pertaining or relating to sheep.

overo *adj.* peach-colored (*applied to horses and cattle*); *Am.* mottled, spotted; *Am.* multicolored; *Am.* **ponerle a uno —** to insult someone.

overol, overoles *m. Am.* overalls.

ovillar v. to ball, wind or form into a ball; **-se** to curl up into a ball.

ovillo m. ball of yarn or thread; tangle; **hacerse uno un —** to curl up into a ball; to become entangled, confused.

oxidado p.p. rusted; adj. rusty.

oxidar v. to oxidize; to rust; **-se** to become oxidized; to rust.

oxígeno m. oxygen

oyente m. & f. listener, auditor, hearer; adj. listening.

P

pabellón m. pavilion; canopy; banner, flag; shelter, covering; external ear.

pabilo m. wick; snuff (of a candle).

pacer[13] v. trr. to pasture; to graze.

paciencia f. patience.

paciente adj. patient; m. & f. patient.

pacienzudo adj. patient, long-suffering.

pacificar[6] v. to pacify; to appease.

pacífico adj. pacific, peaceful, calm.

pacto m. pact, agreement.

padecer[13] v. trr. to suffer.

padecimiento m. suffering.

padrastro m. stepfather; hangnail.

padre m. father; **-s** parents; ancestors; adj. Am. very great, stupendous.

padrenuestro m. paternoster, the Lord's Prayer.

padrino m. godfather; sponsor, patron; second in a duel; best man (at a wedding).

paella f. a popular rice dish with chicken, vegetables, etc.

paga f. payment; pay, salary.

pagadero adj. payable.

pagado p.p. & adj. paid; self-satisfied, conceited; **— de sí mismo** pleased with oneself.

pagador m. payer; paymaster; paying teller (in a bank).

paganismo m. paganism, heathenism.

pagano adj. pagan; m. pagan; payer; dupe, sucker.

pagar[7] v. to pay; to pay for; to requite, return (love); **-se** to be proud of; to boast of; to be pleased with; Am. **-se de palabras** to let oneself be tricked; Am. **— a nueve** to pay in excess.

pagaré m. promissory note; I.O.U.

página f. page.

paginar v. to page.

pago m. payment; prize, reward; country district; Am. one's native farm land or district; adj. paid; Am. **estar -s** to be quits.

país m. nation, country; region.

paisaje m. landscape.

paisanaje m. peasantry, country people; civilians; Am. gang of farm laborers.

paisano m. countryman; peasant; fellow countryman; civilian.

paja f. straw; chaff; rubbish; Am. grass for pasture; **echar -s** to draw lots; **por quítame allá esas -s** for an insignificant reason or pretext; **en un quítame allá esas -s** in a jiffy, in a second; **a humo de -s** thoughtlessly, lightly; **no lo hizo a humo de -s** he did not do it without a special reason or intention.

pajar m. straw loft, barn.

pájaro m. bird; shrewd, cautious person; Am. absent-minded person; Am. person of suspicious conduct; **— carpintero** woodpecker; **— mosca** humming-bird.

paje m. page, valet, attendant.

pajizo adj. made of straw; covered with straw; straw-colored.

pajonal m. plain or field of tall coarse grass.

pala f. shovel; trowel; scoop; paddle; blade of an oar; racket; upper (of a shoe); cunning, craftiness; **meter la —** to deceive with cunning; Am. **hacer la —** to deceive with cunning; to stall, pretend to work; to flatter; **palada** f. scoop, shovelful; stroke of an oar.

palabra f. word; promise; **de —** by word of mouth; **cuatro -s** a few words; **empeñar la —** to promise, pledge; **tener la —** to have the floor; Am. **¡ — !** I mean it, it is true!

palabrero adj. wordy, talkative.

palabrita f. a little word, a few words; a word of advice.

palacio m. palace; **palaciego** m. courtier; adj. relating to a palace or court; court (used as an adj.).

paladar m. palate; taste, relish.

paladear v. to relish, taste with relish.

paladín m. knight; champion, defender.

palanca f. lever; crowbar; bar used for carrying a load.

palangana f. washbowl, basin; Am. platter; Am. large wooden bowl; m. Am. bluffer, charlatan.

palco m. theatre box; **— escénico** stage.

palenque m. palisade, fence; enclosure; Am. hitching post or plank.

paleta f. small flat shovel; mason's trowel; shoulder blade; blade (of a rudder, of a ventilating fan); paddle (of a paddle wheel); painter's palette; Am. candy, sweetmeat or ice cream attached to a stick; Am. a wooden

151

paddle to stir with, or for beating clothes; **en dos -s** in a jiffy, in a second; **paletilla** f. shoulder blade.

palidecer[13] v. irr. to turn pale.

palidez f. pallor, paleness.

pálido adj. pallid, pale.

palillo m. small stick; toothpick; **tocar todos los -s** (Am. **menear uno los -s**) to try every possible means.

paliza f. beating (with a stick), thrashing.

palizada f. palisade; stockade.

palma f. palm tree; palm leaf; palm of the hand; **batir -s** to clap, applaud; **llevarse la —** to triumph, win, carry off the honors; to be the best.

palmada f. slap; clap.

palmario adj. clear, evident.

palmatoria f. small candlestick with handle.

palmear v. to clap, applaud; Am. to pat, clap on the back; Am. to flatter.

palmera f. palm tree.

palmo m. span (about 9 inches); **— a —** slowly, foot by foot.

palmotear v. to clap, applaud.

palo m. stick; pole; log; mast; wood; blow with a stick; suit (in a deck of cards); Am. tree; Am. reprimand, reproof; Am. large swallow of liquor; **— del Brasil** Brazil wood; Am. **— a pique** rail fence, barbed wire fence; Am. **a medio —** half-done; half-drunk; Am. **a — entero** drunk.

paloma f. dove, pigeon; pleasant, mild person; **-s** whitecaps.

palomar m. dovecot (shelter for doves or pigeons).

palomilla f. little dove; moth; small butterfly; **-s** small whitecaps.

palomita f. little dove; **-s** Am. popcorn.

palpable adj. palpable (that can be felt or touched); clear, obvious, evident.

palpar v. to feel; to touch; to grope.

palpitación f. palpitation; beat, throb.

palpitante adj. palpitating, throbbing, trembling; exciting; **la cuestión —** the burning question.

palpitar v. to palpitate; to throb, beat.

palta f. Am. avocado, alligator pear; **palto** m. Am. avocado tree. See **aguacate**.

palúdico adj. marshy; **fiebre palúdica** malarial, or marsh, fever; malaria; **paludismo** m. malaria.

pampa f. Am. pampa (vast treeless plain of South America); Am. prairie; Am. drill field (military); m. & f. pampa Indian of Argentina; m. Am. language of the pampa Indian; adj. Am. pertaining to the pampa Indian; Am. **caballo** **—** horse with head and body of different colors; Am. **trato —** dubious or dishonest deal; Am. **estar a la —** to be in the open; Am. **tener todo a la —** to be ragged or to be indecently exposed; Am. **quedar en —** to be left without clothes; to be left in the lurch.

pampeano adj. Am. of, or pertaining to, the pampa.

pampero adj. Am. of, or pertaining to, the pampas; m. Am. inhabitant of the pampas; Am. violent wind of the pampa.

pan m. bread; loaf of bread; wheat; **-es** fields of grain; breadstuffs; Am. **echar -es** to brag, boast.

pana f. corduroy.

panadería f. bakery.

panadero m. baker; Am. flatterer.

panal m. honeycomb; sweetmeat (made of sugar, egg white, and lemon).

panamericano adj. Pan-American.

pandearse v. to bulge, warp; to sag.

pandeo m. sag; bulge.

pandilla f. gang, band.

panfleto m. pamphlet.

pánico m. panic; adj. panic, panicky.

panne f. accident, car trouble.

panocha f. ear of corn; Am. Mexican raw sugar; Am. a kind of tamale.

panqué m. Am. small cake, cup cake; Am. pancake.

pantalón m. trousers; pants; **un par de -es** a pair of trousers.

pantalla f. light shade; screen; fireplace screen; motion-picture screen; Am. fan, palm leaf fan.

pantano m. swamp; dam; difficulty.

pantanoso adj. swampy, marshy; muddy.

pantera f. panther.

pantorrilla f. calf (of the leg).

pantufla f. bedroom slipper.

panza f. paunch, belly.

panzón, panzudo adj. big-bellied.

pañal m. diaper; **estar en -es** to be in one's infancy; to have little or no knowledge of a thing.

paño m. cloth (any cloth, especially woolen); blotch or spot on the skin; film on the eyeball; Am. parcel of tillable land; Am. kerchief, shawl; **— de manos** towel; **— de mesa** tablecloth; **al —** off-stage; **-s** clothes, garments; **-s menores** underwear; **pañero** m. clothier.

pañolón m. scarf, large kerchief; shawl.

pañuelo m. handkerchief.

papa m. Pope; f. potato; fib, lie; Am. snap, easy job; **-s** pap (soft food for *babies*); soup; *Am.* **cosa** — something good to eat; excellent thing; **echar -s** to fib, lie; *Am.* **importarle a uno una** — not to matter to one a bit; *Am.* **no saber ni** — not to a know a thing; to be completely ignorant.

papá *m.* papa; *Am.* — **grande** grand-father.

papagayo *m.* parrot; talker, chatterer.

papal *adj.* papal.

papalote, papelote *m. Am.* kite.

papamoscas *m.* flycatcher (*a bird*); simpleton, half-wit, dunce.

papanatas *m.* simpleton, fool, dunce.

paparrucha *f.* fib, lie; **paparruchero** *m.* fibber.

papel *m.* paper; sheet of paper; document; role; — **de estraza** brown wrapping paper; — **de lija** sand-paper; — **de seda** tissue paper; — **moneda** paper money; — **secante** blotting. paper; **hacer el** — **de** to play the role of; **hacer buen** (*or* **mal**) — to cut a good (*or* bad) figure.

papelera *f.* folder, file, case or device for keeping papers; *Am.* wastepaper basket; **papelero** *m.* paper manufacturer; *adj.* pertaining to paper; vain, ostentatious.

papelería *f.* stationery store; stationery; lot of papers.

papeleta *f.* card, file card, slip of paper.

papelucho *m.* worthless piece of paper.

papera *f.* goiter; **-s** mumps.

paquete *m.* package; bundle; dandy; packet boat (*mail boat*); *adj. Am.* dolled up, dressed up; *Am.* important, pompous; *Am.* insincere.

par *adj.* even; *m.* pair, couple; peer; **a la** — at par; jointly; at the same time; **al** — **de** on a par with; **bajo** — below par; **sin** — peerless, without an equal, having no equal; **sobre** — above par; **de** — **en** — wide-open.

para *prep.* for; to; toward; in order to; **¿** — **qué?** what for; — **que** so that; — **siempre** forever; — **mis adentros** to myself; **sin qué ni** — **qué** without rhyme or reason; *m. Am.* Paraguayan tobacco; *Am.* Paraguayan (*used as nickname*).

parabién *m.* congratulation; **dar el** — to congratulate.

parabrisa *m.* windshield.

paracaídas *m.* parachute; **paracaidista** *m. & f.* parachutist.

parachoques *m.* bumper.

parada *f.* stop; stopping place; bet, stake; military review; *Am.* parade; *Am.* boastfulness; *Am.* **tener mucha**

— to dress very well.

paradero *m.* stopping place; whereabouts; end.

parado *p.p. & adj.* stopped; unoccupied, unemployed; fixed, motionless; *Am.* standing, erect, straight up; *Am.* stiff, proud; *Am.* cold, unenthusiastic; *Am.* **caer uno** — to land on one's feet; to be lucky; *Am.* **estar bien** — to be well-fixed, well-established; to be lucky; *m. Am.* air, appearance.

paradoja *f.* paradox.

parafina *f.* paraffin.

paraguas *m.* umbrella; **paragüero** *m.* umbrella stand; umbrella maker or seller.

paraguayo *adj. & m.* Paraguayan.

paraíso *m.* paradise, heaven; upper gallery (*in a theater*).

paraje *m.* place; spot; situation.

paralelo *adj.* parallel; similar; *m.* parallel; similarity; **paralela** *f.* parallel line; **paralelismo** *m.* parallelism.

parálisis *f.* paralysis.

paralizar *v.* to paralyze; to stop.

páramo *m.* high, bleak plain; cold region; *Am.* blizzard or a cold drizzle.

parangón *m.* comparison.

parangonar *v.* to compare.

paraninfo *m.* assembly hall, lecture hall, auditorium.

parapeto *m.* parapet.

parar *v.* to stop; to end, end up, come to an end; to parry (*in fencing*); to set up (*type*); *Am.* to stand, place in upright position; — **atención** to notice; — **mientes en** to observe, notice; *Am.* — **las orejas** to prick up one's ears; to pay close attention; **-se** to stop; *Am.* to stand up, get up.

pararrayos *m.* lightning rod.

parásito *m.* parasite; *adj.* parasitic.

parasol *m.* parasol.

parcela *f.* parcel of land; particle, small piece.

parcial *adj.* partial; *m.* follower, partisan; **parcialidad** *f.* partiality; faction, party.

parche *m.* mending patch; sticking plaster; medicated plaster; drum.

pardal *m.* sparrow; linnet; sly fellow.

pardear *v.* to grow dusky; to appear brownish-grey.

pardo *adj.* dark-grey; brown; dark; cloudy; *m.* leopard; *Am.* mulatto; **pardusco** *adj.* greyish; brownish.

parear *v.* to pair, couple, match, mate.

parecer *v. irr.* to seem; to appear, show up; **-se** to resemble each other, look alike; *m.* opinion; appearance, looks; **al —** apparently, seemingly.

parecido *adj.* alike, similar; **bien —** good-looking; *p.p. of* **parecer;** *m.* similarity, likeness, resemblance.

pared *f.* wall; **— maestra** main wall; **— medianera** partition wall.

pareja *f.* pair; couple; match; partner; *Am.* team of two horses; *Am.* horse race.

parejero *m. Am.* race horse; *Am.* overfamiliar person, backslapper, hailfellow-well-met.

parejo *adj.* even; smooth; equal; *adv. Am.* hard.

parentela *f.* relatives, kin.

parentesco *m.* kinship, relationship.

paréntesis *m.* parenthesis; digression; **entre —** by the way.

paria *m. & f.* outcast.

paridad *f.* par, equality.

pariente *m. & f.* relative, relation.

parir *v.* to give birth; to bear (*children*).

parlamentar *v.* to converse; to parley, discuss terms with an enemy.

parlamentario *adj.* parliamentary; *m.* member of parliament; envoy to a parley.

parlamento *m.* speech (*of a character in a play*); parley; parliament, legislative assembly.

parlanchín *adj.* talkative; *m.* talker, chatterer.

parlero *adj.* talkative; gossipy; chattering, chirping.

parlotear *v.* to prate, prattle, chatter, chat.

parloteo *m.* chatter, prattle, idle talk.

paro *m.* work stoppage; lockout; *Am.* throw (*in the game of dice*); *Am.* **— y pinta** game of dice.

parodia *f.* parody, take-off, humorous imitation.

parodiar *v.* to parody, take off, imitate.

parótidas *f. pl.* mumps.

parpadear *v.* to wink; to blink; to flutter the eyelids; to twinkle.

parpadeo *m.* winking; blinking; fluttering of the eyelids; twinkling.

párpado *m.* eyelid.

parque *m.* park; *Am.* ammunition.

parra *f.* grapevine; earthenware jug.

parrafada *f.* chat.

párrafo *m.* paragraph; **echar un — con** to have a chat with.

parranda *f.* revel, orgy, spree; *Am.* gang, band; **andar** (*or* **ir**) **de —** to go on a spree.

parrandear *v.* to revel, make merry, go on a spree.

parrilla *f.* grill, gridiron, broiler; grate.

párroco *m.* parish priest.

parroquia *f.* parish; parish church; clientele, customers.

parroquiano *m.* client, customer; parishioner; *adj.* parochial, of a parish.

parsimonia *f.* thrift, economy; moderation; prudence.

parsimonioso *adj.* thrifty; stingy; cautious; slow.

parte *f.* part; share; place; party (*legal term*); **-s** qualities; *Am.* unnecessary excuses or explanations; **de algún tiempo a esta —** for some time past; **de — de** on behalf of; in favor of; **de — a —** through, from one side to the other; **dar —** to inform; **echar a mala —** to take amiss; **en —** partly; **por todas -s** everywhere; *m.* telegram; message.

partera *f.* midwife.

partición *f.* partition, division.

participación *f.* participation, share; notice.

participante *m. & f.* participant; *adj.* participating, sharing.

participar *v.* to participate, share; to inform, notify.

partícipe *m. & f.* participant; *adj.* participating.

participio *m.* participle.

partícula *f.* particle.

particular *adj.* particular, special; peculiar; private, personal; odd, strange; **en —** specially; **lecciones -es** private lessons; *m.* private citizen; individual; point, detail; matter.

partida *f.* departure, leave; item, entry; record; band, group; squad; shipment; game; set (*in tennis*); *Am.* part in the hair; **— de bautismo** (**de matrimonio** *or* **de defunción**) birth (marriage, *or* death) certificate; **— de campo** picnic; **— de caza** hunting party; **— doble** double-entry bookkeeping; *Am.* **confesar la —** to tell the truth, speak plainly; **jugar una mala —** to play a mean trick.

partidario *m.* partisan, follower, supporter.

partido *m.* party, faction, group; contest, game; profit; district; *Am.* **a** (*or* **al**) **—** in equal shares; *Am.* **dar —** to give a handicap or advantage (*in certain games*); **darse a —** to yield, give up; **sacar — de** to derive advantage from, make the best of; **tomar un —** to decide, make a decision.

partir *v.* to split, divide; to crack, break; to depart, leave; **a — de hoy**

starting today; from this day on; *Am.* **a** (*or* **al**) **—** in equal parts; *Am.* **— a uno por el eje** to ruin someone.

partitura *f.* musical score.

parto *m.* childbirth, delivery; product, offspring; **estar de —** to be in labor.

parvada *f.* pile of unthreshed grain; brood; *Am.* flock (*of birds or children*).

parvedad *f.* smallness; trifle; snack, bit of food.

párvulo *m.* child; *adj.* small; innocent.

pasa *f.* raisin; woolly hair of negroes.

pasada *f.* passing, passage; *Am.* stay; *Am.* embarrassment, shame; **una mala —** a mean trick; **de —** on the way; incidentally, by the way; **dar una — por** to pass by, walk by.

pasadizo *m.* aisle; narrow hall; narrow passageway.

pasado *m.* past; *p.p.* past, gone; *adj.* overripe, spoiled; *Am.* dried (*fruits*); *Am.* thin, bony (*animal*); **— mañana** day after tomorrow; **el año —** last year; **en días -s** in days gone by.

pasaje *m.* passage; fare, ticket; total number of passengers; *Am.* private alley; *Am.* anecdote.

pasajero *adj.* passing, temporary, fleeting, transitory; *m.* passenger.

pasamano *m.* railing, hand rail; gangplank; gangway (*of a ship*).

pasaporte *m.* passport.

pasar *v.* to pass; to cross; to surpass, exceed; to pierce; to go forward; to go over (in, by, to); to enter; to carry over, take across; to happen; to get along; to swallow; to overlook; to tolerate; to suffer; **— las de Caín** to have a hard time; **— por alto** to omit, overlook; **— por las armas** to execute; **-se** to transfer, change over; to get overripe, spoiled; to exceed, go beyond; **se me pasó decirte** I forgot to tell you; *Am.* **pasársela a uno** to deceive someone, break someone's confidence; **un buen —** enough to live on.

pasarela *f.* gangplank.

pasatiempo *m.* pastime; *Am.* cookie.

pascua *f.* Easter; Jewish Passover; **— florida** (*or* **de resurrección**) Easter Sunday; **— de Navidad** Christmas.

pase *m.* pass, permit; thrust (*in fencing*).

pasear *v.* to walk; to take a walk; to ride; **-se** to take a walk; to parade; **-se en automóvil** to take an automobile ride; **-se a caballo** to go horseback riding.

paseo *m.* walk, ride; parade; public park; boulevard; **— en automóvil** automobile ride; **dar un —** to take a walk.

pasillo *m.* aisle; hallway, corridor; short step; short skit; *Am.* a type of dance music; *Am.* runner, hall carpet.

pasión *f.* passion; suffering.

pasivo *adj.* passive; inactive; *m.* liabilities, debts; debit, debit side (*in bookkeeping*).

pasmar *v.* to astound, stun; **-se** to be amazed, stunned; to marvel; to get a sudden chill; to get frostbitten; *Am.* to become dried up, shriveled up; *Am.* to get bruised by the saddle or pack (*said of horses and mules*).

pasmo *m.* amazement, astonishment; wonder, awe.

pasmoso *adj.* astonishing, astounding; marvellous.

paso *m.* pass; step; pace; gait; passage; passing; skit; incident; *Am.* ford; *Am.* ferry, ferryboat wharf; *adv.* slowly; **de —** by the way, in passing; **al — que** while; **salir del —** to get out of a difficulty; *Am.* **marcar el —** to mark step, obey humbly; *adj.* dried (*figs, grapes, prunes, etc.*).

pasta *f.* paste; dough; noodles; book cover, binding; *Am.* cookie, cracker; **de buena —** of good temper or disposition.

pastal *m.* *Am.* range, grazing land, large pasture.

pastar *v.* to pasture, graze.

pastear *v.* *Am.* to graze, pasture.

pastel *m.* pie; pastry roll; filled pastry; trick, fraud; secret pact, plot; pastel crayon; **pintura al —** pastel painting.

pastelería *f.* pastry shop, bakery; pastry.

pastelero *m.* pastry cook; *Am.* turncoat (*person who changes easily from one political party to another*); *Am.* political intriguer.

pasterizar⁹, pasteurizar⁹ *v.* to pasteurize.

pastilla *f.* tablet (*of medicine, candy, etc.*); bar (*of chocolate*); cake (*of soap*).

pastizal *m.* pasture, grassland.

pasto *m.* pasture; grassland; grazing; nourishment; *Am.* grass; **a todo —** without restraint.

pastor *m.* shepherd; pastor.

pastoral *adj.* pastoral; *f.* pastoral play; idyll; pastoral letter; **pastorela** *f.* pastoral, pastoral play; **pastoril** *adj.* pastoral.

pastoso *adj.* pasty, soft; mellow (*said of the voice*); *Am.* grassy.

pastura *f.* pasture; fodder, feed.

pata *f.* foot, leg (*of an animal, table,*

chair, etc.); female duck; — **de gallo** crow's-foot (wrinkle at the corner of the eye); Am. — **de perro** wanderer; Am. **hacer — ancha** to stand firm, face a danger; **meter la —** to put one's foot in it, make an embarrassing blunder; **-s arriba** upside down, head over heels.

patacón m. Am. silver coin worth about one peso.

patada f. kick; stamp (with the foot); footprint; "kick," intoxicating effect; **a -s** with kicks; in great abundance; Am. **en dos -s** in a jiffy, in a second.

patalear v. to kick around; to stamp.

pataleo m. kicking; stamping.

pataleta f. convulsion; fainting fit.

patán m. boor, ill-mannered person; rustic; adj. rude, boorish, ill-mannered.

patata f. potato.

patear v. to kick; to stamp the foot; to tramp about; to trample on; to humiliate; Am. to kick, spring back (as a gun); Am. to have a kick or intoxicating effect.

patentar v. to patent.

patente adj. patent, evident, clear; f. patent; grant; privilege; Am. **de —** excellent, of best quality.

patentizar [9] v. to evidence, reveal, show.

paternal adj. paternal; fatherly.

paternidad f. paternity, fatherhood; authorship.

paterno adj. paternal, fatherly.

patético adj. pathetic.

patibulario adj. harrowing, frightful, hair-raising; criminal.

patíbulo m. scaffold, gallows.

patilla f. small foot or paw; Am. watermelon; Am. stone or brick bench (near a wall); Am. railing of a balcony; Am. slip from a plant; **-s** side whiskers; **Patillas** the Devil.

patín m. skate; a small patio; goosander (a kind of duck); — **de ruedas** roller skate; **patinadero** m. skating rink.

patinar v. to skate; to skid.

patio m. patio, open court, courtyard; Am. railway switchyard; Am. **pasarse uno al —** to take undue liberties.

patituerto adj. crook-legged; knock-kneed; bow-legged.

patizambo adj. knock-kneed.

pato m. duck; **pagar el —** to be the goat; to get the blame; Am. **andar —** to be flat broke, penniless; Am. **hacerse —** to play the fool; Am. **pasarse de —** a **ganso** to take undue liberties; Am. **ser el — de la boda** to be the life of the party; **patito** m. duckling.

patochada f. stupidity, blunder, nonsense.

patraña f. fabulous tale; lie, falsehood.

patria f. fatherland, native country.

patriarca m. patriarch; **patriarcal** adj. patriarchal.

patrimonio m. patrimony; inheritance.

patrio adj. native, of one's native country; paternal, belonging to the father.

patriota m. & f. patriot.

patriótico adj. patriotic.

patriotismo m. patriotism.

patrocinar v. to patronize, favor, sponsor.

patrocinio m. patronage, protection.

patrón m. patron; patron saint; sponsor; master, boss; proprietor, landlord; host; skipper; pattern, standard, model; **patrona** f. landlady; patroness; hostess.

patronato m. board of trustees; foundation (for educational, cultural, or charitable purposes).

patrono m. patron, protector; trustee; patron saint.

patrulla f. patrol; squad, gang.

patrullar v. to patrol.

pausa f. pause, stop, rest.

pausar v. to pause.

pauta f. norm, rule, standard; guide lines (for writing).

pava f. turkey hen; Am. kettle, teapot, teakettle; Am. jest, coarse joke; **pelar la —** to talk by night at the window (said of lovers).

pavesa f. cinder; small firebrand; burnt wick or snuff of a candle; **-s** cinders.

pavimentar v. to pave.

pavimento m. pavement.

pavo m. turkey; Am. sponger, parasite; **— real** peacock; **comer —** to be a wallflower at a dance; adj. silly, foolish; vain.

pavón m. peacock.

pavonearse v. to strut, swagger.

pavoneo m. strut, swagger.

pavor m. awe, dread, terror.

pavoroso adj. frightful, dreadful.

payasada f. clownish act or remark.

payasear v. to clown, play the fool.

payaso m. clown.

paz f. peace.

pazguato adj. simple, dumb, stupid; m. simpleton.

peaje m. toll (for crossing a bridge or ferry).

pealar = **pialar**.

peal = **pial**.

peatón m. pedestrian.

peca f. freckle.

pecado m. sin.

pecador m. sinner; adj. sinful.

pecaminoso adj. sinful.

pecar[6] v. to sin; — **de bueno** to be too good; — **de oscuro** to be exceedingly unclear, too complicated.

pecera f. fish bowl.

pecoso adj. freckly, freckled.

peculado m. embezzlement.

peculiar adj. peculiar; **peculiaridad** f. peculiarity.

pechada f. Am. bump, push, shove with the chest; Am. bumping contest between two riders; Am. overthrowing an animal (by bumping it with the chest of a horse).

pechar v. Am. to bump, push, shove with the chest; Am. to drive one's horse against; Am. to borrow, strike (someone) for a loan.

pechera f. shirtfront; chest protector; bib (of an apron).

pecho m. chest; breast; bosom; heart; courage; **dar el** — to nurse; **tomar a -s** to take to heart; Am. **a todo** — shouting; Am. **en -s de camisa** in shirt sleeves.

pechuga f. breast, breast meat of a fowl; bosom; Am. courage, nerve, audacity, impudence.

pedagogía f. pedagogy, science of education.

pedagógico adj. pedagogic, relating to education or teaching.

pedagogo m. pedagogue, teacher, educator.

pedal m. pedal.

pedalear v. to pedal.

pedante adj. pedantic, affected, vain, superficial; m. pedant; **pedantesco** adj. pedantic.

pedazo m. piece, portion, bit; **hacer -s** to tear or break into pieces; **caerse a -s** to fall into pieces.

pedernal m. flint.

pedestal m. pedestal, base.

pedestre adj. pedestrian, walking, going on foot; commonplace, vulgar, low.

pedido m. commercial order; request, petition; p.p. of **pedir**.

pedigüeño adj. begging, demanding.

pedir[5] v. irr. to ask, beg, petition; to ask for; to demand; to require; to order (merchandise); **a** — **de boca** exactly as desired.

pedrada f. hit or blow with a stone; throw with a stone; mark or bruise made by a stone (thrown); **a -s** by stoning; with stones; **dar una** — to hit

with a stone; **echar a alguien a -s** to stone someone out; **matar a -s** to stone to death.

pedregal m. rocky ground, ground strewn with rocks.

pedregoso adj. rocky, stony, pebbly.

pedrería f. precious stones; precious stone ornament; jewelry.

pedrusco m. boulder.

pedúnculo m. stem (of a leaf, flower or fruit), stalk.

pegajoso adj. sticky; contagious.

pegar[7] v. to hit, strike, slap, beat; to stick, paste, glue; to sew on (a button); to infect; to be becoming; to be fitting, opportune, to the point; Am. to tie, fasten; Am. to yoke; — **fuego** to set on fire; — **un chasco** to play a trick; to surprise, disappoint; — **un susto** to give a scare; — **un salto** (**una carrera**) to take a jump (a run); **-se** to stick, cling; **pegársela a uno** to fool somebody.

pegote m. sticky thing; sticking plaster; clumsy patch; sponger; thick, sticky concoction; clumsy addition or insertion (in a literary or artistic work).

peinado m. coiffure, hairdo; hairdressing; p.p. combed; groomed; adj. effeminate; **bien** — spruce, trim.

peinador m. hairdresser; short wrapper or dressing gown; **peinadora** f. woman hairdresser.

peinar v. to comb; Am. to flatter.

peine m. comb.

peineta f. large ornamental comb.

peladilla f. small pebble.

pelado p.p. & adj. peeled; plucked; skinned; hairless; featherless; barren, treeless, bare; penniless, broke; m. Am. ragged fellow (generally a peon); Am. ill-bred person.

pelafustán m. tramp, vagabond.

pelagatos m. ragged fellow, tramp.

pelaje m. animal's coat, fur; external appearance

pelar v. to cut the hair of; to pluck the feathers or hair from; to peel, shell, skin, husk; to fleece, rob; Am. to beat, thrash; Am. to slander; Am. — **los dientes** to show one's teeth; to smile affectedly; Am. — **los ojos** to keep one's eyes peeled; to open one's eyes wide; **-se** to peel off; to lose one's hair; Am. to be confused; Am. to be careless, unaware; Am. to slip away; Am. to die; **pelárselas por algo** to be dying for something, want something very much.

peldaño m. step (of a staircase).

pelea f. fight, quarrel.
pelear v. to fight; to quarrel.
peletería f. fur store; fur trade; furs; Am. leather goods, leather shop; Am. shoe store.
película f. thin skin; membrane; film; motion-picture film.
peligrar v. to be in danger.
peligro m. danger.
peligroso adj. dangerous.
pelillo m. short, fine hair; -s trouble, nuisance; echar -s a la mar to "bury the hatchet", become reconciled; no pararse en -s not to stop at small details, not to bother about trifles; no tener -s en la lengua to speak frankly.
pelirrojo adj. redheaded, red-haired.
pelo m. hair; nap (of cloth); grain (in wood); al — perfectly; agreed; apropos, to the point; along the grain; eso me viene al — that suits me perfectly; con todos sus -s y señales with every possible detail; Am. por (or en) un — on the point of, almost, by a hair's breadth; montar en — to ride bareback; tomar el — a to kid, make fun of; Am. no aflojar un — not to yield an inch.
pelota f. ball; ball game; Am. boat made of cowhide; en — (or en -s) naked; Am. darle a la — to hit upon by chance; pelotilla f. pellet, little ball.
pelotera f. brawl, row, riot; Am. crowd.
pelotón m. large ball; crowd, gang; heap, pile; platoon of soldiers.
peluca f. wig.
peludo adj. hairy; shaggy; m. plush carpet with shaggy pile; Am. a species of armadillo; Am. agarrar un — to get drunk.
peluquería f. barbershop, hairdresser's shop.
peluquero m. hairdresser, barber.
pelusa f. down; fuzz; nap (of cloth).
pellejo m. hide; skin; peel; salvar el — to save one's skin, escape punishment; Am. jugarse el — to gamble one's life.
pellizcar [6] v. to pinch, nip.
pellizco m. pinching, nipping; pinch, nip.
pena f. penalty; grief, worry; hardship; toil; Am. embarrassment; a duras -s with great difficulty; hardly; me da — it grieves me; Am. it embarrasses me; valer la — to be worth while; tener (or estar con) mucha — to be terribly sorry; Am. to be greatly embarrassed.

penacho m. tuft, crest; plume.
penal adj. penal; código — penal code.
penalidad f. hardship; trouble; penalty.
penar v. to suffer; to worry, fret; to impose a penalty; — por to long for; to suffer because of.
penca f. leaf of a cactus plant; Am. sweetheart; Am. coger una — to get drunk.
penco m. nag, horse; Am. boor.
pendencia f. quarrel; scuffle, fight.
pendenciero adj. quarrelsome.
pender v. to hang; to dangle; to depend.
pendiente f. slope; m. earring; pendant; Am. watch chain; adj. hanging, dangling; pending.
pendón m. banner.
péndulo m. pendulum.
penetración f. penetration; acuteness; keen judgment.
penetrante adj. penetrating; acute; keen.
penetrar v. to penetrate; to pierce; to fathom, comprehend.
península f. peninsula.
peninsular adj. peninsular.
penitencia f. penance.
penitenciaría f. penitentiary.
penitente adj. repentant, penitent; m. & f. penitent.
penoso adj. painful; hard, difficult; embarrassing; fatiguing; Am. timid, shy.
pensador m. thinker; adj. thinking.
pensamiento m. thought; mind; pansy.
pensar [1] v. irr. to think; to think over; to intend.
pensativo adj. pensive.
pensión f. pension; board; scholarship for study; boardinghouse; Am. apprehension, anxiety; — completa room and board.
pensionado m. pensioner (person receiving a pension); adj. & p.p. pensioned.
pensionar v. to pension.
pensionista m. & f. boarder; pensioner (person receiving a pension).
pentagrama m. musical staff.
penúltimo adj. next to the last.
penumbra f. partial shadow, dimness.
penumbroso adj. dim.
peña f. rock, large stone.
peñasco m. large rock; crag.
peñascoso adj. rocky.
peón m. unskilled laborer; foot soldier; spinning top; pawn (in chess); Am. farm hand; Am. apprentice; Am. — de albañil mason's helper.
peonada f. gang of laborers or peons.

peor adj. & adv. worse; worst; — que worse than; — que — that is even worse; tanto — so much the worse.

pepa f. Am. seed (of an apple, melon, etc.); Am. marble (to play with); Pepa nickname for Josefa.

pepenar v. Am. to pick up; Am. to seize, grab.

pepino m. cucumber

pepita f. seed (of an apple, melon, etc.); pip (a disease of birds); nugget (lump of gold or other minerals); Am. fruit stone, pit; Pepita = Josefita dim. of Josefa.

pequeñez f. smallness; childhood; trifle; meanness.

pequeño adj. small, little; young; low, humble; m. child.

pera f. pear; goatee; sinecure, easy job; Am. Peruvian alligator pear (see aguacate); Am. hacerle a uno la — to play a trick on someone; peral m. pear tree; pear orchard.

percal m. percale (fine cotton cloth).

percance m. misfortune, accident; occurrence.

percepción f. perception; idea.

perceptible adj. perceptible, noticeable.

percibir v. to perceive; to collect, receive.

percudido adj. dirty, grimy.

percudir v. to soil, make dirty or grimy; -se to get grimy.

percha f. clothes or hat rack; pole; perch, roost; perch (a fish); perchero m. clothes or hat rack.

perder[1] v. irr. to lose; to squander; to ruin, harm; to miss (a train); — de vista to lose sight of; -se to lose one's way; to get lost; to go astray; to get spoiled; to become ruined.

perdición f. perdition, damnation, hell, ruin.

pérdida f. loss; damage.

perdidamente adv. excessively.

perdido p.p. & adj. lost; strayed; mislaid; ruined; estar — por alguien to be crazy about, or very fond of, someone; m. rake, dissolute fellow; bum, vagabond.

perdigón m. young partridge; bird shot, buckshot; losing gambler.

perdiz f. partridge.

perdón m. pardon; forgiveness; remission.

perdonar v. to pardon; to forgive.

perdulario m. rake, dissolute person; reckless fellow; good-for-nothing; tramp.

perdurable adj. lasting, everlasting.

perdurar v. to last, endure.

perecedero adj. perishable.

perecer[13] v. irr. to perish; to die; -se to long (for), pine (for).

peregrinación f. pilgrimage; long journey

peregrino m. pilgrim; adj. foreign, strange; rare, beautiful, perfect; travelling, wandering; ave peregrina migratory bird, bird of passage.

perejil m. parsley; -es frippery, showy clothes or ornaments.

perenne adj. perennial, enduring, perpetual.

pereza f. laziness; idleness.

perezoso adj. lazy; m. Am. sloth (an animal); Am. safety pin; Am. bed cushion.

perfección f. perfection; a la — to perfection, perfectly.

perfeccionamiento m. perfecting, perfection; completion.

perfeccionar v. to perfect, finish, complete.

perfecto adj. perfect.

perfidia f. perfidy, treachery.

pérfido adj. perfidious, treacherous, faithless.

perfil m. profile; outline; Am. pen or pen point.

perfilar v. to silhouette; to outline; -se to show one's profile; to be silhouetted.

perforación f. perforation, hole; puncture; perforating, boring, drilling.

perforar v. to perforate, pierce; to drill, bore.

perfumar v. to perfume, scent.

perfume m. perfume; fragrance.

perfumería f. perfumery; perfume shop.

pergamino m. parchment.

pericia f. expertness, skill.

perico m. parakeet, small parrot.

perifollos m. pl. frippery, finery, showy ornaments.

perifrasear v. to paraphrase.

perilla f. small pear; pear-shaped ornament, knob; pommel of a saddle; goatee, de — apropos, to the point.

perímetro m. perimeter.

periódico m. newspaper; periodical; adj. periodic, periodical.

periodismo m. journalism; periodista m. & f. journalist; newspaper editor or publisher; periodístico adj. journalistic.

período m. period; cycle; sentence.

peripecia f. vicissitude, change in fortune; unforeseen incident.

peripuesto adj. dressed up, dolled up, decked out.

perito *adj.* learned; experienced; skilful; skilled; *m.* expert.

perjudicar[6] *v.* to damage, impair, harm.

perjudicial *adj.* harmful, injurious.

perjuicio *m.* damage, ruin, mischief; harm.

perjurar *v.* to perjure oneself; to commit perjury; to curse, swear.

perjurio *m.* perjury.

perla *f.* pearl; **de —s** perfectly, just right, to the point.

perlino *adj.* pearly, pearl-colored.

permanecer[13] *v. irr.* to remain, stay.

permanencia *f.* permanence, duration; stability; stay, sojourn.

permanente *adj.* permanent.

permiso *m.* permission; permit.

permitir *v.* to permit, let; to grant.

permuta *f.* exchange, barter.

permutar *v.* to exchange; to barter; to change around.

pernetas : en — barelegged, with bare legs.

pernicioso *adj.* pernicious, harmful.

perno *m.* bolt; spike; **-s** *Am.* tricks, frauds.

pero *conj.* but, except, yet; *m.* objection, exception; defect; a variety of apple tree; a variety of apple; **perón** *m. Am.* a variety of apple.

perogrullada *f.* platitude, trite or commonplace remark.

peroración *f.* peroration, speech, harangue.

perorar *v.* to make an impassioned speech; to declaim, harangue; to plea, make a plea.

perorata *f.* harangue, speech.

perpendicular *adj.*, *m.* & *f.* perpendicular.

perpetuar[18] *v.* to perpetuate.

perpetuo *adj.* perpetual; **perpetua** *f.* everlasting.

perplejidad *f.* perplexity.

perplejo *adj.* perplexed, bewildered.

perra *f.* bitch, female dog; drunkenness; **— chica** five-centime copper coin; **grande** (*or* **gorda**) ten-centime copper coin.

perrada *f.* pack of dogs; **hacer una —** to play a mean trick.

perrera *f.* kennel; toil, hard work, hard job; tantrum; *Am.* brawl, dispute.

perrilla *f. Am.* sty (*on the eyelid*). See **orzuelo**.

perro *m.* dog; **— de busca** hunting dog; **— dogo** bulldog; **— de lanas** poodle; *adj.* dogged, tenacious; *Am.* hard, selfish, mean, stingy.

perruno *adj.* canine, doglike.

persecución *f.* persecution; pursuit.

perseguidor *m.* pursuer; persecutor.

perseguimiento *m.* pursuit; persecution.

perseguir[5, 12] *v. irr.* to pursue; to persecute; to harass, annoy.

perseverancia *f.* perseverance.

perseverar *v.* to persevere.

persiana *f.* Venetian blind; window shade.

persistencia *f.* persistence; **persistente** *adj.* persistent.

persistir *v.* to persist.

persona *f.* person; personage.

personaje *m.* personage; character (*in a book or play*).

personal *adj.* personal; *m.* personnel.

personalidad *f.* personality; individuality; person, personage.

perspectiva *f.* perspective; view; appearance; outlook; prospect.

perspicacia *f.* keenness of mind, penetration, keen insight.

perspicaz *adj.* keen, shrewd.

persuadir . to persuade.

persuasión *f.* persuasion.

persuasivo *adj.* persuasive.

pertenecer[13] *v. irr.* to belong; to pertain to concern.

perteneciente *adj.* pertaining, belonging, concerning.

pértiga *f.* pole, bar, rod.

pertinente *adj.* pertinent, to the point apt, fitting.

pertrechos *m. pl.* military supplies tools, implements.

perturbación *f.* uneasiness, agitation disturbance.

perturbar *v.* to perturb, disturb.

peruano *adj.* & *m.* Peruvian.

perversidad *f.* perversity, wickedness.

perverso *adj.* perverse, wicked; *m.* pervert.

pervertir[3] *v. irr.* to pervert; to corrupt to distort; **-se** to become perverte to go wrong.

pesa *f.* weight (*for scales*); **— de rel** clock weight; **-s y medidas** weight and measures.

pesadez *f.* heaviness; dullness, drows ness; slowness; bother; stubbornnes

pesadilla *f.* nightmàre.

pesado *adj.* heavy; sound (*sleep*); tir some, boring; annoying; slow; dul

pesadumbre *f.* grief, sorrow; weigh heaviness.

pésame *m.* condolence, expression sympathy.

pesantez *f.* gravity; heaviness.

pesar *v.* to weigh; to consider; to hav

weight, value, or importance; to cause grief, sorrow, or regret; *m.* grief, sorrow; a — de in spite of.

pesaroso *adj.* grieved, sad; repentant.

pesca *f.* fishing; catch, fish caught.

pescadería *f.* fish market; **pescadero** *m.* fishmonger, dealer in fish.

pescado *m.* fish (*especially after being caught*); salted codfish.

pescador *m.* fisherman.

pescar[6] *v.* to fish; to catch; to catch unaware, catch in the act.

pescozón *m.* blow on the back of the head or neck.

pescuezo *m.* neck.

pesebre *m.* manger.

peseta *f.* peseta (*monetary unit of Spain*).

pesimismo *m.* pessimism; **pesimista** *m. & f.* pessimist; *adj.* pessimistic.

pésimo *adj.* very bad.

peso *m.* weight; weighing; burden; importance; *Am.* peso (*monetary unit of several Spanish American countries*).

pesquera *f.* fishery (*place for catching fish*); **pesquería** *f.* fishery; fishing.

pesquero *adj.* fishing; **buque** — fishing boat; **industria pesquera** fishing industry.

pesquisa *f.* investigation, inquiry; *m. Am.* police investigator.

pestaña *f.* eyelash; edging, fringe; **quemarse las -s** to burn the midnight oil, study hard at night.

pestañear *v.* to blink; to wink; to flicker.

peste *f.* pest, pestilence, plague; epidemic; stench, stink, foul odor; overabundance, excess; *Am.* smallpox; *Am.* head cold; **echar -s** to utter insults.

pestillo *m.* bolt; latch; lock.

petaca *f.* tobacco pouch; cigar case; leather covered hamper (*used as a pack*); *Am.* leather covered trunk, suitcase; *adj. Am.* heavy, clumsy.

pétalo *m.* petal.

petate *m.* bundle; impostor; *Am.* mat (*of straw or palm leaves*); *Am.* dunce; *Am.* coward; **liar el** — to pack up and go; *Am.* to die; *Am.* **dejar a uno en un** — to ruin a person, leave him penniless.

petición *f.* petition, request.

petirrojo *m.* robin, robin redbreast.

petiso *adj. Am.* small, short, dwarfish; *m. Am.* small horse, pony.

pétreo *adj.* stone, stony.

petróleo *m.* petroleum.

petrolero *m.* oil man; dealer in petroleum; **compañía petrolera** oil company.

petulancia *f.* flippancy; insolence; **petulante** *adj.* pert, impertinent, flippant.

pez *m.* fish; *f.* pitch, tar.

pezón *m.* nipple; stem, stalk (*of a fruit, leaf or flower*); small point of land.

pezuña *f.* hoof.

piadoso *adj.* pious; kind, merciful.

pial *m. Am.* lasso, lariat (*thrown in order to trip an animal*); *Am.* snare, trap.

pialar *v.* to lasso by tripping with a pial.

piano *m.* piano; — **de cola** grand piano; — **vertical** upright piano.

piar[17] *v.* to peep, chirp; to cry, whine.

pica *f.* pike, spear; picador's goad or lance; stonecutter's hammer; *Am.* tapping of rubber trees; *Am.* trail; *Am.* pique, resentment; *Am.* cockfight.

picada *f.* prick; bite (*as of an insect or fish*); puncture; sharp pain; dive (*of a plane*); *Am.* path, trail (*cut through a forest*); *Am.* narrow ford; *Am.* peck.

picadillo *m.* meat and vegetable hash; minced meat, mincemeat.

picador *m.* picador (*mounted bullfighter armed with a goad*); horse-breaker; chopping block; *Am.* tree tapper.

picadura *f.* biting; pricking; bite; prick; sting; puncture; cut tobacco.

picante *adj.* pricking, biting, stinging; spicy; highly seasoned; *m.* strong seasoning; *Am.* highly seasoned sauce (*usually containing chili pepper*).

picapleitos *m.* quarrelsome person (*one who likes to pick a fight*); shyster.

picaporte *m.* latch; latchkey; door knocker.

picar[6] *v.* to prick; to pierce; to bite (*said of fish or insects*); to sting; to peck; to nibble; to mince, chop up; to goad; to stick, poke; to hew, chisel; to pique, vex; to itch, smart, burn; *Am.* to chop (*wood*); *Am.* to open a trail; *Am.* to tap (*a tree*); *Am.* to slaughter (*cattle*); — **muy alto** to aim very high, — **en** to border on, be somewhat of; *Am.* ¡pícale! hurry! **-se** to be piqued, angry; to be moth-eaten; to begin to sour; to begin to rot; *Am.* to get tipsy; **-se de** to boast of.

picardía *f.* roguishness; offensive act or remark; roguish trick; mischief.

picaresco *adj.* picaresque, roguish.

pícaro *m.* rogue, rascal; *adj.* roguish; mischievous; crafty, sly; low, vile; **picarón** *m.* big rascal.

picazón *f.* itch, itching.

pico *m.* beak, bill; sharp point, peak;

pickaxe, pick; spout; mouth; additional amount, a little over; *Am.* a small balance; *Am.* a goodly sum; **tener el — de oro** to be very eloquent; **tener mucho —** to be very talkative.

picotada *f.*, **picotazo** *m.* peck.

picotear *v.* to peck; to chatter; *Am.* to mince, cut into small pieces.

pichel *m.* pitcher; mug.

pichón *m.* pigeon; *Am.* any male bird (*except a rooster*); *Am.* dupe, easy mark; *Am.* novice, inexperienced person, apprentice; *adj. Am.* timid, shy.

pie *m.* foot; leg; stand; stem; base; *Am.* down payment; *Am.* strophe, stanza; *Am.* — **de amigo** wedge; prop; — **de banco** silly remark; **a — juntillas** steadfastly, firmly; **al — de la letra** to the letter, literally, exactly; **de —** (*or* **en —**) standing; **a cuatro -s** on all fours; **dar — to** give an opportunity or occasion; *Am.* **estar a — en** to be ignorant of; **ir a —** to walk.

piececito, piecito *m.* little foot.

piedad *f.* piety; pity; mercy; **monte de — pawnshop**.

piedra *f.* stone; gravel; hailstone; *Am.* piece of a domino set; — **angular** (*or* **fundamental**) cornerstone; — **caliza** limestone; — **pómez** pumice, pumice stone; **a — y lodo** shut tight; **ser — de escándalo** to be an object of scandal.

piel *f.* skin; hide; leather; fur.

piélago *m.* high sea; sea; great abundance, great plenty.

pienso *m.* feed; thought; **ni por — not** even in thought.

pierna *f.* leg; **dormir a — suelta** to sleep like a log, sleep soundly; *Am.* **ser una buena —** to be a good fellow, be always in a good mood.

pieza *f.* piece; part; room; play; **de una —** solid, in one piece; *Am.* **ser de una —** to be an honest, upright man.

pigmento *m.* pigment.

pijama *m.* pajamas.

pila *f.* basin, baptismal font; trough; pile; heap; electric battery; *Am.* fountain; *Am.* hairless dog; *Am.* bald head; **nombre de —** Christian name; *Am.* **andar —** to go naked; *Am.* **tener las -s** (*or* **tener por -s**) to have a lot, have heaps.

pilar *m.* pillar, column; basin of a fountain.

pilcha *f. Am.* any article of clothing; *Am.* mistress; **-s** *Am.* belongings.

píldora *f.* pill.

pilmama *f. Am.* child's nurse, wet nurse.

pilón *m.* basin (*of a fountain*); watering trough; sugar loaf; large wooden or metal mortar (*for grinding grain*); counterpoise; *Am.* an additional amount, premium (*given to a buyer*); *Am.* **de —** to boot, in addition, besides; **piloncillo** *m. Am.* unrefined sugar loaf.

pilotar, pilotear *v.* to pilot.

pilote *m.* pile (*for building*).

piloto *m.* pilot; *Am.* generous entertainer or host.

pillaje *m.* pillage, plunder.

pillar *v.* to pillage, plunder; to pilfer; to seize, snatch, grasp; to catch; *Am.* to surprise, catch in the act.

pillo *adj.* roguish; sly, crafty; *m.* rogue, rascal; *Am.* a species of heron; *Am.* long-legged person; **pilluelo** *m.* little rascal, scamp.

pimentero *m.* pepper plant; pepperbox, pepper shaker.

pimentón *m.* large pepper; cayenne, red pepper; paprika.

pimienta *f.* black pepper.

pimiento *m.* green pepper; red pepper.

pimpollo *m.* rosebud; bud; shoot, sprout; attractive youth.

pináculo *m.* pinnacle, top, summit.

pinar *m.* pine grove.

pincel *m.* artist's brush; **pincelada** *f.* stroke of the brush.

pinchar *v.* to prick; to puncture.

pinchazo *m.* prick; puncture; stab.

pingajo *m.* tag, tatter, rag.

pingo *m. Am.* saddle horse; *Am.* devil.

pingüe *adj.* abundant, copious; fat, greasy.

pino *m.* pine; *Am.* filling for a meat pie; **hacer -s** (*or* **hacer pinitos**) to begin to walk (*said of a baby*); to begin to do things (*said of a novice*).

pinta *f.* spot, mark; outward sign, aspect; pint; *Am.* **hacer —** to play hooky, cut class.

pintar *v.* to paint; to describe, depict; to feign; to begin to turn red, begin to ripen (*said of fruit*); to fancy, imagine *Am.* to play hooky, play truant; *Am.* to fawn, flatter; **no — nada** to be worth nothing, count for nothing; **las cosas no pintaban bien** things did not look well; *Am.* — **venados** to play hooky; **-se** to put on make-up; *Am.* to excel (in); **-se** to praise oneself.

pintarrajear *v.* to daub; to smear with paint or rouge.

pinto *adj. Am.* spotted, speckled.

pintor m. painter, artist; **— de brocha gorda** house painter; poor artist; adj. Am. boastful, conceited.

pintoresco adj. picturesque.

pintura f. painting; picture; paint, color; description

pinzas f. pl. pincers· tweezers· claws (of lobsters, crabs, etc.); Am. pliers, tongs.

piña f. **pineapple**; **pine cone**; **piña cloth**; cluster; Am. pool (a billiard game).

piñata f. pot; hanging pot or other container (filled with candies, fruit, etc.).

piñón m. pine nut; nut pine; pinion.

pío adj. pious, devout; kind, merciful; dappled, spotted (horse), **obras pías** pious works, charitable deeds.

piojo m. louse.

piojoso adj. lousy; mean, stingy.

pipa f. tobacco pipe· keg, barrel; reed pipe (musical instrument), fruit seed (of a lemon, orange, melon); Am. green coconut; Am. potato; Am. **estar —** to be drunk; m. Am. species of green frog.

pipiar[17] v. to peep, chirp.

pipiolo m. novice, beginner; Am. child, youngster

pique m. pique, resentment; chigger (insect), flea; Am. small chili pepper; Am. trail; **a — de** in danger of, on the point of; **echar a —** to sink (a ship), to destroy; **irse a —** to capsize; to sink

piquete m. prick; bite, sting (of insects), small hole, picket, stake; picket (military). Am. small band of musicians; Am. small corral. Am. cutting edge of scissors

piragua f. Am. Indian canoe.

pirámide f. pyramid.

pirata m. pirate

piratear v. to pirate.

piropo m. flattery compliment; a variety of garnet (a precious stone); **echar un —** to "throw a bouquet" to compliment.

pirueta f. whirl· somersault, caper; **hacer -s** to cut capers, to turn somersaults, to do stunts.

pisada f. footstep, footprint; **dar una — to** step on, stamp on; **seguir las -s de** to follow in the footsteps of, to imitate.

pisapapeles m. paperweight.

pisar v. to step on, tread upon; to trample under foot; to pound; to cover (said of a male bird).

piscina f. swimming pool, swimming tank, fish pond.

pise m. Am. rut. Am. tread (of a wheel).

See **rodadura**

piso m. floor; story; pavement; apartment, flat; tread, Am. fee for pasturage rights, Am. table scarf; Am. stool, footstool; Am. small rug.

pisón m. heavy mallet (for pounding, flattening, crushing)

pisotear v. to tramp tramp on, trample; to tread

pisotón m. hard step, stamp (of the foot); **dar un —** to step hard, stamp (upon)

pista f. track, trace, trail; clew; race track; **— de aterrizaje** landing field.

pistola f. pistol, **pistolera** f holster

pistón m. piston, Am. cornet

pita f. Am. agave or century plant; Am. fiber, or thread made from the fiber of the agave or maguey.

pitar v. to toot; to whistle, Am. to smoke, Am. to hiss; Am. to slip away; escape; Am. **-se una cosa** to steal something; Am. **salir pitando** to leave on the run.

pitazo m. toot, whistle, blast.

pitillo m. cigarette; **pitillera** f cigarette case

pito m. whistle; cigarette; Am. tick (an insect); **no vale un —** it is not worth a straw, Am. **no saber ni — de una cosa** not to know anything about a subject.

pizarra f slate, blackboard· **pizarrín** m. slate pencil· **pizarrón** m. blackboard.

pizca f. pinch, small bit, Am. harvest

placa f. badge insignia, plaque, tablet, metal plate; photographic plate; license plate· Am. scab or skin blemish

placentero adj. pleasant agreeable.

placer[38] v. irr to please, content, m. pleasure; sand bank, shoal; placer (place where gold is obtained by washing), Am. pearl fishing.

placero m., **placera** f market vendor

plácido adj. placid, calm.

plaga f. plague, calamity

plagar[7] v. to plague, infest, **-se de** to become plagued or infested with

plagiar v. to plagiarize, steal and use as one's own (the writings, ideas. etc. of another), to kidnap, abduct.

plan m. plan; design, project, drawing, mine floor; Am. clearing; Am building grounds of a ranch.

plana f. page; plain, flat country; mason's trowel, tally sheet, **enmendar la — a uno** to correct a person's mistakes.

plancha f. flatiron, metal plate; gangplank. blunder, Am. railway flatcar;

Am. dental plate; — **de blindaje** armor plate; **hacer una** — to make a ridiculous blunder; **tirarse una** — to place oneself in a ridiculous situation.

planchado *m.* ironing; clothes ironed or to be ironed; *adj Am.* smart, clever; *Am.* brave; *Am* dolled up, dressed up; *Am.* broke, penniless.

planchar *v.* to iron; to smooth out; *Am.* to leave (*someone*) waiting; *Am.* to strike with the flat of a blade; *Am.* to flatter; *Am.* — **el asiento** to be a wallflower at a dance.

planeador *m* glider airplane.

planear *v.* to plan; to glide (*said of an airplane or bird*).

planeo *m* planning; glide, gliding (*of an airplane*)

planeta *m.* planet.

plano *adj.* plane, flat, level; *m.* plane; plan; map, **de** — flatly, clearly, openly; **dar de** — to hit with the flat of anything.

planta *f* plant; plantation; plan; ground plan; sole of the foot; — **baja** ground floor; **buena** — good looks; **echar -s** to brag

plantación *f* plantation; planting.

plantar *v.* to plant; to strike (*a blow*); **-se** to stand firm; to balk; *Am.* to doll up, dress up; **dejar a uno plantado** to "stand someone up," keep someone waiting indefinitely.

plantear *v.* to plan; to establish; to carry out, to state, present (*a problem*); to try

plantío *m.* planting; plantation; recently planted garden; tree nursery

plasma *m.* plasma.

plástico *adj.* plastic.

plata *f* silver; silver money; **hablar en** — to speak in plain language

plataforma *f* platform.

platanal, platanar *m.* grove of banana trees; banana plantation.

plátano *m.* banana; banana tree; plane tree.

platea *f* main floor of a theatre

plateado *adj.* silver-plated; silvery.

platear *v* to silver, plate, cover with silver.

platel *m* platter; tray

platero *m.* silversmith; jeweler

plática *f.* conversation, talk, chat; informal lecture.

platicador *m.* talker; *adj.* talkative.

platicar[6] *v.* to converse, talk, chat.

platillo *m.* saucer; pan (*of a pair of scales*); cymbal; stew.

plato *m.* plate; dish; dinner course.

platón *m.* large plate; platter.

platudo *adj. Am.* wealthy, rich.

playa *f.* beach, shore; *Am.* wide, open space in front of a ranch house; *Am.* — **de estacionamiento** parking lot.

plaza *f* plaza, public square; public market, job, employment; *Am.* park, promenade; — **de armas** parade ground; public square; fortress; — **fuerte** fortress; — **de gallos** cockpit (*for cockfights*); — **de toros** bull ring; **sacar a** — to bring out into the open, make public; **sentar** — to enlist; **plazoleta, plazuela** *f.* small square, court.

plazo *m.* term, time; **a** — on credit; in installments.

pleamar *m.* flood tide, high tide.

plebe *f* rabble; masses

plebeyo *adj* plebeian.

plebiscito *m.* plebiscite, direct vote.

plegadizo *adj.* folding; pliable, easily bent.

plegar[1,7] *v* to fold; to pleat; to crease; **-se** to bend, yield, submit.

plegaria *f* supplication, prayer; prayer hour.

pleito *m.* litigation, lawsuit; dispute; debate; — **de acreedores** bankruptcy proceedings; **pleitista** *m. & f.* quarrelsome person.

plenipotenciario *m.* plenipotentiary (*diplomatic agent having full power or authority*); *adj.* plenipotentiary, having full power.

plenitud *f* plenitude, fullness, completeness; abundance.

pleno *adj.* full, complete; **sesión plena** joint session; **en** — **día** in broad daylight, openly; **en** — **rostro** (or **en plena cara**) right on the face.

pliego *m.* sheet of paper; sealed letter or document.

pliegue *m.* fold, crease, pleat.

plomada *f* plumb, lead weight, plumb bob.

plomazo *m. Am.* shot, bullet.

plomería *f.* plumbing; plumber's shop; lead roof.

plomero *m.* plumber.

plomizo *adj.* leaden, lead-colored.

plomo *m.* lead; plumb, lead weight; bullet; boring person; **a** — vertical; vertically; *adj. Am.* lead-colored.

pluma *f.* feather; plume; quill; pen; — **estilográfica** (or — **fuente**) fountain pen, **plumada** *f* dash, stroke of the pen, flourish; **plumaje** *m.* plumage; plume; **plumero** *m.* feather duster; box for feathers; feather ornament (on *hats, helmets, etc.*); **plumón** *m.* down; feather mattress; **plumoso** *adj.* downy, feathery.

plural *adj.* plural.

pluvial *adj.* rain (*used as adj.*); **capa — cope** (*long cape used by priests during certain religious ceremonies*).

población *f.* population; populating; town, city; *Am.* house.

poblado *m.* inhabited place, village; *p.p.* populated; covered with growth.

poblador *m.* settler (*of a colony*).

poblar² *v. irr.* to populate, people; to to colonize, settle; to stock (*a farm*); to breed; **-se** to become covered (*with leaves or buds*).

pobre *adj.* poor; *m.* poor man; beggar; **pobrete** *m.* poor devil, poor wretch; **pobretón** *m.* poor old fellow, poor wretch.

pobreza *f.* poverty; need; lack, scarcity; barrenness.

pocilga *f.* pigsty, pigpen.

pocillo *m.* cup.

poco *adj.* little, scanty; small; short (*time*); **-s** few, some; *m.* a little, a bit; *adv.* little; **a —** presently, after a short time; **a — rato** (*or* **al — rato**) after a short while; **— a —** slowly, little by little; **a los -s meses** after a few months; **por — me caigo** I almost fell; **tener en —** to hold in low esteem.

podar *v.* to prune, trim, cut off.

podenco *m.* hound.

poder[39] *v. irr* to be able; can; may; **él puede mucho** (*or* **poco**) he has much (*or* little) power; **puede que** it is possible that, it may be that, perhaps; **hasta más no —** to the utmost, to the limit; **no — más** not to be able to do more; to be exhausted; **no puede menos de hacerlo** he cannot help doing it; **no — con la carga** not to be equal to the burden, not to be able to lift the load; *Am.* **-le a uno algo** to be worried or affected by something; *m.* power, authority

poderío *m.* power, dominion; might; wealth.

poderoso *adj.* powerful; wealthy.

podre *f.* pus; decayed matter; **podredumbre** *f.* corruption, decay; pus, rotten matter

podrido *adj.* rotten; *p.p. of* **podrir**.

podrir[16] = **pudrir**[16].

poema *m.* poem.

poesía *f.* poetry; poem.

poeta *m.* poet; **poetastro** *m.* bad poet.

poético *adj.* poetic; **poética** *f.* poetics.

poetisa *f.* poetess.

polaco *adj.* Polish; *m.* Polish, Polish language; Pole.

polaina *f.* legging.

polar *adj.* polar.

polea *f.* pulley

polen *m.* pollen.

policía *f.* police; *m.* policeman.

policial *m. Am.* policeman.

polilla *f.* moth, larva of the moth.

política *f.* politics; policy; *Am.* **— de campanario** politics of a clique.

politicastro *m.* bad or incapable politician.

político *adj.* political; politic; polite; **madre política** mother-in-law; *m.* politician.

póliza *f.* policy, written contract; draft; customhouse certificate; **— de seguros** insurance policy

polizonte *m.* policeman.

polo *m.* pole (*of a magnet or of an axis*), polo (*a game*).

poltrón *adj.* lazy, idle, **silla poltrona** easy chair.

polvareda *f.* cloud of dust; **armar** (*or* **levantar**) **una —** to kick up the dust; to raise a rumpus.

polvera *f.* powder box; compact; powder puff.

polvo *m.* dust, powder; pinch of snuff or powder; **-s** toilet powder; **-s para dientes** tooth powder; **limpio de — y paja** entirely free; net; *Am.* cleaned out, without a penny; *Am.* innocent, ignorant, unaware; *Am.* **tomar el —** to escape, "beat it."

pólvora *f.* gunpowder; fireworks.

polvorear *v.* to powder, sprinkle with powder.

polvoriento *adj.* dusty

polvorín *m.* powder magazine; priming powder; powder flask; *Am.* tick (*parasitic insect*); *Am.* spitfire, quick-tempered person.

polla *f.* pullet (*young hen*); young lass, pool (*in cards*)

pollada *f.* hatch, brood; flock of chicks.

pollera *f.* woman who raises and sells chickens; chicken coop; a bell-shaped basket for chickens; petticoat; *Am.* skirt.

pollino *m.* young donkey, ass.

pollo *m.* young chicken; nestling, young bird; young man; **polluelo** *m.* chick.

pompa *f.* pomp, pageant, procession; bubble; pump.

pomposo *adj.* pompous.

pómulo *m.* cheek bone.

ponche *m.* punch (*a beverage*); **ponchera** *f.* punch bowl.

ponderación f. pondering, careful consideration, weighing; exaggeration.

ponderar v. to ponder, consider, weigh; to exaggerate; to extol.

ponderoso adj. ponderous, heavy

poner[40] v. irr. to put; to place; to set; to lay; to suppose; — **como nuevo a alguien** to cover someone with insults; — **en claro** to clarify; — **en limpio** to recopy, make a clean copy; — **todo de su parte** to do one's best; **pongamos que** ` let us suppose that , -se to place oneself; to become; -se a to begin to; -se al corriente to become informed; -se de pie to stand up; Am. -se bien con alguien to ingratiate oneself with someone, get on his good side; Am. ponérsela to get drunk.

poniente m. west; west wind; **el sol** — the setting sun.

pontón m. pontoon; scow, flat-bottomed boat; log bridge; pontoon bridge.

ponzoña f. venom, poison.

ponzoñoso adj. venomous, poisonous.

popa f. poop, stern; **viento en** — speedily; going well.

popote m. Am. straw for brooms; Am. drinking straw or tube.

populacho m. populace, rabble.

popular adj. popular.

popularidad f. popularity.

populoso adj. populous, densely populated.

poquito adj. very little; Am. timid, shy; m. a small bit; a -a in small quantities.

por prep. by; for; for the sake of, on account of, in behalf of; because of; through; along; in exchange for; in the place of; during; about, around; to, with the idea of; — **ciento** percent; — **consiguiente** consequently; — **entre** among, between; — **escrito** in writing; — **poco se muere** he almost died; **está** — **hacer** it is yet to be done; **él está** — **hacerlo** he is in favor of doing it; **recibir** — **esposa** to receive as a wife; **tener** — to consider, think of as; ¿ — **qué?** interr. adv. why? for what reason?

porcelana f. porcelain, china; enamel.

porcentaje m. percentage.

porción f. portion; part, share, **una** — **de gente** a lot of people.

porche m. porch.

pordiosear v. to beg.

pordiosero m. beggar.

porfía f. stubbornness, obstinacy; persistence, insistence; a — in competition; with great insistence.

porfiado adj. stubborn, obstinate, persistent.

porfiar[17] v. to persist; to insist; to dispute obstinately, to argue.

pormenor m. detail.

pormenorizar[9] v. to detail, tell in detail; to itemize.

poro m. pore.

poroso adj. porous.

poroto m. Am. bean, Am. runt.

porque conj. because, so that.

porqué m. cause, reason, motive.

porquería f. filth, filthy act or word; nasty piece of food, trifle, worthless object.

porra f. club, stick; Am. **mandar a uno a la** — to send someone to the devil; **porrazo** m. blow; knock; bump.

porta f. porthole; cover for a porthole; goal (in football).

portaaviones m. airplane carrier.

portada f. façade, front (of a building); title page.

portador m. carrier; bearer; tray

portal m. portal; entrance, vestibule; portico, porch; Am. Christmas crèche; -es arcades, galleries; **portalón** m. large portal; gangway (of a ship).

portamonedas m. pocketbook, coin purse.

portapapeles m. briefcase.

portaplumas m. penholder

portar v. Am. to carry; -se to behave.

portátil adj. portable.

portavoz m. megaphone; mouthpiece.

portazgo m. toll.

portazo m. bang or slam of a door; **dar un** — to bang or slam the door.

porte m. portage, cost of carriage; freight; postage; manner, bearing; size, capacity; Am. birthday present.

portear v. to carry on one's back; Am. to get out in a hurry.

portento m. portent; wonder, marvel.

portentoso adj. marvelous, extraordinary, amazing, terrifying.

porteño adj. from a port; Am. from Buenos Aires.

portero m. doorkeeper, doorman; janitor.

pórtico m. portico, porch.

portilla f. porthole; small gate or passageway.

portón m. gate.

portugués adj. Portuguese; m. Portuguese, Portuguese language.

porvenir m. future.

pos : en — **de** after; in pursuit of.

posada f. lodging; inn; boardinghouse,

dwelling, home; *Am.* las -e a Christmas festivity lasting nine days; posadero *m.* innkeeper.

posaderas *f. pl.* posterior, buttocks, rump.

posar *v.* to lodge; to rest; to sit down; to pose (*as a model*); to perch (*said of birds*); -se to settle (*said of sediment*); to pomb (*said of birds*)

posdata *f.* postscript.

poseedor *m.* possessor, owner.

poseer[14] *v.* to possess, own; to master, know well; -se to have control of oneself.

posesión *f.* possession.

posesivo *adj. & m.* possessive.

posesor *m.* possessor, owner.

posibilidad *f.* possibility.

posible *adj.* possible; hacer lo — to do one's best; -s *m. pl.* goods, property, means.

posición *f.* position; posture; status, rank, standing; placing.

positivo *adj.* positive; effective; true; practical.

posponer[40] *v. irr.* to postpone, put off; to put after; to subordinate.

pospuesto *p.p. of* posponer.

posta *f.* small bullet; bet, wager; relay (*of post horses*); post station; -s buckshot; por la — posthaste; fast, speedily; *m.* postboy, courier, messenger.

postal *adj.* postal; tarjeta — postcard.

postdata *f.* = posdata.

poste *m.* post, pillar.

postergar[7] *v.* to delay; to postpone; to disregard someone's right.

posteridad *f.* posterity.

posterior *adj.* posterior, back, rear; later.

postigo *m.* wicket, small door or gate; shutter; peep window.

postizo *adj.* false, artificial; *m.* switch, false hair.

postración *f.* prostration, collapse, exhaustion; dejection, lowness of spirits.

postrar *v.* to prostrate; to humiliate; to throw down; to weaken, exhaust; -se to kneel to the ground; to be weakened, exhausted; to collapse.

postre *m.* dessert; a la — at last.

postrer(o) *adj.* last; hindmost, nearest the rear.

postulante *m. & f.* petitioner; applicant, candidate.

póstumo *adj.* posthumous, after one's death.

postura *f.* posture, position; bid; wager; pact, agreement; egg-laying.

potable *adj.* drinkable; agua — drinking water.

potaje *m.* pottage, thick soup; porridge; mixed drink.

pote *m.* pot; jar; jug; *Am.* flask; *Am.* buzzard.

potencia *f.* potency; power; faculty, ability; powerful nation.

potente *adj.* potent, powerful, strong.

potestad *f.* power; dominion, authority.

potranca *f.* filly, young mare.

potrero *m.* herdsman of colts; fenced-in pasture land; *Am.* cattle ranch, stock farm.

potro *m.* colt; rack, torture; *Am.* wild horse; *Am.* stallion.

poyo *m.* stone or brick bench (*usually built against a wall*).

pozo *m.* well; hole, pit; mine shaft; hold of a ship; *Am.* pool, puddle; *Am.* spring, fountain.

práctica *f.* practice; exercise; custom, habit; method.

practicante *m. & f.* doctor's assistant; hospital intern.

practicar[6] *v.* to practice; to put into practice.

práctico *adj.* practical; experienced, skilful; *m.* — de puerto harbor pilot.

pradera *f.* prairie; meadow.

prado *m.* meadow, field; lawn.

preámbulo *m.* preamble, introduction, prologue.

precario *adj.* precarious.

precaución *f.* precaution.

precaver *v.* to guard (against), keep (from); to warn, caution; -se to guard oneself (against); to take precautions.

precavido *adj.* cautious, on guard.

precedencia *f.* precedence; priority.

precedente *adj.* preceding; *m.* precedent.

preceder *v.* to precede; to have precedence.

precepto *m.* precept; rule; order.

preceptor *m.* teacher, tutor.

preciado *adj.* prized, esteemed; precious, valuable.

preciar *v.* to appraise; to value; -se de to boast of, be proud of.

precio *m.* price; value, worth; esteem.

precioso *adj.* precious, valuable; fine, exquisite; beautiful.

precipicio *m.* precipice; ruin.

precipitación *f.* precipitation; rush, haste, hurry.

precipitado *adj.* precipitate, hasty, rash; *m.* precipitate (*chemical term*).

precipitar *v.* to precipitate; to hasten, rush; to hurl, throw headlong; -se to throw oneself headlong; to rush (into).

precipitoso adj. precipitous, steep; rash.

precisar v. to determine precisely; to force, compel, make necessary; Am. to be necessary or urgent; Am. to need.

precisión f. precision, exactness; accuracy; compulsion, force, necessity; Am. haste.

preciso adj. necessary; precise, exact; clear; m. Am. small travelling bag.

precoz adj. precocious.

precursor m. precursor, forerunner.

predecir[27] v. irr. to predict, prophesy, forecast, foretell.

predestinar v. to predestine.

predicación f. preaching.

predicado adj. & m. predicate; p.p. of **predicar**.

predicador m. preacher.

predicar[6] v. to preach.

predicción f. prediction.

predilección f. predilection, preference, liking.

predilecto adj. favorite, preferred.

predisponer[40] v. irr to predispose, bias, prejudice.

predispuesto p.p. of **predisponer** & adj. predisposed, prejudiced, biased.

predominante adj. predominant; prevailing, ruling.

predominar v. to predominate, prevail.

predominio m. predominance; sway, influence.

prefacio m. preface.

prefecto m. prefect (military or civil chief; sometimes a mayor, sometimes governor of a province, as in Peru).

preferencia f. preference; de — with preference; preferably.

preferente adj. preferable; preferred; preferential; **acciones -s** preferred shares.

preferible adj. preferable.

preferir[3] v. irr. to prefer.

prefijar v. to prefix; to set beforehand (as a date).

prefijo m. prefix.

pregonar v. to proclaim, cry out; to make known.

pregunta f. question; **hacer una —** to ask a question.

preguntar v. to ask, inquire.

preguntón adj. inquisitive.

prejuicio m. prejudice.

prelado m. prelate.

preliminar adj. & m. preliminary.

preludiar v. to be the prelude or beginning of; to initiate, introduce; to try out (a musical instrument).

preludio m. prelude; introduction.

prematuro adj. premature, untimely.

premeditado adj. premeditated, deliberate.

premiar v. to reward.

premio m. prize; reward; recompense; premium; **a —** with interest, at interest.

premisa f. premise (either of the first two propositions of a syllogism).

premura f. pressure, urgency, haste.

prenda f. pawn, pledge, security; token; article of clothing; anything valuable; jewel; loved person; **-s** good qualities, gifts, talents; **— de vestir** garment; **juego de -s** game of forfeits; **en — de** as a proof of, as a pledge of.

prendar v. to pawn, pledge; to charm, please; **-se** to get attached to; to fall in love with.

prendedor m. clasp; stickpin; tie pin; brooch; Am. lighter.

prender v. to seize, catch; to bite (said of an insect); to fasten, clasp; to arrest, imprison; to take root; to begin to burn, catch fire; Am. to light (a lamp); Am. to start, begin, undertake; **— el fuego** to start the fire; Am. **-las** to take to one's heels; **-se** to dress up.

prendero m. pawnbroker; second-hand dealer.

prensa f. press; printing press.

prensar v. to press.

preñado adj. pregnant; full.

preñez f. pregnancy.

preocupación f. preoccupation; worry; bias, prejudice.

preocupar v. to preoccupy; to worry; to prejudice; **-se** to be preoccupied; to worry; to be prejudiced.

preparación f. preparation.

preparar v. to prepare; **-se** to get ready; to be prepared.

preparativo adj. preparatory; m. preparation.

preparatorio adj. preparatory.

preposición f. preposition.

prerrogativa f. prerogative, right, privilege.

presa f. prey; dam; fang, tusk; claw; **hacer —** to seize.

presagiar v. to foretell.

presagio m. presage, omen, sign.

presbítero m. priest.

prescindir v. to disregard, set aside, leave aside; to omit; to dispense (with).

prescribir[52] v. to prescribe.

prescrito p.p. of **prescribir**.

presencia f. presence; figure, bearing; **— de ánimo** presence of mind, serenity.

presenciar v. to see, witness; to be

present at.

presentación f. presentation; personal introduction; Am. petition.

presentar v. to present; to introduce; -se to appear, present oneself; to introduce oneself; to offer one's services; Am. to have recourse to justice, file suit.

presente adj. present; m. present, gift; **al** — now, at the present time; **por el (la,** or **lo)** — for the present; **mejorando lo** — present company excepted; **tener** — to bear in mind.

presentimiento m. presentiment, foreboding.

presentir[5] v. irr. to have a presentiment, foreboding or hunch.

preservación f. preservation.

preservar v. to preserve, guard, protect, keep.

presidencia f. presidency; office of president; presidential term; chairmanship.

presidencial adj. presidential.

presidente m. president; chairman; presiding judge.

presidiario m. prisoner, convict.

presidio m. garrison; fortress; penitentiary, prison; **diez años de** — ten years at hard labor (in a prison).

presidir v. to preside; to direct.

presilla f. loop, fastener; clip.

presión f. pressure.

preso m. prisoner; p.p. irr. of **prender** imprisoned.

prestado adj. & p.p. loaned, lent; **dar** — to lend; **pedir** — to borrow.

prestamista m. & f. moneylender.

préstamo m. loan.

prestar v. to loan, lend; Am. to borrow; — **ayuda** to give help; — **atención** to pay attention; Am. **presta acá** give it here, give it to me; -se to lend oneself or itself.

presteza f. promptness, speed.

prestidigitación f. juggling, sleight of hand.

prestidigitador m. juggler.

prestigio m. prestige; influence, authority; good reputation.

presto adj. quick; nimble; prompt; ready; adv. soon, at once; **de** — quickly, promptly.

presumido adj. conceited, presumptuous; p.p. of **presumir**.

presumir v. to presume; to boast; to show off; Am. to court, woo; — **de valiente** to boast of one's valor.

presunción f. presumption, assumption; conceit, arrogance.

presunto adj. presumed; supposed; prospective; **heredero** — heir apparent.

presuntuoso adj. presumptuous, conceited.

presuponer[40] v. irr. to presuppose, take for granted, imply; to estimate.

presupuesto p.p. of **presuponer** presupposed; estimated; m. budget, estimate.

presuroso adj. quick, prompt; hasty.

pretencioso adj. presumptuous; conceited.

pretender v. to pretend; to solicit, seek; to claim; to try; to court.

pretendiente m. pretender, claimant; suitor; office seeker.

pretensión f. pretension; claim; presumption; pretense.

pretérito adj. preterite, past; m. preterite, the past tense.

pretexto m. pretext, pretense, excuse.

pretil m. stone or brick railing; Am. ledge; Am. stone or brick bench (built against a wall).

pretina f. belt, girdle; waistband.

prevalecer[13] v. irr. to prevail.

prevaleciente adj. prevalent, current.

prevención f. prevention; foresight, preparedness; bias, prejudice; provision, supply; admonition, warning; police station; guardhouse.

prevenido adj. & p.p. prepared, ready; forewarned; cautious; supplied.

prevenir[48] v. irr. to prevent, avoid; to prepare beforehand; to foresee; to warn; to predispose; -se to get prepared, get ready.

prever[49] v. irr. to foresee.

previo adj. previous; m. Am. preliminary examination.

previsión f. foresight.

previsto p.p. of **prever**.

prieto adj. dark, black; tight; compact; Am. dark-complexioned, swarthy.

prima f. female cousin; premium; prime (first of the canonical hours).

primacía f. priority, precedence; superiority.

primario adj. primary, principal.

primavera f. spring; primrose; print, flowered silk cloth.

primaveral adj. spring, pertaining to spring.

primer(o) adj. first; former; leading, principal; **primera enseñanza** primary education; **primera materia** raw material; **de buenas a primeras** all of a sudden, unexpectedly; **a primera luz** at dawn; adv. first; rather.

primicia f. first fruit; first profit; **-s** first fruits.

primitivo adj. primitive; primary; original.

primo m. cousin; simpleton, sucker, dupe; **— hermano** (or **— carnal**) first cousin; Am. **coger a uno de —** to deceive someone easily; adj. first; **número —** prime number.

primogénito adj. & m. first-born; **primogenitura** f. birthright; rights of the first-born.

primor m. beauty; excellence; exquisiteness; skill, ability.

primoroso adj. excellent, fine, exquisite; skilful.

prímula f. primrose.

princesa f. princess.

principal adj. principal; renowned, famous; **piso —** main floor (usually, the second floor); m. principal, capital sum; chief, head.

príncipe m. prince; adj. princeps, first (edition).

principiante m. beginner.

principiar v. to begin.

principio m. principle; beginning; origin, source; entrée (main dinner course); **a -s de** towards the beginning of.

prioridad f. priority; precedence.

prisa f. speed, haste; **de** (or **a**) **—** quickly, speedily; **a toda —** with the greatest speed; **eso corre —** that is urgent; **dar — a** to hurry; **darse —** to hurry; **tener** (or **estar de**) **—** to be in a hurry.

prisión f. prison; imprisonment; seizure; shackle; **-es** shackles, fetters, chains.

prisionero m. prisoner.

prisma f. prism.

pristino adj. first, early, former, primitive.

privación f. privation; want, lack; loss.

privado adj. private; personal; unconscious; p.p. deprived; m. favorite.

privar v. to deprive; to enjoy the favor of someone; to be in vogue; **-le a uno del sentido** to stun, daze; **ya no privan esas costumbres** those customs are no longer in vogue or in existence; **-se** to lose consciousness; **-se de** to deprive oneself of.

privativo adj. exclusive; particular, distinctive.

privilegiado adj. privileged.

privilegiar v. to favor; to give a privilege to.

privilegio m. privilege; exemption; patent; copyright; **— de invención** patent on an invention.

pro m. & f. profit, advantage; **en — de** in behalf of; **en — y en contra** pro and con, for and against; **hombre de —** man of worth.

proa f. prow.

probabilidad f. probability.

probable adj. probable.

probar[2] v. irr. to prove; to taste; to test; to try; to try on; to suit, agree with; **no me prueba el clima** the climate does not agree with me.

probeta f. test tube; pressure gauge.

probidad f. integrity, uprightness, honesty.

problema m. problem.

procedente adj. proceeding (from), originating; according to law.

proceder v. to proceed; to originate; to behave; to take action (against); m. behavior, conduct.

procedimiento m. procedure; method; process; conduct.

prócer m. distinguished person; hero; great statesman.

procesado p.p. & adj. relating to, or included in, a lawsuit; accused, prosecuted; m. defendant.

procesar v. to prosecute; to accuse; to indict; to sue.

procesión f. procession; parade.

proceso m. process; lawsuit, legal proceedings; lapse of time; **— verbal** minutes, record.

proclama f. proclamation, ban; marriage banns.

proclamación f. proclamation.

proclamar v. to proclaim.

procurador m. attorney.

procurar v. to procure, obtain, get, acquire; to try, endeavor.

prodigar[7] v. to lavish; to bestow upon; to squander, waste.

prodigio m. prodigy, wonder, marvel; miracle.

prodigioso adj. prodigious, marvelous; fine, exquisite.

pródigo adj. prodigal, wasteful; lavish; generous; m. spendthrift.

producción f. production; produce.

producir[25] v. irr. to produce; to bring about; to yield; **-se** to express oneself, explain oneself; Am. to occur, happen.

productivo adj. productive; fruitful; profitable.

producto m. product; yield; result.

productor m. producer; adj. producing, productive.

proeza f. prowess; Am. boast, exaggeration.

profanación f. profanation.

profanar *v.* to profane; to defile.
profano *adj.* profane, not sacred; irreverent; lay, uninformed (*about a branch of learning*).
profecía *f.* prophecy; prediction.
proferir[3] *v. irr.* to utter, express, speak.
profesar *v.* to profess; to avow, confess.
profesión *f.* profession; avowal, declaration.
profesional *adj.*, *m.* & *f.* professional.
profesionista *m.* & *f.* *Am.* professional.
profesor *m.* professor, teacher; **profesorado** *m.* professorship; faculty; body of teachers; teaching profession.
profeta *m.* prophet.
profético *adj.* prophetic.
profetizar[9] *v.* to prophesy.
proficiente *adj.* proficient, skilled.
profilaxis *f.* prophylaxis (*disease prevention*).
prófugo *adj.* & *m.* fugitive.
profundidad *f.* profundity, depth.
profundizar[9] *v.* to deepen; to go deep into.
profundo *adj.* profound; deep; low.
profuso *adj.* profuse; lavish.
programa *m.* program; plan.
progresar *v.* to progress.
progresista *m.*, *f.* & *adj.* progressive.
progresivo *adj.* progressive.
progreso *m.* progress.
prohibición *f.* prohibition; ban.
prohibir *v.* to prohibit, forbid.
prójimo *m.* neighbor, fellow being; *Am.* **ese** — that fellow.
prole *f.* progeny, offspring.
proletariado *m.* proletariat, working class.
proletario *adj.* proletarian, belonging to the working class; plebeian; *m.* proletarian.
prolijo *adj.* prolix, too long, drawn out, too detailed; boring, tedious.
prologar[7] *v.* to preface, write a preface for.
prólogo *m.* prologue.
prolongación *f.* prolongation, extension; lengthening.
prolongar[7] *v.* to prolong, lengthen, extend.
promediar *v.* to average; to divide or distribute into two equal parts; to mediate; **antes de — el mes** before the middle of the month.
promedio *m.* middle; average.
promesa *f.* promise.
prometedor *adj.* promising hopeful.
prometer *v.* to promise; to show promise; *Am.* to affirm, assure; **-se** to become engaged, betrothed.

prometido *adj.* & *p.p.* betrothed; *m.* fiancé, betrothed; promise.
prominente *adj.* prominent.
promisorio *adj.* promissory.
promoción *f.* promotion, advancement.
promontorio *m.* promontory, headland, cape; anything bulky; bulge.
promotor *m.* promoter.
promovedor *m.* promoter.
promover[1] *v. irr.* to promote; to advance.
promulgación *f.* promulgation, publication, proclamation (*of a law*).
promulgar[7] *v.* to promulgate, proclaim, announce publicly.
pronombre *m.* pronoun.
pronosticar[6] *v.* to prophesy, predict.
pronóstico *m.* forecast; prediction; omen.
prontitud *f.* promptness; quickness.
pronto *adj.* quick, speedy; ready; prompt; *adv.* soon; quickly; **de —** suddenly (*of a law*); **al —** at first; **por de** (or **por lo**) **—** for the present; *m.* sudden impulse.
pronunciación *f.* pronunciation.
pronunciar *v.* to pronounce; to utter; **-se** to rise up in rebellion.
propagación *f.* propagation, spread, spreading.
propaganda *f.* propaganda.
propagar[7] *v.* to propagate, reproduce; to spread.
propalar *v.* to spread (*news*).
propasarse *v.* to overstep one's bounds; to exceed one's authority, go too far.
propensión *f.* tendency, inclination; bent, natural tendency or ability.
propenso *adj.* prone, susceptible, inclined.
propicio *adj.* propitious, favorable.
propiedad *f.* property; ownership; attribute, quality; propriety, appropriateness.
propietario *m.* proprietor, owner.
propina *f.* tip (*voluntary gift of money for service*).
propinar *v.* to give (*something to drink*); to give (*a beating, kick, slap*); *Am.* to tip, give a tip to; **— una paliza** to give a beating.
propio *adj.* proper; suitable; own; same; **amor —** vanity, pride, self-esteem; *m.* messenger.
proponer[40] *v. irr.* to propose; to resolve; to present; **-se** to resolve, make a resolution.
proporción *f.* proportion; dimension; ratio; opportunity, chance.
proporcionar *v.* to proportion; to

adapt, adjust; to furnish, supply; give.

proposición *f.* proposition; proposal; assertion.

propósito *m.* purpose, aim, design; a — apropos, suitable, fitting; by the way; **de** — on purpose; **fuera de** — irrelevant, beside the point.

propuesta *f.* proposal, offer; proposition.

propuesto *p.p.* of **proponer**.

propulsar *v.* to propel.

propulsor *m.* propeller; *adj.* propelling.

prorratear *v.* to prorate, distribute or assess proportionally; to average.

prorrateo *m.* apportionment, proportional distribution.

prórroga *f.* renewal, extension of time.

prorrogar[7] *v.* to put off, postpone; to adjourn; to extend (*time limit*).

prorrumpir *v.* to break forth; — **en llanto** to burst into tears; — **en una carcajada** to let out a big laugh.

prosa *f.* prose.

prosaico *adj.* prosaic; dull; tedious.

proscribir[52] *v.* to proscribe, banish; to outlaw.

proscripción *f.* banishment.

proscripto, proscrito *p.p..* of **proscribir**; *m.* exile, outlaw.

proseguir[5, 12] *v. irr.* to continue; to follow.

prosperar *v.* to prosper.

prosperidad *f.* prosperity; success.

próspero *adj.* prosperous; successful.

prostituir[32] *v.* to prostitute, corrupt.

prostituta *f.* prostitute.

protagonista *m.* & *f.* protagonist (*main character or actor*).

protección *f.* protection; support.

proteccionista *adj.* protective; **tarifa** — protective tariff; *m.* & *f.* protectionist (*follower of the economic principles of protection*).

protector *m.* protector, guardian; *adj.* protecting, protective.

protectorado *m.* protectorate.

proteger[11] *v.* to protect; to shelter; to defend.

proteína *f.* protein.

protesta *f.* protest; protestation.

protestación *f.* protestation, solemn declaration; protest.

protestar *v.* to protest; to assert, assure; to avow publicly; — **una letra** to protest a draft.

protoplasma *m.* protoplasm.

protuberancia *f.* protuberance, bulge.

protuberante *adj.* protuberant, prominent, bulging.

provecho *m.* profit; benefit; utility; advantage; **hombre de** — worthy, useful man.

provechoso *adj.* profitable; useful; beneficial; advantageous.

proveedor *m.* provisioner, provider; supply man.

proveer[14, 52] *v. irr.* to provide; to supply; to confer, bestow; to decide; **-se de** to supply oneself with.

provenir[48] *v. irr.* to originate, arise, come (from).

proverbio *m.* proverb.

providencia *f.* providence; foresight; Providence, God; legal decision, sentence; provision, measure; **tomar una** — to take a step or measure.

providencial *adj.* providential.

provincia *f.* province.

provincial *adj.* provincial.

provinciano *adj.* & *m.* provincial.

provisión *f.* provision; supply, stock.

provisorio *adj.* provisional, temporary.

provisto *p.p. of* **proveer**.

provocación *f.* provocation; dare, defiance.

provocador *adj.* provoking; — provoker.

provocar[6] *v.* to provoke; to excite, rouse; to stimulate.

proximidad *f.* proximity, nearness.

próximo *adj.* next; neighboring; near; **del** — **pasado** of last month.

proyección *f.* projection; jut.

proyectar *v.* to project; to plan; to throw; to cast; **-se** to be cast (*as a shadow*).

proyectil *m.* projectile.

proyectista *m.* & *f.* designer; schemer; planner.

proyecto *m.* project; plan; — **de ley** bill (*in a legislature*).

prudencia *f.* prudence, practical wisdom, discretion.

prudente *adj.* prudent, wise, discreet.

prueba *f.* proof; trial; test; fitting; sample; evidence; *Am.* acrobatic performance, stunt, trick, sleight of hand; **a** — **de incendio** fireproof.

prurito *m.* itch; keen desire.

psicología *f.* psychology.

psicológico *adj.* psychological.

psicólogo *m.* psychologist.

psiquiatra *m.* & *f.* psychiatrist, alienist.

psiquiatría *f.* psychiatry.

púa *f.* prick; barb; prong; thorn; quill (*of a porcupine, etc.*); sharp, cunning person; *Am.* cock's spur; **alambre de -s** barbed wire.

publicación *f.* publication.

publicar[6] *v.* to publish; to reveal; to announce.

publicidad *f.* publicity.

público *adj. & m.* public.

puchero *m.* pot, kettle; meat and vegetable stew; pout; **hacer -s** to pout.

pudiente *adj.* powerful; rich, wealthy; *m.* man of means.

pudín *m.* pudding.

pudor *m.* modesty; shyness.

pudrir[16] *v.* to rot; to vex, annoy; **-se** to rot.

pueblero *m. Am.* townsman (*as opposed to countryman*).

pueblo *m.* town, village; people, race, nation; populace; common people.

puente *m.* bridge; *Am.* dental bridge; *Am.* knife and fork rest; **— colgante** suspension bridge; **— levadizo** drawbridge.

puerca *f.* sow.

puerco *m.* pig, hog; **— espín** porcupine; **— jabalí** wild boar; *adj.* filthy, dirty; coarse, ill-bred.

pueril *adj.* puerile, childish.

puerta *f.* door; gate; entrance; **— accesoria (excusada,** *or* **falsa)** side door; **— de golpe** spring door; trap door; **— franca** open door; free entrance or entry; **— trasera** back door; **a — cerrada** secretly, behind closed doors; *Am.* **en — in** view, in sight, very near.

puerto *m.* port; harbor; refuge; mountain pass; **— franco** free port.

pues *conj.* since, because, for, inasmuch as; then; *adv.* then; well; **— bien** well then, well; **— que** since.

puesta *f.* set, setting (*of a star or planet*); stake at cards; **— de sol** sunset.

puestero *m. Am.* vendor, seller (*at a stand or stall*); *Am.* man in charge of livestock on Argentine ranches.

puesto *p.p. of* **poner** placed, put, set; **mal** (*or* **bien)** — badly (*or* well) dressed; *m.* place; vendor's booth or stand; post, position, office; military post; *Am.* station for watching and taking care of cattle on a ranch; **— de socorros** first-aid station; **— que** *conj.* since.

pugilato *m.* boxing.

pugilista *m.* boxer, prize fighter.

pugna *f.* struggle; conflict; **estar en — con** to be in conflict with; to be opposed to.

pugnar *v.* to fight; to struggle; to strive; to persist.

pujanza *f.* push, force, power.

pujar *v.* to make a strenuous effort; to grope for words; to falter; to outbid (*offer a higher bid than*); *Am.* to grunt; *Am.* to reject; *Am.* to dismiss; *Am.* **—**

para adentro to forbear, keep silent; *Am.* **andar pujado** to go around crestfallen; to be in disgrace.

pujido *m. Am.* grunt (*due to strenuous effort*).

pulcritud *f.* neatness, trimness; excellence, perfection.

pulcro *adj.* neat, trim; beautiful.

pulga *f.* flea; *Am.* small and insignificant person; **tener malas -s** to be illtempered; *Am.* **ser de pocas -s** to be touchy, oversensitive; **pulgón** *m.* blight, plant louse.

pulgada *f.* inch.

pulgar *m.* thumb.

pulido *adj.* polished, refined; polite; neat; exquisite.

pulimentar *v.* to polish.

pulimento *m.* polish; gloss.

pulir *v.* to polish.

pulmón *m.* lung.

pulmonar *adj.* pulmonary, pertaining to the lungs.

pulmonía *f.* pneumonia.

pulpa *f.* pulp.

pulpería *f. Am.* country general store; *Am.* tavern.

pulpero *m. Am.* owner of a country store or tavern.

púlpito *m.* pulpit.

pulque *m. Am.* pulque (*fermented juice of the maguey*).

pulsación *f.* pulsation, beat, throb; pulse, beating.

pulsar *v.* to pulsate, throb, beat; to feel the pulse of; to sound out, examine; to play (*the harp*); *Am.* to judge or try the weight of (*by lifting*).

pulsera *f.* bracelet; wrist bandage; **reloj de —** wrist watch.

pulso *m.* pulse; steadiness; tact; *Am.* bracelet, wrist watch; **un hombre de — a** prudent, steady man; *Am.* **beber a — to** drink straight down, gulp down; **levantar a — to** lift with the strength of the wrist or hand; **sacar a — un negocio** to carry out a deal by sheer perseverance.

pulular *v.* to swarm; to multiply rapidly; to sprout, bud.

pulverizar *v.* to pulverize.

pulla *f.* taunt; mean dig, quip, cutting remark; filthy word or remark.

puma *f.* puma, mountain lion.

puna *f. Am.* cold, arid tableland of the Andes; *Am.* desert; *Am.* sickness caused by high altitude.

pundonor *m.* point of honor.

punta *f.* point, tip; bull's horn; cigar or cigarette butt; *Am.* gang, band, herd, a lot (of things, people, etc.); Am. small leaf of fine tobacco; Am. jeer, cutting remark; -s point lace; scallops; de — on end; de -s (or de puntillas) on tiptoe; Am. a — de by dint of, by means of; estar de — con to be on bad terms with; sacar — a un lápiz to sharpen a pencil; tener sus -s de poeta to be something of a poet.

puntada f. stitch; hint; Am. prick, pricking, sting, sharp pain; no he dado — en este asunto I have left this matter completely untouched.

puntal m. prop; support, basis; bull's horn; Am. snack (between meals).

puntapié m. kick (with the toe of the shoe).

puntazo m. Am. stab, jab.

puntear v. to pluck (the strings of a guitar); to play (a guitar); to make dots; to engrave, draw or paint by means of dots; to stitch; to tack (said of a boat).

puntería f. aim.

puntero m. pointer; chisel; blacksmith's punch; Am. clock or watch hand; Am. leader of a parade; Am. leading ox (or other animal); Am. guide.

puntiagudo adj. sharp, sharp-pointed.

puntilla f. small point; tip; small dagger; tracing point; point lace; Am. penknife; Am. toe rubber; Am. ridge (of a hill); de -s on tiptoe; puntillazo m. stab (with a dagger).

punto m. point; dot; period; stop; stitch; mesh; gun sight; place; moment; — de admiración exclamation mark; — de interrogación question mark; — y coma semicolon; dos -s colon; al — at once, immediately; a — de on the point of; de — knitted, porous knit, stockinet or jersey weave; en — exactly, on the dot; a — fijo with certainty; subir de — to increase or get worse.

puntuación f. punctuation.

puntual adj. punctual, prompt; exact.

puntualidad f. punctuality, promptness; certainty.

puntuar[18] v. to punctuate.

punzada f. puncture; prick; sharp pain.

punzante adj. sharp; pricking; piercing, penetrating.

punzar[9] v. to puncture; to sting; to prick; to punch, perforate.

punzón m. punch, puncher; pick; awl.

puñada f. punch, box, blow with the fist.

puñado m. fistful, handful; a -s abun-

dantly; by handfuls.

puñal m. dagger.

puñalada f. stab; sharp pain; coser a -s to stab to death.

puñetazo m. punch, blow with the fist.

puño m. fist; fistful, handful; cuff; hilt, handle; Am. blow with the fist; a — cerrado firmly; ser como un — to be stingy; tener -s to be strong, courageous.

pupila f. pupil (of the eye).

pupilo m. ward; boarding-school pupil; boarder.

pupitre m. desk, school desk.

puré m. purée, thick soup.

pureza f. purity; chastity.

purga f. purge, laxative, physic.

purgante adj. purgative, laxative; m. purgative, physic, laxative.

purgar[7] v. to purge; to purify; to atone for; -se to purge oneself; to take a laxative.

purgatorio m. purgatory.

purificar[6] v. to purify.

puro adj. pure; clean; chaste; mere, only, sheer; a pura fuerza by sheer force; a puros gritos by just shouting; m. cigar.

púrpura f. purple; purple cloth.

purpúreo adj. purple.

pus m. pus.

puta f. whore, prostitute.

putativo adj. reputed, supposed; padre — foster father.

putrefacción f. putrefaction, decay, rotting.

putrefacto adj. putrid, rotten, decayed.

Q

que rel. pron. that; which; who; whom; el — who; which; the one who; the one which; conj. that; for, because; más (menos) — more (less) than; el mismo — the same as; — (= subj.) let, may you, I hope that; por mucho no matter how much; quieras — no whether you wish or not.

qué interr. adj. & pron. what?; what a! interr. adv. how; ¡ — bonito! how beautiful!; ¿ a — ? what for?; ¿ para — ? what for?; ¿ por — ? why?; ¿ a — tal? how?; hello!; ¡ — más da! what's the difference!; ¡ a mí — ! so what and what's that to me!

quebrada f. ravine; gorge; failure, bankruptcy; Am. brook.

quebradizo adj. breakable; brittle, fragile; delicate.

quebrado adj. broken; weakened; ruptured; bankrupt; rough or rugge-

(ground); m. common fraction; *Am.* navigable waters between reefs.

uebrantar v. to break; to break open; to pound, crush; to violate (*a law*); to weaken; to vex; *Am.* to tame, break in (*a colt*); — el agua to take the chill off the water.

uebranto m. breaking; grief, affliction; discouragement; damage, loss.

uebrar¹ v. irr. to break; to crush; to interrupt; to wither (*said of the complexion*); to become bankrupt; -se to break; to get broken; to be ruptured; -se uno la cabeza to rack one's brain.

uebrazón m. *Am.* breakage, breaking.

uechua adj. *Am.* Quichuan; m. & f. Quichua, Quichuan Indian; m. Quichuan language.

uedar v. to stay; to remain; to be left over; to be left (*in a state or condition*); — en to agree to; *Am.* — de to agree to; — bien to acquit oneself well; to come out well; *Am.* to suit, become (*said of a dress, hat, etc.*); *Am.* — bien con alguien to please someone; -se to remain; -se con una cosa to keep something; to take something (*buy it*); *Am.* -se como si tal cosa to act as if nothing had happened.

uedo adj. quiet, still; gentle; adv. softly; in a low voice; quedito adj. nice and quiet; adv. very softly.

uehacer m. work, occupation; task, duty, chore.

ueja f. complaint; groan, moan; grudge.

uejarse v. to complain; to grumble; to moan; to lament.

uejido m. moan; groan.

uejoso adj. complaining, whining.

uejumbre f. whine, moan; murmur, complaint; -s m. *Am.* grumbler, whiner; quejumbroso adj. whining, complaining.

uemada f. burned forest; *Am.* burn.

uemado m. burned portion of a forest; *Am.* burned field; *Am.* hot alcoholic drink; adj. dark, tan; *Am.* peeved, piqued; *Am.* ruined; p p. of quemar.

uemadura f. burn; scald; smut (*plant disease*).

uemar v. to burn; to scald; to scorch; to sell at a loss; to annoy; *Am.* to deceive, swindle; -se to burn; to be hot.

uemazón f. burn; burning; great heat; fire, conflagration; pique, anger; bargain sale; *Am.* mirage on the pampas.

uerella f. quarrel; complaint; controversy.

uerellarse v. to complain.

querencia f. affection; longing; favorite spot; haunt; stable.

querer⁴¹ v. irr. to want, wish, desire; to will; to be willing; to love; — **decir** to mean; **sin** — unwillingly; **no quiso hacerlo** he refused to do it; **quiere llover** it is trying to rain, it is about to rain; **como quiera** in any way; **como quiera que** since; no matter how; **cuando quiera** whenever, **donde quiera** wherever; anywhere; -se to love each other; *Am.* to be on the point of, be about to; **se quiere caer esa pared** that wall is about to fall.

querido p.p. wanted, desired; adj. beloved, dear; m. lover; querida f. darling; mistress.

quesería f. dairy, creamery, cheese factory; quesera f. dairy, cheese factory; cheese dish; dairymaid, woman cheese vendor or cheesemaker; quesero adj. pertaining to cheese; m. cheesemaker.

queso m. cheese; *Am.* — de higos fig paste.

quicio m. hinge of a door; **sacar a uno de** — to exasperate someone.

quichua = quechua.

quiebra f. break; crack; fissure; fracture; damage, loss; bankruptcy.

quien rel. pron. who, whom; he who, she who; **quién** interr. pron. who? whom?

quienquiera pron. whoever, whosoever, whomsoever.

quieto adj. quiet, still; calm.

quietud f. quiet, stillness, calmness.

quijada f. jaw; jawbone.

quilate m. carat (*twenty-fourth part in weight and value of gold*); unit of weight for precious stones and pearls; -s qualities; degree of perfection or purity.

quilla f. keel.

quimera f. absurd idea, wild fancy.

química f. chemistry.

químico adj. chemical; m. chemist.

quina, quinina f. quinino.

quincalla f. hardware.

quincallería f. hardware; hardware store; hardware trade.

quincena f. fortnight; semimonthly pay.

quinta f. villa, country house; draft, military conscription; sequence of five cards.

quintaesencia f. quintessence, pure essence, purest form.

quiosco m. kiosk, small pavilion.

quirúrgico adj. surgical.

quisquilloso adj. touchy, oversensitive.

quisto : bien — well-liked, well-received, welcome; **mal —** disliked; unwelcome.

quitamanchas *m.* cleaner, stain remover.

quitar *v.* to remove; to take away (off, *or* from); to rob of; to deprive of; to subtract; to parry (*in fencing*); **-se** to take off (*clothing*); to remove oneself, withdraw; **-se de una cosa** to give up something, get rid of something; **-se a alguien de encima** to get rid of someone; ¡**quita allá!** don't tell me that!; ¡**quítese de aquí!** get out of here!

quitasol *m.* large sunshade, parasol.

quite *m.* parry (*in fencing*); dodge, dodging; *Am.* **andar a los -s** to be on the defensive; to take offense easily; to be afraid of one's own shadow; **eso no tiene —** that can't be helped.

quizá, quizás *adv.* perhaps, maybe.

R

rabadilla *f.* end of the spinal column; tail of a fowl; rump.

rábano *m.* radish; **tomar el — por las hojas** to take one thing for another; to misinterpret something.

rabia *f.* rabies; rage; **tener — a alguien** to hate someone; *Am.* **volarse de —** to get furious, angry.

rabiar *v.* to have rabies; to rage; to rave; to suffer a severe pain; **— por** to be dying to or for, be very eager to; **quema que rabia** it burns terribly.

rabieta *f.* tantrum, fit of temper.

rabioso *adj.* rabid (*having rabies*), mad; furious, angry, violent.

rabo *m.* tail; **de cabo a —** from beginning to end; **mirar con el — del ojo** to look out of the corner of one's eye.

racimo *m.* bunch; cluster.

raciocinio *m.* reasoning.

ración *f.* ration; allowance; supply.

racional *adj.* rational; reasonable.

racionamiento *m.* rationing.

racionar *v.* to ration.

radiador *m.* radiator.

radiante *adj.* radiant; shining; beaming.

radiar *v.* to radiate; to radio; to broadcast.

radical *adj.* radical; fundamental; extreme; *m.* radical; root of a word.

radicar[6] *v.* to take root; to be, be found (*in a certain place*); **-se** to take root; to locate, settle.

radio *m.* radius; radium; *m. & f.* radio.

radiodifundir *v.* to broadcast by radio. *See* **difundir.**

radiodifusión *f.* broadcasting. *See* **difu-**

sión.

radiodifusora, radioemisora *f.* broadcasting station.

radioescucha *m. & f.* radio listener.

radiofónico *adj.* radio (*used as adj.*); **estación radiofónica** radio station.

radiografía *f.* radiography, X-ray photography; X-ray picture.

radiografiar[17] *v.* to take X-ray pictures.

radiolocutor *m.* radio announcer. *See* **locutor.**

radiotelefonía *f.* radiotelephony, radio; wireless.

radiotelegrafía *f.* radiotelegraphy, radio, wireless telegraphy.

radioyente = radioescucha.

raer[24] *v. irr.* to scrape off; to rub off; to scratch off; to fray; to erase.

ráfaga *f.* gust of wind; flash of light.

raído *p.p. & adj.* scraped off; rubbed or frayed; worn, threadbare.

raigón *m.* large root; root of a tooth.

raíz *f.* root; origin; foundation; **a — de** close to, right after; **de — by the** roots, completely; **echar raíces** take root, become firmly fixed.

raja *f.* slice; splinter; crack; split; crevice; **hacer -s** to slice; to tear in strips; to cut into splinters; **hacerse uno -s** to wear oneself out (*by dancing, jumping or any violent exercise*).

rajadura *f.* crack, crevice.

rajar *v.* to split; to crack; to cleave; to slice; to chatter; to brag; *Am.* to flunk, fail (*a student*); **-se** to split open; to crack; *Am.* to get afraid, back down.

rajatablas *m. Am.* reprimand, scolding; **a —** in great haste.

ralea *f.* breed, race, stock; species, kind.

ralear *v.* to thin out, make less dense; to become less dense.

ralo *adj.* sparse, thin, thinly scattered.

rallador *m.* grater.

rallar *v.* to grate; to grate on, annoy; *Am.* to goad, spur.

rama *f.* branch, limb; **en — crude**, raw; **andarse por las -s** to beat about the bush, not to stick to the point.

ramada *f.* branches, foliage; arbor; shed, tent.

ramaje *m.* foliage; branches.

ramal *m.* strand (*of a rope, etc.*); branch; branch railway line; halter.

ramera *f.* harlot, prostitute.

ramificarse[6] *v.* to branch off, divide into branches.

ramillete *m.* bouquet; flower cluster.

ramo *m.* bunch (*of flowers*), bouquet; line, branch (*of art, science, industry*) *etc.*); branch, bough; **domingo de -s** Palm Sunday.

ramonear *v.* to cut off twigs or tips of branches; to nibble grass, twigs, or leaves; *Am.* to eat scraps or left-overs.

ramplón *adj.* coarse; crude, uncouth; slovenly.

ramplonería *f.* coarse act or remark; crudeness, coarseness; slovenliness.

rana *f.* frog.

rancio *adj.* rancid, stale; old (*wine*); **linaje —** old, noble lineage.

ranchero *m. Am.* rancher, farmer; **ranchería** *f.* group of huts; *Am.* inn (*for* **arrieros**).

rancho *m.* camp; hamlet; mess (*meal for a group and the group itself*); *Am.* hut; *Am.* country house; *Am.* ranch, small farm (*usually for cattle raising*).

rango *m.* rank, position.

ranura *f.* groove; slot.

rapar *v.* to shave off; to crop (*hair*); to strip bare, rob of everything.

rapaz *adj.* rapacious, grasping, greedy; *m.* lad; **rapaza** *f.* lass, young girl.

rapé *m.* snuff (*pulverized tobacco*).

rapidez *f.* rapidity, speed.

rápido *adj.* rapid, swift; *m.* rapids.

rapiña *f.* plunder; **ave de —** bird of prey.

rapiñar *v.* to plunder; to steal.

raposa *f.* fox.

raptar *v.* to kidnap, abduct.

rapto *m.* abduction, kidnapping; ecstasy, rapture; outburst.

raqueta *f.* racket (*used in games*); tennis.

raquítico *adj.* rickety, feeble, weak, skinny, sickly.

rareza *f.* rarity; oddity; strangeness; freak; curiosity; queer act or remark; peculiarity; **por —** seldom.

raro *adj.* rare; thin, not dense; scarce; strange, odd; ridiculous; **rara vez** (*or* **raras veces**) rarely, seldom.

ras : a — de flush with, even with; **al — con** flush with; **estar — con —** to be flush, perfectly even.

rascacielos *m.* skyscraper.

rascar *v.* to scratch; to scrape; *Am.* to dig up potatoes; *Am.* **— uno para adentro** to seek one's own advantage, look out for oneself.

rasete *m.* sateen.

rasgado *adj.* torn; open; *Am.* generous; -*Am.* outspoken; **ojos -s** large, wide-open eyes.

rasgadura *f.* tear, rip, rent.

rasgar *v.* to tear; to rip.

rasgo *m.* trait, characteristic; stroke of the pen, flourish; feat; *Am.* irrigation

ditch; *Am.* **un — de terreno** a parcel of land; -**s** features; traits.

rasgón *m.* large tear, rent, rip.

rasguñar *v.* to scratch; to claw.

rasguño *m.* scratch.

raso *adj.* plain; flat, smooth; clear, cloudless; *Am.* even, level (*when measuring wheat, corn, etc.*); *Am.* scarce, scanty; **soldado —** private; **al —** in the open air; *m.* satin.

raspadura *f.* scrape; scraping; erasure; shaving (*of wood or metal*).

raspar *v.* to scrape, scrape off; to steal; *Am.* to scold, upbraid.

rastra *f.* drag; sled; large rake; harrow; **a -s** dragging; unwillingly.

rastreador *m.* trailer, tracker, tracer.

rastrear *v.* to trail, track, trace; to rake, harrow; to drag (*a* **dragnet**); to skim, scrape the ground.

rastrero *adj.* low, vile.

rastrillar *v.* to rake; to comb (*flax or hemp*); *Am.* to scrape; *Am.* to shoot; *Am.* to barter, exchange; *Am.* to pilfer, steal (*in stores*).

rastrillo *m.* rake; *Am.* barter, exchange; *Am.* business deal.

rastro *m.* track, trail, scent; trace, sign; rake, harrow; slaughterhouse.

rastrojo *m.* stubble.

rasura *f.* shave, shaving.

rasurar *v.* to shave.

rata *f.* rat; *m.* pickpocket.

ratear *v.* to pilfer; to pick pockets; to creep, crawl.

ratería *f.* petty larceny; meanness.

ratero *m.* pickpocket; *adj.* contemptible, mean.

ratificar *v.* to ratify.

rato *m.* short time, little while; **buen —** pleasant time; long time; -**s perdidos** leisure hours; **a -s** at intervals, from time to time; **pasar el —** to while away the time, kill time; *Am.* **¡hasta cada —!** so long!; see you later!

ratón *m.* mouse; *Am.* **tener un —** to have a hang-over; **ratonera** *f.* mouse trap.

raudal *m.* torrent, downpour, flood; *Am.* rapids.

raudo *adj.* rapid, swift.

raya *f.* line; dash; stripe; boundary line; part in the hair; *Am.* pay, wage; *Am.* **día de —** pay day; **tener a —** to keep within bounds; to hold in check; **pasar de la —** to overstep one's bounds, take undue liberties; *m.* sting ray (*a species of fish*).

rayador *m. Am.* paymaster; *Am.* umpire in a game.

rayar v. to line, make lines on; to streak; to scratch, mark; to cross out; *Am.* to pay or collect wages; *Am.* to stop a horse all of a sudden; *Am.* to spur a horse to run at top speed; — **el alba** to dawn; — **en** to border on; *Am.* **-se uno** to help oneself; to get rich.

rayo m. ray, beam; lightning, thunderbolt; spoke; **-s X** X-rays.

raza f. race; clan; breed; fissure, crevice; **caballo de —** thoroughbred horse.

razón f. reason; right, justice; ratio; account, information, word, message; — **social** firm, firm name; **a — de** at the rate of; **¡con —!** no wonder!; **dar —** to inform; **dar la — a una persona** to admit that a person is right; **perder la — to** lose one's mind; **poner en —** to pacify; **tener — to** be right.

razonable adj. reasonable.

razonamiento m. reasoning.

razonar v. to reason; to discourse, talk; to argue.

reabierto p.p. of reabrir.

reabrir⁵³ v. to reopen.

reacción f. reaction.

reaccionar v. to react.

reaccionario adj. & m. reactionary.

reacio adj. stubborn, obstinate.

reajustar v. to readjust.

reajuste m. readjustment.

real adj. real; royal; m. army camp; fair ground; real (*Spanish coin worth one fourth of a peseta*); **-es** *Am.* money (*in general*); **levantar el —** (*or* **los -es**) to break camp.

realce m. embossment, raised work, relief; prestige; lustre, splendour; **dar —** to enhance; to emphasize.

realeza f. royalty (*royal dignity*).

realidad f. reality; truth; fact; **en —** really, truly, in fact.

realismo m. realism; royalism.

realista adj. realistic; royalist; m. realist; royalist.

realización f. realization, fulfilment; conversion into money, sale.

realizar⁹ v. to realize, fulfill, make real; to convert into money; to sell up.

realzar⁹ v. to emboss; to raise; to enhance; to make stand out; to emphasize.

reanimar v. to revive; to comfort; to cheer; to encourage.

reanudación f. renewal.

reanudar v. to renew, resume, begin again.

reaparecer¹³ v. irr. to reappear.

reasumir v. to resume.

reata f. lariat, rope, lasso.

reavivar v. to revive.

rebaja f. deduction; reduction; discount.

rebajar v. to diminish; to lower, reduce; to tone down (*a painting*); to humiliate; **-se** to lower or humble oneself.

rebanada f. slice.

rebanar v. to slice.

rebaño m. flock; herd.

rebatir v. to beat over and over; to repel, resist; to refute; to rebut (*come back with an argument*); to argue; to parry (*in fencing*).

rebato m. alarm, call to arms; surprise attack.

rebelarse v. to rebel.

rebelde adj. rebellious; m. rebel; defaulter (*one who fails to appear in court*).

rebeldía f. rebelliousness; defiance; default, failure to appear in court; **en — in** revolt.

rebelión f. rebellion, revolt.

rebencazo m. *Am.* crack of a whip; *Am.* lash, stroke with a whip.

rebenque m. rawhide whip.

reborde m. edge, border.

rebosante adj. brimming, overflowing.

rebosar v. to overflow, brim over; to abound.

rebotar v. to rebound, bounce back or again; to make rebound; to repel, reject; to annoy, vex; **-se** to become vexed, upset; *Am.* to become cloudy or muddy (*said of water*); *Am.* **rebotársele a uno la bilis** to get angry, become upset.

rebote m. rebound, bounce; **de —** on the rebound; indirectly.

rebozar⁹ v. to muffle up; **-se** to muffle oneself up; to wrap oneself up.

rebozo m. shawl; sin — frankly, openly.

rebullir³⁰ v. irr. to stir, move; to boil up.

rebusca f. research; search; searching; gleaning; residue.

rebuscar⁶ v. to search thoroughly; to pry into; to glean.

rebuznar v. to bray.

rebuzno m. bray.

recabar v. to obtain, gain by entreaty.

recado m. message; gift; daily food supply, daily marketing; precaution; equipment; *Am.* saddle and trappings; — **de escribir** writing materials; **-s** regards to.

recaer²⁴ v. irr. to fall (upon); to fall again; to relapse; to have a relapse.

recaída f. relapse; falling again.

recalar v. to saturate, soak through; to reach port; to come within sight of land; to land, end up, stop at; Am. — con alguien to "land" on somebody, take it out on somebody.

recalcar[6] v. to emphasize; to harp on; to press down.

recalcitrante adj. obstinate, disobedient, stubborn.

recalentar[1] v. irr. to reheat, warm over; to overheat, heat too much.

recamar v. to embroider (usually with gold or silver).

recámara f. dressing room; Am. bedroom; chamber for an explosive charge.

recapitular v. to recapitulate, sum up, tell briefly.

recargo m. overload; extra load; extra charge; increase (of fever); new charge, new accusation.

recatado adj. cautious, prudent; modest; p.p. concealed.

recatar v. to cover, conceal; -se to show timidity; to be cautious; to hide (from), conceal.

recato m. caution, prudence; reserve, restraint, secrecy; modesty.

recaudación f. collection, collecting; office of tax collector.

recaudador m. tax collector.

recaudar v. to collect (money, taxes, rents, etc.).

recaudo m. collection, collecting; precaution; bond, security; Am. spices, seasonings; Am. daily supply of vegetables; estar a buen — to be ale; poner a buen — to place in safety.

recelar v. to suspect, fear; -se de to be suspicious or afraid of.

recelo m. suspicion, fear.

receloso adj. suspicious, distrustful, fearful.

recepción f. reception; admission.

receptáculo m. receptacle.

receptivo adj. receptive, capable of receiving, quick to receive.

receptor m. receiver; adj. receiving.

receta f. recipe; prescription.

recetar v. to prescribe (a medicine).

recibidor m. receiver; reception room.

recibimiento m. reception; welcome; reception room; parlor.

recibir v. to receive; to admit, accept; to go out to meet; — noticias de to hear from; -se de to receive a title or degree of.

recibo m. reception; receipt; reception room; parlor; sala de — reception room; estar de — to be at home for receiving callers; ser de — to be

acceptable, be fit for use.

reciedumbre f. strength, force, vigor.

recién adv. recently, lately, newly (used before a past participle); Am. just now; Am. a short time ago; Am. — entonces just then.

reciente adj. recent, new.

recinto m. enclosure; precinct.

recio adj. strong, robust; harsh; hard, severe; adv. strongly; harshly; rapidly; hard; loud.

recipiente m. receptacle, container; recipient, receiver (he who receives).

recíproco adj. reciprocal, mutual.

recitación f. recitation, recital.

recital m. musical recital.

recitar v. to recite.

reclamación f. protest, complaint; claim, demand.

reclamador m. claimant; complainer.

reclamante m. & f. claimant; complainer; adj. complaining; claiming.

reclamar v. to claim, demand; to complain, protest (against); to lure, call back (a bird).

reclamo m. protest; claim; advertisement; call; bird call; decoy bird; lure.

reclinar v. to recline, lean; -se to recline, lean back.

recluir[32] v. irr. to seclude, shut up; -se to isolate oneself.

recluso m. recluse, hermit; adj. shut in, shut up.

recluta f. recruiting; Am. roundup of cattle; m. recruit.

reclutamiento m. recruiting; levy, draft.

reclutar v. to recruit, enlist; Am. to round up (cattle).

recobrar v. to recover, regain; -se to recover; to recuperate.

recobro m. recovery.

recodo m. bend, turn; elbow (of a road).

recoger[11] v. to gather; to collect; to pick up; to take in, tighten; to shelter; -se to retire, go home; to withdraw; to seclude oneself; to take shelter.

recogimiento m. seclusion; concentration of thought, composure; retreat; collecting, gathering.

recolección f. collecting, gathering; harvest, crop; summary.

recolectar v. to harvest; to gather.

recomendable adj. praiseworthy, laudable; advisable.

recomendación f. recommendation; request.

recomendar[1] v. irr. to recommend; to commend, praise; to enjoin, urge; to advise.

179

recompensa f. recompense; compensation.

recompensar v. to recompense, reward; to compensate.

reconcentrar v. to concentrate, bring together; to hide in the depth of one's heart; -se to concentrate, become absorbed in thought, collect one's thoughts.

reconciliación f. reconciliation.

reconciliar v. to reconcile; -se to become reconciled.

recóndito adj. hidden, concealed; profound.

reconocer[13] v. irr. to recognize; to admit, acknowledge; to examine carefully; to reconnoiter, scout, explore.

reconocimiento m. recognition; acknowledgment; gratitude; examination; scouting, exploring.

reconstruir[32] v. irr. to reconstruct, rebuild.

recontar[2] v. irr. to recount; to tell, relate.

recopilar v. to compile; to digest, make a digest of.

recordación f. recollection; remembrance.

recordar[2] v. irr. to remember; to recall; to remind; Am. to rouse, awaken; -se to remember; to wake up.

recordativo m. reminder; adj. reminding.

recordatorio m. reminder.

recorrer v. to go over; to travel over; to read over; to look over; to overhaul.

recorrido m. trip, run; mileage, distance traveled.

recortar v. to trim, clip; to shorten; to cut out (figures); to pare off; -se to project itself (as a shadow); to outline itself.

recorte m. clipping; cutting; outline; Am. gossip, slander.

recostar v. to recline, lean; -se to recline, lean back.

recoveco m. turn, bend; nook; sly or underhanded manner.

recreación f. recreation.

recrear v. to entertain, amuse; to gratify, please; -se to amuse oneself; to take delight (in).

recreo m. recreation, entertainment; place of amusement.

recrudecer[13] v. to recur, break out again, flare up, become worse (said of an illness or evil).

rectángulo m. rectangle; adj. rectangular, right-angled.

rectificar[6] v. to rectify, correct, amend;

to refine (liquors).

rectitud f. rectitude, uprightness, righteousness; straightness; accuracy.

recto adj. straight; right; just, honest; ángulo — right angle; m. rectum.

rector m. college or university president; principal; rector, curate, priest.

recua f. drove of pack animals, drove, crowd.

recuento m. recount.

recuerdo m. remembrance; recollection; souvenir, keepsake; memory; -s regards; adj. Am. awake.

reculada f. recoil.

recular v. to recoil, spring back; to fall back, go back, retreat; to yield, back down.

recuperación f. recovery.

recuperar v. to recuperate, recover, regain; -se to recuperate, recover one's health.

recurrir v. to resort (to); to have recourse (to).

recurso m. recourse, resort; petition, appeal; -s means, resources; sin — without remedy; without appeal.

recusar v. to reject, decline.

rechazar[9] v. to reject; to repel, drive back; to rebuff.

rechifla f. hooting; hissing; ridicule.

rechiflar v. to hoot; to hiss; to ridicule.

rechinamiento m. creak; squeak; squeaking; gnashing.

rechinar v. to squeak; to creak; Am. to be furious, angry; Am. to grumble, growl; — los dientes to gnash one's teeth.

rechino = rechinamiento.

rechoncho adj. plump; chubby; squat.

rechuparse v. to smack one's lips.

red f. net; netting; network; snare; **redecilla** f. small net; mesh; hair net.

redacción f. wording; editing; newspaper offices; editorial department; editorial staff.

redactar v. to word, compose; to edit.

redactor m. editor.

redargüir[32] v. irr. to retort, answer back; to contradict, call in question; to reargue.

rededor m. surroundings; al (or en) — around, about.

redención f. redemption.

redentor m. redeemer, savior; el Redentor the Savior.

redil m. sheepfold.

redimir v. to redeem; to ransom; to set free.

rédito m. interest, revenue, yield.

redituar[18] v. to produce, yield (interest).

redoblar *v.* to double; to clinch (*a nail*); to reiterate, repeat; to roll (*a drum*).

redoble *m.* roll (*of a drum*).

redoma *f.* flask, vial.

redomón *m. Am.* half-tame horse or bull; *adj. Am.* half-civilized, rustic.

redonda *f.* surrounding district, neighborhood; whole note (*music*); a la — all around, round about.

redondear *v.* to round, make round; to round off; to round out.

redondel *m.* arena, bull ring; circle.

redondo *adj.* round; whole, entire; clear, evident; *Am.* stupid; *Am.* honest; en — all around.

redopelo : a — against the grain.

redor *m.* round mat; en — around.

reducción *f.* reduction; cut, discount; decrease.

reducido *p.p. & adj.* reduced; compact, small.

reducir[26] *v. irr.* to reduce; to diminish; to convert (into); to reset (*a bone*); -se to adapt oneself, adjust oneself; to be constrained, forced.

reedificar[6] *v.* to rebuild, reconstruct.

reelección *f.* re-election.

reelegir[11] *v.* to re-elect.

reembolsar *v.* to reimburse, refund, repay, pay back.

reembolso *m.* reimbursement, refund.

reemitir *v.* to emit again; to issue again; to rebroadcast; to relay (*a broadcast*).

reemplazable *adj.* replaceable.

reemplazar[9] *v.* to replace; to substitute.

reemplazo *m.* replacement; substitute, substitution.

refacción *f.* light lunch, refreshment; repair, reparation; *Am.* spare part; *Am.* help, aid, loan.

refajo *m.* underskirt; short skirt.

referencia *f.* reference; narration, account.

referente *adj.* referring.

referir[3] *v. irr.* to refer; to narrate; to relate; -se to refer (to), relate (to).

refinamiento *m.* refinement.

refinar *v.* to refine; to purify.

refinería *f.* refinery.

reflector *m.* reflector; floodlight.

reflejar *v.* to reflect; to think over; -se to be reflected.

reflejo *m.* reflection, image; reflex; *adj.* reflected; reflex.

reflexión *f.* reflection; meditation, consideration.

reflexionar *v.* to reflect, meditate, think over.

reflexivo *adj.* reflexive; reflective, thoughtful.

reflujo *m.* ebb; ebb tide.

reforma *f.* reform; reformation; improvement.

reformador *m.* reformer.

reformar *v.* to reform; to correct, amend; to improve; -se to reform.

reformista *m. & f.* reformer.

reforzar[2,9] *v. irr.* to reinforce; to strengthen.

refracción *f.* refraction.

refractario *adj.* refractory; impervious; rebellious, unruly; stubborn.

refrán *m.* popular proverb or saying.

refrenar *v.* to restrain, keep in check; to curb; to rein.

refrendar *v.* to legalize by signing; to countersign (*confirm by another signature*); — un pasaporte to visé a passport.

refrescante *adj.* refreshing.

refrescar[6] *v.* to refresh, renew; to cool; to get cool (*said of the weather*); -se to cool off; to take the fresh air; to take a cooling drink or refreshment; *Am.* to take an afternoon refreshment.

refresco *m.* refreshment.

refresquería *f. Am.* refreshment shop, outdoor refreshment stand.

refriega *f.* strife, fray, scuffle.

refrigeración *f.* refrigeration; light meal or refreshment.

refrigerador *m. Am.* refrigerator, freezer; *adj.* refrigerating, freezing; refreshing.

refrigerio *m.,* refreshment; relief, comfort; coolness.

refuerzo *m.* reinforcement.

refugiado *m.* refugee; *p.p. of refugiar.*

refugiar *v.* to shelter; -se to take shelter or refuge.

refugio *m.* refuge, shelter.

refulgente *adj.* refulgent, radiant, shining.

refundir *v.* to remelt, refound, recast (*metals*); to recast, rewrite, reconstruct.

refunfuñar *v.* to grumble, mumble, growl, mutter.

refunfuño *m.* grumble, growl; refunfuñón *adj.* grouchy; grumbly, grumbling.

refutar *v.* to refute.

regadío *adj.* irrigable, that can be irrigated; irrigated; *m.* irrigated land; tierras de — irrigable lands.

regalar *v.* to give, present as a gift; to regale, entertain; to delight, please; -se to treat oneself well, live a life of ease.

regalo *m.* present, gift; pleasure, delight; dainty, delicacy; luxury, comfort.

regañadientes : a — much against one's wishes; unwillingly.

regañar *v.* to growl; to grumble; to quarrel; to scold.

regaño *m.* scolding, reprimand.

regañón *adj.* grumbling; scolding; quarrelsome; *m.* growler, grumbler, scolder.

regar[1,7] *v. irr.* to irrigate; to water; to sprinkle, scatter, *Am.* to spill, throw off (*said of a horse*); **-se** *Am.* to scatter, disperse (*said of a group, herd, etc.*).

regatear *v.* to haggle, bargain; to dispute; to sell at retail; to race (*in a regatta or boat race*).

regazo *m.* lap.

regentar *v.* to direct, conduct, manage; **— una cátedra** to teach a course (*at a university*).

regente *m.* regent; manager; *adj.* ruling.

regidor *m.* councilman, alderman; *adj.* governing, ruling.

régimen *m.* regime; government, rule, management; **— lácteo** milk diet.

regimiento *m.* regiment; administration; municipal council; position of alderman.

regio *adj.* regal, royal; splendid, magnificent.

región *f.* region.

regir[5,11] *v. irr.* to rule, govern; to direct, manage; to be in force (*said of a law*); to move (*said of the bowels*).

registrador *m.* registrar, recorder; city clerk, official in charge of records; inspector (*in a customhouse*); searcher; *adj.* registering; **caja registradora** cash register.

registrar *v.* to examine, inspect, scrutinize; to register, record; **-se** to register, enroll.

registro *m.* search, inspection; registration; census; registration office; register; record; registration certificate; watch regulator; bookmark; organ stop; *Am.* wholesale textile store.

regla *f.* rule; ruler; order; precept, principle; measure, moderation; menstruation; **en —** in order, in due form; **por — general** as a general rule; usually.

reglamento *m.* regulations, rules; rule, bylaw.

regocijado *adj.* joyful, merry, gay; *p.p. of* regocijar.

regocijar *v.* to gladden, delight; **-se** to be glad; to rejoice.

regocijo *m.* joy; rejoicing.

regordete *adj.* plump.

regresar *v.* to return.

regreso *m.* return; **estar de —** to be back.

reguero *m.* stream, rivulet; trickle; irrigation ditch.

regulación *f.* regulation; adjustment.

regulador *m.* regulator; controller; governor (*of a machine*); *adj.* regulating.

regular *v.* to regulate; to adjust; *adj.* regular, ordinary; moderate; fair, medium; **por lo —** as a rule, usually; *adv.* fairly well.

regularidad *f.* regularity.

regularizar[9] *v.* to regulate, make regular.

rehacer[31] *v. irr.* to remake; to make over; to repair; **-se** to recover one's strength; to rally.

rehén *m.* hostage; **en rehenes** as a hostage.

rehuir[32] *v. irr.* to shun, avoid; to shrink (from).

rehusar *v.* to refuse; **-se a** to refuse to.

reina *f.* queen.

reinado *m.* reign.

reinante *adj.* reigning; prevailing.

reinar *v.* to reign; to rule; to prevail.

reincidir *v.* to relapse, slide back (into).

reino *m.* kingdom.

reintegro *m.* reimbursement, refund.

reír[15] *v. irr.* to laugh; **-se de** to laugh at; *Am.* **— de dientes para afuera** to laugh outwardly, laugh hypocritically.

reiterar *v.* to reiterate, repeat.

reja *f.* grate, grating; plowshare (*blade of the plow*); plowing; *Am.* jail.

rejilla *f.* small grating, lattice; small latticed window; fireplace grate; cane upholstery; *Am.* wire dish-cover.

rejuvenecer[13] *v. irr.* to rejuvenate, make young; **-se** to become rejuvenated.

relación *f.* relation; story, account; long speech in a play, *Am.* verse recited alternately by a couple in a folk dance; **-es** personal relations, connections; acquaintances.

relacionar *v.* to relate, connect; **-se** to be related, connected; to become acquainted, establish friendly connections.

relajación *f.*, **relajamiento** *m.* relaxation; laxity; slackening; hernia.

relajar *v.* to relax; to slacken; to release from a vow or oath; **-se** to get a hernia or rupture; to become weakened; to become lax (*said of laws, customs, etc.*).

relamerse *v.* to lick one's lips; to gloat;

to boast; to slick oneself up.

relámpago m. lightning; flash.

relampaguear v. to lighten; to flash; to sparkle.

relampagueo m. flashing; sheet lightning.

relatar v. to relate, narrate.

relativo adj. relative; — a relative to, regarding.

relato m. narration, account, story.

relegar[7] v. to relegate, banish; to postpone; to set aside, put away.

relente m. night dampness; Am. fresh night breeze.

relevar v. to relieve; to release; to absolve; to replace, substitute; to emboss; to make stand out in relief.

relevo m. relief (from a post or military duty; person who relieves another from the performance of a duty).

relicario m. reliquary (small box or casket for keeping relics); Am. locket.

relieve m. relief, embossment, raised work; -s scraps, leftovers; de — in relief; prominent, outstanding; poner de — to make stand out; to emphasize.

religión f. religion.

religiosidad f. religiousness, piety; faithfulness.

religioso adj. religious; faithful; punctual; m. friar, monk.

relinchar v. to neigh.

relincho m. neigh.

reliquia f. relic; vestige; -s relics, remains.

reloj m. clock; watch; — de pulsera wrist watch; — de sol (or — solar) sundial; — despertador alarm clock.

reluciente adj. shining; sparkling.

relucir[13] v. irr. to glitter, sparkle; to shine.

relumbrante adj. brilliant, flashing; resplendent.

relumbrar v. to glare; to glitter.

relumbre m. glare, glitter.

rellenar v. to refill; to fill up; to pad; to stuff.

relleno adj. stuffed; m. meat stuffing; filling.

remachar v. to clinch; to hammer down; to flatten; to rivet; to fix firmly; -se Am. to be tight-lipped, stubbornly silent.

remache m. clinching; fastening, securing; riveting; rivet.

remanente m. remainder, balance; remnant; residue.

remar v. to row; to struggle.

rematado adj. & p.p. finished; sold at auction; loco — completely crazy.

rematar v. to finish; to end; to give the final or finishing stroke; to auction; to fasten (a stitch); Am. to stop (a horse) suddenly; Am. to buy or sell at auction; -se to be finished, be completely destroyed or ruined.

remate m. finish, end; highest bid at an auction; sale at auction; pinnacle, spire; Am. selvage, edge of a fabric; de — absolutely, without remedy; loco de — completely crazy, stark mad.

remedar v. to imitate; to mimic.

remediar v. to remedy; to help; to avoid.

remedio m. remedy; help; amendment; recourse, resort; sin — without help, unavoidable; no tiene — it can't be helped.

remedo m. imitation; mockery.

remembranza f. remembrance, memory.

rememorar v. to remember, call to mind.

remendar[1] v. irr. to mend, patch; to darn; to repair.

remendón m. cobbler, shoe repairman; mender, patcher.

remero m. rower.

remesa f. shipment; remittance, payment.

remesar v. to remit; to ship.

remiendo m. mend; mending; patch; darn; repair; a -s piecemeal, piece by piece.

remilgado adj. prudish, prim, affected.

remilgo m. prudery, primness, affectation.

reminiscencia f. reminiscence.

remisión f. remission; forgiveness; remittance, remitting; abatement, slackening; Am. anything shipped or sent.

remitente m. & f. sender; shipper.

remitir v. to remit; to send; to pardon; to defer; to refer; to abate; -se to defer, yield (to another's judgment).

remo m. oar; hard and long work; al — at the oar; at hard labor.

remojar v. to soak; to steep; Am. to tip, bribe.

remojo m. soaking; steeping; Am. tip, bribe.

remolacha f. beet.

remolcador m. towboat, tug, tugboat; lancha remolcadora tugboat.

remolcar[6] v. irr. to tow, tug; to take (a person) in tow.

remolino m. swirl, whirl; whirlwind; whirlpool; commotion; Am. pin wheel; Am. ventilating wheel (fan); — de gente throng, crowd.

remolón adj. indolent, lazy.

183

remolque *m.* tow; towrope; **llevar a —** to tow; to take in tow.

remontar *v.* to elevate, raise; to resole; to revamp, patch up, repair; *Am.* to go up; *Am.* to go upstream; **-se** to rise; to soar, fly upward; to date (from), go back (to); *Am.* to take to the woods or hills.

rémora *f.* impediment, obstacle, hindrance.

remordimiento *m.* remorse.

remoto *adj.* remote, distant; improbable.

remover[2] *v. irr.* to remove; to dismiss; to stir.

rempujar *v.* to jostle, push.

rempujón *m.* jostle, push.

remuda *f.* change; substitution; replacement; change of clothes; spare tire; relay of horses; *Am.* spare horse, spare pack animal.

remudar *v.* to change; to replace.

remuneración *f.* remuneration, compensation, pay, reward.

remunerar *v.* to remunerate, compensate, pay, reward (*for services*).

renacer[13] *v. irr.* to be reborn; to spring up, grow up again.

renacimiento *m.* renascence, renaissance; revival; rebirth.

renco *adj.* lame.

rencor *m.* rancor, resentment, hatred, grudge.

rencoroso *adj.* resentful, spiteful.

rendición *f.* surrender; submission; yield, profit.

rendido *p.p. & adj.* tired out, fatigued; devoted; obsequious, servile.

rendija *f.* crack, crevice.

rendimiento *m.* yield, output, profit; surrender, submission; fatigue.

rendir[5] *v. irr.* to subdue; to surrender, hand over; to yield, produce; to fatigue; to render, do (*homage*); *Am.* **— la jornada** to end or suspend the day's work; **-se** to surrender, give up; to become fatigued, worn out.

renegado *m.* renegade, traitor; *adj.* renegade, disloyal; wicked.

renegar[1,7] *v. irr.* to deny insistently; to detest; to blaspheme, cúrse; **— de** to deny, renounce (*one's faith*); *Am.* to hate, protest against.

renglón *m.* line (*written or printed*); item; *Am.* line of business, specialty.

renombrado *adj.* renowned, famous.

renombre *m.* renown, fame.

renovación *f.* renovation, restoration; renewal.

renovar[2] *v. irr.* to renovate; to renew; to replace.

renquear *v.* to limp.

renta *f.* rent, rental; income; revenue.

renuencia *f.* reluctance, unwillingness.

renuente *adj.* reluctant, unwilling.

renuevo *m.* sprout, shoot; renovation, restoration.

renunciar *v.* to renounce; to resign; to refuse; to renege (*fail to follow suit in cards*).

reñidor *adj.* quarrelsome.

reñir[5,19] *v. irr.* to quarrel; to fight; to scold.

reo *adj.* guilty; *m.* culprit, criminal; defendant.

reojo : mirar de — to look out of the corner of one's eye; to look scornfully.

repantigarse[7] *v.* to lounge, stretch out (*in a chair*).

reparación *f.* reparation; repair; indemnity.

reparar *v.* to repair; to regain; to recover; to make amends for, atone for; to remedy; to ward off (*a blow*); *Am.* to rear, buck (*said of horses*); **— en** to observe, notice.

reparo *m.* repair; restoration; observation; notice; doubt, objection; protection; shelter; parry (*fencing*); *Am.* sudden bound or leap of a horse.

repartimiento *m.* distribution, division; assessment.

repartir *v.* to distribute; to allot.

reparto *m.* distribution; mail delivery; cast of characters.

repasar *v.* to review, look over, go over again; to mend (*clothes*); to pass by again.

repaso *m.* review; revision.

repelente *adj.* repellent, repulsive, repugnant.

repeler *v.* to repel; to reject.

repente *m.* sudden movement; *Am.* attack, fit; **de —** suddenly.

repentino *adj.* sudden.

repercutir *v.* to resound, echo back; to rebound; to reflect back (*as light*).

repetición *f.* repetition.

repetido *p.p.* repeated; **repetidas veces** repeatedly, often.

repetir[5] *v. irr.* to repeat; to belch.

repicar[6] *v.* to chime, ring; to mince, chop fine; to sting again, prick again; *Am.* to drum, tap (*with the fingers or heels*); **-se** to be conceited.

repique *m.* chime, ringing, peal; mincing, chopping.

repiquetear *v.* to chime, ring; to jingle; *Am.* to tap (*with fingers or heels*).

repiqueteo *m.* chiming, ringing; jingling, tinkling; *Am.* clicking sound of heels.

repisa *f.* shelf, ledge; sill; wall bracket; — de ventana window sill.

replegar[1, 7] *v. irr.* to fold, pleat; -se to retreat, fall back.

réplica *f.* reply, answer, retort; replica, copy; *Am.* examiner.

replicar[6] *v.* to reply, answer back; to retort.

repliegue *m.* fold, crease, retreat (*of troops*).

repollo *m.* cabbage.

reponer[40] *v. irr.* to replace; to put back; to reply, retort; to restore; -se to recover one's health or fortune; to collect oneself, become calm.

reportaje *m.* newspaper report; reporting.

reportar *v.* to check, control, restrain; to attain, obtain; to bring; to carry; *Am.* to report; -se to control oneself.

reporte *m.* report, news.

repórter, reportero *m.* reporter.

reposado *p.p. & adj.* reposed; quiet, calm; restful.

reposar *v.* to repose; to rest; to lie buried; -se to settle (*said of sediment*).

reposición *f.* replacement; recovery (*of one's health*).

reposo *m.* repose, rest; calm.

repostada *f.* sharp answer, back talk.

reprender *v.* to reprimand, scold.

reprensible *adj.* reprehensible, deserving reproof.

reprensión *f.* reproof, rebuke.

represa *f.* dam; damming, stopping; *Am.* reservoir.

represalia *f.* reprisal.

represar *v.* to bank, dam; to recapture (*a ship*) from the enemy; to repress, check.

representación *f.* representation; play, performance; authority, dignity; petition, plea.

representante *adj.* representing; *m. & f.* representative, actor.

representar *v.* to represent; to declare, state; to express, show; to play, act, perform; -se to imagine, picture to oneself.

representativo *adj.* representative.

represión *f.* repression, control, restraint.

reprimenda *f.* reprimand, rebuke.

reprimir *v.* to repress, check, curb; -se to repress oneself; to refrain.

reprobar[2] *v. irr.* to reprove, blame; to condemn; to flunk, fail.

reprochar *v.* to reproach.

reproche *m.* reproach.

reproducción *f.* reproduction.

reproducir[25] *v. irr.* to reproduce.

reptil *m.* reptile.

república *f.* republic.

republicano *adj. & m.* republican.

repudiar *v.* to repudiate; to disown.

repuesto *m.* stock, supply, provisions; sideboard; de — spare, extra; *p.p.* of **reponer** & *adj.* recovered (*from an illness, loss, fright, etc.*); replaced; restored.

repugnancia *f.* repugnance, disgust; aversion; dislike, reluctance.

repugnante *adj.* repugnant, disgusting, loathsome.

repugnar *v.* to be repugnant; to disgust; to oppose, contradict.

repulido *adj.* polished up, slick; shiny; spruce.

repulsa *f.* repulse; rebuff; rebuke.

repulsar *v.* to repulse, repel, reject.

repulsivo *adj.* repulsive, repugnant.

reputación *f.* reputation.

reputar *v.* to repute.

requebrar[1] *v. irr.* to compliment; to flatter; to flirt with; to court, woo; to break again.

requemado *p.p. & adj.* burned; parched; tanned, sunburnt.

requemar *v.* to parch, dry up; to burn; to overcook; -se to become overheated; to burn inwardly; to get tanned, sunburnt.

requerimiento *m.* requisition; requirement; summons; -s amorous advances, insinuations.

requerir[3] *v. irr.* to require; to need; to summon; to notify; to examine, investigate; — de amores to court, woo.

requesón *m.* cottage cheese.

requiebro *m.* flattery; compliment.

requisito *m.* requirement, requisite; — previo prerequisite.

res *f.* head of cattle; any large animal.

resabio *m.* disagreeable aftertaste; bad habit.

resaca *f.* undertow; surge, surf; redraft (*of a bill of exchange*); *Am.* beating, thrashing; *Am.* mud and slime (*left by a flood*).

resaltar *v.* to stand out; to project, jut out; to rebound, bounce or spring back; to be evident, obvious.

resarcir[10] *v.* to indemnify, compensate, repay; to make amends for; -se to make up for.

resbaladero *m.* slide, slippery place.

resbaladizo *adj.* slippery.

resbalar *v.* to slide; -se to slip; to slide; to skid; **resbalársele a uno una cosa** to let a thing slide off one's back, be impervious to a thing.

resbalón *m.* sudden or violent slip; slide; error; **darse un —** to slip.

resbaloso *adj.* slippery.

rescatar *v.* to ransom; to redeem; to barter, exchange, trade; *Am.* to resell.

rescate *m.* ransom; redemption; barter, exchange.

rescoldo *m.* embers, hot cinders, hot ashes; doubt, scruple.

resecar[6] *v.* to dry up; to parch.

reseco *adj.* very dry; dried up, parched; thin, skinny.

resentimiento *m.* resentment; impairment, damage (*to one's health*).

resentirse[3] *v. irr.* to show resentment, hurt, or grief; to resent; to weaken; to become worse.

reseña *f.* military review; book review; brief account; sign, signal.

reseñar *v.* to review (*a book*); to review (*troops*); to outline briefly, give a short account of.

resero *m. Am.* cowboy, herdsman; *Am.* dealer in livestock.

reserva *f.* reserve; reservation; exception; caution; **a — de** reserving the right to, intending to; **sin —** without reserve, frankly.

reservación *f.* reservation.

reservar *v.* to reserve; to put aside; to postpone; to exempt; to keep secret; **-se** to conserve one's strength, spare oneself (*for another time*).

resfriado *m.* cold (*illness*); *p.p. of* **resfriar**; *adj. Am.* indiscreet.

resfriar[17] *v.* to cool; to chill; **-se** to catch cold; to cool.

resfrío *m.* chill; cold.

resguardar *v.* to guard, defend; to shield; **-se** to guard oneself against; to seek shelter from.

resguardo *m.* defense; security; guarantee; guard.

residencia *f.* residence; office or post of a resident foreign minister; *Am.* luxurious dwelling.

residente *adj.* resident, residing; *m. & f.* resident, dweller; resident foreign minister; *Am.* alien resident.

residir *v.* to reside; to live, dwell; to be inherent, belong (to).

residuo *m.* residue; remainder.

resignación *f.* resignation.

resignar *v.* to resign; to hand over; **-se** to resign oneself.

resina *f.* resin.

resistencia *f.* resistance.

resistente *adj.* resistant; resisting.

resistir *v.* to resist; to tolerate, endure;

-se to resist, struggle.

resolución *f.* resolution; courage, determination; solution; **en —** in brief.

resolver[2, 52] *v. irr.* to resolve, decide; to solve; to dissolve; **-se** to resolve, decide; to be reduced (to), dissolve (into).

resollar[2] *v. irr.* to breathe hard; to pant.

resonar[2] *v. irr.* to resound.

resoplar *v.* to puff, breathe hard; to snort.

resoplido *m.* puff, pant; snort.

resorte *m.* spring; elasticity; means (*to attain an object*); *Am.* elastic, rubber band; *Am.* **no es de mi —** it doesn't concern me.

respaldar *v.* to endorse; to guarantee; *Am.* to back, support; **-se** to lean back; *Am.* to protect one's rear.

respaldo *m.* back (*of a chair or sheet of paper*); protecting wall; endorsement; *Am.* protection, security, guarantee.

respectivo *adj.* respective.

respecto *m.* respect, relation, reference; point, matter; **(con) — a** (*or* **— de**) with respect to, with regard to.

respetable *adj.* respectable.

respetar *v.* to respect.

respeto *m.* respect; reverence, regard; consideration.

respetuoso *adj.* respectful; respectable.

respingar[7] *v.* to buck; to balk (*said of a horse*); to grumble; to curl up (*said of the edge of a garment*).

respingo *m.* buck, balking; muttering, grumbling.

respiración *f.* respiration, breathing.

respirar *v.* to breathe.

respiro *m.* breathing; breath; respite, pause, moment of rest; extension of time (*for payment*).

resplandecer[13] *v. irr.* to shine; to glitter.

resplandeciente *adj.* resplendent, shining.

resplandor *m.* splendor, brilliance, brightness; *Am.* sun's glare.

responder *v.* to respond; to answer; to correspond, harmonize; to answer (for), be responsible (for).

respondón *adj.* saucy, pert, insolent (*in answering*).

responsabilidad *f.* responsibility.

responsable *adj.* responsible.

respuesta *f.* response; answer, reply.

resquebradura, resquebrajadura *f.* fissure, crevice, crack.

resquebrajar = resquebrar.

resquebrar[1] *v. irr.* to crack; to split.

resquicio *m.* crack, slit, crevice; opening; *Am.* vestige, sign, trace.

resta *f.* subtraction (*as an arithmetical*

operation); remainder.

restablecer[13] *v. irr.* to re-establish; to restore; -se to recover.

restante *adj.* remaining; *m.* residue, remainder.

restañar *v.* to stanch (*a wound*); to check the flow of.

restar *v.* to deduct; to subtract; to remain, be left over; to strike back (*a ball*).

restauración *f.* restoration.

restaurante *m.* restaurant.

restaurar *v.* to restore; to recover; to re-establish; to repair.

restitución *f.* restitution, restoration, return.

restituir[32] *v. irr.* to return, give back; to restore.

resto *m.* rest, remainder; stakes at cards; return (*of a tennis ball*); player who returns the ball; -s remains.

restorán *m. Am.* restaurant.

restregar[1,7] *v. irr.* to rub hard; to scrub.

restricción *f.* restriction; restraint; curb; limitation.

restringir[11] *v.* to restrict; to restrain; to limit.

resucitar *v.* to resuscitate, bring to life; to come to life; to revive.

resuelto *p.p. of* **resolver** resolved, determined; *adj.* resolute, bold; quick.

resuello *m.* breath; breathing, panting.

resulta *f.* result; effect, consequence; **de -s** as a result, in consequence.

resultado *m.* result, effect, consequence.

resultante *adj.* resulting; *f.* resultant (*force*).

resultar *v.* to result; to spring, arise as a consequence; to turn out to be; **resulta que** it turns out that.

resumen *m.* résumé, summary; **en —** summing up, in brief.

resumidero *m. Am.* = **sumidero**.

resumir *v.* to summarize, sum up; -se to be reduced or condensed.

resurgir[11] *v.* to arise again; to reappear.

retablo *m.* altarpiece; religious picture hung as a votive offering; series of pictures that tell a story.

retaguardia *f.* rear guard.

retal *m.* remnant.

retar *v.* to challenge, defy; to reprimand, scold; *Am.* to insult.

retardar *v.* to retard, delay.

retazo *m.* remnant; piece; fragment.

retener[45] *v. irr.* to retain; to keep; to withhold; to detain.

retintín *m.* jingle, tinkle; sarcastic tone or ring.

retirada *f.* retreat; withdrawal.

retirado *p.p. & adj.* retired; distant, remote; isolated; pensioned.

retirar *v.* to withdraw; to take away; -se to retire, withdraw; to retreat.

retiro *m.* retreat; retirement; withdrawal; place of refuge; pension of a retired officer.

reto *m.* challenge; defiance; *Am.* scolding; *Am.* insult.

retobado *adj. Am.* saucy; *Am.* stubborn, unruly; *Am.* peevish; *Am.* sly, astute.

retobar *v. Am.* to cover with leather; *Am.* to wrap with leather, oilcloth, or burlap; *Am.* to tan (*leather*); -se *Am.* to rebel, talk back, act saucy; *Am.* to become disagreeable and aloof.

retocar[6] *v.* to retouch; touch up; to finish, perfect.

retoñar *v.* to sprout; to bud; to sprout again; to reappear.

retoño *m.* sprout, shoot; bud.

retoque *m.* retouching; finishing touch.

retorcer[2,10] *v. irr.* to twist; to retort; to distort; -se to wriggle; to squirm.

retorcimiento *m.* twisting; squirming.

retórica *f.* rhetoric.

retornar *v.* to return; to give back.

retorno *m.* return; repayment; barter.

retozar[9] *v.* to gambol, frisk about, frolic, romp; to stir within (*said of passions*).

retozo *m.* frolic; **retozón** *adj.* frisky, playful.

retractarse *v.* to retract, take back one's word.

retraer[46] *v. irr.* to withdraw, draw back, take back; -se de to withdraw from; to keep aloof or away from; to shun.

retraimiento *m.* retirement; reserve, aloofness, shyness.

retranca *f. Am.* brake; **retranquero** *m. Am.* brakeman.

retrancar[6] *v. Am.* to brake, put the brake on; *Am.* **se ha retrancado el asunto** the affair has come to a standstill.

retrasado *p.p. & adj.* behind, behind time; backward; postponed, delayed.

retrasar *v.* to delay, retard; to set back; to go backward; -se to fall behind; to be late, behind time.

retraso *m.* delay.

retratar *v.* to portray; to photograph; to copy, imitate; -se to be portrayed; to be photographed; to be reflected.

retrato *m.* portrait; photograph; copy, imitation; reflection.

retrete *m.* toilet, water closet; place of retreat.

retroceder *v.* to turn back; to fall back,

draw back; to recede.

retroceso *m.* retrogression, backward step; retreat; setback, relapse.

retruécano *m.* pun.

retumbar *v.* to resound; to rumble.

retumbo *m.* loud echo or sound; rumble (*of thunder, cannon, etc.*).

reuma *m. & f.*, **reumatismo** *m.* rheumatism.

reunión *f.* reunion; meeting.

reunir *v.* to reunite; to unite; to group; to gather; to assemble; to collect; -se to meet, assemble; to reunite.

revancha *f.* revenge; return game or match.

revelación *f.* revelation.

revelador *adj.* revealing; *m.* developer (*in photography*).

revelar *v.* to reveal; to. develop (*a film*).

revendedor *m.* retailer; reseller; ticket scalper.

reventa *f.* resale.

reventar[1] *v. irr.* to burst; to burst forth; to explode; to smash; to fatigue, exhaust; to bother; -se to burst; to blow out, explode.

reventón *m.* burst, bursting; blowout; steep hill; hard work, toil; *adj.* bursting.

reverdecer[13] *v. irr.* to grow fresh and green again; to gain new strength and vigor.

reverencia *f.* reverence; bow.

reverenciar *v.* to revere, venerate.

reverendo *adj.* reverend; *Am.* large, big (*ironically*).

reverente *adj.* reverent.

reverso *m.* reverse; back side.

revertir[3] *v. irr.* to revert.

revés *m.* reverse; back, wrong side; back stroke or slap; backhanded thrust (*in fencing*); misfortune; **al —** backwards; wrong side out; in the opposite way; from left to right.

revestir[5] *v. irr.* to dress, clothe; to coat, cover with a coating; -se to dress, put on an outer garment or vestment; to be invested (*with power, authority, etc.*); -se de paciencia to arm oneself with patience.

revisar *v.* to revise; to review; to examine, inspect.

revisión *m.* revision; review (*of a case*), new trial.

revisor *m.* corrector; inspector, overseer.

revista *f.* review; inspection; magazine, journal; second trial or hearing; **pasar —** to pass in review; to examine carefully; to review (*troops*).

revistar *v.* to review, inspect (*troops*).

revivir *v.* to revive.

revocación *f.* repeal, cancellation.

revocar[6] *v.* to revoke, repeal.

revolcar[6] *v.* to knock down; to turn over and over; to floor, defeat; to flunk, fail; -se to wallow; to roll over and over; to flounder.

revolotear *v.* to fly about, flutter around; to hover; to circle around.

revoltijo, **revoltillo** *m.* jumble, mixture, mess; tangle, muddle; **revoltillo de huevos** scrambled eggs.

revoltoso *adj.* turbulent, unruly, rebellious; mischievous; intricate; *m.* agitator, troublemaker; rebel.

revolución *f.* revolution.

revolucionario *adj.* revolutionary; *m.* revolutionist, revolutionary.

revolver[2] *v. irr.* to revolve; to turn over; to stir up; to mix up; to turn around swiftly (*a horse*); -se to move back and forth; to roll over and over; to change (*said of the weather*).

revólver *m.* revolver, pistol.

revuelo *m.* whirl; stir, commotion; flying around.

revuelta *f.* revolt, revolution; second turn; turn, bend; quarrel, fight; *Am.* sudden turning of a horse.

revuelto *p.p. of* **revolver** *& adj.* confused; mixed up; intricate, complicated; choppy (*sea*); changeable (*weather*); **huevos —s** scrambled eggs.

rey *m.* king.

reyerta *f.* quarrel, dispute.

rezagado *adj.* back, behind; *m.* straggler, slow poke, latecomer.

rezagar[7] *v.* to leave behind; to separate (*the weak cattle*) from the herd; *Am.* to reserve, set aside; -se to lag behind.

rezar[9] *v.* to pray; to say or recite (*a prayer*); to mutter, grumble; **así lo reza el libro** so the book says; **eso no reza conmigo** that has nothing to do with me.

rezo *m.* prayer.

rezongar[7] *v.* to grumble, growl, mutter.

rezongón *adj.* growling, grumbling; *m.* grumbler, growler; scolder.

rezumar *v.* to ooze; to leak; **se rezuma** it oozes, it seeps through.

ría *f.* mouth of a river, estuary.

riachuelo *m.* rivulet, brook.

ribazo *m.* bank, ridge.

ribera *f.* shore, bank, beach.

ribereño *adj.* of, pertaining to, or living on, a river bank.

ribete *m.* trimming, border, edge, binding; addition; **tiene sus —s de poeta** he is something of a poet.

ribetear v. to bind, put a binding on; to border, trim the edge or border of.

ricacho adj. quite rich (often said sarcastically); **ricachón** adj. extremely rich, disgustingly rich.

rico adj. rich, wealthy; delicious; exquisite; **ricote** = ricacho.

ridiculizar v. to ridicule, deride.

ridículo adj. ridiculous; queer, strange; m. ridicule; ridiculous situation; **hacer el —** to be ridiculous; to act the fool.

riego m. irrigation; watering.

riel m. rail; **-es** track, railroad track.

rienda f. rein, bridle; moderation, restraint; **a — suelta** with free rein, without restraint; violently, swiftly; **soltar la —** to let loose, act without restraint; **tirar las -s** to draw rein, tighten the reins; to restrain.

riente adj. laughing, smiling.

riesgo m. risk.

rifa f. raffle; scuffle, quarrel.

rifar v. to raffle; to scuffle, quarrel.

rifle m. rifle.

rigidez f. rigidity, stiffness; severity, strictness.

rígido adj. rigid, stiff; severe, strict.

rigor m. rigor; severity; harshness; rigidity, stiffness; **en —** in reality; strictly; **ser de —** to be absolutely indispensable, be required by custom.

rigoroso, riguroso adj. rigorous; harsh; severe; strict.

rima f. rhyme; **-s** poems.

rimar v. to rhyme.

rimbombante adj. high-sounding; resounding.

rimero m. pile, heap.

rincón m. corner; nook; Am. narrow valley.

rinconada f. corner; nook.

rinconera f. corner cupboard, corner table, corner bracket.

ringlera f. tier, row, line.

rinoceronte m. rhinoceros.

riña f. quarrel, dispute, fight.

riñón m. kidney; center, interior.

río m. river.

ripio m. rubble, stone or brick fragments; padding (in a verse, speech, etc.), useless word.

riqueza f. riches; wealth.

risa f. laugh; laughter; **reventar de —** to burst with laughter; **tomar a —** to take lightly to laugh off.

risada f. gale of laughter, loud laugh.

risco m. rocky cliff, crag; honey fritter.

risible adj. laughable, ridiculous.

risotada f. guffaw, big laugh.

ristra f. string (of onions, garlic, etc.); series, row.

risueño adj. smiling; pleasant; delightful.

rítmico adj. rhythmical.

ritmo m. rhythm.

rito m. rite, ceremony.

rival m. & f. rival, competitor; enemy.

rivalidad f. rivalry, competition; enmity.

rivalizar v. to rival, compete.

rizado p.p. curled, adj. wavy, curly; m. curling; curls.

rizar v. to curl; to ripple; to ruffle, gather into ruffles; **-se** to curl one's hair; to curl.

rizo m. curl; adj. curly; **rizoso** adj. curly.

roano adj. roan (red, bay or chestnut-colored, mixed with white; applied to a horse).

robar v. to rob, steal; to abduct, kidnap.

roble m. oak tree; oak wood; **robledal, robledo** m. oak grove.

robo m. robbery, theft; loot, plunder.

robusto adj. robust, vigorous.

roca f. rock, boulder; rocky cliff, crag.

rocalloso adj. rocky.

roce m. graze; friction; contact; **no tener — con** to have no contact with (a person).

rociada f. sprinkling; spray; dew; sprinkle, shower; volley of harsh words.

rociar v. to sprinkle; to spray; to fall (said of dew).

rocín m. nag, hack; draft horse; coarse, ill-bred man; Am. riding horse.

rocío m. dew; sprinkle; shower; spray; adj. Am. reddish, roan (horse).

rocoso adj. rocky.

rodada f. rut, wheel track; Am. tumble, fall.

rodado adj. dapple (horse); p.p. of rodar.

rodadura f. rolling; rut; **— del neumático** tire tread.

rodaja f. disk; small wheel; round slice.

rodar v. irr. to roll; to revolve; to roam, wander about; to fall down (rolling); Am. **— a patadas** to kick down.

rodear v. to go around; to go by a roundabout way; to surround, encircle; Am. to round up (cattle).

rodela f. round shield; Am. padded ring for carrying loads on the head; Am. round slice; Am. kettle lid; Am. hoop; Am. game of rolling a hoop.

rodeo m. detour, roundabout way; circumlocution, roundabout expression; dodge, evasion; corral, stockyard; rodeo, roundup.

rodilla f. knee; **de -s** on one's knees;

hincarse de -s to kneel down.

rodillo *m.* roller; rolling pin; road roller.

roer[51] *v. irr.* to gnaw; to corrode, eat away; to torment, harass.

rogar[2, 7] *v. irr.* to pray, beg, beseech; **hacerse de —** to let oneself be coaxed.

rojez *f.* redness.

rojizo *adj.* reddish.

rojo *adj.* red; red, radical.

rojura *f.* redness.

rollizo *adj.* plump; *m.* log.

rollo *m.* roll; bundle; rolling pin; log.

romadizo *m.* nasal catarrh, head cold.

romance *adj.* Romance, Romanic (*language*); *m.* Romance language; Spanish language; romance, chivalric novel; ballad; eight-syllable meter with even verses rhyming in assonance; **en buen — in** plain language.

románico *adj.* Romanesque (*architecture*); Romance (*language*).

romano *adj.* & *m.* Roman.

romanticismo *m.* romanticism.

romántico *adj.* romantic; sentimental; *m.* romantic; sentimentalist.

romería *f.* pilgrimage.

romero *m.* pilgrim; rosemary (*shrub*).

romo *adj.* blunt; snub-nosed.

rompecabezas *m.* puzzle, riddle.

rompeolas *m.* breakwater, mole.

rompe: de — y rasga resolute, bold; **al —** *Am.* suddenly.

romper[52] *v.* to break; to shatter; to tear; to wear through; *Am.* to leave suddenly or on the run; **— el alba** to dawn; **— a** to start to; **-se** to break.

rompiente *m.* shoal, sand bank, reef; **-s** breakers, surf.

rompimiento *m.* rupture, break; crack; breach; quarrel.

ron *m.* rum.

roncar[6] *v.* to snore; to roar; to brag.

ronco *adj.* hoarse; harsh-sounding.

roncha *f.* hive; welt.

ronda *f.* patrol; night serenaders; round (*of a game, of drinks, etc.*); *Am.* ring-around-a-rosy (*a children's game*); **hacer la —** a to court; *Am.* to surround, trap (*an animal*).

rondar *v.* to go around, hover around; to patrol; to make the rounds; to serenade.

ronquera *f.* hoarseness.

ronquido *m.* snore; snort.

ronronear *v.* to purr.

ronroneo *m.* purr.

ronzal *m.* halter.

roña *f.* scab, mange; filth; infection; stinginess; trickery; *Am.* ill will; grudge; *Am.* **hacer —** to fake an illness.

roñoso *adj.* scabby, mangy; dirty; stingy; *Am.* spiteful; *Am.* faint-hearted, cowardly.

ropa *f.* clothing, clothes; **— blanca** linen; **— vieja** old clothes; stew made from leftover meat; **a quema —** at close range (*when shooting*); suddenly, without warning.

ropaje *m.* clothes, clothing, apparel; robe.

ropero *m.* clothier; wardrobe, clothes-press; wardrobe keeper; *Am.* clothes rack.

roqueño *adj.* rocky; hard, like rock.

rosa *f.* rose; red spot on the skin; rose color; *Am.* rosebush; **— de los vientos** (*or* **— náutica**) mariner's compass.

rosado *adj.* rosy, rose-colored; frosted (*drink*); *Am.* roan, reddish-brown (*horse*).

rosal *m.* rosebush.

rosario *m.* rosary; **— de desdichas** chain of misfortunes.

rosbif *m.* roast beef.

rosca *f.* screw and nut; screw thread; spiral, twist; ring-shaped roll; *Am.* ring-shaped cushion (*for carrying loads on the head*); *Am.* circle of card players.

roseta *f.* rosette; small rose; **-s** popcorn; **rosetón** *m.* large rosette; rose window.

rosillo *adj.* light red; roan (*horse*).

rostro *m.* face; **hacer —** to face.

rota *f.* rout, defeat; ship's course; Rota (*ecclesiastical court*); rattan palm tree.

rotación *f.* rotation.

rotatorio *adj.* rotary.

roto *p.p. irr.* of **romper** & *adj.* broken; shattered; torn; worn out, ragged; *m. Am.* person of the poorer class.

rótulo *m.* title, inscription; label.

rotular *v.* to label; to letter.

rotundo *adj.* round; sonorous; **una negativa rotunda** a flat denial.

rotura *f.* breach, opening; break; tear, rip; rupture; fracture.

roturar *v.* to break ground; to plow (*new ground*).

rozadura *f.* friction; chafe; chafing.

rozamiento *m.* friction; rubbing.

rozar[9] *v.* to graze; to scrape; to chafe; to clear of underbrush; **-se con alguien** to have connections, contact, or dealings with someone.

rozón *m.* graze, sudden or violent scrape; short, broad scythe.

ruano = roano.

rubí *m.* ruby.

rubicundo *adj.* reddish; ruddy, healthy red; reddish-blonde.

rubio *adj.* blond, blonde.

rubor *m.* blush; bashfulness, shyness.

ruborizarse *v.* to blush; to feel ashamed.

rúbrica *f.* scroll, flourish (*added to a signature*); title, heading; **de —** according to ritual, rule or custom.

rucio *adj.* grey (*horse or donkey*); **—rodado** dapple-grey

rudeza *f.* rudeness; coarseness; roughness.

rudo *adj.* rude; coarse; rough; stupid.

rueca *f.* distaff (*used for spinning*).

rueda *f.* wheel; circle, group; round slice; spread of a peacock's tail; **en —** in turn; in a circle; **hacer la — a** to court; to flatter.

ruedo *m.* circuit, tour; border, rim; circumference.

ruego *m.* prayer, supplication, request.

rufián *m.* ruffian; bully.

rugido *m.* roar; rumbling.

rugir[11] *v.* to roar; to bellow.

rugoso *adj.* wrinkled; furrowed.

ruibarbo *m.* rhubarb.

ruidazo *m.* big noise.

ruido *m.* noise; din; dispute; talk, rumor; **hacer** (*o* **meter**) **—** to make a noise; to create a sensation; to cause a disturbance.

ruidoso *adj.* noisy; loud; sensational.

ruin *adj.* vile, base, mean; small, petty; puny; stingy; vicious (*animal*).

ruina *f.* ruin; destruction; downfall.

ruindad *f.* baseness; meanness; stinginess; mean or vile act.

ruinoso *adj.* ruinous; in a state of ruin or decay.

ruiseñor *m.* nightingale.

rumba *f.* *Am.* rumba (*dance and music*); *Am.* spree; *Am.* **irse de —** to go on a spree.

rumbear *v.* *Am.* to head (towards), take a certain direction; *Am.* to cut a path through a forest; *Am.* to go on a spree.

rumbo *m.* direction, course, route; pomp; ostentation; *Am.* cut on the head; *Am.* revel, noisy spree; **hacer — a** to head or sail towards; *Am.* **ir al —** to be going in the right direction, be on the right track.

rumboso *adj.* pompous, ostentatious; generous.

rumiar *v.* to ruminate; to chew the cud; to ponder, meditate.

rumor *m.* rumor, report; murmur; rumble.

runfla *f.* series (*of things of the same kind*); sequence (*in cards*).

runrún *m.* rumor; murmur.

ruptura *f.* rupture; break; fracture.

rural *adj.* rural.

ruso *adj.* Russian; *m.* Russian; Russian language.

rústico *adj.* rustic, rural; crude, coarse; *m.* peasant; **en** (*o* **a la**) **rústica** unbound, paper-bound.

ruta *f.* route, course, way.

rutina *f.* routine.

S

sábado *m.* Saturday.

sábana *f.* bed sheet; altar cloth.

sabana *f.* *Am.* savanna, treeless plain; *Am.* **ponerse en la —** to become suddenly rich.

sabandija *f.* small reptile; small lizard.

sabañón *m.* chilblain.

sabedor *adj.* knowing; aware, informed.

saber[42] *v. irr.* to know; to know how to, be able to; to learn, find out; *Am.* to be in the habit of; **— a** to taste of, taste like; **sabe bien** it tastes good; **a —** namely; that is; *Am.* **¡a — si venga!** who knows whether he will come!; **un no sé qué** an indefinable something; **¿sabe Vd. a la plaza?** do you know the way to the square?; *m.* knowledge, learning.

sabiduría *f.* wisdom; knowledge.

sabiendas : a — consciously, knowingly.

sabio *adj.* wise; judicious; learned; *m.* savant, scholar; sage, wise man.

sable *m.* saber; **sablazo** *m.* blow with a saber; saber wound; **dar un sablazo** to strike for a loan.

sabor *m.* savor, taste, flavor.

saborear *v.* to savor, flavor, season; to relish, taste with pleasure; to enjoy; **-se** to eat or drink with relish; to smack one's lips.

sabotaje *m.* sabotage.

sabotear *v.* to sabotage.

sabroso *adj.* savory, tasty; delicious; delightful.

sabueso *m.* hound.

sacabocados *m.* punch (*tool*).

sacacorchos *m.* corkscrew.

sacamuelas *m. & f.* tooth puller; quack dentist.

sacar[6] *v.* to draw, draw out, pull out, get out, or take out; to get, obtain; to infer; to make (*a copy*); to take (*a snapshot or picture*); to stick out (*one's tongue*); to serve (*a ball*); **— a bailar** to ask to dance, lead on to the dance floor; **— a luz** to publish; **— el cuerpo** to dodge; **— en claro** (*or* **— en limpio**) to deduce, conclude; *Am.* **— el sombrero** to take off one's hat; *Am.* **¡sáquese de allí!** get out of there!

sacerdocio m. priesthood.

sacerdote m. priest.

saciar v. to satiate, satisfy; **-se** to be satiated, satisfied completely.

saco m. sack, bag; sackful, bagful; loose-fitting coat; sack, plundering; *Am.* suit coat; **— de noche** overnight bag, satchel.

sacramento m. sacrament.

sacrificar[6] v. to sacrifice.

sacrificio m. sacrifice.

sacrilegio m. sacrilege.

sacrílego adj. sacrilegious.

sacristán m. sacristan, sexton; *Am.* busybody, meddler.

sacro adj. sacred.

sacrosanto adj. sacrosanct, holy and sacred.

sacudida f. shake, jolt, jerk.

sacudimiento m. shaking; shake, jerk; shock, jolt.

sacudir v. to shake; to jerk; to beat; to beat the dust from; to shake off; **-se** to shake oneself; to brush oneself off; **-se de alguien** to shake someone off, get rid of someone.

sádico adj. sadistic, cruel.

saeta f. arrow, dart.

sagacidad f. sagacity.

sagaz adj. sagacious, shrewd.

sagrado adj. sacred; consecrated; m. asylum, refuge.

sahumar v. to perfume with incense; to fumigate.

sahumerio m. vapor, fume; incense; burning of incense; fumigation.

sainete m. one-act comedy or farce; delicacy, tasty tidbit; flavor, relish; sauce.

sajón adj. & m. Saxon.

sal f. salt; wit, humor; grace; *Am.* misfortune, bad luck.

sala f. parlor; hall, large room; **— de justicia** courtroom.

salado adj. salty; salted; witty; charming; *Am.* costly; *Am.* **estar —** to be unlucky; m. *Am.* salt pit, salt mine.

salar v. to salt; to cure or preserve with salt; *Am.* to bring bad luck (to); *Am.* to dishonor; *Am.* to ruin, spoil; *Am.* to bribe; *Am.* to feed salt to cattle; m. *Am.* salt pit.

salario m. salary, wages.

salchicha f. sausage; **salchichón** m. large sausage.

saldar v. to balance, settle (*an account*).

saldo m. balance, settlement (*of an account*); bargain sale.

saledizo = salidizo.

salero m. saltcellar, saltshaker; place for storing salt; salt lick; wit, grace, charm; *Am.* salt dealer.

salida f. departure; exit; sally; outlet; way out; loophole; outskirts; outcome; jut, projection; outlay, expenditure; witty remark; **— de pie de banco** silly remark, nonsense; **— del sol** sunrise; *Am.* **— de teatro** evening wrap.

salidizo m. jut, ledge, projection; adj. salient, jutting, projecting.

saliente adj. salient, standing out; projecting; m. salient, salient angle; jut, projection.

salina f. salt mine or pit; salt works.

salir[43] v. irr. to go out; to leave, depart; to get out (of); to come out; to sprout; to come (from); to turn out to be; **— bien** to turn out well; to come out well; **— a su padre** to turn out to be or look like his father; *Am.* **— a mano** to come out even; **-se** to get out, slip out; to leak out; **-se con la suya** to get one's own way.

salitral m. saltpeter bed or mine.

salitre m. saltpeter; **salitrera** f. saltpeter mine or bed; **salitroso** adj. nitrous, abounding in saltpeter.

saliva f. saliva.

salmo m. psalm.

salmodiar v. to chant; to talk in a monotone or singsong.

salmón m. salmon.

salmuera f. brine.

salobre adj. briny, salty.

salón m. salon, hall, large room; salted meat or fish.

salpicadura f. spatter, splash.

salpicar[6] v. to sprinkle, spray, spatter.

salpimentar[1] v. irr. to salt and pepper.

salpimienta f. salt and pepper.

salpullido m. rash, skin eruption.

salsa f. sauce; gravy; *Am.* sound whipping or beating; **salsera** f. sauce dish.

saltamontes m. grasshopper.

saltar v. to jump; to jump over; to leap; to bounce; to skip; to burst, break into pieces; to come off; **— a la vista** to be obvious, evident; **— a tierra** to disembark, land; *Am.* **— las trancas** to lose one's patience; to lose one's head.

salteador m. bandit, highway robber.

saltear v. to assault, attack; to hold up, rob; to take by surprise; to jump or skip around.

salto m. jump; leap; precipice; gap; **— de agua** waterfall; **a -s** by jumps; **en un** (*or* **de un**) **—** in a jiffy, quickly; **dar un —** to jump, leap.

saltón adj. jumping, skipping, hopping; jumpy; protruding; Am. half-cooked; ojos -es popeyes, bulging eyes; m. grasshopper.

salubre adj. healthy, healthful.

salubridad f. healthfulness, health; sanitation.

salud f. health; welfare; salvation; ¡ — ! greetings!; your health!

saludable adj. wholesome, healthful, beneficial.

saludador m. greeter; healer; quack.

saludar v. to salute, greet; to fire a salute.

saludo m. salute, nod, greeting.

salutación f. salutation; greeting.

salva f. salvo, salute with guns; greeting, welcome.

salvación f. salvation.

salvado m. bran.

salvador m. savior, rescuer; Savior; adj. saving.

salvaguardar v. to safeguard, defend, protect.

salvaguardia m. safeguard, protection; guard; f. safe-conduct paper, passport; password.

salvajada f. savage act or remark.

salvaje adj. savage; wild; m. savage.

salvajez f. wildness, savagery.

salvajismo m. savagery; Am. savage act or remark. Ses salvajada.

salvamento m. salvation, rescue; place of safety; salvage (rescue of property); bote de — lifeboat.

salvar v. to save; to clear, jump over; to except, exclude; -se to be saved; to save oneself, escape.

salvavidas m. life preserver; lancha — lifeboat.

¡salve! interj. hail!; Salve f. Salve Regina, prayer to the Virgin Mary.

salvia f. sage (a plant).

salvo adj. saved; safe; prep. save, except, but; a — safe, without injury; en — in safety; out of danger.

salvoconducto m. safe-conduct, pass.

san adj. (contr. of santo) saint.

sánalotodo m. cure-all.

sanar v. to heal, cure; to recover, get well.

sanatorio m. sanitarium.

sanción f. sanction.

sancionar v. to sanction; to authorize, ratify.

sandalia f. sandal.

sandez f. stupidity; folly; foolish remark.

sandía f. watermelon.

sandio adj. silly, foolish.

saneamiento m. sanitation; drainage of land.

sanear v. to make sanitary (land, property, etc.); to drain, dry up (land).

sangrar v. to bleed; to drain; to tap (a tree); to pilfer; to exploit (someone); to indent (a line).

sangre f. blood; — fría calmness, coolness of mind; a fría in cold blood.

sangriento adj. bleeding; bloody; bloodstained; bloodthirsty, cruel.

sanguijuela f. leech.

sanguinario adj. bloody, cruel; bloodthirsty, murderous.

sanidad f. health; soundness; healthfulness; sanitation.

sanitario adj. sanitary.

sano adj. sound, healthy; healthful; safe; sane, sensible; whole, unbroken; undamaged; — y salvo safe and sound.

sanseacabó that's all; that's the end.

santiamén en un — in a jiffy.

santidad f. sanctity, holiness, saintliness; su Santidad his Holiness.

santificar v. to sanctify; to consecrate.

santiguar v. to bless; to make the sign of the cross; to beat, hit, punish; -se to cross oneself; to show astonishment (by crossing oneself).

santísimo adj. most holy; m. the Holy Sacrament.

santo adj. saintly, holy; sacred; esperar todo el — día to wait the whole blessed day; — y bueno well and good; Am. ¡santa palabra! that's my final and last word!; m. saint; saint's day; Am. tener el — de espaldas to have a streak of bad luck; santurrón m. religious hypocrite, affectedly pious person.

santuario m. sanctuary; Am. buried treasure; Am. Indian idol.

saña f. fury, rage.

sañudo adj. furious, enraged.

sapo m. toad; Am. despicable little man; Am. chubby person; Am. sly person; echar -s y culebras to swear, curse.

saque m. serve, service (in tennis); server.

saquear v. to sack, plunder, pillage, loot.

saqueo m. sacking, pillaging, plunder; loot, booty.

saquillo m. small bag, handbag, satchel.

sarampión m. measles.

sarao m. soirée, evening party.

sarape m. Am. serape, blanket.

sarcasmo m. sarcasm.

sarcástico adj. sarcastic.

sardina f. sardine.

sargento m. sergeant.

sarmentoso *adj.* vinelike; full of vine shoots; gnarled, knotty.

sarmiento *m.* shoot or branch of a vine.

sarna *f.* itch; mange.

sarnoso *adj.* itchy, scabby, mangy.

sarpullido = **salpullido.**

sarro *m.* tartar (*on teeth*); crust, sediment (*in utensils*).

sarta *f.* string (*of beads*); series.

sartén *f.* frying pan.

sastre *m.* tailor.

satánico *adj.* satanic, devilish.

satélite *m.* satellite.

satén *m.* sateen.

sátira *f.* satire.

satírico *adj.* satirical.

satirizar[9] *v.* to satirize.

satisfacción *f.* satisfaction; apology, excuse; **tomar —** to vindicate oneself; to take revenge; **dar una —** to offer an apology; to apologize.

satisfacer[31] *v. irr.* to satisfy; to pay (*a debt*); **— una letra** to honor a draft; **-se** to be satisfied; to take satisfaction.

satisfactorio *adj.* satisfactory.

satisfecho *p.p.* of **satisfacer** satisfied, gratified; *adj.* content, contented.

saturar *v.* to saturate; to satiate.

sauce *m.* willow.

savia *f.* sap.

saxófono *m.* saxophone.

sazón *f.* season, opportune moment; ripeness; taste, flavor; **a la —** then, at that time; **en —** in season; ripe; opportunely; *adj. Am.* ripe.

sazonado *adj. & p.p.* seasoned; mellow, ripe; expressive (*said of a phrase*).

sazonar *v.* to season; to flavor; **-se** to become seasoned; to ripen, mature.

se *obj. pron.* (*before* **le, la, lo, las,** *and* **los**) to him, to her; to you (*formal*); to them; *refl. pron.* himself, herself, yourself (*formal*), yourselves (*formal*), themselves; *reciprocal pron.* each other, one another.

sebo *m.* tallow, fat.

secante *adj.* drying, blotting; **papel —** blotter; *f.* secant (*math.*).

secar[6] *v.* to dry; to wipe dry; **-se** to dry or wipe oneself; to dry up; to wither; to get thin.

sección *f.* section; division; cutting.

seccionar *v.* to section.

seco *adj.* dry; dried; withered; harsh; abrupt; plain, unadorned; **en —** on dry land, out of the water; **parar en —** to stop short, stop suddenly; **a secas** plain; alone, without anything else; *Am.* simply, straight to the point; **comer pan a secas** to eat just bread;

Am. **bailar a secas** to dance without musical accompaniment.

secreción *f.* secretion.

secretar *v.* to secrete.

secretaría *f.* secretary's office; position of secretary.

secretario *m.* secretary; confidant; **secretaria** *f.* woman secretary; secretary's wife.

secretear *v.* to whisper; **-se** to whisper to each other.

secreto *adj.* secret, hidden; secretive; *m.* secret; secrecy; secret place; **— a voces** open secret; **en —** secretly; **hablar en —** to whisper.

secta *f.* sect.

secuaz *m.* partisan, follower.

secuela *f.* sequel, outcome, consequence.

secuencia *f.* sequence.

secuestrador *m.* kidnapper; confiscator.

secuestrar *v.* to seize; to kidnap; to confiscate.

secuestro *m.* kidnapping; seizure.

secular *adj.* secular; lay, worldly; centennial; *m.* secular, secular priest.

secundar *v.* to second, favor, back up.

secundario *adj.* secondary.

sed *f.* thirst; craving, desire; **tener —** to be thirsty.

seda *f.* silk; **como una —** soft as silk; sweet-tempered; smoothly, easily.

sedán *m.* sedan.

sedativo *adj. & m.* sedative.

sede *f.* seat, see; **Santa Sede** Holy See.

sedentario *adj.* sedentary.

sedeño *adj.* silky, silken.

sedería *f.* silk goods; silk shop.

sedero *m.* silk dealer or weaver; *adj.* silk, pertaining to silk; **industria sedera** silk industry.

sedición *f.* sedition.

sedicioso *adj.* seditious, turbulent.

sediento *adj.* thirsty; dry, parched; anxious, desirous.

sedimento *m.* sediment; dregs, grounds.

sedoso *adj.* silken, silky.

seducción *f.* seduction.

seducir[25] *v. irr.* to seduce; to entice; to charm.

seductivo *adj.* seductive, alluring; inviting, enticing.

seductor *adj.* tempting, fascinating; *m.* seducer; tempter; charming person.

segador *m.* harvester, reaper; **segadora** *f.* harvester, mowing machine; woman reaper.

segar[1,7] *v. irr.* to mow, reap; to cut off.

seglar *adj.* secular, lay; *m.* layman.

segmento *m.* segment.

seguida *f.* succession; series, continuation; **de —** without interruption, continuously; **en —** at once, immediately.

seguido *p.p.* followed; continued; *adj.* continuous; straight, direct; *adv.* without interruption; *Am.* often; *Am.* **de —** at once, immediately.

seguidor *m.* follower.

seguimiento *m.* pursuit.

seguir⁵,¹² *v.irr.* to follow; to continue; to pursue; **-se** to follow as a consequence.

según *prep.* according to; *conj.* as; according to; **— y conforme** (*or* **— y como**) exactly as, just as; that depends.

segundar *v.* to repeat a second time; to second.

segundero *m.* second hand (*of a watch or clock*).

segundo *adj.* & *m.* second.

seguridad *f.* security; safety; certainty; **alfiler de —** safety pin.

seguro *adj.* secure; sure, certain; safe; *Am.* honest, trustworthy; *m.* assurance; insurance; safety device; **a buen —** (**al —**, *or* **de —**) truly, certainly; **en —** in safety; **sobre —** without risk; without taking a chance; *Am.* **irse uno del —** to lose one's temper; *Am.* **a la segura** without risk.

selección *f.* selection, choice.

seleccionar *v.* to select, choose.

selecto *adj.* select, choice.

selva *f.* forest; jungle.

sellar *v.* to seal; to stamp; to conclude; to seal, close tightly.

sello *m.* seal; stamp; *Am.* official stamped paper.

semana *f.* week; week's wages; **días de — —** week days; **entre —** during the week.

semanal *adj.* weekly; **-mente** *adv.* weekly, every week.

semanario *m.* weekly publication; *adj.* weekly.

semblante *m.* countenance; facial expression; appearance.

semblanza *f.* portrait, literary sketch.

sembrado *m.* sown ground; cultivated field.

sembrar¹ *v. irr.* to sow; to scatter.

semejante *adj.* similar, like; such a; *m.* fellow man; **nuestros -s** our fellow men.

semejanza *f.* resemblance, similarity; simile; **a — de** in the manner of.

semejar *v.* to resemble; **-se** to resemble.

semilla *f.* seed.

semillero *m.* seed bed; plant nursery; **— de vicios** hotbed of vice.

seminario *m.* seminary; plant nursery; seed plot.

sempiterno *adj.* everlasting; evergreen.

senado *m.* senate.

senador *m.* senator.

sencillez *f.* simplicity; plainness.

sencillo *adj.* simple; easy; plain; unadorned; unaffected; *m.* loose change, small coins.

senda *f.* path; way, course.

sendero *m.* path.

senectud *f.* senility, old age.

senil *adj.* senile.

seno *m.* cavity, hollow; breast, bosom; womb; lap; cove, bay; innermost recess; sinus (*cavity in a bone*); sine (*math.*).

sensación *f.* sensation.

sensacional *adj.* sensational.

sensatez *f.* prudence, common sense.

sensato *adj.* sensible, wise, prudent.

sensibilidad *f.* sensibility; sensitiveness.

sensible *adj.* sensitive; perceptible; regrettable.

sensitivo *adj.* sensitive.

sensual *adj.* sensual; sensuous.

sensualidad *f.* sensuality; lewdness.

sentada *f.* sitting; **de una —** at one sitting.

sentado *adj.* seated, sitting; **dar por —** to take for granted.

sentar¹ *v. irr.* to seat; to set; to establish; to become, suit, fit; to agree with one (*as food or climate*); **-se** to sit down; to settle down; *Am.* **-se en la palabra** to do all the talking, monopolize the conversation.

sentencia *f.* sentence; verdict; judgment; maxim, proverb.

sentenciar *v.* to sentence; to pass judgment on; to decide.

sentido *p.p.* felt; experienced; *adj.* heartfelt, filled with feeling; sensitive; touchy; **darse por —** to take offense; to have one's feelings hurt; **estar — con alguien** to be offended or peeved at someone; *m.* sense; meaning; judgment; **aguzar el —** to prick up one's ears; **perder el —** to faint.

sentimental *adj.* sentimental.

sentimentalismo *m.* sentimentalism, sentimentality.

sentimiento *m.* sentiment; sensation, feeling; grief, regret.

sentir³ *v. irr.* to feel; to sense; to hear; to regret; **-se** to feel (*well, strong, sad, etc.*); to feel oneself, consider oneself; to feel resentment; to feel a pain; **sin —** without being realized or felt; inadvertently; unnoticed; *m.* feeling; judgment, opinion.

seña *familiar contraction of* **señora.**

seña *f.* sign, mark; signal; password; **-s** address (*name and place of residence*); **por más -s** as an additional proof.

señal *f.* sign, mark; signal; reminder; indication; trace, vestige; scar; token, pledge; *Am.* earmark, brand (*on the ear of livestock*); **en — de** in proof of, in token of.

señalar *v.* to mark; to point out; to indicate; to determine, fix; to appoint; to signal; to assign; *Am.* to earmark, brand (*cattle*); **-se** to distinguish oneself.

señor *m.* mister; sir; owner; master, lord; gentleman; **el Señor** the Lord.

señora *f.* lady; madam; mistress; Mrs.

señorear *v.* to lord it over, domineer; to dominate; to master, control.

señoría *f.* lordship.

señoril *adj.* lordly.

señorío *m.* dominion, rule; domain of a lord; lordship; dignity; mastery, control; body of noblemen.

señorita *f.* miss; young lady.

señorito *m.* master, young gentleman.

señuelo *m.* decoy; lure, bait; *Am.* leading or guiding oxen.

separación *f.* separation.

separado *p.p. & adj.* separate; separated; **por —** separately.

separar *v.* to separate; to set aside; to remove (from); to dismiss (from); **-se** to separate; to retire, resign; to withdraw, leave.

septentrional *adj.* northern.

septiembre *m.* September.

sepulcral *adj.* sepulchral (*pertaining to sepulchers or tombs*); **lápida —** tombstone.

sepulcro *m.* sepulcher, tomb, grave.

sepultar *v.* to bury; to hide.

sepultura *f.* burial; grave; **dar —** to bury.

sequedad *f.* dryness; gruffness.

sequía *f.* drought.

séquito *m.* retinue, following.

ser[14] *v. irr.* to be; to exist; to happen, occur; **— de** (*or* **para**) **ver** to be worth seeing; *m.* being; essence, nature; existence; *Am.* **estar en un —** to be always in the same condition.

serenar *v.* to pacify; to calm down; *Am.* to drizzle, rain gently; **-se** to become serene, calm down; to clear up (*said of the weather*).

serenata *f.* serenade.

serenidad *f.* serenity, calm.

sereno *adj.* serene, calm; clear, cloudless; *m.* night humidity, dew; night watchman; **al —** in the night air.

serie *f.* series.

seriedad *f.* seriousness; gravity; earnestness; dignity.

serio *adj.* serious; grave; earnest; dignified; formal; **en —** seriously.

sermón *m.* sermon; reproof.

sermonear *v.* to preach; to admonish, reprimand.

serpentear *v.* to wind, twist, turn, zigzag.

serpiente *f.* serpent, snake.

serrado *adj.* toothed, notched (*like a saw*); jagged.

serrana *f.* mountain girl; **serranilla** *f.* lyric poem with a rustic theme.

serranía *f.* mountainous region; chain of mountains.

serrano *m.* mountaineer; *adj.* of, pertaining to, or from the mountains.

serrar = **aserrar.**

serrín *m.* sawdust.

serrucho *m.* handsaw.

servible *adj.* serviceable, useful.

servicial *adj.* helpful, obliging.

servicio *m.* service; table service; tea or coffee set; chamber pot; *Am.* toilet, water closet.

servidor *m.* servant; waiter; **— de Vd** at your service; **su seguro —** yours truly.

servidumbre *f.* domestic help, servants; servitude, slavery; service.

servil *adj.* servile; **servilón** *adj.* very servile; *m.* bootlicker, great flatterer.

servilismo *m.* servility, servile behavior or attitude, servile submission.

servilleta *f.* napkin.

servir[5] *v. irr.* to serve; to be of use; **— de** to serve as, act as; to be used as; **— para** to be good for; to be used for; **-se** to serve or help oneself; to be pleased to; **-se de** to make use of; **sírvase Vd. hacerlo** please do it.

sesgado *adj.* slanting, oblique, bias.

sesgar[7] *v.* to slant; to cut on the bias; to follow an oblique line.

sesgo *m.* bias; slant; diagonal cut; turn; **al —** on the bias; diagonally, obliquely.

sesión *f.* session; meeting, conference.

seso *m.* brain; wisdom, intelligence; **devanarse los -s** to rack one's brain.

sestear *v.* to snooze, take a nap.

sesudo *adj.* sensible, wise, prudent; *Am.* stubborn.

seta *f.* mushroom.

seto *m.* fence; hedge.

seudónimo *m.* pseudonym, pen name.

severidad *f.* severity; strictness; seriousness.

severo adj. severe; strict; stern.

sevillano adj. of, from, or pertaining to Seville, Spain.

sexo m. sex.

sexual adj. sexual.

si conj. if; whether; ¡ — ya te lo dije! but I already told you!; — bien although; por — acaso just in case.

sí adv. yes; — que certainly, really, um — es no es a trifle, somewhat; m. assent, consent; refl. pron. (used after a prep.) himself, herself, yourself (formal), themselves; de por — separately, by itself; estar sobre — to be on the alert.

sidra f. cider.

siega f. reaping, mowing; harvesting; harvest, mowing season.

siembra f. sowing; seedtime, sowing time; sown field.

siempre adv. always; Am. in any case, anyway; para (or por) — forever, for always; por — jamás forever and ever; — que whenever; provided that; Am. — sí me voy I've decided to go anyway.

siempreviva f. evergreen; everlasting.

sien f. temple (of the forehead).

sierpe f. serpent, snake.

sierra f. saw; rocky mountain range.

siervo m. serf; slave; servant.

siesta f. siesta, afternoon nap; early afternoon; dormir la — to take an afternoon nap.

sifón m. siphon; siphon bottle.

sigilo m. secret; secrecy.

siglo m. century; period, epoch; the world, worldly matters.

significación f. meaning; significance.

significado m. significance, meaning.

significar[6] v. to signify; to mean; to make known, show; to matter, have importance.

significativo adj. significant.

signo m. sign; mark; symbol.

siguiente adj. following.

sílaba f. syllable.

silabario m. speller, spelling book.

silbar v. to whistle; to hiss.

silbato m. whistle.

silbido m. whistle; hiss.

silenciador m. silencer; muffler (of an automobile).

silencio m. silence; pause; adj. Am. silent, quiet, motionless.

silencioso adj. silent, quiet.

silueta f. silhouette.

silvestre adj. wild; uncultivated.

silvicultor m. forester; silvicultura f. forestry.

silla f. chair; saddle; — de montar saddle; Am. — de balanza rocking chair. See mecedora.

sillón m. large chair; easy chair; Am. — de hamaca rocking chair.

sima f. chasm, abyss.

simbólico adj. symbolic.

simbolismo m. symbolism.

símbolo m. symbol; — de la fe (or de los Apóstoles) the Apostle's creed.

simetría f. symmetry.

simétrico adj. symmetrical.

simiente f. seed.

símil m. simile; similarity; adj. similar.

simpatía f. sympathy; accord, harmony; liking.

simpático adj. sympathetic, congenial; pleasant, agreeable, nice.

simpatizar[9] v. to sympathize (with); to have a liking or sympathy (for); to be congenial (with); no me simpatiza I don't like him.

simple adj. simple; mere; plain; pure, unmixed; naive, innocent; silly, foolish; m. simpleton.

simpleza f. simplicity; simpleness, stupidity, foolishness.

simplicidad f. simplicity; candor.

simplificar[6] v. to simplify.

simplón m. simpleton.

simulacro m. mimic battle, sham or mock battle; image, vision.

simular v. to simulate, feign.

simultáneo adj. simultaneous.

sin prep. without; besides; not counting; — que conj. without; — embargo nevertheless, still, yet; — qué ni para qué without rhyme or reason.

sinapismo m. mustard plaster; irritating person, nuisance, pest, bore.

sincerar v. to square, justify, excuse; -se to square oneself (with), justify oneself (with).

sinceridad f. sincerity.

sincero adj. sincere.

sindicar[6] v. to syndicate; -se to syndicate, form a syndicate.

sindicato m. syndicate.

síndico m. receiver (person appointed to take charge of property under litigation or to liquidate a bankrupt business); trustee.

sinecura f. sinecure (easy and well paid position).

sinfonía f. symphony.

singular adj. singular; unique; striking; odd, strange.

singularizar[9] v. to single out, choose; to distinguish; -se to distinguish oneself; to be singled out.

siniestro *adj.* sinister; left (*side*); *m.* unforeseen loss, damage; **siniestra** *f.* left hand; left-hand side.

sinnúmero *m.* great number, endless number.

sino *conj.* but; *prep.* except; **no hace — lo que le mandan** he only does what he is told; **— que** *conj.* but; *m.* fate, destiny.

sinónimo *m.* synonym; *adj.* synonymous.

sinrazón *f.* injustice, wrong.

sinsabor *m.* displeasure; trouble, grief, distress.

sintaxis *f.* syntax.

síntesis *f.* synthesis; summary.

sintético *adj.* synthetic.

síntoma *m.* symptom; indication, sign.

sintonizar⁹ *v.* to tune in (on).

sinuoso *adj.* sinuous, winding; wavy.

sinvergüenza *m. & f.* shameless person; scoundrel.

siquiera *adv.* at least; even; **ni — not even; *conj.* even though.

sirena *f.* siren; whistle, foghorn.

sirviente *m.* servant; waiter; **sirvienta** *f.* housemaid; waitress.

sisa *f.* petty theft; dart (*made in a garment*).

sisal *m. Am.* sisal or sisal hemp (*fiber used in ropemaking*).

sisar *v.* to take in (*a garment*); to pilfer; to cheat out of, defraud.

sisear *v.* to hiss.

siseo *m.* hiss, hissing.

sistema *m.* system.

sistemático *adj.* systematic.

sitial *m.* chair of a presiding officer; place of honor.

sitiar *v.* to besiege; to surround.

sitio *m.* site, location; place, spot, space; siege; *Am.* cattle ranch; *Am.* taxicab station; **poner — a** to lay siege to.

sito *adj.* situated, located.

situación *f.* situation; position; location; state, condition; *Am.* **hombre de la —** man of the hour, man of influence.

situado *p.p.* situated; placed.

situar¹⁸ *v.* to locate; to place; **-se** to station oneself, place oneself; to be located, placed, situated.

so : **—** capa de under the guise of; **— pena de** under penalty of; **— pretexto de** under the pretext of.

sobaco *m.* armpit.

sobar *v.* to rub; to touch, handle; to knead; to massage; to fondle, pet; to bother; to beat, slap; *Am.* to set bones; *Am.* to flay, skin; *Am.* to win (*in a*

fight); *Am.* to tire out (*a horse*).

soberanía *f.* sovereignty.

soberano *adj. & m.* sovereign.

soberbia *f.* pride, arrogance; ostentation, pomp.

soberbio *adj.* proud, haughty, arrogant; pompous; superb, magnificent; spirited (*horse*).

sobornar *v.* to bribe.

soborno *m.* bribery; bribe; *Am.* overload (*on a pack animal*), extra load.

sobra *f.* surplus, excess; **-s** leftovers, leavings; **de —** more than enough; superfluous, unnecessary.

sobrado *m.* attic; loft; *Am.* pantry shelf; **-s** *Am.* leftovers, leavings; *adj.* leftover; excessive; superfluous; forward, brazen; **sobradas veces** many times, repeatedly.

sobrante *adj.* leftover, surplus, excess, spare; *m.* surplus, excess, remainder.

sobrar *v.* to exceed; to remain, be left over; to be more than enough.

sobre *prep.* over; above; on, upon; about; approximately; besides; **— manera** excessively; **estar — sí** to be cautious, on the alert; **— que** besides, in addition to the fact that; *m.* envelope; address (*on an envelope*).

sobrecama *f.* bedspread.

sobrecarga *f.* overload; overburden.

sobrecargar⁷ *v.* to overload; to overburden.

sobrecoger¹¹ *v.* to surprise, catch unaware; to startle; **-se** to be startled; **-se de miedo** to be seized with fear.

sobreexcitación *f.* overexcitement; thrill.

sobreexcitar *v.* to overexcite.

sobrehumano *adj.* superhuman.

sobrellevar *v.* to endure, bear; to tolerate; to lighten (*another's burden*).

sobremesa *f.* table runner; after dinner conversation at the table; **de —** during the after dinner conversation.

sobrenadar *v.* to float.

sobrenatural *adj.* supernatural.

sobrenombre *m.* surname; nickname.

sobrentender¹ *v. irr.* to assume, understand; **-se** to be assumed, be obvious, be understood.

sobrepasar *v.* to exceed; to excel; **-se** to overstep, go too far.

sobreponer⁴⁰ *v. irr.* to lay on top; **-se** to dominate oneself; **-se a** to overcome; to dominate.

sobrepuesto *p.p. of* **sobreponer**; *m.* appliqué (*trimming laid on a dress*); *Am.* mend, patch.

sobrepujar *v.* to exceed, excel, surpass;

to outweigh.

sobresaliente *adj.* outstanding; projecting; excellent; *m. & f.* substitute (*a person*); understudy (*substitute actor*).

sobresalir⁴³ *v. irr.* to stand out; to project, jut out; to excel.

sobresaltar *v.* to startle, frighten; to assail; to stand out clearly; -se to be startled, frightened.

sobresalto *m.* start, scare, fright, shock; de — suddenly.

sobrescrito *m.* address (*on an envelope*).

sobrestante *m.* overseer, boss, foreman.

sobresueldo *m.* overtime pay, extra pay or wages.

sobretodo *m.* overcoat.

sobrevenir⁴⁸ *v. irr.* to happen, occur, come unexpectedly; to follow, happen after.

sobreviviente *m. & f.* survivor; *adj.* surviving.

sobrevivir *v.* to survive.

sobriedad *f.* sobriety, soberness, temperance, moderation.

sobrina *f.* niece.

sobrino *m.* nephew.

sobrio *adj.* sober, temperate, moderate.

socarrón *adj.* cunning, sly, crafty.

socarronería *f.* craftiness, slyness, cunning.

socavar *v.* to dig under; to undermine.

socavón *m.* tunnel; cave, cavern; underground passageway.

social *adj.* social; sociable, friendly.

socialista *adj.* socialist, socialistic; *m. & f.* socialist.

sociedad *f.* society; partnership; company, firm, corporation; — anónima (*or* — por acciones) stock company.

socio *m.* associate, partner; member.

sociología *f.* sociology.

socorrer *v.* to help, aid, assist.

socorro *m.* help, aid, assistance, relief; *Am.* partial advance payment on a workman's wages.

sodio *m.* sodium.

soez *adj.* low, vile, vulgar; coarse, ill-mannered.

sofá *m.* sofa, davenport.

sofocante *adj.* suffocating, stifling.

sofocar⁶ *v.* to suffocate, choke; to smother; to bother; to embarrass.

sofoco *m.* suffocation, choking, upset, annoyance; embarrassment.

sofrenar *v.* to check; to control; to reprimand.

soga *f.* rope; *Am.* leather lasso or rope.

sojuzgamiento *m.* subjugation, subjection.

sojuzgar⁷ *v.* to subjugate, subdue, subject.

sol *m.* sun; sunshine; sol (*fifth note of the scale*); *Am.* sol (*monetary unit of Peru*); de — a — from sunrise to sunset; hace — it is sunny; tomar el — to bask in the sun; to enjoy the sunshine.

solana *f.* sunny place; sunroom; sun porch; intense sunlight; **solanera** *f.* sunburn; sunny place.

solapa *f.* lapel.

solapado *adj.* sly, crafty, cunning, deceitful, underhanded.

solar *m.* lot, plot of ground; ancestral mansion, manor; *Am.* tenement house; *Am.* back yard; *Am.* town lot, field (*for growing alfalfa, corn, etc.*); *adj.* solar, of the sun.

solar² *v. irr.* to sole (*shoes*); to pave, floor.

solariego *adj.* manorial, pertaining to a manor; casa solariega ancestral manor or mansion.

solaz *m.* solace, comfort; relaxation, recreation.

solazar⁹ *v.* to console, cheer, comfort; -se to seek relaxation or pleasure; to enjoy oneself.

soldado *m.* soldier; — raso private; — de línea regular soldier.

soldadura *f.* soldering; welding; solder.

soldar³ *v. irr.* to solder; to weld.

soleado *adj.* sunny; *p.p.* sunned.

solear = **asolear**.

soledad *f.* solitude; loneliness; homesickness; lonely retreat.

solemne *adj.* solemn; imposing; — disparate downright foolishness, huge blunder.

solemnidad *f.* solemnity; solemn ceremony.

soler²,⁵¹ *v. irr.* to have the custom of, be in the habit of.

solferino *adj.* reddish-purple.

solicitante *m. & f.* solicitor; applicant.

solicitar *v.* to solicit; to apply for; to beg, ask for; to court, woo.

solícito *adj.* solicitous, careful; anxious, concerned, diligent.

solicitud *f.* solicitude; care, concern, anxiety.

solidaridad *f.* solidarity; union; bond, community of interests.

solidez *f.* solidity; compactness.

solidificar⁶ *v.* to solidify.

sólido *adj.* solid; firm; strong; *m.* solid.

soliloquio *m.* soliloquy, monologue.

solista *m. & f.* soloist.

solitaria *f.* tapeworm.

solitario *adj.* solitary; lonely; *m.* recluse, hermit; solitaire (*card game*);

solitaire (*gem set by itself*).

solo *adj.* sole, only; single; alone; lonely; a solas alone; *m.* solo; **sólo** *adv.* only.

solomillo, solomo *m.* sirloin; loin; loin of pork.

soltar² *v. irr.* to loosen, untie, unfasten; to let loose; to set free; to let go; to let out; to utter; -se to set oneself free; to come loose; to lose restraint; to loosen up; -se a to begin to, start to.

soltero *adj.* single, unmarried; *m.* bachelor; **soltera** *f.* spinster; **solterón** *m.* old bachelor; **solterona** *f.* old maid.

soltura *f.* looseness; freedom; facility, ease; agility, nimbleness; release (*of a prisoner*).

solución *f.* solution; loosening, untying.

solventar *v.* to pay (*a bill*), settle (*an account*); to solve (*a problem or difficulty*).

sollozar⁹ *v.* to sob.

sollozo *m.* sob.

sombra *f.* shadow; shade; darkness, shelter, protection; image, reflection (*in the water*); *Am.* guide lines (*under writing paper*); *Am.* awning, sunshade; **hacer** — to shade; to cast a shadow (on).

sombreado *adj.* shady; shaded.

sombrear *v.* to shade; -se *Am.* to seek the shade, stand in the shade.

sombrerería *f.* hat shop.

sombrero *m.* hat; — de copa top hat, high hat; — hongo derby; — de jipijapa Panama hat; *Am.* — de pelo top hat.

sombrilla *f.* parasol, sunshade.

sombrío *adj.* somber, gloomy; shady.

somero *adj.* superficial, shallow; summary, concise.

someter *v.* to submit; to subject; -se to submit.

sometimiento *m.* submission; subjection.

somnolencia *f.* drowsiness, sleepiness; con — sleepily.

son *m.* sound; tune; rumor; en — de guerra in a warlike manner; sin ton ni — without rhyme or reason.

sonaja *f.* jingles, tambourine (*to accompany certain dances*); rattle; **sonajero** *m.* child's rattle.

sonante *adj.* sounding; ringing; sonorous; en dinero — y contante in hard cash.

sonar² *v. irr.* to sound; to ring; to sound familiar; — a to sound like, seem like; -se to blow one's nose; se suena que it is rumored that.

sonda *f.* plumb, string with lead weight

(*for sounding the depth of water*); sounding; surgeon's probe.

sondar = **sondear**.

sondear *v.* to sound, fathom; to sound out; to probe; to examine into.

sondeo *m.* sounding, fathoming.

soneto *m.* sonnet.

sonido *m.* sound.

sonoro *adj.* sonorous; **consonante** sonora voiced consonant.

sonreír¹⁵ *v. irr.* to smile; -se to smile.

sonriente *adj.* smiling, beaming, radiant.

sonrisa *f.* smile.

sonrojarse *v.* to blush.

sonrojo *m.* blush.

sonrosado *adj.* rosy.

sonsacar⁶ *v.* to lure away; to draw (*someone*) out; to extract (*a secret*); to take on the sly.

sonsonete *m.* singsong; rhythmical tapping sound.

soñador *m.* dreamer.

soñar² *v. irr.* to dream; — con (*or — en*) to dream of; — despierto to day-dream.

soñoliento *adj.* sleepy, drowsy.

sopa *f.* soup; sop; estar hecho una — to be sopping wet; *Am.* es un -s he is a fool.

sopapo *m.* chuck, tap, pat (*under the chin*); slap.

sopetón *m.* box, slap; de — all of a sudden, unexpectedly.

soplar *v.* to blow; to blow away; to blow up, inflate; to swipe, steal; to prompt; to "squeal" on, inform against; *Am.* — una bofetada to strike a blow; -se to swell up, puff up; to eat up, gobble up; to gulp down; se sopló el pastel he gobbled up the pie; *Am.* -se a uno to deceive someone, get the best of someone.

soplete *m.* blow torch; blowpipe.

soplo *m.* blowing; puff, gust of wind; breath; whispered warning or advice; "squealing," informing; en un — in a jiffy, in a second.

soplón *m.* informer, "squealer" (*one who tells on someone*), tattletale.

soportal *m.* arcade.

soportar *v.* to support, hold up; bear; to stand, endure, tolerate.

soporte *m.* support.

sorber *v.* to sip; to suck; to swallow; to absorb; to snuff up one's nose.

sorbete *m.* sherbet; fruit ice; *Am.* cone, ice-cream cone; *Am.* silk top hat.

sorbo *m.* sip, swallow, gulp; sniff.

sordera, sordez *f.* deafness.

sórdido *adj.* sordid.

sordina f. mute (of a musical instrument).

sordo adj. deaf; silent, noiseless; dull; muffled; **consonante sorda** voiceless consonant; m. deaf person; **hacerse el —** to pretend not to hear; to turn a deaf ear.

sordomudo adj. deaf and dumb; m. deaf-mute.

sorna f. slyness, cunning; sneer.

soroche m. Am. shortness of breath, sickness caused by high altitude; Am. blush, flush.

sorprendente adj. surprising.

sorprender v. to surprise; -se to be surprised.

sorpresa f. surprise.

sortear v. to draw lots; to raffle; to dodge; to shun; to fight (bulls) skilfully.

sorteo m. drawing or casting of lots; raffle.

sortija f. ring; finger ring; ringlet, curl.

sosa f. soda.

sosegado adj. calm, quiet, peaceful.

sosegar[1,7] v. to calm, quiet; to be quiet; -se to quiet down.

sosiego m. calm, peace, quiet.

soslayo : al — obliquely; slanting; on the bias; **de —** oblique, slanting; at a slant; sideways; **mirada de —** side glance; **pegar de —** to glance, hit at a slant.

soso adj. flat, tasteless, insipid; dull, silly; awkward.

sospecha f. suspicion; mistrust.

sospechar v. to suspect; to mistrust.

sospechoso adj. suspicious; m. suspect.

sostén m. support; prop; supporter; brassière.

sostener[45] v. irr. to sustain; to hold; to support, maintain; to defend, uphold; to endure.

sostenido p.p. & adj. sustained; supported, held up; m. sharp (in music).

sota f. jack (at cards); m. Am. foreman, boss, overseer.

sotana f. cassock (black outer robe of a priest).

sótano m. cellar, basement.

soto m. grove; thicket.

sotreta m. Am. nag, old horse.

soviet m. soviet; **soviético** adj. soviet, of, or pertaining to, soviets.

suave adj. soft; smooth; mild; bland; gentle.

suavidad f. softness; smoothness; mildness; gentleness.

suavizar[9] v. to smooth; to soften.

subalterno adj. & m. subordinate.

subasta f. public auction.

subastar v. to sell at auction.

súbdito m. subject.

subida f. rise; ascent; carrying up; **de — on the way up; muchas -s y bajadas** many ups and downs; much going up and down.

subir v. to ascend, go up, climb; to raise, lift; to carry up; to mount; **— al tren** to board the train, get on the train.

súbito adj. sudden; **de —** suddenly.

sublevación f. revolt, uprising, insurrection.

sublevar v. to excite to rebellion; -se to revolt.

sublime adj. sublime.

submarino m. & adj. submarine.

subordinado adj. & m. subordinate.

subordinar v. to subordinate; to subdue.

subrayar v. to underline; to emphasize.

subsanar v. to mend, remedy, repair (a damage, error, defect, etc.); to make up for (an error, fault, etc.); to excuse (a fault or error).

subscribir = suscribir.

subscripción = suscripción.

subscriptor = suscritor.

subsecretario m. undersecretary.

subsecuente adj. subsequent.

subsiguiente adj. subsequent.

subsistencia f. living, livelihood; sustenance; permanence.

subsistir v. to subsist; to exist; to last.

substancia = sustancia.

substancial = sustancial.

substancioso = sustancioso.

substituible = sustituible.

substantivo = sustantivo.

substitución = sustitución.

substituir = sustituir.

substituto = sustituto.

substracción = sustracción.

substraer = sustraer.

subteniente m. second lieutenant.

subterráneo adj. subterranean, underground; m. underground; cave, tunnel, vault.

suburbano adj. suburban; m. suburban resident.

suburbio m. suburb.

subvención f. subsidy.

subvencionar v. to subsidize.

subyugar v. to subdue.

succión f. suction.

suceder v. to happen, occur; to succeed, follow.

sucesión f. succession; heirs, offspring.

sucesivo adj. successive; **en lo —** hereafter, in the future.

suceso *m.* event; outcome, result.

sucesor *m.* successor.

suciedad *f.* dirt, filth; filthiness; filthy act or remark.

sucinto *adj.* compact, concise, brief.

sucio *adj.* dirty; foul, filthy.

suculento *adj.* juicy.

sucumbir *v.* to succumb; to yield.

sucursal *f.* branch, branch office (*of a post office, bank, etc.*); *adj.* branch (*used as an adj.*).

suche *adj.* *Am.* sour, unripe; *m.* *Am.* pimple; *Am.* office boy, insignificant employee; *Am.* suche (*a tree*).

sud *m.* south; south wind; **sudeste** *m.* & *adj.* southeast; **sudoeste** *m.* & *adj.* southwest.

sudamericano *adj.* & *m.* South American.

sudar *v.* to sweat, perspire; to ooze; to toil.

sudor *m.* sweat, perspiration; toil.

sudoroso *adj.* sweaty, sweating, perspiring.

sueco *adj.* Swedish; *m.* Swede; Swedish language; **hacerse el —** to pretend not to see or understand.

suegra *f.* mother-in-law.

suegro *m.* father-in-law.

suela *f.* sole of a shoe; shoe leather.

sueldo *m.* salary.

suelo *m.* soil, ground; floor; pavement; bottom.

suelto *adj.* loose; free, easy; agile, nimble; blank (*verse*); *m.* small change; short newspaper article, news item.

sueño *m.* sleep; dream; sleepiness, drowsiness; **en -s** in one's sleep; **conciliar el —** to get to sleep; **tener —** to be sleepy.

suero *m.* serum.

suerte *f.* fate; fortune; chance; luck; sort, kind; way, manner; trick; **de — que** so that, in such a way that; and so; **echar -s** to cast lots; **tener — to** be lucky; **tocarle a uno la —** to fall to one's lot; to be lucky.

suéter *m.* *Am.* sweater.

suficiente *adj.* sufficient; competent, able.

sufragar[7] *v.* to defray, pay; to help, aid; *Am.* **— por** to vote for.

sufragio *m.* suffrage; vote; help, aid.

sufrido *adj.* suffering, long-suffering, patient; **mal —** impatient.

sufridor *m.* sufferer; *adj.* suffering.

sufrimiento *m.* suffering; patience, endurance.

sufrir *v.* to suffer; to endure; to allow, permit; to sustain; to undergo; **— un**

examen to take an examination.

sugerencia *f.* *Am.* suggestion, hint.

sugerir[3] *v. irr.* to suggest; to hint.

sugestión *f.* suggestion; hint.

sugestivo *adj.* suggestive.

suicida *m.* & *f.* suicide (*person who commits suicide*).

suicidarse *v.* to commit suicide.

suicidio *m.* suicide (*act of suicide*).

suizo *adj.* & *m.* Swiss.

sujeción *f.* subjection; control; submission.

sujetapapeles *m.* paper clip.

sujetar *v.* to subject; to control; to subdue; to fasten; to grasp, hold; **-se** to subject oneself; to submit; to adhere (to).

sujeto *adj.* subject; liable; fastened; under control; *m.* subject matter; subject; fellow, individual.

sulfato *m.* sulphate.

sulfurarse *v.* to get angry.

sulfúrico *adj.* sulphuric.

sulfuro *m.* sulphide.

sultán *m.* sultan.

suma *f.* sum; addition; substance; summary; **en —** in short.

sumador *adj.* adding; **máquina sumadora** adding machine.

sumar *v.* to add; to add up (to), amount (to); to sum up; **-se a** to join.

sumario *m.* summary; indictment; *adj.* summary, brief, concise; swift (*punishment*).

sumergible *adj.* submergible; *m.* submarine.

sumergir[11] *v.* to submerge, plunge, sink; to immerse; **-se** to submerge; to sink.

sumidero *m.* sink; sewer, drain.

suministrar *v.* to give, supply with, provide with.

sumir *v.* to sink; to submerge; to immerse; *Am.* to dent; **-se** to sink; *Am.* to shrink, shrivel; *Am.* to cower, crouch in fear *Am.* **-se el sombrero hasta las cejas** to pull one's hat over one's eyes.

sumisión *f.* submission; obedience.

sumiso *adj.* submissive; obedient; meek.

sumo *adj.* supreme, highest; high; greatest; **— pontifice** Sovereign Pontiff (*the Pope*); **a lo —** at the most.

suntuoso *adj.* sumptuous, magnificent, luxurious.

superabundancia *f.* superabundance, great abundance, overflow.

superar *v.* to surpass; to exceed; to overcome.

superávit *m.* surplus.

superficial *adj.* superficial; shallow;

frivolous; **superficialidad** *f.* superficiality, shallowness, frivolity.

uperficie *f.* surface; area.

uperfluo *adj.* superfluous.

uperintendente *m.* superintendent; supervisor; overseer.

uperior *adj.* superior; higher; better; upper; *m.* superior; father superior; **superiora** *f.* superior, mother superior.

uperioridad *f.* superiority; excellence.

uperlativo *adj.* & *m.* superlative.

uperstición *f.* superstition.

upersticioso *adj.* superstitious.

upervivencia *f.* survival.

uperviviente = **sobreviviente**.

uplantar *v.* to supplant; to forge (*a document or check*).

uplementar *v.* to supplement.

uplementario *adj.* supplementary, extra.

uplemento *m.* supplement; supply; supplying.

uplente *adj.,* *m.* & *f.* substitute.

úplica *f.* entreaty; request; petition; prayer.

uplicante *adj.* suppliant, beseeching; *m.* & *f.* suppliant; petitioner.

uplicar[6] *v.* to beg, entreat, implore; to pray humbly; to appeal, petition.

uplicio *m.* torture; torment; anguish; execution; instrument of torture; scaffold, gallows.

uplir *v.* to supply; to make up for; to substitute, take the place of (*temporarily*).

uponer[40] *v. irr.* to suppose; to assume; to be important.

uposición *f.* supposition; assumption.

upremacía *f.* supremacy.

upremo *adj.* supreme; final, last.

upresión *f.* suppression; omission; elimination.

uprimir *v.* to suppress; to abolish; to omit.

upuesto *p.p. of* **suponer** supposed, assumed; **— que** supposing that; since; **por —** of course, naturally; *m.* supposition; assumption.

upuración *f.* formation or discharge of pus.

upurar *v.* to fester, form or discharge pus.

ur *m.* south; south wind; **sureste** *m.* southeast; **suroeste** *m.* southwest.

uramericano = **sudamericano**.

urcar[6] *v.* to furrow; to plow; to plow through; to cut through.

urco *m.* furrow; rut; groove; wrinkle.

ureño[11] *adj.* southern, from the south.

urgir[11] *v.* to surge, rise; to spurt; spout;

to appear.

surtido *m.* stock, supply, assortment; *adj.* assorted.

surtidor *m.* supplier; spout, jet.

surtir *v.* to provide, supply, stock (with); to spout, spurt; **— efecto** to produce the desired result; **— un pedido** to fill an order.

susceptible *adj.* susceptible; sensitive; touchy.

suscitar *v.* to raise, stir up, provoke.

suscribir[52] *v.* to subscribe; to endorse; to agree (to); **-se** to subscribe.

suscripción *f.* subscription.

suscrito *p.p. of* **suscribir.**

suscritor *m.* subscriber.

susodicho *adj.* aforesaid, above-mentioned.

suspender *v.* to suspend; to hang; to stop; to defer; to astonish; to flunk, fail; to dismiss temporarily.

suspensión *f.* suspension; postponement, delay; uncertainty; cessation.

suspenso *adj.* suspended; hanging; pending; perplexed, astonished; **en —** in suspense; *m.* failure (*in an examination*).

suspicaz *adj.* suspicious.

suspirar *v.* to sigh; to sigh (for), long (for).

suspiro *m.* sigh; brief pause (*in music*).

sustancia *f.* substance; essence; *Am.* broth.

sustancial *adj.* substantial; nourishing.

sustancioso *adj.* substantial; nourishing.

sustantivo *m.* noun; *adj.* substantive; real; independent.

sustentar *v.* to sustain; to support; to feed, nourish; to maintain, uphold.

sustento *m.* sustenance; food; support.

sustitución *f.* substitution.

sustituible *adj.* replaceable.

sustituir[32] *v. irr.* to substitute.

sustituto *m.* substitute.

susto *m.* scare, fright.

sustracción *f.* subtraction.

sustraer[46] *v. irr.* to subtract; to remove, withdraw; **-se a** to evade, avoid, slip away from.

susurrar *v.* to whisper; to murmur; to rustle; **-se** to be whispered or rumored about.

susurro *m.* whisper; murmur; rustle.

sutil *adj.* subtle; keen; clever; crafty; thin, fine, delicate.

sutileza, sutilidad *f.* subtlety; keenness, cleverness; cunning; thinness, fineness.

suyo *adj.* his, of his; her, of hers; your,

of yours (*formal*); their, of theirs; *pron.* his, hers, yours (*formal*), theirs; **de —** naturally, by nature; **salirse con la suya** to get one's own way; **hacer de las suyas** to be up to one's tricks; **los —s** his (hers, theirs); his (her, their) own people.

T

tabaco *m.* tobacco; cigar; snuff; *Am.* blow with the fist; **tabaquería** *f.* tobacco store, cigar store.

tábano *m.* horsefly, gadfly.

taberna *f.* tavern, bar, liquor store.

tabernáculo *m.* tabernacle.

tabique *m.* partition, partition wall.

tabla *f.* board, plank; plate of metal; slab; table, list; strip of ground; *Am.* chocolate tablet; **-s** draw, tie (*in games*); stage boards, the stage; **a raja —** cost what it may; **hacer — rasa de algo** to disregard, omit, or ignore something; *Am.* to clear away all obstacles in the way of something.

tablado *m.* platform, stage; scaffold; floor boards.

tablero *m.* board; panel; timber, piece of lumber; chessboard, checkerboard; store counter; large work table; gambling table; *Am.* blackboard; **poner al —** to risk, endanger.

tableta *f.* tablet; small thin board; memorandum pad.

tabletear *v.* to rattle; to make a continuous rattling or tapping sound.

tableteo *m.* rattling sound; tapping.

tabilla *f.* tablet; slat, small thin board; splint; small bulletin board; **-s** wooden clappers.

tablón *m.* plank; large, thick board.

taburete *m.* stool; footstool.

tacañería *f.* stinginess, tightness, miserliness.

tacaño *adj.* stingy, tight, miserly; sly.

tácito *adj.* tacit, implied; silent.

taciturno *adj.* taciturn, silent, sullen, sad.

taco *m.* wad; roll; plug, stopper; billiard cue; bite, snack; swear word; *Am.* leather legging; *Am.* short, fat person; *Am.* heel of a shoe; *Am.* pile, heap; **echar -s** to curse, swear; *Am.* **darse uno —** to strut, put on airs.

tacón *m.* heel of a shoe.

taconear *v.* to click the heels, walk hard on one's heels.

taconeo *m.* click, clicking (*of the heels*).

táctica *f.* tactics.

tacto *m.* tact; touch, sense of touch.

tacha *f.* flaw, defect, blemish.

tachar *v.* to cross out; to scratch out; to blot out; to blame; to find fault with; to censure.

tachón *m.* stud; trimming, braid; blot.

tachonar *v.* to stud, ornament with studs; to adorn with trimming.

tachuela *f.* tack, small nail; *Am.* metal dipper; *Am.* runt, "shorty."

tafetán *m.* taffeta; **— inglés** court plaster.

tahur *m.* gambler; cardsharp.

taimado *adj.* sly, crafty; *Am.* sullen, gloomy, gruff.

taita = tatita. See **tata.**

tajada *f.* slice; cut.

tajalápiz *m.* pencil sharpener.

tajar *v.* to slice; to cut; to sharpen (*a pencil*).

tajo *m.* cut; gash; cutting edge; sheer cliff; chopping block.

tal *adj.* such; such a; **— cual** such as; so-so, fair; **— vez** perhaps; **el — Pedro** that fellow Peter; **un — García** a certain García; **— para cual** two of a kind; **— por cual** a nobody; *adv.* just as, in such a way; **estaba — como le dejé** he was just as I left him; **con — (de) que** provided that; **¿qué — ?** how are you?; hello!

talabarte *m.* sword belt.

taladrar *v.* to bore, drill; to pierce; to penetrate.

taladro *m.* auger, drill; bore, drill hole; *Am.* mine tunnel.

tálamo *m.* bridal bed or chamber.

talante *m.* disposition; mood; appearance, manner.

talco *m.* talc (*a soft mineral*); **— en polvo** talcum powder.

talega *f.* money bag, sack.

talento *m.* talent; ability, natural gift.

talentoso *adj.* talented, gifted.

talismán *m.* talisman, charm.

talón *m.* heel; stub, check, coupon.

talonario *m.* stub book; **libro —** stub book.

talonear *v.* to tap with one's heel; walk briskly.

taloneo *m.* tapping with the heel; footsteps.

talla *f.* stature, height; carving; round of a card game; ransom; *Am.* chat; *Am.* thrashing, beating.

tallar *v.* to carve; to cut (*stone*); appraise; to deal (*cards*); *Am.* court, make love; *Am.* to bother, disturb.

tallarín *m.* noodle.

talle *m.* figure, form; waist; fit (*of*

dress); looks, appearance; *Am.* bodice.

taller *m.* workshop; laboratory; studio; factory.

tallo *m.* stalk; stem; shoot, sprout.

tamal *m. Am.* tamale; *Am.* vile trick, intrigue; *Am.* clumsy bundle.

tamaño *m.* size; *adj.* such a; of the size of; **disparate** such a (big) mistake; **— como un elefante** big as an elephant; **tamañito** *adj.* very small; **tamañito así** about this little; **se quedó tamañito** he was (left) astonished, amazed.

tambalearse *v.* to totter, stagger, sway, reel.

también *adv.* also, too; likewise.

tambor *m.* drum; drum-like object; drummer; pair of embroidery hoops; *Am.* bedspring, spring mattress; **tambora** *f.* bass drum; **tamboril** *m.* small drum; **tamborilero** *m.* drummer.

tamborilear *v.* to drum; to extol.

tamiz *m.* fine sieve.

tamizar *v.* to sift; to blend.

tampoco *conj.* either (*after a negative*); **no lo hizo tampoco** he did not do it either; **ni yo —** nor I either.

tan *adv.* (*contr. of* **tanto**) so, as; such a.

tanda *f.* turn; round, bout; task; gang, group; shift, relay; *Am.* section of a theatrical performance.

tangente *adj. & f.* tangent; **salirse por la —** to go off at a tangent; to avoid the issue.

tangible *adj.* tangible.

tango *m.* tango.

tanque *m.* tank; reservoir; *Am.* pond; *Am.* swimming pool.

tantán *m.* clang; knock! knock!; sound of a bell, drum, etc.

tantear *v.* to probe, test; to sound out, feel out; to estimate, calculate approximately; *Am.* to grope, feel one's way; *Am.* to lie in wait; *Am.* to fool, make a fool of; *Am.* **¡tantee Vd.!** just imagine!

tanteo *m.* trial, test; calculation, estimate; score; **al —** by guess; hit or miss.

tanto *adj., pron. & adv.* so much, as much; so; **-s** so many, as many; **certain** amount; counter, chip (*to keep score*); **cuarenta y -s** forty odd; **el — por ciento** percentage, rate; **un —** (*or* **algún —**) somewhat; **— como** as well as; as much as; **— . . .** **como** both . . . and; **— en la ciudad como en el campo** both in the city and in the country; **entre** (*or* **mientras**) **—** meanwhile; **por lo —** therefore.

tañer *v.* to play (*an instrument*); to ring.

tañido *m.* sound, tune; ring; twang (*of a guitar*).

tapa *f.* cover; lid; book cover; heel lift.

tapadera *f.* cover, lid; one who shields another.

tapar *v.* to cover; to plug, stop up; to veil; to hide; *Am.* to fill (*a tooth*); *Am.* to crush, crumple; *Am.* to cover with insults; **-se** to cover up; to wrap oneself up.

tapera *f. Am.* ruins; *Am.* abandoned room or house.

tapete *m.* rug; table scarf.

tapia *f.* adobe wall; wall fence.

tapiar *v.* to wall up; to block up (*a door or window*).

tapicería *f.* tapestry; upholstery; tapestry shop; tapestry making.

tapiz *m.* tapestry.

tapón *m.* plug, stopper, cork; bottle cap.

taquigrafía *f.* shorthand.

taquígrafo *m.* stenographer.

taquilla *f.* ticket office; box office; file (*for letters, papers, etc.*); *Am.* tavern, liquor store.

tararear *v.* to hum.

tarareo *m.* hum, humming.

tarascada *f.* snap, bite; snappy or harsh answer.

tardanza *f.* delay; slowness.

tardar *v.* to delay; to be late; to be long (in); to take long (in); **-se** to delay oneself; to be delayed; **a más —** at the very latest.

tarde *f.* afternoon; *adv.* late; **de — en —** from time to time, now and then.

tardío *adj.* late; slow.

tardo *adj.* slow, lazy; tardy, late; stupid, dull; **tardón** *adj.* very slow; *m.* slow poke, slow person.

tarea *f.* task, job; anxiety, care.

tarifa *f.* tariff; list of duties, taxes, or prices; fare.

tarima *f.* wooden platform; low bench.

tarjeta *f.* card; **— postal** postcard.

tarro *m.* earthen jar; *Am.* horn (*of an animal*); *Am.* can; *Am.* top hat.

tarta *f.* tart.

tartamudear *v.* to stutter, stammer.

tartamudeo *m.* stammer, stammering.

tartamudo *m.* stutterer, stammerer; *adj.* stuttering, stammering.

tartera *f.* griddle; baking pan.

tarugo *m.* wooden block; wooden peg; blockhead, dunce; *adj. Am.* mischievous, devilish.

tasa *f.* measure; standard; rate; appraisal; valuation.

tasación *f.* assessment, valuation, appraisal.

tasajo *m.* piece of jerked beef.

tasar *v.* to measure; to appraise; to rate.

tata *f.* daddy, dad; *Am.* chief (*said by Indians to a superior*); **tatita** *m.* daddy; *Am.* dear chief or daddy (*said by Indians*).

tataranieto *m.* great-great-grandson.

taxear *v.* to taxi (*said of a plane*).

taxi, taxímetro *m.* taxi, taxicab.

taza *f.* cup; bowl; basin of a fountain.

tazón *m.* large cup; bowl; basin of a fountain.

té *m.* tea; *f.* T-square, T-shaped ruler.

te *obj. pron.* you (*fam. sing.*); to you; for you; yourself.

teatral *adj.* theatrical.

teatro *m.* theater; stage; scene, setting; **hacer —** to put on airs, show off.

tecla *f.* key (*of a piano, typewriter, etc.*); **dar uno en la —** to hit the nail on the head, find the right way to do something.

teclado *m.* keyboard.

técnica *f.* technique.

técnico *adj.* technical; *m.* technical expert, technician.

tecolote *m.* Ä*m.* owl.

techado *m.* roof; shed; *p.p. of* **techar**.

techar *v.* to roof.

techo *m.* roof; ceiling.

techumbre *f.* roof; ceiling.

tedio *m.* tediousness; boredom; bother.

tedioso *adj.* tedious, boring, tiresome.

teja *f.* tile; linden tree; *Am.* rear part of a saddle; **de -s abajo** here below, in this world.

tejado *m.* roof; shed.

tejamanil *m.* shingle; small thin board.

tejedor *m.* weaver.

tejer *v.* to weave; to interlace; to braid; to knit.

tejido *m.* textile, fabric; texture; weave; weaving; tissue.

tejón *m.* badger; bar of gold.

tela *f.* cloth; membrane; web; film (*on the surface of liquids*); **— adhesiva** adhesive tape; **— de cebolla** onion skin; flimsy fabric; *Am.* **— emplástica** court plaster; **— metálica** wire screen; **poner en — de juicio** to call in question.

telar *m.* loom.

telaraña *f.* cobweb, spider's web.

telefonear *v.* to telephone.

telefónico *adj.* telephonic, telephone (*used as adj.*); **receptor —** telephone receiver.

teléfono *m.* telephone; **telefonista** *m. & f.* telephone operator.

telegrafía *f.* telegraphy.

telegrafiar[17] *v.* to telegraph.

telegráfico *adj.* telegraphic.

telégrafo *m.* telegraph; **— sin hilos** (*or* **— inalámbrico**) wireless telegraph; **telegrafista** *m. & f.* telegraph operator.

telegrama *m.* telegram.

telescopio *m.* telescope.

televisión *f.* television.

telón *m.* theater curtain; **— de boca** drop curtain; **— de foro** drop scene.

tema *m.* theme; subject; *f.* fixed idea, mania.

temblar[1] *v. irr.* to tremble; to shake; to quiver.

temblón *adj.* tremulous, trembling, shaking, quivering.

temblor *m.* tremor, trembling; shiver; quake; **— de tierra** earthquake.

tembloroso *adj.* trembling, shaking.

temer *v.* to fear; to dread; to suspect.

temerario *adj.* rash, reckless.

temeridad *f.* temerity, recklessness; folly.

temeroso *adj.* fearful; suspicious; timid.

temible *adj.* terrible, dreadful.

temor *m.* fear; dread, suspicion.

témpano *m.* thick slice or chunk (*of anything*); kettledrum; drumhead (*parchment stretched over the end of a drum*); **— de hielo** block of ice; iceberg.

temperamento *m.* temperament; climate.

temperatura *f.* temperature.

tempestad *f.* tempest, storm.

tempestuoso *adj.* tempestuous, stormy.

templado *p.p.* tempered; tuned; *adj.* moderate; temperate; lukewarm; brave; *Am.* in love; *Am.* half-drunk; *Am.* hard, severe; **estar mal —** to be in a bad humor.

templanza *f.* temperance; moderation; mildness.

templar *v.* to temper; to moderate; to calm; to soften; to tune; **-se** to be tempered, moderate; to control oneself; *Am.* to fall in love; *Am.* to take to one's heels; *Am.* to stuff oneself.

temple *m.* temper; temperament; valor; courage; harmony (*of musical instruments*); *Am.* sweetheart; **de mal —** in a bad humor.

templo *m.* temple; church.

temporada *f.* period of time, season; **— de ópera** opera season.

temporal *adj.* temporal; secular; worldly; temporary; *m.* weather; storm; spell of rainy weather.

tempranero *adj.* habitually early or ahead of time; **ser —** to be an early riser.

temprano adj. early; premature; adv. early.

tenacidad f. tenacity; tenaciousness; perseverance.

tenacillas f. pl. small tongs; pincers, tweezers; sugar tongs; curling iron.

tenaz adj. tenacious; firm; strong, resistant; stubborn.

tenazas f. pl. pincers; pliers; tongs; forceps (for pulling teeth); **tenazuelas** f. pl. tweezers, small pincers.

tendedero m. place to hang or spread clothes; clothesline.

tendencia f. tendency, inclination.

tender[1] v. irr. to spread out; to stretch out; to lay out; to tend, have a tendency, move (toward); to hang to dry; Am. to make (a bed); -se to stretch oneself out; to lay all one's cards on the table; to run at full gallop.

ténder m. tender (of a train).

tendero m. storekeeper; tentmaker.

tendón m. tendon, sinew.

tenducho m. wretched little shop.

tenebroso adj. dark, shadowy; gloomy.

tenedor m. table fork; holder, possessor, keeper; **— de libros** bookkeeper.

teneduría f. office and position of bookkeeper; **— de libros** bookkeeping.

tener[45] v. irr. to have; to possess; to hold; **— en mucho** to esteem highly; **— por** to consider, judge; **— que** (+ inf.) to have to; **— gana** (or **ganas**) de to desire, feel like; **— miedo** (**sueño, frío, hambre,** etc.) to be afraid (sleepy, cold, hungry, etc.); **— ... años** to be ... years old; -se to stand firm; to hold on.

tenería f. tannery.

teniente m. first lieutenant; substitute, deputy.

tenis m. tennis.

tenor m. tenor; text, literal meaning; kind, sort, nature.

tensión f. tension; strain.

tenso adj. tense; tight, taut.

tentación f. temptation.

tentáculo m. tentacle, feeler.

tentador adj. tempting; m. tempter; the devil.

tentalear v. to grope, feel around; to finger, touch; to fumble (for something).

tentar[1] v. irr. to tempt; to touch, feel with the fingers; to grope; to attempt, try; to test; to probe, examine with a probe.

tentativa f. attempt, trial.

tentativo adj. tentative.

tenue adj. delicate, thin; flimsy; worthless.

teñir[5,19] v. irr. to dye; to tinge; to darken (the color of a painting).

teologal, teológico adj. theological.

teología f. theology.

teoría f. theory.

teórico adj. theoretical.

tequila m. Am. tequila (liquor made from the maguey plant).

tercero adj. third; m. third person; mediator; go-between; tertiary (member of the third order of St. Francis).

terciar v. to sling across one's shoulders; to divide into three parts; to intervene, mediate; to meddle, join (in); to balance the load on a pack animal; Am. to load or carry on the back; Am. to adulterate, add water to; Am. to mix.

tercio adj. third; m. one third; half of a mule load; military regiment or division; Am. bale, bundle; **hacer uno mal —** to hinder, interfere.

terciopelo m. velvet.

terco adj. obstinate, stubborn; hard; Am. harsh, severe.

tergiversar v. to distort, twist.

terminación f. termination, end; ending.

terminal adj. terminal, final.

terminante adj. closing, ending; decisive, final.

terminar v. to terminate, end; to finish; -se to end.

término m. end; completion; goal, object; boundary, limit; terminal; term; word, phrase; **en otros -s** in other words; **por — medio** on an average; **as a rule; primer —** foreground.

termómetro m. thermometer.

termos f. thermos bottle.

ternera f. calf; veal.

terneza f. tenderness; softness; affection; affectionate word; caress.

terno m. group or combination of three; suit of clothes; Am. set of jewels (earrings, necklace and brooch); Am. cup and saucer; **echar** (or **soltar**) **un —** to utter a bad word; to curse, swear.

ternura f. tenderness.

terquedad f. obstinacy, stubbornness.

terrado m. terrace; flat roof.

terraplén m. railroad embankment.

terrateniente m. & f. landholder.

terraza f. terrace, veranda; flat roof.

terremoto m. earthquake.

terrenal adj. earthly, worldly.

terreno m. land; ground; field; adj. earthly, worldly.

terrestre *adj.* terrestrial; earthly.
terrible *adj.* terrible.
terrífico *adj.* terrific.
territorio *m.* territory.
terrón *m.* clod; lump.
terror *m.* terror.
terso *adj.* polished, smooth.
tertulia *f.* evening party; social gathering; club; conversation; *Am.* theater gallery.
tertuliano, tertulio *m.* member of a tertulia.
tesis *f.* thesis.
tesón *m.* grit, endurance, pluck, persistence.
tesonero *adj. Am.* tenacious, stubborn, persevering, persistent.
tesorería *f.* treasury; **tesorero** *m.* treasurer.
tesoro *m.* treasure; treasury.
testa *f.* head; crown of the head; front.
testamento *m.* testament; will.
testarudez *f.* stubbornness, obstinacy.
testarudo *adj.* stubborn.
testigo *m. & f.* witness; *m.* testimony, proof, evidence; **— de cargo** witness for the prosecution; **— de vista** eyewitness.
testimoniar *v.* to give testimony of; to serve as a witness.
testimonio *m.* testimony; proof, evidence; **levantar falso —** to bear false witness.
testuz *m.* nape; crown of the head (*of certain animals*).
teta *f.* teat, nipple; breast; udder.
tetera *f.* teapot; teakettle; *Am.* nursing bottle.
tétrico *adj.* sad, melancholy, gloomy.
textil *adj.* textile.
texto *m.* text; quotation; textbook.
tez *f.* complexion, skin.
ti *pers. pron.* (*used after prep.*) you; yourself (*fam. sing.*).
tía *f.* aunt; older woman; *Am.* **— rica** pawnshop; **no hay tu —** there is no use or hope; there is no way out of it; **quedarse una para —** to remain an old maid.
tibio *adj.* tepid, lukewarm; indifferent; *Am.* annoyed, angry.
tiburón *m.* shark.
tico *adj. & m. Am.* Costa Rican (*humorous nickname*).
tiempo *m.* time; weather; tense; **a —** in time, on time; **a su —** in due time, at the proper time; **a un —** at one and the same time; **andando el —** in time, as time goes on.
tienda *f.* store; tent; **— de campaña**

camping tent, army tent.
tienta *f.* probe (*surgical instrument*); **a -s** gropingly, feeling one's way; **andar a -s** to grope, feel one's way.
tiento *m.* touch; tact; blind man's stick; steady hand; blow; tentacle, feeler (*of an insect*); *Am.* saddle strap, leather strap, thong; *Am.* snack; *Am.* swallow of liquor; **dar un —** to make a trial or attempt; **hacer algo con mucho —** to do something with great care or caution; **perder el —** to lose one's skill; *Am.* **tener a uno a los -s** to keep someone within sight; *Am.* **tener la vida en un —** to be in great danger.
tierno *adj.* tender; soft; young; recent, new; sensitive; affectionate; *Am.* green, unripe.
tierra *f.* earth; land; ground; soil; native land; **— adentro** inland; **— firme** mainland; solid ground; **dar en — con alguien** to overthrow someone; **echar por —** to knock down; to demolish; **tomar —** to land.
tieso *adj.* stiff, rigid; stuck-up; firm, stubborn.
tiesto *m.* flowerpot; broken piece of earthenware; *Am.* pot.
tiesura *f.* stiffness.
tifo *m.* typhus; **tifoidea** *f.* typhoid fever.
tigre *m.* tiger.
tijera *f.* (*usually* **tijeras**) scissors; sawhorse; **silla de —** folding chair; **tener buena — (or tener buenas -s)** to have a sharp tongue; to be a gossip.
tijeretada *f.*, **tijeretazo** *m.* snip, cut, clip (*with the scissors*).
tijeretear *v.* to snip, cut, clip (*with scissors*); to criticize others, gossip.
tilde *f.* tilde (*mark over an* n); blemish; jot, bit, speck.
timbrar *v.* to stamp, mark with a seal.
timbre *m.* revenue stamp; seal; crest (*on a coat of arms*); call bell; timbre (*quality of tone, tone color*); merit, fame; glorious deed; *Am.* postage stamp.
timidez *f.* timidity; shyness.
tímido *adj.* timid; shy.
timón *m.* helm; rudder; beam of a plow.
timonear *v.* to steer (*a ship*).
timorato *adj.* timorous, timid.
tímpano *m.* eardrum; kettledrum.
tina *f.* large earthen jar; vat, tank, tub; bathtub.
tinaco *m.* tank, vat, tub.
tinaja *f.* large earthen jar.
tinieblas *f. pl.* darkness; obscurity; ignorance, confusion; Tenebrae (*Holy Week religious service*).
tino *m.* acumen, keen insight, good

judgment; tact; accurate aim; good sense of touch; tank, vat.

tinta *f.* ink; dye; tint, hue; -s paints; — **simpática** invisible ink; **saber de buena** — to know on good authority.

tinte *m.* tint, hue; tinge; color; dye; dyeing.

tinterillo *m.* shyster. *See* **picapleitos.**

tintero *m.* inkwell, inkstand; *Am.* writing materials, desk set.

tintinear *v.* to tinkle.

tintineo *m.* tinkle, tinkling.

tinto *adj.* tinged; red (*wine*); *Am.* dark-red; *p.p. irr. of* **teñir.**

tintorería *f.* cleaner's and dyer's shop.

tintorero *m.* dyer.

tintura *f.* tincture; tint, color; dye.

tinturar *v.* to tincture; to tinge; to dye.

tiñoso *adj.* scabby, mangy; stingy.

tío *m.* uncle; old man; good old man; fellow, guy; *Am.* **el cuento del** — deceitful story (*told to extract money*).

tiovivo *m.* merry-go-round.

típico *adj.* typical; *Am.* corrected (*edition*).

tiple *m. & f.* high soprano singer; *m.* treble; soprano voice; treble guitar.

tipo *m.* type; class; model, standard; fellow, guy; *Am.* rate of interest; *Am.* — **de cambio** rate of exchange; **buen** — good-looking fellow.

tipografía *f.* typography, printing; press, printing shop.

tira *f.* strip; stripe; *Am.* **estar hecho -s** to be in rags; *Am.* **sacar a uno las -s** to tan one's hide, beat one to pieces.

tirabuzón *m.* corkscrew.

tirada *f.* throw; issue, edition, printing; *Am.* tirade, long speech; *Am.* sly trick; *Am.* dash (*on horseback*); **de una** — all at once, at one fell swoop.

tirador *m.* shooter; thrower; slingshot; bell cord; handle; printer; *Am.* leather belt with pockets; — **de goma** slingshot.

tiranía *f.* tyranny.

tiránico *adj.* tyrannical.

tirano *adj.* tyrannical; *m.* tyrant.

tirante *adj.* pulling; stretched, taut; strained; *m.* trace (*of a harness*); brace; -s suspenders; supporters (*for stockings*).

tirantez *f.* tension, tightness; strain; pull.

tirar *v.* to throw; to throw away; to shoot, fire; to draw; to print; to attract; *Am.* to cart; — **a** to tend toward; to resemble; to aim at; — **de** to pull, tug; — **bien a la espada** to handle a sword well; **ir tirando** to get along;

a todo (*or* **a más**) — at the most; *Am.* **al** — haphazardly; -**se** to throw oneself; to lie down; *Am.* **tirársela de** to boast of.

tiritar *v.* to shiver.

tiro *m.* throw; shot; piece of artillery; range of a gun; shooting range; charge of a gun; team (*of horses*); chimney draft; mine shaft; *Am.* issue, printing; *Am.* cartage, transport; -**s** *Am.* suspenders; — **al blanco** target practice; *Am.* **al** — at once; *Am.* **de a** (*or* **de al**) — all at once; completely; **caballo de** — draft horse; **ni a -s** absolutely not (*not even if you shoot me*).

tirón *m.* jerk, sudden pull; **de un** — all at once, with one big pull.

tironear *v. Am.* to pull, jerk; *Am.* to attract.

tirotear *v.* to shoot around; to shoot at random; -**se** to exchange shots.

tiroteo *m.* shooting; exchange of shots; skirmish.

tirria *f.* aversion, grudge; **tenerle** — **a una persona** to have a strong dislike for someone; to hold a grudge against someone.

tísico *adj.* tubercular, consumptive.

tisis *f.* tuberculosis, consumption.

títere *m.* puppet; ridiculous little fellow; -**s** puppet show.

titilación *f.* flicker; twinkle; **titileo** *m.* flickering; twinkling; glimmer.

titilar *v.* to flicker; to twinkle.

titubear *v.* to hesitate; to totter, stagger; to grope; to stutter, stammer.

titubeo *m.* hesitation, wavering.

titular *v.* to entitle; to name; -**se** to be called or named; to call oneself; to receive a title; *adj.* titular, in name only.

título *m.* title; heading; sign; inscription; claim, legal right; degree, diploma; credential; titled person; merit; bond, certificate; **a** — **de** under the pretext of; in the capacity of.

tiza *f.* chalk.

tiznado *adj.* sooty, covered with soot; smutty; dirty; *Am.* drunk; *p.p. of* **tiznar.**

tiznar *v.* to smudge, smut; to smear with soot.

tizne *m.* soot; smut; **tiznón** *m.* smudge.

tizón *m.* firebrand (*piece of burning wood*); rust, blight (*on plants*); stain (*on one's honor*).

toalla *f.* towel.

tobillo *m.* ankle.

tocado *m.* headdress; hairdo, coiffure; *adj.* "touched", half-crazy; *p.p. of*

tocar.

tocador *m.* dressing table; boudoir, dressing room; dressing case; player (*of a musical instrument*).

tocar[6] *v.* to touch; to play (*an instrument*); to toll, ring; to knock, rap; — en to stop over in; -le a uno to fall to one's lot; to be one's share; to be one's turn; to concern one; -se to fix one's hair; to become "touched," go slightly crazy.

tocayo *m.* namesake.

tocino *m.* bacon; salt pork; lard.

tocón *m.* stub, stump (*of a tree, arm or leg*).

todavía *adv.* still; yet; even.

todo *adj.* all, whole; every, each; — hombre every man; -s los días every day; a — correr at full or top speed; m. whole; all; everything; -s everybody; ante — first of all; así y — in spite of that; con — in spite of that; del — wholly.

todopoderoso *adj.* almighty.

toga *f.* gown, robe (*worn by a judge, professor, etc.*); Roman toga.

toldería *f. Am.* Indian camp, Indian village.

toldo *m.* awning; pomp, vanity; Am. Indian hut.

tolerancia *f.* tolerance, toleration; **tolerante** *adj.* tolerant.

tolerar *v.* to tolerate; to allow; to overlook, let pass.

tolete *m. Am.* stick, club, cudgel; Am. raft.

toma *f.* taking; seizure, capture; dose; tap (*of a water main*); Am. irrigation ditch; — de corriente plug, electric outlet.

tomar *v.* to take; to grasp, catch; to capture; to drink; — a pechos to take to heart, take seriously; -lo a mal to take it amiss; — el pelo a to make fun of, make a fool of; — por la derecha to turn to the right; -se con to quarrel with.

tomate *m.* tomato.

tomillo *m.* thyme.

tomo *m.* tome, volume; Am. heavy person; Am. dull, silent person; Am. buen — a heavy drinker; de — y lomo bulky; important.

ton: sin — ni son without rhyme or reason.

tonada *f.* tune, song; Am. singsong; Am. local accent; **tonadilla** *f.* little tune; short popular song.

tonel *m.* keg, cask, barrel.

tonelada *f.* ton.

tonelaje *m.* tonnage.

tónico *adj.* & *m.* tonic.

tono *m.* tone; tune; key; pitch; accent; manner; vigor, strength; de buen — of good taste, stylish; subirse de — to put on airs.

tontera = tontería.

tontería *f.* foolishness; stupidity.

tonto *adj.* foolish; stupid; a tontas y a locas recklessly, without thought; *m.* fool; dunce; Am. a game of cards.

topar *v.* to collide with, run into, bump into; to encounter; to find; to run across; to butt; Am. to gamble; Am. to fight with the fists; Am. to meet, greet.

tope *m.* butt, bump, collision; encounter; bumper; hasta el — up to the top; estar hasta los -s to be filled up.

topetada *f.,* **topetazo** *m.* butt; bump, blow on the head; **topetón** *m.* hard bump, collision; butt.

topetear *v.* to butt; to bump.

tópico *m.* topic, subject.

topo *m.* mole (*small animal*); dunce; awkward person.

toque *m.* touch; ringing; beat (*of a drum*); tap; sound (*of a trumpet, clarinet, etc.*); assay; piedra de — touchstone; ¡allí está el — ! there is the difficulty!; there is the real test!

torbellino *m.* whirlwind; rush, bustle, confusion.

torcedura *f.* twist; sprain, strain.

torcer[2,10] *v. irr.* to twist; to turn; to bend; to sprain; to distort; -se to become twisted, bent, or sprained; to get crooked; to go astray; to turn sour (*said of wine*); Am. to get offended, angry.

torcido *p.p.* & *adj.* twisted, turned, bent; crooked; angry, resentful; Am. unfortunate, unlucky; estar — con to be on unfriendly terms with; *m.* twisted roll of candied fruit; coarse silk twist; Am. gesture or look of disdain; Am. lasso made of twisted leather.

tordillo *adj.* greyish, dapple-grey.

tordo *adj.* dapple-grey; *m.* thrush; dapple-grey horse.

torear *v.* to perform in a bullfight; to incite, provoke (*a bull*); to tease.

torero *m.* bullfighter; *adj.* relating to bullfighting.

tormenta *f.* storm, tempest; misfortune.

tormento *m.* torment; torture; rack (*instrument of torture*); anguish; pain.

tornar *v.* to return; to turn; to change, alter; — a hacerlo to do it again.

tornasolado *adj.* iridescent, rainbow-colored; changeable (*silk*).

tornear *v.* to turn in a lathe; to do lathe work; to fight in a tournament.

torneo *m.* tournament.

tornillo *m.* screw; clamp, vise; **faltarle a uno un —** to have little sense, "have a screw loose."

torno *m.* turn; lathe; turnstile; revolving server; winch or windlass (*machine for lifting or pulling, turned by a crank*); **— de hilar** spinning wheel; **en —** around.

toro *m.* bull; *Am.* difficult question; **-s** bullfight; *Am.* **estar en las astas del —** to be in a predicament.

toronja *f.* grapefruit.

torpe *adj.* stupid, dull; clumsy; slow; lewd.

torpedear *v.* to torpedo.

torpedo *m.* torpedo; **torpedero** *m.* torpedo boat.

torpeza *f.* stupidity, dullness; clumsiness; slowness; moral turpitude, lewdness.

torre *f.* tower; turret; castle (*in chess*).

torrente *m.* torrent; flood; **— de voz** powerful voice.

torreón *m.* large tower (*of a fortress, castle, etc.*).

tórrido *adj.* torrid.

torsión *f.* twist; sprain.

torta *f.* torte, round cake; round loaf.

tortilla *f.* omelet; *Am.* tortilla (*flat, thin cornmeal cake*).

tórtola *f.* turtledove.

tortuga *f.* tortoise; turtle.

tortuoso *adj.* tortuous, twisting, winding; sly.

tortura *f.* torture; grief, affliction.

torturar *v.* to torture.

torvo *adj.* grim, stern, severe.

tos *f.* cough; **— ferina** whooping cough.

tosco *adj.* coarse, harsh, rough.

toser *v.* to cough; *Am.* to brag, boast.

tosquedad *f.* coarseness, crudeness, roughness; rudeness.

tostada *f.* toast, toasted bread; *Am.* boring visit or conversation; *Am.* toasted **tortilla; dar** (*or* **pegar**) **una — a uno** to play a mean trick on someone; *Am.* to make someone very angry.

tostado *p.p. & adj.* toasted; roasted; tanned; *Am.* worn out, tired out; *m.* toasting; *Am.* roasted corn.

tostador *m.* toaster.

tostar[2] *v. irr.* to toast; to tan; to overheat; to roast (*coffee*).

tostón *m.* toast dipped in oil; small roasted pig; *Am.* coin worth half a Mexican peso.

total *adj. & m.* total.

totalidad *f.* entirety, whole.

totalitario *adj.* totalitarian.

tóxico *adj.* toxic.

toxina *f.* toxin (*poison produced within animals and plants*).

toza *f.* wooden block; stump; log; piece of bark.

traba *f.* bond, tie; binding or locking device; fastener, fetter, shackle; hindrance, obstacle.

trabado *adj. Am.* tongue-tied; *p.p. of* **trabar.**

trabajador *adj.* industrious; *m.* worker, laborer.

trabajar *v.* to work; to labor; to strive.

trabajo *m.* work; labor; difficulty, obstacle; trouble; hardship.

trabajoso *adj.* laborious, difficult; troublesome; *Am.* unobliging; *Am.* demanding.

trabar *v.* to join, fasten; to clasp; to shackle; to brace; **— amistad con alguien** to become friends with someone; **— batalla** to join in battle; **— conversación** to be engaged in conversation; to engage in conversation; **-se** *Am.* to stammer; **-se de palabras** to get into an argument.

tracción *f.* traction.

tractor *m.* tractor.

tradición *f.* tradition.

tradicional *adj.* traditional.

traducción *f.* translation.

traducir[25] *v. irr.* to translate; to interpret.

traductor *m.* translator.

traer[46] *v. irr.* to bring; to carry; to lead, conduct; to have; to bring about; to wear; **— a uno inquieto** to keep one disturbed; **— a uno a mal —** to mistreat someone; to bother someone; **-se bien** to dress well; to carry oneself well.

trafagar[7] *v.* to traffic, trade; to roam about; to bustle, hustle; to toil.

tráfago *m.* trade, commerce; bustle, hustle; toil.

traficante *m.* trader; dealer; tradesman.

traficar[6] *v.* to traffic, trade; *Am.* to pass or move back and forth (*as traffic*). *See* **transitar.**

tráfico *m.* traffic; trade, commerce.

tragaluz *f.* skylight.

tragar[7] *v.* to swallow; to gulp; to engulf, swallow up.

tragedia *f.* tragedy.

trágico *adj.* tragic.

trago *m.* swallow, gulp; misfortune; *Am.*

brandy, hard liquor; a **-s** slowly, by degrees; **echar un —** to take a drink; **tragón** m. glutton; adj. gluttonous.

traición f. treason; treachery; a **—** treacherously; deceitfully.

traicionar v. to betray.

traicionero adj. treacherous; deceitful; m. traitor.

traído adj. used, old, worn out; **muy —** y **llevado** very worn out; p.p. of traer.

traidor adj. treacherous; m. traitor; betrayer.

traje m. dress; suit; gown; **— de etiqueta** (**— de ceremonia,** or Am. **— de parada**) formal gown; formal suit; dress uniform; **— de luces** bullfighter's costume; Am. **— sastre** woman's tailor-made suit.

trajeado p.p. & adj. dressed, clothed.

trajín m. traffic, going and coming; hustle, bustle, commotion.

trajinar v. to carry, cart back and forth; to go back and forth; to bustle, hustle.

trama f. plot; scheme; conspiracy; woof (horizontal threads of a fabric).

tramar v. to weave; to plot; to scheme.

tramitar v. to transact; to take legal steps; to negotiate.

trámite m. transaction, procedure, step, formality.

tramo m. stretch, lap, span; short distance; regular interval; flight of stairs.

trampa f. trap; snare; hatch, trap door; hinged section of a counter; spring door; fraud; trick.

trampear v. to trick, cheat, swindle.

trampista m. & f. cheat, crook, swindler.

trampolín m. springboard.

tramposo adj. deceitful, tricky; m. swindler, cheat.

tranca f. crossbar, bolt; pole, prop; club, stick; Am. rustic gate; Am. fence with gates; Am. **saltar las -s** to jump over the fence; to lose one's patience, rebel, get angry; Am. **tener una —** to be drunk.

trance m. critical moment; dangerous situation; **el último —** the last moment of life; **a todo —** at any cost, cost what it may.

tranco m. stride, long step; threshold; **a -s** hurriedly; **en dos -s** in a jiffy; Am. **al —** striding, with long steps.

tranquear v. to stride along.

tranquera f. stockade, wooden fence; Am. large gate (made with **trancas**).

tranquilidad f. tranquillity, peacefulness.

tranquilizar[9] v. to quiet, calm down; to

pacify; **-se** to become tranquil, calm down.

tranquilo adj. tranquil, peaceful.

transacción f. transaction, negotiation; compromise.

transar v. Am. to compromise, yield, give in.

transatlántico adj. transatlantic; m. transatlantic steamer.

transbordar = **trasbordar**.

transbordo = **trasbordo**.

transcendencia f. consequence, importance; penetration.

transcendental adj. consequential, important, far-reaching.

transcurrir v. to pass, elapse.

transcurso m. passing, lapse (of time).

transeúnte m. passer-by; pedestrian; transient; adj. transient.

transferencia f. transference, transfer.

transferir[3] v. irr. to transfer.

transformación f. transformation.

transformar v. to transform.

transgredir[51] v. to transgress.

transgresión f. transgression.

transgresor m. transgressor, offender.

transición f. transition.

transigente adj. compromising, yielding, pliable.

transigir[11] v. to compromise, yield, make concessions; to settle by compromise.

transitable adj. passable (road).

transitar v. to pass or move back and forth (as traffic).

tránsito m. transit; traffic; passing; passage; transition; **de —** on the way, in transit, passing through.

transitorio adj. transitory.

transmisión f. transmission.

transmisor m. transmitter; adj. transmitting.

transmitir v. to transmit.

transparencia f. transparency.

transparente adj. transparent; lucid, clear; m. window shade; stained-glass window.

transponer[40] v. irr. to transpose; to transfer; to transplant; to go beyond, go over to the other side; **-se** to hide from view, go behind; to set, go below the horizon.

transportación f. transportation, transport.

transportar v. to transport; to transpose (music); **-se** to be transported, carried away by strong feeling; to be in ecstasy.

transporte m. transport; transportation; transport vessel; ecstasy; **— de locura** fit of madness.

212

transpuesto *p.p. of* **transponer.**

transversal *adj.* transversal, transverse; **sección** — cross section.

transverso *adj.* transverse, cross.

tranvía *m.* streetcar; streetcar track.

trapacear *v.* to swindle, cheat; to racketeer.

trapacería *f.* racket, fraud, swindle.

trapacero *m.* racketeer; cheat, swindler; *adj.* cheating, deceiving.

trapacista *m. & f.* racketeer; swindler, cheat.

trapeador *m. Am.* mopper; *Am.* mop.

trapear *v. Am.* to mop; *Am.* to beat up, give (*someone*) a licking.

trapiche *m.* sugar mill; press (*for extracting juices*); *Am.* grinding machine (*for pulverizing minerals*).

trapisonda *f.* escapade, prank; brawl; noisy spree.

trapo *m.* rag; *Am.* cloth; -**s** clothes; a todo — at full sail; speedily; poner a uno como un — to make one feel like a rag; sacarle a uno los -**s** al sol to exhibit somebody's dirty linen; soltar el — to burst out laughing or crying.

traposo *adj. Am.* ragged, tattered, in rags.

tráquea *f.* trachea, windpipe.

traquetear *v.* to rattle; to shake; to jolt; to crack, crackle.

traqueteo *m.* rattling; shaking; jolting; cracking, crackling; *Am.* uproar, din; *Am.* noisy, disorderly traffic.

tras *prep.* after; in search of; behind, in back of; — **de** behind, after; besides, in addition to; *interj.* ¡ — ! bang!

trasbordar *v.* to transfer.

trasbordo *m.* transfer.

trascendencia = **transcendencia.**

trascendental = **transcendental.**

trasegar[1,7] *v. irr.* to upset, overturn; to change from one place to another; to pour from one container to another.

trasero *adj.* rear, hind, back; *m.* rump.

trasladar *v.* to move, remove; to transfer; to postpone; to translate; to transcribe, copy.

traslado *m.* transfer; transcript, written copy.

traslucirse[13] *v. irr.* to be translucent; to be transparent, clear, evident.

trasnochar *v.* to sit up all night; to stay awake all night; to spend the night out.

traspalar *v.* to shovel.

traspapelar *v.* to mislay, misplace (*a paper, letter, document, etc.*); -**se** to become mislaid among other papers.

traspasar *v.* to pass over, cross over; to go beyond; to pass through; to pierce;

to transfer (*property*); to trespass.

traspaso *m.* transfer; transgression, trespass.

traspié *m.* stumble, slip; **dar un** — to stumble or trip.

trasponer[40] = **transponer.**

trasplantar *v.* to transplant.

trasquila, trasquiladura *f.* shearing, clip, clipping; bad haircut.

trasquilar *v.* to shear; to clip; to crop; to cut badly (*hair*).

trastazo *m.* thump, blow.

traste *m.* fret, stop (*of a guitar*); *Am.* utensil, implement; **dar al** — **con** to destroy, ruin.

trasto *m.* household utensil; piece of junk; rubbish, trash; -**s** utensils; implements; -**s de pescar** fishing tackle.

trastornar *v.* to overturn; to upset; to disturb.

trastorno *m.* upset; disorder; disturbance.

trastrocar[2,6] *v. irr.* to invert, change; to upset.

trasudar *v.* to perspire, sweat slightly.

trasudor *m.* slight perspiration or sweat.

tratable *adj.* friendly, sociable; manageable.

tratado *m.* treaty; treatise.

tratamiento *m.* treatment; title of courtesy; form of address.

tratante *m. & f.* dealer, tradesman, trader.

tratar *v.* to treat; to handle; to discuss; to have social relations with; — **con** to have dealings with; — **de** to try to; to treat of, deal with; -**le a uno de** to address someone as; to treat someone as; — **en** to deal in; -**se bien** to treat oneself well; to behave well; -**se de** to be a question of; **no se trata de eso** that isn't the question, that isn't the point.

trato *m.* treatment; deal, pact; trade; manner, behavior; social relations; dealings; *Am.* — **pampa** unfair deal; ¡ — **hecho!** it's a deal!; **tener buen** — to be affable, sociable.

través *m.* crossbeam; reverse, misfortune; **a** (*or* **al**) — **de** through, across; **de** — across; **dar al** — **con** to ruin, destroy; to squander; **mirar de** — to squint in a sinister manner.

travesaño *m.* crosspiece, crossbar; bolster, long bedpillow; *Am.* railway tie.

travesear *v.* to romp, frisk, frolic; to fool around; to misbehave.

travesía *f.* crossing; sea voyage; wind blowing towards a coast; *Am.* wasteland, desert land; *Am.* partition wall or fence; *Am.* mid-year crop.

travesura *f.* mischief; prank; lively wit.

traviesa *f.* railway tie; rafter, crossbeam.

travieso *adv.* mischievous; lively; restless; **a campo —** (*or* **a campo traviesa**) cross-country.

trayecto *m.* run, stretch, lap, distance (*traveled over*).

trayectoria *f.* path (*of a bullet, missile, etc.*).

traza *f.* plan, design; scheme; plot, invention; appearance; semblance; aspect; indication, sign; **darse -s** to use one's wits or ingenuity; **tener -s de** to have the appearance or signs of; **tiene** (*or* **lleva**) **-s de no acabar nunca** it looks as if he would never end.

trazado *m.* draft, plan, sketch, outline; drawing; *p.p. & adj.* traced, sketched, outlined.

trazar[9] *v.* to trace, sketch; to draw, mark out; to plan.

trébol *m.* clover.

trecho *m.* space, distance; lap (*in a race*); **a -s** by or at intervals; **de — en —** at certain points or intervals; **from time to time**.

tregua *f.* truce; rest, respite.

tremedal *m.* quagmire, bog.

tremendo *adj.* tremendous, huge; terrible.

trementina *f.* turpentine.

tremolar *v.* to flutter, wave (*as a flag*).

trémolo *m.* tremolo (*of the voice*), quaver.

trémulo *adj.* tremulous, trembling, quivering; flickering.

tren *m.* train; *Am.* traffic; **— correo** mail train; **— de aterrizaje** landing gear; *Am.* **— de lavado** laundry; *Am.* **— de mudadas** moving company; **— de recreo** excursion train; **— mixto** freight and passenger train.

trenza *f.* tress; braid; *Am.* string (*of garlic, onions, etc.*); **trencilla** *f.* braid.

trenzar[9] *v.* to braid; **-se** to braid one's hair; *Am.* to fight hand to hand.

trepar *v.* to climb; to clamber; **-se** to climb; to clamber; to perch.

trepidación *f.* jar, vibration; trembling, shaking.

trepidar *v.* to shape, vibrate, tremble, jar.

treta *f.* trick, wile; **malas -s** bad tricks, bad habits.

triángulo *m.* triangle.

tribu *f.* tribe.

tribulación *f.* tribulation, trouble.

tribuna *f.* rostrum (*speaker's platform*).

tribunal *m.* tribunal; court of justice;

body of judges.

tributar *v.* to pay tribute, pay homage

tributario *adj. & m.* tributary.

tributo *m.* tribute; contribution, tax.

trifulca *f.* fight, quarrel, wrangle, row

trigo *m.* wheat.

trigueño *adj.* swarthy; brunet; dark.

trillado *p.p.* beaten; *adj.* trite, hackneyed, commonplace; **camino —** beaten path.

trillar *v.* to thresh; to beat, mistreat *Am.* to cut a path.

trimestre *m.* quarter, period of three months; quarterly payment, income o salary; **trimestral** *adj.* quarterly.

trinar *v.* to trill (*in singing*); to warble to quaver (*said of the voice*); to ge furious.

trinchante *m.* carving fork; carving knife; carver.

trinchar *v.* to carve (*meat*).

trinche *m.* fork; *Am.* carving table *Am.* **plato —** carving platter.

trinchera *f.* trench; ditch; *Am.* stock ade, fence; *Am.* curved knife.

trinchero *m.* carving table; **plato —** carving platter.

trineo *m.* sleigh; sled.

trino *m.* trill (*in singing*).

tripa *f.* intestine, bowel; paunch, belly **-s** entrails, insides.

triple *adj. & m.* triple.

triplicar[6] *v.* to triplicate, triple, treble

tripulación *f.* crew, ship's company.

tripular *v.* to man (*a ship*).

trique *m.* crack, snap; *Am.* utensil trinket; *Am.* clever trick in a game *Am.* drink made from barley; **-s** *Am* poor household utensils, goods, etc.

triscar[6] *v.* to romp, frisk, frolic; t stamp or shuffle the feet; *Am.* t tease, make fun of.

triste *adj.* sad; sorrowful; *Am.* bashful backward; *m. Am.* melancholy lov song.

tristeza *f.* sadness; sorrow; *Am.* tic fever.

tristón *adj.* wistful, quite sad, melan choly.

triunfal *adj.* triumphal.

triunfante *adj.* triumphant.

triunfar *v.* to triumph; to trump (*a cards*).

triunfo *m.* triumph; trump card; trophy

trivial *adj.* trivial, commonplace, trite.

triza *f.* shred, fragment, small piece cord, rope (*for sails*); **hacer -s** to tea into shreds; to tear to pieces.

trocar[2,6] *v. irr.* to change; to barter, ex change; to do one thing instead o another; **-se** to change; **to be transformed;** to exchange.

trocha *f.* path, trail; *Am.* gauge (*of a railway*); *Am.* trot; *Am.* slice or serving of meat.

trofeo *m.* trophy; booty, **spoils.**

troj, troje *m.* barn, **granary.**

trole *m* trolley

tromba *f.* waterspout.

trombón *m.* trombone.

trompa *f.* trumpet; trunk of an elephant; large spinning top; *Am.* snout; *Am.* cowcatcher (*of a locomotive*).

trompada *f.* blow with the fist; bump.

trompeta *f.* trumpet; *m.* trumpeter; useless individual; *Am.* drunk, drunkard; *Am.* bold, shameless fellow.

trompetear *v.* to trumpet, blow the trumpet.

trompo *m.* spinning top; stupid fellow, dunce.

tronada *f.* thunderstorm.

tronar² *v. irr.* to thunder; to explode, burst; *Am.* to execute by shooting; **— los dedos** to snap one's fingers; **por lo que pueda —** just in case.

tronco *m.* tree trunk; log; stem; trunk (*of the human body*); team (*of horses*).

tronchar *v.* to bend or break (*a stalk or trunk*); to chop off; to break off; **-se** to break off or get bent (*said of a stalk or trunk*); *Am.* to get twisted or bent.

tronera *f.* opening; porthole (*through which to shoot*); small, narrow window; pocket of a billiard table; *m.* madcap, reckless fellow.

tronido *m.* thunder; detonation, sharp, sudden sound.

trono *m.* throne.

tropa *f.* troop; crowd; *Am.* herd of cattle, drove of horses (*often* **tropilla**).

tropel *m.* throng; bustle, rush; jumble, confusion.

tropezar¹,⁹ *v. irr.* to stumble; to blunder; **— con** to meet, come across, encounter.

tropezón *m.* stumbling; stumble; slip; **a -es** falteringly, stumbling along clumsily; **darse un —** to stumble, trip.

tropical *adj.* tropical.

trópico *m.* tropic.

tropiezo *m.* stumble; stumbling block; slip, fault; dispute.

tropilla *f.* small troop; *Am.* drove of horses guided by the **madrina;** *Am.* pack of dogs; *Am.* group of spare saddle horses.

tropillero *m. Am.* horse wrangler, herdsman.

trotar *v.* to trot; to hurry.

trote *m.* trot; **al —** quickly.

trovador *m.* troubadour, minstrel.

troza *f.* log.

trozar⁹ *v.* to cut off, break off (*a piece*); to break or cut into pieces.

trozo *m.* piece, bit, fragment; passage, selection.

truco *m.* clever trick; pocketing of a ball (*in the game of pool*); *Am.* blow with the fist; *Am.* a card game; **-s** game of pool (*game similar to billiards*).

truculencia *f.* cruelty, ferocity, ruthlessness.

truculento *adj.* cruel, fierce, ruthless.

trucha *f.* trout; *Am.* vendor's portable stand.

trueno *m.* thunder; explosion, report of a gun; wild youth, troublemaker; *Am.* firecracker, rocket.

trueque, trueco *m.* exchange; barter; *Am.* change, small money; **a** (*or* **en**) **— de** in exchange for.

truhán *m.* scoundrel; swindler; cheat; buffoon, jester.

tu *adj.* thy; your (*fam. sing.*).

tú *pers. pron.* thou; you (*fam. sing.*).

tualet = lavabo.

tuberculosis *f.* tuberculosis; **tuberculoso** *adj.* tuberculous, tubercular.

tubería *f.* tubing, piping; pipe line.

tubo *m.* tube; pipe; lamp chimney; **— de ensayo** test tube.

tuerca *f.* nut (*of a screw*); **llave de -s** wrench.

tuerto· *adj.* one-eyed; blind in one eye; *m.* wrong, injustice; **a — o a derecho** (*or* **a tuertas o a derechas**) rightly or wrongly; thoughtlessly.

tuétano *m.* marrow; pith; innermost part; **mojado hasta los -s** soaked through and through.

tufo *m.* vapor, fume; disagreeable odor; airs, conceit; **tufillo** *m.* whiff, pungent odor.

tul *m.* tulle (*a thin, fine net for veils*); **tul, tule** *m. Am.* a kind of reed or bulrush (*used in the manufacture of seats and backs of chairs*).

tulipán *m.* tulip.

tu·lido *p.p.* crippled; paralyzed; numb.

tullirse²⁰ *v. irr.* to become crippled; to become numb or paralyzed.

tumba *f.* tomb; grave; *Am.* felling of timber; *Am.* forest clearing.

tumbar *v.* to knock down; *Am.* to fell timber; **-se** to lie down.

tumbo *m.* tumble; somersault; **dar -s** to jump, bump along.

tumor *m.* tumor; **tumorcillo** *m.* boil; small tumor.

tumulto *m.* tumult, uproar; mob, throng.

tumultuoso *adj.* tumultuous.

tuna *f.* prickly pear.

tunante *m. & f.* rascal, rogue, scamp; loafer; *Am.* libertine, licentious or lewd person.

tunda *f.* whipping, thrashing; shearing (*the nap of cloth*).

tundir *v.* to lash, beat, whip; to shear (*the nap of cloth*).

túnel *m.* tunnel.

túnica *f.* tunic; gown, robe.

tupido *adj.* dense; compact, thick; blocked, obstructed.

tupir *v.* to press, pack, squeeze together; to stop up, clog; -se to get stopped up; to stuff oneself; to become dense (*as a forest*); *Am.* to get astonished or confused.

turba *f.* mob, throng.

turbación *f.* disturbance, confusion; embarrassment.

turbamulta *f.* throng, mob, crowd.

turbar *v.* to perturb; to disturb; to trouble; -se to get disturbed, confused, embarrassed.

turbio *adj.* muddy; muddled, confused.

turbulento *adj.* turbulent; restless; disorderly.

turco *adj.* Turkish; *m.* Turk; Turkish; Turkish language; *Am.* peddler.

turismo *m.* tourist travel; touring, sightseeing; **oficina de —** travel bureau; **turista** *m. & f.* tourist.

turnar *v.* to alternate; -se to alternate; to take turns.

turno *m.* turn, alternate order.

turrón *m.* nougat, nut confection; almond cake; *Am.* **romper el —** to decide to use the **tú** form of address (*as a mark of close friendship*).

tusa *f. Am.* corn, corncob; *Am.* corn husk; *Am.* corn silk, tassel of an ear of corn.

tusar *v. Am.* to shear; *Am.* to crop, cut badly (*hair*).

tutear *v.* to address familiarly (*using the* **tú** *form*).

tutela *f.* guardianship; guidance, protection.

tutelar *v.* to guide, coach, direct; *adj.* guiding, guardian (*used as adj.*).

tutor *m.* tutor; guardian.

tuyo *poss. adj.* your, of yours (*fam. sing.*); *poss. pron.* yours.

U

u *conj.* (*before words beginning with o or ho*) or.

ubicar[6] *v. Am.* to locate; -se to be situated or located.

ubre *f.* udder.

ufanarse *v.* to glory (in); to be proud (of).

ufano *adj.* proud; gay; self-satisfied.

ujier *m.* usher, doorman.

úlcera *f.* ulcer; sore.

ulterior *adj.* ulterior; further; later.

ultimar *v.* to put an end to; *Am.* to give the finishing blow, kill.

último *adj.* last, final; ultimate; latest; **estar en las últimas** to be on one's last legs; to be at the end of one's rope, be at the end of one's resources.

ultrajar *v.* to outrage, insult; to scorn.

ultraje *m.* outrage, insult.

ultramar *m.* country or place across the sea; **de —** overseas, from across the sea; **en** (*or* **a**) **—** overseas.

ulular *v.* to howl, shriek, hoot.

umbral *m.* threshold.

umbrío *adj.* shady.

un(o) *indef. art.* a, an; -s some, a few; -s **cuantos** a few; **uno** *pron. & num.* one.

unánime *adj.* unanimous.

unanimidad *f.* unanimity, complete accord.

unción *f.* unction (*anointing with oil*); religious fervor; spiritual grace; **Extremaunción** Extreme Unction (*the Last Sacrament of the Church*).

uncir[10] *v.* to yoke.

ungir[11] *v.* to anoint; to consecrate.

ungüento *m.* ointment; salve.

único *adj.* only, sole; unique, singular, rare.

unidad *f.* unity; unit.

unificar[6] *v.* to unify; to unite.

uniformar *v.* to standardize; to make uniform; to furnish with uniforms.

uniforme *adj. & m.* uniform.

uniformidad *f.* uniformity.

unilateral *adj.* unilateral, one-sided.

unión *f.* union.

unir *v.* to unite; to join; to bring together; -se to unite, join together; to wed.

universal *adj.* universal.

universidad *f.* university.

universo *m.* universe.

untar *v.* to anoint; to smear; to oil, grease; to bribe; to corrupt; -se to smear oneself; to get smeared.

unto *m.* grease, fat; ointment.

untuosidad *f.* greasiness; **untuoso** *adj.* unctuous; oily, greasy.

uña *f.* fingernail; toenail; claw; hoof; hook (*on a tool*); **a — de caballo** at

full gallop, at full speed; largo de -s prone to stealing; *Am.* **largas -s** thief; **vivir de sus -s** to live by stealing; *Am.* **echar la — to steal; ser — y carne** to be inseparable friends.

urbanidad *f.* courtesy, politeness; refinement.

urbano *adj.* urban; courteous, polite.

urbe *f.* metropolis, large city.

urdimbre *f.* warp (*of a fabric*); scheme.

urdir *v.* to warp (*in weaving*); to plot, scheme; to invent (*a lie, story, etc.*).

urgencia *f.* urgency; pressing need.

urgente *adj.* urgent, pressing.

urgir[11] *v.* to urge; to be urgent.

urna *f.* urn; — **electoral** ballot box.

urraca *f.* magpie.

usado *p.p.* & *adj.* used;. accustomed; worn; threadbare.

usanza *f.* usage, custom, habit.

usar *v.* to use; to wear; to wear out; to be accustomed; **-se** to be in use, be in vogue.

uso *m.* use; usage; wear; practice, habit; custom; **al — de la época** according to the custom or usage of the period; **estar en buen — to** be in good condition (*said of a thing*).

usted *pers. pron.* (*abbreviated as* Vd., V., *or* Ud.) you.

usual *adj.* usual; ordinary, customary.

usufructo *m.* use, enjoyment; profit.

usufructuar[18] *v.* to enjoy the use of; to make use of.

usura *f.* usury.

usurero *m.* usurer, loan shark.

usurpar *v.* to usurp.

utensilio *m.* utensil; implement, tool.

útero *m.* uterus, womb.

útil *adj.* useful; profitable; **-es** *m. pl.* tools, instruments.

utilidad *f.* utility; profit; usefulness.

utilizar[9] *v.* to utilize; to use.

uva *f.* grape; — **espina** gooseberry; — **pasa** raisin; **estar hecho una — to** be tipsy, drunk.

V

vaca *f.* cow; **carne de — beef; cuero de — cowhide;** *Am.* **hacer — to** play hooky, play truant, cut class; to join in a quick business deal.

vacación *f.* vacation (*usually* **vacaciones**).

vacada *f.* herd of cows.

vacancia *f.* vacancy.

vacante *adj.* vacant, unfilled, unoccupied; *f.* vacancy.

vaciar[17] *v.* to empty; to drain; to cast into a mold;. to hollow out; to flow

(into); **-se** to spill; to empty; to become empty; to flow (into).

vaciedad *f.* emptiness; nonsense, silliness.

vacilación *f.* hesitation; wavering; doubt.

vacilante *adj.* vacillating, hesitating, wavering; unsteady.

vacilar *v.* to vacillate, waver, hesitate; to sway.

vacío *adj.* empty; vacant; unoccupied; hollow; *m.* void; hollow; vacuum; vacancy; gap, blank.

vacuna *f.* vaccine; vaccination; cowpox (*eruptive disease of the cow*); **vacunación** *f.* vaccination.

vacunar *v.* to vaccinate.

vadear *v.* to ford; to wade; to avoid (*a difficulty*).

vado *m.* ford; **no hallar — to** find no way out.

vagabundear *v.* to tramp around, wander, rove; to loiter.

vagabundo *adj.* vagabond, wandering; *m.* vagabond, tramp; vagrant; wanderer.

vagar[7] *v.* to wander, roam; to loiter; to loaf; *m.* leisure; loitering.

vago *adj.* vague; roaming; idle; vagrant; *m.* vagrant, tramp.

vagón *m.* railway car or coach; **vagoneta** *f.* small railway car or tram (*used in mines*); **vagonada** *f.* carload.

vaguear = **vagar**.

vahído *m.* dizziness, dizzy spell.

vaho *m.* vapor, steam, mist; odor.

vaina *f.* sheath, scabbard; case; pod, husk; *Am.* bother, nuisance; *Am.* luck.

vainilla *f.* vanilla.

vaivén *m.* sway; fluctuation, wavering; traffic, coming and going; **-es comings** and goings; ups and downs; inconstancy.

vajilla *f.* tableware; set of dishes; — **de plata** silverware; — **de porcelana** chinaware.

vale *m.* bond, promissory note; voucher; adieu, farewell; *m.* & *f. Am.* comrade, pal, chum.

valedero *adj.* valid, binding, effective.

valedor *m.* defender, protector; *Am.* pal, comrade.

valenciano *adj.* Valencian, of or from Valencia, Spain; *m.* Valencian.

valentía *f.* courage, valor; exploit; boast.

valentón *adj.* blustering, boastful; *m.* bully, braggart.

valer[47] *v. irr.* to favor, protect; to cost; to be worth; to be worthy; to be

217

equivalent to; to be valid; to prevail; to be useful; — la pena to be worth while; — por to be worth; -se de to avail oneself of, make use of; más vale it is better; ¡válgame Dios! heaven help me! good heavens!

valeroso *adj.* valiant, brave; valuable.

valía *f.* worth, value; influence.

validez *f.* validity; stability, soundness.

válido *adj.* valid.

valiente *adj.* valiant, brave; powerful; *m.* brave man; bully.

valija *f.* valise, satchel; mailbag.

valimiento *m.* favor, protection; gozar de — to enjoy protection or favor.

valioso *adj.* valuable, worthy; wealthy.

valor *m.* value; worth; price; significance; valor, courage; boldness, efficacy, power; -es stocks, bonds.

valoración *f.* valuation, appraisal.

valorar *v.* to evaluate, value, appraise.

valorizar[9] *v. Am.* to value, appraise; *Am.* to realize, convert into money.

vals *m.* waltz.

valsar *v.* to waltz.

valuación *f.* valuation, appraisal.

valuar[18] *v.* to value, price, appraise; to rate.

válvula *f.* valve.

valla *f.* stockade, fence; barrier; obstacle; *Am.* cockpit (*for cockfights*).

vallado *m.* stockade, fenced-in place; fence.

valle *m.* valley; vale.

vanagloria *f.* vainglory, boastful vanity.

vanagloriarse[17] *v.* to glory, take great pride (in), boast (of).

vanaglorioso *adj.* vain, boastful, conceited.

vanguardia *f.* vanguard.

vanidad *f.* vanity; conceit; emptiness.

vanidoso *adj.* vain, conceited.

vano *adj.* vain; empty; hollow; *m.* opening in a wall (*for a door or window*).

vapor *m.* vapor, steam, mist; steamer, steamship.

vaporoso *adj.* vaporous, steamy, misty; vaporlike.

vapulear *v.* to beat, whip, thrash.

vapuleo *m.* beating, whipping, thrashing.

vaquería *f.* herd of cows; stable for cows; dairy.

vaquerizo *m.* herdsman; *adj.* pertaining to cows; **vaqueriza** *f.* stable for cows.

vaquero *m.* cowherd, herdsman; cowboy; *Am.* milkman; *adj.* relating to cowherds, cowboys, or cattle.

vaqueta *f.* sole leather; cowhide; *Am.* zurrar a uno la — to tan someone's hide, beat someone up.

vara *f.* twig; stick; rod; wand; staff; yard, yardstick; thrust with a picador's lance.

varadero *m.* shipyard.

varar *v.* to beach (*a boat*); to run aground; to stop, come to a standstill (*said of business*).

varear *v.* to beat; to whip; to sell by the yard; to measure with a vara; *Am.* to exercise (*a horse before a race*).

variable *adj.* variable, unstable, changeable; *f.* variable.

variación *f.* variation.

variado *p.p. & adj.* varied; variegated.

variar[17] *v.* to vary; to change; to shift; to differ.

variedad *f.* variety; variation, change.

varilla *f.* small rod; wand; long, flexible twig; rib (*of an umbrella or fan*); corset stay; *Am.* peddler's wares.

varillero *m. Am.* peddler.

vario *adj.* various; different; changeable; varied; -s various, several.

varón *m.* male, man; *Am.* long beam, timber.

varonil *adj.* manly; strong; brave.

vasallo *adj. & m.* vassal, subject.

vasco, vascongado *adj. & m.* Basque.

vasija *f.* vessel, container, receptacle.

vaso *m.* drinking glass; glassful; vase; vessel; hull of a ship; horse's hoof; — de elección person chosen by God.

vástago *m.* shoot, sprout, stem; scion, offspring; *Am.* stem, trunk of a banana tree.

vasto *adj.* vast, extensive, large.

vate *m.* bard, poet.

vaticinar *v.* to prophesy, predict, foretell.

vaticinio *m.* prophecy, prediction.

vecindad *f.* vicinity; neighborhood neighborliness; casa de — tenement.

vecindario *m.* neighborhood, neighbors vicinity.

vecino *m.* neighbor; resident; citizen *adj.* neighboring; next, near.

vedar *v.* to prohibit; to impede.

vega *f.* fertile lowland or plain; *Am* tobacco plantation.

vegetación *f.* vegetation.

vegetal *adj.* vegetable; *m.* vegetable plant.

vegetar *v.* to vegetate.

vehemente *adj.* vehement, passionate impetuous; violent.

vehículo *m.* vehicle.

veintena *f.* score, twenty.

veintena *f.* score, twenty.

vejestorio *m.* wrinkled old person.

vejete *m.* little old man.

vejez *f.* old age.

vejiga *f.* bladder; blister; smallpox sore; — **de la bilis** (*or* — **de la hiel**) gall bladder.

vela *f.* vigil, watch; night watch; candle; sail; **a toda** — under full sail; **at full** speed; **en** — on watch, without sleep; **hacerse a la** — to set sail.

velada *f.* watch, vigil; evening party; evening function or meeting.

velador *m.* night watchman; keeper, guard; lamp table; bedside table; candlestick; *Am.* lamp shade.

velar *v.* to keep vigil; to stay up at night; to be vigilant; to watch over; to veil; to cover, hide.

velatorio *m.* wake (*vigil over a corpse*). See **velorio**.

veleidoso *adj.* inconstant, fickle, change-able.

velero *m.* sailboat; sailmaker; candle-maker; *adj.* swift-sailing; **buque** — sailboat.

veleta *f.* weathervane, weathercock; *m.* & *f.* fickle person.

velis *m. Am.* valise.

velo *m.* veil; curtain, covering; — **del paladar** velum, soft palate.

velocidad *f.* velocity.

velocímetro *m.* speedometer.

velorio *m. Am.* wake (*vigil over a corpse*); *Am.* dull party.

veloz *adj.* swift, quick, fast.

vello *m.* hair (*on the body*); down, fuzz; nap (*of cloth*).

vellón *m.* fleece; tuft of wool; sheepskin with fleece; silver and copper alloy; an ancient copper coin.

velloso *adj.* hairy; downy, fuzzy.

velludo *adj.* hairy; downy; fuzzy; *m.* plush; velvet.

vena *f.* vein; lode, vein of metal ore; mood, disposition; **estar en** — to be in the mood; to be inspired.

venado *m.* deer; venison, deer meat; *Am.* **pintar** — to play hooky.

vencedor *adj.* conquering, winning, vic-torious; *m.* conqueror, winner, victor.

vencer[10] *v.* to conquer, vanquish; to de-feat; to overcome; to surpass; to win; **-se** to control oneself; to mature, fall due; **se venció el plazo** the time limit expired.

vencido *p.p. & adj.* conquered; defeated; due, fallen due.

vencimiento *m.* conquering, defeat; maturity (*of a debt*), falling due; ex-piration (*of a period of time*).

venda *f.* bandage.

vendaje *m.* bandage.

vendar *v.* to bandage; to blindfold.

vendaval *m.* strong wind, gale.

vendedor *m.* vendor, seller, peddler.

vender *v.* to sell; to betray; **-se** to be sold; to sell oneself, accept a bribe.

vendimia *f.* vintage; profit.

venduta *f. Am.* auction; *Am.* small fruit and vegetable store.

veneno *m.* venom, poison.

venenoso *adj.* poisonous.

venerable *adj.* venerable.

veneración *f.* veneration, reverence.

venerando *adj.* venerable, worthy of respect.

venerar *v.* to venerate, revere; to wor-ship.

venero *m.* water spring; source, origin; lode, layer, seam (*of mineral*).

venezolano *adj.* Venezuelan; *m.* Vene-zuelan; *Am.* Venezuelan silver coin.

vengador *adj.* avenging, revenging; *m.* avenger.

venganza *f.* vengeance, revenge.

vengar[7] *v.* to avenge, revenge; **-se de** to take revenge on.

vengativo *adj.* vindictive, revengeful.

venia *f.* pardon; permission, leave; bow, nod; *Am.* military salute.

venida *f.* arrival; return; river flood, onrush of water; attack (*in fencing*).

venidero *adj.* coming, future; **en lo** — in the future; **-s** *m. pl.* successors.

venir[48] *v. irr.* to come; to arrive; to fit; **-le a uno bien** (*or* **mal**) to be becom-ing (*or* unbecoming); — **a menos** to decline, decay; — **a pelo** to come just at the right moment; to suit perfectly; to be pat, opportune, to the point; — **en** to agree to; — **sobre** to fall upon; **¿a qué viene eso?** what is the point of that?; **-se abajo** to fall down; to collapse; to fail.

venoso *adj.* veined; venous (*of or per-taining to the veins; with veins*).

venta *f.* sale; roadside inn; *Am.* store, vendor's stand; — **pública** auction.

ventaja *f.* advantage; gain, profit; bonus; odds.

ventajoso *adj.* advantageous, beneficial, profitable; *Am.* self-seeking, profiteer-ing.

ventana *f.* window; window shutter; *Am.* clearing (*in a forest*); — (*or* **ventanilla**) **de la nariz** nostril.

ventarrón *m.* gale, strong wind.

ventear *v.* to scent, sniff; to nose around; to air; to blow, be windy; *Am.* to toss in the wind; *Am.* to flee; *Am.* to outrun; **-se** to expel air, break wind; *Am.* to stay outdoors.

ventero *m.* innkeeper.

ventilación f. ventilation.

ventilador m. ventilator; fan (for ventilation).

ventilar v. to ventilate; to air.

ventisca f. blizzard, snowstorm; snowdrift.

ventiscar[6] v. to snow hard and blow (as in a blizzard); to drift (as 'snow in a blizzard).

ventisquero m. blizzard, snowstorm; glacier; snowdrift; snow-capped mountain peak.

ventolera f. gust of wind; pride, vanity; whim; pin wheel; **darle a uno la — de** to take the notion to.

ventoso adj. windy.

ventura f. happiness; fortune, chance; risk, danger; **a la —** at random; **buena — fortune; por —** perchance.

venturoso adj. fortunate, lucky; happy.

ver[49] v. irr. to see; to look; to look at; to look into, examine; **— de** to try to, see to it that; **a más** (or **hasta más**) **—** good-bye; **no — la hora de** to be anxious to; **no tener nada que — con** not to have anything to do with; **-se** to be seen; to be; **-se obligado a** to be obliged to, be forced to; **a mi modo de —** in my opinion; **de buen — good-looking; ser de —** to be worth seeing.

vera f. edge; **a la — del camino** at the edge of the road.

veracidad f. truthfulness.

veraneante m. & f. summer resorter, vacationist, or tourist.

veranear v. to spend the summer.

veraneo m. summering, summer vacation.

veraniego adj. summer, of summer.

verano m. summer.

veras f. pl. reality, truth; **de —** in truth; truly; in earnest.

veraz adj. truthful.

verbal adj. verbal; oral.

verbena f. verbena (a plant); festival or carnival (on eve of a religious holiday).

verbigracia adv. for instance, for example.

verbo m. verb; **el Verbo** the Word (second person of the Trinity).

verboso adj. verbose, wordy.

verdad f. truth; ¿ — ? really?; is that so?; isn't that so?; **— de Perogrullo** truism, evident truth; **de —** (or **a la —**) in truth, in earnest; **en —** really, truly.

verdadero adj. real; true; truthful; sincere.

verde adj. green; unripe; young; off-

color, indecent; m. green; verdure; Am. country, countryside.

verdear v. to grow green; to look green.

verdinegro adj. dark-green.

verdor m. verdure, greenness.

verdoso adj. greenish.

verdugo m. executioner; cruel person; torment; rapier (light sword); lash, whip; welt; shoot of a tree; **verdugón** m. large welt.

verdulera f. woman „vendor of green vegetables; **verdulería** f. green vegetable store or stand.

verdura f. verdure; greenness; green vegetables.

vereda f. path; Am. sidewalk.

veredicto m. verdict.

vergonzoso adj. shameful, disgraceful; shy, bashful; m. species of armadillo.

vergüenza f. shame; disgrace; shyness, bashfulness; **tener —** to have shame; to be ashamed.

vericueto m. rugged, wild place (often rocky).

verídico adj. truthful; true.

verificar[6] v. to verify; to confirm; to test, check; to carry out, fulfill; **-se** to be verified; to take place.

verijas f. pl. Am. groin (hollow between lower part of abdomen and thigh); Am. flanks of a horse.

verja f. grate, grating.

verruga f. wart; nuisance.

versado adj. versed, skilled, expert.

versar v. to deal (with), treat (of); **-se en** to become versed in.

versión f. version; translation.

verso m. verse; meter; **— suelto** (or **— libre**) free or blank verse.

verter[1] v. irr. to pour; to empty; to spill; to translate; to flow down.

vertical adj. vertical.

vértice m. top, apex, summit.

vertiente f. slope; watershed; adj. flowing.

vertiginoso adj. whirling, dizzy, giddy.

vértigo m. dizziness, giddiness; fit of madness.

vestíbulo m. vestibule; lobby.

vestido m. clothing, apparel; dress; garment; suit.

vestidura f. vestment; attire, apparel; raiment.

vestigio m. vestige, sign, trace.

vestir[5] v. irr. to dress; to clothe; to wear; to put on; to adorn; to cover; **-se** to dress, get dressed; to be clothed; to be covered.

vestuario m. wardrobe, apparel; theatrical costumes; cloakroom; dressing room; vestry (*room for church vestments*).

veta *f.* vein, seam (*of mineral*); streak, grain (*in wood*); stripe; *Am.* rope.

veteado *adj.* veined; striped; streaked.

veterano *adj. & m.* veteran.

veterinario *m.* veterinary.

veto *m.* veto.

vetusto *adj.* old, ancient.

vez *f.* time, occasion; turn; **a la —** at the same time; **cada — más** more and more; **cada — que** whenever; **de — en cuando** from time to time; **de una —** all at once; **en — de** instead of; **otra —** again; **una que otra —** rarely, once in a while; **tal —** perhaps; **a veces** sometimes; **raras veces** seldom; **hacer las veces de** to take the place of.

vía *f.* way; road; track; railroad track; conduit; **Vía Crucis** the Way of the Cross; **Vía Láctea** the Milky Way.

viaducto *m.* viaduct.

viajante *m.* traveler; **— de comercio** traveling salesman.

viajar *v.* to travel.

viaje *m.* voyage; trip; travel; **— de ida y vuelta** (or **— redondo**) round trip.

viajero *m.* traveler; *adj.* traveling.

vianda *f.* viands, food; meal.

viandante *m. & f.* wayfarer, walker, pedestrian; passer-by; vagabond.

viático *m.* provisions for a journey; viaticum (*communion given to dying persons*).

víbora *f.* viper.

vibración *f.* vibration.

vibrante *adj.* vibrant, vibrating.

vibrar *v.* to vibrate.

vicepresidente *m.* vice-president.

viceversa *adv.* vice versa, conversely.

viciado *adj.* contaminated, foul; corrupt; *p.p.* of **viciar.**

viciar *v.* to vitiate, corrupt; to adulterate; to falsify; **-se** to become corrupt.

vicio *m.* vice; bad habit; fault; craving; **de — as** a habit; **hablar de —** to talk too much; **-s** *Am.* articles and ingredients used for serving *mate.*

vicioso *adj.* vicious, evil, wicked; having bad habits; licentious; faulty, incorrect (*grammatical construction, reasoning, etc.*).

vicisitud *f.* vicissitude; **-es** vicissitudes, ups and downs, changes of fortune or condition.

víctima *f.* victim.

victoria *f.* victory, triumph; victoria (*carriage*).

victorioso *adj.* victorious.

vicuña *f.* vicuña (*an Andean animal allied to the alpaca and llama*); vicuña wool; vicuña cloth.

vid *f.* vine, grapevine.

vida *f.* life; living; livelihood; **— mía** dearest; **hacer —** to live together; **pasar a mejor —** to die; **tener la — en un hilo** to be in great danger

vidalita *f.* *Am.* melancholy song of Argentina and Chile.

vidente *m.* seer, prophet; *adj.* seeing.

vidriado *m.* glaze; glazed earthenware; *p.p. & adj.* glazed.

vidriar[17] *v.* to glaze (*earthenware*).

vidriera *f.* glass window; glass door; *Am.* show case, show window; **— de colores** stained-glass window.

vidriero *m.* glazier (*one who installs windowpanes*); glass blower; glass maker; glass dealer.

vidrio *m.* glass; any glass article.

vidrioso *adj.* glassy; brittle; slippery, icy; touchy, irritable.

viejo *adj.* old; ancient; worn-out; *m.* old man; **— verde** old man who boasts of his youth and vigor; *Am.* **los -s** the old folks (*applied to one's parents*); **viejota** *f.* old hag.

viento *m.* wind; scent; **hace —** it is windy; **a los cuatro -s** in all directions; **vientecito** *m.* gentle breeze.

vientre *m.* abdomen; belly; bowels; entrails; womb.

viernes *m.* Friday.

viga *f.* beam; rafter.

vigencia *f.* operation (*of a law*); **entrar en —** to take effect (*said of a law*); **estar en —** to be in force (*said of a law*).

vigente *adj.* effective, in force (*as a law*).

vigía *f.* lookout, watchtower; watch (*act of watching*); reef; *m.* lookout, watchman.

vigilancia *f.* vigilance.

vigilante *adj.* vigilant, watchful; *m.* watchman.

vigilar *v.* to keep guard; to watch over.

vigilia *f.* vigil, watch; wakefulness; sleeplessness; night hours (*spent in study*); eve before certain church festivals; vesper service; **día de —** day of abstinence; **comer de —** to abstain from meat.

vigor *m.* vigor; **en — in** force (*said of a law*); **entrar en —** to become effective (*as a law, statute, etc.*).

vigorizar[9] *v.* to invigorate, tone up, give vigor to, strengthen.

vigoroso *adj.* vigorous.

vihuela *f.* guitar.

vil *adj.* vile, base, low, mean.

vileza *f.* villainy; baseness; vile act.

vilipendiar *v.* to revile.

vilo : en — in the air; suspended; undecided; in suspense; **llevar en —** to waft.

villa *f.* village; villa, country house.

villancico *m.* carol; Christmas carol.

villanía *f.* villainy; lowliness.

villano *adj.* rustic, uncouth; villainous, mean, base; *m.* villain; rustic, peasant.

villorrio *m.* small village, hamlet.

vinagre *m.* vinegar; **vinagrera** *f.* vinegar cruet.

vincular *v.* to tie, bind, unite; to entail (*limit the inheritance of property*); to found, base (on).

vínculo *m.* bond, tie, chain; entailed inheritance.

vindicar[6] *v.* to vindicate; to avenge; to defend, assert (*one's rights*); **-se** to avenge oneself; to defend oneself.

vino *m.* wine; **— amontillado** good grade of pale sherry (*originally from Montilla*); **— tinto** dark-red wine; **vinería** *f. Am.* wineshop; **vinero** *adj. Am.* pertaining to wine; **vinoso** *adj.* winy.

viña *f.* vineyard.

viñedo *m.* vineyard.

violación *f.* violation.

violado *adj.* violet; *m.* violet, violet color; *p.p.* violated.

violar *v.* to violate; to rape.

violencia *f.* violence.

violentar *v.* to force; to break into (*a house*); **-se** to force oneself; to get angry.

violento *adj.* violent; impetuous; forced; strained; unnatural.

violeta *f.* violet.

violín *m.* violin; *m. & f.* violinist; *Am.* **estar hecho un —** to be very thin.

violinista *m. & f.* violinist.

virada *f.* tack, change of direction, turn.

virar *v.* to turn, turn around, change direction; to tack (*said of a ship*).

virgen *adj. & f.* virgin.

virginal *adj.* virginal, virgin, pure.

viril *adj.* virile, manly.

virilidad *f.* virility, manhood, manly strength, vigor.

virreinato *m.* viceroyalty (*office or jurisdiction of a viceroy*).

virrey *m.* viceroy.

virtud *f.* virtue.

virtuoso *adj.* virtuous; *m.* virtuoso (*person skilled in an art*).

viruela *f.* smallpox; pock (*mark left by smallpox*); **-s locas** (*or* **-s bastardas**) chicken pox.

viruta *f.* wood shaving.

visa *f.* visa, visé; **visado** *p.p. of* **visar;** *m.* visa, visé.

visaje *m.* grimace; wry face; **hacer -s** to make faces.

visar *v.* to visé; to approve; to O.K.

viscoso *adj.* slimy, sticky.

visera *f.* visor; eye shade; *Am.* blinder (*on a horse's bridle*).

visible *adj.* visible; evident; conspicuous, notable.

visillo *m.* window curtain.

visión *f.* vision; sight; fantasy; apparition; sight (*ridiculous-looking person or thing*).

visionario *adj. & m.* visionary.

visita *f.* visit, call; visitor; callers, company; **— de cumplimiento** (*or* **— de cumplido**) formal courtesy call; **— domiciliaria** police inspection of a house; home call (*of a social worker, doctor, etc.*).

visitación *f.* visitation, visit.

visitador *m.* visitor, caller; inspector.

visitante *m. & f.* caller, visitor; *adj.* visiting.

visitar *v.* to visit; to inspect.

vislumbrar *v.* to catch a glimpse of; to guess, surmise; **-se** to be faintly visible.

vislumbre *f.* glimmer; glimpse; vague idea; faint appearance.

viso *m.* appearance, semblance; pretense, pretext; luster, brilliance, glitter; glass curtain; **a dos -s** with a double view; with a double purpose.

víspera *f.* eve, evening or day before; time just before; **-s** vespers; **en -s de** on the eve of; about to.

vista *f.* sight; vision; view; landscape; look, glance; **a — de** in the presence of; in front of, within view of; **pagadero a la —** payable at sight or upon presentation; **¡hasta la — !** good-bye!; **bajar la —** to lower one's eyes; **conocer de —** to know by sight; **hacer la — gorda** to pretend not to see; **pasar la — por** to glance over; **perder de —** to lose sight of; **tener a la —** to have before one; to have received (*a letter*).

vistazo *m.* glance; **dar un — a** to glance over.

visto *p.p. of* **ver** seen; *adj.* evident, clear; **bien —** well thought of, proper; **mal —** looked down upon, improper; **— bueno** (V°.B° .) approved (O.K.); **dar el — bueno** to approve, O.K.; **— que** whereas, considering that.

222

vistoso *adj.* showy; colorful.
vital *adj.* vital; important, necessary.
vitalicio *adj.* for life; *m.* life-insurance policy; lifetime pension.
vitalidad *f.* vitality.
vitamina *f.* vitamin.
vítor *m.* cheer, applause; ¡ — ! hurrah!
vitorear *v.* to cheer, applaud.
vitrina *f.* glass case; show case; show window.
vituallas *f. pl.* victuals, food, provisions.
vituperar *v.* to revile, insult, call bad names.
vituperio *m.* affront, insult; reproach; censure.
viuda *f.* widow.
viudez *f.* widowhood.
viudo *m.* widower.
vivac, vivaque *m.* bivouac, military encampment; *Am.* police headquarters.
vivacidad *f.* vivacity; brightness; liveliness.
vivaracho *adj.* lively; vivacious, gay.
vivaz *adj.* vivacious, lively; bright, keen, witty.
víveres *m. pl.* food supplies, provisions.
vivero *m.* fish pond, fish hatchery, tree nursery.
viveza *f.* vivacity; animation, liveliness; quickness; brilliance, cleverness.
vívido *adj.* vivid; colorful.
vivienda *f.* dwelling; apartment.
viviente *adj.* living.
vivir *v.* to live; to endure, last; ¡viva! hurrah! long live! ¿quién vive? who goes there?; *m.* existence, living.
vivo *adj.* alive; living, lively; quick; vivid; bright; clever, wide-awake; **tío** — merry-go-round; **al** — vividly; **de viva voz** by word of mouth; **tocar en lo** — to hurt to the quick, touch the most sensitive spot.
vizcacha *f. Am.* viscacha (*South American rodent about the size of a hare*).
vizcachera *f. Am.* viscacha burrow or hole; *Am.* room filled with junk; **vizcacheral** *m. Am.* ground full of viscacha burrows.
vizcaíno *adj.* Biscayan, of or from Biscay, Spain.
vocablo *m.* word, term.
vocabulario *m.* vocabulary.
vocación *f.* vocation; aptness, talent.
vocal *adj.* vocal; oral; vowel; *f.* vowel; *m.* voter (*in an assembly or council*).
vocear *v* to shout; to cry out; to hail.
vocecita *f.* sweet little voice.
vocería *f* clamor, shouting.
vocerío *m* Am. clamor, shouting.
vocero *m* spokesman.

vociferar *v.* to shout, clamor; to yell; to boast loudly of.
vodevil *m.* vaudeville.
volante *adj.* flying; floating; **papel** (*or* **hoja**) — handbill, circular; *m.* ruffle, frill; steering wheel; balance wheel; flywheel.
volar[2] *v. irr.* to fly; to fly away; to explode; to irritate, pique; to rouse (*bird game*); **-se** *Am.* to fly off the handle, lose one's temper.
volátil *adj.* volatile; fickle, changeable; flying.
volcán *m.* volcano; *Am.* precipice; *Am.* swift torrent.
volcánico *adj.* volcanic.
volcar[2,6] *v. irr.* to overturn; to capsize; to upset; to make dizzy; **-se** to upset, get upset.
volear *v.* to volley, hit (*a ball*) in the air.
volición *f.* volition.
voltaje *m.* voltage.
voltear *v.* to turn, turn around; to revolve; to turn inside out; to overturn; to tumble or roll over; to turn a somersault; *Am.* to go prying around; *Am.* — **la espalda** to turn one's back; **-se** to turn over; to change sides.
voltereta *f.* somersault, tumble.
voltio, volt *m.* volt.
voluble *adj.* fickle; moody; changeable; twining (*as a climbing vine*).
volumen *m.* volume.
voluminoso *adj.* voluminous, bulky, very large.
voluntad *f.* will; desire; determination; benevolence, good will; consent; **última** — last will, testament; **de** (*or* **de buena**) — willingly, with pleasure.
voluntario *adj.* voluntary; willful; *m.* volunteer.
voluntarioso *adj.* willful.
voluptuoso *adj.* voluptuous; sensual.
voluta *f.* scroll, spiral-like ornament; **-s de humo** spirals of smoke.
volver[2,52] *v. irr.* to return; to turn; to turn up, over, or inside out; to restore; — **loco** to drive crazy; — **a** (+*inf.*) to do again; — **en sí** to come to, recover one's senses; — **por** to return for; to defend; **-se** to become; to turn; to turn around; to change one's ideas; **-se atrás** to go back; to back out, go back on one's word; **-se loco** to go crazy.
vomitar *v.* to vomit.
vómito *m.* vomit; vomiting.
voracidad *f.* voraciousness, greediness.
vorágine *f.* vortex, whirlpool.
voraz *adj.* voracious, ravenous, greedy.

vórtice *m.* vortex, whirlpool; whirlwind, tornado; center of a cyclone.

votación *f.* voting; vote, total number of votes.

votante *m. & f.* voter.

votar *v.* to vote; to vow; to curse; **¡voto a tal!** by Jove!

voto *m.* vote; vow; prayer; votive offering; oath; wish; — **de confianza** vote of confidence.

voz *f.* voice; sound; shout, outcry; word; rumor; — **común** common rumor or gossip; **a — en cuello** (*or* **a — en grito**) shouting; **at the top of one's lungs; en — alta** aloud; **a voces** shouting, with shouts; **secreto a voces** open secret; **dar voces** to shout, yell.

vozarrón *m.* loud, strong voice.

vuelco *m.* upset; overturning; capsizing; tumble.

vuelo *m.* flight; width, fulness (*of a dress or cloak*); frill, ruffle; jut, projection (*of a building*); **al** (*or* **a**) — on the fly; quickly; **levantar** (*or* **alzar**) **el** — to fly away; to soar.

vuelta *f.* turn; return; repetition; reverse side; cuff, facing of a sleeve; cloak lining; change (*money returned*); **a la** — around the corner; on returning; **a la** — **de los años** within a few years; *Am.* **otra** — again; **dar -s** to turn over and over; to wander about; **dar una** — to take a walk; **estar de** — to be back; **no tiene** — **de hoja** there are no two ways about it.

vuelto *p.p.* of **volver**; *m. Am.* change (*money returned*).

vuestro *poss. adj.* your, of yours (*fam. pl.*); *poss. pron.* yours.

vulgar *adj.* common, ordinary; in common use; low, vile, base.

vulgaridad *f.* vulgarity, coarseness, commonness.

vulgarismo *m.* slang, slang expression, vulgar or ungrammatical expression.

vulgo *m.* populace, the common people; *adv.* commonly, popularly.

Y

y *conj.* and.

ya *adv.* already; now; finally; soon, presently; in time; **¡** — **!** now I see!; **I understand; enough!; ¡** — **lo creo!** I should say so!; yes, of course!; — **no** no longer; — **que** since; although; — **se ve** of course; it is clear; — **voy** I am coming.

yacer[56] *v. irr.* to lie (*in the grave*); to be lying down; to lie, be situated.

yacimiento *m.* bed, layer (*of ore*); — **de**

petróleo oil field.

yanqui *m. & f.* North American, native of the United States; Yankee.

yantar *v.* to eat; *m.* food, meal.

yararás *f. Am.* Argentine poisonous snake.

yarda *f.* yard (*unit of measure*).

yate *m.* yacht.

yedra = **hiedra**.

yegua *f.* mare; *Am.* cigar butt; *adj. Am.* big, large; **yeguada** *f.* herd of mares.

yelmo *m.* helmet.

yema *f.* egg yolk; bud, shoot; candied egg yolk; — **del dedo** finger tip.

yerba = **hierba**.

yerbabuena *f.* mint; peppermint.

yerbero *m. Am.* herb vendor.

yermo *m.* desert, wilderness; *adj.* desert, uninhabited; uncultivated.

yerno *m.* son-in-law.

yerro *m.* error, fault, mistake.

yerto *adj.* stiff, motionless, rigid.

yesca *f.* tinder; anything highly inflammable; incentive (*to passion*); *Am.* **estar hecho una** — to be in great anger.

yeso *m.* gypsum, chalk; plaster; chalk (*for blackboard*); — **blanco** whitewash; — **mate** plaster of Paris; **yesoso** *adj.* chalky.

yo *pers. pron.* I.

yodo *m.* iodine.

yugo *m.* yoke; marriage tie; burden.

yunque *f.* anvil.

yunta *f.* yoke of oxen; pair of draft animals.

yuyo *m. Am.* wild grass, weeds; *Am.* an herb sauce; *Am.* garden stuff; *Am.* **estar** — to be lifeless, insipid; *Am.* **volverse uno** — to faint.

Z

zacate *m. Am.* grass, forage; hay.

zafado *adj.* impudent, brazen, shameless; *Am.* smart, wide-awake, keen; *Am.* "touched", half-crazy; *p.p.* of **zafar**.

zafar *v.* to release, set free; to dislodge; *Am.* to exclude; -**se** to slip away; to dodge; to get rid (of); to get loose; *Am.* to get dislocated (*said of a bone*); *Am.* to go crazy; *Am.* to use foul language.

zafio *adj.* coarse, uncouth, rude.

zafir, zafiro *m.* sapphire.

zafra *f.* sugar-making season; sugar making; sugar crop.

zaga *f.* rear; **a la** — (**a** *or* **en** —) behind.

zagal *m.* young shepherd; lad; **zagala** *f.* young shepherdess; lass, maiden; **zagalejo** *m.* young shepherd; short skirt; petticoat.

zaguán m. vestibule.

zaherir[3] v. irr. to hurt (feelings); to censure, reprove; to reproach.

zaino adj. treacherous; vicious; chestnut-colored (horse).

zalamero m. fawner, flatterer, servile person; **zalamería** f. flattery, scraping and bowing.

zalea f. pelt, undressed sheepskin.

zambo adj. knock-kneed; m. Am. Indian and negro half-breed; Am. a species of South American monkey.

zambullida f. dive, dip, plunge.

zambullir[20] v. to plunge, dip, duck; -se to dive; to plunge.

zambullón m. quick, sudden dip or dive.

zanahoria f. carrot.

zanca f. long leg of any fowl; long leg; long prop; **zancada** f. stride, long step.

zanco m. stilt; **andar en -s** to walk on stilts.

zancón adj. lanky, long-legged; Am. too short (skirt or dress).

zancudo adj. long-legged; m. Am. mosquito.

zángano m. drone; loafer, sponger; Am. rogue, rascal.

zangolotear v. to shake, jiggle; -se to shake; to waddle; to sway from side to side.

zangoloteo m. jiggle, jiggling; shaking; waddling.

zanguanga f. feigned illness; **hacer la —** to pretend to be ill; **zanguango** adj. lazy; silly; m. fool.

zanja f. ditch; trench; Am. irrigation ditch.

zanjar v. to excavate; to dig ditches in; to settle (disputes).

zapapico m. pickaxe.

zapateado m. a Spanish tap dance.

zapatear v. to tap with the feet; to tapdance.

zapateo m. tapping with the feet; Am. a popular tap dance.

zapatería f. shoe store; shoemaker's shop.

zapatero m. shoemaker; shoe dealer.

zapatilla f. slipper, pump.

zapato m. shoe.

zarandajas f. pl. trifles, trinkets, worthless things.

zarandear v. to winnow (separate the chaff from grain); to sift; to sift out; to move (something) quickly, wiggle, jiggle; Am. to whip, lash, mistreat, abuse; -se to wiggle, jiggle; to bump along; to waddle; to strut, swagger.

zarandeo m. jiggle, jiggling; sifting;

waddling; strutting.

zarcillo m. earring; tendril (coil of a climbing vine); Am. earmark (on the ear of an animal).

zarpa f. paw, claw; weighing anchor; **echar la —** to grasp, seize, **zarpada** f. pounce; blow with a paw; **zarpazo** m. blow with the paw; big blow, thud; hard fall.

zarpar v. to weigh anchor; to set sail.

zarza f. bramble; blackberry bush.

zarzamora f. blackberry.

zarzuela f. Spanish musical comedy.

zigzag m. zigzag.

zigzaguear v. to zigzag.

zinc = cinc.

zócalo m. base (of a pedestal); Am. public square.

zodíaco m. zodiac.

zona f. zone; band, girdle; shingles (a disease).

zonzo adj. dull, stupid, silly, foolish.

zoología f. zoology.

zoológico adj. zoological; **jardín — zoo**.

zopenco adj. stupid, dull, thick-headed; m. blockhead, dunce.

zopilote m. Am. buzzard.

zoquete m. block, chunk of wood; hunk of bread; blockhead, dunce, fool; ugly fat person; Am. grease, dirt, filth; Am. slap.

zorra f. fox; foxy person; drunkenness; prostitute; **pillar una —** to get drunk.

zorro m. fox; foxy person; -s fox skins; duster made of cloth or leather strips; **estar hecho un —** to be drowsy; **hacerse uno el —** to pretend to be stupid or not to hear; adj. foxy; **zorrillo, zorrino** m. Am. skunk; **zorruno** adj. foxy.

zorzal m. thrush; crafty fellow; Am. fool, scapegoat, dupe.

zozobra f. foundering; sinking; anxiety; worry.

zozobrar v. to founder; to capsize; to sink; to be in great danger; to fret, worry.

zumbar v. to buzz; to hum; to ring (said of the ears); to scoff at; to strike, hit; Am. to throw out or away; — **una bofetada** to give a slap; -se Am. to slip away, disappear.

zumbido m. buzzing, humming; ringing (in one's ears); hit, blow, whack.

zumbón adj. funny, playful; sarcastic; m. jester.

zumo m. juice; profit; **zumoso** adj. juicy.

zurcido m. darn; darning; p.p. of **zurcir**.

zurcir[10] *v.* to darn; to invent, make up (*lies*).

zurdo *adj.* left-handed; left; **a zurdas** with the left hand; clumsily.

zuro *m.* cob, corncob.

zurra *f.* beating, flogging; tanning (*of leather*).

zurrar *v.* to flog, thrash; to tan (*leather*).

zurrón *m.* pouch; bag; leather bag; *Am.* big coward.

Zutano *m.* so-and-so; a certain person. (*Used often with* **Fulano** *and* **Mengano**).

PARTE SEGUNDA
INGLES-ESPAÑOL

PARTE SEGUNDA
INGLES-ESPAÑOL

AL ESTUDIOSO

EL AUGE que desde el principio de la Guerra Mundial II viene cobrando en la América española el aprendizaje del inglés, nos ha movido a recopilar en este breve Diccionario las voces y locuciones más indispensables de esta lengua tal como se habla y escribe en los Estados Unidos de América.

Al igual que en la Sección española-inglesa hemos antepuesto la abreviatura *Am.* a aquellos vocablos o idiotismos que son de uso exclusivo en alguna región de la América española, o bien de uso frecuentísimo en ésta, aunque ya hayan caído en desuso en la Península. Todo lo cual no excluye la posibilidad de que alguna acepción así designada se oiga en labios de español o sea de uso esporádico en España.

Lo que sí hemos procurado con gran ahinco y anhelamos lograr, presentando al estudioso este caudal indispensable de palabras, es el acercamiento lingüístico de las Américas, como base para nuestra mutua comprensión y como instrumento poderosísimo para nuestra solidaridad.

LOS EDITORES

LISTA DE ABREVIATURAS i
PRONUNCIACIÓN ii
EL SUSTANTIVO vi
EL ADJETIVO Y EL ADVERBIO vii
SUFIJOS COMUNES EN INGLÉS ix
VERBOS IRREGULARES DE LA LENGUA INGLESA xii
NÚMEROS xviii

LISTA DE ABREVIATURAS

adj.	adjectivo	*interr.*	interrogativo
adv.	adverbio	*irr.*	irregular
Am.	Americanismo	*p.p.*	participio pasado o pasivo
art.	artículo	*pers.*	personal

i

art. indef.	artículo indefinido	pl.	plural
aux.	auxiliar	pos.	posesivo
comp.	comparativo	prep.	preposición
conj.	conjunción	pron.	pronombre
contr.	contracción	pron. pers.	pronombre personal
defect.	defectivo	pron. pos.	pronombre posesivo
etc.	etcétera	s.	sustantivo
ger.	gerundio	sing.	singular
gram.	gramatical, gramática	subj.	subjuntivo
imperf.	imperfecto	v.	verbo
indic.	indicativo	v. defect.	verbo defectivo
interj.	interjección	v. irr.	verbo irregular

PRONUNCIACION INGLESA[1]

I. VOCALES

Símbolo fonético	Ortografía inglesa	Ortografía fonética	Explicación de los sonidos
i	see pea	si pi	Equivale a la *i* in *hilo*.
ɪ	bit	bɪt	El sonido más aproximado es la *i* en *virtud*, pero la [ɪ] inglesa es una *i* más abierta tirando a *e* cerrada.
e	late they	let ðe	Equivale aproximadamente a *ei*; la *i* de este diptongo es muy relajada y más abierta que en español.
ɛ	bet	bet	El sonido más aproximado en español es la *e* abierta de *perro*.
æ	sat	sæt	Es una vocal intermedia entre la *a* y la *e*.
ɑ	car	kɑr	Equivale aproximadamente a la *a* en *corgo*.
ɔ	forge	fɔrdʒ	Equivale aproximadamente a la *o* en *corto*, *corre*.
o	mode	mod	Equivale aproximademente a *ou*; la *u* de este diptongo es muy relajada y más abierta que en español.
ʊ	pull	pʊl	El sonido más aproximado en español es la *u* en *turrón*, pero la [ʊ] inglesa es todavía más abierta.

[1] El estudioso puede consultar el importante diccionario de pronunciación norteamericana: Kenyon and Knott, *A Pronouncing Dictionary of American English* (Springfield, Massachusetts: G. & C. Merriam Company, Publishers, 1944).

Símbolo fonético	Ortografía inglesa	Ortografía fonética	Explicación de los sonidos.
u	June moon	dʒuu mun	Equivale aproximadamente a la *u* en *uno*.
ə	cudgel apply	kʌdʒəl əpláɪ	Es una *e* muy relajada. No tiene equivalente en español.
ɚ	teacher	títʃɚ	Es una *e* muy relajada, articulada simultáneamente con la *r*. No tiene equivalente en español.
ɝ	earth fur	ɝθ fɝ	Es un sonido intermedio entre la *e* y la *o* articulado simultáneamente con la *r*. Se acerca más a la *e* que a la *o*. No tiene equivalente en español.
ʌ	duck	dʌk	Es una vocal intermedia entre la *e* muy abierta y la *o*. Se acerca más a la *o* que a la *e*. No tiene equivalente en español.

II. Diptongos

aɪ	aisle nice	aɪl naɪs	Equivale aproximadamente a *ai* en *aire*.
aʊ	now	naʊ	Equivale aproximadamente a *au* en *causa*.
ɔɪ	coy	kɔɪ	Equivale aproximadamente a *oy* en *hoy*. El segundo elemento del diptongo es más abierto y débil, tirando a *e*.
ju	used	juzd	Equivale aproximadamente a *iu* en *ciudad*.
jʊ	cure	kjʊr	Equivale aproximadamente al diptongo *iu*, pero la *u* es más abierta.

III. Consonantes

p	paper	pépə	Equivale aproximadamente a la *p* española, pero es mucho más explosiva.
b	bat	bæt	La *b* inglesa es semejante a la *b* inicial española, pero se pronuncia más explosivamente.

Símbolo fonético	Ortografía inglesa	Ortografía fonética	Explicación de los sonidos.
t	tea	ti	Es bastante diferente de la *t* española. Se articula colocando flojamente la lengua arriba de los dientes incisivos superiores.
d	day	de	Equivale a la *d* inicial española pronunciada con mayor énfasis.
k	cat kill	kæt kɪl	Equivale aproximadamente a la *c* española delante de *a,o,u* pronunciada con mayor énfasis.
g	go gum ago	go gʌm əgó	Equivale aproximadamente a la *g* inicial delante de *a,o,u: goma, guerra, gana;* sólo que la *g* inglesa se pronuncia con mayor explosión.
f	fun affair	fʌn əfér	Equivale aproximadamente a la *f* española.
v	very	vérɪ	No tiene equivalente en español. Es una labiodental que se articula con el labio inferior y los dientes incisivos superiores.
o	thin	ɵɪn	Equivale aproximadamente a la *z* en el castellano *cazar.*
ð	then other	ðɛn ʌ́ðə	Equivale aproximadamente a la *d* española en *pardo.*
s	send case cent	sɛnd kes sɛnt	Equivale aproximadamente a la *s* inicial española: *santo.*
z	rose these zero	roz ðiz zíro	Equivale aproximadamente a la *s* sonora en *mismo,* pero se pronuncia con más sonoridad en inglés.
ʃ	sheet machine nation	ʃit maʃín néʃən	Es una *s* palatal que no tiene equivalente en español. Suena como la *ch* francesa: *chapeau.*
ʒ	vision	víʒən	No tiene equivalente en español. Es una palatal fricativa sonora, semejante a la *y* argentina y uruguaya.
tʃ	chase	tʃes	Equivale aproximadamente a la *ch* en *charla.*

Símbolo fonético	Ortografía inglesa	Ortografía fonética	Explicación de los sonidos.
dʒ	judge gentle	dʒʌdʒ dʒéntļ	No tiene equivalente exacto en español. Se parece a la y de inyectar en la pronunciación de uruguayos y argentinos.
m	much	mʌtʃ	Equivale aproximadamente a la m española.
n	none any	nʌn éni	Equivale aproximadamente a la n española en nada.
n̩	eaten button lesson	ítn̩ bʌtn̩ lésn̩	No tiene equivalente en español. Representa la n sin la articulación de la vocal anterior.
ŋ	ankle angle ring	ǽŋkļ ǽŋgļ rɪŋ	Equivale a la n española en mango, banco.
l	late altar fall folly	let óltɚ fɔl fálɪ	La l inicial equivale aproximadamente a la l española en lado. La l en medio de palabra es más débil que la inicial. La l final se pronuncia a veces de una manera tan relajada en inglés que apenas la percibe el oído español.
ļ	able ankle	ébļ ǽŋkļ	No tiene equivalente en español. Se pronuncia como la l en hábil, pero omitiendo la i.
w	weed well wall	wid wɛl wɔl	Equivale a la u de los diptongos: ui, ue, ua, uo.
h	hat whole	hæt hol	No tiene equivalente exacto en español. Equivale aproximadamente a una j suave que se reduce a una simple aspiración.
hw	where	hwɛr	Equivale a una j suave seguida de una w arriba explicada.
j	year yawn yet	jɪr jon jet	Equivale a la i española en los diptongos ie, ia, io, iu: hiena.
r	rose bear	roz bɛr	No tiene equivalente en español. La punta de la lengua se arrolla hacia atrás sin tocar el paladar. A veces se pierde al grado de vocalizarse.

PRONUNCIACION DE LA S DEL PLURAL[1]

I. La **s** del plural es sorda cuando la palabra termina en las consonantes sordas representadas por los símbolos fonéticos [p], [t], [k], [f], [θ]. Pronúnciase como la *s* de *santo:* **caps** [kæps], **gates** [gets], **cats** [kæts], **books** [buks], **cliffs** [klɪfs], **lengths** [leŋkθs].

Las excepciones más comunes son: **oath** [oθ], **oaths** [oðz]; **leaf** [lif], **leaves** [livz]; **wife** [waɪf], **wives** [waɪvz]; **knife** [naɪf], **knives** [naɪvz]; **calf** [kæf], **calves** [kævz]; **half** [hæf], **halves** [hævz].

II. La **s** del plural es sonora cuando la palabra termina en vocal (incluyendo la **y** que se cambia en **ies**), o en las consonantes sonoras representadas por los símbolos fonéticos [b], [d], [g], [v], [ð], [m], [n], [ŋ], [l]: **cries** [kraɪz], **robes** [robz], **beds** [bɛdz], **logs** [lɔgz], **stoves** [stovz], **lathes** [leðz], **farms** [fɑrmz], **bins** [bɪnz], **kings** [kɪŋz], **falls** [fɔlz], **furs** [fɝz], **papers** [pépɚz], **plows** [plauz].

III. Cuando la palabra termina en las consonantes representadas por los símbolos [s], [ʃ], [tʃ], [z], [ʒ], [dʒ], se añade **es** [ɪz], o **s** [ɪz], si la palabra termina en **-ce, -se, -dge, -ge**: **face** [fes], **faces** [fésɪz]; **kiss** [kɪs], **kisses** [kɪsɪz]; **ash** [æʃ], **ashes** [ǽʃɪz]; **lunch** [lʌntʃ], **lunches** [lʌntʃɪz]; **rose** [roz], **roses** [rózɪz]; **judge** [dʒʌdʒ], **judges** [dʒʌ́dʒɪz].

EL SUSTANTIVO

I. GÉNERO

Son masculinos los nombres de varón o animal macho, y son femeninos los nombres de mujer o animal hembra. Los demás son neutros. El artículo definido **the** se aplica a todos los sustantivos, singular y plural: **the man** el hombre; **the men** los hombres; **the book** el libro; **the books** los libros; **the woman** la mujer; **the women** las mujeres.

En ciertos sustantivos se distingue el género femenino por medio del sufijo **-ess: poet** poeta; **poetess** poetisa. A veces es indispensable indicar el género por medio de las palabras **male** o **female, boy** o **girl, man** o **woman, she** o **he: baby boy** niño; **baby girl** niña; **woman writer** escritora; **she-bear** osa. En otros casos hay una palabra distinta para cada género; **uncle** tío; **aunt** tía.

---

[1] Las mismas reglas se aplican a la pronunciación del genitivo y de la tercera persona del presente de indicativo, singular: **keeps** [kips]; **Kate's** [kets]; **saves** [sevz]; **John's** [dʒɑnz]; **judges** [dʒʌ́dʒɪz]; **Alice's** [ǽlɪsɪz].

II. Plural de Los Sustantivos[1]

1. Generalmente se forma el plural añadiendo **s** al singular: **paper, papers** papel, papeles; **book, books** libro, libros; **chief, chiefs,** jefe, jefes.

2. Los sustantivos que terminan en **ch** (pronunciada como la *ch* española), **ss, x, sh, z,** y o añaden **es** para formar el plural: **arch, arches** arco, arcos; **kiss, kisses** beso, besos; **box, boxes** caja, cajas; **dish, dishes** plato, platos; **buzz, buzzes** zumbido, zumbidos; **hero, heroes** héroe, héroes. Nótese que los sustantivos terminados en **ch** (pronunciada [k]) forman el plural añadiendo **s**: **monarch, monarchs** monarca, monarcas.

3. Los sustantivos que terminan en **fe,** y ciertos sustantivos que terminan en **f,** cambian estas letras en **v** y añaden **es**: **leaf, leaves** hoja, hojas; **life, lives** vida, vidas; **wife, wives** esposa, esposas; **knife, knives** cuchillo, cuchillos.

4. Para formar el plural de los sustantivos terminados en **y** precedida de consonante cámbiase la **y** en **ies**: **fly, flies** mosca, moscas; **cry, cries** grito, gritos; **family, families** familia, familias; **quantity, quantities** cantidad, cantidades. Nótese que los sustantivos terminados en **y** precedida de vocal forman el plural añadiendo **s** al singular: **day, days** día, días.

5. Ciertos sustantivos forman el plural de una manera irregular: **man, men** hombre, hombres; **woman, women** mujer, mujeres; **mouse, mice** ratón, ratones; **louse, lice** piojo, piojos; **goose, geese,** ganso, gansos; **tooth, teeth** diente, dientes; **foot, feet** pie, pies; **ox, oxen** buey, bueyes.

6. Ciertos sustantivos que terminan en **is** forman el pural cambiando la **i** de la terminación en **e**: **axis, axes** eje, ejes; **the crisis, the crises** la crisis, las crisis.

EL ADJETIVO

El adjetivo inglés es invariable en cuanto a género y número. Normalmente se coloca delante del sustantivo: **an interesting book** un libro interesante; **a large table** una mesa grande; **beautiful women** mujeres hermosas.

Los comparativos y superlativos. Aunque no hay una regla general, por lo común los adjetivos monosílabos, los adjetivos acentuados en la última sílaba y algunos bisílabos fácilmente pronunciados forman

---

[1] Véase las reglas para la pronunciación del plural.

el comparativo de aumento y el superlativo añadiendo **-er** y **-est**. Los demás adjetivos van precedidos de **more** y **most**. Nótese que (1) sólo se añaden **-r** y **-st** a los que terminan en e muda; (2) los adjetivos terminados en **-y** cambian esta letra en **i**; (3) los adjetivos terminados en consonante precedida de vocal doblan la consonante:

Positivo	Comparativo	Superlativo
tall alto	**taller** más alto	**the tallest** el más alto
wise sabio	**wiser** más sabio	**the wisest** el más sabio
polite cortés	**politer** más cortés	**the politest** el más cortés
happy feliz	**happier** más feliz	**the happiest** el más feliz
fat gordo	**fatter** más gordo	**the fattest** el más gordo
careful cuidadoso	**more careful** más cuidadoso	**the most careful** el más cuidadoso

El superlativo absoluto se forma anteponiendo **very** y a veces **most**: **very intelligent** muy inteligente; **she is a most beautiful woman** es una mujer hermosísima.

El comparativo y el superlativo de inferioridad se forman con los adverbios **less** y **least**: **less wise** menos sabio; **the least wise** el menos sabio.

El comparativo de igualdad se forma con el adverbio **as**: **as poor as** tan pobre como; **as much as** tanto como; **as much money as** tanto dinero como.

Los adjetivos siguientes forman el comparativo y el superlativo de una manera irregular:

good, well	better	best
bad, ill	worse	worst
little	less, lesser	least
far	farther, further	farthest, furthest
much, many	more	most
old	older, elder	oldest, eldest

EL ADVERBIO

Fórmanse muchos adverbios, añadiendo **-ly** al adjetivo: **courteous** cortés, **courteously** cortésmente; **bold** atrevido, **boldly** atrevidamente. Existen las irregularidades siguientes en la formación de los adverbios que terminan en **-ly**: (1) los adjetivos terminados en **-ble** cambian la **-e** en **-y**: **possible, possibly**; (2) los terminados en **-ic** añaden **-ally**: **poetic, poetically**; (3) los terminados en **-ll** añaden sólo la **-y**: **full, fully**; (4) los terminados en **-ue** pierden la e final: **true, truly**; (5) los terminados en **-y** cambian la y en **i**: **happy, happily**.

Como los adjetivos, la mayor parte de los adverbios forman el *comparativo* y el *superlativo* con los adverbios **more** (más), **most** (más), y **very** (muy). Asimismo los adverbios monosílabos añaden **-er** y **-est**:

Positivo	Comparativo	Superlativo	Superlativo Absoluto
boldly	more boldly	most boldly	very boldly
generously	more generously	most generously	very generously
soon	sooner	soonest	very soon
early	earlier	earliest	very early
late	later	latest	very late
near	nearer	nearest	very near
fast	faster	fastest	very fast

Los adverbios siguientes forman el comparativo y el superlativo de una manera irregular:

well	better	best	very well
badly, ill	worse	worst	very badly
little	less	least	very little
much	more	most	very much
far	farther, further	farthest, furthest	very far

SUFIJOS COMUNES EN INGLES

-dom denota dominio, jurisdicción, estado, condición, etc.: **kingdom** reino; **martyrdom** martirio; **boredom** aburrimiento; **freedom** libertad.

-ed,-d es la terminación del pretérito y del participio pasivo o pasado de los verbos regulares: **I called** llamé; **called** llamado.

-ee indica la persona que recibe la acción: **addressee** destinatario; **employee** empleado.

-eer denota oficio u ocupación: **engineer** ingeniero; **auctioneer** subastador.

-en a) terminación del participio de muchos verbos irregulares: **fallen, broken, shaken;**

b) sufijo que significa *hecho de*: **golden** dorado, de oro; **wooden** de madera; **leaden** de plomo;

c) terminación verbal equivalente a *hacer*: **whiten** hacer blanco, emblanquecer; **darken** hacer obscuro, obscurecer.

-er a) indica la persona que hace o el agente de la acción del verbo: **player** jugador; **talker** hablador;

b) indica el residente de un lugar: **New Yorker** habitante o residente de Nueva York; **islander** isleño;

          c) denota ocupación: **carpenter** carpintero; **baker** panadero;

          d) es la terminación del comparativo de adjetivos y adverbios: **taller** más alto; **faster** más aprisa.

-est   terminación del superlativo: **tallest** el más alto.

-ess   úsase para formar el género femenino de ciertos sustantivos: **patroness** patrona; **poetess** poetisa; **countess** condesa.

-fold   sufijo que significa *veces*: **twofold** dos veces; **hundredfold** cien veces.

-ful   *a)* equivale a *lleno*, y tratándose de adjetivos es igual a *-oso*: **hopeful** lleno de esperanzas; **careful** cuidadoso; **wilful** voluntarioso; **merciful** misericordioso; **glassful** un vaso (*lleno*);

          b) indica a veces hábito o inclinación: **forgetful** olvidadizo;

          c) es a veces equivalente a los sufijos españoles *-ado*, *-ada*: **handful** puñado; **spoonful** cucharada.

-hood   indica estado, condición, carácter, grupo; a menudo equivale a *-dad*: **motherhood** maternidad; **brotherhood** fraternidad; **childhood** niñez; **falsehood** falsedad.

-ician   denota especialidad en cierto ramo: **musician** músico; **technician** técnico; **electrician** electricista.

-ie   sufijo diminutivo: **birdie** pajarito; **Annie** Anita.

-ing   *a)* sufijo del gerundio: **speaking** hablando;

          b) sufijo del participio activo; **threatening** amenazante; **surprising** sorprendente;

          c) úsase a menudo para formar adjetivos: **running water** agua corriente; **drinking water** agua potable; **waiting room** sala de espera; **washing machine** máquina lavadora;

          d) úsase para formar sustantivos: **understanding** entendimiento; **supplying** abastecimiento; **clothing** ropa; **covering** cobertura; equivale al infinitivo castellano: **swimming is good exercise** el nadar es buen ejercicio.

-ish   *a)* úsase para formar ciertos adjetivos de nacionalidad: **Spanish** español; **English** inglés; **Turkish** turco;

          b) indica semejanza: **boyish** como niño, aniñado;

womanish como mujer, mujeril, afeminado; **whitish** blancuzco, medio blanco, que tira a blanco.

-less equivale a *sin, falto de*: **childless** sin hijos; **penniless** sin dinero; en ciertos casos el sufijo inglés se traduce por medio de un prefijo: **countless** innumerable, sin número; **endless** interminable, sin fin

-like significa *semejanza*, y equivale a *como, a manera de*: **lifelike** que parece vivo; **childlike** como niño, infantil; **tigerlike** como tigre.

-ly *a)* sufijo adverbial: **slowly** lentamente; **happily** felizmente; **possibly** posiblemente;

b) añadido a ciertos sustantivos equivale a *como, a la manera de*: **motherly** como madre, materno; **gentlemanly** como caballero, caballeroso; **friendly** amigable; **manly** varonil;

c) equivale a *cada* en estos ejemplos: **daily** cada día; diario; **weekly** cada semana; semanal; **monthly** cada mes; mensual; **yearly** cada año; anual.

-ness úsase para formar sustantivos abstractos: **goodness** bondad; **darkness** obscuridad; **foolishness** tontería; **shamelessness** desvergüenza.

-ship *a)* úsase para formar sustantivos abstractos: **friendship** amistad; **relationship** relación; parentesco;

b) denota arte o destreza: **horsemanship** equitación;

c) expresa dignidad, oficio, cargo, o título: **professorship** profesorado o cátedra; **chairmanship** presidencia (*de un comité, asamblea, etc.*); **lordship** señoría;

d) a veces expresa tan sólo un estado y su duración: **courtship** galanteo, cortejo, noviazgo.

-some expresa en alto grado la cualidad representada por el vocablo al cual se añade: **tiresome** que cansa, cansado; **quarrelsome** dado a riñas, pendenciero; **loathsome** que repugna, asqueroso; **burdensome** gravoso.

-th úsase para formar números ordinales: **fifth** quinto; **tenth** décimo.

-ty *a)* terminación de los múltiples de diez: **twenty** veinte; **thirty** treinta; **forty** cuarenta;

b) terminación de muchos sustantivos abstractos; equivale frecuentemente al sufijo español *-tad* o *-dad*:

beauty beldad; **paternity** paternidad; **falsity** falsedad.

-ward,-wards denotan *hacia*: **homeward** hacia casa; **downward** hacia abajo.

-ways, -wise expresan manera, dirección, posición, etc.: **edgewise** de lado; **sideways** de lado; **lengthwise** a lo largo.

-y *a)* terminación equivalente a los sufijos españoles *-ia, -ía*: **victory** victoria; **glory** gloria; **courtesy** cortesía; **biology** biología. **astronomy** astronomía;

b) sufijo diminutivo: **doggy** perrito; **Johnny** Juanito;

c) denota abundancia, y es a menudo equivalente a *-udo, -oso, -ado*: **rocky** lleno de rocas, rocoso, pedregoso; **rainy** lluvioso; **hairy** lleno de pelo, peludo; **bulky** abultado; **wavy** ondulado; **angry** enojado;

d) expresa semejanza: **rosy** rosado, como una rosa color de rosa.

VERBOS IRREGULARES DE LA LENGUA INGLESA

Se denominan verbos irregulares los que no forman el pretérito o el participio pasivo con la adición de -d o -ed al presente. Obsérvese que en ciertos verbos coexiste la forma regular al lado de la irregular. En otros coexisten dos formas irregulares juntamente con la regular.

Presente	Pretérito	Participio pasivo o pasado
abide	abode	abode
am, is, are	was, were	been
arise	arose	arisen
awake	awoke, awaked	awaked, awoke
bear	bore	born, borne
beat	beat	beat, beaten
become	became	become
befall	befell	befallen
beget	begot	begotten
begin	began	begun
behold	beheld	beheld
bend	bent	bent
bereave	bereft, bereaved	bereft, bereaved
beseech	besought, beseeched	besought, beseeched
beset	beset	beset

Presente	*Pretérito*	*Participio pasivo o pasado*
bet	bet	bet
bid	bid, bade	bidden, bid
bind	bound	bound
bite	bit	bitten, bit
bleed	bled	bled
blow	blew	blown
break	broke	broken
breed	bred	bred
bring	brought	brought
build	built	built
burn	burnt, burned	burnt, burned
burst	burst	burst
buy	bought	bought
can (*verbo defectivo*)	could	—
cast	cast	cast
catch	caught	caught
chide	chided, chid	chided, chidden
choose	chose	chosen
cleave	cleft, clove, cleaved	cleft, cleaved, cloven
cling	clung	clung
clothe	clad, clothed	clad, clothed
come	came	come
cost	cost	cost
creep	crept	crept
crow	crew, crowed	crowed
cut	cut	cut
deal	dealt	dealt
dig	dug, digged	dug, digged
do	did	done
draw	drew	drawn
dream	dreamt, dreamed	dreamt, dreamed
drink	drank	drunk
drive	drove	driven
dwell	dwelt, dwelled	dwelt, dwelled
eat	ate	eaten
fall	fell	fallen
feed	fed	fed
feel	felt	felt
fight	fought	fought
find	found	found
flee	fled	fled
fling	flung	flung
fly	flew	flown
forbear	forbore	forborne
forbid	forbade	forbidden
foresee	foresaw	foreseen
foretell	foretold	foretold

Presente	Pretérito	Participio pasivo o pasado
forget	forgot	forgotten, forgot
forgive	forgave	forgiven
forsake	forsook	forsaken
freeze	froze	frozen
get	got	got, gotten
gild	gilt, gilded	gilt, gilded
gird	girt, girded	girt, girded
give	gave	given
go	went	gone
grind	ground	ground
grow	grew	grown
hang[1]	hung	hung
have, has	had	had
hear	heard	heard
heave	hove, heaved	hove, heaved
hew	hewed	hewn, hewed
hide	hid	hidden, hid
hit	hit	hit
hold	held	held
hurt	hurt	hurt
inlay	inlaid	inlaid
keep	kept	kept
kneel	knelt	knelt
knit	knit, knitted	knit, knitted
know	knew	known
lay	laid	laid
lead	led	led
lean	leaned, leant	leaned, leant
leap	leapt, leaped	leapt, leaped
learn	learned, learnt	learned, learnt
learn	learned, learnt	learned, learnt
leave	left	left
lend	lent	lent
let	let	let
lie[2] (yacer; echarse)	lay	lain
light	lit, lighted	lit, lighted
load	loaded	loaded, laden
lose	lost	lost
make	made	made
may (verbo defectivo)	might	—
mean	meant	meant
meet	met	met
melt	melted	melted, molten
mistake	mistook	mistaken

[1] Es regular cuando significa "ahorcar."
[2] Es regular cuando significa "mentir."

Presente	Pretérito	Participio pasivo o pasado
mow	mowed	mown, mowed
must (verbo defectivo)	—	—
ought (verbo defectivo)	ought	—
pay	paid	paid
put	put	put
quit	quit, quitted	quit, quitted
read [rid]	read [red]	read [red]
rend	rent	rent
rid	rid, ridded	rid, ridded
ride	rode	ridden
ring	rang, rung	rung
rise	rose	risen
run	ran	run
saw	sawed	sawn, sawed
say	said	said
see	saw	seen
seek	sought	sought
sell	sold	sold
send	sent	sent
set	set	set
sew	sewed	sewn, sewed
shake	shook	shaken
shall	should	—
shave	shaved	shaved, shaven
shear	sheared	shorn, sheared
shed	shed	shed
shine[1]	shone	shone
shoe	shod	shod
shoot	shot	shot
show	showed	shown, showed
shred	shred, shredded	shred, shredded
shrink	shrank, shrunk	shrunk, shrunken
shut	shut	shut
sing	sang, sung	sung
sink	sank	sunk
sit	sat	sat
slay	slew	slain
sleep	slept	slept
slide	slid	slid, slidden
sling	slung	slung
slink	slunk	slunk
slit	slit	slit
smell	smelt, smelled	smelt, smelled
smite	smote	smitten
sow	sowed	sown, sowed
speak	spoke	spoken

[1] Es por lo común regular cuando significa "pulir, dar brillo."

Presente	*Pretérito*	*Participio pasivo o pasado*
speed	sped, speeded	sped, speeded
spell	spelled, spelt	spelled, spelt
spend	spent	spent
spill	spilled, spilt	spilled, spilt
spin	spun	spun
spit	spit, spat	spit, spat
split	split	split
spread	spread	spread
spring	sprang, sprung	sprung
stand	stood	stood
stave	staved, stove	staved, stove
steal	stole	stolen
stick	stuck	stuck
sting	stung	stung
stink	stank, stunk	stunk
strew	strewed	strewn, strewed
stride	strode	stridden
strike	struck	struck, striken
string	strung	strung
strive	strove, strived	striven, strived
swear	swore	sworn
sweep	swept	swept
swell	swelled	swollen, swelled
swim	swam	swum
swing	swung	swung
take	took	taken
teach	taught	taught
tear	tore	torn
tell	told	told
think	thought	thought
thrive	throve, thrived	thriven, thrived
throw	threw	thrown
thrust	thrust	thrust
tread	trod	trod, trodden
understand	understood	understood
undertake	undertook	undertaken
undo	undid	undone
uphold	upheld	upheld
upset	upset	upset
wake	woke, waked	waked
wear	wore	worn
weave	wove	woven
wed	wedded	wedded, wed
weep	wept	wept
wet	wet, wetted	wet, wetted
will (*verbo auxiliar*)	would	—
win	won	won

Presente	Pretérito	Participio pasivo o pasado
wind	wound	wound
withdraw	withdrew	withdrawn
withhold	withheld	withheld
withstand	withstood	withstood
work	worked; wrought	worked; wrought
wring	wrung	wrung
write	wrote	written

NUMERALS—NUMEROS

Cardinal Numbers		Números Cardinales	Ordinal Numbers	Números Ordinale
1.......	one	uno, una	first	primero
2.......	two	dos	second	segundo
3.......	three	tres	third	tercero
4.......	four	cuatro	fourth	cuarto
5.......	five	cinco	fifth	quinto
6.......	six	seis	sixth	sexto
7.......	seven	siete	seventh	séptimo
8.......	eight	ocho	eighth	octavo
9.......	nine	nueve	ninth	noveno, nono
10.....	ten	diez	tenth	décimo
11.....	eleven	once	eleventh	undécimo
12.....	twelve	doce	twelfth	duodécimo
13.....	thirteen	trece	thirteenth	décimotercio
14.....	fourteen	catorce	fourteenth	décimocuarto
15.....	fifteen	quince	fifteenth	décimoquinto
16.....	sixteen	dieciseis, diez y seis	sixteenth	décimosexto
17......	seventeen	diecisiete, diez y siete	seventeenth	décimoséptimo
18.....	eighteen	dieciocho, diez y ocho	eighteenth	décimoctavo
19.....	nineteen	diecinueve, diez y nueve	nineteenth	décimonono
20.....	twenty	veinte	twentieth	vigésimo
21.....	twenty-one	veintiuno, veinte y uno	twenty-first	vigésimo prime
30.....	thirty	treinta	thirtieth	trigésimo
40.....	forty	cuarenta	fortieth	cuadragésimo
50.....	fifty	cincuenta	fiftieth	quincuagésimo
60.....	sixty	sesenta	sixtieth	sexagésimo
70.....	seventy	setenta	seventieth	septuagésimo
80.....	eighty	ochenta	eightieth	octogésimo
90.....	ninety	noventa	ninetieth	nonagésimo
100.....	one hundred	ciento	(one) hundredth	centésimo
101.....	one hundred and one	ciento (y) uno	(one) hundred and first	centésimo prim
200.....	two hundred	doscientos	two-hundredth	ducentésimo
300.....	three hundred	trescientos	three-hundredth	tricentésimo
400.....	four hundred	cuatrocientos	four-hundredth	cuadringentésir
500.....	five hundred	quinientos	five-hundredth	quingentésimo
600	six hundred	seiscientos	six-hundredth	sexagésimo
700.....	seven hundred	setecientos	seven-hundredth	septingentésim
800.....	eight hundred	ochocientos	eight-hundredth	octingentésimo
900.....	nine hundred	novecientos	nine-hundredth	noningentésimo
1000	one thousand	mil	(one) thousandth	milésimo
100,000	one hundred thousand	cien mil	(one) hundred thousandth	cienmilésimo
1,000,000	one million	un millón	(one) millionth	millonésimo

A

a [ə, e] *art. indef.* un, una; **what — . . . !** ¡qué . . . !; **such —** tal; tan.

abandon [əbǽndən] *v.* abandonar; dejar; *s.* abandono, desahogo, desenvoltura; entrega.

abandoned [əbǽndənd] *adj.* abandonado; dejado; perverso; inmoral.

abandonment [əbǽndənmənt] *s.* abandono, abandonamiento; desamparo; desenvoltura, desembarazo.

abashed [əbǽʃt] *adj.* humillado, avergonzado.

abate [əbét] *v.* bajar, rebajar; disminuir; acabar con; mitigar(se); calmarse.

abatement [əbétmənt] *s.* diminución, merma; rebaja, descuento; mitigación.

abbey [ǽbi] *s.* abadía, monasterio.

abbot [ǽbət] *s.* abad.

abbreviate [əbríviet] *v.* abreviar, acortar, reducir.

abbreviation [əbriviéʃən] *s.* abreviación, abreviatura.

abdicate [ǽbdəket] *v.* abdicar, renunciar.

abdomen [ǽbdəmən] *s.* abdomen; vientre.

abduct [æbdʌ́kt] *v.* secuestrar, raptar, *Am.* plagiar (*a alguien*).

abduction [æbdʌ́kʃən] *s.* rapto, robo, secuestro (*de una persona*).

aberration [æbəréʃən] *s.* aberración, extravío (*de la mente*).

abhor [əbhór] *v.* aborrecer, odiar, abominar.

abhorrence [əbhórəns] *s.* aborrecimiento, aversión.

abide [əbáid] *v.* quedar, permanecer; morar, habitar; aguardar; soportar, tolerar; **to — by** conformarse a; atenerse a.

ability [əbíləti] *s.* habilidad, capacidad.

abject [æbdʒékt] *adj.* abatido; vil.

able [ébl] *adj.* hábil, capaz; competente; **able-bodied** de cuerpo sano; **to be — to poder;** saber.

ably [ébli] *adv.* hábilmente.

abnormal [æbnórml] *adj.* anormal.

aboard [əbórd] *adv.* a bordo; en el tren; **to go —** embarcarse; **all — !** ¡viajeros al tren!; *Am.* ¡vámonos!

abode [əbód] *s.* morada, domicilio, casa; *pret. & p.p. de* to abide.

abolish [əbáliʃ] *v.* abolir; anular.

abolition [æbəlíʃən] *s.* abolición.

abominable [əbámnəbl] *adj.* abominable, aborrecible.

abortion [əbórʃən] *s.* aborto.

abound [əbáund] *v.* abundar; **to — with** abundar en.

about [əbáut] *prep.* acerca de; tocante a; cerca de; alrededor de; por; *adv.* casi, poco más o menos; **at — ten o'clock** a eso de las diez; **to be — one's business** atender a su negocio; **to be — to** estar para, estar a punto de; **to face —** dar media vuelta; **to have no money — one's person** no llevar dinero consigo.

above [əbʌ́v] *prep.* por encima de; sobre; *adv.* arriba; **— all** sobre todo; **above-mentioned** susodicho, ya mencionado; **from —** de arriba; del cielo, de Dios.

abridge [əbrídʒ] *v.* abreviar; compendiar, condensar; privar (*a uno de sus derechos*).

abroad [əbród] *adv.* en el extranjero; fuera de casa; **to go —** ir al extranjero; **to spread —** divulgar o publicar por todas partes.

abrupt [əbrʌ́pt] *adj.* repentino; precipitado; áspero, brusco; escarpado; **-ly** *adv.* de repente; bruscamente.

abscess [ǽbsɛs] *s.* absceso.

absence [ǽbsn̩s] *s.* ausencia; falta; **— of mind** abstracción; **leave of —** licencia (*para ausentarse*).

absent [ǽbsn̩t] *adj.* ausente; abstraído; distraído; **absent-minded** absorto, abstraído; [æbsént] *v.* **to — oneself** ausentarse.

absolute [ǽbsəlut] *adj.* absoluto; **the — lo** absoluto; **-ly** *adv.* absolutamente; en absoluto.

absolution [æbsəlúʃən] *s.* absolución.

absolve [əbsálv] *v.* absolver, remitir; perdonar, alzar la pena o el castigo.

absorb [əbsórb] *v.* absorber.

absorbent [əbsórbənt] *adj. & s.* absorbente.

absorption [əbsórpʃən] *s.* absorción; abstracción, embebecimiento.

abstain [əbstén] *v.* abstenerse, privarse.

abstinence [ǽbstənəns] *s.* abstinencia.

abstract [ǽbstrækt] *adj.* abstracto; *s.* sumario; extracto; **in the —** en abstracto; [æbstrǽkt] *v.* abstraer; considerar aisladamente; separar, retirar; resumir, compendiar.

abstraction [æbstrǽkʃən] *s.* abstracción; idea abstracta.

absurd [əbsɔ́d] *adj.* absurdo; insensato; ridículo, disparatado.

absurdity [əbsɔ́dəti] *s.* absurdo, disparate.

abundance [əbʌ́ndəns] *s.* abundancia, copia.

abundant [əbʌ́ndənt] *adj.* abundante, copioso.

1

abuse [əbjús] s. abuso; maltrato; ultraje; [əbjúz] v. abusar de; maltratar; injuriar; ultrajar.

abusive [əbjúsɪv] adj. abusivo; insultante, injurioso.

abyss [əbís] s. abismo; sima.

academic [ækədémɪk] adj. académico; escolar.

academy [əkǽdəmɪ] s. academia; colegio, instituto; escuela preparatoria.

accede [æksíd] v. acceder, consentir.

accelerate [æksélərət] v. acelerar(se).

acceleration [ækseləréʃən] s. aceleración.

accelerator [ækséləretə] s. acelerador.

accent [ǽksɛnt] s. acento; [æksént] v. acentuar; recalcar.

accentuate [æksént∫ʊet] v. acentuar; recalcar; realzar.

accept [əksépt] v. aceptar; admitir; acoger; aprobar.

acceptable [əkséptəb]] adj. aceptable; grato; acepto.

acceptance [əkséptəns] s. aceptación; aprobación; buena acogida, recibimiento.

access [ǽksɛs] s. acceso; ataque (de una enfermedad); arrebato (de furia).

accessible [æksésəbl] adj. accessible; asequible, obtenible.

accessory [æksésərɪ] adj. accesorio; adjunto; s. accesorio; cómplice; accessories cosas accesorias, adornos, adminículos.

accident [ǽksədənt] s. accidente; percance, contratiempo; by — por casualidad.

accidental [æksədént] adj. accidental; casual; -ly adv. accidentalmente; por casualidad.

acclaim [əklém] v. aclamar, aplaudir; s. aclamación, aplauso.

acclamation [ækləméʃən] s. aclamación, aplauso.

acclimatize [əkláɪmətaɪz] v. aclimatar(se).

accommodate [əkaməsdét] v. acomodar, ajustar; ayudar, hacer un favor; hospedar, alojar; tener cabida para; to — oneself conformarse, adaptarse.

accommodation [əkaməsdéʃən] s. favor, ayuda; conveniencia; alojamiento (en un hotel, casa, etc.); cabida; adaptación; ajuste.

accompaniment [əkámpənɪmənt] s. acompañamiento.

accompanist [əkámpənɪst] s. acompañador, acompañante.

accompany [əkámpənɪ] v. acompañar.

accomplice [əkámplɪs] s. cómplice.

accomplish [əkámplɪʃ] v. cumplir; completar; lograr, conseguir; realizar, efectuar.

accomplished [əkámplɪʃt] adj. cumplido; realizado; consumado; establecido; diestro; perfecto.

accomplishment [əkámplɪʃmənt] s. cumplimiento; logro, realización; habilidad; perfección; mérito, proeza.

accord [əkɔ́rd] s. acuerdo, convenio; armonía, concierto; of one's own — voluntariamente; espontáneamente; in — with de acuerdo con; with one — unánimemente; v. otorgar, conceder, dar; concordar.

accordance [əkɔ́rdns] s. conformidad, acuerdo; in — with de acuerdo con, de conformidad con.

according [əkɔ́rdɪŋ]: — to según; conforme a; de acuerdo con; — as según (que), a medida que.

accordingly [əkɔ́rdɪŋlɪ] adv. en conformidad; así; como tal; por lo tanto; por consiguiente.

accost [əkɔ́st] v. abordar (a alguien) en la calle, acosar; molestar, perseguir.

account [əkáʊnt] s. cuenta; computación; relato; on — of a causa de; con motivo de; por; on my — por mí; on my own — por mi propia cuenta; on no — de ninguna manera; of no — de ningún valor o importancia; to turn to — aprovechar, hacer útil o provechoso; v. dar cuenta (a); considerar, tener por; to — for dar cuenta o razón de; explicar; how do you — for that? ¿cómo se explica eso?

accountable [əkáʊntəb]] adj. responsable; explicable.

accountant [əkáʊntənt] s. contador, tenedor de libros.

accounting [əkáʊntɪŋ] s. contabilidad, contaduría.

accredit [əkrédɪt] v. acreditar.

accrue [əkrú] v. acumular(se).

accumulate [əkjúmjəlet] v. acumular(se), juntar(se), amontonar(se).

accumulation [əkjumjəléʃən] s. acumulación, amontonamiento.

accuracy [ǽkjərəsɪ] s. precisión, exactitud, esmero.

accurate [ǽkjərɪt] adj. preciso, exacto; correcto; esmerado; cierto; certero; -ly adv. con exactitud; correctamente; con esmero.

accursed [əkɔ́st] adj. maldito; infame.

accusation [ækjəzéʃən] s. acusación.

accuse [əkjúz] v. acusar; denunciar.

accuser [əkjúzə] s. acusador; delator, denunciador.

accustom [əkÁstəm] v. acostumbrar; **to — oneself** acostumbrarse; **to be -ed to** tener la costumbre de, acostumbrar, soler; estar acostumbrado a, estar hecho a.

ace [es] s. as; as, el mejor de su clase (como un aviador excelente); **within an — of** a punto de; muy cerca de.

ache [ek] s. dolor; **tooth— dolor de muelas**; v. doler.

achieve [ətʃív] v. acabar, llevar a cabo; realizar; conseguir, lograr; alcanzar.

achievement [ətʃívmənt] s. logro, realización; proeza, hazaña.

acid [ǽsɪd] adj. ácido; agrio; s. ácido.

acidity [əsídətɪ] s. acidez.

acknowledge [əknálɪdʒ] v. reconocer, admitir; confesar; **to — receipt** acusar recibo.

acknowledgement [əknálɪdʒmənt] s. reconocimiento, expresión de gratitud; confesión, admisión; **— of receipt** acuse de recibo.

acorn [ékɔrn] s. bellota.

acoustics [əkústɪks] s. acústica.

acquaint [əkwént] v. enterar, informar; dar a conocer; familiarizar; **to — oneself with** ponerse al corriente de; enterarse de; **to be -ed with** conocer a (una persona); estar enterado de (algo); conocer (una ciudad, un país, etc.).

acquaintance [əkwéntəns] s. conocimiento; conocido; -s amistades.

acquiesce [ǽkwɪés] v. asentir; consentir, quedar conforme.

acquiescence [ǽkwɪésns] s. asentimiento, consentimiento; conformidad.

acquire [əkwáɪr] v. adquirir; obtener, conseguir; contraer (costumbres, vicios).

acquisition [ǽkwəzíʃən] s. adquisición.

acquit [əkwít] v. absolver, exonerar; pagar, redimir, librar de (una obligación); **to — oneself well** quedar bien; portarse bien.

acquittal [əkwítl] s. absolución

acre [ékə] s. acre (medida de superficie).

acrobat [ǽkrəbæt] s. acróbata.

across [əkrós] prep. a través de; al otro lado de; por; por en medio de; adv. a través, de través; **to go —** atravesar; **to come —, run —** encontrarse con; tropezar con.

act [ækt] s. acto; acción, hecho; v. hacer, desempeñar (un papel); representar (en el teatro); obrar; actuar; portarse; funcionar; **to —** as servir de, estar de.

acting [ǽktɪŋ] s. representación, desempeño (de un papel dramático); acción, actuación; adj. interino, suplente.

action [ǽkʃən] s. acción; acto; actuación;

funcionamiento.

active [ǽktɪv] adj. activo.

activity [æktívətɪ] s. actividad.

actor [ǽktə] s. actor.

actress [ǽktrɪs] s. actriz.

actual [ǽktʃʊəl] adj. verdadero, real; actual (lo que realmente es), existente; **-ly** adv. realmente, en realidad; de hecho, efectivamente.

acumen [əkjúmɪn] s. caletre, tino, perspicacia.

acute [əkjút] adj. agudo; perspicaz; penetrante.

adamant [ǽdəmænt] adj. duro; firme, inflexible.

adapt [ədǽpt] v. adaptar; **to — oneself** adaptarse, acomodarse.

adaptation [ædəptéʃən] s. adaptación.

add [æd] v. sumar; añadir, agregar.

addict [ǽdɪkt] s. adicto (persona adicta al uso de narcóticos); **drug —** morfinómano.

addicted [ədfktɪd] adj. adicto, dado, entregado, habituado.

addition [ədfʃən] s. adición; suma; añadidura, aditamento; **in — to** además de.

additional [ədfʃən] adj. adicional.

address [ədrés] s. dirección, domicilio, señas; sobrescrito; discurso, arenga; destreza; **form of —** tratamiento; v. dirigir, poner la dirección, señas o sobrescrito a; hablar, dirigir la palabra a; dirigirse a; **to — oneself to a task** aplicarse a una tarea.

addressee [ædrɛsí] s. destinatario.

adequate [ǽdəkwɪt] adj. adecuado; proporcionado; suficiente.

adhere [ədhír] v. adherirse; pegarse.

adherence [ədhírəns] s. adherencia.

adhesion [ədhíʒən] s. adhesión.

adhesive [ədhísɪv] adj. adhesivo; pegajoso; **— tape** tela adhesiva, esparadrapo.

adjacent [ədʒésənt] adj. adyacente, contiguo.

adjective [ǽdʒɪktɪv] s. adjetivo.

adjoin [ədʒóɪn] v. estar contiguo o adyacente a, lindar con.

adjourn [ədʒɝn] v. aplazar, diferir; **to — the meeting** suspender o levantar la sesión; **meeting -ed** se levanta la sesión.

adjournment [ədʒɝnmənt] s. aplazamiento, levantamiento (de una sesión).

adjunct [ǽdʒʌŋkt] s. adjunto, aditamento, añadidura; asociado, acompañante; adj. adjunto, unido, subordinado.

adjust [ədʒʌst] v. ajustar; acomodar; arreglar; graduar; **to — oneself** adap-

3

tarse, conformarse.

adjustment [ədʒʌ́stmənt] *s.* ajuste; ajustamiento; arreglo; regulación.

administer [ədmínəstə] *v.* administrar; dirigir, regir, gobernar; aplicar (*remedio, castigo, etc.*); **to — an oath** tomar juramento.

administration [ədmɪnəstréʃən] *s.* administración; dirección, gobierno; gerencia; manejo.

administrative [ədmínəstretɪv] *adj.* administrativo; ejecutivo; gubernativo.

administrator [ədmínəstretə] *s.* administrador.

admirable [ǽdmərəbl] *adj.* admirable; **admirably** *adv.* admirablemente.

admiral [ǽdmərəl] *s.* almirante.

admiration [ædməréʃən] *s.* admiración.

admire [ədmáɪr] *v.* admirar; estimar.

admirer [ədmáɪrə] *s.* admirador; pretendiente.

admission [ədmíʃən] *s.* admisión; confesión; acceso, entrada; precio de entrada o de ingreso.

admit [ədmít] *v.* admitir; aceptar; confesar, reconocer; conceder; dar entrada.

admittance [ədmítns] *s.* entrada; derecho de entrar; admisión.

admonish [ədmóniʃ] *v.* amonestar.

admonition [ædməníʃən] *s.* amonestación, consejo.

ado [ədú] *s.* actividad; bulla; disturbio.

adobe [ədóbɪ] *s.* adobe; casa de adobe.

adolescence [æd]ésns] *s.* adolescencia.

adolescent [æd]ésṇt] *adj. &* *s.* adolescente.

adopt [ədápt] *v.* adoptar.

adoption [ədápʃən] *s.* adopción.

adoration [ædəréʃən] *s.* adoración.

adore [ədór] *v.* adorar.

adorn [ədórn] *v.* adornar; ornar; embellecer.

adornment [ədórnmənt] *s.* adorno.

adrift [ədríft] *adj. &* *adv.* a la deriva, flotando, flotante.

adroit [ədrɔ́ɪt] *adj.* hábil, diestro.

adult [ədʌ́lt] *adj. &* *s.* adulto.

adulterate [ədʌ́ltəret] *v.* adulterar

adulterer [ədʌ́ltərə] *s.* adúltero.

adultery [ədʌ́ltərɪ] *s.* adulterio.

advance [ədvǽns] *v.* avanzar, progresar; adelantar; acelerar; promover; proponer; anticipar, pagar por adelantado; encarecer, subir (*precios*); *s.* avance; progreso; adelanto, anticipo; alza, aumento de precio; **-s** requerimientos, pretensiones, insinuaciones; **in —** por adelantado, con anticipación.

advanced [ədvǽnst] *adj.* avanzado; adelantado; **— in years** entrado en años,

viejo, anciano.

advancement [ədvǽnsmənt] *s.* adelantamiento, mejora, progreso; promoción.

advantage [ədvǽntɪdʒ] *s.* ventaja; beneficio, provecho; **to have the — over** llevar ventaja a; **to take — of** aprovecharse de; **to take — of a person** abusar de la confianza o paciencia de alguien.

advantageous [ædvəntédʒəs] *adj.* ventajoso; provechoso.

advent [ǽdvent] *s.* advenimiento; venida.

adventure [ədvéntʃə] *s.* aventura; riesgo.

adventurer [ədvéntʃərə] *s.* aventurero.

adventurous [ədvéntʃərəs] *adj.* aventurero; atrevido; aventurado, arriesgado.

adverb [ǽdvɜb] *m.* adverbio.

adversary [ǽdvəserɪ] *s.* adversario, antagonista, contrario.

adverse [ədvɜ́s] *adj.* adverso; opuesto, contrario; hostil; desfavorable.

adversity [ədvɜ́sətɪ] *s.* adversidad; infortunio.

advertise [ǽdvətaɪz] *v.* anunciar; avisar, dar aviso.

advertisement [ædvətáɪzmənt] *s.* anuncio, aviso.

advertiser [ǽdvətaɪzə] *s.* anunciador, anunciante.

advertising [ǽdvətaɪzɪŋ] *s.* anuncios; arte o negocio de anunciar.

advice [ədváɪs] *s.* aviso, advertencia; consejo; noticia.

advisable [ədváɪzəbl] *adj.* conveniente; prudente; recomendable.

advise [ədváɪz] *v.* aconsejar; avisar, advertir; informar; **to — with** consultar con; aconsejarse con.

adviser, advisor [ədváɪzə] *s.* consejero, aconsejador.

advocate [ǽdvəkɪt] *s.* abogado; defensor, intercesor; partidario; [ǽdvəket] *v.* abogar por; defender.

aerial [ériəl] *adj.* aéreo; *s.* antena.

aeroplane [ériəplen] = **airplane.**

aesthetic [esθétɪk] *adj.* estético; **-s** *s.* estética.

afar [əfár] *adv.* lejos; **from —** desde lejos.

affable [ǽfəbl] *adj.* afable, amable.

affair [əfér] *s.* asunto; negocio; lance; función, tertulia, convite; cosa; **love —** amorío.

affect [əfékt] *v.* afectar; conmover; fingir; hacer ostentación de.

affectation [æfɪktéʃən] *s.* afectación.

4

affected [əféktɪd] adj. afectado; conmovido, enternecido; fingido; artificioso.

affection [əfékʃən] s. afecto, cariño; inclinación; afección, dolencia.

affectionate [əfékʃənɪt] adj. afectuoso, cariñoso.

affiliate [əflɪet] v. afiliar; afiliarse, unirse, asociarse.

affinity [əfɪnɪtɪ] s. afinidad.

affirm [əfɜ́m] v. afirmar, asegurar, aseverar.

affirmative [əfɜ́mətɪv] adj. afirmativo; s. afirmativa.

affix [əfɪks] v. fijar, pegar; to — one's signature poner su firma, firmar.

afflict [əflɪkt] v. afligir; to be -ed with padecer de, sufrir de, adolecer de.

affliction [əflɪkʃən] s. aflicción; pena, dolor; achaque; angustia; infortunio.

afford [əfórd] v. proveer, proporcionar; I cannot — that expense no puedo hacer ese gasto; he cannot — to waste time no le conviene perder el tiempo; no tiene tiempo que perder; I cannot — that risk no puedo (o no quiero) exponerme a ese riesgo.

affront [əfrʌnt] s. afrenta, agravio, ultraje; v. afrentar, agraviar, ultrajar.

afire [əfáɪr] adj. ardiendo, quemándose.

afloat [əflót] adj. & adv. flotante; flotando; a flote, a flor de agua; a bordo; inundado; a la deriva, sin rumbo; the rumor is — corre la voz.

afoot [əfút] adv. a pie; en marcha, en movimiento.

aforesaid [əfórsed] adj. susodicho, ya dicho.

afraid [əfréd] adj. miedoso, medroso; atemorizado, amedrentado; to be — temer, tener miedo.

afresh [əfréʃ] adv. de nuevo, desde el principio.

African [æfrɪkən] adj. & s. africano; negro.

after [æftæ] prep. después de; tras, tras de; detrás de; en busca de; por; según; adv. después; detrás; conj. después (de) que; adj. subsiguiente; siguiente; — all después de todo; de todos modos; day — tomorrow pasado mañana; after-dinner de sobremesa; —effect consecuencia, resultado; —math consecuencias, resultados (usualmente desastrosos); —thought idea tardía.

afternoon [æftənún] s. tarde.

aftertaste [æftətest] s. dejo, dejillo (sabor que queda en la boca).

afterwards [æftəwədz] adv. después.

again [əgén] adv. otra vez, de nuevo; además; por otra parte; — and — repetidas veces; never — nunca jamás; to come — volver; to do it — volver a hacerlo.

against [əgénst] prep. contra; frente a; en contraste con; — the grain a contrapelo, a redopelo; — a rainy day para cuando llueva.

age [edʒ] s. edad; época; siglo; generación; of — mayor de edad; old — vejez, ancianidad; to become of — llegar a mayor edad; under — menor de edad; v. envejecer(se).

aged [édʒɪd, édʒd] adj. viejo, anciano; añejo; envejecido; — forty years de cuarenta años; — in wood añejado en toneles o barriles (dícese del vino).

agency [édʒənsɪ] s. agencia; medio, intermedio.

agent [édʒənt] s. agente; intermediario, representante; apoderado.

aggrandize [ǽgrəndaɪz] v. engrandecer; agrandar.

aggravate [ǽgrəvet] v. agravar, empeorar; irritar, exasperar.

aggregate [ǽgrɪgɪt] s. agregado, conjunto, colección; adj. agregado, unido; in the — en conjunto.

aggression [əgréʃən] s. agresión.

aggressive [əgrésɪv] adj. agresivo; emprendedor.

aggressor [əgrésə] s. agresor.

aghast [əgést] adj. espantado, pasmado.

agile [ǽdʒəl] adj. ágil.

agility [ədʒílətɪ] s. agilidad.

agitate [ǽdʒətet] v. agitar; turbar, perturbar; alborotar; discutir acaloradamente; maquinar, tramar.

agitation [ædʒətéʃən] s. agitación; alboroto.

agitator [ǽdʒətetə] s. agitador, alborotador, revoltoso.

ago [əgó] adj. & adv. pasado; en el pasado; many years — hace muchos años; much años ha, mucho tiempo ha; long — hace mucho tiempo; ha mucho.

agonize [ǽgənaɪz] v. agonizar; sufrir angustiosamente; retorcerse de dolor; luchar.

agony [ǽgənɪ] s. agonía; angustia; tormento; dolor; lucha.

agree [əgrí] v. acordar, concordar, convenir; consentir; estar de acuerdo; ponerse de acuerdo; sentarle bien a uno (dícese del clima, del alimento, etc.).

agreeable [əgríəbl] adj. agradable, afable; complaciente; conveniente; satisfactorio.

agreement [əgrímənt] *s.* acuerdo, convenio; concordancia, concordia; conformidad; **to be in —** estar de acuerdo; **to come to an —** ponerse de acuerdo.

agricultural [ægrɪkʌ́ltʃərəl] *adj.* agrícola.

agriculture [ǽgrɪkʌltʃə] *s.* agricultura.

agriculturist [ægrɪkʌ́ltʃərɪst] *s.* agricultor.

ahead [əhéd] *adv.* delante, al frente; adelante; **— of time** adelantado; antes de tiempo; **to go —** ir adelante; **to get —** adelantar(se).

aid [ed] *s.* ayuda, auxilio, socorro; ayudante, auxiliar; *v.* ayudar, auxiliar, socorrer.

ail [el] *v.* adolecer, padecer; **what -s you?** ¿qué tienes? ¿qué te aflige?

ailment [élmənt] *s.* achaque, dolencia.

aim [em] *s.* puntería; tino; fin, objeto; proposición; *v.* apuntar (*un arma*); dirigir, asestar; dirigir la puntería; aspirar (a); **to — to please** proponerse (*o tratar de*) agradar.

aimless [émlɪs] *adj.* sin propósito, sin objeto.

air [ɛr] *s.* aire; brisa; tonada; **in the —** en el aire; indeciso, incierto; **in the open —** al raso, al aire libre; **to be on the —** emitir, radiodifundir; **to put on -s** darse tono; *adj.* de aire; aéreo; **— brake** freno neumático; **— line** línea aérea; ruta aérea; **by —mail** por correo aéreo, por vía aérea, por avión; **air-conditioned** de aire acondicionado; *v.* airear; orear; ventilar; publicar, pregonar; ostentar.

aircraft [ɛ́rkræft] *s.* avión, aeroplano; aeronave; aviones.

airplane [ɛ́rplen] *s.* aeroplano, avión; **— carrier** portaaviones.

airport [ɛ́rport] *s.* aeropuerto, aeródromo.

airship [ɛ́rʃɪp] *s.* aeronave.

airtight [ɛ́rtáɪt] *adj.* hermético.

airy [ɛ́rɪ] *adj.* airoso; aireado, ventilado; ligero; tenue.

aisle [aɪl] *s.* pasillo, pasadizo; nave (*de una iglesia*).

ajar [ədʒár] *adj.* entreabierto, entornado.

alarm [əlárm] *s.* alarma; rebato; inquietud; **— clock** despertador; *v.* alarmar; inquietar.

alcohol [ǽlkəhɔl] *s.* alcohol.

alcoholic [ælkəhɔ́lɪk] *adj.* alcohólico.

alcove [ǽlkov] *s.* alcoba.

alderman [ɔ́ldəmən] *s.* concejal, regidor.

ale [el] *s.* cerveza.

alert [ələ́t] *adj.* alerto, vigilante; despierto; vivo; listo; *s.* alarma, rebato **to be on the —** estar alerta.

alfalfa [ælfǽlfə] *s.* alfalfa.

algebra [ǽldʒəbrə] *s.* álgebra.

alien [éljən] *s.* extranjero; residente extranjero; *adj.* extraño, ajeno.

alienate [éljənet] *v.* enajenar; apartar, alejar (*a una persona de otra*).

alienist [éljənɪst] *s.* alienista, psiquiatra

alight [əláɪt] *v.* apearse, desmontarse, bajar(de); posarse (*dícese de pájaros mariposas, etc.*).

alike [əláɪk] *adj.* semejante; parecido **to be —** parecerse, asemejarse; ser iguales; *adv.* del mismo modo.

alive [əláɪv] *adj.* vivo; con vida; viviente; activo; **— with** lleno de.

all [ɔl] *adj.* todo (el); todos (los); *s.* todo; todo el mundo, todos; *adv.* enteramente; **— at once** de una vez; de un tirón; de repente; **— right** bueno; bien; **— the worse** tanto peor; **not at —** de ninguna manera; no hay de qué; **nothing at —** nada en absoluto **— told** (*o* **in —**) en conjunto; **once (and) for —** por última vez; una vez por todas; **to be — in** estar agotado estar rendido de fatiga; **it is — over** se acabó, ha terminado todo.

allay [əlé] *v.* aliviar; calmar.

allegation [æləgéʃən] *s.* alegación, alegato; aseveración.

allege [əlédʒ] *v.* alegar; declarar; sostener, asegurar.

allegiance [əlídʒəns] *s.* lealtad, fidelidad; homenaje.

allergy [ǽlədʒɪ] *s.* alergia (*sensibilidad anormal a ciertos alimentos o sustancias*).

alleviate [əlívɪet] *v.* aliviar.

alley [ǽlɪ] *s.* callejón; callejuela; **blind —** callejón sin salida; **bowling —** boliche, *Am.* bolera.

alliance [əláɪəns] *s.* alianza.

allied [əláɪd] *adj.* aliado; relacionado.

alligator [ǽləgetə] *s.* lagarto; caimán **— pear** aguacate.

allot [əlát] *v.* asignar; repartir.

allow [əláʊ] *v.* permitir, dejar; conceder admitir; asignar; abonar; **to — for certain errors** tener en cuenta ciertos errores.

allowable [əláʊəbl] *adj.* permisible, admisible, lícito.

allowance [əláʊəns] *s.* asignación; abono, pensión; ración; rebaja, descuento; permiso; concesión; **monthly —** mesada, mensualidad; **to make — for** tener en cuenta.

alloy [ǽlɔɪ] *s.* aleación, liga, mezcla (de

6

dos o más metales); [əlɔ́ɪ] *v.* alear, ligar, mezclar (*metales*).

allude [əlúd] *v.* aludir.

allure [əlúr] *v.* seducir, cautivar; atraer, halagar.

allurement [əlúrmənt] *s.* seducción, tentación; atractivo, halago.

alluring [əlúrɪŋ] *adj.* seductivo, halagüeño, encantador.

allusion [əlúʒən] *s.* alusión; indirecta, insinuación.

ally [əláɪ] *v.* unir; aliarse; **to — oneself (itself) with** aliarse con, unirse con; [ǽlaɪ] *s.* aliado.

almanac [ɔ́lmənæk] *s.* almanaque, calendario.

almighty [ɔlmáɪtɪ] *adj.* todopoderoso, omnipotente.

almond [ámənd] *s.* almendra; **— tree** almendro.

almost [ɔ́lmost] *adv.* casi; **I — fell down** por poco me caigo.

alms [amz] *s.* limosna; **— box** cepo o cepillo, alcancía (*para limosnas*).

aloft [əlɔ́ft] *adv.* en alto; arriba.

alone [əlón] *adj.* solo; solitario; único; *adv.* sólo, solamente; **all — a** solas; completamente solo; solito; **to let — no** tocar; no molestar; dejar en paz; no hacer caso de.

along [əlɔ́ŋ] *prep.* a lo largo de; por; al lado de; **— with** junto con; en compañía de; **all —** todo el tiempo; de un extremo a otro; **all — the coast** por toda la costa; **to carry — with one** llevar consigo; **to go — with** acompañar; **to get —** ir bien; **to get — with** llevarse bien con; **get —!** ¡vete! ¡váyase! ¡largo de aquí!

alongside [əlɔ́ŋsáɪd] *prep.* & *adv.* al lado (de); al costado (de); lado a lado.

aloof [əlúf] *adj.* aislado, apartado, retirado; huraño; reservado; *adv.* aparte, lejos.

aloofness [əlúfnɪs] *s.* alejamiento, desapego, aislamiento.

aloud [əláud] *adv.* alto, recio, fuerte, en voz alta.

alphabet [ǽlfəbɛt] *s.* alfabeto.

already [ɔlrɛ́dɪ] *adv.* ya.

also [ɔ́lso] *adv.* también, además, igualmente.

altar [ɔ́ltə] *s.* altar; **high — altar** mayor; **—piece** retablo.

alter [ɔ́ltə] *v.* alterar; cambiar; variar.

alteration [ɔltəréʃən] *s.* alteración, cambio; mudanza; modificación.

alternate [ɔ́ltənɪt] *adj.* alternativo alterno; alternado; *s.* suplente; **-ly** *adv.* alternativamente, por turno;

[ɔ́ltənɛt] *v.* alternar; variar; turnar.

alternative [ɔltɜ́nətɪv] *adj.* alternativo; *s.* alternativa.

although [ɔlðó] *conj.* aunque, si bien, bien que.

altitude [ǽltətjud] *s.* altitud, altura, elevación.

altogether [ɔltəgɛ́ðə] *adv.* del todo, completamente; en conjunto.

aluminum [əlúmɪnəm] *s.* aluminio.

alumnus [əlámnəs] *s.* graduado, exalumno.

always [ɔ́lwɪz] *adv.* siempre.

am [æm] *1ª persona del presente de indic. del verbo* **to be:** soy, estoy.

amalgamate [əmǽlgəmət] *v.* amalgamar; combinar, unir.

amass [əmǽs] *v.* amontonar, acumular, apilar, *Am.* amasar.

amateur [ǽmətʃur] *s.* aficionado; novicio, principiante.

amaze [əméz] *v.* pasmar, maravillar, asombrar.

amazement [əmézmənt] *s.* pasmo, admiración, asombro.

amazing [əmézɪŋ] *adj.* pasmoso, asombroso, maravilloso.

ambassador [æmbǽsədə] *s.* embajador.

amber [ǽmbə] *s.* ámbar; color de ámbar; *adj.* ambarino; de ámbar.

ambiguity [æmbɪgjúətɪ] *s.* ambigüedad.

ambiguous [æmbígjuəs] *adj.* ambiguo.

ambition [æmbíʃən] *s.* ambición; aspiración.

ambitious [æmbíʃəs] *adj.* ambicioso.

amble [ǽmbl] *v.* andar, vagar.

ambulance [ǽmbjələns] *s.* ambulancia.

ambush [ǽmbuʃ] *s.* emboscada; celada; acecho; **to lie in —** estar emboscado, estar al acecho; *v.* emboscar; poner celada a.

amend [əmɛ́nd] *v.* enmendar; rectificar; **-s** *s. pl.* satisfacción, compensación; **to make — for** resarcir, dar satisfacción por, compensar por.

amendment [əmɛ́ndmənt] *s.* enmienda.

American [əmɛ́rəkən] *adj.* & *s.* americano; norteamericano.

amethyst [ǽməɪst] *s.* amatista.

amiable [émɪəbl] *adj.* amable, afable, amistoso.

amicable [ǽmɪkəbl] *adj.* amigable, amistoso.

amid [əmɪ́d] *prep.* en medio de; entre; **amidst** [əmɪ́dst] = **amid.**

amiss [əmɪ́s] *adj.* errado, equivocado, impropio; *adv.* mal; fuera de lugar, impropiamente; **to take —** llevar a mal.

ammonia [əmónjə] *s.* amoníaco.

ammunition [æmjəniʃən] *s.* munición.

amnesty [æmnɛstı] *s.* amnestía.

among [əmʌŋ] *prep.* entre, en medio de; **amongst** [əmʌŋst] = **among.**

amorous [æmərəs] *adj.* amoroso.

amount [əmáunt] *s.* suma; cantidad; total; importe; valor; *v.* montar, subir, importar, ascender (a); valer; **that -s to stealing** eso equivale a robar.

amphitheater [æmfəeiətə] *s.* anfiteatro.

ample [æmpl] *adj.* amplio; abundante; bastante, suficiente.

amputate [æmpjətet] *v.* amputar.

amuse [əmjúz] *v.* divertir, entretener, distraer; **to — oneself** divertirse.

amusement [əmjúzmənt] *s.* diversión, entretenimiento, pasatiempo, recreo, distracción.

amusing [əmjúzıŋ] *adj.* divertido, entretenido; gracioso, chistoso.

an [ən, æn] *art. indef.* un, una.

analogous [ənǽləgəs] *adj.* análogo.

analogy [ənǽlədʒı] *s.* analogía, semejanza.

analysis [ənǽləsıs] *s.* análisis.

analyze [ǽnəlaız] *v.* analizar.

anarchy [ǽnəkı] *s.* anarquía.

anatomy [ənǽtəmı] *s.* anatomía.

ancestor [ǽnsɛstə] *s.* antepassado; **-s** abuelos, antepassados.

ancestral [ænsǽstrəl] *adj.* solariego, de los antepassados; hereditario.

ancestry [ǽnsɛstrı] *s.* linaje, abolengo, ascendencia.

anchor [ǽŋkə] *s.* ancla; **to drop —** anclar, echar anclas, dar fondo, fondear; **to weigh —** levar el ancla; *v.* anclar; echar anclas; fijar, asegurar.

anchovy [ǽntʃovı] *s.* anchoa, anchova.

ancient [énʃənt] *adj.* antiguo; vetusto; **the -s** los antiguos; **la antigüedad.**

and [ənd, ænd] *conj.* y; e (*delante de* i *o* hi); **— so forth** etcétera; y así sucesivamente; **let us try — let us go — see him** vamos a verle.

Andalusian [ændəlúʒən] *adj.* andaluz.

anecdote [ǽnıkdot] *s.* anécdota.

anesthetic [ænəsɛétık] *adj. & s.* anestésico.

anew [ənjú] *adv.* otra vez, de nuevo; nuevamente.

angel [éndʒəl] *s.* ángel.

angelic [ændʒélık] *adj.* angélico.

anger [ǽŋgə] *s.* enojo, enfado, ira, cólera; *v.* enojar, enfadar, encolerizar.

angina [ændʒáınə] *s.* angina; **— pectoris** angina de pecho.

angle [ǽŋgl] *s.* ángulo; rincón; esquina;

punto de vista, aspecto; *v.* pescar.

Anglo-Saxon [ǽnglosǽksn] *adj. & s* anglosajón.

angry [ǽŋgrı] *adj.* enojado; colérico.

anguish [ǽŋgwıʃ] *s.* angustia, ansia, pena, dolor.

angular [ǽŋgjələ] *adj.* angular; anguloso.

animal [ǽnəml] *s. & adj.* animal.

animate [ǽnımıt] *adj.* animado, viviente; [ǽnəmet] *v.* animar; alentar.

animation [ænəméʃən] *s.* animación; viveza.

animosity [ænəmásətı] *s.* animosidad, ojeriza, inquina, rencor.

ankle [ǽŋkl] *s.* tobillo.

annals [ǽnlz] *s. pl.* anales.

annex [ǽnɛks] *s.* anexo; añadidura, aditamento; ala de un edificio; [ənɛ́ks] *v.* anexar.

annexation [ænɛkséʃən] *s.* anexión.

annihilate [ənáıəlet] *v.* aniquilar; anonadar.

anniversary [ænəvə́sərı] *s. & adj.* aniversario.

annotate [ǽnotet] *v.* anotar.

annotation [ænotéʃən] *s.* anotación, acotación, nota.

announce [ənáuns] *v.* anunciar; proclamar.

announcement [ənáunsmənt] *s.* anuncio; aviso; noticia.

announcer [ənáunsə] *s.* anunciador; **radio —** locutor.

annoy [ənɔ́ı] *v.* molestar; fastidiar; incomodar; enfadar.

annoyance [ənɔ́ıəns] *s.* molestia; fastidio; enfado.

annual [ǽnjuəl] *adj.* anual; *s.* anuario; planta anual; **-ly** *adv.* anualmente, cada año, todos los años.

annuity [ənúətı] *s.* anualidad, renta anual.

annul [ənʌ́l] *v.* anular; abolir.

anoint [ənɔ́ınt] *v.* ungir; untar; administrar la Extremaunción.

anon [ənán] *adv.* pronto, luego; otra vez.

anonymous [ənánəməs] *adj.* anónimo.

another [ənʌ́ðə] *adj. & pron.* otro; **one — uno** a otro, unos a otros.

answer [ǽnsə] *s.* respuesta, contestación; réplica; solución; *v.* responder; contestar; replicar; **to — for ser** responsable de (o por); responder de; ser (salir) fiador de; **to — the purpose** ser adecuado, servir para el objeto.

ant [ænt] *s.* hormiga; **—eater** oso hormiguero; **— hill** hormiguero.

antagonism [æntǽgonızm] *s.* antagonismo, oposición, antipatía.

antagonist [æntǽgənıst] *s.* antagonista,

adversario.

antagonize [æntǽgənaɪz] *v.* contrariar, oponerse a, hostilizar.

antecedent [æntəsídn̩t] *adj.* & *s.* antecedente.

antelope [ǽntlop] *s.* antílope.

antenna [æntǽnə] (*pl.* **antennae** [æntǽtníl]) *s.* antena.

anterior [æntíríə] *adj.* anterior; delantero.

anteroom [ǽntɪrum] *s.* antecámara; sala de espera.

anthem [ǽnθəm] *s.* himno.

anthracite [ǽnθrəsaɪt] *s.* antracita.

antiaircraft [æntɪérkræft] *adj.* antiaéreo.

anticipate [æntísəpet] *v.* anticipar(se); prever; esperar.

anticipation [æntɪsəpéʃən] *s.* anticipación; expectación; previsión.

antics [ǽntɪks] *s. pl.* travesuras, cabriolas.

antidote [ǽntɪdot] *s.* antídoto.

antipathy [æntípəθɪ] *s.* antipatía, repugnancia.

antiquated [ǽntəkwetɪd] *adj.* anticuado; desusado.

antique [æntík] *adj.* antiguo; anticuado; *s.* antigualla.

antiquity [æntíkwətɪ] *s.* antigüedad; vejez, ancianidad.

antiseptic [æntəséptɪk] *adj.* & *s.* antiséptico.

antisocial [æntɪsóʃəl] *adj.* antisocial.

antler [ǽntlə] *s.* asta, cuerno (*del venado, ciervo, etc.*).

anvil [ǽnvɪl] *s.* yunque.

anxiety [æŋxáɪətɪ] *s.* ansiedad, zozobra; ansia, anhelo, afán.

anxious [ǽŋkʃəs] *adj.* ansioso; inquieto, preocupado; anheloso, deseoso; **-ly** *adv.* con ansiedad, con ansia, ansiosamente.

any [éni] *adj.* & *pron.* cualquier(a), cualesquier(a); alguno, algunos; **in — case** de todos modos, en todo caso; **I have not — bread** no tengo pan; **she does not sing — more** ya no canta; **he does not want to work — more** no quiere trabajar más.

anybody [énibɑdɪ] *pron.* alguien, alguno; cualquiera; **not . . . — no . . .** nadie, no . . . ninguno; **he does not know —** no conoce a nadie.

anyhow [énihau] *adv.* de todos modos; de cualquier modo.

anyone [éniwan] *pron.* = **anybody**.

anything [éniθiŋ] *pron.* alguna cosa; cualquier cosa; algo; **not . . . — no . . .** nada; **not to know —** no saber nada; **— you wish** todo lo que quiera Vd.

anyway [éniwe] *adv.* de todos modos; en cualquier caso.

anywhere [énihwer] *adv.* dondequiera; en cualquier parte o lugar; en todas partes; **not . . . — no . . .** en (*o a*) ninguna parte; **not to go —** no ir a ninguna parte.

apart [əpárt] *adv.* aparte; separadamente; a un lado; *adj.* aislado, separado; **to take — desarmar, desmontar**; **to tear — despedazar**, hacer pedazos.

apartment [əpártmənt] *s.* departamento, piso, apartamento; vivienda, habitación.

apathy [ǽpəθɪ] *s.* apatía, indiferencia, indolencia.

ape [ep] *s.* mono; *v.* remedar, imitar.

aperture [ǽpətʃə] *s.* abertura.

apex [épeks] *s.* ápice, cumbre.

apiece [əpís] *adv.* cada uno, a cada uno, por persona.

apologetic [əpɑlədʒétɪk] *adj.* que se excusa o disculpa.

apologize [əpɑ́lədʒaɪz] *v.* disculparse, excusarse.

apology [əpɑ́lədʒɪ] *s.* apología; excusa, disculpa, justificación, satisfacción.

apoplexy [ǽpəpleksɪ] *s.* apoplejía.

apostle [əpásl̩] *s.* apóstol.

apostolic [æpəstɑ́lɪk] *adj.* apostólico.

appall [əpɔ́l] *v.* aterrorizar, aterrar; asombrar, espantar.

appalling [əpɔ́lɪŋ] *adj.* aterrador; espantoso, asombroso.

apparatus [æpərétəs] *s.* aparato; aparejo.

apparel [əpǽrəl] *s.* ropa; ropaje; vestidos.

apparent [əpǽrənt] *adj.* aparente; visible; claro, evidente; patente; **heir — heredero presunto**; **-ly** *adv.* aparentemente, al parecer, por lo visto.

apparition [æpərʃən] *s.* aparición; aparecido, espectro, fantasma.

appeal [əpíl] *s.* apelación; recurso; súplica; atracción; atractivo; llamamiento; *v.* apelar; recurrir, acudir; atraer, despertar interés o simpatía; llamar la atención.

appear [əpfr] *v.* aparecer(se); parecer; comparecer.

appearance [əpfrəns] *s.* apariencia, semblante; porte, facha; aparición.

appease [əpíz] *v.* apaciguar, aplacar; pacificar; conciliar; sosegar.

appeasement [əpízmənt] *s.* apaciguamiento; conciliación.

appendix [əpéndɪks] *s.* apéndice.

appertain [æpətén] *v.* pertenecer.

appetite [ǽpətaɪt] *s.* apetito; gana, deseo.

appetizer [ǽpətaɪzə] s. aperitivo.

appetizing [ǽpətaɪzɪŋ] adj. apetecible; apetitoso.

applaud [əplɔ́d] v. aplaudir.

applause [əplɔ́z] s. aplauso.

apple [ǽpl] s. manzana; — tree manzano; Adam's — nuez (de la garganta); Am. manzana; — of my eye niña de mis ojos.

applesauce [ǽplsɔs] s. compota de manzana.

appliance [əpláɪəns] s. utensilio, instrumento; herramienta.

applicant [ǽpləkənt] s. solicitante, aspirante, candidato.

application [ǽpləkéʃən] s. aplicación; solicitud, petición, memorial; Am. ocurso.

applicable [ǽplɪkəbl] adj. aplicable.

applied [əpláɪd] adj. & p.p. aplicado; — for pedido, solicitado.

apply [əpláɪ] v. aplicar(se); to — to dirigirse a, acudir a, recurrir a; to — for solicitar, pedir; to — oneself aplicarse, dedicarse; to — on account acreditar en cuenta.

appoint [əpɔ́ɪnt] v. nombrar; designar; señalar; equipar, amueblar; a well -ed house una casa bien amueblada.

appointment [əpɔ́ɪntmənt] s. nombramiento; designación; cita, compromiso; -s mobiliario, mueblaje; accesorios.

apportion [əpɔ́rʃən] v. repartir proporcionadamente, prorratear.

apportionment [əpɔ́rʃənmənt] s. prorrateo, distribución, repartimiento.

appraisal [əpréz] s. tasa, valuación.

appraise [əpréz] v. avaluar, valuar, tasar.

appreciable [əpríʃɪəbl] adj. apreciable; perceptible.

appreciate [əpríʃɪet] v. apreciar; estimar; agradecer; to — in value subir de valor.

appreciation [əpriʃɪéʃən] s. apreciación; aprecio; valuación; agradecimiento; aumento, alza, subida (de precio).

apprehend [ǽprɪhénd] v. aprehender, asir, prender; comprender; percibir.

apprehension [ǽprɪhénʃən] s. aprehensión, aprensión; recelo, desconfianza, presentimiento; captura.

apprehensive [ǽprɪhénsɪv] adj. aprensivo.

apprentice [əpréntɪs] s. aprendiz; novicio, principiante; v. poner de aprendiz.

apprenticeship [əpréntɪsʃɪp] s. aprendizaje.

approach [əprótʃ] s. acercamiento; aproximación; acceso, entrada; method of — técnica o modo de plantear (un problema); v. acercarse, aproximarse; abordar (a alguien).

approbation [ǽprəbéʃən] s. aprobación.

appropriate [əprópriɪt] adj. apropiado, propio, apto, conveniente, a propósito; [əprópriet] v. apropiarse, apoderarse de; asignar (una suma de dinero).

appropriation [əpropriéʃən] s. apropiación; asignación, suma asignada.

approval [əprúvl] s. aprobación; asentimiento.

approve [əprúv] v. aprobar; asentir a.

approximate [əpráksəmɪt] adj. aproximado; aproximativo; -ly adv. aproximadamente, casi, poco más o menos; [əpráksəmet] v. aproximar; aproximarse, acercarse.

apricot [éprɪkɑt] s. albaricoque; Am. chabacano.

April [éprəl] s. abril.

apron [éprən] s. delantal.

apropos [ǽprəpó] adv. a propósito; adj. oportuno; pertinente; — of a propósito de.

apt [ǽpt] adj. apto, capaz; pertinente, a propósito; — to propenso a.

aptitude [ǽptətjud] s. aptitud, capacidad; habilidad.

aquarium [əkwériəm] s. acuario; pecera.

aquatic [əkwǽtɪk] adj. acuático.

aqueduct [ǽkwɪdʌkt] s. acueducto.

Arab [ǽrəb] adj. & s. árabe.

Aragonese [ǽrəgəniz] adj. & s. aragonés.

arbiter [árbɪtə] s. árbitro, arbitrador, juez árbitro.

arbitrary [árbətrerɪ] adj. arbitrario; despótico.

arbitrate [árbətret] v. arbitrar; decidir; someter al arbitraje.

arbitration [arbətréʃən] s. arbitraje, arbitración.

arbitrator [árbətretə] s. arbitrador, árbitro; medianero.

arbor [árbə] s. emparrado, enramada, glorieta.

arc [ɑrk] s. arco; — lamp lámpara de arco.

arcade [arkéd] s. arcada; galería; soportal.

arch [artʃ] s. arco; bóveda; semicircular — arco de medio punto; — enemy enemigo acérrimo; v. arquear(se); enarcar(se).

archaic [arkéɪk] adj. arcaico, desusado, anticuado.

archbishop [ártʃbíʃəp] s. arzobispo.

archipelago [arkəpélɑgo] s. archipiélago.

architect [árkətɛkt] s. arquitecto.

architectural [ɑrkətéktʃərəl] *adj* arquitectónico.

architecture [árkətektʃə] *s.* arquitectura.

archway [ártʃwe] *s.* pasadizo (*bajo un arco*); arcada, galería abovedada.

arctic [árktɪk] *adj.* ártico.

ardent [árdnt] *adj.* ardiente; apasionado.

ardor [árdə] *s.* ardor; enardecimiento; fervor.

arduous [árdʒʊəs] *adj.* arduo, trabajoso.

are [ɑr] *2ª persona y pl. del presente de indic. del verbo* to be: eres, estás; somos, estamos; sois, estáis; son, están.

area [érɪə] *s.* área, superficie; espacio; región.

arena [ərínə] *s.* arena, redondel, plaza.

Argentine [árdʒəntin] *adj & s.* argentino.

argue [árgjʊ] *v.* argüir; debatir; altercar, **to — into** persuadir a.

argument [árgjəmənt] *s.* argumento; razonamiento; sumario, resumen.

arid [ǽrɪd] *adj.* árido.

arise [əráɪz] *v.* levantarse; elevarse; surgir; provenir.

arisen [ərízn] *p.p. de* to arise.

aristocracy [ǽrəstákrəsɪ] *s.* aristocracia.

aristocrat [ərístəkræt] *s.* aristócrata.

aristocratic [ərɪstəkrǽtɪk] *adj.* aristocrático.

arithmetic [ərîfəmətɪk] *s.* aritmética.

ark [ɑrk] *s.* arca; **— of the covenant** arca del testamento; **Noah's —** arca de Noé.

arm [ɑrm] *s.* brazo; arma, **— in —** de bracete, de bracero; *Am.* de brazo, de brazos; **at —'s length** a una brazada; **with open —s** con los brazos abiertos; *v.* armar(se).

armada [ɑrmádə] *s.* armada, flota.

armament [árməmənt] *s.* armamento.

armature [ármətʃə] *s.* armadura.

armchair [ármtʃer] *s.* silla de brazos, sillón, butaca.

armful [ármfʊl] *s.* brazada.

armistice [árməstɪs] *s.* armisticio.

armor [ármər] *s.* armadura, blindaje, coraza; arnés; *v.* blindar, acorazar.

armored [árməd] *p.p.* blindado, acorazado.

armory [ármərɪ] *s.* armería; arsenal.

armpit [ármpɪt] *s.* sobaco.

army [ármɪ] *s.* ejército; muchedumbre; **— doctor** médico militar; **regular —** tropa de línea.

aroma [ərómə] *s.* aroma, fragancia.

aromatic [ǽrəmǽtɪk] *adj.* aromático.

arose [əróz] *pret. de* to arise.

around [əráʊnd] *adv.* alrededor; en re-

dor; a la redonda; en torno; en derredor; cerca; **all —** por todos lados; *prep.* alrededor de; cerca de; **— here** por aquí; **to go — in circles** dar vueltas, **to go — the world** dar la vuelta al mundo.

arouse [əráʊz] *v.* despertar, *Am.* recordar (*al dormido*); excitar; promover.

arraign [ərén] *v* acusar; procesar (*a un criminal*).

arrange [əréndʒ] *v.* arreglar; disponer; colocar; acomodar, hacer arreglos (para), hacer planes (para).

arrangement [əréndʒmənt] *s.* arreglo; disposición; colocación, orden; convenio.

array [əré] *s.* arreglo, formación, orden; orden (*de batalla*), pompa; gala, atavío, *v.* formar (*tropas*); poner en orden; ataviar, adornar.

arrears [ərírz] *s. pl.* atrasos, pagos o rentas vencidos y no cobrados; **in —** atrasado (*en el pago de una cuenta*).

arrest [ərést] *s.* arresto, captura, aprensión; detención; *v.* aprehender o prender, arrestar; detener; llamar, atraer (*la atención*).

arrival [əráɪvl] *s.* llegada; arribo; venida; **the new —s** los recién llegados.

arrive [əráɪv] *v.* llegar; arribar; **to — at a result** lograr (*o conseguir*) un resultado.

arrogance [ǽrəgəns] *s.* arrogancia.

arrogant [ǽrəgənt] *adj.* arrogante.

arrow [ǽro] *s.* saeta, flecha.

arsenal [ársnəl] *s.* arsenal.

arsenic [ársnɪk] *s.* arsénico.

art [ɑrt] *s.* arte, destreza; astucia, **fine —s** bellas artes, **master of —s** licenciado en letras, maestro en artes.

artery [ártərɪ] *s.* arteria.

artful [ártfəl] *adj* artero, mañero, ladino.

artichoke [ártɪtʃok] *s.* alcachofa.

article [ártɪkl] *s.* artículo; **— of clothing** prenda de vestir; **— of merchandise** mercancía, mercadería.

articulate [ɑrtíkjəlɪt] *adj.* articulado, claro, inteligible; capaz de hablar; [ɑrtíkjəlet] *v.* articular; enunciar; enlazar.

articulation [ɑrtɪkjəléʃən] *s.* articulación; coyuntura.

artifice [ártəfɪs] *s.* artificio; ardid.

artificial [ɑrtəfíʃəl] *adj.* artificial; postizo; afectado, artificioso.

artillery [ɑrtíləri] *s.* artillería; **— man** artillero.

artisan [ártəzn] *s.* artesano; artífice.

artist [ártɪst] *s.* artista.

artistic [ɑrtístɪk] *adj.* artístico; **-ally** *adv.* artísticamente.

as [əz] *adv.*, *conj.*, *prep.* como; mientras; a medida que, según; en el momento en que; **— far —** hasta, hasta donde; **— for (— to)** en cuanto a; **— if** como si; **— it were** por decirlo así; **— large** — tan grande como; **— much** — tanto como; **— well** tan bien; también; **— yet** hasta ahora, todavía; **— long — you wish** todo el tiempo que Vd. quiera; **strong — he is** aunque es tan fuerte, **the same** — lo mismo que.

ascend [əsénd] *v.* ascender; subir; elevarse.

ascension [əsénʃən] *s.* ascensión, subida.

ascent [əsént] *s.* ascenso; subida; ascensión.

ascertain [æsətén] *v.* averiguar, indagar.

ascribe [əskráɪb] *v.* atribuir, imputar, achacar

ash [æʃ] *s.* ceniza; **— tray** cenicero; **— tree** fresno; **Ash Wednesday** miércoles de ceniza; **ash-colored** *adj.* ceniciento, cenizo.

ashamed [əʃémd] *adj.* avergonzado, corrido; **to be —** tener vergüenza; avergonzarse.

ashore [əʃór] *adv.* a tierra, en tierra; **to go —** desembarcar.

Asiatic [eʒɪætɪk] *adj. & s.* asiático.

aside [əsáɪd] *adv.* aparte; a un lado; al lado; *s.* aparte (*en un drama*).

ask [æsk] *v.* preguntar; pedir; rogar; solicitar; invitar; **to — for** pedir; **to — for (about, after)** preguntar por; **to — a question** hacer una pregunta.

askance [əskǽns] *adv.* de soslayo; con recelo, recelosamente; **to look —** mirar con recelo; no aprobar.

asleep [əslíp] *adj.* dormido; **to fall —** dormirse; **my arm is —** se me ha dormido (entumecido *o* entumido) el brazo.

asparagus [əspǽrəgəs] *s.* espárrago.

aspect [ǽspekt] *s.* aspecto.

asphalt [ǽsfɔlt] *s.* asfalto.

aspiration [æspəréʃən] *s.* aspiración; anhelo.

aspire [əspáɪr] *v.* aspirar; anhelar, ambicionar

ass [æs] *s.* asno, burro; pollino.

assail [əsél] *v.* asaltar, acometer, agredir.

assailant [əsélənt] *s.* asaltador, agresor.

assassin [əsǽsɪn] *s.* asesino.

assassinate [əsǽsnet] *v.* asesinar.

assassination [əsæsnéʃən] *s.* asesinato.

assault [əsɔ́lt] *s.* asalto, acometida, ataque; *v* asaltar, acometer, atacar; violar

assay [əsé] *v.* ensayar (*metales*); analizar, examinar; contrastar (*pesas, moneda*); *s.* ensaye (*de metales*); contraste (*de pesas, moneda*).

assemble [əsémbl] *v.* reunir(se), congregar(se), juntar(se); convocar; armar, montar (*maquinaria*).

assembly [əsémblɪ] *s.* asamblea; reunión; montaje (*de maquinaria*); **— hall** salón de sesiones; paraninfo.

assent [əsént] *s.* asentimiento; consentimiento; *v.* asentir; consentir.

assert [əsə́t] *v.* aseverar, asegurar, afirmar; **to — oneself** hacerse valer; obrar con firmeza; vindicarse.

assertion [əsə́ʃən] *s.* aserción, aserto, afirmación.

assess [əsés] *v.* avaluar; tasar; asignar, imponer (*impuestos, multas, contribuciones, etc.*).

assessment [əsésmənt] *s.* avaluación, tasación; imposición (*de contribuciones, multas, etc.*); contribución, impuesto.

asset [ǽset] *s.* cualidad, ventaja; **-s** capital, fondos, caudal; haber, activo; **personal -s** bienes muebles.

assiduous [əsídʒʊəs] *adj.* asiduo, diligente.

assign [əsáɪn] *v.* asignar; señalar, designar; traspasar, ceder a favor de.

assignment [əsáɪnmənt] *s.* asignación; designación; cesión (*de bienes*); tarea (*asignada*); lección (*señalada*).

assimilate [əsímlet] *v.* asimilar(se), absorber(se).

assist [əsíst] *v.* asistir, ayudar.

assistance [əsístəns] *s.* asistencia, ayuda.

assistant [əsístənt] *s.* asistente; ayudante; auxiliar; *adj.* subordinado, auxiliar.

associate [əsóʃɪɪt] *adj.* asociado; *s.* asociado; socio; compañero; colega; [əsóʃɪet] *v.* asociar(se); relacionar.

association [əsosɪéʃən] *s.* asociación; sociedad; conexión, relación.

assorted [əsɔ́rtɪd] *adj.* surtido, mezclado, variado, de todas clases.

assortment [əsɔ́rtmənt] *s.* variedad; clasificación; surtido; colección, grupo.

assume [əsúm] *v.* asumir; tomar; dar por sentado, dar por supuesto; arrogarse, apropiarse.

assumption [əsʌ́mpʃən] *s.* suposición; toma, apropiación; presunción; asunción (*de la Virgen*).

assurance [əʃúrəns] *s.* seguridad, certeza; convicción; confianza; **life —** seguro de vida. *Véase* **insurance.**

assure [əʃúr] *v.* asegurar; afirmar; infundir confianza.

assuredly [əʃúrɪdlɪ] *adv.* seguramente;

sin duda, con seguridad.

asterisk [ǽstərɪsk] s. asterisco.

astonish [əstánɪʃ] v. asombrar, pasmar, espantar.

astonishing [əstánɪʃɪŋ] adj. asombroso, pasmoso, maravilloso.

astonishment [əstánɪʃmənt] s. asombro, pasmo, sorpresa.

astound [əstáund] v. pasmar; aterrar, aturdir.

astray [əstré] adv fuera de camino; adj. desviado, extraviado, descaminado; **to go** — perderse; errar el camino; extraviarse, **to lead** — desviar, extraviar; llevar por mal camino; seducir.

astride [əstráid] adv. a horcajadas.

astronomer [əstránəmə] s. astrónomo.

astronomy [əstránəmɪ] s. astronomía.

Asturian [æstjúrɪən] adj. & s. asturiano.

astute [əstjút] adj. astuto, sagaz.

asunder [əsʌ́ndə] adj. separado; **to cut** — separar, apartar; dividir en dos.

asylum [əsáiləm] s. asilo; hospicio, **orphan** — orfanato, casa de huérfanos, Am. orfanatorio.

at [æt] prep. a; en; en (la) casa de; — **last** por fin, al fin; — **once** al punto; **to be** — **work** estar trabajando; **to enter** — **that door** entrar por aquella puerta.

ate [et] pret. de **to eat**.

atheist [éθɪɪst] s. ateo.

athlete [ǽθolit] s. atleta.

athletic [æolétik] adj. atlético.

athletics [æolétiks] s. gimnasia, atletismo; deportes.

Atlantic [ətlǽntɪk] adj. atlántico; s. el Atlántico.

atlas [ǽtləs] s. atlas.

atmosphere [ǽtməsfɪr] s. atmósfera; ambiente.

atmospheric [ætməsférɪk] adj. atmosférico.

atom [ǽtəm] s. átomo; — **bomb** bomba atómica.

atomic [ətámɪk] adj. atómico.

atone [ətón] v. expiar, purgar; reparar.

atonement [ətónmənt] s. expiación; reparación.

atrocious [ətróʃəs] adj. atroz.

atrocity [ətrásətɪ] s. atrocidad; maldad.

attach [ətǽtʃ] v. unir, juntar; sujetar, pegar, adherir; poner (sello o firma); embargar (bienes); asignar; atribuir.

attachment [ətǽtʃmənt] s. adhesión; apego, afición, cariño; embargo (de bienes); accesorio.

attack [ətǽk] s. ataque, asalto; acceso; v. atacar, acometer, embestir.

attain [ətén] v. lograr, conseguir, alcanzar; llegar a.

attainment [əténmənt] s. logro, consecución; adquisición; dote habilidad.

attempt [ətémpt] s. tentativa; prueba, ensayo; esfuerzo; atentado; v. tentar, intentar; procurar, tratar (de), probar; **to** — **the life of** atentar contra la vida de.

attend [əténd] v. atender, cuidar, mirar por; asistir a; acompañar.

attendance [əténdəns] s. asistencia; presencia; concurrencia.

attendant [əténdənt] s. acompañante; sirviente, servidor; asistente; adj. acompañante.

attention [əténʃən] s. atención; cuidado; fineza; urbanidad; **to pay** — hacer caso, prestar atención.

attentive [əténtɪv] adj. atento; cortés.

attest [ətést] v. atestiguar, atestar; certificar; dar fe.

attic [ǽtɪk] s. desván.

attire [ətáɪr] s. atavío; vestidura; vestido, traje; v. ataviar, adornar.

attitude [ǽtɪtjud] s. actitud; postura.

attorney [ətɔ́nɪ] s. abogado; procurador; apoderado; — **general** fiscal (de una nación o estado); **district** — fiscal de distrito; **power of** — procuración, poder.

attract [ətrǽkt] v. atraer; cautivar; **to** — **attention** llamar la atención.

attraction [ətrǽkʃən] s. atracción; atractivo; -s diversiones; lugares o sitios de interés.

attractive [ətrǽktɪv] adj. atractivo; seductor; simpático.

attractiveness [ətrǽktɪvnɪs] s. atracción; atractivo.

attribute [ǽtrəbjut] s. atributo; propiedad; [ətríbjut] v. atribuir, achacar.

auction [ɔ́kʃən] s. subasta, almoneda, remate, Am. venduta; v. subastar; rematar.

audacious [ɔdéʃəs] adj. audaz, atrevido, osado.

audacity [ɔdǽsətɪ] s. audacia, osadía, descaro.

audible [ɔ́dəbl] adj. audible.

audience [ɔ́dɪəns] s. audiencia; auditorio, público, concurrencia.

audit [ɔ́dɪt] v. intervenir (cuentas); asistir a (una clase) de oyente; s. intervención, comprobación de cuentas.

auditor [ɔ́dɪtə] s. interventor (de cuentas); oyente.

auditorium [ɔdətɔ́rɪəm] s. salón de conferencias o conciertos; paraninfo.

auger [ɔ́gə] s. taladro, barrena.

aught [ɔt] s. algo.

augment [ɔgmént] v. aumentar

augur [ɔ́gə] s. agorero, v. augurar, pronosticar. **to — well** (o **ill**) ser de buen (o mal) agüero

August [ɔ́gəst] s. agosto.

aunt [ænt] s. tía.

auspices [ɔ́spɪsɪz] s. pl. auspicios, protección.

auspicious [ɔspɪ́ʃəs] adj. propicio, favorable.

austere [ɔstír] adj austero, adusto, severo.

austerity [ɔstérətɪ] s. austeridad, severidad

Austrian [ɔ́strɪən] adj. & s. austríaco.

authentic [ɔéntɪk] adj auténtico.

author [ɔ́ɔə] s. autor; escritor

authoritative [əɔ́rətetɪv] adj. autorizado, que tiene autoridad, autoritario.

authority [əɔ́rətɪ] s. autoridad; facultad. **to have on good —** saber de buena tinta.

authorize [ɔ́ɔəraɪz]-v autorizar

auto [ɔ́to] s. auto, automóvil.

automatic [ɔtəmǽtɪk] adj. automático; **-ally** adv automáticamente.

automobile [ɔ́təməbil] s. automóvil.

autonomy [ɔtánəmɪ] s. autonomía.

autumn [ɔ́təm] s. otoño.

autumnal [ɔtʌ́mnl] adj. otoñal.

auxiliary [ɔgzɪ́ljərɪ] adj. & s. auxiliar

avail [əvél] v aprovechar, beneficiar, **to — oneself of** aprovecharse de, s. provecho, ventaja, **of no — de ninguna utilidad o ventaja.

available [əvéləbl] adj. disponible; aprovechable, obtenible.

avalanche [ǽvlæntʃ] s. alud, torrente.

avarice [ǽvərɪs] s. avaricia.

avaricious [ævərɪ́ʃəs] adj. avaro, avariento.

avenge [əvéndʒ] v. vengar; vindicar

avenger [əvéndʒə] s. vengador.

avenue [ǽvənu] s. avenida.

aver [əvɔ́] v afirmar, asegurar.

average [ǽvrɪdʒ] s. promedio, término medio, **on an — por término medio, adj. medio, mediano, ordinario; v. promediar, calcular o sacar el promedio; **to — a loss** prorratear una pérdida; **he -s 20 miles an hour** avanza o recorre un promedio de 20 millas por hora.

averse [əvɔ́s] adj. adverso, renuente.

aversion [əvɔ́ʒən] s. aversión; malquerencia, inquina.

avert [əvɔ́t] v apartar, desviar, evitar; impedir.

aviation [evɪéʃən] s. aviación

aviator [évɪetə] s. aviador.

avocado [ɑvəkádo] s. aguacate.

avoid [əvɔ́ɪd] v evitar, eludir

avow [əváu] v confesar, reconocer, admitir

avowal [əváuəl] s. confesión, admisión.

await [əwét] v. esperar, aguardar

awake [əwék] adj despierto; alerto, **wide-awake** muy despierto, avispado; v. despertar(se)

awaken [əwékən] v despertar(se)

award [əwɔ́rd] s. premio; decisión, sentencia, v asignar, otorgar; conferir, adjudicar (un premio, medalla, etc.)

aware [əwér] adj consciente; enterado, sabedor, cauto, sobre aviso

away [əwé] adv lejos, fuera; adj ausente, **right — ahora mismo, ahorita, **two miles — a diez millas de aquí, **to give — regalar **to go — irse; **to take — quitar.

awe [ɔ] s. pavor, pasmo, **to stand in — quedarse, o estar, pasmado; pasmarse; s. atemorizar. infundir pavor, maravillar

awful [ɔ́fʊl] adj. terrible, horroroso; tremendo, impresionante; **-ly** adv. terriblemente, horrorosamente; muy.

awhile [əhwáɪl] adv (por) un rato, (por) algún tiempo.

awkward [ɔ́kwəd]adj torpe, desmañado, molesto, embarazoso; incómodo; inconveniente.

awl [ɔl] s. lezna, punzón.

awning [ɔ́nɪŋ] s. toldo.

awoke [əwók] pret. & p.p. de to awake.

ax, axe [æks] s hacha.

axis [ǽksɪs] (pl. **axes** [ǽksɪz]) s. eje.

axle [ǽksl] s. eje (de una rueda), **front — eje delantero, **rear — eje trasero

aye [e] adv. sí; s. voto afirmativo.

Aztec [ǽztek] adj & s. azteca.

azure [ǽʒə] adj azul, s azur, azul celeste.

B

babble [bǽbl] s. balbuceo, parloteo, charla, v. balbucear; parlotear, charlar

babe [beb] — baby.

baboon [bæbún] s. mandril (especie de mono).

baby [bébɪ] s. nene, bebé, criatura, adj infantil; de niño; **— girl** nena; v mimar.

bachelor [bǽtʃələ] s. bachiller; soltero.

bacillus [bəsíləs] s. bacilo.

back [bæk] s espalda; lomo; revés, respaldo (de silla), espaldar; **behind one's — a espaldas de uno, a espaldas vueltas; **in — of** detrás de, tras; **to fall on one's — caer de espaldas, caer boca arriba, **to turn one's —

volver las espaldas; *adj.* posterior; trasero; retrasado, atrasado, rezagado; — **pay** sueldo atrasado; — **yard** patio interior; corral; *adv.* atrás, detrás; — **and forth** de aquí para allá; **to come** — volver, regresar, **to give** — devolver; *v.* respaldar, endosar; sostener, apoyar; retroceder; hacer retroceder; **to** — **down** hacerse (para) atrás; retractarse.

backbone [bǽkbón] *s.* espinazo, espina dorsal; firmeza; apoyo, sostén.

backer [bǽkə] *s.* fiador; sostenedor, defensor.

background [bǽkgraʊnd] *s.* fondo; educación; experiencia; **to keep in the** — dejar en último término; quedarse en último término; **mantenerse retirado.**

backhand [bǽkhǽnd] *s.* revés; escritura inclinada a la izquierda, **-ed stroke** revés; **a -ed remark** una ironía; una indirecta.

backing [bǽkɪŋ] *s.* apoyo, garantía, endose, endoso; respaldo.

backward [bǽkwəd] *adj.* atrasado, retrasado, retrógrado; lerdo, tardo; huraño, tímido, esquivo; *adv.* = **backwards.**

backwardness [bǽkwədnɪs] *s.* torpeza, atraso; timidez.

backwards [bǽkwədz] *adv.* hacia (o para) atrás; de espaldas; **to go** — retroceder, andar hacia (o para) atrás.

bacon [békən] *s.* tocino.

bacteria [bæktírɪə] *s. pl.* bacterias.

bacteriology [bæktɪríáledʒɪ] *s.* bacteriología.

bad [bæd] *adj.* malo; perverso, dañoso; podrido; **to go from** — **to worse** ir de mal en peor; **to look** — tener mal cariz, tener mala cara o mal aspecto; **-ly** *adv.* mal, malamente.

bade [bæd] *pret. de* **to bid.**

badge [bædʒ] *s.* insignia, divisa, distintivo.

badger [bǽdʒə] *s.* tejón; *v.* atormentar, acosar, molestar.

badness [bǽdnɪs] *s.* maldad.

baffle [bǽfl] *v.* desconcertar, confundir, frustrar, impedir.

bag [bæg] *s.* saco, bolsa, talega, costal, maleta; zurrón, morral; — **pipe** gaita gallega; *v.* ensacar; cazar; agarrar; adueñarse de; inflarse, abolsarse.

baggage [bǽgɪdʒ] *s.* equipaje; bagaje; — **car** furgón, vagón de equipajes; — **check** talón, contraseña de equipajes; — **tag** marbete, etiqueta.

bail [bel] *s.* fianza, caución, **to let out on** — poner en libertad bajo fianza,

v. dar fianza; salir fiador; achicar (*agua*), vaciar; **to** — **out of a plane** tirarse (*con paracaídas*) de un aeroplano.

bait [bet] *s.* cebo; atractivo, aliciente; *v.* tentar, atraer; cebar; acosar, perseguir.

bake [bek] *v.* hornear, cocer al horno; calcinar.

baker [békə] *s.* panadero, pastelero, hornero.

bakery [békəri] *s.* panadería, pastelería, tahona.

baking [békɪŋ] *s.* hornada; cocimiento; — **powder** levadura.

balance [bǽləns] *s.* balanza, balance; equilibrio, saldo (*de una cuenta*); contrapeso, — **of trade** balanza comercial; — **of power** equilibrio político; **to lose one's** — perder el equilibrio; *v.* contrapesar; pesar; balancear(se); equilibrar, saldar (*una cuenta*).

balcony [bǽlkəni] *s.* balcón, galería (*de teatro*).

bald [bɔld] *adj.* calvo; pelado, sin vegetación; escueto, sin adornos; — **spot** calva.

bale [bel] *s.* bala, fardo (*de mercancías*), *v.* embalar, enfardar, empacar.

balk [bɔk] *v.* oponerse, rebelarse, resistirse; pararse de repente; negarse a seguir; encabritarse; **to** — **someone's plans** frustrar los planes de alguien.

ball [bɔl] *s.* bola, pelota; ovillo (*de estambre, etc.*); bala (*de cañón*); baile; — **bearing** cojinete de bolas; — **game** juego de pelota; beisbol; *v.* ovillar; **to** — **up** enredar, confundir

ballad [bǽləd] *s.* romance, copla, canción, balada.

ballast [bǽləst] *s.* lastre, grava (*usada en terraplenes, caminos, etc.*); *v.* lastrar, poner el lastre a (*una embarcación*).

balloon [bəlún] *s.* globo (*aerostático*).

ballot [bǽlət] *s.* balota, *Am.* boleta, cédula para votar; voto; — **box** urna electoral; *v.* balotar, votar.

balm [bam] *s.* bálsamo.

balmy [bámɪ] *adj.* balsámico, fragante, refrescante, suave; algo loco, chiflado.

balsam [bɔ́lsəm] *s.* bálsamo; especie de abeto.

bamboo [bæmbú] *s.* bambú.

ban [bæn] *s.* bando, proclama, excomunión; prohibición, **marriage -s** (*o* **banns**) amonestaciones; *v.* proscribir, prohibir; condenar.

banana [bənǽnə] *s.* banana; plátano; — **tree** banano; plátano.

band [bænd] *s.* banda; faja, lista, tira;

cinta; partida, pandilla, cuadrilla; **rubber** — liga de goma; *v.* unir, juntar; atar, ligar; **to** — **together** confederarse, juntarse.

bandage [bǽndɪdʒ] *s.* venda, vendaje; *v.* vendar.

bandit [bǽndɪt] *s.* bandido, bandolero.

bang [bæŋ] *s.* golpe, golpazo; estallido; fleco (*de pelo*); **with a** — de golpe, de golpazo, de repente; con estrépito, — ! ¡pum!; *v.* golpear; hacer estrépito; cortar (*el pelo*) en fleco; **to** — **the door** dar un portazo

banish [bǽnɪʃ] *v.* proscribir, desterrar; **to** — **fear** desechar el temor.

banishment [bǽnɪʃmənt] *s.* proscripción; destierro.

banister [bǽnɪstə] *s.* balaustre; barandilla, barandal, pasamano.

bank [bæŋk] *s.* banco, banca; orilla, banda, ribera; montón (*de tierra, etc.*); cuesta, escarpa; bajío, banco de arena; **savings** — caja de ahorros; *adj.* bancario; de banco; *v.* depositar en un banco; amontonar (*tierra o arena*); cubrir con cenizas, tapar (*el fuego*); ladear (*un aeroplano*); **to** — **upon** (*o* on) contar con.

bankbook [bǽŋkbʊk] *s.* libreta de banco.

banker [bǽŋkə] *s.* banquero.

banking [bǽŋkɪŋ] *s.* transacciones bancarias, banca; *adj.* bancario, de banca; — **house** banca, casa de banca.

banknote [bǽŋknot] *s.* billete de banco.

bankrupt [bǽŋkrʌpt] *adj.* en quiebra, arruinado, insolvente; *v.* quebrar; arruinar.

bankruptcy [bǽŋkrʌptsɪ] *s.* bancarrota, quiebra; **to go into** — declararse insolvente; quebrar, hacer bancarrota.

banner [bǽnə] *s.* bandera, estandarte, pendón; *adj.* primero, principal, sobresaliente.

banquet [bǽŋkwɪt] *s.* banquete; *v.* banquetear.

baptism [bǽptɪzəm] *s.* bautismo; bautizo.

Baptist [bǽptɪst] *s.* bautista.

baptize [bæptáɪz] *v.* bautizar.

bar [bar] *s.* barra; barrote, tranca; barrera, obstáculo; barra (*de jabón*); pastilla (*de chocolate*); tribunal; foro; cuerpo de abogados; mostrador de taberna; cantina, taberna; **sand** — banco de arena; **-s reja**; **to be admitted to the** — recibirse de abogado; *v.* atrancar (*la puerta*); estorbar, prohibir; excluir.

barb [barb] *s.* púa.

barbarian [barbérɪən] *s. & adj* bárbaro,

salvaje.

barbarous [bárbərəs] *adj.* bárbaro; salvaje; inculto.

barbecue [bárbɪkju] *s. Am.* barbacoa; *Am.* churrasco; *v.* hacer barbacoa; *Am.* churrasquear.

barbed [barbd] *adj.* con púas; — **wire** alambre de púas.

barber [bárbə] *s.* barbero; peluquero.

barbershop [bárbəʃap] *s.* barbería; peluquería.

bard [bard] *s.* bardo, vate, poeta.

bare [ber] *adj.* desnudo; descubierto; pelado; manifiesto, patente; vacío, desamueblado; — **majority** mayoría escasa; **to lay** — poner de manifiesto, hacer patente, revelar; **to ride** —**back** montar en pelo.

barefoot [bérfʊt] *adj.* descalzo, con los pies desnudos, **-ed** [bérfʊtɪd] = **barefoot.**

bareheaded [bérhédɪd] *adj.* descubierto, sin sombrero.

barelegged [bérlégɪd] *adj.* con las piernas desnudas; sin medias.

barely [bérlɪ] *adv.* apenas; escasamente; — **three pounds** tres libras escasas.

bareness [bérnɪs] *s.* desnudez.

bargain [bárgɪn] *s.* convenio, pacto, negocio, trato; ganga; — **sale** ganga, *Am.* barata; **into the** — por añadidura; de ganancia; **to make a** — cerrar un convenio; *v.* regatear; negociar; **to** — **for** regatear; contar con, esperar.

barge [bardʒ] *s.* lanchón, barca.

bark [bark] *s.* ladrido; corteza (*de árbol*); barco velero; *v.* ladrar; descortezar, quitar la corteza.

barley [bárlɪ] *s.* cebada.

barn [barn] *s.* establo, cuadra, granero, troje; pajar; **streetcar** — cobertizo para tranvías.

barnyard [bárnjard] *s.* corral; — **fowl** aves de corral.

barometer [bərámətə] *s.* barómetro.

baron [bǽrən] *s.* barón.

barracks [bǽrəks] *s. pl.* cuartel.

barrel [bǽrəl] *s.* barril, barrica, tonel, cuba; cañón (*de fusil, pistola, etc.*); *v.* embarrilar (*meter en barril*).

barren [bǽrən] *adj.* árido; estéril.

barrenness [bǽrənnɪs] *s.* aridez; esterilidad.

barrette [bərét] *s.* broche, prendedor (*para sujetar el pelo*).

barricade [bǽrəkéd] *s.* barricada, barrera; *v.* poner barricadas; obstruir el paso con barricadas.

barrier [bǽrɪə] *s.* barrera, valla, obstá-

culo.

barter [bártə] *v.* permutar, trocar, cambiar; *s.* permuta, trueque, cambio.

base [bes] *s.* base; basa; fundamento; *adj.* bajo, vil, ruin; inferior; *v.* basar, fundar; establecer.

baseball [bésból] *s.* baseball o beisbol.

basement [bésmənt] *s.* sótano.

baseness [bésnɪs] *s.* bajeza, ruindad, vileza.

bashful [bǽʃfəl] *adj.* tímido, encogido, vergonzoso.

bashfulness [bǽʃfəlnɪs] *s.* timidez, vergüenza, cortedad, apocamiento.

basic [bésɪk] *adj.* básico; fundamental.

basin [bésṇ] *s.* palangana, jofaina; lebrillo; tazón (*de fuente*); estanque, depósito de agua; **river —** cuenca de río.

basis [bésɪs] (*pl.* **bases** [bésiz]) *s.* base, fundamento.

bask [bæsk] *v.* calentarse (*al sol*), asolearse, tomar el sol.

basket [bǽskɪt] *s.* cesta, cesto, canasta.

basketball [bǽskɪtbɔl] *s.* basquetbol.

bass [bes] *s.* bajo (*en música*) *adj.* bajo, grave; **— drum** tambora, bombo; **— horn** tuba.

bastard [bǽstəd] *s.* & *adj.* bastardo.

baste [best] *v.* hilvanar; pringar (*empapar la carne con grasa*); apalear.

bat [bæt] *s.* palo; *Am.* bate (*de beisbol*); garrote; golpe, garrotazo; murciélago; *v.* apalear; dar palos; *Am.* batear; not **to — an eye** no pestañear.

batch [bætʃ] *s.* hornada; colección, grupo, conjunto.

bath [bæθ] *s.* baño.

bathe [beð] *v.* bañar(se).

bather [béðə] *s.* bañista.

bathhouse [bǽθhaʊs] *s.* casa de baños; bañadero.

bathrobe [bǽθrob] *s.* bata de baño.

bathroom [bǽθrum] *s.* baño, cuarto de baño.

bathtub [bǽθtʌb] *s.* bañera, tina.

battalion [bətǽljən] *s.* batallón.

batter [bǽtə] *s.* batido, masa; *Am.* bateador (*de beisbol*); *v.* golpear; **to — down** derribar, demoler.

battery [bǽtərɪ] *s.* batería; acumulador; asalto.

battle [bǽt̩] *s.* batalla, lucha, combate; *v.* batallar, luchar, combatir.

battlefield [bǽt̩fild] *s.* campo de batalla.

battleship [bǽt̩ʃɪp] *s.* buque de guerra, acorazado.

bawl [bɔl] *s.* aullido, grito, *v.* aullar; gritar, pregonar; **to — out** regañar, reprender.

bay [be] *s.* bahía; ladrido, balido, aullido; **— rum** ron de laurel; **— tree** laurel; **— window** ventana saliente, mirador; **to hold at —** tener a raya; *adj.* bayo; *v.* dar aullidos, ladridos o balidos.

bayonet [béənɪt] *s.* bayoneta; *v.* traspasar; herir con bayoneta.

bazaar [bəzár] *s.* bazar; feria.

be [bi] *v.* ser; estar; quedar(se); hallarse, verse, encontrarse; **— that as it may** sea como sea; **to — cold (warm, hungry, right,** *etc.***)** tener frío (calor, hambre, razón, *etc.*); **to — in a hurry** tener prisa; **he is to —** ha de ser; va a ser; **it is cold (hot, windy,** *etc.***)** hace frío (calor, viento, *etc.*).

beach [bitʃ] *s.* playa, ribera; *v.* varar, poner en seco (*una embarcación*), encallar.

beacon [bíkən] *s.* faro, fanal; boya luminosa, señal.

bead [bid] *s.* cuenta (*de rosario, collar, etc.*); abalorio; glóbulo; gota (*de sudor*); **-s rosario;** collar de cuentas; *v.* adornar con abalorios o cuentecitas.

beak [bik] *s.* pico (*de ave*), espolón (*de nave*).

beam [bim] *s.* rayo (*de luz o de calor*); sonrisa; viga; vigueta; brazo (*de balanza*); **radio —** línea de radiación, radiofaro; *v.* emitir (*luz, rayos*); brillar; sonreír, estar radiante de alegría; radiar, transmitir por radio.

beaming [bímɪŋ] *adj.* radiante, resplandeciente; sonriente.

bean [bin] *s.* judía, habichuela; *Am.* frijol; *Am.* poroto; **coffee —** grano de café; **Lima —** haba; **string —** judía o habichuela verde, *Am.* ejote, poroto.

bear [ber] *s.* oso, osa; bajista (*el que hace bajar los valores en la Bolsa*); *v.* soportar; llevar; sobrellevar; tolerar, aguantar; producir; parir, dar a luz; **to — down** deprimir; apretar; **to — a grudge** guardar rencor; **to — in mind** tener en cuenta, **to — on a subject** tener relación con un asunto, **to — oneself with dignity** portarse con dignidad; **to — out** confirmar; **to — testimony** dar testimonio.

beard [bɪrd] *s.* barba, barbas; aristas (*de trigo o maíz*); **-ed** *adj.* barbado, barbudo.

bearer [bérə] *s.* portador; mensajero.

bearing [bérɪŋ] *s.* porte, presencia, relación, conexión; rumbo, orientación, **ball —** cojinete de bolas, **beyond —** inaguantable, insufrible, **to lose one's -s** perder el rumbo, desorientarse, **fruit-bearing** *adj.* fructífero.

beast [bist] *s.* bestia, animal.

beat [bit] *s.* golpe; toque (*de tambor*); latido, palpitación; compás; ronda (*que hace el policía*); *v.* batir; golpear; azotar; vencer, ganar; marcar (*el compás*); pulsar, latir; sonar (*tambores*); **to — around the bush** andarse por las ramas; valerse de rodeos; *pret. & p.p. de* **to beat.**

beaten [bítn̩] *p.p. de* **to beat** & *adj.* batido; vencido; fatigado; **— path** camino trillado.

beater [bítə] *s.* batidor; molinillo; golpeador; **egg —** batidor de huevos.

beating [bítɪŋ] *s.* paliza, tunda, zurra; latido, pulsación.

beatitude [biǽtɪtjud] *s.* beatitud, bienaventuranza; **the Beatitudes** las bienaventuranzas.

beau [bo] *s.* galán, pretendiente.

beauteous [bjútiəs] *adj.* bello, hermoso.

beautiful [bjútəfəl] *adj.* bello, hermoso.

beautify [bjútəfaɪ] *v.* hermosear, embellecer.

beauty [bjúti] *s.* belleza, hermosura; beldad; **— parlor** salón de belleza.

beaver [bívə] *s.* castor; **— board** cartón para tabiques.

became [bɪkém] *pret. de* **to become.**

because [bɪkɔ́z] *conj.* porque; **— of** *prep.* por, a causa de.

beckon [békən] *s.* seña, llamada; *v.* llamar a señas.

become [bɪkʌ́m] *v.* sentar bien a, quedar bien a; convenir a; hacerse; ponerse; llegar a ser; convertirse en; **to — crazy** volverse loco; enloquecer; **to — angry** enojarse; **to — frightened** asustarse; **to — old** envejecer(se); **what has — of him?** ¿qué ha sido de él? ¿qué se ha hecho él?; *p.p. de* **to become.**

becoming [bɪkʌ́mɪŋ] *adj.* propio, conveniente; decente, decoroso; **that dress is — to you** le sienta bien ese traje.

bed [bɛd] *s.* cama, lecho; cauce (*de un río*); fondo (*de lago o mar*); cuadro (*de jardín*); yacimiento (*mineral*); **to go to —** acostarse; **to put to —** acostar.

bedbug [bédbʌg] *s.* chinche.

bedclothes [bédkloz] *s. pl.* ropa de cama.

bedding [bédɪŋ] = **bedclothes.**

bedroom [bédrum] *s.* cuarto de dormir, alcoba, *Am.* recámara.

bedside [bédsaɪd] **at the —** al lado de la cama; **— table** velador, mesilla de noche.

bedspread [bédsprɛd] *s.* colcha, sobrecama.

bedtime [bédtaɪm] *s.* hora de acostarse, hora de dormir.

bee [bi] *s.* abeja; reunión (*para trabajar o competir*); **to have a — in one's bonnet** tener una idea metida en la cabeza.

beech [bitʃ] *s.* haya; **—nut** nuez de haya, hayuco.

beef [bif] *s.* carne de vaca o toro; vaca, toro (*engordados para matar*); **roast —** rosbif.

beefsteak [bífstek] *s.* bistec, biftec o bisté.

beehive [bíhaɪv] *s.* colmena; abejera.

been [bɪn, bɛn] *p.p. de* **to be.**

beer [bɪr] *s.* cerveza; **— tavern** cervecería.

beet [bit] *s.* remolacha, *Am.* betabel.

beetle [bítl̩] *s.* escarabajo.

befall [bɪfɔ́l] *v.* sobrevenir, acaecer, suceder.

befallen [bɪfɔ́lən] *p.p. de* **befall.**

befell [bɪfél] *pret. de* **befall.**

befit [bɪfít] *v.* convenir.

before [bɪfór] *adv.* antes; delante; al frente; *prep.* antes de; delante de; enfrente de; ante; *conj.* antes (de) que.

beforehand [bɪfórhænd] *adv.* de antemano, por adelantado, con antelación, con anticipación.

befriend [bɪfrénd] *v.* ofrecer o brindar amistad a; favorecer; amparar.

beg [bɛg] *v.* rogar, suplicar, pedir; mendigar, pordiosear; **to — the question** dar por sentado lo mismo que se arguye.

began [bɪgǽn] *pret. de* **to begin.**

beget [bɪgét] *v.* engendrar; causar, producir.

beggar [bégə] *s.* mendigo, pordiosero, pobre; infeliz, miserable.

begin [bɪgín] *v.* comenzar, empezar, principiar.

beginner [bɪgínə] *s.* principiante; novicio.

beginning [bɪgínɪŋ] *s.* principio, comienzo, empiezo; origen; **— with** comenzando con (o por); a partir de; **at the —** al principio.

begot [bɪgát] *pret. & p.p. de* **beget.**

begotten [bɪgátn̩] *p.p. de* **beget.**

beguile [bɪgáɪl] *v.* engañar; defraudar; seducir.

begun [bɪgʌ́n] *p.p. de* **to begin.**

behalf [bɪhǽf] **in (on) — of** por; en nombre de; a favor de; en defensa de; **in my —** en mi nombre; a mi favor, por mí.

18

behave [bɪhév] *v* portarse, conducirse, obrar, proceder (*bien o mal*); — **yourself!** ¡pórtate bien!

behavior [bɪhévjə] *s.* comportamiento, proceder, conducta; funcionamiento; reacción.

behead [bɪhéd] *v* decapitar, degollar, descabezar.

beheld [bɪhéld] *pret. & p.p. de* to behold.

behind [bɪháɪnd] *adv.* detrás, atrás, a la zaga, en zaga; *prep.* detrás de, tras; — **one's back** a espaldas de uno; — **time** atrasado, retrasado; **from** — **por** detrás, **to arrive ten minutes** — **time** llegar con diez minutos de retraso, **to fall** — atrasarse; retrasarse.

behold [bɪhóld] *v.* contemplar, mirar; —! ¡he aquí!

behoove [bɪhúv] *v.* serle necesario a uno, corresponderle a uno; atañerle a uno.

being [bíɪŋ] *s.* ser; ente, esencia, existencia, *ger. de* to be siendo, **for the time** — por ahora; por el momento.

belated [bɪlétɪd] *adj.* tardío; atrasado.

belch [bɛltʃ] *v* eructar, to — **forth** echar, arrojar, vomitar, *s* eructo.

Belgian [béldʒɪən] *adj. & s.* belga.

belief [bəlíf] *s.* creencia, fe, convicción, opinión

believable [bəlívəbl] *adj* creíble

believe [bəlív] *v.* creer, pensar, **to** — **in** creer en, tener fe en, confiar en.

believer [bəlívə] *s* creyente, fiel.

belittle [bɪlítl] *v* menospreciar, apocar, empequeñecer; dar poca importancia a.

bell [bɛl] *s* campana, campanilla, **cow** — cencerro, esquila, **call** — timbre; **jingle** — cascabel, —**flower** campanilla, campánula.

bellboy [bélbɔɪ] *s* mozo de hotel, botones

belle [bɛl] *s* beldad, mujer bella.

belligerent [bəlídʒərənt] *adj & s.* beligerante.

bellow [bélo] *s.* bramido, rugido, *v.* rugir, bramar, berrear; gritar.

bellows [béloz] *s.* (*sing. & pl.*) fuelle.

belly [bélɪ] *s.* barriga, panza, vientre, estómago.

belong [bəlóŋ] *v.* pertenecer, corresponder, **it does not** — **here** está fuera de su sitio, está mal colocado.

belongings [bəlóŋɪŋz] *s. pl.* posesiones, bienes, efectos, cosas.

beloved [bɪlávɪd] *adj* querido, amado

below [bəló] *adv* abajo, bajo; debajo, **here** — aquí abajo, en este mundo, de tejas abajo, *prep.* bajo, debajo de

belt [bɛlt] *s.* cinturón, cintó; correa, zona; s**word** — talabarte; *v* ceñir, fajar.

bemoan [bɪmón] *v* lamentarse de, quejarse de.

bench [bɛntʃ] *s.* banco, banca; tribunal.

bend [bɛnd] *s.* curva; vuelta, recodo; *v.* encorvar(se), doblar(se), *Am.* enchuecar(se); inclinar(se), someter(se), ceder; **to** — **one's efforts** esforzarse (por), dirigir sus esfuerzos.

beneath [bɪníθ] *prep.* debajo de, bajo, indigno de; inferior a.

benediction [bɛnədíkʃən] *s.* bendición

benefactor [bénəfæktə] *s.* benefactor, bienhechor; patrón.

beneficent [bənéfəsnt] *adj.* benéfico.

beneficial [bɛnəfíʃəl] *adj* benéfico; ventajoso, provechoso.

benefit [bénəfɪt] *s.* beneficio; provecho, ventaja; — **performance** función de beneficio, *v* beneficiar; hacer bien, **to** — **by the advice** aprovecharse del consejo, **he** —**ed by the medicine** le hizo bien la medicina.

benevolence [bənévələns] *s* benevolencia.

benevolent [bənévələnt] *adj.* benévolo.

benign [bɪnáɪn] *adj.* benigno, afable

bent [bɛnt] *s.* inclinación; tendencia, propensión, *pret. & p.p de* to bend; *adj.* encorvado, inclinado, doblado, corvo, gacho, **to be** — **on** estar resuelto a.

bequeath [bɪkwíð] *v.* heredar, legar, dejar en testamento

bequest [bɪkwést] *s* legado, donación

berate [bɪrét] *v.* regañar, reñir, reprender

berry [bérɪ] *s* baya (*como mora, fresa, etc.*), grano (*de café*)

berth [bɜθ] *s.* litera (*de un camarote*), **to give a wide** — **to** sacarle el cuerpo a, hacerse a un lado para dejar pasar

beseech [bɪsítʃ] *v.* suplicar, rogar

beset [bɪsét] *v.* atacar; rodear; acosar, *pret. & p.p. de* to beset.

beside [bɪsáɪd] *prep.* al lado de, cerca de, además de, fuera de, **to be** — **oneself** estar fuera de sí, estar loco, **that is** — **the question** eso no hace al caso, no se trata de eso, *adv* además

besides [bɪsáɪdz] *adv* además; *prep.* además de.

besiege [bɪsídʒ] *v* sitiar, cercar, acosar, importunar.

besought [bɪsót] *pret. & p.p. de* to beseech.

best [bɛst] *adj* mejor, *adv* mejor más, **the** — el mejor, lo mejor, — **girl**

novia, querida; — **man** padrino de boda; **at** — a lo más, cuando más; **to do one's** — hacer todo lo posible; **to get the** — **of a person** vencer o ganarle a una persona; **to make the** — **of** sacar el mejor partido de.

bestow [bɪstó] v. otorgar, conferir; **to** — **gifts upon** hacer regalos (o dádivas) a; **time well -ed** tiempo bien empleado.

bet [bet] s. apuesta; v. apostar, *pret. & p.p. de to bet.*

betake [bɪték] v. **to** — **oneself** encaminarse, dirigirse.

betaken [bɪtékən] p.p. de **to betake.**

betook [bɪtúk] *pret. de to betake.*

betray [bɪtré] v. traicionar, vender; hacer traición; revelar, no guardar (*un secreto*); **to** — **one's ignorance** hacer patente su ignorancia.

betrayer [bɪtréə] s. traidor, traicionero.

betrothal [bɪtróθəl] s. esponsales, compromiso, mutua promesa de matrimonio.

betrothed [bɪtróθet] s. prometido, desposado, novio, novia.

better [bétə] adj. mejor, adv mejor, más, — **half** cara mitad; **so much the** — tanto mejor; **to be** — **off** estar mejor así; estar en mejores condiciones, **to change for the** — mejorar(se), **to get** — mejorar(se), restablecerse, aliviarse, v mejorar, **to** — **oneself** mejorarse, mejorar de situación.

betterment [bétəmənt] s. mejoramiento, mejora, mejoría.

between [bətwín] prep. entre, en medio de, adv en medio.

beverage [bévrɪdʒ] s. bebida.

bewail [bɪwél] v. lamentar; quejarse de.

beware [bɪwér] v. guardarse (de), cuidarse (de), — ! ¡cuidado! ¡guárdese!

bewilder [bɪwíldə] v. confundir, turbar, perturbar, dejar perplejo, **to be -ed** estar turbado o perplejo, estar desorientado.

bewilderment [bɪwíldəmənt] s. perplejidad, aturdimiento.

bewitch [bɪwítʃ] v. hechizar, aojar, encantar, cautivar.

beyond [bɪjónd] adv. más allá, más lejos; prep. allende, más allá de, fuera de; — **my reach** fuera de mi alcance.

bias [báɪəs] s. prejuicio; inclinación, tendencia, sesgo, oblicuidad; **on the** — sesgado, al sesgo, de lado; adj. sesgado, oblicuo; v. predisponer, inclinar, influir en.

bib [bɪb] s. babero, pechera (*de delantal*)

Bible [báɪbḷ] s. Biblia.

biblical [bɪblɪkḷ] adj. bíblico.

bicker [bíkə] v. disputar, reñir.

bicycle [báɪsɪkḷ] s. bicicleta; v. andar en bicicleta.

bid [bɪd] s. postura, oferta, envite (*en naipes*), turno (*para envidar*); invitación; v. ofrecer (*precio*); mandar; invitar, convidar; rogar; envidar (*en naipes*), **to** — **fair** parecer muy probable, **to** — **good-bye** decir adiós; despedirse; **to** — **up** alzar, pujar (*la oferta en una subasta*), *pret. & p.p. de to bid.*

bidden [bídn] p.p. de **to bid & to bide.**

bide [baɪd] v. aguardar, **to** — **one's time** esperar una buena oportunidad.

bier [bɪr] s. féretro.

big [bɪg] adj. grande; importante; imponente; — **Dipper** Osa Mayor; — **game** caza mayor; — **sister** hermana mayor; — **with child** encinta, **to talk** — darse bombo, *Am.* darse corte; **big-bellied** panzudo, panzón, barrigón, **big-hearted** magnánimo

bigamy [bígəmɪ] s. bigamia.

bigot [bígət] s. fanático.

bigotry [bígətrɪ] s. fanatismo, intolerancia.

bile [baɪl] s. bilis, hiel, cólera, mal humor

bill [bɪl] s. cuenta, factura, proyecto de ley, cartel, anuncio; programa (*de teatro*), billete de banco; pico (*de ave*), — **of exchange** libranza, letra de cambio, — **of fare** lista de platos; — **of lading** conocimiento de embarque, — **of rights** declaración de derechos, — **of sale** escritura o acta de venta, v cargar en cuenta, enviar una cuenta a, **to** — **and coo** acariciarse y arrullar (*como las palomas*)

billboard [bílbord] s. cartelera.

billfold [bílfold] s. cartera.

billiards [bíljədz] s. billar.

billion [bíljən] s. billón, millón de millones, mil millones (*en los Estados Unidos y Francia*).

billow [bílo] s. oleada; ola grande, v alzarse en ola.

bin [bɪn] s. arcón, depósito, **coal** — carbonera, **grain** — granero.

bind [baɪnd] v. unir, juntar, ligar; amarrar, vendar, ceñir, restringir; obligar, compeler, encuadernar, empastar; ribetear (*con cinta o banda*).

binding [báɪndɪŋ] s. encuadernación, ribete, cinta, **cloth** — encuadernación en tela, **paper** — encuadernación en rústica; adj. obligatorio.

biography [baɪágrəfɪ] s. biografía.

biology [baɪálədʒɪ] s. biología.

birch [bɜtʃ] s. abedul.
bird [bɜd] s. ave; pájaro; persona extraña o mal vista; — **of prey** ave de rapiña; — **seed** alpiste; — **shot** perdigones.
birth [bɜθ] s. nacimiento; parto; linaje; origen, principio; — **certificate** certificado (o fe) de nacimiento; — **control** control de la natalidad; limitación de partos; — **rate** natalidad; **to give** — dar a luz, parir.
birthday [bɜede] s. cumpleaños, natalicio.
birthplace [bɜeples] s. lugar de nacimiento, suelo natal.
birthright [bɜeraıt] s. derechos naturales o de nacimiento; naturalidad; primogenitura.
biscuit [bískɪt] s. bizcocho; galleta; panecillo.
bishop [bíʃəp] s. obispo; alfil (en ajedrez).
bison [báɪsn] s. bisonte, búfalo.
bit [bɪt] s. pedacito, trocito; pizca, miaja, migaja; poquito; bocado (del freno); taladro; **I don't care a** — no me importa un ardite; pret. & p.p. de **to bite**.
bitch [bɪtʃ] s. perra; ramera, prostituta.
bite [baɪt] s. mordedura, mordisco; bocado, bocadito; picadura (de insecto); v. morder; mordiscar; picar.
bitten [bɪtn] p.p. de **to bite**.
bitter [bɪtə] adj. amargo; agrio, acre; áspero; mordaz; **to fight to the** — **end** luchar hasta morir; **-s** s. pl. amargo; **-ly** adv. amargamente; con amargura.
bitterness [bɪtənɪs] s. amargura, amargor; rencor; aspereza.
black [blæk] adj. negro; obscuro; sombrío; **black-and-blue** amoratado, lleno de moretones; — **mark** mancha, estigma, marca de deshonra; s. negro; luto; —**out** obscurecimiento; **to put down in** — **and** white poner por escrito v. teñir de negro; embetunar, dar bola o betún a (los zapatos).
blackberry [blǽkberɪ] s. zarzamora; mora.
blackbird [blǽkbɜd] s. mirlo.
blackboard [blǽkbord] s. encerado; pizarrón; pizarra.
blacken [blǽkən] v. ennegrecer; obscurecer; teñir de negro; denigrar.
blackhead [blǽkhed] s. espinilla.
blackish [blǽkɪʃ] adj. negruzco.
blackmail [blǽkmel] s. chantaje, extorsión; v. ejercer el chantaje, extorsionar.
blackness [blǽknɪs] s. negrura; obscuri-

dad.
blacksmith [blǽksmɪe] s. herrero; -**'s shop** herrería.
bladder [blǽdə] s. vejiga.
blade [bled] s. hoja (de navaja, cuchillo, etc.); hoja (de hierba); espada; pala (de remo); aspa (de hélice); — **shoulder** espaldilla o paletilla.
blame [blem] s. culpa; v. culpar, echar la culpa a; **to be to** — tener la culpa.
blameless [blémlɪs] adj. inculpable.
blanch [blæntʃ] v. blanquear; palidecer; escaldar (almendras).
bland [blænd] adj. blando, suave.
blank [blæŋk] adj. en blanco; vacío; aturdido; — **cartridge** cartucho vacío; — **face** cara sin expresión; — **form** blanco, forma en blanco, Am. esqueleto; — **verse** verso suelto o libre; s. blanco; vacío; hueco, intermedio; papel en blanco; forma en blanco; **application** — forma (o blanco) para memorial o solicitud.
blanket [blǽŋkɪt] s. manta; frazada; cobertor; Am. cobija; Am. sarape, poncho; adj. general, inclusivo, que abarca un grupo o clase.
blare [bler] s. fragor; son de trompetas; clarinada; v. trompetear, proclamar; sonar (las trompetas); hacer estruendo.
blaspheme [blæsfím] v. blasfemar.
blasphemy [blǽsfɪmɪ] s. blasfemia.
blast [blæst] s. ráfaga de viento, golpe de viento; soplo repentino; trompetazo, sonido (de trompeta); silbido; explosión, detonación; carga de dinamita; — **furnace** alto horno; v. volar (con dinamita, etc.); destruir.
blaze [blez] s. llama, llamarada, incendio; resplandor; — **of anger** arranque de ira; v. arder; resplandecer; **to** — **a trail** abrir (o marcar) una senda.
bleach [blitʃ] s. blanqueador; blanqueo; v. blanquear(se); desteñir(se).
bleachers [blítʃəz] s. pl. graderías, Am. glorietas.
bleak [blik] adj. yermo, desierto; helado.
blear [blır] v. nublar (los ojos).
bleary [blírı] adj. nublado, inflamado, lagrimoso, lagañoso.
bleat [blit] s. balido; v. balar.
bled [bled] pret. & p.p. de **to bleed**.
bleed [blid] v. sangrar; desangrar; extorsionar.
blemish [blémɪʃ] s. mancha, tacha, defecto; v. manchar; empañar.
blend [blend] s. mezcla, entremezcla; gradación (de colores, sonidos, etc.); v. mezclar, entremezclar; graduar (colores o sonidos); entremezclarse, fundirse;

armonizar.

bless [bles] v. bendecir; **God — you!** ¡que Dios te bendiga!

blessed [blésɪd] adj. bendito; santo, beato; bienaventurado; **the whole — day** todo el santo día; [blɛst] pret. & p.p. de **to bless.**

blessing [blésɪŋ] s. bendición; gracia, don, beneficio.

blest blest] adj. = **blessed.**

blew [blu] pret. de **to blow.**

blight [blaɪt] s. pulgón (parásito); tizón (honguillo parásito); quemadura (enfermedad de las plantas); roña (de las plantas); malogro; ruina; v. destruir, arruinar; frustrar (esperanzas).

blind [blaɪnd] adj. ciego; tapado, oculto; hecho a ciegas; **— alley** callejón sin salida; **— choice** selección hecha a ciegas; **— flying** vuelo ciego, vuelo a ciegas; **—man** ciego; **—man's buff** juego de la gallina ciega; s. persiana, cortinilla; biombo; venda (para los ojos); anteojera (para resguardar los ojos del caballo); **to be a — for someone** ser tapadera de alguien; v. cegar; ofuscar; encubrir, tapar.

blinder [bláɪndə] s. anteojera, Am. visera (para caballos de tiro).

blindfold [bláɪndfold] v. vendar (los ojos); adj. vendado (de ojos); s. venda (para los ojos).

blindly [bláɪndlɪ] adv. ciegamente; a ciegas.

blindness [bláɪndnɪs] s. ceguera, ceguedad.

blink [blɪŋk] s. pestañeo; parpadeo; guiño; guiñada; v. pestañear; parpadear; guiñar.

bliss [blɪs] s. beatitud, bienaventuranza, gloria; felicidad.

blister [blístə] s. ampolla, vejiga (en la piel o en cualquier superficie); v. ampollar, levantar ampollas; ampollarse.

blizzard [blízəd] s. ventisca; v. ventiscar.

bloat [blot] v. inflar(se); abotagarse.

block [blak] s. bloque, trozo de piedra; zoquete; manzana (de casas), Am. cuadra; horma (para sombrero); estorbo, obstáculo; grupo, sección; **— pulley** polea; **chopping — tajo;** v. estorbar; tapar; bloquear; planchar (sobre horma); parar (una pelota, una jugada); **to — out** esbozar, bosquejar; **to — the door** impedir el paso; **to — up a door** tapiar una puerta.

blockade [blakéd] s. bloqueo; obstrucción; v. bloquear.

blockhead [blákhed] s. zoquete, tonto,

zopenco.

blond(e) [bland] adj. & s. rubio, blondo; Am. huero, güero.

blood [blʌd] s. sangre; **— count** análisis cuantitativo de la sangre; **— pudding** (o **— sausage**) morcilla; **— relative** pariente consanguíneo; **— vessel** vena; arteria; **in cold —** en sangre fría.

bloodshed [blʌ́dʃed] s. matanza; derrame, derramiento o efusión de sangre.

bloodshot [blʌ́dʃat] adj. inyectado de sangre.

bloodthirsty [blʌ́dθɜstɪ] adj. sanguinario.

bloody [blʌ́dɪ] adj. sangriento; ensangrentado; sanguinario, feroz.

bloom [blum] s. flor; florecimiento, floración; lozanía; color rosado (en las mejillas) v. florecer, Am. florear.

blooming [blúmɪŋ] adj. floreciente; fresco, lozano, vigoroso.

blossom [blásəm] s. flor; floración, florecimiento; v. florecer.

blot [blat] s. mancha, borrón; tacha; v. manchar; borrar; secar (con papel secante); emborronar, echar manchas o borrones; **to — out** borrar, tachar; destruir; **this pen -s** esta pluma echa borrones; **blotting paper** papel secante.

blotch [blatʃ] v. emborronar o borronear, manchar, cubrir con manchas; s. mancha, borrón.

blotter [blátə] s. papel secante; libro borrador.

blouse [blaus] s. blusa.

blow [blo] s. golpe; porrazo; sorpresa, choque, desastre; soplo, soplido; fanfarrón; **to come to -s** venir a las manos; v. soplar; ventear; resoplar, sonar (una trompeta); fanfarronear; **to — a fuse** quemar un fusible; **to — one's nose** sonarse; **to — one's brains out** levantarse la tapa de los sesos; **to — open** abrirse; **to — out** apagar(se); estallar, reventar (se) (un neumático); **to—over** pasar; disiparse; **to — up** inflar, hinchar; volar (con dinamita); estallar, reventar.

blower [blóə] s. soplador; fuelle; ventilador, aventador.

blown [blon] p.p. de **to blow** & adj. soplado; inflado; **full-blown rose** rosa abierta.

blowout [blóaut] s. reventón (de neumático); escape violento de gas, aire, etc.

blowpipe [blópaɪp] s. soplete.

blue [blu] adj. azul; triste, melancólico;

s. azul; the **-s** melancolía, morriña, murria; *v.* azular, teñir de azul.

bluebell [blúbel] *s.* campanilla azul (*flor*).

bluebird [blúbɜd] *s.* pájaro azul, *Am.* azulejo.

bluejay [blúdʒe] *s.* gayo, especie de azulejo (*pájaro*).

bluff [blʌf] *s.* acantilado, escarpa, risco; fanfarronada; fanfarrón, farsante; *v.* fanfarronear; alardear, hacer alarde; echar bravatas; embaucar.

bluffer [blʌfɚ] *s.* farsante, fanfarrón.

bluing [blúɪŋ] *s.* añil (*para ropa blanca*).

bluish [blúɪʃ] *adj.* azulado, azulejo.

blunder [blʌndɚ] *s.* disparate, desatino; despropósito; *v.* disparatar, desatinar; equivocarse.

blunt [blʌnt] *adj.* despuntado, embotado; brusco, grosero, *Am.* claridoso; *v.* despuntar, embotar.

blur [blɜ] *s.* mancha; tacha; nube, cosa obscura o confusa; *v.* empañar, borronear, manchar; nublar, ofuscar; empañarse, nublarse.

blush [blʌʃ] *s.* sonrojo; rubor; *v.* sonrojarse, ruborizarse, ponerse colorado.

bluster [blʌstɚ] *v.* ventear o soplar recio (*el viento*); fanfarronear; *s.* ventolera, ventarrón, fuerte golpe de viento; jactancia, fanfarronada.

blustering [blʌstɚɪŋ] *adj.* fanfarrón, jactancioso; **— wind** ventarrón.

boar [bor] *s.* jabalí.

board [bord] *s.* tabla, tablero; mesa; comidas; junta, consejo; cartón; the **-s** las tablas, el teatro; **— and room** cuarto y comida, pensión completa; asistencia; **— of directors** junta directiva; **bulletin —** tablilla para anuncios; **free on —** (f.o.b.) franco a bordo; **on —** a bordo; en el tren; **to go by the —** caer en el mar; perderse; ser descartado; *v.* ir a bordo; subir (*al tren*); entablar, cubrir con tablas; tomar a pupilaje, dar asistencia, pensión o pupilaje; residir o comer (*en casa de huéspedes*).

boarder [bordɚ] *s.* huésped, pupilo, pensionista.

boardinghouse [bordɪŋhaus] *s.* casa de huéspedes, pensión.

boast [bost] *s.* jactancia; alarde; bravata; gloria, orgullo; *v.* jactarse, alardear, hacer alarde de; ostentar.

boastful [bóstfəl] *adj.* jactancioso.

boastfulness [bóstfəlnɪs] *s.* jactancia, ostentación.

boat [bot] *s.* bote; barco, buque; lancha, chalupa.

boathouse [bóthaus] *s.* casilla o cobertizo para botes.

boating [bótɪŋ] *s.* paseo en lancha o bote; **to go —** pasear en bote.

boatman [bótmən] (*pl.* **boatmen** [bótmen]) *s.* barquero.

bob [bab] *s.* meneo, sacudida; pesa (*de metal*); **to wear a —** llevar el pelo corto (o en melena); *v.* menearse; **to — one's hair** cortarse el pelo en melena; **to — up** aparecer de repente; **to — up and down** saltar, brincar; cabecear (*dícese de una embarcación*).

bobwhite [bábhwáit] *s.* codorniz.

bode [bod] *pret. & p.p. de* **to bide**.

bodice [bádɪs] *s.* corpiño, jubón.

bodily [bádlɪ] *adj.* corpóreo; corporal; *adv.* todos juntos, colectivamente; **they rose —** se levantaron todos a una, se levantaron todos juntos.

body [bádɪ] *s.* cuerpo; agregado, conjunto; gremio; carrocería (*de automóvil*); fuselaje (*de aeroplano*); **— of water** extensión de agua; **— politic** grupo político; estado.

bog [bag] *s.* pantano; tremedal; *v.* hundir(se); atascarse.

Bohemian [bohímiən] *adj. & s.* bohemio.

boil [boɪl] *s.* hervor; tumorcillo; **to come to a —** soltar el hervor, hervir; *v.* hervir; cocer; bullir; **to — down** hervir hasta evaporar; abreviar.

boiler [bóɪlɚ] *s.* caldera, marmita; caldera de vapor; calorífero central.

boisterous [bóɪstərəs] *adj.* bullicioso; estrepitoso, ruidoso; tumultuoso.

bold [bold] *adj.* atrevido, osado; arriesgado; audaz; insolente; claro, bien delineado; **— cliff** risco escarpado; **bold-faced** descarado; **bold-faced type** negritas.

boldness [bóldnɪs] *s.* atrevimiento; osadía; audacia; descaro, insolencia.

bologna [bəlóni] *s.* especie de embutido.

Bolshevik [bólʃəvɪk] *adj. & s.* bolchevique.

bolster [bólstɚ] *s.* travesaño, almohada larga (*para la cabecera de la cama*); refuerzo, sostén, soporte; *v.* sostener, apoyar; apuntalar; **to — someone's courage** infundir le ánimo a alguien.

bolt [bolt] *s.* pestillo, cerrojo; perno, tornillo grande; salida de repente; rollo (*de paño, de papel*); **thunder —** rayo; *v.* cerrar con cerrojo; tragar, engullir; romper con (*un partido político*); echarse a correr, lanzarse de repente; caer como rayo; **to — out** salir de golpe.

bomb [bam] *s.* bomba; *v.* bombardear.

bombard [bɑmbárd] v. bombardear, cañonear.

bombardier [bɑmbədfr] s. bombardero.

bombardment [bɑmbárdmənt] s. bombardeo, cañoneo.

bombastic [bɑmbǽstɪk] adj. ampuloso, altisonante.

bomber [bámə] s. bombardero, avión de bombardeo.

bonbon [bánban] s. bombón, confite.

bond [band] s. lazo, vínculo; ligadura; fianza, vale; obligación, bono.

bondage [bándɪdʒ] s. servidumbre, esclavitud.

bondsman [bándzmən] s. fiador.

bone [bon] s. hueso; espina (de pez); -s restos; osamenta; — of contention materia de discordia; to make no -s about it no pararse en pelillos; obrar francamente; v. deshuesar, quitar los huesos o espinas.

bonfire [bánfaɪr] s. hoguera, fogata.

bonnet [bánɪt] s. gorra; sombrero (de mujer).

bonus [bónəs] s. prima, premio, gratificación.

bony [bónɪ] adj. huesudo.

boo [bu] v. mofarse, burlarse (a gritos); — ! interj. ¡bu!; -s s. pl. rechifla, gritos de mofa.

booby [búbɪ] s. bobo, bobalicón.

book [buk] s. libro; The Book la Biblia; cash — libro de caja; memorandum — libreta; on the -s cargado en cuenta; to keep -s llevar los libros o la contabilidad; v. inscribir, asentar (en un libro); to — passage resérvar pasaje.

bookcase [búkkes] s. estante, estantería, armario para libros.

bookkeeper [búkkipə] s. tenedor de libros, contador.

bookkeeping [búkkipɪŋ] s. teneduría de libros, contabilidad; double entry — partida doble.

booklet [búklet] s. librillo, librito, cuaderno, folleto.

bookseller [búksela] s. librero.

bookshelf [búkʃelf] s. estante, repisa para libros.

bookshop [búkʃap] s. librería.

bookstore [búkstor] s. librería.-

boom [bum] s. estampido; alza, auge (en el mercado o bolsa); bonanza, prosperidad momentánea; v. rugir, resonar, hacer estampido; prosperar, medrar, florecer, estar en bonanza; fomentar.

boon [bun] s. don; bendición, gracia, favor; adj. jovial, congenial.

boor [bʊr] s. patán, hombre zafio o grosero.

boorish [bʊrɪʃ] adj. grosero, zafio.

boost [bust] s. empuje, empujón (de abajo arriba); — in prices alza o auge de precios; v. empujar, alzar, levantar; hacer subir.

boot [but] s. bota, calzado; to — por añadidura, de ganancia, Am. de pilón, Am. de ñapa; v. dar un puntapié; to — out echar a puntapiés, echar a patadas.

bootblack [bútblæk] s. limpiabotas.

booth [buɵ] s. casilla, puesto.

bootlegger [bútlegə] s. contrabandista (de licores).

bootlicker [bútlɪkə] s. servilón, zalamero.

booty [bútɪ] s. botín, saqueo.

border [bórdə] s. borde, margen, orilla; orla, franja; ribete; frontera; v. ribetear, guarnecer (el borde); orlar; to — on (o upon) lindar con, confinar con; rayar en; it -s on madness raya en locura.

bore [bor] s. taladro, barreno; agujero (hecho con taladro); calibre (de un cañón, cilindro, etc.); persona o cosa aburrida; v. taladrar, horadar, barrenar; aburrir, fastidiar; pret. de to bear.

bored [bord] adj. cansado, aburrido; p.p. de to bore.

boredom [bórdəm] s. aburrimiento, tedio, hastío, fastidio.

boring [bórɪŋ] adj. aburrido, fastidioso, tedioso.

born [born] p.p. de to bear & adj. nacido; innato; to be — nacer.

borne [born] p.p. to bear.

borough [bɔ́o] s. villa; distrito de municipio.

borrow [bɔ́ro] v. pedir prestado; tomar prestado; tomar fiado.

borrower [bɔ́rəwə] s. el que pide prestado.

bosom [búzəm] s. seno, pecho, corazón; pechera (de camisa); in the — of the family en el seno de la familia; adj querido; — friend amigo íntimo.

boss [bɔs] s. jefe; patrón; mayoral, capataz; political — cacique político; v mandar, dominar, dirigir.

bossy [bɔ́sɪ] adj. mandón, autoritario.

botany [bátnɪ] s. botánica.

both [boɵ] adj. & pron. ambos, entrambos los dos; — this and that tanto est como aquello; — of them ambos ellos dos, los dos; — (of) his friend sus dos amigos, ambos amigos.

bother [báðə] s. molestia; fastidio; in

comodidad; enfado; *v.* molestar(se); fastidiar, enfadar; incomodar; estorbar.

bothersome [báðəsəm] *adj.* molesto.

bottle [bátl] *s.* botella; *v.* embotellar.

bottom [bátəm] *s.* fondo; base; fundamento; asiento (*de silla*); **to be at the — of the class** ser el último de la clase; **what is at the — of all this?** ¿qué hay en el fondo de todo esto!

boudoir [budwár] *s.* tocador

bough [bau] *s.* rama.

bought [bɔt] *pret.* & *p.p.* de **to buy.**

boulder [bóldə] *s.* peña, roca, guijarro grande, pedrusco.

boulevard [búləvard] *s.* bulevar

bounce [bauns] *s.* bote, rebote (*de una pelota*); salto, brinco; *v.* hacer saltar; saltar, brincar; botar; echar, arrojar (*a alguien*); echar, despedir de un empleo.

bound [baund] *s.* salto, brinco; bote, rebote; límite, confín; *adj.* ligado; confinado; obligado; ceñido; encuadernado; **to be — for** ir para, ir con rumbo a; **to be — up in one's work** estar absorto en su trabajo; **it is — to happen** es seguro que sucederá; **I am — to do it** estoy resuelto a hacerlo; *v.* botar, resaltar; saltar, brincar; limitar; ceñir, cercar; *pret.* & *p.p.* de **to bind.**

boundary [báundərɪ] *s.* límite, linde, confín; frontera.

boundless [báundlɪs] *adj.* ilimitado, sin límite, sin término.

bountiful [báuntəfəl] *adj.* generoso, liberal; abundante.

bounty [báuntɪ] *s.* largueza, generosidad; don, favor, gracia; premio, recompensa.

bouquet [buké] *s.* ramillete, ramo de flores; aroma, fragancia.

bourgeois [burʒwá] *adj.* & *s.* burgués.

bout [baut] *s.* combate, lucha, contienda, asalto; **— of pneumonia** un ataque de pulmonía.

bow [bau] *s.* saludo, reverencia, inclinación; proa; *v.* hacer una reverencia, inclinarse (*para saludar*); someterse; **to — one's head** inclinar la cabeza **-ed down** agobiado.

bow [bo] *s.* arco (*para tirar flechas*); arco (*de violín*); curva; lazo, moño (*de cintas*); **bow-legged** *adj.* patizambo, patituerto; *v.* arquear; tocar (*un instrumento*) con arco.

bowels [báuəlz] *s. pl.* intestinos; entrañas; tripas.

bower [báuə] *s.* enramada, ramada, glorieta.

bowl [bol] *s.* cuenco; tazón; jícara; boliche, bola; **wash — palangana, lavamanos; -s** juego de bolos; *v.* bolear; jugar a los bolos, jugar al boliche.

box [baks] *s.* caja; estuche; palco de teatro; casilla; compartimiento; bofetada; **—car** furgón; **— office** taquilla; *v.* encajonar; meter en una caja; abofetear; boxear.

boxer [báksə] *s.* boxeador, pugilista.

boxing [báksɪŋ] *s.* boxeo, pugilato.

boy [bɔɪ] *s.* niño; muchacho; mozo.

boycott [bóɪkat] *v.* boycotear; *s.* boycoteo.

boyhood [bóɪhud] *s.* niñez; mocedad, juventud.

boyish [bóɪɪʃ] *adj.* pueril; juvenil; aniñado.

brace [bres] *s.* traba; tirante; apoyo, refuerzo; corchete ({ }); **carpenter's —** berbiquí; *v.* trabar; apoyar, reforzar; asegurar; estimular, fortalecer; **to — up** animarse, cobrar ánimo.

bracelet [bréslɪt] *s.* brazalete, pulsera.

bracket [brǽkɪt] *s.* ménsula, soporte, sostén; repisa; **-s** paréntesis cuadradas; *v.* colocar entre paréntesis; unir; agrupar.

brag [brǽg] *s.* jactancia; *v.* jactarse (de); hacer alarde de.

braggart [brǽgət] *adj.* & *s.* jactancioso, fanfarrón.

braid [bred] *s.* trenza; galón, trencilla; *v.* trenzar; galonear, guarnecer con galones.

brain [bren] *s.* cerebro; seso; **to rack one's -s** devanarse los sesos, romperse la cabeza; *v.* saltar la tapa de los sesos.

brake [brek] *s.* freno, *Am.* retranca, *Am.* garrote; **— lining** forro de freno; **to apply the -s** frenar; *v.* frenar, enfrenar, *Am.* retrancar, *Am.* dar garrote.

brakeman [brékmən] *s.* guardafrenos, *Am.* retranquero, *Am.* garrotero.

bramble [brǽmbl] *s.* zarza, breña.

bran [brǽn] *s.* salvado.

branch [brǽntʃ] *s.* rama (*de árbol*); ramo (*de la ciencia*); sucursal; bifurcación; sección; tributario (*de un río*); ramificación; **— railway** ramal; *v.* ramificarse; bifurcarse.

brand [brǽnd] *s.* marca; marca de fábrica; hechura; hierro, *Am.* fierro (*de marcar*); estigma; **brand-new** nuevecito, flamante, acabado de hacer o comprar; *v.* marcar; herrar, marcar (*con hierro candente*); difamar; **to — as** motejar de.

brandish [brǽndɪʃ] *v.* blandir; *s.* floreo, molinete.

brandy [brǽndɪ] s. aguardiente; coñac.
brass [bræs] s. latón, bronce; desfachatez, descaro; **-es** utensilios de latón. instrumentos músicos de metal; — **band** banda, murga.
brassière [brəzír] s. corpiño, sostén (*para ceñir los pechos*).
brat [bræt] s. mocoso.
bravado [brəvádo] s. bravata; jactancia.
brave [brev] adj. bravo, valiente, valeroso; v. arrostrar; desafiar, hacer frente a.
bravery [brévərɪ] s. valor, valentía.
brawl [brɔl] v. reyerta, pendencia, riña; alboroto; v. armar una pendencia, alborotar, reñir.
bray [bre] s. rebuzno; v. rebuznar.
brazen [brézn] adj. bronceado; de bronce; de latón; descarado, desvergonzado.
breach [britʃ] s. brecha, abertura; violación, infracción; rompimiento; — **of faith** abuso de confianza; — **of promise** violación de un compromiso; v. abrir brecha.
bread [bred] s. pan; —**box** caja para pan; *Am.* empanizar.
breadth [bredθ] s. anchura, ancho; extensión; amplitud.
break [brek] s. rompimiento; rotura; interrupción, pausa; bajón (*en la bolsa o mercado*); **to have a bad (good) —** tener mala (buena) suerte; to make a bad — cometer un disparate; v. romper(se), quebrantar(se), quebrar(se); amansar, domar; arruinar; **to — away** fugarse, escaparse; **to — into** forzar la entrada en, allanar (*una morada*); **to — loose** escaparse, desprenderse, soltarse; **to — out** estallar (*una guerra*); **to — out of prison** escaparse de la cárcel; **to — a promise** faltar a la palabra; **to — up** desmenuzar, despedazar; disolver; perturbar.
breakable [brékəbl] adj. quebradizo.
breaker [brékə] s. rompiente (*ola*); law — infractor.
breakfast [brékfəst] s. desayuno; **to eat —** tomar el desayuno; v. desayunarse.
breakwater [brékwɔtə] s. rompeolas, malecón.
breast [brest] s. pecho; seno; teta; pechuga (*de ave*); **to make a clean — of** it confesarlo todo.
breath [breθ] s. aliento; resuello; respiro; soplo, hálito; **in the same —** al mismo instante, con el mismo aliento; **out of —** sin aliento, jadeante; **under one's —** en voz baja, entre dientes.
breathe [brið] v. respirar; resollar; tomar aliento; exhalar; **to — into** infundir;

he -ed his last exhaló el último suspiro; **he did not — a word** no dijo palabra.
breathless [bréθlɪs] adj. jadeante; sin aliento.
bred [bred] pret. & p.p. de to breed.
breeches [brítʃɪz] s. pl. bragas, calzones; **riding —** pantalones de montar.
breed [brid] s. casta, raza; ralea, especie; v. criar; procrear, engendrar; educar; producirse; multiplicarse.
breeder [brídə] s. criador; animal de cría.
breeding [brídɪŋ] s. cría, crianza; educación, modales.
breeze [briz] s. brisa, vientecillo.
breezy [brízɪ] adj. airoso, ventilado; refrescado (*por la brisa*); animado, vivaz; **it is —** hace brisa.
brethren [bréðrɪn] s. pl. hermanos (*los fieles de una iglesia o los miembros de una sociedad*).
brevity [brévətɪ] s. brevedad.
brew [bru] s. cerveza; mezcla; v. fermentar, hacer (*licores*); preparar (*té*); fomentar, tramar; fabricar cerveza; amenazar (*una tormenta, calamidad etc.*).
brewery [brúərɪ] s. cervecería, fábrica de cerveza.
briar, brier [bráɪə] s. zarza; rosal silvestre.
bribe [braɪb] s. soborno, cohecho; v. sobornar, cohechar.
bribery [bráɪbərɪ] s. soborno, cohecho.
brick [brɪk] s. ladrillo; ladrillos; v. enladrillar.
brickbat [bríkbæt] s. pedazo de ladrillo insulto.
bridal [bráɪdl] adj. nupcial; de bodas de novia; — **dress** vestido de novia.
bride [braɪd] s. novia, desposada.
bridegroom [bráɪdgrum] s. novio, desposado.
bridesmaid [bráɪdzmed] s. madrina de boda.
bridge [brɪdʒ] s. puente; caballete de la nariz; **draw —** puente levadizo; **suspension —** puente colgante; v. tender un puente; **to — a gap** llenar un vacío
bridle [bráɪdl] s. brida, freno de caballo; freno, restricción; — **path** camino de herradura; v. embridar, enfrenar; reprimir, subyugar; erguirse, erguir la cabeza.
brief [brif] adj. breve, corto, conciso; s. sumario, resumen; informe, memorial breve apostólico; **to hold a — for** abogar por; **-ly** adv. brevemente; en resumen, en breve.

briefcase [brífkes] s. portapapeles, cartera grande.

brigade [brigéd] s. brigada.

bright [brait] adj. brillante, claro, luciente; radiante; alegre; listo, vivo, inteligente; — **color** color subido.

brighten [bráitn] v. abrillantar, pulir, dar lustre; avivar(se); alegrar(se); animar(se); aclararse, despejarse (el cielo).

brightness [bráitnis] s. brillo, lustre, esplendor; claridad; viveza, agudeza, inteligencia.

brilliance [bríljens] s. brillantez, brillo, lustre; resplandor.

brilliant [bríljant] adj. brillante; resplandeciente; espléndido; talentoso; s. brillante; diamante.

brim [brim] s. borde, margen, orilla; ala (de sombrero); **to fill to the** — llenar o arrasar hasta el borde; **to be filled to the** — estar hasta los topes; estar de bote en bote; v. **to** — **over** rebosar.

brine [brain] s. salmuera.

bring [briŋ] v. traer; llevar; ocasionar, causar; **to** — **about** producir, efectuar, ocasionar; **to** — **down** bajar; **to** — **forth** dar a luz; producir; **to** — **to** resucitar; **to** — **up** criar, educar; **to** — **up a subject** traer a discusión un asunto.

brink [briŋk] s. borde, orilla, margen; **on the** — **of** al borde de.

brisk [brisk] adj. vivo, animado; fuerte; rápido; -**ly** adv. aprisa; fuerte.

bristle [brísl] s. cerda; v. erizar(se); **to** — **with** estar erizado (o lleno) de.

bristly [brísli] adj. cerdoso; erizado.

British [brítiʃ] adj. británico; **the** — los ingleses.

brittle [brítl] adj. quebradizo; frágil.

broach [brotʃ] v. traer a colación, comenzar a hablar de (un asunto).

broad [brod] adj. ancho; amplio, vasto, extenso; tolerante; — **hint** insinuación clara; **in** — **daylight** en pleno día; **broad-minded** tolerante, de amplias miras.

broadcast [bródkæst] s. radiodifusión, difusión, emisión; transmisión; v. difundir; radiodifundir, radiar, emitir.

broadcloth [bródklɔθ] s. paño fino de algodón o de lana.

brocade [brokéd] s. brocado.

broil [brɔil] v. asar(se).

broke [brok] pret. de **to break**; adj. quebrado, arruinado; pelado, sin dinero; **to go** — quebrar, arruinarse.

broken [brókən] p.p. de **to break** & adj. roto; rompido; quebrado; quebrantado; arruinado; abatido; — **English**

inglés champurrado o champurreado; inglés mal pronunciado.

broker [brókə] s. corredor, agente; bolsista; **money** — cambista, corredor de cambio.

bronchitis [brankáitis] s. bronquitis.

bronco, broncho [bráŋko] s. potro o caballo bronco, Am. redomón; — **buster** domador.

bronze [bronz] s. bronce, color de bronce; v. broncear.

brooch [brutʃ] s. broche (alfiler de pecho).

brood [brud] s. pollada; nidada; cría; casta; v. empollar; **to** — **over** cavilar.

brook [bruk] s. arroyuelo, riachuelo, Am. quebrada; v. tolerar, aguantar.

broom [brum] s. escoba; retama (arbusto); — **stick** palo o mango de escoba.

broth [brɔθ] s. caldo.

brother [bráðə] s. hermano; cofrade.

brotherhood [bráðəhud] s. hermandad; fraternidad; cofradía.

brother-in-law [bráðərinlɔ] s. cuñado.

brotherly [bráðəli] adj. fraternal.

brought [brɔt] pret. & p.p. de **to bring**.

brow [brau] s. ceja; frente.

brown [braun] adj. moreno; café; castaño; pardo oscuro; tostado; v. tostar(se).

browse [brauz] v. hojear; ramonear, pacer, pastar (el ganado).

bruise [bruz] s. magulladura, cardenal, contusión; v. magullar(se); estropear(se).

brunet, brunette [brunét] adj. moreno, trigueño.

brunt [brʌnt] s. fuerza (de un golpe o ataque); **the** — **of the battle** lo más reñido del combate.

brush [brʌʃ] s. cepillo; brocha; pincel; matorral; roce; encuentro; v. cepillar, acepillar; rozar; **to** — **aside** desechar, echar a un lado; **to** — **up** cepillarse; repasar (una materia, una técnica, etc.).

brushwood [bráʃwud] s. broza; maleza, matorral, zarzal.

brusque [brʌsk] adj. brusco.

brutal [brútl] adj. brutal, bruto.

brutality [brutǽliti] s. brutalidad.

brute [brut] s. bruto, bestia; adj. bruto, brutal; bestial.

bubble [bʌ́bl] s. burbuja; borbollón; ampolla; v. borbotar; hacer espuma; bullir; **to** — **over with joy** rebosar de gozo.

buck [bʌk] s. macho cabrío, cabrón; gamo; macho (del ciervo, antílope, etc.); corveta, respingo (de un caballo); embestida; — **private** soldado raso; **to**

pass the — *Am.* pasar el fardo; *v.* cabriolear, respingar; embestir; encabritarse; bregar con (*el viento*); **to — up** cobrar ánimo; **the horse -ed the rider** el caballo tiró al jinete.

bucket [bʌ́kɪt] *s.* cubo, cubeta, balde.

buckle [bʌ́k|] *s.* hebilla; *v.* abrochar con hebilla; doblarse; abollarse; **to — down to** aplicarse con empeño a; **to — with** luchar con.

buckshot [bʌ́kʃɑt] *s.* posta, perdigón.

buckwheat [bʌ́khwit] *s.* trigo ᴄarraceno.

bud [bʌd] *s.* botón, yema; capullo, pimpollo; retoño; *v.* echar botones o retoños; florecer.

buddy [bʌ́dɪ] *s.* camarada, compañero.

budge [bʌdʒ] *v.* mover(se), menear(se), bullir.

budget [bʌ́dʒɪt] *s.* presupuesto.

buff [bʌf] *s.* piel de ante o búfalo; color de ante; pulidor; **blindman's —** juego de la gallina ciega; *v.* pulir, pulimentar.

buffalo [bʌ́flo] *s.* búfalo.

buffet [bʌféi] *s.* aparador; repostería; mostrador para refrescos; fonda de estación.

buffoon [bʌfún] *s.* bufón; payaso.

bug [bʌg] *s.* insecto; bicho; microbio.

buggy [bʌ́gɪ] *s.* cochecillo.

bugle [bjúg|] *s.* clarín; corneta; trompeta.

build [bɪld] *s.* estructura; talle, forma, hechura; *v.* edificar, construir; fabricar; **to — up one's health** reconstituir su salud.

builder [bɪ́ldə] *s.* constructor.

building [bɪ́ldɪŋ] *s.* edificio; construcción.

built [bɪlt] *pret.* & *p.p. de* **to build.**

bulb [bʌlb] *s.* bulbo (*de la cebolla y otras plantas*); planta bulbosa; **electric light —** bombilla, bujía eléctrica, ampolla, *Am.* foco, bombita.

bulge [bʌldʒ] *s.* bulto; protuberancia; panza; *v.* abultar; combarse.

bulgy [bʌ́ldʒɪ] *adj.* abultado.

bulk [bʌlk] *s.* bulto, volumen; masa; **the — of the army** el grueso del ejército.

bulky [bʌ́lkɪ] *adj.* abultado, voluminoso, grueso.

bull [bʊl] *s.* toro; alcista (*el que hace subir los valores en la bolsa*); disparate, error; **Papal —** bula; **—fight** corrida de toros; **— fighter** torero; **bull's-eye** centro del blanco; tiro perfecto.

bulldog [bʊ́ldɔg] *s.* perro dogo, perro de presa.

bullet [bʊ́lɪt] *s.* bala.

bulletin [bʊ́lətɪn] *s.* boletín; **— board** tablilla para fijar anuncios o avisos.

bullfrog [bʊ́lfrɑg] *s.* rana grande.

bullion [bʊ́ljən] *s.* oro (o plata) en barras; metálico; lingotes de oro o plata.

bully [bʊ́lɪ] *s.* pendenciero, valentón, fanfarrón, matón; *adj.* excelente, magnífico; *v.* intimidar; echar bravatas.

bulwark [bʊ́lwək] *s.* baluarte; defensa

bum [bʌm] *s.* holgazán, vagabundo; gorrón; borracho; **to go on a —** irse de juerga; *adj.* malo, mal hecho, de ínfima calidad; inútil, inservible; **to feel —** estar indispuesto, *v.* holgazanear; vivir de gorra.

bumblebee [bʌ́mb‖bi] *s.* abejorro, abejón.

bump [bʌmp] *s.* tope, choque; golpe; chichón; abolladura; hinchazón; joroba, protuberancia; *v.* topar, topetear; chocar; abollar; **to — along** zarandearse, ir zarandeándose; **to — of** derribar; matar.

bumper [bʌ́mpə] *s.* parachoques, defensa; tope; *adj.* grande, excelente; **— crop** cosecha abundante.

bun [bʌn] *s.* bollo (*de pan*).

bunch [bʌntʃ] *s.* manojo, puñado; racim (*de uvas, plátanos, etc.*); grupo; **— of flowers** ramillete de flores; *v.* juntar(se), agrupar(se).

bundle [bʌ́ndl] *s.* lío, bulto, fardo, hato; haz; paquete; *v.* liar, atar; envolver; **to — up** abrigarse, taparse bien.

bungalow [bʌ́ŋɡəlo] *s.* casita de un piso

bungle [bʌ́ŋɡ|] *v.* chapucear; estropear; echar a perder.

bunion [bʌ́njən] *s.* juanete.

bunk [bʌŋk] *s.* litera, camilla (*fija en la pared*); embuste, tontería, paparruch papa.

bunny [bʌ́nɪ] *s.* conejito.

buoy [bɔɪ] *s.* boya; *v.* boyar, mantener flote; **to — up** sostener, apoyar.

buoyant [bɔ́ɪənt] *adj.* boyante, flotant vivaz, animado, alegre.

burden [bɜ́dn] *s.* carga, peso; cuidad gravamen; *v.* cargar; agobiar.

burdensome [bɜ́dnsəm] *adj.* gravos pesado.

bureau [bjúro] *s.* oficina; despach división, ramo; cómoda; **travel —** oficina de turismo; **weather —** oficin de meteorología, observatorio mete rológico.

burglar [bɜ́glə] *s.* ladrón (*que se mete e casa ajena*).

burglary [bɜ́glərɪ] *s.* robo.

burial [bérɪəl] *s.* entierro; **— plac** cementerio.

burlap [bɜ́læp] *s.* arpillera, tela burd de cáñamo.

burly [bə́lɪ] *adj.* corpulento, voluminoso, grandote.

burn [bɜn] *s.* quemadura; *v.* quemar(se); incendiar; arder; abrasar(se).

burner [bə́nə] *s.* quemador; mechero; hornilla.

burnish [bə́nɪʃ] *v.* bruñir; pulir; *s.* bruñido, pulimento.

burnt [bɜnt] *pret.* & *p.p.* de **to burn.**

burrow [bə́o] *s.* madriguera, conejera; *v.* hacer madrigueras en; escarbar; socavar, minar; esconderse.

burst [bɜst] *s.* reventón, explosión; estallido; — **of laughter** carcajada; *v.* reventar(se); abrirse; estallar; **to** — **into** entrar de repente; **to** — **into tears** prorrumpir en lágrimas; **to** — **with laughter** estallar o reventar de risa; *pret.* & *p.p.* de **to burst.**

bury [bérɪ] *v.* enterrar; sepultar; **to be buried in thought** estar absorto, meditabundo o pensativo.

bus [bʌs] *s.* autobús, ómnibus, *Am.* camión o camioneta, *Am.* guagua.

bush [bʊʃ] *s.* arbusto; mata; matorral, breñal; **rose** — rosal; **to beat around the** — andarse por las ramas.

bushel [bʊ́ʃəl] *s.* fanega (*medida de áridos*).

bushy [bʊ́ʃɪ] *adj.* matoso, espeso; lleno de arbustos.

busily [bɪ́zɪlɪ] *adv.* diligentemente.

business [bɪ́znɪs] *s.* negocio; ocupación; comercio; asunto; — **house** casa de comercio, establecimiento mercantil; — **transaction** negocio, transacción comercial; **to do** — **with** negociar con, comerciar con; **he has no** — **doing it** no tiene derecho a hacerlo; **not to be one's** — no concernirle a uno, no importarle a uno; **to make a** — **deal** hacer un trato.

businesslike [bɪ́znɪslaɪk] *adj.* eficaz, eficiente, práctico; formal.

businessman [bɪ́znɪsmæn] *s.* hombre de negocios, comerciante.

bust [bʌst] *s.* busto; pecho (*de mujer*); **to go out on a** — salir o ir de parranda; *v.* reventar; quebrar; domar (*un potro*).

bustle [bʌ́stl̩] *s.* bulla, bullicio, trajín, alboroto; polisón (*para abultar las caderas*); *v.* bullir(se); menearse; trajinar.

busy [bɪ́zɪ] *adj.* ocupado; activo; —**body** entremetido; — **street** calle de mucho tráfico; *v.* **to** — **oneself** ocuparse.

but [bʌt] *conj.*, *prep.* & *adv.* pero, mas, sino; menos, excepto; sólo, no . . . más que; — **for you** a no ser por Vd.; **not**

only . . . — **also** no sólo . . . sino (que) también; **I cannot help** — no puedo menos de; **she is** — **a child** no es más que una niña.

butcher [bʊ́tʃə] *s.* carnicero; -'s **shop** carnicería; *v.* matar (*reses*); hacer una matanza o carnicería; destrozar.

butchery [bʊ́tʃrɪ] *s.* carnicería, matanza.

butler [bʌ́tlə] *s.* despensero, mayordomo; -'s **pantry** despensa.

butt [bʌt] *s.* culata (*de rifle*); colilla (*de cigarro*); tope, topetazo; cabezada; **the** — **of ridicule** el blanco de las burlas; *v.* topetear, embestir; **to** — **in** entremeterse; **to** — **into a conversation** meter baza, *Am.* meter su cuchara.

butter [bʌ́tə] *s.* manteca, mantequilla; *v.* enmantecar, untar con manteca o mantequilla.

buttercup [bʌ́təkʌp] *s.* botón de oro (*flor*).

butterfly [bʌ́təflaɪ] *s.* mariposa.

buttermilk [bʌ́təmɪlk] *s.* suero de mantequilla.

butterscotch [bʌ́təskátʃ] *s.* confite o jarabe de azúcar y mantequilla.

buttocks [bʌ́təks] *s. pl.* nalgas, asentaderas.

button [bʌ́tn̩] *s.* botón; —**hook** abotonador; *v.* abotonar(se).

buttonhole [bʌ́tnhol] *s.* ojal; *v.* hacer ojales; **to** — **someone** detener, demorar a uno (*charlando*).

buttress [bʌ́trɪs] *s.* contrafuerte; refuerzo, sostén; *v.* sostener, reforzar, poner contrafuerte.

buy [baɪ] *v.* comprar; **to** — **off** sobornar; **to** — **up** acaparar.

buyer [bá́ɪə] *s.* comprador.

buzz [bʌz] *s.* zumbido; murmullo; *v.* zumbar; murmurar; **to** — **the bell** tocar el timbre.

buzzard [bʌ́zəd] *s.* buitre, *Am.* aura, *Am.* zopilote, *Am.* carancho.

by [baɪ] *prep.* por; cerca de; al lado de; junto a; según; — **and** — luego, pronto; — **dint of** a fuerza de; — **far** con mucho; — **night** de noche; — **the way** de paso; a propósito; entre paréntesis; — **two o'clock** para las dos; — **days gone** — días pasados.

bygone [bá́ɪgɒn] *adj.* pasado; **let -s be -s** lo pasado pasado, lo pasado pisado.

bylaw [bá́ɪlɔ] *s.* estatuto; reglamento.

bypath [bá́ɪpæθ] *s.* atajo, vereda.

by-product [bá́ɪprɒdəkt] *s.* producto secundario o accesorio.

bystanders [bá́ɪstændəz] *s.* circunstantes, presentes; mirones.

C

cab [kæb] s. coche de alquiler; taxímetro, taxi; casilla (de una locomotora); — **driver** cochero; chófer.

cabbage [kǽbɪdʒ] s. col, repollo, berza.

cabin [kǽbɪn] s. cabaña, choza, bohío, barraca; camarote (de buque); **airplane** — cabina de aeroplano.

cabinet [kǽbənɪt] s. gabinete; armario; escaparate, vitrina.

cable [kébl] s. cable, amarra; cablegrama; — **address** dirección cablegráfica; v. cablegrafiar.

cablegram [kéblgræm] s. cablegrama.

cabman [kǽbmən] s. cochero; chófer.

cackle [kǽkl] s. cacareo; charla; risotada; v. cacarear; parlotear, charlar.

cactus [kǽktəs] s. (pl. **cacti** [kǽktaɪ]) s. cacto.

cad [kæd] s. canalla (m.); malcriado.

cadence [kédns] s. cadencia.

cadet [kədét] s. cadete.

café [kəfé] s. café, restaurante.

cafeteria [kæfətírɪə] s. restaurante (en donde se sirve uno mismo).

caffein [kǽfiɪn] s. cafeína.

cage [kedʒ] s. jaula; v. enjaular.

cake [kek] s. pastel; bizcocho; bollo; torta; Am. panqué; pastilla (de jabón); — **of ice** témpano de hielo; v. apelmazarse, formar masa compacta.

calamity [kəlǽmətɪ] s. calamidad.

calcium [kǽlsɪəm] s. calcio.

calculate [kǽlkjəlet] v. calcular; **to** — **on** contar con.

calculation [kælkjəléʃən] s. cálculo; cómputo, cuenta.

calculus [kǽlkjələs] s. cálculo.

calendar [kǽləndə] s. calendario, almanaque; — **year** año corriente.

calf [kæf] (pl. **calves** [kævz]) s. ternero, ternera, becerro, becerra; pantorrilla (de la pierna); —**skin** piel de becerro o becerrillo.

caliber [kǽləbə] s. calibre.

calico [kǽləko] s. calicó (tela de algodón).

call [kɔl] s. llamada; llamamiento; visita; demanda, pedido; **within** — al alcance de la voz; v. llamar; gritar; hacer una visita; pasar (lista); **to** — **at a port** hacer escala en un puerto; **to** — **for** ir por; demandar, pedir; **to** — **on** visitar; acudir a (en busca de auxilio); **to** — **to order a meeting** abrir la sesión; **to** — **together** convocar; **to** — **up on the phone** llamar por teléfono.

caller [kɔ́lə] s. visita, visitante; llamador (el que llama).

callous [kǽləs] adj. calloso; duro.

callus [kǽləs] s. callo.

calm [kɑm] s. calma; sosiego; adj. calmo, tranquilo, quieto, sosegado; v. calmar, tranquilizar, sosegar; **to** — **down** calmarse; **-ly** adv. tranquilamente, con calma.

calmness [kɑ́mnɪs] s. calma, sosiego, tranquilidad.

calorie [kǽlorɪ] s. caloría.

calumny [kǽləmnɪ] s. calumnia.

came [kem] pret. de **to come.**

camel [kǽml] s. camello.

camera [kǽmərə] s. cámara fotográfica.

camouflage [kǽməflɑʒ] s. camuflaje; disfraz; v. encubrir, disfrazar.

camp [kæmp] s. campo, campamento; — **chair** silla de tijera; **political** — partido político; v. acampar.

campaign [kæmpén] s. campaña; v. hacer campaña; hacer propaganda.

camphor [kǽmfə] s. alcanfor.

campus [kǽmpəs] s. campo (de una universidad).

can [kæn] s. lata, bote, envase; — **opener** abrelatas; v. envasar, enlatar, v. defect. y aux. (usado sólo en las formas **can** y **could**) poder, saber.

Canadian [kənédɪən] adj. & s. canadiense.

canal [kənǽl] s. canal; **irrigation** — acequia.

canary [kənérɪ] s. canario.

cancel [kǽnsl] v. cancelar; anular; revocar; tachar.

cancellation [kænsléʃən] s. cancelación; anulación; revocación.

cancer [kǽnsə] s. cáncer.

candid [kǽndɪd] adj. cándido, franco, sincero.

candidacy [kǽndədəsɪ] s. candidatura.

candidate [kǽndədet] s. candidato; aspirante.

candle [kǽndl] s. candela, vela; bujía; cirio; — **power** potencia lumínica (en bujías).

candlestick [kǽndlstɪk] s. candelero, palmatoria.

candor [kǽndə] s. candor, sinceridad.

candy [kǽndɪ] s. dulce, confite, bombón; — **shop** confitería, dulcería; v. confitar, azucarar; almibarar, garapiñar; cristalizarse (el almíbar); **candied a** monds almendras garapiñadas.

cane [ken] s. caña; — **plantation** —**field** cañaveral; — **chair** silla de bejuco; **sugar** — caña de azúcar; **walking** — bastón; **to beat with** — **bastonear, apalear.**

canine [kénaɪn] adj. canino, perruno.

canned [kænd] adj. enlatado, envasado,

conservado (*en lata o en vidrio*); — **goods** conservas alimenticias.

cannery [kǽnərɪ] *s.* fábrica de conservas alimenticias.

cannibal [kǽnəbl] *s.* caníbal.

cannon [kǽnən] *s.* cañón.

cannonade [kænənéd] *s.* cañoneo; *v.* cañonear.

cannot [kǽnɒt] = **can not** no puedo, no puede, no podemos, etc.

canoe [kǝnú] *s.* canoa, *Am.* piragua, *Am.* chalupa.

canon [kǽnən] *s.* canon; ley, regla; criterio, norma; canónigo.

canopy [kǽnəpɪ] *s.* dosel, pabellón.

cantaloupe [kǽntlop] *s.* melón.

canteen [kæntín] *s.* cantina; cantimplora.

canton [kǽntən] *s.* cantón, región, distrito.

canvas [kǽnvəs] *s.* lona; lienzo; toldo; cañamazo.

canvass [kǽnvəs] *s.* inspección; escrutinio; indagación, encuesta, pesquisa; solicitación (*de votos*); *v.* examinar, escudriñar; recorrer (*un distrito solicitando algo*); hacer una encuesta; solicitar votos o pedidos comerciales.

canyon [kǽnjən] *s.* cañón, garganta.

cap [kæp] *s.* gorro, gorra; boina; tapa, tapón; cima, cumbre; **percussion —** cápsula fulminante; *v.* tapar, poner tapón a; **that -s the climax** eso es el colmo.

capability [kepəbɪ́lətɪ] *s.* capacidad, aptitud.

capable [képəbl] *adj.* capaz; hábil; competente.

capacious [kəpéʃəs] *adj.* capaz, amplio, espacioso.

capacity [kəpǽsətɪ] *s.* capacidad; cabida; habilidad; aptitud; **in the — of a teacher** en calidad de maestro.

cape [kep] *s.* capa; capote; cabo, promontorio.

caper [képə] *s.* cabriola; voltereta, brinco; **to cut -s** cabriolar, retozar, hacer travesuras; *v.* cabriolar, retozar, juguetear, brincar.

capital [kǽpətl] *s.* capital (*f.*), ciudad principal; capital (*m.*), caudal; chapitel (*de una columna*); letra mayúscula; **to make — of** sacar partido de, aprovecharse de; *adj.* capital; principal; excelente; **— punishment** pena capital, pena de muerte.

capitalism [kǽpətlɪzəm] *s.* capitalismo.

capitalist [kǽpətlɪst] *s.* capitalista; *-ic adj.* capitalista.

capitalization [kæpətləzéʃən] *s.* capitalización.

capitalize [kǽpətlaɪz] *v.* capitalizar; sacar provecho (de); escribir con mayúscula.

capitol [kǽpətl] *s.* capitolio.

caprice [kəprís] *s.* capricho.

capricious [kəpríʃəs] *adj.* caprichoso.

capsize [kæpsáɪz] *v.* zozobrar, volcar(se).

capsule [kǽpsl] *s.* cápsula.

captain [kǽptɪn] *s.* capitán; *v.* capitanear, mandar; servir de capitán.

captivate [kǽptəvet] *v.* cautivar.

captive [kǽptɪv] *s.* & *adj.* cautivo, prisionero.

captivity [kæptívətɪ] *s.* cautiverio, prisión.

captor [kǽptə] *s.* aprehensor o aprensor.

capture [kǽptʃə] *s.* captura; aprensión; presa; toma; *v.* capturar; prender; tomar (*una ciudad*).

car [kar] *s.* coche, automóvil, auto, *Am.* carro; vagón (*de ferrocarril*); camarín (*de ascensor*), ascensor, *Am.* elevador; **dining —** coche comedor; **freight —** furgón, vagón de carga.

caramel [kǽrəml] *s.* caramelo.

carat [kǽrət] *s.* quilate.

caravan [kǽrəvæn] *s.* caravana.

carbolic [karbálɪk] *adj.* carbólico.

carbon [kárbən] *s.* carbono; — **copy** copia en papel carbón; — **paper** papel carbón; — **monoxide** monóxido de carbón.

carburetor [kárbəretə] *s.* carburador.

carcass [kárkəs] *s.* esqueleto; cuerpo descarnado, despojo; res (*muerta*); casco (*de un buque*).

card [kard] *s.* tarjeta; naipe, carta; carda (*para cardar lana*); — **index** índice de fichas; fichero; —**sharp** fullero; **file —** ficha, papeleta; **post —** tarjeta postal; **pack of -s** baraja, naipes; **to play -s** jugar a la baraja, jugar a los naipes; *v.* cardar (*lana*).

cardboard [kárdbord] *s.* cartón; **fine —** cartulina.

cardinal [kárdnəl] *adj.* cardinal; principal, fundamental; rojo, bermellón; — **number** número cardinal; *s.* cardenal (*dignatario eclesiástico*); — **bird** cardenal.

care [kɛr] *s.* cuidado; aflicción; ansiedad; cautela; esmero; cargo, custodia; **to take — of** cuidar de; *v.* tener interés (por); **to — about** tener interés en (o por); preocuparse de; importarle a uno; **to — for** cuidar de; estimar, tenerle cariño a; gustarle a uno; simpatizarle a uno (*una persona*); **to — to** querer, desear, tener ganas de;

what does he — ? ¿a él qué le importa?

career [kərír] s. carrera, profesión.

carefree [kérfri] adj. libre de cuidado, sin cuidados, despreocupado.

careful [kérfəl] adj. cuidadoso; esmerado; cauteloso; **to be —** tener cuidado; **-ly** adv. cuidadosamente, con cuidado; con esmero.

carefulness [kérfəlnıs] s. cuidado; esmero; cautela.

careless [kérlıs] adj. descuidado; negligente; indiferente; **-ly** adv. sin cuidado; sin esmero; descuidadamente.

carelessness [kérlısnıs] s. descuido; falta de esmero; desaliño; negligencia.

caress [kərés] s. caricia; v. acariciar.

caretaker [kértekə] s. cuidador, guardián, vigilante, celador.

carfare [kárfer] s. pasaje de tranvía.

cargo [kárgo] s. carga, cargamento; flete.

caricature [kǽrıkətʃə] s. caricatura; v. caricaturar o caricaturizar.

carload [kárlod] s. furgonada, vagonada, carga de un furgón o vagón.

carnal [kárnl] adj. carnal.

carnation [karnéʃən] s. clavel; color encarnado o rosado.

carnival [kárnəvl] s. carnaval; fiesta, holgorio; feria, verbena.

carnivorous [karnívərəs] adj. carnívoro, carnicero.

carol [kǽrəl] s. villancico; **Christmas —** villancico de Navidad; v. cantar villancicos; celebrar con villancicos.

carouse [kərávz] v. andar de parranda, *Am.* andar de farra; embriagarse.

carpenter [kárpəntə] s. carpintero.

carpentry [kárpəntrı] s. carpintería.

carpet [kárpıt] s. alfombra; **small —** tapete.

carriage [kǽrıdʒ] s. carruaje, coche; acarreo, transporte; porte; **— paid** porte pagado; **good —** buen porte, garbo, manera airosa.

carrier [kǽrıə] s. portador; mensajero; carretero, trajinante; transportador; *Am.* cargador; **airplane —** portaaviones; **disease —** transmisor de gérmenes contagiosos; **mail —** cartero.

carrot [kǽrət] s. zanahoria.

carry [kǽrı] v. llevar; acarrear, transportar; *Am.* cargar; sostener (*una carga*); traer consigo; ganar, lograr (*una elección, un premio, etc.*); **to — away** llevarse; cargar con; entusiasmar, encantar; **to — on** continuar; no parar; **to — oneself well** andar derecho, airoso, garboso; **to — out** llevar a cabo, realizar; sacar.

cart [kart] s. carro, carreta, vagoncillo; v. acarrear.

cartage [kártıdʒ] s. carretaje, acarreo.

carter [kártə] s. carretero; acarreador.

carton [kártn] s. caja de cartón.

cartoon [kartún] s. caricatura.

cartoonist [kartúnıst] s. caricaturista.

cartridge [kártrıdʒ] s. cartucho; **— belt** cartuchera, canana; **— box** cartuchera; **— shell** cápsula.

carve [karv] v. tallar; labrar; cincelar; esculpir; trinchar, tajar (*carne*).

carver [kárvə] s. trinchador; trinchante (*cuchillo*); entallador, escultor.

carving [kárvıŋ] s. talla, obra de escultura, entalladura; **— knife** trinchante.

cascade [kæskéd] s. cascada, salto de agua.

case [kes] s. caso; caja; funda, cubierta, vaina; **window —** marco de ventana; **in — that** caso que, en caso de que, dado que; **in any —** en todo caso; **just in —** por si acaso.

casement [késmənt] s. puerta ventana.

cash [kæʃ] s. dinero contante; **— box** cofre; **— payment** pago al contado; **— on delivery (c.o.d.)** contra reembolso; cóbrese al entregar; **— register** caja registradora (*de dinero*); **to pay —** pagar al contado; v. cambiar, cobrar (*un cheque*).

cashier [kæʃír] s. cajero.

cask [kæsk] s. tonel, barril, cuba.

casket [kǽskıt] s. ataúd; **jewel —** joyero, cofrecillo.

casserole [kǽsərol] s. cacerola.

cassock [kǽsək] s. sotana.

cast [kæst] s. tirada (*al pescar*); molde; matiz; apariencia; defecto (*del ojo*); reparto (*de papeles dramáticos*); actores; **— iron** hierro fundido o colado; v. echar; tirar; arrojar; lanzar; moldear; repartir (*papeles dramáticos*); escoge (*para un papel dramático*); **to — ballot** votar; **to — a statue in bronze** vaciar una estatua en bronce; **to — about** buscar; hacer planes; **to — aside** desechar; **to — lots** echa suertes; **to be — down** estar abatid; *pret. & p.p. de* **to cast.**

castanets [kǽstənets] s. pl. castañuela

caste [kæst] s. casta; **to lose —** perde el prestigio social.

Castilian [kæstíljən] s. & adj. castellano

castle [kǽsl] s. castillo; alcázar; fort leza; torre, roque (*en ajedrez*).

castor oil [kǽstə ɔıl] s. aceite de ricin

casual [kǽʒʊəl] adj. casual; accidenta

casualty [kǽʒʊəltı] s. baja o pérdida (*el ejército*); accidente.

cat [kæt] s. gato; gata.

catalogue [kǽtlɔg] s. catálogo; v. catalogar.

cataract [kǽtərækt] s. catarata.

catarrh [kətúr] s. catarro.

catastrophe [kətǽstrəfɪ] s. catástrofe.

catch [kætʃ] s. presa; botín; pesca; pestillo (*de la puerta*); trampa; cogida (*de la pelota*); — **phrase** frase llamativa; — **question** pregunta tramposa; **he is a good** — es un buen partido; **to play** — jugar a la pelota; v. coger; prender; asir; alcanzar; enganchar; comprender; ser contagioso, pegarse; **to** — **a glimpse of** vislumbrar; **to** — **cold** coger un resfriado, resfriarse; **to** — **on** comprender, caer en la cuenta; **to** — **one's eye** llamarle a uno la atención; **to** — **sight of** avistar; **to** — **unaware** sorprender, coger desprevenido; **to** — **up with** alcanzar a, emparejarse con.

catcher [kǽtʃə] s. cogedor, agarrador; parador, cácher o receptor (*en beisbol*).

catching [kǽtʃɪŋ] adj. pegajoso, contagioso; atractivo.

catechism [kǽtəkɪzəm] s. catecismo.

category [kǽtəgorɪ] s. categoría.

cater [kétə] v. surtir, abastecer, proveer los alimentos (*para banquetes, fiestas, etc.*) **to** — **to** proveer a las necesidades o al gusto de; **to** — **to the taste of** halagar el gusto de.

caterpillar [kǽtəpɪlə] s. oruga; — **tractor** tractor.

cathedral [kəθídrəl] s. catedral.

Catholic [kǽθəlɪk] s. & adj. católico.

Catholicism [kəθúləsɪzəm] s. catolicismo.

catsup [kǽtsəp] s. salsa de tomate.

cattle [kǽtl] s. ganado, ganado vacuno; — **raiser** ganadero, *Am.* estanciero; — **raising** ganadería; — **ranch** hacienda de ganado, *Am.* rancho, *Am.* estancia.

aught [kɔt] pret. & p.p. de **to catch.**

auliflower [kóləflauə] s. coliflor.

ause [kɔz] s. causa; v. causar; originar; **to** — **to** hacer; inducir a.

aution [kóʃən] s. precaución, cautela; aviso, advertencia; — **!** ¡cuidado! ¡atención! v. prevenir, avisar, advertir.

autious [kóʃəs] adj. cauto; cauteloso, cuidadoso; precavido.

avalier [kævəlír] s. caballero; galán; adj. orgulloso, altivo, desdeñoso.

avalry [kǽvlrɪ] s. caballería.

ave [kev] s. cueva; caverna; v. **to** — **in** hundirse; desplomarse.

avern [kǽvən] s. caverna.

avity [kǽvətɪ] s. cavidad, hueco.

caw [kɔ] s. graznido; v. graznar.

cease [sis] v. cesar; parar, desistir; dejar de.

ceaseless [síslɪs] adj. incesante.

cedar [sídə] s. cedro.

cede [sid] v. ceder.

ceiling [sílɪŋ] s. techo (*interior*); cielo máximo (*en aviación*); altura máxima (*en aviación*); — **price** precio máximo.

celebrate [séləbret] v. celebrar.

celebrated [séləbretɪd] adj. célebre, renombrado.

celebration [seləbréʃən] s. celebración; fiesta.

celebrity [səlébrətɪ] s. celebridad; renombre.

celery [sélərɪ] s. apio.

celestial [səléstʃəl] adj. celestial, celeste.

cell [sel] s. celda; célula; pila eléctrica.

cellar [sélə] s. bodega, sótano.

celluloid [séljəlɔɪd] s. celuloide.

cement [səmént] s. cemento; **reinforced** — cemento armado; v. unir, cementar, pegar con cemento; cubrir con cemento.

cemetery [sémətɛrɪ] s. cementerio.

censor [sénsə] s. censor; censurador, crítico; v. censurar (*cartas, periódicos, etc.*).

censorship [sénsəʃɪp] s. censura.

censure [sénʃə] s. censura, crítica, reprobación; v. censurar, criticar, reprobar.

census [sénsəs] s. censo.

cent [sent] s. centavo (*de peso o dólar*), **per** — por ciento.

centennial [senténɪəl] adj. & s. centenario.

center [séntə] s. centro; v. centrar; colocar en el centro; concentrar(se).

centigrade [séntəgred] adj. centígrado.

centipede [séntəpid] s. ciempiés, cientopiés.

central [séntrəl] adj. central; céntrico; s. (la) central de teléfonos.

centralize [séntrəlaɪz] v. centralizar.

century [séntʃərɪ] s. siglo.

cereal [sírɪəl] adj. cereal; s. cereal; grano.

ceremonial [serəmónɪəl] adj. ceremonial; s. ceremonial; rito.

ceremonious [serəmónɪəs] adj. ceremonioso.

ceremony [sérəmonɪ] s. ceremonia; ceremonial.

certain [sótn] adj. cierto, seguro, **-ly** adv. ciertamente; por cierto; de cierto; seguramente; de seguro.

certainty [sótntɪ] s. certeza; certidumbre; seguridad.

certificate [sətífəkɪt] s. certificado; documento; testimonio; — **of stock**

bono, obligación; **birth** — partida de nacimiento; **death** — partida (o certificado) de defunción.

certify [sə́təfaɪ] v. certificar; dar fe, atestiguar.

cessation [sɛséʃən] s. suspensión, paro.

cesspool [séspul] s. cloaca, rezumadero.

chafe [tʃef] s. rozadura; irritación, molestia; v. rozar(se); frotar; irritar(se).

chaff [tʃæf] s. hollejo, cáscara; v. embromar, bromear.

chagrin [ʃəgrín] s. mortificación, desazón, pesar; **-ed** p.p. mortificado, afligido.

chain [tʃen] s. cadena; — **of mountains** cordillera; — **store** tienda sucursal (una entre muchas de una misma empresa); v. encadenar.

chair [tʃer] s. silla; cátedra; presidencia; **arm** — sillón (de brazos); **easy** — butaca, poltrona; **folding** — silla de tijera; **rocking** — mecedora.

chairman [tʃérmən] s. presidente (de una junta).

chairmanship [tʃérmənʃɪp] s. presidencia (de una junta).

chalice [tʃǽlɪs] v. cáliz (vaso sagrado).

chalk [tʃɔk] s. tiza, yeso; greda; v. enyesar; marcar con tiza o yeso; **to — down** apuntar con tiza o yeso (en el pizarrón); **to — out** bosquejar, esbozar con tiza.

chalky [tʃɔ́kɪ] adj. yesoso; blanco.

challenge [tʃǽlɪndʒ] s. desafío; reto; demanda; v. desafiar, retar; disputar, poner a prueba; dar el quienvive.

chamber [tʃémbə] s. cámara; aposento.

chambermaid [tʃémbəmed] s. camarera, sirvienta.

chamois [ʃǽmɪ] s. gamuza.

champion [tʃǽmpɪən] s. campeón; defensor; v. defender.

championship [tʃǽmpɪənʃɪp] s. campeonato.

chance [tʃǽns] s. oportunidad, ocasión; probabilidad, posibilidad; suerte, fortuna; casualidad, azar; riesgo; billete de rifa o lotería; **by** — por casualidad; **game of** — juego de azar; **to run a** — correr riesgo; adj. casual, accidental; v. arriesgar; **to** — acertar a, hacer (algo) por casualidad.

chancellor [tʃǽnsələ] s. canciller; primer ministro; magistrado; rector de universidad.

chandelier [ʃændɪ́f] s. araña de luces, Am. candil.

change [tʃendʒ] s. cambio; mudanza; alteración, vuelta (dinero devuelto), Am. vuelto; suelto, moneda suelta; muda

de ropa; **the** — **of life** la menopausia, v. cambiar; mudar; alterar; **to** — **clothes** mudar de ropa; **to** — **trains** transbordar(se), cambiar de tren.

changeable [tʃéndʒəbl] adj. mudable, variable; inconstante; — **silk** seda tornasolada.

channel [tʃǽnl] s. canal; cauce.

chant [tʃænt] s. canto llano o gregoriano sonsonete; v. cantar (psalmos, himnos, etc.).

chaos [kéas] s. caos; desorden.

chaotic [keátɪk] adj. caótico.

chap [tʃæp] s. grieta, raja, rajadura (en la piel); chico; **what a fine** — **he is** ¡qué buen tipo (o sujeto) es!; v. agrietarse, rajarse (la piel).

chapel [tʃǽpl] s. capilla.

chaperon(e) [ʃǽpəron] s. acompañante, persona de respeto; **to go along as a** — Am. ir de moscón; v. acompañar, servir de acompañante.

chaplain [tʃǽplɪn] s. capellán; **army** — capellán castrense.

chapter [tʃǽptə] s. capítulo; cabildo (de una catedral).

char [tʃar] v. requemar, carbonizar.

character [kǽrɪktə] s. carácter; personaje.

characteristic [kærɪktərístɪk] adj. característico; típico; s. característica, rasgo característico; distintivo; peculiaridad.

characterize [kǽrɪktəraɪz] v. caracterizar.

charcoal [tʃárkol] s. carbón; carboncillo (para dibujar); — **drawing** dibujo al carbón.

charge [tʃardʒ] s. carga; peso; embestida, asalto, ataque; cargo, acusación; cuidado, custodia; encargo; mandato; precio, coste; — **account** cuenta abierta; — **prepaid** porte pagado; **under my** — a mi cargo; **to be in** — **of** estar encargado de; v. cargar; cargar en cuenta; cobrar (precio); mandar; exhortar; atacar, embestir, asaltar; **to** — **with murder** acusar de homicidio.

charger [tʃárdʒə] s. cargador (de batería); caballo de guerra, corcel.

chariot [tʃǽrɪət] s. carroza; carruaje.

charitable [tʃǽrətəbl] adj. caritativo.

charity [tʃǽrɪtɪ] s. caridad; limosna; beneficencia.

charlatan [ʃárlətn] s. charlatán; farsante.

charm [tʃarm] s. encanto; atractivo; hechizo; talismán; **watch** — dije; encantar; cautivar; hechizar.

charming [tʃármɪŋ] adj. encantador

34

atractivo.

chart [tʃɑrt] s. carta (*hidrográfica o de navegar*); mapa; gráfica, representación gráfica; v. cartografiar, delinear mapas o cartas; **to — a course** trazar o planear una ruta o derrotero.

charter [tʃɑ́rtə] s. carta constitucional, constitución, código; título; carta de privilegio; **— member** socio fundador; v. fletar (*un barco*); alquilar (*un ómnibus*).

chase [tʃes] s. caza; persecución; v. cazar; perseguir; **to — away** ahuyentar.

chasm [kǽzəm] s. abismo; vacío.

chaste [tʃest] adj. casto; honesto; puro.

chastise [tʃæstáɪz] v. castigar.

chastisement [tʃæstáɪzmənt] s. castigo, escarmiento.

chastity [tʃǽstətɪ] s. castidad; honestidad; pureza.

chat [tʃæt] s. charla, plática; v. charlar, platicar.

chattels [tʃǽtlz] s. pl. enseres, bienes muebles.

chatter [tʃǽtə] s. charla, parloteo; castañeteo (*de los dientes*); chirrido (*de aves*); v. charlar, parlotear, cotorrear; castañetear (*los dientes*).

chauffeur [ʃófə] s. chófer, cochero de automóvil.

cheap [tʃip] adj. barato; cursi, de mal gusto; **to feel —** sentir vergüenza; **-ly** adv. barato, a poco precio.

cheapen [tʃípən] v. abaratar.

cheapness [tʃípnɪs] s. baratura; cursilería.

cheat [tʃit] s. fraude, engaño; trampa; trampista, tramposo; estafador; embaucador; v. engañar; trampear; embaucar; estafar.

check [tʃek] s. cheque (*de banco*); talón, marbete, contraseña (*de equipajes, etc.*); marca, señal; cuenta (*de restaurante*); restricción, represión; cuadro (*de un tejido o tela*); comprobación; jaque (*en ajedrez*); **—room** vestuario; depósito de equipajes, Am. consigna; v. refrenar, reprimir, restringir; facturar, depositar (*equipajes*); inspeccionar; confrontar, comprobar; marcar (*con una señal*); dar jaque (*en ajedrez*); **to — out of a hotel** desocupar el cuarto o alojamiento de un hotel.

heckbook [tʃékbʊk] s. libreta de cheques; libro talonario.

hecker [tʃékə] s. cuadro; casilla (*de un tablero de ajedrez, etc.*); pieza (*del juego de damas*); comprobador; inspector; **-s** juego de damas; **—board** tablero; v. cuadricular, marcar con cuadritos.

-ed career vida azarosa, vida llena de variedad; **-ed cloth** paño o tela a cuadros.

cheek [tʃik] s. mejilla, carrillo; cachete; descaro, desfachatez; **fat —** mejilla gorda, moflete; **— bone** pómulo.

cheer [tʃɪr] s. alegría; buen ánimo, jovialidad; consuelo; **-s** aplausos, vivas; v. alegrar, alentar, animar; aplaudir, vitorear; **to — up** alentar, dar ánimo; cobrar ánimo, animarse.

cheerful [tʃírfəl] adj. animado, alegre, jovial; **-ly** adv. alegremente, con alegría, con júbilo; de buena gana, de buen grado.

cheerfulness [tʃírfəlnɪs] s. jovialidad, alegría; buen humor.

cheerily [tʃírəlɪ] = **cheerfully**.

cheerless [tʃírlɪs] adj. abatido, desalentado, desanimado; triste, sombrío.

cheery [tʃírɪ] = **cheerful**.

cheese [tʃiz] s. queso; **cottage —** requesón.

chemical [kémɪkl] adj. químico; s. producto químico.

chemist [kémɪst] s. químico.

chemistry [kémɪstrɪ] s. química.

cherish [tʃérɪʃ] v. acariciar, abrigar (*una esperanza, un ideal, etc.*); apreciar.

cherry [tʃérɪ] s. cereza; **— tree** cerezo.

chess [tʃes] s. ajedrez; **—board** tablero de ajedrez.

chest [tʃest] s. cofre, arca, caja; pecho; **— of drawers** cómoda.

chestnut [tʃésnət] s. castaña; **— tree** castaño; adj. castaño; **— horse** caballo zaino.

chew [tʃu] s. mascada, mordisco, bocado; v. mascar, masticar.

chewing gum [tʃúɪŋ gʌm] s. goma de mascar; Am. chicle.

chick [tʃik] s. polluelo, pollito; pajarito; **chick-pea** garbanzo.

chicken [tʃíkɪn] s. pollo; polluelo; **— pox** viruelas locas; **chicken-hearted** cobarde, gallina.

chide [tʃaɪd] v. regañar, reprender, reprobar.

chief [tʃif] s. jefe, caudillo, cacique (*de una tribu*); **commander in —** comandante en jefe; adj. principal; **— clerk** oficial mayor; **— justice** presidente de la corte suprema; **-ly** adv. principalmente, mayormente; sobre todo.

chiffon [ʃifán] s. gasa.

chilblain [tʃílblen] s. sabañón.

child [tʃaɪld] s. niño, niña; hijo, hija; **-'s play** cosa de niños; **to be with —** estar encinta.

childbirth [tʃáɪldbɜə] s. parto, alumbramiento.

childhood [tʃáɪldhʊd] s. niñez, infancia.

childish [tʃáɪldɪʃ] adj. pueril; infantil; — action niñería, niñada.

childless [tʃáɪldlɪs] adj. sin hijos.

childlike [tʃáɪldlaɪk] adj. como niño, aniñado, pueril.

children [tʃíldrən] pl. de child.

Chilean [tʃílɪən] adj. & s. chileno.

chili [tʃílɪ] s. Am. chile, Am. ají.

chill [tʃɪl] s. frío, resfrío; enfriamiento; escalofrío, calofrío; -s and fever escalofríos; adj. frío; v. resfriar(se); enfriar(se); to become -ed resfriarse, escalofriarse.

chilly [tʃílɪ] adj. frío; friolento.

chime [tʃaɪm] s. repique, campaneo; -s órgano de campanas, juego de campanas; v. repicar, campanear; tocar, sonar, tañer (las campanas); to — with estar en armonía con.

chimney [tʃímnɪ] s. chimenea; **lamp** — tubo de lámpara, Am. bombilla.

chin [tʃɪn] s. barba.

china [tʃáɪnə] s. loza de china, porcelana, loza fina; vajilla de porcelana; — closet chinero.

chinaware [tʃáɪnəwer] = **china**.

Chinese [tʃaɪníz] adj. chino; s. chino; idioma chino.

chink [tʃɪŋk] s. grieta, hendidura.

chip [tʃɪp] s. astilla, brizna; fragmento; desconchadura; desportilladura; ficha (de pócar); v. astillar; desconchar(se); descascarar(se); desportillar(se); picar, tajar (con cincel o hacha); to — in contribuir con su cuota.

chipmunk [tʃípmʌŋk] s. especie de ardilla.

chirp [tʃɜp] s. chirrido; pío; gorjeo; v. chirriar; piar; pipiar; gorjear.

chisel [tʃízl] s. cincel; v. cincelar; sisar, estafar.

chivalrous [ʃívlrəs] adj. caballeresco, caballeroso, galante, cortés.

chivalry [ʃívlrɪ] s. caballería; caballerosidad.

chlorine [klórin] s. cloro.

chloroform [klórəfarm] s. cloroformo.

chocolate [tʃɔklɪt] s. chocolate; — pot chocolatera.

choice [tʃɔɪs] s. selección; preferencia; escogimiento; cosa elegida; favorito, preferido; alternativa; to have no other — no tener otra alternativa; adj. selecto; bien escogido; excelente.

choir [kwaɪr] s. coro.

choke [tʃok] s. sofoco, ahogo; tos ahogada; estrangulación; estrangulador, obturador (de automóvil) v. sofocar(se),

ahogar(se); estrangular(se); obstruir, tapar; regularizar (el motor).

cholera [kálərə] s. cólera (m.).

choose [tʃuz] v. escoger; elegir, seleccionar; to — to optar por; preferir; **I do not** — to do it no se me antoja (o no es mi gusto) hacerlo.

chop [tʃɑp] s. chuleta, costilla, tajada (de carne); -s quijadas (usualmente de animal); v. tajar, cortar; picar, desmenuzar (carne).

choppy [tʃápɪ] adj. picado, agitado.

choral [kórəl] adj. coral.

chord [kɔrd] s. cuerda; acorde.

chore [tʃor] s. tarea; quehacer.

chorus [kórəs] s. coro; v. cantar o hablar en coro; contestar a una voz.

chose [tʃoz] pret. de to choose.

chosen [tʃózn] p.p. de to choose.

christen [krísn] v. bautizar.

christening [krísnɪŋ] s. bautizo, bautismo.

Christian [krístʃən] s. & adj. cristiano; — name nombre de pila o bautismo.

Christianity [krɪstʃénətɪ] s. cristiandad, cristianismo.

Christmas [krísməs] s. Navidad, Pascua de Navidad; — Eve Nochebuena; — gift regalo de Navidad; aguinaldo; **Merry** —! ¡Felices Navidades! ¡Felices Pascuas!

chronic [kránɪk] adj. crónico.

chronicle [kránɪk] s. crónica; v. relatar, escribir la crónica de.

chronicler [kránɪklə] s. cronista.

chronological [kranəládʒɪkl] adj. cronológico.

chronometer [krənámətə] s. cronómetro

chrysanthemum [krɪsénɵəməm] s. crisantema, crisantemo.

chubby [tʃʌbɪ] adj. rechoncho; gordiflón

chuck [tʃʌk] s. mamola, golpecito, caricia (debajo de la barba); v. echar, tirar (lo que no sirve); to — under the chin hacer la mamola.

chuckle [tʃʌkl] s. risita; v. reír entre dientes.

chum [tʃʌm] s. compañero, camarada compinche.

chunk [tʃʌŋk] s. trozo; zoquete.

church [tʃɜtʃ] s. iglesia.

churchman [tʃɜtʃmən] s. clérigo, eclesiástico, sacerdote.

churchyard [tʃɜtʃjard] s. patio de iglesia; camposanto, cementerio.

churn [tʃɜn] s. mantequera (para hace manteca); v. batir (en una mantequera) agitar, revolver.

cider [sáɪdə] s. sidra.

cigar [sɪgár] s. cigarro, puro; — stor

tabaquería, estanquillo.

cigarette [sɪgɔrét] s. cigarrillo, pitillo, Am. cigarro; — **case** cigarrera, pitillera; — **holder** boquilla; — **lighter** encendedor.

cinch [sɪntʃ] s. cincha; ganga, cosa fácil; v. cinchar; apretar.

cinder [síndə] s. ceniza; carbón, brasa, ascua; -s cenizas; rescoldo.

cinnamon [sínəmən] s. canela; — **tree** canelo.

cipher [sáɪfə] s. cifra; número; cero.

circle [sɔ́k l] s. círculo; cerco, rueda; v. cercar, circundar; circular, dar vueltas.

circuit [sɔ́kɪt] s. circuito; rodeo, vuelta.

circular [sɔ́kjələ] adj. circular; redondo; s. circular; hoja volante.

circulate [sɔ́kjəlet] v. circular; poner en circulación.

circulation [sɔkjəléʃən] s. circulación.

circumference [səkʌ́mfərəns] s. circunferencia.

circumlocution [sɔkəmlokjúʃən] s. circunlocución, rodeo.

circumscribe [sɔkəmskráɪb] v. circunscribir, limitar.

circumspect [sɔ́kəmspɛkt] adj. circunspecto; prudente.

circumspection [sɔkəmspékʃən] s. circunspección, miramiento, prudencia.

circumstance [sɔ́kəmstæns] s. circunstancia; incidente; ceremonia, pompa.

circus [sɔ́kəs] s. circo.

cistern [sístən] s. cisterna.

citadel [sítədl] s. ciudadela.

citation [saɪtéʃən] s. citación; cita; mención.

cite [saɪt] v. citar; citar a juicio; mencionar.

citizen [sítəzn] s. ciudadano, paisano.

citizenship [sítəznʃɪp] s. ciudadanía.

citron [sítrən] s. acitrón.

city [sítɪ] s. ciudad, población; municipio; adj. municipal; urbano; — **council** ayuntamiento; — **hall** ayuntamiento, casa municipal.

civic [sívɪk] adj. cívico.

civics [sívɪks] s. derecho político.

civil [sívl] adj. civil; cortés; — **engineer** ingeniero civil.

civilian [sɔvɪ́ljən] s. paisano (persona no militar).

civility [səvɪ́lətɪ] s. civilidad, cortesía, urbanidad.

civilization [sɪvləzéʃən] s. civilización.

civilize [sívlaɪz] v. civilizar.

civilized [sívlaɪzd] adj. civilizado.

clad [klæd] pret. & p.p. de **to clothe**.

claim [klem] s. demanda; reclamación; reclamo; derecho; título; pretensión;

miner's — denuncia; v. reclamar; demandar; pedir, exigir; afirmar, sostener; **to** — **a mine** denunciar una mina; **to** — **to be** pretender ser.

claimant [klémənt] s. reclamante o reclamador; pretendiente (a un trono).

clairvoyant [klɛrvóɪənt] adj. clarividente.

clam [klæm] s. almeja.

clamber [klæmbə] v. trepar, encaramarse, subir a gatas, subir gateando.

clamor [klæmə] s. clamor; clamoreo; gritería, vocería; v. clamar; vociferar, gritar.

clamorous [klæmərəs] adj. clamoroso.

clamp [klæmp] s. grapa; tornillo de banco; v. afianzar, sujetar; pisar recio.

clan [klæn] s. clan; tribu.

clandestine [klændéstɪn] adj. clandestino.

clang [klæŋ] s. tantán, retintín; campanada, campanillazo; —! —! ¡tan! ¡tan!; v. sonar, repicar (una campana o timbre); hacer sonar, tocar fuerte.

clap [klæp] s. palmada; golpe seco; — **of thunder** trueno; v. palmear, palmotear, aplaudir, dar palmadas; cerrar de golpe (un libro); dar una palmada, Am. palmear (sobre la espalda); **to** — **in jail** meter (o encajar) en la cárcel.

clarify [klǽrəfaɪ] v. aclarar.

clarinet [klærənɛ́t] s. clarinete.

clarity [klǽrətɪ] s. claridad, luz.

clash [klæʃ] s. choque, encontrón, colisión; riña, conflicto; estruendo; v. chocar; darse un encontrón; hacer crujir; oponerse, estar en conflicto.

clasp [klæsp] s. broche; hebilla; cierre; traba; apretón, apretón de manos; v. abrochar; asir, agarrar; sujetar, asegurar; abrazar; apretar (la mano).

class [klæs] s. clase; v. clasificar.

classic [klǽsɪk] adj. & s. clásico; — **scholar** humanista, erudito clásico.

classical [klǽsɪkl] adj. clásico.

classification [klæsəfəkéʃən] s. clasificación.

classify [klǽsəfaɪ] v. clasificar.

classmate [klǽsmet] s. compañero de clase, condiscípulo.

classroom [klǽsrum] s. clase, aula.

clatter [klǽtə] s. estrépito, boruca; traqueteo; bullicio; alboroto; v. hacer estrépito o boruca; traquetear; meter bulla o alboroto.

clause [kloz] s. cláusula.

claw [klɔ] s. garra; zarpa; uña; pinza (de langosta, cangrejo, etc.); orejas (de un martillo); arañazo; v. desgarrar; arañar; rasgar.

clay [kle] s. barro; arcilla, greda.

clean [klin] adj. limpio; puro; adv. limpiamente; clean-cut bien tallado, de buen talle, de buen parecer; v. limpiar; asear; to — up limpiar(se), asear(se).

cleaner [klínə] s. limpiador; quitamanchas.

cleanliness [klénlɪnɪs] s. limpieza; aseo.

cleanly [klénlɪ] adj. limpio; aseado; [klínlɪ] adv. limpiamente.

cleanness [klínnɪs] s. limpieza; aseo.

cleanse [klɛns] v. limpiar; asear; purificar, depurar.

cleanser [klɛnsə] s. limpiador.

clear [klɪr] adj. claro; patente, manifiesto; límpido; despejado; libre (de culpa, estorbos, deudas, etc.); — profit ganancia neta; to pass — through atravesar, traspasar de lado a lado; to be in the — estar sin deudas; estar libre de culpa; v. aclarar(se); despejar(se); clarificar; quitar (estorbos); desmontar (un terreno); salvar, saltar por encima de; librar (de culpa, deudas, etc.); sacar (una ganancia neta); pasar (un cheque) por un banco de liquidación; liquidar (una cuenta); to — the table levantar la mesa; to — up aclarar(se).

clearance [klírəns] s. espacio (libre entre dos objetos); despacho de aduana; — sale saldo, venta (de liquidación), Am. barata.

clearing [klírɪŋ] s. aclaramiento; claro, terreno desmontado o desarbolado; liquidación de balances; —house banco de liquidación.

clearness [klírnɪs] s. claridad.

cleave [kliv] v. hender(se); tajar; rajar; partir.

cleaver [klívə] s. cuchilla o hacha (de carnicero).

clef [klɛf] s. clave (en música).

cleft [klɛft] s. grieta, hendedura; adj. hendido, partido, rajado; pret. & p.p. de to cleave.

clemency [klɛ́mənsɪ] s. clemencia.

clement [klɛ́mənt] adj. clemente.

clench [klɛntʃ] s. agarro, agarrada, agarrón; apretón; v. agarrar, asir; apretar; apretar (los dientes, el puño).

clergy [klɝ́dʒɪ] s. clero.

clergyman [klɝ́dʒɪmən] s. clérigo, eclesiástico; pastor, sacerdote.

clerical [klɛ́rɪkl] adj. clerical, eclesiástico; oficinesco, de oficina; de dependientes.

clerk [klɝk] s. dependiente; empleado (de oficina); escribiente; archivero (de municipio); law — escribano; v. estar de dependiente.

clever [klɛ́və] adj. diestro, hábil; listo;

talentoso; mañoso; -ly adv. hábilmente; con destreza; con maña.

cleverness [klɛ́vənɪs] s. destreza, habilidad, maña; talento.

clew [klu] s. indicio (que indica el camino para resolver un misterio o problema).

click [klɪk] s. golpecito; chasquido (de la lengua); gatillazo (sonido del gatillo de una pistola); taconeo (sonido de tacones); v. sonar (un pestillo, un broche, un gatillo, etc.); chasquear (la lengua); to — the heels cuadrarse (militarmente); taconear.

client [klárənt] s. cliente.

clientele [klarəntél] s. clientela.

cliff [klɪf] s. risco, precipicio, peñasco, escarpa.

climate [klármɪt] s. clima.

climax [klárməks] s. clímax, culminación; v. culminar; llegar al clímax.

climb [klarm] s. subida, ascenso; v. subir; trepar; encaramarse; to — down bajar a gatas; desprenderse (de un árbol).

climber [klármə] s. trepador; enredadera, planta trepadora.

clime [klarm] s. clima.

clinch [klɪntʃ] v. remachar, redoblar (un clavo); afianzar, sujetar, asegurar bien; cerrar (un trato); abrazarse fuertemente; s. remache; abrazo; agarrón; to be in a — estar agarrados o abrazados.

cling [klɪŋ] v. pegarse, adherirse.

clinic [klínɪk] s. clínica.

clip [klɪp] s. broche, presilla; tijeretada (corta con tijeras); trasquila, trasquiladura; paper — sujetapapeles; to go at a good — ir a paso rápido; andar de prisa; v. recortar; cortar; trasquilar (el pelo o lana de los animales); to — together sujetar.

clipper [klípə] s. clíper (velero o avión de gran velocidad); trasquilador; recortador; -s tijeras; maquinilla (para recortar el pelo).

clipping [klípɪŋ] s. recorte.

cloak [klok] s. capa; manto; v. tapar, embozar, encubrir.

cloakroom [klókrum] s. guardarropa, vestuario.

clock [klak] s. reloj; alarm — despertador.

clockwork [klákwɝk] s. maquinaria de reloj; like — con precisión, puntualmente; sin dificultad.

clod [klad] s. terrón; tonto, necio.

clog [klag] s. estorbo, obstáculo; zueco (zapato de suela gruesa o de madera); — dance zapateado; v. estorbar, em-

38

barazar; obstruir, atorar, tapar; obstruirse, atascarse, azolvarse (*Am.* enzolvarse), atorarse (*un caño, acequia, etc.*).

cloister [klóistə] *s.* claustro; monasterio; convento; *v.* enclaustrar.

close [kloz] *s.* fin, terminación, conclusión; *v.* cerrar(se); concluir; **to — an account** saldar una cuenta; **to — in upon** cercar, rodear; **to — out** liquidar, vender en liquidación.

close [klos] *adj.* cercano, próximo; aproximado; íntimo; estrecho; ajustado; cerrado; mezquino, tacaño; sofocante, opresivo; mal ventilado; **— attention** suma atención; **— questioning** interrogatorio detallado o minucioso; **— translation** traducción fiel; **at — range** de cerca; *adv.* cerca; **-ly** *adv.* aproximadamente; estrechamente; apretadamente; con sumo cuidado a atención.

closeness [klósnis] *s.* cercanía, proximidad; aproximación; estrechez; intimidad; tacañería, avaricia; mala ventilación, falta de aire; fidelidad (*de una traducción*).

closet [klázit] *s.* ropero; alacena, armario; gabinete, retrete, excusado; *v.* encerrar en un cuarto (*para una entrevista secreta*); **to — oneself (themselves)** encerrarse.

clot [klat] *v.* coagular(se), cuajar(se); *s.* coágulo, cuajarón.

cloth [klɔə] *s.* tela, paño, género; trapo; *adj.* de paño; **— binding** encuadernación en tela.

clothe [kloð] *v.* vestir; cubrir; revestir; investir.

clothes [kloz] *s. pl.* ropa; ropaje, vestidos; **suit of —** terno, traje, *Am.* flux; **—line** tendedero; **—pin** pinzas, gancho (*para tender la ropa*).

clothier [klóðjə] *s.* comerciante en ropa o paño; ropero, pañero.

clothing [klóðiŋ] *s.* ropa; ropaje, vestidos.

cloud [klaud] *s.* nube; **storm —** nubarrón; *v.* nublar(se), anublar(se); obscurecer; manchar.

cloudless [kláudlis] *adj.* claro, despejado; sin nubes.

cloudy [kláudi] *adj.* nublado; nubloso; sombrío.

clove [klov] *s.* clavo (*especia*); **— of garlic** diente de ajo.

clover [klóvə] *s.* trébol; **to be in —** estar o vivir en la abundancia; sentirse próspero.

clown [klaun] *s.* payaso, bufón; *v.* payasear, bufonear, hacer el payaso.

cloy [klɔi] *v.* empalagar; hastiar.

club [klʌb] *s.* club, círculo; casino; garrote, porra; palo; basto (*de la baraja*); *v.* golpear, aporrear, apalear; **to — together** formar club; escotar, pagar la cuota que le toca a cada uno, *Am.* cotizar.

clubhouse [klʌbhaus] *s.* club, casino.

cluck [klʌk] *s.* cloqueo; *v.* cloquear.

clue = **clew**

clump [klʌmp] *s.* terrón; pisada fuerte; **— of bushes** matorral; **— of trees** grupo de árboles, arboleda; *v.* apiñar, amontonar; **to — along** andar pesadamente.

clumsy [klʌmzi] *adj.* torpe, desmañado; incómodo; difícil de manejar; mal hecho.

clung [klʌŋ] *pret. & p.p. de* **to cling.**

cluster [klʌstə] *s.* racimo; grupo; *v.* agrupar(se); arracimarse (*formar racimo*).

clutch [klʌtʃ] *s.* apretón fuerte; agarro, agarrón; embrague (*de automóvil*); **-es** garras; uñas; **— pedal** palanca del embrague; **to step on the —** pisar el embrague; desembragar, soltar el embrague; **to throw in the —** embragar; *v.* agarrar, asir; apretar.

clutter [klʌtə] *v.* obstruir; atestar (*de cosas*); poner en desorden; *s.* desorden, confusión.

coach [kotʃ] *s.* coche; entrenador (*en deportes*); maestro particular; *v.* aleccionar; guiar, adiestrar, *Am.* entrenar; **to—with** ser instruido o entrenado por.

coachman [kótʃmən] *s.* cochero.

coagulate [koǽgjəlet] *v.* coagular(se), cuajar(se).

coal [kol] *s.* carbón; ascua, brasa; **hard —** carbón de piedra, antracita; **soft —** hulla; **— bin** carbonera; **— dealer** carbonero; **— oil** kerosina; *v.* cargar de carbón, echar carbón; proveer(se) de carbón.

coalition [koælʃən] *s.* coalición.

coarse [kors] *adj.* tosco; burdo, basto; áspero; rudo, grosero; vulgar; **— sand** arena gruesa.

coarseness [kórsnis] *s.* tosquedad; vulgaridad, grosería, rudeza.

coast [kost] *s.* costa, litoral; **— guard** guardacostas, guarda de costas; *v.* costear, navegar por la costa; deslizar(se), resbalar(se) cuesta abajo.

coastal [kóstl] *adj.* costero, costanero, de la costa.

coastline [kóstlain] *s.* costa, litoral.

coat [kot] *s.* chaqueta, *Am.* saco; lana, pelo (*de un animal*); **lady's —** abrigo de señora; **— hanger** colgador; **— of arms** escudo de armas; **— of paint**

capa de pintura; v. cubrir; revestir, dar una mano (de pintura); **to** — **with sugar** azucarar, bañar en azúcar.

coattail [kóttel] s. faldón.

coax [koks] v. rogar o persuadir con halagos, halagar, tentar.

cob [kab] s. carozo, zuro (de la mazorca del maíz), Am. tusa, Am. olote.

cobbler [káblə] s. remendón (zapatero); pudín de bizcocho y fruta.

cobweb [kábweb] s. telaraña.

cocaine [kokén] s. cocaína.

cock [kak] s. gallo; macho de ave; espita, grifo; martillo (de armas de fuego); —**sure** muy seguro de sí mismo; v. amartillar (un arma de fuego); ladear (la cabeza), ladearse (el sombrero).

cockroach [kákrotʃ] s. cucaracha.

cocktail [káktel] s. coctel; aperitivo (de ostras, almejas, frutas, etc.).

cocky [káki] adj. arrogante, Am. retobado.

cocoa [kóko] s. cacao; bebida de cacao, chocolate.

coconut [kókənət] s. coco (fruta).

cocoon [kəkún] s. capullo (del gusano de seda, etc.).

cod [kad] s. bacalao, abadejo; **cod-liver oil** aceite de hígado de bacalao.

coddle [kádl] v. mimar, consentir.

code [kod] s. código; clave; — **message** comunicación en clave; — **signal** — código de señales.

codfish [kádfiʃ] = **cod**.

coerce [koɜ́s] v. forzar, obligar.

coffee [káfi] s. café; — **shop** café; — **tree** cafeto; **black** — café solo.

coffeepot [káfipat] s. cafetera.

coffer [káfə] s. cofre, arca.

coffin [káfin] s. ataúd, féretro.

coherent [kohírənt] adj. coherente, conexo.

cohesion [kohíʒən] s. cohesión.

coiffure [kwafjúr] s. tocado, peinado.

coil [koil] s. rollo; rosca; espiral de alambre; **electric** — bobina; v. arrollar(se), enrollar(se); enroscar(se).

coin [koin] s. moneda; v. acuñar; inventar, forjar (una frase o palabra).

coinage [kóinidʒ] s. acuñación; sistema monetario; moneda, monedas; invención (de una palabra o frase).

coincide [koinsáid] v. coincidir.

coincidence [koínsədəns] s. coincidencia; casualidad.

coke [kok] s. cok, coque (combustible).

cold [kold] adj. frío; — **cream** crema cosmética; — **meat** fiambre; **to be** — tener frío; **it is** — **today** hace frío hoy; s. frío; catarro, resfriado; **to catch a**

— resfriarse, acatarrarse.

coldness [kóldnis] s. frialdad; indiferencia, despego.

collaborate [kəlǽbəret] v. colaborar.

collaboration [kəlæborésən] s. colaboración.

collapse [kəlǽps] s. desplome, derrumbe, derrumbamiento; hundimiento; postración; v. doblar(se), plegar(se); contraer (el volumen); hundirse, derrumbarse, desplomarse; sufrir una postración.

collar [kálə] s. collar; cuello (de vestido, camisa, etc.); collera (para mulas o caballos de tiro); v. acollarar, poner collar a; coger o agarrar por el cuello; prender.

collateral [kəlǽtərəl] adj. colateral; auxiliar, subsidiario, accesorio; s. garantía (para un préstamo bancario).

colleague [kálig] s. colega.

collect [kəlékt] v. recoger; coleccionar; cobrar; recaudar (impuestos); reunir(se); congregarse; **to** — **oneself** calmarse; sosegarse, reportarse.

collection [kəlékʃən] s. colección; agrupación (de gente); recolección, cobranza, cobro, recaudación; colecta.

collective [kəléktiv] adj. colectivo.

collector [kəléktə] s. colector; coleccionista (de sellos, objetos artísticos, etc.); cobrador (de billetes, deudas, etc.); recaudador (de impuestos).

college [kálidʒ] s. colegio; **medical** — colegio o escuela de medicina.

collide [kəláid] v. chocar; estar en conflicto, oponerse.

collie [káli] s. perro de pastor.

collision [kəlíʒən] s. choque, colisión; oposición, pugna (de intereses, ideas, etc.).

colloquial [kəlókwiəl] adj. familiar; — **expression** locución o frase familiar.

colon [kólən] s. colon (del intestino); dos puntos (signo de puntuación).

colonel [kɜ́nl] s. coronel.

colonial [kólóniəl] adj. colonial.

colonist [kálənist] s. colono, colonizador.

colonization [kələnəzéʃən] s. colonización.

colonize [kálənaiz] v. colonizar; establecerse en colonia.

colony [káləni] s. colonia.

color [kʌ́lə] s. color; colorido; **the** -**s la bandera**; v. colorar; colorear; dar colorido; pintar; teñir; iluminar (una fotografía, grabado, etc.); ruborizarse.

colored [kʌ́ləd] adj. colorado, teñido, colorido, pintado; de color; coloreado; — **person** persona de color.

colorful [kʌ́ləfəl] *adj.* lleno de color; colorido; vistoso; vívido; pintoresco.

coloring [kʌ́lərɪŋ] *s.* colorido; coloración; colorante.

colorless [kʌ́ləlɪs] *adj.* incoloro; descolorido.

colossal [kəlás] *adj.* colosal.

colt [kolt] *s.* potro.

Columbian [kəlʌ́mbɪən] *adj.* colombiano, de Colombia; colombino, referente a Cristóbal Colón.

column [kʌ́ləm] *s.* columna.

comb [kom] *s.* peine; peineta (*de mujer*); cresta (*de gallo*); rastrillo, carda (*para lana*); almohaza (*para caballos*); panal (*de miel*); *v.* peinar; rastrillar, cardar (*lana*); escudriñar; **to — one's hair** peinarse.

combat [kámbæt] *s.* combate, pelea; *v.* combatir.

combatant [kámbətənt] *adj.* & *s.* combatiente.

combination [kambənéʃən] *s.* combinación.

combine [kəmbáin] *v.* combinar(se), unir(se).

combustible [kəmbástəbl] *adj.* & *s.* combustible.

combustion [kəmbástʃən] *s.* combustión.

come [kʌm] *v.* venir; llegar; provenir; **to — about** suceder; **to — again** volver, volver a venir; **to — back** volver, regresar; **to — downstairs** bajar; **to — in** entrar; **to — out** salir; **to — of age** llegar a mayor edad; **to — off** soltarse, zafarse; **to — to** volver en sí; **to — to terms** ponerse de acuerdo, ajustarse; **to — up** subir; surgir (*una cuestión*); *p.p.* **de to come.**

comedian [kəmídiən] *s.* cómico, comediante.

comedy [kámədɪ] *s.* comedia.

comely [kʌ́mlɪ] *adj.* agradable a la vista, gentil, bien parecido.

comet [kámɪt] *s.* cometa.

comfort [kʌ́mfət] *s.* comodidad; bienestar; alivio, consuelo; *v.* consolar, confortar, aliviar.

comfortable [kʌ́mfətəbl] *adj.* cómodo; confortable; **— life** vida holgada; **— income** un buen pasar, renta suficiente; **comfortably** *adv.* cómodamente; con comodidad; holgadamente.

comforter [kʌ́mfətə] *s.* consolador; edredón, cobertor acolchado.

comfortless [kʌ́mfətlɪs] *adj.* incómodo; desconsolado.

comic [kámɪk] *adj.* cómico; chistoso; gracioso; **-s** *pl.* caricaturas, historietas cómicas.

comical [kámɪkl] *adj.* cómico, gracioso.

coming [kʌ́mɪŋ] *adj.* que viene, que llega; próximo; venidero; *s.* venida, llegada; **— of Christ** advenimiento de Cristo.

comma [kámə] *s.* coma.

command [kəmǽnd] *s.* mando; mandato, orden; mandamiento; comandancia; comando; dominio; **at your — a** la orden de Vd., a la disposición de Vd.; **he has a good — of English** domina bien el inglés; *v.* mandar; ordenar; dominar; comandar, **to — respect** inspirar respeto, imponerse.

commander [kəmǽndə] *s.* jefe; comandante; teniente de navío; comendador (*de ciertas órdenes*); **— in chief** comandante en jefe; general en jefe.

commandment [kəmǽndmənt] *s.* mandamiento; mandato, orden.

commemorate [kəmémərət] *v.* conmemorar.

commence [kəméns] *v.* comenzar.

commencement [kəménsmənt] *s.* comienzo, principio; acto de distribución de diplomas.

commend [kəménd] *v.* alabar, elogiar; encomendar, encargar; recomendar.

commendation [kaməndéʃən] *s.* encomio, alabanza.

comment [kámənt] *s.* comentario, observación, nota; *v.* comentar; hacer observaciones; hacer comentarios.

commentary [kámənterɪ] *s.* comentario.

commentator [káməntetə] *s.* comentador; comentarista; **radio —** comentarista radial.

commerce [káməs] *s.* comercio.

commercial [kəmə́ʃəl] *adj.* comercial.

commiseration [kəmɪzəréʃən] *s.* compasión.

commissary [káməserɪ] *s.* comisario.

commission [kəmíʃən] *s.* comisión; encargo; junta; nombramiento; **to put out of —** inutilizar; descomponer, quebrar; retirar del servicio (*un navío*); *v.* comisionar; encargar; nombrar; poner en servicio (*un navío*); **-ed officer** oficial comisionado (*alférez u oficial superior a éste*).

commissioner [kəmíʃənə] *s.* comisionado; comisario; **police —** comisario de policía.

commit [kəmít] *v.* cometer; encargar; **to — to memory** aprender de memoria; **to — to prison** encarcelar; **to — oneself** dar o expresar su opinión, expresarse abiertamente, comprometerse.

committee [kəmítɪ] *s.* comité; comisión,

junta; — **of one** comisionado o delegado único.

commodity [kəmádətɪ] s. mercancía; género, mercadería, artículo de comercio, producto.

common [kámən] adj. común; general; corriente; vulgar, ordinario; público; — **law** derecho consuetudinario; — **sense** sentido común; — **soldier** soldado raso; **-s** s. pl. refectorio (de un colegio o universidad); ejido, campo común; **-ly** adv. comúnmente, por lo común.

commonness [kámənnɪs] s. vulgaridad, ordinariez; frecuencia.

commonplace [kámənples] adj. común, trivial; s. lugar común.

commonwealth [kámənwɛlθ] s. estado; república; pueblo, colectividad.

commotion [kəmóʃən] s. conmoción; tumulto; bullicio; levantamiento.

commune [kəmjún] v. comunicarse (con); comulgar.

communicate [kəmjúnəket] v. comunicar(se); transmitir.

communication [kəmjunəkéʃən] s. comunicación.

communicative [kəmjúnəketɪv] adj. comunicativo.

communion [kəmjúnjən] s. comunión.

communism [kámjunɪzəm] s. comunismo.

communist [kámjunɪst] s. & adj. comunista.

community [kəmjúnɪtɪ] s. comunidad; sociedad; vecindario, barrio; — **chest** caja de beneficencia, fondos de beneficencia.

compact [kəmpǽkt] adj. compacto; denso; apretado; conciso, sucinto; [kámpækt] s. pacto, trato, convenio; polvera.

compactness [kəmpǽktnɪs] s. solidez; densidad; concisión.

companion [kəmpǽnjən] s. compañero; acompañante.

companionship [kəmpǽnjənʃɪp] s. compañerismo, camaradería; compañía.

company [kámpənɪ] s. compañía; sociedad; visita; **ship's** — tripulación; **to keep** — with acompañar a; cortejar a; tener relaciones con, frecuentar la compañía de.

comparable [kámpərəbļ] adj. comparable.

comparative [kəmpǽrətɪv] adj. comparativo.

compare [kəmpér] v. comparar; cotejar; confrontar; contrastar; **beyond** — incomparable, sin par, sin igual, sin

comparación.

comparison [kəmpǽrəsn] s. comparación; símil; **beyond** — incomparable, sin comparación; **in** — **with** comparado con.

compartment [kəmpártmənt] s. compartimiento, sección, división; departamento.

compass [kámpəs] s. compás (para dibujar); brújula; área, ámbito; alcance.

compassion [kəmpǽʃən] s. compasión, lástima.

compassionate [kəmpǽʃənɪt] adj. compasivo, misericordioso.

compatible [kəmpǽtəbļ] adj. compatible.

compatriot [kəmpétrɪət] s. compatriota.

compel [kəmpél] v. compeler, obligar; exigir.

compensate [kámpənset] v. compensar; recompensar; remunerar.

compensation [kámpənséʃən] s. compensación; recompensa; remuneración.

compete [kəmpít] v. competir.

competence [kámpətəns] s. competencia, aptitud, capacidad.

competent [kámpətənt] adj. competente; calificado; capaz.

competition [kampətíʃən] s. competencia; concurso, certamen; contienda.

competitive [kəmpétətɪv] adj. en competencia; — **examination** oposición, concurso.

competitor [kəmpétətə] s. competidor; rival; opositor.

compile [kəmpáɪl] v. compilar, recopilar.

complacency [kəmplésnsɪ] s. complacencia, contentamiento.

complacent [kəmplésṇt] adj. complaciente, satisfecho.

complain [kəmplén] v. quejarse; querellarse.

complaint [kəmplént] s. queja; quejido, lamento; dolencia, enfermedad; **to lodge a** — hacer una reclamación.

complement [kámpləmənt] s. complemento; [kámpləment] v. complementar, completar.

complete [kəmplít] adj. completo; v. completar; terminar; **-ly** adv. completamente, por completo.

completeness [kəmplítnɪs] s. perfección; minuciosidad; lo completo; lo cabal; lo acabado.

completion [kəmplíʃən] s. completamiento; terminación, conclusión; cumplimiento.

complex [kámplɛks] s. complejo; [kəmpléks] adj. complejo; compuesto;

complicado.

complexion [kəmplékʃən] *s.* cutis, tez; aspecto.

complexity [kəmpléksəti] *s.* complejidad.

compliance [kəmpláɪəns] *s.* complacencia; condescendencia; conformidad; cumplimiento; **in** — **with** — **to conform to** de acuerdo con, conforme a.

complicate [kámpləket] *v.* complicar.

complicated [kámpləketɪd] *adj.* complicado.

complication [kampləkéʃən] *s.* complicación.

compliment [kámpləmənt] *s.* cumplido, cumplimiento; requiebro, lisonja, galantería; **to send one's** -**s** enviar saludos; [kámpləment] *v.* cumplimentar; requebrar; lisonjear; alabar.

comply [kəmpláɪ] *v.* consentir, conformarse (con), obrar de acuerdo (con); cumplir (con).

component [kəmpónənt] *adj. & s.* componente.

compose [kəmpóz] *v.* componer; **to** — **oneself** sosegarse, serenarse, calmarse.

composed [kəmpózd] *adj.* compuesto; tranquilo, sereno, sosegado; **to be** — **of** estar compuesto de, componerse de, constar de.

composer [kəmpózə] *s.* compositor; autor.

composite [kəmpázɪt] *adj.* compuesto; *s.* compuesto; mezcla.

composition [kampəzíʃən] *s.* composición; arreglo; compuesto.

composure [kəmpóʒə] *s.* compostura, calma, serenidad.

compound [kámpaund] *adj. & s.* compuesto; [kampáund] *v.* componer; mezclar, combinar; **to** — **interest** calcular el interés compuesto.

comprehend [kamprɪhénd] *v.* comprender; abarcar, abrazar, incluir.

comprehensible [kamprɪhénsəbl] *adj.* comprensible, inteligible.

comprehension [kamprɪhénʃən] *s.* comprensión.

comprehensive [kamprɪhénsɪv] *adj.* comprensivo; inclusivo.

compress [kámpres] *s.* compresa; [kəmprés] *v.* comprimir, apretar, condensar.

compression [kəmpréʃən] *s.* compresión.

comprise [kəmpráɪz] *v.* comprender, abarcar, incluir, abrazar; constar de.

compromise [kámprəmaɪz] *s.* compromiso; arreglo; avenencia; término medio; *v.* comprometer; avenirse, transigir, *Am.* transar.

comptroller [kəntrólə] *s.* interventor, *Am.* contralor.

compulsion [kəmpʌlʃən] *s.* compulsión, coacción.

compulsory [kəmpʌlsərɪ] *adj.* obligatorio.

computation [kampjətéʃən] *s.* cómputo, cálculo.

compute [kəmpjút] *v.* computar.

comrade [kámræd] *s.* camarada, compañero.

concave [kankév] *adj.* cóncavo.

conceal [kənsíl] *v.* encubrir, ocultar, esconder.

concealment [kənsílmənt] *s.* encubrimiento.

concede [kənsíd] *v.* conceder; otorgar; admitir, reconocer.

conceit [kənsít] *s.* presunción, amor propio, vanagloria; concepto, agudeza.

conceited [kənsítɪd] *adj.* presuntuoso, presumido, vanidoso, engreído.

conceivable [kənsívəbl] *adj.* concebible, imaginable, comprensible.

conceive [kənsív] *v.* concebir; imaginar.

concentrate [kánsn̩tret] *v.* concentrar(se), reconcentrar(se).

concentration [kansn̩tréʃən] *s.* concentración; reconcentración.

concept [kánsept] *s.* concepto, idea; opinión.

conception [kənsépʃən] *s.* concepción; concepto, idea.

concern [kənsɜ́n] *s.* compañía, negociación; negocio, ocupación; establecimiento mercantil; interés; cuidado, preocupación; **to be of no** — no ser de consecuencia; *v.* concernir, importar, interesar; preocupar; **in all that** -**s him** en cuanto le atañe, en cuanto le concierne.

concerned [kənsɜ́nd] *adj.* interesado; preocupado, intranquilo, inquieto, ansioso; **to be** — **about** interesarse por, preocuparse por; **as far as I am** — por lo que me concierne, por lo que me toca, en cuanto a mí me atañe.

concerning [kənsɜ́nɪŋ] *prep.* tocante a, respecto a, acerca de.

concert [kánsɜt] *s.* concierto; [kənsɜ́t] *v.* concertar, arreglar (*un plan*).

concession [kənséʃən] *s.* concesión.

conciliate [kənsílɪet] *v.* conciliar, poner en armonía; ganar la voluntad de.

concise [kənsáɪs] *adj.* conciso, sucinto.

conciseness [kənsáɪsnɪs] *s.* concisión, brevedad.

conclude [kənklúd] *v.* concluir; acabar, terminar; deducir; decidir.

conclusion [kənklúʒən] *s.* conclusión.

conclusive [kənklúsɪv] *adj.* conclusivo, concluyente.

concoct [kənkákt] *v.* confeccionar; preparar *(combinando diversos ingredientes)*; inventar, urdir.

concoction [kənkákʃən] *s.* cocimiento, menjurje; mezcla.

concord [kánkɔrd] *s.* concordia, conformidad, acuerdo; convenio, pacto.

concrete [kankrít] *adj.* concreto; de hormigón, de cemento; *s.* hormigón, cemento, *Am.* concreto.

concur [kənkɔ́] *v.* estar de acuerdo, ser del mismo parecer; unirse.

condemn [kəndém] *v.* condenar; **to — a building** condenar un edificio.

condemnation [kandemnéʃən] *s.* condenación.

condensation [kandɛnséʃən] *s.* condensación; resumen, compendio.

condense [kəndéns] *v.* condensar(se).

condescend [kandɪsénd] *v.* condescender.

condescension [kandɪsénʃən] *s.* condescendencia.

condiment [kándəmənt] *s.* condimento.

condition [kəndíʃən] *s.* condición; estado; nota o calificación provisional; **on — that** a condición de que, con tal que; *v.* acondicionar; poner en buena condición; estipular; reprobar provisionalmente *(a un estudiante)*.

conditional [kəndíʃən] *adj.* condicional.

condole [kəndól] *v.* condolerse; **to — with** dar el pésame a; consolar a.

condolence [kəndóləns] *s.* pésame.

conduce [kəndjús] *v.* conducir.

conducive [kəndjúsɪv] *adj.* conducente.

conduct [kándʌkt] *s.* conducta; comportamiento, proceder; dirección, manejo; [kəndʌ́kt] *v.* conducir; dirigir; manejar; **to — oneself well** portarse bien.

conductor [kəndʌ́ktə] *s.* conductor; guía; **orchestra —** director de orquesta; **train —** revisor; cobrador, *Am.* conductor.

conduit [kándɪt] *s.* conducto; caño; cañería, tubería.

cone [kon] *s.* cono; **paper —** cucurucho; **pine —** piña.

confection [kənfékʃən] *s.* confección; confitura; confite, dulce.

confectionery [kənfékʃənɪ] *s.* confitería; dulcería; confites, dulces.

confederacy [kənfédərəsɪ] *s.* confederación.

confederate [kənfédərɪt] *adj. & s.* confederado; [kənfédəret] *v.* confederar(se).

confederation [kənfɛdəréʃən] *s.* confederación.

confer [kənfɔ́] *v.* conferir, conceder; conferenciar, consultar.

conference [kánfərəns] *s.* conferencia; consulta, junta, sesión.

confess [kənfés] *v.* confesar(se); reconocer, admitir.

confession [kənféʃən] *s.* confesión.

confessional [kənféʃən] *s.* confesionario.

confessor [kənfésə] *s.* confesor.

confidant [kanfədǽnt] *s.* confidente.

confide [kənfáid] *v.* confiar; fiar.

confidence [kánfədəns] *s.* confianza; confidencia; **— game** estafa; **— man** estafador.

confident [kánfədənt] *adj.* confiado; seguro, cierto; **-ly** *adv.* confiadamente, con toda seguridad.

confidential [kanfədénʃəl] *adj.* confidencial; íntimo; secreto; **-ly** *adv.* en confianza.

confine [kánfain] *s.* confín; [kənfáin] *v.* confinar; encerrar; **to — oneself to** limitarse a; **to be -ed in bed** estar encamado, guardar cama.

confinement [kənfáinmənt] *s.* encerramiento; encierro; prisión, encarcelación.

confirm [kənfɔ́m] *v.* confirmar.

confirmation [kanfəméʃən] *s.* confirmación.

confiscate [kánfɪsket] *v.* confiscar.

conflagration [kanfləgréʃən] *s.* conflagración, incendio.

conflict [kánflɪkt] *s.* conflicto, oposición, choque; lucha, combate; [kənflíkt] *v.* chocar, oponerse, estar en conflicto.

conform [kənfɔ́rm] *v.* conformar(se).

conformity [kənfɔ́rmətɪ] *s.* conformidad.

confound [kanfáund] *v.* confundir, perturbar, desconcertar, aturdir; **— it!** ¡caramba!

confront [kənfrʌ́nt] *v.* confrontar; carear, poner cara a cara *(a dos reos)*; encararse con, afrontar, hacer frente a, arrostrar.

confuse [kənfjúz] *v.* confundir; trastornar; embrollar; desconcertar.

confused [kənfjúzd] *adj.* confuso; revuelto; desconcertado, perplejo; **to become —** confundirse; desconcertarse.

confusing [kənfjúzɪŋ] *adj.* confuso, revuelto; desconcertante.

confusion [kənfjúʒən] *s.* confusión; desorden; tumulto; perplejidad.

congeal [kəndʒíl] *v.* congelar(se), helar(se), cuajar(se).

congenial [kəndʒínjəl] *adj.* congenial;

simpático; **to be — with** congeniar con, simpatizar con.

congestion [kəndʒéstʃən] s. congestión; aglomeración.

conglomeration [kənglɑməréʃən] s. aglomeración.

congratulate [kəngrǽtʃələt] v. congratular, felicitar, dar el parabién.

congratulation [kəngrætʃəléʃən] s. congratulación, felicitación, parabién, enhorabuena.

congregate [kɑ́ŋgrɪget] v. congregar(se), juntar(se), reunir(se).

congregation [kɑŋgrigéʃən] s. congregación; asamblea, reunión; colección, agregado; fieles, feligreses (de una iglesia).

congress [kɑ́ŋgrəs] s. congreso; asamblea.

congressional [kəngréʃənl] adj. perteneciente al congreso.

congressman [kɑ́ŋgrəsmən] s. congresista, diputado, representante.

conjecture [kəndʒéktʃə] s. conjetura, suposición; v. conjeturar, suponer.

conjugate [kɑ́ndʒəget] v. conjugar.

conjugation [kɑndʒəgéʃən] s. conjugación.

conjunction [kəndʒʌ́ŋkʃən] s. conjunción.

conjure [kʌ́ndʒə] v. conjurar; **to — up** evocar; [kəndʒúr] rogar, implorar.

connect [kənékt] v. conectar; unir(se), juntar(se); enlazar(se); relacionar(se); acoplar.

connection [kənékʃən] s. conexión; enlace; vínculo; unión; relación; **-s** parientes; amigos, amistades.

conniption [kənípʃən] s. pataleta; **to have a —** darle a uno una pataleta.

connive [kənáɪv] v. conspirar; disimular; hacerse cómplice.

connoisseur [kɑnəsʒ́] s. conocedor, perito.

conquer [kɑ́ŋkə] v. conquistar; vencer.

conqueror [kɑ́ŋkərə] s. conquistador; vencedor.

conquest [kɑ́ŋkwest] s. conquista.

conscience [kɑ́nʃəns] s. conciencia.

conscientious [kɑnʃiénʃəs] adj. concienzudo.

conscious [kɑ́nʃəs] adj. consciente; sabedor; **-ly** adv. conscientemente; a sabiendas.

consciousness [kɑ́nʃəsnɪs] s. conciencia, estado consciente; **to lose —** perder el sentido o conocimiento.

conscript [kɑnskrípt] v. reclutar; [kɑ́nskrɪpt] s. recluta.

consecrate [kɑ́nsɪkret] v. consagrar; dedicar.

consecration [kɑnsɪkréʃən] s. consagración; dedicación.

consecutive [kənsékjətɪv] adj. consecutivo.

consent [kənsént] s. consentimiento; permiso, asentimiento; v. consentir; permitir, asentir.

consequence [kɑ́nsəkwens] s. consecuencia.

consequent [kɑ́nsəkwent] adj. consecuente; consiguiente; s. consecuente, consiguiente, consecuencia; **-ly** adv. por consiguiente, por consecuencia.

conservation [kɑnsəvéʃən] s. conservación; preservación.

conservative [kənsʒ́vətɪv] adj. conservador; conservativo; s. conservador.

conservatory [kənsʒ́vatorɪ] s. conservatorio; invernadero.

conserve [kənsʒ́v] s. conserva, dulce; v. conservar; preservar.

consider [kənsídə] v. considerar.

considerable [kənsídərəbl] adj. considerable; cuantioso; **considerably** adv. considerablemente; **considerably older** bastante más viejo.

considerate [kənsídərɪt] adj. considerado.

consideration [kənsɪdəréʃən] s. consideración; respeto; importancia; remuneración; **in — of** en atención a, teniendo en cuenta, en razón de, en vista de.

considering [kənsídərɪŋ] prep. en razón de, en vista de; en atención a, en consideración de.

consign [kənsáɪn] v. consignar; enviar; entregar.

consist [kənsíst] v. consistir (en); constar (de).

consistency [kənsístənsɪ] s. consecuencia; consistencia, firmeza, solidez.

consistent [kənsístənt] adj. consecuente, lógico; compatible; consistente, coherente.

consolation [kɑnsəléʃən] s. consolación; consuelo.

console [kənsól] v. consolar.

consolidate [kənsɑ́lədet] v. consolidar(se); unir(se), combinar(se).

consonant [kɑ́nsənənt] adj. consonante; conforme; s. consonante.

consort [kɑ́nsərt] s. consorte; [kənsɔ́rt] v. **to — with** asociarse con.

conspicuous [kɑnspíkjʊəs] adj. conspicuo, notorio; manifiesto, sobresaliente.

conspiracy [kənspírəsɪ] s. conspiración, conjuración.

conspirator [kənspírətə] s. conspirador,

conjurado.

conspire [kənspáɪr] v. conspirar; tramar, maquinar.

constable [kánstəb]] s. alguacil, policía; condestable (*título*).

constancy [kánstənsɪ] s. constancia.

constant [kánstənt] adj. constante; s. constante, cantidad constante; **-ly** adv. constantemente, continuamente, siempre; a menudo.

constellation [kanstəléʃən] s. constelación.

consternation [kanstənéʃən] s. consternación.

constipate [kánstəpet] v. estreñir.

constipation [kanstəpéʃən] s. estreñimiento.

constituent [kənstítʃuənt] adj. constituyente; constitutivo; componente; s. componente, elemento; elector, votante.

constitute [kánstətjut] v. constituir; componer; establecer.

constitution [kanstətjúʃən] s. constitución.

constitutional [kanstətjúʃən]] adj. constitucional; s. paseo a pie, caminata (*para hacer ejercicio*).

constrain [kənstrén] v. constreñir; obligar, forzar; apretar, comprimir.

construct [kənstrʌ́kt] v. construir, fabricar.

construction [kənstrʌ́kʃən] s. construcción; estructura; interpretación.

constructive [kənstrʌ́ktɪv] adj. constructivo; de utilidad positiva; provechoso.

construe [kənstrú] v. interpretar, explicar.

consul [kánsḷ] s. cónsul.

consulate [kánsḷɪt] s. consulado.

consult [kənsʌ́lt] v. consultar.

consultation [kansḷtéʃən] s. consulta.

consume [kənsúm] v. consumir; gastar; perder (*el tiempo*).

consumer [kənsúmə] s. consumidor.

consummate [kánsəmet] v. consumar, completar; [kənsʌ́mɪt] adj. consumado, perfecto, completo.

consumption [kənsʌ́mpʃən] s. consumo, gasto; consunción; tisis, tuberculosis.

consumptive [kənsʌ́mptɪv] adj. tísico.

contact [kántækt] s. contacto; v. tocar; poner(se) en contacto con; estar en contacto con.

contagion [kəntédʒən] s. contagio.

contagious [kəntédʒəs] adj. contagioso.

contain [kəntén] v. contener; encerrar; tener cabida para; reprimir, refrenar; **to — oneself** centenerse, refrenarse.

container [kənténə] s. envase, caja, recipiente.

contaminate [kəntǽmənet] v. contaminar, viciar, inficionar.

contemplate [kántəmplet] v. contemplar; meditar; tener la intención de; proyectar.

contemplation [kantəmpléʃən] s. contemplación; meditación; intención, propósito.

contemporary [kəntémpərerɪ] adj. contemporáneo; coetáneo.

contempt [kəntémpt] s. desdén, menosprecio; desprecio; **— of court** contumacia.

contemptible [kəntémptəb]] adj. despreciable, vil.

contemptuous [kəntémptʃuəs] adj. desdeñoso.

contend [kənténd] v. contender; competir; argüir; altercar; sostener, afirmar.

content [kántent] s. contenido; sustancia; capacidad, volumen; **-s** contenido; **table of -s** tabla de materias, índice general.

content [kəntént] adj. contento; satisfecho; s. contento; satisfacción; **to one's heart's —** a pedir de boca; hasta saciarse; a su entera satisfacción; v. contentar; satisfacer.

contented [kənténtɪd] adj. contento, satisfecho.

contention [kənténʃən] s. contención, contienda, disputa, controversia; tema, argumento; aseveración.

contentment [kənténtmənt] s. contentamiento, contento.

contest [kántest] s. concurso, certamen; debate; contienda; torneo; [kəntést] v. contender; disputar; luchar por; **to — with** competir con.

context [kántekst] s. contexto.

contiguous [kəntígjuəs] adj. contiguo; adyacente.

continent [kántənənt] s. continente; adj. continente, casto, moderado.

continental [kantənént]] adj. & s. continental.

contingency [kəntíndʒənsɪ] s. contingencia, eventualidad.

contingent [kəntíndʒənt] adj. & s. contingente.

continual [kəntínjuəl] adj. continuo; frecuente; **-ly** adv. de continuo, continuamente, frecuentemente.

continuance [kəntínjuəns] s. continuación; aplazamiento.

continuation [kəntɪnjuéʃən] s. continuación.

continue [kəntínju] v. continuar.

continuity [kɑntənúetɪ] *s.* continuidad.

continuous [kəntínjʊəs] *adj.* continuo, sin parar, sin cesar.

contortion [kɛntɔ́rʃən] *s.* contorsión.

contour [kɑ́ntʊr] *s.* contorno; perímetro.

contraband [kɑ́ntrəbænd] *s.* contrabando.

contract [kɑ́ntɹækt] *s.* contrato, pacto, convenio; contrata; **marriage — es**ponsales; [kəntrǽkt] *v.* contratar; contraer(se), encoger(se); **to — an ill**ness contraer una enfermedad; **to — the brows** fruncir las cejas.

contraction [kɛntrǽkʃən] *s.* contracción.

contractor [kɑntrǽktə] *s.* contratista.

contradict [kɑntrədíkt] *v.* contradecir; contrariar.

contradiction [kɑntrədíkʃən] *s.* contradicción; contrariedad.

contradictory [kɑntrədíktərɪ] *adj.* contradictorio; opuesto, contrario.

contrary [kɑ́ntrerɪ] *adj.* contrario; opuesto; testarudo, obstinado; *s.* contrario; **on the —** al contrario.

contrast [kɑ́ntræst] *s.* contraste; [kəntrǽst] *v.* contrastar.

contribute [kəntríbjʊt] *v.* contribuir.

contribution [kɑntrəbjúʃən] *s.* contribución; aportación; cuota; dádiva.

contributor [kəntríbjətə] *s.* contribuidor; colaborador.

contrite [kɑ́ntraɪt] *adj.* contrito.

contrivance [kɛntrɑ́ɪvəns] *s.* traza, maquinación; artificio, invención; designio; artefacto, aparato, máquina.

contrive [kəntrɑ́ɪv] *v.* tramar, maquinar, inventar, idear; proyectar; **to — to** buscar el medio de, tratar de, procurar.

control [kəntróɫ] *s.* mando, manejo, dirección; freno, restricción; regulador; *Am.* control, **—s** mandos, controles; **stick** palanca (*de un aeroplano*); **to** lose **— of one's** temper perder la paciencia; *v.* gobernar, manejar, *Am.* controlar; regular, regularizar; restringir; contener, reprimir; tener a raya; **to — oneself** contenerse, dominarse.

controller [kəntrólə] *s.* interventor, registrador, *Am.* contralor, *Am.* controlador; regulador; aparato de manejo y control.

controversy [kɑ́ntrəvɜsɪ] *s.* controversia, debate, disputa.

conundrum [kənʌ́ndrəm] *s.* adivinanza, acertijo.

convalesce [kɑnvəlés] *v.* convalescer.

convene [kənvín] *v.* juntar, convocar; reunirse.

convenience [kənvínjəns] *s.* conveniencia, comodidad; **at one's —** cuando

le convenga a uno, cuando tenga oportunidad, cuando buenamente pueda.

convenient [kənvínjənt] *adj.* conveniente; oportuno; cómodo; a propósito; **-ly** *adv.* convenientemente, cómodamente.

convent [kɑ́nvent] *s.* convento.

convention [kənvénʃən] *s.* convención; congreso, asamblea; convenio; costumbre, regla.

conventional [kənvénʃənl] *adj.* convencional; tradicional.

converge [kənvɜ́dʒ] *v.* converger o convergir.

conversant [kɑ́nvəsənt] : **— with** versado en.

conversation [kɑnvəséʃən] *s.* conversación.

converse [kənvɜ́s] *v.* conversar, hablar, platicar.

conversion [kənvɜ́ʃən] *s.* conversión.

convert [kɑ́nvɜt] *s.* converso, persona convertida; catecúmeno (*de una reciente*); [kənvɜ́t] *v.* convertir(se).

convex [kɑnvéks] *adj.* convexo.

convey [kənvé] *v.* llevar; transportar; transferir, traspasar; transmitir; comunicar; **to — thanks** expresar agradecimiento, dar las gracias.

conveyance [kənvéəns] *s.* vehículo; transporte; transmisión; entrega; comunicación; traspaso; escritura de propiedad o traspaso.

convict [kɑ́nvɪkt] *s.* presidiario; reo; [kənvíkt] *v.* convencer (*de un delito*), declarar culpable; probar la culpabilidad de.

conviction [kənvíkʃən] *s.* convicción; convencimiento; prueba de culpabilidad.

convince [kənvíns] *v.* convencer.

convincing [kənvínsɪŋ] *adj.* convincente.

convocation [kɑnvokéʃən] *s.* convocación; asamblea.

convoke [kənvók] *v.* convocar.

convoy [kɑ́nvɔɪ] *s.* convoy, escolta, guardia; [kənvɔ́ɪ] *v.* convoyar.

convulsion [kənvʌ́lʃən] *s.* convulsión, agitación.

coo [ku] *s.* arrullo; *v.* arrullar.

cook [kʊk] *s.* cocinero, cocinera; *v.* cocinar, guisar; cocer; **to — up a plan** urdir un plan.

cookery [kʊ́kərɪ] *s.* cocina, arte de cocinar.

cookie, cooky [kʊ́kɪ] *s.* bizcochito, bollito.

cooking [kʊ́kɪŋ] *s.* cocina, arte culinaria; **— stove** cocina de gas, cocina eléctrica, estufa; **— utensils** batería de cocina, trastos de cocina.

cool [kul] *adj.* fresco; frío, indiferente; calmo, sereno; *s.* fresco, frescura; *v.* refrescar; enfriar; templar, calmar; **to — off** enfriarse; calmarse.

coolness [kúlnıs] *s.* fresco, frescura; frialdad, indiferencia.

coon [kun] *s.* coatí (*cuadrúpedo carnívoro*); negro; **a -'s age** una eternidad, mucho tiempo.

coop [kup] *s.* jaula; **chicken —** gallinero; *v.* enjaular; **to — up** encerrar.

cooperate [koápəret] *v.* cooperar.

cooperation [koapəréʃən] *s.* cooperación.

cooperative [koápəretıv] *adj.* cooperativo; *s.* cooperativa, sociedad cooperativa.

coördinate [koórdnet] *v.* coordinar; [koórdnıt] *adj.* coordinado.

coördination [koordnéʃən] *s.* coordinación.

cop [kap] *s.* polizonte, policía.

cope [kop] *v.* **to — with** tener suficiente fuerza para; **I cannot — with this** no puedo con esto, no puedo dar abasto a esto.

copious [kópıəs] *adj.* copioso, abundante.

copper [kápə] *s.* cobre; polizonte, policía; **— coin** moneda de cobre, centavo; **— kettle** marmita o caldera de cobre; *adj.* cobrizo.

copy [kápı] *s.* copia; ejemplar (*de un libro*); manuscrito (*para el impresor*); *v.* copiar; imitar; remedar.

copyright [kápıraıt] *s.* derecho de propiedad literaria; *v.* registrar, obtener patente de propiedad literaria.

coquette [kokét] *s.* coqueta.

coral [kórəl] *s.* coral; *adj.* coralino, de coral.

cord [kord] *s.* cuerda; cordón, cordel; cuerda (*medida de leña*); tendón; **-s pantalones de pana; spinal —** espinazo, espina dorsal.

cordial [kórdʒəl] *adj.* & *s.* cordial.

corduroy [kórdəróı] *s.* pana; **-s pantalones de pana; — road** camino de troncos o maderos.

core [kor] *s.* corazón, centro; núcleo; esencia; *v.* cortar el centro o corazón de; despepitar (*una manzana*).

cork [kork] *s.* corcho; tapón; **— tree** alcornoque; *v.* tapar con corcho.

corkscrew [kórkskru] *s.* tirabuzón, sacacorchos; *adj.* espiral, de forma espiral.

corn [korn] *s.* maíz; grano, cereal; callo (*de los pies o manos*); **— bread** pan de maíz; **— meal** harina de maíz; *v.* salar, curar, acecinar.

corned beef [kórnd bif] *s.* carne de vaca curada (*en salmuera y salitre*).

corner [kórnə] *s.* rincón; ángulo; esquina; rinconada; monopolio; **—stone** piedra angular; **— table (— shelf, — bracket)** rinconera; *v.* arrinconar; acorralar; acaparar, monopolizar.

cornet [kornét] *s.* corneta.

cornfield [kórnfıld] *s.* maizal, *Am.* milpa.

cornice [kórnıs] *s.* cornisa.

coronation [korənéʃən] *s.* coronación.

coronet [kóronıt] *s.* coronilla, guirnalda.

corporal [kórpərəl] *adj.* corporal; corpóreo; *s.* cabo (*militar*).

corporation [korpəréʃən] *s.* corporación; sociedad mercantil.

corps [kor] *s.* cuerpo (*grupo organizado*); **air —** cuerpo de aviación; **army —** cuerpo de ejército.

corpse [korps] *s.* cadáver.

corpulent [kórpjələnt] *adj.* corpulento.

corpuscle [kórpəs] *s.* corpúsculo.

corral [korél] *s.* corral; *v.* acorralar.

correct [kərékt] *v.* corregir; *adj.* correcto; **it is —** está bien; **-ly** *adv.* correctamente; **-ly done** bien hecho.

correction [kərékʃən] *s.* corrección.

correctness [kəréktnıs] *s.* corrección.

corrector [kəréktə] *s.* corregidor, corrector.

correlate [kórəlet] *v.* correlacionar.

correspond [kərəspánd] *v.* corresponder; corresponderse, cartearse, escribirse.

correspondence [korəspándəns] *s.* correspondencia.

correspondent [korəspándənt] *adj.* correspondiente; *s.* correspondiente; corresponsal.

corresponding [korəspándıŋ] *adj.* correspondiente; conforme.

corridor [kórədə] *s.* corredor, pasillo, pasadizo.

corroborate [kərábəret] *v.* corroborar.

corrode [kəród] *v.* corroer(se).

corrupt [kərÁpt] *adj.* corrompido; perverso, depravado; **to become —** corromperse; *v.* corromper; pervertir; sobornar.

corruption [kərÁpʃən] *s.* corrupción; soborno; descomposición.

corset [kórsıt] *s.* corsé.

cosmetic [kazmétık] *adj.* & *s.* cosmético.

cosmopolitan [kazməpálətn] *adj.* cosmopolita.

cost [kost] *s.* coste, costa o costo; **at all -s** a toda costa; **to sell at —** vender al costo; *v.* costar; *pret.* & *p.p.* de **to cost.**

costly [kóstlı] *adj.* costoso.

costume [kástjum] *s.* vestuario, traje,

vestido; atavío; indumentaria.

cot [kɑt] *s.* catre; **folding** — catre de tijera.

cottage [kátɪdʒ] *s.* casita, caseta; casa de campo; — **cheese** requesón.

cotton [kátṇ] *s.* algodón; —**seed** semilla de algodón; — **wool** algodón en rama; — **yarn** hilaza.

couch [kautʃ] *s.* canapé, diván; *v.* expresar; estar escondido o en acecho; **-ed in difficult language** expresado en lenguaje difícil.

cough [kɔf] *s.* tos; — **drop** pastilla para la tos; **whooping** — tosferina; *v.* toser; **to — up** expectorar.

could [kud] *pret. del. v. defect.* can.

council [káunsḷ] *s.* concilio; consejo; **city** — consejo municipal.

councilman [káunsḷmən] *s.* concejal.

councilor [káunsḷə] *s.* concejal.

counsel [káunsḷ] *s.* consejo; parecer, dictamen; abogado consultor; *v.* aconsejar; recomendar.

counselor [káunsḷə] *s.* consejero; abogado consultor.

count [kaunt] *s.* cuenta, cálculo; cómputo; cargo, acusación; conde; *v.* contar; valer, tener importancia; **to — on** contar con, confiar en.

countenance [káuntənəns] *s.* semblante, aspecto; **to give — to** favorecer, apoyar; aprobar; *v.* aprobar; favorecer, apoyar; tolerar.

counter [káuntə] *s.* contador; mostrador; tablero; ficha; *adj.* contrario, opuesto; *adv.* al contrario; **to run — to** ser contrario a, oponerse a; *v.* oponerse; contradecir; **to — a blow** devolver un golpe.

counteract [kauntərǽkt] *v.* contrarrestar, neutralizar.

counterbalance [kauntəbǽləns] *v.* contrapesar; equilibrar; [káuntəbæləns] *s.* contrapeso.

counterfeit [káuntəfɪt] *s.* falsificación; *adj.* falso; falsificado, falseado; contrahecho; — **money** moneda falsa; *v.* contrahacer, falsificar, falsear.

countermand [káuntəmænd] *s.* contraorden, contramando, revocación, cancelación; [kauntəmǽnd] *v.* contramandar, revocar, cancelar.

counterpart [káuntəpart] *s.* contraparte.

counterpoise [káuntəpoɪz] *s.* contrapeso; *v.* contrapesar.

countess [káuntɪs] *s.* condesa.

countless [káuntlɪs] *adj.* incontable, innumerable.

country [kántrɪ] *s.* país; tierra; patria; campo; *adj.* campestre; rural; rústico;

campesino.

countryman [kántrɪmən] *s.* compatriota, paisano; campesino, *Am.* ranchero, *Am.* jíbaro, *Am.* guajiro.

countryside [kántrɪsaɪd] *s.* campiña, campo.

county [káuntɪ] *s.* condado (*división de un estado*).

coupé [kupé, kup] *s.* cupé.

couple [kʌpḷ] *s.* par; pareja; *v.* parear; unir; acoplar.

couplet [kʌplɪt] *s.* copla, versos pareados.

coupling [kʌplɪŋ] *s.* unión, conexión; acoplamiento; enganche.

coupon [kúpαn] *s.* cupón; talón.

courage [kɜ́rɪdʒ] *s.* coraje, ánimo, valor.

courageous [kərédʒəs] *adj.* valeroso, valiente, animoso.

courier [kúrɪə] *s.* mensajero.

course [kors] *s.* curso; rumbo, trayecto; marcha, progreso; método; asignatura; plato (*de una comida*); — **of conduct** conducta, proceder; **golf** — campo o cancha de golf; **race** — hipódromo, pista; **in the — of a year** en el transcurso de un año; **of** — claro, por supuesto; **to follow a straight** — seguir una línea recta.

court [kort] *s.* patio; plazuela, plazoleta; juzgado, tribunal de justicia; corte; **tennis** — cancha para tenis; — **plaster** tela adhesiva, tafetán inglés, esparadrapo; **to pay** — to hacer la corte a, cortejar, galantear; *v.* cortejar; galantear; buscar; **to — danger** exponerse al peligro.

courteous [kɜ́rtɪəs] *adj.* cortés.

courtesy [kɜ́rtɪsɪ] *s.* cortesía; fineza, atención; reverencia.

courtier [kórtɪə] *s.* cortesano, palaciego.

court-martial [kórtmárʃəl] *s.* consejo de guerra; *v.* someter a consejo de guerra.

courtship [kórtʃɪp] *s.* cortejo, galanteo.

courtyard [kórtjard] *s.* patio.

cousin [kʌ́zṇ] *s.* primo; prima; **first** — primo hermano, primo carnal.

cove [kov] *s.* cala, ensenada.

covenant [kʌ́vənənt] *s.* convenio, pacto; contrato.

cover [kʌ́və] *s.* cubierta, tapa, tapadera; cobija; cobertor; encuadernación; envoltura; funda; albergue, abrigo; **table** — tapete; **to send under separate** — enviar por separado; *v.* cubrir; tapar; encubrir; abrigar, proteger; abarcar; **to — a distance** recorrer una distancia.

covering [kʌ́vərɪŋ] *s.* cubierta, cobertura; envoltura; cobija, abrigo.

covet [kʌ́vɪt] *v.* codiciar; ambicionar.

covetous [kʌ́vɪtəs] *adj.* codicioso.

cow [kau] s. vaca; hembra (de elefante y otros cuadrúpedos); v. atemorizar, acobardar.

coward [káuəd] adj. & s. cobarde.

cowardice [káuədɪs] s. cobardía.

cowardliness [káuədlɪnɪs] s. cobardía.

cowardly [káuədlɪ] adj. cobarde; adv. cobardemente.

cowboy [káubɔɪ] s. vaquero, Am. gaucho.

cower [káuə] v. agacharse (de miedo o vergüenza), achicarse, encogerse (de miedo), acobardarse.

cowhide [káuhaɪd] s. cuero de vaca, vaqueta.

cowl [kaul] s. capucha.

coy [kɔɪ] adj. recatado, esquivo, modesto; tímido; gazmoño.

coyote [káɪot, kaɪóti] s. coyote.

cozy [kózɪ] adj. cómodo y abrigado; cómodo y agradable.

crab [kræb] s. cangrejo; cascarrabias (persona de mal genio); — **apple** manzana silvestre.

crack [kræk] s. raja, grieta, rendija; crujido; estallido; trueno, estampido; golpe; pulla, chanza; **at the — of dawn** al romper el alba; adj. excelente; v. rajar(se), hender(se), agrietarse; crujir; estallar; **to — a joke** soltar un chiste; **to — nuts** cascar nueces.

cracked [krækt] adj. agrietado, rajado; quebrado; chiflado, loco.

cracker [krækə] s. galleta.

crackle [krækl] s. crujido; crepitación; chasquido; v. crujir, crepitar.

cradle [krédl] s. cuna.

craft [kræft] s. maña, destreza; astucia, artificio, cautela; arte, oficio; embarcación; embarcaciones.

craftsman [kræftsmən] s. artesano, artífice.

crafty [kræftɪ] adj. mañoso, astuto, cauteloso, taimado.

crag [kræg] s. risco, peñasco.

cram [kræm] v. rellenar; atestar; atracar(se), hartar(se); engullir.

cramp [kræmp] s. calambre; grapa; v. comprimir, apretar, estrechar; afianzar, sujetar (con grapa).

cranberry [krænberɪ] s. arándano.

crane [kren] s. grulla (ave); grúa (máquina para levantar pesos); v. **to — one's neck** estirar el cuello.

cranium [krénɪəm] s. cráneo.

crank [kræŋk] s. cigüeña, manubrio, manija, manivela; **he is a —** es un maniático; v. voltear el manubrio o la cigüeña.

cranky [kræŋkɪ] adj. cascarrabias; maniático; enojadizo.

cranny [krænɪ] s. grieta, rendija.

crape [krep] s. crespón; crespón negro.

crash [kræʃ] s. estallido, golpazo, estruendo; choque; fracaso; quiebra, bancarrota; v. estrellar(se); estallar; chocar; **to — an airplane** aterrizar de golpe un aeroplano; **to — into** chocar con, estrellarse contra.

crate [kret] s. canasto, cesta, jaula (para el transporte de mercancías, etc.); Am. huacal; v. embalar en jaula.

crater [krétə] s. cráter.

cravat [krəvǽt] s. corbata.

crave [krev] v. ansiar, anhelar, apetecer; **to — mercy (pardon)** pedir misericordia (perdón).

crawl [krɔl] s. marcha lenta; natación a la marinera; v. arrastrarse; gatear, andar a gatas; marchar lentamente; **to be -ing with ants** hormiguear, estar lleno de hormigas.

crayon [kréon] s. lápiz de color, Am. creyón; pastel; tiza, yeso.

craze [krez] s. manía, locura; moda; antojo; v. enloquecer.

crazy [krézɪ] adj. loco; trastornado; **to go —** volverse loco, perder el juicio.

creak [krik] s. crujido, rechino, rechinamiento; v. crujir, rechinar.

cream [krim] s. crema; nata; — **of tomato soup** puré de tomate; **cold —** crema cosmética; **ice —** helado; v. desnatar; batir, mezclar (azúcar y mantequilla); preparar (legumbres) con salsa de crema.

creamery [krímərɪ] s. lechería, quesería, Am. mantequillería.

creamy [krímɪ] adj. natoso; lleno de crema o nata.

crease [kris] s. pliegue; arruga; v. plegar, hacer pliegues; arrugar.

create [krɪét] v. crear.

creation [krɪéʃən] s. creación; obra.

creative [krɪétɪv] adj. creativo, creador.

creator [krɪétə] s. creador.

creature [krítʃə] s. criatura; ser viviente; animalejo.

credence [krídn̩s] s. creencia, crédito.

credentials [krɪdénʃəlz] s. pl. credenciales.

credible [krédəbl] adj. creíble.

credit [krédɪt] s. crédito; buena fama; — **and debit** haber y deber; activo y pasivo; **on —** a crédito, al fiado, a plazo; **to give —** dar crédito, creer; acreditar, abonar; **that does him —** eso le acredita; v. acreditar; abonar en cuenta; creer, dar crédito; atribuir.

creditable [krédɪtəbl] adj. loable.

creditor [krédɪtə] s. acreedor.

credulous [krédʒələs] *adj.* crédulo.

creed [krid] *s.* credo; creencia.

creek [krik, krɪk] *s.* riachuelo, arroyo.

creep [krip] *v.* arrastrarse; gatear, andar a gatas; trepar (*las plantas*); andar lentamente; deslizarse; sentir hormigueo (*en el cuerpo*); *s. pl.* hormigueo; aprensión, horror.

creeper [krípə] *s.* enredadera, planta trepadora.

crepe [krep] = **crape.**

crept [krept] *pret. & p.p. de* to creep.

crescent [krésnt] *adj.* creciente; *s.* luna creciente; media luna (*emblema de turcos y mahometanos*).

crest [krest] *s.* cresta; penacho; copete; cima, cumbre; timbre (*de un escudo de armas*).

crestfallen [kréstfolən] *adj.* cabizbajo, alicaído, abatido.

cretonne [krítən] *s.* cretona.

crevice [krévɪs] *s.* grieta, hendedura.

crew [kru] *s.* tripulación; cuadrilla (*de obreros*); *pret. de* to crow.

crib [krɪb] *s.* camita de niño; pesebre; granero, arcón; armazón (*usado en la construcción de edificios*); traducción o clave fraudulenta (*en un examen*); *v.* enjaular; usar traducción o clave fraudulenta (*en un examen*).

cricket [kríkɪt] *s.* grillo; vilorta (*juego*).

crime [kraɪm] *s.* crimen.

criminal [krímɪnəl] *adj. & s.* criminal.

crimp [krɪmp] *v.* rizar; *s.* rizo.

crimson [krímsŋ] *adj. & s.* carmesí.

cripple [krípl] *s.* cojo, manco; tullido; baldado, inválido; *v.* estropear; mutilar, derrengar; baldar; incapacitar.

crisis [kráɪsɪs] *s.* crisis.

crisp [krɪsp] *adj.* crespo, encrespado; tieso; bien tostado; quebradizo; — answer contestación aguda; — wind brisa refrescante; *v.* encrespar.

criterion [kraɪtírɪən] *s.* criterio.

critic [krítɪk] *s.* crítico; criticón.

critical [krítɪkl] *adj.* crítico; criticador, criticón.

criticism [krítǝsɪzǝm] *s.* crítica; criticismo.

criticize [krítǝsaɪz] *v.* criticar; censurar.

croak [krok] *v.* croar; graznar; *s.* canto de ranas; graznido.

crochet [kroʃé] *s.* labor de gancho; — hook aguja de gancho; *v.* hacer labor de gancho.

crock [krak] *s.* vasija de loza, jarra.

crockery [krókǝrɪ] *s.* loza.

crocodile [krákǝdaɪl] *s.* cocodrilo, *Am.* caimán.

crony [krónɪ] *s.* compadre, compinche,

camarada, compañero.

crook [kruk] *s.* falsario; estafador; maleante, pícaro; curva, vuelta; recodo; gancho; **shepherd's** — cayado; *v.* torcer(se); to — one's arm doblar el brazo o codo.

crooked [krúkɪd] *adj.* torcido; curvo, encorvado, *Am.* chueco; falso, fraudulento.

croon [krun] *v.* cantar "tristes" (*con exagerado patetismo*).

crop [krap] *s.* cosecha; buche (*de ave*); látigo, *Am.* cuarta; — of hair cabellera; *v.* segar; recortar; rapar; to — out aparecer, asomar; to — up brotar, manifestarse inesperadamente.

cross [kros] *s.* cruz; cruce; cruzamiento (*de razas*); mezcla; *v.* cruzar(se); atravesar(se); santiguar(se); encontrarse; contrariar; *adj.* en cruz, cruzado, transversal; malhumorado; **cross-country** try a campo traviesa; **cross-examine** *v.* interrogar, repreguntar; **cross-eyed** bizco; —word puzzle crucigrama.

crossbar [krósbar] *s.* travesaño.

crossing [krósɪŋ] *s.* cruce; cruzamiento; encrucijada, crucero; travesía; **railroad** — cruce; **river** — vado.

crossroad [krósrod] *s.* vía transversal, encrucijada, crucero.

crouch [krautʃ] *v.* agacharse, agazaparse.

crow [kro] *s.* cuervo; canto del gallo; **crow's-foot** pata de gallo (*arrugas en el rabo del ojo*); *v.* cantar (*el gallo*); cacarear; jactarse, hacer alarde.

crowbar [króbar] *s.* barra, palanca de hierro.

crowd [kraud] *s.* muchedumbre; gentío, gente; cuadrilla, pandilla; grupo; *v.* agolparse, apiñar(se); estrujar, empujar.

crowded [kráudɪd] *adj.* atestado, lleno, apiñado.

crown [kraun] *s.* corona; copa (*de sombrero*); cima; *v.* coronar.

crucible [krúsǝbl] *s.* crisol.

crucifix [krúsǝfɪks] *s.* crucifijo.

crucify [krúsǝfaɪ] *v.* crucificar.

crude [krud] *adj.* basto, tosco, rudo; inculto; — oil petróleo crudo; — sugar azúcar bruto, azúcar crudo.

cruel [krúǝl] *adj.* cruel.

cruelty [krúǝltɪ] *s.* crueldad.

cruet [krúɪt] *s.* ampolla (*pequeña vasija de cristal*); vinajera (*para servir vino en la misa*); **oil** — aceitera; **vinegar** — vinagrera.

cruise [kruz] *s.* travesía, viaje por mar; excursión; *v.* navegar.

cruiser [krúzǝ] *s.* crucero (*buque*).

crumb [krʌm] s. migaja; miga; mendrugo; v. desmenuzar, desmigajar.

crumble [krámbl] v. desmenuzar(se); desmoronarse.

crumple [krámpl] v. arrugar(se); ajar, apabullar.

crunch [krʌntʃ] v. crujir; mascullar.

crusade [kruséd] s. cruzada; v. hacer una campaña; hacer una cruzada.

crusader [kruséda] s. cruzado.

crush [krʌʃ] s. compresión, presión; estrujamiento, apiñamiento de gente; v. estrujar; aplastar; majar; subyugar; **to — stone** moler piedra.

crust [krʌst] s. corteza (de pan, queso, etc.); costra; mendrugo; v. encostrarse, cubrir(se) de costra.

crusty [krʌsti] adj. costroso.

crutch [krʌtʃ] s. muleta.

cry [kraɪ] s. grito; lloro, lamento; **a far — from** muy distante de, muy lejos de; v. gritar; llorar; clamar; exclamar; vocear; **to — for help** pedir socorro.

crystal [krístl] s. cristal; **— clear** cristalino.

crystalline [krístlɪn] adj. cristalino.

crystallize [krístlaɪz] v. cristalizar(se).

cub [kʌb] s. cachorro (de oso, tigre, lobo, león); **— reporter** reportero novato.

Cuban [kjúban] adj. & s. cubano.

cube [kjub] s. cubo; **— root** raíz cúbica.

cubic [kjúbɪk] adj. cúbico.

cuckoo [kúku] s. cuco, cuclillo; adj. tocado, chiflado, medio loco.

cucumber [kjúkʌmbə] s. pepino.

cud [kʌd] s. rumia; **to chew the —** rumiar.

cuddle [kʌdl] v. abrazar, tener en brazos; estar abrazados.

cudgel [kʌdʒəl] s. garrote; porra; v. aporrear, apalear.

cue [kju] s. señal, indicación; pie (últimas palabras de un parlamento que sirven de señal en el teatro); **billiard — taco** de billar.

cuff [kʌf] s. puño (de camisa o de vestido); doblez (del pantalón); bofetada; v. abofetear, dar de bofetadas.

culminate [kʌlmənet] v. culminar.

culprit [kʌlprɪt] s. reo, delincuente, culpable.

cult [kʌlt] s. culto; secta religiosa.

cultivate [kʌltəvet] v. cultivar; labrar, barbechar.

cultivated [kʌltəvetɪd] adj. cultivado; culto.

cultivation [kʌltəvéʃən] s. cultivación, cultivo; cultura.

cultivator [kʌltəvetə] s. cultivador; máquina cultivadora.

culture [kʌltʃə] s. cultura; cultivo.

cultured [kʌltʃəd] adj. culto; cultivado.

cumbersome [kámbəsəm] adj. engorroso, embarazoso, incómodo.

cunning [kánɪŋ] adj. astuto, socarrón, sagaz, taimado; diestro; cuco, mono, gracioso; s. astucia, maña, sagacidad.

cup [kʌp] s. taza, pocillo; copa (trofeo).

cupboard [kábəd] s. armario, aparador; alacena.

cur [kɜ] s. perro mestizo, Am. perro chusco; villano, vil, cobarde.

curate [kjúrɪt] s. cura.

curb [kɜb] s. reborde, encintado (de la acera), Am. cordón de la acera; freno, restricción; barbada (del freno de un caballo); brocal de pozo; v. refrenar, reprimir.

curd [kɜd] s. cuajada; v. cuajar(se), coagular(se).

curdle [kɜdl] v. cuajar(se), coagular(se).

cure [kjur] s. cura, curación; remedio; v. curar(se); sanar.

curio [kjúrɪo] s. curiosidad, objeto raro y curioso.

curiosity [kjurɪásəti] s. curiosidad; rareza.

curious [kjúrɪəs] adj. curioso; extraño, raro.

curl [kɜl] s. rizo, bucle; espiral (de humo); v. rizar(se); ensortijar(se); enroscar(se); retorcerse, alzarse en espirales (el humo).

curly [kɜlɪ] adj. rizo, rizoso, rizado, crespo, Am. chino.

currant [kɜənt] s. grosella; **— bush** grosellero.

currency [kɜənsɪ] s. moneda corriente; circulación; **paper — papel** moneda.

current [kɜənt] adj. corriente; común, prevaleciente, en boga; s. corriente.

curse [kɜs] s. maldición; calamidad; v. maldecir.

cursed [kɜst] adj. maldito.

curt [kɜt] adj. corto; brusco.

curtail [kɜtél] v. cercenar; acortar; restringir, reducir.

curtain [kɜtn] s. cortina; telón (de teatro); v. poner cortinas.

curvature [kɜvətʃə] s. curvatura.

curve [kɜv] s. curva; v. encorvar(se), torcer(se); doblar(se).

curved [kɜvd] adj. encorvado; torcido, curvo, corvo, Am. chueco.

cushion [kúʃən] s. cojín; almohadilla, almohadón; amortiguador (para amortiguar un sonido o golpe); v. acojinar; amortiguar (un choque).

custard [kástəd] s. flan, natillas.

custody [kástədɪ] s. custodia, cargo,

cuidado; **to hold in** — custodiar.

custom [kʌ́stəm] s. costumbre, hábito, uso, usanza; **-s** derechos de aduana; **— made** hecho a la medida; **— tailor** maestro sastre.

customary [kʌ́stəmerɪ] adj. acostumbrado, habitual, usual, de costumbre.

customer [kʌ́stəməl] s. parroquiano, cliente, marchante.

customhouse [kʌ́stəmhaʊs] s. aduana; **— official** aduanero; **— mark** marchamo.

cut [kʌt] s. corte (m.); cortadura, Am. cortada; rebanada, tajada, rebaja, reducción (de precios, sueldos); hechura (de un traje); ausencia (de la clase); grabado; **short** — atajo, camino corto; v. cortar; tajar; labrar, tallar; segar; rebajar, reducir (precios, sueldos); negar el saludo a; alzar (los naipes); **to — across** cruzar, atravesar; **to — capers** hacer cabriolas, cabriolar; **to — class** faltar a la clase; **to — out** recortar; excluir; **to be — out for** estar hecho para, tener vocación para; pret.& p.p. de to cut.

cute [[kjut] adj. mono, cuco; astuto.

cuticle [kjútɪk] s. cutícula.

cutlery [kʌ́tlərɪ] s. cuchillería; cuchillos.

cutlet [kʌ́tlɪt] s. chuleta.

cutter [kʌ́tə] s. cortador; máquina para cortar; trineo; **wood** — leñador; **coast guard** — barco guardacostas.

cutting [kʌ́tɪŋ] adj. cortante; penetrante; mordaz, sarcástico.

cycle [sáɪk] s. ciclo.

cyclone [sáɪklon] s. ciclón; huracán.

cylinder [sílɪndə] s. cilindro.

cylindrical [sɪlíndrɪl.] adj. cilíndrico.

cymbal [símbl] s. címbalo, platillo; **to play the -s** tocar los platillos.

cynic [sínɪk] s. cínico.

cynical [sínɪk] adj. cínico.

cynicism [sínəsɪzəm] s. cinismo.

cypress [sáɪprəs] s. ciprés.

D

dad [dæd] s. papá, tata; **daddy** s. papaíto o papacito, tata, tatita, Am. taita.

daffodil [dǽfədɪl] s. narciso.

dagger [dǽgə] s. daga; puñal; **to look -s at** traspasar con la mirada.

daily [délɪ] adj. diario; adv. diariamente; s. diario, periódico.

dainty [déntɪ] adj. delicado, fino, primoroso, exquisito; s. golosina, manjar exquisito.

dairy [dérɪ] s. lechería, vaquería; quesería, quesera.

daisy [dézɪ] s. margarita, maya.

dale [del] s. cañada.

dally [dǽlɪ] v. juguetear; holgazanear; entretenerse, tardar; malgastar el tiempo.

dam [dæm] s. presa, represa; v. represar, estancar.

damage [dǽmɪdʒ] s. daño; perjuicio; avería; **to pay for -s** indemnizar, pagar los daños y perjuicios; v. dañar(se); averiar(se).

dame [dem] s. dama, señora; **old —** vieja.

damn [dæm] v. maldecir; condenar; blasfemar; **— i l !** ¡maldito sea!

damnation [dæmnéʃən] s. condenación, perdición.

damp [dæmp] adj. húmedo; mojado; s. humedad; v. humedecer, mojar.

dampen [dǽmpən] v. mojar, humedecer; desalentar; amortiguar.

dampness [dǽmpnɪs] s. humedad.

damsel [dǽmzl] s. damisela.

dance [dæns] s. baile; danza; **— music** música de baile; v. bailar; danzar.

dancer [dǽnsə] s. bailador; bailarín, bailarina; danzante.

dandelion [dǽndlaɪən] s. diente de león.

dandruff [dǽndrəf] s. caspa.

dandy [dǽndɪ] s. currutaco, majo, afectado; chulo; adj. elegante, excelente.

danger [déndʒə] s. peligro, riesgo.

dangerous [déndʒərəs] adj. peligroso; arriesgado; **-ly** adv. peligrosamente; **-ly ill** gravemente enfermo.

dangle [dǽŋgl] v. pender, colgar, bambolear(se) (en el aire).

dapple(d) [dǽpl(d)] adj. rodado, con manchas (dícese de los caballos);. **dapple-grey** rucio rodado, tordo, tordillo.

dare [der] s. desafío, reto, provocación; **— devil** atrevido, osado; v. atreverse, osar; desafiar.

daring [dérɪŋ] s. atrevimiento, osadía; adj. osado, atrevido, arrojado.

dark [dɑrk] adj. obscuro; sombrío; **— horse** caballo desconocido (que gana inesperadamente la carrera); candidato nombrado inesperadamente; **— secret** secreto profundo; enigma; **dark-skinned** moreno, trigueño; s. obscuridad; sombra.

darken [dɑ́rkən] v. obscurecer(se); nublarse.

darkness [dɑ́rknɪs] s. obscuridad; tinieblas; sombra.

darky [dɑ́rkɪ] s. negro (persona).

darling [dɑ́rlɪŋ] adj. & s. amado, querido; **my —** vida mía (o mi vida), amor mío.

darn [dɑrn] s. zurcido; **it is not worth**

a — no vale un comino, no vale un pito; v. zurcir; — ¡caramba! ¡canastos!; -ing needle aguja de zurcir.

dart [dart] s. dardo, flecha; sisa (en un vestido); movimiento rápido; v. lanzar(se); flechar; to — out salir como una flecha; to — in and out entrar y salir precipitadamente.

dash [dæʃ] s. raya; carrera corta; ímpetu; garbo; pizca (de sal, azúcar, etc.); rociada (de agua); —board tablero de instrumentos; with a — of the pen de una plumada; v. lanzar(se); echar(se); estrellar(se); salpicar; frustrar (esperanzas); to — by pasar corriendo; to — out salir a la carrera; to — off a letter escribir de prisa una carta.

data [déta] s. pl. datos.

date [det] s. fecha; data; cita, compromiso; dátil; out of — anticuado, desusado; fuera de moda; up to — al día, moderno; up to this — hasta ahora, hasta la fecha; v. fechar; to — from datar de; remontarse a.

daub [dob] s. embarrar, untar; pintarrajear.

daughter [dóta] s. hija; daughter-in-law nuera.

daunt [dont] v. intimidar, asustar, espantar; desanimar.

dauntless [dóntlis] adj. denodado, intrépido.

davenport [dévenport] s. sofá.

dawn [dɔn] s. alba; amanecer, madrugada; v. amanecer; alborear, rayar (el día); it just -ed upon me acabo de darme cuenta.

day [de] s. día; — after tomorrow pasado mañana; — before yesterday anteayer o antier; — laborer jornalero; by — de día; by the — por día; eight-hour — jornada de ocho horas; to win the — ganar la jornada, triunfar.

daybreak [débrek] s. amanecer, alba, at — al amanecer, al romper el día, al rayar el día.

daylight [délait] s. luz del día.

daytime [détaim] s. día (tiempo de luz natural); in the — durante el día, de día.

daze [des] s. aturdimiento; deslumbramiento; to be in a — estar aturdido; v. aturdir; ofuscar; deslumbrar.

dazzle [dæz] s. brillantes; v. deslumbrar, ofuscar.

deacon [díkən] s. diácono.

dead [ded] adj. muerto; — air aire viciado o estancado; — letter carta no reclamada; — loss pérdida absoluta,

adv. completamente, absolutamente; sumamente, muy; — sure completamente seguro; — tired muerto de cansancio; s. the — los muertos; in the — of the night en el sigilo de la noche; in the — of winter en lo más crudo del invierno.

deaden [dédn] v. amortiguar.

deadly [dédli] adj. mortal; fatal; como la muerte, cadavérico; adv. mortalmente; — dull sumamente aburrido.

deaf [def] adj. sordo; deaf-mute s. & adj. sordomudo.

deafen [défen] v. ensordecer; amortiguar, apagar (un sonido).

deafening [défəniŋ] adj. ensordecedor, estruendoso.

deafness [défnis] s. sordera.

deal [dil] s. trato, negocio; mano (en el juego de naipes); distribución, reparto (de los naipes); a great — of una gran cantidad de, mucho; to give a square — tratar con equidad; v. tallar (en juegos de naipes); distribuir, repartir; dar (un golpe); to — in comerciar en; to — with tratar de (un asunto); tratar con; negociar con.

dealer [díla] s. negociante, comerciante; tratante; tallador (en el juego de naipes).

dealings [dílms] s. pl. relaciones (comerciales o amistosas); comercio, tratos; negocios.

dealt [delt] pret. & p.p. de to deal.

dean [din] s. deán (dignidad eclesiástica); decano (de universidad).

dear [dir] adj. querido, amado; caro, costoso; adv. caro; — me! ¡Dios mío! oh —! ¡ay!; my — querido mío; Dear Sir Muy señor mío; -ly adv. cariñosamente; a precio alto; my -ly beloved muy amado mío; muy amados míos.

dearth [dɜə] s. escasez, carestía, insuficiencia.

death [deə] s. muerte; mortandad; — rate mortalidad.

deathbed [déebed] s. lecho de muerte.

debase [dibés] v. rebajar el valor de; degradar, humillar, envilecer.

debatable [dibétəbl] adj discutible, disputable.

debate [dibét] s. debate, discusión; v. debatir, discutir; considerar; deliberar.

debit [débit] s. débito, adeudo, cargo, debe (de una cuenta); pasivo (en contabilidad); v. adeudar, cargar en cuenta.

debris [dəbrí] s. escombros; ruinas.

debt [det] s. deuda; adeudo; débito; bad — cuenta incobrable; to run into — adeudarse, entramparse, cargarse de deudas.

debtor [détə] s. deudor.

debut [dıbjú] s. estreno; **to make a —** debutar, estrenarse.

decade [déked] s. década, decenio.

decadence [dıkédns] s. decadencia.

decanter [dıkéntə] s. garrafa; **large —** garrafón.

decay [dıké] s. decaimiento; decadencia, ruina; podredumbre; caries (de la dentadura); v. decaer; venir a menos; pudrir(se) o podrir(se).

decease [dısís] s. muerte, fallecimiento; v. morir, fallecer.

deceased [dısíst] adj. & s. muerto, difunto.

deceit [dısít] s. engaño; fraude; trampa.

deceitful [dısítfəl] adj. engañador; tramposo; engañoso.

deceive [dısív] v. engañar.

December [dısémbə] s. diciembre.

decency [dísnsı] s. decencia.

decent [dísnt] adj. decente; decoroso.

decide [dısáıd] v. decidir, resolver, determinar; **to —** to resolverse a, decidirse a.

decided [dısáıdıd] adj. decidido, resuelto.

decimal [désəml] adj. decimal; s. decimal, fracción decimal.

decipher [dısáıfə] v. descifrar.

decision [dısíʒən] s. decisión, resolución.

decisive [dısáısıv] adj. decisivo; terminante.

deck [dɛk] s. cubierta (de un buque); baraja; v. cubrir; ataviar; **to — oneself out** emperifollarse.

declaration [dɛkləréʃən] s. declaración.

declare [dıklǽr] v. declarar; afirmar.

decline [dıkláın] s. declinación; decadencia; mengua; baja (de precios); v. declinar; decaer; rehusar; **to — to do something** negarse a hacer algo.

declivity [dıklívətı] s. declive.

decompose [dikəmpóz] v. descomponer(se); corromper(se), pudrir(se).

decorate [dékəret] v. decorar, adornar; condecorar.

decoration [dɛkəréʃən] s. decoración; adorno, insignia, condecoración.

decorative [dékəretıv] adj. decorativo; ornamental.

decorum [dıkórəm] s. decoro; circunspección.

decoy [dıkóı] s. reclamo, señuelo, figura de ave (que sirve para atraer aves); cebo (artificio para atraer con engaño); trampa, lazo; v. atraer con señuelo o engaño.

decrease [díkrıs] s. disminución o diminución; merma; mengua; [dıkrís] v.

disminuir(se); mermar; menguar.

decree [dıkrí] s. decreto; v. decretar; mandar.

decrepit [dıkrépıt] adj. decrépito.

dedicate [dédəket] v. dedicar.

dedication [dedəkéʃən] s. dedicación; dedicatoria.

deduce [dıdjús] v. deducir, inferir.

deduct [dıdʌkt] v. deducir, descontar, rebajar.

deduction [dıdʌkʃən] s. deducción; rebaja, descuento.

deed [dıd] s. hecho, acción, acto; hazaña; escritura (de venta o compra).

deem [dim] v. juzgar, creer, considerar.

deep [dip] adj. hondo; profundo; obscuro; bajo, grave; **— in debt** cargado de deudas; **— in thought** absorto; **— mourning** luto riguroso; **to go off the — end** echarse a pique; caer en el abismo; **— into the night** en las tinieblas de la noche; **s. the —** el mar; **-ly** adv. profundamente, hondamente; intensamente.

deepen [dípən] v. ahondar, profundizar.

deer [dır] s. ciervo, venado; **—skin** piel o cuero de venado.

deface [dıfés] v. desfigurar, estropear, mutilar.

defame [dıfém] v. difamar, calumniar, denigrar.

default [dıfólt] s. falla, falta, negligencia (de un deber, pago, obligación); deficiencia; v. fallar, faltar (en el cumplimiento de un deber, pago, obligación; no comparecer a la cita de un tribunal).

defeat [dıfít] s. derrota, vencimiento; frustración (de un plan); v. vencer, derrotar; frustrar.

defect [dıfékt] s. defecto.

defective [dıféktıv] adj. defectuoso; incompleto; subnormal, falto de inteligencia; — **verb** verbo defectivo.

defend [dıfénd] v. defender.

defendant [dıféndənt] s. acusado, demandado, procesado.

defender [dıféndə] s. defensor; abogado defensor.

defense [dıféns] s. defensa.

defenseless [dıfénslıs] adj. indefenso, inerme.

defensive [dıfénsıv] adj. defensivo; s. defensiva.

defer [dıfʒ́] v. diferir, posponer, aplazar; **to — to another's opinion** remitirse o ceder al dictamen de otro.

defiance [dıfáıəns] s. reto, desafío, provocación; oposición; **in —** of en abierta oposición con, a despecho de.

deficiency [dıfíʃənsı] s. deficiencia; defecto; déficit.

deficient [dɪffʃənt] *adj.* deficiente; defectuoso.

deficit [défəsɪt] *s.* déficit.

defile [dɪfáɪl] *v.* viciar, corromper; profanar; manchar, ensuciar.

define [dɪfáɪn] *v.* definir.

definite [défənɪt] *adj.* definido; claro, preciso; fijo; — **article** artículo determinado o definido; **-ly** *adv.* definidamente; claramente; **-ly not** terminantemente no.

definition [defənʃ́ən] *s.* definición.

definitive [dɪfínətɪv] *adj.* definitivo.

deform [dɪfɔ́rm] *v.* deformar; desfigurar, afear.

deformed [dɪfɔ́rmd] *adj.* deforme, disforme; deformado; desfigurado.

deformity [dɪfɔ́rmətɪ] *s.* deformidad; deformación.

defraud [dɪfrɔ́d] *v.* defraudar.

defray [dɪfré] *v.* sufragar, costear, pagar (*gastos*).

deft [dɛft] *adj.* diestro, ágil.

defy [dɪfáɪ] *v.* desafiar; retar; oponerse a, resistirse a.

degenerate [dɪdʒénərɪt] *adj.* & *s.* degenerado; [dɪdʒénəret] *v.* degenerar.

degradation [degrədéʃən] *s.* degradación; envilecimiento.

degrade [dɪgréd] *v.* degradar; envilecer, rebajar.

degree [dɪgrí] *s.* grado; rango; **by -s** gradualmente; **to get a — graduarse.**

deign [den] *v.* dignarse, condescender.

deity [díətɪ] *s.* deidad.

dejected [dɪdʒéktɪd] *adj.* abatido.

dejection [dɪdʒékʃən] *s.* abatimiento, melancolía, depresión.

delay [dɪlé] *s.* demora, tardanza, dilación, retraso; *v.* demorar; retardar, dilatar; diferir; tardarse.

delegate [déləget] *s.* delegado, representante; *v.* delegar, diputar.

delegation [deləgéʃən] *s.* delegación, diputación.

deliberate [dɪlíbərɪt] *adj.* deliberado, premeditado; cauto, prudente; lento; **-ly** *adv.* deliberadamente; con premeditación; [dɪlíbəret] *v.* deliberar.

deliberation [dɪlɪbəréʃən] *s.* deliberación.

delicacy [déləkəsɪ] *s.* delicadeza; sensibilidad; finura; golosina.

delicate [déləkət] *adj.* delicado; frágil; exquisito.

delicatessen [deləkətésṇ] *s.* tienda de fiambres, queso, ensaladas, etc.

delicious [dɪlíʃəs] *adj.* delicioso.

delight [dɪláɪt] *s.* deleite; delicia; *v.*

deleitar(se); encantar; agradar; **to —** **in** gozarse en, deleitarse en.

delighted [dɪláɪtɪd] *adj.* encantado; **to be — to** alegrarse de, tener mucho gusto en (o de).

delightful [dɪláɪtfəl] *adj.* deleitoso; delicioso; ameno, agradable.

delineate [dɪlínɪet] *v.* delinear, trazar.

delinquent [dɪlíŋkwənt] *adj.* & *s.* delincuente.

delirious [dɪlírɪəs] *adj.* delirante; **to be — delirar, desvariar.**

delirium [dɪlírɪəm] *s.* delirio, desvarío.

deliver [dɪlívə] *v.* entregar; librar, libertar; pronunciar (*un discurso*); dar (*un golpe*).

deliverance [dɪlívərəns] *s.* liberación, rescate.

deliverer [dɪlívərə] *s.* libertador; portador, mensajero.

delivery [dɪlívərɪ] *s.* entrega; liberación; parto; elocuencia, manera de pronunciar un discurso; **— service** servicio de entrega; **— truck** camión (o camioneta) de reparto; **mail —** reparto de correo.

dell [del] *s.* cañada, hondonada.

delude [dɪlúd] *v.* engañar.

deluge [déljudʒ] *s.* diluvio; *v.* inundar; abrumar.

delusion [dɪlúʒən] *s.* ilusión; engaño, error.

demand [dɪmǽnd] *s.* demanda; exigencia; solicitud; **on — a** solicitud; *v.* demandar, reclamar; exigir.

demanding [dɪmǽndɪŋ] *adj.* exigente.

demeanor [dɪmínə] *s.* conducta, comportamiento, proceder.

demented [dɪméntɪd] *adj.* demente.

demobilize [dɪmóblaɪz] *v.* demovilizar.

democracy [dəmákrəsɪ] *s.* democracia.

democrat [déməkræt] *s.* demócrata.

democratic [deməkrǽtɪk] *adj.* democrático.

demolish [dɪmálɪʃ] *v.* demoler.

demon [dímən] *s.* demonio.

demonstrate [démənstret] *v.* demostrar.

demonstration [demənstréʃən] *s.* demostración; prueba.

demonstrative [dɪmánstrətɪv] *adj.* demostrativo; efusivo.

den [dɛn] *s.* guarida; escondrijo; cueva, lugar de retiro.

denial [dɪnáɪəl] *s.* negación; negativa; **self-denial** abnegación.

denomination [dɪnamənéʃən] *s.* denominación; nombre, título, designación; secta religiosa.

denote [dɪnót] *v.* denotar.

denounce [dɪnáʊns] *v.* denunciar; delatar, acusar.

dense [dɛns] *adj.* denso; espeso, apretado; estúpido.

density [dɛnsɔtɪ] s. densidad; estupidez.

dent [dɛnt] *s.* abolladura; mella; *v.* abollar; mellar.

dental [dɛ́ntl] *adj.* dental; *s.* dental, consonante dental.

dentist [dɛ́ntɪst] *v.* dentista.

denunciation [dɪnʌnsɪéʃən] *s.* denuncia, acusación.

deny [dɪnáɪ] *v.* negar; rehusar; **to — oneself** sacrificarse, abnegarse; **to — oneself to callers** negarse a recibir visitas.

depart [dɪpárt] *v.* partir, salir, irse; desviarse, apartarse.

departed [dɪpártɪd] *adj.* ido; ausente; difunto.

department [dɪpártmənt] *s.* departamento; distrito; ramo, división; **— store** almacén.

departure [dɪpártʃə] *s.* salida, partida; desviación.

depend [dɪpénd] *v.* depender; **to — on** depender de; contar con, confiar en.

dependable [dɪpéndəbl] *adj.* seguro, fidedigno, digno de confianza.

dependence [dɪpéndəns] *s.* dependencia; confianza.

dependency [dɪpéndənsɪ] *s.* dependencia; sucursal.

dependent [dɪpéndənt] *adj.* dependiente; subordinado; *s.* dependiente, familiar.

depict [dɪpíkt] *v.* pintar, describir; representar.

deplete [dɪplít] *v.* agotar; vaciar.

deplorable [dɪplórəbl] *adj.* deplorable, lamentable.

deplore [dɪplór] *v.* deplorar.

deport [dɪpórt] *v.* deportar; **to — oneself well** portarse bien.

deportment [dɪpórtmənt] *s.* comportamiento, conducta.

depose [dɪpóz] *v.* deponer; declarar; atestiguar.

deposit [dɪpázɪt] *s.* depósito; *v.* depositar.

deposition [depəzíʃən] *s.* deposición; declaración.

depositor [dɪpázɪtə] *s.* depositador.

depot [dípo] *s.* depósito; almacén; estación de ferrocarril.

depreciate [dɪpríʃɪet] *v.* depreciar; bajar de precio; abaratar(se); menospreciar.

depress [dɪprés] *v.* deprimir; abatir; desanimar; depreciar, rebajar el valor de.

depressed [dɪprést] *adj.* abatido, decaído.

depressing [dɪprésɪŋ] *adj.* deprimente.

depression [dɪpréʃən] *s.* depresión; decaimiento, abatimiento; rebaja (*de precios*).

deprive [dɪpráɪv] *v.* privar.

depth [depɵ] *s.* profundidad; hondura; fondo; longitud (*de un solar*); gravedad (*de los sonidos*); viveza (*de los colores*); **in the — of the night** en las tinieblas de la noche; **in the — of winter** en lo más crudo del invierno.

deputation [depjətéʃən] *s.* diputación, delegación; comisión.

depute [dɪpjút] *v.* diputar, delegar.

deputy [dépjətɪ] *s.* diputado; agente; delegado.

derange [dɪréndʒ] *v.* trastornar, desordenar.

derby [dɔ́bɪ] *s.* sombrero hongo, *Am.* sombrero de bola.

deride [dɪráɪd] *v.* escarnecer, ridiculizar, mofarse de, burlarse de.

derision [dɪríʒən] *s.* mofa, escarnio.

derive [dəráɪv] *v.* derivar(se); provenir; sacar (*provecho*); recibir (*placer*).

derrick [dérɪk] *s.* grúa; armazón (*para la explotación del petróleo*).

descend [dɪsénd] *v.* descender; bajar; **to — upon** caer sobre, acometer.

descendant [dɪséndənt] *adj. & s.* descendiente.

descent [dɪsént] *s.* descenso; bajada; descendencia, linaje; descendimiento; declive.

describe [dɪskráɪb] *v.* describir; trazar.

description [dɪskrípʃən] *s.* descripción; **of all —s** de todas clases.

descriptive [dɪskríptɪv] *adj.* descriptivo.

desert [dézət] *adj.* desierto, despoblado; estéril; *s.* desierto, yermo; páramo; [dɪzɔ́t] *v.* abandonar, desamparar; desertar.

deserter [dɪzɔ́tə] *s.* desertor.

desertion [dɪzɔ́ʃən] *s.* deserción, abandono, desamparo.

deserve [dɪzɔ́v] *v.* merecer.

deserving [dɪzɔ́vɪŋ] *adj.* meritorio; merecedor.

design [dɪzáɪn] *s.* designio, propósito, intención; plan, proyecto; diseño, dibujo; *v.* diseñar, trazar; proyectar; idear.

designate [dézɪgnet] *v.* designar; señalar, indicar, nombrar.

designer [dɪzáɪnə] *s.* diseñador; dibujante; proyectista; intrigante.

desirability [dɪzaɪrəbflətɪ] *s.* conveniencia, utilidad.

desirable [dɪzáɪrəbl] *adj.* deseable; agradable; conveniente.

desire [dɪzáɪr] *s.* deseo; anhelo, ansia; *v.* desear; anhelar, ansiar.

desirous [dɪzáɪrəs] *adj.* deseoso.

desist [dɪzíst] *v.* desistir.

desk [desk] *s.* escritorio, bufete, pupitre, mesa de escribir.

desolate [désɪt] *adj.* desolado; despoblado, desierto; solitario; [désəlet] *v.* desolar; asolar, arrasar; despoblar.

desolation [desléʃən] *s.* desolación; soledad.

despair [dɪspér] *s.* desesperación; desesperanza; *v.* desesperarse, perder la esperanza.

despairing [dɪspérɪŋ] *adj.* desesperado, sin esperanza.

despatch [dɪspǽtʃ] = **dispatch**.

desperate [désprɪt] *adj.* desesperado; arriesgado, temerario; — **illness** enfermedad gravísima; **-ly** *adv.* desesperadamente; **-ly ill** gravísimamente enfermo.

desperation [despəréʃən] *s.* desesperación; temeridad.

despise [dɪspáɪz] *v.* despreciar; desdeñar; menospreciar.

despite [dɪspáɪt] *s.* despecho; *prep.* a despecho de, a pesar de.

despoil [dɪspóɪl] *v.* despojar.

despondency [dɪspándənsɪ] *s.* abatimiento, desaliento, descaecimiento o decaimiento del ánimo.

despondent [dɪspándənt] *adj.* abatido, descaecido o decaído de ánimo, desalentado, desesperanzado.

despot [déspət] *s.* déspota.

despotic [dɪspátɪk] *adj.* despótico.

despotism [déspətɪzəm] *s.* despotismo.

dessert [dɪzɔ́rt] *s.* postre.

destination [destənéʃən] *s.* destinación, destino; paradero.

destine [déstɪn] *v.* destinar; **-ed** for con rumbo a, con destinación a; destinado a.

destiny [déstənɪ] *s.* destino, sino, hado.

destitute [déstətjut] *adj.* destituido, necesitado; falto, desprovisto.

destroy [dɪstróɪ] *v.* destruir.

destroyer [dɪstróɪə] *s.* destruidor; destructor, cazatorpedero, destroyer.

destruction [dɪstrʌkʃən] *s.* destrucción; ruina.

destructive [dɪstrʌktɪv] *adj.* destructivo.

detach [dɪtǽtʃ] *v.* separar, despegar, desprender; destacar (*una porción de tropa*).

detachment [dɪtǽtʃmənt] *s.* separación; desprendimiento; despego, desapego, alejamiento; destacamento (*militar*).

detail [dítel] *s.* detalle; pormenor; destacamento (*militar*); **to go into** — de-

tallar, pormenorizar; [dɪtél] *v.* detallar; pormenorizar; destacar, asignar.

detain [dɪtén] *v.* detener; entretener, demorar, retardar.

detect [dɪtékt] *v.* descubrir.

detective [dɪtéktɪv] *s.* detective, detectivo, policía secreto.

detention [dɪténʃən] *s.* detención.

deteriorate [dɪtíriəret] *v.* deteriorar(se).

deterioration [dɪtɪriəréʃən] *s.* deterioro.

determination [dɪtɜmənéʃən] *s.* determinación; decisión; resolución, firmeza.

determine [dɪtɜ́mɪn] *v.* determinar; decidir; **to** — **to** determinarse a, decidirse a, resolverse a.

determined [dɪtɜ́mɪnd] *adj.* determinado, decidido, resuelto.

detest [dɪtést] *v.* detestar, aborrecer.

detour [dítur] *s.* rodeo, desvío, desviación, vuelta; *v.* dar o hacer un rodeo.

devastate [dévəstet] *v.* devastar, arruinar, asolar.

develop [dɪvéləp] *v.* desarrollar(se); desenvolver(se); revelar (*una película o placa fotográfica*); explotar (*una mina*).

development [dɪvéləpmənt] *s.* desarrollo; desenvolvimiento; crecimiento; fomento; explotación; revelamiento (*de una película*).

deviate [dívɪet] *v.* desviar(se).

deviation [dívɪéʃən] *s.* desviación; desvío, extravío.

device [dɪváɪs] *s.* artificio; mecanismo, aparato; ardid, recurso; divisa; **left to one's own** **-s** abandonado a sus propios recursos.

devil [dévl] *s.* diablo; demonio.

devilish [dévlɪʃ] *adj.* diabólico; endiablado; travieso.

deviltry [dévltrɪ] *s.* diablura.

devious [dívɪəs] *adj.* desviado; tortuoso; indirecto.

devise [dɪváɪz] *v.* idear, trazar, urdir.

devoid [dɪvóɪd] *adj.* exento, libre, falto, privado, desprovisto.

devote [dɪvót] *v.* dedicar; consagrar; **to** — **oneself** to dedicarse a, consagrarse a, aplicarse a.

devoted [dɪvótɪd] *adj.* dedicado, consagrado; apegado; — **friend** amigo fiel o leal.

devotion [dɪvóʃən] *s.* devoción; piedad; afecto; lealtad.

devour [dɪváur] *v.* devorar.

devout [dɪváut] *adj.* devoto, piadoso; sincero.

dew [dju] *s.* rocío, sereno; *v.* rociar; caer (*el rocío*).

dewdrop [djúdrap] *s.* gota de rocío.

dewy [djúɪ] *adj.* rociado, húmedo de

rocío.

dexterity [dɛkstérətɪ] s. destreza.

dexterous [dɛkstrəs] adj. diestro.

diadem [dáɪədɛm] s. diadema.

diagnose [daɪəgnós] v. diagnosticar.

diagonal [daɪǽgənl] adj. diagonal, oblicuo; s. diagonal.

diagram [dáɪəgræm] s. diagrama.

dial [dáɪəl] s. esfera; muestra (del reloj), Am. carátula; — **telephone** teléfono automático; v. sintonizar o captar (una estación radiotelefónica).

dialect [dáɪəlɛkt] s. dialecto.

dialogue [dáɪələg] s. diálogo; v. dialogar.

diameter [daɪǽmətə] s. diámetro.

diamond [dáɪmənd] s. diamante; rombo (figura geométrica).

diaper [dáɪəpə] s. pañal.

diarrhea [daɪəríə] s. diarrea.

diary [dáɪərɪ] s. diario.

dice [daɪs] s. pl. de die dados; v. cuadricular, cortar en cuarterones o cubos.

dictate [dɪktet] s. dictado, precepto; v. dictar.

dictation [dɪktéʃən] s. dictado; mando absoluto; **to take**—escribir al dictado.

dictator [dɪktétə] s. dictador.

dictatorship [dɪktétəʃɪp] s. dictadura.

diction [dɪkʃən] s. dicción.

dictionary [dɪkʃənɛrɪ] s. diccionario.

did [dɪd] pret. de to do.

die [daɪ] s. (pl. dice) dado (para jugar); (pl. dies) matriz, molde; cuño (sello para acuñar moneda).

die [daɪ] v. morir(se); marchitarse, secarse (las flores, plantas, etc.); **to — out** morirse, extinguirse, apagarse.

diet [dáɪət] s. dieta; régimen; **to be on a — estar a dieta; to put on a —** adietar, poner a dieta; v. ponerse a dieta; estar a dieta.

differ [dɪfə] v. diferir, diferenciarse, distinguirse; disentir; **to — with** no convenir con, no estar de acuerdo con.

difference [dɪfrəns] s. diferencia; distinción; discordia, controversia; **it makes no** — no importa, es igual, da lo mismo.

different [dɪfrənt] adj. diferente; distinto.

differentiate [dɪfərénʃɪet] v. diferenciar(se); distinguir(se).

difficult [dɪfəkʌlt] adj. difícil; dificultoso, trabajoso, penoso.

difficulty [dɪfəkʌltɪ] s. dificultad; apuro, aprieto.

diffidence [dɪfədəns] s. timidez; desconfianza de sí propio.

diffident [dɪfədənt] adj. huraño; tímido.

diffuse [dɪfjús] adj. difuso; prolijo; [dɪf-

júz] v. difundir.

diffusion [dɪfjúʒən] s. difusión; diseminación.

dig [dɪg] v. cavar; excavar; ahondar; escarbar; trabajar duro; **to — under** socavar; **to — up** desenterrar; s. piquete; pulla, sarcasmo.

digest [dáɪdʒɛst] s. sumario, compendio; recopilación; código; [dədʒést] v. digerir; recopilar.

digestible [dədʒéstəbl] adj. digestible, digerible.

digestion [dədʒéstʃən] s. digestión.

digestive [dədʒéstɪv] adj. digestivo.

dignified [dɪgnəfaɪd] adj. digno, mesurado; serio, grave.

dignitary [dɪgnətɛrɪ] s. dignatario.

dignity [dɪgnətɪ] s. dignidad.

digress [dəgrés] v. divagar.

digression [dəgréʃən] s. digresión, divagación.

dike [daɪk] s. dique, represa; zanja.

dilate [daɪlét] v. dilatar(se), extender(se), ensanchar(se).

diligence [dɪlədʒəns] s. diligencia; aplicación, esmero.

diligent [dɪlədʒənt] adj. diligente, activo, aplicado.

dilute [dɪlút] v. diluir, desleír; aguar; adj. diluido.

dim [dɪm] adj. penumbroso, obscuro; nublado; confuso; indistinto; deslustrado, sin brillo; v. obscurecer; anublar, ofuscar; atenuar.

dime [daɪm] s. moneda de diez centavos.

dimension [dəménʃən] s. dimensión.

diminish [dəmínɪʃ] v. disminuir; rebajar.

diminution [dɪmənjúʃən] s. diminución, mengua.

diminutive [dəmínjətɪv] adj. diminuto; diminutivo; s. diminutivo.

dimness [dɪmnɪs] s. semi-obscuridad, penumbra; ofuscamiento.

dimple [dɪmpl] s. hoyuelo.

din [dɪn] s. estruendo, fragor, estrépito.

dine [daɪn] v. comer; festejar u obsequiar con una comida.

diner [dáɪnə] s. coche-comedor; comensal (persona que come a la mesa).

dingy [dɪndʒɪ] adj. negruzco; manchado, sucio.

dining [dáɪnɪŋ] ger. de to dine; — **car** coche-comedor; — **room** comedor.

dinner [dɪnə] s. comida; — **coat** smoking o esmoquin.

dint [dɪnt] s.: **by — of** a fuerza de.

dip [dɪp] s. zambullida; inmersión; bajada; declive; depresión; v. meter(se); zambullirse; mojar (la pluma en el tintero); teñir; agachar (la cabeza); saludar (*con la bandera*); inclinarse (*un camino*); dar un bajón (*un avión*); hundirse (*el sol en el horizonte*); **to — out** vaciar (*con cucharón o cazo*).

diphtheria [dɪféfrɪə] *s.* difteria.

diploma [dɪplómə] *s.* diploma.

diplomacy [dɪplóməsɪ] *s.* diplomacia.

diplomat [dɪpləmæt] *s.* diplomático.

diplomatic [dɪpləmǽtɪk] *adj.* diplomático.

dipper [dípə] *s.* cucharón, cazo; **the Big Dipper** la Osa Mayor.

dire [daɪr] *adj.* extremo; horrendo; fatal, de mal agüero.

direct [dərékt] *adj.* directo; derecho, en línea recta; inmediato; **— current** corriente continua; **— object** acusativo; *adv.* directamente; **-ly** *adv.* directamente; inmediatamente; en seguida; *v.* dirigir; guiar; encaminar; dar direcciones ú ordenes.

direction [dərékʃən] *s.* dirección; administración; gerencia; rumbo.

directive [dəréktɪv] *adj.* directivo; *s.* orden, mandato.

directness [dəréktnɪs] *s.* derechura; franqueza; lo directo; **with —** sin rodeos.

director [dəréktə] *s.* director; gerente.

directory [dəréktərɪ] *s.* directorio; junta directiva; **telephone —** guía telefónica.

dirigible [dírədʒəbl] *adj. & s.* dirigible.

dirt [dɜrt] *s.* suciedad; mugre; tierra, polvo, lodo.

dirty [dɜrtɪ] *adj.* sucio; mugriento; cochino; enlodado; manchado; *v.* ensuciar; manchar; enlodar.

disable [dɪsébl] *v.* incapacitar.

disadvantage [dɪsədvǽntɪdʒ] *s.* desventaja; **to be at a —** estar en una situación desventajosa.

disagree [dɪsəgrí] *v.* diferir, disentir; no convenir, no estar de acuerdo; no sentarle a uno bien (*el clima, la comida, etc.*).

disagreeable [dɪsəgríəbl] *adj.* desagradable; áspero, de mal genio.

disagreement [dɪsəgrímənt] *s.* desavenencia, desacuerdo; disensión; discordia; discordancia.

disappear [dɪsəpír] *v.* desaparecer.

disappearance [dɪsəpírəns] *s.* desaparición.

disappoint [dɪsəpóɪnt] *v.* chasquear; contrariar; decepcionar; faltar a lo prometido; desilusionar; **to be —ed** estar desilusionado o decepcionado; estar desengañado; quedar contrariado.

disappointing [dɪsəpóɪntɪŋ] *adj.* desi-

lusionante, desengañador, decepcionante.

disappointment [dɪsəpóɪntmənt] *s.* desilusión, desengaño, decepción; chasco; contrariedad.

disapproval [dɪsəprúvl] *s.* desaprobación.

disapprove [dɪsəprúv] *v.* desaprobar.

disarm [dɪsárm] *v.* desarmar(se).

disarmament [dɪsárməmənt] *s.* desarme.

disarray [dɪsəré] *s.* desarreglo, confusión, desorden; *v.* desarreglar, desordenar.

disaster [dɪzǽstə] *s.* desastre.

disastrous [dɪzǽstrəs] *adj.* desastroso.

disband [dɪsbǽnd] *v.* dispersar; licenciar (*las tropas*); desbandarse.

disbelieve [dɪsbəlív] *v.* descreer, no creer.

disburse [dɪsbɜ́s] *v.* desembolsar.

disbursement [dɪsbɜ́smənt] *s.* desembolso; gasto.

disc [dɪsk] = **disk.**

discard [dɪskard] *s.* descarte; desecho, cosa desechada; [dɪskárd] *v.* descartar; desechar.

discern [dɪsɜ́n] *v.* discernir, distinguir; percibir.

discernment [dɪsɜ́nmənt] *s.* discernimiento.

discharge [dɪstʃárdʒ] *s.* descarga (*de artillería*); descargo (*de una obligación*); desempeño (*de un deber*); exoneración; despedida; licencia (*militar*); pago (*de una deuda*); derrame, desagüe; supuración; *v.* descargar; exonerar; poner en libertad; despedir, echar, deponer; dar de baja (*a un soldado*); pagar (*una deuda*); arrojar, supurar; desaguar.

disciple [dɪsáɪpl] *s.* discípulo.

discipline [dísəplɪn] *s.* disciplina; *v.* disciplinar.

disclose [dɪsklóz] *v.* descubrir; revelar.

discolor [dɪskÁlə] *v.* descolorar(se), desteñir(se).

discomfort [dɪskÁmfət] *s.* incomodidad; malestar.

disconcert [dɪskənsɜ́t] *v.* desconcertar.

disconnect [dɪskənékt] *v.* desconectar; desunir, separar.

disconnected [dɪskənéktɪd] *p.p. & adj.* desconectado; desunido; inconexo, incoherente.

disconsolate [dɪskánslɪt] *adj.* desconsolado.

discontent [dɪskəntént] *s.* descontento; *v.* descontentar.

discontented [dɪskənténtɪd] *adj.* descontento; descontentadizo.

discontinue [dɪskəntínju] *v.* descontinuar; parar; suspender, interrumpir; abandonar.

discord [dískord] *s.* discordia; disonancia, discordancia; desavenencia.

discount [dískaunt] *s.* descuento; rebaja; — rate tipo de descuento; *v.* descontar; rebajar.

discourage [dıskʌridʒ] *v.* desanimar, desalentar, abatir; to — from disuadir de.

discouragement [dıskʌridʒmənt] *s.* desaliento, abatimiento.

discourse [dískors] *s.* discurso; conversación; [dıskórs] *v.* disertar, discurrir, hablar.

discourteous [dıskə́rtıəs] *adj.* descortés, desatento.

discourtesy [dıskə́rtəsı] *s.* descortesía, desatención.

discover [dıskʌvə] *v.* descubrir.

discoverer [dıskʌvərə] *s.* descubridor.

discovery [dıskʌvrı] *s.* descubrimiento.

discredit [dıskrédıt] *s.* descrédito; deshonra; *v.* desacreditar; deshonrar; no creer.

discreet [dıskrít] *adj.* discreto, prudente.

discrepancy [dıskrépənsı] *s.* discrepancia, diferencia, variación.

discretion [dıskréʃən] *s.* discreción; prudencia; at one's own — a discreción.

discriminate [dıskrímənət] *v.* discernir, distinguir; hacer distinciones, hacer favoritismos; to — against hacer favoritismos en perjuicio de.

discuss [dıskʌs] *v.* discutir.

discussion [dıskʌʃən] *s.* discusión.

disdain [dısdén] *s.* desdén, menosprecio; *v.* desdeñar, menospreciar; desdeñarse de.

disdainful [dısdénfəl] *adj.* desdeñoso.

disease [dızíz] *s.* enfermedad.

diseased [dızízd] *adj.* enfermo.

disembark [dısımbárk] *v.* desembarcar.

disentangle [dısın.ǽŋgl] *v.* desenredar, desenmarañar, deshacer (*una maraña o enredo*).

disfigure [dısfígjə] *v.* desfigurar; afear.

disgrace [dısgrés] *s.* ignominia, deshonra; vergüenza; to be in — estar desacreditado, haber perdido la gracia o el favor; *v.* deshonrar; degradar; desacreditar; avergonzar.

disgraceful [dısgrésfəl] *adj.* vergonzoso.

disguise [dısgáız] *v.* disfraz; *v.* disfrazar.

disgust [dısgʌ́st] *s.* asco; repugnancia; disgusto; *v.* disgustar, dar asco; repugnar.

disgusted [dısgʌ́stıd] *adj.* disgustado, descontento; asqueado.

disgusting [dısgʌ́stıŋ] *adj.* asqueroso, repugnante.

dish [dıʃ] *s.* plato; manjar, vianda; -es vajilla; *v.* servir.

dishearten [dıshártn] *v.* desalentar, desanimar, descorazonar.

disheveled [dıʃévld] *adj.* desgreñado; desaliñado, desaseado.

dishonest [dısánıst] *adj.* engañoso, falso, tramposo, falto de honradez, fraudulento.

dishonesty [dısánıstı] *s.* fraude, falta de honradez.

dishonor [dısánə] *s.* deshonra; afrenta; *v.* deshonrar; recusar (*un giro o cheque*).

dishonorable [dısánərəbl] *adj.* deshonroso; infame.

disillusion [dısılúʒən] *s.* desilusión, decepción, desengaño; *v.* desilusionar, decepcionar, desengañar.

disinfect [dısınfékt] *v.* desinfectar.

disinfectant [dısınféktənt] *s.* desinfectante.

disinterested [dısíntərəstıd] *adj.* desinteresado..

disk [dısk] *s.* disco.

dislike [dısláık] *s.* antipatía, aversión; *v.* sentir o tener aversión por; I — it me repugna, no me gusta, me desagrada.

dislocate [dísloket] *v.* dislocar, descoyuntar.

dislodge [dıslʌdʒ] *v.* desalojar.

disloyal [dıslóıəl] *adj.* desleal.

dismal [dízml] *adj.* lúgubre, sombrío, tétrico.

dismantle [dısmǽntl] *v.* desmantelar; desmontar, desarmar.

dismay [dısmé] *s.* desmayo, desaliento, pavor; *v.* desalentar, desanimar; atemorizar.

dismiss [dısmís] *v.* despedir, expulsar, destituir; desechar; licenciar, dar de baja; dar por terminado (*un pleito o caso jurídico*); to — the meeting disolver la junta, levantar la sesión.

dismissal [dısmísl] *s.* despedida, expulsión, destitución (*de un cargo*).

dismount [dısmáunt] *v.* desmontar; apear(se); desarmar (*un cañón, una máquina*); desengastar (*joyas*).

disobedience [dısəbídıəns] *s.* desobediencia.

disobedient [dısəbídıənt] *adj.* desobediente.

disobey [dısəbé] *v.* desobedecer.

disorder [dısórdə] *s.* desorden; trastorno; confusión; enfermedad; *v.* desordenar; trastornar; desarreglar.

disorderly [dısórdəlı] *adj.* desordenado; desarreglado; revoltoso; escandaloso;

adv. desordenadamente.

disown [dɪsón] *v.* repudiar; desconocer, negar.

dispassionate [dɪspǽʃənɪt] *adj.* desapasionado.

dispatch [dɪspǽtʃ] *s.* despacho; envío; parte (*m.*), comunicación, mensaje; prontitud, expedición; *v.* despachar; enviar, expedir; matar.

dispel [dɪspél] *v.* disipar; dispersar.

dispensary [dɪspénsərɪ] *s.* dispensario.

dispensation [dɪspənséʃən] *s.* dispensa, exención; dispensación; distribución.

dispense [dɪspéns] *v.* dispensar, dar; repartir, distribuir; administrar (*la justicia*); despachar (*recetas, medicamentos*); **to — from** eximir de, dispensar de; **to — with** omitir; pasarse sin, prescindir de.

dispersal [dɪspə́s] *s.* dispersión; desbandada.

disperse [dɪspə́s] *v.* dispersar(se), disipar(se), esparcir(se).

displace [dɪsplés] *v.* desalojar; desplazar; poner fuera de su lugar; suplantar.

display [dɪsplé] *s.* manifestación, exhibición; ostentación; *v.* exhibir; mostrar, manifestar; desplegar.

displease [dɪsplíz] *v.* desagradar; disgustar, fastidiar.

displeasure [dɪspléʒə] *s.* desagrado, disgusto, descontento.

disposal [dɪspóz] *s.* disposición; arreglo; venta (*de bienes*).

dispose [dɪspóz] *v.* disponer; arreglar; influir; **to — of** deshacerse de.

disposition [dɪspozíʃən] *s.* disposición; arreglo; aptitud, inclinación; venta; **good (bad) —** buen (mal) genio.

disprove [dɪsprúv] *v.* refutar.

dispute [dɪspjút] *s.* disputa; *v.* disputar.

disqualify [dɪskwálɪfaɪ] *v.* inhabilitar, incapacitar, descalificar.

disregard [dɪsrɪgárd] *s.* desatención, falta de atención, negligencia, descuido; falta de respeto o consideración; *v.* desatender, no hacer caso de, desentenderse de.

disrespect [dɪsrɪspékt] *s.* desacato, falta de respeto.

disrespectful [dɪsrɪspéktfəl] *adj.* irrespetuoso.

dissatisfied [dɪssǽtɪsfaɪd] *adj.* descontento, malcontento, mal satisfecho.

dissatisfy [dɪssǽtɪsfaɪ] *v.* descontentar, no satisfacer.

dissect [dɪsékt] *v.* disecar, hacer una disección; analizar.

dissemble [dɪsémbl] *v.* disimular, fingir.

dissension [dɪsénʃən] *s.* disensión, discordia.

dissent [dɪsént] *v.* disentir; *s.* desacuerdo; disensión, desavenencia.

dissimulation [dɪsɪmjəléʃən] *s.* disimulo.

dissipate [dɪsəpet] *v.* disipar(se).

dissipation [dɪsəpéʃən] *s.* disipación.

dissolute [dɪsəlut] *adj.* disoluto.

dissolution [dɪsəlúʃən] *s.* disolución.

dissolve [dɪzálv] *v.* disolver(se); anular.

dissuade [dɪswéd] *v.* disuadir.

distaff [dɪstǽf] *s.* rueca.

distance [dístəns] *s.* distancia; lejanía, alejamiento; **in the —** a lo lejos, en lontananza.

distant [dístənt] *adj.* distante; apartado, lejano, remoto; esquivo; **to be — from** distar de; **-ly** *adv.* de lejos; remotamente; a distancia; en lontananza.

distaste [dɪstést] *s.* disgusto, aversión, repugnancia.

distasteful [dɪstéstfəl] *adj.* desagradable, repugnante.

distend [dɪsténd] *v.* dilatar, ensanchar.

distil [dɪstíl] *v.* destilar.

distillation [dɪstɪléʃən] *s.* destilación.

distillery [dɪstílərɪ] *s.* destilería.

distinct [dɪstíŋkt] *adj.* distinto, claro diferente; **-ly** *adv.* distintamente, claramente, con claridad.

distinction [dɪstíŋkʃən] *s.* distinción.

distinctive [dɪstíŋktɪv] *adj.* distintivo

distinguish [dɪstíŋgwɪʃ] *v.* distinguir discernir.

distinguished [dɪstíŋgwɪʃt] *adj.* distinguido.

distinguishing [dɪstíŋgwɪʃɪŋ] *adj.* distintivo, característico.

distort [dɪstórt] *v.* desfigurar, deformar torcer, falsear; tergiversar.

distract [dɪstrǽkt] *v.* distraer; perturbar

distraction [dɪstrǽkʃən] *s.* distracción diversión; perturbación; **to drive to — volver loco.**

distress [dɪstrés] *s.* angustia, aflicción congoja; dolor; **to be in —** tener un aflicción; estar apurado; estar en zozobra (*un navío*); *v.* angustiar, acongojar, afligir; **to be -ed** estar afligido o apurado.

distribute [dɪstríbjut] *v.* distribuir, repartir.

distribution [dɪstrəbjúʃən] *s.* distribución; repartimiento.

distributor [dɪstríbjətə] *s.* distribuidor

district [dístrɪkt] *s.* distrito; **— attorney** fiscal de distrito.

distrust [dɪstrÁst] *s.* desconfianza; recelo; *v.* desconfiar; recelar.

distrustful [dɪstrÁstfəl] *adj.* descon

fiado, sospechoso, receloso.

disturb [dɪstɜ́b] v. turbar, perturbar, inquietar; desarreglar; incomodar, molestar; **don't — yourself!** ¡no se moleste Vd.!

disturbance [dɪstɜ́bəns] s. disturbio; perturbación; desorden; alboroto; molestia.

disuse [dɪsjús] s. desuso; **to fall into —** caer en desuso; caducar.

ditch [dɪtʃ] s. zanja; foso; **irrigation —** acequia; v. zanjar, abrir zanjas; meter en la zanja; **to — someone** deshacerse de alguien.

ditto [dɪ́to] s. ídem, lo mismo.

divan [dáɪvæn] s. diván.

dive [daɪv] s. zambullida (echándose de cabeza), buceada, chapuz; picada (descenso rápido de un avión); garito, leonera; v. echarse de cabeza; zambullirse (de cabeza); bucear; sumergirse (un submarino); **to — into someone** abalanzarse sobre alguien.

diver [dáɪvə] s. buzo; zambullidor.

diverge [dəvɜ́dʒ] v. divergir, irse apartando, separarse; diferir.

divergence [dəvɜ́dʒəns] s. divergencia; diferencia (de opiniones).

divers [dáɪvəz] adj. diversos, varios.

diverse [dəvɜ́s] adj. diverso; diferente.

diversion [dəvɜ́ʒən] s. diversión, recreo; desviación.

diversity [dəvɜ́sɪtɪ] s. diversidad, diferencia, variedad.

divert [dəvɜ́t] v. divertir, entretener; distraer; desviar, apartar.

divide [dəváɪd] v. dividir(se); partir.

dividend [dɪ́vədend] s. dividendo.

divine [dəváɪn] adj. divino; v. adivinar.

divinity [dəvɪ́nətɪ] s. divinidad; deidad; teología.

division [dəvɪ́ʒən] s. división.

divorce [dəvɔ́rs] s. divorcio; v. divorciar(se).

divulge [dəvʌ́ldʒ] v. divulgar.

dizziness [dɪ́zɪnɪs] s. vahído o vaguido, desvanecimiento, mareo, vértigo.

dizzy [dɪ́zɪ] adj. desvanecido, mareado; confuso; aturdido; **— speed** velocidad vertiginosa.

do [du] v. hacer; **to — away with** deshacerse de; prescindir de; **to — a lesson** estudiar una lección; **to — one's hair** peinarse, arreglarse el pelo; **to — the dishes** lavar los platos; **to — up** envolver; limpiar; arreglar; lavar o planchar; **to — well in business** prosperar en los negocios; **to — without** pasarse sin; **to have nothing to — with** no tener nada que ver con; **that**

will — basta, bastará; that won't — eso no sirve; eso no resultará así; **this will have to —** habrá que conformarse con esto; **how — you — ?** ¿cómo está Vd.?; **— you hear me?** ¿me oye Vd.?; **yes, I — sí,** le oigo; **I — say it** sí lo digo.

docile [dásl] adj. dócil.

dock [dak] s. muelle, desembarcadero; dársena; **dry — carenero,** dique de carena; v. entrar en el muelle; atracar, meter (una embarcación) en el muelle o dique; **to — the wages** rebajar la paga.

doctor [dáktə] s. doctor; médico, facultativo; v. medicinar, curar; **to — oneself** medicinarse, tomar medicinas.

doctrine [dáktrɪn] s. doctrina.

document [dákjəmənt] s. documento; [dákjəment] v. documentar.

dodge [dadʒ] s. evasión, evasiva; v. evadir(se); escabullirse; hurtar el cuerpo; **to — around a corner** dar un esquinazo.

doe [do] s. cierva; hembra (del antílope, del gamo, de la liebre).

dog [dɔg] s. perro, perra; can; **hot — salchicha caliente,** Am. perro caliente; **to put on a lot of —** emperifollarse; darse mucho tono, Am. darse mucho corte; v. seguir la pista de, perseguir, acosar; adv. sumamente, completamente; **dog-tired** cansadísimo.

dogma [dɔ́gmə] s. dogma.

dogmatic [dɔgmǽtɪk] adj. dogmático.

doily [dɔ́ɪlɪ] s. mantelito (para platos, vasos, lámparas, etc.).

doings [dúɪŋz] s. pl. hechos, acciones, acontecimientos; **great —** mucha actividad, fiesta, función.

dole [dol] s. reparto gratuito (de dinero o alimento); ración, limosna; v. repartir gratuitamente.

doleful [dólfəl] adj. lúgubre, triste, lastimoso.

doll [dal] s. muñeca, muñeco; v. **to — up** emperifollarse, ataviarse; **dolly** s. muñequita.

dollar [dálə] s. dólar.

domain [domén] s. dominio; heredad.

dome [dom] s. cúpula; media naranja (de iglesia).

domestic [dəméstɪk] adj. doméstico; hogareño; nacional, del país, Am. criollo; s. criado, sirviente.

dominant [dámənənt] adj. dominante.

dominate [dámənet] v. dominar.

domination [damənéʃən] s. dominación, dominio.

domineer [damənír] v. dominar, señorear.

domineering [dɑmənírɪŋ] *adj.* dominador, mandón, imperioso, tiránico.

dominion [dəmínjən] *s.* dominio.

domino [dáməno] *s.* dominó, traje de máscara; disfraz; ficha (*de dominó*); **dominoes** dominó (*juego*).

don [dɑn] *s.* don (*título*); caballero; *v.* ponerse, vestirse.

donate [dónet] *v.* donar, regalar, hacer donación.

donation [donéʃən] *s.* donación; regalo, dádiva.

done [dʌn] *p.p. de* to do hecho; terminado, acabado; **to be — in** estar rendido de cansancio; **the meat is well —** está bien asada la carne.

donkey [dáŋkɪ] *s.* burro, asno.

doom [dum] *s.* hado, sino, destino; mala suerte, perdición, ruina; **the day of —** el día del juicio final; *v.* condenar, sentenciar; predestinar; **to be -ed to failure** estar predestinado al fracaso.

door [dor] *s.* puerta; entrada.

doorbell [dórbel] *s.* campanilla o timbre (*de llamada*).

doorknob [dórnɑb] *s.* tirador de puerta, perilla, manija.

doorman [dórmæn] *s.* portero.

doorstep [dórstep] *s.* escalón de la puerta; umbral.

doorway [dórwe] *s.* puerta, entrada; vano (*de la puerta*).

dope [dop] *s.* opio; narcótico; droga, menjurje, medicamento; información; **— fiend** morfinómano; **he is a —** es un zoquete; *v.* narcotizar; **to —** adivinar, conjeturar; **to — oneself up** medicinarse demasiado.

dormitory [dórmətɔrɪ] *s.* dormitorio.

dose [dos] *s.* dosis; *v.* medicinar; **to — oneself** medicinarse.

dot [dɑt] *s.* punto; **on the —** en punto; *v.* marcar con puntos; poner el punto (*sobre la* i).

dotage [dótɪdʒ] *s.* chochez; **to be in one's —** chochear.

dote [dot] *v.* chochear; **to — on** estar loco por.

double [dʌbl] *adj.* doble; doblado; **— boiler** baño de María; **— deal** trato doble; **— s** juego de dobles (*en tenis*); *adv.* doblemente; **doublebreasted** cruzado; **double-faced** de dos caras; *v.* doblar(se); duplicar(se); **to — up** doblarse; **doubly** *adv.* doblemente; por duplicado.

doubt [daʊt] *s.* duda; *v.* dudar.

doubtful [dáʊtfəl] *adj.* dudoso; dudable.

doubtless [dáʊtlɪs] *adj.* indudable, cierto,

seguro; *adv.* sin duda; indudablemente; probablemente.

douche [duʃ] *s.* ducha; jeringa.

dough [do] *s.* pasta, masa; dinero.

doughnut [dónət] *s.* bollito o buñuelo en rosca.

dove [dʌv] *s.* paloma.

dove [dov] *pret. de* to dive.

down [daʊn] *adv.* abajo, hacia abajo; **— to** hasta; **— East** en el este; **— the street** calle abajo; **to cut — prices** reducir o rebajar precios; **to get — to work** aplicarse; **to go (o come) — bajar**; **to pay —** pagar al contado; **to put —** poner; anotar, apuntar, poner por escrito; *adj.* abatido, descorazonado; **— grade** declive, pendiente; **prices are —** han bajado los precios; **to be — on someone** tenerle ojeriza a alguien; **— plumón**; vello; pelusa; *v.* echar por tierra, derribar; rebajar (*precios*).

downcast [dáʊnkæst] *adj.* cabizbajo, abatido; **with — eyes** con los ojos bajos.

downfall [dáʊnfɔl] *s.* caída; ruina.

downpour [dáʊnpor] *s.* aguacero, chaparrón.

downright [dáʊnraɪt] *adj.* claro, positivo, categórico, absoluto; **— foolishness** solemne disparate; *adv.* enteramente; absolutamente.

downstairs [dáʊnstérz] *adv.* abajo; en el piso bajo; *adj.* del piso bajo; *s.* piso bajo, piso inferior.

downstream [dáʊnstrím] *adv.* río abajo, aguas abajo; con la corriente.

downtown [dáʊntáʊn] *adv.* al centro, en el centro (*de una población*); *adj.* del centro; *s.* centro.

downward [dáʊnwəd] *adj.* descendente; inclinado; *adv.* (= **downwards**) hacia abajo.

downy [dáʊnɪ] *adj.* suave, blando; velloso; plumoso.

dowry [dáʊrɪ] *s.* dote.

doze [doz] *s.* siestecita, sueño ligero; *v.* dormitar.

dozen [dʌzn] *s.* docena.

drab [dræb] *adj.* pardo, pardusco; monótono.

draft [dræft] *s.* corriente de aire; trago; libranza, letra de cambio, giro bancario; trazado; plan; leva (*militar*), conscripción; tiro (*de estufa, hogar, etc.*); calado (*de un barco*); **— beer** cerveza de barril; **— horse** caballo de tiro; **— rough** croquis, borrador; *v.* trazar, dibujar, delinear; reclutar, echar leva; redactar (*un documento*).

draftsman [dráftsmən] *s.* dibujante.

drag [dræg] *s.* rastra; traba, obstáculo; **to have a — with someone** tener buenas aldabas con alguien; *v.* arrastrar(se); rastrear; moverse despacio; **to — on and on** prolongarse demasiado, prolongarse hasta el fastidio.

dragon [drǽgən] *s.* dragón.

drain [dren] *s.* desagüe, desaguadero, conducto; agotamiento; consumo; *v.* desaguar(se); apurar (*un vaso*); agotar, consumir; escurrir(se), secar(se); desecar (*un terreno*), *Am.* drenar.

drainage [drénidʒ] *s.* desagüe, *Am.* drenaje; desaguadero; sistema de desaguaderos; desecamiento, desecación (*de un terreno, laguna, etc.*).

drake [drek] *s.* pato.

drama [drámə] *s.* drama.

dramatic [drəmǽtɪk] *adj.* dramático.

dramatist [drǽmətɪst] *s.* dramaturgo, dramático.

dramatize [drǽmətaɪz] *v.* dramatizar.

drank [dræŋk] *pret. de to* **drink**.

drape [drep] *s.* colgadura, cortina, tapiz; *v.* colgar, entapizar, adornar con tapices; cubrir, revestir.

drapery [drépərɪ] *s.* tapicería, colgaduras, cortinas; pañería, paños, géneros.

drastic [drǽstɪk] *adj.* extremo, fuerte, violento; **to take — steps** tomar medidas enérgicas.

draught [dræft] *véase* **draft**.

draw [dro] *v.* tirar; estirar; jalar (halar); atraer; sacar; dibujar, trazar; girar, librar (*una libranza*); hacer (*una comparación*); correr (*la cortina*); **to — aside** apartar(se); **to — a breath** aspirar, tomar aliento; **to — lots** echar suertes, sortear; **to — near** acercarse; **to — out** sacar; sonsacar (*a una persona*); alargar, prolongar; **to — up** acercar(se); redactar (*un documento*); *s.* empate (*en deportes o juegos*); número sacado (*en una rifa*); atracción; **—bridge** puente levadizo.

drawback [dróbæk] *s.* desventaja; obstáculo, inconveniente.

drawer [dror] *s.* cajón, gaveta; **-s** calzoncillos.

drawer [dróə] *s.* librador, girador; dibujante.

drawing [dróɪŋ] *s.* dibujo; delineación, trazado; sorteo; **— paper** papel de dibujo; **— room** sala de recibo, recibidor, recibimiento.

drawn [dron] *p.p. de to* **draw**.

dread [dred] *s.* pavor, temor, aprensión; *adj.* terrible; temido; *v.* temer; sentir aprensión de.

dreadful [drédfəl] *adj.* horrendo; espantoso.

dream [drim] *s.* sueño; ensueño; *v.* soñar; **to — of** soñar con, soñar en.

dreamer [drímə] *s.* soñador.

dreamland [drímlænd] *s.* tierra del ensueño; región de los sueños.

dreamt [drempt] = **dreamed**.

dreamy [drimɪ] *adj.* soñoliento; soñador; melancólico; como un sueño; **a — recollection** un vago recuerdo.

dreary [drírɪ] *adj.* sombrío; melancólico.

dredge [dredʒ] *s.* draga; *v.* dragar.

dregs [dregz] *s. pl.* heces, sedimento.

drench [drentʃ] *s.* mojada, mojadura, empapada; *v.* empapar; mojar; remojar.

dress [dres] *s.* vestido, traje; vestidura, ropaje, atavío; **— rehearsal** ensayo general y último (*antes de una función*); **— suit** traje de etiqueta; *v.* vestir(se); arreglarse, componerse; aderezar; adobar (*carne o pieles*); curar (*heridas*); alinear, formar (*las tropas*); **to — down** reprender, regañar; **to — up** emperifollarse, acicalarse, ataviarse.

dresser [drésə] *s.* tocador, cómoda (*con espejo*); **she is a good —** viste con elegancia o buen gusto.

dressing [drésɪŋ] *s.* aderezo; salsa (*para ensaladas*); relleno (*para carne, pollo, etc.*); medicamento, vendajes (*para heridas*); **a — down** regaño; **— gown** bata; **— room** tocador; **— table** tocador.

dressmaker [drésmekə] *s.* modista.

drew [dru] *pret. de to* **draw**.

dribble [drɪbl] *v.* gotear; dejar caer en gotas; babear; *s.* goteo; chorrito.

driblet [drɪblɪt] *s.* gota, gotita; **in -s** gota a gota; en pequeñas cantidades.

dried [draɪd] *pret. & p.p. de to* **dry**; *adj.* seco; paso; **— fig** higo paso.

drift [drɪft] *s.* dirección, rumbo, tendencia; montón, amontonameinto (*de arena, nieve, etc.*); deriva, desvío (*de un barco o avión*); **to get the — of a conversation** enterarse a medias de una conversación; *v.* flotar; ir(se) a la deriva; dejarse llevar por la corriente; amontonarse (*la nieve, la arena*); esparcirse (*la arena, la nieve, las nubes*).

driftwood [drɪftwʊd] *s.* madera o leña flotante; madera de playa.

drill [drɪl] *s.* taladro, barrena; ejercicio; adiestramiento, *Am.* entrenamiento; disciplina; dril (*tela*); *v.* taladrar, barrenar, perforar; hacer ejercicio; aleccionar; disciplinar (*un ejército*); adiestrar(se), *Am.* entrenar(se).

drily [dráɪlɪ] *adv.* secamente.

drink [driŋk] *s.* bebida; trago; *v.* beber; **to — a toast** to beber a la salud de, brindar por; **— it down!** ¡bébaselo! ¡trágueselo.

drinkable [dríŋkəbl] *adj.* potable.

drip [drip] *s.* goteo; *v.* gotear, caer gota a gota; dejar caer gota a gota.

drive [draiv] *s.* paseo en coche o automóvil; calzada, carretera; campaña; empuje; tiro, tirada (*de una pelota*); *v.* impulsar, impeler, empujar; arrear (*animales*); conducir, guiar o manejar (*un auto*); forzar; encajar, clavar (*una estaca, cuña, o clavo*); tirar, lanzar (*una pelota*); dar un paseo en auto; llevar (*a alguien*) en auto; cavar (*un pozo, túnel, etc.*); **to — away** ahuyentar; **to — a good bargain** hacer un buen trato; **to — mad** volver loco; **what are you driving at?** ¿qué quieres decir con eso?

drivel [drivl] *s.* baba; ñoñería, tontería; *v.* babear; chochear, decir ñoñerías.

driveling [drivliŋ] *adj.* baboso.

driven [drivn] *p.p. de* to drive.

driver [dráivə] *s.* cochero, chófer, mecánico, conductor (*de automóvil*); arriero (*de animales*); uno de los palos de golf; **pile —** martinete (*para clavar pilotes*); **slave —** mandón, tirano; **truck —** carretero, camionero.

driveway [dráivwe] *s.* calzada de entrada, carretera de entrada.

drizzle [drizl] *v.* lloviznar; *s.* llovizna.

drone [dron] *s.* zángano; holgazán; zumbido; *v.* zumbar; hablar con monotonía; holgazanear, perder el tiempo.

droop [drup] *v.* doblarse, andar o estar alicaído; estar abatido; languidecer; marchitarse; bajar (*los hombros, los párpados*); **his shoulders —** tiene los hombros caídos; **-ing eyelids** párpados caídos.

drop [drɑp] *s.* gota; declive; baja; caída; **cough —** pastilla para la tos; **letter —** buzón; **— curtain** telón (*de teatro*); **— hammer** martinete *v.* dejar caer, soltar; gotear; caer; dejar (*un asunto, una amistad*); **to — a line** poner unos renglones; **to — asleep** quedarse dormido, dormirse; **to — behind** dejar atrás; quedarse atrás; **to — in** hacer una visita inesperada, *Am.* descolgarse; **to — in a mailbox** echar al buzón; **to — out** retirarse; desaparecer; **to — the curtain** bajar el telón.

drought [draut] *s.* sequía.

drove [drov] *s.* manada, recua, rebaño; tropel; *pret. de* to drive.

drown [draun] *v.* ahogar(se), anegar(se);

apagar, ahogar (*un sonido*).

drowse [drauz] *v.* dormitar; estar amodorrado.

drowsiness [dráuzinis] *s.* modorra, somnolencia.

drowsy [dráuzi] *adj.* soñoliento; adormilado, amodorrado; **to become —** amodorrarse.

drudge [drʌdʒ] *v.* afanarse, atarearse; *s.* trabajador, esclavo del trabajo.

drug [drʌg] *s.* droga; narcótico; **to be a — on the market** ser invendible (*una mercancía*); *v.* jaropar (*administrar drogas en demasía*); narcotizar.

druggist [drʌgist] *s.* boticario, droguista, droguero, farmacéutico.

drugstore [drʌgstor] *s.* botica, droguería, farmacia.

drum [drʌm] *s.* tambor; tímpano (*del oído*); barril, tonel; **bass —** tambora, bombo; **—stick** bolillo de tambor; *v.* tocar el tambor; tamborilear; **to — a lesson into someone** meterle a uno la lección en la cabeza; **to — up trade** solicitar o fomentar ventas.

drummer [drʌmə] *s.* tambor, tamborilero; viajante de comercio, agente.

drunk [drʌŋk] *p.p. de* to drink; *adj.* borracho, ebrio, emborrachado, bebido; **to get —** emborracharse, embriagarse.

drunkard [drʌŋkəd] *s.* borracho, borrachín, beodo, bebedor.

drunken [drʌŋkən] *adj.* borracho, ebrio.

drunkenness [drʌŋkənnis] *s.* borrachera, embriaguez.

dry [drai] *adj.* seco; árido; **a — book** un libro aburrido; **— cleaner** quitamanchas; tintorero; **— cleaning** lavado o limpieza al seco; **— goods** lencería, géneros, tejidos, telas; **— measure** medida para áridos; *v.* secar(se); enjugar; **to — up** secarse, resecarse.

dryness [dráinis] *s.* sequedad; aridez.

dubious [djúbiəs] *adj.* dudoso.

duchess [dátʃis] *s.* duquesa.

duck [dʌk] *s.* pato, pata; ánade; dril (*género*); zambullida, chapuz; agachada rápida (*para evitar un golpe*); *v.* zambullir(se), chapuzar(se); agachar(se); agachar (*la cabeza*).

duckling [dʌkliŋ] *s.* patito, anadeja.

due [dju] *adj.* debido; vencido, pagadero; **in — time** a su debido tiempo; **the bill is —** se ha vencido la cuenta; **the train is — at two o'clock** el tren debe llegar a las dos; *adv.* directamente; **— east** hacia el este, rumbo al oriente; *s.* derecho, privilegio; **-s** cuota.

duel [djúəl] *s.* duelo, desafío, combate; *v.* batirse en duelo.

duet [djuét] *s.* duo, dueto.

dug [dʌg] *pret. & p.p. de* **to dig.**

duke [djuk] *s.* duque.

dukedom [djúkdəm] *s.* ducado.

dull [dʌl] *adj.* opaco, empañado, mate; sin brillo; aburrido; embotado, sin punta, sin filo; torpe, tardo; para dolor sordo; — sound sonido sordo o apagado; *v.* embotar(se); empañar(se); ofuscar; amortiguar (*un dolor o sonido*).

dullness [dʌlnɪs] *s.* falta de brillo; estupidez, torpeza; falta de punta o filo; aburrimiento; embotamiento (*de los sentidos o inteligencia*); pesadez.

duly [djúlɪ] *adv.* debidamente.

dumb [dʌm] *adj.* mudo; silencioso, callado; estúpido, torpe; — creature animal.

dumbness [dʌmnɪs] *s.* mudez; mutismo; estupidez.

dummy [dʌmɪ] *s.* maniquí, figurón, muñeco; zoquete, tonto; *adj.* falso, fingido.

dump [dʌmp] *s.* montón (*de tierra, carbón, etc.*); terrero, vaciadero, escorial; garbage — muladar; basurero; to be in the —s estar abatido; *v.* echar, vaciar, descargar; echar a la basura.

dunce [dʌns] *s.* zopenco, zoquete, tonto.

dune [djun] *s.* duna o médano.

dung [dʌŋ] *s.* boñiga, estiércol.

dungeon [dʌndʒən] *s.* mazmorra, calabozo.

dunghill [dʌŋhɪl] *s.* muladar, estercolero.

dupe [djup] *s.* inocentón, incauto, víctima (*de un engaño*); *v.* embaucar.

duplicate [djúpləkɪt] *adj. & s.* doble, duplicado; [djúpləket] *v.* duplicar, copiar.

duplicity [djuplísətɪ] *s.* duplicidad, doblez.

durable [djúrəbl] *adj.* durable, duradero.

duration [djuréʃən] *s.* duración.

during [dúrɪŋ] *prep.* durante.

dusk [dʌsk] *s.* crepúsculo (*vespertino*), anochecida; caída de la tarde; sombra, oscuridad; at — al atardecer.

dusky [dʌskɪ] *adj.* obscuro, negruzco; sombrío.

dust [dʌst] *s.* polvo; tierra; cloud of — polvareda; *v.* sacudir el polvo, desempolvar, quitar el polvo; empolvar, llenar de polvo; espolvorear.

duster [dʌstə] *s.* limpiador; quitapolvo; feather — plumero.

dusty [dʌstɪ] *adj.* polvoriento; empolvado, lleno de polvo.

Dutch [dʌtʃ] *adj. & s.* holandés; — treat convite a escote.

Dutchman [dʌtʃmən] *s.* holandés.

duty [djútɪ] *s.* deber, obligación; derechos aduanales; impuesto; — free libre de derechos aduanales.

dwarf [dwɔrf] *s. & adj.* enano; *v.* achicar, empequeñecer; impedir el desarrollo o crecimiento de.

dwell [dwel] *v.* residir, morar, habitar vivir; to — on a subject espaciarse o dilatarse en un asunto.

dweller [dwélə] *s.* habitante, morador.

dwelling [dwélɪŋ] *s.* morada, habitación, domicilio.

dwelt [dwelt] *pret. & p.p. de* **to dwell.**

dwindle [dwíndl] *v.* menguar, mermar; disminuir(se); gastarse.

dye [daɪ] *s.* tinte, tintura; *v.* teñir, tinturar.

dyer [dáɪə] *s.* tintorero; -'s shop tintorería.

dying [dáɪɪŋ] *adj.* moribundo; agonizante.

dynamic [daɪnǽmɪk] *adj.* dinámico; enérgico; -s *s.* dinámica.

dynamite [dáɪnəmaɪt] *s.* dinamita; *v.* dinamitar, volar con dinamita.

dynamo [dáɪnəmo] *s.* dínamo.

dynasty [dáɪnæstɪ] *s.* dinastía.

dysentery [dísəntɪ] *s.* disentería.

E

each [itʃ] *adj.* cada; *pron.* cada uno; — other el uno al otro, uno(s) a otro(s).

eager [ígə] *adj.* anhelante, ansioso, deseoso; -ly *adv.* con anhelo; con ahinco; ansiosamente.

eagerness [ígənɪs] *s.* anhelo, ansia, deseo vehemente; ahinco; ardor.

eagle [ígl] *s.* águila.

ear [ɪr] *s.* oreja; oído; —drum tímpano; — muff orejera; — of corn mazorca; — of wheat espiga; by — de oído; within —shot al alcance del oído.

earl [ɜl] *s.* conde.

early [ɜlɪ] *adv.* temprano; *adj.* temprano; primitivo, remoto; — riser madrugador, tempranero, mañanero; at an — date en fecha próxima.

earn [ɜn] *v.* ganar; merecer.

earnest [ɜnɪst] *adj.* serio, formal; ardiente; in — en serio, con toda formalidad; de buena fe; -ly *adv.* seriamente; con ahinco; encarecidamente, ansiosamente.

earnestness [ɜnɪstnɪs] *s.* seriedad; celo; solicitud; sinceridad; in all — con todo ahinco; con toda formalidad; con toda sinceridad.

earnings [ə́nɪŋz] s. ganancias; sueldo, salario, paga.

earring [írrɪŋ] s. arete, zarcillo, pendiente, arracada.

earth [ɜθ] s. tierra; suelo.

earthen [ɜ́ən] adj. de tierra; de barro.

earthenware [ɜ́ənwer] s. loza de barro; trastos, cacharros.

earthly [ɜ́lɪ] adj. terrenal, terrestre, mundano; terreno; **to be of no — use** no servir para nada.

earthquake [ɜ́kwek] s. terremoto, temblor de tierra.

earthworm [ɜ́wɜm] s. lombriz.

ease [iz] s. facilidad; naturalidad; soltura; comodidad; tranquilidad; **at —** tranquilo; cómodo; v. facilitar; aliviar; mitigar; tranquilizar; aligerar (el peso); aflojar.

easel [íz] s. caballete (de pintor).

easily [ízəlɪ] adv. fácilmente; sin dificultad; cómodamente.

east [ist] s. este; oriente, levante; adj. del este, oriental; adv. al este, hacia el este; en el este.

Easter [ístə] s. Pascuas, Pascua Florida; **— Sunday** Domingo de Resurrección o de Pascuas.

eastern [ístən] adj. oriental; del este.

eastward [ístwəd] adv. & adj. hacia el este u oriente.

easy [ízɪ] adj. fácil; cómodo; dócil; tranquilo; **— chair** silla cómoda, poltrona, butaca; **easy-going man** hombre cachazudo o calmo; **at an —** pace a paso moderado; **within — reach** al alcance; a la mano.

eat [it] v. comer; **to — away** corroer, destruir; **to — breakfast** desayunarse, tomar el desayuno; **to — dinner** tomar la comida, comer; **to — supper** tomar la cena, cenar; **to — one's heart out** sufrir en silencio; **to — one's words** retractarse.

eaten [ítŋ] p.p. de **to eat.**

eaves [ivz] s. pl. alero (de un tejado).

ebb [ɛb] s. reflujo; decadencia; **— tide** marea menguante; **to be at a low —** estar decaído; v. menguar, decaer.

ebony [ɛ́bənɪ] s. ébano.

eccentric [ɪksɛ́ntrɪk] adj. & s. excéntrico.

ecclesiastic [ɪklizɪǽstɪk] adj. & s. eclesiástico.

echo [ɛ́ko] s. eco; v. hacer eco, repetir; resonar, repercutir.

eclipse [ɪklɪ́ps] s. eclipse; v. eclipsar.

economic [ikənámɪk] adj. económico.

economical [ikənámɪk] adj. económico.

economics [ikənámɪks] s. economía política.

economist [ikánəmɪst] s. economista.

economize [ikánəmaɪz] v. economizar

economy [ikánəmɪ] s. economía; parsimonia.

ecstasy [ɛ́kstəsɪ] s. éxtasis.

eddy [ɛ́dɪ] s. remolino; v. arremolinarse.

Eden [ídŋ] s. Edén; paraíso.

edge [ɛdʒ] s. orilla, borde; filo; **to be on — estar** nervioso.

edgewise [ɛ́dʒwaɪz] adv. de lado; de filo.

edible [ɛ́dəbl] adj. & s. comestible.

edifice [ɛ́dəfɪs] s. edificio.

edify [ɛ́dəfaɪ] v. edificar (moral y espiritualmente).

edit [ɛ́dɪt] v. redactar; preparar o corregir (un manuscrito) para la imprenta; cuidar (una edición).

edition [ɪdɪ́ʃən] s. edición.

editor [ɛ́dɪtə] s. redactor; director de un periódico; revisor (de manuscritos).

editorial [ɛdətórɪəl] adj. editorial; s. editorial (m.), artículo de fondo.

educate [ɛ́dʒəket] v. educar; instruir.

education [ɛdʒəkéʃən] s. educación; crianza; instrucción, enseñanza; pedagogía.

educational [ɛdʒəkéʃənl] adj. educativo, docente; pedagógico.

educator [ɛ́dʒəketə] s. educador.

eel [il] s. anguila.

effect [əfɛ́kt] s. efecto; **-s** bienes, efectos; **to go into —** hacerse vigente, ponerse en operación (una ley); v. efectuar; ejecutar; realizar.

effective [əfɛ́ktɪv] adj. efectivo, eficaz; vigente (una ley), **-ly** adv. eficazmente.

effectual [əfɛ́ktʃʊəl] adj. eficaz.

effeminate [əfɛ́mənɪt] adj. afeminado.

efficacy [ɛ́fəkəsɪ] s. eficacia.

efficiency [əffɛ́ənsɪ] s. eficiencia; eficacia.

efficient [əffɛ́ənt] adj. eficiente; eficaz.

effort [ɛ́fət] s. esfuerzo; empeño.

effrontery [əfrʌ́ntərɪ] s. descaro, desvergüenza, desfachatez.

effusive [əfjúsɪv] adj. efusivo, demostrativo, expansivo.

egg [ɛg] s. huevo; **fried —** huevo frito o estrellado; **hard-boiled —** huevo cocido, huevo duro; **scrambled -s** huevos revueltos; **soft-boiled —** huevos pasados por agua; v. **to — on** incitar.

eggplant [ɛ́gplænt] s. berenjena.

egotism [ígətɪzəm] s. egotismo; egoísmo.

Egyptian [ɪdʒɪ́pʃən] adj. & s egipcio.

either [íðə] adj. & pron. uno u otro; **— of the two** cualquiera de los dos, **in — case** en ambos casos; adv. tampoco, **nor I —** ni yo tampoco; conj. o

eject [ɪdʒɛ́kt] v. echar, arrojar, expulsar.

elaborate [ɪlǽbərɪt] adj. elaborado, primoroso; esmerado; [ɪlǽbəret] v. elaborar.

elapse [ɪlǽps] v. transcurrir, pasar.

elastic [ɪlǽstɪk]·adj. elástico; s. elástico; goma elástica; cordón elástico; liga elástica.

elasticity [ɪlæstfsətɪ] s. elasticidad.

elated [ɪlétɪd] adj. exaltado, gozoso, alborozado.

elbow [ɛlbó] s. codo; recodo, ángulo; to be within — reach estar a la mano; v. codear, dar codazos; to — one's way through abrirse paso a codazos.

elder [ɛ́ldə] adj. mayor, más grande, más viejo, de más edad; s. mayor; anciano; dignatario (en ciertas iglesias); our —s nuestros mayores; nuestros antepasados.

elderly [ɛ́ldəlɪ] adj. viejo, anciano.

eldest [ɛ́ldɪst] adj. mayor.

elect [ɪlɛ́kt] adj. & s. electo; elegido; v. elegir.

election [ɪlɛ́kʃən] s. elección.

elector [ɪlɛ́ktə] s. elector.

electoral [ɪlɛ́ktərəl] adj. electoral.

electric [ɪlɛ́ktrɪk] adj. eléctrico; — meter electrómetro, contador eléctrico; — storm tronada, tempestad; s. tranvía o ferrocarril eléctrico.

electrical [ɪlɛ́ktrɪk] adj. eléctrico; — engineering electrotecnia, ingeniería eléctrica; — engineer ingeniero electricista; electrotécnico.

electrician [ɪlɛktrɪ́ʃən] s. electricista.

electricity [ɪlɛktrɪ́sətɪ] s. electricidad.

electrify [ɪlɛ́ktrəfaɪ] v. electrizar; electrificar.

electrocute [ɪlɛ́ktrəkjut] v. electrocutar.

elegance [ɛ́ləgəns] s. elegancia.

elegant [ɛ́ləgənt] adj. elegante.

element [ɛ́ləmənt] s. elemento.

elemental [ɛləmɛ́ntl] adj. elemental.

elementary [ɛləmɛ́ntərɪ] adj. elemental.

elephant [ɛ́ləfənt] s. elefante.

elevate [ɛ́ləvet] v. elevar; alzar, levantar.

elevation [ɛləvéʃən] s. elevación; altura; exaltación.

elevator [ɛ́ləvetə] s. ascensor, Am. elevador; grain — almacén de granos.

elicit [ɪlɪ́sɪt] v. extraer, sonsacar; to — admiration despertar admiración; to — applause suscitar el aplauso o los aplausos.

eligible [ɛ́lɪdʒəbl] adj. elegible.

eliminate [ɪlɪ́mənet] v. eliminar.

elimination [ɪlɪmənéʃən] s. eliminación.

elk [ɛlk] s. ante.

elm [ɛlm] s. olmo.

elope [ɪlóp] v. fugarse (con su novio).

eloquence [ɛ́ləkwəns] s. elocuencia.

eloquent [ɛ́ləkwənt] adj. elocuente.

else [ɛls] adj. & adv. otro (úsase sólo en ciertas combinaciones); más, además; or — de otro modo; si no; nobody — ningún otro; nothing — nada más; somebody — algún otro, otra persona; what — ? ¿qué más?

elsewhere [ɛ́lʃwer] adv. en otra parte, a otra parte.

elucidate [ɪlúsədet] v. elucidar, esclarecer, aclarar, clarificar.

elucidation [ɪlusədéʃən] s. elucidación, esclarecimiento, explicación.

elude [ɪlúd] v. eludir, evadir.

emaciated [ɪméʃɪetɪd] adj. demacrado, escuálido, macilento.

emanate [ɛ́mənet] v. emanar, brotar.

emanation [ɛmənéʃən] s. emanación; efluvio.

emancipate [ɪmǽnsəpet] v. emancipar.

emancipation [ɪmænsəpéʃən] s. emancipación.

embalm [ɪmbám] v. embalsamar.

embankment [ɪmbǽŋkmənt] s. terraplén; dique.

embargo [ɪmbárgo] s. embargo; prohibición; to put an — on embargar.

embark [ɪmbárk] v. embarcar(se).

embarrass [ɪmbǽrəs] v. turbar, desconcertar; apenar; avergonzar; embarazar; to be financially -ed encontrarse escaso de fondos.

embarrassing [ɪmbǽrəsɪŋ] adj. embarazoso, penoso; desconcertante; angustioso.

embarrassment [ɪmbǽrəsmənt] s. turbación, vergüenza, desconcierto; aprieto, apuro, dificultad; estorbo, embarazo.

embassy [ɛ́mbəsɪ] s. embajada.

embellish [ɪmbɛ́lɪʃ] v. embellecer, hermosear.

ember [ɛ́mbə] s. ascua; -s ascuas, rescoldo.

embezzle [ɪmbɛ́zl] v. desfalcar.

embezzlement [ɪmbɛ́zlmənt] s. desfalco, peculado.

embitter [ɪmbɪ́tə] v. amargar.

emblem [ɛ́mbləm] s. emblema.

embody [ɪmbádɪ] v. encarnar, dar cuerpo a; incorporar, abarcar.

emboss [ɪmbós] v. realzar, grabar en relieve.

embrace [ɪmbrés] s. abrazo; v. abrazar(se); abarcar.

embroider [ɪmbróɪdə] v. bordar; recamar; ornar, embellecer.

embroidery [ɪmbróɪdərɪ] s. bordado; bordadura; recamo.

emerald [ɛ́mərəld] s. esmeralda.

emerge [ɪmɜ́dʒ] v. emerger; surtir.

emergency [ɪmɜ́dʒənsɪ] s. caso fortuito; aprieto; urgencia; emergencia.

emigrant [émɑgrənt] adj. & s. emigrante.

emigrate [émɑgret] v. emigrar.

emigration [emɑgréʃən] s. emigración.

eminence [émənəns] s. eminencia.

eminent [émənənt] adj. eminente.

emit [ɪmft] v. emitir; exhalar, arrojar; despedir (olor, humo, etc.).

emotion [ɪmóʃən] s. emoción.

emotional [ɪmóʃən] adj. emocional; emotivo; sentimental; sensible.

emperor [émpərə] s. emperador.

emphasis [émfəsɪs] s. énfasis.

emphasize [émfəsaɪz] v. dar énfasis; hacer hincapié en; subrayar, recalcar; acentuar.

emphatic [ɪmfǽtɪk] adj. enfático; recalcado; **-ally** adv. enfáticamente.

empire [émpaɪr] s. imperio.

employ [ɪmplóɪ] v. emplear; dar empleo a; ocupar; **to be in his —** ser su empleado; trabajar a sus órdenes.

employee [ɪmplóɪí] s. empleado.

employer [ɪmplóɪə] s. patrón, amo, principal.

employment [ɪmplóɪmənt] s. empleo; ocupación.

empower [ɪmpáʊə] v. autorizar; apoderar (dar poder a un abogado).

empress [émprɪs] s. emperatriz.

emptiness [émptɪnɪs] s. vaciedad; futilidad, vanidad.

empty [émptɪ] adj. vacío; vacante, desocupado; vano; v. vaciar; desaguar, desembocar.

enable [ɪnébl] v. capacitar, hacer capaz; habilitar, dar poder; facilitar; hacer posible.

enact [ɪnǽkt] v. decretar, promulgar; hacer el papel de.

enamel [ɪnǽml] s. esmalte; v. esmaltar.

enamor [ɪnǽmə] v. enamorar, mover a amar; encantar; **to be -ed of** estar enamorado de.

encamp [ɪnkǽmp] v. acampar.

enchant [ɪntʃǽnt] v. encantar; embelesar; hechizar.

enchanter [ɪntʃǽntə] s. encantador; hechichero, mago, brujo.

enchantment [ɪntʃǽntmənt] s. encanto; encantamiento; hechicería.

enchantress [ɪntʃǽntrɪs] s. encantadora; hechicera, bruja.

encircle [ɪnsɜ́kl] v. cercar, rodear, ceñir.

enclose [ɪnklóz] v. encerrar; cercar, rodear, circundar; incluir.

enclosure [ɪnklóʒə] s. recinto, cercado, vallado; remesa, lo remitido (dentro de una carta), lo adjunto; encerramiento.

encompass [ɪnkʌ́mpəs] v. abarcar; encuadrar; rodear, ceñir, circundar.

encounter [ɪnkáʊntə] s. encuentro; combate; v. encontrar(se); encontrarse con; tropezar con.

encourage [ɪnkɜ́ɪdʒ] v. alentar, animar; fomentar.

encouragement [ɪnkɜ́ɪdʒmənt] s. aliento, ánimo; estímulo; fomento.

encroach [ɪnkrótʃ] v. **to — upon** usurpar, invadir, meterse en, quitar (el tiempo).

encyclopedia [ɪnsaɪkləpídɪə] s. enciclopedia.

end [ɛnd] s. fin; cabo; término; extremo; **no — of things** un sin fin de cosas; **odds and -s** retazos; **on — de punta**; **to put an — to** acabar con, poner fin a; v. acabar; terminar; concluir, dar fin.

endanger [ɪndéndʒə] v. poner en peligro, arriesgar.

endear [ɪndfr] v. hacer amar, hacer querer; **to — oneself** hacerse querer.

endeavor [ɪndévə] s. esfuerzo, empeño; tentativa; tarea; v. procurar, tratar de, intentar; esforzarse por o en.

ending [éndɪŋ] s. final; terminación; conclusión.

endless [éndlɪs] adj. sin fin, interminable, inacabable; eterno.

endorse = indorse.

endorsement = indorsement.

endow [ɪndáʊ] v. dotar.

endowment [ɪndáʊmənt] s. dotación; dote, don.

endurance [ɪndjúrəns] s. resistencia; aguante; paciencia; duración.

endure [ɪndjúr] v. aguantar, soportar; sufrir; durar, perdurar.

enema [énəmə] s. lavativa.

enemy [énəmɪ] s. enemigo.

energetic [enədʒétɪk] adj. enérgico.

energy [énədʒɪ] s. energía.

enervate [énəvet] v. enervar, debilitar.

enfold = infold.

enforce [ɪnfórs] v. dar fuerza a; hacer cumplir (una ley); **to — obedience** hacer obedecer, imponer obediencia.

enforcement [ɪnfórsmənt] s. coacción; cumplimiento forzoso (de una ley).

engage [ɪngédʒ] v. ocupar; emplear, contratar; atraer (la atención); alquilar; engranar, acoplar; **to — in battle** trabar batalla; **to — (oneself) to do it** comprometerse a hacerlo; **to be -ed in something** estar ocupado en algo; **to be -ed to be married** estar comprometido para casarse.

engagement [ɪngédʒmənt] s. compromiso; cita; noviazgo; convenio, contrato; pelea; traba, engrane, acoplamiento (*de maquinaria*).

engender [ɪndʒéndə] v. engendrar, producir.

engine [éndʒən] s. máquina; motor; locomotora.

engineer [endʒənír] s. ingeniero; maquinista (*de locomotora*); v. dirigir, planear.

engineering [endʒənírɪŋ] s. ingeniería; manejo, planeo.

English [íŋglɪʃ] adj. inglés; s. inglés, idioma inglés; **the — los** ingleses.

Englishman [íŋglɪʃmən] s. inglés.

engrave [ɪngrév] v. grabar, esculpir.

engraving [ɪngrévɪŋ] s. grabado; estampa, lámina; **wood — grabado** en madera.

engrossed [ɪngróst] adj. absorto, ensimismado.

engulf [ɪngʌ́lf] v. engolfar, absorber, tragar.

enhance [ɪnhǽns] v. realzar; engrandecer.

enigma [ɪnígmə] s. enigma.

enjoin [ɪndʒɔ́ɪn] v. mandar, ordenar; **to — from** prohibir, vedar.

enjoy [ɪndʒɔ́ɪ] v. gozar de; disfrutar de; **to — oneself** divertirse, gozar, deleitarse; **to — the use of** usufructuar.

enjoyable [ɪndʒɔ́ɪəbl] adj. agradable, deleitable.

enjoyment [ɪndʒɔ́ɪmənt] s. placer, goce, disfrute; usufructo.

enlarge [ɪnlárdʒ] v. agrandar(se); ensanchar; ampliar; **to — upon** explayarse en, extenderse en; comentar.

enlighten [ɪnláɪtn] v. alumbrar; iluminar; ilustrar, instruir.

enlist [ɪnlíst] v. alistar(se); sentar plaza (*de soldado*); reclutar.

enlistment [ɪnlístmənt] s. reclutamiento; alistamiento.

enliven [ɪnláɪvən] v. avivar, animar, alegrar.

enmity [énməti] s. enemistad.

ennoble [ɪnóbl] v. ennoblecer.

enormous [ɪnórməs] adj. enorme.

enough [ənʌ́f] adj. & adv. bastante; s. lo bastante, lo suficiente; **that is — eso** basta, con eso basta; **—! ¡**basta!.

enquire = **inquire**.

enrage [ɪnrédʒ] v. enrabiar, hacer rabiar; enfurecer.

enrapture [ɪnrǽptʃə] v. extasiar, embelesar, enajenar.

enrich [ɪnrítʃ] v. enriquecer.

enroll [ɪnról] v. alistar(se); matricular(se); inscribir(se); hacerse miembro.

enrollment [ɪnrólmənt] s. alistamiento; registro, matrícula.

ensign [énsn] s. alférez (*de la marina*); [énsaɪn] bandera; insignia.

enslave [ɪnslév] v. esclavizar.

ensnare [ensnér] v. enredar, entrampar, embaucar.

ensue [ensú] v. sobrevenir, seguir(se), resultar.

entail [ɪntél] v. envolver, ocasionar; vincular (*una herencia*).

entangle [ɪntǽŋgl] v. enredar, enmarañar, embrollar.

enter [éntə] v. entrar en; ingresar en; asentar (*una partida, cantidad, etc.*); registrar; salir (*al escenario*).

enterprise [éntəpraɪz] s. empresa.

enterprising [éntəpraɪzɪŋ] adj. emprendedor.

entertain [entətén] v. divertir; agasajar; obsequiar; banquetear; acariciar (*una idea*); abrigar (*una esperanza, un rencor*); **she -s a great deal** es muy fiestera u obsequiosa.

entertaining [entəténɪŋ] adj. entretenido, divertido, chistoso.

entertainment [entəténmənt] s. entretenimiento; pasatiempo; diversión; fiesta; convite.

enthusiasm [ɪnejúziæzəm] s. entusiasmo.

enthusiast [ɪnejúziæst] s. entusiasta.

enthusiastic [ɪnejuziǽstɪk] adj. entusiasta, entusiástico; **to be — estar** estusiasmado.

entice [ɪntáɪs] v. atraer, tentar, seducir, halagar.

entire [ɪntáɪr] adj. entero, cabal; **the — world** todo el mundo; **-ly** adv. enteramente, por entero.

entirety [ɪntáɪrtɪ] s. totalidad, entereza; conjunto; todo.

entitle [ɪntáɪtl] v. titular, intitular; autorizar, dar derecho.

entity [éntəti] s. entidad; ente, ser.

entrails [éntrəlz] s. pl. entrañas; tripas.

entrance [éntrəns] s. entrada; ingreso.

entreat [ɪntrít] v. suplicar, rogar; instar.

entreaty [ɪntrítɪ] s. súplica, ruego; instancia.

entrench = **intrench**.

entrust [ɪntrʌ́st] v. confiar; depositar, entregar.

entry [éntrɪ] s. entrada; ingreso; partida, registro, anotación; **double — partida** doble (*en teneduría*).

enumerate [ɪnjúmərɛt] v. enumerar.

enunciate [ɪnʌ́nsɪɛt] v. articular; enunciar, declarar.

envelop [ɪnvéləp] v. envolver.

71

envelope [énvəlop] s. sobre, cubierta (*de una carta*).

enviable [énviəbl] adj. envidiable.

envious [énviəs] adj. envidioso.

environment [ınváırənmənt] s. ambiente, medio ambiente.

environs [ınváırənz] s. pl. cercanías, contornos, alrededores.

envoy [énvɔı] s. enviado.

envy [énvı] s. envidia; v. envidiar.

epic [épık] s. epopeya, poema épico; adj. épico.

epidemic [epədémık] s. epidemia; peste; adj. epidémico.

episode [épəsod] s. episodio.

epistle [ıpísl] s. epístola, carta.

epitaph [épətæf] s. epitafio.

epoch [épək] s. época.

equal [íkwəl] adj. igual; **to be — to a task** ser competente (*o* tener suficientes fuerzas) para una tarea; s. igual; cantidad igual; v. igualar; ser igual a; **-ly** adv. igualmente; por igual.

equality [ıkwálətı] s. igualdad.

equalize [íkwəlaız] v. igualar; emparejar; equilibrar; nivelar.

equation [ıkwéʒən] s. ecuación.

equator [ıkwétə] s. ecuador.

equilibrium [ıkwəlíbrıəm] s. equilibrio.

equip [ıkwíp] v. equipar; proveer; habilitar.

equipment [ıkwípmənt] s. equipo; aparatos; avíos; habilitación.

equity [ékwətı] s. equidad; justicia.

equivalent [ıkwívələnt] adj. & s. equivalente.

equivocal [ıkwívəkl] adj. equívoco, ambiguo.

era [írə] s. era, época.

eradicate [ırǽdıket] v. desarraigar; extirpar.

erase [ırés] v. borrar; tachar.

eraser [ırésə] s. goma, *Am.* borrador; **blackboard —** cepillo.

erasure [ıréʒə] s. borradura, raspadura.

ere [er] prep. antes de; conj. antes (de) que.

erect [ırékt] adj. erguido; derecho; levantado; *Am.* parado; v. erigir; levantar; alzar.

ermine [ʒ́mın] s. armiño.

erosion [ıróʒən] s. erosión; desgaste.

err [ʒ] v. errar; equivocarse; descarriarse.

errand [érənd] s. mandado, recado, encargo; **— boy** mandadero.

errant [érənt] adj. errante; **knight-errant** caballero andante.

erroneous [əróniəs] adj. erróneo, errado.

error [érə] s. error.

erudition [erudíʃən] s. erudición.

eruption [ırʌ́pʃən] s. erupción.

escapade [éskəped] s. trapisonda, travesura.

escape [əskép] s. escape; fuga, huída; escapada; escapatoria; v. escapar(se); fugarse; huir(se); eludir, evadir; **it -s me** se me escapa.

escort [éskɔrt] s. escolta; acompañante; convoy; [ıskɔ́rt] v. escoltar; convoyar; acompañar.

escutcheon [ıskʌ́tʃən] s. escudo de armas, blasón.

especial [əspéʃəl] adj. especial; **-ly** adv. especialmente.

espionage [éspıanıdʒ] s. espionaje.

essay [ése] s. ensayo; [esé] v. ensayar.

essence [ésns] s. esencia.

essential [əsénʃəl] adj. esencial.

establish [əstǽblıʃ] v. establecer.

establishment [əstǽblıʃmənt] s. establecimiento.

estate [əstét] s. hacienda, heredad; bienes, propiedades; estado, condición; **country —** finca rural.

esteem [əstím] s. estima, estimación, aprecio; v. estimar, apreciar; considerar, juzgar.

estimable [éstəməbl] adj. estimable.

estimate [éstəmıt] s. tasa, cálculo aproximado; presupuesto; opinión; [éstəmet] v. estimar, tasar, calcular aproximadamente; hacer un presupuesto; juzgar, opinar.

estimation [estəméʃən] s. juicio, opinión; estima; estimación.

estuary [éstʃuerı] s. estuario o estero, desembocadura de un río.

etch [etʃ] v. grabar al agua fuerte.

etching [étʃıŋ] s. agua fuerte, grabado al agua fuerte.

eternal [ıtʒ́nl] adj. eterno.

eternity [ıtʒ́nətı] s. eternidad.

ether [íθə] s. éter.

ethereal [ıθíriəl] adj. etéreo.

ethical [éθıkl] adj. ético, moral.

ethics [éθıks] s. ética, moral.

etiquette [étıket] s. etiqueta (*regla de conducta social*).

etymology [etəmálədʒı] s. etimología.

eucalyptus [jukəlíptəs] s. eucalipto.

European [jurəpíən] adj. & s. europeo.

evacuate [ıvǽkjuet] v. evacuar; desocupar.

evade [ıvéd] v. evadir.

evaluate [ıvǽljuet] v. valorar, avaluar.

evaporate [ıvǽpəret] v. evaporar(se).

evaporation [ıvæpəréʃən] s. evaporación.

evasion [ıvéʒən] s. evasión, evasiva.

evasive [ıvésıv] adj. evasivo.

eve [iv] s. víspera, vigilia; **Christmas**

Eve Nochebuena; **New Year's Eve** víspera del Año Nuevo; **on the — of** en vísperas de.

even [ívən] *adj.* liso, plano, llano; igual; parejo; a nivel; uniforme; **— dozen** docena cabal; **— number** número par; **— temper** genio apacible; **to be — with someone** estar mano a mano (o estar a mano) con alguien; **to get — with someone** desquitarse de alguien; *adv.* aun, hasta; **— if** (o **— though**) aun cuando; **— so** aun así; **not —** ni siquiera, ni aun; *v.* allanar; nivelar(se); igualar(se); emparejar; **-ly** *adv.* igualmente; de un modo igual; con uniformidad; con suavidad.

evening [ívnıŋ] *s.* tarde; noche (*las primeras horas*); **— gown** vestido de etiqueta; **— star** estrella vespertina, lucero de la tarde.

evenness [ívənnıs] *s.* lisura; igualdad; **— of temper** apacibilidad o suavidad de genio.

event [ivént] *s.* suceso, acontecimiento; incidente, evento; resultado, consecuencia; **in any —** en todo caso; **in the —** of en caso de.

eventful [ivéntfəl] *adj.* lleno de sucesos; importante, memorable.

eventual [ivéntʃuəl] *adj.* eventual; último, final, terminal; **-ly** *adv.* finalmente, por fin, con el tiempo; eventualmente.

ever [évə] *adv.* siempre; jamás; alguna vez; **— so much** muchísimo; **for — and —** por (o para) siempre jamás; **hardly —** casi nunca, apenas; **if —** si alguna vez; **more than —** más que nunca; **the best friend I — had** el mejor amigo que en mi vida he tenido.

evergreen [évəgrin] *s.* siempreviva, sempiterna; *adj.* siempre verde.

everlasting [evəlǽstıŋ] *adj.* sempiterno, eterno, perpetuo; duradero; *s.* eternidad; sempiterna (*planta*); siempreviva; perpetua, flor perpetua.

evermore [cvəmór] *adv.* para siempre; **for —** para siempre jamás.

every [évrı] *adj.* cada; todo; todos los, todas las; **— bit of it** todo, todito; **— day** todos los días; **— once in a while** de vez en cuando; **— one of them** todos ellos; **— other day** cada dos días, un día sí y otro no.

everybody [évrıbadı] *pron.* todos, todo el mundo.

everyday [évrıdé] *adj.* diario, cuotidiano, de todos los días; ordinario.

everyone [évrıwʌn] *pron.* todos; todo el mundo; cada uno.

everything [évrıɵıŋ] *pron.* todo.

everywhere [évrıhwer] *adv.* por (o en) todas partes; a todas partes.

evict [ivíkt] *v.* desalojar; expulsar.

evidence [évədəns] *s.* evidencia; prueba; demostración, señal; testimonio; **to be in —** mostrarse; *v.* hacer evidente, evidenciar; patentizar, revelar, mostrar.

evident [évədənt] *adj.* evidente, patente.

evil [ívl] *adj.* malo, malvado, maligno; aciago, de mal agüero; **to cast the — eye** aojar; **the Evil One** el Diablo; *s.* mal; maldad; *adv.* mal.

evildoer [ívldúə] *s.* malhechor.

evoke [ivók] *v.* evocar; **to — laughter** provocar a risa.

evolution [evəlúʃən] *s.* evolución.

evolve [iválv] *v.* desarrollar(se), desenvolver(se); urdir; evolucionar.

ewe [ju] *s.* oveja.

exact [igzǽkt] *adj.* exacto; *v.* exigir; **-ly** *adv.* exactamente; en punto.

exacting [igzǽktıŋ] *adj.* exigente.

exaggerate [igzǽdʒəret] *v.* exagerar.

exalt [igzólt] *v.* exaltar, ensalzar.

exaltation [egzoltéʃən] *s.* exaltación.

examination [igzæmənéʃən] *s.* examen; reconocimiento (*médico*).

examine [igzǽmın] *v.* examinar; reconocer (*dícese del médico*).

example [igzǽmpl] *s.* ejemplo.

exasperate [igzǽspəret] *v.* exasperar, irritar.

excavate [ékskəvet] *v.* excavar.

exceed [iksíd] *v.* exceder; sobrepasar; propasarse.

exceedingly [iksídıŋlı] *adv.* sumamente, extremamente; **— well** extremamente bien.

excel [iksél] *v.* sobresalir (en o entre); sobrepujar (a).

excellence [éksləns] *s.* excelencia.

excellency [ékslənsı] *s.* excelencia.

excellent [ékslənt] *adj.* excelente.

except [iksépt] *prep.* excepto, menos; *v.* exceptuar.

excepting [ikséptıŋ] *prep.* excepto, salvo, menos, exceptuando.

exception [iksépʃən] *s.* excepción; objeción; **with the — of** a excepción de, con excepción de; **to take —** objetar; ofenderse.

exceptional [iksépʃənl] *adj.* excepcional.

excess [iksés] *s.* exceso; sobrante; **— baggage (weight)** exceso de equipaje (de peso); **to drink to —** beber en exceso.

excessive [iksésıv] *adj.* excesivo; **-ly** *adv.* excesivamente, en exceso, demasiado.

exchange [ikstʃéndʒ] *s.* cambio; trueque;

intercambio, canje (de publicaciones, prisioneros); lonja, bolsa; **rate of —** cambio, Am. tipo de cambio; **telephone —** central de teléfonos; v. cambiar; trocar; canjear (publicaciones, prisioneros); **to — greetings** saludarse; mandarse felicitaciones.

excite [ıksáıt] v. excitar; acalorar; agitar.

excited [ıksáıtıd] adj. excitado, acalorado; animado; **to get —** entusiasmarse; sobreexcitarse; acalorarse; **-ly** adv. acaloradamente, agitadamente.

excitement [ıksáıtmənt] s. excitación; acaloramiento; agitación, alboroto; animación.

exciting [ıksáıtıŋ] adj. excitante, excitador; estimulante.

exclaim [ıksklém] v. exclamar.

exclamation [ɛkskləméʃən] s. exclamación; **— point** punto de admiración.

exclude [ıksklúd] v. excluir.

exclusion [ıksklúʒən] s. exclusión.

exclusive [ıksklúsıv] adj. exclusivo; privativo; **— of** sin contar.

excommunicate [ɛkskəmjúnəket] v. excomunicar.

excommunication [ɛkskəmjunəkéʃən] s. excomunión.

excrement [ɛ́kskrımənt] s. excremento.

excursion [ıkskɜ́ʒən] s. excursión; correría; expedición.

excusable [ıkskjúzəbl] adj. excusable, disculpable.

excuse [ıkskjús] s. excusa; disculpa; [ıkskjúz] v. excusar; disculpar; perdonar, dispensar; eximir; **— me!** ¡dispense Vd.!; ¡perdone Vd.!

execute [ɛ́ksıkjut] v. ejecutar; ajusticiar; llevar a cabo.

execution [ɛksıkjúʃən] s. ejecución; desempeño.

executioner [ɛksıkjúʃənə] s. verdugo.

executive [ıgzɛ́kjʊtıv] adj. ejecutivo; s. ejecutivo, poder ejecutivo; gerente, administrador.

executor [ıgzɛ́kjətə] s. albacea, ejecutor testamentario; [ɛ́ksıkjutə] ejecutor.

exemplary [ıgzɛ́mplərı] adj. ejemplar.

exempt [ıgzɛ́mpt] adj. exento, libre; v. eximir, exentar.

exemption [ıgzɛ́mpʃən] s. exención.

exercise [ɛ́ksəsaız] s. ejercicio; v. ejercitar(se); ejercer (poder o autoridad); hacer ejercicio, hacer gimnasia; **to be -d about something** estar preocupado o sobreexcitado por algo.

exert [ıgzɜ́t] v. ejercer; **to — oneself** esforzarse, hacer esfuerzos, empeñarse.

exertion [ıgzɜ́ʃən] s. ejercicio; esfuerzo, empeño.

exhale [ɛkshél] v. exhalar, emitir; espirar, soplar.

exhaust [ıgzɔ́st] s. escape (de gas o vapor); v. agotar; consumir; debilitar, fatigar; **I am -ed** no puedo más; estoy agotado.

exhaustion [ıgzɔ́stʃən] s. agotamiento; fatiga, postración.

exhibit [ıgzíbıt] v. exhibir; mostrar, exponer.

exhibition [ɛksəbíʃən] s. exhibición; exposición, manifestación.

exhilarate [ıgzílərət] v. alborozar, excitar, animar, entusiasmar.

exhort [ıgzɔ́rt] v. exhortar.

exile [ɛ́gzaıl] s. destierro, exilio; desterrado; v. desterrar; expatriar.

exist [ıgzíst] v. existir.

existence [ıgzístəns] s. existencia.

existent [ıgzístənt] adj. existente.

exit [ɛ́gzıt] s. salida; salida (del foro); v. vase o vanse (un personaje o personajes al fin de una escena).

exodus [ɛ́ksədəs] s. éxodo.

exonerate [ıgzánəret] v. exonerar.

exorbitant [ıgzɔ́rbətənt] adj. exorbitante.

exotic [ıgzátık] adj. exótico; raro, extraño.

expand [ıkspǽnd] v. ensanchar(se); dilatar(se); extender(se); agrandar(se); desarrollar (una ecuación).

expanse [ıkspǽns] s. espacio, extensión.

expansion [ıkspǽnʃən] s. expansión; ensanche; desarrollo (de una ecuación).

expansive [ıkspǽnsıv] adj. expansivo; efusivo.

expect [ıkspɛ́kt] v. esperar; contar con; **I — so** supongo que sí.

expectation [ɛkspɛktéʃən] s. expectación; expectativa; esperanza.

expectorate [ıkspɛ́ktəret] v. expectorar, desgarrar.

expedient [ıkspídıənt] adj. conveniente, oportuno; ventajoso; prudente; s. expediente, medio.

expedition [ɛkspıdíʃən] s. expedición.

expeditionary [ɛkspıdíʃənɛrı] adj. expedicionario.

expel [ıkspɛ́l] v. expeler; expulsar.

expend [ıkspɛ́nd] v. gastar; consumir.

expenditure [ıkspɛ́ndıtʃə] s. gasto; desembolso.

expense [ıkspɛ́ns] s. gasto; coste, costa o costo.

expensive [ıkspɛ́nsıv] adj. costoso.

expensiveness [ıkspɛ́nsıvnıs] s. precio subido, coste elevado.

experience [ıkspfríəns] s. experiencia; aventura, lance; v. experimentar; pasar (*penas, sufrimientos*); sentir.

experienced [ɪkspfrɪənst] *adj.* experimentado; ducho, perito, experto.

experiment [ɪkspérəmənt] *s.* experimento, prueba; *v.* experimentar, hacer un experimento.

experimental [ɪkspérəméntl]] *adj.* experimental.

expert [ékspɜːt] *s.* experto, perito; [ɪkspɜːt] *adj.* experto, perito, experimentado.

expiration [ɛkspəréʃən] *s.* terminación; vencimiento (*de un plazo*); espiración (*del aire*).

expire [ɪkspáɪr] *v.* expirar, morir; acabar; vencerse (*un plazo*); expeler (*el aire aspirado*).

explain [ɪksplén] *v.* explicar.

explainable [ɪksplénəbl] *adj.* explicable.

explanation [ɛksplənéʃən] *s.* explicación.

explanatory [ɪksplǽnətorɪ] *adj.* explicativo.

explode [ɪksplód] *v.* estallar, hacer explosión, *Am.* explotar; reventar; volar (*con dinamita*); desacreditar (*una teoría*).

exploit [éksplɔɪt] *s.* hazaña, proeza; [ɪksplɔ́ɪt] *v.* explotar; sacar partido de, abusar de.

exploitation [ɛksplɔɪtéʃən] *s.* explotación.

exploration [ɛkspləréʃən] *s.* exploración.

explore [ɪksplór] *v.* explorar.

explorer [ɪksplórə] *s.* explorador.

explosion [ɪksplóʒən] *s.* explosión, estallido.

explosive [ɪksplósɪv] *adj. & s.* explosivo.

export [éksport] *s.* exportación; artículo exportado, mercancía exportada; [ɪkspórt] *v.* exportar.

exportation [ɛkspɔrtéʃən] *s.* exportación.

expose [ɪkspóz] *v.* exponer; exhibir, mostrar, poner a la vista; revelar; desenmascarar.

exposition [ɛkspəzíʃən] *s.* exposición; exhibición.

exposure [ɪkspóʒə] *s.* exposición; revelación; **to die of** — morir a efecto de la intemperie.

expound [ɪkspáʊnd] *v.* exponer, explicar.

express [ɪksprés] *adj.* expreso; explícito, claro; **— company** compañía de expreso; expreso, *Am.* exprés; **— train** tren expreso; *adv.* por expreso, por exprés; *s.* expreso; tren expreso, *Am.* exprés; *v.* expresar; enviar por expreso (*o* por exprés).

expression [ɪkspréʃən] *s.* expresión.

expressive [ɪksprésɪv] *adj.* expresivo.

expulsion [ɪkspʌ́lʃən] *s.* expulsión.

exquisite [ɛkskwízɪt] *adj.* exquisito.

exquisiteness [ɛkskwízɪtnɪs] *s.* exquisitez; primor.

extant [ɪkstǽnt] *adj.* existente.

extend [ɪksténd] *v.* extender(se); tender; prolongar(se); alargar(se); agrandar; dilatar, prorrogar (*un plazo*); dar (*el pésame, el parabién, ayuda, etc.*).

extended [ɪksténdɪd] *adj.* extenso; prolongado; extendido.

extension [ɪksténʃən] *s.* extensión; prolongación; prórroga (*de un plazo*); añadidura, anexo.

extensive [ɪksténsɪv] *adj.* extenso, ancho, dilatado; extensivo; **-ly** *adv.* extensamente, por extenso; extensivamente; **-ly used** de uso general o común.

extent [ɪkstént] *s.* extensión; grado; **to a great** — en gran parte, generalmente; **to such an** — that a tal grado que; **to the** — of one's ability en proporción a su habilidad; **up to a certain** — hasta cierto punto.

extenuate [ɪksténjʊet] *v.* atenuar, mitigar.

exterior [ɪkstírɪə] *adj.* exterior; externo; *s.* exterioridad; exterior, porte, aspecto.

exterminate [ɪkstɜːmənet] *v.* exterminar, destruir por completo, extirpar.

extermination [ɪkstɜːmənéʃən] *s.* exterminio.

external [ɪkstɜːnl]] *adj.* externo; exterior; *s.* exterioridad; lo externo.

extinct [ɪkstíŋkt] *adj.* extinto; extinguido, apagado.

extinguish [ɪkstíŋgwíʃ] *v.* extinguir; apagar.

extol [ɪkstól] *v.* enaltecer; ensalzar.

extort [ɪkstórt] *v.* obtener por fuerza o amenaza, exigir (*dinero, promesa, etc.*), *Am.* extorsionar.

extortion [ɪkstórʃən] *s.* extorsión.

extra [ékstrə] *adj.* extraordinario; de sobra, de más, adicional; suplementario; **— tire** neumático de repuesto o de recambio; **— workman** obrero supernumerario; *adv.* extraordinariamente; *s.* extra; extraordinario (*de un periódico*); suplemento; gasto extraordinario; recargo (*cargo adicional*); actor suplente o supernumerario.

extract [ékstrækt] *s.* extracto; cita, trozo (*entresacado de un libro*); resumen; [ɪkstrǽkt] *v.* extraer; seleccionar; citar.

extraordinary [ɪkstrórdnerɪ] *adj.* extraordinario; **extraordinarily** *adv.* extraordinariamente; de manera extraordinaria.

extravagance [ɪkstrǽvəgəns] *s.* despilfarro, derroche, gasto excesivo; lujo excesivo; extravagancia, capricho.

extravagant [ɪkstrǽvəgənt] adj. gastador, despilfarrado; extravagante, disparatado; — **praise** elogios excesivos; — **prices** precios exorbitantes.

extreme [ɪkstrím] adj. extremo; último; más remoto; excesivo; riguroso; radical; — **opinions** opiniones extremadas; s. extremo; cabo; **to go to -s** extremar, exagerar; hacer extremos; tomar las medidas más extremas; **-ly** adv. extremamente, en extremo.

extremity [ɪkstrémətɪ] s. extremidad, extremo; medida extrema; **in —** en gran peligro; en un apuro.

exuberant [ɪgzjúbərənt] adj. exuberante.

exult [ɪgzʌ́lt] v. alborozarse, regocijarse.

eye [aɪ] s. ojo; — **shade** visera; **in a twinkling of an —** en un abrir y cerrar de ojos; **hook and —** macho y hembra; **to catch one's —** llamar la atención; **to have good -s** tener buena vista; **to have before one's -s** tener a (o tener ante) la vista; **to keep an — on** cuidar, vigilar; **to see — to —** estar completamente de acuerdo; v. mirar, observar.

eyeball [áɪbɔl] s. globo del ojo.

eyebrow [áɪbraʊ] s. ceja.

eyeglass [áɪglæs] s. lente, cristal (de anteojo); ocular (de microscopio o telescopio); **-es** lentes, anteojos.

eyelash [áɪlæʃ] s. pestaña.

eyelid [áɪlɪd] s. párpado.

eyesight [áɪsaɪt] s. vista; **poor —** mala vista.

F

fable [fébl] s. fábula.

fabric [fǽbrɪk] s. género, tela; tejido; textura; estructura.

fabulous [fǽbjələs] adj. fabuloso.

façade [fəsád] s. fachada.

face [fes] s. cara, rostro; fachada, frente (m.); haz, superficie; muestra (de reloj); Am. carátula; — **value** valor nominal; **in the — of** en presencia de, ante, frente a; **to lose —** perder prestigio; **to make -s** hacer muecas o gestos; **to save one's —** salvar el amor propio; v. encararse con; enfrentarse con; hacer frente a; mirar hacia; forrar; **to — about** volverse, Am. voltearse; **to — danger** afrontar o arrostrar el peligro; **to — with marble** revestir de mármol; **it -s the street** da a la calle.

facilitate [fəsɪ́lətet] v. facilitar.

facility [fəsɪ́lətɪ] s. facilidad.

fact [fækt] s. hecho; dato; verdad, realidad; **in — de** hecho; en realidad.

faction [fǽkʃən] s. facción, bando, partido, pandilla.

factor [fǽktə] s. factor; elemento; agente; v. descomponer en factores.

factory [fǽktrɪ] s. fábrica.

faculty [fǽkḷtɪ] s. facultad.

fad [fæd] s. novedad; manía; moda.

fade [fed] v. descolorar(se), desteñir(se); marchitar(se); apagarse (un sonido); desvanecerse.

fagged [fægd] adj. agotado, rendido de cansancio.

fail [fel] v. faltar; fallar; fracasar; decaer debilitarse; quebrar, hacer bancarrota no tener éxito; **to — in an examination** fallar en un examen, salir mal en un examen; **to — a student** reproba o suspender a un estudiante; **to do it** dejar de hacerlo, no hacerlo **don't — to come** no deje Vd. de venir; **without —** sin falta.

failure [féljə] s. fracaso; malogro; falta descuido, negligencia; quiebra, banca rrota; debilitamiento.

faint [fent] adj. débil; lánguido; cas imperceptible, tenue, vago, indistin to; **to feel —** sentirse desvanecido **—hearted** tímido, cobarde; s. des mayo; v. desmayarse; languidecer; **-l** adv. débilmente; lánguidamente; in distintamente, vagamente, tenuemen te; apenas.

faintness [féntnɪs] s. languidez, debili dad, desfallecimiento; falta de clari dad; vaguedad.

fair [fer] adj. justo, recto, honrado; im parcial; equitativo; regular, mediano rubio, blondo; bello; despejado, clar — **chance of success** buena probabi lidad de éxito; — **complexion** te blanca; — **hair** pelo rubio; — **nam** reputación sin mancilla; — **play** jueg limpio; — **sex** sexo bello; — **weathe** buen tiempo, tiempo bonancible; t **act —** obrar con imparcialidad (o co equidad); **to play —** jugar limpio; a feria; mercado; exposición; **-ly** ad justamente; imparcialmente; mediana mente; **-ly difficult** medianament difícil; **-ly well** regular, bastante bier

fairness [férnɪs] s. justicia, equidad, im parcialidad; blancura (de la tez) belleza.

fairy [férɪ] s. hada; — **godmother** had madrina; — **tale** cuento de hadas.

fairyland [férɪlænd] s. tierra de la hadas.

faith [feθ] s. fe; fidelidad; **in good — d** buena fe; **to have — in** tener fe o con fianza en; **to keep —** cumplir con l palabra.

faithful [féəfəl] *adj.* fiel; leal; **-ly** *adv.* fielmente; con fidelidad; puntualmente; **-ly yours** suyo afectísimo; siempre suyo.

faithfulness [féəfəlnıs] *s.* fidelidad; lealtad; exactitud.

faithless [féəlıs] *adj.* infiel; sin fe; desleal; falso.

fake [fek] *s.* fraude, trampa, falsedad; embustero; *adj.* falso, fingido; *v.* falsear; fingir; simular.

falcon [fólkən] *s.* halcón.

fall [fɔl] *s.* caída; bajada; ruina; baja (*de precios*); otoño; **-s** cascada, catarata, salto de agua; *v.* caer(se); decaer; bajar; **to** — **asleep** dormirse, quedarse dormido; **to** — **back** retroceder; **to** — **behind** atrasarse, rezagarse, quedarse atrás; **to** — **in love** enamorarse; **to** — **out with** reñir con, enemistarse con; **to** — **to** **one** tocarle a uno, corresponderle a uno; **his plans fell through** fracasaron (*o* se malograron) sus planes.

fallen [fólən] *p.p. de* **to fall.**

fallow [fǽlo] *adj.* baldío; *s.* barbecho, *v.* barbechar.

false [fɔls] *adj.* falso; postizo (*dientes, barba, etc.*); fingido, simulado.

falsehood [fólshʊd] *s.* falsedad, mentira.

falseness [fólsnıs] *s.* falsedad.

falsify [fólsəfaı] *v.* falsificar, falsear; mentir.

falsity [fólsətı] *s.* falsedad; mentira.

falter [fóltə] *v.* vacilar; titubear; tambalearse; bambolearse; **to** — **an excuse** balbucear una excusa; *s.* temblor, vacilación.

fame [fem] *s.* fama.

famed [femd] *adj.* afamado, famoso, renombrado.

familiar [fəmíljə] *adj.* familiar, íntimo; confianzudo; **to be** — **with a subject** conocer bien, estar versado en oser conocedor de una materia; *s.* familiar.

familiarity [fəmılıǽrətı] *s.* familiaridad; confianza, franqueza.

family [fǽmlı] *s.* familia; — **name** apellido; — **tree** árbol genealógico; **to be in the** — **way** estar encinta.

famine [fǽmın] *s.* hambre; escasez, carestía.

famished [fǽmıʃt] *adj.* hambriento, muerto de hambre; **to be** — morirse de hambre.

famous [féməs] *adj.* famoso.

fan [fæn] *s.* abanico; aventador; ventilador; aficionado (*a deportes*); admirador; *v.* abanicar; ventilar.

fanatic [fənǽtık] *adj. & s.* fanático.

fanaticism [fənǽtəsızəm] *s.* fanatismo.

fanciful [fǽnsıfəl] *adj.* fantástico; caprichoso; imaginario.

fancy [fǽnsı] *s.* fantasía, antojo, capricho; imaginación; afición, gusto; **to have a** — **for** tener afición a; **to strike one's** — antojársele a uno; **to take a** — **to a person** caerle a uno bien (*o* simpatizarle a uno) una persona; *adj.* fantástico, de fantasía; de adorno; elegante; — **ball** baile de fantasía o disfraces; — **free** libre de cuidados; — **work** labor; bordado fino; *v.* imaginar(se); fantasear; forjar, concebir (*una idea*); **to** — **oneself** imaginarse; **just** — **the idea!** ¡figúrate qué idea! **I don't** — **the idea of** no me gusta la idea de.

fang [fæŋ] *s.* colmillo (*de ciertos animales*).

fantastic [fæntǽstık] *adj.* fantástico; extravagante.

fantasy [fǽntəsı] *s.* fantasía.

far [far] *adv.* lejos; — **away** muy lejos; — **and wide** por todas partes; — **better** mucho mejor; — **off** muy lejos; a lo lejos; **by** — con mucho; **as** — **as** hasta; en cuanto a; **as** — **as I know** según parece; a lo que parece; que yo sepa; **so** — hasta ahora; hasta aquí; hasta entonces; **how** — ? ¿hasta dónde? *adj.* lejano, distante, remoto; — **journey** largo viaje; **it is a** — **cry from** dista mucho de.

faraway [fárəwé] *adj.* muy lejano, distante, remoto; abstraído.

farce [fars] *s.* farsa.

fare [fɛr] *s.* pasaje, tarifa de pasajes; pasajero; comida, alimento; *v.* pasarla (*bien o mal*); irle a uno (*bien o mal*); **to** — **forth** salir.

farewell [fɛrwél] *s.* despedida, adiós; **to bid** — **to** despedirse de; —! ¡adiós!

farfetched [fárfétʃt] *adj.* traído de muy lejos; forzado; traído por los cabellos; que no hace al caso, improbable, poco creíble.

farm [farm] *s.* hacienda, granja, *Am.* estancia, *Am.* rancho; — **produce** productos agrícolas; *v.* cultivar, labrar (*la tierra*); **to** — **out** dar en arriendo; repartir.

farmer [fármə] *s.* labrador; granjero; agricultor; *Am.* ranchero, *Am.* estanciero, *Am.* hacendado.

farmhouse [fármhaʊs] *s.* alquería, finca.

farming [fármıŋ] *s.* labranza, agricultura, cultivo de los campos; *adj.* agrícola.

farmyard [fármjard] *s.* corral (*de una*

alquería).

far-off [fárɔ́f] *adj.* distante, remoto.

farther [fárðə] *adv.* más lejos; más; **— on** más adelante; *adj.* más remoto, más lejano.

farthest [fárðɪst] *adj.* más lejano; más remoto; *adv.* más lejos.

fascinate [fǽsɳet] *v.* fascinar.

fascination [fæsɳéʃən] *s.* fascinación.

fashion [fǽʃən] *s.* moda, boga; estilo; manera; **— plate** figurín; **the latest —** la última moda (*o* novedad); **after a —** medianamente, no muy bien; **to be in —** estar de moda; estilarse; *v.* forjar, hacer, formar; idear.

fashionable [fǽʃnəbl] *adj.* de moda; de buen tono; elegante.

fast [fæst] *adj.* rápido, veloz; adelantado (*dícese del reloj*); firme; fiel (*amigo*); fijo; disipado, disoluto; *adv.* aprisa, de prisa; firmemente, fijamente; **—asleep** profundamente dormido; *s.* ayuno; *v.* ayunar.

fasten [fǽsɳ] *v.* fijar(se); sujetar(se), asegurar(se); atar, unir; abrochar(se).

fastener [fǽsɳə] *s.* broche; abrochador.

fastidious [fæstídɪəs] *adj.* melindroso.

fat [fæt] *adj.* gordo; grasiento; mantecoso; **— profits** ganancias pingües; *s.* grasa, manteca; gordura; **the — of the land** lo mejor y más rico de la tierra.

fatal [fétl] *adj.* fatal.

fatality [fətǽlətɪ] *s.* fatalidad; muerte.

fate [fet] *s.* hado, sino, destino; fortuna, suerte.

father [fáðə] *s.* padre.

fatherhood [fáðəhʊd] *s.* paternidad.

father-in-law [fáðərɪnlɔ] *s.* suegro.

fatherland [fáðəlænd] *s.* patria.

fatherly [fáðəlɪ] *adv.* paternal.

fathom [fǽðəm] *v.* sondar, sondear; penetrar; *s.* braza (*medida de profundidad*).

fathomless [fǽðəmlɪs] *adj.* insondable.

fatigue [fətíg] *s.* fatiga, cansancio; *v.* fatigar(se), cansar(se).

fatness [fǽtnɪs] *s.* gordura.

fatten [fǽtn] *v.* engordar.

faucet [fɔ́sɪt] *s.* grifo, llave, espita, canilla, *Am.* bitoque.

fault [fɔlt] *s.* falta; defecto, tacha; culpa; falla (*grieta o quiebra geológica*); **to a —** excesivamente; **to be at —** ser culpable; **to find — with** criticar a.

faultfinder [fɔ́ltfaɪndə] *s.* criticón, criticador.

faultless [fɔ́ltlɪs] *adj.* intachable, sin tacha, perfecto.

faulty [fɔ́ltɪ] *adj.* defectuoso, imperfecto.

favor [févə] *s.* favor; **your — of the . . .** su grata (carta) del . . .; *v.* favorecer.

favorable [févrəbl] *adj.* favorable; **favorably** *adv.* favorablemente.

favorite [févrɪt] *adj.* & *s.* favorito.

favoritism [févrɪtɪzəm] *s.* favoritismo.

fawn [fɔn] *s.* cervato; color de cervato; *v.* adular; halagar.

fear [fɪr] *s.* temor, miedo; pavor; *v.* temer.

fearful [fírfəl] *adj.* terrible, espantoso; temible, temeroso; miedoso.

fearless [fírlɪs] *adj.* sin temor, intrépido, atrevido, arrojado.

fearlessness [fírlɪsnɪs] *s.* intrepidez, arrojo, osadía, atrevimiento.

feasible [fízəbl] *adj.* factible, hacedero, dable.

feast [fist] *s.* fiesta; festín, banquete; *v.* festejar, obsequiar; banquetear; **to — one's eyes on** deleitar la vista en.

feat [fit] *s.* proeza, hazaña; acto de destreza; suerte (*en el circo*).

feather [féðə] *s.* pluma; **-s** plumaje; **a — in one's cap** un triunfo para uno; **— weight** de peso mínimo; *v.* emplumar.

feathery [féðərɪ] *adj.* plumoso, ligero, como una pluma.

feature [fítʃə] *s.* facción, rasgo distintivo; película principal (*en el cine*); **-s** facciones (*de la cara*); **— article** artículo sobresaliente o principal; *v.* destacar, hacer sobresalir; dar realce a; mostrar, exhibir (*como cosa principal*), hacer resaltar.

February [fébrʊerɪ] *s.* febrero.

fed [fed] *pret.* & *p. p. de* **to feed**; **to be up** estar harto; estar hasta la coronilla; estar hasta el copete.

federal [fédərəl] *adj.* federal.

federation [fedəréʃən] *s.* federación, confederación, liga.

fee [fi] *s.* honorario (honorarios); derechos; cuota; **admission —** derechos de entrada; precio de entrada.

feeble [fíbl] *adj.* débil, endeble; **feebly** *adv.* débilmente.

feed [fid] *s.* forraje, pasto, pienso (*para los caballos*); comida; *v.* alimentar(se); dar de comer; pacer, pastar; **to — coal** echar carbón.

feel [fil] *v.* sentir; tocar, tentar; palpar; **to — better (sad, happy,** *etc.*) sentirse mejor (triste, feliz, *etc.*); **to — one's way** tantear el camino; **to — for someone** compadecer a alguien; **it -s soft** está suave; **it -s hot in here** se siente calor aquí; *s.* tacto, sentido del tacto; **this cloth has a nice —** esta tela es suave al tacto.

feeler [fílə] *s.* tentáculo, antena (*de los*

78

insectos); tiento; propuesta (*para averiguar la inclinación o pensamiento de alguien*).

feeling [fílɪŋ] *s.* sensación; tacto; sentimiento; emoción; pasión; compasión; ternura; **to hurt someone's -s** ofender la sensibilidad de alguien; *adj.* sensible, compasivo.

feet [fit] *pl. de* **foot.**

feign [fen] *v.* fingir.

fell [fɛl] *v.* derribar, echar abajo; cortar (*un árbol*); *pret. de* **to fall.**

fellow [félo] *s.* socio, miembro (*de una sociedad, colegio, etc.*); becario (*estudiante que disfruta una beca*); camarada; compañero; individuo, tipo, sujeto, hombre; **— citizen** conciudadano; **— man** prójimo; **— member** consocio; colega; **— student** condiscípulo.

fellowship [féloʃɪp] *s.* compañerismo; unión; confraternidad; sociedad; beca; **to get a —** obtener una beca.

felony [félənɪ] *s.* crimen.

felt [fɛlt] *s.* fieltro; *adj.* de fieltro; *pret. & p.p. de* **to feel.**

female [fímel] *s.* hembra; *adj.* hembra; femenino, mujeril, de la mujer; **— cat** (**dog,** *etc.*) gata (perra, *etc.*); **— screw** tuerca, hembra de tornillo.

feminine [fémənɪn] *adj.* femenino, femenil.

fence [fɛns] *s.* cerca, valla, vallado; receptor de cosas robadas; **to be on the —** estar indeciso; *v.* esgrimir; **to — in** cercar, rodear con cerca.

fencing [fénsɪŋ] *s.* esgrima; cercado.

fender [féndə] *s.* guardabarros, guardafango; *Am.* trompa (*de locomotora*).

ferment [fə́mənt] *s.* fermento; fermentación; [fəmént] *v.* fermentar; hacer fermentar.

fermentation [fɜməntéʃən] *s.* fermentación.

fern [fɜn] *s.* helecho.

ferocious [fəróʃəs] *adj.* feroz, fiero.

ferocity [fərásətɪ] *s.* ferocidad, fiereza.

ferret [férɪt] *v.* **to — out** buscar, cazar; escudriñar, indagar.

ferry [férɪ] *s.* barca de pasaje (*a través de un río o bahía*); embarcadero; *v.* transportar de una orilla a otra; atravesar (*un río*) en barca de pasaje.

fertile [fɜ́tl] *adj.* fértil; fecundo.

fertility [fɜtílətɪ] *s.* fertilidad.

fertilize [fɜ́tlaɪz] *v.* fertilizar; abonar; fecundar.

fertilizer [fɜ́tlaɪzə] *s.* abono (*para la tierra*).

fervent [fɜ́vənt] *adj.* ferviente; fervoroso.

fervor [fɜ́və] *s.* fervor; ardor.

fester [féstə] *v.* supurar; enconarse (*una llaga*); *s.* llaga, úlcera.

festival [féstəvl] *s.* fiesta.

festive [féstɪv] *adj.* festivo; alegre.

festivity [festívətɪ] *s.* júbilo, regocijo; festividad.

fetch [fɛtʃ] *v.* ir a buscar, traer.

fete [fet] *s.* fiesta; *v.* festejar; agasajar.

fetter [fétə] *v.* engrillar, meter en grillos, encadenar; **-s** *s. pl.* grillos, cadenas, trabas.

feud [fjud] *s.* riña, pelea, contienda; **old —** enemistad antigua (*entre dos personas o familias*).

feudal [fjúdl] *adj.* feudal.

fever [fívə] *s.* fiebre, calentura.

feverish [fívərɪʃ] *adj.* calenturiento, febril.

feverishness [fívərɪʃnɪs] *s.* calentura; agitación febril.

few [fju] *adj. & pron.* pocos; **a —** unos pocos, unos cuantos.

fiancé [fiənsé] *s.* novio; **fiancée** *f.* novia.

fib [fɪb] *s.* bola, mentirilla, paparrucha, papa; *v.* echar papas, decir o contar paparruchas.

fibber [fɪbə] *s.* paparruchero, cuentero, mentirosillo.

fiber [fáibə] *s.* fibra.

fibrous [fáibrəs] *adj.* fibroso.

fickle [fɪkl] *adj.* inconstante, voluble, veleidoso, mudable.

fiction [fɪkʃən] *s.* ficción.

fictional [fɪkʃənl] *adj.* novelesco; ficticio.

fictitious [fɪktíʃəs] *adj.* ficticio.

fiddle [fɪdl] *s.* violín; *v.* tocar el violín; **to — around** malgastar el tiempo; juguetear.

fidelity [faidélətɪ] *s.* fidelidad.

fidget [fɪdʒɪt] *v.* estar inquieto; agitarse, menearse nerviosamente.

field [fild] *s.* campo; campo o cancha (*de deportes*); **— artillery** artillería de campaña; **— glasses** anteojos de larga vista.

fiend [find] *s.* demonio, diablo; **dope —** morfinómano.

fiendish [fíndɪʃ] *adj.* diabólico.

fierce [fɪrs] *adj.* feroz, fiero; furioso, espantoso.

fierceness [fírsnɪs] *s.* ferocidad; fiereza; vehemencia.

fiery [fáirɪ] *adj.* fogoso, ardiente; vehemente.

fig [fɪg] *s.* higo; **— tree** higuera.

fight [fait] *s.* lucha; pelea; riña, pleito; **he has a lot of — left** le sobra fuerza para luchar; *v.* luchar (con); pelear;

79

combatir; reñir; batirse; **to — it out** decidirlo a golpes o con argumentos; **to — one's way through** abrirse camino a la fuerza.

fighter [fáɪtə] s. luchador; combatiente; guerrero; **— airplane** aeroplano de combate.

fighting [fáɪtɪŋ] s. lucha, combate, pelea; adj. combatiente; luchador.

figure [fígjə] s. figura; forma; talle (de una persona); cifra, número; valor, precio; **-s** cuentas, cálculos; **— of speech** figura de dicción; **to be good at -s** saber hacer bien las cuentas; ser listo en aritmética; **to cut a poor —** tener mala facha, hacer el ridículo; v. figurar; imaginarse, figurarse; adornar con dibujos; calcular; **to — on** contar con, confiar en; tener la intención de, proponerse; tomar en cuenta; **to — out** descifrar, resolver.

filament [fíləmənt] s. filamento.

file [faɪl] s. fichero; archivo; registro, lista; guardapapeles; fila; lima (para cortar o pulir); **— card** ficha, papeleta; v. archivar; guardar en el fichero; registrar, asentar en el registro; limar; desfilar, marchar en fila.

filial [fíliəl] adj. filial.

fill [fɪl] v. llenar(se); ocupar (un puesto); empastar (un diente); servir, atender, despachar (un pedido); inflar (un neumático); tapar (un agujero); **to — out a blank** llenar un formulario (forma o esqueleto).

fillet [fɪlé] s. filete; [fflɪt] cinta, lista de adorno.

filling [fílɪŋ] s. relleno; empaste (dental); **gold —** orificación.

filly [fíli] s. potranca.

film [fɪlm] s. película; membrana; tela (formada sobre la superficie de un líquido); nube (en el ojo); v. filmar (cinematografiar); **her eyes -ed with tears** se le arrasaron los ojos de lágrimas.

filter [fíltə] s. filtro; v. filtrar(se).

filth [fɪlθ] s. suciedad; porquería; mugre.

filthiness [fílθɪnɪs] s. suciedad, porquería.

filthy [fílθɪ] adj. sucio, puerco, cochino; mugriento.

fin [fɪn] s. aleta (de pez).

final [fáɪnḷ] adj. final; terminante; definitivo; **-ly** adv. finalmente; en fin, por fin.

finance [fənǽns] s. teoría bancaria, Am. finanza; **-s** fondos, recursos monetarios; negocios bancarios, Am. finanzas; v. hacer operaciones bancarias; fomentar (un negocio o empresa), Am. financiar.

financial [fənǽnʃəl] adj. financiero; monetario.

financier [fɪnənsír] s. financiero, Am. financista.

financing [fənǽnsɪŋ] s. Am. financiamiento.

find [faɪnd] v. hallar; encontrar; declarar; **to — fault with** criticar a, censurar a; **to — guilty** declarar o encontrar culpable; **to — out** descubrir; averiguar; s. hallazgo.

finding [fáɪndɪŋ] s. descubrimiento; hallazgo; fallo, decisión; **-s** resultados, datos (de una investigación).

fine [faɪn] adj. fino; perfecto, excelente; superior; primoroso; **— arts** bellas artes; **— sand** arena fina o menuda; **— weather** tiempo claro o despejado; **to feel —** sentirse muy bien de salud; **to have a — time** pasar un rato muy divertido; **fine-looking** bien parecido, guapo; s. multa; **in —** finalmente, en fin, en resumen; v. multar; **-ly** adv. finamente; con primor; excelentemente; muy bien, perfectamente.

fineness [fáɪnnɪs] s. finura; fineza; primor; excelencia, perfección.

finery [fáɪnərɪ] s. galas; atavíos, adornos.

finger [fíŋgə] s. dedo (de la mano); **—print** impresión digital; **the little —** el dedo meñique; **middle —** dedo del corazón, dedo de enmedio; **ring —** dedo anular; v. tocar; manosear.

fingernail [fíŋgənel] s. uña.

finicky [fínɪkɪ] adj. melindroso.

finish [fínɪʃ] s. fin, término, conclusión; pulimento; **to have a rough —** estar sin pulir, sin pulimento o al natural; v. acabar, acabar con, terminar, finalizar; pulir, pulimentar.

finished [fínɪʃt] adj. acabado; pulido, pulimentado; excelente.

fir [fɜ] s. abeto.

fire [faɪr] s. fuego; lumbre; quemazón; incendio; ardor; **— alarm** alarma de incendios; **— department** cuerpo o servicio de bomberos; servicio de incendios **— engine** bomba (para incendios); **— escape** escalera de salvamento; **— insurance** seguro contra incendios; **to be on —** estar ardiendo, estar quemándose; **to catch —** incendiarse, quemarse; **to set on —** pegar fuego, incendiar; **to be under enemy —** estar expuesto al fuego del enemigo; v. incendiar; pegar fuego; inflamar; disparar; **to — an employee** despedir (o expulsar) a un empleado.

firearm [fáɪrɑrm] s. arma de fuego.

firebrand [fáirbrænd] s. tizón; pavesa.

firecracker [fáirkrækə] s. triquitraque.

firefly [fáirflai] s. luciérnaga.

fireman [fáirmən] s. bombero; fogonero.

fireplace [fáirples] s. chimenea, hogar.

fireproof [fáirpruf] adj. incombustible; a prueba de incendio; v. hacer incombustible.

fireside [fáirsaid] s. hogar.

firewood [fáirwʊd] s. leña.

fireworks [fáirwɜːks] s. fuegos artificiales.

firm [fɜːm] adj. firme; fijo; estable; s. firma, razón social (*nombre de una casa comercial*); compañía (*comercial o industrial*); **-ly** adv. firmemente, con firmeza.

firmament [fɜːməmənt] s. firmamento.

firmness [fɜːmnɪs] s. firmeza, estabilidad.

first [fɜːst] adj. primero; adv. primero, en primer lugar, al principio; **from the —** desde el principio; **first-born** primogénito; **first-class** de primera clase; **first-cousin** primo hermano; **first-rate** de primera clase; muy bien; **—hand** de primera mano.

fish [fɪʃ] s. pez; pescado; **— market** pescadería; **— story** patraña, cuento extravagante o increíble; **neither — nor fowl** ni chicha ni limonada; v. pescar.

fisher [fɪʃə] s. pescador.

fisherman [fɪʃərmən] s. pescador.

fishery [fɪʃərɪ] s. pesquera; pesquería, pesca.

fishhook [fɪʃhʊk] s. anzuelo.

fishing [fɪʃɪŋ] s. pesca, pesquería; **— rod** caña de pescar; **— tackle** avíos o enseres de pescar; **to go —** ir de pesca.

fissure [fɪʃə] s. grieta, hendedura, *Am.* rajadura.

fist [fɪst] s. puño; **to shake one's —** amenazar con el puño.

fit [fɪt] adj. apto; a propósito, propio, conveniente; capaz; sano, de buena salud, en buen estado; **— to be tied** frenético; **not to see —** to do it no tener a bien hacerlo; s. talle (*de un traje*); ajuste; encaje (*de una pieza en otra*); ataque, convulsión; **— of anger** acceso, arrebato o arranque de cólera; **by -s and starts** espasmódicamente; **that suit is a good —** ese traje le entalla (o le viene) bien; v. ajustar(se); adaptar; encajar(se), caber (en); acomodar; entallar (*un vestido*); venir bien (*un vestido, zapatos, sombrero, etc.*); ser a propósito para, ser propio para; capacitar, preparar; **to — in with** armonizar con; llevarse bien con; **to — out** equipar, proveer; **it does not**

— the facts no está de acuerdo con los hechos; no hace al caso.

fitness [fítnɪs] s. aptitud; capacidad; conveniencia; propiedad (*de una idea, de una palabra, etc.*); **physical —** buena salud.

fitting [fítɪŋ] adj. propio, apropiado; a propósito, conveniente; s. ajuste; **dress —** prueba de un vestido; s. avíos, guarniciones, accesorios.

fix [fɪks] v. fijar; asegurar; arreglar; ajustar; remendar; componer; reparar; **to — up** arreglar(se); componer(se); s. apuro, aprieto.

fixed [fɪkst] adj. fijo, firme.

fixture [fíkstʃə] s. accesorio fijo; persona firmemente establecida (*en un sitio o empleo*); **electric light -s** instalaciones eléctricas (*como brazos de lámparas, arañas*).

flabby [flǽbɪ] adj. blanducho.

flag [flæg] s. bandera; banderola; **— lily** flor de lis; **—stone** losa; v. hacer señas con banderola; adornar con banderas; decaer, debilitarse, menguar, flaquear.

flagrant [flégrənt] adv. flagrante, notorio, escandaloso.

flagstaff [flǽgstæf] s. asta de bandera.

flair [flɛr] s. instinto, penetración, cacumen, disposición o aptitud natural.

flake [flek] s. copo (*de nieve*); escama; hojuela; **corn -s** hojuelas de maíz; v. descostrarse, descascararse.

flame [flem] s. llama; flama; v. llamear, flamear, echar llamas; inflamar(se); enardecer(se).

flaming [flémɪŋ] adj. llameante; flameante; encendido; ardiente, apasionado; **— red** rojo encendido.

flank [flæŋk] s. flanco; costado; lado; ijar (*de un animal*); v. flanquear; rodear.

flannel [flǽnl] s. franela.

flap [flæp] s. aleta; cartera; cubierta (*de bolsillo*); golpeteo; aleteo; v. golpetear; aletear, batir (*las alas*); hojear con violencia (*las páginas*).

flare [flɛr] s. llamarada; llama; arranque (*de ira*); vuelo (*de una falda*); v. llamear, echar llamaradas; tener vuelo (*una falda*); **to — up** enfurecerse; encenderse; **the illness -ed up** recudeció la enfermedad.

flash [flæʃ] s. rayo; destello, llamarada; fogonazo; **— of hope** rayo de esperanza; **— of lightning** relámpago; **— of wit** agudeza; **in a —** en un instante; **news —** última noticia (*enviada por radio o telégrafo*); v. relampaguear; destellar; brillar; centellear; radiar o telegrafiar (*noticias*); **to — by** pasar como un relámpago.

flashing [flǽʃɪŋ] *s.* relampagueo, centelleo; *adj.* relumbrante; flameante.

flashlight [flǽʃlaɪt] *s.* linterna eléctrica.

flashy [flǽʃɪ] *adj.* relumbrante; llamativo, de relumbrón, ostentoso; chillante, chillón (*dícese de los colores*).

flask [flæsk] *s.* frasco.

flat [flæt] *adj.* plano, llano; chato; aplastado; insípido; monótono; desinflado; **— denial** negativa terminante; **— note** nota desentonada; **— rate** precio o número redondo; **D —** re bemol (*nota musical*); **—car** vagón de plataforma; **to be — broke** estar completamente pelado, estar sin dinero; **to fall — caer** de plano; caer mal (*un discurso, chiste, etc.*); **to sing —** desafinarse, cantar desentonadamente; **to refuse -ly** negarse absolutamente; *s.* plano; palma (*de la mano*); apartamento, departamento, piso; bemol (*en música*).

flatiron [flǽtaɪən] *s.* plancha.

flatness [flǽtnɪs] *s.* llanura; lisura; insipidez; desafinamiento (*en música*).

flatten [flǽtn̩] *v.* aplastar(se); aplanar(se); allanar(se).

flatter [flǽtə] *v.* lisonjear; adular.

flatterer [flǽtərə] *s.* lisonjero, adulador.

flattering [flǽtərɪŋ] *adj.* lisonjero, halagüeño, adulador.

flattery [flǽtərɪ] *s.* lisonja, halago; adulación.

flavor [flévə] *s.* sabor; gusto; condimento; *v.* sazonar; dar sabor a; condimentar.

flavorless [flévəlɪs] *adj.* insípido, sin sabor.

flaw [flɔ] *s.* defecto; falta; tacha; imperfección.

flawless [flɔ́lɪs] *adj.* sin tacha; intachable, irreprochable; perfecto.

flax [flæks] *s.* lino.

flay [fle] *v.* desollar.

flea [fli] *s.* pulga.

fled [flɛd] *pret. & p.p.* de **to flee.**

flee [fli] *v.* huir; huir de.

fleece [flis] *s.* vellón, lana; *v.* trasquilar, esquilar; despojar, estafar, defraudar.

fleet [flit] *s.* flota; armada; *adj.* veloz.

fleeting [flítɪŋ] *adj.* fugaz, transitorio, pasajero, efímero.

Flemish [flémɪʃ] *adj.* flamenco; *s.* flamenco, idioma flamenco; **the —** los flamencos.

flesh [flɛʃ] *s.* carne; **— and blood** carne y hueso; **— color** color encarnado; **in the —** en persona.

fleshy [flɛ́ʃɪ] *adj.* carnoso; gordo, gordiflón.

flew [flu] *pret. de* **to fly.**

flexibility [flɛksəbɪ́lətɪ] *s.* flexibilidad.

flexible [flɛ́ksəbl̩] *adj.* flexible.

flicker [flɪ́kə] *s.* titilación, parpadeo, luz trémula; temblor momentáneo (*de emoción*); aleteo; especie de pájaro carpintero; *v.* titilar; temblar; parpadear; vacilar; aletear; **to — one's eyelash** pestañear.

flier [flá ɪə] *s.* volador; aviador; tren rápido.

flight [flaɪt] *s.* vuelo; bandada (*de pájaros*); escuadrilla (*de aviones*); fuga, huída; **— of stairs** tramo de escalera; **to put to —** poner en fuga.

flimsy [flɪ́mzɪ] *adj.* endeble, débil; tenue; quebradizo; frágil; baladí; **a — excuse** una excusa baladí.

fling [flɪŋ] *v.* arrojar(se), lanzar(se); tirar; echar; **to — open (shut)** abrir (cerrar) de golpe; *s.* tiro; tirada, lanzamiento; tentativa; **to go out on a —** irse a echar una cana al aire.

flint [flɪnt] *s.* pedernal.

flip [flɪp] *v.* arrojar, lanzar al aire; sacudir; dar un dedazo.

flippancy [flɪ́pənsɪ] *s.* ligereza; frivolidad; impertinencia; petulancia.

flippant [flɪ́pənt] *adj.* ligero (*en sus acciones y modales*), ligero de cascos; frívolo; impertinente; petulante.

flirt [flɝt] *s.* coqueta; coquetón, coquetona; *v.* coquetear.

flirtation [flɝtéʃən] *s.* coquetería; **to carry on a —** coquetear.

flit [flɪt] *v.* pasar velozmente; volar; revolotear.

float [flot] *s.* boya; cosa flotante, flotador; corcho (*de una caña de pescar*); balsa; carro o carroza (*de procesiones, fiestas, etc.*); *v.* flotar; sobrenadar; boyar; poner a flote; lanzar al mercado (*una nueva emisión de valores, bonos, etc.*).

flock [flak] *s.* bandada (*de pájaros, niños, etc.*); rebaño, grey; manada (*de animales*); grupo; **— of people** gentío, muchedumbre; *v.* agruparse, congregarse; **to — to** acudir juntos (*o* en bandadas) a; **to — together** andar juntos, volar en bandadas, ir en grupo.

flog [flag] *v.* azotar.

flood [flʌd] *s.* inundación; diluvio; avenida (*de agua*), crecida; creciente; torrente; **—gate** compuerta (*de una presa*); esclusa (*de un canal*); **— light** reflector; proyector de luz; **— tide** flujo (*o* marea ascendiente); *v.* inundar.

82

floor [flor] *s.* suelo; piso; plan, fondo (*de un buque*); fondo (*del mar*); **to have the —** tener la palabra; *v.* solar; entarimar, enladrillar, enlosar; echar al suelo, derribar; asombrar.

flop [flɑp] *v.* caer o colgar flojamente; aletear; menearse (*una cosa*) de uno a otro lado; echar, lanzar, dejar caer; fracasar, fallar; **to — down** dejarse caer; desplomarse, tumbarse; **to — over** voltear(se); dar vueltas; *s.* fracaso.

florist [flóɾɪst] *s.* florero, florera; **-'s shop** florería.

floss [flɔs] *s.* seda floja; pelusa; fibra sedosa; **dental —** seda dental.

flounder [fláundə] *v.* patalear (*en el lodo, nieve, etc.*); forcejear (*por salir del lodo, nieve, o cualquier aprieto*); revolcarse; tropezar, cometer errores; *s.* lenguado (*pez*).

flour [flauɾ] *s.* harina.

flourish [flɜ́ɪʃ] *v.* florecer, prosperar, medrar; blandir (*una espada o bastón*); agitar en el aire; *s.* floreo; adorno o rasgo caprichoso; ostentación.

floury [fláuɾɪ] *adj.* harinoso.

flow [flo] *s.* flujo; corriente; **— of words** torrente de palabras; *v.* fluir; correr; flotar, ondear; **to — into** desembocar en; **to be -ing with riches** nadar en la abundancia.

flower [fláuə] *s.* flor; **— bed** cuadro de jardín; **— vase** florero; *v.* florecer, *Am.* florear.

flowerpot [fláuɾpɑt] *s.* tiesto, maceta.

flowery [fláuɾɪ] *adj.* florido.

flowing [flóɪŋ] *adj.* flúido, corriente, fluente; suelto, ondeante.

flown [flon] *p.p. de* **to fly.**

flu [flu] *s.* influenza, gripe.

fluctuate [flʌ́ktʃuet] *v.* fluctuar.

fluctuation [flʌktʃuéʃən] *s.* fluctuación.

flue [flu] *s.* cañón de chimenea); tubo de escape.

fluency [flúənsɪ] *s.* fluidez; labia.

fluent [flúənt] *adj.* fluente, flúido; **to speak -ly** hablar con facilidad.

fluff [flʌf] *v.* mullir; esponjar.

fluffy [flʌ́fɪ] *adj.* mullido, suave, blando; cubierto de vello o plumón; **— hair** pelo esponjado o esponjoso.

fluid [flúɪd] *adj. & s.* flúido.

flung [flʌŋ] *pret. & p.p. de* **to fling.**

flunk [flʌŋk] *s.* reprobación (*en un examen o asignatura*); *v.* reprobar, suspender (*en un examen*); salir mal, fracasar o fallar (*en un examen*).

flunky [flʌ́ŋkɪ] *s.* lacayo; ayudante servil; zalamero, persona servil.

flush [flʌʃ] *s.* sonrojo, rubor; bochorno;

flujo rápido; flux (*de naipes*); *adj.* lleno; rico; parejo, al mismo nivel; **— with** a flor de, a ras de; *v.* sonrojar(se), ruborizar(se), poner(se) colorado; hacer rebosar (*de agua*); **to — out** vaciar (*un depósito*), enjuagar.

flute [flut] *s.* flauta; estría (*de una columna*); *v.* acanalar, estriar (*una columna*).

flutter [flʌ́tə] *s.* aleteo; agitación; alboroto; vuelco (*del corazón*); *v.* aletear; revolotear; agitar(se); palpitar; menear(se); tremolar (*una bandera*).

flux [flʌks] *s.* flujo.

fly [flaɪ] *s.* mosca; pliegue (*para cubrir botones*); bragueta (*abertura de los pantalones*); **on the —** al vuelo; **to hit a —** pegar una planchita o elevar una palomita (*en beisbol*); *v.* volar; pasar velozmente; huir; ondear; enarbolar (*una bandera*); **to — at** lanzarse sobre; **to — away** volar, irse, escaparse; **to — off the handle** perder los estribos (o la paciencia; **to — open (shut)** abrirse (cerrarse) de repente; **to — up in anger** montar en cólera.

flyer = flier.

flyleaf [fláɪlif] *s.* guarda (*hoja en blanco al principio y al fin de un libro*).

foam [fom] *s.* espuma; *v.* espumar, hacer espuma.

focus [fókəs] *s.* foco; distancia focal; *v.* enfocar(se).

fodder [fádə] *s.* forraje.

foe [fo] *s.* enemigo.

fog [fɑg] *s.* niebla, neblina, bruma; velo, nube (*en una película o fotografía*); **—horn** sirena; *v.* anublar, ofuscar, obscurecer; ponerse brumoso; velar(se) (*una película*).

foggy [fɑ́gɪ] *adj.* brumoso, nublado; obscuro, confuso.

foil [fɔɪl] *s.* oropel, hojuela, laminita de metal; florete (*de esgrima*); realce, contraste; **tin —** hojuela de estaño; *v.* frustrar.

fold [fold] *s.* pliegue, doblez, redil; grey; **three—** tres veces; **hundred—** cien veces; *v.* doblar(se), plegar(se); envolver; **to — one's arms** cruzarse de brazos.

folder [fóldə] *s.* folleto, circular; papelera; plegador (*el que pliega*); plegadera (*máquina para plegar*).

folding [fóldɪŋ] *adj.* plegadizo; **— chair** silla plegadiza, silla de tijera; **— machine** plegadera, máquina plegadora; **— screen** biombo.

foliage [fóliɪdʒ] *s.* follaje, fronda.

folio [fólio] *s.* folio; infolio, libro en folio; pliego; **— edition** edición en folio.

folk [fok] s. gente; pueblo; **-s** parientes, allegados; familia; personas; amigos (*vocativo familiar*); adj. popular, del pueblo; —**dance** danza o baile tradicional; —**lore** folklore; cuentos, leyendas y tradiciones populares; — **song** canción popular, canción típica o tradicional.

follow [fálo] v. seguir; ejercer (*un oficio o profesión*); seguir el hilo de (*un argumento*); seguirse (*como consecuencia*); **to** — **suit** jugar el mismo palo (*en naipes*); seguir el ejemplo, imitar.

follower [fáləwə] s. seguidor; imitador; partidario.

following [fáləwɪŋ] s. séquito, comitiva, partidarios; adj. siguiente; subsiguiente.

folly [fálɪ] s. locura; necedad, tontería; desatino.

foment [fomént] v. fomentar.

fond [fand] adj. aficionado (a); amigo (de), amante (de), encariñado (con); cariñoso, afectuoso; tierno; **to be** — **of** querer a (*una persona*); estar encariñado con, ser aficionado a; gustar de (*algo*); **-ly** adv. cariñosamente, afectuosamente.

fondle [fándl] v. acariciar.

fondness [fándnɪs] s. cariño, afecto, afición.

font [fant] s. pila bautismal; fuente.

food [fud] s. alimento, sustento; comida.

foodstuff [fúdstʌf] s. alimento; producto alimenticio; comestibles.

fool [ful] s. tonto, necio, zonzo; payaso; **to play the** — payasear, hacer el payaso; v. chasquear, chancear(se); bromear, embromar; engañar; **to** — **away time** malgastar el tiempo.

foolish [fúlɪʃ] adj. tonto; necio, bobo, zonzo.

foolishness [fúlɪʃnɪs] s. tontería, necedad, bobería.

foot [fut] s. pie; pata (*de animal*); **on** — a pie; — **soldier** soldado de infantería; **to put one's** — **in it** meter la pata; v. andar a pie; **to** — **it** andar a pie; **to** — **the bill** pagar la cuenta; sufragar los gastos.

football [fútbol] s. futbol, football.

footing [fútɪŋ] s. base; posición firme; **to be on a friendly** — **with** tener relaciones amistosas con; **to lose one's** — perder pie.

footlights [fútlaɪts] s. pl. candilejas (*del teatro*); tablas, teatro.

footman [fútmən] s. lacayo.

footnote [fútnot] s. nota al pie de una página.

footpath [fútpæθ] s. vereda, senda, trocha (*para gente de a pie*).

footprint [fútprɪnt] s. huella, pisada.

footstep [fútstɛp] s. pisada, paso, huella; **to follow in the** **-s of** seguir las pisadas o huellas de.

footstool [fútstul] s. banquillo, taburete, escabel.

fop [fap] s. currutaco.

for [for] prep. por; para; — **all of her intelligence** a pesar de su inteligencia; — **fear that** por miedo (de) que; — **the present** por el presente, por ahora; **as** — **him** en cuanto a él; **to know** — **a fact** saber de cierto, saber de hecho; **to pay him** — **it** pagárselo; **to thank him** — **it** agradecérselo; conj. porque, pues.

forage [fórɪdʒ] s. forraje; v. forrajear; dar forraje a.

foray [fóre] s. correría, incursión; saqueo; v. pillar, saquear.

forbade [fəbæd] pret. de **to forbid.**

forbear [forbɛr] s. antepasado; [forbér] v. abstenerse de; tener paciencia.

forbid [fəbíd] v. prohibir; vedar.

forbidden [fəbídn] adj. prohibido; vedado; p.p. de **to forbid.**

forbidding [fəbídɪŋ] adj. austero, reservado; pavoroso; impenetrable.

forbore [forbór] pret. de **to forbear.**

forborne [forbórn] p.p. de **to forbear.**

force [fors] s. fuerza; cuerpo (*de policía, de empleados, etc.*) **in** — en vigor, vigente; **armed** — **s** fuerzas armadas; v. forzar, obligar; **to** — **one's way** abrirse paso por fuerza; **to** — **out** echar por fuerza, echar a la fuerza.

forced [forst] adj. forzado.

forceful [fórsfəl] adj. vigoroso; enérgico.

forceps [fórsəps] s. gatillo (*tenazas para sacar muelas*); pinzas.

forcible [fórsəbl] adj. fuerte, enérgico; potente; violento; eficaz; hecho a la fuerza; **forcibly** adv. fuertemente; con energía; forzosamente; por fuerza.

ford [ford] s. vado; v. vadear.

fore [for] adj. anterior, delantero; de proa; s. frente; puesto delantero; adv. delante, hacia adelante; interj. ¡cuidado! (*dícese en el campo de golf*).

forearm [fórarm] s. antebrazo.

forebode [forbód] v. presagiar; presentir.

foreboding [forbódɪŋ] s. presentimiento; presagio.

forecast [fórkæst] s. pronóstico; [forkæst] v. pronosticar; predecir; pret & p.p. de **to forecast.**

forefather [fórfaðə] s. antepasado.

forefinger [fórfɪŋgə] s. (dedo) índice.

forefoot [fórfʌt] s. pata delantera, mano (de cuadrúpedo).

forego [forgó] v. abstenerse de.

foregone [forgón] p.p. de **to forego; a — conclusion** una conclusión inevitable.

foreground [fórgraund] s. frente, primer plano, primer término.

forehead [fórid] s. frente (f.).

foreign [fórin] adj. extranjero; foráneo; extraño; — **to his nature** ajeno a su índole; — **office** ministerio de relaciones exteriores; departamento de negocios extranjeros; — **trade** comercio exterior; **foreign-born** extranjero de nacimiento.

foreigner [fórinə] s. extranjero; forastero.

forelock [fórlak] s. guedeja.

foreman [fórmən] s. capataz; presidente (de un jurado); Am. caporal (de un rancho o hacienda).

foremost [fórmost] adj. primero; delantero; principal, más notable, más distinguido.

forenoon [fornún] s. (la) mañana.

forerunner [forrʌnə] s. precursor; presagio.

foresaw [forsó] pret. de **to foresee.**

foresee [forsí] v. prever.

foreseen [forsín] p.p. de **to foresee** previsto.

foresight [fórsait] s. previsión.

forest [fórist] s. bosque, selva; — **ranger** guardabosques; v. arbolar, plantar de árboles.

forester [fóristə] s. guardabosques; silvicultor; habitante de un bosque.

forestry [fóristri] s. silvicultura.

foretell [fortél] v. predecir, pronosticar, presagiar.

foretold [fortóld] pret. & p.p. de **to foretell.**

forever [fəévə] adv. por (o para) siempre.

forfeit [fórfit] s. multa; pena; prenda perdida; **game of -s** juego de prendas; v. perder, perder el derecho a.

forgave [fəgév] pret. de **to forgive.**

forge [fordʒ] s. fragua; forja; v. fraguar; forjar; falsear, falsificar; **to — ahead** abrirse paso; avanzar.

forgery [fórdʒəri] s. falsificación.

forget [fəgét] v. olvidar; olvidarse de; **to — oneself** cometer un desmán impensadamente; perder el tino o la paciencia.

forgetful [fəgétfəl] adj. olvidadizo; negligente.

forgetfulness [fəgétfəlnis] s. olvido; negligencia.

forget-me-not [fəgétminat] s. nomeol-

vides.

forgive [fəgív] v. perdonar.

forgiven [fəgívən] p.p. de **to forgive.**

forgiveness [fəgívnis] s. perdón.

forgiving [fəgívin] adj. perdonador, misericordioso, de buen corazón.

forgot [fəgát] pret. & p.p. de **to forget.**

forgotten [fəgátn] p.p. de **to forget.**

fork [fork] s. tenedor; horca; horquilla (para heno); horcón; bifurcación; v. bifurcarse; levantar o arrojar (heno) con horquilla.

forlorn [fəlórn] adj. desamparado, desdichado.

form [form] s. forma; condición; estado; **blank —** blanco, forma en blanco, Am. esqueleto; v. formar(se).

formal [fórml] adj. formal, perteneciente a la forma, convencional; ceremonioso; — **party** reunión de etiqueta; **-ly** adv. formalmente, con ceremonia, solemnemente.

formality [formǽləti] s. formalidad, ceremonia; formalismo.

formation [forméʃən] s. formación.

former [fórmə] adj. primero, precedente, anterior; antiguo; **in — times** en otro tiempo, en días de antaño, antiguamente, anteriormente; **the —** aquél (aquélla, aquéllos, aquéllas); **-ly** adv. anteriormente; antes, en tiempos pasados.

formidable [fórmidəbl] adj. formidable.

formula [fórmjələ] s. fórmula.

formulate [fórmjəlet] v. formular.

forsake [fəsék] v. desamparar; abandonar.

forsaken [fəsékən] p.p. de **to forsake** & adj. desamparado, abandonado.

forsook [fəsúk] pret. de **to forsake.**

fort [fort] s. fuerte, fortín, fortaleza.

forth [forθ] adv. adelante; hacia adelante; **to go —** salir; **and so —** etcétera, y así sucesivamente.

forthcoming [fórθkʌmin] adj. venidero, próximo; **funds will not be —** until no habrá fondos disponibles hasta.

forthwith [forθwiθ] adv. en seguida, pronto, al punto.

fortification [fortəfəkéʃən] s. fortificación.

fortify [fórtəfai] v. fortificar; fortalecer.

fortitude [fórtətjud] s. fortaleza.

fortnight [fórtnait] s. quincena, quince días, dos semanas.

fortress [fórtris] s. fortaleza, fuerte.

fortuitous [fortjúətəs] adj. fortuito; inopinado, inesperado.

fortunate [fórtʃənit] adj. afortunado; **-ly** adv. afortunadamente, por fortuna.

fortune [fórtʃən] s. fortuna; **—teller**

agorero, adivino.

forum [fórəm] *s.* foro; tribunal.

forward [fórwəd] *adj.* delantero; precoz; progresista; atrevido; descarado; *adv.* adelante, hacia adelante; *v.* transmitir; despachar; reenviar; **to — a plan** fomentar un plan.

fossil [fás] *adj.* fósil; anticuado; *s.* fósil.

foster [fóstə] *v.* criar, nutrir; fomentar, promover; *adj.* putativo; adoptivo.

fought [fɔt] *pret.* & *p.p. de* **to fight.**

foul [faul] *adj.* sucio; asqueroso; puerco, cochino; fétido; vil; injusto; **— air** aire viciado; **— ball** pelota foul (*en beisbol*); **—mouthed** mal hablado, obsceno; **— play** juego sucio; fraude; violencia; **— weather** mal tiempo; *s.* mala jugada (*contraria a las reglas del juego*), trampa, *Am.* chapuza, foul; *v.* ensuciar; violar (*las reglas de un juego*); *Am.* pegar un foul (*en beisbol*).

found [faund] *v.* fundar, establecer; *pret.* & *p.p. de* **to find.**

foundation [faundéʃən] *s.* fundación; base, fundamento; dotación.

founder [fáundə] *s.* fundador; fundidor (*de metales*); *v.* zozobrar, irse a pique; fracasar; tropezar; hacer zozobrar.

foundry [fáundrɪ] *s.* fundición.

fountain [fáuntɪ] *s.* fuente; manantial; **— pen** pluma (de) fuente, pluma estilográfica.

fourscore [fórskór] *adj.* cuatro veintenas, ochenta.

fourth [forθ] *adj.* cuarto; *s.* cuarto, cuarta parte; **the — of July** el cuatro de julio.

fowl [faul] *s.* ave; gallo, gallina; pollo.

fox [faks] *s.* zorra; zorro; persona astuta.

foxy [fáksɪ] *adj.* zorro, zorruno, astuto.

fraction [frǽkʃən] *s.* fracción; quebrado.

fracture [frǽktʃə] *s.* fractura; quiebra; rotura; *v.* fracturar; quebrar, romper.

fragile [frǽdʒəl] *adj.* frágil.

fragment [frǽgmənt] *s.* fragmento.

fragrance [frégrəns] *s.* fragancia.

fragrant [frégrənt] *adj.* fragante, oloroso.

frail [frel] *adj.* frágil; endeble, débil.

frailty [fréltɪ] *s.* debilidad, flaqueza.

frame [frem] *s.* armazón, armadura, esqueleto; estructura; marco (*de un cuadro, ventana, espejo, etc.*); disposición (*de ánimo*); **embroidery —** bastidor para bordar; **— house** casa con armazón de madera; *v.* formar, forjar; fabricar; enmarcar (*poner en marco*); inventar; **to — someone** conspirar contra una persona; **to — up a charge** forjar un cargo o acusación.

framework [frémwɜk] *s.* armazón, es-

queleto; estructura.

franc [fræŋk] *s.* franco (*moneda francesa*).

franchise [frǽntʃaɪz] *s.* franquicia; derecho o privilegio político; sufragio, voto.

frank [fræŋk] *adj.* franco, sincero; **very — francote;** *s.* sello de franqueo; franquicia de correos; *v.* franquear, despachar, enviar (*carta*) exenta de franqueo.

frankfurter [frǽŋkfətə] *s.* salchicha.

frankness [frǽŋknɪs] *s.* franqueza, sinceridad.

frantic [frǽntɪk] *adj.* frenético; **-ally** *adv.* frenéticamente.

fraternal [frətɜ́n]] *adj.* fraternal.

fraternity [frətɜ́nətɪ] *s.* fraternidad; confraternidad.

fraud [frɔd] *s.* fraude, engaño; trampa, *Am.* chapuza; trampista, tramposo.

fraudulent [frɔ́dʒələnt] *adj.* fraudulento.

fray [fre] *s.* reyerta, riña, pelea, alboroto; raedura; *v.* raer(se); deshilacharse.

frayed [fred] *adj.* raído, deshilachado.

freak [frik] *s.* capricho; rareza, hombre o cosa rara; monstruosidad, fenómeno.

freckle [frék] *s.* peca; *v.* ponerse pecoso.

freckled [frékld] *adj.* pecoso.

freckly [fréklɪ] *adj.* pecoso.

free [fri] *adj.* libre; suelto; gratuito; exento, liberal, generoso; **— of charge** gratis; **— on board (f.o.b.)** libre a bordo; **— port** puerto franco; **— postage** franco de porte; **to give someone a hand** dar rienda suelta o libertad de acción a una persona; **—hand drawing** dibujo a pulso, dibujo a mano; *adv.* libremente; gratis, de balde; *v.* librar; libertar; soltar; eximir; **-ly** *adv.* libremente; con soltura.

freedom [frídəm] *s.* libertad; libre uso; exención.

freeze [friz] *v.* helar(se); congelar(se).

freezing [frízɪŋ] *adj.* helado, glacial; **— point** punto de congelación.

freight [fret] *s.* flete; carga; **— train** tren de carga, tren de mercancías; **by — por** carga; *v.* fletar, cargar; enviar por carga.

French [frentʃ] *adj.* francés; **to take — leave** marcharse a la francesa, irse sin despedirse; *s.* francés, idioma francés; **the —** los franceses.

Frenchman [fréntʃmən] *s.* francés.

frenzy [frénzɪ] *s.* frenesí.

frequency [fríkwənsɪ] *s.* frecuencia.

frequent [fríkwənt] *adj.* frecuente; *v.* frecuentar; **-ly** *adv.* frecuentemente, a menudo.

fresh [freʃ] *adj.* fresco; reciente; nuevo; impertinente, entremetido; **— water**

agua dulce; -ly *adv.* frescamente; con frescura; nuevamente, recientemente; -ly painted recién pintado, acabado de pintar.

freshen [fréʃən] *v.* refrescar(se).

freshman [fréʃmən] *s.* novato, novicio, estudiante del primer año.

freshness [fréʃnɪs] *s.* frescura; frescor, fresco; descaro.

fret [fret] *v.* irritar(se); apurarse; estar nervioso; agitarse; *s.* agitación, apuro, preocupación; traste (*de guitarra, mandolina, etc.*); —work calado.

fretful [frétfəl] *adj.* descontentadizo, malhumorado, enojadizo; nervioso.

friar [fráɪə] *s.* fraile.

friction [frɪkʃən] *s.* fricción; rozamiento; frotación; desavenencia.

Friday [fráɪdɪ] *s.* viernes.

fried [fraɪd] *adj.* frito; freído; *p.p. de* **to fry**.

friend [frend] *s.* amigo, amiga.

friendless [fréndlɪs] *adj.* sin amigos, solo.

friendliness [fréndlɪnɪs] *s.* afabilidad; amistad.

friendly [fréndlɪ] *adj.* amistoso, afable, amigable; propicio, favorable; *adv.* amistosamente.

friendship [fréndʃɪp] *s.* amistad.

frigate [frɪgɪt] *s.* fragata.

fright [fraɪt] *s.* espanto, susto; terror; espantajo, she is a — es un adefesio.

frighten [fráɪtn] *v.* espantar, asustar, atemorizar; to — away espantar, ahuyentar; to get -ed espantarse, asustarse.

frightened [fráɪtnd] *adj.* espantado, asustado.

frightful [fráɪtfəl] *adj.* espantoso, terrible, horroroso.

frigid [frɪdʒɪd] *adj.* frígido, frío.

fringe [frɪndʒ] *s.* fleco; flequillo; orla; *v.* adornar con fleco; orlar.

frippery [frɪpərɪ] *s.* perifollos, moños, perejiles; cursilería.

frisk [frɪsk] *v.* retozar, cabriolar, saltar, brincar; registrar (*los bolsillos*), *Am.* esculcar.

frisky [frɪskɪ] *adj.* retozón, juguetón.

fritter [frɪtə] *s.* fritura, fruta de sartén; *v.* to — away malgastar, desperdiciar poco a poco.

frivolity [frɪválətɪ] *s.* frivolidad.

frivolous [frɪvələs] *adj.* frívolo.

fro [fro] : to and — de una parte a otra; de aquí para allá.

frock [frak] *s.* vestido (*de mujer*); — coat levita.

frog [frag] *s.* rana; broche (*de cordoncillos o galones*); — in the throat gallo en la garganta.

frolic [frálɪk] *s.* retozo, juego; holgorio, diversión; *v.* retozar, travesear, juguetear.

from [frʌm, frʌm] *prep.* de; desde; to take something away — a person quitarle algo a una persona.

front [frʌnt] *s.* frente (*m.*); fachada; frontispicio, in — of enfrente de; delante de; — shirt — pechera; *adj.* delantero; frontal; frontero; *v.* hacer frente a; to — towards mirar hacia; dar a, caer a.

frontier [frʌntír] *s.* frontera; *adj.* fronterizo.

frost [frɔst] *s.* escarcha; helada; *v.* escarchar; helar; cubrir de escarcha.

frosting [frɔstɪŋ] *s.* escarcha, confitura (*para cubrir un pastel*).

frosty [frɔstɪ] *adj.* escarchado, cubierto de escarcha; helado.

froth [frɔθ] *s.* espuma; *v.* espumar, hacer espuma; echar espuma o espumarajos; to — at the mouth echar espumarajos por la boca; enfurecerse.

frown [fraʊn] *s.* ceño; entrecejo; *v.* fruncir el ceño o las cejas; to — at mirar con ceño; desaprobar (*algo*).

froze [froz] *pret. de* **to freeze**.

frozen [frózn] *p.p. de* **to freeze**.

frugal [frúgl] *adj.* frugal.

fruit [frut] *s.* fruto (*en general*); fruta (*comestible*); to eat — comer fruta; — tree árbol frutal; *v.* fructificar, producir frutas.

fruitful [frútfəl] *adj.* fructuoso; productivo; provechoso.

fruitless [frútlɪs] *adj.* infructuoso, improductivo, estéril.

frustrate [frʌstret] *v.* frustrar.

frustration [frʌstréʃən] *s.* frustración.

fry [fraɪ] *v.* freír(se); *s.* fritada; small — pececillos; gente menuda; **French fries** patatas fritas a la francesa; -ing pan sartén.

fudge [fʌdʒ] *s.* dulce (*usualmente de chocolate y nueces*).

fuel [fjúəl] *s.* combustible; incentivo.

fugitive [fjúdʒətɪv] *adj.* fugitivo; transitorio; *s.* fugitivo, prófugo.

fulfill [fʊlfíl] *v.* cumplir; cumplir con; realizar; llevar a cabo; llenar (*un requisito*).

fulfillment [fʊlfílmənt] *s.* cumplimiento.

full [fʊl] *adj.* lleno; completo; harto; pleno; — dress traje de etiqueta; — moon plenilunio, luna llena; — skirt falda de vuelo entero; — of fun muy divertido, muy chistoso; at — speed a toda velocidad; in — completamente;

por completo; **to the —** por completo, por entero, totalmente; *adv.* completamente, enteramente; **to know — well** saber perfectamente, saber a ciencia cierta; **full-blooded** de raza pura; **full-fledged** hecho y derecho; maduro; completo; **-y** *adv.* completamente, enteramente, por completo.

fullness [fúlnɪs] *s.* plenitud; llenura.

fumble [fʌmbl] *v.* tentalear, buscar a tientas; chapucear, no coger la pelota o soltarla al correr.

fume [fjum] *v.* exhalar vapor o gas; rabiar; **-s** *s. pl.* vapores, emanaciones, gases.

fumigate [fjúməget] *v.* fumigar, sahumar, *Am.* humear.

fun [fʌn] *s.* diversión; burla, broma, chanza, *Am.* choteo; **for —** en (o de) broma; de chanza; de chiste; **full of —** muy divertido; **to have —** divertirse; **to make — of** burlarse de, chancearse con, *Am.* chotear, chotearse con.

function [fʌŋkʃən] *s.* función; *v.* funcionar.

fund [fʌnd] *s.* fondo, caudal; **-s** fondos, recursos; *v.* consolidar (*una deuda*); prorrogar el plazo de (*una deuda*).

fundamental [fʌndəméntl] *adj.* fundamental; *s.* fundamento, principio.

funeral [fjúnərəl] *adj.* funeral, fúnebre; *s.* funeral, exequias, funerales.

fungus [fʌŋgəs] *s.* hongo; fungosidad.

funnel [fʌnl] *s.* embudo; humero (*cañón de chimenea*).

funny [fʌnɪ] *adj.* chistoso, cómico, gracioso, divertido; extraño, raro; **the funnies** la sección cómica (*de un periódico*).

fur [fɜ] *s.* piel (*de animales peludos o lanudos*); sarro (*en la lengua*); **— coat** abrigo de pieles; *v.* forrar, cubrir o adornar con pieles.

furious [fjúrɪəs] *adj.* furioso.

furl [fɜl] *v.* arrollar, enrollar; plegar.

furlough [fɜlo] *s.* licencia militar; *v.* dar licencia militar.

furnace [fɜnɪs] *s.* horno.

furnish [fɜnɪʃ] *v.* proveer, suministrar, surtir; equipar; proporcionar; **to — a room** amueblar un cuarto.

furniture [fɜnɪtʃə] *s.* muebles, mobiliario, moblaje, mueblaje.

furrow [fɜro] *s.* surco, arruga; *v.* surcar, arar.

further [fɜðə] *adj.* adicional; más lejano, más remoto; *adv.* además; más; más lejos; *v.* promover, fomentar, adelantar.

furthermore [fɜðəmor] *adv.* además.

furthest [fɜðɪst] *adj.* (el) más lejano, (el) más remoto; *adv.* más lejos.

furtive [fɜtɪv] *adj.* furtivo.

fury [fjúrɪ] *s.* furia; frenesí.

fuse [fjuz] *s.* fusible; mecha; *v.* fundir(se).

fuselage [fjúzlɪdʒ] *s.* fuselaje.

fuss [fʌs] *s.* melindre, preocupación inútil; bulla innecesaria; **to make a — over someone** darle a alguien demasiada importancia, desvivirse por alguien; *v.* hacer melindres, inquietarse (*por bagatelas*).

fussy [fʌsɪ] *adj.* melindroso; minucioso (*en demasía*); inquieto, nervioso; **— dress** vestido con demasiados adornos.

futile [fjútl] *adj.* fútil; vano.

future [fjútʃə] *adj.* futuro; *s.* futuro; porvenir.

fuzz [fʌz] *s.* vello; pelusa.

fuzzy [fʌzɪ] *adj.* velloso; cubierto de plumón fino; cubierto de pelusa.

G

gab [gæb] *v.* charlar, parlotear; *s.* charla; **gift of —** labia, facundia.

gabardine [gǽbədɪn] *s.* gabardina (*paño*).

gabble [gǽbl] *s.* charla, cotorreo; *v.* charlar, cotorrear.

gable [gébl] *s.* gablete (*de un tejado*); **— roof** tejado de caballete o de dos aguas; **— window** ventana con gablete.

gad [gæd] *v.* vagar, callejear; andar de aquí para allá.

gadget [gǽdʒɪt] *s.* adminículo, artefacto, chisme.

gag [gæg] *s.* mordaza; broma, burla; morcilla, chiste (*improvisado por un actor*); *v.* amordazar; dar náuseas, hacer vomitar, basquear; interpolar chistes (*en la escena*).

gage *véase* **gauge.**

gaiety [géətɪ] *s.* alegría, viveza, alborozo.

gaily [gélɪ] *adv.* alegremente; vistosamente.

gain [gen] *s.* ganancia, provecho; *v.* ganar.

gait [get] *s.* paso, andadura, marcha.

gale [gel] *s.* ventarrón; **— of laughter** risotada, carcajada, risada.

gall [gɔl] *s.* bilis, hiel; amargura; odio; descaro; **— bladder** vejiga de la bilis; *v.* irritar.

gallant [gǽlənt] *adj.* valiente; noble; vistoso; [gəlǽnt] *adj.* galante, atento, cortés; galanteador; *s.* galán.

gallantry [gǽləntrɪ] *s.* galantería; gallardía, valor.

gallery [gǽlərɪ] *s.* galería; paraíso, gallinero (*del teatro*).

galley [gǽlɪ] *s.* galera; cocina (*de un*

buque); — **proof** galerada; — **slave** galeote.

gallon [gǽlən] *s.* galón (*aproximadamente cuatro litros*).

gallop [gǽləp] *s.* galope; *v.* galopar, galopear; ir a galope.

gallows [gǽloz] *s.* horca.

galoshes [gəlúʃɪz] *s. pl.* chanclos, zapatos fuertes, zapatones.

gamble [gǽmbļ] *v.* jugar, apostar, aventurar (*algo*) en el juego; to — away perder en el juego; to — everything jugar el todo por el todo; arriesgarlo todo; *s.* jugada (*en juegos de azar*), apuesta; riesgo.

gambol [gǽmbəl] *v.* retozar; cabriolar; juguetear; *s.* retozo, cabriola.

game [gem] *s.* juego; deporte; caza (*animales de caza y su carne*); to make — of mofarse de, burlarse de; *adj.* valiente, atrevido; resuelto; — bird ave de caza.

gander [gǽndə] *s.* ánsar, ganso.

gang [gæŋ] *s.* cuadrilla; pandilla; juego (*de herramientas o máquinas*); *v.* agrupar(se); to — up against conspirar contra.

gangplank [gǽŋplæŋk] *s.* plancha, pasamano (*de un buque*), pasarela.

gangrene [gǽŋgrin] *s.* gangrena; *v.* gangrenar(se).

gangster [gǽŋstə] *s.* bandolero, bandido, maleante, atracador.

gangway [gǽŋwe] *s.* paso, pasadizo; plancha, pasamano; portalón (*de un barco*); —! ¡a un lado! ¡ábranse!

gantlet = **gauntlet**.

gap [gæp] *s.* brecha, abertura; boquete; hueco; intervalo.

gape [gep] *v.* brecha, abertura; bostezo; boqueada; *v.* boquear, abrir la boca; estar boquiabierto (*mirando*), estar embobado; bostezar.

garage [gərɑ́ʒ] *s.* garaje.

garb [garb] *s.* vestido; vestidura; aspecto, apariencia; *v.* vestir, ataviar.

garbage [gárbɪdʒ] *s.* desperdicios, basura.

garden [gárdn] *s.* jardín; huerta; huerto; *v.* cultivar un jardín.

gardener [gárdnə] *s.* jardinero, hortelano; horticultor.

gargle [gárgḷ] *s.* gargarismo, *Am.* gárgaras; *v.* gargarizar, hacer gárgaras, *Am.* gargarear.

garland [gárlənd] *s.* guirnalda.

garlic [gárlɪk] *s.* ajo.

garment [gármənt] *s.* prenda (*de vestir*).

garnish [gárnɪʃ] *s.* aderezo; adorno; *v.* aderezar, adornar, guarnecer.

garret [gǽrɪt] *s.* desván, buhardilla.

garrison [gǽrəsṇ] *s.* guarnición; *v.* guarnecer o guarnicionar (*una fortaleza*).

garter [gártə] *s.* liga (*para sujetar las medias*); *v.* sujetar con liga.

gas [gæs] *s.* gas; gasolina; — **burner** mechero; — **stove** estufa o cocina de gas; **tear** — gas lacrimante o lacrimógeno; *v.* asfixiar con gas; envenenar con gas.

gaseous [gǽsɪəs] *adj.* gaseoso.

gash [gæʃ] *s.* cuchillada, herida, incisión; *v.* dar una cuchillada, acuchillar.

gasoline [gǽsəlɪn] *s.* gasolina.

gasp [gæsp] *s.* boqueada; grito sofocado; *v.* boquear; jadear; sofocarse; abrir la boca (*de asombro*).

gate [get] *s.* portón, entrada; puerta; *Am.* tranquera (*puerta de trancas*).

gateway [gétwe] *s.* paso, entrada.

gather [gǽðə] *v.* recoger; coger; reunir(se), juntar(se); deducir, colegir; fruncir (*en pliegues*); cobrar (*fuerzas*); to — dust llenarse de polvo, empolvarse; *s.* pliegue.

gathering [gǽðərɪŋ] *s.* asamblea, reunión; muchedumbre; pliegue.

gaudy [gódɪ] *adj.* vistoso, llamativo, chillón, chillante.

gauge [gedʒ] *s.* calibrador; indicador; instrumento para medir; medida; calibre (*de un cañón, pistola, etc.*); ancho (*del ferrocarril*), *Am.* trocha; *v.* medir; calibrar; estimar, calcular.

gaunt [gont] *adj.* macilento, demacrado, flaco.

gauntlet [góntlɪt] *s.* guantelete; manopla; to throw down the — retar, desafiar.

gauze [goz] *s.* gasa; cendal.

gave [gev] *pret. de* to give.

gawk [gɔk] *v.* bobear, mirar embobado; *s.* simplón, bobo.

gawky [gókɪ] *adj.* torpe, desmañado; bobo.

gay [ge] *adj.* alegre; vivo; vistoso; festivo.

gayety *véase* gaiety.

gaze [gez] *s.* mirada (fija); *v.* contemplar, mirar con fijeza, clavar la mirada.

gazette [gəzét] *s.* gaceta.

gear [gɪr] *s.* aperos; herramientas; aparejo; equipo; rueda dentada; engranaje (*de ruedas dentadas*); **foot** — calzado; **low** — primera velocidad; **steering** — mecanismo de dirección; **to be in** — estar engranado; **to shift** — cambiar de engrane o velocidad; **to throw in** — engranar; **to throw out of** — desengranar; —**shift lever** palanca de engrane, palanca de cambios; *v.* engranar.

geese [gis] *pl. de* **goose.**

gelatin [dʒélətn] *s.* gelatina, jaletina.

gem [dʒem] *s.* gema, piedra preciosa; joya, alhaja; panecillo, bollo.

gender [dʒéndə] *s.* género.

general [dʒénərəl] *adj. & s.* general; **in — en** general, por lo común, por lo general.

generality [dʒenərǽlətɪ] *s.* generalidad.

generalize [dʒénərəlaɪz] *v.* generalizar.

generate [dʒénəret] *v.* engendrar; producir; originar.

generation [dʒenəréʃən] *s.* generación; producción.

generosity [dʒenərásətɪ] *s.* generosidad.

generous [dʒénərəs] *adj.* generoso; magnánimo, liberal; amplio; abundante.

genial [dʒínjəl] *adj.* genial, afable.

genius [dʒínjəs] *s.* genio; ingenio, talento.

genteel [dʒɛntíl] *adj.* gentil, cortés; elegante; gallardo.

gentile [dʒéntaɪl] *adj. & s.* gentil.

gentle [dʒéntl] *adj.* suave; afable; apacible; manso; gentil.

gentleman [dʒéntlmən] *s.* caballero; **gentlemen** *pl.* caballeros; señores.

gentlemanly [dʒéntlmənlɪ] *adj.* caballeroso, caballero, cortés.

gentleness [dʒéntlnɪs] *s.* suavidad, dulzura, apacibilidad; mansedumbre.

gently [dʒéntlɪ] *adv.* suavemente, despacio; dulcemente; con ternura; mansamente.

genuine [dʒénjʊɪn] *adj.* genuino; sincero.

geographical [dʒiəgrǽfɪk] *adj.* geográfico.

geography [dʒiágrəfɪ] *s.* geografía.

geological [dʒiəlúdʒɪkl] *adj.* geológico.

geology [dʒiálədʒɪ] *s.* geología.

geometric [dʒiəmétrɪk] *adj.* geométrico.

geometry [dʒiámətrɪ] *s.* geometría.

geranium [dʒəréniəm] *s.* geranio.

germ [dʒɜm] *s.* germen; microbio.

German [dʒɜmən] *adj. & s.* alemán.

germinate [dʒɜmənet] *v.* germinar.

gesticulate [dʒɛstíkjəlet] *v.* gesticular, hacer gestos o ademanes, accionar, manotear.

gesture [dʒéstʃə] *s.* gesto; ademán; a **mere —** una pura formalidad; *v.* gesticular, hacer gestos.

get [get] *v.* obtener, adquirir, lograr, conseguir; recibir, ganar; llegar (a); traer; coger, atrapar; preparar (*la lección, la comida, etc.*); **to — along** llevarse bien (*con alguien*); ir pasándola (*o* ir pasándola); **to — angry** ponerse enojado, enojarse; **to — away** escaparse; irse; **to — down** bajar; **to — ill** ponerse

enfermo, enfermar(se); **to — in** entrar; meter(se); llegar; **to — married** casarse; **to — off the train** bajar del tren; apearse del tren; **to — old** envejecer(se); **to — on** subir a; montar; **to — out** salir; irse; sacar; divulgarse (*un secreto*); **to — over** pasar por encima de; recuperarse de (*una enfermedad*); olvidar (*una ofensa*); pasársele a uno (*el susto*); **to — ready** preparar(se); alistar(se); **to — rich** enriquecerse, hacerse rico; **to — rid of** deshacerse de, desprenderse de; **to — through** pasar; terminar; **to — together** juntar(se), reunir(se); ponerse de acuerdo; **to — up** levantarse; **I got him to do it** le persuadí a que lo hiciese; **I (have) got to do it** tengo que hacerlo; **I don't — it** no lo comprendo; **that's what -s me** (*or* **-s my goat**) eso es lo que me irrita.

ghastly [gǽstlɪ] *adj.* horrible; pálido, lívido, cadavérico.

ghost [gost] *s.* espectro, fantasma; **the Holy Ghost** el Espíritu Santo; **not to have the — of a notion of** no tener la más remota idea de.

ghostly [góstlɪ] *adj.* como un espectro; de espectros, de aparecidos.

giant [dʒáɪənt] *s.* gigante; *adj.* gigantesco; enorme.

giddy [gídɪ] *adj.* ligero de cascos, frívolo; voluble, inconstante; desvanecido, **— speed** velocidad vertiginosa.

gift [gɪft] *s.* regalo; dádiva; don; dote, talento, prenda; donación.

gifted [gíftɪd] *adj.* talentoso, de talento.

gigantic [dʒaɪgǽntɪk] *adj.* gigantesco.

giggle [gígl] *s.* risita, risilla; risa falsa; *v.* reírse falsamente; reírse sofocando la voz; reír con una risilla afectada.

gild [gɪld] *v.* dorar.

gill [gɪl] *s.* agalla (*de pez*).

gilt [gɪlt] *adj. & s.* dorado; *pret. & p.p. de* **to gild.**

gin [dʒɪn] *s.* ginebra (*licor*).

ginger [dʒíndʒə] *s.* jengibre; **— ale** cerveza de jengibre.

gingerbread [dʒíndʒəbred] *s.* pan de jengibre; ornato de mal gusto.

gingham [gíŋəm] *s.* guinga (*tela de algodón*).

gipsy *véase* **gypsy.**

giraffe [dʒərǽf] *s.* jirafa.

gird [gɜd] *v.* ceñir; rodear; **to — oneself for** prepararse para.

girdle [gɜdl] *s.* ceñidor; cinto; faja; *v.* ceñir; fajar; cercar.

girl [gɜl] *s.* niña; muchacha; joven, chica, moza; criada.

girlhood [gə́lhʊd] s. niñez; mocedad, juventud.

girlish [gə́lıʃ] adj. pueril; de niña, de muchacha; juvenil.

girt [gɜt] pret. & p.p. de to gird; v. véase gird.

girth [gɜə] s. circunferencia; cincha (para caballos); faja; v. cinchar; ceñir.

gist [dʒıst] s. substancia, esencia.

give [gıv] v. dar; regalar; ceder, dar de sí; to — away regalar; entregar; revelar (un secreto); to — back devolver; to — birth dar a luz, parir; to — in ceder; darse por vencido; to — off emitir; to — out divulgar; repartir; agotarse; to — up abandonar; desistir; renunciar a; perder la esperanza; rendir(se); ceder, darse por vencido; s. elasticidad.

given [gívən] p.p. de to give; adj. dado; regalado; adicto, entregado; dispuesto, inclinado; — name nombre de pila, nombre de bautismo; — time hora determinada;—that dado que, supuesto que.

giver [gívə] s. dador, donador.

glacial [gléʃəl] adj. glacial.

glacier [gléʃə] s. glaciar, helero.

glad [glæd] adj. alegre; contento; to be — to alegrarse de, tener mucho gusto en (o de); -ly adv. alegremente; con mucho gusto; de buena gana.

gladden [glǽdn] v. regocijar, alegrar.

glade [gled] s. claro herboso (en un bosque).

gladness [glǽdnıs] s. alegría, gozo.

glamour [glǽmə] s. encanto, hechizo; fascinación, embrujo; — girl niña hechicera.

glamorous [glǽmərəs] adj. fascinador, hechicero.

glance [glæns] s. mirada, vistazo, ojeada; vislumbre; v. echar (o dar) un vistazo; vislumbrar; pegar de soslayo; to — off rebotar de soslayo (o de lado).

gland [glænd] s. glándula.

glare [gler] s. resplandor, relumbre; mirada furiosa; v. resplandecer, relumbrar; to — at mirar enfurecido a.

glass [glæs] s. vidrio; cristal; vaso; copa (de cristal); lente; looking — espejo; -es anteojos, lentes, gafas; adj. de vidrio; — blower vidriero, soplador de vidrio; — case escaparate.

glassware [glǽswer] s. vajilla de cristal, cristalería; — shop cristalería.

glassy [glǽsı] adj. vidrioso.

glaze [glez] s. vidriado; lustre; superficie lustrosa o glaseada; v. vidriar; glasear; lustrar; poner vidrios a.

glazier [gléʒə] s. vidriero.

gleam [glim] s. destello, rayo, fulgor, viso; v. destellar, fulgurar, centellear.

glean [glin] v. recoger; espigar.

glee [gli] s. regocijo; júbilo; — club orfeón, masa coral.

glib [glıb] adj. locuaz; de mucha labia; — excuse excusa fácil.

glide [glaıd] s. deslizamiento; ligadura (en música); planeo (de un aeroplano); v. deslizarse; resbalarse; planear (un aeroplano).

glider [gláıdə] s. deslizador, planeador (aeroplano).

glimmer [glímə] s. vislumbre; viso; titileo; — of hope rayo de esperanza; v. titilar, centellear.

glimpse [glımps] s. vislumbre; vistazo, ojeada; to catch a — of vislumbrar; v. vislumbrar.

glint [glınt] s. fulgor, rayo, destello.

glisten [glísn] v. relucir, brillar.

glitter [glítə] s. lustre, brillo, resplandor; v. relumbrar, relucir, brillar.

gloat [glot] v. gozarse (en), deleitarse (en); relamerse (de gusto).

globe [glob] s. globo; esfera.

gloom [glum] s. lobreguez, sombra; abatimiento, tristeza, melancolía.

gloomy [glúmı] adj. lóbrego, sombrío; triste, melancólico; abatido.

glorify [glórəfaı] v. glorificar.

glorious [glórıəs] adj. glorioso; espléndido.

glory [glórı] s. gloria; v. gloriarse; vanagloriarse.

gloss [glɔs] s. lustre, brillo; pulimento; glosa, comentario; v. lustrar, dar brillo a; pulir; glosar, comentar; to — over encubrir, dar colorido de bueno (a algo que no lo es).

glossary [glósərı] s. glosario.

glossy [glósı] adj. lustroso; pulido.

glove [glʌv] s. guante; v. enguantar, poner guantes.

glow [glo] s. incandescencia; brillo (de un ascua); calor vivo; fosforescencia v. lucir, brillar (como un ascua); fosforecer; estar encendido o enardecido.

glowing [glóıŋ] adj. encendido, ardiente.

glowworm [glówɜm] s. luciérnaga.

glue [glu] s. cola (para pegar); v. encolar, pegar (con cola).

glutton [glʌtn] s. glotón.

gluttonous [glʌtnəs] adj. glotón; goloso.

gluttony [glʌtnı] s. gula, glotonería.

gnarled [narld] adj. nudoso, torcido.

gnash [næʃ] v. crujir, rechinar (los dientes).

gnat [næt] s. jején (insecto).

gnaw [nɔ] v. roer.

go [go] v. ir(se); andar; marchar, funcionar; acudir; **to — around** andar alrededor de; dar vueltas; **to —** away irse; **to — back on one's word** faltar a la palabra; **to — by** pasar por; guiarse por (una regla); **to — down** bajar; **to — insane** volverse loco; **to — into** entrar en; investigar; caber en; **to — off** hacer explosión; dispararse; irse, salir disparado; **to — on** proseguir, continuar; **to — out** salir; apagarse; **to — over** pasar por encima de; examinar con cuidado; releer; repasar; recorrer; **to — to sleep** dormirse; **to — under** ir o pasar por debajo de; hundirse; **to — up** subir; **to let —** soltar; **there is not enough to —** around no hay (bastante) para todos; s. empuje, energía; **it is a —** trato hecho; **to be on the —** estar en continuo movimiento.

goad [god] s. aguijón; v. aguijonear; aguijar, incitar.

goal [gol] s. meta; fin, objetivo.

goat [got] s. cabra; **male — macho** cabrío; **to be the —** ser la víctima, pagar el pato.

goatee [gotí] s. perilla.

gobble [gáb] v. tragar, engullir; **to — up** engullirse.

gobbler [gáblɚ] s. pavo.

go-between [góbɪtwɪn] s. medianero.

goblet [gáblɪt] s. copa grande.

goblin [gáblɪn] s. duende.

god [gɑd] s. dios; **God** Dios.

godchild [gɑ́dtʃaɪld] s. ahijado, ahijada.

goddess [gádɪs] s. diosa.

godfather [gɑ́dfɑðɚ] s. padrino.

godless [gɑ́dlɪs] adj. impío, ateo.

godlike [gɑ́dlaɪk] adj. como Dios; divino.

godly [gɑ́dlɪ] adj. pío, devoto; divino.

godmother [gɑ́dmʌðɚ] s. madrina.

goggles [gɑ́glz] s. pl. antiparras, gafas.

going [góɪŋ] ger. & adj. que anda, marcha o funciona bien; **to be —** ir, irse; s. ida, partida; **comings and -s** idas y venidas.

goiter [góɪtɚ] s. papera, Am. buche.

gold [gold] s. oro; **— standard** patrón de oro.

golden [góldn̩] adj. de oro; áureo; dorado.

goldfinch [góldfɪntʃ] s. jilguero amarillo.

goldfish [góldfɪʃ] s. carpa dorada.

goldsmith [góldsmɪθ] s. orfebre.

golf [gɑlf] s. golf.

gondola [gándələ] s. góndola; cabina (de una aeronave); **— car** vagón de mercancías (sin techo), Am. jaula.

gone [gɔn] p.p. de **to go** & adj. ido; perdido; **he is —** se fué; **it is all —** se acabó; ya no hay más.

gong [gɔŋ] s. gong, batintín.

good [gʊd] adj. bueno; válido; valedero; **— afternoon** buenas tardes; **— day** buenos días; adiós; **— evening** buenas noches; **— morning** buenos días; **— night** buenas noches; **Good Friday** Viernes Santo; **for —** para siempre, permanentemente; **to have a — time** pasar un buen rato; divertirse; **to make —** pagar, compensar; cumplir (una promesa); salir bien, tener buen éxito; s. bien; beneficio, provecho, ventaja; **-s** bienes, efectos; mercancías.

good-bye [gʊdbáɪ] s. & interj. adiós.

good-looking [gúdlúkɪŋ] adj. bien parecido, guapo.

goodly [gúdlɪ] adj. grande, considerable; de buena apariencia.

good-natured [gʊdnétʃəd] adj. de buen genio, bonachón, afable.

goodness [gúdnɪs] s. bondad; **—! ¡Dios mío! ¡cielos!**

goody [gúdɪ] s. golosina, bonbón, dulce; interj. ¡qué gusto!; **goody-goody** beatuco (el que afecta virtud), papanatas.

goose [gus] s. ganso; bobo, tonto; **—** flesh carne de gallina.

gooseberry [gúsberɪ] s. grosella; grosellero (arbusto).

gopher [gófɚ] s. roedor semejante a la ardilla.

gore [gor] s. cuajarón de sangre; cuchillo (Am. cuchilla), sesga (tira de lienzo en figura de cuchilla); v. acornear, herir con los cuernos; hacer una sesga en (un traje).

gorge [gɔrdʒ] s. cañada, barranco, barranca; v. engullir(se), atracarse.

gorgeous [gɔ́rdʒəs] adj. primoroso, vistoso, hermosísimo.

gorilla [gərɪ́lə] s. gorila.

gory [górɪ] adj. sangriento, ensangrentado.

gospel [gáspl̩] s. evangelio; **it is the — truth** es la pura verdad.

gossip [gásɪp] s. chisme, chismería; murmuración; hablilla; murmurador, chismero o chismoso; v. chismear, murmurar.

gossipy [gásəpɪ] adj. chismero, chismoso.

got [gɑt] pret. & p.p. de **to get**.

Gothic [gáɪk] adj. gótico; s. gótico (idioma de los godos); estilo gótico.

gotten [gátn̩] p.p. de **to get**.

gouge [gaʊdʒ] s. gubia (especie de for-

món o escoplo curvo); *v.* excavar con gubia, formón o escoplo; **to — some-one's eyes out** sacarle los ojos a alguien.

gourd [gord] *s.* calabaza.

gout [gaut] *s.* gota (*enfermedad*).

govern [gÁvən] *v.* gobernar; regir.

governess [gÁvənɪs] *s.* institutriz.

government [gÁvəmənt] *s.* gobierno.

governmental [gʌvəméntl] *adj.* gubernativo.

governor [gÁvənə] *s.* gobernador; regulador (*de una máquina*).

gown [gaun] *s.* vestido (*de mujer*); toga (*de un juez, profesor, etc.*); **dressing — bata**.

grab [græb] *v.* agarrar, asir; arrebatar; *s.* arrebatiña; agarro, agarrón; presa.

grace [gres] *s.* gracia; favor; donaire, garbo; **to say —** bendecir la mesa, dar gracias; **to be in the good —s of someone** gozar del favor de uno; *v.* agraciar, adornar.

graceful [grésfəl] *adj.* gracioso, agraciado, garboso; **-ly** *adv.* graciosamente, con gracia, con garbo.

gracefulness [grésfəlnɪs] *s.* gracia, donaire, gallardía, garbo.

gracious [gréʃəs] *adj.* afable; cortés; **—!** ¡válgame Dios!

gradation [gredéʃən] *s.* graduación; gradación; grado.

grade [gred] *s.* grado; nota, calificación; cuesta, declive, pendiente, *Am.* gradiente; **— crossing** cruce a nivel (*de un ferrocarril con una carretera*); **the —s** escuela primaria; *v.* graduar, clasificar; calificar, dar una calificación; nivelar (*un camino*).

gradual [grédʒuəl] *adj.* gradual; **-ly** *adv.* gradualmente, poco a poco.

graduate [grédʒuɪt] *adj.* graduado, que ha recibido un grado académico; **to do — work** cursar asignaturas superiores (*al bachillerato*); *s.* estudiante graduado (*que estudia para licenciado o doctor*); [grédʒuet] *v.* graduar(se).

graduation [grædʒuéʃən] *s.* graduación.

graft [græft] *s.* injerto; tejido injertado; sisa, malversación (*de caudales públicos*); ganancia ilegal, *Am.* mordida; *v.* injertar; malversar fondos ajenos; sisar, exigir pago ilegal, *Am.* morder.

grafter [græftə] *s.* malversador (*de fondos públicos*), estafador, *Am.* coyote, *Am.* mordelón.

grain [gren] *s.* grano; fibra (*de la madera*), veta (*del mármol o madera*); **against the —** a (*o* al) redopelo, a contrapelo.

gram [græm] *s.* gramo.

grammar [græmə] *s.* gramática; **— school** escuela primaria.

grammatical [grəmǽtɪkl] *adj.* gramatical, gramático.

granary [grǽnərɪ] *s.* granero.

grand [grænd] *adj.* grande; grandioso, admirable; magnífico.

grandchild [grǽntʃaɪld] *s.* nieto.

grandchildren [grǽntʃɪldrən] *s. pl.* nietos.

granddaughter [grǽndɔtə] *s.* nieta.

grandeur [grǽndʒə] *s.* grandeza, grandiosidad; majestad.

grandfather [grǽnfaðə] *s.* abuelo.

grandiose [grǽndɪos] *adj.* grandioso, magnífico.

grandma [grǽnma] *s.* abuela, abuelita, *Am.* mamá grande.

grandmother [grǽnmʌðə] *s.* abuela.

grandness [grǽndnɪs] *s.* grandeza; grandiosidad; magnificencia.

grandpa [grǽnpa] *s.* abuelo, abuelito, *Am.* papá grande.

grandparent [grǽnperənt] *s.* abuelo, abuela; **-s** abuelos.

grandson [grǽnsʌn] *s.* nieto.

grandstand [grǽnstænd] *s.* andanada, gradería cubierta.

grange [grendʒ] *s.* granja; asociación de agricultores.

granite [grǽnɪt] *s.* granito (*roca*).

granny [grǽnɪ] *s.* abuelita; viejecita, viejita.

grant [grænt] *s.* concesión; subvención; donación; transferencia de propiedad (*mediante escritura*); *v.* conceder; otorgar; ceder, transferir (*derechos, propiedad, etc.*); **to take for -ed** dar por supuesto, dar por sentado.

granulate [grǽnjəlet] *v.* granular(se).

grape [grep] *s.* uva.

grapefruit [grépfrut] *s.* toronja.

grapevine [grépvaɪn] *s.* vid; parra.

graph [græf] *s.* diagrama, gráfica; *v.* hacer una gráfica o diagrama.

graphic [grǽfɪk] *adj.* gráfico.

graphite [grǽfaɪt] *s.* grafito.

grapple [grǽpl] *v.* luchar, pelear **cuerpo** a cuerpo; aferrar, agarrar.

grasp [græsp] *v.* agarrar; asir; apretar; abarcar; comprender; *s.* agarro, asimiento; apretón de manos; **to be within one's —** estar al alcance de uno; **to have a good — of a subject** estar fuerte en una materia, saber a fondo una materia.

grass [græs] *s.* hierba; césped; pasto.

grasshopper [grǽshapə] *s.* saltamontes, saltón, *Am.* chapulín.

93

grassy [grǽsɪ] adj. herboso, Am. pastoso.

grate [gret] s. reja, verja, enrejado; parrilla, brasero; v. enrejar, poner enrejado; crujir, rechinar (los dientes); rallar (queso); **to — on** molestar, irritar.

grateful [grétfəl] adj. agradecido; grato, agradable.

grater [grétə] s. rallador.

gratify [grǽtəfaɪ] v. complacer, dar gusto, agradar; satisfacer.

grating [grétɪŋ] s. reja, enrejado, verja; adj. rechinante; molesto, áspero.

gratis [grétɪs] adv. gratis, de balde.

gratitude [grǽtətjud] s. gratitud.

gratuitous [grətjúətəs] adj. gratuito; sin fundamento; **— statement** afirmación arbitraria.

grave [grev] adj. grave; serio; s. tumba, sepulcro, sepultura; acento grave; **—stone** losa o lápida sepulcral.

gravel [grǽvl] s. grava, guijo, cascajo; cálculos (en los riñones, la vejiga, etc.); mal de piedra; v. cubrir con grava.

graveyard [grévjard] s. cementerio.

gravity [grǽvətɪ] s. gravedad; seriedad.

gravy [grévɪ] s. salsa; jugo (de carne).

gray [gre] adj. gris; cano; entrecano (que empieza a encanecer); **— horse** rucio, tordo, tordillo; **— matter** seso; **gray-headed** canoso; **s.** gris, color gris; v. encanecer; poner(se) gris.

grayish [gréɪʃ] adj. grisáceo, pardusco; **— hair** pelo entrecano.

grayness [grénɪs] s. grisura, gris, calidad de gris; encanecimiento.

graze [grez] v. pacer; apacentar, Am. pastear, pastar; rozar; raspar; s. roce, rozón, raspadura.

grease [gris] s. grasa; v. engrasar; untar; lubricar; **to — the palm** untar la mano, sobornar.

greasy [grísɪ] adj. grasiento, grasoso.

great [gret] adj. gran(de); eminente; magnífico, excelente; **a — deal** una gran cantidad; muchos; mucho; **a — many** muchos; **a — while** un largo rato o tiempo; **-ly** adv. grandemente; mucho; muy; en gran parte; sobremanera.

great-grandchild [grétgrǽntʃaɪld] s. biznieto.

great-grandfather [grétgrǽnfɑðə] s. bisabuelo.

great-grandmother [grétgrǽnmʌðə] s. bisabuela.

greatness [grétnɪs] s. grandeza.

Grecian [gríʃən] adj. & s. griego.

greed [grid] s. codicia; avaricia; gula.

greedily [grídɪlɪ] adv. vorazmente; con avaricia; con gula.

greediness [grídɪnɪs] s. codicia; avaricia; gula; voracidad.

greedy [grídɪ] adj. codicioso; avaro; goloso; voraz.

Greek [grik] adj. & s. griego.

green [grin] adj. verde; novato, inexperto; **to grow —** verdear; **the fields look —** verdean los campos; s. verde, verdor; césped, prado; campo de golf; **-s** verduras, hortalizas.

greenhouse [grínhaʊs] s. invernáculo, invernadero.

greenish [grínɪʃ] adj. verdoso.

greenness [grínnɪs] s. verdor, verdura; inmadurez; falta de experiencia, impericia.

greet [grit] v. saludar; **to — each other** saludarse.

greeting [grítɪŋ] s. saludo; salutación; **-s!** ¡salud! ¡saludos!

grenade [grinéd] s. granada, bomba pequeña.

grew [gru] pret. de **to grow.**

grey = **gray.**

greyish = **gray.**

greyness = **grayness.**

greyhound [gréhaʊnd] s. lebrel, galgo.

griddle [grídl] s. tartera; plancha (para tapar el hornillo).

grief [grif] s. dolor, pesar; **to come to —** sobrevenirle a uno una desgracia; fracasar.

grievance [grívəns] s. queja; resentimiento; motivo de queja, injusticia, ofensa.

grieve [griv] v. afligir(se); lamentar(se) acongojar(se).

grievous [grívəs] adj. doloroso, penoso grave, atroz.

grill [grɪl] s. parrilla; **men's —** restaurante para hombres; v. asar en parrillas; interrogar (a un sospechoso).

grim [grɪm] adj. austero, áspero; fiero torvo, siniestro.

grimace [grimés] s. mueca, gesto; v. hacer muecas o gestos.

grime [graɪm] s. mugre; v. ensuciar.

grimy [gráɪmɪ] adj. mugriento.

grin [grɪn] s. sonrisa abierta; sonrisa maliciosa; sonrisa canina; v. sonreír (mostrando mucho los dientes).

grind [graɪnd] v. moler; machacar; afilar, amolar; afanarse demasiado, estudiar con desmasiado empeño, machacar la lección; **to — a hand organ** tocar el organillo; **to — one's teeth** rechinar los dientes; s. molienda faena, trabajo penoso; estudiante te sonero; **the daily** — la rutina diaria.

grinder [gráɪndə] s. moledor; molinillo (*para moler café*); amolador, afilador; muela (*piedra para afilar*); muela (*diente molar*).

grip [grɪp] v. agarrar; asir; apretar; impresionar, conmover; s. agarro; asimiento; apretón; asidero, asa; valija, maletín, saco de mano; **to have a on someone** tener agarrado a alguien.

grippe [grɪp] s. gripe, influenza.

grit [grɪt] s. arenilla, arena; piedra arenisca; firmeza, tesón; **-s** maíz, avena, o trigo a medio moler; v. rechinar, crujir.

gritty [grítɪ] adj. arenoso; valeroso, firme.

grizzly [grízlɪ] adj. grisáceo, pardusco; **— bear** oso pardo.

groan [gron] s. gemido, quejido; v. gemir; quejarse; crujir (*por exceso de peso*).

grocer [grósə] s. abacero, Am. abarrotero, Am. bodeguero.

grocery [grósərɪ] s. abacería, tienda de comestibles, Am. abarrotería, Am. tienda de abarrotes; Am. bodega; **groceries** comestibles, Am. abarrotes.

groom [grum] s. novio; caballerizo, mozo de caballeriza; establero; v. almohazar, limpiar con la almohaza (*a los caballos*), cuidar (*a los caballos*); **to — oneself** asearse, peinarse, componerse; **well-groomed** bien vestido, aseado, limpio.

groove [gruv] s. estría, ranura, acanaladura; surco (*en un camino*); muesca, encaje; v. acanalar, estriar.

grope [grop] v. tentalear, tentar, andar a tientas; **to — for** buscar tentando, buscar a tientas.

gross [gros] adj. grueso; burdo; tosco; grosero; **— earnings** ganancias totales; **— ignorance** ignorancia crasa; **— weight** peso bruto; s. grueso, totalidad; gruesa (*doce docenas*).

grotesque [grotésk] adj. & s. grotesco.

grotto [gráto] s. gruta.

grouch [grautʃ] s. mal humor; gruñón, refunfuñón, cascarrabias; **to have a against someone** tenerle ojeriza (*o mala voluntad*) a una persona; guardarle rencor a alguien; v. gruñir, refunfuñar; estar de mal humor.

grouchy [gráutʃɪ] adj. gruñón, refunfuñón, malhumorado, cascarrabias.

ground [graʊnd] s. suelo, tierra; terreno; motivo, razón; fundamento, base; **-s** heces, desperdicios, sedimento; **— floor** piso bajo, planta baja; **to break —** ro-

turar, arar; cavar; **to give** — retroceder, ceder; **to hold one's** — mantenerse firme; v. conectar (*un alambre*) con la tierra; encallar (*una embarcación*); aterrizar (*un aeroplano*); **to be well -ed** poseer las bases o principios fundamentales; *pret. & p.p. de* **to grind**.

groundless [gráʊndlɪs] adj. infundado.

group [grup] s. grupo; v. agrupar.

grove [grov] s. arboleda, bosquecillo.

grow [gro] v. crecer; brotar; cultivar; criar; producir; **to — angry** ponerse enojado o enfadado, enfadarse, enojarse; **to — better** ponerse mejor, mejorar; **to — difficult** dificultarse, hacerse difícil; **to — late** hacerse tarde; **to — old** ponerse viejo, envejecer; **to — out of a habit** perder la costumbre; **to — pale** ponerse pálido, palidecer; **to — tired** cansarse.

growl [graʊl] s. gruñido; v. gruñir.

growler [gráʊlə] s. angry; regañón.

grown [gron] p.p. de **to grow** & adj. crecido; desarrollado; **— man** hombre maduro, hombre hecho; **— with trees** poblado de árboles.

grown-up [grónʌp] adj. crecido, adulto; s. adulto.

growth [groθ] s. crecimiento, acrecentamiento; aumento; desarrollo; vegetación; tumor, lobanillo, excrecencia.

grudge [grʌdʒ] s. inquina, rencor, resentimiento, mala voluntad; v. tener inquina, envidia o mala voluntad; dar de mala gana.

gruff [grʌf] adj. áspero, rudo; grosero.

grumble [grʌmbl] s. refunfuño, gruñido, queja; v. refunfuñar, gruñir, quejarse.

grumbler [grʌmblə] s. gruñón; regañón.

grumpy [grʌmpɪ] adj. malhumorado; gruñón.

grunt [grʌnt] s. gruñido, Am. pujido; v. gruñir, Am. pujar.

guarantee [gærəntí] s. garantía; fianza; fiador; v. garantizar; dar fianza; salir fiador de.

guarantor [gérəntə] s. fiador.

guaranty [gérəntɪ] s. garantía; fianza; fiador; v. *véase* **guarantee.**

guard [gard] s. guarda; guardia; resguardo; **to be on —** estar alerta; estar en guardia; **to keep —** vigilar; v. guardar; resguardar; vigilar; **to — (oneself) against** guardarse de.

guardian [gárdɪən] s. guardián, custodio; tutor; **— angel** ángel custodio, ángel de la guarda.

guardianship [gárdɪənʃɪp] s. tutela; guarda, custodia.

Guatemalan [gwatəmálən] adj. & s.

guatemalteco.

guess [ges] *s.* conjetura, suposición; adivinación; *v.* adivinar; suponer, creer.

guest [gest] *s.* convidado; visita; huésped, pensionista, inquilino.

guffaw [gʌfɔ́] *s.* risotada, carcajada.

guidance [gáidns] *s.* guía, dirección.

guide [gaid] *s.* guía.

guidebook [gáidbuk] *s.* guía del viajero; **railway** — guía de ferrocarriles.

guild [gild] *s.* gremio; cofradía; asociación.

guile [gail] *s.* engaño, astucia.

guilt [gilt] *s.* culpa, delito; culpabilidad.

guiltless [gíltlis] *adj.* libre de culpa; inocente.

guilty [gílti] *adj.* culpable; reo, delincuente.

guise [gaiz] *s.* aspecto, apariencia; modo; **under the** — **of** so capa de; disfrazado de.

guitar [gitár] *s.* guitarra.

gulf [gʌlf] *s.* golfo; abismo.

gull [gʌl] *s.* gaviota.

gullet [gʌ́lit] *s.* gaznate.

gully [gʌ́li] *s.* barranco, barranca; hondonada.

gulp [gʌlp] *s.* trago; *v.* tragar; engullir; **to** — **it down** tragárselo.

gum [gʌm] *s.* goma; encía; **chewing** — goma de mascar, *Am.* chicle; — **tree** árbol gomífero, *Am.* gomero; *v.* engomar, pegar con goma.

gun [gʌn] *s.* arma de fuego; cañón; fusil, escopeta; pistola, revólver; **a 21** — **salute** una salva de 21 cañonazos.

gunboat [gʌ́nbot] *s.* cañonero, lancha cañonera.

gunner [gʌ́nə] *s.* artillero, cañonero; ametrallador.

gunpowder [gʌ́npaudə] *s.* pólvora.

gurgle [gɝ́gl] *v.* borbotar, hacer borbollones; *s.* borbollón, borbotón.

gush [gʌʃ] *s.* chorro; borbollón, borbotón; efusión (*de cariño o entusiasmo*); *v.* chorrear, borbotar, borbollar, borbollonear; brotar; ser demasiado efusivo.

gust [gʌst] *s.* ráfaga, ventolera.

gut [gʌt] *s.* tripa, intestino; cuerda de tripa; **to have -s** tener agallas (*ánimo*).

gutter [gʌ́tə] *s.* arroyo (*de la calle o de un camino*); gotera (*del techo*); zanja.

guy [gai] *s.* sujeto, tipo, individuo; tirante, alambre, cadena (*para sostener algo*); *v.* sostener (*algo*) con tirantes; burlarse de, mofarse de.

gymnasium [dʒimnéziəm] *s.* gimnasio.

gymnastics [dʒimnǽstiks] *s. pl.* gimnasia.

gypsy [dʒípsi] *s.* & *adj.* gitano.

H

habit [hǽbit] *s.* hábito; costumbre; **drinking** — vicio de la bebida; **riding** — traje de montar.

habitual [həbítʃʊəl] *adj.* habitual; acostumbrado.

hack [hæk] *s.* tajo; tos seca; caballo de alquiler; rocín; escritor mercenario; *v.* tajar, picar; toser con tos seca.

hackneyed [hǽknid] *adj.* trillado, muy común.

had [hæd] *pret.* & *p.p. de* **to have**; **you** — **better do it** es bueno que Vd. lo haga; **sería bueno que Vd. lo hiciese**; **I** — **rather go than stay** preferiría irme a quedarme.

hag [hæg] *s.* hechicera, bruja; viejota.

haggard [hǽgəd] *adj.* macilento, flaco.

haggle [hǽgl] *v.* regatear.

hail [hel] *s.* granizo; saludo; llamada, grito; **Hail Mary Ave María**; *interj.* ¡salud!; ¡salve!; *v.* granizar; saludar; llamar; aclamar; **to** — **from** proceder de, ser oriundo de.

hailstorm [hélstɔrm] *s.* granizada.

hair [her] *s.* pelo; cabello; vello; filamento (*de las plantas*); — **net** red para el cabello.

hairbrush [hérbrʌʃ] *s.* cepillo para el cabello.

haircut [hérkʌt] *s.* corte de pelo; **to have a** — hacerse cortar el pelo.

hairdo [hérdu] *s.* peinado.

hairdresser [hérdresə] *s.* peluquero; peinadora.

hairless [hérlis] *adj.* sin pelo; pelado; lampiño.

hairpin [hérpin] *s.* horquilla, *Am.* gancho (*para el pelo*).

hairy [héri] *adj.* peludo, cabelludo; hirsuto, velloso, velludo.

hale [hel] *adj.* sano, fuerte, robusto; *v.* llevar (*a una persona*) por fuerza.

half [hæf] *s.* mitad; — **an apple media manzana**; *adj.* medio; — **brother hermanastro**; — **cooked a medio cocer, medio cocido**; **half-past one la una y media**.

half-breed [hǽfbrid] *adj.* & *s.* mestizo.

half-hour [hǽfáʊr] *s.* media hora; *adj.* de media hora.

half-mast [hǽfmǽst] *s.* media asta; *v.* poner a media asta (*la bandera*).

half-open [hǽfópən] *adj.* entreabierto; medio abierto, entornado.

halfway [hǽfwe] *adj.* & *adv.* a medio camino; parcial, incompleto; — **between** equidistante de; — **finished a medio**

acabar; **to do something** — hacer algo a medias.
half-witted [hǽfwɪtɪd] adj. imbécil, zonzo.
halibut [hǽləbət] s. mero, hipogloso (pez).
hall [hɔl] s. salón (para asambleas, funciones, etc.); edificio (de un colegio o universidad); vestíbulo; corredor, pasillo; **town** — ayuntamiento.
hallo = hello.
hallow [hǽlo] v. santificar; consagrar.
Halloween [hæloin] s. víspera de Todos los Santos.
halo [hélo] s. halo; aureola.
halt [hɔlt] s. alto, parada; v. parar(se), detener(se); hacer alto; vacilar.
halter [hɔltə] s. ronzal, cabestro.
halting [hɔltɪŋ] adj. vacilante; **-ly** adv. con vacilación.
halve [hæv] v. partir por la mitad; partir en dos.
halves [hævz] pl. de **half**; **to go** — ir a medias.
ham [hæm] s. jamón.
hamburger [hǽmbɜgə] s. carne picada de vaca; bocadillo o emparedado de carne picada, Am. hamburguesa.
hamlet [hǽmlɪt] s. caserío, aldehuela.
hammer [hǽmə] s. martillo; martinete (de piano); **sledge** — macho; v. martillar; machacar; clavar.
hammock [hǽmək] s. hamaca, Am. chinchorro.
hamper [hǽmpə] s. canasto, cesto grande, cuévano; v. estorbar, impedir, embarazar.
hand [hænd] s. mano; manecilla (de reloj); obrero; letra (modo de escribir); — **and glove** uña y carne; — **in** (cogidos) de la mano; **at** — a la mano, cerca; **made by** — hecho a mano; on — disponible; en existencia; listo; a la mano, presente; **on the other** — en cambio, por otra parte; **to have one's** -**s full** estar ocupadísimo; v. entregar, dar; **to** — **down** bajar (una cosa para dársela a alguien); transmitir (de una a otra generación); pronunciar (un fallo); **to** — **in** entregar; **to** — **over** entregar.
handbag [hǽndbæg] s. bolsa o bolso, saco de noche, maletín.
handball [hǽndbɔl] s. pelota; juego de pelota.
handbill [hǽndbɪl] s. hoja volante (anuncio).
handcuff [hǽndkʌf] v. maniatar; **-s** s. pl. esposas, manillas de hierro.
handful [hǽndfəl] s. manojo, puñado.
handicap [hǽndɪkæp] s. desventaja, es-

torbo, impedimento, obstáculo; ventaja o desventaja (impuesta en ciertas contiendas); — **race** carrera de handicap; v. estorbar, poner trabas a.
handiwork [hǽndɪwɜk] s. labor, trabajo hecho a mano; artefacto.
handkerchief [hǽŋkətʃɪf] s. pañuelo.
handle [hǽndl] s. mango, asa; tirador (de puerta o cajón); puño (de espada); manubrio (de bicicleta, organillo, etc.); v. manejar; manipular; manosear, tocar; comerciar en; **-s easily** se maneja con facilidad, es muy manuable.
handmade [hǽndméd] adj. hecho a mano.
handsaw [hǽndsɔ] s. serrucho.
handshake [hǽndʃek] s. apretón de manos.
handsome [hǽnsəm] adj. hermoso, guapo, bien parecido; generoso; **a** — **sum** una suma considerable.
handwriting [hǽndraɪtɪŋ] s. letra (modo de escribir), escritura.
handy [hǽndɪ] adj. a la mano, próximo; hábil, diestro; manuable, fácil de manejar.
hang [hæŋ] v. colgar; suspender; ahorcar; inclinar (la cabeza); **sentenced to** — condenado a la horca; **to** — **around** andar holgazaneando por un sitio; rondar; esperar sin hacer nada; **to** — **on** colgarse de; depender de; estar pendiente de; persistir; **to** — **paper on a wall** empapelar una pared; **to** — **with tapestries** entapizar; s. modo de caerle la ropa a una persona; modo de manejar (un mecanismo); modo de resolver (un problema); significado (de un argumento); **I don't care a** — no me importa un ardite.
hangar [hǽŋə] s. hangar, cobertizo.
hanger [hǽŋə] s. colgadero; percha, clavijero; **paper** — empapelador.
hanging [hǽŋɪŋ] s. muerte en la horca; **-s** colgaduras; adj. colgante; colgado.
hangman [hǽŋmən] s. verdugo.
hangnail [hǽŋnel] s. padrastro (pedacito de pellejo que se levanta junto a las uñas).
hang-over [hǽŋovə] s. sobrante, remanente, resto; **to have a** — Am. tener un ratón o estar enratonado (tras una borrachera), Am. estar crudo o tener una cruda.
haphazard [hæphǽzəd] adv. al azar, al acaso, a la ventura, a la buena de Dios; adj. casual; impensado.
haphazardly [hæphǽzədlɪ] adv. = haphazard.
hapless [hǽplɪs] adj. desventurado, desgraciado.

happen [hǽpən] v. suceder, pasar, acontecer, sobrevenir, acaecer; **to — to hear** (do, be, etc.) oír (hacer, estar, etc.) por casualidad; **to — to pass by** acertar a pasar; **to — on** (upon) encontrarse con, tropezar con.

happening [hǽpəniŋ] s. acontecimiento, suceso.

happily [hǽpli] adv. felizmente; afortunadamente.

happiness [hǽpinis] s. felicidad, dicha, contento.

happy [hǽpi] adj. feliz; dichoso, alegre; afortunado; **to be — to** alegrarse de.

harangue [hərǽŋ] s. arenga, perorata; v. arengar, perorar.

harass [hǽrəs] v. acosar, hostigar, molestar.

harbor [hárbə] s. puerto; asilo, refugio, abrigo; v. abrigar; hospedar; albergar.

hard [hard] adj. duro; tieso; arduo, difícil; **— cash** dinero contante y sonante, metálico; **— coal** antracita; **— liquor** licor espiritoso (aguardiente, ron, etc.); **— luck** mala suerte; **— of hearing** medio sordo; **— water** agua cruda; adv. fuerte, recio, con fuerza; con empeño, con ahínco; **— by** muy cerca; **—hearted** de corazón duro; **hardworking** muy trabajador, industrioso, aplicado.

harden [hárdn] v. endurecer(se).

hardening [hárdniŋ] s. endurecimiento.

hardly [hárdli] adv. apenas; a duras penas; difícilmente; duramente, con aspereza; probablemente no.

hardness [hárdnis] s. dureza; aspereza; dificultad.

hardship [hárdʃip] s. apuro, aflicción; trabajo, penalidad.

hardware [hárdwer] s. quincalla, quincallería; **— shop** quincallería, ferretería.

hardy [hárdi] adj. robusto, fuerte, recio; atrevido.

hare [her] s. liebre.

harebrained [hérbrénd] adj. atolondrado, ligero de cascos.

harlot [hárlət] s. ramera, prostituta.

harm [harm] s. daño; mal; perjuicio; v. dañar; hacer mal, hacer daño; perjudicar.

harmful [hármfəl] adj. dañoso; dañino, nocivo, perjudicial.

harmless [hármlis] adj. innocuo; inofensivo; no dañoso, inocente.

harmlessness [hármlisnis] s. innocuidad; inocencia, falta de malicia.

harmonic [harmánikl] adj. armónico.

harmonious [harmóniəs] adj. armonioso.

harmonize [hármənaiz] v. armonizar; concordar; congeniar.

harmony [hárməni] s. armonía.

harness [hárnis] s. guarniciones (de caballerías); jaez, aparejo; **to get back in —** volver al servicio activo, volver a trabajar; volver a la rutina; v. enjaezar, poner guarniciones a (un caballo, mula, etc.).

harp [harp] s. arpa; v. tocar el arpa; **to — on** repetir constantemente (una nota, palabra, tema, etc.); porfiar en.

harpoon [harpún] s. arpón; v. arponear, pescar con arpón.

harrow [hǽro] s. rastro, rastrillo, grada; v. rastrear, rastrillar; atormentar; horrorizar.

harrowing [hǽrowiŋ] adj. horrendo, horripilante, que pone los cabellos de punta.

harry [hǽri] v. acosar, molestar; asolar.

harsh [harʃ] adj. tosco, áspero; severo, austero.

harshness [hárʃnis] s. aspereza; tosquedad; severidad.

harvest [hárvist] s. cosecha; siega, agosto; recolección; v. cosechar; segar.

hash [hæʃ] s. picadillo.

haste [hest] s. prisa; apresuramiento; **in — de prisa**; **to make —** darse prisa, apresurarse.

hasten [hésn] v. apresurar(se), precipitar(se); darse prisa.

hastily [héstli] adv. aprisa, de prisa, apresuradamente, precipitadamente.

hasty [hésti] adj. apresurado; precipitado.

hat [hæt] s. sombrero.

hatch [hætʃ] v. empollar; criar pollos; idear, maquinar; s. cría, nidada, pollada; escotillón, trampa (puerta en el suelo); **—way** escotilla.

hatchet [hǽtʃit] s. hacha; **to bury the —** echar pelillos a la mar, olvidar rencores o enemistades.

hate [het] s. odio; aborrecimiento; v. odiar; aborrecer; detestar.

hateful [hétfəl] adj. odioso, aborrecible.

hatred [hétrid] s. odio, aversión.

haughtily [hótli] adv. con altivez, altaneramente, arrogantemente.

haughtiness [hótinis] s. altanería, altivez.

haughty [hóti] adj. altivo, altanero, arrogante.

haul [hol] v. acarrear, transportar; jalar (halar); tirar de; arrastrar; **to — down the flag** arriar (o bajar) la bandera; s. acarreo; transporte; tirón, estirón; buena pesca; ganancia, botín.

haunch [hɔntʃ] s. anca.

haunt [hɔnt] v. frecuentar a menudo; andar por, vagar por (como fantasma o espectro); **that idea -s me** me persigue esa idea; **-ed house** casa de espantos, fantasmas o aparecidos; s. guarida.

have [hæv] v. tener; poseer; haber (v. aux.); **to — a suit made** mandar hacer un traje; **to — a look at** dar un vistazo a, echar una mirada a; **to — to tener que; deber; I'll not — it** so no lo toleraré, no lo permitiré; **what did she — on?** ¿qué vestido llevaba (puesto)?

haven [hévən] s. asilo, abrigo, refugio; puerto.

havoc [hævək] s. estrago, estropicio, ruina; **to cause —** hacer estragos.

hawk [hɔk] s. halcón; v. pregonar (mercancías).

hawthorn [hɔ́əorn] s. espino.

hay [he] s. heno, paja, hierba seca; **— fever** catarro asmático.

hayloft [hélɔft] s. henil, pajar.

haystack [héstæk] s. montón de heno o paja.

hazard [hǽzəd] s. azar; riesgo, peligro; estorbo, obstáculo (en el campo de golf); v. arriesgar, aventurar.

hazardous [hǽzədəs] adj. peligroso.

haze [hez] s. bruma, neblina, niebla; v. atormentar, hostigar (con bromas estudiantiles).

hazel [hézl] s. avellano; **—nut** avellana; adj. de avellano; avellanado, color de avellana.

hazy [hézɪ] adj. nublado, brumoso; confuso.

he [hi] pron. pers. él; **— who** el que, quien; **he-goat** macho cabrío.

head [hed] s. cabeza; cabecera (de cama); jefe; **— of hair** cabellera; **game of -s or tails** juego de cara y cruz, juego de las chapas, Am. juego de cara y sello; **to be out of one's —** delirar, estar delirante; **to come to a —** madurar; supurar (un absceso); **to keep one's —** conservar la calma, no perder la cabeza; **it goes to his —** le desvanece; se le sube a la cabeza; adj. principal, primero; de proa, de frente; **head-on** de frente; v. encabezar; ir a la cabeza de; acaudillar; mandar, dirigir; **to — off** atajar; detener, refrenar; **to — towards** dirigirse a, encaminarse a.

headache [hédek] s. dolor de cabeza.

headdress [héddres] s. tocado, adorno para la cabeza.

headgear [hédgɪr] s. sombrero, gorro, gorra; tocado, toca (de mujer); cabezada (de guarnición para caballo).

heading [hédɪŋ] s. encabezamiento, título.

headland [hédlənd] s. cabo, promontorio.

headlight [hédlaɪt] s. linterna delantera, faro delantero.

headline [hédlaɪn] s. título, encabezado.

headlong [hédlɔ́ŋ] adv. de cabeza; precipitadamente.

headquarters [hédkwɔ́rtəz] s. cuartel general; jefatura; oficina principal.

headstrong [hédstrɔŋ] adj. testarudo, porfiado, obstinado.

headway [hédwe] s. progreso, avance; **to make —** avanzar, adelantar, progresar.

heal [hil] v. curar; sanar; cicatrizar.

health [helθ] s. salud; sanidad; salubridad.

healthful [hélθfəl] adj. sano; salubre; saludable.

healthfulness [hélθfəlnɪs] s. salubridad; sanidad.

healthy [hélθɪ] adj. sano; saludable.

heap [hip] s. montón; pila; v. amontonar; apilar.

hear [hɪr] v. oír; escuchar; tener noticias; **to — about someone** oír hablar de alguien; **to — from someone** tener noticias de alguien; **to — of** saber de, tener noticias de, oír hablar de; **I -d that . . .** oí decir que . . .

heard [hɜd] pret. & p.p. de **to hear.**

hearer [hírə] s. oyente.

hearing [hírɪŋ] s. oído; audiencia; examen de testigos; **hard of —** medio sordo, algo sordo; **within —** al alcance del oído.

hearsay [hírse] s. hablilla, rumor; **by —** de oídas.

hearse [hɜs] s. carroza fúnebre.

heart [hart] s. corazón; ánimo; **at — en realidad, en el fondo; from the bottom of one's —** de corazón, con toda el alma; con toda sinceridad; **to learn by —** aprender de memoria; **to take — cobrar ánimo; to take to —** tomar en serio; tomar a pechos.

heartache [hártek] s. dolor del corazón; angustia, pesar, congoja.

heartbroken [hártbrokən] adj. traspasado de dolor, acongojado, angustiado; desengañado.

hearten [hártn] v. animar.

heartfelt [hártfelt] adj. sentido, cordial, sincero; **my — sympathy** mi más sentido pésame.

hearth [harθ] s. hogar; fogón.

heartily [hártɪlɪ] *adv.* de corazón; cordialmente; de buena gana; **to eat** — comer con apetito; comer bien (*o mucho*).

heartless [hártlɪs] *adj.* de mal corazón; cruel; insensible.

heart-rending [hártrendɪŋ] *adj.* angustioso; agudo.

hearty [hártɪ] *adj.* sincero, cordial; sano, fuerte; — **food** alimento nutritivo; a — **laugh** una buena carcajada; — **meal** comida abundante.

heat [hit] *s.* calor; ardor; vehemencia; celo (*ardor sexual de la hembra*); calefacción (*para las habitaciones*); corrida, carrera (*de prueba*); *v.* calentar(se); acalorar(se).

heater [hítə] *s.* calentador; calorífero.

heathen [híðən] *s.* pagano, gentil, idólatra; paganos; *adj.* pagano; irreligioso.

heating [hítɪŋ] *s.* calefacción.

heave [hiv] *v.* levantar, alzar (*con esfuerzo*); arrojar, lanzar; exhalar (*un suspiro*); jalar (*un cable*); jadear; basquear, hacer esfuerzos por vomitar.

heaven [hévən] *s.* cielo.

heavenly [hévənlɪ] *adj.* celeste; celestial; divino.

heavily [hévlɪ] *adv.* pesadamente, lentamente; copiosamente, excesivamente.

heaviness [hévɪnɪs] *s.* pesadez, pesantez; opresión, abatimiento.

heavy [hévɪ] *adj.* pesado; grueso; burdo, opresivo; — **rain** aguacero recio o fuerte; **with a** — **heart** abatido, acongojado.

hectic [héktɪk] *adj.* febril; inquieto.

hedge [hedʒ] *s.* seto; vallado, barrera; *v.* cercar; poner valla o seto a; evitar o evadir contestaciones.

hedgehog [hédʒhɑg] *s.* erizo.

heed [hid] *v.* atender; hacer caso; prestar atención; *s.* atención, cuidado; **to pay** — to prestar atención a; hacer caso de.

heedless [hídlɪs] *adj.* descuidado; desatento.

heel [hil] *s.* talón (*del pie o de una media*); tacón (*del zapato*); **head over** —**s** patas arriba; *v.* poner tacón a; poner talón a.

heifer [héfə] *s.* novilla, vaquilla.

height [haɪt] *s.* altura; elevación; — **of folly** colmo de la locura.

heighten [háɪtṇ] *v.* avivar; aumentar(se); realzar.

heinous [hénəs] *adj.* aborrecible, odioso; malvado.

heir [er] *s.* heredero.

heiress [érɪs] *s.* heredera.

held [held] *pret. & p.p.* de **to hold**.

hell [hel] *s.* infierno.

hello [heló] *interj.* ¡hola!; ¡halo!.

helm [helm] *s.* timón.

helmet [hélmɪt] *s.* yelmo.

help [help] *s.* ayuda; auxilio; remedio; alivio; criado o criados, sirviente o sirvientes; empleado o empleados; *v.* ayudar, asistir; auxiliar; remediar; servir (*algo de comer*); **to** — **down** ayudar a bajar — **yourself** sírvase Vd. (*de comer o beber*); tómelo Vd., está a la disposición de Vd.; **he cannot** — **it** no puede evitarlo; **he cannot** — **doing it** no puede menos de hacerlo; **he cannot** — **but come** no puede menos de venir.

helper [hélpə] *s.* ayudante, asistente.

helpful [hélpfəl] *adj.* útil, servicial; provechoso.

helping [hélpɪŋ] *s.* ayuda; porción (*que se sirve en la mesa*).

helpless [hélplɪs] *adj.* desamparado; desvalido; imposibilitado; incapaz; perplejo, indeciso (*sin saber qué hacer*); a — **situation** una situación irremediable.

helplessness [hélplɪsnɪs] *s.* incapacidad; incompetencia; impotencia, debilidad; abandono, desamparo.

hem [hem] *s.* dobladillo, bastilla; *v.* dobladillar, bastillar, hacer dobladillos en (*la ropa*); **to** — **in** rodear, cercar; **to** — **and haw** toser y retoser (*fingidamente*); tartamudear, vacilar.

hemisphere [hémɪsfɪr] *s.* hemisferio.

hemlock [hémlɑk] *s.* cicuta (*hierba venenosa*); abeto americano.

hemp [hemp] *s.* cáñamo, *Am.* sisal.

hemstitch [hémstɪtʃ] *s.* dobladillo de ojo; *v.* hacer o (echar) dobladillo de ojo

hen [hen] *s.* gallina; ave hembra.

hence [hens] *adv.* de (*o* desde) aquí; desde ahora; por lo tanto, por consiguiente; a **week** — de hoy en ocho días; de aquí a una semana.

henceforth [hensfóre] *adv.* de aquí en adelante; de hoy en adelante; desde ahora.

her [hɜ] *pron.* la; le, a ella; ella (*con preposición*); *adj.* su (sus), de ella.

herald [hérəld] *s.* heraldo; anunciador, proclamador; precursor; *v.* anunciar, proclamar, publicar.

herb [ɜb] *s.* hierba (yerba).

herd [hɜd] *s.* hato, rebaño; ganado; manada; tropel, muchedumbre; **the common** — el populacho, la chusma; *v.* reunir, juntar (*el ganado*); ir en manadas, ir juntos.

herdsman [hɜdzmən] *s.* vaquero, vaquerizo; pastor.

here [hɪr] *adv.* aquí; acá; — **it is** aquí está, helo aquí, aquí lo tiene Vd.; — **is to you!** ¡a la salud de Vd.!; **that is neither — nor there** eso no viene al caso.

hereafter [hɪréftɚ] *adv.* de aquí (o de hoy) en adelante; desde ahora en adelante; en lo futuro; *s.* **the —** la otra vida.

hereby [hɪrbái] *adv.* por este medio; mediante la presente, por la presente; con estas palabras.

hereditary [hɪrédɪtɚɪ] *adj.* hereditario.

heredity [hɪrédɪtɪ] *s.* herencia.

herein [hɪrín] *adv.* aquí dentro; en esto.

heresy [hérəsɪ] *s.* herejía.

heretic [hérətɪk] *s.* hereje.

heretofore [hɪrtəfɔ́r] *adv.* hasta ahora, hasta el presente.

herewith [hɪrwíθ] *adv.* aquí dentro, con esto, adjunto, incluso.

heritage [hérətɪdʒ] *s.* herencia.

hermit [hɜ́mɪt] *s.* ermitaño.

hernia [hɜ́nɪə] *s.* hernia, ruptura, relajamiento.

hero [hfro] *s.* héroe; protagonista.

heroic [hɪrɔ́ɪk] *adj.* heroico.

heroine [hérɔɪn] *s.* heroína.

heroism [hérɔɪzəm] *s.* heroísmo.

heron [hérən] *s.* garza.

herring [hérɪŋ] *s.* arenque.

hers [hɜz] *pron. pos.* suyo (suya, suyos, suyas), de ella; el suyo (la suya, los suyos, las suyas); el (la, los, las) de ella; **a friend of —** un amigo suyo.

herself [hɚsélf] *pron.* ella misma; se *(como reflexivo)*; **by —** sola; por sí (sola); **she — did it** ella misma lo hizo; **she talks to —** ella habla para sí, habla consigo misma, habla para sus adentros, habla sola.

hesitant [hézətənt] = **hesitating**.

hesitate [hézətet] *v.* vacilar; titubear; dudar.

hesitating [hésətetɪŋ] *adj.* vacilante; indeciso; irresoluto; **-ly** *adv.* con vacilación.

hesitation [hezətéʃən] *s.* vacilación; titubeo, duda.

hew [hju] *v.* tajar, cortar; picar *(piedra)*; labrar *(madera, piedra)*.

hewn [hjun] *p.p.* de **to hew**.

hey [he] *interj.* ¡he!; ¡oiga!; ¡oye!

hiccup, hiccough [hfkʌp] *s.* hipo; *v.* hipar, tener hipo.

hickory [hfkɔrɪ] *s.* nogal americano; — **nut** nuez *(del nogal americano)*.

hid [hɪd] *pret. & p.p.* de **to hide**.

hidden [hfdṇ] *p.p.* de **to hide**; *adj.* oculto, escondido.

hide [haɪd] *v.* ocultar(se); esconder(se); **to — from** esconderse de, recatarse de; *s.* cuero, piel; **to play — and seek** jugar al escondite.

hideous [hfdɪəs] *adj.* horrendo, horripilante, feote.

high [haɪ] *adj.* alto; — **altar** altar mayor; — **and dry** enjuto; **en seco; — antiquity** antigüedad remota; — **explosive** explosivo de gran potencia; — **tide** pleamar; — **wind** ventarrón, viento fuerte; **in — gear** en directa, en tercera velocidad; **two feet** — dos pies de alto; **it is — time that** ya es hora de que; **to be in — spirits** estar muy animado; *adv.* alto; **a precio subido; en alto; to look — and low** buscar por todas partes; **high-grade** de calidad superior; **high-handed** arbitrario, despótico; **high-minded** magnánimo, orgulloso; **high-sounding** altisonante, rimbombante; **high-strung** muy tenso.

highland [háɪlənd] *s.* tierra montañosa; **the Highlands** las montañas de Escocia.

highly [háɪlɪ] *adv.* altamente; sumamente, muy; — **paid** muy bien pagado.

highness [háɪnɪs] *s.* altura; elevación; Alteza *(título)*.

highway [háɪwe] *s.* camino real; carretera, calzada.

highwayman [háɪwemən] *s.* forajido, salteador de caminos, bandido.

hike [haɪk] *s.* caminata, paseo largo, *Am.* andada; *v.* dar *(o echar)* una caminata.

hill [hɪl] *s.* colina, collado, cerro; montoncillo de tierra; **ant —** hormiguero; **down —** cuesta abajo; **up —** cuesta arriba.

hillock [hflək] *s.* collado, otero, montecillo.

hillside [hflsaɪd] *s.* ladera.

hilltop [hfltɒp] *s.* cumbre, cima *(de una colina)*.

hilly [hflɪ] *adj.* montuoso; accidentado.

hilt [hɪlt] *s.* empuñadura, puño *(de una espada o daga)*.

him [hɪm] *pron.* le; lo; él *(con preposición)*.

himself [hɪmsélf] *pron.* él mismo; se *(como reflexivo)*; a sí mismo; *véase* **herself**.

hind [haɪnd] *adj.* trasero; posterior; *s.* cierva; **most** *adj.* último, postrero.

hinder [hfndɚ] *v.* estorbar, impedir, obstruir.

hindrance [hfndrəns] *s.* estorbo, obstáculo, impedimento.

hinge [hɪndʒ] *s.* gozne; bisagra; *v.* engoznar, poner goznes; **to — on** girar sobre; depender de.

hint [hɪnt] *s.* indirecta, insinuación; sugestión; **not to take the —** no darse por entendido; *v.* insinuar, intimar, sugerir indirectamente.

hip [hɪp] *s.* cadera.

hippopotamus [hɪpəpátəməs] *s.* hipopótamo.

hire [haɪr] *s.* alquiler; paga, sueldo; *v.* alquilar; emplear; dar empleo, *Am.* enganchar, *Am.* conchabar; **to — out** alquilarse, ponerse a servir a otro.

his [hɪz] *pron. pos.* suyo (suya, suyos, suyas), de él; el suyo (la suya, los suyos, las suyas); el (la, los, las) de él; **a friend of —** un amigo suyo; *adj.* su (sus), de él.

hiss [hɪs] *s.* silbido, chiflido; siseo; *v.* sisear, silbar, chiflar.

historian [hɪstɔ́rɪən] *s.* historiador.

historic [hɪstɔ́rɪk] *adj.* histórico.

historical [hɪstɔ́rɪkl] *adj.* histórico.

history [hɪ́strɪ] *s.* historia.

hit [hɪt] *v.* pegar, golpear; dar (*un golpe*); dar en (*o* con); chocar; **they — it off well** se llevan bien, congenian; **to — the mark** acertar, atinar, dar en el blanco; **to — upon** dar con; encontrarse con, encontrar por casualidad; *pret. & p.p. de* to hit; *s.* golpe; choque; golpe de fortuna; pulla, dicharacho; **to be a great —** ser un gran éxito; **to make a — with someone** caerle en gracia a una persona.

hitch [hɪtʃ] *v.* atar, amarrar; enganchar; uncir (*bueyes*); dar un tirón; **to — one's chair nearer to** acercar su silla a; *s.* tirón; obstáculo, impedimento, tropiezo; enganche, enganchamiento.

hitchhike [hɪ́tʃhaɪk] *v.* viajar de gorra (*en automóvil*), *Am.* irse o viajar de mosca.

hither [hɪ́ðə] *adv.* acá; **— and thither** acá y allá.

hitherto [hɪ́ðətú] *adv.* hasta aquí, hasta ahora, hasta hoy.

hive [haɪv] *s.* colmena; enjambre; **-s** ronchas (*de la piel*).

hoard [hord] *s.* tesoro escondido; acumulamiento secreto de provisiones; *v.* atesorar, guardar (*con avaricia*); acumular secretamente.

hoarse [hors] *adj.* bronco, áspero, ronco.

hoarseness [hɔ́rsnɪs] *s.* ronquera; carraspera.

hoary [hórɪ] *adj.* cano, encanecido, canoso.

hobble [háb] *v.* cojear, renquear; maniatar o manear (*un animal*); impedir,

estorbar; *s.* cojera; traba, maniota o manea (*cuerda con que se atan las manos de una bestia*).

hobby [hábɪ] *s.* afición; trabajo hecho por afición (*no por obligación*).

hobo [hóbo] *s.* vagabundo.

hodgepodge [hádʒpadʒ] *s.* mezcolanza, baturrillo.

hoe [ho] *s.* azada, azadón; *v.* cavar, escardar, limpiar con azadón.

hog [hag] *s.* puerco, cerdo, cochino; *v.* apropiárselo todo.

hoist [hɔɪst] *v.* alzar, levantar; izar (*la bandera, las velas*); *s.* elevador, *Am.* malacate.

hold [hold] *v.* tener(se); retener; detener; tener cabida para; sostener; mantener(se); opinar; celebrar (*una reunión, etc.*); ocupar (*un puesto*); ser válido (*un argumento o regla*); **to — back someone** detener (*o* refrenar) a alguien; **to — forth** perorar, hablar largamente; **to — in place** sujetar; **to — off** mantener(se) a distancia; mantenerse alejado; **to — on** agarrar(se); asir(se); persistir; **— on!** ¡agárrese bien! ¡deténgase! ¡pare!; **to — someone responsible** hacerle a uno responsable; **to — someone to his word** obligar a uno a cumplir su palabra; **to — oneself erect** tenerse o andar derecho; **to — one's own** mantenerse firme; **to — one's tongue** callarse; **to — out** continuar, durar; mantenerse firme; **to — over** aplazar; durar; continuar en un cargo; **to — still** estarse quieto o callado; **to — tight** apretar; **to — to one's promise** cumplir con la promesa; **to — up** levantar, alzar; detener; asaltar, atracar (*para robar*); **how much does it — ?** ¿cuánto le cabe? *s.* agarro; dominio; influencia; autoridad; bodega (*de un barco*); cabina de carga (*de un aeroplano*); **to get — of** asir, agarrar; atrapar; **to take — of** coger, agarrar, asir.

holder [hóldə] *s.* tenedor, posesor; receptáculo; cojinillo (*para coger un trasto caliente*); **cigarette —** boquilla; **pen—** portaplumas.

holdup [hóldʌp] *s.* asalto, atraco.

hole [hol] *s.* agujero; abertura; hoyo, hueco, cavidad; bache (*de un camino*); **swimming —** charco, remanso; **to be in a —** hallarse en un apuro o aprieto.

holiday [hálədɛ] *s.* día de fiesta, día festivo, festividad; **-s** días de fiesta; vacaciones.

holiness [hólɪnɪs] *s.* santidad.

HOL—HOR

hollow [hálo] *adj.* hueco; vacío; cóncavo; hundido; falso; *s.* hueco; hoyo; cavidad; concavidad; depresión; cañada, hondonada; *v.* ahuecar; excavar; ahondar.

holly [hálɪ] *s.* agrifolio, acebo.

holster [hólstə] *s.* pistolera, funda (*de pistola*).

holy [hólɪ] *adj.* santo; sagrado, sacro; — water agua bendita.

homage [hámɪdʒ] *s.* homenaje; reverencia, acatamiento; to do — acatar, rendir homenaje, honrar.

home [hom] *s.* casa, hogar; habitación, domicilio; at — en casa; *adj.* doméstico; casero; — office oficina matriz o central; — rule autonomía; — run *Am.* jonrón (*en beisbol*); — stretch último trecho (*de una carrera*); *adv.* a casa; en casa; to strike — herir en lo vivo; dar en el clavo o en el blanco.

homeland [hómlænd] *s.* tierra natal, suelo patrio.

homeless [hómlɪs] *adj.* sin casa; destituido.

homelike [hómlaɪk] *adj.* hogareño, cómodo.

homely [hómlɪ] *adj.* feo; llano, sencillo; casero, doméstico.

homemade [hómméd] *adj.* hecho en casa; doméstico, nacional, del país.

homesick [hómsɪk] *adj.* nostálgico.

homesickness [hómsɪknɪs] *s.* nostalgia.

homestead [hómstɛd] *s.* heredad; casa y terrenos adyacentes.

homeward [hómwəd] *adv.* a casa; hacia la patria; — voyage retorno, viaje de vuelta.

homework [hómwɜk] *s.* trabajo de casa; trabajo hecho en casa.

homicide [hámsaɪd] *s.* homicidio; homicida, asesino.

homogeneous [homədʒínɪəs] *adj.* homogéneo.

hone [hon] *v.* amolar, asentar, afilar; *s.* piedra de afilar.

honest [ánɪst] *adj.* honrado, recto; genuino; — goods mercancías genuinas; -ly *adv.* honradamente; de veras.

honesty [ánɪstɪ] *s.* honradez, rectitud.

honey [hánɪ] *s.* miel; dulzura; querido, querida.

honeycomb [hánɪkom] *s.* panal.

honeyed [hánɪd] *adj.* meloso; dulce; melifluo.

honeymoon [hánɪmun] *s.* luna de miel; viaje de novios, viaje de bodas; *v.* pasar la luna de miel.

honeysuckle [hánɪsʌkl] *s.* madreselva.

honk [hɔŋk] *s.* pitazo (*de automóvil*);

graznido (*voz del ganso*); *v.* sonar la bocina; graznar.

honor [ánə] *s.* honor; honra; señoría (*título*); upon my — sobre mi palabra; *v.* honrar; dar honra.

honorable [ánərəbl] *adj.* honorable; honroso; honrado.

honorary [ánərerɪ] *adj.* honorario, honorífico.

hood [hud] *s.* capucha, caperuza; capirote, cubierta (*del motor*); *v.* encapuchar, encapirotar.

hoof [huf] *s.* casco, pezuña; pata (*de caballo, toro, etc.*).

hook [huk] *s.* gancho, garfio; anzuelo (*para pescar*); — and eye corchete; macho y hembra, by — or crook por la buena o por la mala, por angas o por mangas; on his own — por su propia cuenta; *v.* enganchar(se); abrochar(se); pescar, coger con anzuelo; robar, hurtar.

hooky [húkɪ] : to play — hacer novillos, *Am.* capear la escuela, *Am.* pintar venado, *Am.* jubilarse.

hoop [hup] *s.* aro; argolla; *v.* poner aro a; ceñir, cercar.

hoot [hut] *v.* ulular (*dícese del buho, lechuza, etc.*); rechiflar, ridiculizar; *s.* alarido, chillido.

hooting [hútɪŋ] *s.* grita, rechifla.

hop [hap] *s.* salto, brinco; baile; *v.* saltar; brincar.

hope [hop] *s.* esperanza; *v.* esperar; to — for esperar; to — against — esperar desesperando; esperar lo que no puede ser, esperar lo imposible.

hopeful [hópfəl] *adj.* esperanzado, lleno de esperanza; a young — un joven prometedor; -ly *adv.* con esperanza; con ansia; lleno de esperanza.

hopeless [hóplɪs] *adj.* sin esperanza, falto de esperanza, desesperanzado; desesperado; irremediable; — cause causa perdida; — illness enfermedad incurable; it is — no tiene remedio; -ly *adv.* sin esperanza, sin remedio.

hopelessness [hóplɪsnɪs] *s.* falta de esperanza; falta de remedio; desesperanza, desaliento.

horde [hord] *s.* horda; muchedumbre, gentío; enjambre.

horizon [həráɪzn] *s.* horizonte.

horizontal [horəzántl] *adj.* horizontal.

horn [hɔrn] *s.* cuerno; asta; bocina, trompa (*de un automóvil*); corneta; trompeta; — of plenty cuerno de la abundancia; *v.* acornear, dar cornadas; to — in entrometerse.

hornet [hórnɪt] *s.* avispón; -'s nest avis-

103

pero.

horrible [hórəbl] *adj.* horrible; **horribly** *adv.* horriblemente.

horrid [hórɪd] *adj.* horrendo, horrible.

horrify [hórəfaɪ] *v.* horrorizar, aterrorizar, espantar.

horror [hórə] *s.* horror.

horse [hors] *s.* caballo; caballete (*de madera*), borriquete (*de carpinteros*); **saddle —** caballo de silla; **— dealer** chalán; **— race** carrera de caballos; **— sense** sentido común.

horseback [hórsbæk] *s.* lomo de caballo; **to ride —** montar a caballo, cabalgar, jinetear.

horsefly [hórsflaɪ] *s.* tábano, mosca de caballo.

horselaugh [hórslæf] *s.* carcajada, risotada.

horseman [hórsmən] *s.* jinete.

horsemanship [hórsmənʃɪp] *s.* equitación.

horsepower [hórspauə] *s.* caballo de fuerza.

horseradish [hórsrædɪʃ] *s.* rábano picante.

horseshoe [hórʃʃu] *s.* herradura.

hose [hoz] *s.* medias; manga o manguera (*para regar*); **men's —** calcetines.

hosiery [hóʒrɪ] *s.* medias; calcetines; calcetería (*negocio*); **shop** calcetería.

hospitable [hóspɪtəbl] *adj.* hospitalario.

hospital [háspɪt] *s.* hospital.

hospitality [haspɪtǽlətɪ] *s.* hospitalidad.

host [host] *s.* huésped (*el que hospeda*), anfitrión (*el que convida*); hospedero, mesonero; hueste; ejército, multitud; hostia; **sacred —** hostia consagrada.

hostage [hástɪdʒ] *s.* rehén (*persona que queda como prenda en poder del enemigo*).

hostess [hóstɪs] *s.* huéspeda (*la que hospeda o convida*).

hostile [hást]] *adj.* hostil.

hostility [hastílətɪ] *s.* hostilidad.

hot [hat] *adj.* caliente; caluroso; cálido; picante (*como el pimentón, chile, ají, etc.*); furioso; fresco, reciente; **—bed** semillero; **hot-headed** enojadizo, impetuoso; exaltado; **— house** invernáculo, invernadero; **it is — today** hace calor hoy.

hotel [hotél] *s.* hotel.

hotel-keeper [hotélkípə] *s.* hotelero.

hotly [hátlɪ] *adv.* calurosamente, con vehemencia.

hound [haund] *s.* perro de busca, lebrel, galgo, sabueso, podenco; *v.* acosar, perseguir; azuzar, incitar.

hour [aur] *s.* hora; **— hand** horario.

hourly [áurlɪ] *adv.* por horas; a cada hora; a menudo; *adj.* frecuente; por horas.

house [haus] *s.* casa; cámara, asamblea legislativa; **country —** casa de campo; **a full —** un lleno completo (*en el teatro*); [hauz] *v.* alojar; hospedar.

household [háushold] *s.* casa, familia; *adj.* casero; doméstico.

housekeeper [háuskipə] *s.* casera; ama de llaves; **to be a good —** ser una mujer hacendosa.

housekeeping [háuskipɪŋ] *s.* gobierno de casa; quehaceres domésticos.

housetop [háustap] *s.* techumbre, tejado.

housewife [háuswaɪf] *s.* mujer de su casa; madre de familia.

housework [háuswɜk] *s.* trabajo de casa; quehaceres domésticos.

hove [hov] *pret. & p.p. de* **heave**.

hovel [hʌvl] *s.* choza, cabaña, *Am.* bohío, *Am.* jacal; cobertizo.

hover [hʌvə] *v.* cernerse (*como un pájaro*); vacilar; **to — around** revolotear; rondar.

how [hau] *adv.* cómo; **— beautiful!** ¡qué hermoso!; **— early (late, soon)?** ¿cuándo? ¿a qué hora? **— far is it?** ¿a qué distancia está? ¿cuánto dista de aquí? **— long?** ¿cuánto tiempo? **— many?** ¿cuántos? **— much is it?** ¿cuánto es? ¿a cómo se vende? ¿cuál es el precio? **— old are you?** ¿cuántos años tiene Vd.? **— no matter —** much por mucho que; **he knows — difficult it is** él sabe lo difícil que es; él sabe cuán difícil es.

however [hauévə] *adv. & conj.* sin embargo, no obstante, con todo, empero; **— difficult it may be** por muy difícil que sea; **— much** por mucho que.

howl [haul] *s.* aullido, alarido, chillido, grito; *v.* aullar; chillar, dar alaridos; gritar.

hub [hʌb] *s.* cubo (*de una rueda*); eje, centro de actividad.

hubbub [hʌbʌb] *s.* ajetreo; barullo.

huckster [hʌkstə] *s.* vendedor ambulante.

huddle [hʌdl] *s.* montón, confusión, tropel; **to be in a —** estar agrupados (*en futbol para planear una jugada*); **to get in a —** agruparse (*para aconsejarse o planear algo*); *v.* amontonar(se); acurrucarse.

hue [hju] *s.* tinte, matiz.

huff [hʌf] *s.* enojo, rabieta; **to get into a —** enojarse.

hug [hʌg] *v.* abrazar, estrechar; **to — the coast** costear; *s.* abrazo fuerte.

huge [hjudʒ] *adj.* enorme; descomunal.

hull [hʌl] *s.* casco (*de una nave*); armazón (*de una aeronave*); vaina, hollejo (*de ciertas legumbres*); *v.* mondar, pelar, desvainar, deshollejar.

hum [hʌm] *v.* canturrear (*o* canturriar), tararear; zumbar (*dícese de insectos, máquinaria, etc.*); **to — to sleep** arrullar; *s.* canturreo, tarareo; zumbido; *interj.* ¡hum!; ¡ejém!

human [hjúmən] *adj.* humano; *s.* ser humano.

humane [hjumén] *adj.* humano; humanitario.

humanitarian [hjumænətérɪən] *adj.* humanitario; *s.* filántropo.

humanity [hjumǽnɪtɪ] *s.* humanidad.

humble [hʌ́mbl] *adj.* humilde; *v.* humillar; **humbly** *adv.* humildemente, con humildad.

humbleness [hʌ́mblnɪs] *s.* humildad.

humid [hjúmɪd] *adj.* húmedo.

humidity [hjumídətɪ] *s.* humedad.

humiliate [hjumílɪeɪt] *v.* humillar.

humiliation [hjumɪlɪéʃən] *s.* humillación.

humility [hjumílətɪ] *s.* humildad.

hummingbird [hʌ́mɪŋbɜd] *s.* colibrí, pájaro mosca, *Am.* chuparrosa, *Am.* chupaflor, *Am.* guainumbí.

humor [hjúmə] *s.* humor, humorismo, gracia; capricho; **out of —** de mal humor, malhumorado, disgustado; *v.* seguir el humor (*a una persona*), complacer; mimar.

humorous [hjúmərəs] *adj.* humorístico, gracioso, cómico, chistoso.

hump [hʌmp] *s.* joroba, corcova, giba; *v.* encorvar.

humpback [hʌ́mpbæk] **= hunchback.**

hunch [hʌntʃ] *s.* joroba, corcova, giba; presentimiento, corazonada; *v.* encorvar (*la espalda*).

hunchback [hʌ́ntʃbæk] *s.* joroba; jorobado.

hundred [hʌ́ndrəd] *adj.* cien(to); *s.* ciento; **-s** centenares, cientos.

hundredth [hʌ́ndrədθ] *adj.* centésimo.

hung [hʌŋ] *pret. & p.p. de* **to hang.**

hunger [hʌ́ŋgə] *s.* hambre; *v.* tener hambre, estar hambriento; **to — for** ansiar, anhelar.

hungrily [hʌ́ŋgrɪlɪ] *adv.* con hambre, hambrientamente.

hungry [hʌ́ŋgrɪ] *adj.* hambriento; **to be — tener hambre.**

hunk [hʌŋk] *s.* pedazo grande; mendrugo (*de pan*).

hunt [hʌnt] *v.* cazar; perseguir; buscar; escudriñar; **to — down** dar caza a;

seguir la pista de; **to — for** buscar; *s.* caza, cacería; busca, búsqueda; perseguimiento.

hunter [hʌ́ntə] *s.* cazador; buscador; perro de caza, perro de busca.

huntsman [hʌ́ntsmən] *s.* cazador.

hurl [hɜl] *v.* arrojar, lanzar.

hurrah [hərɔ́] *interj.* ¡hurra! ¡viva!; *v.* vitorear.

hurricane [hɜ́rɪken] *s.* huracán.

hurried [hɜ́rɪd] *adj.* apresurado; **-ly** *adv.* de prisa, apresuradamente, a escape.

hurry [hɜ́rɪ] *v.* apresurar(se); precipitar(se); dar(se) prisa; apurarse; correr; **to — in (out)** entrar (salir) de prisa; **to — up** apresurar(se); dar(se) prisa; *s.* prisa; precipitación; **to be in a —** tener prisa, ir de prisa, estar de prisa.

hurt [hɜt] *v.* hacer daño; dañar; perjudicar; herir; lastimar; doler; **to — one's feelings** darle a uno que sentir; lastimar a uno; **my tooth -s** me duele la muela; *pret. & p.p. de* **to hurt**; *s.* daño; herida; lesión; dolor.

husband [hʌ́zbənd] *s.* marido, esposo.

hush [hʌʃ] *v.* acallar, aquietar; callar(se); **—!** ¡chitón! ¡silencio! ¡cállese! ¡quieto!; **to — up a scandal** encubrir un escándalo; *s.* silencio, quietud.

husk [hʌsk] *s.* cáscara, hollejo, vaina; *v.* mondar, pelar, deshollejar.

husky [hʌ́skɪ] *adj.* ronco; forzudo, fuerte; cascarudo.

hustle [hʌ́sl] *v.* apresurar(se); apurarse; menear(se); atropellar; *s.* prisa, apresuramiento, meneo; actividad; **— and bustle** vaivén.

hut [hʌt] *s.* choza, cabaña, *Am.* bohío.

hyacinth [háɪəsɪnθ] *s.* jacinto.

hybrid [háɪbrɪd] *adj.* híbrido.

hydraulic [haɪdrɔ́lɪk] *adj.* hidráulico.

hydrogen [háɪdrədʒən] *s.* hidrógeno.

hydroplane [háɪdrəplen] *s.* hidroplano, hidroavión.

hygiene [háɪdʒin] *s.* higiene.

hymn [hɪm] *s.* himno.

hyphen [háɪfən] *s.* guión.

hypocrisy [hɪpɑ́krəsɪ] *s.* hipocresía.

hypocrite [hípəkrɪt] *s.* hipócrita.

hypocritical [hɪpəkrítɪkəl] *adj.* hipócrita.

hypothesis [haɪpɑ́θəsɪs] *s.* hipótesis.

hysterical [hɪstérɪkl] *adj.* histérico.

I

I [aɪ] *pron. pers.* yo.

Iberian [aɪbírɪən] *adj.* ibérico, íbero.

ice [aɪs] *s.* hielo; helado, sorbete; **— cream** helado; **ice-cream parlor** *Am.* heladería; **— skates** patines de cuchilla; **— water** agua helada; *v.* helar;

escarchar, alfeñicar, cubrir con escarcha (*un pastel*).

iceberg [áisbɜg] *s.* montaña de hielo, témpano.

icebox [áisbaks] *s.* nevera, *Am.* refrigerador.

iceman [áismæn] *s.* vendedor de hielo.

icicle [áisik:l] *s.* carámbano.

icy [áisi] *adj.* helado, frío; congelado; cubierto de hielo.

idea [aidíə] *s.* idea.

ideal [aidíəl] *adj.* & *s.* ideal.

idealism [aidíəlizəm] *s.* idealismo.

idealist [aidíəlist] *s.* idealista.

idealistic [aidiəlístik] *adj.* idealista.

identical [aidéntik:l] *adj.* idéntico.

identify [aidénɪfai] *v.* identificar.

identity [aidéntəti] *s.* identidad.

idiom [ídiəm] *s.* modismo, idiotismo.

idiot [ídiət] *s.* idiota.

idiotic [idiátik] *adj.* idiota.

idle [áid:l] *adj.* ocioso; perezoso, holgazán; vano; desocupado; *v.* holgazanear; perder el tiempo; funcionar (*el motor solo, sin engranar*); **idly** *adv.* ociosamente; inútilmente; perezosamente.

idleness [áid:lnis] *s.* ociosidad; ocio, desocupación; pereza, holgazanería.

idler [áid:lə] *s.* holgazán, haragán.

idol [áid:l] *s.* ídolo.

idolatry [aidálətri] *s.* idolatría.

idolize [áid:laiz] *v.* idolatrar.

idyl [áid:l] *s.* idilio.

if [if] *conj.* si.

ignite [ignáit] *v.* encender(se), inflamar(se); prender, pegar fuego a.

ignition [igníʃən] *s.* ignición, encendido (*de un motor*); — **switch** interruptor de encendido, *Am.* switch de ignición.

ignoble [ignóbl] *adj.* innoble; bajo, vil.

ignorance [ígnərəns] *s.* ignorancia.

ignorant [ígnərənt] *adj.* ignorante.

ignore [ignór] *v.* no hacer caso de, desatender; desairar.

ill [il] *adj.* enfermo; malo; — **nature** mal genio, mala índole; — **will** mala voluntad, ojeriza, inquina; *s.* mal; enfermedad; calamidad, infortunio; *adv.* mal, malamente; — **at ease** inquieto, intranquilo; **ill-bred** mal criado; **ill-clad** mal vestido; **ill-humored** malhumorado; **ill-mannered** descortés, grosero; **ill-natured** de mala índole, *Am.* mal genioso.

illegal [ilígl] *adj.* ilegal; ilícito.

illegitimate [ilidʒítəmit] *adj.* ilegítimo; bastardo.

illicit [ilísit] *adj.* ilícito.

illiteracy [ilítərəsi] *s.* analfabetismo.

illiterate [ilítərit] *adj.* & *s.* analfabeto.

illness [ílnis] *s.* mal, enfermedad.

illuminate [ilúmənet] *v.* iluminar; alumbrar; esclarecer.

illumination [ilumənéʃən] *s.* iluminación; alumbrado.

illusion [ilúʒən] *s.* ilusión.

illusive [ilúsiv] *adj.* ilusorio, ilusivo, falaz.

illusory [ilúsəri] *adj.* ilusorio, ilusivo, engañoso.

illustrate [iləstrét] *v.* ilustrar; esclarecer.

illustration [iləstréʃən] *s.* ilustración; grabado, estampa; aclaración, esclarecimiento.

illustrator [íləstretə] *s.* ilustrador.

illustrious [ilástriəs] *adj.* ilustre.

image [ímidʒ] *s.* imagen.

imagery [ímidʒri] *s.* conjunto de imágenes, figuras; fantasía.

imaginary [imædʒəncri] *adj.* imaginario.

imagination [imædʒənéʃən] *s.* imaginación; imaginativa.

imaginative [imædʒənetiv] *adj.* imaginativo.

imagine [imædʒin] *v.* imaginar(se); figurarse.

imbecile [ímbəsil] *adj.* & *s.* imbécil.

imbibe [imbáib] *v.* embeber, absorber; beber.

imbue [imbjú] *v.* imbuir, infundir; impregnar, empapar.

imitate [ímətet] *v.* imitar; remedar.

imitation [imitéʃən] *s.* imitación; remedo; *adj.* imitado, de imitación.

imitator [ímətetə] *s.* imitador; remedador.

immaculate [imækjəlit] *adj.* inmaculado, sin mancha.

immaterial [imətírial] *adj.* inmaterial, espiritual; **it is — to me** me es indiferente.

immediate [imídiit] *adj.* inmediato; próximo; **-ly** *adv.* inmediatamente; en seguida; al punto, en el acto, al instante.

immense [iméns] *adj.* inmenso.

immensity [ménsəti] *s.* inmensidad.

immerse [imɜs] *v.* sumergir, sumir.

immigrant [ímigrənt] *adj.* & *s.* inmigrante.

immigrate [ímigret] *v.* inmigrar.

immigration [imigréʃən] *s.* inmigración.

imminent [ímənənt] *adj.* inminente.

immodest [imádist] *adj.* deshonesto, impúdico, indecente.

immoral [imórəl] *adj.* inmoral; licencioso.

immorality [imərǽləti] *s.* inmoralidad.

immortal [imórtl] *adj.* & *s.* inmortal.

immortality [imortǽləti] *s.* inmortalidad.

immovable [ɪmúvəbl] *adj.* inmovible (*o* inamovible); inmóvil; inmutable.

immune [ɪmjún] *adj.* inmune.

immunity [ɪmjúnətɪ] *s.* inmunidad.

imp [ɪmp] *s.* diablillo.

impair [ɪmpɛ́r] *v.* dañar, perjudicar, menoscabar, desvirtuar, debilitar.

impairment [ɪmpɛ́rmənt] *s.* menoscabo; perjuicio, deterioro.

impart [ɪmpárt] *v.* impartir, dar, comunicar.

impartial [ɪmpárʃəl] *adj.* imparcial.

impartiality [ɪmparʃǽlətɪ] *s.* imparcialidad.

impassible [ɪmpǽsəbl] *adj.* impasible.

impassioned [ɪmpǽʃənd] *adj.* apasionado, vehemente, ardiente.

impassive [ɪmpǽsɪv] *adj.* impasible.

impatience [ɪmpéʃəns] *s.* impaciencia.

impatient [ɪmpéʃənt] *adj.* impaciente.

impeach [ɪmpítʃ] *v.* demandar o acusar formalmente (*a un alto funcionario de gobierno*); **to — a person's honor** poner en tela de juicio el honor de uno.

impede [ɪmpíd] *v.* impedir, estorbar, obstruir.

impediment [ɪmpédəmənt] *s.* impedimento, obstáculo, estorbo; traba.

impel [ɪmpél] *v.* impeler, impulsar.

impending [ɪmpéndɪŋ] *adj.* inminente, amenazador.

imperative [ɪmpérətɪv] *adj.* imperativo; imperioso, urgente; *s.* imperativo.

imperceptible [ɪmpəséptəbl] *adj.* imperceptible.

imperfect [ɪmpə́fɪkt] *adj.* imperfecto; defectuoso; *s.* imperfecto (*tiempo del verbo*).

imperial [ɪmpírɪəl] *adj.* imperial.

imperil [ɪmpérəl] *v.* poner en peligro, arriesgar.

imperious [ɪmpírɪəs] *adj.* imperioso; urgente.

impersonal [ɪmpə́spl] *adj.* impersonal.

impersonate [ɪmpə́snet] *v.* representar (*un personaje*); remedar, imitar; fingirse otro, pretender ser otro.

impertinence [ɪmpə́tnəns] *s.* impertinencia; insolencia, descaro.

impertinent [ɪmpə́tnənt] *adj.* impertinente; insolente, descarado.

impervious [ɪmpə́vɪəs] *adj.* impermeable; impenetrable; **— to reason** refractario, testarudo.

impetuous [ɪmpétʃʊəs] *adj.* impetuoso.

impetus [ɪmpətəs] *s.* ímpetu.

impious [ɪmpɪəs] *adj.* impío.

implacable [ɪmplékəbl] *adj.* implacable.

implant [ɪmplǽnt] *v.* implantar, plan-

tar; inculcar, infundir.

implement [ɪmpləmənt] *s.* herramienta, instrumento; **-s** utensilios, aperos, enseres.

implicate [ɪmplɪket] *v.* implicar, envolver, enredar.

implore [ɪmplór] *v.* implorar, rogar; suplicar.

imply [ɪmplái] *v.* implicar; querer decir; insinuar.

impolite [ɪmpəláɪt] *adj.* descortés.

import [ɪmpórt] *s.* significado, significación, sentido; importancia; **-s** artículos importados; [ɪmpórt] *v.* importar; significar, querer decir.

importance [ɪmpórtns] *s.* importancia.

important [ɪmpórtnt] *adj.* importante.

impose [ɪmpóz] *v.* imponer; **to — upon** abusar de (*la amistad, hospitalidad, confianza de alguien*); engañar.

imposing [ɪmpózɪŋ] *adj.* imponente; impresionante.

imposition [ɪmpəzíʃən] *s.* imposición; carga, impuesto; abuso (*de confianza*).

impossibility [ɪmpasəbíˈlətɪ] *s.* imposibilidad.

impossible [ɪmpásəbl] *adj.* imposible.

impostor [ɪmpástə] *s.* impostor, embaucador.

imposture [ɪmpástʃə] *s.* impostura, fraude, engaño.

impotence [ɪmpətəns] *s.* impotencia.

impotent [ɪmpətənt] *adj.* impotente.

impoverish [ɪmpávərɪʃ] *v.* empobrecer.

impregnate [ɪmprégnet] *v.* impregnar; empapar; empreñar.

impress [ɪmprés] *s.* impresión, marca, señal, huella; [ɪmprés] *v.* imprimir, estampar, marcar, grabar; impresionar.

impression [ɪmpréʃən] *s.* impresión; marca.

impressive [ɪmprésɪv] *adj.* impresionante; imponente.

imprint [ɪmprɪnt] *s.* impresión; pie de imprenta; [ɪmprɪnt] *v.* imprimir; estampar.

imprison [ɪmprísn] *v.* aprisionar, encarcelar.

imprisonment [ɪmpríznmənt] *s.* prisión, encarcelación o encarcelamiento.

improbable [ɪmprábəbl] *adj.* improbable.

improper [ɪmprápə] *adj.* impropio.

improve [ɪmprúv] *v.* mejorar(se); **to — upon** mejorar; **to — one's time** aprovechar el tiempo.

improvement [ɪmprúvmənt] *s.* mejoramiento; mejora; progreso, adelanto; mejoría (*de una enfermedad*).

improvise [ɪmprəvaɪz] *v.* improvisar.

imprudent [imprúdņt] *adj.* imprudente.
impudence [ímpjədəns] *s.* impudencia, descaro, insolencia.
impudent [ímpjədənt] *adj.* impudente, descarado, insolente.
impulse [ímpʌls] *s.* impulso; ímpetu; inclinación; **to act on —** obrar impulsivamente.
impunity [impjúnəti] *s.* impunidad, falta o exención de castigo.
impure [impjúr] *adj.* impuro; sucio; adulterado.
impurity [impjúrəti] *s.* impureza.
impute [impjút] *v.* imputar, achacar, atribuir.
in [in] *prep.* en; dentro de; de (*después de un superlativo*); — **haste** de prisa; — **the morning** por (o en) la mañana; — **writing** por escrito; **at two — the morning** a las dos de la mañana; **dressed — white** vestido de blanco; **the tallest — his class** el más alto de su clase; **to come — a week** venir de hoy en ocho días, venir dentro de ocho días; *adv.* dentro; adentro; en casa; **to be — and out** estar entrando y saliendo; **to be all —** no poder más, estar rendido de cansancio; **to be — with someone** estar asociado con alguien; disfrutar el aprecio de una persona; **to come —** entrar; **to have it — for someone** tenerle ojeriza a una persona; **to put —** meter; **is the train — ?** ¿ha llegado el tren?
inability [inəbíləti] *s.* inhabilidad, incapacidad.
inaccessible [inəksésəbļ] *adj.* inaccesible; inasequible.
inaccurate [inékjərit] *adj.* inexacto, impreciso, incorrecto.
inactive [inéktiv] *adj.* inactivo; inerte.
inactivity [inæktívəti] *s.* inactividad, inacción, inercia.
inadequate [inédəkwit] *adj.* inadecuado; insuficiente.
inadvertent [inədvэ́tņt] *adj.* inadvertido; descuidado; **-ly** *adv.* inadvertidamente; descuidadamente.
inanimate [inénəmit] *adj.* inanimado.
inasmuch [inəzmʌ́tʃ] : **— as** visto que, puesto que; en cuanto.
inattentive [inəténtiv] *adj.* desatento.
inaugurate [inɔ́gjəret] *v.* inaugurar, iniciar; investir de una dignidad o cargo.
inauguration [inɔgjəréʃən] *s.* inauguración.
inborn [inbɔ́rn] *adj.* innato, connatural.
incandescent [inkəndésņt] *adj.* incandescente, candente.
incapable [inképəbļ] *adj.* incapaz.

incense [ínsɛns] *s.* incienso; [inséns] *v.* inflamar, exasperar.
incentive [inséntiv] *s.* incentivo, estímulo.
incessant [insésņt] *adj.* incesante, continuo.
inch [intʃ] *s.* pulgada (2.54 *centímetros*); **by -es** poco a poco, gradualmente; **every — a man** nada menos que todo un hombre; **to be within an — of** estar a dos pulgadas de, estar muy cerca de; *v.* avanzar muy despacio (*por pulgadas*).
incident [ínsədənt] *s.* incidente, suceso, acontecimiento.
incidental [insədéntļ] *adj.* incidental; accidental; contingente; **-s** *pl.* gastos imprevistos; **-ly** *adv.* incidentalmente; de paso.
incision [insíʒən] *s.* incisión.
incite [insáit] *v.* incitar.
inclination [inklənéʃən] *s.* inclinación.
incline [ínklain] *s.* declive, pendiente, cuesta; [inkláin] *v.* inclinar(se).
inclose = **enclose**.
inclosure = **enclosure**.
include [inklúd] *v.* incluir, encerrar; abarcar.
inclusive [inklúsiv] *adj.* inclusivo; **from Monday to Friday —** del lunes al viernes inclusive.
incoherent [inkohfrənt] *adj.* incoherente, inconexo.
income [ínkʌm] *s.* renta, rédito, ingreso, entrada; **— tax** impuesto sobre rentas.
incomparable [inkámpərəb[[]] *adj.* incomparable, sin par, sin igual.
incompatible [inkəmpétəbļ] *adj.* incompatible.
incompetent [inkámpətənt] *adj.* incompetente.
incomplete [inkəmplít] *adj.* incompleto.
incomprehensible [inkɑmprihénsəbļ] *adj.* incomprensible.
inconsiderate [inkənsídərit] *adj.* inconsiderado, falto de miramiento.
inconsistency [inkənsístənsi] *s.* inconsecuencia; falta de uniformidad (*en la aplicación de una regla o principio*).
inconsistent [inkənsístənt] *adj.* inconsecuente; falto de uniformidad.
inconstancy [inkánstənsi] *s.* inconstancia, mudanza.
inconstant [inkánstənt] *adj.* inconstante, mudable, voluble.
inconvenience [inkənvínjəns] *s.* inconveniencia; molestia; *v.* incomodar; molestar.
inconvenient [inkənvínjənt] *adj.* inconveniente; inoportuno.

incorporate [ɪnkɔ́rpərɪt] *adj.* incorporado; asociado; [ɪnkɔ́rpəret] *v.* incorporar; incorporarse, asociarse (*para formar un cuerpo*).

incorrect [ɪnkərékt] *adj.* incorrecto.

increase [ɪ́nkris] *s.* aumento; acrecentamiento; crecimiento; incremento; [ɪnkrís] *v.* aumentar(se); acrecentar(se), crecer.

increasingly [ɪnkrísɪŋlɪ] *adv.* más y más; cada vez más.

incredible [ɪnkrédəbl] *adj.* increíble.

incredulity [ɪnkrədúlətɪ] *s.* incredulidad.

incredulous [ɪnkrédʒələs] *adj.* incrédulo, descreído.

inculcate [ɪnkʌ́lket] *v.* inculcar, infundir.

incur [ɪnkɜ́] *v.* incurrir en.

incurable [ɪnkjúrəbl] *adj.* incurable, irremediable; *s.* incurable.

indebted [ɪndétɪd] *adj.* adeudado, endeudado; obligado, agradecido.

indebtedness [ɪndétɪdnɪs] *s.* deuda; obligación.

indecency [ɪndísnsɪ] *s.* indecencia.

indecent [ɪndísnt] *adj.* indecente.

indeed [ɪndíd] *adv.* en verdad, a la verdad; de veras; realmente.

indefinite [ɪndéfənɪt] *adj.* indefinido.

indelible [ɪndéləbl] *adj.* indeleble.

indelicate [ɪndéləkət] *adj.* indelicado, indecoroso.

indemnify [ɪndémnəfaɪ] *v.* indemnizar.

indemnity [ɪndémnətɪ] *s.* indemnización.

indent [ɪndént] *v.* dentar, endentar; sangrar (*comenzar un renglón más adentro que los otros*).

independence [ɪndɪpéndəns] *s.* independencia.

independent [ɪndɪpéndənt] *adj.* independiente.

indescribable [ɪndɪskráɪbəbl] *adj.* indescriptible.

index [índeks] *s.* índice; *v.* alfabetizar, ordenar alfabéticamente; poner en un índice.

indian [índɪən] *adj. & s.* indio; — **Ocean** Océano Indico.

indicate [índəket] *v.* indicar.

indication [ɪndəkéʃən] *s.* indicación.

indicative [ɪndíkətɪv] *adj. & s.* indicativo.

indict [ɪndáɪt] *v.* procesar, demandar (*ante un juez*); enjuiciar, formar causa a.

indictment [ɪndáɪtmənt] *s.* acusación (*hecha por el Gran Jurado*), denuncia, proceso judicial.

indifference [ɪndífrəns] *s.* indiferencia; apatía.

indifferent [ɪndífrənt] *adj.* indiferente; apático.

indigenous [ɪndídʒənəs] *adj.* indígena, autóctono, nativo.

indigestion [ɪndədʒéstʃən] *s.* indigestión.

indignant [ɪndígnənt] *adj.* indignado; **-ly** *adv.* con indignación.

indignation [ɪndɪgnéʃən] *s.* indignación.

indignity [ɪndígnətɪ] *s.* indignidad, afrenta.

indigo [índɪgo] *s.* índigo, añil; — **blue** azul de añil.

indirect [ɪndərékt] *adj.* indirecto.

indiscreet [ɪndɪskrít] *adj.* indiscreto.

indiscretion [ɪndɪskréʃən] *s.* indiscreción.

indispensable [ɪndɪspénsəbl] *adj.* indispensable.

indispose [ɪndɪspóz] *v.* indisponer.

indisposed [ɪndɪspózd] *adj.* indispuesto

indisposition [ɪndɪspəzíʃən] *s.* indisposición; malestar.

indistinct [ɪndɪstíŋkt] *adj.* indistinto.

individual [ɪndəvídʒuəl] *adj.* individual; *s.* individuo, sujeto, persona.

individuality [ɪndəvɪdʒuǽlətɪ] *s.* individualidad; individuo, persona.

indivisible [ɪndəvízəbl] *adj.* indivisible.

indoctrinate [ɪndáktrɪnet] *v.* adoctrinar.

indolence [índələns] *s.* indolencia, desidia, apatía.

indolent [índələnt] *adj.* indolente, desidioso, apático.

indomitable [ɪndámətəbl] *adj.* indomable.

indoor [índor] *adj.* interior, de casa.

indoors [índorz] *adv.* dentro, en casa; adentro; **to go** — entrar; ir adentro.

indorse [ɪndórs] *v.* endosar; respaldar; apoyar, garantizar.

indorsement [ɪndórsmənt] *s.* endose, endoso; respaldo; garantía, apoyo.

indorser [ɪndórsə] *s.* endosante.

induce [ɪndjús] *v.* inducir.

inducement [ɪndjúsmənt] *s.* aliciente, incentivo.

induct [ɪndʌ́kt] *v.* introducir; iniciar; instalar (*en un cargo*).

induction [ɪndʌ́kʃən] *s.* inducción; instalación (*en un cargo*).

indulge [ɪndʌ́ldʒ] *v.* gratificar, complacer; seguir el humor a (*una persona*); mimar, consentir (*a un niño*); **to** — **in** darse a, entregarse a (*un placer*); darse el lujo de, permitirse el placer de.

indulgence [ɪndʌ́ldʒəns] s. indulgencia; complacencia (*en el vicio o placer*).

indulgent [ɪndʌ́ldʒənt] adj. indulgente.

industrial [ɪndʌ́strɪəl] adj. industrial.

industrialist [ɪndʌ́strɪəlɪst] s. industrial; fabricante.

industrious [ɪndʌ́strɪəs] adj. industrioso, aplicado, diligente.

industry [índəstrɪ] s. industria; aplicación, diligencia.

ineffable [ɪnéfəbl] adj. inefable.

ineffective [ɪnəféktɪv] adj. inefectivo, ineficaz.

inequality [ɪnɪkwálətɪ] s. desigualdad; disparidad.

inert [ɪnɜ́t] adj. inerte.

inertia [ɪnɜ́ʃə] s. inercia.

inestimable [ɪnéstəməbl] adj. inestimable.

inevitable [ɪnévətəbl] adj. inevitable.

inexhaustible [ɪnɪgzɔ́stəbl] adj. inagotable.

inexpensive [ɪnɪkspénsɪv] adj. económico, barato.

inexperience [ɪnɪkspírɪəns] s. inexperiencia, falta de experiencia.

inexperienced [ɪnɪkspírɪənst] adj. inexperto, falto de experiencia.

inexplicable [ɪnéksplɪkəbl] adj. inexplicable.

inexpressible [ɪnɪkspɪˈrésəbl] adj. inexpresable, indecible, inefable.

infallible [ɪnfǽləbl] adj. infalible.

infamous [ínfəməs] adj. infame, ignominioso.

infamy [ínfəmɪ] s. infamia.

infancy [ínfənsɪ] s. infancia.

infant [ínfənt] s. infante, bebé, criatura, nene.

infantile [ínfəntaɪl] adj. infantil.

infantry [ínfəntrɪ] s. infantería.

infect [ɪnfékt] v. infectar, inficionar; contagiar; contaminar.

infection [ɪnfékʃən] s. infección; contagio.

infectious [ɪnfékʃəs] adj. infeccioso; contagioso.

infer [ɪnfɜ́] v. inferir, deducir, colegir.

inference [ínfərəns] s. inferencia, deducción.

inferior [ɪnfírɪə] adj. & s. inferior.

inferiority [ɪnfɪrɪɔ́rətɪ] s. inferioridad.

infernal [ɪnfɜ́nl] adj. infernal.

inferno [ɪnfɜ́no] s. infierno.

infest [ɪnfést] v. infestar, plagar.

infidel [ínfədl] adj. & s. infiel.

infinite [ínfənɪt] adj. & s. infinito.

infinitive [ɪnfínətɪv] adj. & s. infinitivo.

infinity [ɪnfínətɪ] s. infinidad; infinito.

infirm [ɪnfɜ́m] adj. enfermizo, achacoso, débil.

infirmary [ɪnfɜ́mərɪ] s. enfermería.

infirmity [ɪnfɜ́mətɪ] s. enfermedad, achaque; flaqueza.

inflame [ɪnflém] v. inflamar(se); enardecer(se).

inflammation [ɪnfləméʃən] s. inflamación.

inflate [ɪnflét] v. inflar; hinchar.

inflation [ɪnfléʃən] s. inflación; hinchazón.

inflection [ɪnflékʃən] s. inflexión.

inflict [ɪnflíkt] v. infligir, imponer.

influence [ínfluəns] s. influencia, influjo; v. influir en; ejercer influencia o influjo sobre.

influential [ɪnfluénʃəl] adj. influyente.

influenza [ɪnfluénzə] s. influenza, gripe.

influx [ínflʌks] s. entrada, afluencia (*de gente*).

infold [ɪnfóld] v. envolver; abrazar abarcar.

inform [ɪnfɔ́rm] v. informar; enterar avisar; **to — against** delatar a, denunciar a.

informal [ɪnfɔ́rml] adj. informal, sin ceremonia; **— visit** visita de confianza; **-ly** adv. informalmente, sin ceremonia de confianza.

information [ɪnfəméʃən] s. información; informe; noticias; conocimientos, saber.

infringe [ɪnfrínd͡ʒ] v. infringir, violar; **— upon** violar.

infuriate [ɪnfjúrɪet] v. enfurecer.

infuse [ɪnfjúz] v. infundir; inculcar.

ingenious [ɪnd͡ʒínjəs] adj. ingenioso.

ingenuity [ɪnd͡ʒənúətɪ] s. ingeniosidad

ingratitude [ɪnɡrǽtətjud] s. ingratitud

ingredient [ɪnɡrídɪənt] s. ingrediente.

inhabit [ɪnhǽbɪt] v. habitar, vivir en residir en.

inhabitant [ɪnhǽbətənt] s. habitante.

inhale [ɪnhél] v. inhalar, aspirar, inspirar.

inherent [ɪnhírənt] adj. inherente.

inherit [ɪnhérɪt] v. heredar.

inheritance [ɪnhérətəns] s. herencia.

inhibit [ɪnhíbɪt] v. inhibir, cohibir, refrenar, reprimir; impedir.

inhibition [ɪnɪbíʃən] s. inhibición, cohibición; prohibición, restricción.

inhospitable [ɪnháspɪtəbl] adj. inhospitalario.

inhuman [ɪnhjúmən] adj. inhumano.

inimitable [ɪnímətəbl] adj. inimitable

iniquity [ɪníkwətɪ] s. iniquidad, maldad

initial [ɪníʃəl] adj. & s. inicial; v. marcar o firmar con iniciales.

initiate [ɪníʃɪet] v. iniciar.

initiative [ɪnfʃɪetɪv] s. iniciativa.

ject [ɪndʒékt] v. inyectar; injerir, introducir.

jection [ɪndʒékʃən] s. inyección.

junction [ɪndʒʌ́ŋkʃən] s. mandato, orden; entredicho.

jure [ɪndʒɚ] v. dañar; herir, lesionar; lastimar.

jurious [ɪndʒúrɪəs] adj. dañoso, dañino, perjudicial.

jury [ɪndʒəri] s. daño; herida, lesión; perjuicio.

justice [ɪndʒʌ́stɪs] s. injusticia.

k [ɪŋk] s. tinta; v. entintar; teñir o manchar con tinta.

kling [íŋklɪŋ] s. indicación, indicio, idea, sospecha, noción vaga.

kstand [íŋkstænd] s. tintero.

kwell [íŋkwel] s. tintero.

laid [ɪnléd] adj. incrustado, embutido; — work embutido, incrustación; pret. & p.p. de to inlay.

land [ɪnlənd] s. interior (de un país); adj. interior, del interior de un país; adv. tierra adentro.

lay [ɪnlé] v. incrustar, embutir; [ɪnle] s. embutido.

mate [ɪnmet] s. residente, asilado (de un hospicio, asilo, casa de corrección, etc.); presidiario; hospiciano.

most [ɪnmost] adj. más interior, más íntimo, más secreto o recóndito; más profundo.

n [ɪn] s. posada, mesón, fonda.

nate [ɪnét] adj. innato, connatural.

ner [ɪnɚ] adj. interior; íntimo, recóndito; —most = inmost.

ning [ínɪŋ] s. entrada, cuadro (en beisbol); turno (del bateador en beisbol y otros juegos).

keeper [ínkɪpɚ] s. ventero, mesonero, posadero.

nocence [ínəsŋs] s. inocencia.

nocent [ínəsŋt] adj. & s. inocente.

nocuous [ɪnákjʊəs] adj. innocuo, inofensivo.

novation [ɪnəvéʃən] s. innovación.

nuendo [ɪnjʊéndo] s. insinuación, indirecta.

numerable [ɪnjúmərəbl] adj. innumerable.

oculate [ɪnákjəlet] v. inocular; contaminar.

offensive [ɪnəfénsɪv] adj. inofensivo.

opportune [ɪnapətjún] adj. inoportuno.

quire [ɪnkwáɪr] v. inquirir, indagar; preguntar; to — about preguntar por; to — into indagar, investigar.

quiry [ɪnkwáɪrɪ] s. indagación; investigación; pregunta; interrogatorio.

inquisition [ɪnkwəzíʃən] s. inquisición; indagación.

inquisitive [ɪnkwízətɪv] adj. inquisitivo, investigador; preguntón; curioso.

inroad [ínrod] s. incursión, invasión, ataque; to make -s upon atacar; mermar.

insane [ɪnsén] adj. insano, loco; — asylum manicomio, casa de locos.

insanity [ɪnsǽnətɪ] s. locura.

insatiable [ɪnséʃɪəbl] adj. insaciable.

inscribe [ɪnskráɪb] v. inscribir.

inscription [ɪnskrípʃən] s. inscripción; letrero.

insect [ínsɛkt] s. insecto.

insecure [ɪnsɪkjúr] adj. inseguro.

insensible [ɪnsénsəbl] adj. insensible.

insensitive [ɪnsénsətɪv] adj. insensible.

inseparable [ɪnsépərəbl] adj. inseparable.

insert [ínsɚt] s. inserción; intercalación; hoja (insertada en un libro); circular, folleto (insertado en un periódico); [ɪnsɚt] v. insertar; intercalar; encajar; meter.

insertion [ɪnsɚ́ʃən] s. inserción; introducción.

inside [ínsáɪd] s. interior; -s entrañas; adj. interior, interno; secreto; adv. dentro; adentro; to turn — out volver(se) al revés; prep. dentro de.

insight [ínsaɪt] s. penetración, discernimiento; intuición; perspicacia; comprensión.

insignia [ɪnsígnɪə] s. pl. insignias.

insignificant [ɪnsɪgnɪfəkənt] adj. insignificante.

insinuate [ɪnsínjʊet] v. insinuar.

insinuation [ɪnsɪnjʊéʃən] s. insinuación; indirecta.

insipid [ɪnsípɪd] adj. insípido.

insist [ɪnsíst] v. insistir en; empeñarse (en); porfiar, persistir.

insistence [ɪnsístəns] s. insistencia, empeño, porfía.

insistent [ɪnsístənt] adj. insistente; porfiado, persistente.

insolence [ínsələns] s. insolencia.

insolent [ínsələnt] adj. insolente.

inspect [ɪnspékt] v. inspeccionar; examinar, registrar.

inspection [ɪnspékʃən] s. inspección; registro.

inspector [ɪnspéktɚ] s. inspector.

inspiration [ɪnspəréʃən] s. inspiración.

inspire [ɪnspáɪr] v. inspirar.

install [ɪnstɔ́l] v. instalar.

installation [ɪnstəléʃən] s. instalación.

installment, instalment [ɪnstɔ́lmənt]

s. instalación; abono (*pago*); entrega o continuación (*semanal o mensual de una novela*); **to pay in** -**s** pagar por plazos; pagar en abonos.

instance [ínstəns] **s.** ejemplo, caso; vez, ocasión; instancia; **for —** por ejemplo.

instant [ínstənt] **s.** instante; *adj.* inmediato; urgente; **the 10th —** el 10 del (mes) corriente; **-ly** *adv.* al instante, inmediatamente.

instantaneous [instənténíəs] *adj.* instantáneo.

instead [instéd] *adv.* en lugar de ello (eso, él, ella, *etc.*); **— of** en lugar de, en vez de.

instep [ínstep] **s.** empeine (*del pie, del zapato*).

instigate [ínstəget] **v.** instigar.

instill [instíl] **v.** inculcar, infundir.

instinct [ínstiŋkt] **s.** instinto.

instinctive [instíŋktiv] *adj.* instintivo.

institute [ínstətjut] **s.** instituto; *v.* instituir.

institution [instətjúʃən] **s.** institución.

instruct [instrákt] *v.* instruir; dar instrucciones.

instruction [instrákʃən] **s.** instrucción; enseñanza; **lack of —** falta de saber o conocimientos; **-s** órdenes, instrucciones.

instructive [instráktiv] *adj.* instructivo.

instructor [instráktə] **s.** instructor.

instrument [ínstrəmənt] **s.** instrumento.

instrumental [instrəméntl] *adj.* instrumental; **to be — in** ayudar a, servir de instrumento para.

insufferable [insáfrəbl] *adj.* insufrible, inaguantable.

insufficiency [insəffíʃənsi] **s.** insuficiencia; incompetencia; falta, escasez.

insufficient [insəffíʃənt] *adj.* insuficiente; inadecuado.

insulate [ínsəlet] **v.** aislar.

insulation [insəléʃən] **s.** aislamiento; aislación.

insulator [ínsəletə] **s.** aislador.

insult [ínsʌlt] **s.** insulto; [insʌlt] **v.** insultar.

insurance [inʃúrəns] **s.** aseguramiento; seguro; prima, premio (*de una póliza de seguro*); **— agent** agente de seguros; **— company** compañía de seguros; **— policy** póliza de seguro; **accident —** seguro contra accidentes; **fire —** seguro contra incendios; **life —** seguro sobre la vida.

insure [inʃúr] *v.* asegurar; asegurarse de.

insurgent [insə́dʒənt] *adj.* & **s.** insurgente, insurrecto.

insurmountable [insəmáʊntəbl] *adj.*

insuperable.

insurrection [insərékʃən] **s.** insurrección, rebelión, alzamiento.

intact [intǽkt] *adj.* intacto.

integral [íntəgrəl] *adj.* integral; integrante; **s.** integral.

integrity [intégrəti] **s.** integridad, entereza.

intellect [íntlekt] **s.** intelecto; entendimiento.

intellectual [intléktʃuəl] *adj.* & **s.** intelectual.

intelligence [intélədʒəns] **s.** inteligencia; información, noticias; policía secreta.

intelligent [intélədʒənt] *adj.* inteligente.

intemperance [intémpərəns] **s.** intemperancia.

intend [inténd] *v.* intentar, pensar, tener la intención de; proponerse; destinar; **to — to do it** pensar hacerlo.

intense [inténs] *adj.* intenso.

intensity [inténsəti] **s.** intensidad.

intensive [inténsiv] *adj.* intenso; intensivo.

intent [intént] **s.** intento, intención, propósito; significado; **to all -s and purposes** en todo caso, en todos sentidos en realidad; *adj.* atento; **— on** absorto en, reconcentrado en; resuelto a, decidido a.

intention [inténʃən] **s.** intención.

intentional [inténʃən] *adj.* intencional; **-ly** *adv.* intencionalmente, adrede, propósito.

inter [intə́] *v.* enterrar, sepultar.

intercede [intəsíd] *v.* interceder.

intercept [intəsépt] *v.* interceptar; atajar.

interception [intəsépʃən] **s.** intercepción.

intercession [intəséʃən] **s.** intercesión.

interchange [íntətʃendʒ] **s.** intercambio, cambio, trueque; [intətʃéndʒ] *v.* cambiar, trocar; permutar; alternar.

intercourse [íntəkors] **s.** comunicación comercio, trato; intercambio (*de ideas sentimientos, etc.*).

interest [íntərist] **s.** interés, rédito; participación (*en un negocio*); *v.* interesar.

interested [íntəristid] *adj.* interesado; **to be — in** interesarse (*o por*).

interesting [íntəristiŋ] *adj.* interesante.

interfere [intəfír] *v.* intervenir; interponerse, entremeterse; estorbar; **to with** estorbar, frustrar; dificultar.

interference [intəffrəns] **s.** intervención; obstáculo; interferencia (*en radio*).

interior [ɪntíriə] *adj.* interior; interno; *s.* interior.

interjection [ɪntədʒékʃən] *s.* interjección, exclamación; intercalación.

interlace [ɪntəlés] *v.* entrelazar, enlazar, entretejer.

interlock [ɪntəlák] *v.* entrelazar(se); trabar(se).

intermediate [ɪntəmídɪɪt] *adj.* intermedio.

interminable [ɪntə́mɪnəb!] *adj.* interminable, inacabable.

intermingle [ɪntəmíŋg!] *v.* entremezclar(se), entreverar(se); mezclar(se).

intermission [ɪntəmíʃən] *s.* intermisión; intermedio, entreacto.

intermittent [ɪntəmítn̩t] *adj.* intermitente.

intern [ɪntə́n] *v.* internar, confinar, encerrar; [íntən] *s.* practicante (*de medicina en un hospital*).

internal [ɪntə́n!] *adj.* interno; interior.

international [ɪntənǽʃən!] *adj.* internacional.

interoceanic [ɪntəoʃɪǽnɪk] *adj.* interoceánico.

interpose [ɪntəpóz] *v.* interponer(se).

interpret [ɪntə́prɪt] *v.* interpretar.

interpretation [ɪntəprɪtéʃən] *s.* interpretación.

interpreter [ɪntə́prɪtə] *s.* intérprete.

interrogate [ɪntérəget] *v.* interrogar.

interrogation [ɪnterəgéʃən] *s.* interrogación.

interrogative [ɪntərágətɪv] *adj.* interrogativo; *s.* pronombre o palabra interrogativa.

interrupt [ɪntərʌ́pt] *v.* interrumpir.

interruption [ɪntərʌ́pʃən] *s.* interrupción.

intersect [ɪntəsékt] *v.* cortar(se); cruzar(se).

intersection [ɪntəsékʃən] *s.* intersección; street — bocacalle.

intersperse [ɪntəspə́s] *v.* entremezclar, esparcir.

intertwine [ɪntətwáɪn] *v.* entrelazar, entretejer, trenzar.

interval [íntəvl] *s.* intervalo.

intervene [ɪntəvín] *v.* intervenir; interponerse; mediar.

intervention [ɪntəvénʃən] *s.* intervención.

interview [íntəvju] *s.* entrevista; *v.* entrevistar, entrevistarse con.

intestine [ɪntéstɪn] *s.* intestino; *adj.* intestino, interno.

intimacy [íntəməsɪ] *s.* intimidad.

intimate [íntəmɪt] *adj.* íntimo; *s.* amigo íntimo; [íntəmet] *v.* intimar, insinuar;

indicar, dar a entender.

intimation [ɪntəméʃən] *s.* intimación, insinuación.

intimidate [ɪntímədet] *v.* intimidar, acobardar, infundir miedo.

into [íntʊ, íntə] *prep.* en; dentro de; hacia el interior.

intolerable [ɪntálərəb!] *adj.* intolerable, inaguantable.

intolerance [ɪntálərəns] *s.* intolerancia.

intolerant [ɪntálərənt] *adj.* intolerante.

intonation [ɪntonéʃən] *s.* entonación.

intoxicate [ɪntáksəket] *v.* embriagar; emborrachar.

intoxication [ɪntaksəkéʃən] *s.* embriaguez; envenenamiento, intoxicación (*estado tóxico o envenenamiento parcial*).

intravenous [ɪntrəvínəs] *adj.* intravenoso.

intrench [ɪntréntʃ] *v.* atrincherer; to — oneself atrincherarse; to — upon another's rights infringir los derechos ajenos; to be -ed estar atrincherado; estar firmemente establecido.

intrepid [ɪntrépɪd] *adj.* intrépido.

intricate [íntrəkɪt] *adj.* intrincado, enredado.

intrigue [ɪntríg] *s.* intriga; enredo; trama; lío, embrollo; *v.* intrigar; tramar, maquinar.

intriguer [ɪntrígə] *s.* intrigante.

introduce [ɪntrədjús] *v.* introducir; presentar.

introduction [ɪntrədʌ́kʃən] *s.* introducción; presentación.

intrude [ɪntrúd] *v.* entremeterse (*o* entrometerse); introducir, meter.

intruder [ɪntrúdə] *s.* intruso, entremetido.

intrusion [ɪntrúʒən] *s.* intrusión, entremetimiento.

intrusive [ɪntrúsɪv] *adj.* intruso.

intrust = **entrust**.

intuition [ɪntʊíʃən] *s.* intuición.

inundate [ínəndet] *v.* inundar.

inure [ɪnjúr] *v.* habituar, acostumbrar.

invade [ɪnvéd] *v.* invadir.

invader [ɪnvédə] *s.* invasor.

invalid [ɪnvǽlɪd] *adj.* inválido (*que no vale*), nulo, de ningún valor.

invalid [ínvəlɪd] *adj.* inválido, enfermizo, achacoso; — diet dieta para inválidos; *s.* inválido.

invaluable [ɪnvǽljəb!] *adj.* de gran precio o valor, inapreciable, inestimable.

invariable [ɪnvérɪəb!] *adj.* invariable; **invariably** *adv.* invariablemente; sin falta, sin excepción.

invasion [ɪnvéʒən] *s.* invasión.

invent [ɪnvént] v. inventar.

invention [ɪnvénʃən] s. invención; invento; inventiva, facultad para inventar.

inventive [ɪnvéntɪv] adj. inventivo.

inventiveness [ɪnvéntɪvnɪs] s. inventiva.

inventor [ɪnvéntə] s. inventor.

inventory [ínvəntorɪ] s. inventario; v. inventariar.

inverse [ɪnvɜ́s] adj. inverso.

invert [ɪnvɜ́t] v. invertir; trastrocar; volver al revés.

invest [ɪnvɜ́st] v. invertir, colocar (fondos); investir (de una dignidad o cargo); revestir (de autoridad); sitiar.

investigate [ɪnvéstəget] v. investigar, indagar.

investigation [ɪnvestəgéʃən] s. investigación; indagación.

investigator [ɪnvéstəgetə] s. investigador; indagador.

investment [ɪnvéstmənt] s. inversión (de fondos).

investor [ɪnvéstə] s. el que invierte fondos.

invigorate [ɪnvígəret] v. vigorizar, fortalecer.

invincible [ɪnvínsəbl] adj. invencible.

invisible [ɪnvízəbl] adj. invisible.

invitation [ɪnvətéʃən] s. invitación.

invite [ɪnváɪt] v. invitar; convidar.

inviting [ɪnváɪtɪŋ] adj. atractivo; seductivo, tentador.

invoice [ɪnvɔɪs] s. factura; envío, mercancías enviadas; v. facturar.

invoke [ɪnvók] v. invocar.

involuntary [ɪnváləntɛrɪ] adj. involuntario.

involve [ɪnválv] v. complicar, enredar; envolver; implicar; comprometer; **to get -d in difficulties** embrollarse, meterse en embrollos.

inward [ínwəd] adj. interior; interno; secreto; adv. hacia el interior; hacia dentro, adentro, para dentro; **-s** adv. = inward.

iodine [áɪodaɪn] s. yodo.

ire [aɪr] s. ira.

iridescent [ɪrədésn̩t] adj. iridiscente, tornasolado, irisado.

iris [áɪrɪs] s. iris; arco iris; flor de lis.

Irish [áɪrɪʃ] adj. irlandés; s. irlandés, idioma irlandés; **the —** los irlandeses.

irksome [ɜ́ksəm] adj. fastidioso, engorroso, molesto, tedioso.

iron [áɪən] s. hierro; plancha (de planchar ropa); adj. férreo, de hierro; **—work** herraje, trabajo en hierro; **—works** herrería; fábrica de hierro;

v. planchar; **to — out a difficul**[t]
allanar una dificultad.

ironical [aɪránɪk] adj. irónico.

ironing [áɪənɪŋ] s. planchado.

irony [áɪrənɪ] s. ironía.

irregular [ɪrégjələ] adj. irregular.

irrelevant [ɪréləvənt] adj. fuera de pr[o]pósito, inaplicable al caso, inoportun[o] que no viene (o no hace) al caso.

irreligious [ɪrɪlídʒəs] adj. irreligios[o] impío.

irremediable [ɪrɪmídɪəbl] adj. irrem[e]diable; incurable.

irreproachable [ɪrɪprótʃəbl] adj. irrepr[o]chable, intachable.

irresistible [ɪrɪzístəbl] adj. irresistib[le]

irresolute [ɪrézəlut] adj. irresoluto, [in]deciso.

irreverence [ɪrévərəns] s. irreverenci[a] desacato.

irreverent [ɪrévərənt] adj. irreveren[te]

irrigate [íəget] v. regar; irrigar, baña[r]

irrigation [ɪrəgéʃən] s. riego; irrigació[n] **— canal** acequia, canal de irrigació[n]

irritable [írətəbl] adj irritable; coléri[co]

irritate [írətet] v. irritar.

irritating [írətɪŋ] adj. irritante.

irritation [ɪrətéʃən] s. irritación.

island [áɪlənd] s. isla.

islander [áɪləndə] s. isleño.

isle [aɪl] s. isla, ínsula.

isolate [áɪslet] v. aislar.

isolation [aɪsléʃən] s. aislamiento.

isolationism [aɪsléʃənɪzm̩] s. aisla[mi]ento.

issue [íʃʊ] s. tirada, impresión; emisi[ón] (de valores, acciones, etc.); problem[a] argumento; resultado, consecuenc[ia] **without —** sin prole, sin sucesión; **take — with** disentir o diferir de; publicar, dar a luz; dar, promulgar (*[un] decreto*); emitir (*valores, acciones, et[c.]*); emanar; fluir; salir; brotar; proven[ir]

isthmus [ísməs] s. istmo.

it [ɪt] pron. neutro lo, la (acusativo); [él], ella (después de una preposici[ón] por lo general no se traduce cuando [es] sujeto del verbo: **— is there** está a[hí] **— is I soy yo; — is raining** llue[ve] está lloviendo **what time is — ?** ¿q[ué] hora es?; **— is two o'clock** son [las] dos; **how goes — ?** ¿qué tal?

Italian [ɪtǽljən] adj. & s. italiano.

italic [ɪtǽlɪk] adj. itálico; **-s** s. le[tra] bastardilla.

italicize [ɪtǽləsaɪz] v. poner en le[tra] bastardilla.

itch [ɪtʃ] s. comezón; picazón; sarna [en]*fermedad de la piel*); v. picar, dar[le a] uno comezón; sentir comezón; **to**

114

-ing to tener ansias de.

itchy [ítʃɪ] *adj.* sarnoso, *Am.* sarniento; **to feel —** sentir comezón.

item [áɪtəm] *s.* artículo; detalle; noticia, suelto (*de un periódico*); partida (*de una lista*).

itemize [áɪtəmaɪz] *v.* pormenorizar, detallar; hacer una lista de.

itinerary [aɪtínərɛrɪ] *s.* itinerario; ruta; guía de viajeros.

its [ɪts] *pos. neutro* su (sus), de él, de ella, de ello.

itself [ɪtsélf] *pron. neutro* mismo, misma; **by —** por sí, de por sí, por sí solo; solo, aislado; **in —** en sí.

ivory [áɪvrɪ] *s.* marfil.

ivy [áɪvɪ] *s.* hiedra (yedra).

J

jab [dʒæb] *v.* picar; pinchar; *s.* piquete, pinchazo.

jack [dʒæk] *s.* gato (*para alzar cosas pesadas*); sota (*en naipes*); macho (*del burro y otros animales*); bandera de proa; **— of all trades** aprendiz de todo y oficial de nada; **— pot** premio gordo, premio mayor; **— rabbit** liebre americana; *v.* **to — up** solevantar, alzar con gato (*un objeto pesado*).

jackass [dʒǽkæs] *s.* asno, burro.

jacket [dʒǽkɪt] *s.* chaqueta; envoltura; forro (*de un libro*); hollejo (*de la patata*).

jackknife [dʒǽknaɪf] *s.* navaja.

jagged [dʒǽgɪd] *adj.* serrado, dentado.

jail [dʒel] *s.* cárcel; *v.* encarcelar.

jailer [dʒélə] *s.* carcelero.

jam [dʒæm] *v.* estrujar, apachurrar; atorar(se); obstruir(se), atascar(se); apiñar(se), agolpar(se); **to — on the brakes** frenar de golpe; **to — one's fingers** machucarse los dedos; **to — through** forzar por, meter a la fuerza; *s.* conserva, compota; apretura; atascamiento; **traffic —** aglomeración de transeúntes o automóviles, *Am.* bola; **to be in a —** estar en un aprieto.

janitor [dʒǽnətə] *s.* conserje; portero; casero (*encargado de un edificio*).

January [dʒǽnjuɛrɪ] *s.* enero.

Japanese [dʒæpənízz] *adj. & s.* japonés.

jar [dʒɑr] *s.* jarra, jarro; tarro; choque; sacudida; trepidación, vibración; **large earthen —** tinaja; *v.* trepidar; hacer vibrar; hacer temblar; menear; **to — on one's nerves** ponerle a uno los nervios de punta.

jargon [dʒárgən] *s.* jerga, jerigonza.

jasmine [dʒǽzmɪn] *s.* jazmín.

jasper [dʒǽspə] *s.* jaspe.

jaunt [dʒɔnt] *s.* caminata, excursión; *v.*

dar un paseíto, hacer una corta caminata.

jaw [dʒɔ] *s.* quijada, mandíbula, *Am.* carretilla; **-s** grapa (*de herramienta*).

jawbone [dʒɔ́bón] *s.* mandíbula, quijada.

jay [dʒe] *s.* grajo; rústico, bobo; **blue —** azulejo; **-walker** el que cruza las bocacalles descuidadamente.

jazz [dʒæz] *s.* jazz (*cierta clase de música sincopada*); *v.* tocar el jazz; bailar el jazz; **to — up** sincopar; animar, alegrar.

jealous [dʒéləs] *adj.* celoso; envidioso; **to be — of someone** tener celos de una persona, tenerle celos a una persona.

jealousy [dʒéləsɪ] *s.* celos; envidia.

jeer [dʒɪr] *s.* mofa, befa, escarnio, *Am.* choteo; *v.* mofar, befar, *Am.* chotear; **to —** at mofarse de.

jelly [dʒélɪ] *s.* jalea; *v.* convertir(se) en jalea, hacer(se) gelatinoso.

jerk [dʒɜrk] *s.* tirón; sacudida, *Am.* jalón; espasmo muscular; *v.* sacudir(se); dar un tirón; atasajar (*la carne*); **to — out** sacar de un tirón; **-ed beef** tasajo, *Am.* charqui.

jersey [dʒɜ́rzɪ] *s.* tejido de punto, tejido elástico, *Am.* jersey; chaqueta, blusa, camisa (*de punto*), *Am.* jersey.

jest [dʒɛst] *s.* broma; chanza; chiste; *v.* bromear; chancearse.

jester [dʒéstə] *s.* chancero, burlón; bufón.

Jesuit [dʒéʒuɪt] *s.* jesuita.

jet [dʒɛt] *s.* chorro; surtidor (*de fuente*); azabache; **gas —** mechero de gas; *adj.* de azabache; **jet-black** negro como el azabache; *v.* chorrear, salir en chorro.

Jew [dʒu] *s.* judío.

jewel [dʒúəl] *s.* joya, alhaja; gema; **— box** estuche, joyero.

jeweler [dʒúələ] *s.* joyero; **-'s shop** joyería.

jewelry [dʒúəlrɪ] *s.* joyas, alhajas, pedrería; **— store** joyería.

Jewish [dʒúɪʃ] *adj.* judío.

jiffy [dʒífɪ] *s.* instante; **in a —** en un instante, en dos paletas, en un decir Jesús, en un santiamén.

jig [dʒɪg] *s.* jiga (*música y baile*); **— saw** sierra mecánica (*para recortar figuras*); **-saw puzzle** rompecabezas (*de recortes*); *v.* tocar una jiga; bailar una jiga; bailotear; menear(se).

jiggle [dʒígl] *v.* zangolotear(se), zarandear(se), menear(se); *s.* zarandeo, meneo, zangoloteo.

jilt [dʒɪlt] *v.* desairar, dar calabazas, dejar plantado.

jingle [dʒíŋgl] *s.* retintín; verso o rima infantil; **— bell** cascabel; *v.* hacer retintín.

job [dʒɑb] s. tarea, faena; trabajo; empleo, ocupación; **to be out of a —** estar sin trabajo; estar desocupado.

jockey [dʒɑkɪ] s. jockey; v. maniobrar (*para sacar ventaja o ganar un puesto*).

join [dʒɔɪn] v. juntar(se); enlazar(se); acoplar; unirse a, asociarse a.

joint [dʒɔɪnt] s. juntura; coyuntura, articulación; conexión; bisagra; garito (*casa de juego*); fonducho, restaurante de mala muerte; **out of —** descoyuntado; desunido; adj. unido, asociado, copartícipe; colectivo; **— account** cuenta en común; **— action** acción colectiva; **— committee** comisión mixta; **— creditor** acreedor copartícipe; **— heir** coheredero; **— session** sesión plena; **-ly** adv. juntamente, juntos, unidamente, colectivamente.

joke [dʒok] s. broma; chiste, chanza; v. bromear; chancear(se), Am. chotear.

joker [dʒókə] s. bromista, chancero, guasón, Am. choteador; naipe especial (*que no pertenece a ningún palo*).

jokingly [dʒókɪŋlɪ] adv. en (o de) chanza, en (o de) broma; de chiste.

jolly [dʒálɪ] adj. jovial; alegre; festivo; v. bromear, chancearse.

jolt [dʒolt] s. sacudida; sacudimiento; choque; v. sacudir.

jostle [dʒásl] v. rempujar o empujar, dar empellones; codear; s. rempujón, empujón, empellón.

jot [dʒɑt] v. **to — down** apuntar, tomar apuntes; s. jota, pizca.

journal [dʒɜn] s. diario; periódico; revista; acta (*de una junta o concilio*).

journalism [dʒɜnɪzəm] s. periodismo.

journalist [dʒɜnlɪst] s. periodista.

journalistic [dʒɜnlístɪk] adj. periodístico.

journey [dʒɜnɪ] s. viaje; jornada; v. viajar.

joy [dʒɔɪ] s. júbilo, regocijo; alegría, gusto, deleite; felicidad.

joyful [dʒɔ́ɪfəl] adj. regocijado, jubiloso; alegre; **-ly** adv. con regocijo, regocijadamente, con júbilo, alegremente.

joyous [dʒɔ́ɪəs] adj. jubiloso, alegre, gozoso.

jubilant [dʒúbələnt] adj. jubiloso, alegre.

jubilee [dʒúblɪ] s. jubileo; júbilo.

judge [dʒʌdʒ] s. juez; **— advocate** auditor de un consejo militar; v. juzgar.

judgment [dʒʌ́dʒmənt] s. juicio; sentencia, fallo; opinión; discernimiento; **— day** día del juicio final.

judicial [dʒudíʃəl] adj. judicial.

judicious [dʒudíʃəs] adj. juicioso, cuerdo.

jug [dʒʌg] s. cántaro; jarro, jarra; botija, chirona (*cárcel*) Am. chirola.

juggle [dʒʌ́gl] v. hacer juegos de manos, hacer suertes; **to — the accounts** barajar (o manipular) las cuentas; s. juego de manos, suerte; trampa.

juggler [dʒʌ́glə] s. prestidigitador, malabarista.

juice [dʒus] s. jugo; zumo.

juiciness [dʒúsɪnɪs] s. jugosidad.

juicy [dʒúsɪ] adj. jugoso, zumoso; suculento; **a — story** un cuento picante

July [dʒulɑ́ɪ] s. julio.

jumble [dʒʌ́mbl] v. revolver(se), barajar, mezclar(se); s. mezcolanza, revoltijo; confusión.

jump [dʒʌmp] v. saltar; brincar; salvar (*de un salto*); hacer saltar; comerse una pieza (*en el juego de damas*); **to — at the chance** asir o aprovechar la oportunidad; **to — bail** perder la fianza por evasión; **to — over** saltar por encima de, salvar de un salto; **to — the track** descarrilarse; **to — to conclusions** hacer deducciones precipitadas; s. salto; brinco; subida repentina (*del precio*); **to be always on the —** andar siempre de aquí para allá, trajinar, trafagar, ser muy activo.

jumper [dʒʌ́mpə] s. saltador; chaquetón holgado (*de obrero*); vestido sin mangas (*puesto sobre la blusa de mujer*); traje de juego (*para niños*).

jumpy [dʒʌ́mpɪ] adj. saltón; asustadizo nervioso.

junction [dʒʌ́ŋkʃən] s. unión, juntura confluencia (*de dos ríos*); empalme (*de ferrocarriles*).

juncture [dʒʌ́ŋktʃəs] s. juntura; coyuntura; **at this —** a esta sazón, en este coyuntura.

June [dʒun] s. junio.

jungle [dʒʌ́ŋgl] s. selva; matorral; Am jungla; Am. manigua.

junior [dʒúnjə] adj. menor, más joven; **— college** colegio para los dos primeros años del bachillerato; **John Smith Junior (Jr.)** John Smith, hijo; estudiante del tercer año (*en escuela superior, colegio o universidad*).

junk [dʒʌŋk] s. basura, desperdicio; trastos viejos; cosa inservible; Chinese **— junco** chino (*embarcación pequeña* v. desechar, echar a la basura.

jurisdiction [dʒurɪsdíkʃən] s. jurisdicción.

jurisprudence [dʒurɪsprúdn̩s] s. jurisprudencia, derecho.

juror [dʒúrə] s. jurado, miembro de u jurado.

jury [dʒúrɪ] s. jurado; **grand —** jurado de acusación.

just [dʒʌst] adj. justo; recto; exacto; adv. ni más ni menos, exactamente, justamente; precisamente; sólo, no más, nada más; apenas; **— now** ahora mismo; **he is — a little girl** no es más que una niña, es una niña no más; **to have — açabar de**

justice [dʒʌstɪs] s. justicia; juez; magistrado.

justification [dʒʌstəfəkéʃən] s. justificación.

justify [dʒʌstəfaɪ] v. justificar.

justly [dʒʌstlɪ] adv. justamente; con razón.

jut [dʒʌt] v. sobresalir, proyectarse, extenderse; s. salidizo, proyección.

juvenile [dʒúvənɪl] adj. juvenil.

K

kangaroo [kæŋgərú] s. canguro.

keel [kil] s. quilla; v. dar de quilla (voltear un barco); **to — over** volcar(se); zozobrar; caerse patas arriba, desplomarse.

keen [kin] adj. agudo; afilado; perspicaz; ansioso.

keenness [kínnɪs] s. agudeza; perspicacia; anhelo, ansia.

keep [kip] v. guardar; tener guardado; tener; retener; conservar(se); preservar(se); mantener(se); **to — accounts** llevar las cuentas; **to — at it** persistir, seguir dale que dale; **to — away** mantener(se) alejado; **to — back** tener a raya; detener; reprimir, restringir; **to — from** impedir; guardar(se) de; abstenerse de; **to — going** seguir andando, seguir adelante; seguir viviendo; **to — off** no arrimarse, no acercarse; no entrar; mantener(se) a distancia; **to — one's hands off** no tocar; **to — one's temper** contenerse, refrenarse, reprimirse; **to — quiet** estarse quieto o callado; **to — something up** seguir o continuar haciendo algo; **to — to the right** seguir a la derecha; mantenerse a la derecha; **to — track of** llevar la cuenta de; no perder de vista; s. manutención, subsistencia; **for —s** para siempre; para guardar; dado, no prestado.

keeper [kípə] s. guardián, custodio; **jail —** carcelero.

keeping [kípɪŋ] s. custodia; mantenimiento; preservación, conservación; **in — with** en armonía con.

keepsake [kípsek] s. prenda, recuerdo, regalo.

keg [keg] s. tonel, barril.

kennel [kénl] s. perrera.

kept [kept] pret. & p.p. de **to keep**.

kerchief [kɔ́tʃɪf] s. pañuelo, pañolón.

kernel [kɔ́nl] s. simiente; grano (de trigo o maíz); meollo (de ciertas frutas como la nuez); núcleo.

kerosene [kérəsin] s. kerosina, petróleo para lámparas.

kettle [kétl] s. caldera; **—drum** tímpano; **tea—** marmita, tetera, Am. pava (para el mate).

key [ki] s. llave; clave; tecla (de piano, órgano o máquina de escribir); cayo, isleta; **— ring** llavero; **to be in —** estar a tono, estar templado; estar en armonía; v. poner a tono, afinar, templar (con llave); armonizar; **to — up** elevar el tono de; **to be all -ed up** estar sobreexcitado, estar en tensión nerviosa.

keyboard [kíbord] s. teclado.

keyhole [kíhol] s. ojo de la cerradura.

keynote [kínot] s. nota tónica; idea o principio fundamental.

keystone [kíston] s. clave (de un arco); base, fundamento principal.

khaki [kákɪ] s. kaki, caqui; adj. de kaki.

kick [kɪk] s. coz; patada; puntapié; queja; protesta; fuerza (de una bebida); estímulo; **to have a — Am.** patear (dícese del licor); v. cocear; dar coces o patadas; dar puntapiés; patear; quejarse, protestar; **to — out** echar a patadas; echar, expulsar; **to — the bucket** estirar la pata, morir, Am. patear el balde; **to — up a lot of dust** levantar una polvareda.

kid [kɪd] s. cabrito; cabritilla (piel curtida de cabrito); niño, niña; **— gloves** guantes de cabritilla; v. bromear, embromar; chancearse con, Am. chotear.

kidnap [kídnæp] v. secuestrar, raptar.

kidnapper [kídnæpə] s. secuestrador; robachicos, ladrón de niños.

kidnapping [kídnæpɪŋ] s. rapto, secuestro.

kidney [kídnɪ] s. riñón; **— bean** judía, frijol; **— stones** cálculos.

kill [kɪl] v. matar; destruir; amortiguar; parar (el motor); s. animal o animales matados (en la caza).

killer [kílə] s. matador; asesino.

kiln [kɪln] s. horno.

kilo [kílo], **kilogram** [kíləgræm] s. kilo, kilogramo.

kilometer [kíləmitə] s. kilómetro.

kimono [kəmónə] s. quimono; bata.

kin [kɪn] s. parentela, parientes, familia; **to notify the nearest of —** avisar al pariente o deudo más cercano.

kind [kaɪnd] *adj.* bondadoso; benévolo; amable; tc send one's — regards to enviar afectuosos saludos a; **kind-hearted** de buen corazón; — of tired algo cansado; *s.* clase, especie, género; **to pay in** — pagar en especie; pagar en la misma moneda.

kindergarten [kíndəgartṇ] *s.* escuela de párvulos.

kindle [kíndḷ] *v.* encender(se); inflamar(se); incitar; prender (*el fuego*).

kindling [kíndlɪŋ] *s.* encendimiento; leña ligera, astillas, *Am.* charamuscas.

kindly [káɪndlɪ] *adj.* bondadoso; benigno; benévolo; amable, apacible; *adv.* bondadosamente, amablemente; con benevolencia; por favor; **not to take** — **to** criticism no aceptar de buen grado las correcciones.

kindness [káɪndnɪs] *s.* bondad, amabilidad; gentileza; benevolencia; favor.

kindred [kíndrɪd] *adj.* emparentado; allegado; semejante; — **facts** hechos relacionados; — **spirits** espíritus afines.

king [kɪŋ] *s.* rey; rey (*en ajedrez*); dama (*en el juego de damas*).

kingdom [kíŋdəm] *s.* reino.

kingly [kíŋlɪ] *adj.* regio, real; majestuoso; *adv.* regiamente; majestuosamente.

kinky [kíŋkɪ] *adj.* crespo, ensortijado, *Am.* grifo.

kinship [kínʃɪp] *s.* parentesco; afinidad; semejanza.

kinsman [kínzmən] *s.* pariente, deudo.

kiss [kɪs] *s.* beso; *v.* besar.

kit [kɪt] *s.* estuche, caja de herramientas; saco, envoltura (*para guardar instrumentos, herramientas, etc.*); gatito; **medicine** — botiquín; **soldier's** — mochila.

kitchen [kítʃɪn] *s.* cocina; **—ware** trastos de cocina.

kite [kaɪt] *s.* cometa (*f.*), *Am.* papalote; milano (*pájaro*).

kitten [kítṇ] *s.* gatito.

kitty [kítɪ] *s.* gatito, mínino.

knack [næk] *s.* destreza, maña, habilidad.

knapsack [nǽpsæk] *s.* mochila, morral, alforja.

knave [nev] *s.* bribón, bellaco, pícaro; sota (*de naipes*).

knead [nid] *v.* amasar, sobar.

knee [ni] *s.* rodilla; **knee-deep** hasta la rodilla; metido hasta las rodillas.

kneel [nil] *v.* arrodillarse; hincarse.

knell [nɛl] *s.* doble (*toque de campanas por los difuntos*); *v.* doblar, tocar a muerto.

knelt [nɛlt] *pret. & p.p. de* **to kneel.**

knew [nju] *pret. de* **to know.**

knickknack [nȋknæk] *s.* chuchería, baratija, chisme.

knife [naɪf] *s.* cuchillo; cuchilla; **carving** — trinchante; **pocket** — cortaplumas; navaja; *v.* acuchillar.

knight [naɪt] *s.* caballero; campeón; caballo (*en ajedrez*); — **errant** caballero andante; *v.* armar caballero.

knighthood [nȃɪthʊd] *s.* caballería, orden de la caballería.

knit [nɪt] *v.* tejer (*a punto de aguja*); hacer calceta o malla; enlazar; soldarse (*un hueso*) **to** — one's brow fruncir las cejas, arrugar la frente; *pret. & p.p. de* **to knit.**

knitting [nítɪŋ] *s.* labor de punto; — **needle** aguja de media.

knives [naɪvz] *pl. de* **knife.**

knob [nɑb] *s.* perilla, botón, tirador (*de puerta, cajón, etc.*); protuberancia.

knock [nɑk] *v.* golpear; golpetear; llamaro tocar a la puerta; criticar, censuraro hablar mal de; **to** — **down** derribar; desmontar (*una máquina o aparato*); **to** — **off** suspender (*el trabajo*); rebajar (*del precio*); derribar, echar abajo; **to** — **out** aplastar de un golpe, poner fuera de combate; dejar sin sentido; *s.* golpe; golpeteo; toque, llamada, aldabonazo; crítica, censura; **knock-kneed** zambo, patizambo.

knocker [nɑ́kə] *s.* llamador, aldaba, aldabón; criticón, murmurador.

knoll [nol] *s.* colina, loma; eminencia.

knot [nɑt] *s.* nudo; lazo; *v.* anudar(se).

knotty [nátɪ] *adj.* nudoso; dificultoso, enredado.

know [no] *v.* conocer; saber; reconocer; distinguir; **to** — **how to** swim saber nadar; **to** — **of** saber de; tener conocimiento de; tener noticias de; estar enterado de.

knowingly [nóɪŋlɪ] *adv.* a sabiendas; adrede.

knowledge [nálɪdʒ] *s.* conocimiento; saber, sabiduría; pericia; **not to my** — no que yo sepa.

known [non] *p.p. de* **to know.**

knuckle [nΛkḷ] *s.* nudillo; coyuntura, articulación; *v.* someterse; **to** — **down** someterse; aplicarse con empeño al trabajo.

L

label [lébḷ] *s.* marbete, etiqueta, rótulo; *v.* marcar, rotular; apodar, llamar.

labor [lébə] *s.* trabajo; labor; obra; mano de obra; la clase obrera; — **union**

unión de obreros; **to be in** — estar de parto; *v.* trabajar; afanarse; estar de parto; elaborar (*un punto*).

laboratory [lǽbrətɔrɪ] *s.* laboratorio.

laborer [lébərə] *s.* trabajador, obrero; jornalero, peón.

laborious [labórɪəs] *adj.* laborioso, trabajoso, penoso; industrioso.

labyrinth [lǽbərɪnθ] *s.* laberinto.

lace [les] *s.* encaje; cordón, cordoncillo, cinta (*de zapato, de corsé, etc.*); **gold** — galón de oro (*para guarnecer uniformes*); *v.* atar con cinta o córdón; guarnecer con encajes; enlazar, entrelazar.

lack [læk] *s.* falta; escasez, carencia; deficiencia; *v.* carecer de, faltarle a uno; necesitar; **he -s courage** le falta ánimo.

lacking [lǽkɪŋ] *adj.* falto, carente.

lacquer [lǽkə] *s.* laca; *v.* barnizar con laca.

lad [læd] *s.* rapaz, chico.

ladder [lǽdə] *s.* escalera de mano.

laden [lédn] *adj.* cargado; agobiado, abrumado; *v.* cargar; agobiar.

ladies [lédɪz] *pl. de* **lady.**

ladle [lédl] *s.* cucharón; *v.* servir (*sopa*) con cucharón.

lady [lédɪ] *s.* señora; dama; **—like** como señora, muy fina, elegante; **—love** amada, querida.

lag [læg] *v.* rezagarse, quedarse atrás, atrasarse; andar lentamente; *s.* retardo o retardación, retraso.

lagoon [ləgún] *s.* laguna.

laid [led] *pret. & p.p. de* **to lay; to be** — estar incapacitado o estropeado.

lain [len] *p.p. de* **to lie.**

lair [lɛr] *s.* guarida; cueva de fieras.

lake [lek] *s.* lago.

lamb [læm] *cordero;* **—kin** corderito.

lame [læm] *adj.* cojo; lisiado, estropeado; **— excuse** disculpa falsa; *v.* hacer cojo; estropear, incapacitar.

lament [ləmént] *s.* lamento; *v.* lamentar(se).

lamentable [lǽməntəbl] *adj.* lamentable; doloroso.

lamentation [læməntéʃən] *s.* lamentación, lamento.

lamp [læmp] *s.* lámpara; linterna; farol; **—post** poste (de farol); **—shade** pantalla de lámpara.

lance [læns] *s.* lanza; *v.* alancear, lancear, herir con lanza; picar con bisturí.

land [lænd] *s.* tierra; terreno; suelo; *v.* desembarcar; aterrizar (*un avión*); llegar; coger (*un pez*); **to** — **a job** conseguir una colocación, lograr un

empleo.

landholder [lǽndholdə] *s.* terrateniente, propietario, hacendado.

landing [lǽndɪŋ] *s.* desembarco, desembarque; aterrizaje (*de un avión*); desembarcadero; descanso (*de escalera*); **— field** campo de aterrizaje; aeropuerto; **— strip** pista de aterrizaje.

landlady [lǽndledɪ] *s.* patrona, casera, dueña (*de la casa*).

landlord [lǽndlɔrd] *s.* amo, patrón, propietario, dueño; casero.

landmark [lǽndmark] *s.* mojón, señal (*para fijar los confines*); marca; suceso culminante.

landowner [lǽndɔnə] *s.* terrateniente, propietario, hacendado.

landscape [lǽndskeɹ] *s.* paisaje.

landslide [lǽndslaɪd] *s.* derrumbe, derrumbamiento, desplome; gran mayoría de votos.

lane [len] *s.* senda, vereda; callejuela; ruta, derrotero (*de vapores o aviones*).

language [lǽŋgwɪdʒ] *s.* lengua; idioma; lenguaje.

languid [lǽŋgwɪd] *adj.* lánguido.

languish [lǽŋgwɪʃ] *v.* languidecer.

languor [lǽŋgə] *s.* languidez.

lank [læŋk] *adj.* alto y delgado, largucho.

lanky [lǽŋkɪ] *adj.* largucho, zancón, zancudo.

lantern [lǽntən] *s.* linterna; farol.

lap [læp] *s.* falda, regazo; aleta; etapa, trecho (*de una carrera*); *v.* lamer; **to** — **over** cruzar(se) sobre, entrecruzar(se).

lapel [ləpél] *s.* solapa.

lapse [læps] *s.* lapso; transcurso; desliz, error; *v.* deslizarse; pasar, transcurrir; caer en un desliz; decaer (*el entusiasmo, el interés, etc.*); caducar (*un plazo, un contrato, etc.*).

larboard [lárbəd] *s.* babor; *adj.* de babor; **— side** banda de babor.

larceny [lársnɪ] *s.* latrocinio, hurto, ratería.

lard [lard] *s.* lardo, manteca de puerco; *v.* mechar.

large [lardʒ] *adj.* grande; **at** — suelto, libre; sin trabas; en general; **-ly** *adv.* grandemente, en gran parte.

lariat [lǽrɪət] *s.* reata.

lark [lark] *s.* alondra; diversión, holgorio, jarana; **to go on a** — ir o andar de jarana.

larva [lárvə] *s.* larva.

larynx [lǽrɪŋks] *s.* laringe.

lascivious [ləsívɪəs] *adj.* lascivo.

lash [læʃ] *s.* látigo; azote, latigazo; pestaña; *v.* fustigar; azotar; censurar, reprender; amarrar.

lass [læs] *s.* moza, muchacha, doncella.

lassitude [lǽsɔtjud] *s.* dejadez, flojedad, decaimiento de fuerzas.

lasso [lǽso] *s.* lazo, reata, mangana, *Am.* guaso; *v.* lazar, *Am.* enlazar.

last [læst] *adj.* último; final; pasado; — **night** anoche; — **year** el año pasado; **at** — por fin, finalmente, al fin; **next to the** — penúltimo; **to arrive** — llegar el último; *s.* fin, término; horma (*de zapato*); *v.* durar; perdurar; **-ly** *adv.* finalmente, en conclusión.

lasting [lǽstɪŋ] *adj.* duradero; perdurable.

latch [lætʃ] *s.* pestillo, picaporte, aldaba, cerrojo; *v.* cerrar con aldaba.

late [let] *adj.* tardío; tardo; reciente; último; —**comer** recién llegado; rezagado; **a** — **hour** una hora avanzada; **the** — **Mr. X** el finado (*o* difunto) Sr. X; **to have a** — **supper** cenar tarde; *adv.* tarde; — **in the night** a una hora avanzada de la noche; — **into the night** a deshoras de la noche; — **in the week** a fines de la semana; *of* — últimamente, recientemente; hace poco; **to be** — ser tarde; llegar tarde; estar atrasado, venir o llegar con retraso (*el tren*); **the train was ten minutes** — el tren llegó con diez minutos de retraso; **-ly** últimamente, recientemente; hace poco, poco ha.

latent [létnt] *adj.* latente.

later [léta] *adv. & adj.* (*comp. de* **late**) más tarde; después, luego; más reciente; posterior.

lateral [lǽtərəl] *adj.* lateral.

latest [létɪst] *adv. & adj.* (*superl. de* **late**) más tarde; más reciente, más nuevo; último; **the** — **fashion** la última moda, las últimas novedades; **the** — **news** las últimas novedades, las noticias más recientes; **at the** — a más tardar.

lathe [leð] *s.* torno (*de carpintero o mecánico*).

lather [lǽðə] *s.* jabonadura, espuma de jabón; *v.* jabonar, enjabonar; espumar, hacer espuma.

Latin [lǽtn] *adj.* latino; *s.* latín.

latitude [lǽtɪtjud] *s.* latitud; libertad; amplitud.

latter [lǽtə] *adj.* último; **towards the** — **part of the week** a (*o* hacia) fines de la semana; **the** — éste (ésta, esto, etc.).

lattice [lǽtɪs] *s.* celosía; enrejado, rejilla.

laud [lɔd] *v.* loar, encomiar, alabar.

laudable [lɔ́dəbl] *adj.* laudable, loable.

laugh [læf] *v.* reír(se); **to** — **at** reírse de;

to — **loudly** reírse a carcajadas; **to** — **in one's sleeve** reírse para sus adentros; **she** — **-ed in his face** se rió en sus barbas; *s.* risa; **loud** — risotada, carcajada, risada.

laughable [lǽfəbl] *adj.* risible; ridículo.

laughter [lǽftə] *s.* risa.

launch [lɔntʃ] *v.* botar o echar (*un barco*) al agua; lanzar; empezar, poner en operación; **to** — **forth** lanzarse; **to** — **forth on a journey** emprender un viaje; *s.* lancha.

launder [lɔ́ndə] *v.* lavar y planchar (*la ropa*).

laundress [lɔ́ndrɪs] *s.* lavandera.

laundry [lɔ́ndrɪ] *s.* lavandería; lavado; ropa (lavada).

laurel [lɔ́rəl] *s.* laurel; gloria, honor.

lava [lávə] *s.* lava.

lavatory [lǽvətorɪ] *s.* lavabo; lavamanos; lavatorio.

lavender [lǽvəndə] *s.* espliego, lavándula; *adj.* lila, morado claro.

lavish [lǽvɪʃ] *adj.* gastador, pródigo, dadivoso; abundante, copioso; profuso; lujoso; *v.* prodigar; malgastar, despilfarrar; **to** — **praise upon** colmar de alabanzas a; **-ly** pródigamente; copiosamente; lujosamente.

law [lɔ] *s.* ley; derecho, jurisprudencia; regla; — **student** estudiante de leyes, estudiante de derecho; **law-abiding** observante de la ley.

lawbreaker [lɔ́brekə] *s.* infractor, transgresor.

lawful [lɔ́fəl] *adj.* legal; lícito; válido; permitido.

lawless [lɔ́lɪs] *adj.* sin ley; ilegal; desenfrenado; revoltoso; licencioso.

lawmaker [lɔ́mekə] *s.* legislador.

lawn [lɔn] *s.* césped, prado; linón (*tela de hilo o algodón*); — **mower** cortadora de césped.

lawsuit [lɔ́sut] *s.* pleito, litigio.

lawyer [lɔ́jə] *s.* abogado, jurisconsulto.

lax [læks] *adj.* flojo; suelto; relajado.

laxative [lǽksətɪv] *adj. & s.* laxante, purgante.

laxity [lǽksətɪ] *s.* flojedad, flojera; relajamiento (*de una regla, ley, etc.*).

lay [le] *pret. de* **lie**.

lay [le] *v.* colocar; poner; tender, extender; poner (*huevos*); echar (*la culpa*); atribuir (*la responsabilidad*); presentar, exponer; asentar (*el polvo*); **to** — **a wager** apostar; **to** — **aside** poner a un lado; ahorrar; **to** — **away** (*o* **by**) guardar; **to** — **bare** revelar; exponer; **to** — **down** poner, colocar; rendir (*las armas*); **to** — **down the law** mandar, dictar; **to — hold of** asir, agarrar; **to — off a workman** suspender a un obrero; **to — open** exponer a la vista; **to — out a plan** trazar un plan; **to — up** almacenar; guardar, ahorrar; **to be laid up** estar incapacitado o estropeado; **to — waste** asolar; *s.* lay, balada, canción; situación, orientación (*del terreno*); *adj.* lego, laico; profano (*no iniciado en una ciencia*).

layer [léə] *s.* capa; estrato; gallina ponedora.

layman [lémən] *s.* lego, seglar, laico.

lazily [lézɪlɪ] *adv.* perezosamente.

laziness [lézɪnɪs] *s.* pereza.

lazy [lézɪ] *adj.* perezoso, holgazán.

lead [lɛd] *s.* plomo; plomada, pesa de plomo.

lead [lid] *v.* guiar, dirigir; llevar; conducir; mandar (*un ejército*); ir a la cabeza de; sobresalir entre; ser mano (*en el juego de naipes*); **to — an orchestra** dirigir una orquesta, llevar la batuta; **to — astray** llevar por mal camino, extraviar, descarriar; **to — the way** ir por delante, mostrar el camino; *s.* delantera, primer lugar; mando, dirección; indicio; papel principal; primer actor.

leaden [lédṇ] *adj.* plomizo; aplomado, color de plomo; pesado.

leader [lídə] *s.* jefe, caudillo, *Am.* líder; director; guía; caballo delantero; **-s** puntos suspensivos.

leadership [lídəʃɪp] *s.* dirección, mando; iniciativa.

leading [lídɪŋ] *adj.* principal; delantero; **— man** primer actor.

leaf [lif] *s.* hoja; *v.* echar hojas (*un árbol*), cubrirse de hojas; **to — through a book** hojear un libro.

leafless [líflɪs] *adj.* sin hojas, deshojado.

leaflet [líflɪt] *s.* hojilla; folleto, hoja volante, papel volante, circular.

leafy [lífɪ] *adj.* frondoso.

league [lig] *s.* liga, confederación; sociedad; legua; *v.* asociar(se); ligarse, coligarse.

leak [lik] *s.* gotera (*en un techo*); agujero, grieta (*por donde se escapa el agua o el gas*); escape (*de gas, vapor, electricidad, etc.*); *v.* gotear(se); rezumar(se); hacer agua (*dícese de un barco*); salirse, escaparse (*el gas, el vapor, etc.*).

lean [lin] *v.* inclinar(se); recostar(se), reclinar(se), apoyar(se); *adj.* magro; flaco; **— year** año estéril, año improductivo.

leant [lɛnt] = **leaned.**

leap [lip] *v.* saltar; brincar; *s.* salto, brin-

co; **— year** año bisiesto.

leapt [lɛpt] *pret. & p.p. de* **to leap.**

learn [lɜn] *v.* aprender; saber, averiguar, enterarse de.

learned [lɜnɪd] *adj.* erudito; docto.

learner [lɜnə] *s.* aprendedor; estudiante, estudioso.

learning [lɜnɪŋ] *s.* erudición, saber; aprendizaje.

learnt [lɜnt] *pret. & p.p. de* **to learn.**

lease [lis] *v.* arrendar, dar o tomar en arriendo; *s.* arriendo, contrato de arrendamiento.

least [list] *adj.* (el) mínimo, (el) más pequeño; *adv.* menos; **at —** al menos, a lo menos, por lo menos; **the —** lo (el, la) menos.

leather [léðə] *s.* cuero, piel; *adj.* de cuero, de piel; **— strap** correa.

leave [liv] *v.* dejar; abandonar; salir (de); partir; irse; **to — out** dejar fuera; omitir; *s.* permiso, licencia; **— of absence** licencia; **to take — of** despedirse de.

leaven [lévən] *s.* levadura, fermento; *v.* fermentar (*la masa*).

leaves [livz] *pl. de* **leaf.**

leavings [lívɪŋz] *s.* sobras, desperdicios.

lecture [léktʃə] *s.* conferencia, discurso; reprensión; *v.* dar una conferencia; explicar; reprender.

lecturer [léktʃərə] *s.* conferenciante; lector (*de universidad*).

led [lɛd] *pret. & p.p. de* **to lead.**

ledge [lɛdʒ] *s.* borde; salidizo.

ledger [lédʒə] *s.* libro mayor (*en contabilidad*).

leech [litʃ] *s.* sanguijuela.

leer [lɪr] *s.* mirada de soslayo, mirada lujuriosa; *v.* mirar de soslayo; mirar con lujuria.

left [lɛft] *pret. & p.p. de* **to leave; I have two books —** me quedan dos libros; *adj.* izquierdo; *s.* izquierda; **mano izquierda; at (on, to) the —** a la izquierda.

left-handed [léfthǽndɪd] *adj.* zurdo; a la izquierda; torpe; malicioso, insincero; **— compliment** alabanza irónica.

leftist [léftɪst] *s.* izquierdista.

leftover [léftovə] *adj.* sobrante; **-s** *s. pl.* sobras.

leg [lɛg] *s.* pierna; pata (*de animal, mesa, etc.*); pie o pata (*de banquillo, silla, etc.*); etapa, trecho (*de una carrera o viaje*); **to be on one's last -s** estar en las últimas.

legacy [légəsɪ] *s.* legado, herencia.

legal [lígḷ] *adj.* legal; lícito.

legalize [líglaɪz] *v.* legalizar; sancionar,

autorizar.

legate [légit] *s.* legado; delegado.

legation [ligéʃən] *s.* legación; embajada.

legend [lédʒənd] *s.* leyenda; letrero, inscripción.

legendary [lédʒəndərɪ] *adj.* legendario.

leggings [légɪŋz] *s. pl.* polainas.

legion [lídʒən] *s.* legión.

legislate [lédʒɪslet] *v.* legislar.

legislation [ledʒɪsléʃən] *s.* legislación.

legislative [lédʒɪsletɪv] *adj.* legislativo.

legislator [lédʒɪsletə] *s.* legislador.

legislature [lédʒɪsletʃə] *s.* legislatura, asamblea legislativa.

legitimate [lɪdʒítɪmɪt] *adj.* legítimo.

leisure [líʒə] *s.* ocio; — **hours** horas de ocio; **to be at** — **estar ocioso**; estar libre o desocupado; **do it at your** — hágalo Vd. cuando pueda o le convenga; hágalo Vd. en sus ratos de ocio.

leisurely [líʒəlɪ] *adj:* lento, deliberado, pausado; *adv.* sin prisa, despacio, a sus (mis, tus, *etc.*) anchas.

lemon [lémən] *s.* limón; — **tree** limonero; *adj.* de limón; — **color** cetrino.

lemonade [lemonéd] *s.* limonada.

lend [lend] *v.* prestar.

lender [léndə] *s.* prestador; **money** — prestamista.

length [leŋkθ] *s.* largo, largor, largura, longitud; duración; cantidad (*de una sílaba*); **at** — largamente, detenidamente; al fin; **to go to any** — hacer cuanto esté de su parte.

lengthen [léŋkθeən] *v.* alargar(se); prolongar(se).

lengthwise [léŋkθwaɪz] *adv.* a lo largo; longitudinalmente; *adj.* longitudinal.

lengthy [léŋkθɪ] *adj.* largo, prolongado.

lenient [línɪənt] *adj.* indulgente, clemente, poco severo.

lens [lenz] *s.* lente; cristalino (*del ojo*).

lent [lent] *pret. & p.p. de* to lend.

Lent [lent] *s.* cuaresma.

leopard [lépəd] *s.* leopardo.

less [les] *adj.* menor; *adv. & prep.* menos; — **and** — cada vez menos.

lessen [lésn] *v.* aminorar(se), disminuir(se), reducir(se); mermar.

lesser [lésə] *adj.* menor, más pequeño.

lesson [lésn] *s.* lección.

lest [lest] *conj.* no sea que, por miedo de que.

let [let] *v.* dejar, permitir; alquilar, arrendar; — **us** (*o* let's) **do it** vamos a hacerlo, hagámoslo; — **him come** que venga; **to** — **be** no molestar, dejar en paz; no tocar; **to** — **down** bajar; desilusionar; **to** — **go** soltar; **to** — **in** dejar entrar, admitir; **to** —

know avisar, enterar, hacer saber; **to** — **off** soltar; dejar libre; **to** — **through** dejar pasar; **to** — **up** disminuir; *pret. & p.p. de* to let.

lethargy [léθədʒɪ] *s.* letargo; **to fall into** a — aletargarse.

letter [létə] *s.* letra; carta; — **box** buzón; — **carrier** cartero; —**head** membrete; *v.* rotular, hacer a mano letras de molde.

lettuce [létɪs] *s.* lechuga.

level [lévl] *adj.* llano, plano; **a nivel;** igual; parejo; **level-headed** bien equilibrado, sensato; *adv.* a nivel; a ras; **s.** nivel; **to be on the** — obrar rectamente, obrar sin engaño; ser o decir la pura verdad; *v.* nivelar; igualar; allanar; apuntar, asestar (*un arma*); **to** — **to the ground** arrasar, echar por tierra.

lever [lévə] *s.* palanca; **control** — palanca de mando.

levy [lévɪ] *s.* imposición, recaudación (*de tributos, impuestos, etc.*); leva, enganche, reclutamiento; embargo (*de propiedad*); *v.* imponer, exigir, recaudar (*tributos o multas*); reclutar; **to** — **on someone's property** embargar la propiedad de alguien.

lewd [lud] *adj.* lujurioso, lascivo, deshonesto.

lewdness [lúdnɪs] *s.* lascivia, lujuria.

liability [laɪəbílɪtɪ] *s.* responsabilidad; obligación; desventaga; **liabilities** obligaciones, deudas; pasivo.

liable [láɪəbl] *adj.* responsable, obligado; sujeto, expuesto; propenso; probable.

liar [láɪə] *s.* mentiroso, embustero.

libel [láɪbl] *s.* libelo; difamación; *v.* difamar.

liberal [líbərəl] *adj. & s.* liberal.

liberality [lɪbərélətɪ] *s.* liberalidad; largueza, generosidad.

liberate [líbəret] *v.* libertar, librar; soltar.

liberation [lɪbəréʃən] *s.* liberación.

liberator [líbəretə] *s.* libertador.

libertine [líbətin] *adj. & s.* libertino.

liberty [líbətɪ] *s.* libertad; **at** — libre.

librarian [laɪbrérɪən] *s.* bibliotecario.

library [láɪbrerɪ] *s.* biblioteca.

lice [laɪs] *pl. de* louse.

license, licence [láɪsns] *s.* licencia; permiso; título; **driver's** — licencia (pase, certificado o patente) de chófer; título de conductor; licencia para manejar; — **plate** placa (*o* chapa) de numeración, chapa de circulación, chapa de matrícula; *v.* licenciar, dar licencia a; permitir, autorizar.

licentious [laisénʃəs] *adj.* licencioso, disoluto.

lick [lɪk] *v.* lamer; dar una tunda o zurra; vencer; **to — someone's boots** adular a uno con servilismo; **to — the dust** morder el polvo; adular; *s.* lamedura, *Am.* lamida; lengüetada; **salt** — lamedero (*lugar salino donde lame el ganado*); **not to do a — of work** no hacer absolutamente nada.

licking [lɪkɪŋ] *s.* zurra, tunda.

lid [lɪd] *s.* tapadera, tapa; **eye —** párpado.

lie [lai] *s.* mentira; embuste; **to give the — to** desmentir, dar un mentís; *v.* mentir (*pret. & p.p.* lied); tenderse, acostarse; yacer; estar; estar situado; consistir (en); **to — back** recostarse, echarse hacia atrás; **to — down** acostarse, echarse, tenderse; **to — in wait** acechar, espiar.

lieutenant [luténənt] *s.* teniente; **second — subteniente.**

life [laif] *s.* vida; **from — del natural; still — naturaleza muerta; —boat** bote de salvamento, lancha salvavidas; **— imprisonment** prisión perpetua; **— insurance** seguro sobre la vida; **— pension** pensión vitalicia; **— preserver** salvavidas, cinto o chaqueta de salvamento.

lifeless [láiflis] *adj.* sin vida; muerto; exánime, inanimado; desanimado.

lifelessness [láiflisnis] *s.* falta de vida; inercia; falta de animación.

lifelike [láiflaik] *adj.* como la vida; natural, que parece vivo.

lifelong [láiflóŋ] *adj.* perpetuo, de toda la vida.

lifetime [láiftaim] *s.* vida, transcurso de la vida.

lift [lɪft] *v.* levantar; alzar; elevar; disiparse (*las nubes, la niebla, las tinieblas*); **to — one's hat** quitarse el sombrero (*para saludar*); *s.* elevación; exaltación de ánimo; alzamiento, levantamiento; carga; ayuda (*para levantar una carga*); alza (*de un zapato*); ascensor, *Am.* elevador; **to give someone a — in a car** llevar a alguien en el auto.

light [lait] *s.* luz; lumbre; **tail — Am.** farito trasero, *Am.* farol de cola, *Am.* calavera; *adj.* claro; con luz; de tez blanca; ligero; leve; frívolo; **— drink** bebida suave; **—headed** frívolo, ligero de cascos; **—hearted** alegre; **— opera** opereta; **to make — of** dar poca importancia a; *v.* encender(se); iluminar, alumbrar; **to — upon caer**

sobre; posarse en (*dícese de los pájaros, mariposas, etc.*).

lighten [láitn] *v.* aligerar; iluminar; aclarar; relampaguear; alegrar.

lighter [láitə] *s.* encendedor.

lighthouse [láithaus] *s.* faro.

lighting [láitiŋ] *s.* iluminación; alumbrado.

lightly [láitli] *adv.* ligeramente; levemente; frívolamente; sin seriedad.

lightness [láitnis] *s.* ligereza; frivolidad; claridad.

lightning [láitniŋ] *s.* relampagueo; relámpago; **— rod** pararrayos.

likable [láikəbl] *adj.* agradable, simpático, placentero.

like [laik] *adv. & prep.* como; del mismo modo que; semejante a; *adj.* semejante, parecido; **in — manner de manera semejante, del mismo modo; to feel — going** tener ganas de ir; **to look — someone** parecerse a alguien; **it looks — rain** parece que va a llover, quiere llover; *s.* semejante, igual; **-s** gustos; preferencias; *v.* gustarle a uno; **he -s books** le gustan los libros; **do whatever you —** haz lo que gustes.

likely [láikli] *adj.* probable, creíble; prometedor; **— place** lugar a propósito; **it is — to happen** es probable que suceda; *adv.* probablemente.

liken [láikən] *v.* asemejar, comparar.

likeness [láiknis] *s.* semejanza; parecido; retrato.

likewise [láikwaiz] *adv.* igualmente, asimismo; del mismo modo; también.

liking [láikiŋ] *s.* simpatía; afición; preferencia, gusto.

lilac [láilək] *s.* lila; *adj.* lila, morado claro.

lily [líli] *s.* lirio; azucena.

limb [lim] *s.* rama (*de árbol*); miembro (*del cuerpo*), pierna, brazo.

limber [límbə] *adj.* flexible; ágil; *v.* hacer flexible; **to — up** agilitar(se), hacer(se) flexible.

lime [laim] *s.* cal; lima (*fruta*); liga (*para cazar pájaros*).

limelight [láimlait] *s.* luz de calcio; proscenio; **to be in the — estar a la vista del público.**

limestone [láimston] *s.* piedra caliza.

limit [límit] *s.* límite; confín; *v.* limitar.

limitation [limitéʃən] *s.* limitación; restricción.

limited [límitid] *adj.* limitado; restringido.

limitless [límitlis] *adj.* ilimitado, sin límites.

limp [limp] *s.* cojera; *v.* cojear; renquear;

adj. flojo; flexible.

limpid [límpɪd] *adj.* límpido; claro, transparente.

line [laɪn] *s.* línea; renglón; raya; cuerda; ramo, giro (*de negocios*); especialidad; — **of goods** surtido, línea (*Am.* renglón) de mercancías; **branch railway** — ramal; **pipe** — cañería, tubería; **to bring into** — alinear; obligar a proceder de acuerdo con un plan; poner de acuerdo; **to get in** — meterse en fila, hacer (*o* formar) cola; *v.* linear, rayar; alinear; forrar; **to** — **up** alinear(se); formarse, formar fila.

lineage [línɪɪdʒ] *s.* linaje.

linear [línɪə] *adj.* lineal.

lined [laɪnd] *adj.* rayado; forrado.

linen [línɪn] *s.* lino; ropa blanca.

liner [láɪnə] *s.* vapor, buque; **air** — avión, transporte aéreo.

linger [língə] *v.* tardar(se), demorarse, dilatarse; andar ocioso, vagar; perdurar; prolongarse.

lingerie [lɛnʒəri] *s.* ropa interior de mujer.

lining [láɪnɪŋ] *s.* forro.

link [lɪŋk] *s.* eslabón; enlace; **cuff** -s gemelos; *v.* eslabonar(se); enlazar(se).

linnet [línɪt] *s.* jilguero.

linoleum [linólɪəm] *s.* linóleo (*tela impermeable para cubrir el suelo*).

linseed [línsɪd] *s.* linaza; — **oil** aceite de linaza.

lint [lɪnt] *s.* hilas; hilachas.

lion [láɪən] *s.* león.

lioness [láɪənɪs] *s.* leona.

lip [lɪp] *s.* labio.

lipstick [lípstɪk] *s.* lápiz para los labios.

liquid [líkwɪd] *adj.* líquido; — **assets** valores líquidos (*o* realizables); — **measure** medida para líquidos; *s.* líquido.

liquidate [líkwɪdet] *v.* liquidar, saldar (*cuentas*); poner término a.

liquidation [lɪkwɪdéʃən] *s.* liquidación; saldo de cuentas.

liquor [líkə] *s.* licor; bebida espiritosa (*como aguardiente, ron, etc.*).

lisp [lɪsp] *s.* ceceo; *v.* cecear; balbucir.

list [lɪst] *s.* lista; registro; escora (*inclinación de un barco*); *v.* alistar, registrar, poner o apuntar en una lista; hacer una lista de; escorar, inclinarse a la banda.

listen [lísṇ] *v.* escuchar; atender, dar oídos, prestar atención; — ! ¡oye! ¡escucha! ¡oiga! ¡escuche!; **to** — **in** escuchar por radio; escuchar a hurtadillas (*una conversación*).

listener [lísṇə] *s.* escuchador, oyente;

radio — radioescucha, radioyente.

listless [lístlɪs] *adj.* abstraído; indiferente; indolente; desatento.

listlessness [lístlɪsnɪs] *s.* indiferencia, inatención, abstracción.

lit [lɪt] *pret.* & *p.p. de* **to light**; *adj.* alumbrado; algo borracho.

literal [lítərəl] *adj.* literal; -**ly** *adv.* al pie de la letra, literalmente.

literary [lítərɛrɪ] *adj.* literario.

literature [lítərətʃʊr] *s.* literatura; impresos, folletos, circulares.

litigation [lɪtəgéʃən] *s.* litigio, pleito.

litter [lítə] *s.* camada, cría; litera; camilla; cama de paja (*para animales*); cosas esparcidas en desorden; desorden, revoltillo; *v.* desarreglar, revolver, esparcir cosas por.

little [lítḷ] *adj.* pequeño; poco; — **Bear** Osa Menor; **a** — **coffee** un poco de café; **a** — **while** un ratito (*o* ratico), un poco; *adv.* & *s.* poco; — **by** — poco a poco.

live [lɪv] *v.* vivir; **to** — **down** hacer olvidar, borrar (*el pasado*); **to** — **up to** vivir en conformidad con, vivir de acuerdo con.

live [laɪv] *adj.* vivo; enérgico, activo; — **coal** ascua encendida; — **oak** encina; — **question** cuestión palpitante, cuestión de actualidad; — **wire** alambre cargado; persona muy activa.

livelihood [láɪvlɪhʌd] *s.* vida, alimento, subsistencia, manutención.

liveliness [láɪvlɪnɪs] *s.* viveza, animación; agilidad.

lively [láɪvlɪ] *adj.* vivo; vivaz; animado, alegre; airoso; — **horse** caballo brioso; *adv.* vivamente; de prisa.

liver [lívə] *s.* hígado; vividor.

livery [lívərɪ] *s.* librea; caballeriza (*para caballos de alquiler*); **auto** — **garage** para autos de alquiler.

lives [laɪvz] *pl. de* **life**.

livestock [láɪvstak] *s.* ganado.

livid [lívɪd] *adj.* lívido; amoratado.

living [lívɪŋ] *s.* vida; manutención, subsistencia; *adj.* vivo; viviente; — **room** sala; — **wage** sueldo suficiente para vivir; **the** — los vivos.

lizard [lízəd] *s.* lagarto; **small** — lagartija.

load [lod] *s.* carga; **ship** — cargamento; -**s of** gran cantidad de; montones de; *v.* cargar; agobiar; colmar.

loaf [lof] *s.* hogaza de pan; **sugar** — azúcar de pilón; *v.* holgazanear, haraganear.

loafer [lófə] *s.* holgazán, haragán, zángano.

oan [lon] s. préstamo; empréstito; — **shark** usurero; v. prestar (dinero).

oath [loe] adj. maldispuesto, renuente; **to be —** to repugnarle a uno.

oathe [loð] v. repugnarle a uno; abominar.

oathsome [lóðsəm] adj. repugnante, asqueroso; aborrecible.

oaves [lovz] pl. de loaf.

obby [lábi] s. vestíbulo; antecámara; salón de entrada; camarilla (que busca ventajas ante un cuerpo legislativo); **hotel —** vestíbulo o patio del hotel; v. cabildear (procurar ventajas o partidarios en una asamblea).

obster [lábstə] s. langosta de mar.

ocal [lókl] adj. local; — **train** tren ordinario.

ocality [lokélətɪ]s. localidad; comarca.

ocalize [lóklaɪz] v. localizar.

ocate [lóket] v. situar, establecer; localizar, averiguar la posición de; avecindarse, radicarse, establecerse.

ocation [lokéʃən] s. situación, sitio, localidad.

ock [lak] s. cerradura; esclusa (de un canal); llave (de un arma de fuego); guedeja (de pelo); bucle, rizo; v. cerrar con llave; trabar(se), juntar(se); entrelazar(se); **to —** in encerrar; **to — out** cerrar la puerta (a alguien), dejar afuera; **to — up** encerrar; encarcelar.

ocket [lákɪt] s. guardapelo.

ockout [lákaut] s. paro (suspensión del trabajo por parte de los empresarios); cierre de fábrica.

ocksmith [láksmɪe] s. cerrajero.

ocomotive [lokəmótɪv] s. locomotora; — **engineer** maquinista.

ocust [lókəst] s. langosta, saltamontes; cigarra; — **tree** algarrobo; acacia falsa.

odge [ladʒ] s. logia; casita accesoria; casa de campo; v. alojar(se); hospedar(se); colocar; **to — a complaint** presentar una queja.

odger [ládʒə] s. huésped, inquilino.

odging [ládʒɪŋ] s. alojamiento, hospedaje; vivienda.

oft [loft] s. desván; galería, balcón interior (de un templo); **choir —** coro; **hay —** pajar.

ofty [lófti] adj. elevado; sublime; altivo.

og [lɔg] s. leño, troza, tronco aserrado; corredera (aparato para medir las millas que anda la nave); diario de navegación; — **cabin** cabaña de troncos; v. cortar (árboles); cortar leños y transportarlos; registrar (en el diario de navegación).

logic [ládʒɪk] s. lógica.

logical [ládʒɪkl] adj. lógico.

loin [lɔɪn] s. ijada, ijar, lomo.

loiter [lóɪtə] v. holgazanear, vagar, malgastar el tiempo; **to — behind** rezagarse.

loll [lal] v. arrellanarse o repantigarse, recostarse con toda comodidad.

lone [lon] adj. solo, solitario.

loneliness [lónlɪnɪs] s. soledad.

lonely [lónlɪ] adj. solo, solitario; triste, desamparado.

lonesome [lónsəm] adj. solo, solitario; triste, nostálgico.

long [lɔŋ] adj. largo; **the whole day —** todo el santo día; **three feet —** tres pies de largo; **to be — in coming** tardar en venir; adv. mucho, mucho tiempo; — **ago** hace mucho tiempo; **as** (o so) **—** en tanto que, mientras que; **how — is it since . . . ?** ¿cuánto tiempo hace que . . . ?; **so —** ! ¡hasta luego! ¡adiós!; **long-suffering** sufrido, paciente; **long-winded** prolijo, largo (en hablar); v. anhelar; ansiar; **to — for** anhelar; suspirar por.

longer [lóŋgə] adj. más largo; adv. más, más tiempo; **no —** ya no; **not . . . any —** ya no; no . . . más.

longevity [landʒévətɪ] s. longevidad.

longing [lóŋɪŋ] s. anhelo, añoranza, nostalgia; adj. anhelante, anheloso, nostálgico; **-ly** adv. con anhelo anhelosamente, con ansia.

longitude [lándʒətjud] s. longitud.

longshoreman [lóŋʃormən] s. estibador (de barco o muelle), cargador.

look [luk] v. mirar; parecer; **it -s well on you** le cae (o le sienta) bien; **to — after** atender, cuidar; **to — alike** parecerse; asemejarse; **to — down on a person** mirar con desprecio (o menospreciar) a alguien; **to — for** buscar; esperar; **to — forward to** anticipar con placer; **to — into** examinar, investigar; — **out!** ¡cuidado!; ¡tenga cuidado!; **to — out of** asomarse a; **to — over** examinar; dar un vistazo a; **to — up** levantar la vista; buscar; **to — up to** admirar, mirar con respeto; s. mirada, vistazo; **-s** apariencia, aspecto; **to have good -s** ser bien parecido.

looking glass [lúkɪnglæs] s. espejo.

lookout [lúkaut] s. vigía; atalaya; mirador; vista, perspectiva; **that is your —** ¡eso a usted!; **to be on the —** estar alerta.

loom [lum] s. telar; v. destacarse, descollar; asomar(se), aparecer.

loop [lup] s. lazo, gaza, presilla; vuelta, curva; circuito; v. hacer una gaza (con o en); atar con gaza o presilla; hacer un circuito.

loophole [lúphol] s. agujero, abertura; salida; escapatoria.

loose [lus] adj. suelto; flojo; holgado; desatado; disoluto; — **change** suelto, moneda suelta; **to let** — soltar; v. soltar; desatar; aflojar; -**ly** adv. sueltamente; flojamente; con poca exactitud, sin fundamento.

loosen [lúsn] v. soltar(se); aflojar(se); desatar(se); **to** — **one's hold** desasirse, soltarse.

looseness [lúsnɪs] s. soltura; flojedad, flojera; holgura; relajación; flujo (de vientre).

loot [lut] s. botín, pillaje, saqueo; v. saquear, pillar, robar.

lop [lɑp] v. tronchar, desmochar (Am. mochar).

loquacious [lokwéʃɔs] adj. locuaz, hablador, lenguaraz.

lord [lord] s. señor; dueño, amo; lord; **Lord's Prayer** Padre Nuestro; **Our Lord** Nuestro Señor; v. señorear, mandar; **to** — **it over** señorear, dominar.

lordly [lórdlɪ] adj. señoril; noble; altivo; despótico; adv. altivamente, imperiosamente.

lordship [lórdʃɪp] s. señoría (título); señorío, dominio.

lose [luz] v. perder; **to** — **sight of** perder de vista.

loss [lɔs] s. pérdida; **to be at a** — estar perplejo; no saber qué hacer; **to sell at a** — vender con pérdida.

lost [lɔst] pret. & p.p. de **to lose**; adj. perdido; extraviado; — **in thought** absorto, abstraído; **to get** — perderse, extraviarse.

lot [lɑt] s. lote; parte, porción; suerte; solar, porción de terreno; **a** — **of** (o -**s of**) una gran cantidad de; mucho; muchos; **to draw** -**s** echar suertes; **to fall to one's** — tocarle a uno, caerle en suerte; adv. mucho; **a** — **better** mucho mejor.

lotion [lóʃən] s. loción.

lottery [látərɪ] s. lotería.

loud [laʊd] adj. ruidoso; recio, fuerte; chillón (dícese también de los colores); adv. ruidosamente, fuerte, recio; alto, en voz alta.

loud-speaker [láʊdspíkɔ] s. altavoz, altoparlante.

lounge [laʊndʒ] s. sala de descanso; sofá, diván, canapé; v. arrellanarse,

repantigarse, recostarse cómodamente; sestear; holgazanear.

louse [laʊs] s. piojo.

lousy [láʊzɪ] adj. piojoso; asqueroso.

lovable [lʌvəbl] adj. amable.

love [lʌv] s. amor; cariño; afición; — **affair** amorío; **to be in** — estar enamorado; **to fall in** — **with** enamorarse de; **to make** — to enamorar a; amar, querer; gustar mucho de, gustarle a uno mucho; encantarle a uno algo.

loveliness [lʌvlɪnɪs] s. belleza, hermosura; amabilidad.

lovely [lʌvlɪ] adj. amable; lindo, bello, exquisito; encantador; ameno.

lover [lʌvɔ] s. amante; **music** — aficionado a (o amante de) la música.

loving [lʌvɪŋ] adj. amante, amoroso, cariñoso, afectuoso; -**ly** adv. cariñosamente, afectuosamente.

low [lo] adj. bajo; vil; humilde; abatido; débil; gravemente enfermo; deficiente; — **comedy** farsa, sainete; — **gear** primera velocidad; — **Mass** misa rezada; **dress with a** — nec vestido escotado (o con escote); **to b** — **on something** estar escaso d algo; **to be in** — **spirits** estar abatido o desanimado; adv. bajo; en voz baja quedo, quedito; con bajeza, a prec bajo vilmente; s. mugido; v. mugir.

lower [lóɔ] adj. más bajo; inferior; — **case letter** letra minúscula; — **man** estudiante de los dos primeros años; — **house** cámara de diputado v. bajar; disminuir; rebajar; abati humillar.

lowland [lólænd] s. tierra baja.

lowliness [lólɪnɪs] s. bajeza; humilda

lowly [lólɪ] adj. bajo, humilde; inferic adv. humildemente.

lowness [lónɪs] s. bajeza; humilda abatimiento; gravedad (de tono); d bilidad (de un sonido); baratura.

loyal [lɔ́ɪəl] adj. leal, fiel.

loyalty [lɔ́ɪəltɪ] s. lealtad, fidelidad.

lubricant [lúbrɪkənt] adj. & s. l bricante.

lubricate [lúbrɪket] v. lubricar.

lucid [lúsɪd] adj. lúcido; claro; lucient

luck [lʌk] s. suerte; fortuna; **in** — buena suerte; **in bad** — de ma suerte.

luckily [lʌ́kɪlɪ] adv. afortunadamente, p fortuna.

lucky [lʌ́kɪ] adj. afortunado, feliz; **to** — tener suerte, tocarle a uno la suert

lucrative [lúkrətɪv] adj. lucrativo.

ludicrous [lúdɪkrəs] adj. ridículo.

ug [lʌg] v. llevar, traer, Am. cargar; to — away cargar con, llevarse (una cosa pesada).

uggage [lʌ́gɪdʒ] s. equipaje.

ukewarm [lúkwɔ́rm] adj. tibio, templado; indiferente.

ull [lʌl] v. arrullar; sosegar; calmar(se); s. calma, momento de calma.

ullaby [lʌ́ləbaɪ] s. arrullo, canción de cuna.

umber [lʌ́mbə] s. madera, maderaje; —man maderero, negociante en madera; —yard depósito de maderas; v. cortar y aserrar madera; explotar los bosques; moverse pesadamente.

uminous [lúmənəs] adj. luminoso.

ump [lʌmp] s. terrón; bulto; hinchazón, chichón; protuberancia; — of sugar terrón de azúcar; v. amontonar; consolidar (gastos); apelotonarse, aterronarse, formar terrones.

umpy [lʌ́mpɪ] adj. aterronado.

unatic [lúnətɪk] adj. & s. lunático, loco.

unch [lʌntʃ] s. almuerzo; merienda; —room merendero, Am. lonchería; v. almorzar; merendar; Am. tomar el lonche.

uncheon [lʌ́ntʃən] s. almuerzo; merienda.

ung [lʌŋ] s. pulmón.

urch [lɝtʃ] s. sacudida; tambaleo repentino; to give a — tambalearse; to leave someone in the — dejar a uno plantado, dejar a uno a buenas noches; v. tambalearse; dar un tambaleo repentino.

ure [lʊr] s. aliciente, atractivo; tentación; cebo o reclamo (para atraer); v. atraer; seducir; atraer (con cebo o reclamo).

urk [lɝk] v. estar oculto; estar en acecho; moverse furtivamente.

uscious [lʌ́ʃəs] adj. exquisito, delicioso, sabroso.

ust [lʌst] s. lujuria; deseo vehemente; codicia; v. to — after codiciar.

uster [lʌ́stə] s. lustre, brillo.

ustrous [lʌ́strəs] adj. lustroso.

usty [lʌ́stɪ] adj. vigoroso, fornido, robusto.

ute [lut] s. laúd.

uxuriant [lʌgʒúrɪənt] adj. lozano, frondoso, exuberante.

uxurious [lʌgʒúrɪəs] adj. lujoso; dado al lujo; frondoso.

uxury [lʌ́kʃərɪ] s. lujo.

ye [laɪ] s. lejía.

ing [láɪɪŋ] ger. de to lie; adj. mentiroso; lying-in hospital casa de maternidad.

lynch [lɪntʃ] v. linchar.

lynx [lɪŋks] s. lince.

lyre [laɪr] s. lira.

lyric [lɪ́rɪk] s. poema lírico; adj. lírico.

lyrical [lɪ́rɪkl] adj. lírico.

lyricism [lɪ́rəsɪʒəm] s. lirismo.

M

macaroni [mækərónɪ] s. macarrón o macarrones.

macaroon [mækərún] s. macarrón, almendrado, bollito de almendra.

machine [məʃín] s. máquina; automóvil; — gun ametralladora; — made hecho a máquina; political — camarilla política; sewing — máquina para coser.

machinery [məʃínərɪ] s. maquinaria.

machinist [məʃínɪst] s. mecánico, maquinista.

mackerel [mækərəl] s. escombro, caballa (pez).

mad [mæd] adj. loco; rabioso; furioso, enojado; to drive — enloquecer, volver loco; to get — encolerizarse; to go — volverse loco, enloquecerse; -ly adv. locamente.

madam, madame [mædəm] s. madama, señora.

madcap [mædkæp] s. calavera (m.), adj. temerario; temerario; atolondrado.

madden [mædn] v. enloquecer(se).

made [med] pret. & p.p. de to make; to be — of estar hecho de; ser de; to have something — mandar hacer algo; made-up fingido, falso; artificial, pintado (con afeites).

madman [mædmæn] s. loco.

madness [mædnɪs] s. locura; rabia.

magazine [mægəzín] s. revista; almacén (especialmente para provisiones militares); powder — polvorín.

magic [mædʒɪk] s. magia; adj. mágico.

magician [mədʒíʃən] s. mágico; brujo.

magistrate [mædʒɪstret] s. magistrado.

magnanimous [mægnǽnəməs] adj. magnánimo.

magnet [mægnɪt] s. imán.

magnetic [mægnétɪk] adj. magnético.

magnificence [mægnífəsns] s. magnificencia.

magnificent [mægnífəsnt] adj. magnífico.

magnify [mægnəfaɪ] v. agrandar, engrandecer; amplificar; exagerar.

magnitude [mægnətjud] s. magnitud.

magpie [mægpaɪ] s. urraca; cotorra, hablador, habladora.

mahogany [məhágənɪ] s. caoba.

maid [med] s. criada, sirvienta, camarera, Am. recamarera, Am. mucama; doncella; — of honor doncella de honor; old — solterona.

maiden [médṇ] s. doncella; virgen; mozuela; soltera; — **lady** mujer soltera; — **voyage** primer viaje (*de un vapor*).

mail [mel] s. correo; correspondencia; **air** — correo aéreo; **coat of** — malla; **—bag** valija; — **train** tren correo; v. echar al correo.

mailbox [mélboks] s. buzón.

mailman [mélmæn] s. cartero.

maim [mem] v. mutilar, estropear.

main [men] adj. principal, mayor, de mayor importancia; s. tubería, cañería principal (*de agua o gas*); alta mar, océano; **in the** — en su mayor parte; en general, en conjunto; **-ly** adv. principalmente.

mainland [ménlænd] s. continente, tierra firme.

maintain [mentén] v. mantener; sostener, afirmar; guardar.

maintenance [méntənəns] s. mantenimiento; sustento; manutención; sostén, sostenimiento.

maize [mez] s. maíz.

majestic [mədʒéstik] adj. majestuoso.

majesty [mædʒɪstɪ] s. majestad.

major [médʒə] adj. mayor, más grande; principal; — **key** tono mayor; s. comandante; mayor, mayor de edad; curso o asignatura de especialización (*en la universidad*); v. especializarse (*en un curso de estudios*).

majority [mədʒɔ́rətɪ] s. mayoría; mayor edad.

make [mek] v. hacer; fabricar; formar; pronunciar (*un discurso*); **to** — **a clean breast of** confesar; **to** — **a train** alcanzar un tren; **to** — **a turn** dar vuelta; **to** — **away with** llevarse, robar; matar; **to** — **fast** asegurar, afianzar; **to** — **headway** progresar, adelantar, avanzar; **to** — **much of** dar mucha importancia a; **to** — **neither head nor tail of** no comprender nada de; **to** — **nothing out of** no comprender nada de, no sacar nada en limpio; **to** — **out in the distance** distinguir a lo lejos; **to** — **over** rehacer, alterar (*un traje*); **to** — **sure** asegurarse; **to** — **toward** dirigirse a, encaminarse a; **to** — **up a story** inventar un cuento; **to** — **up after a quarrel** hacer las paces; **to** — **up for a loss** compensar por una pérdida; **to** — **up one's face** pintarse la cara; **to** — **up one's mind** resolverse, decidirse; s. hechura, forma; marca (*de fábrica*); manufactura.

maker [mékə] s. hacedor; fabricante; artífice.

make-up [mékʌp] s. compostura, composición, hechura; naturaleza, carácter; facial — afeite, cosmético.

malady [mælədɪ] s. mal, enfermedad.

malaria [məlérɪə] s. malaria, fiebre palúdica, paludismo.

malcontent [mælkəntent] adj. & s. malcontento.

male [mel] adj. macho; varón; masculino; varonil; de hombres, de varones; s. macho; varón; hombre.

malice [mælɪs] s. malicia.

malicious [məlíʃəs] adj. malicioso, perverso, malévolo.

malign [məláɪn] v. calumniar, difamar; adj. maligno; pernicioso.

malignant [məlígnənt] adj. maligno, malévolo.

mallet [mælɪt] s. mazo, maceta.

malt [molt] s. malta; **-ed milk** leche malteada.

mama, mamma [múmə] s. mamá.

mammal [mæml] s. mamífero.

mammoth [mæmə] adj. gigantesco, enorme.

mammy [mæmɪ] s. mamita; niñera negra; criada negra.

man [mæn] s. hombre; varón; pieza (*del ajedrez*); — **and wife** marido y mujer; **to a** — unánimemente, todos a una; **officers and men** oficiales y soldados; **man-of-war** buque de guerra; — **cook** cocinero; v. armar, proveer de gente armada; guarnecer (*una fortaleza*); tripular (*una embarcación*).

manage [mænɪdʒ] v. manejar; gobernar; dirigir; gestionar; **to** — **to do something** arreglárselas para hacer algo.

manageable [mænɪdʒəbl] adj. manejable; domable, dócil.

management [mænɪdʒmənt] s. manejo; dirección; gobierno, administración; gerencia.

manager [mænɪdʒə] s. gerente; director, administrador; empresario.

mandate [mændet] s. mandato; asignar por mandato.

mane [men] s. melena (*del león*), crin (*del caballo*).

maneuver [mənúvə] s. maniobra; gestión; v. maniobrar; manipular, manejar.

manful [mænfəl] adj. varonil; viril.

manganese [mæŋgənis] s. manganeso.

mange [mendʒ] s. sarna, roña.

manger [méndʒə] s. pesebre.

mangle [mæŋgl] v. magullar, mutilar, destrozar, estropear; planchar con máquina de planchar; s. planchadora (*máquina de planchar*).

mangy [méndʒɪ] *adj.* sarnoso, *Am.* sarniento.

manhood [ménhʊd] *s.* virilidad; edad viril; hombres.

mania [ménɪa] *s.* manía.

manicure [ménɪkjʊr] *s.* manicura; *v.* manicurar,

manifest [ménəfɛst] *adj.* manifiesto; *v.* manifiesto (*lista de la carga de un buque*); *v.* manifestar; poner de manifiesto; declarar.

manifestation [mænəfɛstéʃən] *s.* manifestación.

manifesto [mænɪfésto] *s.* manifiesto, bando, proclama.

manifold [ménəfold] *adj.* múltiple; numeroso, diverso.

manikin [ménəkɪn] *s.* maniquí; muñeco; hombrecillo.

manila [mənílə] *s.* abacá (*cáñamo de Manila*); — **paper** papel de Manila.

manipulate [mənípjəlet] *v.* manipular; manejar.

manipulation [mənɪpjəléʃən] *s.* manipulación.

mankind [mænkáɪnd] *s.* humanidad, género humano; los hombres.

manly [ménlɪ] *adj.* varonil, viril; *adv.* varonilmente.

manner [ménə] *s.* manera; modo; género; aire, ademán; **-s** maneras, modales, costumbres; **after the —** a la manera de; **by no — of means de** ningún modo.

mannish [ménɪʃ] *adj.* hombruno.

manoeuvre = maneuver.

manor [ménə] *s.* solar, casa solariega.

mansion [ménʃən] *s.* mansión; palacio.

manslaughter [ménslɔtə] *s.* homicidio impremeditado o casual.

mantel [méntl̩] *s.* manto (*de una chimenea*); repisa de chimenea.

mantle [méntl̩] *s.* manto; capa.

manual [ménjʊəl] *adj.* manual; — **training school** escuela de artes y oficios; *s.* manual; teclado de órgano.

manufacture [mænjəfæktʃə]' *s.* fabricación; manufactura; *v.* fabricar, manufacturar.

manufacturer [mænjəfæktʃərə] *s.* fabricante.

manufacturing [mænjəfæktʃərɪŋ] *s.* fabricación; *adj.* fabril, manufacturero.

manure [mənʊr] *s.* estiércol; abono; *v.* estercolar, abonar (*la tierra*).

manuscript [ménjəskrɪpt] *adj.* & *s.* manuscrito.

many [ménɪ] *adj.* muchos; — **a time**

muchas veces; **a great —** muchísimos; **as — as** tantos como; cuantos; **as — as five** hasta cinco; **how — ?** ¿cuántos?; **three books too —** tres libros de más; **too —** demasiados.

map [mæp] *s.* mapa; *v.* trazar un mapa de; **to — out** proyectar, planear.

maple [mépl̩] *s.* arce, *Am.* meple.

mar [mar] *v.* desfigurar, estropear

marble [márbl̩] *s.* mármol; canica (*para jugar*); **to play -s** jugar a las canicas; *adj.* de mármol; marmóreo.

march [martʃ] *s.* marcha; *v.* marchar, caminar; hacer marchar; **to — in** entrar marchando; **to — out** marcharse; salirse marchando.

March [martʃ] *s.* marzo.

mare [mɛr] *s.* yegua.

margin [márdʒɪn] *s.* margen; orilla; sobrante; reserva (*fondos*).

marginal [márdʒɪnl̩] *adj.* marginal; — **note** nota marginal, acotación.

marigold [mérɪgold] *s.* caléndula, maravilla.

marine [mərín] *adj.* marino; marítimo; — **corps** cuerpo de marinos; *s.* marino; soldado de marina; **merchant —** marina mercante.

mariner [mérənə] *s.* marinero.

maritime [mérətaɪm] *adj.* marítimo.

mark [mark] *s.* marca; señal, seña; nota, calificación; **question —** punto de interrogación; **to come up to the —** alcanzar la norma requerida; **to hit the —** dar en el blanco; **to make one's —** distinguirse; **to miss one's —** fallar; errar el tiro; fracasar; *v.* marcar; señalar; notar; observar; calificar; **— my words!** ¡advierte lo que te digo!; **to — down** anotar, apuntar; rebajar el precio de.

marker [márkə] *s.* marcador; marca, señal; jalón.

market [márkɪt] *s.* mercado, plaza; — **place** mercado, plaza; — **price** precio corriente; **meat —** carnicería; **stock —** mercado de valores, bolsa; *v.* vender; vender o comprar en el mercado; **to go -ing** ir de compras.

marmalade [mármled] *s.* mermelada.

maroon [mərún] *s.* & *adj.* rojo obscuro.

marooned [mərúnd] *adj.* abandonado (*en lugar desierto*) aislado; **to get —** encontrarse aislado, perdido o incomunicado.

marquis [márkwɪs] *s.* marqués.

marquise [markíz] *s.* marquesa.

marriage [mérɪdʒ] *s.* matrimonio; casamiento, boda; unión, enlace; — **license** licencia para casarse.

married [mǽrɪd] adj. casado; conyugal. **— couple** matrimonio, cónyuges; pareja de casados; **to get —** casarse.

marrow [mǽro] s. meollo, tuétano, medula (de los huesos).

marry [mǽrɪ] v. casar; casarse; casarse con.

marsh [marʃ] s. pantano; ciénaga.

marshal [márʃəl] s. mariscal; alguacil; jefe de policía (en ciertas regiones); maestro de ceremonia; **fire —** jefe de bomberos; v. ordenar, arreglar; guiar, conducir con ceremonia.

marshmallow [márʃmælo] s. pastilla o bombón de altea.

marshy [márʃɪ] adj. pantanoso, cenagoso.

mart [mart] s. mercado.

martial [márʃəl] adj marcial; **— law** estado de guerra.

martin [mártɪn] s. avión (pájaro).

martyr [mártə] s. mártir; v. martirizar, torturar, atormentar.

martyrdom [mártədəm] s. martirio.

marvel [márvl̩] s. maravilla; v. maravillarse.

marvelous [márvləs] adj. maravilloso.

masculine [mǽskjəlɪn] adj masculino; varonil; hombruno.

mash [mæʃ] v. majar, amasar; machacar, magullar; **-ed potatoes** puré de papas (o patatas); .patatas majadas.

mask [mæsk] s. máscara; disfraz; careta; v. disfrazar, enmascarar; encubrir; **-ed ball** baile de máscaras.

mason [mésn̩] s. albañil; **Mason** masón, francmasón.

masonry [mésn̩rɪ] s. albañilería; mampostería; **Masonry** masonería, francmasonería.

masquerade [mæskəréd] s. mascarada; disfraz, máscara; v. enmascararse, disfrazarse; andar disfrazado.

mass [mæs] s, masa; montón; mole; mayoría, mayor parte; misa; **— meeting** mitin popular; **the -es** las masas, el pueblo; v. juntar(se) en masa.

massacre [mǽsəkə] s. hecatombe, matanza, carnicería, destrozo; v. hacer matanza o hecatombe, destrozar.

massage [məsáʒ] v. friccionar, dar masaje; s. masaje.

massive [mǽsɪv] adj. sólido, macizo; voluminoso, imponente.

mast [mæst] s. mástil, palo.

master [mǽstə] s. amo, dueño, señor; maestro; patrón; experto, perito; **— band —** director de la banda; **— of arts** maestro en artes, licenciado; **-'s degree** licenciatura, grado de licencia-do; adj. maestro; **— builder** maestro de obras; **— key** llave maestra; v. do-minar; domar; gobernar; **to — a language** dominar un idioma.

masterful [mǽstəfəl] adj. magistral; dominante.

masterly [mǽstəlɪ] adj. magistral; adv. magistralmente.

masterpiece [mǽstəpis] s. obra maestra.

mastery [mǽstərɪ] s. maestría, arte; destreza; dominio.

mastiff [mǽstɪf] s. mastín, alano.

mat [mæt] s. estera; esterilla; felpudo; tapete; colchoncillo (de gimnasia); borde de cartón (para hacer resaltar una pintura).

match [mætʃ] s. fósforo, cerilla Am. cerillo; pareja; partida, contienda, juego; **he has no —** no tiene igual; **he is a good —** es un buen partido; **the hat and coat are a good —** el abrigo y el sombrero hacen juego; v. igualar, aparear; hacer juego, armonizar; **to one's strength** medir uno sus fuerzas; **these colors do not — well** estos colores no casan bien.

matchless [mǽtʃlɪs] adj. sin par, sin igual, incomparable.

mate [met] s. compañero, compañera; consorte; macho o hembra (entre animales o aves); piloto (el segundo de un buque mercante); oficial subalterno (en la marina); v. aparear(se).

material [mətíriəl] adj. material; esencial; s. material; tejido, género; materia; **raw —** materia prima.

maternal [mətśn̩l] adj. maternal, materno.

maternity [mətśnətɪ] s. maternidad.

mathematical [mæɵəmǽtɪk]l] adj.matemático.

mathematician [mæɵəmətíʃən] s. matemático.

mathematics [mæɵəmǽtɪks] s. matemáticas.

matinée [mætəné] s. función de la tarde Am. matiné.

matriculate [mətríkjəlet] v. matricular(se).

matriculation [mətrɪkjəléʃən] s. matriculación, matrícula.

matrimony [mǽtrəmonɪ] s. matrimonio, casamiento.

matrix [métrɪks] s. matriz; molde.

matron [métrən] s. matrona, madre de familia; ama de llaves; vigilante, cuidadora (de un asilo, cárcel para mujeres, etc.).

matter [mǽtə] s. materia; material, sustancia; asunto, cuestión; cosa; pu-

— for complaint motivo de queja; — of two minutes cosa de dos minutos; as a — of fact de hecho; en verdad, en realidad; business -s negocios; printed — impresos; serious — cosa seria; it is of no — no tiene importancia; to do something as a — of course hacer algo por rutina; what is the — ? ¿qué pasa?; ¿qué tiene Vd.?; matter-of-fact person persona de poca imaginación; *v.* importar; supurar; it does not — no importa, no le hace.

mattress [métris] *s.* colchón; spring — colchón de muelles.

mature [mətjúr] *adj.* maduro; a note un pagaré vencido; *v.* madurar(se); vencerse, hacerse cobrable o pagadero (*un pagaré, una deuda*).

maturity [mətjúrəti] *s.* madurez; vencimiento (*de una deuda u obligación*).

maul [mol] *v.* magullar; maltratar; manejar rudamente; golpear.

maxim [mǽksɪm] *s.* máxima.

maximum [mǽksəməm] *adj.* & *s.* máximo.

may [me] *v. irr y defect.* poder; tener permiso para, serle permitido a uno; ser posible; — I sit down? ¿puedo sentarme?; — you have a good time que se divierta Vd.; it — be that puede ser que, tal vez sea que; it — rain puede (ser) que llueva, es posible que llueva; she — be late puede (ser) que llegue ella tarde.

May [me] *s.* mayo, mes de mayo; — Day primero de mayo; —pole mayo; — Queen maya (*reina de la fiesta del primero de mayo*).

maybe [mébɪ] *adv.* quizás, tal vez, acaso.

mayonnaise [meənéz] *s.* mayonesa.

mayor [méə] *s.* alcalde, alcalde mayor.

maze [mez] *s.* laberinto; confusión; to be in a — estar confuso o perplejo.

me [mi] *pron. pers.* me; mí (*después de preposición*); give it to — démelo (a mí); for — para mí; with — conmigo.

meadow [médo] *s.* pradera, prado; — lark alondra de los prados.

meager [mígə] *adj.* escaso, insuficiente; magro, flaco.

meal [mil] *s.* comida; harina (*a medio moler*); corn — harina de maíz; —time hora de comer.

mean [min] *adj.* ruin, bajo, humilde; vil; mezquino, tacaño (*de mal genio*); malo, indispuesto; mediano; medio; intermedio; — distance distancia media; *s.* medio; término medio; — in medios; recursos; a man of -s un hombre

pudiente o rico; by -s of por medio de; by all -s de todos modos; a toda costa; por supuesto; by no -s de ningún modo; *v.* querer decir, significar; pensar, proponerse, tener la intención de; intentar; destinar; he -s well tiene buenas intenciones.

meaning [mínɪŋ] *s.* significado, sentido; significación; propósito, intención; *adj.* significativo; well-meaning bien intencionado.

meaningless [mínɪŋlɪs] *adj.* sin sentido, vacío de sentido.

meanness [mínnɪs] *s.* ruindad, vileza, bajeza; mezquindad.

meant [ment] *pret.* & *p.p. de* to mean.

meantime [míntaɪm] *adv.* mientras tanto, entretanto; *s.* ínterin, entretanto; in the — en el ínterin, mientras tanto.

meanwhile [mínhwaɪl] = meantime.

measles [mízlz] *s.* sarampión.

measurable [méʒrəbl] *adj.* medible, mensurable; measurably *adv.* marcadamente.

measure [méʒə] *s.* medida; compás (*de música*); cadencia, ritmo; proyecto de ley; ley; beyond — sobremanera; con exceso; dry — medida para áridos; in large — en gran parte, en gran manera; *v.* medir.

measured [méʒəd] *adj.* medido; moderado; acompasado.

measurement [méʒəmənt] *s.* medida; dimensión; tamaño; medición.

meat [mit] *s.* carne; meollo, sustancia; — ball albóndiga; — market carnicería; cold — fiambre.

meaty [mítɪ] *adj.* carnoso; sustancioso.

mechanic [məkǽnɪk] *adj.* & *s.* mecánico; -s *s.* mecánica.

mechanical [məkǽnɪkl] *adj.* mecánico; maquinal.

mechanism [mékənɪzəm] *s.* mecanismo.

medal [médl] *s.* medalla.

meddle [médl] *v* entrometerse o entremeterse; meterse.

meddler [médlə] *s.* entremetido.

meddlesome [médlsəm] *adj.* entremetido.

median [mídɪən] *adj.* mediano, del medio; *s.* punto, línea o número del medio; mediana.

mediate [mídɪet] *v.* mediar; intervenir; arbitrar.

mediation [mídɪéʃən] *s.* mediación, intervención, intercesión.

mediator [mídɪetə] *s.* mediador, medianero, árbitro.

medical [médɪkl] *adj.* médico; — school

escuela de medicina.

medicine [médəsɲ] s. medicina; medicamento; **— ball** pelota grande de cuero; **— cabinet** botiquín; **— man** curandero indio.

medieval [midiívl] adj. medioeval o medieval.

mediocre [midiókə] adj. mediocre, mediano; ordinario.

mediocrity [midiákrətı] s. mediocridad, medianía.

meditate [médətet] v. meditar.

meditation [medətéʃən] s. meditación.

medium [mídiəm] s. medio; medio ambiente; adj. mediano; intermedio; a medio cocer, a medio asar.

medley [médlı] s. baturrillo, mezcla, mezcolanza.

meek [mik] adj. manso, dócil, paciente, sufrido.

meekness [míknıs] s. mansedumbre, docilidad.

meet [mit] v. encontrar(se); reunirse; conocer (personalmente), ser presentado a; ir a esperar (un tren, vapor, o a alguien); satisfacer (deseos, requisitos, etc.); pagar (una deuda); sufragar (gastos); responder a (una acusación); **to — in battle** trabar batalla; **to — with** encontrarse con; tropezar con; topar con; reunirse con; s. concurso, contienda (tratándose de deportes); **track —** competencia de atletas.

meeting [mítın] s. reunión; mitin; sesión; asamblea; encuentro.

megaphone [mégəfon] s. megáfono, portavoz, bocina.

melancholy [mélənkalı] s. melancolía; adj. melancólico.

mellow [mélo] adj. maduro, sazonado; dulce, blando, suave; v. madurar(se), sazonar(se); ablandar(se), suavizar(se).

melodious [məlódıəs] adj. melodioso.

melody [mélədı] s. melodía.

melon [mélən] s. melón.

melt [melt] v. derretir(se); disolver(se); fundir(se).

member [mémbə] s. miembro; socio.

membership [mémbəʃıp] s. número de miembros o socios; asociación; (los) miembros (de un club o sociedad).

membrane [mémbren] s. membrana.

memento [mıménto] s. memento, memoria, recuerdo.

memoir [mémwar] s. memoria, apuntaciones; -s memorias; autobiografía.

memorable [mémərəbl] adj. memorable.

memorandum [memərændəm] s. memorándum; memoria, apunte; —

book memorándum, librito de apuntes, memorial.

memorial [məmórıəl] s. monumento conmemorativo; obra o fiesta conmemorativa; memorial, petición; adj. conmemorativo.

memorize [mémərarz] v. aprender de memoria.

memory [mémərı] s. memoria; recuerdo.

men [men] pl. de **man**.

menace [ménıs] s. amenaza; v. amenazar.

mend [mend] v. remendar; reparar; componer; enmendar; **to — one's ways** enmendarse, reformarse; s. remiendo; reparación; **to be on the —** ir mejorando.

menial [mínıəl] adj. servil, bajo.

menstruation [menstruéʃən] s. menstruo o menstruación.

mental [méntl] adj. mental.

mentality [mentǽlətı] s. mentalidad; ingenio.

mention [ménʃən] s. mención; alusión; v. mencionar, mentar; **don't —** no hay de qué (contestación a "thank you").

menu [ménju] s. menú, lista de platos.

meow [mjau] = **mew**.

mercantile [mɜ́kəntıl] adj. mercantil.

mercenary [mɜ́snɛrı] adj. mercenario.

merchandise [mɜ́tʃəndaız] s. mercancías, mercaderías; **piece of —** mercancía.

merchant [mɜ́tʃənt] s. comerciante; negociante; mercader; adj. mercantil; **— marine** marina mercante.

merciful [mɜ́sıfəl] adj. misericordioso, piadoso.

merciless [mɜ́sılıs] adj. sin piedad, despiadado, incompasivo.

mercury [mɜ́kjərı] s. mercurio; azogue.

mercy [mɜ́sı] s. merced; favor, gracia; misericordia, piedad, compasión; **to be at the — of** estar a merced de.

mere [mır] adj. mero; simple, puro; **a formality** una pura formalidad, nada más que una formalidad, una formalidad no más; **a — trifle** una nonada; **-ly** adv. meramente; sólo, solamente, simplemente.

merge [mɜdʒ] v. combinar(se), unir(se), absorber(se); fundirse.

meridian [mərídıən] adj. & s. meridiano.

merit [mérıt] s. mérito; v. merecer.

meritorious [merətórıəs] adj. meritorio.

merrily [mérəlı] adv. alegremente, con regocijo.

merriment [mérımənt] s. alegría, regocijo.

cijo, júbilo.

merry [mérɪ] *adj.* alegre; jovial; divertido; festivo; — **Christmas** Felices Navidades, Felices Pascuas; **to make — divertirse.**

merry-go-round [mérɪgəraʊnd] *s.* tío vivo, *Am.* los caballitos.

merrymaker [mérɪmekə] *s.* fiestero; **ferguista.**

merrymaking [mérɪmekɪŋ] *s.* regocijo; jaleo, juerga, jolgorio; *adj.* regocijado, alegre, festivo, fiestero.

mesh [meʃ] *s.* malla; red; -**es** red, redes; *v.* enredar, coger con red; **to — gears** engranar.

mess [mes] *s.* rancho, comida (*en el ejército o la marina*); lío, confusión; suciedad; — **of fish** plato o ración de pescado; **to make a — of** revolver, confundir; ensuciar; echar a perder; *v.* revolver, confundir; ensuciar, echar a perder (*generalmente:* **to — up**); **to — around** revolver o mezclar las cosas; entrometerse; **messy** [mésɪ] *adj.* desordenado, desarreglado; sucio.

message [mésɪdʒ] *s.* mensaje; parte (*m.*), comunicación; recado.

messenger [mésndʒə] *s.* mensajero; mandadero.

met [met] *pret. & p.p. de* **to meet.**

metal [métl] *s.* metal; *adj.* de metal, metálico.

metallic [mətǽlɪk] *adj.* metálico.

metallurgy [métlɜdʒɪ] *s.* metalurgia.

metaphor [métəfə] *s.* metáfora.

meteor [mítɪə] *s.* meteoro; estrella fugaz.

meteorological [mitɪərələdʒɪk]] *adj.* meteorológico.

meteorology [mitɪərálədʒɪ] *s.* meteorología.

meter [mítə] *s.* metro; contador (*de gas, agua, electricidad, etc.*).

method [méθəd] *s.* método; técnica.

methodical [məθádɪk]] *adj.* metódico.

metre = meter.

metric [métrɪk] *adj.* métrico.

metropolis [mətrápļɪs] *s.* metrópoli.

metropolitan [metrəpálətņ] *adj.* metropolitano.

mettle [métl] *s.* temple, brío, ánimo, valor.

mew [mju] *s.* maullido, maúllo, miau; *v.* maullar.

Mexican [méksɪkən] *adj. & s.* mejicano o mexicano.

mezzanine [mézənin] *s.* entresuelo.

mice [maɪs] *pl. de* **mouse.**

microbe [máɪkrob] *s.* microbio.

microphone [máɪkrəfon] *s.* micrófono.

microscope [máɪkrəskop] *s.* microscopio.

microscopic [maɪkrəskápɪk] *adj.* microscópico.

mid [mɪd] *adj.* medio (*úsase por lo general en composición*); **in — air** en el aire; *prep.* en medio de, entre.

midday [mídde] *s.* mediodía; *adj.* del mediodía.

middle [mídl] *adj.* medio; intermedio; **Middle Ages** Edad Media; — **finger** dedo de en medio, dedo del corazón; — **size** tamaño mediano; *s.* medio, centro, mitad; **in the — of** en medio de, a la mitad de; **towards the — of the month** a mediados del mes.

middle-aged [mídléʒd] *adj.* de edad mediana, de edad madura.

middleman [mídlmæn] *s.* revendedor; medianero, corredor, agente.

middle-sized [mídlsáɪzd] *adj.* de mediano tamaño, de mediana estatura.

middy [mídɪ] *s.* guardiamarina (*m.*); — **blouse** blusa a la marinera.

midget [mídʒɪt] *s.* enanillo.

midnight [mídnaɪt] *s.* medianoche; *adj.* de (la) medianoche; — **blue** azul oscuro; — **Mass** misa del gallo.

midshipman [mídʃɪpmən] *s.* guardiamarina (*m.*)

midst [mɪdst] *s.* medio, centro; **in the — of** en medio de, entre; **in our — entre nosotros.**

midstream [mídstrim] *s.* el medio (o el centro) de la corriente.

midsummer [mídsámə] *s.* pleno verano, solsticio estival, la mitad del verano.

midterm [mídtɜm]; — **examination** examen a mitad del curso.

midway [mídwé] *adj.* situado a medio camino; equidistante; *adv.* a medio camino; en medio del camino.

midwife [mídwaɪf] *s.* partera, comadrona.

mien [min] *s.* facha, aspecto.

might [maɪt] *imperf. de* **may** podía; podría; pudiera, pudiese; *s.* poder, poderío, fuerza.

mighty [máɪtɪ] *adj.* poderoso, potente, fuerte; *adv.* muy, sumamente.

migrate [máɪgret] *v.* emigrar.

migration [maɪgréʃən] *s.* migración.

mike [maɪk] **= microphone.**

mild [maɪld] *adj.* suave; blando; apacible; templado, moderado.

mildness [máɪldnɪs] *s.* suavidad; mansedumbre; apacibilidad; templanza, dulzura.

mile [maɪl] *s.* milla; —**stone** mojón.

mileage [máɪlɪdʒ] *s.* millaje, número de millas; recorrido (*en millas*). *Compárese* kilometraje, número de kilómetros.

military [mílǝterɪ] adj. militar; de guerra; s. **the —** el ejército; los militares.

militia [mɪlíʃǝ] s. milicia.

milk [mɪlk] s leche; **— diet** régimen lácteo; v. ordeñar.

milkmaid [mílkmed] s. lechera.

milkman [mílkmǝn] s. lechero, Am. vaquero.

milky [mílkɪ] adj. lácteo; lechoso; **Milky Way Vía Láctea.**

mill [mɪl] s. molino; fábrica; la milésima parte de un dólar; **saw —** aserradero; **spinning —** hilandería; **sugar — ingenio** de azúcar; **textile — fábrica** de tejidos; v. moler; aserrar (*madera*); fabricar; acordonar (*el canto de la moneda*); **to — around** arremolinarse (*una muchedumbre*).

miller [mílǝ] s. molinero; mariposa nocturna.

milliner [mílǝnǝ] s. modista (*de sombreros para señoras*).

millinery [mílǝnerɪ] s. sombreros de señora; artículos para sombreros de señora; oficio de modista; **— shop** sombrerería.

million [míljǝn] s. millón; **a — dollars** un millón de dólares.

millionaire [mɪljǝnér] adj. & s. millonario.

millionth [míljǝnθ] adj. & s. millonésimo.

millstone [mílston] s. muela o piedra de molino; carga pesada.

mimic [mímɪk] adj. mímico, imitativo; **— battle** simulacro; s. imitador, remedador; v. imitar, remedar.

mince [mɪns] v. picar, desmenuzar; **not to — words** hablar con toda franqueza.

mincemeat [mínsmit] s. picadillo (*especialmente el de carne, pasas, manzanas y especias*).

mind [maɪnd] s. mente; pensamiento; inteligencia; ánimo, espíritu; propósito, intención; parecer, opinión; **to be out of one's —** estar loco, haber perdido el juicio; **to change one's —** cambiar de parecer; **to give someone a piece of one's —** cantarle a alguien la verdad; echarle a alguien un buen regaño; **to have a — to** estar por; sentir ganas de; **to make up one's —** decidirse, resolverse; **to my —** a mi modo de ver; **to speak one's — freely** hablar con toda franqueza; v. cuidar; atender a, hacer caso de, obedecer; **I don't —** no tengo inconveniente en ello; **never —** no importa; no se

preocupe; no se moleste; no haga Vd. caso; **to — one's own business** atender a lo suyo, no meterse en lo ajeno.

mindful [máɪndfǝl] adj. atento (a); cuidadoso (de).

mine [maɪn] pron. pos. mío (mía, míos, mías); el mío (la mía, los míos, las mías); **a book of —** un libro mío.

mine [maɪn] s. mina; **— sweeper** dragaminas; v. minar; explotar (*una mina*); extraer (*mineral*).

miner [máɪnǝ] s. minero.

mineral [mínǝrǝl] adj. & s. mineral.

mingle [mɪ́ŋgl] v. mezclar(se); entremezclar(se); confundir(se); juntarse.

miniature [mínɪtʃǝ] s. miniatura; adj. en miniatura; diminuto.

minimize [mínǝmaɪz] v. empequeñecer.

minimum [mínǝmǝm] adj. & s. mínimo.

mining [máɪnɪŋ] s. minería, explotación de minas; adj. minero; **— engineer** ingeniero de minas.

minister [mínɪstǝ] s. ministro; pastor, clérigo; v. ministrar; atender; proveer, socorrer.

ministry [mínɪstrɪ] s. ministerio; socorro, ayuda.

mink [mɪŋk] s. visón.

minnow [míno] s. pececillo de río.

minor [máɪnǝ] adj. menor; de menor edad; secundario; **— key** tono menor; s. menor de edad; premisa menor (*de un silogismo*); tono menor; curso o asignatura menor.

minority [mǝnórǝtɪ] s. minoría; minoridad, menor edad; menor parte.

minstrel [mínstrǝl] s. trovador; bardo, vate; actor cómico que remeda al negro norteamericano.

mint [mɪnt] s. menta, hierbabuena (yerbabuena); pastilla o bombón de menta; casa de moneda; **a — of money** un montón de dinero, la mar de dinero; v. acuñar.

minuet [mɪnjuét] s. minué.

minus [máɪnǝs] adj. negativo; sin, falto de; **seven — four** siete menos cuatro; s. menos, signo menos.

minute [mínɪt] s. minuto; **-s** acta (*de una junta*); **— hand** minutero.

minute [mǝnjút] adj. menudo, diminuto; minucioso, detallado.

miracle [mírǝk] s. milagro.

miraculous [mǝrǽkjǝlǝs] adj. milagroso.

mirage [mǝráʒ] s. espejismo.

mire [maɪr] s. cieno, fango, lodo; v. atascar(se) en el fango; enlodar(se).

mirror [mírǝ] s. espejo; v. reflejar.

mirth [mɜe] s. júbilo, regocijo, alegría.

mirthful [mɜefəl] adj. jubiloso, regocijado, gozoso, alegre.

miry [máɪrɪ] adj. cenagoso, fangoso, lodoso.

misbehave [mɪsbihév] v. portarse mal, obrar mal.

miscarriage [mɪskǽrɪdʒ] s. aborto, malparto; mal éxito; extravío (de una carta, papel, etc.).

miscarry [mɪskǽrɪ] v. malograrse, frustrarse; abortar; extraviarse (una carta).

miscellaneous [mɪsləénɪəs] adj. misceláneo, diverso.

mischief [mɪstʃɪf] s. travesura; diablura; mal, daño; diablillo, persona traviesa.

mischievous [mɪstʃɪvəs] adj. travieso; malicioso; dañino.

misconduct [mɪskándʌkt] s. mala conducta; mala administración; [mɪskəndʌ́kt] v. maladministrar, manejar mal; **to — oneself** portarse mal, conducirse mal.

misdeed [mɪsdíd] s. fechoría, mala acción.

misdemeanor [mɪsdɪmínə] s. mal comportamiento; fechoría.

miser [máɪzə] s. avaro, avariento.

miserable [mízrəbl] adj. miserable; infeliz, desdichado.

miserly [máɪzəlɪ] adj. avariento, avaro; tacaño, mezquino.

misery [mízrɪ] s. miseria, desgracia; estrechez, pobreza; dolor.

misfortune [mɪsfórtʃən] s. infortunio, desgracia, desastre.

misgiving [mɪsgívɪŋ] s. mal presentimiento, aprensión, recelo, temor.

mishap [mɪshǽp] s. desgracia, contratiempo, accidente.

mislaid [mɪsléd] pret. & p.p. de to mislay.

mislay [mɪslé] v. extraviar, perder; poner fuera de su sitio, colocar mal; traspapelar (una carta, documento, etc.).

mislead [mɪslíd] v. guiar por mal camino; extraviar, descarriar; engañar.

misled [mɪsléd] pret. & p.p. de to mislead.

misplace [mɪsplés] v. extraviar, poner fuera de su sitio, colocar mal; traspapelar (una carta, documento, etc.).

misprint [mɪsprínt] s. errata, error tipográfico, error de imprenta.

misrepresent [mɪsreprɪzént] v. falsear, falsificar; tergiversar.

miss [mɪs] v. errar, no acertar; fallar; equivocar; perder (una oportunidad, un tren, etc.); faltar a; echar de menos,

Am. extrañar; **he just -ed being killed** por poco le matan; s. error; falla, falta.

miss [mɪs] s. señorita; **Miss Smith** la señorita Smith.

missile [mɪsl] s. proyectil; arma arrojadiza; adj. arrojadizo, que se puede arrojar o tirar.

missing [mɪsɪŋ] adj. ausente; perdido; **one book is —** falta un libro.

mission [mɪʃən] s. misión.

missionary [mɪʃənerɪ] adj. & s. misionero.

misspell [mɪsspél] v. escribir con mala ortografía, deletrear mal.

mist [mɪst] s. neblina, niebla; llovizna, *Am.* garúa; v. lloviznar; anublar.

mistake [məsték] s. error, yerro, equivocación; errata (de imprenta); **to make a —** equivocarse; v. equivocar.

mistaken [məstékən] p.p. de to mistake & adj. equivocado; errado; erróneo, incorrecto; **to be —** estar equivocado, equivocarse, errar.

mister [mɪstə] s. señor.

mistook [mɪstʊ́k] pret. de to mistake.

mistreat [mɪstrít] v. maltratar.

mistress [mɪstrɪs] s. señora; ama, dueña; querida, amante; **school—** maestra.

mistrust [mɪstrʌ́st] s. desconfianza; v. desconfiar de.

mistrustful [mɪstrʌ́stfəl] adj. desconfiado, sospechoso, receloso.

misty [mɪstɪ] adj. brumoso; nublado; empañado; vago, indistinto.

misunderstand [mɪsʌndəstǽnd] v. comprender mal; entender mal; interpretar mal; no comprender.

misunderstanding [mɪsʌndəstǽndɪŋ] s. equivocación; mala interpretación, mala inteligencia; desavenencia.

misunderstood [mɪsʌndəstʊ́d] pret. & p.p. de to misunderstand.

misuse [mɪsjús] s. abuso; mal uso; malversación (de fondos); [mɪsjúz] v. abusar de; maltratar; usar o emplear mal; malversar (fondos).

mite [maɪt] s. óbolo, friolera, pequeñez; criatura.

miter [máɪtə] s. mitra; dignidad de obispo.

mitigate [mítəget] v. mitigar.

mitten [mítn] s. mitón (guante de una pieza y sin dedos).

mix [mɪks] v. mezclar(se); unir(se), juntar(se), asociar(se); **to — someone up** confundir a uno; s. mezcla; confusión, lío.

mixture [mɪkstʃə] s. mezcla; mezcolanza.

moan [mon] s. quejido, gemido; v. gemir; quejarse; lamentar(se).

moat [mot] s. foso.

mob [mab] s. populacho; muchedumbre, gentío, *Am.* bola (*de gente*); v. atropellar; apiñarse o agolparse alrededor de.

mobile [móbl] adj. móvil; movible; movedizo.

mobilization [mobləzéʃən] s. movilización.

mobilize [móblaɪz] v. movilizar.

moccasin [mákəsn] s. *Am.* mocasín (*zapato burdo de cuero*); *Am.* mocasín (*víbora venenosa*).

mock [mak] v. mofar, mofarse de; remedar, imitar; **to — at** mofarse de; burlarse de; s. mofa, burla, escarnio; mímica; remedo; adj. falso, ficticio, imitado; **— battle** simulacro, batalla fingida.

mockery [mókərɪ] s. burla, mofa, escarnio; remedo.

mode [mod] s. modo; manera; moda.

model [mádl] s. modelo; patrón; figurín, maniquí; adj. ejemplar, modelo; **— school** escuela modelo; v. modelar; moldear, formar; posar, servir de modelo.

moderate [mádərɪt] adj. moderado; templado; módico; [mádəret] v. moderar(se); templar(se).

moderation [madəréʃən] s. moderación; templanza.

modern [mádən] adj. moderno.

modernize [mádənaɪz] v. modernizar.

modest [mádɪst] adj. modesto.

modesty [mádəstɪ] s. modestia.

modification [madəfəkéʃən] s. modificación.

modify [mádəfaɪ] v. modificar.

modulate [mádʒəlet] v. modular.

Mohammedan [mohǽmədən] adj. & s. mahometano.

moist [mɔɪst] adj. húmedo; mojado.

moisten [mɔɪsn] v. humedecer; mojar.

moisture [mɔɪstʃə] s. humedad.

molar [mólə] adj. molar; s. muela.

molasses [məlǽsɪz] s. melaza, miel de caña.

mold [mold] s. molde, matriz; moho; tierra vegetal; v. moldear, amoldar; modelar; enmohecer(se), cubrir(se) de moho.

molder [móldə] v. desmoronarse.

molding [móldɪŋ] s. moldura; moldeamiento.

moldy [móldɪ] adj. mohoso.

mole [mol] s. lunar; topo (*animal*); dique, malecón, rompeolas.

molecule [máləkjul] s. molécula.

molest [məlést] v. molestar.

molten [móltn] adj. derretido, fundido, en fusión.

moment [mómənt] s. momento; importancia, consecuencia.

momentary [mómənterɪ] adj. momentáneo.

momentous [moméntəs] adj. importante.

momentum [mómentəm] s. momento (*de una fuerza*); ímpetu.

monarch [mánək] s. monarca.

monarchy [mánəkɪ] s. monarquía.

monastery [mánəsterɪ] s. monasterio.

Monday [mándɪ] s. lunes.

monetary [mánəterɪ] adj. monetario.

money [mánɪ] s. dinero; **— changer** cambista; **— order** giro postal; **paper —** papel moneda; **silver —** moneda de plata; **money-making** lucrativo, provechoso, ganancioso.

mongrel [máŋgrəl] adj. & s. mestizo, mixto, cruzado, *Am.* chusco (*perro*).

monk [mʌŋk] s. monje.

monkey [mʌŋkɪ] s. mono; **—shine** monada, monería; **— wrench** llave inglesa; v. juguetear; hacer monerías; payasear; entremeterse; **to — with** juguetear con; meterse con.

monogram [mánəgræm] s. monograma.

monologue [mánlɔg] s. monólogo, soliloquio.

monopolize [mənáplaɪz] v. monopolizar, acaparar.

monopoly [mənáplɪ] s. monopolio.

monosyllable [mánəsɪləbl] s. monosílabo.

monotonous [mənátnəs] adj. monótono.

monotony [mənátnɪ] s. monotonía.

monster [mánstə] s. monstruo; adj enorme.

monstrosity [manstrásətɪ] s. monstruosidad; monstruo.

monstrous [mánstrəs] adj. monstruoso

month [mʌnθ] s. mes.

monthly [mánθlɪ] adj. mensual; s. publicación mensual; adv. mensualmente

monument [mánjəmənt] s. monumento

monumental [manjəméntl] adj. monumental; colosal, grandioso.

moo [mu] s. mugido; v. mugir.

mood [mud] s. humor, disposición de ánimo; modo (*del verbo*); **to be in** good **—** estar de buen humor; **to be in the —** to estar dispuesto a, tene gana de.

moody [múdɪ] adj. caprichoso, voluble mudable; melancólico, mohíno.

moon [mun] s. luna; mes lunar; once

in a blue — de Pascuas a San Juan, muy rara vez, *Am.* por campanada de vacante, *Am.* a cada muerte de (*o* por la muerte de un) obispo.

moonlight [múnlaɪt] *s.* luz de la luna; **— dance** baile a la luz de la luna; **— night** noche de luna.

moor [mur] *v.* amarrar, atracar (*un buque*); anclar; estar anclado; *s.* terreno inculto o baldío.

Moor [mur] *s.* moro.

Moorish [múrɪʃ] *adj.* morisco, moro.

mop [map] *s. Am.* trapeador; **dust —** limpiapolvo; **— of hair** greñas, cabellera abundante; *v.* limpiar (*el suelo*), *Am.* trapear; **to — one's brow** limpiarse (*o* secarse) la frente; **to — up** limpiar; vencer; acabar con.

mope [mop] *v.* andar quejumbroso o abatido.

moral [mórəl] *adj.* moral; **— philosophy** ética, moral; *s.* moraleja; **-s** moral, ética.

morale [mərél] *s.* moral, entereza de ánimo.

moralist [mórəlɪst] *s.* moralista.

morality [mərǽləti] *s.* moralidad.

moralize [mórəlaɪz] *v.* moralizar.

morbid [mórbɪd] *adj.* mórbido, morboso; malsano.

more [mor] *adj.* & *adv.* más; **— and —** cada vez más, más y más; **— or less** poco más o menos; **there is no —** no hay más, ya no hay; **se** acabó.

moreover [moróvə] *adv.* además.

morning [mórnɪŋ] *s.* mañana; **good — !** ¡buenos días!; **tomorrow —** mañana por la mañana; *adj.* de la mañana; matutino, matinal; **morning-glory** dondiego de día; **— star** lucero del alba.

morphine [mórfin] *s.* morfina.

morrow [móro] : **on the —** el día de mañana; mañana.

morsel [mórsl] *s.* bocado; manjar sabroso.

mortal [mórtl] *adj.* & *s.* mortal.

mortality [mortǽləti] *s.* mortalidad; mortandad.

mortar [mórtə] *s.* mortero; argamasa, mezcla; **metal —** almirez.

mortgage [mórgɪdʒ] *s.* hipoteca, gravamen; *v.* hipotecar.

mortify [mórtəfaɪ] *v.* mortificar; avergonzar.

mosaic [mozéɪk] *adj.* & *s.* mosaico.

mosquito [məskíto] *s.* mosquito; **— net** mosquitero.

moss [mɔs] *s.* musgo; **moss-grown** musgoso, cubierto de musgo; anticua-

do.

mossy [mósɪ] *adj.* musgoso.

most [most] *adv.* más; sumamente, muy; *s.* la mayoría, la mayor parte, el mayor número o cantidad; los más; **— people** la mayoría (*o* la mayor parte) de la gente; **at the —** a lo más, a lo sumo; **for the — part** por la mayor parte; generalmente, mayormente; **the that I can do** lo más que puedo hacer; **the — votes** el mayor número de votos, los más votos.

mostly [móstlɪ] *adv.* por la mayor parte; mayormente, principalmente.

moth [mɔθ] *s.* polilla; mariposa nocturna; **— ball** bolita de naftalina; **moth-eaten** apolillado.

mother [mʌðə] *s.* madre; **mother-of-pearl** madreperla, nácar; *adj.* de madre; materno, maternal; nativo, natal; **— country** madre patria; país natal; **— Superior** superiora; **— tongue** lengua materna; *v.* servir de madre a, cuidar de.

motherhood [mʌðəhud] *s.* maternidad.

mother-in-law [mʌðərɪnlo] *s.* suegra.

motherly [mʌðəlɪ] *adj.* maternal, materno.

motif [motíf] *s.* motivo, tema.

motion [móʃən] *s.* moción; movimiento; ademán; señal, seña; *v.* hacer una seña o señas; indicar.

motionless [móʃənlɪs] *adj.* inmóvil, inmoble.

motion picture [móʃənpfktʃə] *s.* cine o cinematógrafo; película; fotografía cinematográfica; **motion-picture** *adj.* cinematográfico.

motive [mótɪv] *s.* motivo; tema; *adj.* motriz.

motley [mátlɪ] *adj.* abigarrado, multicolor, de diversos colores; variado, mezclado; *s.* mezcla, mezcolanza.

motor [mótə] *s.* motor; automóvil; *v.* pasear o ir en automóvil.

motorboat [mótəbot] *s.* autobote, lancha de gasolina, bote de motor.

motorcar [mótəkar] *s.* automóvil.

motorcoach [mótəkotʃ] *s.* autobús, ómnibus, *Am.* camión, *Am.* guagua.

motorcycle [mótəsaɪkl] *s.* motocicleta.

motorist [mótərɪst] *s.* motorista, automovilista.

motorman [mótəmən] *s.* motorista.

mottled [mátld] *adj.* moteado; jaspeado, manchado.

motto [máto] *s.* mote, divisa, lema.

mould = **mold.**

moulder = **molder.**

moulding = **molding.**

mouldy = moldy.

mound [maʊnd] s. montecillo, montículo, montón de tierra.

mount [maʊnt] s. monte; montura, cabalgadura, caballo; v. montar; montar a caballo; subir, ascender; armar (*una máquina*); engastar (*joyas*).

mountain [máʊntn] s. montaña; adj. montañés; de montaña; — **goat** cabra montés; — **lion** puma; — **range** cordillera, cadena de montañas.

mountaineer [maʊntnír] s. montañés.

mountainous [máʊntnəs] adj. montañoso.

mourn [mɔrn] v. lamentar; deplorar; **to — for** llorar a; estar de duelo por.

mournful [mɔ́rnfəl] adj. fúnebre; lúgubre; lastimero; triste.

mourning [mɔ́rnɪŋ] s. luto; duelo; lamentación; **to be in —** estar de luto, estar de duelo; adj. de luto.

mouse [maʊs] s. ratón; — **trap** ratonera.

moustache = mustache.

mouth [maʊθ] s. boca; abertura; desembocadura, embocadura (*de un río*).

mouthful [máʊθfəl] s. bocado.

mouthpiece [máʊθpis] s. boquilla (*de un instrumento de viento*); portavoz.

movable [múvəbl] adj. movible, móvil; **-s** s. pl. muebles, bienes muebles.

move [muv] v. mover(se); mudarse, mudar de casa; menear(se); conmover; inducir; proponer, hacer la moción de (*en una asamblea*); andar; hacer una jugada (*en ajedrez o damas*); — **away** irse; alejarse; apartarse; **to — forward** avanzar; **to — on** seguir adelante, caminar; **to — out** irse, mudarse, mudar de casa; s. movimiento; mudanza (*de una casa a otra*); paso, trámite (*para conseguir algo*); jugada, turno (*en juegos*); **get a — on there!** ¡ande! ¡dése prisa! Am. ¡ándele!

movement [múvmənt] s. movimiento; maniobra; meneo; acción; mecanismo, movimiento (*de un reloj*); evacuación (*del vientre*).

movie [múvɪ] s. cine, película; **-s** cine.

mow [mo] v. segar; cortar (*césped*).

mower [móə] s. segador; segadora, cortadora mecánica; máquina segadora.

mown [mon] adj. & p.p. segado.

Mr. [místə] Sr., señor; **Mrs.** [mísɪz] Sra., señora.

much [mʌtʃ] adj., adv. & s. mucho; — **the same** casi lo mismo; **as — as** tanto como; **how —?** ¿cuánto?; **not — of a book** un libro de poco valor; **not — of a poet** un poetastro; **so —**

that tanto que; **too —** demasiado; **very —** muchísimo; **to make — of** dar mucha importancia a.

muck [mʌk] s. estiércol húmedo; cieno; porquería, suciedad.

mucous [mjúkəs] adj. mucoso; — **membrane** membrana mucosa.

mud [mʌd] s. lodo, fango, cieno; — **wall** tapia.

muddle [mʌdl] v. enturbiar; confundir; embrollar; s. confusión, embrollo, lío, desorden.

muddy [mʌdɪ] adj. fangoso, lodoso; turbio; confuso; v. enlodar, ensuciar; enturbiar.

muff [mʌf] s. manguito (*para las manos*); falla, error (*en ciertos juegos*); v. no coger, dejar escapar (*un sonido*).

muffin [mʌfɪn] s. bollo, panecillo.

muffle [mʌfl] v. embozar; tapar; apagar, amortiguar (*un sonido*).

muffler [mʌflə] s. bufanda; silenciador (*para maquinaria*).

mug [mʌg] s. pichel, vaso con asa.

mulatto [məláto] s. mulato.

mulberry [mʌlberɪ] s. mora; — **tree** moral.

mule [mjul] s. mulo, mula; **muleteer** [mjuletír] s. arriero.

mull [mʌl] v. meditar, ponderar, revolver en la mente; calentar (*vino, sidra etc.*) con azúcar y especias.

multiple [mʌltəpl] s. múltiplo; adj. múltiple.

multiplication [mʌltəpləkéʃən] s. multiplicación; — **table** tabla de multiplicar.

multiplicity [mʌltəplísətɪ] s. multiplicidad.

multiply [mʌltəplaɪ] v. multiplicar(se).

multitude [mʌltətjud] s. multitud.

mum [mʌm] adj. callado, silencioso; **to keep —** estarse (*o quedarse*) callado.

mumble [mʌmbl] v. murmurar, hablar entre dientes; mascullar; s. murmullo; **to talk in a —** mascullar las palabras, hablar entre dientes.

mummy [mʌmɪ] s. momia.

mumps [mʌmps] s. parótidas, paperas.

munch [mʌntʃ] v. mascar ruidosamente, mascular.

municipal [mjunísəpl] adj. municipal.

municipality [mjunɪsəpǽlətɪ] s. municipio; municipalidad.

munition [mjuníʃən] s. munición; — **plant** fábrica de municiones, arsenal; v. guarnecer, abastecer de municiones.

mural [mjúrəl] adj. & s. mural.

murder [mɜ́də] s. asesinato, homicidio; v. asesinar.

murderer [mɜ́dərə] s. asesino, homicida.

murderess [mɜ́dəris] s. asesina, homicida.

murderous [mɜ́dərəs] adj. asesino, homicida.

murmur [mɜ́mə] s. murmullo; susurro; queja; v. murmurar; susurrar; quejarse.

muscle [mʌ́sl] s. músculo.

muscular [mʌ́skjələ] adj. muscular; musculoso.

muse [mjuz] v. meditar; s. meditación; Muse musa.

museum [mjuzíəm] s. museo.

mush [mʌʃ] s. potaje espeso de maíz; masa de maíz; cualquier masa blanda; sentimentalismo.

mushroom [mʌ́ʃrum] s. seta, hongo.

music [mjúzik] s. música; — stand atril.

musical [mjúzik]] adj. musical, músico; melodioso; armonioso; aficionado a la música; — comedy zarzuela, comedia musical.

musician [mjuzíʃən] s. músico.

muskmelon [mʌ́skmelən] s. melón.

muskrat [mʌ́skræt] s. almizclera (roedor semejante a la rata).

muslin [mʌ́zlɪn] s. muselina.

muss [mʌs] v. desarreglar, desordenar; arrugar.

must [mʌst] v. defect. (por lo general se usa sólo en el presente) deber; deber de, haber de; tener que.

mustache [mʌ́stæʃ] s. bigote, mostacho.

mustard [mʌ́stəd] s. mostaza; — plaster sinapismo.

muster [mʌ́stə] v. pasar lista o revista; juntarse para una formación militar; reunir(se); to — out dar de baja; to — up one's courage cobrar valor o ánimo; s. revista (de soldados o marinos); to pass — pasar lista o revista; ser aceptable (en una inspección).

musty [mʌ́stɪ] adj. mohoso; rancio, añejo.

mute [mjut] adj. mudo; s. mudo; letra muda; sordina (de violín).

mutilate [mjútʃlet] v. mutilar.

mutiny [mjútʃnɪ] s. motín; v. amotinarse.

mutter [mʌ́tə] v. murmurar, refunfuñar; hablar entre dientes; s. murmullo, refunfuño.

mutton [mʌ́tɲ] s. carne de carnero; — chop chuleta de carnero.

mutual [mjútʃʊəl] adj. mutuo.

muzzle [mʌ́zl] s. hocico; bozal (para el hocico); boca (de arma de fuego); v. abozalar, poner bozal a; amordazar; hacer callar.

my [maɪ] adj. mi (mis).

myriad [mírɪəd] s. miríada, diez mil; millares, gran cantidad.

myrtle [mɜ́tl] s. mirto, arrayán.

myself [mɑsélf] pron. yo mismo; me (como reflexivo); a mí mismo; by — solo; I — did it yo mismo lo hice; I talk to — hablo conmigo mismo, hablo para mis adentros.

mysterious [mɪstíriəs] adj. misterioso.

mystery [místrɪ] s. misterio.

mystic [místɪk] adj. & s. místico.

mystical [místɪk]] adj. místico.

myth [mɪə] s. mito, fábula.

mythology [mɪəálədʒɪ] s. mitología.

N

nab [næb] v. agarrar, coger; arrestar.

nag [næg] s. rocín, caballejo, jaco; v. importunar, irritar (con repetidos regaños).

nail [nel] s. clavo; uña (del dedo); — file lima (para las uñas); v. clavar; clavetear; agarrar, atrapar.

naive [naív] adj. simple, ingenuo, cándido.

naked [nékɪd] adj. desnudo.

nakedness [nékɪdnɪs] s. desnudez.

name [nem] s. nombre; renombre, fama; —sake tocayo; by the — of nombrado, llamado; apellidado; family — apellido; to call someone -s motejar o decirle groserías a uno; ponerle apodos a uno; to make a — for oneself ganar fama; what is your — ? ¿cómo se llama Vd.?; v. nombrar; mentar, mencionar; llamar.

nameless [némlɪs] adj. sin nombre; anónimo.

namely [némlɪ] adv. a saber, esto es, es decir.

nap [næp] s. siesta; pelo (de un tejido); to take a — echar un sueño, echar una siesta; v. dormitar; echar un sueño; sestear.

nape [nep] s. nuca, cogote.

naphtha [næpeə] s. nafta.

napkin [næpkɪn] s. servilleta.

narcissus [narsísəs] s. narciso.

narcotic [narkátɪk] adj. & s. narcótico.

narrate [nærét] v. narrar.

narration [næréʃən] s. narración.

narrative [nérətɪv] adj. narrativo; s. narración; narrativa; relato.

narrow [néro] adj. estrecho; angosto; limitado; intolerante; — escape trance difícil, escapada difícil; — search búsqueda esmerada; narrow-minded fanático, intolerante; -s pl. desfiladero, paso; estrecho o estrechos;

v. angostar(se), estrechar(se); limitar, restringir, reducir; **-ly** *adv.* estrechamente; **he -ly escaped** por poco no se escapa.

narrowness [nǽrənɪs] *s.* estrechez, estrechura, angostura, limitación; intolerancia.

nasal [nézl] *adj.* nasal.

nastiness [nǽstɪnɪs] *s.* suciedad, porquería; grosería.

nasturtium [nəstə́ʃəm] *s.* mastuerzo.

nasty [nǽstɪ] *adj.* sucio, asqueroso; feo; indecente; grosero; **a — fall** una caída terrible; **a — disposition** un genio horrible.

nation [néʃən] *s.* nación.

national [nǽʃən] *adj.* nacional; *s.* nacional, ciudadano.

nationality [næʃənǽlətɪ] *s.* nacionalidad.

native [nétɪv] *adj.* nativo; natal; natural; indígena; del país, *Am.* criollo; **— of** oriundo de, natural de; *s.* nativo, natural, indígena; habitante.

nativity [netívətɪ] *s.* nacimiento; natividad (*de la Virgen María*); **the Nativity** la Navidad.

natural [nǽtʃərəl] *adj.* natural; sencillo, sin afectación; *s.* becuadro (*signo musical*); **he is a — for that job** tiene aptitud natural para ese puesto; **-ly** *adv.* naturalmente; con naturalidad.

naturalism [nǽtʃərəlɪzəm] *s.* naturalismo.

naturalist [nǽtʃərəlɪst] *s.* naturalista.

naturalization [nætʃərəlezéʃən] *s.* naturalización.

naturalize [nǽtʃərəlaɪz] *v.* naturalizar.

naturalness [nǽtʃərəlnɪs] *s.* naturalidad.

nature [nétʃə] *s.* naturaleza; natural, genio, índole; instinto; especie; **to copy from —** copiar del natural.

naught [nɔt] *s.* cero; nada.

naughty [nɔ́tɪ] *adj.* malo, desobediente; travieso, pícaro; malicioso.

nausea [nɔ́zɪə] *s.* náusea.

nauseate [nɔ́zɪet] *v.* dar náuseas, dar bascas, asquear; dar asco; sentir náusea; **to be -ed** tener náuseas.

nauseating [nɔ́zɪetɪŋ] *adj.* nauseabundo, asqueroso.

naval [névl] *adj.* naval; **— officer** oficial de marina.

nave [nev] *s.* nave (*de una iglesia*).

navel [névl] *s.* ombligo; **— orange** naranja california (*sin semillas*).

navigable [nǽvəgəbl] *adj.* navegable.

navigate [nǽvəget] *v.* navegar.

navigation [nævəgéʃən] *s.* navegación;

náutica.

navigator [nǽvəgetə] *s.* navegador, navegante.

navy [névɪ] *s.* marina de guerra; armada; **— blue** azul marino; **— yard** astillero, arsenal.

nay [ne] *adv.* no; no sólo ... sino (que) también; *s.* no, voto negativo.

near [nɪr] *adv.* cerca; casi; **— at hand** cerca, a la mano; **I came — forgetting to do it** por poco se me olvida hacerlo; **to come (go, draw) —** acercarse; **—sighted** miope; *prep.* cerca de; **— the end of the month** hacia fines del mes; *adj.* cercano, próximo; estrecho, íntimo; **— silk** seda imitada; **I had a — accident** por poco me sucede un accidente; *v.* acercarse (a).

near-by [nírbáɪ] *adj.* cerca, a la mano; *adj.* cercano, próximo.

nearly [nírlɪ] *adv.* casi, cerca de; aproximadamente, próximamente; **I — did it** estuve al punto de hacerlo, estuve para hacerlo.

nearness [nírnɪs] *s.* cercanía, proximidad.

neat [nit] *adj.* pulcro, aseado, limpio, ordenado; esmerado; hábil, diestro; **-ly** *adv.* aseadamente; esmeradamente; ordenadamente; hábilmente.

neatness [nítnɪs] *s.* pulcritud, aseo; limpieza; esmero; claridad.

necessarily [nésəserəlɪ] *adv.* necesariamente.

necessary [nésəserɪ] *adj.* necesario; **necessaries** *s. pl.* necesidades, requisitos.

necessitate [nəsésətet] *v.* necesitar, precisar.

necessity [nəsésətɪ] *s.* necesidad.

neck [nɛk] *s.* cuello; pescuezo; garganta; **— of land** istmo; **low —** escote; **— and —** parejos (*en una carrera*).

necklace [néklɪs] *s.* collar; gargantilla.

necktie [néktaɪ] *s.* corbata.

need [nid] *s.* necesidad; pobreza; **for — of** por falta de; **if — be** si fuere menester, en caso de necesidad; *v.* necesitar; tener necesidad de; hacerle falta a uno; tener que.

needful [nídfəl] *adj.* necesario; necesitado.

needle [nídl] *s.* aguja.

needless [nídlɪs] *adj.* innecesario, inútil.

needlework [nídlwɜk] *s.* labor, bordado costura.

needy [nídɪ] *adj.* necesitado, menesteroso.

ne'er [nɛr] *adv.* contr. de **never;** ne'er-

do-well s. persona incompetente; haragán.

negation [nɪgéʃən] s. negación; negativa.

negative [négətɪv] adj. negativo; s. negativa; negación, partícula o voz negativa; negativa (de una fotografía).

neglect [nɪglékt] s. negligencia; descuido; abandono; v. descuidar; desatender; abandonar; **to — to** dejar de, olvidar, olvidarse de.

neglectful [nɪgléktfəl] adj. negligente, descuidado.

negligence [néglədʒəns] s. negligencia.

negligent [néglədʒənt] adj. negligente, descuidado.

negotiate [nɪgóʃɪet] v. negociar; agenciar; vencer (un obstáculo o dificultad), dar cima a.

negotiation [nɪgoʃéʃən] s. negociación.

negro [nígro] s. & adj. negro.

neigh [ne] s. relincho; v. relinchar.

neighbor [nébə] s. vecino; prójimo; adj. vecino; cercano.

neighborhood [nébəhʊd] s. vecindad; vecindario; inmediación; **in the — of a hundred dollars** cerca de cien dólares.

neighboring [nébərɪŋ] adj. vecino; cercano; colindante.

neither [níðə] pron. ninguno, ni (el) uno ni (el) otro; **— of the two** ninguno de los dos; adj. ninguno; **— one of us** ninguno de nosotros; conj. ni; **— . . . nor** ni . . . ni; **— will I** tampoco yo, ni yo tampoco.

nephew [néfju] s. sobrino.

nerve [nɜv] s. nervio; valor, ánimo; audacia; descaro; **-s** nervios; nerviosidad; **to strain every —** esforzarse hasta más no poder, poner el mayor empeño posible.

nervous [nɜvəs] adj. nervioso.

nervousness [nɜvəsnɪs] s. nerviosidad; agitación.

nest [nɛst] s. nido; nidada; **— egg** nidal; ahorros; **— of baskets** (boxes, tables) juego graduado de cestas (cajas, mesitas); **wasp's —** avispero; v. anidar.

nestle [nésl] v. acurrucarse; abrigar(se); anidar.

net [net] s. red; malla; tejido de mallas; adj. de mallas, de punto de malla; v. redar, enredar, coger con red; cubrir con una red.

net [net] adj. neto; **— price** precio neto; **— profit** ganancia neta o líquida; v. producir una ganancia neta o líquida; obtener una ganancia líquida.

nettle [nétl] s. ortiga; v. picar, irritar, enfadar.

network [nétwɜk] s. red; malla; **radio —** red de estaciones radiofónicas.

neuter [njútə] adj. neutro.

neutral [njútrəl] adj. neutral; neutro.

neutrality [njutrǽlətɪ] s. neutralidad.

neutralize [njútrəlaɪz] v. neutralizar.

never [névə] adv. nunca, jamás; **— mind** no importa; no haga Vd. caso; no se moleste Vd.; **never-ending** perpetuo, eterno; de nunca acabar.

nevertheless [nevəðəlés] adv. & conj. sin embargo, no obstante, con todo, empero.

new [nju] adj. nuevo; reciente; moderno; fresco; adv. recién; **—born baby** criatura recién nacida.

newcomer [njúkʌmə] s. recién llegado.

newly [njúlɪ] adv. nuevamente, recientemente; **— arrived** recién llegado; **— wed** recién casado.

newness [njúnɪs] s. novedad, calidad de nuevo.

news [njuz] s. noticias, nuevas; novedades; **piece of —** noticia, nueva; **—boy** vendedor de periódicos; **—reel** película noticiera; película de noticias mundiales; **—stand** puesto de periódicos.

newsmonger [njúzmʌŋgə] s. chismoso, chismero, gacetilla.

newspaper [njúzpepə] s. periódico.

next [nɛkst] adj. próximo; entrante, que viene; siguiente; contiguo; **in the — life** en la otra vida; **to be — in turn** tocarle a uno, ser su turno; adv. después, luego; **— best** segundo en cualidad o importancia; prep.; **— to** junto a; al lado de; después de.

nibble [nɪbl] s. mordisco; v. mordiscar, mordisquear; picar, morder.

nice [naɪs] adj. fino; bueno; amable, simpático; lindo; primoroso; refinado, esmerado; preciso, exacto; **-ly** adv. con esmero; con finura o primor; sutilmente, con delicadeza; amablemente; bien; **to get along -ly with** llevarse bien con.

nicety [náɪsətɪ] s. fineza, finura; delicadeza; exactitud.

niche [nɪtʃ] s. nicho.

nick [nɪk] s. mella, desportilladura; **in the — of time** en el momento crítico; v. mellar, desportillar.

nickel [nɪkl] s. níquel; moneda de cinco centavos; **nickel-plated** niquelado.

nickname [níknem] s. mote, apodo; v. apodar, poner apodo a.

niece [nis] s. sobrina.

niggardly [nígədlı] *adj.* mezquino, ruin, tacaño; *adv.* mezquinamente, ruinmente.

night [naɪt] *s.* noche; **good —** ! ¡buenas noches!; **tomorrow —** mañana por la noche; *adj.* nocturno; de noche; **— owl** buho; trasnochador; **— watchman** sereno, vigilante nocturno.

nightfall [náɪtfɔl] *s.* anochecer, caída de la tarde, anochecida.

nightgown [náɪtgaun] *s.* camisa de dormir, camisa de noche, *Am.* camisón.

nightingale [náɪtŋgel] *s.* ruiseñor.

nightly [náɪtlɪ] *adv.* cada noche, todas las noches; *adj.* nocturno, de noche.

nightmare [náɪtmer] *s.* pesadilla.

nimble [nɪmbl] *adj.* ágil, ligero; listo.

nip [nɪp] *v.* pellizcar; mordiscar; marchitar, helar (*por la acción del frío*); **to — in the bud** cortar en germen, destruir al nacer; **to — off** despuntar; podar; *s.* pellizco; mordisco; trago.

nipple [nɪpl] *s.* teta, tetilla, pezón; pezón de goma.

nitrate [náɪtret] *s.* nitrato.

nitrogen [náɪtrɔdʒən] *s.* nitrógeno.

no [no] *adv.* no; **— longer** ya no; **there is — more** no hay más; *adj.* ningún(o); **— matter how much** por mucho que; **— one** ninguno, nadie; **— smoking** se prohibe fumar; **I have — friend** no tengo ningún amigo; **of — use** inútil, sin provecho; *s.* no, voto negativo.

nobility [nobílətɪ] *s.* nobleza.

noble [nóbl] *s.* & *adj.* noble.

nobleman [nóblmən] *s.* noble.

nobleness [nóblnɪs] *s.* nobleza.

nobly [nóblɪ] *adv.* noblemente.

nobody [nóbadɪ] *pron.* nadie, ninguno.

nod [nad] *v.* inclinar la cabeza (*para hacer una seña, saludar, o asentir*); cabecear, dar cabezadas (*dormitando*); *s.* inclinación de cabeza, saludo; señal de asentimiento (*con la cabeza*).

noise [nɔɪz] *s.* ruido; barullo; sonido; *v.* divulgar; **it is being -d about that** corre el rumor que.

noiseless [nɔ́ɪzlɪs] *adj.* sin ruido, silencioso, quieto; **-ly** *adv.* sin ruido, silenciosamente.

noisily [nɔ́ɪzɪlɪ] *adv.* ruidosamente.

noisy [nɔ́ɪzɪ] *adj.* ruidoso.

nominal [námənl] *adj.* nominal.

nominate [námənet] *v.* nombrar, designar.

nomination [namənéʃən] *s.* nombramiento, nominación.

none [nʌn] *pron.* ninguno; ningunos; nada; **I want — of that** no quiero

nada de eso; **that is — of his business** no le importa a él eso; *adv.* no, de ningún modo; **— the less** no menos; **to be — the happier for that** no estar por eso más contento.

nonentity [nanéntətɪ] *s.* nulidad, persona o cosa inútil.

nonsense [nánsens] *s.* tontería, necedad; disparate, desatino.

noodle [núdl] *s.* tallarín, fideo, pasta (*para sopa*).

nook [nuk] *s.* rincón; **breakfast —** desayunador.

noon [nun] *s.* mediodía.

noonday [núnde] *s.* mediodía; *adj.* meridiano, de mediodía; **— meal** comida de mediodía.

noontide [núntaɪd] *s.* mediodía.

noontime [núntaɪm] *s.* mediodía.

noose [nus] *s.* dogal; lazo, nudo corredizo, *Am.* gaza; *v.* lazar, coger con lazo; hacer un lazo corredizo en.

nor [nɔr] *conj.* ni; **neither . . . —** ni . . . ni.

norm [nɔrm] *s.* norma.

normal [nɔ́rml] *adj.* normal; *s.* norma; **normal, línea perpendicular.

north [nɔrθ] *s.* norte; *adj.* septentrional; norteño; del norte; **— pole** polo norte, polo ártico; **— wind** cierzo, norte; **North American** norteamericano; *adv.* al norte, hacia el norte.

northeast [nɔreíst] *adj.* & *s.* nordeste; *adv.* hacia el nordeste, rumbo al nordeste.

northeastern [nɔreístən] *adj.* del nordeste, nordeste.

northern [nɔ́rðən] *adj.* septentrional; norteño; del norte; hacia el norte; **— lights** aurora boreal.

northerner [nɔ́rðənə] *s.* norteño, habitante del norte.

northward [nɔ́rewəd] *adv.* hacia el norte, rumbo al norte.

northwest [nɔrewést] *adj.* & *s.* noroeste; *adv.* hacia el noroeste.

northwestern [nɔrowéstən] *adj.* noroeste del noroeste.

Norwegian [nɔrwídʒən] *adj.* & *s.* noruego.

nose [noz] *s.* nariz; proa (*de un barco*); **— dive** picada (*de un avión*); *v.* olfatear; **to — around** husmear, curiosear.

nostalgia [nastældʒɪə] *s.* nostalgia, añoranza.

nostrils [nástrəlz] *s. pl.* narices, ventanas de la nariz.

not [nat] *adv.* no; **— at all** de ningún modo; de nada (*contestación a* "thank you"); **— at all sure** nada seguro; **— even a word** ni siquiera una palabra.

notable [nótəbl] *adj.* notable.

notary [nótərɪ] *s.* notario.

notation [notéʃən] *s.* notación; apunte; anotación.

notch [natʃ] *s.* muesca, ranura; hendidura; *v.* ranurar, hacer una ranura en.

note [not] *s.* nota; apunte, apuntación; **bank —** billete de banco; **promissory —** pagaré, abonaré; *v.* notar, observar, reparar; **to — down** apuntar.

notebook [nótbʊk] *s.* libreta; cuaderno, libro de apuntes.

noted [nótɪd] *adj.* notable, célebre, famoso.

noteworthy [nótwɜ̃ðɪ] *adj.* notable, célebre.

nothing [nʌθɪŋ] *s.* nada; cero; **for —** por nada; inútilmente; de balde, gratis.

notice [nótɪs] *s.* noticia; aviso, advertencia, anuncio; mención; **to give a short —** avisar a última hora; **to take — of** hacer caso de, prestar atención a; *v.* notar, observar; prestar atención a; hacer caso a (o de); notificar.

noticeable [nótɪsəbl] *adj.* notable; conspicuo; perceptible.

notify [nótəfaɪ] *v.* notificar, avisar.

notion [nóʃən] *s.* noción; idea; capricho; **-s** mercería, artículos menudos (*como alfileres, botones, etc.*), chucherías.

notorious [notórɪəs] *adj.* notorio.

notwithstanding [natwɪθstǽndɪŋ] *prep.* a pesar de; *adv.* & *conj.* no obstante, sin embargo; **— that** a pesar de que.

nought = naught.

noun [naʊn] *s.* nombre, sustantivo.

nourish [nɜ̃rɪʃ] *v.* nutrir, alimentar.

nourishing [nɜ̃rɪʃɪŋ] *adj.* nutritivo, alimenticio.

nourishment [nɜ̃rɪʃmənt] *s.* nutrimento, sustento, alimento; nutrición.

novel [nɑ́vl] *s.* novela; *adj.* novel, nuevo; raro, original.

novelist [nɑ́vlɪst] *s.* novelista.

novelty [nɑ́vltɪ] *s.* novedad; innovación; **novelties** novedades.

November [novémbə] *s.* noviembre.

novice [nɑ́vɪs] *s.* novicio; novato, principiante.

now [naʊ] *adv.* ahora; ya; **— . . . —** ya . . . ya, ora . . . ora; **— and then** de vez en cuando, de cuando en cuando; **— that** ahora que; **— then** ahora bien; **he left just —** salió hace poco,

Am. salió recién.

nowadays [náʊədez] *adv.* hoy día.

nowhere [nóhwer] *adv.* en ninguna parte, a ninguna parte.

noxious [nɑ́kʃəs] *adj.* nocivo.

nucleus [njúklɪəs] *s.* núcleo.

nude [njud] *adj.* desnudo.

nudge [nʌdʒ] *v.* codear, tocar con el codo; *s.* codazo ligero.

nuisance [njúsns] *s.* molestia; lata, fastidio; persona o cosa fastidiosa.

null [nʌl] *adj.* nulo; **— and void** nulo e inválido.

numb [nʌm] *adj.* entumecido o entumido, aterido; **to become —** entumecerse, entumirse, aterirse; *v.* entumecer.

number [nʌ́mbə] *s.* número; *v.* numerar; ascender a (*cierto número*); **to — him among one's friends** contarle entre sus amigos.

numberless [nʌ́mbəlɪs] *adj.* innumerable, sin número.

numeral [njúmrəl] *s.* número, cifra; guarismo; *adj.* numeral.

numerical [njumérɪkl] *adj.* numérico.

numerous [njúmrəs] *adj.* numeroso; numerosos, muchos.

nun [nʌn] *s.* monja.

nuptial [nʌ́pʃəl] *adj.* nupcial; **-s** *s. pl.* nupcias, bodas.

nurse [nɜs] *s.* enfermera, enfermero; niñera, aya, *Am.* nana, *Am.* manejadora, *Am.* pilmama; **wet —** nodriza, ama de cría; *v.* criar, amamantar, dar de mamar, lactar; mamar; cuidar (a *un enfermo*); abrigar (*rencor*).

nursery [nɜ́rsrɪ] *s.* cuarto para niños; criadero, semillero (*de plantas*); **day —** sala donde se cuida y divierte a los niños.

nurture [nɜ́rtʃə] *s.* crianza; nutrimento; *v.* criar; nutrir; cuidar; fomentar.

nut [nʌt] *s.* nuez. (*nombre genérico de varias frutas como la almendra, la castaña, la avellana, etc.*); tuerca; loco, tipo raro o extravagante.

nutcracker [nʌ́tkrækə] *s.* cascanueces.

nutmeg [nʌ́tmeg] *s.* nuez moscada.

nutrition [njutríʃən] *s.* nutrición; nutrimento, alimento.

nutritious [njutríʃəs] *adj.* nutritivo, alimenticio.

nutritive [njútrɪtɪv] *adj.* nutritivo.

nutshell [nʌ́tʃel] *s.* cáscara de nuez (*o de otro fruto semejante*); **in a —** en suma, en breve, en pocas palabras.

nymph [nɪmf] *s.* ninfa.

O

oak [ok] s. roble; encina; — **grove** robledo o robledal; **live** — encina siempreverde.

oar [or] s. remo; v. remar, bogar.

oasis [oésɪs] s. oasis. .

oat [ot] s. avena (planta); **-s** avena, granos de avena.

oath [oθ] s. juramento; blasfemia, reniego.

oatmeal [ótmil] s. harina de avena; gachas de avena.

obedience [əbídɪəns] s. obediencia.

obedient [əbídɪənt] adj. obediente.

obesity [obísətɪ] s. obesidad, gordura.

obey [əbé] v. obedecer.

object [ábdʒɪkt] s. objeto; cosa; complemento (del verbo); [əbdʒékt] v. objetar; oponerse; tener inconveniente.

objection [əbdʒékʃən] s. objeción, reparo; inconveniente.

objective [əbdʒéktɪv] adj. objetivo; — **case** caso complementario; s. objetivo; fin, propósito.

obligate [ábləget] v. obligar, constreñir, comprometer.

obligation [abləgéʃən] s. obligación; deber; deuda; **to be under** — **to** estar obligado a; estar agradecido a, deber favores a.

obligatory [əblígətorɪ] adj. obligatorio.

oblige [əblái.ʒ] v. obligar; complacer; **much -ed!** ¡muchas gracias! ¡muy agradecido!; **to be very much -ed to someone** quedar muy agradecido con alguien.

obliging [əbláɪdʒɪŋ] adj. complaciente, obsequioso, comedido, cortés.

oblique [əblík] adj. oblicuo.

obliterate [əblítəret] v. borrar; arrasar, destruir.

oblivion [əblívɪən] s. olvido.

oblivious [əblívɪəs] adj. olvidado, abstraído.

obnoxious [əbnákʃəs] adj. ofensivo; molesto; odioso.

obscene [əbsín] adj. obsceno.

obscenity [əbsénətɪ] s. obscenidad, indecencia.

obscure [əbskjúr] adj. obscuro; v. obscurecer; ofuscar.

obscurity [əbskjúrətɪ] s. obscuridad.

obsequies [ábsɪkwɪz] s. exequias, honras, funerales.

obsequious [əbsíkwɪəs] adj. obsequioso; servil, zalamero.

observance [əbzɔ́rvəns] s. observancia; ceremonia, rito.

observant [əbzɔ́rvənt] adj. observador; observante.

observation [abzɜvéʃən] s. observación.

observatory [əbzɔ́rvətorɪ] s. observatorio; mirador.

observe [əbzɔ́rv] v. observar; guardar (las fiestas religiosas); celebrar (una fiesta).

observer [əbzɔ́rvə] s. observador.

obsess [əbsés] v. obsesionar, causar obsesión.

obsession [əbséʃən] s. obsesión; idea fija.

obsolete [ábsəlit] adj. anticuado; desusado.

obstacle [ábstək] s. obstáculo.

obstinacy [ábstənəsɪ] s. obstinación, terquedad, porfía.

obstinate [ábstənɪt] adj. obstinado, terco, porfiado.

obstruct [əbstrʌkt] v. obstruir.

obstruction [əbstrʌkʃən] s. obstrucción; impedimento, estorbo.

obtain [əbtén] v. obtener, conseguir, alcanzar, adquirir.

obtainable [əbténəbl] adj. obtenible, asequible.

obviate [ábvɪet] v. obviar; allanar (una dificultad).

obvious [ábvɪəs] adj. obvio, evidente.

occasion [əkéʒən] s. ocasión; oportunidad; causa, motivo; acontecimiento; v. ocasionar, causar.

occasional [əkéʒənl] adj. ocasional; infrecuente, poco frecuente; **-ly** adv. de vez en cuando, a veces.

occidental [aksədéntl] adj. & s. occidental.

occupant [ákjəpənt] s. ocupante; inquilino.

occupation [akjəpéʃən] s. ocupación trabajo, empleo, oficio.

occupy [ákjəpaɪ] v. ocupar.

occur [əkɔ́] v. ocurrir, suceder; **to** — **to one** ocurrírsele a uno, venirle a la mente.

occurrence [əkɔ́əns] s. ocurrencia, suceso, caso, acontecimiento.

ocean [óʃən] s. océano.

o'clock [əklák] contr. de **of the clock it is two** — son las dos.

October [aktóbə] s. octubre.

oculist [ákjəlɪst] s. oculista.

odd [ad] adj. extraño, singular, raro non o impar; — **change** suelto, cambio sobrante; — **moments** momento libres, momentos de ocio; — **shoe** zapato suelto (sin compañero); — **volume** tomo suelto; **thirty** — treinta tantos, treinta y pico; **-ly**; adv. extrañamente, de un modo raro.

oddity [ádətı] *s.* rareza.

odds [adz] *s. pl. o sing.* diferencia, disparidad (*en apuestas*): ventaja, puntos de ventaja (*en apuestas*); — **and ends** retazos, trozos sobrantes, pedacitos varios; **the — are against me** la suerte me es contraria, estoy de mala suerte; **to be at -s with** estar reñido o enemistado con.

ode [od] *s.* oda.

odious [ódıəs] *adj.* odioso.

odor [ódə] *s.* olor; **bad — mal** olor, hedor.

odorous [ódərəs] *adj.* oloroso.

o'er [or] *contr. de* over.

of [av, ʌv] *prep.* de; — **course** por supuesto, claro, ya se ve; — **late** últimamente; **a quarter — five** las cinco menos cuarto; **to smell —** oler a; **to taste —** saber a.

off [ɔf] *adv.* lejos, fuera, a distancia; (*equivale al reflexivo* se *en ciertos verbos*: marcharse, irse, *etc.*); — **and on** de vez en cuando; a intervalos; **ten cents —** rebaja de diez centavos; **ten miles —** a una distancia de diez millas; **to take a day —** ausentarse por un día; descansar por un día; *adj.* ausente; distante, más remoto; quitado; **the — side** el lado más remoto; **with his hat —** con el sombrero quitado; **the electricity is —** está cortada la electricidad; **to be — in one's accounts** estar errado en sus cuentas; **to be — to war** haberse ido a la guerra; **to be well —** ser persona acomodada, estar en buenas circunstancias; *prep.* lejos de; **off-color** de mal color; verde (*indecente*); — **shore** a vista de la costa; — **standard** de calidad inferior; — **the road** desviado, descarriado; a un lado del camino; **to be — duty** no estar de turno; estar libre.

offend [əfénd] *v.* ofender.

offender [əféndə] *s.* ofensor; transgresor, delincuente.

offense [əféns] *s.* ofensa; agravio; delito, culpa; **no — was meant** lo hice (*o* lo dije) sin malicia; **weapon of —** arma ofensiva.

offensive [əfénsıv] *adj.* ofensivo; *s.* ofensiva.

offer [ɔ́fə] *v.* ofrecer; **to — to do it** ofrecerse a hacerlo; *s.* oferta; ofrecimiento; promesa; propuesta.

offering [ɔ́fərıŋ] *s.* ofrenda; oferta; ofrecimiento.

offhand [ɔ́fhǽnd] *adv.* de improviso, por el momento, sin pensarlo, impensadamente; *adj.* impensado, hecho de im-

proviso; **in an — manner** con indiferencia; descuidadamente; sin plan.

office [ɔ́fıs] *s.* oficio; cargo; función; oficina, despacho; — **building** edificio para oficinas; **post — correo; box — taquilla**, *Am.* boletería; **through the good -s of** por el intermedio de.

officer [ɔ́fəsə] *s.* oficial; funcionario; policía, agente de policía; **— commander**, dirigir (*como oficial*); proveer de oficiales.

official [əfíʃəl] *adj.* oficial; *s.* oficial, funcionario; empleado público.

officiate [əfíʃıet] *v.* oficiar.

officious [əfíʃəs] *adj.* oficioso, intruso, entremetido.

offset [ɔfsét] *v.* compensar por; contrapesar.

offspring [ɔ́fsprıŋ] *s.* prole, hijos, descendientes; hijo, vástago; resultado, consecuencia.

oft [ɔft] = **often.**

often [ɔ́fən] *adv.* muchas veces, con frecuencia, frecuentemente, a menudo; **how — ?** ¿cuántas veces?; ¿cada cuándo?

ogre [ógə] *s.* ogro, gigante, monstruo.

oil [ɔıl] *s.* aceite; óleo; petróleo; — **can** alcuza; — **painting** pintura al óleo; — **well** pozo de petróleo; **motor — aceite** para motores; *v.* aceitar, engrasar, lubricar; untar.

oilcloth [ɔ́ılklɔə] *s.* hule, tela de hule.

oily [ɔ́ılı] *adj.* aceitoso, oleoso; grasiento.

ointment [ɔ́ıntmənt] *s.* ungüento.

O.K. [óké] *adj.* bueno; corriente, convenido; *adv.* bien; **it's — está** bien; **to give one's — dar el** V°. B°, (visto bueno); *v.* dar el V°. B°., aprobar.

old [old] *adj.* viejo; antiguo; añejo; — **maid** solterona; — **man** anciano, viejo; — **wine** vino añejo; **days of — días** de antaño; **how — are you?** ¿cuántos años tiene Vd.? ¿qué edad tiene Vd.?; **to be — enough to ...** tener bastante edad para ... ; **to be an — hand** at ser ducho en, ser muy perito o experto en.

olden [óldn] *adj.* viejo, antiguo, de antaño.

old-fashioned [óldfǽʃənd] *adj.* pasado de moda; anticuado; chapado a la antigua.

old-time [óldtáım] *adj.* vetusto, de tiempos antiguos; de antaño.

old-timer [óldtáımə] *s.* antiguo residente.

olive [álıv] *s.* oliva, aceituna; — **grove** olivar; — **oil** aceite de oliva; — **tree** olivo; *adj.* aceitunado, verde aceituna.

omelet [ámlɪt] s. tortilla de huevos.

omen [ómən] s. agüero, presagio.

ominous [ámənəs] adj. siniestro, de mal agüero, amenazador.

omission [omíʃən] s. omisión.

omit [omít] v. omitir; dejar de.

omnipotent [amnípətənt] adj. omnipotente, todopoderoso.

on [an] prep. en; a; sobre, encima de; — all sides por todos lados; — arriving al llegar; — board a bordo; en el tren; — condition that con la condición de que; — credit al fiado; — foot a pie; — horseback a caballo; — Monday el lunes; — purpose a propósito, adrede; — sale de venta; — time a tiempo; a plazo; adv. adelante; farther — más adelante; later — después; — and — sin parar, sin cesar, continuamente; adj. puesto; his hat is — lleva puesto el sombrero; the light is — está encendida la luz.

once [wʌns] adv. una vez; en otro tiempo; — and for all una vez por todas, definitivamente; — in a while de vez en cuando; — upon a time érase que se era; en otro tiempo; at — al punto; a un mismo tiempo; just this — siquiera esta vez, sólo esta vez; conj. una vez que, cuando; luego que.

one [wʌn] adj. un, uno; — hundred cien, ciento; — thousand mil; his — chance su única oportunidad; the — and only el único; one-armed manco; one-eyed tuerto; one-sided de un solo lado; unilateral; parcial; desigual; s. & pron. uno; — another uno a otro; — by — uno a uno; uno por uno; the — who el que, la que; the green — el verde; this — éste, ésta.

oneself [wʌnsélf] pron. se (reflexivo); to speak to — hablar consigo mismo; by — solo; por sí, por sí solo.

onion [ʌnjən] s. cebolla.

onlooker [ánlukə] s. espectador, mirón.

only [ónlɪ] adj. solo, único; adv. sólo, solamente; conj. sólo'que.

onset [ánset] s. embestida, ataque; impulso inicial, primer ímpetu; arranque.

onto [ántu] prep. a; sobre.

onward [ánwəd] adv. adelante; hacia adelante.

ooze [uz] v. rezumar(se), escurrir(se).

opal [óp!] s. ópalo.

opaque [opék] adj. opaco; mate.

open [ópən] v. abrir(se); to — into comunicarse con, tener paso a; to — onto dar a, caer a, mirar a; adj. abierto; franco, sincero; expuesto (a); — country campo raso, campo abierto;

— question cuestión discutible; — to temptation expuesto a caer en la tentación; — winter invierno sin nieve; in the — al aire al (o en el) aire libre; open-minded receptivo; de amplias miras; —mouthed boquiabierto, con la boca abierta; s. campo raso, aire libre.

opening [ópənɪŋ] s. abertura; apertura, comienzo; claro (en un bosque); puesto vacante; oportunidad; adj. primero; — night of a play estreno de una comedia; the — number el primer número (de un programa).

opera [ápərə] s. ópera; — glasses gemelos; — house ópera, teatro de la ópera; comic — ópera cómica, zarzuela.

operate [ápəret] v. operar; funcionar; obrar; maniobrar; manejar; to — on a person operar a una persona.

operation [apəréʃən] s. operación; funcionamiento; manipulación; manejo; maniobra; to be in — funcionar, estar funcionando.

operator [ápəretə] s. operador, cirujano; maquinista, mecánico, operario; especulador (en la Bolsa); mine — explotador de minas; telegraph — telegrafista; telephone — telefonista.

operetta [apərétə] s. opereta, zarzuela.

opinion [əpínjən] s. opinión, parecer.

opium [ópɪəm] s. opio.

opponent [əpónənt] s. contrario, adversario, antagonista.

opportune [apətjún] adj. oportuno; a propósito.

opportunity [apətjúnətɪ] s. oportunidad; ocasión.

oppose [əpóz] v. oponer(se); oponerse a.

opposing [əpózɪŋ] adj. opuesto, contrario.

opposite [ápəzɪt] adj. opuesto; contrario; frontero, de enfrente; — to frente a; prep. frente a, en frente de; s. contrario; the — lo opuesto, lo contrario.

opposition [apəzíʃən] s. oposición; resistencia.

oppress [əprés] v. oprimir; agobiar.

oppression [əpréʃən] s. opresión.

oppressive [əprésɪv] adj. opresivo; abrumador; gravoso; bochornoso, sofocante.

oppressor [əprésə] s. opresor.

optic [áptɪk] adj. óptico; -s s. óptica.

optical [áptɪk!] adj. óptico.

optician [aptíʃən] s. óptico.

optimism [áptəmɪzəm] s. optimismo.

optimist [áptəmɪst] s. optimista.

optimistic [aptəmístik] *adj.* optimista.
option [ápʃən] *s.* opción, derecho de escoger; alternativa.
optional [ápʃənl] *adj.* discrecional.
opulence [ápjələns] *s.* opulencia, riqueza, abundancia.
opulent [ápjələnt] *adj.* opulento, rico; abundante.
or [ər] *conj.* o, u (*delante de* o, ho).
oracle [órək] *s.* oráculo.
oral [órəl] *adj.* oral; bucal.
orange [órɪndʒ] *s.* naranja; — **blossom** azahar; — **grove** naranjal; — **tree** naranjo; *adj.* de naranja; anaranjado.
orangeade [orɪndʒéd] *s.* naranjada.
oration [oréʃən] *s.* discurso, peroración, arenga.
orator [órətə] *s.* orador.
oratory [órətorɪ] *s.* oratoria, elocuencia; oratorio, capilla.
orb [orb] *s.* orbe.
orbit [órbɪt] *s.* órbita.
orchard [órtʃəd] *s.* huerto.
orchestra [órkɪstrə] *s.* orquesta; — **seat** butaca, luneta, *Am.* platea (*de orquesta*).
orchid [órkɪd] *s.* orquídea.
ordain [ordén] *v.* ordenar; decretar.
ordeal [ordíl] *s.* prueba penosa.
order [órdə] *s.* orden; pedido; clase; **holy -s** órdenes sagradas; **in — en** orden; en buen estado; en regla; **in — to** para, a fin de; **in — that** para que, a fin de que; **made to —** mandado hacer, hecho a la medida; **to be out of —** estar descompuesto; estar desordenado; no estar en regla; *v.* ordenar, mandar; arreglar; pedir (*hacer un pedido*); **to — away** echar, despedir, expulsar.
orderly [órdəlɪ] *adj.* ordenado; en orden, bien arreglado; bien disciplinado; *s.* ordenanza (*soldado*); asistente de hospital.
ordinance [órdnəns] *s.* ordenanza, ley, reglamento.
ordinarily [órdnerəlɪ] *adv.* ordinariamente, por lo común.
ordinary [órdnerɪ] *adj.* ordinario.
ore [or] *s.* mineral.
organ [órgən] *s.* órgano; **hand —** organillo.
organic [orgénɪk] *adj.* orgánico; constitutivo, fundamental.
organism [órgənɪzəm] *s.* organismo.
organist [órgənɪst] *s.* organista.
organization [orgənəzéʃən] *s.* organización; organismo; entidad; sociedad.
organize [órgənaɪz] *v.* organizar(se).
organizer [órgənaɪzə] *s.* organizador.

orgy [órdʒɪ] *s.* orgía.
orient [órɪent] *s.* oriente; *v.* orientar.
oriental [orɪéntl] *adj.* & *s.* oriental.
orientate [órɪentet] *v.* orientar.
orifice [órəfɪs] *s.* orificio.
origin [órədʒɪn] *s.* origen.
original [ərídʒənl] *adj.* & *s.* original; **-ly** *adv.* originalmente, originariamente; en el principio, al principio.
originality [orɪdʒənǽlətɪ] *s.* originalidad.
originate [ərídʒənet] *v.* originar(se).
oriole [órɪol] *s.* oriol (*pájaro*).
ornament [órnəmənt] *s.* ornamento, adorno; [órnəment] *v.* ornamentar, adornar, ornar.
ornamental [órnəméntl] *adj.* ornamental, de adorno, decorativo.
ornate [ornét] *adj.* ornado, adornado en exceso; — **style** estilo florido.
orphan [órfən] *adj.* & *s.* huérfano; — **asylum** hospicio, orfanato, asilo de huérfanos; *v.* dejar huérfano a.
ostentation [astəntéʃən] *s.* ostentación, boato.
ostentatious [astəntéʃəs] *adj.* ostentoso.
ostrich [óstrɪtʃ] *s.* avestruz.
other [ʌ́ðə] *adj.* & *s.* otro; — **than** otra cosa que; más que; **every — day** cada dos días, un día sí y otro no; **some — day** otro día.
otherwise [ʌ́ðəwaɪz] *adv.* de otro modo; en otros respetos; *adj.* otro, diferente.
otter [átə] *s.* nutria; piel de nutria.
ought [ɔt] *v. defect.* (*por lo general se traduce por el presente y el condicional de* deber) debo, debes, etc.; debería, deberías, etc.; debiera, debieras, etc.
ounce [auns] *s.* onza.
our [aur] *adj.* nuestro (nuestra, nuestros, nuestras).
ours [aurz] *pron. pos.* nuestro (nuestra, nuestros, nuestras); el nuestro (la nuestra, los nuestros, las nuestras); a **friend of —** un amigo nuestro.
ourselves [aursélvz] *pron.* nosotros mismos; nos (*reflexivo*); a nosotros mismos; **we —** nosotros mismos; **by —** solos; por nosotros; *véase* **herself.**
oust [aust] *v.* echar, expulsar.
out [aut] *adv.* fuera; afuera; hacia fuera; — **of fear** por miedo, de miedo; — **of humor** malhumorado; — **of money** sin dinero; — **of print** agotado; — **of touch with** aislado de, sin contacto con; — **of tune** desentonado; **made — of** hecho de; **to fight it —** decidirlo luchando; **to have it — with** habérselas con; **to speak —** hablar francamente; *adj.* ausente; apagado; — **and — criminal** crimi-

nal empedernido; — **and** — **refusal** una negativa redonda; — **size** tamaño poco común o extraordinario; **before the week is** — antes de que termine la semana; **the book is just** — acaba de publicarse el libro; **the secret is** — se ha divulgado el secreto.

outbreak [áutbrek] s. erupción; ataque; arranque (de ira); motín, insurrección, tumulto; **at the** — **of the war** al estallar la guerra.

outburst [áutbəst] s. explosión; estallido; arranque (de pasión); erupción.

outcast [áutkæst] adj. excluido, desechado; desterrado; s. paria (persona excluida de la sociedad).

outcome [áutkʌm] s. resultado, consecuencia.

outcry [áutkrai] s. grito; clamor.

outdoor [áutdor] adj. externo, fuera de la casa; — **games** juegos al aire libre.

outdoors [autdórz] adv. puertas afuera, fuera de casa, al aire libre, al raso; s. aire libre, campo raso, campiña.

outer [áutə] adj. exterior, externo.

outfit [áutfit] s. equipo; pertrechos; v. equipar, habilitar, aviar.

outing [áutiŋ] s. excursión, gira (jira), caminata.

outlaw [áutlɔ] s. forajido, bandido; prófugo, fugitivo; v. proscribir; declarar ilegal.

outlay [áutle] s. gasto, desembolso; [autlé] v. gastar, desembolsar.

outlet [áutlet] s. salida; desaguadero, desagüe.

outline [áutlain] s. bosquejo, esbozo; contorno; v. bosquejar, esbozar; delinear.

outlive [autlív] v. sobrevivir.

outlook [áutluk] s. vista; perspectiva.

outlying [áutlaiiŋ] adj. circundante, exterior, remoto (del centro).

out-of-date [áutəvdét] adj. fuera de moda, anticuado.

outpost [áutpost] s. avanzada.

output [áutput] s. rendimiento; producción total.

outrage [áutredʒ] s. ultraje; v. ultrajar.

outrageous [autrédʒəs] adj. afrentoso; atroz.

outran [autrǽn] pret. de to outrun.

outrun [autrʌ́n] v. aventajar (en una carrera); dejar atrás; p.p. de to outrun.

outset [áutset] s. comienzo, principio.

outshine [autʃáin] v. eclipsar, sobrepasar (en brillo o lucidez).

outshone [autʃón] pret. & p.p. de to outshine.

outside [áutsáid] adj. exterior, externo; foráneo; adv. fuera, afuera; fuera de casa; prep. fuera de; s. exterior, parte exterior; superficie; lado de afuera; **in a week, at the** — en una semana, a lo sumo; **to close on the** — cerrar por fuera.

outsider [autsáidə] s. foráneo, persona de fuera; extraño.

outskirts [áutskəts] s. pl. alrededores, arrabales, cercanías.

outspoken [áutspókən] adj. franco, francote, Am. claridoso.

outstanding [áutstǽndiŋ] adj. sobresaliente; destacado, notable; — **bills** cuentas por cobrar; — **debts** deudas por pagar.

outstretched [áutstrétʃt] adj. extendido; **with** — **arms** con los brazos abiertos.

outward [áutwəd] adj. exterior, externo; aparente; superficial; adv. fuera, hacia fuera; — **bound** que sale, de salida; para fuera, para el extranjero; **-ly** adv. exteriormente; por fuera; aparentemente.

outweigh [autwé] v. exceder en peso o valor; sobrepujar.

oval [óvl] adj. oval, ovalado; s. óvalo.

ovation [ovéʃən] s. ovación.

oven [ʌ́vən] s. horno.

over [óvə] prep. sobre; por; por encima de; encima de; a través de; al otro lado de; más de; — **night** por la noche, durante la noche; (véase overnight); — **to** a; **all** — **the city** por toda la ciudad; adv. encima; al otro lado; otra vez, de nuevo; — **again** otra vez, de nuevo; — **against** en contraste con; — **and** — una y otra vez, repetidas veces; — **curious** demasiado curioso; — **generous** demasiado generoso; — **here** acá, aquí; — **there** allá, allí; **two years and** — más de dos años; **to do it** — hacerlo otra vez; volver a hacerlo; adj. excesivo; **it is all** — ya se acabó, se ha acabado; ha pasado.

overalls [óvəɔlz] s. pl. Am. overol, overoles (pantalones de trabajo).

overate [ovét] pret. de to overeat.

overboard [óvəbord] adv. al mar, al agua.

overcame [ovəkém] pret. de to overcome.

overcast [óvəkæst] adj. encapotado, nublado; **to become** — encapotarse, nublarse; [óvəkæst] v. nublar o anublar; sobrehilar (dar puntadas sobre el borde de una tela); pret. & p.p. de to overcast.

overcoat [óvəkot] s. sobretodo, abrigo.

overcome [ovəkám] v. vencer; rendir; p.p. & adj. vencido; rendido; agobiado; to be — by weariness estar rendido de fatiga.

overeat [ovít] v. hartarse.

overeaten [ovítn] p.p. de to overeat.

overexcite [óvərıksáıt] v. sobreexcitar.

overflow [óvəflo] s. derrame, desbordamiento, inundación; superabundancia; [ovəfló] v. derramarse, desbordarse; rebosar; inundar.

overgrown [óvəgrón] adj. denso, frondoso, poblado (de follaje, herbaje, etc.); — boy muchachón, muchacho demasiado crecido para su edad.

overhang [ovəhéŋ] v. colgar por encima de; proyectarse o sobresalir por encima de; adornar con colgaduras; amenazar (dícese de un desastre o calamidad).

overhaul [ovəhól] v. reparar (de cabo a rabo); remendar; alcanzar (en una carrera).

overhead [óvəhed] s. gastos generales (renta, seguro, alumbrado, calefacción, etc.); adj. de arriba; elevado; — expenses gastos generales; [óvəhéd] adv. encima de la cabeza, arriba; en lo alto.

overhear [ovəhír] v. oír por casualidad, alcanzar a oír, acertar a oír.

overheard [ovəhɜ́d] pret. & p.p. de to overhear.

overheat [ovəhít] v. recalentar(se); calentar(se) demasiado.

overhung [ovəháŋ] pret. & p.p. de to overhang.

overland [óvəlænd] adv. & adj. por tierra.

overload [ovəlód] v. sobrecargar; [óvəlod] s. sobrecarga.

overlook [ovəlúk] v. mirar a (desde lo alto); dar a, tener vista a; pasar por alto, omitir; perdonar (faltas); descuidar, no notar; inspeccionar, examinar.

overly [óvəlı] adv. excesivamente.

overnight [óvənáıt] adv. durante la noche; toda la noche; adj. de noche; nocturno; — bag saco de noche; — trip viaje de una noche.

overpower [ovəpáuə] v. subyugar, abrumar, vencer.

overran [ovərén] pret. de to overrun.

overrun [ovərán] v. desbordarse, inundar; sobrepasar; infestar, invadir; p.p. de to overrun.

overseas [óvəsíz] adv. en ultramar, allende los mares; adj. de ultramar.

oversee [ovəsí] v. dirigir; vigilar.

overseer [óvəsır] s. sobrestante, capataz; inspector, superintendente.

overshoe [óvəʃu] s. chanclo; zapato de goma, caucho o hule.

oversight [óvəsaıt] s. inadvertencia, negligencia, descuido.

overstep [ovəstép] v. sobrepasarse, propasarse; traspasar; to — the bounds traspasar los límites; propasarse.

overtake [ovəték] v. alcanzar.

overtaken [ovətékən] p.p. de to overtake.

overthrew [ovəθrú] pret. de to overthrow.

overthrow [óvəθro] s. derrocamiento, derrota, destrucción; caída; [ovəθró] v. derrocar; derribar, echar abajo, volcar; destronar.

overthrown [ovəθrón] p.p. de to overthrow.

overtime [óvətaım] adv. & adj. en exceso de las horas estipuladas; — pay sobresueldo.

overtook [ovətúk] pret. de to overtake.

overture [óvətʃə] s. obertura, preludio; propuesta, proposición.

overturn [ovətɜ́n] v. volcar(se); trastornar; derribar; echar abajo.

overwhelm [ovəhwélm] v. abrumar, agobiar; oprimir; arrollar.

overwhelming [ovəhwélmıŋ] adj. abrumador; opresivo; arrollador, irresistible, poderoso.

overwork [óvəwɜ́k] v. atarearse, afanarse más de lo debido, trabajar demasiado; s. exceso de trabajo.

owe [o] v. deber, adeudar.

owing [óıŋ] adj. debido; — to debido a.

owl [aul] s. lechuza, buho, Am. tecolote.

own [on] adj. propio; a house of his — una casa suya; his — people los suyos; to be on one's — no estar a merced ajena; trabajar por su propia cuenta; to come into one's — entrar en posesión de lo suyo; to hold one's — mantenerse firme; v. poseer, tener; admitir, reconocer; to — to confesar; to — up confesar.

owner [ónə] s. dueño, amo; propietario; poseedor.

ownership [ónəʃıp] s. posesión, propiedad.

ox [aks] (pl. oxen [áksn]) s. buey.

oxygen [áksədʒən] s. oxígeno.

oyster [óıstə] s. ostra, ostión.

P

pace [pes] s. paso; v. pasear, andar; andar al paso; marchar; medir a pasos.

149

pacific [pəsífɪk] *adj.* pacífico.

pacify [pǽsəfaɪ] *v.* pacificar, apaciguar; calmar.

pack [pæk] *s.* fardo, lío, carga; manada (*de lobos*); cuadrilla, pandilla (*de ladrones*); jauría (*de perros*); muchedumbre; baraja (*de naipes*); — **animal** acémila, bestia de carga; *v.* empacar, empaquetar; embalar; enlatar; envasar; apiñar(se); cargar (*una bestia*); hacer (*el baúl, la maleta*); **to — off** despedir de repente; echar a la calle; largarse, irse.

package [pǽkɪdʒ] *s.* paquete; fardo, bulto; cajetilla (*de cigarrillos*).

packer [pǽkə] *s.* empacador; embalador, envasador.

packet [pǽkɪt] *s.* paquetillo; cajetilla.

packing [pǽkɪŋ] *s.* embalaje; envase; relleno; — **box** caja para embalar o empacar; — **house** establecimiento frigorífico, fábrica para envasar o enlatar comestibles.

pact [pækt] *s.* pacto, convenio.

pad [pæd] *s.* almohadilla, cojincillo; tableta, bloc de papel; *v.* rellenar; forrar; acolchar.

padding [pǽdɪŋ] *s.* relleno (*de pelo, algodón, paja, etc.*), *Am.* guata; ripio; palabras o frases inútiles.

paddle [pǽdl] *s.* pala; remo de canoa; — **wheel** rueda de paleta; *v.* remar con pala; apalear; chapotear (*en el agua*).

padlock [pǽdlak] *s.* candado; *v.* cerrar con candado.

pagan [pégən] *s.* & *adj.* pagano.

paganism [pégənɪzəm] *s.* paganismo.

page [pedʒ] *s.* página; paje; "botones" (*de hotel*), mensajero; *v.* paginar; vocear, llamar a voces.

pageant [pǽdʒənt] *s.* manifestación, desfile, procesión, pompa; representación al aire libre.

paid [ped] *pret.* & *p.p. de* **to pay.**

pail [pel] *s.* balde, cubo, cubeta.

pain [pen] *s.* dolor; sufrimiento; **-s** esmero; **on** (**under**) — **of** so pena de; **to be in** — estar sufriendo, tener dolores; **to take -s** esmerarse, extremarse; *v.* doler; causar dolor; afligir.

painful [pénfəl] *adj.* doloroso; penoso; arduo.

painless [pénlɪs] *adj.* sin dolor; libre de dolor.

painstaking [pénztekɪŋ] *adj.* esmerado, cuidadoso; aplicado.

paint [pent] *s.* pintura, color; colorete; *v.* pintar; pintarse (*la cara*); **to — the town red** irse de juerga o de parranda,

Am. irse de farra.

paintbrush [péntbrʌʃ] *s.* pincel; brocha.

painter [péntə] *s.* pintor.

painting [péntɪŋ] *s.* pintura.

pair [per] *s.* par; pareja; **a — of scissors** unas tijeras; *v.* aparear(se); hacer pareja, hacer pares; **to — off** aparear(se).

pajamas [pədʒǽməz] *s. pl.* pijama.

pal [pæl] *s.* compañero, camarada.

palace [pǽlɪs] *s.* palacio.

palate [pǽlɪt] *s.* paladar.

pale [pel] *adj.* pálido; descolorido; *v.* palidecer, ponerse pálido o descolorido.

paleness [pélnɪs] *s.* palidez.

palisade [pæləséd] *s.* palizada, estacada; **-s** riscos, acantilados.

pall [pol] *v.* empalagar; aburrir; **it -s on me me empalaga**; me aburre; *s.* paño de ataúd; palia (*lienzo que se pone encima del cáliz*).

pallid [pǽlɪd] *adj.* pálido.

pallor [pǽlə] *s.* palidez.

palm [pam] *s.* palma; palmera; — **Sunday** Domingo de Ramos; — **tree** palma, palmera; *v.* **to — something off on someone** pasar o dar algo indeseable a una persona (*sin que se dé cuenta de ello*).

palpable [pǽlpəbl] *adj.* palpable, tangible; evidente.

palpitate [pǽlpətet] *v.* palpitar, latir.

palpitation [pælpətéʃən] *s.* palpitación; latido.

paltry [póltrɪ] *adj.* mezquino, miserable, despreciable, insignificante.

pamper [pǽmpə] *v.* mimar, consentir (*a un niño*).

pamphlet [pǽmflɪt] *s.* folleto, *Am.* panfleto.

pan [pæn] *s.* cazuela, cacerola; cazo; platillo (*de balanza*); **dish —** cazo para lavar platos; **frying —** sartén; *v.* **to — out** (**well**) salir bien, dar buen resultado.

Pan-American [pænəmérəkən] *adj.* panamericano.

pancake [pǽnkek] *s.* tortita de harina, *Am.* panqué.

pander [pǽndə] *s.* alcahuete, encubridor; *v.* alcahuetear, servir de alcahuete.

pane [pen] *s.* vidrio, cristal (*de ventana o puerta*); cuadro (*de vidrio*).

panel [pǽnl] *s.* panel, tablero; cuarterón (*de puerta, ventana, etc.*); tabla (*doble pliegue de una falda o vestido*); **jury —** jurado; *v.* proveer de (*o adornar con*) paneles.

pang [pæŋ] *s.* dolor agudo; angustia,

tormento.

panic [pǽnɪk] *adj. & s.* pánico; **panic-stricken** sobrecogido de pánico.

pansy [pǽnzɪ] *s.* pensamiento (*flor*).

pant [pænt] *v.* jadear; palpitar; **to —** anhelar, ansiar.

panther [pǽnɵə] *s.* pantera.

panting [pǽntɪŋ] *s.* jadeo, palpitación; *adj.* jadeante.

pantry [pǽntrɪ] *s.* despensa

pants [pænts] *s. pl.* pantalones.

papa [pápə] *s.* papá.

papal [pépl] *adj.* papal.

paper [pépə] *s.* papel; periódico; tema, ensayo, **-s** papeles, documentos, credenciales; **naturalization -s** carta de naturaleza, certificado de ciudadanía; **— of pins** cartón de alfileres; **on —** escrito; por escrito; *adj.* de papel; **para papel; — doll** muñeca de papel; **— money** papel moneda; **—weight** pisapapeles; *v.* empapelar.

paprika [pǽprɪkə] *s.* pimentón.

par [par] *s.* paridad, igualdad; valor nominal; **— value** valor a la par; **above —** sobre par, a premio, con prima; **at —** a la par; **below —** bajo par, a descuento; **on a —** **with** al par de, al nivel de, igual a; **to feel above —** sentirse mejor que de ordinario; **to feel below —** sentirse menos bien que de ordinario.

parable [pǽrəbl] *s.* parábola (*alegoría bíblica*).

parachute [pǽrəʃut] *s.* paracaídas.

parachutist [pǽrəʃutɪst] *s.* paracaidista.

parade [pəréd] *s.* parada, desfile, procesión; paseo; **— ground** campo de maniobras; **to make a —** **of** ostentar, hacer ostentación de; *v.* desfilar, pasar en desfile; marchar en parada; hacer ostentación de.

paradise [pǽrədais] *s.* paraíso.

paradox [pǽrədaks] *s.* paradoja.

paraffin [pǽrəfɪn] *s.* parafina.

paragraph [pǽrəgræf] *s.* párrafo; *v.* dividir en párrafos.

Paraguayan [pærəgwáiən] *adj. & s.* paraguayo.

parallel [pǽrəlel] *adj. & s.* paralelo; *v.* ser (o correr) paralelo a; comparar, cotejar.

paralysis [pərǽləsɪs] *s.* parálisis.

paralyze [pǽrəlaɪz] *v.* paralizar.

paramount [pǽrəmaunt] *adj.* importantísimo, superior, supremo, máximo.

parapet [pǽrəpɪt] *s.* parapeto.

parasite [pǽrəsaɪt] *s.* parásito.

parasol [pǽrəsɔl] *s.* parasol, sombrilla.

parcel [pársl] *s.* paquete; parcela, por-

ción, lote (*de terreno*); **— post** paquete postal; *v.* parcelar, dividir en porciones o parcelas; hacer paquetes; **to — out** repartir.

parch [partʃ] *v.* resecar(se); tostar(se).

parchment [pártʃmənt] *s.* pergamino.

pardon [párdn] *s.* perdón; indulto; **I beg your —** perdone Vd.; dispense Vd.; *v.* perdonar; dispensar; indultar.

pare [per] *v.* mondar, pelar (*manzanas, patatas, etc.*); cortar, recortar; **to — down expenditures** reducir gastos.

parent [pérənt] *s.* padre, madre; origen; **-s** padres.

parentage [pérəntɪdʒ] *s.* linaje; padres.

parenthesis [pərénɵəsɪs] (*pl.* **parentheses** [pərénəsiz]) *s.* paréntesis.

parish [pǽrɪʃ] *s.* parroquia.

parishioner [pərʃǿənə] *s.* parroquiano, feligrés; **-s** fieles, feligreses.

park [park] *s.* parque; *v.* estacionar, dejar (*un automóvil*); estacionarse; **-ing lot** *Am.* playa de estacionamiento; **-ing space** sitio o lugar para estacionarse; **free -ing** estacionamiento gratis; **no -ing** se prohibe estacionarse; no estacionarse.

parley [párlɪ] *s.* parlamento, discusión, conferencia; *v.* parlamentar, discutir.

parliament [párləmənt] *s.* parlamento.

parliamentary [parləméntərɪ] *adj.* parlamentario.

parlor [párlə] *s.* sala, salón; sala de recibo; **— car** coche salón; **beauty —** salón de belleza.

parochial [pərókɪəl] *adj.* parroquial.

parody [pǽrədɪ] *s.* parodia; *v.* parodiar.

parole [pəról] *s.* palabra de honor; **to put on —** dejar libre (*a un prisionero*) bajo palabra de honor; *v.* dejar libre bajo palabra de honor.

parrot [pǽrət] *s.* cotorra, loro, perico, papagayo; *v.* remedar, repetir como loro.

parry [pǽrɪ] *v.* parar, quitar o reparar (*un golpe*), *s.* quite, reparo.

parsley [párslɪ] *s.* perejil.

parsnip [pársnəp] *s.* chirivía (*legumbre*).

parson [pársn] *s.* pastor, clérigo.

part [part] *s.* parte (*f.*); papel (*dramático*); raya (*del cabello*); **— and parcel** parte esencial o inherente; **— owner** condueño, dueño en parte; **— time** parte del tiempo; **in foreign -s** en el extranjero, en países extranjeros; **spare -s** piezas accesorias, piezas de repuesto (o de refacción); **to do your —** haga Vd. cuanto esté de su parte; *v.* partir(se); separar(se); **to — company** separarse; **to — from** separarse de, despedirse de; **to — one's hair** hacerse la raya; **to — with** separarse de, despedirse de, deshacerse de.

partake [parték] v. tomar parte, tener parte, participar.

partaken [partékən] p.p. de **to partake.**

partial [párʃəl] adj. parcial; **-ly** adv. parcialmente, en parte; con parcialidad.

partiality [parʃǽlətɪ] s. parcialidad.

participant [partísəpənt] adj. & s. participante, partícipe, copartícipe.

participate [partísəpet] v. participar.

participation [partɪsəpéʃən] s. participación.

participle [pártəsəpl] s. participio; **present — gerundio.**

particle [pártɪkl] s. partícula.

particular [partíkjələ] adj. particular; peculiar, esmerado, exacto; escrupuloso; quisquilloso, exigente; s. particular, detalle, circunstancia; **in —** en particular, especialmente; **-ly** adv. particularmente; en particular.

parting [pártɪŋ] s. despedida; separación; bifurcación; **the — of the ways** encrucijada, bifurcación, cruce de caminos; adj. de despedida, último.

partisan [pártəzn] adj. partidario; parcial; s. partidario; secuaz, seguidor.

partition [partíʃən] s. partición; división, separación; tabique, Am. medianía; v. partir, dividir; repartir.

partly [pártlɪ] adv. en parte.

partner [pártnə] s. socio, consocio; compañero; **dancing —** pareja de baile.

partnership [pártnəʃɪp] s. sociedad, compañía.

partook [partúk] pret. de **to partake.**

partridge [pártrɪdʒ] s. perdiz.

party [pártɪ] s. tertulia, reunión, fiesta; grupo, partida (de gente) parte (en un pleito, contrato); **hunting —** partida de caza; **political —** partido político.

pass [pæs] s. paso; pase, permiso de entrar; aprobación (en un examen); trance, situación; **— key** llave maestra; **to come to —** suceder; v. pasar; pasar por; pronunciar (sentencia), dar (un juicio o parecer); aprobar (a un estudiante); adoptar (una ley); ser aprobado en (un examen); **to — away** pasar a mejor vida, morir; desaparecer; pasar (el tiempo).

passable [pǽsəbl] adj. pasable, transitable; pasadero, regular, mediano.

passage [pǽsɪdʒ] s. pasaje; paso, tránsito; transcurso (del tiempo); pasillo, pasadizo; travesía, viaje por mar; aprobación (de un proyecto de ley); adopción (de una ley).

passenger [pǽsndʒə] s. pasajero; **the -s** los pasajeros; el pasaje.

passer-by [pǽsəbáɪ] s. transeúnte, viandante.

passion [pǽʃən] s. pasión; **Passion play** drama de la Pasión; **to fly into a —** montar en cólera, encolerizarse.

passionate [pǽʃənɪt] adj. apasionado.

passive [pǽsɪv] adj. pasivo; s. voz pasiva.

passport [pǽsport] s. pasaporte.

password [pǽswɜd] s. consigna, contraseña, santo y seña.

past [pæst] adj. pasado; último; **— master** perito; **the — president** el expresidente, el último presidente; **— tense** tiempo pasado; pretérito; **for some time —** desde hace algún tiempo, de poco tiempo a esta parte; prep. **— bearing** insoportable; **— understanding** incomprensible; **half — two** las dos y media; **woman — forty** cuarentona, mujer de más de cuarenta años; **to go — the house** pasar por (o por enfrente de) la casa; s. pasado; pretérito; pretérito imperfecto; **man with a —** hombre de dudosos antecedentes.

paste [pest] s. pasta; engrudo; v. pegar (con engrudo).

pasteboard [péstbord] s. cartón; **— box** caja de cartón.

pasteurize [péstəraɪz] v. pasterizar (o pasteurizar).

pastime [péstaɪm] s. pasatiempo.

pastor [péstə] s. pastor, clérigo, cura.

pastoral [péstərəl] adj. pastoril; pastoral; s. pastoral, carta pastoral; écloga; pastorela, idilio.

pastry [péstrɪ] s. pastelería, pasteles; **— cook** pastelero; **— shop** pastelería.

pasture [péstʃə] s. pastura, pasto; dehesa; v. pastar, pacer; apacentar(se).

pat [pæt] adj. apto, oportuno; **to have a lesson —** saber al dedillo la lección; **to stand —** mantenerse firme; adv. a propósito; oportunamente; de molde; s. palmadita, caricia, golpecito; **— of butter** cuadrito de mantequilla; v. dar palmaditas a; acariciar; pasar la mano (para alisar o acariciar).

patch [pætʃ] s. remiendo; parche; mancha; pedazo (de terreno); sembrado; v. remendar; **to — up a quarrel** hacer las paces.

pate [pet] s. coronilla (de la cabeza); **bald —** calva.

patent [pǽtnt] adj. patente, evidente, manifiesto; de patente; **— leather** charol; **— medicine** medicina de

PAT—PED

patente; — right patente; s..patente;
v. patentar.
paternal [pətə́nl] adj. paternal, paterno.
paternity.[pətə́nətɪ] s. paternidad.
path [pæθ] s. senda, sendero; vereda;
ruta; trayectoria (de una bala).
pathetic [pəθέtɪk] adj. patético.
pathos [péθɑs] s. patetismo, cualidad
patética.
pathway [pǽθwe] s. senda, vereda, vía.
patience [péʃəns] s. paciencia.
patient [péʃənt] adj. paciente; pacienzudo; s. paciente, enfermo.
patriarch [pétrɪɑrk] s. patriarca.
patriarchal [petrɪárkl] adj. patriarcal.
patrimony [pǽtrəmonɪ] s. patrimonio.
patriot [pétrɪət] s. patriota.
patriotic [petrɪɑtɪk] adj. patriótico.
patriotism [pétrɪətɪzəm] s. patriotismo.
patrol [pətról] s. patrulla; ronda; v.
patrullar, rondar.
patron [pétrən] s. patrón, patrono; benefactor; cliente, parroquiano; —
saint santo patrón.
patronage [pétrənɪdʒ] s. patrocinio,
amparo; clientela; condescendencia;
political — control de nombramien-
tos políticos.
patroness [pétrənɪs] s. patrona, pro-
tectora.
patronize [pétrənaɪz] v. patrocinar, amparar; tratar con condescendencia;
favorecer, ser parroquiano de.
patter [pǽtə] v. golpetear ligeramente;
talonear; charlar, parlotear; s. golpeteo; golpecitos; taloneo; charla, parloteo.
pattern [pǽtən] s. modelo; dechado;
muestra; ejemplo; patrón, molde;
diseño, dibujo (en tejidos, telas, etc.);
v. to — oneself after seguir el
ejemplo de; to — something after
(on, upon) forjar o modelar algo a
imitación de.
paunch [pɔntʃ] s. panza, barriga.
pause [pɔz] s. pausa; v. pausar, hacer
pausa; detenerse, parar.
pave [pev] v. pavimentar; to — the
way for preparar o abrir el camino
para; to — with bricks enladrillar;
to — with flagstones enlosar.
pavement — enladrillado.
pavilion [pəvɪljən] s. pabellón.
paw [pɔ] s. garra, zarpa; v. echar la
zarpa; arañar; manosear; to — the
ground patear la tierra (dícese del
caballo).
pawn [pɔn] s. prenda, empeño; peón
(de ajedrez); —broker prestamista,

prendero; —shop empeño, casa de empeños, montepío; in — en prenda; v. empeñar, dejar en prenda.
pay [pe] v. pagar; costear; ser prove-choso; valer la pena; to — attention prestar atención; to — back resti-tuir, devolver; to — court hacer la corte; to — down pagar al contado; to — homage hacer o rendir home-naje; to — one's respects presentar sus respetos; to — a visit hacer una visita; s. pago; recompensa; paga; sueldo; —day día de pagos, Am. día de raya; —master pagador, Am. rayador; — roll nómina.
payable [péəbl] adj. pagadero.
payment [pémənt] s. pago; paga; — in full pago total.
pea [pi] s. guisante, chícharo; sweet — guisante de olor.
peace [pis] s. paz.
peaceable [písəbl] adj. pacífico, tran-quilo.
peaceful [písfəl] adj. pacífico; tranquilo, quieto, sosegado.
peach [pitʃ] s. melocotón, durazno; per-sona bella o admirable; — tree duraz-no, duraznero, melocotonero.
peacock [píkɑk] s. pavón, pavo real; to act like a — pavonearse, hacer ostentación.
peak [pik] s. pico, cumbre, cima; cús-pide; punto máximo.
peal [pil] s. repique (de campanas); — of laughter carcajada, risotada; — of thunder trueno; v. repicar (las campanas).
peanut [pínət] s. cacahuate, Am. maní.
pear [per] s. pera; — tree peral; alli-gator — aguacate, Am. palta (variedad sudamericana).
pearl [pɜrl] s. perla; — necklace collar de perlas; mother-of-pearl nácar, madreperla.
pearly [pɜ́rlɪ] adj. perlino; nacarado; aperlado.
peasant [péznt] adj. & s. campesino, rústico, Am. jíbaro, Am. guajiro.
pebble [pébl] s. guija, china, guijarro, piedrecilla.
peck [pek] v. picar, picotear; s. picotazo, picotada; medida de áridos (aproxi-madamente 9 litros); a — of trouble la mar de disgustos o molestias.
peculiar [pɪkjúljə] adj. peculiar; raro, singular, extraño.
peculiarity. [pɪkjulɪǽrətɪ] s. peculiari-dad; particularidad; rareza.
pedagogue [pédəgɑg] s. pedagogo, dó-mine.

153

pedal [pédl] s. pedal; v. pedalear, mover los pedales.

pedant [pédnt] s. pedante.

pedantic [pɪdǽntɪk] adj. pedante, pedantesco.

peddle [pédl] v. ir vendiendo de puerta en puerta; **to — gossip** chismear

peddler [pédlɚ] s. buhonero, vendedor ambulante.

pedestal [pédɪstl] s. pedestal.

pedestrian [pədéstrɪən] s. peatón, transeúnte, viandante; adj. pedestre.

pedigree [pédəgri] s. linaje, genealogía.

peek [pik] v. atisbar, espiar; s. atisbo.

peel [pil] s corteza, cáscara (de algunas frutas); pellejo (de patatas); v. pelar(se), descortezar(se), deshollejar(se); **to keep one's eye -ed** tener los ojos muy abiertos, estar alerta.

peep [pip] v. atisbar, espiar; asomar(se); pipiar, piar; s. atisbo; ojeada; pío (de pollo o ave).

peer [pɪr] s. par, igual; noble; v. mirar con atención, atisbar; asomar; **to — into other people's business** fisgar, curiosear.

peeve [piv] v. irritar, poner de mal humor; **to get -d** amoscarse, ponerse de mal humor.

peevish [pívɪʃ] adj. enojadizo; malhumorado.

peg [peg] s. espiga, clavo de madera, estaquilla; clavija (de violín); **to take a person down a** — rebajar o humillar a alguien; v. clavar, clavetear; poner estaquillas; **to — along** atarearse, trabajar con tesón.

pellet [pélɪt] s. pelotilla; píldora; bola.

pell-mell [pélmél] adj. confuso, tumultuoso; adv. a trochemoche, atropelladamente, en tumulto.

pelt [pelt] s. zalea, cuero (especialmente de oveja); piel; v. golpear; **to — with stones** apedrear, arrojar piedras a.

pen [pɛn] s. pluma (para escribir); corral; redil; **—holder** mango de pluma, portapluma; **— name** nombre de pluma; **fountain —** pluma fuente, pluma estilográfica; **pig —** pocilga; v. escribir (con pluma); acorralar, encerrar.

penal [pínl] adj. penal.

penalty [pénlti] s. pena, castigo; multa.

penance [pénəns] s. penitencia.

pencil [pénsl] s. lápiz; lapicero; **— sharpener** tajalápiz.

pendant [péndənt] s. pendiente (adorno que cuelga); adj. pendiente.

pending [péndɪŋ] adj. pendiente; colgado; prep. durante.

pendulum [péndʒələm] s. péndulo.

penetrate [pénətret] v. penetrar.

penetrating [pénətretɪŋ] adj. penetrante.

penetration [penətréʃən] s. penetración.

peninsula [pənínsələ] s. península.

penitent [pénətənt] adj. arrepentido, penitente; s. penitente.

penitentiary [penəténʃɚɪ] s. penitenciaría, presidio.

penknife [pénnaɪf] s. cortaplumas; navaja.

penmanship [pénmənʃɪp] s. escritura, caligrafía.

pennant [pénənt] s. banderola, gallardete.

penniless [pénɪlɪs] adj. pobre, sin dinero.

penny [péni] s. centavo (de dólar); **to cost a pretty —** costar un ojo de la cara, costar un dineral.

pension [pénʃən] s. pensión; retiro (de un militar); v. pensionar.

pensive [pénsɪv] adj. pensativo.

pent [pent] adj. encerrado; acorralado; **pent-up emotions** sentimientos reprimidos.

people [pípl] s. gente; pueblo; v. poblar.

pepper [pépɚ] s. pimienta; **— plant** pimentero; **— shaker** pimentero; **green -s** pimientos verdes; **red —** pimentón, chile, Am. ají; v. sazonar con pimienta; **to — with bullets** acribillar a balazos.

peppermint [pépɚmɪnt] s. menta; pastilla o bombón de menta.

per [pɚ] prep. por; **— capita** por cabeza; **— cent** por ciento; **— year** al año; **ten cents — dozen** diez centavos por docena (o diez centavos la docena).

percale [pɚkél] s. percal.

perceive [pɚsív] v. percibir.

percentage [pɚséntɪdʒ] s. porcentaje, tanto por ciento.

perceptible [pɚséptəbl] adj. perceptible.

perception [pɚsépʃən] s. percepción.

perch [pɚtʃ] s. percha (para pájaros); perca (pez); v. encaramar(se); posarse (en una percha o rama).

perchance [pɚtʃǽns] adv. por ventura, acaso, quizás, tal vez.

percolate [pɚkəlet] v. filtrar(se), colar(se); rezumarse; penetrar.

perdition [pɚdíʃən] s. perdición.

perennial [pɚénɪəl] adj. perenne; continuo; perpetuo.

perfect [pɚfɪkt] adj. perfecto; completo; s. tiempo perfecto (del verbo); [pɚfékt]

v. perfeccionar.
perfection [pəfékʃən] *s.* perfección.
perfidious [pəffdɪəs] *adj.* pérfido.
perfidy [pɜ́fɪdɪ] *s.* perfidia.
perforate [pɜ́fəret] *v.* perforar.
perform [pəfɔ́rm] *v.* ejecutar; llevar a cabo, cumplir, hacer; funcionar (*una máquina*); desempeñar o representar un papel.
performance [pəfɔ́rməns] *s.* ejecución; desempeño, cumplimiento, funcionamiento (*de una máquina o motor*); función, representación; acto, acción.
perfume [pɜ́fjum] *s.* perfume; [pəfjúm] *v.* perfumar.
perfumery [pəfjúmərɪ] *s.* perfumería; perfumes.
perhaps [pəhǽps] *adv.* acaso, tal vez, quizá (*o* quizás), puede ser.
peril [pérəl] *s.* peligro; riesgo, *v.* poner en peligro.
perilous [pérələs] *adj.* peligroso.
perimeter [perímətə] *s.* perímetro.
period [pírɪəd] *s.* período; punto final; fin, término.
periodic [pɪrɪádɪk] *adj.* periódico.
periodical [pɪrɪádɪk] *adj.* periódico; *s.* revista, publicación periódica.
perish [périʃ] *v.* perecer.
perishable [périʃəbl] *adj.* perecedero; deleznable.
perjure [pɜ́dʒə] *v.* **to — oneself** perjurar.
perjury [pɜ́dʒrɪ] *s.* perjurio, juramento falso.
permanence [pɜ́mənəns] *s.* permanencia.
permanent [pɜ́mənənt] *adj.* permanente; duradero.
permeate [pɜ́mɪet] *v.* penetrar, saturar; difundirse por, filtrarse por.
permissible [pəmfsəbl] *adj.* lícito.
permission [pəmfʃən] *s.* permiso, licencia.
permit [pɜ́mɪt] *s.* permiso, pase; licencia; [pəmft] *v.* permitir.
pernicious [pənfʃəs] *adj.* pernicioso.
perpendicular [pɜpəndfkjələ] *adj. & s.* perpendicular.
perpetrate [pɜ́pətret] *v.* perpetrar, cometer.
perpetual [pəpétʃʊəl] *adj.* perpetuo.
perpetuate [pəpétʃʊet] *v.* perpetuar.
perplex [pəpléks] *v.* confundir, turbar, aturdir.
perplexed [pəplékst] *adj.* perplejo, confuso.
perplexity [pəpléksətɪ] *s.* perplejidad, confusión.
persecute [pɜ́sɪkjut] *v.* perseguir, aco-

sar.
persecution [pɜsɪkjúʃən] *s.* persecución.
persecutor [pɜ́sɪkjutə] *s.* perseguidor.
perseverance [pɜsəvfrəns] *s.* perseverancia.
persevere [pɜsəvfr] *v.* perseverar; persistir.
persist [pəzfst] *v.* persistir; porfiar.
persistence [pəzfstəns] *s.* persistencia, porfía.
persistent [pəzfstənt] *adj.* persistente; porfiado.
person [pɜ́sn] *s.* persona.
personage [pɜ́snɪdʒ] *s.* personaje.
personal [pɜ́snl] *adj.* personal; en persona.
personality [pɜsnǽlətɪ] *s.* personalidad; persona, personaje; alusión personal.
personnel [pɜsnél] *s.* personal.
perspective [pəspéktɪv] *s.* perspectiva; **— drawing** dibujo en perspectiva.
perspiration [pɜspəréʃən] *s.* sudor.
perspire [pəspáɪr] *v.* sudar.
persuade [pəswéd] *v.* persuadir.
persuasion [pəswéʒən] *s.* persuasión; creencia.
persuasive [pəswésɪv] *adj.* persuasivo.
pert [pɜt] *adj.* insolente, descarado, atrevido, *Am.* retobado.
pertain [pətén] *v.* pertenecer; atañer.
pertinent [pɜ́tnənt] *adj.* pertinente, a propósito, al caso.
perturb [pətɜ́b] *v.* perturbar.
peruse [pərúz] *v.* leer con cuidado.
Peruvian [pərúvɪən] *adj. & s.* peruano.
pervade [pəvéd] *v.* llenar, penetrar, difundirse por.
perverse [pəvɜ́s] *adj.* perverso; terco, obstinado.
pervert [pəvɜ́t] *v.* pervertir; falsear; [pɜ́vɜt] *s.* perverso.
pessimism [pésəmɪzəm] *s.* pesimismo.
pessimist [pésəmɪst] *s.* pesimista; **-ic** *adj.* pesimista.
pest [pest] *s.* peste, plaga; pestilencia.
pester [péstə] *v.* importunar, molestar.
pestilence [péstləns] *s.* pestilencia.
pet [pet] *s.* animal mimado, animal casero o doméstico; niño mimado; favorito; *adj.* favorito; mimado; **— name** nombre de cariño (*por lo general diminutivo*); *v.* mimar, acariciar.
petal [pétl] *s.* pétalo.
petition [pətfʃən] *s.* petición, súplica; instancia, memorial, solicitud, *Am.* ocurso; *v.* solicitar, pedir, dirigir una instancia o memorial a; suplicar, rogar.
petroleum [pətrólɪəm] *s.* petróleo.

petticoat [pétɪkot] s. enaguas.
petty [pétɪ] adj. insignificante, pequeño; mezquino; inferior, subordinado; — **cash** fondos para gastos menores; — **larceny** ratería; — **officer** oficial subordinado (en la marina); — **treason** traición menor.
pew [pju] s. banco de iglesia.
phantom [fǽntəm] s. fantasma.
pharmacist [fάrməsɪst] s. farmacéutico, boticario.
pharmacy [fάrməsɪ] s. farmacia, botica.
phase [fez] s. fase.
phenomena [fənάmənə] pl. de phenomenon.
phenomenon [fənάmənən] s. fenómeno.
philosopher [fəlάsəfə] s. filósofo.
philosophical [fɪləsάfɪk]] adj. filosófico.
philosophy [fəlάsəfɪ] s. filosofía.
phone [fon] s. teléfono; v. telefonear.
phonetics [fonétɪks] s. fonética.
phonograph [fónəgræf] s. fonógrafo.
phosphate [fάsfet] s. fosfato.
phosphorus [fάsfərəs] s. fósforo (elemento químico).
photo [fóto] s. fotografía, retrato.
photograph [fótəgræf] s. fotografía, retrato; v. fotografiar, retratar.
photographer [fətάgrəfə] s. fotógrafo.
photography [fətάgrəfɪ] s. fotografía.
phrase [frez] s. frase; expresión, locución; v. frasear; expresar, formular.
physic [fɪzɪk] s. purga, purgante; v. purgar.
physical [fɪzɪk] adj. físico.
physician [fəzíʃən] s. médico.
physicist [fɪzəsɪst] s. físico.
physics [fɪzɪks] s. física.
physiological [fɪzɪəlάdʒɪk]] adj. fisiológico.
physiology [fɪzɪάladʒɪ] s. fisiología.
physique [fɪzík] s. físico, constitución física, talle, cuerpo.
piano [pɪǽno] s. piano; — **bench** banqueta de piano; — **stool** taburete de piano; **grand** — piano de cola; **upright** — piano vertical.
picaresque [pɪkərésk] adj. picaresco.
pick [pɪk] v. escoger; coger; picar; mondarse, limpiarse (los dientes); desplumar (un ave); roer (un hueso); falsear (una cerradura); armar (una pendencia); **to** — **flaws** criticar, censurar; **to** — **out** escoger; **to** — **pockets** ratear; **to** — **up** recoger; **to** — **up speed** acelerar la marcha; s. pico (herramienta); selección; lo selecto, lo mejor; recolección, cosecha; **ice** — punzón para romper hielo; **tooth**— mondadientes, palillo de dientes.

pickaxe [pɪkæks] s. pico, zapapico.
picket [pɪkɪt] s. piquete (estaca o palo clavado en la tierra); piquete (vigilante huelguista); piquete de soldados; v. estacionar piquetes cerca de (una fábrica, campamento, etc.); vigilar (por medio de piquetes); estar de guardia.
pickle [pɪk]] s. encurtido; **to be in a** — hallarse en un aprieto; v. encurtir, escabechar; **-ed cucumbers** pepinillos encurtidos; **-ed fish** escabeche, pescado en escabeche.
pickpocket [pɪkpɑkɪt] s. rata (m.), ratero.
picnic [pɪknɪk] s. partida de campo, día de campo, comida campestre, Am picnic; v. hacer una comida campestre; ir a un picnic.
picture [pɪktʃə] s. cuadro, pintura retrato; fotografía; lámina, grabado película; — **frame** marco; — **gallery** museo o galería de pinturas; v. pintar dibujar; describir; imaginar(se).
picturesque [pɪktʃərésk] adj. pintoresco
pie [paɪ] s. pastel; empanada.
piece [pis] s. pieza; pedazo; trozo; parte sección; — **of advice** consejo; — **o land** parcela; — **of money** moneda — **of news** noticia; — **of nonsens** tontería; —**meal** en pedazos, a peda zos, por partes; v. remendar; **to** — **between meals** comer a deshoras; **to** — — **on** to juntar a, pegar a; **to** — **to gether** unir, pegar, juntar.
pier [pɪr] s. muelle, embarcadero; rom peolas; pilar (de puente o arco).
pierce [pɪrs] v. atravesar, traspasar taladrar; agujerear, perforar.
piety [pάɪətɪ] s. piedad, religiosidad.
pig [pɪg] s. puerco, cerdo, cochino; - **iron** hierro en lingotes; —**heade** cabezón, testarudo; **guinea** — cone jillo de Indias.
pigeon [pídʒən] s. pichón; paloma.
pigeonhole [pídʒənhol] s. casilla; encasillar.
pigment [pɪgmənt] s. pigmento, color.
pike [paɪk] s. pica, lanza; lucio (pez).
pile [paɪl] s. pila, montón; pelo (d ciertos tejidos); pilote; **-s** almorran (enfermedad); —**driver** martinete (pa ra clavar pilotes); v. apilar(se), amon tonar(se); acumular(se).
pilfer [pɪlfə] v. pillar, ratear, hurta sisar.
pilgrim [pɪlgrɪm] s. peregrino, romer
pilgrimage [pɪlgrəmɪdʒ] s. peregrin ción, romería.
pill [pɪl] s. píldora; persona fastidiosa.
pillage [pɪlɪdʒ] v. pillar, saquear; pillaje, saqueo.

pillar [pílə] *s.* pilar, columna; **to go from — to post** ir de Ceca en Meca.

pillow [pílo] *s.* almohada; cojín.

pillowcase [pílokes] *s.* funda de almohada.

pilot [páilət] *s.* piloto; guía; **— light** (*o* **— burner**) mechero, encendedor (*de una cocina o estufa de gas*); **harbor —** práctico de puerto; *v.* pilotar o pilotear; dirigir, guiar.

pimple [pímpl] *s.* grano, barro.

pin [pin] *s.* alfiler; prendedor; espiga; bolo (*del juego de bolos*); **— money** dinero para alfileres; **— wheel** molinete, *Am.* remolino; **breast —** broche; *v.* prender (*con alfiler*); asegurar, fijar, clavar; **to — down** fijar, inmovilizar; hacer dar una contestación definitiva; **to — one's hope** to poner toda su esperanza en; **to — up** prender con alfileres; colgar (*un dibujo o retrato*), fijar con tachuelas.

pincers [pínsəz] *s. pl.* pinzas; tenazas; **small —** tenacillas.

pinch [pintʃ] *v.* pellizcar; apretar; escatimar, economizar; prender, arrestar; **to — one's finger in the door** machucarse el dedo en la puerta; *s.* pellizco; pizca, porción pequeña; punzada, dolor agudo; aprieto, apuro; **— hitter** suplente, sustituto.

pinchers [píntʃəz] = **pincers.**

pine [pain] *s.* pino; **— cone** piña; **— grove** pinar; **— nut** piñón; *v.* languidecer; **to — away** consumirse; **to — for** anhelar, suspirar por.

pineapple [páinæpl] *s.* piña, ananá o ananás.

pink [piŋk] *s.* clavel; color de rosa; **in the — of condition** en la mejor condición; *adj.* rosado, color de rosa.

pinnacle [pínəkl] *s.* pináculo, cumbre.

pint [paint] *s.* pinta (*aproximadamente medio litro*).

pioneer [paiənír] *s.* explorador, colonizador; fundador, iniciador, precursor; *v.* explorar, colonizar; fundar, promover.

pious [páiəs] *adj.* pío, piadoso.

pipe [paip] *s.* pipa (*de fumar*); tubo, caño; cañón (*de órgano*); caramillo, flauta; **— line** cañería, tubería; *v.* conducir por cañerías; desaguar por cañería; proveer de tuberías o cañerías; chillar; **to — down** bajar la voz.

piper [páipə] *s.* gaitero, flautista.

piping [páipiŋ] *s.* cañería, tubería; cordoncillo (*de adorno para costuras*); chillido, silbido; *adj.* agudo, chillón; **— hot** muy caliente; hirviendo.

pippin [pípin] *s.* camuesa.

pique [pik] *o.* enojo, resentimiento; *v.* picar, excitar; enojar, irritar; **to — oneself on** picarse de, preciarse de.

pirate [páirət] *s.* pirata; *v.* piratear; plagiar.

pistol [pístl] *s.* pistola; revólver.

piston [pístn] *s.* pistón, émbolo; **— ring** aro de pistón; **— rod** vástago del émbolo.

pit [pit] *s.* hoyo; foso; hueso (*de ciertas frutas*); **— of the stomach** boca del estómago.

pitch [pitʃ] *s.* tiro, lanzamiento (*de una pelota*); cabezada (*de un barco*); diapasón, tono; grado, declive, grado de inclinación; pez (*f.*), brea; resina; **— dark** oscurísimo; *v.* tirar, lanzar, arrojar; cabecear (*un barco*); graduar el tono de (*un instrumento o voz*); echarse de cabeza; inclinarse; **to — a tent** armar una tienda de campaña; acampar; **to — into** arremeter contra, reprender, regañar; **— in!** ¡manos a la obra!

pitcher [pítʃə] *s.* cántaro, jarro o jarra; tirador, lanzador (*en beisbol*).

pitchfork [pítʃfork] *s.* horca, horquilla (*para hacinar las mieses, levantar la paja, etc.*).

piteous [pítiəs] *adj.* lastimero, lastimoso.

pith [piθ] *s.* meollo, médula; esencia, sustancia.

pitiful [pítifəl] *adj.* lastimoso; lamentable; miserable.

pitiless [pítilis] *adj.* despiadado, incompasivo, cruel.

pity [píti] *s.* piedad; lástima; compasión; **for —'s sake** por piedad, por Dios; **what a —!** ¡qué lástima!; *v.* compadecer; tener lástima por; apiadarse de, tener piedad de.

placard [plǽkard] *s.* letrero, cartel; *v.* fijar carteles.

place [ples] *s.* lugar, sitio; puesto; empleo; posición; localidad; **— of business** oficina; **— despacho; — of worship** templo, iglesia; **market —** plaza, mercado; **in — of** en lugar de, en vez de; **it is not my —** to do it no es mi deber hacerlo, no me toca a mí hacerlo; *v.* colocar; situar; poner; acomodar, dar empleo a.

placid [plǽsid] *adj.* plácido, apacible, sosegado.

plague [pleg] *s.* plaga; peste, pestilencia; calamidad; *v.* plagar, infestar; importunar.

plaid [plæd] *s.* tartán, tela a cuadros; manta escocesa a cuadros; diseño a cuadros; *adj.* a cuadros.

plain [plen] *adj.* llano, sencillo, claro; franco; ordinario; **—** **fool tonto de capirote; — woman** mujer sin atractivo; **in — sight** en plena vista, **plain-clothes man** detectivo, *adv.* claramente; **—** **stupid** completamente estúpido; **plain-spoken** franco, francote, sincero, *s.* llano, llanura.

plaintiff [pléntɪf] *s.* demandante.

plaintive [pléntɪv] *adj.* lastimero, triste.

plan [plæn] *s.* plan; proyecto; plano (*dibujo o mapa*), *v.* planear; proyectar, idear; pensar, proponerse.

plane [plen] *s.* plano, superficie plana; aeroplano; cepillo (*de carpintero*) *adj.* plano, llano; **— tree** plátano falso; *v.* acepillar, alisar con cepillo (*la madera o los metales*).

planet [plǽnɪt] *s.* planeta.

plank [plæŋk] *s.* tabla, tablón; principio, base (*del programa de un partido político*); *v.* entablar, entarimar, cubrir con tablas; asar (*carne*) en una tabla.

plant [plænt] *s.* planta; fábrica, taller; *v.* plantar; sembrar; implantar; establecer.

plantation [plæntéʃən] *s.* plantación; plantío; sembrado; **coffee —** cafetal; **cotton —** algodonal; **rubber —** cauchal, **sugar —** ingenio de azúcar.

planter [plæntə] *s.* plantador, cultivador.

plaque [plæk] *s.* placa.

plasma [plǽzmə] *s.* plasma.

plaster [plǽstə] *s.* yeso; emplasto, **— of Paris** yeso, yeso mate; **court —** esparadrapo, tafetán inglés; **mustard —** sinapismo; *v.* enyesar, emplastar, poner emplastos a; pegar (*carteles, anuncios*); embarrar.

plastic [plǽstɪk] *adj.* plástico.

plat [plæt] *s.* plano; parcela; *v.* levantar o trazar un plano.

plate [plet] *s.* plato; placa; plancha; lámina, **dental —** dentadura postiza; *v.* platear; dorar; niquelar; blindar, proteger con planchas de metal.

plateau [platô] *s.* altiplanicie, mesa, meseta.

plateful [plétful] *s.* plato, plato lleno.

platform [plǽtfɔrm] *s.* plataforma; tablado; programa de un partido político; **railway —** andén.

platinum [plǽtnəm] *s.* platino.

platitude [plǽtətjud] *s.* lugar común, perogrullada.

platter [plǽtə] *s.* platel, platón.

play [ple] *v.* jugar; juguetear; tocar

(*música*); representar; hacer, desempeñar (*un papel*); manipular (*un instrumento, radio, fonógrafo, etc.*); to **— a joke** hacer una broma, dar un chasco, to **— cards** jugar a los naipes, jugar a la baraja, to **— havoc** hacer estragos, causar daño; to **— tennis** jugar al tenis; to **— the fool** hacer el tonto, fingirse tonto; **to be all -ed out** no poder más, estar agotado; *s.* juego, jugada (*acción, movimiento en un juego*); pieza, drama, comedia, representación; recreación, diversión; **— on words** juego de palabras, equívoco; **to give full — to** dar rienda suelta a.

player [pléə] *s.* jugador; músico; cómico, actor; **— piano** piano mecánico, pianola; **piano —** pianista; **violin —** violinista.

playful [pléfəl] *adj.* juguetón, retozón; bromista.

playground [plégraund] *s.* campo o patio de recreo.

playmate [plémet] *s.* compañero de juego.

plaything [pléθɪŋ] *s.* juguete.

playwright [plérait] *s.* dramático, dramaturgo.

plea [pli] *s.* súplica, ruego; alegato, defensa; pretexto; **on the — that** con el pretexto de que.

plead [plid] *v.* abogar; suplicar; argüir; alegar; defender (*una causa*); to **— guilty** declararse o confesarse culpable.

pleasant [pléznt] *adj.* grato; agradable; simpático.

pleasantry [plézntrɪ] *s.* chanza, broma, chiste, humorada.

please [pliz] *v.* agradar, gustar, dar gusto a; complacer; **— do it** haga Vd. el favor de hacerlo, tenga Vd. la bondad de hacerlo, sírvase hacerlo; **as you —** como Vd. quiera, como Vd. guste; **if you —** si me hace Vd. (el) favor; to **be -ed to** complacerse en, tener gusto en; alegrarse de; **to be -ed with** gustarle a uno, estar satisfecho de (*o con*).

pleasing [plízɪŋ] *adj.* agradable.

pleasure [pléʒə] *s.* placer, gusto; deleite, alegría, gozo; **— trip** viaje de recreo; **what is your —?** ¿qué deseaba Vd.? ¿en qué puedo servirle?

pleat [plit] *s.* pliegue, doblez; *v.* plegar, hacer pliegues con.

plebeian [plɪbíən] *adj.* & *s.* plebeyo.

pledge [pledʒ] *s.* promesa; prenda (*garantía*); fianza; **as a — of** en prenda de; *v.* prometer; empeñar, dar en pren-

da; hacer firmar una promesa; **to —
one's word** empeñar (o dar) su palabra; **to — to secrecy** exigir promesa
de sigilo.

plenipotentiary [plenəpətén∫ərı] *adj.*
& s. plenipotenciario.

plentiful [pléntıfəl] *adj.* abundante,
copioso.

plenty [pléntı] *s.* abundancia, copia; —
of time bastante tiempo; that is
con eso basta; basta.

pliable [pláıəbl] *adj.* flexible; manejable,
dócil; transigente.

pliant [pláıənt] *adj.* flexible; dócil,
sumiso.

pliers [pláıəz] *s. pl.* alicates, tenazas.

plight [plaıt] *s.* apuro, aprieto, situación difícil.

plod [plad] *v.* bregar, trafagar, afanarse,
trabajar asiduamente.

plot [plat] *s.* trama, enredo; complot,
conspiración; parcela (de tierra), solar;
plano, diagrama; *v.* tramar, urdir;
maquinar, conspirar; hacer el plano o
diagrama de; **to — a curve** hacer
una gráfica.

plotter [plátə] *s.* conspirador; tramador;
conjurado.

plough = plow.

plow [plau] *s.* arado; **—share** reja de
arado; *v.* arar; surcar.

pluck [plʌk] *v.* coger; arrancar; desplumar (un ave); puntear (las cuerdas de una guitarra); **to —** al tirar de;
to — up arrancar; cobrar ánimo;
s. ánimo, valor; tirón.

plucky [plʌkı] *adj.* valeroso, animoso.

plug [plʌg] *s.* taco, tapón; caballejo,
penco; elogio incidental (de un producto comercial o de una persona); —
of tobacco tableta de tabaco; **electric
— clavija** de conexión; **fire —** boca de agua para incendios; **spark —**
bujía; *v.* tapar; **to — along** afanarse,
atarearse; **to — in** enchufar, conectar;
to — up tapar, obstruir.

plum [plʌm] *s.* ciruela; la cosa mejor; la
mejor colocación; — **pudding** pudín
inglés con pasas; **— tree** ciruelo.

plumage [plúmıd3] *s.* plumaje.

plumb [plʌm] *s.* plomo, pesa de plomo;
sonda; **out of —** no vertical; *adj.*
vertical, a plomo, recto; **— bob** plomo,
plomada; *adv.* a plomo, verticalmente;
— crazy completamente loco; *v.* sondear; aplomar (una pared).

plumber [plʌmə] *s.* plomero.

plumbing [plʌmıŋ] *s.* plomería; cañerías (de un edificio); oficio de plomero.

plume [plum] *s.* pluma; plumaje; pena-

cho; *v.* adornar con plumas; **to — its
wing** alisarse o componerse el plumaje del ala.

plump [plʌmp] *adj.* rechoncho, regordete, rollizo; *adv.* de golpe; *v.* **to —
down** dejar(se) caer; desplomarse, sentarse de golpe.

plunder [plʌndə] *s.* pillaje, saqueo;
botín; *v.* pillar; saquear.

plunge [plʌnd3] *v.* zambullir(se), sumer-
gir(se); hundir(se); lanzar(se), arro-
jar(se), precipitar(se); **to — headlong** echarse de cabeza; *s.* zambullida;
salto (de arriba abajo).

plural [plúrəl] *adj. & s.* plural.

plus [plʌs] *s.* más, signo más; **— quantity** cantidad positiva; **two — three**
dos más tres.

plush [plʌ∫] *s.* felpa; velludo.

ply [plaı] *v.* manejar con tesón (un instrumento o herramienta); importunar (con
preguntas); hacer con regularidad un
recorrido (entre dos puntos); **to — a
trade** seguir o ejercer un oficio; **to —
oneself with** saturarse de, rellenarse
de; *s.* doblez, pliegue; capa (de tejido,
goma, etc.).

pneumatic [njumǽtık] *adj.* neumático.

pneumonia [njumónjə] *s.* pulmonía.

poach [pot∫] *v.* escalfar (huevos); invadir
(un vedado); cazar o pescar en vedado;
robar caza o pesca (de un vedado).

pocket [pákıt] *s.* bolsillo, faltriquera,
Am. bolsa; tronera (de billar); cavidad; hoyo; *v.* embolsarse; apropiarse;
ocultar (el orgullo o rencor); aguantar
(un insulto).

pocketbook [pákıtbuk] *s.* cartera; portamonedas; **woman's —** bolsa.

pocketknife [pákıtnaıf] *s.* navaja; cortaplumas.

pod [pad] *s.* vaina (de guisante, frijol,
etc.).

poem [póım] *s.* poema, poesía.

poet [póıt] *s.* poeta; vate.

poetess [póıtıs] *s.* poetisa.

poetic [poétık] *adj.* poético; **-s** *s.* arte
poética, poética.

poetical [poétık] *adj.* poético.

poetry [póıtrı] *s.* poesía.

point [poınt] *s.* punto; punta (de lápiz,
espada, tierra, etc.); **it is not to the —**
no viene al caso; **not to see the —**
no caer en la cuenta; no ver el chiste,
propósito o intención; **on the — of —**
a punto de; *v.* apuntar; señalar; indicar; **to — out** señalar, mostrar,
indicar.

pointed [póıntıd] *adj.* puntiagudo, agudo; satírico; apto, a propósito, al caso;

— **arch** arco apuntado, arco ojival.

pointer [póintə] s. puntero; indicador; señalador; perro de punta y vuelta; indicación, consejo.

poise [poiz] s. equilibrio; porte, compostura; v. equilibrar(se); balancear(se).

poison [póizn̩] s. veneno; ponzoña; v. envenenar, emponzoñar.

poisonous [póizn̩əs] adj. venenoso, ponzoñoso.

poke [pok] v. atizar, remover (el fuego); picar (con el dedo o cualquier objeto puntiagudo); **to — along** andar perezosamente; **to — around** husmear, curiosear; **to — fun at** burlarse de; **to — into** meter en; **to — out** sacar; proyectarse; s. pinchazo; piquete; codazo; aguijonada; **slow** — tardón.

polar [póla] adj. polar; — **bear** oso blanco.

pole [pol] s. poste; pértiga, palo largo; asta (de bandera); garrocha; polo; **Pole** polaco; **north** — polo norte, polo ártico; **south** — polo sur, polo antártico; — **vault** salto con garrocha.

police [pəlís] s. policía; v. vigilar; guardar el orden.

policeman [pəlísmən] s. policía (m.), guardia de policía, polizonte, Am. vigilante, Am. gendarme.

policy [páləsɪ] s. política; **insurance —** póliza de seguro.

Polish [pólɪʃ] adj. polaco; s. polaco, idioma polaco.

polish [pálɪʃ] s. pulimento; lustre, brillo; urbanidad, cultura; **shoe —** betún, bola; v. pulir, pulimentar; dar brillo o lustre a; embolar, dar bola o brillo a (zapatos).

polite [pəláɪt] adj. cortés, fino, urbano, político.

politeness [pəláɪtnɪs] s. cortesía; fineza, urbanidad.

politic [pálətɪk] adj. político, prudente; conveniente.

political [pəlítɪkl̩] adj. político.

politician [palətíʃən] s. político; politicastro.

politics [pálətɪks] s. política.

poll [pol] s. votación; lista electoral; **-s** comicios; urnas electorales; casilla (donde se vota); — **tax** impuesto (de tanto por cabeza); v. registrar los votos de; votar; recibir (votos).

pollen [pálɪn] s. polen.

pomegranate [pʌmgrǽnɪt] s. granada; — **tree** granado.

pomp [pamp] s. pompa, boato.

pompous [pámpəs] adj. pomposo, os-

tentoso.

pond [pand] s. charca; estanque; **fish —** vivero.

ponder [pándə] v. ponderar, pesar, examinar; **to — over** reflexionar.

ponderous [pándərəs] adj. ponderoso; pesado.

pontoon [pantún] s. pontón, chata, barco chato; flotador (de hidroavión); — **bridge** pontón, puente flotante.

pony [pónɪ] s. caballito, potrillo; clave o traducción (usada ilícitamente en un examen).

poodle [púdl̩] s. perro de lanas.

pool [pul] s. charco; charca; trucos (juego parecido al billar); polla o puesta (en ciertos juegos); fondos en común, combinación de fondos (para una empresa o para especular); "trust"; **swimming —** piscina; v. formar una polla; combinar fondos.

poor [pur] adj. pobre; malo; de mala calidad; — **student** estudiante pobre; mal estudiante; — **little thing** pobrecito; **the —** los pobres; **-ly** adv. pobremente; mal.

poorhouse [púrhaus] s. hospicio, casa de pobres.

pop [pap] s. tronido, trueno, estallido; detonación; — **of a cork** taponazo; **soda —** gaseosa; v. reventar, estallar; detonar; saltar (un tapón); **to — a question** espetar una pregunta; **to — corn** hacer palomitas de maíz, hacer rosetas de maíz; **to — in and out** entrar y salir de sopetón; **to — one's head out** sacar o asomar de repente la cabeza.

popcorn [pápkɔrn] s. rosetas, palomitas de maíz, Am. alborotos.

Pope [pop] s. Papa.

popeyed [pápaid] adj. de ojos saltones, Am. desorbitado.

poplar [páplə] s. álamo; **black —** chopo; — **grove** alameda.

poppy [pápɪ] s. amapola.

populace [pápjəlɪs] s. pueblo, populacho.

popular [pápjələ] adj. popular.

popularity [papjəlǽrɪtɪ] s. popularidad.

populate [pápjələt] v. poblar.

population [papjəléʃən] s. población.

populous [pápjələs] adj. populoso.

porcelain [pɔ́rslɪn] s. porcelana.

porch [pɔrtʃ] s. pórtico, porche; galería.

porcupine [pɔ́rkjəpain] s. puerco espín.

pore [por] s. poro; v. **to — over a book** engolfarse en la lectura.

pork [pɔrk] s. puerco, carne de puerco; — **chop** chuleta de puerco; **salt —** tocino salado.

porous [pórəs] *adj.* poroso.
porridge [pórɪdʒ] *s.* potaje, gachas.
port [pɔrt] *s.* puerto; vino de Oporto; babor (*lado izquierdo de un barco*); —**hole** porta, portilla.
portable [pórtəbl] *adj.* portátil.
portal [pórtl] *s.* portal.
portent [pórtent] *s.* portento, presagio, agüero.
portentous [porténtəs] *adj.* portentoso; prodigioso; de mal agüero.
porter [pórtə] *s.* mozo de cordel, *Am.* cargador; camarero (*en un coche-cama*); portero.
portfolio [portfólɪo] *s.* portafolio, cartera; carpeta; ministerio.
portion [pórʃən] *s.* porción; *v.* repartir.
portly [pórtlɪ] *adj.* corpulento.
portrait [pórtret] *s.* retrato.
portray [portré] *v.* retratar, pintar, dibujar, representar.
portrayal [portréəl] *s.* retrato, delineación, delineamiento, representación.
Portuguese [pórtʃəgiz] *adj. & s.* portugués.
pose [poz] *s.* postura, actitud; afectación; *v.* posar (*como modelo*); colocar(se) en cierta postura; afectar una actitud o postura; proponer, plantear (*una cuestión o problema*); **to — as** fingirse, hacerse pasar por.
position [pəzíʃən] *s.* posición; postura; situación, empleo, puesto.
positive [pázətɪv] *adj.* positivo; cierto, seguro; categórico; dogmático.
possess [pəzés] *v.* poseer.
possession [pəzéʃən] *s.* posesión.
possessive [pəzésɪv] *adj. & s.* posesivo.
possessor [pəzésə] *s.* poseedor, posesor, dueño.
possibility [pasəbíləti] *s.* posibilidad.
possible [pásəbl] *adj.* posible; **possibly** *adv.* posiblemente; acaso, tal vez.
post [post] *s.* poste, pilar; puesto; empleo; **army —** guarnición militar; **—haste** por la posta, rápidamente; **— office** correo, casa de correos; **post-office box** apartado, casilla postal; **—paid** porte pagado, franco de porte; *v.* fijar (*anuncios, carteles*); anunciar; poner en lista; apostar, situar; echar al correo; **to — an entry** asentar o hacer un asiento (*en teneduría*); **to be well -ed** estar al corriente, estar bien enterado.
postage [póstɪdʒ] *s.* porte, franqueo; **— stamp** sello de correo, *Am.* estampilla, *Am.* timbre.
postal [póstl] *adj.* postal; **— card** tarjeta postal; **— money order** giro postal.

postcard [póstkard] *s.* tarjeta postal.
poster [póstə] *s.* cartel, cartelón; fijador de carteles.
posterior [pastírɪə] *adj.* posterior; trasero.
posterity [pastérəti] *s.* posteridad.
posthumous [pástʃuməs] *adj.* póstumo.
postman [póstmən] *s.* cartero.
postmaster [póstmæstə] *s.* administrador de correos.
postpone [postpón] *v.* posponer; aplazar, diferir; postergar.
postponement [postpónmənt] *s.* aplazamiento.
postscript [pósskrɪpt] *s.* posdata.
posture [pástʃə] *s.* postura, actitud; posición; *v.* adoptar una postura.
posy [pózɪ] *s.* flor.
pot [pat] *s.* pote; olla, puchero, cacharro (*de cocina*); bacín, bacinica (*de cámara o recámara*); **flower —** tiesto, maceta; **—bellied** panzudo, barrigón.
potassium [pətǽsɪəm] *s.* potasio.
potato [pətéto] *s.* patata, papa; **sweet —** batata, *Am.* camote, *Am.* boniato.
potency [pótnsɪ] *s.* potencia, poder, fuerza.
potent [pótnt] *adj.* potente, poderoso, fuerte.
potential [pəténʃəl] *adj. & s.* potencial.
pottage [pátɪdʒ] *s.* potaje.
potter [pátə] *s.* alfarero, fabricante de vasijas o cacharros de barro; **—'s field** cementerio de pobres y desconocidos.
pottery [pátərɪ] *s.* cerámica, alfarería, vasijas de barro.
pouch [pautʃ] *s.* bolsa, saquillo; **mail —** valija; **tobacco —** tabaquera, petaca.
poultice [póltɪs] *s.* emplasto.
poultry [póltrɪ] *s.* aves de corral.
pounce [pauns] *s.* salto (*para agarrar*); zarpada; *v.* **to — into** entrar de sopetón; **to — upon** abalanzarse sobre, saltar sobre, agarrar.
pound [paund] *s.* libra; golpazo; **— sterling** libra esterlina; *v.* golpear, machacar, martillar.
pour [por] *v.* vaciar, verter; servir (*una taza de té*); fluir; llover a cántaros, llover recio.
pout [paut] *v.* hacer pucheros, lloriquear; poner cara de enfado; *s.* puchero, pucherito.
poverty [pávətɪ] *s.* pobreza.
powder [páudə] *s.* polvo; pólvora (*explosivo*); polvos (*de tocador*); **— compact** polvera; **— magazine** polvorín; **— puff** polvera, borla, *Am.* cisne, *Am.* mota; *v.* empolvar(se); polvorear; pulverizar(se); **to — one's face** empolvarse la cara, ponerse pol-

vos.

power [páuə] s. poder; poderío; potencia; fuerza; **motive — fuerza motriz; — of attorney** poder; **— plant** planta de fuerza motriz.

powerful [páuəfəl] adj. poderoso.

powerless [páuəlıs] adj. impotente.

practicable [prǽktıkəb] adj. practicable; factible, hacedero; práctico; **— road** camino transitable.

practical [prǽktık] adj. práctico; **— joke** chasco, burla pesada; **-ly** adv. casi, virtualmente; realmente, en realidad; prácticamente.

practice [prǽktıs] s. práctica; ejercicio (de una profesión); método; regla, costumbre; clientela; v. practicar; ejercer (una profesión); ejercitarse.

practiced [prǽktıst] adj. práctico, experimentado; experto, perito.

prairie [prérı] s. pradera, llanura.

praise [prez] s. alabanza; elogio; encomio; v. alabar; elogiar; encomiar.

praiseworthy [prézwɜðı] adj. laudable.

prance [prǽns] v. cabriolar, hacer cabriolas.

prank [prǽŋk] s. travesura, burla; **to play -s** hacer travesuras.

prate [pret] v. parlotear, charlar; s. parloteo, charla.

prattle [prǽt] v. parlotear, charlar; s. parloteo, charla.

pray [pre] v. orar, rezar; rogar, suplicar; **— tell me** dígame por favor, le ruego que me diga.

prayer [prer] s. oración, rezo; ruego, súplica; **— book** devocionario; **Lord's —** Padre Nuestro.

preach [pritʃ] v. predicar; sermonear.

preacher [pritʃə] s. predicador.

preaching [pritʃıŋ] s. predicación; sermón; sermoneo.

preamble [príæmbl] s. preámbulo.

prearranged [priərændʒd] adj. arreglado de antemano.

precarious [prıkérıəs] adj. precario; inseguro.

precaution [prıkóʃən] s. precaución.

precede [prısíd] v. preceder.

precedence [prısídns] s. precedencia; prioridad.

precedent [présədənt] s. precedente.

preceding [prısídıŋ] adj. precedente, anterior.

precept [písept] s. precepto.

precinct [prísıŋkt] s. distrito; recinto; **-s** límites, inmediaciones.

precious [préʃəs] adj. precioso; querido, amado, caro; **— little** poquísimo, muy poco.

precipice [présəpıs] s. precipicio.

precipitate [prısípətet] v. precipitar(se), adj. precipitado, apresurado, atropellado; s. precipitado.

precipitation [prısıpətéʃən] s. precipitación; lluvia (o nieve, rocío, granizo, etc.); cantidad de agua pluvial.

precipitous [prısípətəs] adj. precipitoso, escarpado; precipitado.

precise [prısáıs] adj. preciso, exacto.

precision [prısíʒən] s. precisión, exactitud.

preclude [prıklúd] v. excluir; impedir.

precocious [prıkóʃəs] adj. precoz.

predecessor [predısésə] s. predecesor.

predestine [prıdéstın] v. predestinar.

predicament [prıdíkəmənt] s. aprieto, apuro, dificultad.

predicate [prédıkıt] adj. & s. predicado.

predict [prıdíkt] v. predecir, vaticinar.

prediction [prıdíkʃən] s. predicción, pronóstico, vaticinio.

predilection [prıdılékʃən] s. predilección, preferencia.

predispose [prıdıspóz] v. predisponer.

predominance [prıdámənəns] s. predominio; ascendiente.

predominant [prıdámənənt] adj. predominante.

predominate [prıdámənet] v. predominar.

preface [préfıs] s. prefacio; prólogo; v. prologar.

prefer [prıfɜ́] v. preferir; **to — a claim** presentar una demanda.

preferable [préfrəb] adj. preferible; preferente; **preferably** adv. preferiblemente; preferentemente, de preferencia.

preference [préfrəns] s. preferencia.

preferred [prıfɜ́d] p.p. & adj. preferido; **— shares** acciones preferentes.

prefix [prífıks] s. prefijo; [priffks] v. prefijar, anteponer.

pregnancy [prégnənsı] s. preñez, embarazo.

pregnant [prégnənt] adj. preñado; lleno, repleto; encinta.

prejudice [prédʒədıs] s. prejuicio, prevención; daño; v. predisponer, prevenir; perjudicar.

prelate [prélıt] s. prelado.

preliminary [prılímənerı] adj. & s. preliminar.

prelude [préljud] s. preludio; v. preludiar.

premature [primətjúr] adj. prematuro.

premeditated [prımédətetıd] adj. premeditado.

premier [prímıə] s. primer ministro;

adj. primero; principal.
premise [prémɪs] *s.* premisa; **-s** terrenos; local.
premium [prímɪəm] *s.* premio; **at a —** muy escaso, muy caro; **insurance —** prima de seguro.
preoccupy [priákjəpaɪ] *v.* preocupar; ocupar de antemano.
prepaid [pripéd] *adj.* pagado de antemano; **to send —** enviar porte pagado, enviar franco de porte.
preparation [prepəréʃən] *s.* preparación; preparativo.
preparatory [prɪpǽrətorɪ] *adj.* preparatorio.
prepare [pripér] *v.* preparar(se).
preparedness [prɪpérɪdnɪs] *s.* preparación, prevención.
preposition [prepəzɪʃən] *s.* preposición.
preposterous [prɪpástrəs] *adj.* absurdo, insensato.
prerequisite [prirékwəzɪt] *s.* requisito previo.
prerogative [prɪrágətɪv] *s.* prerrogativa.
presage [présɪdʒ] *s.* presagio; [priségʒ] *v.* presagiar.
prescribe [prɪskráɪb] *v.* prescribir; recetar.
prescription [prɪskrípʃən] *s.* receta; prescripción, precepto, mandato.
presence [prézns] *s.* presencia; **— of mind** aplomo, serenidad.
present [prézɲt] *s.* presente; regalo; **at — al** presente, ahora; **for the —** por ahora; *adj.* presente; corriente, actual; **— company excepted** mejorando lo presente; **— participle** gerundio; **to be —** asistir, estar presente; [prɪzént] *v.* presentar; regalar, obsequiar.
presentation [prezɲtéʃən] *s.* presentación; regalo, obsequio.
presentiment [prɪzéntəmənt] *s.* presentimiento; corazonada.
presently [prézɲtlɪ] *adv.* luego, pronto, dentro de poco.
preservation [prezərvéʃən] *s.* preservación; conservación.
preserve [prɪzɝv] *v.* preservar, guardar; conservar; mantener; *s.* conserva, compota; **forest —** vedado.
preside [prɪzáɪd] *v.* presidir; **to — at (— over)** a meeting presidir una junta.
presidency [prézədənsɪ] *s.* presidencia.
president [prézədənt] *s.* presidente.
presidential [prezədénʃəl] *adj.* presidencial.
press [pres] *v.* prensar; apretar; comprimir; planchar (*ropa*); forzar; apremiar; urgir; empujar; **to — forward**

empujar hacia adelante; avanzar, ganar terreno; **to — one's point** porfiar; insistir en su argumento; **to — through the crowd** abrirse paso por entre la multitud; **to be hard -ed by work** estar abrumado de trabajo; **to be hard -ed for money** estar escaso de fondos; *s.* prensa; imprenta.
pressing [présɪŋ] *adj.* apremiante, urgente.
pressure [préʃə] *s.* presión; apremio, urgencia; **— cooker** cocinilla de presión; **— gauge** manómetro.
prestige [prestíʃ] *s.* prestigio.
presumable [prɪsúməbl] *adj.* presumible, probable.
presume [prɪzúm] *v.* presumir; suponer; **to — on (upon)** abusar de; **to — to** atreverse a.
presumption [prɪzʌmpʃən] *s.* presunción; pretensión; suposición.
presumptuous [prɪzʌmptʃʊəs] *adj.* presuntuoso, pretencioso, presumido.
presuppose [prisəpóz] *v.* presuponer.
pretend [prɪténd] *v.* pretender; fingir.
pretense [prɪténs] *s.* pretensión; presunción; ostentación; apariencia; pretexto; **under — of** so pretexto de.
pretension [prɪténʃən] *s.* pretensión; pretexto.
pretext [prítekst] *s.* pretexto.
prettily [prítɪlɪ] *adv.* lindamente; agradablemente.
prettiness [prítɪnɪs] *s.* lindeza, gracia.
pretty [prítɪ] *adj.* lindo, bonito, bello, *Am.* chulo; *adv.* medianamente; bastante; un poco, algo; **— well** regular, así así; bastante bien, medianamente.
prevail [prɪvél] *v.* prevalecer; **to — on (upon)** persuadir.
prevailing [prɪvélɪŋ] *adj.* predominante; en boga.
prevalent [prévələnt] *adj.* prevaleciente; común, corriente.
prevent [prɪvént] *v.* prevenir, evitar; impedir; estorbar.
prevention [prɪvénʃən] *s.* prevención; precaución.
previous [prívɪəs] *adj.* previo; **-ly** *adv.* previamente; antes; de antemano.
prey [pre] *s.* presa; víctima; **birds of —** aves de rapiña; *v.* **to — on** cazar; rapiñar, pillar; robar; **it -s upon my mind** me tiene preocupado, me tiene en zozobra.
price [praɪs] *s.* precio; valor; costo (*coste o costa*); **at any —** a toda costa, a todo trance; *v.* apreciar, valuar, fijar el precio de; averiguar el precio de.
priceless [práɪslɪs] *adj.* sin precio, in-

apreciable.

prick [prɪk] *v.* picar; pinchar; punzar; sentir comezón; sentir picazón; **to —** **up one's ears** aguzar las orejas; *s.* picadura; punzada; pinchazo; piquete; aguijón; púa.

prickly [príklɪ] *adj.* espinoso, lleno de espinas; lleno de púas; **— heat** picazón causada por el calor; **— pear** tuna *(de nopal).*

pride [praɪd] *s.* orgullo; soberbia; *v.* **to — oneself on (upon)** enorgullecerse de, preciarse de.

priest [prist] *s.* sacerdote.

priesthood [prísthʊd] *s.* sacerdocio.

prim [prɪm] *adj.* remilgado; repulido; peripuesto; estirado.

primarily [praɪmérəlɪ] *adv.* primariamente, principalmente; en primer lugar.

primary [práɪmerɪ] *adj.* primario; primero; fundamental; principal; **— colors** colores elementales; **— election** elección primaria; **— school** escuela primaria.

prime [praɪm] *adj.* primero; principal; primario; selecto, de primera calidad; **— minister** primer ministro; **— number** número primo; *s.* flor *(de la vida o de la edad);* la flor y nata *(lo mejor);* plenitud; número primo; **to be in one's —** estar en la flor de la edad; *v.* preparar, informar, instruir de antemano; cebar *(un carburador, bomba o arma de fuego).*

primer [prímə] *s.* abecedario, cartilla de lectura; compendio.

primeval [praɪmívl] *adj.* primitivo.

primitive [prímətɪv] *adj.* primitivo.

primness [prímnɪs] *s.* remilgo, tiesura, demasiada formalidad, dengue, afectación.

primp [prɪmp] *v.* acicalar(se), adornar-(se), arreglar(se).

primrose [prímroz] *s.* prímula o primavera *(flor);* color amarillo pálido.

prince [prɪns] *s.* príncipe.

princely [prínslɪ] *adj.* noble, regio, magnífico, propio de un príncipe.

princess [prínsɪs] *s.* princesa.

principal [prínsəpl] *adj.* principal; *s.* principal, capital; principal, jefe, director.

principle [prínsəpl] *s.* principio; regla; ley; fundamento, base.

print [prɪnt] *s.* tipo, letra de molde; estampa; lámina, grabado; estampado *(tejido estampado);* diseño *(estampado);* impresión; **in —** impreso, publicado; **out of —** agotado; *v.* imprimir; estam-

par; escribir en letra de molde; **-ed fabric** estampado.

printer [príntə] *s.* impresor.

printing [príntɪŋ] *s.* imprenta; impresión; tipografía; **— office** imprenta; **— press** prensa.

prior [práɪə] *adj.* previo, anterior, precedente; **— to** anterior a, con antelación a; *s.* prior *(de un monasterio).*

priority [praɪɔ́rətɪ] *s.* prioridad, precedencia, antelación.

prism [prízəm] *s.* prisma.

prison [prízn] *s.* prisión, cárcel; *v.* encarcelar.

prisoner [prízṇə] *s.* prisionero, preso.

privacy [práɪvəsɪ] *s.* secreto, reserva; retiro; **to have no —** carecer de sitio privado; estar a la vista del público.

private [práɪvɪt] *adj.* privado; personal; particular; secreto; confidencial; **a — citizen** un particular; **— school** escuela particular; *s.* soldado raso; **in —** en secreto; a solas, privadamente.

privation [praɪvéʃən] *s.* privación.

privilege [prívlɪdʒ] *s.* privilegio.

privileged [prívlɪdʒd] *adj.* privilegiado; **to be —** tener el privilegio de.

prize [praɪz] *s.* premio, galardón; presa, botín de guerra; **— fight** boxeo público, pugilato; **— fighter** boxeador, pugilista; **— medal** medalla de premio; *v.* apreciar, estimar, tener en gran estima.

probability [prɑbəbílətɪ] *s.* probabilidad.

probable [prábəbl] *adj.* probable; **probably** *adv.* probablemente.

probation [probéʃən] *s.* probación; noviciado; prueba; **to put a prisoner on —** poner a un prisionero en libertad bajo la vigilancia de un juez.

probe [prob] *v.* tentar, reconocer, sondear *(una herida);* escudriñar, examinar a fondo; indagar; *s.* tienta *(instrumento de cirujano);* indagación.

problem [prábləm] *s.* problema.

procedure [prəsídʒə] *s.* procedimiento; proceder.

proceed [prəsíd] *v.* proceder; proseguir; seguir adelante; **to —** proceder a, comenzar a, ponerse a.

proceeding [prəsídɪŋ] *s.* procedimiento; transacción; **-s** transacciones; actas; proceso.

proceeds [prósidz] *s. pl.* producto, ganancia.

process [práses] *s.* proceso; procedimiento; método; **in — of time** con el transcurso del tiempo, con el tiempo, andando el tiempo; **in the — of being made** en vía de preparación; *v.*

preparar mediante un procedimiento especial, someter a un procedimiento; procesar (ante un juez).

procession [prəséʃən] s. procesión; desfile; **funeral** — cortejo fúnebre.

proclaim [proklém] v. proclamar; promulgar.

proclamation [prakləméʃən] s. proclamación; proclama.

procure [prokiúr] v. procurar, conseguir, obtener.

prod [prad] v. aguijonear; picar.

prodigal [prádɪgl] adj. & s. pródigo, gastador.

prodigious [prədídʒəs] adj. prodigioso.

prodigy [prádədʒɪ] s. prodigio.

produce [prádjus] s. producto; productos agrícolas; [prədjús] v. producir.

producer [prədjúsə] s. productor; **theatrical** — empresario.

product [prádəkt] s. producto.

production [prədʌ́kʃən] s. producción; producto; obra, composición; representación teatral.

productive [prədʌ́ktɪv] adj. productivo.

profanation [prafənéʃən] s. profanación, desacato.

profane [prəfén] adj. profano; v. profanar.

profess [prəfés] v. profesar; pretender.

profession [prəféʃən] s. profesión.

professional [prəféʃənl] adj. profesional; s. profesional, Am. profesionista.

professor [prəfésə] s. profesor, catedrático.

proffer [práfə] s. oferta, propuesta; v. ofrecer, proponer.

proficiency [prəfíʃənsɪ] s. pericia, destreza.

proficient [prəfíʃənt] adj. proficiente, perito, experto.

profile [prófaɪl] s. perfil; contorno.

profit [práfɪt] s. provecho, utilidad, beneficio; ganancia; lucro; — **and loss** pérdidas y ganancias; **net** — ganancia neta o líquida; v. aprovechar; ganar, sacar provecho; **to** — **by** aprovecharse de, sacar provecho de.

profitable [práfɪtəbl] adj. provechoso; lucrativo.

profiteer [prafətír] s. extorsionista, carero, explotador, logrero; v. extorsionar, explotar, cobrar más de lo justo.

profound [prəfáund] adj. profundo.

profuse [prəfjús] adj. profuso, abundante; pródigo.

progeny [prádʒənɪ] s. prole.

program [prógræm] s. programa; plan.

progress [prágrɛs] s. progreso; [prəgrés] v. progresar.

progressive [prəgrésɪv] adj. progresivo; progresista; s. progresista.

prohibit [prohíbɪt] v. prohibir; vedar.

prohibition [proəbíʃən] s. prohibición.

project [prádʒɛkt] s. proyecto, plan; [prədʒɛ́kt] v. proyectar(se); extenderse, sobresalir.

projectile [prədʒɛ́ktl] s. proyectil; adj. arrojadizo; — **weapon** arma arrojadiza.

projection [prədʒɛ́kʃən] s. proyección; saliente, salidizo.

proletarian [prolətérɪən] adj. & s. proletario.

proletariat [prolətérɪət] s. proletariado.

prologue [prólɔg] s. prólogo.

prolong [prəlɔ́ŋ] v. prolongar.

prolongation [proləŋgéʃən] s. prolongación.

promenade [praménéd] s. paseo; baile (usualmente prom); v. pasearse.

prominent [prámənənt] adj. prominente; notable; saliente; conspicuo.

promiscuous [prəmískjʊəs] adj. promiscuo.

promise [prámɪs] s. promesa; v. prometer; **Promised Land** Tierra de Promisión.

promising [prámɪsɪŋ] adj. prometedor.

promissory [práməsorɪ] adj. promisorio; — **note** pagaré.

promontory [práməntorɪ] s. promontorio.

promote [prəmót] v. promover; fomentar; explotar; adelantar, ascender; elevar (a un empleo o dignidad superior).

promoter [prəmótə] s. promotor, promovedor.

promotion [prəmóʃən] s. promoción; ascenso; adelantamiento.

prompt [prampt] adj. pronto, puntual; listo, presto; v. mover, incitar, inducir; apuntar (servir de apuntador en el teatro); soplar (sugerir a otro lo que debe decir en una clase o junta).

promptly [prámptlɪ] adv. pronto, prontamente, presto; puntualmente; con prontitud, con presteza.

promptness [prámptnɪs] s. prontitud, presteza; puntualidad.

promulgate [prəmʌ́lget] v. promulgar.

prone [pron] adj. inclinado; propenso, dispuesto; boca abajo; postrado.

prong [prɔŋ] s. púa, punta.

pronoun [prónaun] s. pronombre.

pronounce [prənáuns] v. pronunciar; declarar.

pronounced [prənáunst] adj. pronunciado, marcado; — **opinions** opiniones decididas.

pronunciation [prənʌnsıéʃən] s. pronunciación.

proof[pruf]s. prueba;comprobación; adj. impenetrable, resistente; — against a prueba de; —reader corrector de pruebas de imprenta; — sheet prueba, pliego de prueba; galley — galerada; bomb— a prueba de bomba; fire — a prueba de incendios; water— impermeable.

prop [prɑp] s. puntal; sostén, apoyo; v apuntalar, sostener.

propaganda [prɑpəgǽndə] s. propaganda.

propagate [prápəget] v. propagar(se).

propagation [prɑpəgéʃən] s. propagación; diseminación.

propel [prəpél] v. propulsar, impeler.

propeller [prəpélə] s. hélice (de un buque o avión); propulsor, impulsor.

proper [prápə] adj. propio; conveniente, a propósito; justo; correcto; — noun nombre propio; -ly adv. propiamente; con propiedad, correctamente.

property [prápətɪ] s. propiedad; posesión; posesiones, bienes.

prophecy [práfəsɪ] s. profecía.

prophesy [práfəsaɪ] v. profetizar, predecir, pronosticar, augurar.

prophet [práfɪt] s. profeta.

prophetic [prəfétɪk] adj. profético.

propitious [prəpíʃəs] adj. propicio, favorable.

proportion [prəpórʃən] s. proporción; out of— desproporcionado; v. proporcionar; well -ed bien proporcionado.

proposal [prəpózl] s. propuesta; proposición; declaración (de amor).

propose [prəpóz] v. proponer; declararse, hacer propuesta de matrimonio; to — to do something proponerse hacer algo.

proposition [prɑpəzíʃən] s. proposición; propuesta; asunto.

proprietor [prəpráɪətə] s. propietario, dueño.

propriety [prəpráɪətɪ] s. propiedad, corrección; decoro.

prorate [prorét] v. prorratear, repartir proporcionalmente.

prosaic [prozéɪk] adj. prosaico.

prose [proz] s. prosa; adj. prosaico.

prosecute [prásɪkjut] v. procesar, enjuiciar, demandar ante un juez; llevar adelante (un negocio, empresa, demanda, etc.).

prosecution [prɑsɪkjúʃən] s. prosecución, seguimiento; parte acusadora (en un pleito).

prosecutor [prásɪkjutə] s. fiscal; acusador.

prospect [práspekt]s. perspectiva, vista; esperanza; espectativa; cliente (candidato o comprador) probable; probabilidad de éxito (para un negocio, empleo, etc.); v. explorar, andar en busca de.

prospective [prəspéktɪv] adj. probable, posible, esperado; presunto.

prospector [prəspéktə] s. explorador, buscador (de minas, petróleo, etc.).

prosper [práspə] v. prosperar, medrar.

prosperity [praspérətɪ] s. prosperidad.

prosperous [prásprəs] adj. próspero.

prostitute [prástətjut] s. ramera, prostituta; v. prostituir.

prostrate [prástret] adj. postrado; abatido; v. postrar; abatir.

protect [prətékt] v. proteger.

protection [prətékʃən] s. protección; amparo.

protective [prətéktɪv] adj. protector; — tariff tarifa proteccionista.

protector [prətéktə] s. protector.

protectorate [prətéktrɪt] s. protectorado.

protégé [prótəge] s. protegido.

protein [prótiɪn] s. proteína.

protest [prótɛst] s. protesta, protestación; [prətést] v. protestar.

protestant [prátɪstənt] adj. & s. protestante.

protestation [pratəstéʃən] s. protestación, protesta.

protoplasm [prótəplæzəm] s. protoplasma.

protract [protrǽkt] v. alargar, extender, prolongar.

protrude [protrúd] v. sobresalir; resaltar; proyectar(se).

protuberance [protjúbərəns] s. protuberancia.

proud [praud] adj. orgulloso; soberbio.

prove [pruv] v. probar; demostrar; comprobar; resultar.

proverb [právəb] s. proverbio; refrán.

provide [prəváɪd] v. proveer; abastecer; suplir; estipular; to — for hacer provisión para; to — with proveer de.

provided [prəváɪdɪd] conj. con tal (de) que, a condición (de) que; — that con tal (de) que.

providence [právədəns] s. providencia.

providential [pravədénʃəl] adj. providencial.

provider [prəváɪdə] s. proveedor.

province [právɪns] s. provincia; jurisdicción; it isn't within my — no está dentro de mi jurisdicción; no es de mi incumbencia.

provincial [prəvínʃəl] *adj.* provincial; *s.* provinciano.

provision [prəvíʒən] *s.* provisión; abastecimiento; estipulación; -**s** provisiones; víveres; **to make the necessary** -**s** tomar las medidas (o precauciones) necesarias.

proviso [prəváizo] *s.* condición, estipulación.

provocation [prəvəkéʃən] *s.* provocación.

provoke [prəvók] *v.* provocar; irritar; enfadar.

prow [prau] *s.* proa.

prowess [práuis] *s.* proeza.

prowl [praul] *v.* rondar en acecho; fisgonear.

proximity [praksíməti] *s.* proximidad.

proxy [práksi] *s.* apoderado, substituto, delegado; **by** — mediante apoderado.

prude [prud] *s.* mojigato, persona gazmoña.

prudence [prúdn̩s] *s.* prudencia.

prudent [prúdn̩t] *adj.* prudente.

prudery [prúdərɪ] *s.* mojigatería, gazmoñería, remilgo.

prudish [prúdɪʃ] *adj.* gazmoño, remilgado.

prune [prun] *s.* ciruela; ciruela pasa; *v.* podar, recortar.

pry [prai] *v.* atisbar, espiar; fisgar, fisgonear; curiosear; **to** — **a secret out** extraer (o arrancar) un secreto; **to** — **apart** separar por fuerza; **to** — **into other people's affairs** entremeterse en lo ajeno; **to** — **open** abrir a la fuerza; **to** — **up** levantar con una palanca.

psalm [sam] *s.* salmo.

pseudonym [sjúdn̩ɪm] *s.* seudónimo.

psychiatrist [saɪkáɪətrɪst] *s.* psiquiatra, alienista.

psychiatry [saɪkáɪətrɪ] *s.* psiquiatría.

psychological [saɪkəládʒɪk|] *adj.* psicológico.

psychologist [saɪkúlədʒɪst] *s.* psicólogo.

psychology [saɪkúlədʒɪ] *s.* psicología.

public [páblɪk] *adj.* público; — **prosecutor** fiscal; *s.* público.

publication [pʌblɪkéʃən] *s.* publicación.

publicity [pʌblísətɪ] *s.* publicidad, propaganda.

publish [páblɪʃ] *v.* publicar; editar; -**ing house** editorial o editora.

publisher [páblɪʃə] *s.* publicador; editor.

pucker [pʌkə] *v.* fruncir.

pudding [púdɪŋ] *s.* budín, pudín.

puddle [pʌdl] *s.* charco.

puff [pʌf] *s.* resoplido; bocanada (de

humo, vapor, *etc.*); bullón (*de vestido*); — **of wind** ráfaga, soplo; — **paste** hojaldre; **cream** — bollo de crema; **powder** — polvera, borla, *Am.* mota; *v.* resoplar, jadear; echar bocanadas; **to** — **up** inflar(se); ahuecar(se); hinchar(se).

pug [pʌg] *s.* perro dogo; — **nose** nariz chata, ñata o respingada.

pull [pul] *v.* tirar de; jalar (halar), sacar; arrancar; estirar; **to** — **apart** desgarrar; despedazar; descomponer; desmontar; **to** — **down the curtain** bajar la cortinilla; **to** — **oneself together** componerse, serenarse; **to** — **over to the right** hacerse a la derecha, desviarse hacia la derecha; **to** — **up** arrancar; parar (*un caballo, un auto*); parar, hacer alto; **to** — **through** salir de un apuro; sacar (*a alguien*) de un apuro; **to** — **in·to the station** el tren llegó a la estación; *s.* tirón; estirón; ascenso difícil; esfuerzo (*para subir*); **to have** — tener buenas aldabas, tener influencia.

pullet [púlɪt] *s.* polla.

pulley [púlɪ] *s.* polea; garrucha.

pulp [pʌlp] *s.* pulpa.

pulpit [púlpɪt] *s.* púlpito.

pulsate [pálset] *v.* pulsar, latir.

pulse [pʌls] *s.* pulso; pulsación.

pulverize [pálvəraɪz] *v.* pulverizar.

pumice [pámɪs] *s.* piedra pómez.

pump [pʌmp] *s.* bomba (*para sacar agua*); zapatilla; **gasoline** — bomba de gasolina; **hand** — bomba de mano; **tire** — bomba para neumáticos; *v.* manejar la bomba, *Am.* bombear; inflar (*un neumático*); **to** — **someone** sacarle (o sonsacarle) a una persona la verdad o un secreto.

pumpkin [pámpkɪn] *s.* calabaza.

pun [pʌn] *s.* equívoco, retruécano, juego de palabras; *v.* decir retruécanos o equívocos, jugar del vocablo.

punch [pʌntʃ] *s.* puñetazo, puñada; ponche (*bebida*); punzón, sacabocados; empuje, fuerza, vitalidad; — **bowl** ponchera; *v.* dar un puñetazo, dar una puñada; punzar, horadar, perforar; **to** — **a hole** hacer un agujero o perforación.

punctual [pʌ́ŋktʃʊəl] *adj.* puntual.

punctuality [pʌŋktʃʊǽlətɪ] *s.* puntualidad.

punctuate [pʌ́ŋktʃʊet] *v.* puntuar.

punctuation [pʌŋktʃʊéʃən] *s.* puntuación.

puncture [pʌ́ŋktʃə] *v.* picar, punzar, pinchar; agujerear, perforar; -**d tire**

neumático picado; *s.* picadura; pinchazo; perforación; **to have a tire** — tener un neumático picado, tener una llanta o goma picada.

punish [pʌnɪʃ] *v.* castigar.

punishment [pʌnɪʃmənt] *s.* castigo.

puny [pjúnɪ] *adj.* endeble, débil, flaco, enfermizo; insignificante.

pup [pʌp] *s.* cachorro.

pupil [pjúpl] *s.* discípulo; — **of the eye** pupila, niña del ojo.

puppet [pʌpɪt] *s.* títere, muñeco, monigote; — **show** títeres.

puppy [pʌpɪ] *s.* cachorrito.

purchase [pɔ́tʃəs] *v.* comprar; mercar; *s.* compra; merca; **to get a** — **upon** agarrarse fuerte a.

purchaser [pɔ́tʃəsə] *s.* comprador, marchante.

pure [pjur] *adj.* puro; **-ly** *adv.* puramente; meramente.

purée [pjuré] *s.* puré.

purgative [pɔ́gətɪv] *adj.* purgante; *s.* purga, purgante.

purgatory [pɔ́gətorɪ] *s.* purgatorio.

purge [pɔdʒ] *v.* purgar(se); limpiar; purificar(se); *s.* purga, purgante.

purify [pjúrəfaɪ] *v.* purificar(se); depurar.

purity [pjúrətɪ] *s.* pureza.

purple [pɔ́pl] *s.* púrpura; *adj.* purpúreo, morado.

purport [pɔ́port] *s.* significado; tenor, sustancia; [pəpórt] *v.* pretender, aparentar.

purpose [pɔ́pəs] *s.* propósito, intención; fin, objeto; **for no** — sin objeto, inútilmente, en vano, para nada; **on** — adrede, de propósito; *v.* proponerse.

purr [pɔ] *s.* ronroneo (*del gato*); zumbido (*del motor*); *v.* ronronear (*el gato*).

purse [pɔs] *s.* bolsillo, portamonedas, bolsa; *v.* **to** — **one's lips** fruncir los labios.

pursue [pəsú] *v.* perseguir; seguir; dedicarse a (*una carrera, un estudio*).

pursuer [pəsúə] *s.* perseguidor.

pursuit [pəsút] *s.* perseguimiento; busca; ocupación; ejercicio (*de una profesión, cargo, etc.*); **in** — **of** a caza de, en seguimiento de, en busca de.

pus [pʌs] *s.* pus, podre.

push [pʊʃ] *v.* empujar; fomentar, promover; apresurar; **to** — **aside** hacer a un lado, rechazar, apartar; **to** — **forward** empujar, abrirse paso; avanzar; **to** — **through** encajar (*por un agujero o rendija*); abrirse paso a empujones; *s.* empuje; empujón, empellón; — **button** botón eléctrico.

pushcart [pʊ́ʃkart] *s.* carretilla de mano.

pussy [pʊ́sɪ] *s.* minino, gatito; — **willow** especie de sauce americano.

put [pʊt] *v.* poner; colocar; **to** — **a question** hacer una pregunta; **to** — **across an idea** darse a entender bien; hacer aceptar una idea; **to** — **away** apartar; guardar; **to** — **before** poner delante, anteponer; proponer ante; **to** — **by money** ahorrar o guardar dinero; **to** — **down** apuntar, anotar; sofocar (*una revolución*); rebajar (*los precios*); **to** — **in words** expresar; **to** — **in writing** poner por escrito; **to** — **off** aplazar, posponer; diferir; **to** — **on** ponerse (*ropa*); **to** — **on airs** darse tono o ínfulas; **to** — **on weight** engordar; **to** — **out** apagar, extinguir; **to** — **someone out** echar o expulsar a alguien; molestar o incomodar a alguien; **to** — **to shame** avergonzar; **to** — **up** enlatar, envasar (*frutas, legumbres*); apostar (*dinero*); alojar(se); erigir; **to** — **up for sale** poner de venta; **to** — **up with** aguantar, tolerar; *pret. & p.p. de* **to put**.

putrefy [pjútrəfaɪ] *v.* podrir (o pudrir), corromper.

putrid [pjútrɪd] *adj.* putrefacto, podrido.

putter [pʌtə] *v.* trabajar sin orden ni sistema; ocuparse en cosas de poca monta; malgastar el tiempo.

putty [pʌtɪ] *s.* masilla; *v.* tapar o rellenar con masilla.

puzzle [pʌzl] *s.* rompecabezas, acertijo enigma; **crossword** — crucigrama; *v.* embrollar, poner perplejo, confundir **to** — **out** desenredar, descifrar; **to** — **over** ponderar; tratar de resolver o descifrar; **to be** — **d** estar perplejo.

pyramid [pírəmɪd] *s.* pirámide.

Q

quack [kwæk] *s.* graznido (*del pato*) curandero, matasanos, medicastro charlatán; *adj.* falso; *v.* graznar.

quagmire [kwǽgmaɪr] *s.* tremedal cenagal.

quail [kwel] *s.* codorniz.

quaint [kwent] *adj.* raro, extraño; pintoresco.

quake [kwek] *s.* temblor; terremoto; *v* temblar.

qualification [kwɑləfəkéʃən] *s.* calificación; cualidad, calidad; requisito aptitud.

qualify [kwálɪfaɪ] *v.* calificar; capacitar **to** — **for a position** estar capacitado para una posición; **his studies** —

him for the.job sus estudios le capacitan para el puesto.

quality [kwálətɪ] s. cualidad; calidad.

qualm [kwɑm] s. escrúpulo.

quantity [kwántətɪ] s. cantidad.

quarantine [kwɔ́rəntin] s. cuarentena; v. poner en cuarentena, aislar.

quarrel [kwɔ́rəl] s. riña, reyerta, pendencia; querella; v. reñir; pelear, disputar.

quarrelsome [kwɔ́rəlsəm] adj. reñidor, pendenciero.

quarry [kwɔ́rɪ] s. cantera; presa, caza (animal perseguido); v. explotar (una cantera); trabajar en una cantera.

quart [kwort] s. cuarto de galón (0.9463 de un litro).

quarter [kwɔ́rtə] s. cuarto, cuarta parte; moneda de 25 centavos; trimestre (cuarta parte de un año); barrio, distrito; -s morada, vivienda; alojamiento; **from all -s** de todas partes; **to give no — to the enemy** no dar cuartel al enemigo; adj. cuarto; v. cuartear, dividir en cuartos; descuartizar; acuartelar, acantonar, alojar (tropas).

quarterly [kwɔ́rtəlɪ] adv. trimestralmente, por trimestres; adj. trimestral; s. publicación trimestral.

quartet [kwortét] s. cuarteto.

quartz [kworts] s. cuarzo.

quaver [kwévə] v. temblar; s. temblor; trémolo (de la voz).

quay [ki] s. muelle, embarcadero.

queen [kwin] s. reina.

queer [kwir] adj.. raro, extraño, singular; excéntrico; **to feel —** sentirse raro, no sentirse bien; v. poner en ridículo, comprometer; **to — oneself with** quedar mal con, ponerse mal con.

quell [kwɛl] v. reprimir; sofocar (una revuelta); calmar.

quench [kwɛntʃ] v. apagar (el fuego, la sed); reprimir, sofocar, ahogar, templar el ardor de.

query [kwírɪ] s. pregunta; interrogación, signo de interrogación; duda; v. preguntar, expresar duda; marcar con signo de interrogación.

quest [kwɛst] s. busca; pesquisa.

question [kwɛ́stʃən] s. pregunta; cuestión; problema; duda; proposición; **— mark** signo de interrogación; **beyond — fuera de duda; that is out of the —** ¡imposible!; ¡ ni pensar en ello!; v. preguntar; interrogar; dudar.

questionable [kwɛ́stʃənəbl] adj. dudoso; discutible.

questioner [kwɛ́stʃənə] s. interrogador,

preguntador.

questioning [kwɛ́stʃənɪŋ] s. interrogatorio; adj. interrogador.

questionnaire [kwɛstʃonér] s. cuestionario, lista de preguntas, interrogatorio.

quibble [kwíbl] v. sutilizar, valerse de argucias o sutilezas; andar en dimes y diretes; s. sutileza, argucia.

quick [kwɪk] adj. pronto, presto, listo; rápido, veloz; agudo; **— temper** genio violento; **— wit** mente aguda; adv. rápidamente, de prisa, con prisa, pronto; s. carne viva; **to cut to the —** herir en lo vivo, herir en el alma.

quicken [kwíkən] v. acelerar(se); avivar(se); aguzar (la mente, el entendimiento).

quickly [kwíklɪ] adv. pronto, presto, de prisa, aprisa, rápidamente.

quickness [kwíknɪs] s. rapidez; presteza, prontitud; viveza; agudeza (de ingenio).

quicksand [kwíksænd] s. arena movediza.

quicksilver [kwíksɪlvə] s. mercurio, azogue.

quiet [kwáɪət] adj. quieto; callado; tranquilo; en calma; reposado; s. quietud; sosiego, reposo; calma; silencio; v. aquietar; sosegar; calmar, tranquilizar; **to — down** aquietarse; calmarse; **-ly** adv. quietamente, con quietud; calladamente; tranquilamente.

quietness [kwáɪətnɪs] s. quietud; sosiego, calma.

quill [kwɪl] s. pluma; cañón (de pluma de ave); púa (de puerco espín).

quilt [kwɪlt] s. colcha; v. acolchar.

quince [kwɪns] s. membrillo.

quinine [kwáɪnaɪn] s. quinina.

quip [kwɪp] s. pulla, dicharacho; agudeza.

quirk [kwɝk] s. chifladura, extravagancia, capricho; peculiaridad mental.

quit [kwɪt] v. dejar, abandonar; irse; parar, cesar; **to — doing something** dejar de hacer algo; -s adj. desquitado; **we are -s** no nos debemos nada, estamos desquitados, Am. estamos a mano; pret. & p.p. de to quit.

quite [kwaɪt] adv. bastante; del todo, enteramente; **— a person** una persona admirable; **— so** así es, en efecto; **it's — the fashion** está muy en boga.

quitter [kwítə] s. el que deja fácilmente lo empezado, el que se da fácilmente por vencido; evasor; desertor.

quiver [kwívə] v. temblar; estremecerse;

169

s. temblor; estremecimiento.

quiz [kwɪz] *s.* examen; interrogatorio; cuestionario; *v.* examinar, interrogar, hacer preguntas.

quota [kwóta] *s.* cuota.

quotation [kwotéʃən] *s.* citación, cita; cotización (*de precios*); **— marks** comillas.

quote [kwot] *v.* citar; cotizar (*precios*); **to — from** citar a, entresacar una cita de; *s.* cita, citación; **-s** comillas; **in -s** entre comillas.

quotient [kwóʃənt] *s.* cociente.

R

rabbi [ræbaɪ] *s.* rabí, rabino.

rabbit [ræbɪt] *s.* conejo.

rabble [ræbl] *s.* populacho, plebe; canalla.

rabies [rébɪz] *s.* rabia, hidrofobia.

raccoon [rækún] *s. Am.* mapache.

race [res] *s.* raza; corrida, carrera; contienda; **— track** (*o* **— course**) pista; **boat — regata**; *v.* correr; competir en una carrera; ir corriendo; regatear (*competir en una regata*); acelerar (*un motor*).

racer [résə] *s.* corredor; caballo de carrera; auto de carrera.

racial [réʃəl] *adj.* racial.

rack [ræk] *s.* percha, colgadero, clavijero; potro de tormento; **baggage — red; towel — toallero; to fall into — and ruin** caer en un estado de ruina total; *v.* atormentar; **to — one's brain** devanarse los sesos, quebrarse uno la cabeza.

racket [rǽkɪt] *s.* raqueta (*de tenis*); boruca, estrépito, baraúnda; bullicio; trapacería.

racketeer [rǽkɪtɪr] *s.* trapacista, trapacero, extorsionista; *v.* trapacear, extorsionar.

radiance [rédɪəns] *s.* resplandor, brillo.

radiant [rédɪənt] *adj.* radiante; resplandeciente, brillante.

radiate [rédɪet] *v.* irradiar; radiar.

radiator [rédɪetə] *s.* radiador; calorífero.

radical [rǽdɪkl] *adj. & s.* radical.

radio [rédɪo] *s.* radio (*m. o f.*); radiotelefonía; radiotelegrafía; **— commentator** comentarista radial; **— listener** radioescucha, radioyente; **— program** programa radiofónico; **by — por radio**; *v.* radiar, emitir, transmitir, radiodifundir o difundir.

radish [rǽdɪʃ] *s.* rábano.

radium [rédɪəm] *s.* radio (*elemento químico*).

radius [rédɪəs] *s.* radio (*de un círculo*).

raffle [rǽfl] *s.* rifa, sorteo; *v.* rifar, sortear.

raft [ræft] *s.* balsa; **a — of things** un montón (*o la mar*) de cosas.

rafter [rǽftə] *s.* viga (*del techo*).

rag [ræg] *s.* trapo; harapo, andrajo, *Am.* hilacho; **— doll** muñeca de trapo; **to be in -s** estar hecho andrajos, *Am.* estar hecho tiras.

ragamuffin [rǽgəmʌfɪn] *s.* pelagatos, golfo; granuja, pilluelo.

rage [redʒ] *s.* rabia, furor; ira; **to be all the —** estar en boga, estar de moda; *v.* rabiar; enfurecerse; estar enfurecido; bramar; **to — with anger** bramar de ira.

ragged [rǽgid] *adj.* andrajoso, haraposo, harapiento, desharrapado, roto; **— edge** borde raído o deshilachado; **to be on the —** edge estar al borde del precipicio; estar muy nervioso.

raid [red] *s.* incursión, invasión repentina; allanamiento (*de un local*); **air — ataque** aéreo, bombardeo aéreo; *v.* hacer una incursión; invadir de repente; caer sobre; allanar (*un local*), entrar a la fuerza.

rail [rel] *s.* riel, carril; ferrocarril; barandal, barandilla;.**— fence** empalizada, estacada; **by —** por ferrocarril.

railing [rélɪŋ] *s.* baranda, barandilla; pasamano (*de escalera*), balaustrada, barrera; rieles.

railroad [rélrod] *s.* ferrocarril; *adj.* ferroviario; de ferrocarril.

railway [rélwe] *s.* ferrocarril; *adj.* ferroviario; de ferrocarril; **— crossing** cruce, crucero.

raiment [rémənt] *s.* vestidura, ropaje.

rain [ren] *s.* lluvia; **— water** agua llovediza; *v.* llover; **— or shine** que llueva o no; llueva o truene; a todo trance.

rainbow [rénbo] *s.* arco iris.

raincoat [rénkot] *s.* impermeable; *Am.* capa de agua, *Am.* manga o capa de hule.

raindrop [réndrap] **•** gota de agua.

rainfall [rénfɔl] *s.* lluvia, lluvias; cantidad de agua pluvial; aguacero.

rainy [réni] *adj.* lluvioso.

raise [res] *v.* levantar, alzar; subir; erigir; criar; cultivar; reunir (*dinero*); reclutar (*un ejército*); fermentar; **to — a question** hacer una observación o suscitar una duda; **to — a racket** armar un alboroto; *s.* aumento de sueldo.

raisin [rézn] *s.* pasa, uva seca.

rake [rek] *s.* rastro, rastrillo; libertino, perdulario; *v.* rastrear, rastrillar (*la tierra*); raspar; barrer (*con rastrillo*);

atizar (*el fuego*).

rally [ráli] *v.* juntar(se); recobrarse; mejorar (*de salud*); fortalecerse; revivir; tomar nueva vida; **to — to the side of** acudir al lado de; *s.* junta popular, junta libre; recuperación.

ram [ræm] *s.* carnero; ariete o martillo hidráulico; espolón de buque; **battering — ariete;** *v.* apisonar, aplanar a golpes; aplastar *de un cheque*; rellenar, atestar; **to — a boat** chocar con un barco; arremeter contra un barco.

ramble [rémbl] *v.* vagar; divagar; callejear; *s.* paseo, andanza.

rampart [rémpart] *s.* baluarte, muralla.

ran [ræn] *pret. de* **to run.**

ranch [rænt∫] *s.* hacienda, *Am.* rancho; **cattle — hacienda** de ganado, *Am.* rancho, *Am.* estancia.

rancid [ránsid] *adj.* rancio, acedo.

rancor [ránkə] *s.* rencor, encono.

random [rándəm] *adj.* impensado; fortuito, al azar; **at — al azar, a la ventura.**

rang [ræŋ] *pret. de* **to ring.**

range [rendʒ] *v.* alinear; poner en fila; arreglar; rondar, vagar por; fluctuar; **to — ten miles** tener un alcance de diez millas (*un arma de fuego*); *s.* fila, hilera; alcance; extensión; fluctuación, variación (*dentro de ciertos* límites); distancia; pastizal, *Am.* pastal; estufa; **gas — cocina** de gas; **— of mountains** cordillera, cadena de montañas; **— of vision** campo de visión; **in — with** en línea con; **shooting — campo** de práctica para tirar.

rank [ræŋk] *s.* rango, categoría; orden; calidad; grado; fila; línea, hilera; **the — and file** el pueblo, la gente ordinaria; la tropa; *v.* poner en fila; ordenar, arreglar; clasificar; **to — above** sobresalir a; ser de grado superior a; **to — high** tener un alto rango, categoría o renombre; ser tenido en alta estima; **to — second** tener el segundo lugar; **to — with** estar al nivel de, tener el mismo grado que; **he -s high in athletics** sobresale en los deportes.

ransack [ránsæk] *v.* escudriñar; saquear.

ransom [ránsəm] *s.* rescate; *v.* rescatar; redimir.

rant [rænt] *v.* desvariar; disparatar; gritar necedades.

rap [ræp] *v.* golpear, dar un golpe; criticar, censurar; **to — on the door** llamar o tocar a la puerta; *s.* golpe; **not to care a — no** importarle a uno un ardite.

rapacious [rəpé∫əs] *adj.* rapaz.

rape [rep] *s.* estupro, violación (*de una mujer*); *v.* forzar, violar (*a una mujer*).

rapid [rápid] *adj.* rápido; **-s** *s. pl.* raudal, rápidos (*de un río*).

rapidity [rəpídəti] *s.* rapidez, velocidad.

rapt [ræpt] *adj.* extasiado; absorto.

rapture [rápt∫ə] *s.* éxtasis, rapto.

rare [rer] *adj* raro; precioso; extraordinario, extraño; a medio asar, a medio freír, medio crudo, **-ly** *adv.* rara vez, raras veces; raramente; extraordinariamente.

rarity [rérəti] *s.* rareza; enrarecimiento (*de la atmósfera*).

rascal [rásk∫l] *s.* bribón, bellaco, pícaro.

rash [ræ∫] *adj.* temerario, atrevido; precipitado; imprudente; *s.* salpullido, erupción (*de la piel*).

rashness [ræ∫nis] *s.* temeridad.

rasp [ræsp] *v.* chirriar; irritar; *s.* chirrido, sonido áspero; ronquera, carraspera.

raspberry [rázberi] *s.* frambuesa; **— bush** frambueso.

raspy [ráspi] *adj.* ronco; áspero.

rat [ræt] *s.* rata; postizo (*para el pelo*).

rate [ret] *s.* proporción; porcentaje; tanto por ciento, *Am.* tipo (*de interés*); tarifa; precio; **— of exchange** cambio, *Am.* tipo de cambio; **— of increase** incremento proporcional; **of increase** incremento proporcional; **at any — en** todo caso, de todos modos; **at that — a ese** paso; en esa proporción; **at the — of a** razón de; **first — de** primera clase o calidad; muy bien; *v.* calificar, clasificar, considerar; tasar, valuar; **he -s as the best** se le considera como el mejor; **he -s high** se le tiene en alta estima.

rather [ráðə] *adv.* algo, un poco, un tanto; más bien; mejor, mejor dicho; **— than más** bien que; **I would — die than** prefiero antes la muerte que; **I would — not go** preferiría no ir.

ratify [rátifai] *s.* ratificar.

rating [rétiŋ] *s.* clasificación; rango, grado; clase.

ratio [ré∫o] *s.* razón, proporción; relación.

ration [ré∫ən] *s.* ración; *v.* racionar.

rational [ré∫ənl] *adj.* racional.

rationing [ré∫əniŋ] *s.* racionamiento.

rattle [rátl] *v.* traquetear; golpetear; sacudir ruidosamente; confundir, desconcertar; **to — off** decir de corrido (*o decir muy aprisa*); *s.* traqueteo; golpeteo; **child's — sonaja,** sonajero; **death — estertor** de la muerte.

rattlesnake [rátlsnek] *s.* culebra de

cascabel, *Am.* cascabel o cascabela.

raucous [rókəs] *adj.* ronco; estentóreo.

ravage [rǽvidʒ] *s.* estrago, ruina, destrucción, asolamiento; saqueo, pillaje; *v.* asolar, arruinar; pillar, saquear.

rave [rev] *v.* desvariar, delirar, disparatar; bramar; **to — about someone** deshacerse en elogios de alguien.

raven [révən] *s.* cuervo; *adj.* negro lustroso.

ravenous [rǽvənəs] *adj.* voraz; devorador; **to be —** tener un hambre canina.

ravine [rəvín] *s.* quebrada, hondonada, barranco (*o* barranca).

ravish [rǽviʃ] *v.* encantar; arrebatar; violar (*a una mujer*).

raw [rɔ] *adj.* crudo; áspero; pelado, descarnado; inexperto, nuevo; **— material** materia prima; **— recruit** recluta nuevo; **— silk** seda en rama, seda cruda; **— sugar** azúcar bruto, azúcar crudo.

rawhide [róhaid] *s.* cuero crudo; **— whip** rebenque.

ray [re] *s.* rayo; raya (*especie de pez*).

rayon [réɑn] *s.* rayón, seda artificial.

raze [rez] *v.* arrasar, asolar.

razor [rézə] *s.* navaja de afeitar; **— blade** hoja de afeitar; **safety —** navaja de seguridad.

reach [ritʃ] *v.* llegar a; alcanzar; tocar; extenderse; **to — for** tratar de coger; echar mano a; **to — into** meter la mano en; penetrar en; **to — out one's hand** alargar o tender la mano; *s.* alcance; extensión; **beyond his —** fuera de su alcance; **within his —** a su alcance.

react [riǽkt] *v.* reaccionar.

reaction [riǽkʃən] *s.* reacción.

reactionary [riǽkʃənɛri] *adj.* & *s.* reaccionario.

read [rid] *v.* leer; indicar (*dícese de un contador, termómetro, etc.*); **to — law** estudiar derecho; **it -s thus** dice así, reza así; **it -s easily** se lee fácilmente o sin esfuerzo.

read [red] *pret.* & *p.p. de* **to read.**

reader [rídə] *s.* lector; libro de lectura.

readily [rédili] *adv.* pronto, con presteza; fácilmente, sin esfuerzo.

readiness [rédinis] *s.* prontitud, presteza, facilidad; buena disposición; **to be in —** estar preparado, estar listo.

reading [rídiŋ] *s.* lectura; indicación (*de un barómetro, termómetro, etc.*); **— room** sala o salón de lectura.

readjust [riədʒást] *v.* reajustar, ajustar de nuevo; arreglar de nuevo; readap-

tar.

readjustment [riədʒástmənt] *s.* reajuste; readaptación; nuevo arreglo.

ready [rédi] *adj.* pronto, listo; preparado; propenso; dispuesto; **— cash** fondos disponibles; dinero a la mano.

ready-made [rédiméd] *adj.* hecho, ya hecho.

real [rəl] *adj.* real, verdadero; **— estate** bienes raíces, bienes inmuebles; **-ly** *adv.* realmente, verdaderamente.

realism [ríəlizəm] *s.* realismo.

realist [ríəlist] *s.* realista; **-ic** *adj.* realista, vivo, natural.

reality [riǽləti] *s.* realidad.

realization [riələzéʃən] *s.* realización; comprensión.

realize [ríəlaiz] *v.* darse cuenta de, hacerse cargo de; realizar, efectuar; convertir en dinero.

realm [rɛlm] *s.* reino; dominio, región.

reap [rip] *v.* segar; cosechar; recoger; obtener, sacar (*provecho, fruto, etc.*).

reaper [rípə] *s.* segador; segadora, máquina segadora.

reappear [riəpír] *v.* reaparecer.

rear [rir] *adj.* trasero, posterior; de atrás; **— admiral** contraalmirante; **— guard** retaguardia; *s.* espalda, parte de atrás; trasero; fondo (*de una sala, salón, etc.*); cola (*de una fila*); **in the —** detrás, atrás, a la espalda; *v.* criar, educar; encabritarse, empinarse (*el caballo*).

reason [rízn] *s.* razón; causa, motivo; **by — of** a causa de; **it stands to —** es razonable; *v.* razonar; **to — out** discurrir, razonar.

reasonable [ríznəbl] *adj.* razonable, justo; racional; módico, moderado; **reasonably** *adv.* razonablemente; con razón; bastante.

reasoning [ríznıŋ] *s.* razonamiento, raciocinio.

reassure [riəʃúr] *v.* tranquilizar, restaurar la confianza a; asegurar de nuevo.

rebate [ríbet] *s.* rebaja (*de precio*); *v.* rebajar (*precio*).

rebel [rébl] *s.* & *adj.* rebelde; [ribél] *v.* rebelarse.

rebellion [ribéljən] *s.* rebelión.

rebellious [ribéljəs] *adj.* rebelde.

rebirth [ribə́ɵ] *s.* renacimiento.

rebound [ribáund] *v.* rebotar; repercutir; [ribáund] *s.* rebote; **on the —** de rebote.

rebuff [ribʌ́f] *s.* desaire; repulsa; *v.* desairar; rechazar.

rebuild [ribfld] *v.* reconstruir, reedificar.

rebuilt [ribílt] *pret. & p.p. de* **to rebuild**.

rebuke [ribjúk] *s.* reprensión, reproche, reprimenda, repulsa; *v.* reprender, reprochar.

recall [rík̇ɔl] *s.* llamada, aviso (*para hacer volver*); retirada (*de un diplomático*); revocación; [rikɔ́l] *v.* recordar; retirar; revocar.

recede [risíd] *v.* retroceder; retirarse.

receipt [risít] *s.* recibo; fórmula, receta; —s entradas, ingresos; **on — of** al recibo de; **we are in — of** your kind **letter . . .** obra en nuestro poder su grata . . . ; *v.* sellar (*con el recibí*), dar recibo.

receive [risív] *v.* recibir.

receiver [risívə] *s.* receptor; recibidor, depositario, síndico; recipiente, receptáculo.

recent [rísn̩t] *adj.* reciente; **-ly** *adv.* recientemente, *Am.* recién (*como en* salió recién); **-ly married** recién casados.

receptacle [riséptək̇l] *s.* receptáculo.

reception [risépʃən] *s.* recepción; recibimiento; acogida, acogimiento.

recess [risés] *s.* nicho, hueco; tregua, intermisión; hora de recreo o asueto; **in the -es of** en lo más recóndito de; *v.* suspender el trabajo; levantar (*por corto tiempo*) una sesión; hacer un hueco o nicho en (*la pared*).

recipe [résəpi] *s.* receta, fórmula.

recipient [risípiənt] *s.* recipiente, recibidor; *adj.* receptivo.

reciprocal [risíprək̇l] *adj.* recíproco, mutuo.

reciprocate [risíprək̇et] *v.* corresponder.

recital [risáit̩l] *s.* recitación; relación, narración; recital (*músico*).

recitation [resətéʃən] *s.* recitación.

recite [risáit] *v.* recitar; relatar; decir o dar la lección.

reckless [réklis] *adj.* temerario, atrevido; precipitado; descuidado; **— with one's money** derrochador.

recklessness [réklisnis] *s.* temeridad, osadía, descuido.

reckon [rékən] *v.* contar, computar, calcular; juzgar; suponer; **to — on** contar con.

reckoning [rékəniŋ] *s.* cuenta; ajuste de cuentas; cálculo; **the day of —** el día del juicio.

reclaim [riklém] *v.* recobrar, aprovechar (*tierras baldías*); aprovechar o utilizar (*el hule usado*); pedir la devolución de, tratar de recobrar.

recline [rikláin] *v.* reclinar(se), recostar(se).

recluse [riklús] *adj.* recluso, solitario; *s.* recluso, solitario, ermitaño.

recognition [rekəgníʃən] *s.* reconocimiento.

recognize [rékəgnaiz] *v.* reconocer.

recoil [rikɔ́il] *v.* recular, *Am.* patear (*un arma de fuego*); retroceder, retirarse; *s.* reculada; rebote.

recollect [rekəlékt] *v.* recordar; [rikəlékt] recobrar, volver a cobrar; recoger, reunir.

recollection [rekəlékʃən] *s.* recuerdo.

recommend [rekəménd] *v.* recomendar.

recommendation [rekəmendéʃən] *s.* recomendación.

recompense [rékəmpens] *v.* recompensar; *s.* recompensa.

reconcile [rékənsail] *v.* reconciliar; ajustar, conciliar; **to — oneself to** resignarse a, conformarse con.

reconciliation [rekənsiliéʃən] *f.* reconciliación; ajuste, conciliación; conformidad, resignación.

reconnoiter [rikənɔ́itə] *v.* reconocer, explorar; hacer un reconocimiento o exploración.

reconsider [rikənsídə] *v.* reconsiderar.

reconstruct [rikənstrʌ́kt] *v.* reconstruir, reedificar.

reconstruction [rikənstrʌ́kʃən] *s.* reconstrucción.

record [rékəd] *s.* registro; copia oficial de un documento; memoria; historial (*de una persona*), hoja de servicios; disco (*fonográfico*); record (*en deportes*); **to break the speed —** batir el record de velocidad; **an off-the-record remark** una observación que no ha de constar en el acta; observación hecha en confianza; *adj.* notable, extraordinario; sobresaliente; [rikɔ́rd] *v.* registrar; asentar, apuntar; inscribir; grabar en disco fonográfico.

recount [rikáunt] *s.* recuento, segunda cuenta; [rikáunt] *v.* contar, narrar, relatar, referir; [rikáunt] recontar, volver a contar.

recourse [ríkors] *s.* recurso, refugio, auxilio; **to have —** to recurrir a.

recover [rikʌ́və] *v.* recobrar(se), recuperar(se); recobrar la salud; reponerse; [rikʌ́və] volver a cubrir.

recovery [rikʌ́vri] *s.* recobro; recuperación; cobranza.

recreation [rekriéʃən] *s.* recreación, recreo.

recruit [rikrút] *v.* reclutar; alistar; *s.* recluta; novato, nuevo miembro (*de una organización*).

rectangle [réktæŋ̇l] *s.* rectángulo.

173

rectify [réktəfaɪ] v. rectificar.

rector [réktə] s. rector.

rectum [réktəm] s. recto.

recuperate [rɪkjúpəret] v. recuperar, recobrar; recobrar la salud.

recur [rɪkɜ́] v. volver a ocurrir; repetirse; **to — to a matter** volver a un asunto.

red [red] adj. rojo; colorado, encarnado; **red-hot** candente; enfurecido, furioso; muy caliente; **— tape** formalismo, trámites enojosos; **— wine** vino tinto; **to see —** enfurecerse; s. color rojo; rojo.

redden [rédn] v. enrojecer(se); ruborizarse, ponerse rojo; teñir de rojo.

reddish [rédɪʃ] adj. rojizo.

redeem [rɪdím] v. redimir; rescatar; desempeñar (una prenda); cumplir (una promesa).

redeemer [rɪdímə] s. salvador, redentor; **the Redeemer** el Redentor.

redemption [rɪdémpʃən] s. redención; rescate; **— of a note** pago de una obligación.

redness [rédnɪs] s. rojez o rojura; inflamación.

redouble [rɪdʌ́bl] v. redoblar; repetir; repercutir.

redress [rídres] s. reparación, enmienda, compensación; desagravio; [rɪdrés] v. enmendar, rectificar, remediar, reparar; desagraviar.

reduce [rɪdjús] v. reducir; mermar; rebajar; adelgazar(se); subyugar.

reduction [rɪdʌ́kʃən] s. reducción; merma; rebaja.

redwood [rédwud] s. Am. secoya o secuoya (árbol gigantesco de California); madera roja de la secoya.

reed [rid] s. caña; junco, junquillo; lengüeta, boquilla (de ciertos instrumentos de viento); caramillo.

reef [rif] s. arrecife, escollo; banco de arena (en el mar).

reek [rik] v. exhalar, echar (vaho o vapor); heder, oler mal; s. hedor, mal olor.

reel [ril] s. carrete; carretel; cinta cinematográfica; v. aspar, enredar (en carretel); bambolearse, tambalearse; **to — off stories** ensartar cuento tras cuento.

re-elect [rialékt] v. reelegir.

re-election [rialékʃən] s. reelección.

re-enter [riéntə] v. volver a entrar.

re-establish [riəstéblɪʃ] v. restablecer.

refer [rɪfɜ́] v. referir; transmitir, remitir; dejar al juicio o decisión de; referirse, aludir; acudir, recurrir (a un tratado, diccionario, etc.).

referee [refərí] s. árbitro; v. arbitrar.

reference [réfrəns] s. referencia, mención, alusión; fiador, el que recomienda a otro; **— book** libro de referencia, libro de consulta; **commercial -s** fiadores, referencias comerciales; **letter of —** carta de recomendación; **with — to** con respecto a, respecto de, en cuanto a.

refill [rifíl] v. rellenar.

refine [rɪfáɪn] v. refinar, purificar; pulir; perfeccionar.

refined [rɪfáɪnd] adj. refinado; pulido, fino, culto.

refinement [rɪfáɪnmənt] s. refinamiento, finura; buena crianza; refinación, purificación; perfeccionamiento.

refinery [rɪfáɪnərɪ] s. refinería.

reflect [rɪflékt] v. reflejar (luz, calor); reflexionar; meditar; **to — on one's character** desdecir del carácter de uno.

reflection [rɪflékʃən] s. reflexión; reflejo, imagen; tacha, discrédito; **on —** después de reflexionarlo.

reflex [rífleks] adj. reflejo; s. reflejo; acción refleja.

reflexive [rɪfléksɪv] adj. reflexivo.

reform [rɪfɔ́rm] v. reformar(se); s. reforma.

reformation [refəméʃən] s. reforma.

reformer [rɪfɔ́rmə] s. reformador; reformista.

refraction [rɪfrékʃən] s. refracción.

refractory [rɪfrǽktərɪ] adj. refractario, terco, obstinado, rebelde.

refrain [rɪfrén] v. refrenarse, abstenerse; s. estribillo.

refresh [rɪfréʃ] v. refrescar(se); renovar.

refreshing [rɪfréʃɪŋ] adj. refrescante; renovador, que renueva; placentero.

refreshment [rɪfréʃmənt] s. refresco.

refrigeration [rɪfrɪdʒəréʃən] s. refrigeración, enfriamiento.

refrigerator [rɪfrídʒəretə] s. nevera, Am refrigerador.

refuge [réfjudʒ] s. refugio, asilo, amparo.

refugee [refjudʒí] s. refugiado.

refund [rɪfʌ́nd] s. reembolso, reintegro [rɪfʌ́nd] v. reembolsar, restituir, reintegrar; [rɪfʌ́nd] consolidar (una deuda).

refusal [rɪfjúzl] s. negativa; desaire; opción (derecho de recusar un convenio provisional).

refuse [rɪfjúz] v. rehusar; negar; desechar; rechazar; **to — to** rehusarse a negarse a.

refuse [réfjus] s. desechos, basura, sobras, desperdicios.

refute [rɪfjút] v. refutar.

regain [rɪgén] v. recobrar; ganar de nuevo.

regal [rígl] adj. regio, real.

regale [rɪgél] v. regalar, agasajar; recrear.

regalia [rɪgélɪə] s. pl. galas, decoraciones, insignias.

regard [rɪgárd] v. mirar; considerar; juzgar; estimar; **as —s this** tocante a esto, en cuanto a esto; por lo que toca a esto; s. miramiento, consideración; respeto; estima; mirada; **—s** recuerdos, memorias; **in** (o **with**) **—** to con respecto a, tocante a, respecto de.

regarding [rɪgárdɪŋ] prep. tocante a, con respecto a, respecto de, relativo a.

regardless [rɪgárdlɪs]: **— of** sin hacer caso de, prescindiendo de.

regent [rídʒənt] s. regente.

regime [rɪʒím] s. régimen.

regiment [rédʒəmənt] s. regimiento.

region [rídʒən] s. región.

register [rédʒɪstɚ] s. registro; matrícula; archivo; lista; contador, indicador; registro (del órgano, de la voz); **cash —** caja registradora; v. registrar; matricular(se); inscribir(se); marcar, indicar; mostrar, manifestar; certificar (una carta).

registrar [rédʒɪstrɑr] s. registrador, archivero.

registration [rɛdʒɪstréʃən] s. registro; asiento (en un libro); matrícula; inscripción.

regret [rɪgrét] s. pesadumbre, dolor; sentimiento, remordimiento; **to send —s** enviar sus excusas (al rehusar una invitación); v. sentir, lamentar; arrepentirse de.

regrettable [rɪgrétəbl] adj. lamentable.

regular [régjələ] adj. regular; metódico, ordenado; **a — fool** un verdadero necio, un tonto de capirote; **— price** precio corriente; **— soldier** soldado de línea.

regularity [rɛgjəlǽrətɪ] s. regularidad.

regulate [régjəlet] v. regular, regularizar.

regulation [rɛgjəléʃən] s. regulación; regla, orden; **—s** reglamento; **— uniform** uniforme de regla, uniforme de ordenanza.

regulator [régjəletə] s. regulador; registro (de reloj).

rehearsal [rɪhɜ́sl] s. ensayo (de un drama, concierto, etc.); enumeración, repetición.

rehearse [rɪhɜ́s] v. ensayar; repetir, repasar.

reign [ren] s. reino, reinado; v. reinar.

reimburse [riɪmbɜ́s] v. reembolsar.

reimbursement [riɪmbɜ́smənt] s. reembolso, reintegro.

rein [ren] s. rienda; v. guiar, gobernar; refrenar (un caballo).

reindeer [réndɪr] s. reno (especie de ciervo).

reinforce [riɪnfɔ́rs] v. reforzar.

reinforcement [riɪnfɔ́rsmənt] s. refuerzo.

reiterate [riítəret] v. reiterar, repetir.

reject [rɪdʒɛ́kt] v. rechazar; desechar; descartar; rehusar.

rejoice [rɪdʒɔ́ɪs] v. regocijar(se).

rejoicing [rɪdʒɔ́ɪsɪŋ] s. regocijo, júbilo.

rejoin [rɪdʒɔ́ɪn] v. reunirse con; volver(se) a unir; [rɪdʒɔ́ɪn] replicar.

rejuvenate [rɪdʒúvənet] v. rejuvenecer.

relapse [rɪlǽps] s. recaída; v. recaer, reincidir.

relate [rɪlét] v. relatar, narrar; relacionar; **it —s to** se relaciona con, se refiere a.

related [rɪlétɪd] adj. relatado, narrado; relacionado; **to become — by marriage** emparentar; **we are —** somos parientes; estamos emparentados.

relation [rɪléʃən] s. relación; narración; parentesco; pariente; **—s** parientes, parentela; **with — to** con relación a, con respecto a, tocante a.

relationship [rɪléʃənʃɪp] s. relación; parentesco.

relative [rélətɪv] adj. relativo; s. relativo, pronombre relativo; pariente, deudo; **— to** relativo a; tocante a; referente a.

relax [rɪlǽks] v. relajar; aflojar; mitigar(se); esparcirse, recrearse.

relaxation [rilækséʃən] s. esparcimiento, expansión, solaz, recreo, recreación; aflojamiento o relajamiento (de músculos); **— of discipline** relajación de la disciplina; **— of one's mind** esparcimiento del ánimo.

relay [ríle] s. relevo, remuda; **— race** carrera de relevo; **electric —** relevador; [rílé] v. transmitir, despachar; hacer cundir (una noticia); **to — a broadcast** reemitir (o redifundir) un programa de radio.

release [rɪlís] v. soltar; librar; poner en libertad; relevar; aliviar; **to — a piece of news** hacer pública una nueva; **to — from blame** exonerar; s. liberación; alivio; exoneración; escape.

relegate [réləget] v. relegar; **to — to a corner** arrinconar, arrumbar.

relent [rɪlént] v. mitigar(se); ceder; aplacarse.

relentless [rɪléntlɪs] adj. implacable.

reliability [rɪlaɪəbílətɪ] s. formalidad; puntualidad; integridad.

reliable [rɪláɪəbl] *adj.* formal; puntual; digno de confianza.

reliance [rɪláɪəns] *s.* confianza; **self-reliance** confianza en sí, confianza en sus propias fuerzas.

relic [rélɪk] *s.* reliquia.

relief [rɪlíf] *s.* alivio; descanso, consuelo; ayuda, socorro; relieve, realce; **low —** bajo relieve; **to be on —** recibir manutención gratuita; **to put in —** realzar, poner en relieve.

relieve [rɪlíːv] *v.* relevar; librar; ayudar; aliviar; mitigar.

religion [rɪlídʒən] *s.* religión.

religious [rɪlídʒəs] *adj.* & *s.* religioso.

relinquish [rɪlíŋkwɪʃ] *v.* abandonar, dejar.

relish [rélɪʃ] *s.* buen sabor; gusto; apetito; goce; condimento; entremés (*aceitunas, encurtidos, etc.*); *v.* saborear; paladear; gustarle a uno, agradarle a uno.

reluctance [rɪlʌ́ktəns] *s.* repugnancia, renuencia, aversión, desgana.

reluctant [rɪlʌ́ktənt] *adj.* renuente, refractario, opuesto; **-ly** *adv.* renuentemente, con renuencia, de mala gana, a redopelo.

rely [rɪláɪ] *v.* **to — on** contar con, confiar en, fiarse de.

remain [rɪmén] *v.* quedar(se), permanecer, estarse, restar, faltar.

remainder [rɪméndə] *s.* resto; restante; residuo.

remains [rɪménz] *s. pl.* restos; reliquias; sobras.

remake [rimék] *v.* rehacer, hacer de nuevo.

remark [rɪmárk] *s.* observación, nota, reparo; *v.* notar, observar; **to — on** comentar; aludir a.

remarkable [rɪmárkəbl] *adj.* notable; extraordinario; **remarkably** *adv.* notablemente; extraordinariamente.

remedy [rémədɪ] *s.* remedio; cura; *v.* remediar; curar.

remember [rɪmémbə] *v.* recordar; acordarse; **— me to him** déle Vd. recuerdos (*o* memorias) de mi parte.

remembrance [rɪmémbrəns] *s.* recuerdo; recordación; memoria; **-s** recuerdos, saludos.

remind [rɪmáɪnd] *v.* recordar.

reminder [rɪmáɪndə] *s.* recordatorio, recordativo, memorándum, memoria; advertencia.

reminiscence [remənísns] *s.* reminiscencia, memoria, recuerdo.

remiss [rɪmís] *adj.* descuidado, negligente.

remission [rɪmíʃən] *s.* remisión, perdón.

remit [rɪmít] *v.* remitir; remesar, enviar una remesa; perdonar, absolver.

remittance [rɪmítns] *s.* remisión, envío, remesa (*de fondos*).

remnant [rémnənt] *s.* resto; residuo; retazo (*de tela, paño, etc.*); vestigio.

remodel [rimádl] *v.* rehacer, reconstruir; modelar de nuevo.

remorse [rɪmɔ́rs] *s.* remordimiento.

remote [rɪmót] *adj.* remoto; lejano.

removal [rɪmúːvl] *s.* mudanza, traslado; deposición (*de un empleo*); eliminación; extracción; alejamiento.

remove [rɪmúːv] *v.* remover; mudar(se), trasladar(se); quitar; eliminar; extirpar; sacar, extraer; deponer (*de un empleo*); apartar; alejar.

removed [rɪmúːvd] *adj.* remoto, distante.

renaissance [renəsáns] *s.* renacimiento.

renascence [rɪnǽsns] *s.* renacimiento.

rend [rend] *v.* desgarrar, rasgar; rajar.

render [réndə] *v.* dar; entregar; hacer; ejecutar, interpretar (*música o un papel dramático*); traducir; **to — an account of** rendir o dar cuenta de; **to — homage** rendir homenaje; **to — thanks** rendir gracias, dar las gracias; **to — useless** inutilizar, incapacitar.

renew [rɪnjú] *v.* renovar; restaurar; reanudar; prorrogar (*un préstamo*).

renewal [rɪnjúəl] *s.* renovación; reanudación; prórroga.

renounce [rɪnáuns] *v.* renunciar.

renovate [rénəvet] *v.* renovar.

renown [rɪnáun] *s.* renombre.

renowned [rɪnáund] *adj.* renombrado.

rent [rent] *s.* alquiler; renta, arrendamiento; **it is for —** se alquila, se arrienda; *v.* alquilar, arrendar.

rent [rent] *pret.* & *p.p. de* to rend; *s.* grieta, hendidura; rasgadura, rotura.

rental [réntl] *s.* renta, alquiler.

reopen [ríópən] *v.* reabrir(se), volver a abrir(se).

repair [rɪpér] *v.* reparar; remendar; componer; restaurar; **to — to** dirigirse a; *s.* reparo, reparación; remiendo; compostura; **in — en** buen estado; compuesto.

reparation [repəréʃən] *s.* reparación, desagravio.

repay [rɪpé] *v.* resarcir; compensar; reembolsar; pagar.

repayment [rɪpémənt] *s.* reintegro, pago, devolución, restitución.

repeal [rɪpíl] *v.* derogar, abrogar, revocar, abolir (*una ley*); *s.* abrogación, derogación, revocación, abolición (*de una ley*).

repeat [rɪpít] v. repetir; s. repetición.

repeated [rɪpítɪd] adj. repetido; -ly adv. repetidamente; repetidas veces, una y otra vez.

repel [rɪpél] v. repeler; rechazar; repugnar; **that idea -s me** me me repugna (o me es repugnante) esa idea.

repent [rɪpént] v. arrepentirse (de).

repentance [rɪpéntəns] s. arrepentimiento.

repentant [rɪpéntənt] adj. arrepentido; penitente.

repetition [repɪtíʃən] s. repetición.

replace [rɪplés] v. reponer, volver a colocar; reemplazar; restituir; remudar.

replaceable [rɪplésəbl] adj. reemplazable; substituible.

replacement [rɪplésmənt] s. reposición; reemplazo; devolución, restitución; substitución.

replenish [rɪplénɪʃ] v. reabastecer; rellenar, llenar.

replete [rɪplít] adj. repleto, atestado.

replica [réplɪkə] s. reproducción, copia exacta.

reply [rɪplái] v. replicar, contestar, responder; s. réplica, contestación, respuesta.

report [rɪpórt] v. dar cuenta de; avisar; informar; presentar un informe; rendir informe; hacer un reportaje, Am. reportar; denunciar, delatar; presentarse; **to — for duty** presentarse; **it is -ed that** dizque, se dice que, corre la voz que; s. noticia, reporte; informe; memorial, relación; rumor; estallido, disparo; **news — reportaje.**

reporter [rɪpórtə] s. reportero, repórter.

repose [rɪpóz] v. reposar, decansar; **to — one's confidence in** confiar en; depositar su confianza en; s. reposo.

represent [reprɪzént] v. representar.

representation [reprɪzentéʃən] s. representación.

representative [reprɪzéntətɪv] adj. representativo; representante; típico; s. representante; delegado, diputado.

repress [rɪprés] v. reprimir; refrenar, restringir; cohibir.

repression [rɪpréʃən] s. represión.

reprimand [réprəmænd] v. reprender, regañar; s. reprimenda, reprensión, regaño.

reprisal [rɪpráɪzl] s. represalia.

reproach [rɪprótʃ] v. reprochar; censurar, criticar; echar en cara; s. reproche, reprimenda; censura.

reproduce [riprədjús] v. reproducir.

reproduction [riprədʌkʃən] s. reproduc-

ción.

reproof [rɪprúf] s. reprensión, reproche, regaño.

reprove [rɪprúv] v. reprobar, reprender, censurar.

reptile [réptl] s. reptil.

republic [rɪpʌblɪk] s. república.

republican [rɪpʌblɪkən] adj. & s. republicano.

repudiate [rɪpjúdɪet] v. repudiar.

repugnance [rɪpʌgnəns] s. repugnancia; aversión.

repugnant [rɪpʌgnənt] adj. repugnante; antipático.

repulse [rɪpʌls] v. repulsar, repeler; rechazar; s. repulsa; desaire.

repulsive [rɪpʌlsɪv] adj. repulsivo, repugnante.

reputable [répjətəbl] adj. de buena reputación.

reputation [repjətéʃən] s. reputación, renombre.

repute [rɪpjút] v. reputar; estimar, considerar; s. reputación; renombre, fama; **of ill —** de mala fama.

request [rɪkwést] s. solicitud, petición, demanda; súplica, ruego; **at the —** **of** a solicitud de, a instancias de; v. solicitar, pedir, rogar, suplicar.

require [rɪkwáɪr] v. requerir; exigir, demandar.

requirement [rɪkwáɪrmənt] s. requerimiento, requisito; exigencia; necesidad.

requisite [rékwəzɪt] s. requisito; adj. requerido, necesario.

requisition [rekwəzíʃən] s. requisición, demanda, orden; v. demandar, pedir, ordenar.

rescue [réskjʊ] v. rescatar; librar; salvar; s. rescate, salvamento, salvación, socorro; **to go to the —** **of** acudir al socorro de, ir a salvar a.

research [rɪsɜtʃ] s. rebusca, búsqueda, investigación; [rɪsɜtʃ] v. rebuscar, investigar.

resemblance [rɪzémbləns] s. semejanza, parecido.

resemble [rɪzémbl] v. asemejarse a, semejar, parecerse a.

resent [rɪzént] v. resentirse de, sentirse de, darse por agraviado de.

resentful [rɪzéntfəl] adj. resentido; rencoroso.

resentment [rɪzéntmənt] s. resentimiento.

reservation [rezəvéʃən] s. reservación; reserva.

reserve [rɪzɜv] v. reservar; s. reserva.

reservoir [rézəvɔr] s. depósito (de agua,

aceite, gas, provisiones, etc.); receptáculo; **water —** alberca, aljibe, tanque, estanque.

reside [rɪzáɪd] *v.* residir, vivir.

residence [rézədəns] *s.* residencia; domicilio.

resident [rézədənt] *adj. & s.* residente.

residue [rézdju] *s.* residuo, resto.

resign [rızáɪn] *v.* renunciar; dimitir; **to — oneself to** resignarse a.

resignation [rezıgnéʃən] *s.* renuncia, dimisión; resignación.

resin [rézɲ] *s.* resina.

resist [rızíst] *v.* resistir; oponerse, resistirse a.

resistance [rızístəns] *s.* resistencia.

resistant [rızístənt] *adj.* resistente.

resolute [rézəlut] *adj.* resuelto.

resolution [rezəlúʃən] *s.* resolución; acuerdo.

resolve [rızálv] *v.* resolver(se); **to — into** resolverse en, reducirse a, transformarse en; **to —** to acordar; proponerse, resolverse a.

resort [rızórt] *v.* recurrir, acudir; **to — to force** recurrir a la fuerza; *s.* refugio; morada; **as a last —** como último recurso; **summer —** lugar de veraneo; **vice —** garito; casa de mala fama; **to have — to** recurrir a.

resorter [rızórtə] *s.* **summer —** veraneante.

resound [rızáʊnd] *v.* resonar; repercutir; retumbar.

resource [rısórs] *s.* recurso; **natural -s** recursos o riquezas naturales.

respect [rıspékt] *v.* respetar; **as -s** por lo que respecta a, por lo que toca a, tocante a; *s.* respeto; consideración; **with — to** (con) respecto a, respecto de; por lo que atañe a.

respectable [rıspéktəbl] *adj.* respetable.

respectful [rıspéktfəl] *adj.* respetuoso.

respecting [rıspéktıŋ] *prep.* con respecto a, tocante a.

respective [rıspéktɪv] *adj.* respectivo.

respiration [respəréʃən] *s.* respiración, respiro.

respite [réspɪt] *s.* tregua, pausa, descanso; intervalo; prórroga.

resplendent [rɪspléndənt] *adj.* resplandeciente.

respond [rıspánd] *v.* responder; corresponder; reaccionar.

response [rıspáns] *s.* respuesta, contestación; reacción.

responsibility [rıspansəbflətı] *s.* responsabilidad.

responsible [rıspánsəbl] *adj.* responsable; formal, digno de confianza.

rest [rest] *s.* descanso; reposo; quietud; tregua; pausa; apoyo; **at —** en reposo; tranquilo; **the —** el resto; los demás; *v.* descansar; reposar; apoyar; **to — on** descansar sobre; apoyar(se) en; basar(se) en; contar con, confiar en, depender de.

restaurant [réstərənt] *s.* restaurante, *Am.* restorán.

restful [réstfəl] *adj.* reposado, sosegado, tranquilo.

restitution [restətjúʃən] *s.* restitución; devolución.

restless [réstlıs] *adj.* inquieto, intranquilo.

restlessness [réstlısnıs] *s.* inquietud, desasosiego, intranquilidad.

restoration [restəréʃən] *s.* restauración; restitución; renovación.

restore [rıstór] *v.* restaurar; renovar; restituir; restablecer.

restrain [rıstrén] *v.* refrenar, contener, cohibir, reprimir, coartar; restringir.

restraint [rıstrént] *s.* restricción; reserva, circunspección; moderación; cohibición.

restrict [rıstríkt] *v.* restringir, limitar.

restriction [rıstríkʃən] *s.* restricción.

result [rızʌ́lt] *v.* resultar; **to — from** resultar de; **to — in** parar en; causar; dar por resultado; *s.* resulta, resultado; **as a —** de resultas, como resultado.

resume [rızúm] *v.* reasumir, volver a tomar; recomenzar; reanudar, continuar.

résumé [rézumé] *s.* resumen, sumario.

resuscitate [rısʌ́sətet] *v.* resucitar; revivir.

retail [rítel] *s.* venta al por menor; **at — al** por menor; **— merchant** detallista, comerciante al por menor; **— price** precio al por menor; *v.* detallar; vender al menudeo (*o* vender al por menor), *Am.* menudear.

retailer [rítélə] *s.* detallista, revendedor, comerciante al por menor.

retain [rıtén] *v.* retener; emplear.

retaliate [rıtǽliet] *v.* desquitarse, vengarse.

retaliation [rıtæliéʃən] *s.* desquite; desagravio; represalia, venganza.

retard [rıtárd] *v.* retardar, retrasar atrasar.

retinue [rétnju] *s.* comitiva, séquito acompañamiento.

retire [rıtáɪr] *v.* retirar(se); jubilar(se) acostarse; apartarse.

retirement [rıtáɪrmənt] *s.* retiro; jubilación.

retort [rıtórt] *v.* replicar; redargüir; *s*

réplica.

retouch [ritʌ́tʃ] v. retocar; s. retoque.

retrace [ritrés] v. repasar; volver a trazar; to — one's steps volver sobre sus pasos, retroceder.

retract [ritrǽkt] v. retractar, retractarse de; desdecirse (de); retraer.

retreat [ritrít] s. retiro, refugio, asilo; retirada; retreta (toque de retirada); v. retirarse; retroceder.

retrench [ritréntʃ] v. cercenar, reducir, disminuir; economizar.

retrieve [ritrív] v. cobrar (la caza); recobrar, recuperar; reparar (una pérdida).

return [ritə́n] v. volver, regresar; retornar; devolver; replicar; redituar; producir; restar (la pelota en tenis); to — a favor corresponder a un favor; to — a report rendir un informe; s. vuelta, regreso; retorno; recompensa; restitución; desvolución; réplica; resto (en un juego de pelota); rédito, ganancia; informe; — game desquite, juego de desquite; — ticket boleto de vuelta; by — mail a vuelta de correo; election —s reportaje de elecciones; in — en cambio; in — for a cambio de, a trueque de; income tax — declaración de rentas; many happy —s muchas felicidades (en su día).

reunion [rijńjən] s. reunión; junta.

reunite [rijunáit] v. reunir(se), volver a unirse; reconciliar(se).

reveal [rivíl] v. revelar.

revel [révl] v. deleitarse, gozarse; parrandear, Am. farrear; andar de parranda, Am. andar de farra; — parranda, juerga, jarana.

revelation [revləʃən] s. revelación; Revelation(s) Apocalipsis.

revelry [révlri] s. jaleo, juerga, jarana.

revenge [rivéndʒ] v. vengar, vindicar; s. venganza; desquite.

revengeful [rivéndʒfəl] adj. vengativo.

revenue [révənju] s. renta; rédito; rentas públicas, ingresos.

revere [rivír] v. venerar.

reverence [révrəns] s. reverencia; veneración; v. reverenciar, venerar.

reverend [révrənd] adj. reverendo; venerable.

reverent [révrənt] adj. reverente.

reverie, revery [révəri] s. ensueño; arrobamiento.

reverse [rivə́s] adj. inverso, invertido; contrario, opuesto; s. revés, reverso, dorso; lo contrario; contratiempo; v. invertir; voltear; revocar (una sentencia).

revert [rivə́t] v. revertir, volver atrás, retroceder.

review [rivjú] v. repasar; revisar; revistar, pasar revista a (las tropas); reseñar, hacer una reseña de (un libro); s. revista; repaso; reseña, crítica (de un libro, drama, etc.); revisión (de un caso jurídico, sentencia, etc.).

revile [riváil] v. vilipendiar, vituperar, denigrar.

revise [riváiz] v. revisar, repasar, releer (para corregir); corregir, enmendar.

revision [rivíʒən] s. revisión; enmienda; edición enmendada o mejorada.

revival [riváivl] s. renovación; revivificación; renacimiento; nueva presentación (de una pieza u obra); — meeting junta para revivir el fervor religioso; religious — despertamiento (o nuevo fervor) religioso.

revive [riváiv] v. revivir, resucitar; volver en sí; renacer; reavivar, reanimar(se); avivar.

revoke [rivók] v. revocar, abrogar, anular; renunciar (en los juegos de naipes).

revolt [rivólt] v. revuelta, rebelión, sublevación; v. rebelarse, sublevarse; it —s me me da asco, me repugna.

revolution [revəlúʃən] s. revolución; vuelta (que da una rueda).

revolutionary [revəlúʃəneri] adj. & s. revolucionario.

revolutionist [revəlúʃənist] s. revolucionario.

revolve [riválv] v. girar, dar vueltas; rodar; voltear, dar vueltas a; to — in one's mind revolver en la mente, ponderar, reflexionar.

revolver [riválvə] s. revólver.

reward [riwɔ́rd] v. premiar; recompensar; s. premio, gratificación, recompensa, galardón; albricias (por haber hallado algún objeto perdido).

rewrite [riráit] v. volver a escribir; refundir (un escrito).

rhetoric [rétərik] s. retórica.

rheumatism [rúmətizəm] s. reumatismo, reuma.

rhinoceros [rainásərəs] s. rinoceronte.

rhubarb [rúbarb] s. ruibarbo.

rhyme [raim] s. rima; without — or reason sin ton ni son; v. rimar.

rhythm [ríðəm] s. ritmo.

rhythmical [ríðmikl] adj. rítmico, acompasado, cadencioso.

rib [rib] s. costilla; varilla (de paraguas); cordoncillo (de ciertos tejidos).

ribbon [ríbən] s. cinta; listón, banda; tira.

rice [rais] s. arroz; — field arrozal.

rich [rɪtʃ] *adj.* rico; costoso, suntuoso; sabroso; — color color vivo; — food alimento muy mantecoso o dulce.

riches [rɪtʃɪz] *s. pl.* riqueza, riquezas.

rickety [rɪkɪtɪ] *adj.* desvencijado; raquítico.

rid [rɪd] *v.* librar, desembarazar; to get — of librarse de, deshacerse de, desembarazarse de; *pret. & p.p. de* to rid.

ridden [rɪdn] *p.p. de* to ride.

riddle [rɪdl] *s.* acertijo, adivinanza, enigma; *v.* acribillar, perforar; to — with bullets acribillar a balazos.

ride [raɪd] *v.* cabalgar, montar; pasear (*en automóvil, a caballo*); ir en tranvía, automóvil, tren, etc.; to — a bicycle andar o montar en bicicleta; to — a horse montar un caballo; to — horseback montar a caballo; to — over a country pasar o viajar por un país (*en auto, a caballo o por tren*); to — someone dominar a alguien; burlarse de alguien; *s.* paseo (*a caballo o en automóvil*); viaje (*a caballo, en automóvil, por ferrocarril, etc.*).

rider [raɪdə] *s.* jinete; pasajero (*de automóvil*); biciclista; motociclista; aditamento, cláusula añadida (*a un proyecto de ley*).

ridge [rɪdʒ] *s.* espinazo, lomo (*entre dos surcos*); arista, intersección (*de dos planos*); cordillera; cerro; caballete (*de tejado*); cordoncillo (*de ciertos tejidos*).

ridicule [rɪdɪkjul] *s.* ridículo; burla, mofa; *v.* ridiculizar, poner en ridículo.

ridiculous [rɪdɪkjələs] *adj.* ridículo.

rifle [raɪfl] *s.* rifle; *v.* pillar, robar; despojar.

rig [rɪg] *v.* aparejar, equipar; enjarciar (*un barco de vela*); to — oneself up emperifollarse, ataviarse; *s.* aparejo, equipo; aparato; atavío, traje.

rigging [rɪgɪŋ] *s.* jarcia, aparejo.

right [raɪt] *adj.* derecho; diestro; recto; justo; propio; adecuado; correcto; — angle ángulo recto; — side lado derecho; derecho (*de un tejido, traje, etc.*); it is — that está bien que, es justo que; to be — tener razón; to be all — estar bien; estar bien de salud; to be in one's — mind estar, estar en sus cabales; *adv.* derecho, directamente; rectamente; justamente; bien; correctamente; a la derecha; — aboutface media vuelta; — hungry muy hambriento; — now ahora mismo, inmediatamente; — there allí mismo, *Am.* allí mero; go — home! ¡vete derechito a casa! it is — where you

left it está exactamente (*o* en el mero lugar) donde lo dejaste; to hit — in the eye dar de lleno en el ojo, *Am.* dar en el mero ojo; *s.* derecho; autoridad; privilegio; — of way derecho de vía; by — (by -s) justamente, con justicia; según la ley; from — to left de derecha a izquierda; to the — a la derecha; to be in the — tener razón; *v.* enderezar; corregir.

righteous [raɪtʃəs] *adj.* recto, justo, virtuoso.

righteousness [raɪtʃəsnɪs] *s.* rectitud, virtud.

rightful [raɪtfəl] *adj.* justo; legítimo.

right-hand [raɪthænd] *adj.* derecho, de la mano derecha; — man brazo derecho.

rightist [raɪtɪst] *s.* derechista.

rightly [raɪtlɪ] *adv.* con razón; justamente, rectamente; propiamente, aptamente, debidamente.

rigid [rɪdʒɪd] *adj.* rígido.

rigidity [rɪdʒɪdətɪ] *s.* rigidez; tiesura.

rigor [rɪgə] *s.* rigor; rigidez; severidad.

rigorous [rɪgəəs] *adj.* rigoroso (*o* riguroso), severo.

rim [rɪm] *s.* borde, orilla; aro.

rime = rhyme.

rind [raɪnd] *s.* corteza, cáscara.

ring [rɪŋ] *s.* anillo, sortija; argolla; aro, círculo; arena (*de un circo*); campo de combate; pista (*de un hipódromo*); toque; tañido; repique; sonido metálico — leader cabecilla; — of defiance tono de reto; — of shouts gritería; — of a telephone llamada de teléfono; ring-shaped en forma de anillo, anular; key—llavero; sarcastic—retintín *v.* tocar (*un timbre, una campanill* *o campana*); sonar; tañer, repicar resonar; zumbar (*los oídos*); to — fo something llamar para pedir algo to — the nose of an animal ponerl una argolla en la nariz a un animal to — up on the phone llamar po teléfono.

ringlet [rɪŋlɪt] *s.* rizo, bucle; pequeñ sortija.

rink [[rɪŋk] *s.* patinadero (*cancha par patinar*).

rinse [rɪns] *v.* enjuagar; lavar; aclara (*la ropa*); *s.* enjuague.

riot [raɪət] *s.* motín, desorden, alborot tumulto, *Am.* bola; — color r queza o exceso de colores chillant *v.* amotinarse, alborotar, armar u tumulto.

rip [rɪp] *v.* rasgar(se), romper(se); des coser(se); to — off rasgar, arranca cortar; **to — out a seam** descoser una costura; *s.* rasgón, rasgadura, rotura; descosido.

ripe [ráip] *adj.* maduro, sazonado; en sazón; **— for** maduro para, sazonado para; bien preparado para, listo para.

ripen [ráipən] *v.* madurar(se), sazonar-(se).

ripeness [ráipnis] *s.* madurez, sazón.

ripple [rípl] *v.* rizar(se), agitar(se), ondear, temblar (*la superficie del agua*); murmurar (*un arroyo*); *s.* onda, temblor, ondulación (*en la superficie del agua*); murmullo (*de un arroyo*).

rise [raiz] *v.* subir; ascender; alzarse, levantarse; elevarse; surgir; salir (*el sol, la luna, un astro*); hincharse (*la masa del pan*); **to — up in rebellion** sublevarse, levantarse, alzarse (en rebelión); *s.* subida; ascenso; pendiente; elevación; salida (*del sol, de la luna, etc.*); subida, alza (*de precios*).

risen [rízn] *p.p. de* to rise.

risk [risk] *s.* riesgo; *v.* arriesgar, aventurar, poner en peligro; exponerse a; **to — defeat** correr el riesgo de perder, exponerse a perder.

risky [ríski] *adj.* arriesgado, peligroso, aventurado.

rite [rait] *s.* rito, ceremonia.

ritual [rítʃuəl] *adj. & s.* ritual, ceremonial.

rival [ráivl] *s.* rival, competidor, émulo; *adj.* competidor; **the — party** el partido opuesto; *v.* rivalizar con, competir con.

rivalry [ráivlri] *s.* rivalidad.

river [rívə] *s.* río.

rivet [rívit] *s.* remache; *v.* remachar; fijar.

rivulet [rívjəlit] *s.* riachuelo, arroyuelo.

road [rod] *s.* camino; carretera; vía.

roadside [ródsaid] *s.* borde del camino.

roadway [ródwe] *s.* camino, carretera.

roam [rom] *v.* vagar, errar, andar errante.

roar [ior] *v.* rugir, bramar; **to — with laughter** reír a carcajadas; *s.* rugido, bramido; **— of laughter** risotada, carcajada.

roast [rost] *v.* asar(se); tostar (*café, maíz, etc.*); ridiculizar, criticar; *s.* asado, carne asada; *adj.* asado; **— beef** rosbif, rosbí.

rob [rob] *v.* robar, hurtar; **to — someone of something** robarle algo a alguien.

robber [rábə] *s.* ladrón; **highway —** salteador.

robbery [rábri] *s.* robo, hurto.

robe [rob] *s.* manto, traje talar, túnica, toga (*de un juez, letrado, etc.*); bata; **automobile — manta de automóvil.**

robin [rábin] *s.* petirrojo.

robust [róbʌst] *adj.* robusto, fuerte.

rock [rak] *s.* roca, peña; peñasco; **— crystal** cristal de roca; **— salt** sal de piedra, sal gema o sal mineral; **to go on the —s** tropezar en un escollo, *Am.* escollar; *v.* mecer(se), balancear(se); bambolear(se); estremecer; **to — to sleep** adormecer (*meciendo*), arrullar.

rocker [rákə] *s.* mecedora; arco de una mecedora o cuna.

rocket [rákit] *s.* cohete.

rocking [rákŋ] *s.* balanceo; *adj.* oscilante — **chair silla** mecedora.

rocky [ráki] *adj.* roqueño, rocoso, rocalloso, peñascoso; pedregoso; movedizo; tembloroso; débil desvanecido.

rod [rad] *s.* vara, varilla; medida de longitud (*aproximadamente 5 metros*); **fishing —** caña de pescar.

rode [rod] *pret. de* to ride.

rogue [rog] *s.* pícaro, bribón, tunante, pillo; **-s' gallery** colección policíaca de retratos de criminales.

roguish [rógʃ] *adj.* pícaro, pillo, picaresco; travieso.

role [rol] *s.* papel, parte.

roll [rol] *v.* rodar; girar; balancearse (*un barco*); bambolearse; ondular, retumbar (*el trueno, un cañón*); aplanar, alisar con rodillo; arrollar, enrollar, hacer un rollo o bola; envolver; redoblar (*un tambor*); pronunciar (*la rr doble*); **to — over in the snow** revolverse o revolcarse en la nieve; **to — up** arrollar, enrollar, envolver; *s.* rollo (*de papel, paño, tela, etc.*); balanceo (*de un barco*); retumbo (*del trueno, de un cañón*); redoble (*de un tambor*); lista; ondulación; oleaje; bollo, rosca, panecillo; **to call the —** pasar lista.

roller [rólə] *s.* rodillo, cilindro (*para aplanar o alisar*); rollo (*rodillo de pastelero*); oleada; **— coaster** montaña rusa; **— skate** patín de ruedas.

Roman [rómən] *adj. & s.* romano; **— nose** nariz aguileña.

romance [roméns] *s.* romance; novela (*de caballerías o de aventuras*); cuento, fábula; aventura romántica; amorío, lance amoroso; *v.* contar o fingir fábulas; andar en amoríos o aventuras; **Romance** *adj.* romance, románico, neolatino.

romantic [roméntik] *adj.* romántico; novelesco.

romanticism [roméntəsizəm] *s.* romanticismo.

romanticist [romǽntəsɪst] s. romántico, escritor romántico.

romp [rɑmp] v. triscar, juguetear, retozar, travesear.

roof [ruf] s. techo, techumbre, techado; tejado; — garden azotea-jardín; — of the mouth paladar; flat — azotea; v. techar.

room [rum] s. cuarto, pieza, sala, habitación; espacio; lugar, sitio; there is no — for more no cabe(n) más, no hay lugar o cabida para más; to make — hacer lugar; —mate compañero de cuarto; v. vivir, hospedarse, alojarse.

roomer [rúmə] s. inquilino.

roominess [rúminɪs] s. holgura.

roomy [rúmɪ] adj. espacioso, amplio, holgado.

roost [rust] s. gallinero; percha de gallinero; v. acurrucarse (las aves en la percha); pasar la noche.

rooster [rústə] s. gallo.

root [rut] s. raíz; v. arraigar(se); echar raíces; hocicar, hozar (dícese de los cerdos); to — for vitorear, aclamar; to — out (o — up) desarraigar, arrancar de raíz; to become —ed arraigarse.

rope [rop] s. soga, cuerda; resta, lazo; to be at the end of one's — haber agotado el último recurso; estar (o andar) en las últimas; no saber qué hacer; to know the —s saber todas las tretas de un asunto o negocio; v. amarrar; lazar, enlazar; to — off acordelar, poner cuerdas tirantes alrededor de (un sitio); to — someone in embaucar a alguien.

rosary [rózərɪ] s. rosario.

rose [roz] pret. de to rise.

rose [roz] s. rosa; color de rosa; —bush rosal; — window rosetón.

rosebud [rózbʌd] s. capullo o botón de rosa, yema, pimpollo.

rosette [rozét] s. roseta; rosetón.

roetrum [rústrəm] s. tribuna.

rosy [rózɪ] adj. rosado; color de rosa; alegre, risueño; — future porvenir risueño.

rot [rɑt] v. pudrir(se); corromperse; s. podre, podredumbre, putrefacción.

rotary [rótərɪ] adj. rotatorio, giratorio, rotativo.

rotate [rótet] v. girar, dar vueltas; hacer girar; turnarse; cultivar en rotación.

rotation [rotéʃən] s. rotación, vuelta; — of crops rotación de cultivos.

rote [rot] s. rutina, repetición maquinal; by — maquinalmente.

rotten [rátn̩] adj. podrido, putrefacto;

hediondo; corrompido, córrupto.

rouge [ruʒ] s. colorete; v. pintar(se), poner(se) colorete.

rough [rʌf] adj. áspero; tosco; brusco; grosero; fragoso, escabroso; borrascoso, tempestuoso; — diamond diamante en bruto; — draft borrador; bosquejo; — estimate cálculo aproximativo, tanteo; — ground terreno escabroso; — idea idea aproximada; — sea mar picado; — weather tiempo borrascoso; adv. véase roughly; v. to — it vivir sin lujos ni comodidades, hacer vida campestre.

roughen [rʌfən] v. hacer o poner áspero; picar, rascar (una superficie); rajarse, agrietarse (la piel).

roughly [rʌflɪ] adv. ásperamente; groseramente, rudamente; aproximadamente; to — estimate — tantear.

roughness [rʌfnɪs] s. aspereza; escabrosidad; rudeza; tosquedad; the — of the sea lo picado del mar; the — of the weather lo borrascoso del tiempo.

round [raʊnd] adj. redondo; rotundo; circular; — trip viaje redondo, viaje de ida y vuelta; round-trip ticket boleto (o billete) de ida y vuelta; s. vuelta, rotación, revolución; ronda; vuelta (en el juego de naipes); tanda, turno (en ciertos deportes); escalón, travesaño (de escalera de mano); danza en rueda; — of ammunition carga de municiones; descarga; — of applause explosión de aplausos; — of pleasures sucesión de placeres; to make the —s rondar; prep. & adv. véase around; — about a la redonda; por todos lados; round-shouldered cargado de espaldas; to come — again volver otra vez; to go — a corner doblar una esquina; v. redondear; dar vuelta a; to — a corner doblar una esquina; to — out redondear; completar; to — up cattle juntar el ganado, Am. rodear el ganado.

roundabout [ráʊndəbaʊt] adj. indirecto.

roundup [ráʊndʌp] s. rodeo (de ganado).

rouse [raʊz] v. despertar(se), Am. recordar; excitar; incitar, provocar; levantar (la caza).

rout [raʊt] s. derrota, fuga desordenada; v. derrotar; poner en fuga; to — out echar, hacer salir a toda prisa.

route [rut] s. ruta, camino, vía; itinerario; v. dirigir o enviar por cierta ruta.

routine [rutín] s. rutina.

rove [rov] v. vagar, errar, andar errante.

rover [róvə] s. vagabundo.

row [raʊ] s. riña, pelea, pelotera; v. pelearse, reñir, armar una riña o pelotera.

row [roʊ] s. fila, hilera; paseo en lancha; v. remar, bogar; llevar en lancha o bote.

rowboat [róʊbət] s. bote de remos, lancha.

rower [róə] s. remero.

royal [róɪəl] adj. real, regio.

royalist [róɪəlɪst] s. realista.

royalty [róɪəltɪ] s. realeza, soberanía real; persona o personas reales; derechos (pagados a un autor o inventor).

rub [rʌb] v. frotar; restregar; fregar; raspar; irritar; **to — out** borrar; **to — someone the wrong way** irritar, contrariar, llevarle a uno la contraria; s. fricción, friega, frotación; roce; sarcasmo; **there is the —** allí está la dificultad.

rubber [rʌbə] s. caucho, goma, Am. hule; goma elástica; goma de borrar; partida (en ciertos juegos de naipes); jugada decisiva (en ciertos juegos de naipes); **-s** chanclos, zapatos de goma o hule; adj. de caucho, de goma, Am. de hule; **— band** faja o banda de goma; **— plantation** cauchal; **— tree** Am. caucho, Am. gomero.

rubbish [rʌbɪʃ] s. basura, desechos, desperdicios; tonterías.

rubble [rʌbl̩] s. escombros; ripio, cascajo, fragmentos de ladrillos o piedras; piedra en bruto, piedra sin labrar.

ruby [rúbɪ] s. rubí.

rudder [rʌdə] s. timón.

ruddy [rʌdɪ] adj. rojo; rojizo; rubicundo.

rude [rud] adj. rudo; grosero; áspero; brusco; tosco.

rudeness [rúdnɪs] s. rudeza; grosería, descortesía; tosquedad.

rueful [rúfəl] adj. triste; lastimoso, lamentable.

ruffian [rʌfɪən] s. rufián, hombre brutal.

ruffle [rʌfl̩] v. rizar, fruncir (tela); arrugar; desarreglar; rizar (la superficie del agua); perturbar; molestar; s. volante (de un traje); frunce, pliegue; ondulación (en el agua).

rug [rʌg] s. alfombra, tapete.

rugged [rʌgɪd] adj. escabroso, fragoso; áspero; recio, robusto; tosco; borrascoso, tempestuoso.

ruin [rúɪn] s. ruina; **to go to —** arruinarse, caer en ruinas, venir a menos; v. arruinar; echar a perder; estropear.

ruinous [rúɪnəs] adj. ruinoso; desastroso.

rule [rul] s. regla; reglamento; precepto; gobierno, mando; **as a —** por regla general; v. regir, gobernar; mandar; dirigir, guiar; dominar; fallar, decidir; rayar (con regla); **to — out** excluir; **to — over** regir, gobernar.

ruler [rúlə] s. gobernante; soberano; regla (para medir o trazar líneas).

ruling [rúlɪŋ] s. fallo, decisión; gobierno; adj. predominante, prevaleciente; principal.

rum [rʌm] s. ron.

rumble [rʌmbl̩] v. retumbar, hacer estruendo, rugir; s. retumbo, estruendo, rumor, ruido sordo; **— seat** asiento trasero (de cupé).

ruminate [rúmənet] v. rumiar; reflexionar, meditar.

rummage [rʌmɪdʒ] v. escudriñar revolviéndolo todo; s. búsqueda desordenada; **— sale** venta de prendas usadas (para beneficencia).

rumor [rúmə] s. rumor; runrún; v. murmurar; **it is -ed that** corre la voz que.

rump [rʌmp] s. anca; trasero.

rumple [rʌmpl̩] v. estrujar, ajar; arrugar; s. arruga (en un traje).

rumpus [rʌmpəs] s. barullo, alharaca, boruca, batahola.

run [rʌn] v. correr; andar (una máquina, un reloj, etc.), funcionar, marchar; fluir; chorrear; recorrer; dirigir, manejar (un negocio, empresa, máquina, casa, etc.); extenderse (de un punto a otro); correrse (los colores); ser candidato (a un puesto político); **to — a fever** tener calentura; **to — away** huir; fugarse, escaparse; **to — across a person** encontrarse o tropezar con una persona; **to — down** dejar de funcionar (una máquina, reloj, etc.); aprehender a (un criminal); hablar mal de; atropellar; **to get — down in health** quebrantársele a uno la salud; **to — dry** secarse; **to — into** tropezar con, encontrárse con; chocar con; **to — into debt** adeudarse; **to — something into** meter algo en, clavar algo en; **to — out** salirse; **to — out of money** acabársele a uno el dinero; **to — over** derramarse (un líquido); atropellar, pasar por encima de; repasar, echar un vistazo a (la lección, un libro, etc.); **to — through a book** hojear un libro; **the play ran for three months se dió la comedia durante tres meses**; s. carrera, corrida; curso, marcha; recorrido; manejo; **— of good luck** serie de repetidos éxitos; **— of performances** serie de representaciones; **— on a bank** corrida, demanda extraordinaria de fondos bancarios; **in the long — a la larga**; **stocking — carrera**; **the common — of mankind** el común de las gentes; **to have the — of** tener el libre uso de; p.p. de **to run**.

runaway [ránəwe] *adj.* fugitivo; — **horse** caballo desbocado; — **marriage** casamiento de escapatoria; *s.* fugitivo; caballo desbocado; fuga.

rung [rʌŋ] *s.* barrote, travesaño (*de silla, escalera de mano, etc.*); *pret.* & *p.p. de* to ring.

runner [ránə]· *s.* corredor; tapete (*para un pasillo o mesa*), *Am.* pasillo; carrera (*en una media*); cuchilla (*de patín o de trineo*); contrabandista.

running [rániŋ] *s.* corrida, carrera; manejo, dirección; flujo; **to be out of the** — estar fuera de combate; *adj.* corriente; — **board** estribo; — **expenses** gastos corrientes; — **knot** nudo corredizo; — **water** agua corriente; **in** — **condition** en buen estado; **for ten days** — por diez días seguidos.

runt [rʌnt] *s.* enano; hombrecillo.

runway [ránwe] *s.* senda; vía; pista (*de aterrizaje*).

rupture [ráptʃə] *s.* ruptura; rompimiento, rotura; hernia; *v.* romper(se); reventar.

rural [rúrəl] *adj.* rural, campestre.

rush [rʌʃ] *v.* lanzar(se), precipitar(se); apresurar(se); despachar con prontitud; abalanzarse; acometer; empujar; **to** — **out** salir a todo correr; **to** — **past** pasar a toda prisa; *s.* precipitación, prisa; acometida; junco; — **chair** silla de junco; — **of business** gran movimiento comercial; — **of people** tropel de gente; — **order** pedido urgente.

Russian [ráʃən] *adj.* & *s.* ruso.

rust [rʌst] *s.* moho, orín; tizón (*enfermedad de las plantas*); — **color** color rojizo; *v.* enmohecer(se), oxidar(se).

rustic [rástik] *adj.* & *s.* rústico, campesino.

rustle [rástl] *v.* susurrar, crujir; menear; **to** — **cattle** robar ganado; *s.* susurro, crujido.

rusty [rásti] *adj.* mohoso, cubierto de orín, oxidado; rojizo; entorpecido, falto de uso; falto de práctica.

rut [rʌt] *s.* rodada; rutina, método rutinario; **to be in a** — hacer una cosa por rutina, ser esclavo de la rutina.

ruthless [rúelɪs] *adj.* despiadado, cruel, brutal.

ruthlessness [rúelɪsnɪs] *s.* fiereza, falta de miramiento, truculencia, crueldad.

rye [rai] *s.* centeno.

S

saber [sébə] *s.* sable.

sabotage [sǽbətɑʒ] *s.* sabotaje; *v.* sabo-

tear.

sack [sæk] *s.* saco; costal; saqueo, pillaje; *v.* ensacar, meter en un saco; saquear, pillar.

sacrament [sǽkrəmənt] *s.* sacramento.

sacred [sékrɪd] *adj.* sagrado, sacro.

sacredness [sékrɪdnɪs] *s.* santidad; lo sagrado.

sacrifice [sǽkrəfaɪs] *s.* sacrificio; **to sell at a** — vender con pérdida; *v.* sacrificar.

sacrilege [sǽkrəlɪdʒ] *s.* sacrilegio.

sacrilegious [sækrɪlíḑʒəs] *adj.* sacrílego.

sad [sæd] *adj.* triste.

sadden [sǽdn] *v.* entristecer(se).

saddle [sǽdl] *s.* silla de montar; silla de bicicleta o motocicleta; —**bag** alforja; — **horse** caballo de silla; —**tree** arzón; *v.* ensillar; **to** — **someone with responsibilities** cargar a alguien de responsabilidades.

sadistic [sædístɪk] *adj.* sádico, cruel.

sadness [sǽdnɪs] *s.* tristeza.

safe [sef] *adj.* seguro; salvo; sin riesgo, sin peligro; digno de confianza; — **and sound** sano y salvo; **safe-conduct** salvoconducto; **to be** — no correr peligro, estar a salvo; *s.* caja fuerte; **-ly** *adv.* seguramente; con seguridad; sin peligro; **to arrive -ly** llegar bien, llegar sin contratiempo alguno.

safeguard [séfgard] *s.* salvaguardia; resguardo, defensa; *v.* resguardar, proteger, salvaguardar.

safety [séfti] *s.* seguridad; protección; **in** — con seguridad; sin peligro; *adj.* de seguridad; — **device** mecanismo de seguridad; — **pin** imperdible, alfiler de seguridad.

saffron [sǽfrən] *s.* azafrán; *adj.* azafranado, color de azafrán.

sag [sæg] *v.* combarse, pandearse; doblegarse; deprimirse, hundirse (*en el centro*); encorvarse; **his shoulders** — tiene las espaldas caídas; *s.* pandeo, flexión, depresión; concavidad.

sagacious [səgéʃəs] *adj.* sagaz, ladino, astuto.

sagacity [səgǽsəti] *s.* sagacidad; astucia.

sage [sedʒ] *adj.* sabio; cuerdo, prudente; *s.* sabio; salvia (*planta*).

said [sed] *pret.* & *p.p. de* to say.

sail [sel] *s.* vela (*de barco*); viaje o paseo en barco de vela; **under full** — a toda vela; **to set** — hacerse a la vela; *v.* navegar; hacerse a la vela; zarpar, salir (*un buque*); viajar, ir (*en barco, bote, etc.*); pasear en bote de vela; **to** — **a kite** volar una cometa o papalote; **to** — **along** deslizarse; navegar; ir bien;

to — along the coast costear.

sailboat [sélbot] s. bote o barco de vela.

sailor [séla] s. marinero; marino.

saint [sent] s. santo; adj. santo; san (delante de nombres masculinos excepto: Santo Tomás, Santo Domingo, Santo Toribio); v. canonizar.

saintly [séntlɪ] adj. santo; pío, devoto.

sake [sek]: **for the — of** por; por amor a; por consideración a; **for my —** por mí; **for pity's —** por piedad; ¡caramba!; **for the — of argument** por vía de argumento.

salad [séləd] s. ensalada; **— dressing** aderezo (para ensalada).

salary [sélərɪ] s. salario, sueldo.

sale [sel] s. venta; saldo, Am. barata; **— by auction** almoneda, subasta; **-s tax** impuesto sobre ventas; **for (on) —** de venta.

salesman [sélzmən] s. vendedor; dependiente (de tienda); **traveling —** agente viajero, viajante de comercio.

saleswoman [sélzwumən] s. vendedora; dependienta (de tienda).

salient [sélɪənt] adj. saliente, sobresaliente; prominente.

saliva [sɔláɪvə] s. saliva.

sallow [sélo] adj. amarillento, pálido.

sally [sélɪ] s. salida; agudeza, chiste agudo; v. salir, hacer una salida; **to — forth** salir.

salmon [sémən] s. salmón.

saloon [səlún] s. salón (de un vapor); taberna, Am. cantina; **dining — of a ship** salón-comedor de un vapor.

salt [sɔlt] s. sal; chiste, agudeza; **smelling -s** sales aromáticas; **the — of the earth** la flor y nata de la humanidad; adj. salado; salobre; **—cellar** salero; **— mine** salina; **— pork** tocino salado; **— shaker** salero; **— water** agua salada, agua de mar; v. salar; **to — one's money away** guardar o ahorrar su dinero.

saltpeter [sɔ́ltpítə] s. salitre, nitro; **— mine** salitral, salitrera.

salty [sɔ́ltɪ] adj. salado; salobre.

salutation [sæljɔtéʃən] s. salutación, saludo.

salute [səlút] s. saludo; **gun —** salva; v. saludar; cuadrarse (militarmente).

salvation [sælvéʃən] s. salvación.

salve [sæv] s. untura, ungüento; alivio; v. aliviar, aquietar, calmar; untar.

same [sem] adj. mismo; igual; idéntico; **it is all the — to me** me es igual, me da lo mismo; **the —** lo mismo; el mismo (la misma, los mismos, las mismas).

sample [sémpl] s. muestra, prueba; **book of -s** muestrario; v. probar; calar.

sanctify [sénktɔfaɪ] v. santificar.

sanction [sénkʃən] s. sanción; aprobación, autorización; v. sancionar; ratificar; aprobar, autorizar.

sanctity [sénktɪtɪ] s. santidad.

sanctuary [sénktʃuɛrɪ] s. santuario; asilo.

sand [sænd] s. arena; **— pit** arenal; v. enarenar, cubrir de arena; mezclar con arena; refregar con arena.

sandal [séndl] s. sandalia; alpargata; Am. guarache (huarache).

sandpaper [séndpepə] s. papel de lija; v. lijar, pulir o alisar con papel de lija.

sandstone [séndston] s. piedra arenisca.

sandwich [séndwɪtʃ] s. bocadillo, emparedado, sandwich; v. intercalar, meter (entre).

sandy [séndɪ] adj. arenoso; arenisco; **— hair** pelo rojizo.

sane [sen] adj. sano, sensato; cuerdo.

sang [sæŋ] pret. de to sing.

sanitarium [sænɔtérɪəm] s. sanatorio.

sanitary [sénɔterɪ] adj. sanitario.

sanitation [sænɔtéʃən] s. saneamiento; salubridad.

sanity [sénɔtɪ] s. cordura.

sank [sæŋk] pret. de to sink.

sap [sæp] s. savia; tonto, bobo; v. agotar, debilitar, minar.

sapling [séplɪŋ] s. vástago, renuevo; arbolillo.

sapphire [séfaɪr] s. zafiro; color de zafiro.

sarcasm [sárkæzəm] s. sarcasmo.

sarcastic [sarkéstɪk] adj. sarcástico.

sardine [sardín] s. sardina.

sash [sæʃ] s. faja (cinturón de lana, seda o algodón); banda, cinta ancha; **window — bastidor** (o marco) de ventana.

sat [sæt] pret. & p.p. de to sit.

satchel [sétʃəl] s. valija, maletín, maleta, saco.

sate [set] v. saciar.

sateen [sætín] s. satén o rasete (raso de inferior calidad).

satellite [sétlaɪt] s. satélite.

satiate [séʃɪet] v. saciar, hartar.

satin [sétɪ̩] s. raso.

satire [sétaɪr] s. sátira.

satirical [sɔtírɪkl] adj. satírico.

satirize [sétɔraɪz] v. satirizar.

satisfaction [sætɪsfékʃən] s. satisfacción.

satisfactorily [sætɪsféktrɪlɪ] adv. satisfactoriamente.

satisfactory [sætɪsféktrɪ] adj. satisfactorio.

satisfied [sétɪsfaɪd] adj. satisfecho, contento.

satisfy [sǽtɪsfaɪ] v. satisfacer.

saturate [sǽtʃəret] v. saturar, empapar.

Saturday [sǽtədɪ] s. sábado.

sauce [sɔs] s. salsa; — dish salsera; v. aderezar con salsa; sazonar, condimentar; insolentarse con.

saucepan [sɔ́spæn] s. cacerola.

saucer [sɔ́sə] s. platillo.

sauciness [sɔ́sɪnɪs] s. descaro, insolencia.

saucy [sɔ́sɪ] adj. descarado, respondón, insolente, Am. retobado.

saunter [sɔ́ntə] v. pasearse, vagar.

sausage [sɔ́sɪdʒ] s. salchicha, salchichón; longaniza; chorizo.

savage [sǽvɪdʒ] adj. salvaje; fiero; bárbaro, brutal, feroz; s. salvaje.

savagery [sǽvɪdʒrɪ] s. salvajismo; crueldad, fiereza.

savant [səvánt] s. sabio.

save [sev] v. salvar; ahorrar; economizar; guardar; resguardar; to — from librar de; to — one's eyes cuidarse la vista; prep. salvo, menos, excepto.

saver [sévə] s. salvador; libertador; ahorrador; life— salvavidas.

saving [sévɪŋ] adj. salvador; ahorrativo, económico; frugal; s. ahorro, economía; -s ahorros; -s bank caja o banco de ahorros; prep. salvo, excepto, con excepción de.

savior [sévjə] s. salvador.

savor [sévə] s. sabor; dejo; v. saborear; sazonar; to — of saber a, tener el sabor de; it -s of treason huele a traición.

savory [sévərɪ] adj. sabroso.

saw [sɔ] s. sierra; —horse caballete; v. aserrar, serrar; it -s easily es fácil de aserrar; pret. de to see.

sawdust [sɔ́dʌst] s. aserrín, serrín.

sawmill [sɔ́mɪl] s. aserradero.

sawn [sɔn] p.p. de to saw.

Saxon [sǽksn] adj. & s. sajón.

saxophone [sǽksəfon] s. saxófono.

say [se] v. decir; declarar; —! ¡diga! ¡oiga usted!; that is to — es decir; to — one's prayers rezar, decir o recitar sus oraciones; to — the least por lo menos; it is said that dizque, se dice que, dicen que; s. afirmación, aserto; the final — la autoridad decisiva; to have a — in a matter tener voz y voto en un asunto; to have one's — expresarse, dar su opinión.

saying [séɪŋ] s. dicho, refrán; aserto; as the — goes como dice el refrán.

scab [skæb] s. costra (de una herida); roña; esquirol (obrero que sustituye a un huelguista); obrero que acepta un

jornal inferior; v. encostrarse (una herida), cubrirse de una costra.

scabbard [skǽbəd] s. vaina, funda (de espada, puñal, etc.).

scabby [skǽbɪ] adj. costroso; roñoso, sarnoso, tiñoso.

scabrous [skébrəs] adj. escabroso.

scaffold [skǽfld] s. andamio, tablado; patíbulo, cadalso.

scaffolding [skǽfldɪŋ] s. andamiada (Am. andamiaje), andamios.

scald [skɔld] v. escaldar; to — milk calentar la leche hasta que suelte el hervor; s. escaldadura, quemadura.

scale [skel] s. escala; platillo de balanza; balanza; escama (de pez o de la piel); costra; pair of -s balanza; platform — báscula; v. escalar; subir, trepar por; graduar (a escala); medir según escala; pesar; escamar, quitar las escamas a; pelarse, despellejarse; descostrar(se); to — down prices rebajar proporcionalmente los precios.

scallop [skáləp] s. onda, pico (adorno); molusco bivalvo; -s festón (recortes en forma de ondas o picos); v. festonear, recortar en forma de ondas o picos; asar con salsa o migas de pan.

scalp [skælp] s. cuero cabelludo; v. desollar el cráneo; revender (boletos, billetes) a precio subido.

scaly [skélɪ] adj. escamoso, lleno de escamas; — with rust mohoso.

scamp [skæmp] s. pícaro, bribón, bellaco.

scamper [skǽmpə] v. correr, escabullirse, escaparse; s. escabullida, carrera, corrida.

scan [skæn] v. escudriñar; examinar, mirar detenidamente; echar un vistazo a (en el habla popular); medir (el verso).

scandal [skǽndl] s. escándalo; maledicencia, murmuración.

scandalize [skǽndlaɪz] v. escandalizar, dar escándalo.

scandalous [skǽndləs] adj. escandaloso; difamatorio; vergonzoso.

scant [skænt] adj. escaso; corto, insuficiente; v. escatimar, limitar.

scanty [skǽntɪ] adj. escaso; insuficiente.

scar [skɑr] s. cicatriz; costurón; raya, marca (en una superficie pulida); v. marcar, rayar; hacer o dejar una cicatriz en.

scarce [skɛrs] adj. escaso; raro, -ly adv. escasamente; apenas.

scarcity [skérsətɪ] s. escasez; carestía, insuficiencia.

scare [skɛr] v. espantar, asustar; alarmar, sobresaltar; he -s easily se asusta fácilmente; to — away ahuyentar, espantar; s. susto, sobresalto.

scarecrow [skérkro] s. espantajo; espantapájaros.

scarf [skarf] s. bufanda; mantilla; pañuelo (*para el cuello o la cabeza*); tapete (*para una mesa, tocador, etc.*).

scarlet [skárlιt] s. escarlata; *adj.* de color escarlata; — **fever** escarlata, escarlatina.

scary [skérι] *adj.* espantadizo, asustadizo, miedoso.

scatter [skǽtǝ] *v.* esparcir(se); desparramar(se); dispersar(se); —**brained** ligero de cascos, aturdido.

scene [sin] s. escena; escenario; decoración; vista; **to make a** — causar un escándalo.

scenery [sínǝrι] s. paisaje, vista; **stage** — decoraciones.

scent [sɛnt] s. olor; perfume; pista, rastro; **to be on the** — **of** seguir el rastro de; **to have a keen** — tener buen olfato; *v.* oler, olfatear, ventear, husmear; perfumar.

scepter [sɛ́ptǝ] s. cetro.

sceptic [skɛ́ptιk] *adj. & s.* escéptico.

scepticism [skɛ́ptǝsιzǝm] s. escepticismo.

schedule [skɛ́dʒʊl] s. horario; itinerario (*de trenes*); lista, inventario (*adjunto a un documento*); *v.* fijar el día y la hora (*para una clase, conferencia, etc.*); establecer el itinerario para (*un tren o trenes*).

scheme [skim] s. esquema, plan, proyecto; empresa; ardid, trama, maquinación; **color** — combinación de colores; **metrical** — sistema de versificación; *v.* proyectar, urdir; maquinar, intrigar, tramar.

schemer [skímǝ] s. maquinador, intrigante; proyectista.

scheming [skímιŋ] *adj.* maquinador, intrigante; s. maquinación.

scholar [skálǝ] s. escolar, estudiante; becario (*el que disfruta de una beca*); erudito, docto.

scholarly [skálǝlι] *adj.* erudito, sabio, docto; *adv.* eruditamente, doctamente.

scholarship [skálǝʃιp] s. saber; erudición; beca; **to have a** — disfrutar una beca.

scholastic [skolǽstιk] *adj.* escolástico; escolar.

school [skul] s. escuela; — **of fish** banco de peces; *adj.* de escuela; — **day** día de escuela; — **board** consejo de enseñanza; *v.* enseñar, educar, instruir, aleccionar.

schoolboy [skúlbɔι] s. muchacho de escuela.

schoolgirl [skúlgɜl] s. muchacha de escuela.

schoolhouse [skúlhaʊs] s. escuela.

schooling [skúlιŋ] s. instrucción; enseñanza, educación.

schoolmaster [skúlmæstǝ] s. maestro de escuela.

schoolmate [skúlmet] s. condiscípulo, compañero de escuela.

schoolroom [skúlrum] s. clase, aula.

schoolteacher [skúltitʃǝ] s. maestro de escuela.

schooner [skúnǝ] s. goleta; vaso grande para cerveza; **prairie** — galera con toldo.

science [sáιǝns] s. ciencia.

scientific [saιǝntífιk] *adj.* científico; -**ally** *adv.* científicamente.

scientist [sáιǝntιst] s. científico, hombre de ciencia.

scion [sáιǝn] s. vástago.

scissors [sízǝz] s. *pl.* tijeras.

scoff [skɔf] s. mofa, burla, befa, escarnio; *v.* escarnecer; mofarse; **to** — **at** mofarse de, burlarse de, escarnecer a.

scold [skold] *v.* reñir, reprender, regañar; s. regañón, persona regañona.

scolding [skóldιŋ] s. regaño, reprensión; *adj.* regañón.

scoop [skup] s. cuchara, cucharón; pala; palada, cucharada; buena ganancia; **newspaper** — primera publicación de una noticia; *v.* cavar, excavar; ahuecar; cucharear, sacar con cucharón o pala; achicar (*agua*); **to** — **in a good profit** sacar buena ganancia.

scoot [skut] *v.* escabullirse, correr, irse a toda prisa; —¡largo de aquí!

scope [skop] s. alcance, extensión; esfera, campo.

scorch [skɔrtʃ] *v.* chamuscar; resecar, agostar; *s.* chamusquina, *Am.* chamuscada o chamuscadura.

score [skor] s. cuenta; escor (*en el juego*); raya, línea; calificación (*expresada numéricamente*); veintena; **musical** — partitura; **on that** — a ese respecto; **on the** — **of** a causa de, con motivo de; **to keep the** — llevar la cuenta; **to settle old** -**s** desquitarse; *v.* marcar el escor, señalar los tantos en un juego; calificar (*numéricamente*); instrumentar (*música*); rayar, marcar con rayas; **to** — **a point** ganar un punto o tanto; **to** — **a success** lograr éxito, obtener un triunfo.

scorn [skɔrn] s. desdén, menosprecio; *v.* desdeñar, menospreciar.

scornful [skɔ́rnfǝl] *adj.* desdeñoso.

scorpion [skɔ́rpιǝn] s. escorpión, alacrán.

Scotch [skɑtʃ] *adj.* escocés; **the —** los escoceses, el pueblo escocés.

scoundrel [skáundrəl] *s.* bellaco, bribón, pícaro.

scour [skaur] *v.* fregar, restregar, limpiar; pulir; **to — the country** recorrer la comarca (*en busca de algo*).

scourge [skɜdʒ] *s.* azote; *v.* azotar; castigar.

scout [skaut] *s.* explorador (*usualmente military*); **a good —** un buen explorador; una buena persona, un buen compañero; *v.* explorar; reconocer.

scowl [skaul] *s.* ceño; *v.* fruncir el ceño, mirar con ceño; poner mala cara.

scramble [skræmbl] *v.* hacer un revoltillo de (*huevos*); revolver, mezclar confusamente; **to — for something** forcejear por coger algo; pelearse por coger algo; **to — up** trepar o subir a gatas (*una cuesta*); **-d eggs** revoltillo, huevos revueltos; *s.* revoltillo, confusión; pelea.

scrap [skræp] *s.* fragmento, pedacito; migaja; riña, reyerta; **-s** sobras; desperdicios; desechos; retales; **—book** álbum de recortes; **— iron** recortes o desechos de hierro, *v.* desechar; tirar a la basura; descartar; pelear, reñir.

scrape [skrep] *v.* raspar; rasguñar; rascar, raer; rozar; **to — along** ir tirando, ir pasándola; **to — together** recoger o acumular poco a poco; **to bow and —** ser muy servil; *s.* raspadura; rasguño; aprieto, dificultad, lío.

scraper [skrépə] *s.* raspador: persona ahorrativa y tacaña.

scratch [skrætʃ] *v.* arañar, rasguñar; rascar; raspar; rayar; escarbar; hacer garabatos, escribir mal; **to — out** borrar, tachar; sacar (*los ojos*) con las uñas; *s.* arañazo, araño, rasguño; raya, marca; **to start from —** empezar sin nada; empezar desde el principio; empezar sin ventaja.

scrawl [skrɔl] *s.* garabato; *v.* hacer garabatos, escribir mal.

scrawny [skrɔ́nɪ] *adj.* huesudo, flaco.

scream [skrim] *s.* chillido, alarido, grito; **he's a —** es muy cómico o chistoso; *v.* chillar, gritar.

screech [skritʃ] *s.* chillido; **— owl** lechuza; *v.* chillar.

screen [skrin] *s.* pantalla; mampara; biombo; resguardo; tamiz, cedazo; **— door** antepuerta de tela metálica; **motion-picture —** pantalla de cinematógrafo; **wire —** pantalla de tela metálica; *v.* tapar; resguardar, proteger con una pantalla o biombo; cerner;

proyectar sobre la pantalla, filmar; **to — windows** proteger las ventanas con tela metálica.

screw [skru] *s.* tornillo; **— eye** armella; **— nut** tuerca; **— propeller** hélice; **— thread** rosca; *v.* atornillar; torcer, retorcer; **to — a lid on** atornillar una tapa; **to — up one's courage** cobrar ánimo.

screwdriver [skrúdraɪvə] *s.* destornillador.

scribble [skríbl] *v.* garrapatear, hacer garabatos, borronear, escribir mal o de prisa; *s.* garabato.

script [skrɪpt] *s.* letra cursiva, escritura; manuscrito (*de un drama, de una película*).

scripture [skrɪptʃə] *s.* escritura sagrada; **the Scriptures** la Sagrada Escritura, la Biblia.

scroll [skrol] *s.* rollo de pergamino o papel; voluta, adorno en espiral; rúbrica (*de una firma*).

scrub [skrʌb] *v.* fregar; restregar; *s.* friega, fregado; *adj.* achaparrado; bajo, inferior; **— oak** chaparro, **— pine** pino achaparrado; **— team** equipo de jugadores suplentes o menos bien entrenados; **— woman** fregona.

scruple [skrúpl] *s.* escrúpulo; *v.* escrupulizar, tener escrúpulos.

scrupulous [skrúpjələs] *adj.* escrupuloso.

scrutinize [skrútnaɪz] *v.* escudriñar, escrutar

scrutiny [skrútnɪ] *s.* escrutinio.

scuff [skʌf] *v.* raspar; arrastrar los pies.

scuffle [skʌfl] *s.* refriega, riña, pelea; *v.* forcejear; luchar, pelear; arrastrar los pies.

sculptor [skʌlptə] *s.* escultor

sculpture [skʌlptʃə] *s.* escultura, *v.* esculpir, cincelar, tallar.

scum [skʌm] *s.* nata, capa, espuma, escoria; residuo; desechos; canalla, gente baja; *v.* espumar.

scurry [skɜ́ɪ] *v.* escabullirse; echar a correr; apresurarse; *s.* apresuramiento; corrida, carrera.

scuttle [skʌtl] *v.* echar a correr; barrenar (*un buque*); echar a pique; *s.* escotilla, escotillón; balde (*para carbón*).

scythe [saɪð] *s.* guadaña.

sea [si] *s.* mar; **to be at —** estar en el mar; estar perplejo o confuso; **to put to —** hacerse a la mar; *adj.* marino, marítimo, de mar; **— biscuit** galleta; **— green** verdemar; **— gull** gaviota; **— level** nivel del mar; **— lion** león marino, foca; **— power** potencia naval.

seaboard [síbord] *s.* costa, litoral; *adj.*

188

costanero, litoral.

seacoast [síkost] *s.* posta, litoral.

seal [sil] *s.* sello; timbre; foca, león marino; **to set one's — to** sellar; aprobar; *v.* sellar; estampar; cerrar; tapar; **to — in** encerrar, cerrar herméticamente; **to — with sealing wax** lacrar.

sealing wax [sílɪŋ wæks] *s.* lacre.

seam [sim] *s.* costura; juntura; cicatriz; filón, veta; *v.* echar una costura, coser.

seaman [símon] *s.* marino, marinero.

seamstress [símstrɪs] *s.* costurera.

seaplane [síplen] *s.* hidroavión.

seaport [síport] *s.* puerto de mar.

sear [sɪr] *v.* chamuscar(se), tostar(se), resecar(se); herrar, marcar con hierro candente; *adj.* reseco, marchito.

search [sɜrtʃ] *v.* buscar; escudriñar; registrar; examinar; **to — a prisoner** registrar a un prisionero; **to — for something** buscar algo; **to — into** investigar, indagar; *s.* busca, búsqueda; registro, inspección; investigación, pesquisa, indagación; **— warrant** mandato judicial de practicar un registro; **in — of** en busca de.

seashore [síʃor] *s.* costa, playa, orilla o ribera del mar.

seasick [síʃor] *adj.* mareado; **to get —** marearse.

seasickness [sísɪknɪs] *s.* mareo.

seaside [sísaɪd] *s.* costa, litoral; playa.

season [sízn] *s.* estación (*del año*); temporada; sazón, ocasión, tiempo; **— ticket** billete de abono; **Christmas —** navidades; **harvest —** siega, tiempo de la cosecha; **opera —** temporada de la ópera; **to arrive in good —** llegar en sazón, llegar a tiempo; *v.* sazonar; condimentar; aclimatar.

seasoning [síznɪŋ] *s.* condimento; salsa; desecación (*de la madera*).

seat [sit] *s.* asiento; silla; sitio; residencia; sede (*episcopal, del gobierno, etc*); nalgas; fondillos, parte trasera (*de los pantalones o calzones*); **— of learning** centro de estudios, centro de erudición; *v.* sentar; asentar; dar asiento a; **to — oneself** sentarse; **it -s a thousand people** tiene cabida para mil personas.

seaweed [síwid] *s.* alga marina.

secede [sisíd] *v.* separarse (*de una federación o unión*).

seclude [siklúd] *v.* recluir, apartar, aislar; **to — oneself from** recluirse de, apartarse de.

secluded [siklúdɪd] *adj.* apartado, aislado; solitario.

seclusion [siklúʒən] *s.* apartamiento, soledad, aislamiento; retiro.

second [sékənd] *adj.* segundo; inferior; **— hand** segundero (*de reloj*); **— lieutenant** subteniente; **second-rate de** segunda clase; mediocre, inferior; **on — thought** después de pensarlo bien; *s.* segundo; padrino (*en un desafío*); ayudante; mercancía de segunda calidad; mercancía defectuosa; *v.* secundar (*o segundar*), apoyar; apadrinar.

secondary [sékəndɛrɪ] *adj.* secundario; **— education** segunda enseñanza; **— school** escuela secundaria, escuela de segunda enseñanza.

second-hand [sékəndhǽnd] *adj.* de segunda mano; usado; indirecto, por intermedio de otro.

secondly [sékəndlɪ] *adv.* en segundo lugar.

secrecy [síkrəsɪ] *s.* secreto, sigilo, reserva.

secret [síkrɪt] *s.* secreto; *adj.* secreto; escondido, oculto; **— service** policía secreta; **-ly** *adv.* secretamente, en secreto.

secretary [sékrətɛrɪ] *s.* secretario; escritorio (*con estantes para libros*).

secrete [sikrít] *v.* secretar (*una secreción*); esconder, ocultar.

secretion [sikríʃən] *s.* secreción.

secretive [sikrítɪv] *adj.* reservado, callado; **— gland** glándula secretoria.

sect [sɛkt] *s.* secta.

section [sékʃən] *s.* sección; trozo; tajada; región; barrio; *v.* seccionar, dividir en secciones.

secular [sékjələ] *adj. & s.* secular.

secure [sikjúr] *adj.* seguro; firme; *v.* asegurar; afianzar; obtener; resguardar; **-ly** *adv.* seguramente, con seguridad; firmemente.

security [sikjúrətɪ] *s.* seguridad; fianza, garantía, prenda; resguardo, protección; **securities** bonos, obligaciones, acciones, valores.

sedan [sɪdǽn] *s.* sedán.

sedate [sɪdét] *adj.* sosegado; tranquilo, sereno; serio.

sedative [sédətɪv] *adj. & s.* calmante, sedativo.

sedentary [sédntɛrɪ] *adj.* sedentario; inactivo.

sediment [sédəmənt] *s.* sedimento, heces, residuo.

sedition [sɪdíʃən] *s.* sedición.

seditious [sɪdíʃəs] *adj.* sedicioso.

seduce [sɪdjús] *v.* seducir.

seduction [sɪdʌ́kʃən] *s.* seducción.

see [si] *v.* ver; **— that you do it no** deje Vd. de hacerlo; tenga Vd. cuidado de hacerlo; **I'll — to it** me encargaré de ello; **let me — a ver; to — a person home** acompañar a una persona a casa; **to — a person off** ir a la estación para despedir a una persona; **to — a person through a difficulty** ayudar a una persona a salir de un apuro; **to — through a person** adivinar lo que piensa una persona, darse cuenta de sus intenciones; **to — to one's affairs** atender a sus asuntos; **to have seen military service** haber servido en el ejército; *s.* sede, silla; **Holy See** Santa Sede.

seed [sid] *s.* semilla, simiente; pepita; **to go to —** producir semillas; decaer, declinar; descuidar de su persona, andar desaseado; *v.* sembrar; despepitar, quitar las pepitas o semillas de; producir semillas.

seedling [sídlɪŋ] *s.* planta de semillero; arbolillo (*de menos de tres pies de altura*).

seedy [sídɪ] *adj.* semilloso, lleno de semillas; raído; desaseado.

seek [sik] *v.* buscar; pedir, solicitar; **to — after** buscar; **to — to** tratar de, esforzarse por.

seem [sim] *v.* parecer; **it -s to me** me parece.

seemingly [símɪŋlɪ] *adv.* aparentemente, en apariencia, al parecer.

seemly [símlɪ] *adj.* propio, decente, decoroso.

seen [sin] *p.p. de* **to see.**

seep [sip] *v.* escurrirse, rezumarse, colarse, filtrarse.

seer [sɪr] *s.* vidente, adivino, profeta.

seethe [sið] *v.* bullir, hervir; burbujear.

segment [ségmənt] *s.* segmento.

seize [siz] *v.* asir, coger, agarrar; apoderarse de; prender o aprehender; aprovecharse de (*una oportunidad*); embargar, secuestrar; **to — upon** asir; **to become -d with fear** sobrecogerse de miedo.

seizure [síʒɚ] *s.* cogida; captura; aprehensión (*de un criminal*); secuestro, embargo (*de bienes*); ataque (*de una enfermedad*).

seldom [séldəm] *adv.* rara vez, raras veces, raramente.

select [səlékt] *adj.* selecto, escogido; *v.* elegir, escoger; entresacar.

selection [səlékʃən] *s.* selección, elección.

self [sɛlf] **: by one —** por sí, por sí mismo; **for one—** para sí; **one's other —** su otro yo; **his wife and —** su esposa y él (*véase* **herself, himself, ourselves, themselves,** *etc.*); **self-centered** egoísta, egocéntrico; **self-conscious** consciente de sí, cohibido, tímido; **self-control** dominio de sí mismo (o de sí propio); **self-defense** defensa propia; **self-denial** abnegación; **self-evident** patente, manifiesto; **self-esteem** respeto de sí mismo; amor propio; **self-government** gobierno autónomo, autonomía; gobierno democrático; **self-interest** propio interés; egoísmo; **self-love** amor propio; **self-possessed** sereno, dueño de sí, tranquilo; **self-sacrifice** abnegación; **self-satisfied** pagado de sí, satisfecho de sí.

selfish [sɛlfɪʃ] *adj.* egoísta; **-ly** *adv.* con egoísmo, por egoísmo.

selfishness [sɛlfɪʃnɪs] *s.* egoísmo.

selfsame [sɛlfsém] *adj.* mismo, idéntico, mismísimo.

sell [sɛl] *v.* vender; venderse, estar de venta; **to — at auction** vender en almoneda o subasta, subastar; **to — out** venderlo todo.

seller [sɛlɚ] *s.* vendedor.

selves [sɛlvz] *pl. de* **self.**

semblance [sémbləns] *s.* semejanza; apariencia.

semicircle [séməsɜkl] *s.* semicírculo.

semicolon [séməkolən] *s.* punto y coma.

seminary [sémənɛrɪ] *s.* seminario.

senate [sénɪt] *s.* senado.

senator [sénɪtɚ] *s.* senador.

send [sɛnd] *v.* enviar; mandar; despachar; remitir, expedir; lanzar (*una flecha, pelota, etc.*); **to — away** despedir, despachar; **to — forth** despachar, enviar; emitir; exhalar; echar; **to — someone up for 15 years** condenar a un reo a 15 años de prisión; **to — word** avisar, mandar decir, mandar recado.

sender [séndɚ] *s.* remitente; transmisor.

senile [sínaɪl] *adj.* senil, caduco; chocho.

senility [sənílɪtɪ] *s.* senectud; chochera o chochez.

senior [sínjɚ] *adj.* mayor, de más edad; más antiguo, superior en dignidad o rango; **— class** clase del cuarto año; *s.* persona o socio más antiguo; estudiante del último año; **to be somebody's — by two years** ser dos años mayor que alguien.

sensation [sɛnséʃən] *s.* sensación.

sensational [sɛnséʃənl] *adj.* sensacional; emociante.

sense [sɛns] *s.* sentido; sentimiento; sensación; juicio, sensatez; significado; **common —** sentido común; **to make —** tener sentido; **to be out of one's -s** estar fuera de sí, estar loco; *v.* percibir, sentir; darse cuenta de.

senseless [sénslɪs] *adj.* sin sentido; insensato, absurdo; insensible, privado de sentido.

sensibility [sensəbíʃlətɪ] *s.* sensibilidad.

sensible [sénsəbl] *adj.* sensato, razonable, cuerdo; sensible, perceptible; **sensibly** *adv.* sensatamente, con sensatez, con sentido común; sensiblemente, perceptiblemente.

sensitive [sénsətɪv] *adj.* sensitivo; sensible; quisquilloso, susceptible.

sensitiveness [sénsətɪvnɪs] *s.* sensibilidad.

sensual [sénʃuəl] *adj.* sensual, carnal, lujurioso.

sensuality [senʃuǽlətɪ] *s.* sensualidad; lujuria.

sent [sɛnt] *pret. & p.p. de* to send.

sentence [séntəns] *s.* sentencia, fallo, decisión; oración (*gramatical*); **death —** pena capital; *v.* sentenciar.

sentiment [séntəmənt] *s.* sentimiento; sentido.

sentimental [sentəméntl] *adj.* sentimental.

sentimentality [sentəmentǽlətɪ] *s.* sentimentalismo, sentimentalidad.

sentinel [séntənl] *s.* centinela.

sentry [séntrɪ] *s.* centinela.

separate [sépɪrt] *adj.* separado; apartado, solitario; distinto, diferente; **-ly** *adv.* separadamente, por separado, aparte; [sépəret] *v.* separar(se); apartar(se).

separation [sepəréʃən] *s.* separación.

September [septémbə] *s.* septiembre.

sepulcher [sépʃkə] *s.* sepulcro, sepultura.

sequel [síkwəl] *s.* secuela; continuación, consecuencia; resultado.

sequence [síkwəns] *s.* secuencia, sucesión; serie, continuación; consecuencia, resultado; runfla (*serie de tres o más naipes de un mismo palo*).

serenade [sɛrənéd] *s.* serenata; *v.* dar serenata a.

serene [sərín] *adj.* sereno; tranquilo; claro, despejado.

serenity [sərénətɪ] *s.* serenidad; calma.

sergeant [sárdʒənt] *s.* sargento; **— at arms** oficial que guarda el orden (*en un cuerpo legislativo*).

serial [sírɪəl] *s.* cuento o novela por entregas; *adj.* consecutivo, en serie; **— novel** novela por entregas.

series [sírɪz] *s.* serie; series.

serious [sírɪəs] *adj.* serio; grave; **-ly** *adv.* seriamente, con seriedad, en serio; gravemente.

seriousness [sírɪəsnɪs] *s.* seriedad; gravedad.

sermon [sɔ́mən] *s.* sermón.

serpent [sɔ́pənt] *s.* serpiente; sierpe.

serum [sírəm] *s.* suero.

servant [sɔ́vənt] *s.* sirviente; criado; servidor; **— girl** criada, *Am.* mucama.

serve [sɔv] *v.* servir; surtir, abastecer; **to — a term in prison** cumplir una condena; **to — a warrant** entregar una citación; **to — as** servir de; **to — for** servir de, servir para; **to — notice on** notificar, avisar, advertir; **to — one's purpose** servir para el caso o propósito; **it -s me right** bien me lo merezco; *s.* saque (*de la pelota en tenis*).

server [sɔ́və] *s.* servidor; saque (*el que saca la pelota en el juego de tenis*); bandeja; mesa de servicio.

service [sɔ́vɪs] *s.* servicio; saque (*de la pelota en tenis*); entrega (*de una citación judicial*); **at your —** a la disposición de Vd., servidor de Vd.; **funeral —** honras fúnebres, funerales, exequias; **mail —** servicio de correos; **table —** servicio de mesa, vajilla; **tea —** juego o servicio de té; **— entrance** entrada para el servicio; **— man** militar; **— station** estación de servicio; *v.* servir; reparar; surtir (*una tienda*).

serviceable [sɔ́vɪsəbl] *adj.* servible; útil; duradero.

servile [sɔ́vl] *adj.* servil.

servitude [sɔ́vətjud] *s.* servidumbre; esclavitud.

session [séʃən] *s.* sesión.

set [sɛt] *v.* poner; colocar, asentar; fijar; establecer; ajustar; engastar (*piedras preciosas*); solidificar(se), endurecer(se) (*el cemento, yeso, etc.*); ponerse (*el sol, la luna*); empollar; **to — a bone** componer un hueso dislocado; **to — a trap** armar una trampa; **to — about** ponerse a; **to — an example** dar ejemplo; **to — aside** poner a un lado, poner aparte; apartar; ahorrar; **to — back** retrasar, atrasar; **to — forth** exponer, expresar; manifestar; **to — forth on a journey** ponerse en camino; **to — off** disparar, hacer estallar (*un explosivo*); hacer resaltar; salir; **to — on fire** pegar o poner fuego a, incendiar; **to — one's jaw** apretar las quijadas; **to — one's heart on** tener la esperanza puesta en; **to — one's mind on** resolverse a, aplicarse a; **to — out for** partir para, salir para; **to — out** to empezar a; **to — right** colocar bien; enderezar; rectificar; **to — sail** hacerse a la vela; **to — the**

brake frenar, apretar el freno; **to —
up** erigir, levantar; armar, montar
(*una máquina*); parar (*tipo de imprenta*); establecer, poner (*una tienda,
un negocio*); **to — upon someone**
acometer, asaltar a alguien; *pret. &
p.p. de* **to set**; *adj.* fijo; firme; sólido;
resuelto; rígido; puesto; establecido;
engastado; **— to go** listo para partir;
s. juego, colección; serie; grupo, clase;
partida (*de tenis*); **— of dishes** servicio de mesa, vajilla; **— of teeth**
dentadura; **radio —** radio, radiorre-
ceptor; **tea —** servicio para té.

setback [sétbæk] *s.* atraso, revés, retroceso inesperado.

settee [setí] *s.* canapé.

setting [sétɪŋ] *s.* engaste (*de una joya*);
escena, escenario; puesta (*del sol, de
un astro*); **— sun** sol poniente.

settle [sétl] *v.* colonizar, poblar; estable-
cer(se); fijar(se); asentar(se); arreglar,
poner en orden, ajustar (*cuentas*); zanjar (*una disputa*); pagar, liquidar, saldar; **to — down**; formalizarse; asen-
tarse; calmarse; poner casa; **to — on**
a date fijar o señalar una fecha; **to —
property on (upon)** asignar bienes o
propiedad a; **to — the matter** decidir
el asunto, concluir con el asunto.

settlement [sétlmənt] *s.* establecimiento; colonia; poblado; colonización;
asignación o traspaso (*de propiedad*);
ajuste, arreglo; pago; saldo, finiquito,
liquidación; **— house** casa de beneficencia; **marriage —** dote.

settler [sétlə] *s.* colono, poblador; **— of
disputes** zanjador de disputas.

sever [sévə] *v.* desunir(se), partir(se), di-
vidir(se), separar(se); cortar, romper.

several [sévrəl] *adj.* varios, diversos;
distintos, diferentes.

severe [səvír] *adj.* severo; áspero, austero; rígido; riguroso; grave; recio,
fuerte.

severity [səvérətɪ] *s.* severidad; austeridad; rigidez; gravedad; rigor.

sew [so] *v.* coser.

sewer [sjúə] *s.* albañal, cloaca.

sewing [sóɪŋ] *s.* costura; modo de coser;
— machine máquina de coser; **—
room** cuarto de costura.

sewn [son] *p.p. de* **to sew.**

sex [sɛks] *s.* sexo.

sexton [sékstən] *s.* sacristán.

sexual [sékʃʊəl] *adj.* sexual.

shabby [ʃæbɪ] *adj.* raído, gastado; andrajoso; mal vestido; vil, injusto; **to treat
someone shabbily** tratar a alguien
injustamente o con menosprecio.

shack [ʃæk] *s.* cabaña, choza, *Am.* bohío,
Am. jacal.

shackle [ʃækl] *v.* encadenar; trabar,
echar trabas a, poner grillos a; estorbar; **-s** *s. pl.* cadenas, trabas, grillos,
esposas; estorbo.

shade [ʃed] *s.* sombra; tinte, matiz;
visillo, cortinilla; pantalla (*de lámpara*), visera (*para los ojos*); **a —
longer** un poco más largo; **— of
meaning** matiz; **in the —** of a la
sombra de; *v.* sombrear; dar sombra;
resguardar de la luz; matizar.

shadow [ʃædo] *s.* sombra; obscuridad,
espectro; **under the —** of al abrigo
de, a la sombra de; **without a —** of
doubt sin sombra de duda; *v.* sombrear; obscurecer; **to — someone**
espiarle a alguien los pasos, seguirle
por todas partes.

shadowy [ʃædowɪ] *adj.* lleno de sombras;
tenebroso; vago, indistinto.

shady [ʃédɪ] *adj.* sombrío, sombreado,
umbrío; **— business** negocio sospechoso; **— character** persona de carácter dudoso, persona de mala fama.

shaft [ʃæft] *s.* pozo o tiro (*de mina, de
elevador*); cañón de chimenea; columna; eje, árbol (*de maquinaria*); flecha.

shaggy [ʃægɪ] *adj.* peludo, velludo; lanudo; desaseado; áspero.

shake [ʃek] *v.* menear(se); estremecer-
(se); temblar; sacudir(se); agitar(se);
titubear, vacilar; hacer vacilar; dar,
estrechar (*la mano*); **to — hands** dar
un apretón de manos, darse la mano;
to — one's head mover o menear
la cabeza; cabecear; **to — with cold**
tiritar de frío, estremecerse de frío;
to — with fear temblar de miedo,
estremecerse de miedo; *s.* sacudida,
sacudimiento; estremecimiento, temblor, apretón (*de manos*); **hand—**
apretón de manos.

shaken [ʃékən] *p.p. de* **to shake.**

shaky [ʃékɪ] *adj.* tembloroso; vacilante.

shall [ʃæl] *v. aux. del futuro del indicativo
en las primeras personas* (**I, we**); *en
las demás expresa mayor énfasis, mandato u obligación,* **he — not !do it**
no lo hará, no ha de hacerlo; **thou
shalt not steal** no hurtarás.

shallow [ʃælo] *adj.* bajo, poco profundo;
superficial; ligero de cascos.

shallowness [ʃælonɪs] *s.* poca hondura;
poca profundidad; superficialidad; ligereza de juicio.

sham [ʃæm] *s.* fingimiento, falsedad,
farsa; *adj.* fingido, simulado; falso; **—
battle** simulacro, batalla fingida; *v.*

fingir, simular.

shame [Sem] s. vergüenza; deshonra; — on you! ¡qué vergüenza!; it is a — es una vergüenza; es una lástima; **to bring — upon** deshonrar; v. avergonzar; deshonrar.

shameful [Sémfəl] adj. vergonzoso.

shameless [Sémlıs] adj. desvergonzado, descarado.

shamelessness [Sémlısnıs] s. desvergüenza; descaro, desfachatez.

shampoo [Sæmpú] s. champú, lavado de la cabeza; v. dar un champú, lavar (la cabeza).

shamrock [Sémrak] s. trébol.

shank [Sæŋk] s. canilla (parte inferior de la pierna); zanca.

shanty [Sæntı] s. choza, cabaña, casucha.

shape [Sep] s. forma; figura; estado, condición; **to be in a bad —** estar mal; **to put into —** arreglar, poner en orden, ordenar; v. formar, dar forma a; tomar forma; **to — one's life** dar forma a, ajustar o disponer su vida; **his plan is shaping well** va desarrollándose bien su plan.

shapeless [Séplıs] adj. informe, sin forma.

share [Ser] s. porción, parte; participación; acción (participación en el capital de una compañía); v. compartir; repartir; participar; **to — in** participar en, tener parte en; **to — a thing with** compartir una cosa con.

shareholder [Sérholdə] s. accionista.

shark [Sark] s. tiburón; estafador; perito, experto; **loan —** usurero; **to be a —** at ser un águila (o ser muy listo) para.

sharp [Sarp] adj. agudo; puntiagudo cortante; punzante; mordaz; picante; astuto; claro, distinto, bien marcado; repentino; **— curve** curva curva abrupta, curva pronunciada o muy cerrada; **— ear** oído fino;—**features** facciones bien marcadas; **— struggle** lucha violenta; **— taste** sabor acre; **— temper** genio áspero; **— turn** vuelta repentina; s. sostenido (en música); **card —** tahur, fullero; adv. véase **sharply**; **at ten o'clock —** a las diez en punto.

sharpen [Sárpən] v. afilar(se); sacar punta a; aguzar(se); amolar.

sharply [Sárplı] adv. agudamente; mordazmente, ásperamente; repentinamente; claramente; **to arrive —** llegar en punto.

sharpness [Sárpnıs] s. agudeza; sutileza; mordacidad; rigor; aspereza; acidez.

shatter [Sétə] v. estrellar(se), astillar(se), hacer(se) añicos; quebrar(se), romper(se); **to — one's hopes** frustrar

sus esperanzas; **his health was —ed** se le quebrantó la salud; **—s** s. pl. pedazos, trozos, añicos, fragmentos; **to break into —** hacer(se) añicos.

shave [Sev] v. afeitar(se), rasurar(se); rapar(se); acepillar (madera); s. rasura, Am. afeitada; **he had a close —** por poco no se escapa; se salvó por milagro.

shaven [Sévən] p.p. de **to shave**; **clean-shaven** bien afeitado.

shaving [Sévıŋ] s. rasura, Am. afeitada; **wood —s** virutas; **— brush** brocha de afeitar; **— soap** jabón de afeitar.

shawl [Sol] s. mantón, chal.

she [Si] pron. pers. ella; **— who** la que; s. hembra; **she-bear** osa; **she-goat** cabra.

sheaf [Sif] s. haz, gavilla, manojo; lío; v. hacer gavillas.

shear [Sır] v. trasquilar, esquilar (las ovejas); cortar (con tijeras grandes).

shears [Sırz] s. pl. tijeras grandes.

sheath [Sie] s. vaina; funda, envoltura.

sheathe [Sið] v. envainar.

sheaves [Sivz] pl. de **sheaf**.

shed [Sed] s. cobertizo; tejadillo; Am. galpón (de una estancia); v. derramar; difundir; esparcir; mudar (de piel, plumas, etc.); **be impermeable** (un paño, abrigo, sombrero, etc.); **to — leaves** deshojarse; pret. & p.p. de **to shed**.

sheen [Sin] s. lustre, viso.

sheep [Sip] s. oveja; carnero; ovejas; **— dog** perro de pastor; **—fold** redil; **—skin** zalea; badana; pergamino; diploma (de pergamino).

sheepish [Sípıs] adj. vergonzoso, encogido, tímido.

sheer [Sır] adj. puro; completo; fino, delgado, transparente, diáfano; escarpado, cortado a pico; **by — force a** pura fuerza.

sheet [Sit] s. sábana; hoja, pliego (de papel); lámina (de metal); extensión (de agua, hielo); **— lightning** relampagueo.

shelf [Self] s. estante, anaquel; repisa; saliente de roca.

shell [Sel] s. concha; cáscara (de huevo, nuez, etc.); vaina (de guisantes, frijoles, garbanzos, etc.); casco (de una embarcación); armazón (de un edificio); granada, bomba, cápsula (para cartuchos); v. cascar (nueces); desvainar, quitar la vaina a, pelar; desgranar (maíz, trigo, etc.); bombardear.

shellac [Sɔlæk] s. laca; v. barnizar con laca.

shellfish [Sélfıs] s. marisco; mariscos.

shelter [Séltə] s. abrigo, refugio, asilo;

resguardo, protección; **to take** — refugiarse, abrigarse; *v.* abrigar, refugiar, guarecer; proteger, amparar.

shelve [ʃelv] *v.* poner o guardar en un estante; poner a un lado, arrinconar, arrumbar.

shelves [ʃelvz] *s. pl.* estantes, anaqueles; estantería.

shepherd [ʃépəd] *s.* pastor; zagal; — **dog** perro de pastor.

sherbet [ʃə́bɪt] *s.* sorbete.

sheriff [ʃérɪf] *s.* alguacil mayor (*de un condado en los Estados Unidos*).

sherry [ʃérɪ] *s.* jerez, vino de Jerez.

shield [ʃild] *s.* escudo, rodela, broquel; resguardo, defensa; *v.* escudar, resguardar, proteger.

shift [ʃɪft] *v.* cambiar; mudar(se); alternar(se); variar; desviar(se); trasladar, transferir; **to — for oneself** valerse o mirar por sí mismo; **to — gears** cambiar de marcha; **to — the blame** echar a otro su propia culpa; *s.* cambio; desvío, desviación; tanda, grupo de obreros; turno; **gear**— cambio de marcha.

shiftless [ʃíftlɪs] *adj.* negligente; holgazán.

shilling [ʃɪ́lɪŋ] *s.* chelín.

shin [ʃɪn] *s.* espinilla (*de la pierna*); *v.* **to — up** trepar.

shine [ʃaɪn] *v.* brillar, resplandecer, lucir; pulir; dar brillo, lustre o bola, embolar (*zapatos*); *s.* brillo, lustre, resplandor; **rain or** — llueva o truene; **to give a shoe** — dar bola (brillo o lustre) a los zapatos; embolar o embetunar los zapatos; limpiar el calzado.

shingle [ʃɪŋgl] *s.* ripia, tabla delgada, *Am.* tejamanil o tejamaní; pelo corto escalonado; letrero de oficina; **-s** zona (*erupción de la piel*); *v.* cubrir con tejamaniles; techar con tejamaniles.

shining [ʃáɪnɪŋ] *adj.* brillante; resplandeciente.

shiny [ʃáɪnɪ] *adj.* brillante; lustroso.

ship [ʃɪp] *s.* buque, barco, navío, nave; aeronave, avión; —**builder** ingeniero naval, constructor de buques; —**mate** camarada a bordo; —**yard** astillero; **on** —**board** a bordo; *v.* embarcar(se); despachar, enviar; remesar; transportar; alistarse como marino.

shipment [ʃípmənt] *s.* embarque; cargamento; despacho, envío; remesa.

shipper [ʃípə] *s.* embarcador; remitente.

shipping [ʃípɪŋ] *s.* embarque; despacho, envío; —**charges** gastos de embarque; — **clerk** dependiente de muelle; dependiente encargado de embarques.

shipwreck [ʃíprek] *s.* naufragio; *v.* echar a pique, hacer naufragar; naufragar, irse a pique.

shirk [ʃɜk] *v.* evadir, evitar.

shirt [ʃɜt] *s.* camisa; —**waist** blusa; **in** — **sleeves** en camisa, en mangas de camisa.

shiver [ʃívə] *v.* tiritar; temblar; estremecerse; *s.* escalofrío, temblor, estremecimiento.

shoal [ʃol] *s.* bajío, banco de arena; banco (*de peces*).

shock [ʃak] *s.* choque; sacudida; sacudimiento; golpe; sobresalto; — **absorber** amortiguador; — **of grain** hacina o gavilla de mieses; — **of hair** guedeja, greña; — **troops** tropas de asalto; *v.* chocar, ofender; escandalizar; causar fuerte impresión; horrorizar; sacudir; conmover; hacinar, hacer gavillas de (*mieses*).

shocking [ʃákɪŋ] *adj.* chocante, ofensivo, repugnante; espantoso, escandaloso.

shod [ʃad] *pret. & p.p. de* **to shoe.**

shoe [ʃu] *s.* zapato; botín; **brake** — zapata de freno; **horse**— herradura; — **blacking** betún, bola; — **polish** brillo, lustre, bola; — **store** zapatería, *Am.* peletería; *v.* calzar; herrar (*un caballo*).

shoeblack [ʃúblæk] *s.* limpiabotas.

shoehorn [ʃúhɔrn] *s.* calzador.

shoelace [ʃúles] *s.* lazo, cinta, cordón de zapato.

shoemaker [ʃúmekə] *s.* zapatero.

shoestring [ʃústrɪŋ] *s.* lazo, cinta, cordón de zapato.

shone [ʃon] *pret. & p.p. de* **to shine.**

shook [ʃuk] *pret. de* **to shake.**

shoot [ʃut] *v.* tirar, disparar, descargar; hacer fuego; fusilar; dar un balazo; lanzar; disparar (*una instantánea*); fotografiar, filmar (*una escena*); echar (*los dados*); brotar (*las plantas*); **to — by** pasar rápidamente; **to — forth** brotar, salir; germinar; lanzarse; **to — it out with someone** pelearse a balazos; **to — up a place** entrarse a balazos por un lugar; *s.* vástago, retoño, renuevo; **to go out for a** — salir a tirar; ir de caza.

shooter [ʃútə] *s.* tirador.

shooting [ʃútɪŋ] *s.* tiroteo; — **match** certamen de tiradores (*o de tiro al blanco*); — **pain** punzada, dolor agudo; — **star** estrella fugaz.

shop [ʃap] *s.* tienda; taller; —**window** escaparate, vitrina, aparador, *Am.* vidriera; **barber**— barbería; **beauty** — salón de belleza; **to talk** — hablar uno de su oficio o profesión; v. ir de tiendas; ir de compras, comprar.

shopkeeper [ʃápkipə] s. tendero.

shopper [ʃápə] s. comprador.

shopping [ʃápiŋ] s. compra, compras; **to go —** ir de compras, ir de tiendas.

shore [ʃor] s. costa, playa, orilla, ribera; puntal; **ten miles off —** a diez millas de la costa; v. **to — up** apuntalar, poner puntales.

shorn [ʃorn] p.p. de **to shear.**

short [ʃort] adj. corto; breve; bajo, Am. chaparro; escaso; brusco; **— cut** atajo; método corto; **short-legged** de piernas cortas; **— loan** préstamo a corto plazo; **for —** para abreviar; **in —** en resumen, en suma, en conclusión; **in — order** rápidamente, prontamente; **in a — time** en poco tiempo; **al poco tiempo; to be — of** estar falto o escaso de; **to cut —** acortar, abreviar, terminar de repente; **to run — of something** acabársele (írsele acabando) a uno algo; **to stop —** parar de repente, parar en seco.

shortage [ʃórtidʒ] s. escasez, carestía; déficit; falta.

shortcoming [ʃórtkʌmiŋ] s. falta, defecto.

shorten [ʃórtṇ] v. acortar(se), abreviar(se), disminuir(se).

shortening [ʃórtniŋ] s. manteca, grasa (para hacer pasteles); acortamiento; abreviación.

shorthand [ʃórthænd] s. taquigrafía.

shortly [ʃórtlɪ] adv. brevemente; en breve; al instante, pronto, luego; bruscamente, secamente.

shortness [ʃórtnɪs] s. cortedad; brevedad; pequeñez; escasez, deficiencia.

shorts [ʃorts] s. pl. calzoncillos, calzones cortos.

shortsighted [ʃórtsáɪtɪd] adj. miope; corto de vista.

shot [ʃat] pret. & p.p. de **to shoot**; s. tiro; disparo; balazo; cañonazo; balas; inyección; tirada (en ciertos juegos); **of liquor** trago de aguardiente; **buck—** municiones, postas; **not by a long —** ni con mucho, ni por pienso, nada de eso; **he is a good —** es buen tirador, tiene buen tino; **to take a —** at disparar un tiro a; hacer una tentativa de; **within rifle —** a tiro de rifle.

shotgun [ʃátɡʌn] s. escopeta.

should [ʃud] v. aux. del condicional en las primeras personas (I, we) : **I said that I —** go dije que iría; equivale al imperfecto de subjuntivo: **if it — rain**

si lloviera; se usa con la significación de deber: **you — not do it** no debieras (o no debería) hacerlo.

shoulder [ʃóldə] s. hombro; lomo, pernil (de puerco, cordero); borde, saliente (de un camino); **—s** espalda, espaldas; **— blade** espaldilla, paletilla; **straight from the —** con toda franqueza; **to turn a cold —** to volver las espaldas a, tratar fríamente; v. cargar al hombro, echarse sobre las espaldas; cargar con, asumir; empujar con el hombro.

shout [ʃaut] v. gritar; vocear; s. grito.

shove [ʃʌv] v. empujar, dar empellones; **to — aside** echar a un lado, rechazar; **to — off** partir, zarpar (un buque); salir, irse; s. empujón, empellón; empuje.

shovel [ʃʌvl] s. pala; v. traspalar.

show [ʃo] v. mostrar; enseñar; exhibir; probar, demostrar; indicar; verse; asomarse; **— him in** que pase, hágale entrar; **to — off** alardear, hacer ostentación de; lucirse; **to — up** aparecer, presentarse; **to — someone up** hacer subir a alguien; mostrarle el camino (para subir); desenmascarar a alguien, poner a alguien en la evidencia; s. exhibición; demostración; ostentación; espectáculo; representación, función; apariencia; **window** escaparate, vitrina, aparador, Am. vidriera; **to go to the —** ir al teatro, al cine; **to make a — of oneself** exhibirse, hacer ostentación.

showcase [ʃókes] s. vitrina, aparador.

shower [ʃávə] s. aguacero, chubasco, chaparrón; lluvia; ducha, baño de ducha; **bridal —** tertulia para obsequiar a una novia; v. llover; caer un aguacero.

shown [ʃon] p.p. de **to show**.

showy [ʃóɪ] adj. ostentoso; vistoso, chillón.

shrank [ʃræŋk] pret. de **to shrink**.

shred [ʃred] s. tira, triza; andrajo; fragmento; pizca; **to be in —s** estar raído; estar andrajoso; estar hecho trizas; **to tear to —s** hacer trizas; v. desmenuzar; hacer trizas, hacer tiras; pret. & p.p. de **to shred**.

shrew [ʃru] s. arpía, mujer brava, mujer de mal genio.

shrewd [ʃrud] adj. astuto, sagaz, agudo.

shriek [ʃrik] v. chillar, gritar; s. chillido, grito.

shrill [ʃrɪl] adj. agudo, penetrante, chillón; v. chillar.

shrimp [ʃrɪmp] s. camarón; hombrecillo insignificante.

shrine [ʃraɪn] *s.* santuário; altar; lugar venerado.

shrink [ʃrɪŋk] *v.* encoger(se); contraer-(se); disminuir; **to — back** retroceder; **to — from** retroceder ante, apartarse de; huir de, rehuir.

shrinkage [ʃrínkɪdʒ] *s.* encogimiento; contracción; merma.

shrivel [ʃrívl] *v.* encoger(se); fruncir(se), marchitar(se); disminuir(se).

shroud [ʃraud] *s.* mortaja; *v.* amortajar; cubrir, ocultar.

shrub [ʃrʌb] *s.* arbusto.

shrubbery [ʃrʌ́bərɪ] *s.* arbustos.

shrug [ʃrʌg] *v.* encogerse de hombros; *s.* encogimiento de hombros.

shrunk [ʃrʌŋk] *pret. & p.p. de* **to shrink.**

shrunken [ʃrʌ́ŋkən] *p.p. de* **to shrink.**

shudder [ʃʌ́də] *v.* temblar, estremecerse; *s.* temblor, estremecimiento.

shuffle [ʃʌ́fl] *v.* barajar; revolver, mezclar; arrastrar *(los pies)*; **to — along** ir arrastrando los pies; *s.* mezcla, confusión; evasiva; **— of feet** arrastramiento de pies; **it is your —** a Vd. le toca barajar.

shun [ʃʌn] *v.* esquivar, evadir, rehuir, evitar.

shut [ʃʌt] *v.* cerrar(se); **to — down** parar el trabajo; cerrar *(una fábrica)*; **to — in** encerrar; **to — off** cortar *(el gas, la electricidad, el agua, etc.)*; **to — off from** incomunicar, aislar de, cortar la comunicación con; excluir; **to — out** impedir la entrada de; cerrar la puerta a; **to — up** cerrar bien; tapar; encerrar; tapar la boca, hacer callar; callarse; *pret. & p.p. de* **to shut;** *adj.* cerrado.

shutter [ʃʌ́tə] *s.* contraventana; postigo *(de ventana)*; cerrador; obturador *(de una cámara fotográfica)*.

shuttle [ʃʌ́tl] *s.* lanzadera; *v.* ir y venir acompasadamente *(como una lanzadera)*.

shy [ʃaɪ] *adj.* tímido, apocado, vergonzoso; asustadizo; esquivo; **to be — on** estar escaso de; **to be — two cents** faltarle a uno dos centavos; *v.* esquivarse, hacerse a un lado; asustarse; **— at something** retroceder ante algo; respingar *(un caballo)* al ver algo; espantarse con algo; **to — away** esquivarse de repente; respingar *(un caballo)*; desviarse, apartarse.

shyness [ʃáɪnɪs] *s.* apocamiento, timidez, vergüenza.

shyster [ʃáɪstə] *s.* leguleyo, abogadillo tramposo, picapleitos.

sick [sɪk] *adj.* enfermo, malo; nauseado; angustiado; **— leave** licencia por enfermedad; **to be — for** languidecer por, suspirar por; **to be — of** estar cansado de; estar harto de; **to be — to** *(o* **at***)* **one's stomach** tener náuseas; **to make —** enfermar; dar pena, dar lástima; *s.* **the —** los enfermos; *v.* incitar, azuzar *(a un perro)* **— him** ¡síguele!

sicken [síkən] *v.* enfermar(se), poner(se) enfermo; dar asco; tener asco; sentir náuseas.

sickening [síknɪŋ] *adj.* nauseabundo, repugnante; lastimoso.

sickle [síkl] *s.* hoz.

sickly [síklɪ] *adj.* enfermizo; achacoso, enclenque; malsano.

sickness [síknɪs] *s.* enfermedad; malestar; náusea.

side [saɪd] *s.* lado; cara; costado; ladera, falda *(de una colina)*; partido, facción; **— by —** lado a lado; **by his — a** su lado; **by the — of** al lado de; **on all —s** por todos lados; **to take —s with** ser partidario de, ponerse al lado de; *adj.* lateral; de lado; oblicuo; incidental; secundario, de menos importancia; **— glance** mirada de soslayo, de través *o* de reojo; **— issue** cuestión secundaria; **— light** luz lateral; noticia, detalle *o* ilustración incidental; *v.* **to — with** estar por, ser partidario de, apoyar a, opinar con.

sideboard [sáɪdbord] *s.* aparador.

sidetrack [sáɪdtræk] *v.* desviar; echar a un lado.

sidewalk [sáɪdwɔk] *s.* acera, *Am.* banqueta, *Am.* vereda.

sideways [sáɪdwez] *adv.* de lado, de costado; oblicuamente; hacia un lado; *adj.* lateral, de lado, oblicuo.

siege [sidʒ] *s.* cerco, sitio, asedio; **to lay — to** sitiar, cercar.

sieve [sɪv] *s.* tamiz, cedazo; criba; *v. véase* **sift.**

sift [sɪft] *v.* cerner, tamizar; cribar.

sigh [saɪ] *v.* suspirar; *s.* suspiro.

sight [saɪt] *s.* vista; visión; espectáculo; escena; mira *(de un arma de fuego)*; **in — of** a vista de; **payable at —** pagadero a la vista; **he is a —** un adefesio o mamarracho; **this room is a —** este cuarto es un horror; **to catch — of** vislumbrar, avistar; **to know by —** conocer de vista; **to lose — of** perder de vista; **to see the —s** ver o visitar los puntos de interés; *v.* avistar; ver.

sightseeing [sáɪtsiɪŋ] *s.* turismo; **— tour** paseo en auto para ver puntos de interés.

sign [saɪn] *s.* signo; seña, señal; muestra; letrero; —**board** cartel; tablero (*para fijar anuncios*); *v.* firmar; contratar, hacer firmar; **to** — **over property** ceder una propiedad mediante escritura, hacer cesión legal de propiedad; **to** — **up for a job** firmar el contrato para un empleo; contratar para un empleo.

signal [sígnl] *s.* señal, seña; *v.* señalar, indicar, hacer seña, dar la señal; *adj.* señalado, notable; extraordinario; — **beacon** faro; — **code** código de señales.

signature [sígnətʃə] *s.* firma.

signer [sáɪnə] *s.* firmante.

significance [sɪgnífəkəns] *s.* significación; significado.

significant [sɪgnífəkənt] *adj.* significativo.

signify [sígnəfaɪ] *v.* significar.

silence [sáɪləns] *s.* silencio; *v.* acallar, apagar (*un sonido*); aquietar, sosegar.

silent [sáɪlənt] *adj.* silencioso; callado; tácito; — **partner** socio comanditario (*que no tiene voz ni voto*).

silhouette [sɪluét] *s.* silueta; *v.* perfilar; **to be -d against** perfilarse contra.

silk [sɪlk] *s.* seda; *adj.* de seda; — **industry** industria sedera; — **ribbon** cinta de seda.

silken [sɪlkən] *adj.* sedoso; de seda.

silkworm [sɪlkwɜrm] *s.* gusano de seda.

silky [sɪlkɪ] *adj.* sedoso, sedeño; de seda.

sill [sɪl] *s.* umbral; **window** — antepecho de ventana.

silly [sɪlɪ] *adj.* necio, tonto, bobo, simple; absurdo, insensato.

silver [sɪlvə] *s.* plata; vajilla de plata; color de plata; *adj.* de plata; plateado; argentino; — **wedding** bodas de plata; *v.* platear; argentar; **to** — **a mirror** azogar un espejo.

silversmith [sɪlvəsmɪθ] *s.* platero.

silverware [sɪlvəwɛr].*s.* vajilla de plata, vajilla plateada; cuchillos, cucharas y tenedores (*por lo general de plata o plateados*).

silvery [sɪlvərɪ] *adj.* plateado; argentino.

similar [sɪmələ] *adj.* semejante; **-ly** *adv.* semejantemente, de la misma manera.

similarity [sɪmələrətɪ] *s.* semejanza, parecido:

simile [sɪməlɪ] *s.* símil.

simmer [sɪmə] *v.* hervir a fuego lento.

simple [sɪmpl] *adj.* simple; sencillo; llano; tonto, mentecato; **simple-minded** ingenuo, simple, simplón; *s.* simple.

simpleton [sɪmpltən] *s.* simplón, papanatas, papamoscas.

simplicity [sɪmplísətɪ] *s.* sencillez; simplicidad; simpleza; ingenuidad.

simplify [sɪmpləfaɪ] *v.* simplificar.

simply [sɪmplɪ] *adv.* simplemente; sencillamente; solamente.

simultaneous [saɪmltènɪəs] *adj.* simultáneo.

sin [sɪn] *s.* pecado, culpa; *v.* pecar.

since [sɪns] *conj.* desde que; después (de) que; puesto que, como, visto que; dado que; *prep.* desde, despues de; *adv.* desde entonces; **ever** — desde entonces; **he died long** — murió hace mucho tiempo; **we have been here** — **five** estamos aquí desde las cinco.

sincere [sɪnsír] *adj.* sincero.

sincerity [sɪnsérətɪ] *s.* sinceridad.

sinecure [sínɪkjur] *s.* sinecura (*trabajo fácil y bien pagado*).

sinew [sínju] *s.* tendón; fibra, vigor.

sinewy [sínjəwɪ] *adj.* nervudo, nervioso o nervoso; fuerte, vigoroso.

sinful [sínfəl] *adj.* pecaminoso; pecador.

sing [sɪŋ] *v.* cantar; **to** — **out of tune** desentonar(se), desafinar; **to** — **to sleep** arrullar.

singe [sɪndʒ] *v.* chamuscar; *s.* chamusquina, *Am.* chamuscada, *Am.* chamuscadura.

singer [síŋə] *s.* cantor; cantora, cantatriz.

single [síŋgl] *adj.* solo; individual; particular; soltero; — **entry bookkeeping** teneduría por partida simple; — **room** cuarto para uno; — **woman** mujer soltera; **not a** — **word** ni una sola palabra; *s.* billete de un dólar; *v.* **to** — **out** singularizar, distinguir, escoger; entresacar.

singlehanded [síŋglhǽndɪd] *adj.* solo, sin ayuda.

singsong [síŋsɔŋ] *s.* sonsonete, cadencia monótona.

singular [síŋgjələ] *adj.* singular; raro, extraordinario; *s.* singular, número singular.

sinister [sínɪstə] *adj.* siniestro, aciago, funesto.

sink [sɪŋk] *v.* hundir(se); sumir(se), sumergir(se); echar a pique; irse a pique, naufragar; cavar (*un pozo*); enterrar, clavar (*un puntal o poste*); **to** — **into one's mind** grabarse en la memoria; **to** — **one's teeth into** clavar el diente en; **to** — **to sleep** caer en el sueño; *s.* sumidero; fregadero.

sinner [sínə] *s.* pecador.

sinuous [sínjuəs] *adj.* sinuoso, tortuoso; con vueltas y rodeos.

sinus [sáɪnəs] *s.* seno, cavidad (*en un*

hueso); **frontal** — seno frontal.

sip [sɪp] *v.* sorber; chupar; *s.* sorbo.

siphon [sáɪfən] *s.* sifón; *v.* sacar (*agua*) con sifón.

sir [83] *s.* señor.

siren [sáɪrən] *s.* sirena.

sirloin [sɜ́loɪn] *s.* solomillo, solomo.

sirup [sírəp] *s.* jarabe.

sissy [sísɪ] *adj. & s.* afeminado, maricón.

sister [sístə] *s.* hermana; **Sister Mary** Sor María.

sister-in-law [sístərɪnlò] *s.* cuñada, hermana política.

sit [sɪt] *v.* sentar(se); colocar, asentar; posarse (*un pájaro*); estar sentado; estar situado; empollar (*las gallinas*); apoyarse; reunirse, celebrar sesión (*un cuerpo legislativo, un tribunal*); sentar, venir o caer (*bien o mal un traje*); **to — down** sentarse; **to — out a dance** quedarse sentado durante una pieza de baile; **to — still** estarse quieto; **to — tight** mantenerse firme en su puesto; **to — up** incorporarse; **to — up all night** velar toda la noche; **to — up and take notice** despabilarse.

site [saɪt] *s.* sitio, local, situación.

sitting [sítɪŋ] *s.* sesión (*de un cuerpo legislativo, tribunal, etc.*); sentada; **at one** — de una sentada; *adj.* sentado; **— hen** gallina ponedora; **— room** sala (de descanso); sala de espera; antesala.

situated [sítʃvetɪd] *adj.* situado, sito, ubicado, colocado.

situation [sɪtʃʋéʃən] *s.* situación; colocación, empleo; posición.

size [saɪz] *s.* tamaño; medida; *v.* clasificar según el tamaño; **to — up** tantear, formarse una idea de, juzgar.

sizzle [sízļ] *v.* chirriar (*aplícase al sonido que hace la carne al freírse*); *s.* chirrido (*de la carne al freírse*).

skate [sket] *s.* patín; **ice —** patín de hielo, patín de cuchilla; **roller —** patín de ruedas; *v.* patinar.

skein [sken] *s.* madeja.

skeleton [skélətņ] *s.* esqueleto; armazón; **— key** llave maestra.

skeptic = sceptic.

sketch [skɛtʃ] *s.* boceto; diseño; croquis, esbozo; *v.* bosquejar; delinear; esbozar, dibujar.

ski [ski] *s.* esquí; *v.* esquiar, patinar con esquís.

skid [skɪd] *v.* patinar, resbalar(se) patinar (*una rueda*); deslizarse.

skill [skɪl] *s.* destreza, maña, habilidad, pericia.

skilled [skɪld] *adj.* experto, práctico, ex-

perimentado, hábil.

skillet [skílɪt] *s.* sartén; cacerola.

skillful, skilful [skílfəl] *adj.* experto, diestro, ducho, hábil, perito.

skim [skɪm] *v.* desnatar, quitar la nata a; espumar, quitar la espuma a; leer superficialmente; **to — over the surface** rozar la superficie.

skimp [skɪmp] *v.* escatimar; economizar; ser tacaño; hacer (*las cosas*) con descuido.

skin [skɪn] *s.* piel; cutis; pellejo; cuero; cáscara, hollejo; **to save one's —** salvar el pellejo; **skin-deep** superficial; *v.* desollar; pelar; **to — someone (out of his money)** desplumar a una persona, quitarle a uno el dinero.

skinny [skínɪ] *adj.* flaco; descarnado.

skip [skɪp] *v.* saltar; brincar; saltarse (*unos renglones, un párrafo, etc.*), omitir; saltar por encima de, saltar de un brinco; **to — out** salir a escape, escabullirse, escaparse; *s.* salto, brinco omisión.

skipper [skípə] *s.* patrón (*de barco*); capitán; saltador, brincador.

skirmish [skɜ́mɪʃ] *s.* escaramuza; *v.* escaramuzar, sostener una escaramuza.

skirt [skɜt] *s.* falda, *Am.* pollera; orilla, borde; **under —** enaguas; *v.* bordear, orillar, ir por la orilla de; circundar; **to — along a coast** costear.

skit [skɪt] *s.* parodia, juguete o paso cómico; boceto satírico o burlesco.

skull [skʌl] *s.* cráneo; calavera.

skunk [skʌŋk] *s. Am.* zorrillo o zorrino, *Am.* mapurite.

sky [skaɪ] *s.* cielo; **— blue** azul celeste.

skylark [skáɪlork] *s.* alondra, calandria.

skylight [skáɪlaɪt] *s.* claraboya, tragaluz.

skyrocket [skáɪrakɪt] *s.* cohete.

skyscraper [skáɪskrepə] *s.* rascacielos.

slab [slæb] *s.* tabla, plancha, losa; tajada gruesa; **marble —** losa de mármol.

slack [slæk] *adj.* flojo; tardo, lento; inactivo; **— season** temporada inactiva; *s.* flojedad, flojera; inactividad; **to take up the —** apretar, estirar; **—s** pantalones anchos con pliegues, *v.* véase **slacken**.

slacken [slǽkən] *v.* aflojar(se); flojear, retardar(se); disminuir.

slag [slæg] *s.* escoria.

slain [slen] *p.p. de* **slay.**

slam [slæm] *v.* cerrar(se) de golpe; dejar caer de golpe; **to — someone** decirle a alguien una claridad o grosería; **to — the door** dar un portazo; *s.* golpazo; claridad, grosería; **— of a door**

portazo; **to make a grand —** ganar todas las bazas (*en el juego de bridye*).

slander [slǽndə] *s.* calumnia, maledicencia; *v.* calumniar.

slanderous [slǽndərəs] *adj.* calumnioso.

slang [slæŋ] *s.* jerga, jerigonza; vulgarismo.

slant [slænt] *s.* sesgo; inclinación; punto de vista; *adj.* sesgado; inclinado; oblicuo; *v.* sesgar; inclinar(se); ladear.

slap [slæp] *s.* palmada, manazo, manotada; insulto, desaire; *v.* dar una palmada a, dar un manazo a.

slash [slæʃ] *v.* acuchillar; dar cuchilladas o tajos; cortar; hacer fuerte rebaja de (*precios, sueldos*); *s.* cuchillada; tajo, tajada, cortadura.

slat [slæt] *s.* tabla, tablilla.

slate [slet] *s.* pizarra; color de pizarra; lista de candidatos; **— pencil** pizarrín.

slaughter [slótə] *s.* carnicería, matanza, *Am.* carneada; **—house** matadero, *Am.* matanza; *v.* matar; *Am.* carnear; hacer una matanza; destrozar.

slave [slev] *s.* esclavo; **— driver** capataz de esclavos; persona que agobia de trabajo a otra; **— labor** trabajo de esclavos; trabajadores forzados; *v.* trabajar como esclavo.

slaver [slǽvə] *s.* baba; *v.* babosear, babear.

slavery [slévrɪ] *s.* esclavitud.

slavish [slévɪʃ] *adj.* servil.

slay [sle] *v.* matar.

sled [slɛd] *s.* trineo, rastra.

sleek [slik] *adj.* liso; pulido, resbaloso; suave; artero, mañoso; *v.* alisar; pulir.

sleep [slip] *v.* dormir; **to — it off** dormir la mona; **to — off a headache** curarse con sueño un dolor de cabeza; **to — on it** consultarlo con la almohada; *s.* sueño; **to go to —** dormirse, quedarse dormido; **to put to —** adormecer; arrullar (*al nene*).

sleeper [slípə] *s.* durmiente; coche-cama, coche-dormitorio.

sleepily [slípɪlɪ] *adv.* con somnolencia.

sleepiness [slípɪnɪs] *s.* sueño, modorra, somnolencia.

sleeping [slípɪŋ] *adj.* durmiente; dormido; **— car** coche-cama, coche-dormitorio; **— pills** píldoras para dormir; **— sickness** encefalitis letárgica.

sleepless [slíplɪs] *adj.* desvelado, insomne, sin sueño.

sleepy [slípɪ] *adj.* soñoliento; amodorrado; **to be —** tener sueño.

sleet [slit] *s.* cellisca; *v.* cellisquear.

sleeve [sliv] *s.* manga.

sleigh [sle] *s.* trineo; **— bell** cascabel; *v.* pasearse en trineo.

sleight [slait] : **— of hand** juego de manos; prestidigitación, escamoteo.

slender [slɛ́ndə] *adj.* delgado; tenue; escaso, insuficiente.

slept [slɛpt] *pret. & p.p. de* **to sleep.**

sleuth [sluə] *s.* detective (*o* detectivo).

slew [slu] *pret. de* **to slay.**

slice [slaɪs] *s.* rebanada, tajada; lonja; *v.* rebanar, tajar; cortar.

slick [slɪk] *v.* alisar; pulir; **to — up** alisar bien, pulir bien; pulirse, acicalarse, componerse; *adj.* liso; meloso, suave; aceitoso; astuto, mañoso.

slicker [slɪ́kə] *s.* impermeable de hule (*o* de caucho); embaucador.

slid [slɪd] *pret. & p.p. de* **to slide.**

slidden [slídn] *p.p. de* **to slide.**

slide [slaɪd] *v.* resbalar(se); deslizar(se); hacer resbalar; patinar; **to — into** meter(se) en; **to — out** (*o* **— away**) deslizarse, colarse, escabullirse, escaparse; **to let something —** dejar pasar algo; no hacer caso de algo; *s.* resbalón; resbaladero, lugar resbaladizo; ligado (*en música*); *véase* **landslide; — cover** tapa corrediza; **— rule** regla de cálculo; **microscope —** platina.

slight [slaɪt] *s.* desaire, menosprecio, desdén; desatención; *v.* desairar, menospreciar; descuidar, desatender; *adj.* delgado; delicado; leve, ligero; pequeño; insignificante; escaso; **-ly** *adv.* escasamente; ligeramente; un poco, apenas.

slim [slɪm] *adj.* delgado; esbelto; escaso.

slime [slaɪm] *s.* limo, cieno, fango; baba, secreción viscosa.

slimy [slaɪmɪ] *adj.* viscoso, mucoso, fangoso; baboso.

sling [slɪŋ] *s.* honda (*para tirar piedras*); cabestrillo (*para sostener el brazo*); eslinga (*maroma provista de ganchos para levantar pesos*); **—shot** tirador de goma *o* hule; *v.* tirar, arrojar; **to — a rifle over one's shoulder** echarse el rifle al hombro.

slink [slɪŋk] *v.* andar furtivamente, **to — away** escurrirse, escabullirse, deslizarse.

slip [slɪp] *v.* deslizar(se); resbalar(se); cometer un desliz; equivocarse; **to — away** escaparse, escabullirse, escurrirse; **to — in** meter(se); **to — one's dress on** ponerse de prisa el vestido; **to — out** salirse; sacar a hurtadillas; **to — out of joint** dislocarse, *Am.* zafarse (*un hueso*); **to — something**

off quitar(se) algo; **to let an opportunity** — dejar pasar una oportunidad; **it slipped my mind** se me olvidó, se me pasó; **it slipped off** se zafó; s. desliz; resbalón; error, equivocación; funda (de muebles, de almohada); combinación-enagua; pedazo (de papel), papeleta; embarcadero; guía, sarmiento (para transplantar); — **knot** nudo corredizo.

slipper [slípə] s. zapatilla; babucha; pantufla.

slippery [slípri] adj. resbaloso, resbaladizo; evasivo.

slit [slit] v. cortar, hacer una rendija, abertura o incisión; **to — into strips** cortar en tiras; pret. & p.p. de **to slit**; s. abertura, hendedura, rendija; cortada, incisión.

slobber [slábə] s. baba; v. babosear, babear.

slobbering [slábərɪŋ] adj. baboso.

slogan [slógən] s. lema, mote.

sloop [slup] s. chalupa.

slop [slap] v. ensuciar, salpicar; derramar(se); s. fango, suciedad; **—s** lavazas, agua sucia; desperdicios.

slope [slop] v. inclinar(se); s. inclinación; declive; falda, ladera, cuesta, bajada; vertiente.

sloppy [slápi] adj. puerco, sucio, cochino; desaseado; mal hecho.

slot [slat] s. abertura, hendedura, ranura (en que se introduce una moneda); **— machine** máquina automática que funciona por medio de una moneda, "traganíqueles", "tragamonedas"; v. hacer una abertura o hendedura.

sloth [sloθ] s. pereza; perezoso (cuadrúpedo).

slouch [slautʃ] s. persona perezosa o desaseada; postura muy relajada o floja; **— hat** sombrero gacho; **to walk with a** — andar con los hombros caídos y la cabeza inclinada; v. andar agachado; andar caído de hombros; andar alicaído; arrellanarse, repantigarse (en una silla).

sloveliness [slávənlɪnɪs] s. desaseo, desaliño; suciedad.

slovenly [slávənlɪ] adj. desaseado, desaliñado; desarreglado.

slow [slo] adj. lento, despacioso; tardo; atrasado; lerdo, torpe; adv. lentamente, despacio; v. **to — down** (o **up**) retardar, disminuir (el paso, la marcha, la velocidad); aflojar el paso; **-ly** adv. despacio, lentamente.

slowness [slónɪs] s. lentitud; torpeza; cachaza.

slug [slʌg] s. bala; porrazo, puñetazo; babosa (molusco sin concha); haragán; trago (de aguardiente); lingote (de imprenta); v. aporrear, abofetear, dar puñetazos.

sluggard [slʌgəd] s. holgazán, haragán.

sluggish [slʌgɪʃ] adj. tardo; inactivo.

sluice [slus] s. compuerta; caño, canal; **—gate** compuerta.

slum [slʌm] s. barrio bajo; v. visitar los barrios bajos.

slumber [slʌmbə] v. dormitar; dormir; s. sueño, sueño ligero.

slump [slʌmp] v. hundirse; desplomarse; bajar repentinamente (los precios o valores); s. desplome, hundimiento, bajón, baja repentina (de precios, valores, etc.).

slung [slʌŋ] pret. & p.p. de **to sling**.

slunk [slʌŋk] pret. & p.p. de **to slink**.

slush [slʌʃ] s. nieve a medio derretir; lodazal, fango; sentimentalismo; desperdicios.

sly [slaɪ] adj. astuto, socarrón, zorro, taimado; **on the** — a hurtadillas, a escondidas.

slyness [sláɪnɪs] s. disimulo, astucia.

smack [smæk] s. sabor, dejo; beso ruidoso; chasquido (de látigo); palmada, manotada; **a — of something** una pizca de algo; v. dar un beso ruidoso; chasquear (un látigo); dar un manazo; **to — of** saber a, tener el sabor de; oler a; **to — one's lips** chuparse los labios; saborearse, rechuparse, relamerse.

small [smɔl] adj. pequeño, chico; bajo; insignificante; mezquino; **— change** dinero menudo, suelto; **— hours** primeras horas de la mañana; **— letters** letras minúsculas; **— talk** conversación insubstancial, charladuría; **— voice** vocecita; **to feel** — sentirse pequeño o insignificante.

smallness [smólnɪs] s. pequeñez; bajeza.

smallpox [smólpaks] s. viruelas.

smart [smart] adj. listo, vivo, inteligente; ladino; astuto; agudo; elegante; **— remark** observación aguda o penetrante; **— set** gente de buen tono; s. escozor, Am. ardor; v. picar, escocer, Am. arder.

smash [smæʃ] v. quebrantar, quebrar, romper; destrozar; aplastar; **to — into** chocar con; topar con, darse un tope contra; s. quebrazón, quiebra; fracaso; choque o tope violento; derrota completa.

smattering [smætərɪŋ] s. conocimiento superficial y rudimental.

smear [smɪr] v. embarrar, untar, manchar; **to —— with paint** pintorrear, pintarrajear; *s.* mancha.

smell [smɛl] *v.* oler; **to —— of** oler a; *s.* olor; olfato; **—— of olor a; to take a ——** oler.

smelly [smɛ́li] *adj.* oloroso; hediondo.

smelt [smɛlt] *v.* fundir *(metales); pret. & p.p. de* to smell.

smile [smaɪl] *v.* sonreír(se); *s.* sonrisa.

smiling [smaɪ́lɪŋ] *adj.* risueño, sonriente; **-ly** *adv.* sonriendo, con cara risueña.

smite [smaɪt] *v.* golpear; herir; castigar; afligir; *véase* smitten.

smith [smɪθ] *s.* forjador; *véase* blacksmith, goldsmith, silversmith.

smithy [smɪ́θɪ] *s.* herrería, fragua, forja.

smitten [smɪ́tn̩] *p.p. de* to smite & *adj.* afligido; castigado; enamorado; **to be —— with a disease** darle a uno una enfermedad.

smock [smɑk] *s.* bata corta, batín.

smoke [smok] *s.* humo; **cloud of ——** humareda; **to have a ——** dar una fumada, fumar; *v.* fumar, *Am.* chupar *(un cigarro);* humear; ahumar; **to —— out** ahuyentar o echar fuera con humo.

smoker [smókə] *s.* fumador; vagón de fumar; reunión o tertulia de fumadores.

smokestack [smókstæk] *s.* chimenea.

smoking [smókɪŋ] *adj.* humeante; de fumar; para fumadores; **—— car** vagón de fumar; **—— room** fumadero, cuarto de fumar.

smoky [smókɪ] *adj.* humeante; humoso, lleno de humo; ahumado.

smooth [smuð] *adj.* liso; terso; igual, parejo; plano, llano; suave; tranquilo; sagaz; **—— disposition** genio afable; **—— manners** maneras o modales afables; **—— style** estilo fluido y fácil; **—— talker** hablador melifluo y sagaz; *v.* alisar; allanar; pulir; emparejar; **to —— over** allanar, alisar, arreglar; **-ly** *adv.* suavemente; blandamente; fácilmente, con facilidad.

smoothness [smúðnɪs] *s.* lisura; igualdad, uniformidad; suavidad; afabilidad; tranquilidad; facilidad, fluidez.

smote [smot] *pret. de* to smite.

smother [smʌ́ðə] *v.* ahogar(se); sofocar(se); asfixiar(se).

smudge [smʌdʒ] *v.* tiznar, manchar o ensuciar con tizne; ahumar; *s.* tiznón, mancha *(hecha con tizne);* humareda, nube espesa de humo.

smuggle [smʌ́gl̩] *v.* contrabandear, hacer contrabando; **to —— in** meter de contrabando; **to —— out** sacar de contrabando.

smuggler [smʌ́glə] *s.* contrabandista.

smut [smʌt] *s.* tizne; suciedad, mancha; obscenidad, dicho obsceno o indecente; tizón *(enfermedad de ciertas plantas); v.* tiznar; ensuciar, manchar.

smutty [smʌ́tɪ] *adj.* tiznado, manchado de tizne; sucio.

snack [snæk] *s.* bocado, bocadillo, tentempié, bocadito; merienda, comida ligera.

snag [snæg] *s.* tocón *(tronco cortado casi a flor de tierra);* raigón; tropiezo, obstáculo; **to hit a ——** tropezar con un obstáculo; *v.* rasgar; enredar.

snail [snel] *s.* caracol.

snake [snek] *s.* culebra, víbora; *v.* culebrear.

snap [snæp] *v.* chasquear, dar un chasquido; estallar; quebrar(se); fotografiar instantáneamente; **his eyes —— le** chispean los ojos; **to —— at** echar una mordida o mordisco a; dar una tarascada a, morder; asir *(una oportunidad);* **to —— back** al tirar una mordida a; dar una respuesta grosera a; **to —— off** soltarse, saltar; quebrar(se); **to —— one's fingers** tronar los dedos, castañetear con los dedos; **to —— shut** cerrar(se) de golpe; **to —— together** apretar, abrochar; **to —— up** agarrar, asir; morder; *s.* chasquido; estallido; mordida, mordisco, dentellada; broche de presión; energía, vigor; galleta; cosa fácil, ganga; **cold ——** nortazo; repentino descenso de temperatura; **not to care a ——** no importarle a uno un ardite o un comino; *adj.* hecho de prisa, impensado; instantáneo; **—— fastener** broche de presión; **—— judgment** decisión atolondrada; **—— lock** cerradura de golpe.

snappy [snǽpɪ] *adj.* mordedor, *Am.* mordelón; enojadizo, *Am.* enojón; violento, vivo; elegante; **—— cheese** queso acre o picante; **—— eyes** ojos chispeantes.

snapshot [snǽpʃɑt] *s.* instantánea, fotografía instantánea; *v.* sacar una instantánea.

snare [snɛr] *s.* trampa, lazo; acechanza; red; *v.* enredar; atrapar, coger con trampa; tender lazos a.

snarl [snɑrl] *v.* gruñir; enmarañar(se), enredar(se); *s.* gruñido; maraña, enredo; pelo enmarañado.

snatch [snætʃ] *v.* arrebatar; agarrar; **to —— at** tratar de asir o agarrar; *s.* arrebatiña, arrebatamiento; trozo, pedacito; **to make a —— at** tratar de arrebatar, tratar de agarrarse a.

sneak [snik] *v.* andar furtivamente; obrar solapadamente; **to — in** meter(se) a escondidas; colarse; **to — out** escurrirse, salirse a hurtadillas; sacar, llevarse (*algo*) a escondidas; *s.* persona solapada.

sneer [snɪr] *v.* sonreír con sorna; hacer un gesto de desdén; mofarse; **to — at** mofarse de; *s.* sorna, mofa, rechifla; gesto desdeñoso.

sneeze [sniz] *v.* estornudar; *s.* estornudo.

sniff [snɪf] *v.* husmear, olfatear; sorber (*por las narices*); resollar para adentro; **to — at** husmear; menospreciar; *s.* husmeo, olfateo; sorbo (*por las narices*).

sniffle [snɪfl] *v.* sorber por las narices.

snip [snɪp] *v.* tijeretear; **to — off** cortar de un tijeretazo, recortar; *s.* tijeretada, tijeretazo; pedacito, recorte.

snipe [snaɪp] *v.* tirar, disparar desde un escondite.

snitch [snɪtʃ] *v.* arrebatar; ratear, hurtar.

snoop [snup] *v.* fisgar, fisgonear, curiosear; *s.* curioso, fisgón.

snooze [snuz] *v.* dormitar, sestear; *s.* siestecita, siestita; **to take a —** echar un sueñecito o siestita; descabezar el sueño.

snore [snor] *v.* roncar; *s.* ronquido.

snort [snɔrt] *v.* resoplar; bufar; *s.* resoplido, bufido.

snout [snaut] *s.* hocico, jeta.

snow [sno] *s.* nieve; *v.* nevar; **to be -ed under** estar totalmente cubierto por la nevada.

snowball [snóbɔl] *s.* bola de nieve; *v.* tirar bolas de nieve.

snowdrift [snódrɪft] *s.* ventisca, ventisquero, montón de nieve.

snowfall [snófɔl] *s.* nevada.

snowflake [snóflek] *s.* copo de nieve.

snowstorm [snóstɔrm] *s.* fuerte nevada, nevasca.

snowy [snóɪ] *adj.* nevado; níveo, blanco como la nieve.

snub [snʌb] *v.* desairar, menospreciar; *s.* desaire; **snub-nosed** chato, *Am.* ñato.

snuff [snʌf] *v.* olfatear, husmear, ventear; aspirar (*por la nariz*); despabilar (*una candela*); **to — at** olfatear, ventear; **to — out** apagar, extinguir; **to — up** sorber (*por las narices*); *s.* sorbo (*por la nariz*); rapé, tabaco en polvo; pabilo, mecha quemada (*de una vela*).

snug [snʌg] *adj.* apretado; ajustado; compacto; abrigado; cómodo.

so [so] *adv.* así; tan, muy; tanto; **so-so** regular; **so-and-so** Fulano (de tal); **— as to** para; **— far** tan lejos; hasta ahora, hasta aquí; **— many** tantos; **— much** tanto; **— much for that** basta por ese lado; **— much the better** tanto mejor; **— that** de modo que; para que; a fin de que; de suerte que; **— then** conque, pues bien, así pues; **and — forth** etcétera; y así sucesivamente; **I believe —** así lo creo; **is that — ?** ¿de veras? ¿de verdad? ¡no diga!; **ten minutes or —** poco más o menos diez minutos, como diez minutos.

soak [sok] *v.* remojar(se); empapar(se); **to — up** absorber, embeber; chupar; **to be -ed through** estar empapado; estar calado hasta los huesos; *s.* remojo, mojada; borrachín; golpe, puñetazo.

soap [sop] *s.* jabón; **— bubble** pompa de jabón, *Am.* bombita; burbuja de jabón; **— dish** jabonera; **soft —** jabón blando; lisonja, adulación; *v.* enjabonar.

soapy [sópɪ] *adj.* lleno de jabón.

soar [sor] *v.* remontarse; encumbrarse; subir muy alto; remontar el vuelo.

sob [sab] *v.* sollozar; *s.* sollozo.

sober [sóbə] *adj.* sobrio; moderado, templado; serio, grave; cuerdo, sensato; tranquilo, sereno; **to be —** estar en su juicio, no estar borracho; *v.* **to — down** sosegar(se), calmar(se); formalizarse; **to — up** desembriagarse, desemborracharse; bajársele a uno la borrachera.

soberly [sóbəlɪ] *adv.* sobriamente; cuerdamente, con sensatez; seriamente.

soberness [sóbənɪs] *s.* sobriedad; seriedad.

sobriety [səbráɪətɪ] *s.* sobriedad; cordura.

so-called [sókɔld] *adj.* así llamado, llamado.

sociable [sóʃəbl] *adj.* sociable, social, tratable.

social [sóʃəl] *adj.* social; sociable; tratable, de buen trato; *s.* reunión social, tertulia.

socialism [sóʃəlɪzəm] *s.* socialismo.

socialist [sóʃəlɪst] *adj.* & *s.* socialista.

society [səsáɪətɪ] *s.* sociedad; compañía.

sociology [soʃɪáládʒɪ] *s.* sociología.

sock [sak] *s.* calcetín; porrazo, golpe; *v.* pegar, apalear, golpear; *Am.* batear (*una pelota*).

socket [sákɪt] *s.* cuenca (*del ojo*); portalámparas, enchufe, *Am.* sóquet.

sod [sad] *s.* césped; terrón (*de tierra*

sembrada de césped); v. cubrir de césped.

soda [sóde] s. soda, sosa; — **fountain** Am. fuente de soda; — **water** agua gaseosa; **baking** — bicarbonato de sodio.

sodium [sódɪəm] s. sodio.

sofa [sófə] s. sofá.

soft [sɔft] adj. blando; muelle; suave; tierno; dulce; **soft-boiled eggs** huevos pasados por agua; — **coal** carbón bituminoso; — **drink** bebida no alcohólica; — **metal** metal dulce, metal maleable; — **soap** jabón blando; adulación; — **water** agua dulce; adv. *véase* **softly**.

soften [sɔfən] v. ablandar(se); suavizar(se); enternecer(se); templar(se); **to** — **one's voice** bajar la voz, hablar quedo (o quedito).

softly [sɔftlɪ] adv. blandamente; suavemente; quedo, quedito.

softness [sɔftnɪs] s. blandura; molicie; suavidad; ternura; dulzura.

soil [sɔɪl] s. suelo; terreno, tierra; mancha; v. ensuciar(se); manchar(se).

sojourn [sódʒɜn] s. estada, estancia, permanencia, Am. estadía; [sodʒɜn] v. permanecer; estarse, residir por una temporada.

solace [sálɪs] s. solaz; v. solazar.

solar [sólə] adj. solar, del sol.

sold [sold] pret. & p.p. de **to sell; to be** — **on an idea** estar bien convencido de una idea.

solder [sádə] v. soldar; s. soldadura.

soldier [sóldʒə] s. soldado.

sole [sol] adj. solo, único; exclusivo; suela (*del zapato*); planta (*del pie*); lenguado (*pez*); v. solar, echar suelas a; **to half-sole** echar o poner medias suelas a.

solely [sóllɪ] adv. sólamente, únicamente.

solemn [sáləm] adj. solemne.

solemnity [sɔlémnɪtɪ] s. solemnidad.

solicit [səlɪsɪt] v. solicitar.

solicitor [səlɪsɪtə] s. solicitador, agente.

solicitous [səlɪsɪtəs] adj. solícito.

solicitude [səlɪsətjud] s. solicitud, cuidado.

solid [sálɪd] s. sólido; adj. sólido; firme; macizo; sensato; unánime; — **blue** todo azul; — **gold** oro puro; **for one** — **hour** por una hora entera, por una hora sin parar; **the country is** — **for** el país está firmemente unido en favor de.

solidarity [sɑlədǽrətɪ] s. solidaridad.

solidify [səlɪdəfaɪ] v. solidificar(se).

solidity [səlɪdətɪ] s. solidez.

soliloquy [səlɪləkwɪ] s. soliloquio.

solitary [sálətɛrɪ] adj. solitario; solo; s. solitario, ermitaño.

solitude [sálətjud] s. soledad.

solo [sólo] s. solo.

soloist [sólоɪst] s. solista.

soluble [sóljəbl] adj. soluble, que se disuelve fácilmente.

solution [səlúʃən] s. solución.

solve [salv] v. resolver; explicar, aclarar, desenredar.

somber [sámbə] adj. sombrío.

some [sʌm] adj. algún, alguno; algunos, unos; algo de, un poco de; — **one** alguien, alguno; — **twenty people** unas veinte personas; pron. algunos, unos; algo, un poco; una parte.

somebody [sámbʌdɪ] pron. alguien; a — un personaje de importancia.

somehow [sámhaʊ] adv. de algún modo, de alguna manera; — **or other** de una manera u otra; por alguna razón.

someone [sámwʌn] pron. alguno, alguien.

somersault [sáməsɔlt] s. voltereta; v. dar una voltereta.

something [sámθɪŋ] s. algo, alguna cosa; un poco; — **else** alguna otra cosa, otra cosa.

sometime [sámtaɪm] adv. algún día; alguna vez; en algún tiempo; —**s** adv. a veces, algunas veces, de vez en cuando.

somewhat [sámhwɑt] s. algo, alguna cosa, un poco; adv. algo, un tanto.

somewhere [sámhwɛr] adv. en alguna parte; — **else** en alguna otra parte.

son [sʌn] s. hijo.

song [sɔŋ] s. canción, canto; **the Song of Songs** el Cantar de los Cantares; — **bird** ave canora, pájaro cantor; **to buy something for a** — comprar algo muy barato.

son-in-law [sánɪnlɔ] s. yerno, hijo político.

sonnet [sánɪt] s. soneto.

sonorous [sənórəs] adj. sonoro.

soon [sun] adv. pronto, presto; luego; — **after** poco después (de); **al poco tiempo; as** — **as** tan pronto como; luego que, así que; **how** — ? ¿cuándo?

soot [sʊt] s. hollín; tizne.

soothe [suð] v. calmar, sosegar; aliviar.

soothsayer [súseə] s. adivino.

sooty [sútɪ] adj. tiznado, cubierto de hollín.

sop [sap] v. empapar; **to** — **up** absorber; **to be sopping wet** estar hecho una sopa, estar mojado hasta los huesos; s. sopa (*pan u otra cosa empapada en leche, caldo, etc.*); soborno, regalo (*para* *acallar, conciliar, o sobornar*).

sophomore [sófəmor] *s.* estudiante de segundo año.

soprano [səpráno] *s.* soprano; **high** — tiple; — **voice** voz de soprano.

sorcerer [sórsərə] *s.* brujo, hechicero.

sordid [sórdɪd] *adj.* sórdido; vil, indecente; mezquino.

sore [sor] *adj.* dolorido; inflamado, enconado; afligido, apenado; lastimado, ofendido, picado; — **eyes** mal de ojos; **to be** — **at** estar enojado con; **to have a** — **throat** tener mal de garganta, dolerle a uno la garganta; *s.* úlcera, llaga; inflamación; lastimadura; pena, aflicción; **-ly** *adv.* dolorosamente, penosamente; **to be -ly in need of** necesitar con urgencia.

soreness [sórnɪs] *s.* dolor, dolencia; inflamación.

sorrel [sórəl] *adj.* alazán (*rojo canela*); *s.* color alazán; caballo alazán.

sorrow [sáro] *s.* dolor, pena, pesar; pesadumbre; arrepentimiento; *v.* apenarse, afligirse, sentir pena.

sorrowful [sórəfəl] *adj.* pesaroso, doloroso, lastimoso, afligido; **-ly** *adv.* tristemente, dolorosamente, con pena, desconsoladamente.

sorry [sórɪ] *adj.* triste, pesaroso, afligido, arrepentido; lastimoso; **I am** — lo siento; me pesa; **I am** — **for her** la compadezco.

sort [sort] *s.* suerte, clase, especie; — **of tired** algo cansado, un tanto cansado; **all -s of** toda suerte de, toda clase de; **out of** - **s** de mal humor, malhumorado; indispuesto; *v.* clasificar, ordenar, arreglar; **to** — **out** separar, clasificar; entresacar; escoger.

sought [sɔt] *pret. & p.p. de* **seek**.

soul [sol] *s.* alma; **not a** — nadie, ni un alma.

sound [saund] *adj.* sano; cuerdo; sensato; firme, sólido; ileso; **a** — **beating** una buena zurra o tunda; — **business** buen negocio, negocio bien organizado; — **reasoning** raciocinio sólido; — **sleep** sueño profundo; — **title** título válido o legal; **of** — **mind** en su juicio cabal; **safe and** — sano y salvo; **to sleep** — dormir profundamente; *s.* son, sonido; tono; brazo de mar; — **wave** onda sonora; *v.* sonar, tocar; sondear; tantear; auscultar (*el pecho, los pulmones*); cantar, entonar (*alabanzas*); **to** — **out** tantear, sondear.

soundness [sáundnɪs] *s.* solidez; cordura, buen juicio; rectitud; validez; — **of body** buena salud corporal.

soup [sup] *s.* sopa.

sour [saur] *adj.* agrio; desabrido; acre; ácido; rancio; malhumorado; — **milk** leche cortada; *v.* agriar(se); cortarse (*la leche*); fermentar; poner(se) de mal humor.

source [sors] *s.* origen; manantial, fuente.

sourness [sáurnɪs] *s.* acidez, agrura, desabrimiento.

south [sauθ] *s.* sur, sud; *adj.* meridional; del sur; austral; **South American** sudamericano; suramericano; — **pole** polo sur, polo antártico; *adv.* hacia el sur.

southeast [sauθíst] *s. & adj.* sudeste, *adv.* hacia el sudeste.

southeastern [sauθístən] *adj.* del sudeste, sudeste.

southern [sʌðən] *adj.* meridional, del sur, austral, sureño; — **Cross** Cruz del Sur.

southerner [sʌðənə] *s.* sureño, meridional, habitante del sur.

southward [sáuəwəd] *adv.* hacia el sur, rumbo al sur.

southwest [sauəwést] *s. & adj.* sudoeste (*o suroeste*); *adv.* hacia el sudoeste.

southwestern [sauəwéstən] *adj.* sudoeste (*o suroeste*), del sudoeste.

souvenir [suvənír] *s.* recuerdo, memoria.

sovereign [sávrɪn] *s. & adj.* soberano.

sovereignty [sávrɪntɪ] *s.* soberanía.

soviet [sóvɪt] *s.* sóviet; *adj.* soviético.

sow [sau] *s.* puerca.

sow [so] *v.* sembrar.

sown [son] *p.p. de* **sow**.

space [spes] *s.* espacio; *v.* espaciar.

spacious [spéʃəs] *adj.* espacioso; dilatado, vasto.

spade [sped] *s.* azada, azadón; espada (*del juego de naipes*); *r.* cavar con la azada.

span [spæn] *s.* palmo; espacio; tramo; arco u ojo (*de puente*); envergadura (*de un aeroplano*); — **of life** longevidad; *v.* medir a palmos; atravesar.

spangle [spǽŋgl] *s.* lentejuela; *v.* adornar con lentejuelas; brillar, centellear; **-d with stars** estrellado, sembrado (*o tachonado*) de estrellas.

Spaniard [spǽnjəd] *s.* español.

spaniel [spǽnjəl] *s.* perro de aguas.

Spanish [spǽnɪʃ] *adj.* español; *s.* español, idioma español.

spank [spæŋk] *v.* zurrar, dar una tunda, dar nalgadas; *s.* palmada, nalgada.

spanking [spǽŋkɪŋ] *s.* zurra, tunda, nalgadas.

spare [sper] *v.* ahorrar; evitar (*molestias, trabajo, etc.*); perdonar; **I cannot**

— **another dollar** no dispongo de otro dólar, no tengo más dinero disponible; **I cannot — the car today** no puedo pasarme hoy sin el automóvil; **to — no expense** no escatimar gastos; **to — the enemy** usar de clemencia con el enemigo; **to have time to —** tener tiempo de sobra; *adj.* flaco, descarnado; escaso, frugal; mezquino; sobrante; de sobra; de repuesto; **— cash** dinero disponible o de sobra; **— time** tiempo libre, tiempo disponible; **— tire** neumático de repuesto.

spark [spark] *s.* chispa; **— plug** bujía; *v.* chispear, echar chispas, chisporrotear.

sparkle [spárkl] *s.* chispa, centella; brillo, centelleo; viveza, animación; *v.* centellear; chispear; relucir, brillar.

sparkling [spárklɪŋ] *adj.* centelleante; reluciente; chispeante; **— wine** vino espumoso.

sparrow [spǽro] *s.* gorrión, pardal.

sparse [spars] *adj.* escaso; esparcido; poco denso, poco poblado; **— hair** pelo ralo.

spasm [spǽzəm] *s.* espasmo.

spat [spæt] *pret. & p.p. de* **to spit**; *v.* reñir, disputar; dar un manazo o sopapo; *s.* sopapo, manotada; riña, desavenencia; **-s** polainas cortas.

spatter [spǽtə] *v.* salpicar; rociar; manchar; *s.* salpicadura; rociada.

speak [spik] *v.* hablar; decir; recitar; **— to the point!** ¡vamos al grano!; **so to —** por decirlo así; **to — for** hablar por, hablar en nombre o en favor de; pedir, solicitar; apalabrar, reservar; **to — one's mind** hablar sin rodeos, decir claramente lo que se piensa; **to — out** (*o* **— up**) hablar claro; hablar con toda franqueza; hablar en voz alta.

speaker [spíkə] *s.* orador; conferenciante, conferencista; el que habla; **— of the House** presidente de la cámara de representantes; **loud-speaker** altavoz, altoparlante.

spear [spɪr] *s.* lanza; arpón (*para pescar*); brote, retoño, hoja (*de hierba*); *v.* alancear, lancear, herir con lanza.

spearmint [spírmɪnt] *s.* yerbabuena (hierbabuena), menta.

special [spéʃəl] *adj.* especial; particular; **— delivery** entrega especial de correo; *s.* tren o autobús especial; carta urgente, entrega especial; **-ly** *adv.* especialmente; en especial; sobre todo.

specialist [spéʃəlɪst] *s.* especialista.

specialize [spéʃəlaɪz] *v.* especializarse.

specialty [spéʃəltɪ] *s.* especialidad.

species [spíʃɪz] *s.* especie; especies.

specific [spɪsífɪk] *adj.* específico; peculiar, característico; **— gravity** peso específico; *s.* específico; **-ally** *adv.* específicamente; especificadamente; particularmente, en particular.

specify [spésəfaɪ] *v.* especificar; estipular.

specimen [spésəmən] *s.* espécimen, muestra, ejemplar.

speck [spek] *s.* mota; manchita; partícula; **not a —** ni pizca; *v. véase* **speckle**.

speckle [spékl] *s.* manchita; mota; *v.* motear, salpicar de motas o manchas; manchar.

speckled [spékld] *adj.* moteado; **— with freckles** pecoso.

spectacle [spéktəkl] *s.* espectáculo; **-s** gafas, anteojos; **to make a — of oneself** ponerse en la evidencia, ponerse en ridículo.

spectacular [spektǽkjələ] *adj.* espectacular, ostentoso, aparatoso.

spectator [spéktetə] *s.* espectador.

specter [spéktə] *s.* espectro, fantasma, aparecido.

spectrum [spéktrəm] *s.* espectro.

speculate [spékjəlet] *v.* especular; reflexionar.

speculation [spekjəléʃən] *s.* especulación; reflexión.

speculative [spékjəletɪv] *adj.* especulativo; teórico.

speculator [spékjəletə] *s.* especulador.

sped [sped] *pret. & p.p. de* **to speed**.

speech [spitʃ] *s.* habla; lenguaje, idioma; discurso, arenga; conferencia; parlamento (*de un actor*); **to make a —** pronunciar un discurso, hacer una perorata.

speechless [spítʃlɪs] *adj.* sin habla; mudo; estupefacto.

speed [spid] *s.* velocidad; rapidez; presteza, prontitud; **— limit** velocidad máxima; **at full —** a toda velocidad; *v.* apresurar(se), acelerar(se), dar(se) prisa; correr; ir con exceso de velocidad; despachar.

speedily [spídɪlɪ] *adv.* velozmente, rápidamente; a todo correr; de prisa, con prontitud.

speedometer [spidámətə] *s.* velocímetro.

speedy [spídɪ] *adj.* veloz, rápido.

spell [spel] *s.* hechizo, encanto; temporada, corto período; ataque (*de una enfermedad*); **to put under a —** aojar; hechizar, encantar; *v.* deletrear;

significar, indicar; **how is it -ed?**
¿cómo se escribe?

speller [spélə] *s.* silabario; deletreador.

spelling [spélɪŋ] *s.* ortografía; deletreo;
— **book** silabario.

spelt [spelt] *pret. & p.p. de* to spell.

spend [spend] *v.* gastar; usar, agotar,
consumir; **to — a day** pasar un día.

spendthrift [spéndərɪft] *s.* derrochador,
gastador, pródigo.

spent [spent] *pret. & p.p. de* to spend.

sphere [sfɪr] *s.* esfera; globo, orbe.

spherical [sférɪk] *adj.* esférico.

spice [spaɪs] *s.* especia; picante; aroma;
v. condimentar, sazonar con especias.

spicy [spáɪsɪ] *adj.* sazonado con especias;
picante; aromático.

spider [spáɪdə] *s.* araña; sartén; — **web**
telaraña.

spigot [spígət] *s.* espita, grifo, canilla.

spike [spaɪk] *s.* espiga; perno; clavo largo;
alcayata; pico; *v.* clavar; clavetear.

spill [spɪl] *v.* verter; derramar(se) des-
parramar(se); hacer caer (*de un caballo*); revelar (*una noticia, un secreto*);
s. derrame, derramamiento; vuelco;
caída (*de un caballo*).

spilt [spɪlt] *pret. & p.p. de* to spill.

spin [spɪn] *v.* hilar; girar, dar vueltas,
rodar; bailar (*un trompo*); **to — out**
prolongar, alargar; **to — yarns** contar
cuentos; *s.* giro, vuelta; paseo (*en
automóvil, bicicleta, etc.*); barrena (*hablando de aeroplanos*).

spinach [spínɪtʃ] *s.* espinaca.

spinal [spáɪnl] *adj.* espinal; — **column**
columna vertebral, espina dorsal.

spindle [spíndl] *s.* huso; eje.

spine [spaɪn] *s.* espina; espinazo, espina
dorsal, columna vertebral.

spinner [spínə] *s.* hilandero, hilandera;
máquina de hilar.

spinning [spínɪŋ] *s.* hilandería, arte de
hilar; — **machine** aparato para hilar,
máquina de hilar; — **mill** hilandería;
— **top** trompo; — **wheel** torno de
hilar.

spinster [spínstə] *s.* soltera; solterona.

spiral [spáɪrəl] *adj.* espiral; — **staircase**
caracol, escalera espiral; *s.* espiral.

spire [spaɪr] *s.* aguja, chapitel de torre;
cúspide, ápice; punto más alto; — **of
grass** brizna de hierba.

spirit [spírɪt] *s.* espíritu; temple; viveza,
animación; ánimo; **low -s** abatimiento; **to be in good -s** estar de buen
humor; **to be out of -s** estar triste
o abatido; *v.* **to — away** llevarse mis-
teriosamente.

spirited [spírɪtɪd] *adj.* vivo, brioso, fo-

goso.

spiritual [spírɪtʃʊəl] *adj.* espiritual; *s.*
espiritual (*tonada religiosa de los negros
del sur de los Estados Unidos*).

spit [spɪt] *v.* escupir; expectorar; *pret. &
p.p. de* to spit; *s.* esputo, saliva;
asador.

spite [spaɪt] *s.* despecho, rencor, inquina,
ojeriza; **in — of** a despecho de, a
pesar de; **out of —** por despecho; *v.*
picar, irritar, hacer rabiar.

spiteful [spáɪtfəl] *adj.* rencoroso.

splash [splæʃ] *v.* salpicar; rociar; enlodar,
manchar; chapotear (*en el agua*); *s.*
salpicadura; rociada; chapoteo.

spleen [splin] *s.* bazo; mal humor, rencor.

splendid [spléndɪd] *adj.* espléndido.

splendor [spléndə] *s.* esplendor; esplendidez.

splice [splaɪs] *v.* empalmar, unir, juntar;
s. empalme; junta.

splint [splɪnt] *s.* tablilla; astilla; *v.* entablillar.

splinter [splíntə] *s.* astilla; raja; *v.* as-
tillar(se), hacer(se) astillas; romper(se)
en astillas.

split [splɪt] *v.* hender(se), rajar(se); res-
quebrajar(se); partir(se), dividir(se);
to — hairs pararse en pelillos; **to —
one's sides with laughter** desternillarse de risa, reventar de risa; **to —
the difference** partir la diferencia;
pret. & p.p. de to split; *adj.* partido,
hendido, rajado; dividido; resquebra-
jado; *s.* raja, hendedura, grieta; cisma,
rompimiento.

spoil [spoɪl] *v.* dañar(se), echar(se) a
perder, podrir(se) o pudrir(se), co-
rromper(se); estropear(se); arruinar
consentir, mimar; *s.* botín, presa; —
of war botín o despojos de guerra.

spoke [spok] *s.* rayo (*de rueda*); *pret. de*
to speak.

spoken [spókən] *p.p. de* to speak.

spokesman [spóksmən] *s.* portavoz, vocero.

sponge [spʌndʒ] *s.* esponja; gorrón
parásito; *v.* lavar o limpiar con esponja; vivir de gorra, vivir a costa
ajena; **to — up** chupar, absorber.

spongecake [spʌndʒkek] *s.* bizcocho esponjoso.

sponger [spʌndʒə] *s.* esponja, gorrón
pegote, parásito, *Am.* pavo.

spongy [spʌndʒɪ] *adj.* esponjoso, esponjado.

sponsor [spánsə] *s.* padrino, madrina
patrón (*el que patrocina una empresa*)
defensor; fiador; fomentador, promo-

vedor; *v.* apadrinar; promover, fomentar; patrocinar; ser fiador de.

spontaneity [spɒntənɪəti] *s.* espontaneidad.

spontaneous [spɒnténiəs] *adj.* espontáneo.

spook [spuk] *s.* espectro, fantasma, aparecido.

spool [spul] *s.* carrete, carretel; *v.* devanar, enredar (*hilo*) en carrete.

spoon [spun] *s.* cuchara; *v.* cucharear, sacar con cuchara.

spoonful [spúnfəl] *s.* cucharada.

sport [sport] *s.* deporte; **in — en broma, de burla; to make — of** reírse de, burlarse de; **to be a good —** ser buen perdedor (*en el juego*); ser un buen compañero; *v.* jugar; divertirse; bromear, chancearse; **to — a new dress** lucir un traje nuevo; **-(s)** *adj.* deportivo; **— clothes** trajes deportivos.

sportsman [spórtsmən] *s.* deportista; jugador generoso, buen perdedor (*en deportes*).

spot [spɒt] *s.* mancha; mota; sitio, lugar; **in -s** aquí y allí; aquí y allá; **on the — allí** mismo; al punto; **to pay — cash** pagar al contado; *v.* manchar, ensuciar; motear; echar de ver, distinguir; avistar; localizar.

spotless [spɒtlɪs] *adj.* sin mancha, limpio.

spotted [spɒtɪd] *adj.* manchado; moteado.

spouse [spauz] *s.* esposo, esposa.

spout [spaut] *v.* chorrear; brotar; salir en chorro; emitir; declamar, perorar; hablar mucho; *s.* chorro; surtidor; pico (*de tetera, cafetera, jarra, etc.*); espita.

sprain [spren] *v.* torcer (*una coyuntura o músculo*); **to — one's ankle** torcerse el tobillo; *s.* torsión, torcedura.

sprang [spræŋ] *pret. de* to spring.

sprawl [sprɒl] *v.* despatarrarse; estar despatarrado; tenderse; **to — one's legs** abrir las piernas; *s.* postura floja (*abiertos los brazos y piernas*).

spray [spre] *s.* rocío, rociada; líquido para rociar; ramita; **sea — espuma** del mar; *v.* rociar.

spread [spred] *v.* extender(se); desparramar(se); esparcir(se); difundir(se), diseminar(se), dispersar(se); propalar(se) (*noticias, rumores, etc.*), propagar(se); **to — apart** abrir(se), separar(se); **to — butter on** poner mantequilla en; **to — out the tablecloth** tender el mantel; **to — paint on** dar una mano de pintura a; **to — with** cubrir de; untar con; *s.* extensión; amplitud, anchura; envergadura (*de un aeroplano*).

difusión; diseminación; propagación; cubierta, sobrecama; festín; mantequilla, queso, etc., que se le unta al pan; *pret. & p.p. de* to spread.

spree [spri] *s.* juerga, parranda, holgorio; **to go on a — andar** (*o* ir) de parranda o juerga, *Am.* ir de farra.

sprig [sprɪg] *s.* ramita.

sprightly [spráɪtlɪ] *adj.* vivo, animado, brioso; alegre.

spring [sprɪŋ] *v.* saltar, brincar; hacer saltar; **to — a leak** hacer agua (*un barco*); comenzar a gotearse (*la cañería, el techo, etc.*); formarse una gotera; **to — a trap** hacer saltar una trampa; **to — at** abalanzarse sobre; **to — from** salir de, nacer de, brotar de; **to — news or a surprise** dar de sopetón una noticia o sorpresa; **to — something open** abrir algo a la fuerza; **to — to one's feet** levantarse de un salto; **to — up** brotar; surgir; crecer; levantarse de un salto; *s.* primavera; muelle (*de metal*); resorte; elasticidad; salto, brinco; manantial, fuente; origen; *adj.* primaveral; **— board** trampolín; **— mattress** colchón de muelles; **— water** agua de manantial.

springtime [sprɪŋtaɪm] *s.* primavera.

sprinkle [sprɪŋkl] *v.* rociar; regar; espolvorear; salpicar; lloviznar; *s.* rociada, rocío; llovizna; **— of salt** pizca de sal.

sprint [sprɪnt] *v.* echar una carrera; *s.* carrera, carrerilla, corrida corta.

sprout [spraut] *v.* brotar; retoñar, germinar; hacer germinar o brotar; *s.* retoño, renuevo; **Brussels -s** bretones, coles de Bruselas.

spruce [sprus] *s.* abeto; *adj.* pulcro, aseado, pulido; elegante; *v.* **to — up** asearse, componerse, emperifollarse.

sprung [sprʌŋ] *pret. & p.p. de* to spring.

spun [spʌn] *pret. & p.p. de* to spin.

spur [spɜ] *s.* espuela; acicate; aguijón, estímulo; espolón (*del gallo*); estribación (*de una montaña*); **— track** ramal corto (*de ferrocarril*); **on the — of the moment** impensadamente, sin la reflexión debida; por el momento; *v.* espolear, aguijar, picar, incitar; **to — on** animar, incitar a obrar o a seguir adelante.

spurn [spɜn] *v.* rechazar, desdeñar, menospreciar.

spurt [spɜt] *v.* salir a borbotones; chorrear; echar chorros; hacer un repentino esfuerzo (*para ganar una carrera*); *s.* borbotón, chorrazo, chorro repentino; esfuerzo repentino; **— of anger** arranque de ira; **-s of flame** llamaradas.

sputter [spʌ́tə] v. chisporrotear; refunfuñar; s. chisporroteo; refunfuño.

sputum [spjútəm] s. esputo.

spy [spaɪ] s. espía; v. espiar; acechar; atisbar; **to — on** espiar, atisbar.

spyglass [spáɪglæs] s. anteojo de larga vista.

squabble [skwábl] s. reyerta; v. reñir, disputar.

squad [skwɑd] s. escuadra, patrulla, partida.

squadron [skwádrən] s. escuadra; escuadrón.

squalid [skwálɪd] adj. escuálido.

squall [skwɔl] s. chubasco; chillido; v. chillar.

squander [skwándə] v. despilfarrar, derrochar, malgastar, disipar.

square [skwer] s. cuadro; cuadrado; plaza; manzana de casas; escuadra (de carpintero); casilla (de tablero de ajedrez, damas, etc.); **he is on the —** obra de buena fe; v. cuadrar; ajustar, arreglar, saldar (cuentas); justificar; cuadricular; **to — one's shoulders** enderezar los hombros; cuadrarse; **to — oneself with** sincerarse con, justificarse ante; **to — a person with another** poner bien a una persona con otra; adj. cuadrado, en cuadro, a escuadra, en ángulo recto; saldado; justo, recto, equitativo; franco; **— corner** esquina en ángulo recto; **— dance** cuadrilla; **— meal** comida completa, comida en regla; **— mile** milla cuadrada; **— root** raíz cuadrada; **to be — with someone** estar en paz con alguien, no deberle nada, Am. estar a mano; adv. véase **squarely**.

squarely [skwérlɪ] adv. equitativamente, honradamente; firmemente; de buena fe; derecho, derechamente; **to hit the target — in the middle** pegar de lleno en el blanco.

squash [skwɑʃ] s. calabaza; v. aplastar, despachurrar o apachurrar.

squat [skwɑt] v. agazaparse, sentarse en cuclillas; ocupar tierras baldías para ganar título de propietario; adj. agazapado, sentado en cuclillas; rechoncho, achaparrado, Am. chaparro.

squawk [skwɔk] v. graznar; chillar; quejarse; s. graznido; chillido; queja.

squeak [skwik] v. rechinar, chirriar; chillar; s. rechinamiento; chirrido, chillido.

squeal [skwil] v. chillar; quejarse, pro-

testar; soplar, delatar; s. chillido.

squeeze [skwiz] v. estrujar; despachurrar o apachurrar; exprimir; prensar; apretar; **to — into** meter(se) a estrujones, encajar(se) en; **to — out the juice** exprimir el jugo; **to — through a crowd** abrirse paso a estrujones por entre la muchedumbre; s. estrujón; apretón; abrazo fuerte; apretura.

squelch [skweltʃ] v. aplastar; acallar, imponer silencio; reprender; **to — a revolt** sofocar o apagar una revuelta.

squint [skwɪnt] v. mirar de través; mirar de soslayo; mirar achicando los ojos; mirar furtivamente; bizquear (mirar bizco); s. mirada de soslayo; mirada bizca; mirada furtiva; **squint-eyed** adj. bisojo o bizco.

squire [skwaɪr] s. escudero; v. acompañar, escoltar.

squirm [skwɝm] v. retorcerse; **to — out of a difficulty** forcejear para salir de un aprieto.

squirrel [skwɝl] s. ardilla.

squirt [skwɝt] v. jeringar; echar un chisguete; salir a chorritos (o a chisguetes); s. jeringazo; chisguete.

stab [stæb] v. apuñalar, dar una puñalada, dar de puñaladas, acuchillar; pinchar; s. puñalada, cuchillada, estocada; pinchazo.

stability [stəbílətɪ] s. estabilidad.

stable [stébl] adj. estable; s. establo, cuadra; caballeriza; v. poner (los animales) en la caballeriza.

stack [stæk] s. pila, montón, rimero; hacina (de paja o heno); chimenea, cañón de chimenea; **library -s** estanterías o anaqueles de biblioteca; v. amontonar, apilar.

stadium [stédɪəm] s. estadio.

staff [stæf] s. báculo, cayado, bastón, vara; asta (de bandera, de lanza); cuerpo, consejo administrativo; **— of life** sostén de la vida; **— officer** oficial de estado mayor; **army — estado mayor; editorial — redacción; musical — pentagrama; teaching — cuerpo docente; v. proveer de funcionarios y empleados (una organización).

stag [stæg] s. venado, ciervo; macho, hombre; **— dinner** banquete exclusivo para hombres.

stage [stedʒ] s. tablado; tablas, escenario; escena; teatro; etapa, tramo; período; parada; **—coach** ómnibus, autobús; **— hand** tramoyista; **by way -s** por grados, gradualmente; v. representar, poner en escena; **to — a hold-up** hacer un asalto, atracar; **to — a**

surprise dar una sorpresa.

stagger[stǽgə] v. tambalearse, trastabillar, bambolearse; hacer tambalear; azorar, asombrar; **to — working hours** escalonar las horas de trabajo; s. tambaleo, bamboleo.

stagnant [stǽgnənt] adj. estancado; **to become —** estancarse.

staid [sted] adj. grave, serio.

stain [sten] v. manchar; teñir; colorar; **stained-glass window** vidriera de colores; s. mancha, mancilla; tinte, tintura; materia colorante.

stainless [sténlɪs] adj. sin mancha, inmaculado, limpio; **— steel** acero inempañable o inoxidable.

stair [ster] s. peldaño, escalón; **-s** escalera.

staircase [stérkes] s. escalera.

stairway [stérwe] s. escalera.

stake [stek] s. estaca; puesta, apuesta; **his future is at —** su porvenir está en peligro o riesgo; **to die at the —** morir en la hoguera; **to have a — in the future of** tener ínterés en el porvenir de; **to have much at —** irle a uno mucho en una cosa; haber aventurado mucho; v. estacar; atar a una estaca; apostar; arriesgar, aventurar; **to — off** señalar con estacas (un perímetro).

stale [stel] adj. viejo; rancio; gastado, improductivo.

stalk [stɔk] s. tallo; caña.

stall [stɔl] s. casilla, puesto (de un mercado o feria); casilla o sección de un establo; v. encasillar, meter en casilla; atascarse (un auto); pararse (el motor); **he is -ing** está haciendo la pala; **to be -ed in the mud** estar atascado en el lodo.

stallion [stǽljən] s. caballo de cría, caballo padre, Am. padrillo, garañón.

stammer [stǽmə] v. tartamudear, balbucear; s. tartamudeo, balbuceo.

stammerer [stǽmərə] s. tartamudo.

stammering [stǽmərɪŋ] s. tartamudeo; adj. tartamudo.

stamp [stæmp] v. sellar; timbrar; poner un sello a; estampar; imprimir; marcar, señalar; patear, patalear; **to — one's foot** dar patadas en el suelo; **to — out** extirpar, borrar; s. sello; timbre, estampilla; estampa; marca, impresión; patada (en el suelo); **postage —** sello, Am. estampilla, Am. timbre; **revenue —** timbre.

stampede [stæmpíd] s. estampida; huída en desorden; tropel; éxodo repentino; v. arrancar, huir en tropel; ir en tropel;

ahuyentar, hacer huir en desorden.

stanch [stɑntʃ] v. restañar, estancar; adj. fuerte, firme; leal, constante, fiel.

stand [stænd] v. poner derecho, colocar verticalmente, Am. parar; ponerse de pie, levantarse; estar de pie; estar (situado); pararse; aguantar, sufrir, tolerar; **to — a chance of** tener probabilidad de; **to — an expense** sufragar un gasto; **to — aside** apartarse; mantenerse apartado; **to — back of** colocarse detrás de; salir fiador de, garantizar a, respaldar a; **to — by** mantenerse a corta distancia; apoyar, defender; estar alerta; **to — for** significar; estar por, apoyar; tolerar; **to — in the way** estorbar; **to — on end** poner(se) de punta; erizarse (el pelo); **to — one's ground** mantenerse firme; **to — out** resaltar, destacarse; sobresalir; **to — six feet** tener seis pies de altura; **to — up for** apoyar, defender; **it -s to reason** es razonable, es lógico; s. puesto; mesilla; pedestal; posición, actitud; alto, parada (para resistir); quiosco; **grand—** andanada, gradería cubierta (para espectadores); **music —** atril; **umbrella —** paragüero.

standard [stǽndəd] s. norma; nivel normal; modelo, patrón, Am. estándar; criterio; base, sostén, pedestal; estandarte; **gold —** patrón de oro; **to be up to —** satisfacer las normas requeridas; adj. normal, que sirve de norma; de uso general; corriente; **standard-bearer** portaestandarte.

standardization [stændədəzéʃən] s. normalización, uniformación, igualación.

standardize [stǽndədaɪz] v. normalizar, uniformar, Am. estandarizar.

standing [stǽndɪŋ] s. posición; reputación; **of long —** que ha prevalecido largo tiempo; muy antiguo; adj. derecho, en pie; de pie; establecido, permanente; **— water** agua estancada; **there is — room only** no quedan asientos.

standpoint [stǽndpɔɪnt] s. punto de vista.

standstill [stǽndstɪl] s. alto; pausa; **to come to a —** pararse; hacer alto.

stank [stæŋk] pret. de **to stink**.

stanza [stǽnzə] s. estrofa.

staple [stépl] s. broche de alambre (para sujetar papeles); grapa, argolla, armella; artículo principal; **-s** artículos de necesidad prima; adj. principal; de uso corriente; indispensable; v. asegurar (papeles) con broche de alambre; sujetar con armellas.

star [star] *s.* estrella; asterisco: **star-spangled** estrellado; *adj.* sobresaliente, excelente; *v.* estrellar, adornar o señalar con estrellas; marcar con asterisco: presentar como estrella (*a un actor*): lucir(se) en las tablas o el cine, hacer el papel principal.

starboard [stárbord] *s.* estribor; *adj.* de estribor; — **side** banda de estribor; *adv.* a estribor.

starch [startʃ] *s.* almidón; fécula; *v.* almidonar.

stare [ster] *v.* mirar, mirar con fijeza o curiosidad; mirar azorado; clavar la mirada, fijar la vista; *s.* mirada fija, mirada persistente.

starfish [stárfiʃ] *s.* estrella de mar.

stark [stark] *adj.* tieso; escueto; — **folly** pura tontería; — **in death** tieso, muerto; — **narrative** narración escueta, sin adornos; *adv.* completamente, totalmente; — **mad** loco de remate; — **naked** enteramente desnudo, en cueros, *Am.* encuerado.

starlight [stárlaɪt] *s.* luz estelar, luz de las estrellas.

starry [stárɪ] *adj.* estrellado, sembrado de estrellas; como estrellas, brillante.

start [start] *v.* comenzar, empezar, principiar; poner(se) en marcha; partir, salir; dar un salto, sobresaltarse; **the motor -s** el motor arranca; **to — after someone** salir en busca de alguien; **to — off** salir, partir; dar principio a; **to — out on a trip** empezar una jornada, emprender un viaje; **to — the motor** hacer arrancar el motor; *s.* comienzo, empiezo, principio; sobresalto, respingo (*de un caballo*); arranque; ventaja (*en una carrera*).

starter [stártə] *s.* arranque, arrancador; iniciador; primero de una serie; **self-starter** arranque automático.

startle [stártl] *v.* asustar(se), sobresaltar(se), espantar(se).

startling [stártlɪŋ] *adj.* sobresaltante, pasmoso, asombroso, sorprendente.

starvation [starvéʃən] *s.* inanición, hambre.

starve [starv] *v.* morir(se) de hambre; hambrear; matar de hambre.

state [stet] *s.* estado; condición, situación; **in great** — con gran pompa; *adj.* de estado; del estado; de ceremonia; *v.* declarar, decir; expresar, exponer.

stately [stétlɪ] *adj.* majestuoso, imponente.

statement [stétmənt] *s.* declaración; exposición; informe, relato; cuenta,

estado de cuenta.

stateroom [stétrum] *s.* camarote (*de un buque*).

statesman [stétsmən] *s.* estadista, hombre de estado.

static [stǽtɪk] *adj.* estático; *s.* estática.

station [stéʃən] *s.* estación; paradero, puesto; estado, posición social; **broadcasting** — transmisora o emisora; *v.* estacionar, colocar, apostar.

stationary [stéʃənerɪ] *adj.* estacionario; fijo.

stationery [stéʃənerɪ] *s.* papelería.

statistics [statístɪks] *s.* estadística; datos estadísticos.

statuary [stǽtʃʊerɪ] *s.* estatuaria, arte de hacer estatuas; colección de estatuas.

statue [stǽtʃu] *s.* estatua.

stature [stǽtʃə] *s.* estatura.

status [stétəs] *s.* estado, condición; posición social o profesional.

statute [stǽtʃʊt] *s.* estatuto, ordenanza.

staunch = **stanch**.

stave [stev] *s.* duela de barril; *v.* poner duelas (*a un barril*); **to — off** mantener a distancia; evitar; rechazar.

stay [ste] *v.* quedarse, permanecer; parar(se); detener(se); hospedarse, alojarse; resistir; **to — an execution** diferir o aplazar una ejecución; **to — one's hunger** engañar el hambre; **to — up all night** velar toda la noche; *s.* estada, estancia, permanencia; suspensión; sostén, apoyo; varilla o ballena de corsé; **to grant a —** conceder una prórroga.

stead [sted] : **in her (his) —** en su lugar; **to stand one in good —** servirle a uno, ser de provecho para uno.

steadfast [stédfæst] *adj.* fijo, firme; constante.

steadily [stédɪlɪ] *adv.* constantemente; firmemente; sin parar, de continuo; sin vacilar.

steadiness [stédɪnɪs] *s.* firmeza; constancia; estabilidad.

steady [stédɪ] *adj.* firme; estable; invariable, constante; continuo; *v.* afianzar, mantener firme, asegurar; calmar (*los nervios*).

steak [stek] *s.* bistec o bisté; tajada (*para asar o freír*).

steal [stil] *v.* robar, hurtar; andar furtivamente; **to — away** colarse, escabullirse, escaparse; **to — into a room** meterse a hurtadillas en un cuarto; **to — out of a room** salirse a escondidas de un cuarto, colarse, escabullirse; *s.*

robo, hurto.

stealth [stɛlθ] : **by —** a hurtadillas, a escondidas, con cautela.

stealthy [stɛ́lθɪ] adj. cauteloso, furtivo, secreto.

steam [stim] s. vapor; vaho; adj. de vapor; por vapor; — **engine** máquina de vapor; — **heat** calefacción por vapor; v. cocer al vapor; dar un baño de vapor; saturar de vapor; echar vapor; **to — into port** llegar a puerto (un vapor).

steamboat [stímbot] s. buque de vapor.

steamer [stímə] s. vapor, buque de vapor.

steamship [stímʃɪp] s. vapor, buque de vapor.

steed [stid] s. corcel, caballo de combate; caballo brioso.

steel [stil] s. acero; adj. acerado, de acero; v. acerar, revestir de acero; **to — oneself against** fortalecerse contra.

steep [stip] adj. empinado, escarpado, pendiente; muy alto; — **price** precio alto o excesivo; v. remojar, empapar; saturar; poner o estar en infusión.

steeple [stípl̩] s. aguja, chapitel; cúspide.

steepness [stípnɪs] s. inclinación abrupta; lo empinado, lo escarpado; altura (de precios).

steer [stɪr] s. novillo; buey; v. guiar, conducir, manejar, gobernar; timonear; **to — a course** seguir un rumbo; **the car —s easily** se maneja fácilmente el auto, es de fácil manejo.

stem [stɛm] s. tallo; tronco; pedúnculo (de hoja, flor o fruto); raíz (de una palabra); pie (de copa); cañón (de pipa de fumar); proa; v. estancar, represar; resistir, refrenar; contraponerse a; **to — from** provenir de.

stench [stɛntʃ] s. hedor, hediondez.

stenographer [stənógrəfə] s. estenógrafo, taquígrafo, mecanógrafo.

step [stɛp] s. paso; pisada; peldaño, escalón, grada; grado; gestión; — **by — paso a paso; to be in — with** marchar a compás con; estar de acuerdo con; **to take —s** dar pasos; tomar medidas; gestionar; v. andar, caminar; dar un paso; **to — aside** hacerse a un lado, apartarse; **to — back** dar un paso o pasos atrás; retroceder; **to — down** bajar; **to — off a distance** medir a pasos una distancia; **to — on** pisar, pisotear; **to — on the gas** pisar el acelerador; darse prisa; **to — out** salir; **to — up** subir; acelerar.

stepfather [stépfaðə] s. padrastro.

stepmother [stépmʌðə] s. madrastra.

steppe [stɛp] s. estepa.

sterile [stɛ́rəl] adj. estéril.

sterility [stərflɪtɪ] s. esterilidad.

sterilize [stɛ́rəlaɪz] v. esterilizar.

sterling [stɜ́lɪŋ] s. vajilla de plata esterlina; adj. genuino; de ley; — **silver** plata de ley, plata esterlina; **pound —** libra esterlina.

stern [stɜn] adj. austero, severo; firme; s. popa.

sternness [stɜ́nnɪs] s. austeridad, severidad; firmeza.

stethoscope [stéθəskop] s. estetoscopio.

stevedore [stívədor] s. estibador, cargador.

stew [stju] v. estofar; preocuparse, apurarse; s. estofado, guisado; **to be in a — estar preocupado o apurado.**

steward [stjúwəd] s. mayordomo; camarero (de buque o avión).

stewardess [stjúwədɪs] s. camarera (de buque o avión).

stick [stɪk] s. palo; vara; garrote; raja de leña; — **of dynamite** barra de dinamita; **control —** palanca (de aeroplano); **walking —** bastón; **stick-up** atraco (para robar), asalto; v. pegar(se), adherir(se); permanecer; estar pegado; picar, pinchar; herir (con cuchillo, puñal, etc.); fijar (con clavos, alfileres, tachuelas, etc.); atascarse (en el fango un carro, auto, etc.); **to — something in** (o **into**) clavar o meter algo en; encajar en; **to — out** salir, sobresalir; proyectarse; **to — out one's head** asomar la cabeza; **to — out one's tongue** sacar la lengua; **to — to a job** perseverar (o persistir) en una tarea; **to — up** sobresalir; destacarse; estar de punta (el pelo); **to — one's hands up** alzar las manos; **to — someone up** asaltar o atracar a alguien (para robar); véase **stuck.**

sticker [stíkə] s. marbete engomado.

sticky [stíkɪ] adk. pegajoso.

stiff [stɪf] adj. tieso; rígido; entumido, duro; terco; fuerte; — **climb** subida ardua o difícil; — **price** precio alto o subido; **stiff-necked** terco, obstinado; **scared —** yerto, muerto de miedo; s. cadáver.

stiffen [stífən] v. atiesar(se), poner(se) tieso; entumir(se); endurecer(se); espesar(se); subir de punto, aumentar (la resistencia).

stiffness [stífnɪs] s. tiesura; rigidez; dureza; rigor; terquedad.

stifle [stáɪfl̩] v. ahogar(se), asfixiar(se), sofocar(se); apagar, extinguir.

stigma [stígmə] s. estigma; baldón.

still [stɪl] adj. quieto; callado, silencioso; tranquilo; inmóvil; **—born** nacido muerto; **— life** naturaleza muerta; v. aquietar; calmar; acallar; adv. todavía, aún; conj. empero, no obstante, sin embargo; s. destiladera, alambique; silencio.

stillness [stílnɪs] s. quietud, calma, silencio.

stilt [stɪlt] s. zanco; pilote, puntal, soporte.

stilted [stíltɪd] adj. tieso, afectado, pomposo.

stimulant [stímjələnt] adj. & s. estimulante.

stimulate [stímjəlet] v. estimular.

stimulation [stɪmjəléʃən] s. estimulación, estímulo.

stimulus [stímjələs] s. estímulo.

sting [stɪŋ] v. picar; pinchar, aguijonear; escocer (Am. arder); embaucar; s. picadura, piquete, mordedura, picazón; aguijón; escozor; **— of remorse** remordimiento.

stinginess [stíndʒɪnɪs] s. tacañería, mezquindad.

stingy [stíndʒɪ] adj. mezquino, ruin, tacaño; escaso.

stink [stɪŋk] v. heder, oler mal; apestar; s. hedor, mal olor, hediondez.

stint [stɪnt] v. escatimar; ser frugal o económico; **to — oneself** privarse de lo necesario, economizar demasiado; s. tarea, faena; **without —** sin límite; sin escatimar. generosamente.

stipulate [stípjəlet] v. estipular.

stipulation [stɪpjəléʃən] s. estipulación, condición.

stir [stɜ] v. menear(se); mover(se), bullir(se); atizar (el fuego); incitar; conmover; perturbar; revolver; **to — up** incitar; conmover; revolver; suscitar (un argumento, pelea, etc.); s. meneo, agitación, movimiento; alboroto.

stirring [stɜ́ɪŋ] adj. conmovedor.

stirrup [stírəp] s. estribo.

stitch [stɪtʃ] v. coser; dar puntadas; s. puntada; punzada; **to be in —s** desternillarse de risa.

stock [stak] s. surtido; existencias, provisión; ganado; cepa, linaje, estirpe; acciones, valores; **in —** en existencia; **live—** ganado; **meat —** caldo de carne; adj. en existencia, existente, disponible; común, trivial; **— answer** contestación corriente, común o trivial; **— company** sociedad anónima; compañía teatral; **— exchange** bolsa; **— farm** hacienda de ganado, Am.

rancho, Am. estancia; **— market** mercado de valores, bolsa; **— room** almacén; **— size** tamaño ordinario (regularmente en existencia); **—yard** matadero; v. surtir, abastecer; tener en existencia (para vender); **to — a farm** surtir o proveer de ganado un rancho, **to — up with** surtirse de, acumular.

stockade [stakéd] s. estacada, empalizada; vallado; v. empalizar, rodear de empalizadas.

stockbroker [stákbrokə] s. bolsista, corredor de bolsa.

stockholder [stákholdə] s. accionista.

stocking [stákɪŋ] s. media.

stoic [stóɪk] adj. & s. estoico.

stoke [stok] v. atizar (el fuego); cebar, alimentar (un horno).

stole [stol] pret. de **to steal**.

stolen [stólən] p.p. de **to steal**.

stolid [stálɪd] adj. estólido, insensible.

stomach [stámək] s. estómago; v. aguantar, tolerar.

stone [ston] s. piedra; hueso (de las frutas); **within a —'s throw** a tiro de piedra; adj. pétreo, de piedra; **Stone Age** Edad de Piedra; **stone-deaf** totalmente sordo, sordo como una tapia; v. apedrear; deshuesar (las frutas).

stony [stóni] adj. pedregoso; pétreo, de piedra; duro.

stood [stud] pret. & p.p. de **to stand**.

stool [stul] s. taburete, banquillo; bacín, bacinica; excremento; **— pigeon** soplón (el que delata a otro).

stoop [stup] v. agacharse; doblarse, inclinarse; encorvarse; andar encorvado o caído de hombros; rebajarse, humillarse, abajarse; s. encorvamiento, inclinación (de espaldas); **to walk with a —** andar encorvado o caído de hombros; **stoop-shouldered** cargado de espaldas, encorvado.

stop [stap] v. parar(se), hacer alto, detener(se); acabar(se); cesar; parar de, dejar de; atajar; reprimir; suspender; obstruir, tapar; **to — at a hotel** hospedarse o alojarse en un hotel; **to — at nothing** no pararse en escrúpulos; **to — from** impedir; **to — over at** hacer escala en; **to — short** parar(se) de sopetón, parar(se) en seco; **to — up** tapar, obstruir; atascar; s. parada; alto, pausa; estada, estancia; detención; suspensión; llave (de instrumento de viento); traste (de guitarra); registro (de órgano); **— consonant** consonante explosiva.

stopover [stápovə] s. parada, escala; **to make a —** in hacer escala en.

stoppage [stápɪdʒ] *s.* detención; obstrucción; **work —** paro.

stopper [stápə] *s.* tapón.

storage [stórɪdʒ] *s.* almacenaje; **— battery** acumulador; **to keep in —** almacenar.

store [stor] *s.* tienda; almacén; depósito; acopio; **-s** provisiones; bastimentos; víveres; **department —** almacén; **dry-goods —** lencería, *Am.* mercería, *Am.* cajón de ropa; **fruit —** frutería; hat **— sombrerería; grocery —** abacería, tienda de comestibles, *Am.* tienda de abarrotes, *Am.* bodega; **shoe —** zapatería; **to have in —** tener guardado; *v.* almacenar; guardar; abastecer; **to — up** acumular.

storehouse [stórhaus] *s.* almacén, depósito.

storekeeper [stórkipə] *s.* tendero; almacenista; guardalmacén.

storeroom [stórrum] *s.* almacén; bodega; despensa.

stork [stork] *s.* cigüeña.

storm [storm] *s.* tormenta, tempestad, borrasca, temporal; tumulto; asalto; **— troops** tropas de asalto; **hail—** granizada; **snow—** nevasca; **wind—** vendaval; *v.* asaltar, atacar; rabiar; **it is -ing** hay tormenta, hay tempestad.

stormy [stórmɪ] *adj.* tempestuoso, borrascoso; turbulento.

story [stórɪ] *s.* cuento, historia, historieta; relato; chisme; rumor; argumento, trama; piso (*de un edificio*); **newspaper —** artículo de periódico, gacetilla.

stout [staut] *adj.* corpulento, robusto, fornido; fuerte; firme; leal; valiente.

stove [stov] *s.* estufa; cocina de gas, cocina eléctrica; *pret. & p.p. de* **stave.**

stow [sto] *v.* meter, guardar; esconder; estibar, acomodar la carga de un barco; rellenar; **to — away on a ship** embarcarse clandestinamente, esconderse en un barco.

straddle [strǽdl] *v.* ponerse o estar a horcajadas, ponerse a caballo, cabalgar; favorecer ambos lados (*de un pleito, controversia, etc.*).

straggle [strǽgl] *v.* vagar, desviarse; extraviarse; andar perdido; dispersarse; **to — behind** rezagarse.

straight [stret] *adj.* recto; derecho; directo; recto; honrado; franco; erguido; correcto; en orden; **— face** cara seria; **— hair** pelo lacio; **— hand of five cards** runfla de cinco naipes del mismo palo; **— rum** ron puro, sin mezcla; **for two hours —** por dos horas segui-

das, por dos horas sin parar; **to set a person —** dar consejo a una persona; mostrarle el camino, modo o manera de hacer algo; *adv.* directamente, derecho, en línea recta; francamente; honradamente; **— away** (*o* **— off** en seguida, al punto; **to talk — from the shoulder** hablar con toda franqueza o sinceridad.

straighten [strétn] *v.* enderezar(se); arreglar, poner en orden.

straightforward [stretfórwəd] *adj.* derecho, recto; honrado; franco, sincero; *adv.* directamente, en línea recta.

straightness [strétnɪs] *s.* derechura; rectitud; honradez.

straightway [strétwe] *adv.* luego, inmediatamente, en seguida.

strain [stren] *v.* estirar demasiado, hacer fuerza; poner tirante; violentar, forzar (*los músculos, los nervios, la vista, etc.*); colar, tamizar; **to — one's wrist** torcerse la muñeca; *s.* tensión excesiva; tirantez; torcedura; esfuerzo excesivo; linaje, rasgo racial; aire, tonada.

strainer [strénə] *s.* coladera; cedazo.

strait [stret] *s.* estrecho; **-s** estrecho; aprieto, apuro; **— jacket** camisa de fuerza.

strand [strænd] *v.* encallar; dejar perdido (*sin medios de salir*), dejar aislado, extraviar; **to be -ed** estar encallado; estar extraviado (*sin medios de salir*), estar aislado, andar perdido; *s.* ribera, playa; ramal (*de cuerda, cable, etc.*); hebra, hilo; **— of hair** guedeja; trenza; **— of pearls** hilera de perlas.

strange [strendʒ] *adj.* extraño; raro, singular; desconocido.

strangeness [stréndʒnɪs] *s.* extrañeza, rareza.

stranger [stréndʒə] *s.* extraño, desconocido; forastero.

strangle [strǽŋgl] *v.* estrangular(se).

strap [stræp] *s.* correa; tira de cuero o de tela; correón; tirante; **metal —** banda de metal; *v.* amarrar o atar con correas; azotar (*con correa*); *véase* **strop.**

stratagem [strǽtədʒəm] *s.* estratagema.

strategic [strətídʒɪk] *adj.* estratégico.

strategy [strǽtədʒɪ] *s.* estrategia.

stratosphere [strǽtəsfɪr] *s.* estratosfera.

straw [strɔ] *s.* paja; **I don't care a —** no me importa un comino; *adj.* de paja; pajizo; **straw-colored** pajizo, color de paja; **— hat** sombrero de paja; **— vote** voto no oficial (*para averiguar la opinión pública*).

strawberry [stróberɪ] *s.* fresa.

stray [stre] v. extraviarse, descarriarse, desviarse; perderse, errar el camino; vagar; adj. extraviado, perdido; — **remark** observación aislada; s. animal perdido o extraviado.

streak [strik] s. raya, línea, lista; veta, vena; rasgo; rayo (de luz); — **of lightning** relámpago, rayo; v. rayar, Am. listar, hacer rayas o listas en.

stream [strim] s. corriente, chorro, río, arroyo, arroyuelo; — **of cars** desfile de autos; **down**— río abajo, agua abajo, con la corriente; **up**— río arriba, agua arriba, contra la corriente; v. correr (el agua), fluir; brotar, manar; derramarse; flotar (en el viento), ondear; to— **out of** salir a torrentes de.

streamer [strímɚ] s. banderola; gallardete; listón, cinta (que flota en el aire)

street [strit] s. calle.

streetcar [strítkɚ] s. tranvía.

strength [strεŋkθ] s. fuerza; poder; potencia; fortaleza; **on the** — **of his promise** fundado en su promesa.

strengthen [strέŋkθɚn] v. fortalecer(se). reforzar(se).

strenuous [strέnjʊəs] adj. arduo; enérgico, vigoroso.

stress [strɛs] s. fuerza, esfuerzo; tensión, torsión, compresión; urgencia; énfasis; acento; v. acentuar; recalcar, dar énfasis a, hacer hincapié en.

stretch [strɛtʃ] v. estirar(se); alargar(se); tender(se); ensanchar; to — **oneself** estirarse, desperezarse; to — **out one's hand** tender o alargar la mano; s. trecho, distancia; extensión; período de tiempo; elasticidad; tensión; esfuerzo (de la imaginación); estirón; tensión; **home** — último trecho (de una carrera).

stretcher [strέtʃɚ] s. estirador, ensanchador, dilatador; camilla (para los heridos).

strew [stru] v. regar, esparcir.

strewn [strun] p.p. de to strew; — **with** regado de, cubierto de.

stricken [stríkɚn] p.p. de to strike; adj. herido; afligido; agobiado; atacado.

strict [strɪkt] adj. estricto; **in** — **confidence** en absoluta confianza, con toda reserva.

stridden [strídɚn] p.p. de to stride.

stride [straɪd] v. tranquear, caminar a paso largo, dar zancadas, andar a trancos; s. zancada, tranco, paso largo.

strife [straɪf] s. refriega, contienda, pleito.

strike [straɪk] v. dar, golpear, pegar; dar (un golpe); azotar; herir; atacar; chocar con; dar con, encontrar (oro, pe-

tróleo, etc.); ocurrírsele a uno (una idea); asumir, afectar (una postura, una actitud); dar (la hora un reloj); encender (un fósforo); acuñar (moneda); declararse o estar en huelga, to — **at** amagar; acometer; to — **off** borrar, tachar; cortar; to — **one's attention** atraer o llamar la atención; to — **one's fancy** antojársele a uno; to — **one's head against** darse un cabezazo contra; to — **out in a certain direction** tomar cierto rumbo, encaminarse o irse en cierta dirección; to — **someone for a loan** darle un sablazo a alguien; to — **up a friendship** trabar amistad, to — **with terror** sobrecoger de terror, **how does she — you?** ¿qué tal le parece?, ¿qué piensa Vd. de ella?; s. golpe; huelga, descubrimiento repentino (de petróleo, de una mina, etc.); —**breaker** esquirol (obrero que sustituye a un huelguista).

striker [stráɪkɚ] s. huelguista; golpeador.

striking [stráɪkɪŋ] adj. notable; llamativo; conspicuo, manifiesto; sorprendente; extraordinario; que está en huelga.

string [strɪŋ] s. cuerda; cordel, cinta, cordón; sarta (de perlas, cuentas, etc.); fibra (de habichuelas, porotos, etc.); fila, hilera; — **bean** habichuela, judía verde, Am. ejote, Am. poroto; — **of lies** sarta de mentiras; v. ensartar; tender (un cable, un alambre); desfibrar, quitar las fibras a; encordar (una raqueta, un violín); encordelar, atar con cordeles, lazos o cuerdas, tomar el pelo, engañar; to — **out** extender(se), prolongar(se); to — **up** colgar.

strip [strɪp] v. despojar; robar; desnudar(se); desvestir(se); desmantelar; to — **the gears** estropear el engranaje; to — **the skin from** desollar, pelar; s. tira, lista, listón; — **of land** faja de tierra.

stripe [straɪp] s. franja, raya, lista, tira; banda, galón; tipo, índole; v. rayar, Am. listar, adornar con listas.

striped [stráɪpɪd, straɪpt] adj. listado.

strive [straɪv] v. esforzarse; luchar, forcejear; hacer lo posible; to — **to** esforzarse por.

striven [strívɚn] p.p. de to strive.

strode [strod] pret. de to stride.

stroke [strok] s. golpe; ataque, apoplejía; — **of a bell** campanada; — **of a painter's brush** pincelada; — **of lightning** rayo; — **of the hand** caricia; — **of the pen** plumada; **at the** — **of ten** al dar las diez; v. frotar suavemente, pasar suavemente la mano, acariciar; alisar.

stroll [strol] v. dar un paseo, pasearse; vagar; **to — the streets** callejear; s. paseo, paseíto.

strong [strɔŋ] adj. fuerte; forzudo, fornido; vigoroso; recio; enérgico; firme; bien marcado; acérrimo; **— chance** buena probabilidad; **— coffee** café cargado; **— market** mercado firme; **strong-willed** de voluntad fuerte, decidido; adv. fuertemente; firmemente.

stronghold [strɔ́nhold] s. fuerte, plaza fuerte.

strop [strap] v. asentar (navajas de afeitar); s. asentador de navajas.

strove [strov] pret. de **to strive**.

struck [strʌk] pret. & p.p. de **to strike**; **to be — with a disease** darle a uno una enfermedad; **to be — with terror** estar o quedar sobrecogido de terror.

structural [strʌ́ktʃərəl] adj. estructural, relativo a la estructura.

structure [strʌ́ktʃə] s. estructura; construcción; edificio.

struggle [strʌ́gl] v. bregar, luchar, pugnar; forcejear; esforzarse; s. esfuerzo; contienda; lucha, pugna.

strung [strʌŋ] pret. & p.p. de **to string**.

strut [strʌt] v. pavonearse, contonearse; s. contoneo; tirante, puntal.

stub [stʌb] s. trozo, fragmento, pedazo mochado; tocón (de árbol); talón (de libro talonario, boleto, etc.); **— book** libro talonario; **— pen** pluma de punta mocha; v. **to — one's foot** dar(se) un tropezón.

stubble [stʌ́bl] s. rastrojo; cañones (de la barba).

stubborn [stʌ́bən] adj. terco, testarudo, obstinado, porfiado, cabezón.

stubbornness [stʌ́bənnɪs] s. terquedad, testarudez, porfía, obstinación.

stucco [stʌ́ko] s. estuco; v. estucar, cubrir de estuco.

stuck [stʌk] pret. & p.p. de **to stick** pegado; atorado; atascado; **— full of holes** agujereado; **stuck-up** tieso, estirado, orgulloso.

stud [stʌd] s. tachón, tachuela de adorno; botón postizo para camisa; perno; **—horse** caballo padre; v. tachonar; clavetear.

student [stjúdn̩t] s. estudiante.

studied [stʌ́dɪd] adj. estudiado.

studio [stjúdɪo] s. estudio, taller.

studious [stjúdɪəs] adj. estudioso; aplicado; estudiado.

study [stʌ́dɪ] s. estudio; cuidado, solici-

tud; gabinete de estudio; v. estudiar.

stuff [stʌf] s. materia; material; género, tela; cosa; cosas; menjurje, medicina; cachivaches, baratijas; **of good — de** buena estofa; v. rellenar; henchir; hartar(se), atracar(se), atiborrar(se).

stuffing [stʌ́fɪŋ] s. relleno; material para rellenar.

stumble [stʌ́mbl] v. tropezar, dar(se) un tropezón; dar un traspié; hablar o recitar equivocándose a cada paso; **to — upon** tropezar con; s. tropiezo, tropezón, traspié.

stump [stʌmp] s. tocón (tronco que queda de un árbol); raigón (de muela); muñón (de brazo o pierna cortada); **— of a tail** rabo; **to be up a —** hallarse en un apuro, estar perplejo; v. trozar el tronco de (un árbol); renquear, cojear; dejar confuso, confundir; **to — the country** recorrer el país pronunciando discursos políticos.

stumpy [stʌ́mpɪ] adj. rechoncho, Am. chaparro; lleno de tocones.

stun [stʌn] v. aturdir, pasmar; atolondrar.

stung [stʌŋ] pret. & p.p. de **to sting**.

stunk [stʌŋk] pret. & p.p. de **to stink**.

stunning [stʌ́nɪŋ] adj. aplastante; elegante, bellísimo.

stunt [stʌnt] v. achaparrar, impedir el desarrollo de, no dejar crecer; hacer suertes; hacer piruetas; s. suerte; pirueta, suerte acrobática, maniobra gimnástica; hazaña sensacional.

stupefy [stjúpəfaɪ] v. atontar; entorpecer; aturdir, atolondrar, pasmar, dejar estupefacto.

stupendous [stjupéndəs] adj. estupendo.

stupid [stjúpɪd] adj. estúpido; atontado.

stupidity [stjupídətɪ] s. estupidez.

stupor [stjúpə] s. letargo, modorra; aturdimiento; **in a —** aletargado.

sturdy [stɔ́dɪ] adj. fornido, fuerte, robusto; firme.

stutter [stʌ́tə] v. tartamudear; s. tartamudeo; tartamudez.

stutterer [stʌ́tərə] s. tartamudo.

stuttering [stʌ́tərɪŋ] adj. tartamudo; s. tartamudeo.

sty [staɪ] s. pocilga; orzuelo (en el párpado), Am. perrilla.

style [staɪl] s. estilo; moda; **to be in —** estar de moda, estilarse; v. intitular, nombrar; **to — a dress** cortar un vestido a la moda.

stylish [staɪlɪʃ] adj. elegante; a la moda.

subdivision [sʌbdəvíʒən] s. subdivisión; parcelación de terrenos.

subdue [səbdjú] v. subyugar, someter;

sujetar, dominar; amansar, domar.

subdued [səbdjúd] *p.p. de* **to subdue**; *adj.* sumiso; sujeto; manso; suave; tenue; — **light** luz tenue.

subject [sʌ́bdʒɪkt] *s.* súbdito; sujeto; asunto, tema, materia; *adj.* sujeto; sometido; inclinado, propenso; expuesto; [səbdʒékt] *v.* sujetar; someter; subyugar, sojuzgar.

subjection [səbdʒékʃən] *s.* sujeción; dominación; sumisión.

subjugate [sʌ́bdʒəget] *v.* subyugar, sojuzgar.

sublime [səbláɪm] *adj.* sublime.

submarine [sʌbmərín] *adj.* submarino; [sʌ́bmərin] *s.* submarino.

submerge [səbmə́dʒ] *v.* sumergir(se), hundir(se), sumir(se).

submission [səbmíʃən] *s.* sumisión, sometimiento.

submissive [səbmísɪv] *adj.* sumiso.

submit [səbmít] *v.* someter; **to** — **a report** someter (presentar *o* rendir) un informe; **to** — **to punishment** someterse a un castigo.

subordinate [səbɔ́rdṇɪt] *adj.* & *s.* subordinado; subalterno; dependiente; [səbɔ́rdṇet] *v.* subordinar.

subscribe [səbskráɪb] *v.* subscribir(se); firmar; **to** — **five dollars** prometer una cuota o subscripción de cinco dólares; **to** — **for** subscribirse a, abonarse a; **to** — **to a plan** subscribirse a (*o* aprobar) un plan.

subscriber [səbskráɪbə] *s.* suscritor, abonado; infrascrito (*que firma un documento*), firmante.

subscription [səbskrípʃən] *s.* subscripción, abono.

subsequent [sʌ́bsɪkwent] *adj.* subsiguiente, subsecuente, posterior; **-ly** *adv.* después, posteriormente; subsiguientemente.

subservient [səbsə́vɪənt] *adj.* servil, servilón.

subside [səbsáɪd] *v.* menguar, disminuir; bajar (*de nivel*); calmarse, aquietarse.

subsidize [sʌ́bsədaɪz] *v.* subvencionar.

subsidy [sʌ́bsədɪ] *s.* subvención.

subsist [səbsíst] *v.* subsistir.

substance [sʌ́bstəns] *s.* substancia (sustancia).

substantial [səbstǽnʃəl] *adj.* substancial, substancioso; sólido; considerable; importante; **to be in** — **agreement** estar en substancia de acuerdo.

substantive [sʌ́bstəntɪv] *adj.* & *s.* sustantivo.

substitute [sʌ́bstətjut] *v.* sustituir (substituir); reemplazar; *s.* sustituto, su-

plente; reemplazo.

substitution [sʌbstətjúʃən] *s.* sustitución (substitución); reemplazo.

subterranean [sʌbtərénɪən] *adj.* subterráneo.

subtle [sʌ́tḷ] *adj.* sutil.

subtlety [sʌ́tḷtɪ] *s.* sutileza; agudeza.

subtract [səbtrǽkt] *v.* sustraer (substraer); restar.

subtraction [səbtrǽkʃən] *s.* sustracción (substracción), resta.

suburb [sʌ́bɝb] *s.* suburbio, arrabal.

suburban [səbɝ́bən] *adj.* & *s.* suburbano.

subversive [səbvɝ́sɪv] *adj.* subversivo (*en contra de la autoridad constituida*); trastornador, destructivo.

subway [sʌ́bwe] *s.* subterráneo, túnel; metro, ferrocarril subterráneo.

succeed [səksíd] *v.* suceder a; medrar, tener buen éxito, salir bien.

success [səksɛ́s] *s.* éxito, buen éxito; triunfo.

successful [səksɛ́sfəl] *adj.* afortunado; próspero; **to be** — tener buen éxito; **-ly** *adv.* con buen éxito, prósperamente.

succession [səksɛ́ʃən] *s.* sucesión.

successive [səksɛ́sɪv] *adj.* sucesivo.

successor [səksɛ́sə] *s.* sucesor; heredero.

succor [sʌ́kə] *s.* socorro; *v.* socorrer.

succumb [səkʌ́m] *v.* sucumbir.

such [sʌtʃ] *adj.* tal; semejante; — **a tal**, semejante; — **a good man** un hombre tan bueno; — **as** tal como, tales como; **at** — **an hour** a tal hora; **at** — **and** — **a place** en tal o cual lugar.

suck [sʌk] *v.* chupar; mamar; **to** — **up** chupar; sorber; *s.* chupada; mamada.

sucker [sʌ́kə] *s.* chupador; mamón, mamantón; dulce (*que se chupa*); primo (*persona demasiado crédula*).

suckle [sʌ́kḷ] *v.* mamar; amamantar, dar de mamar.

suction [sʌ́kʃən] *s.* succión; chupada, aspiración.

sudden [sʌ́dṇ] *adj.* súbito, repentino; precipitado; inesperado; **all of a** — de súbito, de repente, de sopetón; **-ly** *adv.* de súbito, de repente, de sopetón.

suddenness [sʌ́dnnɪs] *s.* precipitación; rapidez.

suds [sʌdz] *s.* espuma, jabonadura.

sue [su] *v.* demandar; **to** — **for damages** demandar por daños y perjuicios; **to** — **for peace** pedir la paz.

suet [súɪt] *s.* sebo, gordo, grasa.

suffer [sʌ́fə] *v.* sufrir; padecer.

sufferer [sʌ́fərə] *s.* sufridor.

suffering [sʌ́fərɪŋ] *s.* sufrimiento, padecimiento; *adj.* doliente; sufrido, paciente.

suffice [səfáıs] v. bastar, ser bastante o suficiente.

sufficient [səffÇənt] adj. suficiente, bastante; **-ly** adv. suficientemente, bastante.

suffocate [sÁfəket] v. sofocar(se), ahogar(se), asfixiar(se).

suffocation [səfəkéʃən] s. asfixia, sofoco.

suffrage [sÁfrıdʒ] s. sufragio; voto.

sugar [ʃúgə] s. azúcar; — **bowl** azucarera; — **cane** caña de azúcar; **lump of** — terrón de azúcar; v. azucarar; cristalizarse (el almíbar), Am. azucararse.

suggest [səgdʒést] v. sugerir, indicar.

suggestion [səgdʒéstʃən] s. sugestión, Am. sugerencia; indicación.

suggestive [səgdʒéstıv] adj. sugestivo.

suicide [súəsaıd] s. suicidio; suicida; **to commit** — suicidarse.

suit [sut] s. traje, terno, Am. flux (o flus); palo (de la baraja); demanda, pleito; petición; galanteo; v. adaptar, acomodar; agradar; satisfacer; sentar bien, venir bien; caer bien; convenir; ser a propósito; — **yourself** haz lo que quieras, haga Vd. lo que guste.

suitable [sútəbl] adj. propio, conveniente, debido, a propósito, apropiado, adecuado.

suitably [sútəblı] adv. propiamente, adecuadamente, convenientemente.

suitcase [sútkes] s. maleta, valija.

suite [swit] s. serie; comitiva, acompañamiento; — **of rooms** vivienda, apartamento, habitación; **bedroom** — juego de muebles para alcoba.

suitor [sútə] s. pretendiente, galán; demandante (en un pleito).

sulk [sʌlk] v. tener murria, estar hosco o malhumorado; s. murria.

sulky [sÁlkı] adj. malcontento, hosco, malhumorado; **to be** — tener murria.

sullen [sÁlın] adj. hosco, sombrío, tétrico; malhumorado, taciturno.

sully [sÁlı] v. manchar, ensuciar; empañar.

sulphate [sÁlfet] s. sulfato.

sulphide [sÁlfaıd] s. sulfuro.

sulphur [sÁlfə] s. azufre.

sulphuric [sʌlfjúrık] adj. sulfúrico.

sultan [sÁltn] s. sultán.

sultry [sÁltrı] adj. bochornoso, sofocante; — **heat** bochorno, calor sofocante.

sum [sʌm] s. suma; cantidad; esencia, substancia; — **total** total; v. sumar; **to** — **up** resumir, recapitular.

summarize [sÁməraız] v. resumir, compendiar.

summary [sÁmərı] s. sumario, resumen;

compendio; adj. sumario; breve.

summer [sÁmə] s. verano; estío; adj. veraniego, estival, de verano; — **resort** balneario, lugar de veraneo; v. veranear.

summit [sÁmıt] s. cima, cúspide, cumbre.

summon [sÁmən] v. citar; convocar, llamar; **-s** s. notificación; cita judicial, citación, emplazamiento.

sumptuous [sÁmptʃʊəs] adj. suntuoso.

sun [sʌn] s. sol; — **bath** baño de sol; — **porch** solana; v. asolear; **to** — **oneself** asolearse, tomar el sol.

sunbeam [sÁnbim] s. rayo de sol.

sunburn [sÁnbɜn] s. quemadura de sol; v. asolear(se); quemar(se) al sol, tostar(se) al sol.

Sunday [sÁndı] s. domingo.

sundial [sÁndaıəl] s. cuadrante solar, reloj de sol.

sundown [sÁndaun] s. puesta del sol.

sundry [sÁndrı] adj. varios, diversos.

sunflower [sÁnflauə] s. girasol.

sung [sʌŋ] pret. & p.p. de **to sing.**

sunk [sʌŋk] pret. & p.p. de **to sink.**

sunken [sÁŋkən] adj. hundido, sumido.

sunlight [sÁnlaıt] s. luz del sol, luz solar.

sunny [sÁnı] adj. asoleado o soleado; alegre, risueño, resplandeciente; — **day** día de sol.

sunrise [sÁnraız] s. salida del sol, amanecer, amanecida.

sunset [sÁnset] s. puesta del sol.

sunshine [sÁnʃaın] s. luz del sol, solana.

sunstroke [sÁnstrok] s. insolación.

sup [sʌp] v. cenar.

superb [supɝb] adj. soberbio.

superficial [supəfíʃəl] adj. superficial.

superfluous [supɝflʊəs] adj. superfluo.

superhuman [supəhjúmən] adj. sobrehumano.

superintend [suprınténd] v. dirigir, inspeccionar, vigilar.

superintendent [suprınténdənt] s. superintendente; inspector; capataz.

superior [səpírıə] adj. & s. superior.

superiority [səpırıórətı] s. superioridad.

superlative [səpɝlətıv] adj. & s. superlativo.

supernatural [supənætʃrəl] adj. sobrenatural; **the** — lo sobrenatural.

supersede [supəsíd] v. reemplazar.

superstition [supəstíʃən] s. superstición.

superstitious [supəstíʃəs] adj. supersticioso.

supervise [supəváız] v. dirigir, inspeccionar, vigilar.

supervision [supəvíʒən] s. inspección,

vigilancia.

supervisor [supəváizə] s. superintendente, inspector; interventor.

supper [sápə] s. cena.

supplant [səplǽnt] v. suplantar; reemplazar.

supple [sápl] adj. flexible; dócil.

supplement [sápləmənt] s. suplemento; apéndice; [sápləment] v. suplementar, completar.

suppliant [sápliənt] adj. & s. suplicante.

supplication [sʌplikéʃən] s. súplica, plegaria; ruego.

supply [səplái] v. proveer; abastecer, surtir; suplir; dar, suministrar; s. provisión, abastecimiento; bastimento; abasto; surtido; **supplies** provisiones; materiales; víveres; pertrechos; — **pipe** cañería o caño de abastecimiento; tubería o tubo de suministro.

support [səpórt] v. sostener; apoyar; mantener; sustentar; soportar, aguantar; s. apoyo; sostén, soporte, puntal; sustento, manutención; amparo.

supporter [səpórtə] s. defensor; partidario; mantenedor; sostén, apoyo; tirante (para medias).

suppose [səpóz] v. suponer.

supposed [səpózd] adj. supuesto; presunto; -ly adv. supuestamente.

supposition [sʌpəzíʃən] s. suposición.

suppress [səprés] v. suprimir; reprimir; parar, suspender; **to — a revolt** sofocar una revuelta o motín.

suppression [səpréʃən] s. supresión; represión.

supremacy [səpréməsɪ] s. supremacía.

supreme [səprím] adj. supremo.

sure [ʃur] adj. seguro; cierto; estable; adv. véase **surely**; **be — and do it** hágalo sin falta, no deje Vd. de hacerlo; -ly adv. seguramente; ciertamente; con toda seguridad; sin falta.

surety [ʃúrtɪ] s. seguridad; garantía, fianza; fiador.

surf [sɜf] s. oleaje, rompientes; resaca.

surface [sɜfɪs] s. superficie; cara; v. alisar, allanar; poner superficie.

surfeit [sɜfɪt] s. hastío, exceso; v. hastiar; empalagar.

surge [sɜdʒ] s. oleada, oleaje; v. agitarse, hinchar(se) (el mar); surgir.

surgeon [sɜdʒən] s. cirujano.

surgery [sɜdʒərɪ] s. cirujía.

surgical [sɜdʒɪkl] adj. quirúrgico.

surly [sɜlɪ] adj. rudo, hosco, malhumorado.

surmise [səmáɪz] v. conjeturar, suponer, presumir; s. conjetura, suposición.

surmount [səmáunt] v. superar, vencer; coronar.

surname [sɜnem] s. sobrenombre, apellido; v. apellidar, llamar.

surpass [səpǽs] v. sobrepasar, superar, sobrepujar, exceder, aventajar.

surpassing [səpǽsɪŋ] adj. sobresaliente, excelente.

surplus [sɜplʌs] s. sobra, sobrante, exceso, excedente; superávit; adj. sobrante, excedente, de sobra.

surprise [səpráɪz] s. sorpresa; v. sorprender.

surprising [səpráɪzɪŋ] adj. sorprendente.

surrender [səréndə] v. rendir(se), entregar(se), darse; ceder; s. rendición; entrega; cesión; sumisión.

surround [səráund] v. rodear, cercar, circundar.

surrounding [səráundɪŋ] adj. circundante, circunvecino, circunstante.

surroundings [səráundɪŋz] s. pl. alrededores, inmediaciones, cercanías; ambiente.

survey [sɜve] s. examen, reconocimiento, inspección, estudio; medición, agrimensura (de un terreno); plano (de un terreno); bosquejo o esbozo general (de historia, literatura, etc.); — **course** curso general o comprensivo; [səvé] v. examinar, inspeccionar, reconocer medir (un terreno), levantar un plano (el agrimensor).

surveyor [səvéə] s. agrimensor.

survival [səvávɪl] s. supervivencia; sobrevivente; resto.

survive [səváɪv] v. sobrevivir; quedar vivo, salvarse.

survivor [səvávə] s. sobreviviente.

susceptible [səséptəbl] adj. susceptible; — **of proof** capaz de probarse; — **to** propenso a.

suspect [sáspekt] s. sospechoso; [səspékt] v. sospechar.

suspend [səspénd] v. suspender.

suspenders [səspéndəz] s. tirantes (de pantalón).

suspense [səspéns] s. suspensión, incertidumbre; ansiedad; **to keep in —** tener en suspenso, tener en ascuas.

suspension [səspénʃən] s. suspensión; — **bridge** puente colgante.

suspicion [səspíʃən] s. sospecha.

suspicious [səspíʃəs] adj. sospechoso; suspicaz.

sustain [səstén] v. sostener; mantener; sustentar; aguantar; sufrir (un daño o pérdida); apoyar, defender.

sustenance [sástənəns] s. sustento; subsistencia; alimentos; mantenimiento.

swagger [swǽgə] v. pavonearse, contonearse; fanfarronear; *s.* pavoneo, contoneo; fanfarronada.

swain [swen] *s.* galán.

swallow [swálo] *s.* golondrina; trago; *v.* tragar; deglutir.

swam [swæm] *pret. de* to swim.

swamp [swamp] *s.* pantano; ciénaga; — **land** cenagal, terreno pantanoso; *v.* inundar(se); sumergir(se); **to be -ed with work** estar abrumado de trabajo.

swampy [swámpɪ] *adj.* pantanoso, cenagoso, fangoso.

swan [swan] *s.* cisne.

swap [swap] *v.* cambalachear, cambiar, trocar; *s.* cambalache, cambio, trueque.

swarm [sworm] *s.* enjambre; *v.* pulular; bullir, hervir, hormiguear.

swarthy [swórðɪ] *adj.* trigueño, moreno, *Am.* prieto.

swat [swat] *v.* pegar, aporrear; aplastar de un golpe (*una mosca*); *s.* golpe.

sway [swe] *v.* mecer(se); cimbrar(se); balancearse; ladear(se) oscilar; tambalear; influir; *s.* oscilación; vaivén; balanceo; influjo, influencia; mando; predominio.

swear [swer] *v.* jurar; renegar, blasfemar, echar maldiciones; juramentar, tomar juramento; **to — by** jurar por; poner toda su confianza en; **to — in** juramentar; **to — off** smoking jurar no fumar más, renunciar al tabaco.

sweat [swet] *v.* sudar; trasudar; hacer sudar; *s.* sudor; trasudor.

sweater [swétə] *s. Am.* suéter; sudador, el que suda.

sweaty [swétɪ] *adj.* sudoroso.

Swede [swid] *s.* sueco.

Swedish [swídɪʃ] *adj.* sueco; *s.* sueco, idioma sueco.

sweep [swip] *v.* barrer; dragar (*puertos, ríos, etc.*); extenderse; **to — down upon** caer sobre; asolar; **to — everything away** barrer con todo; **she swept into the room** entró garbosamente en la sala; *s.* barrida; extensión; soplo (*del viento*).

sweeper [swípə] *s.* barrendero; **carpet —** escoba mecánica.

sweeping [swípɪŋ] *s.* barrido; **-s** basura; *adj.* abarcador, que lo abarca todo, vasto; asolador; **— victory** victoria completa.

sweet [swit] *adj.* dulce; oloroso; fresco; **— butter** mantequilla sin sal; **— corn** maíz tierno; **— milk** leche fresca; **— pea** guisante de olor; **— potato** batata, *Am.* camote, *Am.* boniato; **to have a — tooth** ser goloso, gustarle

a uno los dulces; *s.* dulce, golosina; **my —** mi vida, mi alma.

sweeten [switn] *v.* endulzar(se), dulcificar(se); suavizar.

sweetheart [swíthart] *s.* querida, novia, prometida; amante, querido, galán, novio.

sweetmeat [swítmit] *s.* confite, confitura, dulce, golosina.

sweetness [swítnɪs] *s.* dulzura; melosidad; suavidad.

swell [swel] *v.* hinchar(se), henchir(se), inflar(se); dilatar(se), abultar(se); acrecentar; *s.* hinchazón; protuberancia; oleaje; *adj.* elegante; muy bueno, excelente, magnífico; **to have a — head** creerse gran cosa; ser vanidoso.

swelling [swélɪŋ] *s.* hinchazón; chichón, .bulto; protuberancia.

swept [swept] *pret. & p.p. de* to sweep.

swerve [swɜv] *v.* desviar(se); torcer; cambiar repentinamente de rumbo; *s.* desvío brusco, cambio repentino de dirección; **to make a — to the right** torcer a la derecha.

swift [swɪft] *adj.* veloz, rápido.

swiftness [swíftnɪs] *s.* velocidad, rapidez, presteza, prontitud.

swim [swɪm] *v.* nadar; flotar; **to — across** pasar a nado, atravesar nadando; **my head is swimming** tengo vértigo, se me va la cabeza, estoy desvanecido; *s.* nadada; **— suit** traje de baño o natación.

swimmer [swímə] *s.* nadador.

swindle [swíndl] *v.* estafar; *s.* estafa.

swine [swaɪn] *s.* marrano, puerco, cerdo, cochino; marranos, puercos, cerdos.

swing [swɪŋ] *v.* columpiar(se), mecer(se), balancear(se); oscilar; hacer oscilar; blandir (*un bastón, espada, etc.*); colgar; girar; hacer girar; **to — a deal** llevar a cabo un negocio; **to — around** dar vuelta, girar; **to — one's arms** girar o menear los brazos; **to — open** abrirse de pronto (*una puerta*); *s.* columpio; hamaca; balanceo; vaivén; compás, ritmo; golpe, guantada, puñetazo; **— door** puerta giratoria; **in full —** en su apogeo, en pleno movimiento; **to give someone full —** darle a alguien completa libertad de acción.

swipe [swaɪp] *v.* hurtar, sisar.

swirl [swɜl] *v.* arremolinarse; girar, dar vueltas; *s.* remolino; torbellino; vuelta, movimiento giratorio.

Swiss [swɪs] *adj. & s.* suizo.

switch [swɪtʃ] *s.* látigo, azote, *Am.* chicote, *Am.* rebenque; latigazo; pelo postizo; cambio; **electric —** interruptor,

T

conmutador; **railway** — aguja, cambio; —**man** guardagujas, *Am.* cambiavía; *v.* azotar; desviar(se); cambiar(se); **to** — **off** cortar (*la comunicación o la corriente eléctrica*); apagar (*la luz eléctrica*); **to** — **on the light** encender la luz.

switchboard [swítʃbord] *s.* cuadro o tablero de distribución; cuadro conmutador.

swollen [swólən] *p.p.* de **to swell**.

swoon [swun] *v.* desvanecerse, desmayarse; *s.* desmayo.

swoop [swup] *v.* **to** — **down upon** caer de súbito sobre; abalanzarse sobre; acometer; **to** — **off** cortar de un golpe; **to** — **up** agarrar, arrebatar; *s.* descenso súbito; arremetida; **at one** — de un golpe.

sword [sord] *s.* espada; — **belt** talabarte.

swore [swor] *pret.* de **to swear**.

sworn [sworn] *p.p.* de **to swear**.

swum [swʌm] *p.p.* de **to swim**.

swung [swʌŋ] *pret. & p.p.* de **to swing**.

syllable [síləbl] *s.* sílaba.

symbol [símbl] *s.* símbolo.

symbolic [simbálik] *adj.* simbólico.

symbolism [símblizəm] *s.* simbolismo.

symmetrical [simétrikl] *adj.* simétrico.

symmetry [símitri] *s.* simetría.

sympathetic [simpəθétik] *adj.* simpático; que simpatiza o siente simpatía; compasivo; — **towards** favorablemente dispuesto a (*o hacia*).

sympathize [símpəθaiz] *v.* simpatizar; compadecerse, condolerse.

sympathy [símpəθi] *s.* simpatía; armonía; lástima, compasión; **to extend one's** — dar el pésame.

symphony [símfəni] *s.* sinfonía; — **orchestra** orquesta sinfónica.

symptom [símptəm] *s.* síntoma.

syndicate [síndikit] *s.* sindicato; **newspaper** — sindicato periodístico; [síndiket] *v.* sindicar, formar un sindicato; sindicarse, combinarse para formar un sindicato; vender (*un cuento, caricatura, serie de artículos, etc.*) a un sindicato.

synonym [sínənim] *s.* sinónimo.

synonymous [sinánəməs] *adj.* sinónimo.

syntax [síntæks] *s.* sintaxis.

synthesis [sínθəsis] *s.* síntesis.

synthetic [sinétik] *adj.* sintético.

syringe [sírindʒ] *s.* jeringa.

syrup = **sirup**.

system [sístəm] *s.* sistema.

systematic [sistəmétik] *adj.* sistemático.

tabernacle [tébənækl] *s.* tabernáculo.

table [tébl] *s.* mesa; tabla (*de materias, de multiplicar, etc.*); — **cover** tapete, cubremesa; —**land** mesa, meseta; *v.* poner sobre la mesa; formar tabla o índice; **to** — **a motion** dar carpetazo a una moción, aplazar la discusión de una moción.

tablecloth [téblklɔθ] *s.* mantel.

tablespoon [téblspun] *s.* cuchara grande.

tablespoonful [téblspunful] *s.* cucharada.

tablet [téblit] *s.* tableta; tablilla, pastilla; bloc de papel; lápida, placa.

tableware [téblwer] *s.* vajilla, servicio de mesa.

tabulate [tébjəlet] *v.* formar tablas o listas.

tacit [tésit] *adj.* tácito.

taciturn [tésətɜn] *adj.* taciturno, silencioso.

tack [tæk] *s.* tachuela; hilván; virada o cambio de rumbo (*de una embarcación*); amura, jarcia (*para sostener el ángulo de una vela*); **to change** — cambiar de amura, cambiar de rumbo; *v.* clavetear con tachuelas; coser, hilvanar; pegar, clavar; juntar, unir; virar, cambiar de rumbo; zigzaguear (*un barco de vela*).

tackle [tékl] *s.* aparejo, equipo; enseres, avíos; agarrada (*en futbol*); atajador (*en futbol*); **fishing** — avíos de pescar; *v.* agarrar, asir, atajar (*en futbol*); atacar (*un problema*); acometer (*una empresa*).

tact [tækt] *s.* tacto, tino, tiento.

tactful [téktfəl] *adj.* cauto, prudente, diplomático.

tactics [téktiks] *s.* táctica.

tactless [téktlis] *adj.* falto de tacto o de tino; imprudente, incauto.

taffeta [téfitə] *s.* tafetán.

tag [tæg] *s.* marbete, etiqueta; cartela; pingajo, rabito, cabo; **to play** — jugar al tócame tú, jugar a la pega; *v.* pegar un marbete a, marcar; **to** — **after** seguir de cerca, pisar los talones a; **to** — **something on to** juntar, añadir o agregar algo a.

tail [tel] *s.* cola, rabo; cabo, extremo, extremidad; — **light** farol trasero, farol de cola; — **spin** barrena.

tailor [télə] *s.* sastre.

taint [tent] *s.* tacha, mancha; corrupción; *v.* manchar; corromper(se), inficionar(se).

take [tek] *v.* tomar; coger; llevar; conducir; dar (*un paseo, vuelta, paso, salto*); hacer (*un viaje*); asumir; sacar o tomar (*una fotografía*); **to — a chance** aventurarse, correr un riesgo; **to — a fancy** to caerle en gracia a uno; aficionarse a; antojársele a uno; **to — a look** to mirar a, echar una mirada a; **to — a notion** to antojársele a uno; **to — after** salir a, parecerse a; seguir el ejemplo de; **to — amiss** interpretar mal, echar a mala parte; **to — an oath** prestar juramento; **to — apart** desarmar, desmontar; **to — away** llevarse; **to — back one's words** desdecirse, retractarse; **to — back to** devolver (*algo*) a; **to — by surprise** coger desprevenido, coger de sorpresa; **to — care of** cuidar de, atender a; **to — charge of** encargarse de; **to — cold** resfriarse, acatarrarse; **to — down in writing** poner por escrito, apuntar; **to — effect** surtir efecto, dar resultado; entrar en vigencia (*una ley*); **to — exercise** hacer ejercicio; hacer gimnasia; **to — from** quitar a; sustraer de, restar de; **to — in** meter en; recibir; abarcar; embaucar; reducir, achicar (*un vestido*); **to — leave** decir adiós, despedirse; **to — off** quitar; descontar, rebajar; despegar (*un aeroplano*); remedar, parodiar (*a alguien*); **to — offense** ofenderse, darse por ofendido; **to — on a responsibility** asumir una responsabilidad; **to — out** sacar; por ej.; **to — place** tener lugar, suceder, ocurrir; **to — stock** hacer inventario; **to — stock in** creer, tener confianza en; **to — the floor** tomar la palabra; **to — to heart** tomar a pechos, tomar en serio; **to — to one's heels** poner pies en polvorosa; **to — to task** reprender, regañar; **to — up a matter** tratar un asunto; **to — up space** ocupar espacio; **I — it that** supongo que; **s.** toma; **take-off** despegue (*de un aeroplano*); remedo, parodia.

aken [tékən] *p.p. de* **to take; to be — ill** caer enfermo.

alcum [tǽlkəm] *s.* talco; **— powder** talco en polvo.

ale [tel] *s.* cuento, relato, fábula; chisme; **to tell —s** contar cuentos o chismes; chismear, murmurar.

alebearer [télbɛrə] *s.* soplón, chismoso.

alent [tǽlənt] *s.* talento.

alented [tǽləntɪd] *adj.* talentoso.

alk [tɔk] *v.* hablar; charlar, platicar, conversar; **to — into** inducir o persuadir a; **to — nonsense** decir tonterías, hablar disparates; **to — out of** disuadir de; **to — over** discutir; **to — up** alabar; hablar claro o recio, hablar en voz alta; *s.* charla, conversación, plática; habla; discurso; conferencia; rumor; **— of the town** comidilla, tema de murmuración.

talkative [tɔ́kətɪv] *adj.* hablador, locuaz, platicador.

talker [tɔ́kə] *s.* hablador; conversador; platicador; orador.

tall [tɔl] *adj.* alto; **— tale** cuento exagerado o increíble; **six feet —** seis pies de altura o de alto.

tallow [tǽlo] *s.* sebo.

tally [tǽlɪ] *s.* cuenta; **— sheet** plana para llevar la cuenta; *v.* llevar la cuenta; **to — up** contar, sumar; **to — with** corresponder con, concordar con.

tame [tem] *adj.* manso; dócil; **— amusement** diversión poco animada o desabrida; *v.* amansar, domar, domeñar; domesticar.

tamper [tǽmpə] *v.* **to — with** meterse con, juguetear con; falsificar (*un documento*); **to — with a lock** tratar de forzar una cerradura.

tan [tæn] *v.* curtir, adobar (*pieles*); zurrar, azotar; tostar(se), requemar(se); *adj.* tostado, requemado; color de canela; bayo, amarillento; *s.* color moreno, de canela o café con leche.

tangent [tǽndʒənt] *adj. & s.* tangente; **to go off at a —** salirse por la tangente.

tangerine [tǽndʒərin] *s.* naranja tangerina o mandarina.

tangible [tǽndʒəbl] *adj.* tangible, palpable; corpóreo.

tangle [tǽngl] *v.* enredar(se), enmarañar(se); confundir(se), embrollar(se); *s.* enredo, maraña, embrollo; confusión.

tank [tæŋk] *s.* tanque; depósito; **swimming —** piscina.

tanner [tǽnə] *s.* curtidor.

tannery [tǽnərɪ] *s.* curtiduría, tenería.

tantalize [tǽntlaɪz] *v.* molestar; hacer desesperar; exasperar.

tantrum [tǽntrəm] *s.* berrinche.

tap [tæp] *s.* palmadita; golpecito; espita, grifo; **— dance** zapateado, *Am.* zapateo; **—room** bar; **beer on —** cerveza del barril, cerveza de sifón; *v.* tocar, golpear ligeramente; dar una palmadita o golpecito; taladrar; extraer; **to — a tree** sangrar un árbol.

tape [tep] *s.* cinta, cintilla; **— measure** cinta para medir; **—worm** solitaria; **adhesive —** tela adhesiva, esparadrapo; v. atar o vendar con cinta; medir con cinta.

taper [tépə] s. velita, candela; adelgazamiento gradual (*de un objeto*); v. adelgazar, disminuir gradualmente; **to — off** ahusar(se), ir disminuyendo (*hasta rematar en punta*).

tapestry [tǽpɪstrɪ] s. tapiz, colgadura; tapicería; tela (*para forrar muebles*).

tapioca [tæpɪókə] s. tapioca.

tar [tar] s. alquitrán, brea, pez (*f.*); v. alquitranar, embrear, poner brea o alquitrán.

tardy [tárdɪ] adj. tardo, tardío, **to be — ** llegar tarde o retrasado.

target [tárgɪt] s. blanco; **— practice** tiro al blanco.

tariff [tǽrɪf] s. tarifa; arancel, impuesto.

tarnish [tárnɪʃ] v. empañar(se); manchar; perder el lustre; s. deslustre, falta de lustre, empañamiento; mancha.

tarry [tǽrɪ] v. demorarse, tardar(se).

tart [tɑrt] adj. acre, agridulce; agrio; picante; **— reply** respuesta mordaz o agria; s. tarta, torta rellena con dulce de frutas.

task [tæsk] s. faena, tarea, quehacer; **to take to —** reprender, regañar.

tassel [tǽsl] s. borla.

taste [test] v. gustar; probar, saborear, paladear; **to — of onion** saber a cebolla; **it -s sour** sabe agrio, tiene un sabor o gusto agrio; s. gusto; sabor, prueba; afición; **after—** dejo; **in good —** de buen gusto, **to take a — of** probar.

tasteless [téstlɪs] adj. insípido; desabrido; de mal gusto.

tasty [téstɪ] adj. sabroso, gustoso; de buen gusto.

tatter [tǽtə] s. harapo, Am hilacho.

tattered [tǽtəd] adj roto, harapiento, andrajoso.

tattle [tǽtl] v chismear, murmurar; s. habladuría, murmuración, hablilla; **—tale** chismoso, soplón.

taught [tɔt] pret. & p.p. de **to teach.**

taunt [tɔnt] v. mofarse de, echar pullas; reprochar; s. mofa, pulla.

tavern [tǽvən] s. taberna; posada.

tax [tæks] s. impuesto, contribución; esfuerzo; v. imponer contribuciones a; tasar; abrumar; reprender, reprobar; cobrar (*un precio*); **to — one's patience** abusar de la paciencia.

taxation [tækséʃən] s. impuestos, contribuciones; imposición de contribuciones.

taxi [tǽksɪ] s. taxímetro, taxi, automóvil de alquiler; v. ir en taxímetro; taxear

(*un aeroplano*).

taxicab [tǽksɪkæb] = **taxi.**

taxpayer [tǽkspeə] s. contribuyente.

tea [ti] s. té.

teach [titʃ] v. enseñar; instruir.

teacher [títʃə] s. maestro, maestra.

teaching [títʃɪŋ] s. enseñanza; instrucción; doctrina.

teacup [tíkʌp] s. taza para té.

teakettle [tíketl] · s. marmita, tetera Am. pava (*para el mate*).

team [tim] s. equipo (*de jugadores*) partido, grupo; tronco (*de caballos mulas, etc.*); yunta (*de bueyes*); **—work** cooperación; v. uncir, enganchar; formar pareja; acarrear, transportar; **te — up** unirse, formar un equipo.

teamster [tímstə] s. carretero.

teapot [típɑt] s. tetera.

tear [tɪr] s. lágrima; **— gas** gas lácri mógeno o lacrimante; **to burst into -s** romper a llorar; deshacerse en lágrimas.

tear [ter] v. rasgar(se); desgarrar, romper; **to — along** ir a toda velocidad andar aprisa, correr; **to — apar** desarmar, desmontar; separar, apar tar; **to — away** arrancar; irse; **to — down** demoler, derribar (*un edificio* desarmar, desmontar (*una máquina*) **to — off in a hurry** salir corriendo salir a la carrera; **to — one's hai** mesarse los cabellos; s. desgarradura rasgadura; rasgón, rotura, prisa; wea **and —** desgaste.

tearful [tírfəl] adj. lloroso.

tease [tiz] v. embromar; molestar; im portunar.

teaspoon [tíspun] s. cucharilla, cucha rita.

teaspoonful [tíspunfʊl] s. cucharadita

teat [tit] s. teta.

technical [téknɪk] adj. técnico.

technician [teknɪʃən] s. técnico.

technique [teknɪk] s. técnica.

tedious [tídɪəs] adj. tedioso, pesado, abu rrido, fastidioso.

tediousness [tídɪəsnɪs] s. tedio.

teem [tim] v. **to — with** abundar en estar lleno de.

teens [tinz] s. pl. edad de trece a diecı nueve años; números de trece a dieci nueve; **to be in one's —** tener d trece a diecinueve años.

teeth [tie] s. pl. de **tooth; he escape by the skin of his —** por poco no s escapa, se escapó por milagro.

telegram [téləgræm] s. telegrama.

telegraph [téləgræf] s. telégrafo; v. tele grafiar.

telegraphic [teləgrǽfɪk] *adj.* telegráfico.
telegraphy [təlégrəfɪ] *s.* telegrafía.
telephone [téləfon] *s.* teléfono; — **booth** casilla de teléfono; — **operator** telefonista; — **receiver** receptor telefónico; *v.* telefonear, llamar por teléfono.
telescope [téləskop] *s.* telescopio; *v.* enchufar(se), encajar(se) un objeto en otro.
television [téləvɪʒən] *s.* televisión.
tell [tel] *v.* decir; contar; expresar; explicar; adivinar; decidir; **to — on someone** delatar a alguien, contar chismes de alguien; **to — someone off** decirle a alguien cuatro verdades; **his age is beginning to —** ya comienza a notársele la edad.
teller [télə] *s.* narrador, relator; pagador o recibidor (*de un banco*); escrutador de votos.
temerity [təmérətɪ] *s.* temeridad.
temper [témpə] *v.* templar; *s.* temple (*de un metal*); genio, temple, humor; mal genio; **to keep one's —** contenerse, dominarse; **to lose one's —** perder la calma, encolerizarse.
temperament [témprəmənt] *s.* temperamento; disposición; temple.
temperance [témprəns] *s.* templanza, sobriedad.
temperate [témprɪt] *adj.* templado, moderado; sobrio.
temperature [témprətʃə] *s.* temperatura; **to have a —** tener calentura o fiebre.
tempest [témpɪst] *s.* tempestad.
tempestuous [tempéstʃʊəs] *adj.* tempestuoso, borrascoso.
temple [témpl] *s.* templo; sien.
temporal [témpərəl] *adj.* temporal.
temporarily [témpərerəlɪ] *adv.* temporalmente.
temporary [témpəreri] *adj.* temporal, transitorio, provisorio; interino.
tempt [tempt] *v.* tentar; incitar; provocar; atraer.
temptation [temptéʃən] *s.* tentación.
tempter [témptə] *s.* tentador.
tempting [témptɪŋ] *adj.* tentador, atractivo.
tenacious [tɪnéʃəs] *adj.* tenaz, aferrado.
tenacity [tɪnǽsətɪ] *s.* tenacidad; aferramiento; tesón.
tenant [ténənt] *s.* inquilino, arrendatario.
tend [tend] *v.* cuidar, vigilar, guardar; atender; tender, inclinarse.
tendency [téndənsɪ] *s.* tendencia; propensión.
tender [téndə] *adj.* tierno; delicado;

sensible; **tender-hearted** de corazón tierno; *s.* oferta, ofrecimiento; ténder (*de un tren*); lancha (*de auxilio*); cuidador, vigilante; **legal —** moneda corriente; *v.* ofrecer.
tenderloin [téndəlɔɪn] *s.* filete.
tenderness [téndənɪs] *s.* ternura, terneza; delicadeza.
tendon [téndən] *s.* tendón.
tendril [téndrɪl] *s.* zarcillo (*tallito de una planta trepadora*).
tenement [ténəmənt] *s.* casa de vecindad.
tennis [ténɪs] *s.* tenis; — **court** cancha de tenis.
tenor [ténə] *s.* tenor; significado; — **voice** voz de tenor.
tense [tens] *adj.* tenso; tirante; *s.* tiempo (*del verbo*).
tension [ténʃən] *s.* tensión; tirantez.
tent [tent] *s.* tienda de campaña; pabellón; *v.* acampar.
tentacle [téntək] *s.* tentáculo.
tentative [téntətɪv] *adj.* tentativo.
tepid [tépɪd] *adj.* tibio.
term [tɜm] *s.* término; período; plazo; sesión; -**s** términos, expresiones, palabras; condiciones; **to be on good —s** estar en buenas relaciones; **not to be on speaking —s** no hablarse, no dirigirse la palabra; **to come to —s** ajustarse, ponerse de acuerdo; *v.* nombrar, llamar, denominar.
terminal [tɜmən] *adj.* terminal, final, último; *s.* término, fin; estación terminal; **electric —** toma de corriente, borne (*de aparato eléctrico*).
terminate [tɜmənet] *v.* terminar, acabar.
termination [tɜmənéʃən] *s.* terminación, fin; desinencia (*gramatical*).
terrace [térɪs] *s.* terraplén; terraza, terrado; *v.* terraplenar.
terrestrial [təréstrɪəl] *adj.* terrestre, terreno, terrenal.
terrible [térəbl] *adj.* terrible; **terribly** *adv.* terriblemente.
terrier [térɪə] *s.* perro de busca.
terrific [tərífɪk] *adj.* terrífico.
terrify [térəfaɪ] *v.* aterrar, aterrorizar.
territory [tératorɪ] *s.* territorio.
terror [térə] *s.* terror, espanto.
test [test] *s.* prueba, ensayo, experimento; comprobación; examen; — **tube** probeta, tubo de ensayo; **to undergo a —** sufrir una prueba; *v.* probar, ensayar, comprobar, experimentar; poner a prueba; examinar.
testament [téstəmənt] *s.* testamento.
testify [téstəfaɪ] *v.* atestiguar, atestar.
testimony [téstəmonɪ] *s.* testimonio.

text [tɛkst] s. texto.

textbook [tɛkstbʊk] s. texto, libro de texto.

textile [tékstl] adj. textil; de tejidos; — **mill** fábrica de tejidos; s. tejido, materia textil.

texture [tékstʃɚ] s. textura, contextura; tejido.

than [ðæn] conj. que; **more — once** más de una vez; **more — he knows** más de lo que él sabe.

thank [θæŋk] v. dar gracias, agradecer; **— heaven!** ¡gracias a Dios!; **— you** gracias; **to have oneself to — for** tener la culpa de; ser responsable de; **-s** s. pl. gracias.

thankful [θǽŋkfəl] adj. agradecido; **-ly** adv. agradecidamente, con agradecimiento, con gratitud.

thankfulness [θǽŋkfəlnɪs] s. gratitud, agradecimiento.

thankless [θǽŋklɪs] adj. ingrato; **— task** tarea ingrata o infructuosa.

thanksgiving [θæŋksgívɪŋ] s. acción de gracias; **— Day** día de acción de gracias.

that [ðæt] adj. ese, esa, aquel, aquella; **— one** ése, ésa, aquél, aquélla; pron. ése, ésa, eso, aquél, aquélla, aquello; pron. rel. que; **— is** es decir; **— of** el de, la de, lo de; **— which** el que, la que, lo que; conj. que; para que, a fin de que; **so —** para que; de modo que, a fin de que, de suerte que, de tal manera que; adv. tan; **— far** tan lejos; hasta allá, hasta allí; **— long** así de largo; de este tamaño; tanto tiempo.

thatch [θætʃ] s. paja (para techar); v. techar con paja; **-ed roof** techumbre o techo de paja.

thaw [θɔ] v. deshelar(se), derretir(se); volverse más tratable o amistoso; s. deshielo, derretimiento.

the [delante de consonante ðə; delante de vocal ðɪ] art. el, la; lo; los, las; adv. **— more . . . — less** cuanto más . . . tanto menos; mientras más . . . tanto menos.

theater [θíətɚ] s. teatro.

theatrical [θɪætrɪk̩l] adj. teatral.

thee [ðɪ] pron. te.

theft [θɛft] s. hurto, robo.

their [ðɛr] adj. su (sus), de ellos, de ellas.

theirs [ðɛrz] pron. pos. suyo (suya, suyos, suyas), de ellos, de ellas; el suyo (la suya, los suyos, las suyas); el (la, los, las) de ellos; **a friend of —** un amigo suyo, un amigo de ellos.

them [ðɛm] pron. los, las; les; ellos, ellas (con preposición).

theme [θim] s. tema; ensayo.

themselves [ðəmsélvz] pron. ellos mismos, ellas mismas; se (como reflexivo); **to —** a sí mismos; véase herself.

then [ðɛn] adv. entonces; en aquel tiempo; en aquella ocasión; después, luego, en seguida; conj. pues, en tal caso; **now —** ahora bien; **now and —** de vez en cuando, de cuando en cuando; **now . . . — ** ora . . . ora; ya . . . ya; **well —** conque, pues entonces; ahora bien.

thence [ðɛns] adv. desde allí, de allí; desde entonces, desde aquel tiempo; por eso, por esa razón; **—forth** de allí en adelante, desde entonces.

theological [θɪəlɑ́dʒɪk̩l] adj. teológico; teologal.

theology [θɪɑ́ləɑdʒɪ] s. teología.

theoretical [θiərɛ́tɪk̩l] adj. teórico.

theory [θíərɪ] s. teoría.

there [ðɛr] adv. allí, allá, ahí; **— is, — are** hay; **— followed an argument** siguió una disputa.

thereabouts [ðɛrəbáʊts] adv. por allí, por ahí; aproximadamente.

thereafter [ðɛrǽftɚ] adv. después de eso, de allí en adelante.

thereby [ðɛrbái] adv. en relación con eso; así, de ese modo; por allí cerca.

therefore [ðɛ́rfor] adv. por eso, por consiguiente, por lo tanto.

therein [ðɛrín] adv. en eso, en ello; allí dentro.

thereof [ðɛrɑ́v] adv. de eso, de ello.

thereon [ðɛrɑ́n] adv. encima; encima de (o sobre) él, ella, ello, etc.

thereupon [ðɛrəpɑ́n] adv. luego, después, en eso, en esto; por consiguiente, por eso, por lo tanto; encima de (o sobre) él, ella, ello, etc.

therewith [ðɛrwíθ] adv. con eso, con ello, con esto; luego, en seguida.

thermometer [θəmɑ́mətɚ] s. termómetro.

thermos [θɚ́məs] : **— bottle** termos.

these [ðiz] adj. estos, estas; pron. éstos, éstas.

thesis [θísɪs] s. tesis.

they [ðe] pron. ellos, ellas.

thick [θɪk] adj. espeso; denso; tupido; grueso; torpe, estúpido; **— voice** voz ronca; **one inch —** una pulgada de espesor; adv. véase **thickly**; **thick-headed** cabezudo, testarudo; estúpido; **thick-set** grueso, rechoncho; **thick-skinned** insensible; que no se avergüenza fácilmente; s. espesor; densidad, lo más denso; **the — of the crowd** lo más denso de la muchedumbre; **the — of the fight** lo más reñido del combate; **through — and thin** por toda suerte de penalidades.

thicken [ɵíkən] v. espesar(se); engrosar; **the plot -s** se complica el enredo.

thicket [ɵíkɪt] s. espesura, maleza, matorral, *Am.* manigua.

thickly [ɵíklɪ] adv. espesamente; densamente.

thickness [ɵíknɪs] s. espesor; espesura, grueso, grosor; densidad.

thief [ɵif] s. ladrón.

thieve [ɵiv] v. hurtar, robar.

thieves [ɵivz] pl. de **thief.**

thigh [ɵaɪ] s. muslo.

thimble [ɵímbl] s. dedal.

thin [ɵɪn] adj. delgado; flaco; ralo; escaso; tenue, fino; transparente; débil; aguado; **— broth** caldo aguado; **— hair** pelo ralo; v. adelgazar(se); enflaquecer; aguar (*el caldo*); **to — out** realear (*el pelo*); ralear o aclarar (*un bosque*).

thine [ðaɪn] pron. pos. tuyo (tuya, tuyos, tuyas); el tuyo (la tuya, los tuyos, las tuyas); adj. tu, tus.

thing [ɵɪŋ] s. cosa; **no such —** nada de eso; **that is the —** to do eso es lo que debe hacerse; eso es lo debido.

think [ɵɪŋk] v. pensar; creer, juzgar; opinar; **to — it over** pensarlo; **to — of** pensar en; pensar de; **to — up an excuse** urdir una excusa; **to — well of** tener buena opinión de; **— nothing of it** no haga Vd. caso de ello, no le dé Vd. importancia; **what do you — of her?** ¿qué piensa Vd. de ella?; **to my way of —ing** a mi modo de ver.

thinker [ɵíŋkə] s. pensador.

thinly [ɵínlɪ] adv. delgadamente; escasamente.

thinness [ɵínnɪs] s. delgadez; flacura; raleza (*del cabello*); enrarecimiento (*del aire*).

third [ɵɜd] adj. tercero; s. tercio, tercera parte.

thirst [ɵɜst] s. sed; anhelo, ansia; v. tener sed; **to — for** tener sed de; anhelar, ansiar.

thirsty [ɵɜ́stɪ] adj. sediento; **to be —** tener sed.

this [ðɪs] adj. este, esta; pron. éste, ésta, esto.

thistle [ɵísl] s. abrojo; cardo.

thither [ɵíðə] adv. allá, hacia allá, para allá.

tho [ðo] = **though.**

thong [ɵɔŋ] s. correa, tira de cuero, *Am.* guasca.

thorn [ɵɔrn] s. espina, púa; espino; abro-

jo.

thorny [ɵɔ́rnɪ] adj. espinoso; arduo, difícil.

thorough [ɵɜ́o] adj. completo, entero, cabal, cumplido, acabado; esmerado.

thoroughbred [ɵɜ́obred] adj. de casta pura, de raza pura; bien nacido; s. animal o persona de casta; caballo de casta.

thoroughfare [ɵɜ́ofer] s. vía pública, carretera, camino real; pasaje.

thoroughly [ɵɜ́olɪ] adj. completamente, enteramente, cabalmente; a fondo.

those [ðoz] adj. esos, esas, aquellos, aquellas; pron. ésos, ésas, aquéllos, aquéllas; **— of** los de, las de; **— which** los que, las que; aquellos que; **— who** los que, las que, quienes.

thou [ðaʊ] pron. tú.

though [ðo] conj. aunque, si bien, bien que; aun cuando; sin embargo; **as —** como si.

thought [ɵɔt] s. pensamiento; idea, intención; reflexión, meditación; consideración; cuidado; **to be lost in —** estar abstraído; **to give it no —** no pensar en ello, no darle importancia, no hacerle caso; pret. & p.p. de **think.**

thoughtful [ɵɔ́tfəl] adj. pensativo; considerado; atento, solícito, cuidadoso; **to be — of others** pensar en los demás, tener consideración o solicitud por los demás; **-ly** adv. con reflexión; consideradamente, con consideración; con solicitud.

thoughtfulness [ɵɔ́tfəlnɪs] s. consideración, atención, cuidado, solicitud.

thoughtless [ɵɔ́tlɪs] adj. inconsiderado; descuidado; irreflexivo, atolondrado; **-ly** adv. inconsideradamente, sin consideración; sin reflexión; sin pensar; descuidadamente, irreflexivamente, atolondradamente.

thoughtlessness [ɵɔ́tlɪsnɪs] s. irreflexión, inadvertencia, descuido; atolondramiento.

thrash [ɵræʃ] v. trillar, desgranar (*las mieses*); zurrar, azotar; **to — around** revolcarse, agitarse, menearse; **to — out a matter** ventilar un asunto.

thread [ɵred] s. hilo; hebra, fibra; **screw —** rosca de tornillo; v. ensartar, enhebrar; **to — a screw** roscar un tornillo; **to — one's way through a crowd** colarse por entre la muchedumbre.

threadbare [ɵrédber] adj. raído, gastado.

threat [ɵret] s. amenaza; amago.

threaten [ərétn] v. amenazar; amagar.

threatening [ərétnıŋ] adj. amenazante, amenazador.

thresh [ərɛʃ] véase **thrash**.

threshold [əréʃold] s. umbral, entrada.

threw [əru] pret. de to **throw**.

thrice [ərais] adv. tres veces.

thrift [ərift] s. economía, frugalidad.

thrifty [əríftı] adj. económico, frugal; próspero.

thrill [əril] v. emocionar(se), conmover-(se); estremecerse de emoción, sobre-excitarse; s. emoción viva, estremecimiento emotivo, sobreexcitación.

thrive [əraıv] v. medrar, prosperar; florecer.

thriven [ərívən] p.p. de to **thrive**.

throat [ərot] s. garganta.

throb [ərɑb] v. latir, pulsar, palpitar; s. latido, palpitación.

throe [əro] s. agonía; congoja.

throne [əron] s. trono.

throng [ərɔŋ] s. muchedumbre, multitud, tropel, gentío; v. agolparse, apiñarse; atestar.

throttle [ərɑ́tl] s. válvula reguladora, obturador, regulador; — lever palanca del obturador o regulador; v. ahogar; estrangular; to — down disminuir o reducir la velocidad.

through [əru] prep. por; a través de; por medio de; por conducto de; por entre; adv. de un lado a otro; de parte a parte, a través; de cabo a cabo; desde el principio hasta el fin; completamente, enteramente; loyal — and — leal a toda prueba; to be wet — estar empapado; estar mojado hasta los tuétanos; to carry a plan — llevar a cabo un plan; adj. directo, continuo; — ticket billete (Am. boleto) directo; — train tren rápido, tren de servicio directo; to be — with haber acabado con; no querer ocuparse más de.

throughout [əruáut] prep. por todo, por todas partes de; desde el principio hasta el fin de; — the year durante todo el año; adv. por todas partes; en todas partes; en todo, en todos respetos; desde el principio hasta el fin.

throve [ərov] pret. de to **thrive**.

throw [əro] v. tirar, arrojar, lanzar; echar; to — away tirar, arrojar; malgastar; to — down arrojar, echar por tierra, derribar; to — in gear engranar; to — in the clutch embragar; to — off a burden librarse o deshacerse de una carga; to — out echar fuera; expeler; to — out of gear

engranar; to — out of work privar de trabajo, quitar el empleo a; to — out the clutch desembragar; to — overboard echar al agua; to — up vomitar; s. tiro, tirada.

thrown [əron] p.p. de to **throw**.

thrush [ərʌʃ] s. tordo, zorzal.

thrust [ərʌst] s. meter; hincar, clavar; encajar; empujar; to — a task upon someone imponer una tarea a una persona, obligar a alguien a desempeñar un quehacer; to — aside echar o empujar a un lado; rechazar; to — in (o into) meter en, encajar en, intercalar en; to — out sacar; echar fuera; to — someone through with a sword atravesar a alguien de parte a parte con la espada; pret. & p.p. de to thrust; s. estocada, cuchillada, puñalada, lanzada; empuje, empujón o empellón; arremetida, acometida.

thud [əʌd] s. porrazo, golpazo, golpe sordo.

thug [əʌg] s. ladrón, salteador.

thumb [əʌm] s. pulgar; under the — of bajo el poder o influencia de; v. hojear (con el pulgar).

thumbtack [əʌ́mtæk] s. chinche.

thump [əʌmp] s. golpazo, porrazo, trastazo; golpe sordo; v. golpear, golpetear, aporrear, dar un porrazo.

thunder [əʌ́ndə] s. trueno; tronido; estruendo; v. tronar.

thunderbolt [əʌ́ndəbolt] s. rayo.

thundering [əʌ́ndərıŋ] adj. atronador.

thunderous [əʌ́ndərəs] adj. atronador, estruendoso.

thunderstorm [əʌ́ndəstɔrm] s. tronada, tormenta o tempestad de truenos.

Thursday [əɜ́zdı] s. jueves.

thus [ðʌs] adv. así; — far hasta aquí, hasta ahora, hasta hoy.

thwart [əwɔrt] v. frustrar; estorbar; impedir.

thy [ðaı] adj. tu, tus.

thyme [taım] s. tomillo.

thyself [ðaısélf] pron. tú mismo; a tí mismo; te (como reflexivo); véase herself.

tick [tık] s. tic tac; funda (de colchón o almohada); garrapata (insecto parásito); v. hacer tic tac (como un reloj); latir (el corazón); to — off marcar.

ticket [tíkıt] s. billete, Am. boleto; lista de candidatos (de un partido); balota (para votar); — office taquilla; despacho de boletos, Am. boletería.

tickle [tíkl] v. cosquillear, hacer cosquillas; sentir o tener cosquillas; halagar, gustarle a uno; to be -d to death morirse de gusto, estar muy contento; *s.* cosquilleo, cosquillas.

ticklish [tíklɪʃ] *adj.* cosquilloso; delicado, arriesgado, difícil.

tidbit [tídbɪt] *s.* bocado, bocadito, golosina.

tide [taɪd] *s.* marea; corriente; **Christmas** — navidades, temporada de navidad; *v.* **to** — **someone over a difficulty** ayudar a alguien durante una crisis o dificultad.

tidings [táɪdɪŋz] *s. pl.* noticias, nuevas.

tidy [táɪdɪ] *adj.* aseado, limpio, ordenado; **a** — **sum** una suma considerable; *v.* asear, arreglar, poner en orden; **to** — **oneself up** asearse.

tie [taɪ] *v.* atar, liar, ligar, amarrar; enlazar, vincular; empatar (*en juegos, carreras, etc.*); **to** — **tight** amarrar bien, apretar fuerte; **to** — **up the traffic** obstruir el tráfico; *s.* lazo, ligadura, atadura; enlace, vínculo; corbata; empate (*en carreras, juegos, etc.*); **railway** — traviesa, *Am.* durmiente o travesaño.

tier [tɪr] *s.* fila, hilera, ringlera.

tiger [táɪgə] *s.* tigre; — **cat** gato montés.

tight [taɪt] *adj.* apretado, ajustado, estrecho; hermético; firme, tieso, tirante; mezquino, tacaño; borracho; **to be in a** — **spot** estar en un aprieto; **to close** — apretar, cerrar herméticamente; **to hold on** — agarrarse bien; **it fits** — está muy estrecho o ajustado.

tighten [táɪtn] *v.* apretar; estrechar; estirar, poner tirante.

tightness [táɪtnɪs] *s.* estrechez; tirantez, tensión; mezquindad, tacañería.

tigress [táɪgrɪs] *s.* tigre hembra.

tile [taɪl] *s.* teja; baldosa, azulejo; — **roof** tejado; *v.* tejar, cubrir con tejas; cubrir con azulejos, embaldosar.

till [tɪl] *prep.* hasta; *conj.* hasta que; *v.* cultivar, labrar, arar; *s.* gaveta o cajón para el dinero.

tillage [tíləd̮ʒ] *s.* labranza, cultivo, labor.

tilt [tɪlt] *v.* ladeo, inclinación; declive; altercación, disputa; **at full** — **s** a toda velocidad; *v.* ladear(se), inclinar(se).

timber [tímbə] *s.* madera de construcción; maderaje; madero; viga.

time [taɪm] *s.* tiempo; hora; vez; plazo; **at** — **s** a veces; **at one and the same** — **s** a la vez; **at this** — ahora, al presente; **behind** — atrasado, retrasado; **from** — **to** — de vez en cuando; **in** — a tiempo; andando el tiempo; **on** — puntual; con puntualidad; **a tiempo;** a la hora debida; **several** — **s** varias veces; **to beat** — marcar el compás;

to buy on — comprar a plazo; **to have a good** — divertirse, pasar un buen rato; **what** — **is it?** ¿qué hora es?; *v.* cronometrar, medir el tiempo de; regular, poner en punto (*el reloj, el motor*); escoger el momento oportuno para.

timely [táɪmlɪ] *adj.* oportuno.

timepiece [táɪmpis] *s.* reloj; cronómetro.

timetable [táɪmtebl] *s.* itinerario, horario.

timid [tímɪd] *adj.* tímido.

timidity [tɪmídətɪ] *s.* timidez.

timorous [tímərəs] *adj.* timorato, tímido, miedoso.

tin [tɪn] *s.* estaño; hojalata, lata; cosa de hojalata; — **can** lata; — **foil** hoja de estaño; *v.* estañar, cubrir con estaño; enlatar.

tincture [tíŋktʃə] *s.* tintura; tinte; — **of iodine** tintura de yodo; *v.* tinturar, teñir.

tinder [tíndə] *s.* yesca.

tinge [tɪnd̮ʒ] *v.* teñir; matizar; *s.* tinte, matiz; dejo, saborcillo.

tingle [tíŋgl] *v.* hormiguear, sentir hormigueo; **to** — **with excitement** estremecerse de entusiasmo; *s.* hormigueo, picazón, comezón.

tinkle [tíŋkl] *v.* tintinear; hacer retintín; *s.* tintineo; retintín.

tinsel [tínsl] *s.* oropel; *adj.* de oropel.

tint [tɪnt] *s.* tinte, matiz; *v.* teñir, matizar.

tiny [táɪnɪ] *adj.* diminuto, menudo, chiquito, chiquitín.

tip [tɪp] *s.* punta, extremo, extremidad; propina; noticia o aviso secreto; *v.* ladear(se), inclinar(se); dar propina (a); **to** — **a person off** dar aviso secreto a; **to** — **one's hat** tocarse el sombrero; **to** — **over** volcar(se), voltear(se).

tipsy [típsɪ] *adj.* alumbrado, algo borracho; ladeado.

tiptoe [típto] *s.* punta del pie; **on** — de puntillas; *v.* andar de puntillas.

tire [taɪr] *s.* llanta, neumático, goma; **flat** — llanta o goma reventada; *v.* cansar(se), fatigar(se).

tired [taɪrd] *adj.* cansado, fatigado; — **out** extenuado de fatiga, rendido.

tireless [táɪrlɪs] *adj.* incansable, infatigable.

tiresome [táɪrsəm] *adj.* cansado, aburrido, pesado.

tissue [tíʃʊ] *s.* tejido; — **paper** papel de seda.

tithe [taɪð] *s.* diezmo.

title [táɪtl] *s.* título; — **page** portada.

to [tu] *prep.* a; hasta; hacia; para; — **try** — tratar de; esforzarse por; **a quarter** — **five** las cinco menos cuarto; **bills** — **be paid** cuentas por pagar; **frightened** — **death** muerto de susto; **from house** — **house** de casa en casa; **he has** — **go** tiene que ir; **near** — cerca de; **not** — **my knowledge** no que yo sepa; *adv.* — **and fro de acá para allá; to come** — volver en sí.

toad [tod] *s.* sapo o escuerzo.

toast [tost] *v.* tostar(se); brindar por, beber a la salud de; *s.* tostada; brindis.

toaster [tóstə] *s.* tostador.

tobacco [təbǽko] *s.* tabaco.

today [tədé] *adv.* hoy; hoy día.

toe [to] *s.* dedo del pie; punta (*de la media, del zapato, etc.*); *v.* **to** — **in** andar con la punta de los pies para dentro.

toenail [tónel] *s.* uña del dedo del pie.

together [təgéðə] *adv.* juntamente; a un mismo tiempo, a la vez; juntos; — **with** junto con; **all** — juntos; **en junto; to call** — convocar, juntar; **to come** — juntarse, unirse; ponerse de acuerdo; **to walk** — andar juntos.

toil [toil] *v.* afanarse, trafagar, atarearse; *s.* esfuerzo, trabajo, faena, fatiga.

toilet [tóilit] *s.* retrete, excusado, común, *Am.* inodoro; — **articles** artículos de tocador; — **case** neceser; — **paper** papel de excusado, papel higiénico.

token [tókən] *s.* señal, símbolo; prenda; recuerdo; prueba, muestra; ficha (*de metal*); — **payment** pago nominal.

told [told] *pret.* & *p.p.* de **to tell**.

tolerance [tólərəns] *s.* tolerancia.

tolerant [tólərənt] *adj.* tolerante.

tolerate [tóləret] *v.* tolerar.

toleration [tóləréʃən] *s.* tolerancia.

toll [tol] *s.* doble, tañido (*de las campanas*); peaje; portazgo; — **bridge** puente de peaje; —**gate** barrera de peaje; **to pay** — pagar peaje o portazgo; *v.* tañer, doblar (*las campanas*).

tomato [təméto] *s.* tomate, *Am.* jitomate.

tomb [tum] *s.* tumba.

tombstone [túmston] *s.* lápida sepulcral.

tomcat [támkæt] *s.* gato.

tomorrow [təmóro] *adv.* mañana; — **morning** mañana por la mañana; — **noon** mañana al mediodía; **day after** — pasado mañana.

ton [tʌn] *s.* tonelada.

tone [ton] *s.* tono; sonido; timbre; *v.* dar tono a, modificar el tono de; **to** — **down** bajar de tono; suavizar; **to** — **down one's voice** moderar la voz; **to** — **in well with** armonizar con, entonar bien con; **to** — **up** subir de tono; tonificar, vigorizar.

tongs [tɔŋz] *s. pl.* tenazas.

tongue [tʌŋ] *s.* lengua; idioma; **to be tongue-tied** tener trabada la lengua.

tonic [tánik] *s.* & *adj.* tónico.

tonight [tənáit] *adv.* esta noche, a la noche.

tonnage [tʌnidʒ] *s.* tonelaje.

tonsil [táns] *s.* amígdala.

tonsilitis [tansəláitis] *s.* amigdalitis.

too [tu] *adv.* también; demasiado; — **many** demasiados; — **much** demasiado; **it is** — **bad!** ¡es una lástima!

took [tuk] *pret.* de **to take**.

tool [tul] *s.* instrumento; herramienta.

toot [tut] *v.* tocar o sonar la bocina; pitar; tocar (*un cuerno, trompa o trompeta*); **to** — **one's own horn** alabarse, cantar sus propias alabanzas; *s.* toque o sonido (*de bocina, trompeta, etc.*); silbido, pitido; pitazo (*de locomotora*).

tooth [tuθ] *s.* diente; muela; — **mark** dentellada; **to fight** — **and nail** luchar a brazo partido; **to have a sweet** — ser amigo de golosinas.

toothache [túeek] *s.* dolor de muelas.

toothbrush [túebrʌʃ] *s.* cepillo de dientes.

toothed [tuθt] *adj.* dentado.

toothless [túθlis] *adj.* desdentado.

toothpaste [túθpest] *s.* pasta para los dientes, pasta dentífrica.

toothpick [túθpik] *s.* mondadientes, palillo de dientes.

top [tap] *s.* cumbre, cima; copete; cúspide; tope; pináculo; remate; cabeza; superficie; copa (*de árbol*); tapa, cubierta; trompo; **at the** — **of his class** a la cabeza de su clase; **at the** — **of one's voice** a voz en cuello; **filled up to the** — lleno hasta el tope; **from** — **to bottom** de arriba abajo; **from** — **to toe** de pies a cabeza; **on** — **of** encima de, sobre; *adj.* superior; más alto; —**coat** abrigo, sobretodo; **at** — **speed** a velocidad máxima; *v.* coronar; exceder; sobresalir, sobrepujar; rematar; **to** — **off** rematar; terminar.

topaz [tópæz] *s.* topacio.

toper [tópə] *s.* bebedor, borrachín.

topic [tápik] *s.* tema, asunto, materia, tópico.

topmost [tápmost] *adj.* más alto; superior.

topple [tápl] *v.* echar abajo, derribar; volcar; **to** — **over** venirse abajo; volcarse.

topsy-turvy [tápsitʌvi] *adj.* & *adv.* patas arriba; en confusión; trastornado; enrevesado, al revés.

torch [tortʃ] s. antorcha; **blow** — soplete.

tore [tor] pret. de to tear.

torment [tórment] s. tormento; [tɔrmént] v. atormentar; afligir.

torn [torn] p.p. de to tear roto, rompido, rasgado.

tornado [tornédo] s. tornado.

torpedo [torpído] s. torpedo; — **boat** torpedero; v. torpedear.

torrent [tɔ́rənt] s. torrente.

torrid [tɔ́rɪd] adj. tórrido.

tortoise [tɔ́rtəs] s. tortuga.

tortuous [tɔ́rtʃʊəs] adj. tortuoso.

torture [tɔ́rtʃər] s. tortura, tormento; v. torturar, atormentar.

toss [tɔs] v. tirar, echar, arrojar, lanzar; menear(se); cabecear (un buque); **to** — **aside** echar a un lado; desechar; **to** — **up** echar para arriba; aventar; s. tiro, tirada; meneo, sacudida.

tot [tɔt] s. chiquitín, chiquitina, chiquitico, chiquitica, niñito, niñita, nene, nena.

total [tótl] adj. & s. total.

totalitarian [totælətériən] adj. totalitario.

totter [tátə] v. tambalear(se), bambolear(se); estar para desplomarse.

touch [tʌtʃ] v. tocar; palpar, tentar; conmover, enternecer; compararse con, igualar; **to** — **at a port** hacer escala en un puerto; **to** — **off an explosive** prender la mecha de un explosivo; **to** — **up** retocar; s. toque; tacto, sentido del tacto; tiento; —**stone** piedra de toque; **a** — **of fever** algo de calentura; **to keep in** — **with** mantener(se) en comunicación con.

touching [tʌ́tʃɪŋ] adj. conmovedor, enternecedor.

touchy [tʌ́tʃɪ] adj. quisquilloso, susceptible, sensible, sensitivo.

tough [tʌf] adj. correoso; fuerte; firme; duro; arduo, difícil; terco; empedernido, malvado.

toughen [tʌ́fn] v. curtir(se); endurecer(se), empedernir(se); hacer(se) correoso.

toughness [tʌ́fnɪs] s. dureza; correosidad; flexibilidad; tenacidad; resistencia; dificultad.

tour [tʊr] s. viaje, excursión; vuelta; jira; v. viajar por; recorrer; hacer una jira; hacer un viaje de turismo.

tourist [túrɪst] s. turista.

tournament [túrnəmənt] s. torneo; certamen, concurso.

tow [to] v. remolcar; s. remolque; —**boat** remolcador; —**rope** cuerda de remolque; **to take in** — remolcar, llevar a remolque.

toward [tord] prep. hacia; rumbo a; alrededor de; para, para con; — **four o'clock** a eso de las cuatro.

towards [tordz] = **toward.**

towel [táʊl] s. toalla.

tower [táʊə] s. torre; torreón; **bell** — campanario; v. sobresalir, sobrepujar; destacarse, descollar; elevarse.

towering [táʊrɪŋ] adj. encumbrado; elevado, muy alto; sobresaliente.

town [taʊn] s. población, ciudad, pueblo, aldea; municipio; — **hall** ayuntamiento.

township [táʊnʃɪp] s. unidad primaria de gobierno local; sección de seis millas cuadradas (en terrenos públicos).

toxin [táksɪn] s. toxina.

toy [tɔɪ] s. juguete; adj. de juego, de juguete; pequeñito; v. jugar, juguetear.

trace [tres] s. señal, indicio, vestigio; huella, rastro; tirante (de una guarnición); v. trazar; calcar; rastrear, seguir la huella de; rebuscar, investigar; **to** — **the source of** remontarse al origen de, buscar el origen de.

trachea [trékɪə] s. tráquea.

track [træk] s. pista, huella, rastro; pisada; vereda, senda; vía; — **sports** deportes de pista; **race** — pista; **railroad** — rieles, vía del tren, vía férrea o ferrovía; **to be off the** — estar extraviado, estar descarrilado; **to be on the** — **of** rastrear, ir siguiendo la pista de; **to keep** — **of** llevar la cuenta de; no perder de vista; v. rastrear, seguir la huella de; **to** — **down** coger, atrapar; descubrir; **to** — **in mud** traer lodo en los pies, entrar con los pies enlodados.

tract [trækt] s. área; terreno; folleto; **digestive** — canal digestivo.

traction [trǽkʃən] s. tracción.

tractor [trǽktə] s. tractor.

trade [tred] s. comercio; trato, negocio; trueque, cambio; oficio; clientela, parroquianos; — **school** escuela de artes y oficios; — **union** gremio obrero o de obreros; v. comerciar, negociar, traficar, tratar; trocar, cambiar.

trademark [trédmark] s. marca de fábrica.

trader [tréda] s. mercader, comerciante, negociante, traficante.

tradesman [trédzmən] s. mercader, comerciante, traficante; tendero.

tradition [trədíʃən] s. tradición.

traditional [trədíʃənl] adj. tradicional.

traffic [trǽfɪk] s. tráfico; tráfago; tránsito; circulación; v. traficar, comerciar, negociar.

tragedy [trǽdʒədɪ] s. tragedia.

tragic [trǽdʒɪk] adj. trágico.

trail [trel] s. pista, rastro, huella; senda, sendero, trocha, vereda; cola (de vestido); v. arrastrar(se); rastrear, seguir la pista de; andar detrás de; **to — behind** ir rezagado, rezagarse.

train [tren] s. tren; cola (de vestido); séquito, comitiva; v. amaestrar(se), ejercitar(se); adiestrar(se) o adestrar(se), Am. entrenar(se); educar; disciplinar (tropas); apuntar (un cañón).

trainer [trénə] s. amaestrador; Am. entrenador.

training [trénɪŋ] s. adiestramiento, disciplina, Am. entrenamiento; educación; **— camp** campo de entrenamiento o práctica.

trait [tret] s. rasgo, característica; cualidad.

traitor [trétə] s. traidor.

tram [træm] s. vagoneta (de una mina de carbón).

tramp [træmp] v. pisotear; andar a pie; vagabundear; s. vago, vagabundo; caminata, marcha; pisadas.

trample [trǽmpl] v. pisar, hollar, pisotear; **to — on** pisotear, hollar; s. pisadas.

trance [træns] s. rapto, arrobamiento, enajenamiento, éxtasis; **to be in a —** estar arrobado, estar enajenado; estar distraído o ensimismado.

tranquil [trǽnkwɪl] adj. tranquilo.

tranquillity [trænkwílətɪ] s. tranquilidad.

transact [trænsǽkt] v. tramitar, despachar, llevar a cabo.

transaction [trænsǽkʃən] s. transacción, trato, negocio; trámite; negociación; **-s actas;** memorias.

transatlantic [trænsətlǽntɪk] adj. transatlántico.

transcend [trænsénd] v. trascender, ir más allá de.

transcontinental [trænskɑntənéntl] adj. transcontinental.

transcribe [trænskráɪb] v. transcribir.

transcript [trǽnskrɪpt] s. transcripción, copia.

transfer [trǽnsfɜ] s. transferencia; traslado; traspaso; transbordo; **— of ownership** cesión o traspaso de propiedad; **streetcar —** transferencia, contraseña, cupón de pasaje; [trænsfɜ́] v. transferir; trasbordar (de un tren a otro), cambiar (de tren, de tranvía); traspasar (propiedad), trasladar.

transfigure [trænsfígjə] v. transfigurar.

transform [trænsfórm] v. transformar(se).

transformation [trænsfəméʃən] s. transformación.

transgress [trænsgrés] v. transgredir, violar, quebrantar (una ley); pecar; **to — the bounds of** traspasar los límites de.

transgression [trænsgréʃən] s. transgresión; violación de una ley; pecado.

transgressor [trænsgrésə] s. transgresor.

transient [trǽnʃənt] s. transeúnte; adj. transeúnte; transitorio, pasajero.

transit [trǽnsɪt] s. tránsito; **in —** en tránsito, de paso.

transition [trænzíʃən] s. transición; tránsito, paso.

transitive [trǽnsətɪv] adj. transitivo.

transitory [trǽnsətɔrɪ] adj. transitorio, pasajero.

translate [trænslét] v. traducir, verter, trasladar.

translation [trænsléʃən] s. traducción, versión; translación (de un lugar a otro).

translator [trænslétə] s. traductor.

translucent [trænslúsnt] adj. translúcido; **to be —** traslucirse.

transmission [trænsmíʃən] s. transmisión; caja de velocidades.

transmit [trænsmít] v. transmitir; emitir.

transmitter [trænsmítə] s. transmisor; emisor.

transom [trǽnsəm] s. montante.

transparent [trænspérənt] adj. transparente.

transplant [trænsplént] v. trasplantar.

transport [trǽnsport] s. transporte; acarreo; éxtasis; **— plane** aeroplano de transporte; [trænspórt] v. transportar acarrear; **to be -ed with joy** estar enajenado de placer.

transportation [trænspətéʃən] s. transportación, transporte; boleto, pasaje.

transpose [trænspóz] v. transponer.

transverse [trænsvɜ́s] adj. transverso, transversal, puesto de través.

trap [træp] s. trampa, lazo, red; **— door** trampa; **mouse —** ratonera; v. entrampar, coger con trampa; atrapar.

trapeze [træpíz] s. trapecio.

trappings [trǽpɪŋz] s. pl. arreos, jaeces, guarniciones.

trash [træʃ] s. basura; hojarasca; cachivaches; gentuza, plebe.

travel [trǽvl] v. viajar; viajar por; recorrer; s. viaje; tráfico.

traveler [trǽvlə] s. viajero.

traveling [trǽvlɪŋ] adj. de viaje, para

viaje; — **expenses** gastos de viaje; — **salesman** agente viajero, viajante de comercio.

traverse [trǽvəs] v. atravesar, cruzar; recorrer; s. travesaño.

travesty [trǽvɪstɪ] s. parodia; v. parodiar, falsear.

tray [tre] s. bandeja; batea.

treacherous [trétʃərəs] adj. traicionero, traidor, alevoso.

treachery [trétʃərɪ] s. traición, perfidia, alevosía.

tread [trɛd] v. pisar, hollar; pisotear; andar á pie, caminar; s. paso; pisada, huella; Am. pise (de una rueda); tire — rodadura del neumático, Am. banda rodante.

treason [trízn̩] s. traición.

treasonable [tríznəbl] adj. traidor, traicionero.

treasure [tréʒə] s. tesoro; v. atesorar.

treasurer [tréʒərə] s. tesorero.

treasury [tréʒərɪ] s. tesorería; tesoro, erario; **Secretary of the Treasury** ministro de hacienda.

treat [trit] v. tratar; curar; convidar, invitar; s. obsequio, agasajo, convite; placer, gusto.

treatise [trítɪs] s. tratado.

treatment [trítmənt] s. trato; **medical** — tratamiento médico.

treaty [trítɪ] s. tratado, pacto, convenio.

treble [trébl] adj. triple; — **voice** voz atiplada; s. tiple; v. triplicar.

tree [tri] s. árbol; **apple** — manzano; **family** — árbol genealógico; **shoe** — horma de zapato; **to be up a** — estar subido a un árbol; estar en un gran aprieto; estar perplejo.

treeless [trílɪs] adj. pelado, sin árboles, despoblado de árboles.

treetop [trítɑp] s. copa de árbol.

trellis [trélɪs] s. emparrado, enrejado.

tremble [trémbl] v. temblar; estremecerse; s. temblor; estremecimiento.

tremendous [triméndəs] adj. tremendo.

tremor [trémə] s. temblor.

tremulous [trémjələs] adj. trémulo; tembloroso.

trench [trentʃ] s. trinchera; zanja, foso.

trend [trend] s. tendencia; rumbo, dirección.

trespass [tréspəs] v. invadir, traspasar; violar, infringir; pecar; **to — on property** meterse sin derecho en la propiedad ajena; **no -ing** prohibida la entrada; s. transgresión; pecado.

tress [tres] s. trenza; bucle.

trial [tráɪəl] s. ensayo, prueba; tentativa; aflicción; juicio, proceso; — **flight** vuelo de prueba.

triangle [tráɪæŋgl] s. triángulo.

triangular [traɪǽŋgjələ] adj. triangular.

tribe [traɪb] s. tribu.

tribulation [trɪbjəléʃən] s. tribulación.

tribunal [trɪbjún̩] s. tribunal, juzgado.

tributary [trɪbjətɛrɪ] adj. & s. tributario.

tribute [trɪbjut] s. tributo; homenaje.

trick [trɪk] s. treta; suerte; maña, ardid, trampa; travesura; baza (en el juego de naipes); **to be up to one's old -s** hacer de las suyas; v. embaucar, trampear, hacer trampa; burlar; **to — oneself up** componerse, emperifollarse.

trickery [trɪkərɪ] s. engaños, malas mañas, astucia.

trickle [trɪkl] v. gotear; escurrir; s. goteo.

tricky [trɪkɪ] adj. tramposo, Am. mañero; intrincado, complicado.

tried [traɪd] p.p. de to try & adj. probado.

trifle [tráɪfl] s. fruslería, friolera, nadería, nonada; bagatela; v. chancear(se), bromear; jugar, juguetear.

trigger [trɪgə] s. gatillo (de pistola, rifle, etc.).

trill [trɪl] v. trinar; **to — the r** pronunciar la erre doble; s. trino.

trim [trɪm] v. guarnecer, adornar; recortar; podar, mondar; despabilar (una vela); ganarle a uno (en el juego); **to — up** adornar, componer; adj. aseado, limpio, pulcro, acicalado; s. adorno, franja, ribete, guarnición; **to be in — for** estar en buena salud para; estar bien entrenado para.

trimming [trɪmɪŋ] s. adorno, aderezo, guarnición; orla, ribete, franja; paliza, zurra; **-s** adornos; accesorios; recortes.

trinket [trɪŋkɪt] s. chuchería, baratija.

trip [trɪp] s. viaje, travesía; recorrido, jira; tropezón; v. tropezar; dar un traspié; equivocarse; hacer tropezar, hacer caer; saltar, brincar, corretear.

triple [trɪpl] adj. & s. triple; v. triplicar.

trite [traɪt] adj. trillado, trivial, vulgar.

triumph [tráɪəmf] s. triunfo; v. triunfar.

triumphal [traɪʌmfl] adj. triunfal.

triumphant [traɪʌmfənt] adj. triunfante; **-ly** adv. triunfantemente, en triunfo.

trivial [trɪvjəl] adj. trivial, insignificante.

trod [trɑd] pret. & p.p. de to tread.

trodden [trɑdn̩] p.p. de to tread.

trolley [trɑlɪ] s. trole; tranvía de trole.

trombone [trɑmbon] s. trombón.

troop [trup] s. tropa; cuadrilla.

trophy [trófɪ] s. trofeo.

tropic [trɑpɪk] s. trópico; adj. tropical.

tropical [trápɪkl̩] *adj.* tropical.

trot [trat] *v.* trotar; hacer trotar; *s.* trote.

trouble [trʌ́bl̩] *v.* perturbar, turbar; molestar, incomodar; afligir; preocupar(se); **don't — to come** no se moleste Vd. en venir; *s.* pena, aflicción; inquietud, perturbación; dificultad; molestia; **panne**, avería, accidente (*a un mecanismo*); **heart —** enfermedad del corazón; **to be in —** estar en un aprieto o apuro; **it is not worth the —** no vale la pena.

troublemaker [trʌ́blmekə] *s.* agitador, alborotador, malcontento.

troublesome [trʌ́blsəm] *adj.* molesto, fastidioso, enfadoso, dificultoso; penoso

trough [trɔf] *s.* comedero; artesa; batea; **eaves —** canal, gotera del tejado; **drinking —** abrevadero.

trousers [tráuzəz] *s. pl.* pantalones.

trousseau [trúso] *s.* ajuar de novia.

trout [traut] *s.* trucha.

trowel [tráuəl] *s.* llana, *Am.* cuchara (*de albañil*).

truant [trúənt] *s.* novillero, holgazán (*que se ausenta de la escuela*); **to play — hacer novillos**, *Am.* capear la escuela, *Am.* pintar venado, *Am.* jubilarse; *adj.* vago, perezoso.

truce [trus] *s.* tregua.

truck [trʌk] *s.* camión; carretón; carreta; basura; baratijas; **garden —** hortalizas, legumbres y verduras; **— garden** hortaliza, huerta de legumbres; *v.* acarrear, transportar en camión o carretón.

trudge [trʌdʒ] *v.* caminar, caminar con esfuerzo; *s.* caminata.

true [tru] *adj.* verdadero; cierto; verídico; fiel; exacto, preciso; legítimo.

truly [trúlɪ] *adv.* verdaderamente, en verdad; en realidad; exactamente, correctamente; fielmente; **very — yours** su seguro servidor.

trump [trʌmp] *s.* triunfo (*en el juego de naipes*); *v.* matar con un triunfo (*en el juego de naipes*); **to — up an excuse** forjar o inventar una excusa.

trumpet [trʌ́mpɪt] *s.* trompeta; clarín; **ear —** trompetilla acústica; *v.* trompetear, tocar la trompeta; pregonar, divulgar.

trunk [trʌŋk] *s.* tronco; baúl; trompa (*de elefante*); **-s** calzones cortos (*para deportes*); **— line** línea principal.

trust [trʌst] *s.* confianza, fe; crédito; custodia; cargo; depósito; trust, sindicato o combinación monopolista; *v.* confiar; fiar en, tener confianza en, fiarse de; esperar; dar crédito a.

trustee [trʌstí] *s.* fideicomisario, depositario; **university -s** regentes universitarios; **board of -s** patronato consejo.

trustful [trʌ́stfəl] *adj.* confiado.

trusting [trʌ́stɪŋ] *adj.* confiado.

trustworthy [trʌ́stwɚðɪ] *adj.* fidedigno digno de confianza.

trusty [trʌ́stɪ] *adj.* fidedigno; honrado leal; *s.* presidiario fidedigno (*a quien se le conceden ciertos privilegios*).

truth [truθ] *s.* verdad.

truthful [trúθfəl] *adj.* verdadero; verídico; veraz.

truthfulness [trúθfəlnɪs] *s.* veracidad.

try [traɪ] *v.* probar, ensayar; hacer la prueba; poner a prueba; intentar, procurar; procesar, enjuiciar, formar causa (*a un acusado*); ver (*una causa*); **to — on** a suit probarse un traje; **to — one's luck** probar fortuna; **to — someone's patience** poner a prueba la paciencia de alguien; **to — to** tratar de, procurar, intentar; *s.* prueba, tentativa, ensayo.

trying [tráɪŋ] *adj.* molesto; penoso, irritante.

tub [tʌb] *s.* tina; bañera; baño; batea cuba; *v.* lavar en tina o cuba.

tube [tjub] *s.* tubo; inner **— cámara** (*de un neumático*); **radio —** lámpara o tubo de radio.

tubercular [tjubɚ́kjələ] *adj.* tuberculoso, tísico.

tuberculosis [tjubɚkjəlósɪs] *s.* tuberculosis.

tuck [tʌk] *v.* alforzar, hacer o echar alforzas; **to — in** meter en; **to — in bed** arropar; **to — under one's arm** meter bajo el brazo; **to — up** arremangar, recoger; **to — up one's sleeves** arremangarse; *s.* alforza.

Tuesday [tjúzdɪ] *s.* martes.

tuft [tʌft] *s.* penacho, copete; borla macizo (*de plantas*).

tug [tʌg] *v.* remolcar; jalar (halar) arrastrar; trabajar con esfuerzo; **to — at** tirar de, jalar; *s.* tirón, estirón, *Am.* jalón; remolcador; **—boat** remolcador **— of war** lucha a tirones de cuerda

tuition [tjuʃən] *s.* derechos de enseñanza, *Am.* colegiatura.

tulip [tjúləp] *s.* tulipán.

tumble [tʌ́mbl̩] *v.* caer(se); voltear; dar volteretas; **to — down** caerse; desplomarse; **to — into someone** tropezar con alguien; **to — over** volcar, tumbar, derribar; venirse abajo; *s.* caída, tumbo, vuelco, voltereta, *Am.* rodada; desorden.

tumbler [tʌmblə] s. vaso (de mesa); acróbata.

tumor [tjúmə] s. tumor.

tumult [tjúmʌlt] s. tumulto.

tumultuous [tjumʌltʃʊəs] adj. tumultuoso.

tuna [túnə] s. atún (pez).

tune [tjun] s. tonada; tono; armonía; **to be in** — estar a tono, estar afinado o templado; estar entonado; **to be out of** — estar desentonado o desafinado; desentonar; v. afinar, templar; armonizar; **to** — **in** sintonizar; **to** — **up the motor** poner al punto el motor.

tunic [tjúnɪk] s. túnica.

tunnel [tʌnl] s. túnel; socavón; v. socavar; abrir un túnel.

turbulent [tɜbjələnt] adj. turbulento; revoltoso.

turf [tɜf] s. césped; terrón de tierra (con césped); hipódromo, pista (para carreras).

Turk [tɜk] s. turco.

turkey [tɜkɪ] s. pavo, Am. guajolote (o guajalote).

Turkish [tɜkɪʃ] adj. turco; s. turco, idioma turco.

turmoil [tɜmɔɪl] s. alboroto; confusión.

turn [tɜn] v. volver(se); voltear(se); girar, dar vueltas, rodar, virar; tornear, labrar al torno; ponerse (pálido, rojo, etc.); **to** — **back** volver atrás; volverse, retroceder; devolver; **to** — **down** en entregar; recogerse, acostarse; **to** — **inside out** voltear o volver al revés; **to** — **into** convertir(se) en; **to** — **off** apagar (la luz); cortar (el agua, el gas, etc.); **to** — **off the main road** salirse o desviarse de la carretera; **to** — **on encender** (la luz); abrir la llave (del gas, del agua); **to** — **on someone** volverse contra, acometer o caer sobre alguien; **to** — **out** apagar (la luz); echar, expulsar, arrojar; producir; **to** — **out well** salir o resultar bien; **to** — **over** volcar(se), voltear(se); doblar; revolver (en la mente); entregar; **to** — **over and over** dar repetidas vueltas; **to** — **sour** agriarse, fermentarse; **to** — **the corner** doblar la esquina; **to** — **to** acudir a; volverse a; dirigirse a; convertir(se) en; **to** — **to the left** doblar o torcer a la izquierda; **to** — **up** aparecer; **to** — **up one's nose at** desdeñar; hacer ascos a; **to** — **up one's sleeves** arremangarse; **to** — **upside down** trastornar; volcar; **it** — **s my stomach** me da asco o náusea;

s. vuelta; revolución; giro; recodo (del camino); turno; virada, cambio de rumbo; — **of mind** actitud mental; **at every** — a cada paso; **to be one's** — tocarle a uno; **to do one a good** — hacerle a uno un favor; **to take** —**s** turnarse.

turnip [tɜnəp] s. nabo.

turnover [tɜnovə] s. vuelco (de un coche); cambio (de empleados); **business** — movimiento de mercancías, número de transacciones; **labor** — movimiento de obreros, cambio frecuente de trabajadores; **apple** — pastel de manzana; — **collar** cuello doblado.

turpentine [tɜpəntaɪn] s. trementina; aguarrás.

turpitude [tɜpətjud] s. torpeza, vileza.

turquoise [tɜkwɔɪz] s. turquesa.

turret [tɜɪt] s. torrecilla; torre blindada; alminar.

turtle [tɜtl] s. tortuga; —**dove** tórtola.

tusk [tʌsk] s. colmillo.

tutor [tútə] s. tutor, maestro particular; v. enseñar, instruir.

tuxedo [tʌksído] s. esmoquin.

twang [twæŋ] s. tañido (de una cuerda de guitarra); nasalidad, tonillo gangoso; v. puntear, tañer (una cuerda); hablar con voz nasal, hablar con tonillo gangoso.

twangy [twæŋɪ] adj. gangoso, nasal.

tweed [twid] s. mezclilla de lana; — **suit** traje de mezclilla.

tweezers [twízəz] s. pl. pinzas, tenacillas.

twice [twaɪs] adv. dos veces.

twig [twɪg] s. ramita; varita.

twilight [twáɪlaɪt] s. crepúsculo; **at** — entre dos luces; adj. crepuscular.

twin [twɪn] adj. & s. gemelo, mellizo, Am. cuate.

twine [twaɪn] s. cuerda, cordel; v. enroscar(se), torcer(se), retorcer(se); entrelazar.

twinge [twɪndʒ] s. punzada (dolor agudo); v. punzar.

twinkle [twɪŋkl] v. titilar, parpadear, pestañear; chispear; s. titilación, parpadeo; pestañeo; guiño, guiñada; **in the** — **of an eye** en un abrir y cerrar de ojos.

twirl [twɜl] v. girar; dar vueltas; s. giro, vuelta; molinete, floreo.

twist [twɪst] v. torcer(se); retorcer(se), enroscar(se); s. torsión, torcedura; torzal, cordoncillo (hecho de varias hebras torcidas); curva, recodo, vuelta; rosca (de pan); **mental** — sesgo de la mente, sesgo mental.

twitch [twitʃ] v. crisparse, contraerse, torcerse convulsivamente (un músculo); temblar (los párpados); dar un tirón; s. temblor, ligera convulsión, contracción nerviosa; tirón.

twitter [twítə] v. gorjear (los pájaros); temblar; agitarse; s. gorjeo; agitación, estremecimiento nervioso.

twofold [túfóld] adj. doble.

type [taɪp] s. tipo; v. escribir a máquina.

typewrite [táɪpraɪt] v. escribir a máquina.

typewriter [táɪpraɪtə] s. máquina de escribir.

typewriting [táɪpraɪtɪŋ] s. mecanografía; trabajo de mecanógrafo.

typewritten [táɪprɪtn̩] adj. escrito a máquina.

typhoid [táɪfɔɪd] s. tifoidea, fiebre tifoidea.

typhus [táɪfəs] s. tifo.

typical [típɪkl̩] adj. típico.

typist [táɪpɪst] s. mecanógrafo; mecanógrafa.

tyrannical [tɪrǽnɪkl̩] adj. tiránico, tirano.

tyranny [tírənɪ] s. tiranía.

tyrant [táɪrənt] s. tirano.

U

udder [ʌ́də] s. ubre.

ugliness [ʌ́glɪnɪs] s. fealdad; fiereza.

ugly [ʌ́glɪ] adj. feo; fiero; repugnante; de mal genio; desagradable.

ulcer [ʌ́lsə] s. úlcera.

ulterior [ʌltíːrɪə] adj. ulterior.

ultimate [ʌ́ltəmɪt] adj. último; final; fundamental; -ly adv. finalmente, a la larga.

umbrella [ʌmbrélə] s. paraguas; sombrilla.

umpire [ʌ́mpaɪr] s. árbitro, arbitrador; v. arbitrar.

un- [ʌn-] prefijo negativo equivalente a: sin, no, in-, des-.

unable [ʌnébl̩] adj. incapaz, inhábil; to be — to come no poder venir.

unaccustomed [ʌnəkʌ́stəmd] adj. desacostumbrado; insólito, inusitado.

unaffected [ʌnəféktɪd] adj. inafectado, sin afectación, natural, sincero.

unalterable [ʌnɔ́ltərəbl̩] adj. inalterable.

unanimity [junənímətɪ] s. unanimidad.

unanimous [junǽnəməs] adj. unánime.

unarmed [ʌnármd] adj. desarmado.

unavoidable [ʌnəvɔ́ɪdəbl̩] adj. inevitable, ineludible.

unaware [ʌnəwér] adj. desprevenido, inadvertido; ignorante; incauto; -s adv. inesperadamente, inopinadamente; impensadamente.

unbalanced [ʌnbǽlənst] adj. desequilibrado; — account cuenta no saldada.

unbearable [ʌnbérəbl̩] adj. inaguantable, insoportable.

unbecoming [ʌnbɪkʌ́mɪŋ] adj. impropio; an — dress un vestido que no sienta bien o que cae mal.

unbelief [ʌnbəlíf] s. incredulidad.

unbelievable [ʌnbəlívəbl̩] adj. increíble.

unbeliever [ʌnbəlívə] s. descreído, incrédulo.

unbelieving [ʌnbəlívɪŋ] adj. descreído, incrédulo.

unbending [ʌnbéndɪŋ] adj. inflexible.

unbiassed [ʌnbáɪəst] adj. imparcial, libre de prejuicio.

unbosom [ʌnbúzəm] v. revelar, confesar, descubrir (secretos); to — oneself desahogarse con alguien, revelar sus más íntimos secretos.

unbound [ʌnbáund] adj. desencuadernado, no encuadernado; suelto, desligado.

unbroken [ʌnbrókən] adj. intacto, entero; indómito; ininterrumpido, continuo.

unbutton [ʌnbʌ́tn̩] v. desabotonar, desabrochar.

uncanny [ʌnkǽnɪ] adj. extraño, raro, misterioso.

unceasing [ʌnsísɪŋ] adj. incesante.

uncertain [ʌnsə́tn̩] adj. incierto; dudoso; indeciso.

uncertainty [ʌnsə́tn̩tɪ] s. incertidumbre; falta de certeza.

unchangeable [ʌntʃéndʒəbl̩] adj. inmutable, inalterable, invariable.

unchanged [ʌntʃéndʒd] adj. inalterado, igual.

uncharitable [ʌntʃǽrətəbl̩] adj. duro, falto de caridad.

uncle [ʌ́ŋkl̩] s. tío.

unclean [ʌnklín] adj. inmundo, sucio, impuro.

uncomfortable [ʌnkʌ́mfətəbl̩] adj. incómodo, molesto.

uncommon [ʌnkámən] adj. poco común, insólito, raro.

uncompromising [ʌnkámprəmaɪzɪŋ] adj. intransigente; inflexible.

unconcern [ʌnkənsə́n] s. indiferencia.

unconditional [ʌnkəndíʃən̩l] adj. incondicional; absoluto.

uncongenial [ʌnkəndʒínjəl] adj. que no congenia, incompatible.

unconquerable [ʌnkáŋkərəbl̩] adj. invencible, inconquistable.

unconquered [ʌnkáŋkəd] adj. no conquistado, no vencido.

unconscious [ʌnkánʃəs] adj. inconsciente; privado.

unconsciousness [ʌnkʌ́nʃəsnɪs] *s.* inconsciencia; insensibilidad.

uncontrollable [ʌnkəntróləbl] *adj.* irrefrenable, ingobernable.

unconventional [ʌnkənvénʃən]] *adj.* despreocupado, libre de trabas o reglas.

uncouth [ʌnkúθ] *adj.* rudo, tosco, inculto, grosero; desmañado.

uncover [ʌnkʌ́və] *v.* descubrir(se); revelar; destapar(se); desabrigar(se).

unction [ʌ́ŋkʃən] *s.* unción; fervor; **Extreme Unction** Extremaunción.

unctuous [ʌ́ŋkʃəs] *adj.* untuoso.

uncultivated [ʌnkʌ́ltəvetɪd] *adj.* inculto; baldío.

uncultured [ʌnkʌ́ltʃəd] *adj.* inculto; grosero.

undecided [ʌndɪsáɪdɪd] *adj.* indeciso.

undeniable [ʌndɪnáɪəbl] *adj.* innegable.

under [ʌ́ndə] *prep.* bajo; debajo de; menos de; **— age** menor de edad; **— cover** a cubierto; **— the cover of** al abrigo de, al amparo de; **— pretense of** so pretexto de; **— twelve** menos de doce; **to be — obligation to** deber favores a; *adv.* debajo; abajo; menos; *adj.* inferior, de abajo (*en ciertas combinaciones*); **— dose** dosis escasa o corta; **— secretary** subsecretario; **— side** lado de abajo, lado inferior; **the — dogs** los de abajo.

underbrush [ʌ́ndəbrʌʃ] *s.* maleza.

underclothes [ʌ́ndəkloz] *s. pl.* ropa interior.

underestimate [ʌ́ndəéstəmet] *v.* menospreciar, apreciar en menos de lo justo; salir corto en un cálculo.

underfed [ʌ́ndəféd] *adj.* malnutrido.

undergo [ʌndəgó] *v.* sufrir, aguantar, padecer.

undergone [ʌndəgón] *p.p. de* **to undergo.**

undergraduate [ʌndəgrǽdʒuɪt] *s.* estudiante del bachillerato; **— course** cursos o asignaturas para el bachillerato.

underground [ʌ́ndəgraund] *adj.* subterráneo; *v.* subterráneo; *adv.* bajo tierra; en secreto; ocultamente.

underhanded [ʌ́ndəhǽndɪd] *adj.* socarrón, secreto, disimulado, clandestino.

underline [ʌ́ndəlaɪn] *v.* subrayar.

underlying [ʌndəláɪɪŋ] *adj.* fundamental.

undermine [ʌndəmáɪn] *v.* minar, socavar.

underneath [ʌndəníθ] *prep.* bajo, debajo de; *adv.* debajo.

underpay [ʌndəpé] *v.* malpagar; esca-

timar la paga.

undersell [ʌndəsél] *v.* malbaratar; vender a menos precio que.

undershirt [ʌ́ndəʃət] *s.* camiseta.

undersigned [ʌndəsáɪnd] *s.* firmante, infrascrito; **the —** el infrascrito, los infrascritos.

undersized [ʌndəsáɪzd] *adj.* achaparrado, de tamaño inferior al normal.

underskirt [ʌ́ndəskət] *s.* enaguas, refajo.

understand [ʌndəstǽnd] *v.* entender; comprender; sobrentender.

understandable [ʌndəstǽndəbl] *adj.* comprensible.

understanding [ʌndəstǽndɪŋ] *s.* comprensión; entendimiento, inteligencia; acuerdo; *adj.* comprensivo.

understood [ʌndəstúd] *pret. & p.p. de* **to understand;** *adj.* entendido; convenido; sobrentendido.

understudy [ʌ́ndəstʌdɪ] *s.* sobresaliente, actor suplente; *v.* servir de sobresaliente o actor suplente.

undertake [ʌndəték] *v.* emprender; tratar de, intentar; comprometerse a.

undertaken [ʌndətékən] *p.p. de* **to undertake.**

undertaker [ʌ́ndətekə] *s.* director de funeraria; embalsamador.

undertaking [ʌndətékɪŋ] *s.* empresa.

undertook [ʌndətúk] *pret. de* **to undertake.**

undertow [ʌ́ndəto] *s.* resaca.

underwear [ʌ́ndəwer] *s.* ropa interior.

underwent [ʌndəwént] *pret. de* **to undergo.**

underworld [ʌ́ndəwɜld] *s.* hampa, bajos fondos de la sociedad; clase criminal.

undesirable [ʌndɪzáɪrəbl] *adj.* indeseable; inconveniente.

undid [ʌndíd] *pret. de* **to undo.**

undisturbed [ʌndɪstɜ́bd] *adj.* impasible; sereno, tranquilo; intacto.

undo [ʌndú] *v.* deshacer; desatar; desabrochar; desenredar; anular; **to — one's hair** soltarse el cabello.

undone [ʌndʌ́n] *p.p. de* **to undo;** inacabado, sin hacer; sin terminar; **it is still —** está todavía por hacer, está inacabado; **to come —** desatarse.

undoubtedly [ʌndáutɪdlɪ] *adv.* indudablemente, sin duda.

undress [ʌndrés] *v.* desnudar(se), desvestir(se).

undue [ʌndjú] *adj.* indebido; impropio; excesivo.

undulate [ʌ́ndjəlet] *v.* ondular, ondear.

unduly [ʌndjúlɪ] *adv.* indebidamente.

undying [ʌndáɪɪŋ] *adj.* imperecedero, eterno.

unearth [ʌnɜ́ə] *v.* desenterrar.

uneasily [ʌníːɪt] *adv.* intranquilamente, inquietamente, con inquietud; incómodamente.

uneasiness [ʌníːzɪnɪs] *s.* malestar, inquietud, intranquilidad, desasosiego.

uneasy [ʌníːsɪ] *adj.* ansioso, inquieto, intranquilo; cohibido; incómodo.

uneducated [ʌnédʒəkeɪtɪd] *adj.* inculto, indocto, falto de instrucción, ignorante.

unemployed [ʌnɪmplɔ́ɪd] *adj.* desocupado, desempleado, cesante; ocioso; — funds fondos no invertidos o inactivos.

unemployment [ʌnɪmplɔ́ɪmənt] *s.* desempleo, cesantía, falta de empleo, desocupación.

unending [ʌnéndɪŋ] *adj.* inacabable, interminable.

unequal [ʌníːkwəl] *adj.* desigual; insuficiente, ineficaz.

uneven [ʌníːvən] *adj.* desigual, disparejo; irregular, accidentado; — numbers números impares o nones.

unevenness [ʌníːvənnɪs] *s.* desigualdad; desnivel; irregularidad, escabrosidad (*del terreno*).

unexpected [ʌnɪkspéktɪd] *adj.* inesperado; -ly *adv.* de improviso, inesperadamente.

unfailing [ʌnféɪlɪŋ] *adj.* que nunca falta, constante, indefectible; infalible.

unfair [ʌnféɪr] *adj.* injusto; tramposo; to act -ly obrar de mala fe.

unfaithful [ʌnféɪθfəl] *adj.* infiel; desleal.

unfamiliar [ʌnfəmíljə] *adj.* poco familiar; desconocido; to be — with no tener conocimiento de; no estar al tanto de, ignorar; no conocer bien.

unfasten [ʌnfǽsn] *v.* desabrochar; desatar; aflojar.

unfavorable [ʌnféɪvrəbl] *adj.* desfavorable, contrario, adverso.

unfeeling [ʌnfíːlɪŋ] *adj.* insensible; incompasivo.

unfinished [ʌnfínɪʃt] *adj.* inacabado, sin terminar, sin acabar; sin barnizar o pulir.

unfit [ʌnfít] *adj.* incompetente, inepto, incapaz; inservible; impropio; *v.* incapacitar.

unfold [ʌnfóld] *v.* desenvolver(se), desarrollar(se); desdoblar; revelar.

unforeseen [ʌnforsín] *adj.* imprevisto.

unforgettable [ʌnfəgétəbl] *adj.* inolvidable.

unfortunate [ʌnfɔ́rtʃənɪt] *adj.* desventurado, infeliz, desgraciado, desdichado; -ly *adv.* desgraciadamente, por desgracia.

unfriendly [ʌnfréndlɪ] *adj.* hostil, enemigo; poco amistoso; *adv.* hostilmente.

unfurl [ʌnfɜ́l] *v.* desplegar.

unfurnished [ʌnfɜ́nɪʃt] *adj.* desamueblado.

ungrateful [ʌngrétfəl] *adj.* ingrato, desagradecido.

unhappy [ʌnhǽpɪ] *adj.* infeliz; desgraciado, desventurado, desdichado.

unharmed [ʌnhɑ́rmd] *adj.* sin daño, ileso.

unhealthy [ʌnhéləɪ] *adj.* malsano; insalubre; enfermizo.

unheard-of [ʌnhɜ́dəv] *adj.* inaudito; desconocido.

unhitch [ʌnhítʃ] *v.* desenganchar; desatar.

unhook [ʌnhúk] *v.* desenganchar; desabrochar.

unhurt [ʌnhɜ́t] *adj.* ileso.

uniform [júnəfɔrm] *adj.* & *s.* uniforme.

uniformity [junəfɔ́rmətɪ] *s.* uniformidad.

unify [júnəfaɪ] *v.* unificar, unir.

unimportant [ʌnɪmpɔ́rtṇt] *adj.* insignificante, poco importante.

union [júnjən] *s.* unión; — leader jefe de un gremio obrero; — trade-union gremio obrero.

unique [juník] *adj.* único, singular.

unison [júnəzṇ] : in — al unísono (*en el mismo tono*); al compás.

unit [júnɪt] *s.* unidad.

unite [junáɪt] *v.* unir(se).

unity [júnətɪ] *s.* unidad; unión.

universal [junəvɜ́əl] *adj.* universal.

universe [júnəvɜs] *s.* universo.

university [junəvɜ́sətɪ] *s.* universidad.

unjust [ʌndʒʌ́st] *adj.* injusto.

unjustifiable [ʌndʒʌ́stəfaɪəbl] *adj.* injustificable, injustificado.

unkempt [ʌnkémpt] *adj.* desaseado, desaliñado; desgreñado.

unkind [ʌnkáɪnd] *adj.* falto de bondad descortés; cruel.

unknown [ʌnnón] *adj.* desconocido; no sabido; ignoto; — quantity incógnita, it is — se ignora, no se sabe, se desconoce.

unlawful [ʌnlɔ́fəl] *adj.* ilegal, ilícito.

unless [ənlés] *conj.* a menos que, a no ser que.

unlike [ʌnláɪk] *adj.* desemejante, distinto, diferente; *prep.* a diferencia de.

unlikely [ʌnláɪklɪ] *adj.* improbable, inverosímil.

unlimited [ʌnlímɪtɪd] *adj.* ilimitado.

unload [ʌnlód] *v.* descargar; vaciar; deshacerse de (*acciones, mercancías*).

unlock [ʌnlák] v. abrir (*con llave*); soltar, destrabar; revelar, penetrar (*secretos*).

unlucky [ʌnlʌ́ki] adj. desdichado, desventurado, desgraciado, desafortunado; aciago, de mal agüero, funesto; **an — number** un número de mala suerte.

unmanageable [ʌnmǽnɪdʒəb] adj. inmanejable, ingobernable, intratable, indomable.

unmarried [ʌnmǽrɪd] adj. soltero.

unmerciful [ʌnmɜ́sɪfəl] adj. despiadado, inclemente.

unmistakable [ʌnməstékəb] adj. inequívoco, claro, inconfundible.

unmoved [ʌnmúvd] adj. fijo; inmutable, impasible, indiferente.

unnatural [ʌnnǽtʃərəl] adj. afectado, artificial; anormal; **an — mother** una madre desnaturalizada.

unnecessary [ʌnnɛ́səsɛrɪ] adj. innecesario.

unnoticed [ʌnnótɪst] adj. inadvertido.

unobliging [ʌnəbláɪdʒɪŋ] adj. poco complaciente, descortés, descomedido.

unobserved [ʌnəbzɜ́vd] adj. inadvertido; sin ser visto.

unobtainable [ʌnəbténəb] adj. inobtenible, inasequible, inaccesible.

unoccupied [ʌnákjəpaɪd] adj. desocupado; vacío; desalquilado.

unpack [ʌnpǽk] v. desempacar, desembalar.

unpaid [ʌnpéd] adj. no pagado; sin pagar; **— bills** cuentas por pagar.

unpleasant [ʌnplɛ́zn̩t] adj. desagradable.

unpleasantness [ʌnplɛ́zn̩tnɪs] s. manera desagradable; desazón; desavenencia; **the — of a situation** lo desagradable de una situación; **to have an — with** tener una desavenencia con.

unprecedented [ʌnprésədɛntɪd] adj. sin precedente; inaudito.

unprepared [ʌnprɪpérd] adj. desprevenido; no preparado; no listo.

unpublished [ʌnpʌ́blɪʃt] adj. inédito, no publicado.

unquenchable [ʌnkwɛ́ntʃəb] adj. inapagable, inextinguible.

unquestionable [ʌnkwɛ́stʃənəb] adj. indisputable, indudable; irreprochable.

unravel [ʌnrǽv] v. desenredar; desenmarañar; deshilachar(se); deshilar.

unreal [ʌnríəl] adj. irreal; ilusorio, imaginario.

unreasonable [ʌnríznəb] adj. desrazonable, fuera de razón; irracional.

unrecognizable [ʌnrékəgnaɪzəb] adj. irreconocible, no conocible, incapaz de reconocerse; desconocido.

unrefined [ʌnrɪfáɪnd] adj. no refinado; inculto, grosero.

unrest [ʌnrést] s. inquietud, desasosiego.

unroll [ʌnról] v. desenrollar(se), desenvolver(se).

unruly [ʌnrúlɪ] adj. indómito; indócil; desobediente.

unsafe [ʌnséf] adj. inseguro, peligroso.

unsalable [ʌnséləb] adj. invendible.

unsatisfactory [ʌnsætɪsfǽktrɪ] adj. no satisfactorio, inaceptable.

unseen [ʌnsín] adj. no visto, oculto; invisible.

unselfish [ʌnsélfɪʃ] adj. desinteresado.

unselfishness [ʌnsélfɪʃnɪs] s. desinterés, abnegación.

unsettled [ʌnsétl̩d] adj. desordenado, en desorden; turbio; inestable; incierto; indeciso; deshabitado; no establecido; **— bills** cuentas no liquidadas, cuentas pendientes; **— weather** tiempo variable; **an — liquid** un líquido revuelto o turbio.

unshaken [ʌnʃékən] adj. inmóvil, inmovible, firme.

unsightly [ʌnsáɪtlɪ] adj. feo, desagradable a la vista.

unskilled [ʌnskíld] adj. inexperto.

unskillful [ʌnskílfəl] adj. inhábil, desmañado, inexperto.

unsociable [ʌnsóʃəb] adj. insociable, huraño, intratable, arisco.

unspeakable [ʌnspíkəb] adj. indecible; inefable; atroz.

unstable [ʌnstéb] adj. inestable.

unsteady [ʌnstédɪ] adj. inseguro, inestable; movedizo; variable, inconstante.

unsuccessful [ʌnsəksésfəl] adj. sin éxito; desafortunado; **to be — no** tener éxito.

unsuitable [ʌnsútəb] adj. impropio, inapropiado; inepto; inconveniente; incongruente; incompatible.

unsuspected [ʌnsəspéktɪd] adj. insospechado.

untidy [ʌntáɪdɪ] adj. desaliñado, desaseado; desarreglado, en desorden.

untie [ʌntáɪ] v. desatar(se); desamarrar; deshacer (*un nudo o lazo*).

until [ʌntfl] prep. hasta; conj. hasta que.

untimely [ʌntáɪmlɪ] adj. inoportuno; prematuro; adv. inoportunamente; fuera de sazón; demasiado pronto.

untiring [ʌntáɪrɪŋ] adj. incansable.

untold [ʌntóld] adj. indecible, innumerable, incalculable, inestimable.

untouched [ʌntátʃt] *adj.* intacto, no tocado, íntegro; impasible, no conmovido; **to leave** — no tocar, dejar intacto; dejar impasible, no conmover.

untried [ʌntráɪd] *adj.* no probado, no ensayado, no experimentado; — **law case** causa todavía no vista.

untroubled [ʌntrʌ́bld] *adj* sosegado, tranquilo, quieto.

untrue [ʌntrú] *adj.* falso; infiel; desleal; mentiroso.

untruth [ʌntrúθ] *s.* falsedad; mentira.

untrained [ʌntrénd] *adj.* indisciplinado, falto de disciplina; sin educación; inexperto.

unused [ʌnjúzd] *adj.* no usado; desacostumbrado; — **to** no hecho a, desacostumbrado a.

unusual [ʌnjúʒʊəl] *adj.* inusitado, insólito; desusado; raro, extraño; extraordinario.

unveil [ʌnvél] *v.* quitar el velo a; revelar, descubrir.

unwary [ʌnwéri] *adj.* incauto.

unwashed [ʌnwáʃt] *adj.* no lavado, sin lavar; sucio.

unwelcome [ʌnwélkəm] *adj.* indeseable, no deseado; mal acogido, mal recibido, mal quisto.

unwholesome [ʌnhólsəm] *adj.* malsano; insalubre, dañino.

unwieldy [ʌnwíldi] *adj.* inmanejable, difícil de manejar, embarazoso, engorroso.

unwilling [ʌnwílɪŋ] *adj.* renuente, maldispuesto, reacio; **to be** — **to** no querer, no estar dispuesto a; **-ly** *adv.* de mala gana, sin querer.

unwillingness [ʌnwílɪŋnɪs] *s.* renuencia, falta de voluntad; mala gana.

unwise [ʌnwáɪz] *adj.* imprudente, indiscreto; necio.

unworthy [ʌnwə́ði] *adj.* indigno.

unwrap [ʌnræp] *v.* desenvolver.

up [ʌp] *adv.* arriba, hacia arriba, en lo alto; de pie; *adj.* levantado; derecho, erecto; terminado, concluido; — **and down** de arriba abajo; de acá para allá; **-s and downs** altibajos; fluctuaciones, vaivenes; — **the river** río arriba; — **to now** hasta ahora; **his time is** — ha expirado su tiempo; se ha cumplido su plazo; **prices are** — los precios han subido; **that is** — **to you** queda a la discreción de Vd.; eso es cosa suya; **to be** — **against it** estar perplejo, no saber qué hacer, estar en un aprieto; **to be** — **on the news** estar al corriente (*o* al tanto) de las noticias); **to be** — **to one's old tricks**

hacer de las suyas; **to eat it** — comérselo; **what's** — ? ¿qué pasa?; *v.* levantar, alzar.

upbraid [ʌpbréd] *v.* reprender, regañar

upheld [ʌphéld] *pret. & p.p. de* **to uphold.**

uphill [ʌphíl] *adv.* cuesta arriba; *adj.* ascendente; trabajoso, arduo.

uphold [ʌphóld] *v.* sostener; apoyar

upholster [ʌphólstə] *v.* entapizar y rellenar (*muebles*).

upholstery [ʌphólstrɪ] *s.* tapicería.

upkeep [ʌpkip] *s.* manutención.

upland [ʌplənd] *s.* altiplanicie, tierra alta.

uplift [ʌplíft] *s.* elevación; edificación (*espiritual*); [ʌplíft] *v.* elevar; edificar (*espiritualmente*).

upon [əpán] *prep.* en, sobre, encima de; — **arriving** al llegar.

upper [ʌpə] *adj.* superior; alto; — **berth** litera alta, cama alta (*de un coche dormitorio*); **to have the** — **hand** ejercer dominio o mando; llevar la ventaja; *s.* litera alta, cama alta; **pala** (*parte superior del calzado*).

upright [ʌpraɪt] *adj.* recto; derecho; vertical; justo, honrado; — **piano** piano vertical; *s.* poste; puntal; piano vertical.

uprightness [ʌpraɪtnɪs] *s.* rectitud.

uprising [ʌpráɪzɪŋ] *s.* alzamiento, levantamiento; revuelta.

uproar [ʌpror] *s.* tumulto, alboroto, bulla, gritería.

uproarious [ʌprórɪəs] *adj.* estruendoso, bullicioso, tumultuoso.

uproot [ʌprút] *v.* desarraigar, arrancar de raíz.

upset [ʌpsét] *v.* volcar; trastornar; tumbar; perturbar, turbar; **to become** — volcarse; turbarse; trastornársele a uno el estómago; *pret. & p.p. de* **to upset**; *adj.* indispuesto, descompuesto; desarreglado, trastornado; [ʌpsɛt] *s.* vuelco; trastorno; desorden; indisposición.

upshot [ʌpʃat] *s.* resultado, fin.

upside [ʌpsáɪd] *s.* lado o parte superior; — **down** al revés; patas arriba; en desorden.

upstairs [ʌpstérz] *adv.* arriba, en el piso de arriba; *adj.* de arriba; *s.* piso (*o* pisos) de arriba.

upstart [ʌpstart] *s.* advenedizo, principiante presuntuoso.

up-to-date [ʌptədét] *adj.* moderno; al corriente, al tanto.

upturn [ʌptɜn] *s.* alza, subida (*de precios*); mejora.

upward [ʌpwəd] *adv.* arriba, para arriba,

hacia arriba; más; — of más de; *adj.* ascendente, hacia arriba, para arriba.

upwards [Ápwədz] *adv.* – **upward.**

urban [ə́bən] *adj.* urbano.

urchin [ə́tʃɪn] *s.* granuja, pilluelo; **sea —** erizo de mar.

urge [ədʒ] *v.* urgir, instar; exhortar; recomendar o solicitar con instancia; apremiar, incitar, estimular; *s.* impulso; gana, ganas; estímulo.

urgency [ə́dʒənsɪ] *s.* urgencia; apremio.

urgent [ə́dʒənt] *adj.* urgente, apremiante.

urinate [júrənet] *v.* orinar.

urine [júrɪn] *s.* orina, (los) orines.

urn [ɜn] *s.* urna; **coffee —** cafetera.

us [ʌs] *pron.* nos; nosotros (*con preposición*).

usage [júsɪdʒ] *s.* usanza; uso; **hard —** uso constante.

use [jus] *s.* uso; empleo; utilidad; **it is of no —** es inútil; no sirve; **out of —** desusado, ya no usado; pasado de moda; **to have no further —** for ya no necesitar, ya no tener necesidad de; **what is the — of it?** ¿para qué sirve? ¿qué ventaja tiene?; ¿qué objeto tiene?; [juz] *v.* usar; emplear; servirse de, hacer uso de; acostumbrar, soler, *Am.* saber; **— your judgment** haz lo que te parezca; **to — up** gastar, agotar; consumir; **to be -d to** estar hecho, acostumbrado o habituado a; **he -d to do it** solía hacerlo, lo hacía.

useful [júsfəl] *adj.* útil.

usefulness [júsfəlnɪs] *s.* utilidad.

useless [júslɪs] *adj.* inútil; inservible.

uselessness [júslɪsnɪs] *s.* inutilidad.

usher [ʌ́ʃə] *s.* acomodador (*en un teatro o iglesia*); ujier; *v.* conducir, llevar, acompañar; introducir.

usual [júʒʊəl] *adj.* usual; corriente, común, general; **-ly** *adv.* usualmente, generalmente, por lo general.

usurer [júʒərə] *s.* usurero.

usurp [juzɜ́p] *v.* usurpar.

usury [júʒərɪ] *s.* usura.

utensil [jutɛ́nsl] *s.* utensilio.

uterus [jútərəs] *s.* útero.

utility [jutílətɪ] *s.* utilidad; servicio.

utilize [jútlaɪz] *v.* utilizar; aprovechar.

utmost [Átmost] *adj.* sumo, extremo; más distante; más grande, mayor; más alto; último; **he did his —** hizo cuanto pudo; **to the —** hasta más no poder.

utter [Átə] *v.* proferir; decir, expresar; **to — a cry** dar un grito; *adj.* completo, total; absoluto.

utterance [Átərəns] *s.* declaración; expresión; modo de hablar.

uttermost [Átəmost] **= utmost.**

uvula [júvjələ] *s.* campanilla, galillo de la garganta.

V

vacancy [vékənsɪ] *s.* vacante, empleo vacante; vacío; habitación o apartamento desocupado.

vacant [vékənt] *adj.* vacante; vacío; desocupado; libre.

vacate [véket] *v.* desocupar, dejar vacío; dejar vacante.

vacation [vekéʃən] *s.* vacación; vacaciones.

vaccinate [væksnet] *v.* vacunar.

vaccination [væksnéʃən] *s.* vacunación.

vaccine [væksin] *s.* vacuna.

vacillate [væslet] *v.* vacilar.

vacuum [vǽkjʊəm] *s.* vacío; **— cleaner** escoba eléctrica.

vagabond [vǽgəbɑnd] *adj.* & *s.* vagabundo.

vagrant [végrənt] *adj.* vago, vagabundo, errante; *s.* vago, vagabundo.

vague [veg] *adj.* vago.

vain [ven] *adj.* vano; vanidoso; **in —** en vano.

vainglory [venglórɪ] *s.* vanagloria.

vale [vel] *s.* valle; cañada.

valentine [vǽləntaɪn] *s.* tarjeta o regalo del día de San Valentín (*el día de los enamorados*); **to my —** a mi querido, a mi querida.

valet [vǽlɪt] *s.* criado, camarero; planchador de trajes.

valiant [vǽljənt] *adj.* valiente, valeroso.

valid [vǽlɪd] *adj.* válido, valedero.

validity [vəlídətɪ] *s.* validez.

valise [vəlís] *s.* valija, maleta, *Am.* velís, *Am.* petaca.

valley [vǽlɪ] *s.* valle.

valor [vǽlə] *s.* valor, ánimo, valentía.

valorous [vǽlərəs] *adj.* valeroso, valiente.

valuable [vǽljəbl] *adj.* valioso; precioso; preciado; **-s** *s. pl.* objetos de valor, joyas, alhajas.

valuation [væljʊéʃən] *s.* valuación, valoración; avalúo; tasa.

value [vǽlju] *s.* valor; precio; mérito; estimación, aprecio; *v.* valorar, avaluar, valuar; apreciar, estimar.

valueless [vǽljʊlɪs] *adj.* sin valor.

valve [vælv] *s.* válvula; valva (*de los moluscos*); **safety —** válvula de seguridad.

van [væn] *s.* camión (*para transportar muebles*); **—guard** vanguardia.

vane [ven] *s.* veleta; aspa (*de molino de viento*); paleta (*de hélice*).

vanilla [vənílə] s. vainilla.

vanish [vǽnɪʃ] v. desvanecerse, desaparecer(se).

vanity [vǽnɪtɪ] s. vanidad; — case neceser; — table tocador.

vanquish [vǽnkwɪʃ] v. vencer.

vantage [vǽntɪdʒ] s. ventaja; point of — lugar estratégico.

vapor [vépə] s. vapor; vaho.

variable [vérɪəbl] adj. & s. variable.

variance [vérɪəns] s. variación, cambio; desavenencia; to be at — estar desavenidos; no estar de acuerdo.

variation [vərɪéʃən] s. variación; variedad.

varied [vérɪd] adj. variado, vario.

variegated [vérɪgetɪd] adj. abigarrado.

variety [vəráɪətɪ] s. variedad.

various [vérɪəs] adj. varios; diferentes, distintos.

varnish [várnɪʃ] s. barniz; v. barnizar.

vary [vérɪ] v. variar; cambiar.

vase [ves] s. vaso, jarrón.

vassal [vǽsl] adj. & s. vasallo.

vast [vǽst] adj. vasto; inmenso; anchuroso; -ly adv. vastamente, sumamente, muy.

vastness [vǽstnɪs] s. inmensidad.

vat [vǽt] s. tina, tanque.

vaudeville [vódəvɪl] s. vodevil, función de variedades.

vault [vɔlt] s. bóveda; tumba; bank — caja fuerte; depósito; pole — salto con garrocha; v. abovedar, edificar una bóveda; dar figura de bóveda; saltar con garrocha; saltar por encima de.

vaunt [vɔnt] v. jactarse; ostentar, alardear; s. jactancia.

veal [vil] s. carne de ternera; — cutlet chuleta de ternera.

veer [vɪr] v. virar; s. virada.

vegetable [védʒtəbl] s. vegetal, planta; legumbre; -s hortaliza, legumbres; green -s verduras; adj. vegetal; de legumbres, de hortaliza; — garden hortaliza.

vegetate [védʒətet] v. vegetar.

vegetation [vedʒətéʃən] s. vegetación.

vehemence [víəməns] s. vehemencia.

vehement [víəmənt] adj. vehemente.

vehicle [víɪkl] s. vehículo.

veil [vel] s. velo; v. velar; tapar, encubrir.

vein [ven] s. vena; veta, filón.

veined [vend] adj. veteado, jaspeado; venoso.

velocity [vəlásətɪ] s. velocidad.

velvet [vélvɪt] s. terciopelo; velludo; adj. de terciopelo; aterciopelado.

velvety [vélvɪtɪ] adj. aterciopelado.

vendor [véndə] s. vendedor; buhonero, vendedor ambulante.

veneer [vənír] s. chapa; v. chapar o chapear, Am. enchapar.

venerable [vénərəbl] adj. venerable; venerando.

venerate [vénəret] v. venerar.

veneration [venəréʃən] s. veneración.

Venezuelan [venəzwílən] adj. & s. venezolano.

vengeance [véndʒəns] s. venganza; with a — con furia; con violencia.

venison [vénəzn] s. venado, carne de venado.

venom [vénəm] s. veneno, ponzoña.

venomous [vénəməs] adj. venenoso, ponzoñoso.

vent [vent] s. abertura; escape; desahogo; fogón (de arma de fuego); to give — to anger desahogar la ira, dar desahogo a la cólera; v. dar salida o desahogo; desahogar, descargar.

ventilate [véntlet] v. ventilar.

ventilation [ventléʃən] s. ventilación.

ventilator [véntletə] s. ventilador.

venture [véntʃə] s. ventura, riesgo; business — especulación; empresa o negocio arriesgado; v. aventurar, arriesgar; to — outside aventurarse a salir; to — to aventurarse a, atreverse a, osar.

venturous [véntʃərəs] adj. aventurado.

veranda [vərǽndə] s. galería; terraza; balcón corrido.

verb [vɜb] s. verbo.

verbal [vɜ́bl] adj. verbal; oral.

verbose [vəbós] adj. verboso; palabrero.

verdict [vɜ́dɪkt] s. veredicto; fallo, decisión, sentencia; — of "not guilty" veredicto de inculpabilidad.

verdure [vɜ́dʒə] s. verdura, verdor, verde.

verge [vɜdʒ] s. borde, margen, orilla; on the — of al borde de; a punto de; v. to — on rayar en, estar al margen de; to — toward tender a, inclinarse a.

verify [vérəfaɪ] v. verificar; comprobar.

verily [vérəlɪ] adv. en verdad.

veritable [vérətəbl] adj. verdadero.

verse [vɜs] s. verso.

versed [vɜst] adj. versado, experto, perito.

version [vɜ́ʒən] versión.

vertical [vɜ́tɪk̩l] adj. vertical.

very [vérɪ] adv. muy; — much muchísimo; — many muchísimos; it is — cold today hace mucho frío hoy; adj. mismo; mismísimo; mero; the — man el mismísimo hombre; the — thought of la mera idea de.

vespers [véspəz] *s. pl.* vísperas.

vessel [vésl] *s.* vasija; vaso; barco, embarcación; **blood** — vaso, vena, arteria.

vest [vest] *s.* chaleco; *v.* conferir; **to** — **with power** revestir de autoridad, conferir poder a.

vestibule [véstəbjul] *s.* vestíbulo; zaguán.

vestige [véstɪdʒ] *s.* vestigio.

vestment [véstmənt] *s.* vestidura.

veteran [vétərən] *adj. & s.* veterano.

veterinary [vétrənɛrɪ] *s.* veterinario o albéitar.

veto [víto] *s.* veto; prohibición; *v.* vedar, prohibir; poner el veto a; negarse a aprobar.

vex [veks] *v.* molestar, hostigar; incomodar, enfadar; perturbar.

vexation [vekséʃən] *s.* molestia, incomodidad; enojo.

via [váɪə] *prep.* por, por la vía de.

viaduct [váɪədʌkt] *s.* viaducto.

vial [váɪəl] *s.* frasco, redoma; **small** — ampolleta.

viands [váɪəndz] *s. pl.* vianda, alimentos, comida.

vibrate [váɪbret] *v.* vibrar.

vibration [vaɪbréʃən] *s.* vibración.

vice [vaɪs] *s.* vicio; falta, defecto.

vice-president [váɪsprézədənt] *s.* vicepresidente.

viceroy [váɪsrɔɪ] *s.* virrey.

vice versa [váɪsɪvə́sə] viceversa.

vicinity [vəsínətɪ] *s.* vecindad; cercanía; inmediaciones.

vicious [víʃəs] *adj.* vicioso; malo; maligno; malicioso; — **dog** perro mordedor, perro bravo.

vicissitude [vəsísətjud] *s.* vicisitud, peripecia.

victim [víktɪm] *s.* víctima.

victor [víktə] *s.* vencedor.

victorious [vɪktórɪəs] *adj.* victorioso.

victory [víktrɪ] *s.* victoria.

victuals [vítlz] *s. pl.* vituallas, víveres.

vie [vaɪ] *v.* competir.

view [vju] *s.* vista; paisaje; parecer, opinión; inspección; mira, propósito; **in** — **of** en vista de; **to be within** — estar al alcance de la vista; **with a** — **to** con el propósito de; con la esperanza o expectación de; con la mira puesta en; *v.* mirar; examinar.

viewpoint [vjúpɔɪnt] *s.* punto de vista.

vigil [vídʒəl] *s.* vigilia, velada; **to keep** — velar.

vigilance [vídʒələns] *s.* vigilancia, desvelo.

vigilant [vídʒələnt] *adj.* vigilante.

vigor [vígə] *s.* vigor.

vigorous [vígərəs] *adj.* vigoroso.

vile [vaɪl] *adj.* vil, bajo, ruin; pésimo.

villa [vílə] *s.* quinta, casa de campo.

village [vílɪdʒ] *s.* villa, aldea.

villager [vílɪdʒə] *s.* aldeano.

villain [vílən] *s.* villano, malvado, bellaco.

villainous [vílənəs] *adj.* villano, ruin, vil, bellaco.

villainy [vílənɪ] *s.* villanía, vileza.

vim [vɪm] *s.* vigor, fuerza, energía.

vindicate [víndəket] *v.* vindicar, vengar.

vindictive [vɪndíktɪv] *adj.* vengativo.

vine [vaɪn] *s.* vid, parra; enredadera.

vinegar [vínɪgə] *s.* vinagre.

vineyard [vínjəd] *s.* viña, viñedo.

vintage [víntɪdʒ] *s.* vendimia; edad, época.

violate [váɪəlet] *v.* violar; infringir.

violation [vaɪəléʃən] *s.* violación; infracción.

violence [váɪələns] *s.* violencia.

violent [váɪələnt] *adj.* violento.

violet [váɪəlɪt] *s.* violeta; violado, color de violeta; *adj.* violado.

violin [vaɪəlín] *s.* violín.

violinist [vaɪəlínɪst] *s.* violinista.

viper [váɪpə] *s.* víbora.

virgin [vʒ́dʒɪn] *adj. & s.* virgen.

virginal [vʒ́dʒɪnl] *adj.* virginal.

virtual [vʒ́tʃʊəl] *adj.* virtual; **-ly** *adv.* virtualmente.

virtue [vʒ́tʃʊ] *s.* virtud.

virtuous [vʒ́tʃʊəs] *adj.* virtuoso.

visa [vízə] *s.* visa, visado; *v.* visar, refrendar.

visé = visa.

vise [vaɪs] *s.* tornillo de banco.

visible [vízəbl] *adj.* visible.

vision [víʒən] *s.* visión; vista.

visionary [víʒənɛrɪ] *adj.* visionario; imaginario; *s.* visionario, iluso, soñador.

visit [vízɪt] *v.* visitar; **to** — **punishment upon** mandar un castigo a, castigar a; *s.* visita.

visitation [vɪzətéʃən] *s.* visitación, visita; castigo, calamidad.

visitor [vízɪtə] *s.* visita; visitador.

visor [váɪzə] *s.* visera.

vista [vístə] *s.* vista, paisaje.

vital [váɪtl] *adj.* vital.

vitality [vaɪtǽlətɪ] *s.* vitalidad.

vitamin [váɪtəmɪn] *s.* vitamina.

vivacious [vaɪvéʃəs] *adj.* vivaz, vivaracho, vivo, alegre, animado.

vivacity [vaɪvǽsətɪ] *s.* viveza, vivacidad.

vivid [vívɪd] *adj.* vívido, vivo; animado.

vocabulary [vokǽbjələrɪ] *s.* vocabulario.

vocal [vókl] *adj.* vocal; oral; **to be**

— hablar, expresarse.

vocation [vokéʃən] s. vocación.

vogue [vog] s. boga, moda; **in —** en boga, de moda.

voice [vɔɪs] s. voz; habla; voto; v. expresar, decir; **-d consonant** consonante sonora.

voiceless [vɔ́ɪslɪs] adj. mudo; sin voz; **— consonant** consonante sorda.

void [vɔɪd] adj. vacío; nulo, inválido; **— of** falto de, desprovisto de; s. vacío; v. vaciar, evacuar; anular, invalidar.

volatile [válətl] adj. volátil; inconstante.

volcanic [valkǽnɪk] adj. volcánico.

volcano [valkéno] s. volcán.

volition [volíʃən] s. volición; voluntad.

volley [válɪ] s. descarga, lluvia (de piedras, flechas, balas, etc.); voleo (de la pelota); v. descargar una lluvia de proyectiles; volear una pelota.

volt [volt] s. voltio.

voltage [vóltɪdʒ] s. voltaje.

volume [váljəm] s. volumen; tomo; bulto; suma, cantidad.

voluminous [vəlámənəs] adj. voluminoso.

voluntary [váləntɛrɪ] adj. voluntario.

volunteer [valəntír] s. voluntario; adj. voluntario; de voluntarios; v. ofrecer, dar voluntariamente; ofrecerse.

voluptuous [vəláptʃʊəs] adj. voluptuoso.

vomit [vámɪt] s. vómito; v. vomitar, Am. deponer.

voracious [vɔréʃəs] adj. voraz.

vote [vot] s. voto; votación; v. votar; votar por.

voter [vótə] s. votante, elector.

vouch [vautʃ] v. **to — for** dar fe de; garantizar, responder de; salir fiador de.

voucher [váutʃə] s. comprobante, justificante; recibo; fiador.

vouchsafe [vautʃséf] v. otorgar, conceder.

vow [vau] s. voto; juramento; v. votar, jurar, hacer voto de.

vowel [váuəl] s. & adj. vocal.

voyage [vɔ́ɪɪdʒ] s. viaje; travesía; v. viajar.

vulgar [válgə] adj. soez, ordinario, grosero; vulgar.

vulture [váltʃə] s. buitre, Am. cóndor.

W

wabble [wábl] v. tambalear(se), bambolear(se); vacilar; temblar; s. tambaleo, bamboleo; balanceo.

wad [wad] s. taco; bodoque; pelotilla, bolita, rollo; **— of money** rollo de

billetes (de banco); dinero; v. atacar (un arma de fuego); rellenar; hacer una pelotilla de.

waddle [wádl] v. anadear; contonearse, zarandearse (al andar); s. anadeo; zarandeo, contoneo.

wade [wed] v. vadear; chapotear; andar descalzo por la orilla del agua; **to — through a book** leer con dificultad un libro.

wafer [wéfə] s. oblea; hostia (consagrada).

waft [wæft] v. llevar en vilo, llevar por el aire; llevar a flote; s. ráfaga de aire; movimiento (de la mano).

wag [wæg] v. menear; sacudir; **to — the tail** colear, menear la cola; s. meneo; bromista, farsante.

wage [wedʒ] v. hacer (guerra); dar (batalla); s. (usualmente wages) paga, jornal; **— earner** jornalero, obrero; trabajador.

wager [wédʒə] s. apuesta; v. apostar.

wagon [wǽgən] s. carro, carreta; carretón.

wail [wel] v. gemir, lamentar; s. gemido, lamento.

waist [west] s. cintura; talle; blusa; **—band** pretina.

waistcoat [wéstkot] s. chaleco.

wait [wet] v. esperar, aguardar; servir; **to — for** esperar, aguardar; **to — on** (**upon**) servir a; atender a; **to — table** servir la mesa, servir de mozo o camarero (en un restaurante); s. espera; **to lie in — for** estar en acecho de.

waiter [wétə] s. mozo, camarero, sirviente, Am. mesero.

waiting [wétɪŋ] s. espera; **— room** sala de espera.

waitress [wétrɪs] s. camarera, moza, Am. mesera.

waive [wev] v. renunciar a; **to — one's right** renunciar voluntariamente a sus derechos.

wake [wek] v. despertar(se); **to — up** despertar(se); despabilarse; s. velatorio (acto de velar a un muerto), Am. velorio; estela (huella que deja un barco en el agua); **in the — of** después de, detrás de.

wakeful [wékfəl] adj. desvelado, despierto; insomne.

waken [wékən] v. despertar(se); Am. recordar (a una persona que está dormida).

walk [wɔk] v. andar, caminar, ir a pie; recorrer a pie; pasear; **to — away** irse, marcharse; **to — back home**

volverse a casa (a pie); **to — down** bajar; **to — in** entrar; **to — out** salirse, irse; parar el trabajo, declararse en huelga; **to — the streets** callejear; **to — up** subir; *s.* paseo; senda, vereda; acera; paso (*del caballo*); manera de andar; **— of life** vocación; **a ten minutes'** — una caminata de diez minutos.

wall [wɔl] *s.* pared; muro; muralla; **low mud — tapia; to drive to the —** poner entre la espada y la pared, poner en un aprieto.

wallet [wálɪt] *s.* cartera.

wallflower [wólflauə] *s.* alelí; **to be a — at a dance** comer pavo, *Am.* planchar el asiento.

wallop [wáləp] *v.* pegar, zurrar, golpear; *s.* guantada, bofetón, golpazo.

wallow [wálo] *v.* revolcarse; chapalear o chapotear (*en el lodo*).

wallpaper [wólpepə] *s.* papel (de empapelar).

walnut [wólnət] *s.* nuez de nogal; nogal; **— tree** nogal.

waltz [wɔlts] *s.* vals; *v.* valsar, bailar el vals.

wan [wan] *adj.* pálido, enfermizo, enclenque; lánguido.

wand [wand] *s.* vara, varita; **magic —** varita de virtud.

wander [wándə] *v.* vagar, errar; **to — away** extraviarse; **to — away from** apartarse de, desviarse de; **my mind —s easily** me distraigo fácilmente.

wanderer [wándərə] *s.* vago, vagabundo.

wane [wen] *v.* menguar; decaer; *s.* mengua; diminución; **to be on the —** ir menguando; ir desapareciendo.

want [wɑnt] *v.* querer, desear; necesitar; *s.* falta; necesidad; escasez, carencia; **to be in —** estar necesitado.

wanting [wántɪŋ] *adj.* falto; deficiente; necesitado.

wanton [wántən] *adj.* desenfrenado, libre; licencioso; inconsiderado; temerario.

war [wɔr] *s.* guerra; *v.* guerrear, hacer guerra; **to — on** guerrear con.

warble [wórbl] *v.* gorjear; trinar; *s.* gorjeo; trino.

warbler [wórblə] *s.* cantor; pájaro gorjeador.

ward [wɔrd] *s.* pupilo, menor o huérfano (*bajo tutela*); cuadra (*de hospital, prisión, etc.*); distrito (*de una ciudad*); *v.* **to — off** resguardarse de; evitar; parar (*un golpe*).

warden [wórdn] *s.* guardián; alcaide; **prison —** alcaide de una prisión.

wardrobe [wórdrob] *s.* guardarropa, ropero, armario; vestuario; ropa.

warehouse [wérhaus] *s.* almacén, depósito.

wares [werz] *s. pl.* artículos, mercancías, mercaderías, efectos.

warfare [wórfɛr] *s.* guerra.

warlike [wórlaɪk] *adj.* guerrero, bélico.

warm [wɔrm] *adj.* caliente, cálido, caluroso; acalorado; cordial; reciente; **—hearted** de buen corazón; **he is —** tiene calor; **it is — today** hace calor hoy; *v.* calentar(se); **to — over** recalentar; **to — up** calentar(se); acalorarse; entusiasmarse.

warmth [wɔrmθ] *s.* calor; cordialidad.

warn [wɔrn] *v.* avisar, advertir, amonestar; prevenir, precaver.

warning [wórnɪŋ] *s.* aviso, advertencia, amonestación; escarmiento; **let that be a —** to you que te sirva de escarmiento.

warp [wɔrp] *s.* urdimbre (*de un tejido*); torcedura, deformación; comba; *v.* combar(se), deformar(se), torcer(se); urdir (*los hilos de un telar*).

warrant [wórent] *s.* autorización; garantía, justificación; comprobante; orden, mandato, citación (*ante un juez*); *v.* autorizar; garantizar; justificar.

warrior [wórɪə] *s.* guerrero.

warship [wórʃɪp] *s.* buque de guerra, acorazado.

wart [wɔrt] *s.* verruga.

wary [wérɪ] *adj.* cauteloso, cauto, precavido, prevenido; **to be — of** desconfiar de.

was [waz] *pret. de* **to be** (*primera y tercera persona del singular*).

wash [waʃ] *v.* lavar(se); **to — away** deslavar(se); **to be -ed away by the waves** ser arrastrado por las olas; *s.* lavado; lavadura; lavatorio; lavazas, agua sucia; **mouth —** enjuague o enjuagatorio; **—bowl** lavabo, palangana, lavamanos; **—cloth** paño para lavarse; **— dress** vestido lavable; **— room** lavabo, lavatorio.

washable [wáʃəbl] *adj.* lavable.

washed-out [wáʃtáut] *adj.* desteñido; agotado, sin fuerzas.

washer [wáʃə] *s.* lavador; máquina de lavar; arandela (*para una tuerca*); **—woman** lavandera.

washing [wáʃɪŋ] *s.* lavado; ropa sucia o para lavar; ropa lavada; **— machine** lavadora, máquina de lavar.

wasp [wasp] *s.* avispa.

waste [west] *v.* gastar; desgastar; malgastar, desperdiciar, derrochar; disipar; **to — away** gastarse, consumirse; desgastarse; *s.* desperdicio; gasto inútil; **desgaste**; desechos, desperdicios; terreno baldío, desierto; *adj.* inútil, desechado; desierto; baldío, **— of time** pérdida de tiempo; **—basket** cesto para papeles; **— land** terreno baldío; **—paper** papeles inútiles, papel de desecho; **to go to —** gastarse, perderse; malgastarse, desperdiciarse; **to lay —** asolar, arruinar.

wasteful [wéstfəl] *adj.* despilfarrado, gastador; desperdiciado; ineconómico.

watch [watʃ] *v.* mirar, observar; vigilar; velar; cuidar; **— out!** ¡cuidado!; **to — out for** tener cuidado con; cuidar; vigilar; *s.* reloj (de bolsillo); vela, vigilia; guardia; centinela, vigilante; **—chain** cadena de reloj, *Am.* leontina; **— charm** dije; **wrist —** reloj de pulsera; **to be on the —** tener cuidado; estar alerta; **to keep —** over vigilar a.

watchful [wátʃfəl] *adj.* alerto, vigilante, despierto, atento.

watchman [wátʃmən] *s.* vigilante, guardia, sereno.

watchtower [wátʃtauə] *s.* atalaya, mirador.

watchword [wátʃwɜd] *s.* contraseña, santo y seña, consigna; lema.

water [wótə] *s.* agua; **— color** acuarela; color para acuarela; **— power** fuerza hidráulica; **—shed** vertiente; **—sports** deportes acuáticos; **— supply** abastecimiento de agua; *v.* regar; aguar, diluir con agua; abrevar, dar de beber (*al ganado*); dar agua (*el ganado*); tomar agua (*un barco, locomotora, etc.*); **my eyes —** me lloran los ojos; **my mouth -s** se me hace agua la boca.

waterfall [wótəfɔl] *s.* cascada, catarata, caída de agua.

watermelon [wótəmelən] *s.* sandía.

waterproof [wótəpruf] *adj. & s.* impermeable; *v.* hacer impermeable.

waterspout [wótəspaut] *s.* surtidor; tromba, manga de agua.

waterway [wótəwe] *s.* vía de agua, río navegable, canal.

watery [wótəri] *adj.* aguado; acuoso; mojado, húmedo.

wave [wev] *v.* ondear; ondular; agitar; blandir (*una espada, bastón, etc.*); **to — aside** apartar, rechazar; **to — good-bye** hacer una seña o ademán de despedida; **to — hair** ondular el pelo; **to — one's hand** hacer una seña o señas con la mano; mover la mano; *s.* onda; ola; ondulación; **— of the hand** ademán, movimiento de la mano; **permanent —** ondulación permanente.

waver [wévə] *v.* oscilar, vacilar, titubear; tambalear(se); *s.* vacilación, titubeo.

wavy [wévɪ] *adj.* rizado, ondulado; ondulante.

wax [wæks] *s.* cera; **— candle** vela de cera; **— paper** papel encerado; *v.* encerar; pulir con cera; hacerse, ponerse; crecer (*la luna*).

way [we] *s.* vía; camino; ruta; senda; modo, manera; **— in** entrada; **— out** salida; **— through** paso, pasaje; **a long — off** muy lejos, a una larga distancia; **by — of** por, por vía de; **by — of comparison** a modo de comparación; **by the —** de paso; **in no — de** ningún modo; **on the — to** camino de, rumbo a; **out of the — fuera** del camino; apartado; a un lado; impropio; extraordinario; **to be in a bad —** hallarse en mal estado; **to be well under —** estar (*un trabajo*) ya bastante avanzado; **to give — ceder**; quebrarse; **to have one's —** hacer su capricho, salirse con la suya; **to make — for** abrir paso para.

waylay [welé] *v.* estar en acecho de (*alguien*); asaltar; detener (*a una persona*).

wayside [wésaid] *s.* borde del camino; **— inn** posada al borde del camino.

wayward [wéwəd] *adj.* voluntarioso, desobediente.

we [wi] *pron.* nosotros, nosotras.

weak [wik] *adj.* débil; flaco; endeble; **— market** mercado flojo; **weak-minded** de voluntad débil; simple; **— tea** té claro o suave.

weaken [wíkən] *v.* debilitar(se); desmayar, flaquear, perder ánimo.

weakly [wíklɪ] *adv.* débilmente; *adj.* enfermizo, débil, enclenque.

weakness [wíknɪs] *s.* debilidad; flaqueza.

wealth [wɛlθ] *s.* riqueza; copia, abundancia.

wealthy [wélθɪ] *adj.* rico.

wean [win] *v.* destetar; apartar gradualmente (*de un hábito, de una amistad*).

weapon [wépən] *s.* arma.

wear [wɛr] *v.* llevar, tener o traer puesto; usar; gastar, desgastar; **to — away** gastar(se), desgastar(se); consumir(se); **to — off** desgastar(se), gastar(se); borrarse; **to — out** gastar(se); desgastar(se), consumir(se); agotar; cansar; **it -s well** es duradero; dura mucho; **as the day wore on** a medida que pasaba el día; *s.* uso, gasto; durabilidad; — **and tear** desgaste; uso; **men's** — ropa para hombres; **clothes for summer** — ropa de verano.

wearily [wírɪlɪ] *adv.* penosamente, con cansancio, con fatiga, fatigadamente.

weariness [wírɪnɪs] *s.* cansancio, fatiga.

wearing [wérɪŋ] *adj.* cansado, aburrido, fastidioso.

wearisome [wírɪsəm] *adj.* fatigoso, molesto, fastidioso.

weary [wírɪ] *adj.* cansado, fatigado, aburrido; *v.* cansar(se), fatigar(se).

weasel [wíźl] *s.* comadreja.

weather [wéðɚ] *s.* tiempo; **weatherbeaten** desgastado o curtido por la intemperie; — **bureau** oficina meteorológica; — **conditions** condiciones atmosféricas; —**vane** veleta; **it is fine** — hace buen tiempo; **to be under the** — estar enfermo; estar indispuesto; *v.* exponer a la intemperie; orear, secar al aire; **to** — **a storm** aguantar un chubasco; salir ileso de una tormenta.

weave [wiv] *v.* tejer, entretejer; urdir; **to** — **together** entretejer, entrelazar; combinar; *s.* tejido.

weaver [wívɚ] *s.* tejedor.

web [web] *s.* tela; membrana (*entre los dedos de los pájaros acuáticos*); **spider's** — telaraña.

wed [wed] *v.* casarse; casarse con; casar; *p.p. de* **to wed**.

wedded [wédɪd] *p.p. & adj.* casado; unido; — **to an idea** aferrado a una idea.

wedding [wédɪŋ] *s.* boda, casamiento, nupcias, enlace; — **day** día de bodas; — **trip** viaje de novios; **silver** — bodas de plata.

wedge [wedʒ] *s.* cuña; **entering** — cuña, entrada, medio de entrar, modo de penetrar; *v.* acuñar, meter cuñas; **to be -d between** estar encajado entre.

Wednesday [wénzdɪ] *s.* miércoles.

wee [wi] *adj.* diminuto, chiquitico, pequeñito.

weed [wid] *s.* cizaña, mala hierba; *v.* desherbar (o desyerbar), quitar o arrancar la mala hierba; **to** — **a garden** desherbar un huerto; **to** — **out** escardar; eliminar, arrancar, entresacar.

weedy [wídɪ] *adj.* herboso, lleno de malas hierbas.

week [wik] *s.* semana; —**day** día de trabajo, día laborable, día hábil; —**end** fin de semana; **a** — **from today** de hoy en ocho días.

weekly [wíklɪ] *adj.* semanal, semanario; *adv.* semanalmente, por semana; *s.* semanario, periódico o revista semanal.

weep [wip] *v.* llorar.

weeping [wípɪŋ] *adj.* llorón; lloroso; — **willow** sauce llorón; *s.* llanto, lloro, lágrimas.

weevil [wívl] *s.* gorgojo.

weigh [we] *v.* pesar; ponderar, considerar; **to** — **anchor** zarpar, levar el ancla; **to** — **down** agobiar; abrumar; **to** — **on one's conscience** serle a uno gravoso, pesarle a uno.

weight [wet] *s.* peso; pesa (*de reloj o medida para pesar*); carga; **paper**—pisapapeles; *v.* cargar, sobrecargar; añadir peso a; asignar un peso o valor relativo a.

weighty [wétɪ] *adj.* grave, ponderoso; de mucho peso; importante.

weird [wɪrd] *adj.* extraño, raro, misterioso, fantástico.

welcome [wélkəm] *s.* bienvenida; buena acogida; *adj.* grato, agradable; bien acogido, bien quisto; bienvenido; bien recibido; — **home!** ¡bienvenido!; — **rest** grato reposo o descanso; **you are** — no hay de qué, de nada (*para contestar a* "thank you"); **you are** — **here** está Vd. en su casa; **you are** — **to use it** se lo presto con todo gusto; está a su disposición; *v.* dar la bienvenida a; acoger o recibir con gusto.

weld [weld] *v.* soldar(se); *s.* soldadura.

welfare [wélfɛr] *s.* bienestar; bien; felicidad; — **work** labor social o de beneficencia.

well [wel] *adv.* bien; **he is** — **over fifty** tiene mucho más de cincuenta años; — **then** pues bien, ahora bien, conque; **well-bred** bien criado; bien educado, **well-meaning** bien intencionado; **well-nigh** casi, muy cerca de; *adj.* bueno; bien de salud, sano; conveniente; — **and good** santo y muy bueno; **well-being** bienestar; **well-off** acomodado, adinerado; en buenas condiciones; **well-to-do** próspero, adinerado; **all is** — no hay novedad, todo va bien; **it is** — **to do it** conviene hacerlo, es conveniente hacerlo.

well [wel] *s.* pozo; cisterna; manantial; **artesian** — pozo artesiano; *v.* manar; **tears -ed up in her eyes** se le arrasaron los ojos de lágrimas.

welt [welt] *s.* verdugo, verdugón, roncha.

went [went] *pret. de* **to go.**

wept [wept] *pret. & p.p. de* **to weep.**

were [wɜ] *pret. de* **to be** (*en el plural y en la segunda persona del singular del* *indicativo; es además el imperfecto del subjuntivo);* if **I — you** si yo fuera Vd.; **there —** había, hubo.

we**st** [west] *s.* oeste, occidente, ocaso; *adj.* occidental, del oeste; **West Indies** Antillas; *adv.* hacia el oeste, al oeste; en el oeste.

western [wéstən] *adj.* occidental, del oeste.

westerner [wéstənə] *s.* natural del oeste, habitante del oeste, occidental.

westward [wéstwəd] *adv.* hacia el oeste; *adj.* occidental, oeste.

wet [wet] *adj.* húmedo; mojado; **— nurse** nodriza, ama de leche; *s.* humedad; antiprohibicionista (*el que favorece la venta de bebidas alcohólicas*); *v.* mojar; humedecer; *pret. & p.p. de* to wet.

wetness [wétnis] *s.* humedad.

whack [hwæk] *v.* golpear, pegar; *s.* golpe; golpazo; tentativa, prueba.

whale [hwel] *s.* ballena; *v.* pescar ballenas.

wharf [hwɔrf] *s.* muelle, embarcadero.

what [hwɑt] *pron. interr.* qué; qué cosa; cuál; *pron. rel.* lo que; **— for?** ¿para qué? *adj.* qué; **— book?** ¿qué libro? **— a man!** ¡qué hombre!; **— happy children!** ¡qué niños más (*o* tan) felices!; **take — books you need** tome Vd. los libros que necesite.

whatever [hwɑtévə] *pron.* cualquiera cosa que, lo que, cuanto, todo lo que; **— do you mean?** ¿qué quiere Vd. decir?; **do it,** — happens hágalo suceda lo que suceda; *adj.* cualquiera; **any person** — una persona cualquiera; **no money** — nada de dinero.

whatsoever [hwɑtsoévə] = whatever.

wheat [hwit] *s.* trigo; **cream of —** crema de trigo.

wheel [hwil] *s.* rueda; rodaja; disco; bicicleta; timón; **— chair** silla rodante, silla de ruedas; **steering —** volante (*de automóvil*); rueda del timón; *v.* rodar; hacer rodar; girar; acarrear; andar en bicicleta; **to — around** dar una vuelta; girar sobre los talones; **to — the baby** pasear al bebé en su cochecito.

wheelbarrow [hwílbæro] *s.* carretilla.

when [hwen] *adv. & conj.* cuando; *adv. interr.* ¿cuándo?

whence [hwens] *adv.* de donde; de que.

whenever [hwenévə] *adj. & conj.* cuando, siempre que, cada vez que.

where [hwer] *adv.* donde; adonde; en donde; por donde; **—?** ¿dónde?; ¿adónde?

whereabouts [hwérəbaùts] *s.* paradero;

adv. interr. ¿dónde?

whereas [hwerǽz] *conj.* mientras que puesto que, visto que, considerando que.

whereby [hwerbái] *adv.* por donde, por lo cual; con lo cual.

wherefore [hwérfor] *adv.* por qué; por lo cual; por eso, por lo tanto.

wherein [hwerín] *adv.* en qué; en donde en lo cual.

whereof [hweráv] *adv.* de que; de donde de quien, de quienes.

whereupon [hwerəpán] *adv.* después de lo cual; entonces.

wherever [hwerévə] *adv.* dondequiera que, adondequiera que, por dondequiera que.

wherewithal [hwérwiðɔl] *s.* medios, fondos; dinero.

whet [hwet] *v.* amolar, afilar; aguzar estimular.

whether [hwéðə] *conj.* si; ya sea que sea que; **— we escape or not** ya sea que escapemos o no; **I doubt —** dudo (de) que.

which [hwitʃ] *pron. interr.* ¿cuál?; ¿cuáles?; *pron. rel.* que; el cual, la cual los cuales, las cuales; el que, la que los que, las que; *adj. interr.* qué; **— boy has it?** ¿cuál de los muchachos lo tiene? ¿qué muchacho lo tiene?; — way did he go? ¿por qué camino se fué?; ¿por dónde se fué? **during —** time tiempo durante el cual.

whichever [hwitʃévə] *pron. & adj.* cualquiera (que), cualesquiera (que); el que, la que; **— road you take** cualquier camino que Vd. siga.

whiff [hwif] *s.* soplo; fumada, bocanada repentino olor o hedor; *v* soplar; echar bocanadas.

while [hwail] *s.* rato; tiempo, temporada **a short —** un ratito; **a short — ago** hace poco, hace poco rato; **to be worth —** valer la pena; *conj.* mientras mientras que; *v.* **to — away the time** pasar el tiempo.

whilst [hwailst] *conj.* mientras, mientras que.

whim [hwim] *s.* capricho, antojo.

whimper [hwímpə] *v.* lloriquear, gimotear; quejarse; *s.* lloriqueo, gimoteo quejido.

whimsical [hwímzikl] *adj.* caprichoso.

whine [hwain] *v.* lloriquear; quejarse *s.* gemido, quejido.

whiner [hwáinə] *s.* llorón, persona quejosa, *Am.* quejumbres.

whip [hwip] *v.* azotar, fustigar; zurrar; dar una paliza a, dar latigazos a;

batir (*crema*, *huevos*); vencer; **to —
up** batir; coger o asir de repente;
hacer de prisa; *s.* azote, látigo, fuete;
batido.

whipping [hwípiŋ] *s.* tunda, zurra, paliza; **— cream** crema para batir.

whir [hwɜ] *v.* zumbar; *s.* zumbido.

whirl [hwɜl] *v.* girar, dar vueltas; arremolinarse; **my head -s** siento vértigo,
estoy desvanecido; *s.* giro, vuelta; remolino; espiral (*de humo*); confusión.

whirlpool [hwɜlpul] *s.* remolino, vorágine, vórtice.

whirlwind [hwɜlwind] *s.* remolino, torbellino.

whisk [hwɪsk] *v.* barrer; desempolvar
(*con escobilla*); batir (*huevos*); **to —
away** barrer de prisa; llevarse de prisa, arrebatar; irse de prisa, escaparse;
to — something out of sight escamotear algo, esconder algo de prisa;
s. **— broom** escobilla; **with a — of
the broom** de un escobillazo.

whisker [hwískə] *s.* pelo de la barba;
-s barbas; patillas; bigotes (*del gato*).

whiskey [hwíski] *s.* whisky (*aguardiente
de maíz, centeno, etc.*).

whisper [hwíspə] *v.* cuchichear, hablar
en secreto; soplar, decir al oído; susurrar; secretearse; **it is -ed that** corre
la voz que; dízque, dicen que; *s.* cuchicheo, secreteo; susurro; murmullo;
to talk in a — hablar en secreto;
susurrar.

whistle [hwísl] *v.* silbar; chiflar; pitar;
to — for someone llamar a uno con
un silbido; *s.* silbido, chiflido; sibato,
pito.

whit [hwɪt] *s.* jota, pizca.

white [hwaɪt] *adj.* blanco; puro; inocente; honrado, recto; **—caps** cabrillas o
palomas (*olas con crestas blancas*); **—
lead** albayalde; **— lie** mentirilla, mentira venial; **white-livered** cobarde; **to
show the — feather** mostrar cobardía, portarse como cobarde; *s.* blanco; clara (*del huevo*).

whiten [hwaɪtn] *v.* blanquear; emblanquecer(se), poner(se) blanco.

whiteness [hwaɪtnɪs] *s.* blancura; palidez; pureza.

whitewash [hwaɪtwaʃ] *v.* blanquear, enjalbegar; encubrir, disimular (*faltas,
errores*); absolver (*sin justicia*); *s.* lechada.

whither [hwíðə] *adv.* adonde; **—?** ¿adónde?

whitish [hwaɪtɪʃ] *adj.* blancuzco, blanquecino, blanquizco.

whittle [hwítl] *v.* cortar, mondar, tallar;

tajar, sacar punta a (*un lápiz*); **to —
down expenses** cercenar o reducir los
gastos.

whiz [hwɪz] *v.* zumbar; *s.* zumbido, silbido; **to be a —** ser un águila, ser
muy listo.

who [hu] *pron. rel.* quien, quienes, que,
el que, la que, los que, las que; **he —**
el que, quien; *pron. interr.* ¿quién?;
¿quiénes?; **— is it?** ¿quién es?

whoever [huévə] *pron.* quienquiera que,
cualquiera que; el que.

whole [hol] *adj.* todo; entero; íntegro;
the — day todo el día; **—hearted**
sincero, cordial; **—heartedly** de todo
corazón; con todo ánimo; *s.* todo,
total, totalidad; **as a —** en conjunto;
on the — en general, en conjunto.

wholesale [hólsel] *s.* venta al por mayor,
Am. mayoreo; **by —** al por mayor;
adj. al por mayor; en grandes cantidades; **— dealer** comerciante al por
mayor, *Am.* mayorista; **— slaughter**
matanza; gran hecatombe; **— trade**
comercio al por mayor, *Am.* comercio
mayorista; *adv.* al por mayor, por
mayor; *v.* vender al por mayor, *Am.*
mayorear.

wholesome [hólsəm] *adj.* saludable,
sano; salubre; **— man** hombre normalmente bueno o de buena índole.

wholly [hólɪ] *adv.* enteramente, completamente, totalmente.

whom [hum] *pron. pers.* a quien, a
quienes; que; al que (a la que, a los
que, *etc.*); al cual (a la cual, a los
cuales, *etc.*); for **— para quien; **— did
you see?** ¿a quién vió Vd.?

whoop [hup] *s.* grito, chillido, alarido;
respiro convulsivo (*que acompaña a la
tos ferina*); *v.* gritar, vocear, echar
gritos; respirar convulsivamente (*al
toser*); **to — it up** armar una gritería,
gritar; **whooping cough** tos ferina.

whore [hor] *s.* ramera, puta, prostituta.

whose [huz] *pron.* cuyo, cuya, cuyos,
cuyas; *pron. interr.* ¿de quién?; ¿de
quiénes?; **— book is this?** ¿de quién
es este libro?

why [hwaɪ] *adv.* ¿por qué?; **the reason
—** la razón por la que (*o* la cual); **—,
of course!** ¡sí, por supuesto!; ¡claro
que sí!; **—, that is not true!** ¡si esò
no es verdad! *s.* porqué, causa, razón,
motivo.

wick [wɪk] *s.* mecha, pabilo.

wicked [wíkɪd] *adj.* malvado, malo, inicuo.

wickedness [wíkɪdnɪs] *s.* maldad, iniquidad, perversidad.

wicker [wíkə] s. mimbre; — **chair** silla de mimbre.

wicket [wíkɪt] s. postigo; ventanilla.

wide [waɪd] adj. ancho; amplio; vasto; extenso; — **apart** muy apartados; **wide-awake** muy despierto; alerta, vigilante; — **of the mark** muy lejos del blanco; — **open** muy abierto; abierto de par en par; **far and** — por todas partes, extensamente; **to open** — abrir mucho; abrir (la puerta) de par en par; **two feet** — dos pies de ancho (o de anchura).

widely [wáɪdlɪ] adv. ampliamente; extensamente; muy; mucho.

widen [wáɪdn] v. ensanchar(se), ampliar(se), dilatar(se).

widespread [wáɪdspréd] adj. muy esparcid.., muy extensivo; bien difundido; extendido; general, extendido por todas partes.

widow [wído] s. viuda.

widower [wídəwə] s. viudo.

width [wídə] s. ancho, anchura.

wield [wild] v. manejar; esgrimir (la espada o la pluma); ejercer (el poder).

wife [waɪf] s. esposa.

wig [wɪg] s. peluca.

wiggle [wígl] v. menear(se); s. meneo.

wigwam [wígwam] s. choza de los indios norteños.

wild [waɪld] adj. salvaje; feroz, fiero; montaraz; silvestre; indómito; Am. cimarrón; impetuoso, desenfrenado; bullicioso; violento; loco; enojado; desatinado; ansioso; **to talk** — disparatar, desatinar; s. yermo, desierto, monte.

wildcat [wáɪldkæt] s. gato montés; — **scheme** empresa arriesgada.

wilderness [wíldənɪs] s. yermo, desierto, monte; inmensidad.

wildness [wáɪldnɪs] s. salvajez; ferocidad, fiereza; locura.

wile [waɪl] s. ardid, engaño; astucia.

wilful, willful [wílfəl] adj. voluntarioso, testarudo, caprichudo; intencional.

will [wɪl] v. querer, decidir; ordenar, mandar; legar; v. defect. y aux. querer; rigurosamente debe usarse para formar el futuro en las segundas y terceras personas : **she** — **go** ella irá; en las primeras personas indica voluntad o determinación : **I** — **not do it** no lo haré, no quiero hacerlo.

will [wɪl] s. voluntad; albedrío; testamento; **free** — libre albedrío; **ill** — mala voluntad, malquerencia.

willing [wílɪŋ] adj. bien dispuesto, deseoso, complaciente; voluntario; **-ly** adv. con gusto, de buena gana, de buena voluntad; voluntariamente.

willingness [wílɪŋnɪs] s. buena voluntad, buena gana.

willow [wílo] s. sauce; mimbrera; **weeping** — sauce llorón.

wilt [wɪlt] v. marchitar(se); ajar(se); desmayar; languidecer.

wily [wáɪlɪ] adj. astuto, artero.

win [wɪn] v. ganar; lograr, obtener; persuadir; alcanzar; **to** — **out** ganar, triunfar; salirse con la suya; **to** — **over** persuadir; atraer; alcanzar o ganar el favor de.

wince [wɪns] v. cejar (ante una dificultad o peligro); encogerse (de dolor, susto, etc.).

winch [wɪntʃ] s. malacate.

wind [wɪnd] s. viento, aire; resuello; — **instrument** instrumento de viento; **to get** — **of** barruntar; tener noticia de.

wind [waɪnd] v. enredar; devanar, ovillar; dar cuerda a (un reloj); serpentear (un camino); dar vueltas; **to** — **someone around one's finger** manejar fácilmente a alguien, gobernarle; **to** — **up one's affairs** terminar o concluir uno sus negocios; s. vuelta; recodo.

windbag [wíndbæg] s. fuelle, parlanchín, hablador.

windfall [wíndfol] s. golpe de fortuna, ganancia repentina, herencia inesperada.

winding [wáɪndɪŋ] adj. sinuoso, tortuoso, que da vueltas; — **staircase** escalera de caracol.

windmill [wíndmɪl] s. molino de viento.

window [wíndo] s. ventana; **show** — escaparate, vitrina, aparador, Am. vidriera; — **shade** visillo, cortinilla; — **sill** antepecho, repisa de ventana.

windowpane [wíndopen] s. cristal de ventana, vidriera.

windpipe [wíndpaɪp] s. tráquea, gaznate.

windshield [wíndʃild] s. parabrisa, guardabrisa.

windy [wíndɪ] adj. airoso; ventoso; **it is** — hace aire, ventea, sopla el viento.

wine [waɪn] s. vino; — **cellar** bodega.

wing [wɪŋ] s. ala; bastidor (de escenario); **under the** — **of** bajo la tutela de; **to take** — levantar el vuelo.

winged [wɪŋd, wíŋɪd] adj. alado.

wink [wɪŋk] v. guiñar; pestañear, parpadear, s. guiño, guiñada· **I didn't sleep a** — no pegué los ojos en toda la noche.

winner [wínə] s. ganador; vencedor; —

of a prize agraciado, premiado.

winning [wínɪŋ] *adj.* ganancioso; triunfante, victorioso; atractivo, encantador; **-s** *s. pl.* ganancias.

winsome [wínsəm] *adj.* simpático, atractivo, gracioso.

winter [wíntə] *s.* invierno; **— clothes** ropa de invierno; *v.* invernar, pasar el invierno.

wintry [wíntrɪ] *adj.* invernal, de invierno; frío, helado.

wipe [waɪp] *v.* secar; enjugar; limpiar; **to — away one's tears** limpiarse las lágrimas; **to — off** borrar; limpiar; **to — out a regiment** destruir o aniquilar un regimiento.

wire [waɪr] *s.* alambre; telegrama; **by —** por telégrafo; **— entanglement** alambrada; **— fence** alambrado; **— netting** tela metálica, alambrado; **to pull -s** mover los hilos; *v.* poner alambrado, instalar alambrado eléctrico; atar con alambre; telegrafiar.

wireless [wáɪrlɪs] *adj.* inalámbrico, sin hilos; **— telegraphy** radiotelegrafía; *s.* radio, radiotelegrafía; telegrafía sin hilos; radiotelefonía; radiograma.

wiry [wáɪrɪ] *adj.* de alambre; como alambre; nervudo.

wisdom [wízdəm] *s.* sabiduría, saber; cordura; prudencia; **— tooth** muela del juicio.

wise [waɪz] *adj.* sabio, cuerdo, sensato; discreto, prudente; **the Three Wise Men** los Tres Reyes Magos; **to get — to** darse cuenta de; *s.* modo, manera; **in no —** de ningún modo.

wisecrack [wáɪzkræk] *s.* bufonada, dicho agudo o chocarrero, dicharacho.

wish [wɪʃ] *v.* desear, querer; **to — for** desear; anhelar; **I — it were true!** ¡ojalá (que) fuera verdad!; *s.* deseo.

wistful [wístfəl] *adj.* anhelante, anheloso, ansioso; tristón, melancólico.

wit [wɪt] *s.* agudeza, sal, chiste; ingenio; hombre agudo o de ingenio; **to be at one's wit's end** haber agotado todo su ingenio; **to be out of one's -s** estar fuera de sí, estar loco; **to lose one's -s** perder el juicio; **to use one's -s** valerse de su industria ó ingenio.

witch [wɪtʃ] *s.* hechicera; bruja.

witchcraft [wítʃkræft] *s.* hechicería.

with [wɪð, wɪθ] *prep.* con; para con; en compañía de; **filled —** lleno de; **ill —** enfermo de; **the one — the black hat** el del (o la del) sombrero negro.

withdraw [wɪðdrɔ́] *v.* retirar(se); apartar(se); separar(se); **to — a statement** retractarse.

withdrawal [wɪðdrɔ́əl] *s.* retirada, retiro.

withdrawn [wɪðdrɔ́n] *p.p. de* **to withdraw.**

withdrew [wɪðdrú] *pret. de* **to withdraw.**

wither [wíðə] *v.* marchitar(se); ajar(se); secar(se).

withheld [wɪðhéld] *pret. & p.p. de* **to withhold.**

withhold [wɪðhóld] *v.* retener; detener; **to — one's consent** negarse a dar su consentimiento.

within [wɪðín] *prep.* dentro de; **— call** al alcance de la voz; **— five miles** a poco menos de cinco millas; **it is — my power** está en mi mano; *adv.* dentro, adentro.

without [wɪðáut] *prep.* sin; **— my seeing him** sin que yo le viera; *adv.* fuera, afuera.

withstand [wɪðstǽnd] *v.* resistir; aguantar, padecer.

withstood [wɪðstúd] *pret. & p.p. de* **to withstand.**

witness [wítnɪs] *s.* testigo; testimonio; *v.* ver, presenciar; ser testigo de; atestiguar, dar fe de.

witticism [wítəsɪzəm] *s.* ocurrencia, agudeza, dicho agudo.

witty [wítɪ] *adj.* agudo, ocurrente, gracioso, divertido, chistoso; **— remark** dicho agudo, agudeza, ocurrencia.

wives [waɪvz] *s. pl. de* **wife.**

wizard [wízəd] *s.* genio, hombre de ingenio; mago, mágico.

woe [wo] *s.* miseria, aflicción, infortunio; **— is me!** ¡miserable de mí!

woke [wok] *pret. de* **to wake.**

wolf [wʊlf] (*pl.* **wolves** [wʊlvz] *s.* lobo.

woman [wúmən] (*pl.* **women** [wímɪn]) *s.* mujer; **— writer** escritora.

womanhood [wúmənhʊd] *s.* estado de mujer; la mujer (las mujeres); integridad femenil; feminidad.

womankind [wúmənkaɪnd] *s.* la mujer, las mujeres, el sexo femenino.

womanly [wúmənlɪ] *adj.* femenil, mujeril, femenino; *adv.* femenilmente, como mujer.

womb [wuml] *s.* vientre, entrañas; útero, matriz.

won [wʌn] *pret. & p.p. de* **to win.**

wonder [wʌ́ndə] *s.* maravilla; prodigio; admiración; **in —** maravillado; **no — that** no es mucho que; no es extraño que; *v.* asombrarse, maravillarse, pasmarse, admirarse; **to — at** admirarse de, maravillarse de; **I — what time it is** ¿qué hora será? **I — when he came** ¿cuándo vendría? **I should not — if** no me extrañaría que.

wonderful [wˈʌndəfəl] *adj.* maravilloso, admirable; **-ly** *adv.* maravillosamente, admirablemente, a las mil maravillas: **-ly well** sumamente bien.

wondrous [wˈʌndrəs] *adj.* maravilloso, pasmoso, extraño.

wont [wʌnt] *adj.* acostumbrado; **to be — to** soler, acostumbrar, *Am.* saber; *s.* costumbre, hábito, uso.

woo [wu] *v.* cortejar, enamorar, galantear.

wood [wʊd] *s.* madera, palo; leña, **-s** bosque; selva, **— engraving** grabado en madera; **—shed** leñera, cobertizo para leña; **fire—** leña; **piece of fire—** leño.

woodcutter [wˈʊdkʌtə] *s.* leñador.

wooded [wˈʊdɪd] *adj.* arbolado, poblado de árboles.

wooden [wˈʊdn̩] *adj.* de madera, de palo; tieso.

woodland [wˈʊdlænd] *s.* monte, bosque, selva.

woodman [wˈʊdmən] *s.* leñador; habitante del bosque.

woodpecker [wˈʊdpɛkə] *s.* pájaro carpintero.

woodwork [wˈʊdwɜk] *s.* maderamen; labrado en madera; obra de carpintería.

woof [wuf] *s.* trama (*de un tejido*); tejido.

wool [wʊl] *s.* lana; *adj.* de lana; lanar; **wool-bearing** lanar; **— dress** vestido de lana.

woolen [wˈʊlɪn] *adj.* de lana; lanudo; **— mill** fábrica de tejidos de lana; *s.* tejido de lana; género o paño de lana.

woolly [wˈʊlɪ] *adj.* lanudo; de lana.

word [wɜd] *s.* palabra; vocablo, voz; noticia, aviso; mandato, orden; **pass—** contraseña; **by — of mouth** de palabra, verbalmente; *v.* expresar; redactar, formular.

wordy [wˈɜdɪ] *adj.* palabrero, verboso, ampuloso.

wore [wor] *pret. de* to wear.

work [wɜk] *s.* trabajo; obra; faena; tarea; empleo, ocupación; labor; **-s** taller, fábrica; maquinaria, mecanismo; **at —** trabajando; ocupado; *v.* trabajar; funcionar; obrar; surtir efecto; manejar, manipular; resolver (*un problema*); explotar (*una mina*); hacer trabajar; **to — havoc** hacer estropicios, causar daño; **to — loose** soltarse, aflojarse; **to — one's way through college** sufragar los gastos universitarios con su trabajo; **to — one's way up** subir por sus propios esfuerzos; **to — out a plan** urdir un plan; **to be all -ed up** estar sobreexcitado; **it didn't — out** no dió resultado; **the plan -ed well** tuvo buen éxito el plan.

worker [wˈɜkə] *s.* trabajador; obrero; operario.

working [wˈɜkɪŋ] *s.* funcionamiento, operación; cálculo (*de un problema*); explotación (*de una mina*); *adj.* obrero, trabajador; **— class** clase obrera o trabajadora; **— hours** horas de trabajo; **a hard-working man** un hombre muy trabajador.

workingman [wˈɜkɪŋmæn] *s.* trabajador; obrero.

workman [wˈɜkmən] *s.* trabajador, obrero, operario.

workmanship [wˈɜkmənʃɪp] *s.* hechura; trabajo; mano de obra.

workshop [wˈɜkʃɑp] *s.* taller.

world [wɜld] *s.* mundo; **the World War** la Guerra Mundial.

worldly [wˈɜldlɪ] *adj.* mundano, mundanal, terreno, terrenal.

worm [wɜm] *s.* gusano; lombriz; **worm-eaten** comido de gusanos; carcomido, apolillado; *v.* **to — a secret out of someone** extraerle o sonsacarle un secreto a una persona; **to — oneself into** insinuarse en, meterse en.

worn [worn] *p.p. de* to wear; **worn-out** gastado, roto; rendido de fatiga.

worry [wˈɜɪ] *s.* inquietud, ansiedad, cuidado, preocupación, apuro, apuración; *v.* inquietar(se), preocupar(se), afligir(se), apurar(se).

worse [wɜs] *adj.* peor; más malo; *adv.* peor; **— and —** cada vez peor; **than ever** peor que nunca; **from bad to —** de mal en peor; **so much the —** tanto peor; **to be — off** estar peor que antes; **to change for the —** empeorar(se); **to get —** empeorar(se).

worship [wˈɜʃəp] *s.* adoración, culto, veneración; *v.* adorar; reverenciar.

worshiper [wˈɜʃəpə] *s.* adorador; **the -s** los fieles.

worst [wɜst] *adj.* peor, *adv.* peor; **the — el** peor; la peor; lo peor; *v.* derrotar.

worth [wɜθ] *s.* valor, valía, mérito; precio; **ten cent's — of** diez centavos de; **to get one's money's — out of** sacar todo el provecho posible del dinero gastado en; *adj.* digno de; **— hearing** digno de oírse; **to be — valer;** **to be — doing** valer la pena de hacerse; **to be — while** valer la pena.

worthless [wˈɜθlɪs] *adj.* sin valor; inútil;

despreciable.

worthy [wɜ́ði] *adj.* digno; valioso, apreciable; meritorio, merecedor; *s.* benemérito, hombre ilustre.

would [wʊd] *imperf. de indic. y de subj. del verbo defect.* **will: she — come every day** solía venir (o venía) todos los días; **if you — do it** si lo hiciera Vd.; *expresa a veces deseo:* **— that I knew it!** ¡quién lo supiera!; ¡ojalá que yo lo supiera!; *v. aux. del condicional* : **she said she — go** dijo que iría.

wound [wund] *s.* herida; llaga, lesión; *v.* herir; lastimar; agraviar.

wound [waʊnd] *pret. & p.p. de to wind.*

wove [wov] *pret. de to weave.*

woven [wóvən] *p.p. de to weave.*

wrangle [rǽŋgl] *v.* altercar, disputar, reñir; juntar, *Am.* rodear (*el ganado*); *s.* riña, pendencia.

wrap [ræp] *v.* envolver; enrollar, arrollar, **to — up** envolver(se); abrigar(se), tapar(se); **to be wrapped up in** estar envuelto en; estar absorto en; *s.* abrigo, manto.

wrapper [rǽpə] *s.* envoltura, cubierta; **woman's —** bata.

wrapping [rǽpɪŋ] *s.* envoltura; **— paper** papel de envolver.

wrath [ræθ] *s.* ira, cólera, rabia.

wrathful [rǽθfəl] *adj.* colérico, rabioso, iracundo.

wreath [riθ] *s.* guirnalda, corona; **— of smoke** espiral de humo.

wreathe [rið] *v.* hacer guirnaldas; adornar con guirnaldas; **-d in smiles** sonriente.

wreck [rek] *s.* ruina; destrucción; naufragio; accidente; destrozos, despojos (*de un naufragio*); *v.* arruinar; naufragar; echar a pique; destrozar, demoler; **to — a train** descarrilar un tren.

wrench [rentʃ] *v.* torcer, retorcer; arrancar, arrebatar; *s.* torcedura; torsión; tirón, arranque, *Am.* jalón; llave de tuercas; **monkey —** llave inglesa.

wrest [rest] *v.* arrebatar, arrancar; usurpar.

wrestle [résl] *v.* luchar a brazo partido; luchar; *s.* lucha a brazo partido.

wrestler [réslə] *s.* luchador (*a brazo partido*).

wretch [retʃ] *s.* miserable, infeliz; villano.

wretched [rétʃɪd] *adj.* miserable; desdichado, infeliz; afligido; bajo, vil; malísimo; **a — piece of work** un trabajo pésimo o malísimo.

wriggle [rɪ́gl] *v.* menear(se); retorcer(se); **to — out of** salirse de, escaparse de; escabullirse de.

wring [rɪŋ] *v.* torcer, retorcer; exprimir, estrujar; **to — money from someone** arrancar dinero a alguien; **to — out** exprimir (*la ropa*).

wrinkle [rɪ́ŋkl] *s.* arruga; surco, **the latest — in style** la última novedad; *v.* arrugar(se).

wrist [rɪst] *s.* muñeca, **— watch** reloj de pulsera.

writ [rɪt] *s.* auto, orden judicial, mandato jurídico; **the Holy Writ** la Sagrada Escritura.

write [raɪt] *v.* escribir; **to — back** contestar por carta; **to — down** apuntar, poner por escrito, **to — off** cancelar (*una deuda*); **to — out** poner por escrito; escribir por entero; **to — up** relatar, describir; redactar.

writer [ráɪtə] *s.* escritor; autor.

writhe [raɪð] *v.* retorcerse.

writing [ráɪtɪŋ] *s.* escritura; escrito; composición literaria; forma o estilo literario; **hand—** letra; **— desk** escritorio; **— paper** papel de escribir; **to put in —** poner por escrito.

written [rɪ́tn] *p.p. de to write.*

wrong [rɒŋ] *adj.* falso, incorrecto; malo; injusto; equivocado; mal hecho; inoportuno; inconveniente; **the — side of a fabric** el envés o el revés de un tejido; **the — side of the road** el lado izquierdo o contrario del camino; **that is the — book** ése no es el libro; **it is in the — place** no está en su sitio, está mal colocado; *adv.* mal; al revés; **to go —** extraviarse, descaminarse; resultar mal; *s.* mal, daño, perjuicio; injusticia; agravio; **to be in the —** no tener razón, estar equivocado; **to do —** hacer mal; *v.* perjudicar; agraviar; hacer mal a.

wrote [rot] *pret. de to write.*

wrought [rɒt] *pret. & p.p. irr. de to work; adj.* labrado; forjado; **— iron** hierro forjado, **— silver** plata labrada; **to be wrought-up** estar sobreexcitado.

wrung [rʌŋ] *pret. & p.p. de to wring.*

wry [raɪ] *adj.* torcido; **to make a — face** hacer una mueca.

Y

yacht [jɑt] *s.* yate, *v.* navegar en yate.

Yankee [jǽŋki] *adj. y s.* yanqui.

yard [jɑrd] *s.* yarda (*medida de longitud*); patio; cercado; terreno (*adyacente a una casa*); **back —** corral; **barn—**

corral; **navy** — arsenal; **ship**— astillero.

yardstick [járdstɪk] s. yarda (*de medir*); medida (*metro, vara, etc.*); patrón, norma.

yarn [jarn] s. estambre; hilado, hilaza; cuento enredado y poco probable.

yawn [jɔn] v. bostezar; s. bostezo.

yea [je] adv. sí; s. sí, voto afirmativo.

year [jɪr] s. año, —**book** anuario; -**'s income** renta anual; **by the** — por año; **leap** — año bisiesto.

yearly [jɪrlɪ] adj. anual; adv. anualmente; una vez al año, cada año.

yearn [jɜn] v. anhelar, **to** — **for** anhelar; suspirar por.

yearning [jɜnɪŋ] s. anhelo.

yeast [jist] s. levadura, fermento.

yell [jel] v. gritar, dar gritos, vociferar; s. grito, alarido.

yellow [jélo] adj. amarillo; cobarde; — **fever** fiebre amarilla; s. amarillo; v. poner(se) amarillo.

yellowish [jéloʃ] adj. amarillento.

yelp [jelp] v. aullar, ladrar; s. aullido, ladrido.

yes [jes] adv. sí.

yesterday [jéstədɪ] adv. & s. ayer; **day before** — anteayer o antier.

yet [jet] adv. & conj. todavía, aún; con todo, sin embargo; no obstante; **as** — todavía, aún; **not** — todavía no.

yield [jild] v. ceder, rendir, producir; someterse; **to** — **five percent** redituar el cinco por ciento; s. rendimiento, rendición; rédito.

yoke [jok] s. yugo, yunta (*de bueyes, mulas, etc.*); v. uncir; unir.

yolk [jok] s. yema (*de huevo*)

yonder [jándə] adj. aquel, aquella, aquellos, aquellas; adv. allá, allí, más allá, acullá.

yore [jor] : **in days of** — antaño, en días de antaño.

you [ju] pron. pers. tú, usted, vosotros, ustedes; te, le, lo, la, os, las, los; **to** — a ti, a usted, a vosotros a ustedes; te, le, les; pron. impers. se, uno.

young [jʌŋ] adj. joven; nuevo; — **leaves** hojas tiernas; — **man** joven; **her** — **ones** sus niños, sus hijitos; **the** — **people** la gente joven, los jóvenes, la

juventud; s. jóvenes; cría, hijuelos (*de los animales*).

youngster [jʌŋstə] s. muchacho, niño, jovencito, chiquillo.

your [jʊr] adj. tu (tus), vuestro (vuestra, vuestros, vuestras), su (sus), de usted, de ustedes.

yours [jʊrz] pron. pos. tuyo (tuya, tuyos, tuyas); vuestro (vuestra, vuestros, vuestras); suyo (suya, suyos, suyas) de usted, de ustedes; el tuyo (la tuya, los tuyos, las tuyas); el suyo (la suya los suyos, las suyas); el (la, los, las) de usted; el (la, los, las) de ustedes; **a friend of** — un amigo tuyo, un amigo vuestro; un amigo suyo, un amigo de usted o ustedes.

yourself [jʊrsélf] pron. te, se (*como reflexivo*); **to** — a ti mismo; a usted mismo; **you** — tú mismo; usted mismo; véase **herself**.

yourselves [jʊrsélvz] pron. os, se (*com reflexivo*); **to** — a vosotros mismos; ustedes mismos; **you** — vosotros mismos; ustedes mismos.

youth [juθ] s. joven; juventud; jóvenes.

youthful [júθfəl] adj. joven; juvenil.

Yuletide [júltaɪd] s. Pascua de Navidad; Navidades.

Z

zeal [zil] s. celo, fervor, ardor, entusiasmo.

zealot [zélət] s. fanático.

zealous [zéləs] adj. celoso, ardiente, fervoroso.

zenith [zínɪθ] s. cenit, cumbre.

zephyr [zéfə] s. céfiro.

zero [zíro] s. cero.

zest [zest] s. entusiasmo, buen sabor.

zigzag [zígzæg] s. zigzag; adj. & adv. en zigzag; v. zigzaguear, culebrear, andar en zigzag, serpentear.

zinc [zɪŋk] s. cinc (zinc).

zipper [zípə] s. cierre relámpago, abrochador corredizo o de corredera, *Am* riqui.

zodiac [zódɪæk] s. zodíaco.

zone [zon] s. zona; v. dividir en zonas.

zoo [zu] s. jardín zoológico.

zoological [zoəládʒɪkl] adj. zoológico.

zoology [zoálədʒɪ] s. zoología.

NOTES

NOTES

Pocket Books, Inc., proudly presents to readers the world over the latest list of books for language students:

THE MERRIAM-WEBSTER POCKET DICTIONARY (C-5). Contains 25,000 vocabulary entries and gives the meaning, spelling, and pronunciation of each word. Here are also synonyms and antonyms, abbreviations, foreign words, and population figures for the United States and Canada. (35c)

LAROUSSE'S FRENCH-ENGLISH, ENGLISH-FRENCH DICTIONARY (GC-24). Over 25,000 vocabulary entries plus a Pronunciation Guide for French and English. This book was written and edited under the auspices of the world's foremost authorities on the French language. (50c)

LANGENSCHEIDT'S GERMAN-ENGLISH, ENGLISH-GERMAN DICTIONARY (GC-7). Over 30,000 entries in 528 pages. Listing of abbreviations, weights and measures, irregular verbs, and many other helpful tables. (50c)

MONDADORI'S POCKET ITALIAN-ENGLISH, ENGLISH-ITALIAN DICTIONARY (GC-47). More than 25,000 vocabulary entries, over 600 pages. A comprehensive but compact explanation of grammar, including tables of irregular verbs; keys to pronunciation; up-to-date technical terms; slang and idioms. (50c)

THESE SYMBOLS GUARANTEE
THE BEST IN READING

POCKET BOOKS, INC., is the largest publisher of books in the world today in terms of the number of copies it has sold and is currently selling. Over 750,000,000 copies have carried the symbol of "Gertrude," the little kangaroo, or the perky cardinal, or the stylized anchor and dolphin—all trademarks guaranteeing you books of exceptional merit and value.

Only genuine POCKET BOOK, CARDINAL and PERMABOOK editions carry these symbols. The titles are carefully chosen from the lists of all leading publishers and present the most distinguished and most widely diversified group offered today by any publisher of paper-bound books. Watch for these symbols. They are your guarantee of the best in reading at the lowest possible price.

rrible. Go back to sleep. We can talk
Ms. Slaight turned toward the door.

No, said the little voice in Marnie's head. It, at
ast, was sounding stronger. *Talk now! What kind
f kidnapping is this? Doesn't she need to take a pic-
ure or video with today's paper, at least? Or is she
just psycho? Please, please let her be planning a ransom note.*

Dizzily Marnie got herself up on one elbow.
"Wait a minute," she croaked.

The door closed, and locked, behind Ms. Slaight.
Marnie collapsed back on the cot, her mind
whirling faster, now, than the room.

THE LIKES OF ME, *Randall Beth Pl...*

BROKEN CHORDS, *Barbara Snow Gilbert*

THE HERMIT THRUSH SINGS, *Susan Butler*

ONE THOUSAND PAPER CRANES, *Takayuki Ishii*